ARTIST'S
& GRAPHIC DESIGNERS
MARKET 2016

ArtistsMarketOnline.com

Where & How to Sell What You Create

THE ULTIMATE MARKET RESEARCH TOOL FOR ARTISTS AND DESIGNERS

To register your *2016 Artist's & Graphic Designer's Market* book and **start your FREE 1-year online subscription**, scratch off the block below to reveal your activation code*, then go to www.ArtistsMarketOnline.com. Click on "Sign Up Now" and enter your contact information and activation code. It's that easy!

Carefully scratch off the block with a coin. **Do not use a key.**

UPDATED MARKET LISTINGS
EASY-TO-USE SEARCHABLE DATABASE • RECORD-KEEPING TOOLS
INDUSTRY NEWS • PROFESSIONAL TIPS & ADVICE

*Valid through 12/31/16

ArtistsMarketOnline.com
Where & How to Sell What You Create

Activate your FREE ArtistsMarketOnline.com subscription to get instant access to:

- **UPDATED MARKET LISTINGS** — Find additional listings, updated contact information and more. ArtistsMarketOnline.com provides the most comprehensive database of verified markets available anywhere.

- **EASY-TO-USE SEARCHABLE DATABASE** — Looking for a specific magazine or book publisher? Just type in its name or other relevant keywords. Or widen your prospects with the Advanced Search. You can also receive notifications for listings that have been recently updated!

- **PERSONALIZED TOOLS** — Store your best-bet markets, and use our popular record-keeping tools to track your submissions. Plus, get new and updated market listings, query reminders, and more—every time you log in!

- **PROFESSIONAL TIPS & ADVICE** — From pricing information to sample query letters, and from how-to articles to Q&As, we have the resources creative freelancers need.

YOU'LL GET ALL OF THIS WITH YOUR FREE SUBSCRIPTION TO

ArtistsMarketOnline.com
Where & How to Sell What You Create

AGDM16

41ST ANNUAL EDITION

ARTIST'S
& GRAPHIC DESIGNER'S
MARKET 2016

HOW TO SELL YOUR ART AND MAKE A LIVING

Mary Burzlaff Bostic, Editor

NORTH LIGHT BOOKS
CINCINNATI, OHIO
artistsmarketonline.com

Publisher and Community Leader, Fine Art Community: Jamie Markle
Senior Content Director, North Light Books: Mona Clough
Market Books Assistant, North Light Books: Keeyana Avery

Artist's Market Online website: artistsmarketonline.com
Artist's Network website: artistsnetwork.com
North Light Shop website: northlightshop.com

Distributed in Canada by Fraser Direct
100 Armstrong Avenue
Georgetown, ON, Canada L7G 5S4
Tel: (905) 877-4411

Distributed in the U.K. and Europe by F&W Media International, LTD
Brunel House, Forde Close, Newton Abbot, TQ12 4PU, UK
Tel: (+44) 1626 323200, Fax: (+44) 1626 323319
E-mail: enquiries@fwmedia.com

Distributed in Australia by Capricorn Link
P.O. Box 704, S. Windsor NSW, 2756 Australia
Tel: (02) 4560-1600, Fax: (02) 4577-5288
E-mail: books@capricornlink.com.au

ISSN: 1075-0894
ISBN-13: 978-1-4403-4261-5
ISBN-10: 1-4403-4261-X

Cover design by Geoffrey Raker
Interior design by Claudean Wheeler
Interior layout by Hanna Firestone and Geoffrey Raker
Production coordinated by Debbie Thomas

Attention Booksellers: This is an annual directory of F+W Media, Inc. Return deadline for this edition is December 31, 2016.

a content + ecommerce company

CONTENTS

© Mark Crilley

© Richard McLaughlin

MARKETS

Find record label markets exclusively on ArtistsMarketOnline.com with your FREE subscription.

© Rami Niemi

FROM THE EDITOR

Love it or hate it, dealing with money is a key component of running a successful creative business. While your passion for creating is why you became an artist or designer, competently handling your income and outgo allows you to keep doing what you love.

If handling money isn't your strength, we're here to help. This edition of *Artist's & Graphic Designer's Market* includes articles on selling without begging, obtaining micro funding for your business, beginning a Kickstarter campaign, and options for accepting payment from your clients.

You'll also find features on a variety of topics to help keep your business running smoothly and inspiring interviews with five successful creatives. And, as always, we've included more than 1,800 individually verified market contacts (complete with payment information!).

So, what's holding you back? Keep creating and good luck!

Mary Burzlaff Bostic

Mary Burzlaff Bostic
art.design@fwmedia.com
www.artistsmarketonline.com

P.S. Don't forget to register at **Artist's Market Online, which you get FREE for a year with the purchase of this book**. With your free 1-year subscription, you'll be able to search market contacts, track your submissions, read up on the latest market news, and much more. Use the activation code from the front insert to access your free subscription today.

HOW TO USE THIS BOOK

If you're picking up this book for the first time, you might not know quite how to start using it. Your first impulse might be to flip through and quickly make a mailing list, submitting to everyone with hopes that *someone* might like your work. Resist that urge. First you have to narrow down the names in this book to those who need your particular art style. That's what this book is all about. We provide the names and addresses of art buyers along with plenty of marketing tips. You provide the hard work, creativity, and patience necessary to hang in there until work starts coming your way.

Listings

The book is divided into market sections, from galleries to art fairs. (See the Table of Contents for a complete list.) Each section begins with an introduction containing information and advice to help you break into that specific market. Listings are the meat of this book. In a nutshell, listings are names, addresses, and contact information for places that buy or commission artwork, along with a description of the type of art they need and their submission preferences.

Articles and Interviews

Throughout this book you will find helpful articles and interviews with working artists and experts from the art world. These articles give you a richer understanding of the marketplace by sharing the featured artists' personal experiences and insights. Their stories, and the lessons you can learn from other artists' feats and follies, give you an important edge over competition.

HOW ARTIST'S & GRAPHIC DESIGNER'S MARKET WORKS

Following the instructions in the listings, we suggest you send samples of your work (not originals) to a dozen (or more) targeted markets. The more companies you send to, the greater your chances of a positive response. Establish a system to keep track of whom you submit your work to and send follow-up mailings to your target markets at least twice a year.

How to Read Listings

The first thing you'll notice about many of the listings in this book is the group of symbols that appears before the name of each company. (You'll find a quick-reference key to the symbols on the back inside cover of the book.) Here's what each symbol stands for:

- ✚ Market new to this edition
- ☯ Canadian market
- ➒ International market
- ⍟ Market prefers to work with local artists/designers

Each listing contains a description of the artwork and/or services the company prefers. The information often reveals how much freelance artwork is used, whether computer skills are needed, and which software programs are preferred.

In some sections, additional subheads help you identify potential markets. Magazine listings specify needs for cartoons and illustrations. Galleries specify media and style.

Editorial comments, denoted by ◖, give you extra information about markets, such as company awards, mergers and insight into a company's staff or procedures.

It might take a while to get accustomed to the layout and language in the listings. In the beginning, you will encounter some terms and symbols that might be unfamiliar to you. Refer to the Glossary to help you with terms you don't understand.

Working With Listings

1. Read the entire listing to decide whether to submit your samples. Do not use this book simply as a mailing list of names and addresses. Reading listings carefully helps you narrow your mailing list and submit appropriate material.

2. Read the description of the company or gallery in the first paragraph of the listing. Then jump to the **Needs** or **Media** heading to find out what type of artwork is preferred. Is it the type of artwork you create? This is the first step to narrowing your target market. You should send your samples only to places that need the kind of work you create.

3. Send appropriate submissions. It seems like common sense to research what kind of samples a listing wants before sending off just any artwork you have on hand. But believe it or not, some artists skip this step. Some art directors have pulled their listings from *Artist's & Graphic Designer's Market* because they've received too many inappropriate submissions. Look under the **First Contact & Terms** heading to find out how to contact the market and

FREQUENTLY ASKED QUESTIONS

1 **How do companies get listed in the book?** No company pays to be included—all listings are free. Every company has to fill out a detailed questionnaire about their art needs. All questionnaires are screened to make sure the companies meet our requirements. Each year we contact every company in the book and ask them to update their information.

2 **Why aren't other companies I know about listed in this book?** We may have sent these companies a questionnaire, but they never returned it. Or if they did return a questionnaire, we may have decided not to include them based on our requirements. If you know of a market you'd like to see in the book, send an e-mail request to art.design@fwmedia.com.

3 **I sent some samples to a company that stated they were open to reviewing the type of work I do, but I have not heard from them yet, and they have not returned my materials. What should I do?** At the time we contacted the company, they were open to receiving such submissions. However, things can change. It's a good idea to contact any company listed in this book to check on their policy before sending them anything. Perhaps they have not had time to review your submission yet. If the listing states that they respond to queries in one month, and more than a month has passed, you can send a brief e-mail to the company to inquire about the status of your submission. Some companies receive a large volume of submissions, so you must be patient. Never send originals when you are querying—always send copies. If for any reason your samples are never returned, you will not have lost forever the opportunity to sell an important image. It is a good idea to include a SASE (self-addressed, stamped envelope) with your submissions, even if the listing does not specifically request that you do so. This may facilitate getting your work back.

4 **A company says they want to publish my artwork, but first they will need a fee from me. Is this a standard business practice?** No, it is not a standard business practice. You should never have to pay to have your art reviewed or accepted for publication. If you suspect that a company may not be reputable, do some research before you submit anything or pay their fees. The exception to this rule is art fairs. Most art fairs have an application fee, and usually there is a fee for renting booth space. Some galleries may also require a fee for renting space to exhibit your work (see the gallery market section for more information).

what to send. Some companies and publishers are very picky about what kinds of samples they like to see; others are more flexible.

What's an inappropriate submission? Here's an example: Suppose you want to be a children's book illustrator. Don't send samples of your cute animal art to *Business Law Today* magazine—they would rather see law-related subjects. Use the Niche Marketing Index to find listings that accept children's illustrations. You'd be surprised how many illustrators waste their postage sending the wrong samples—which, of course, alienates art directors. Make sure all your mailings are *appropriate ones*.

4. Consider your competition. Under the **Needs** heading, compare the number of free-lancers who contact the company with the number they actually work with. You'll have a better chance with listings that use a lot of artwork or work with many artists.

5. Look for what they pay. In most sections, you can find this information under **First Contact & Terms**. In the Book Publishers section publishers list pay rates under headings pertaining to the type of work they assign, such as **Text Illustration** or **Book Design**.

At first, try not to be too picky about how much a listing pays. After you have a couple of assignments under your belt, you might decide to send samples only to medium- or high-paying markets.

6. Be sure to read the Tips. This is where art directors describe their pet peeves and give clues for how to impress them. Artists say the information within the **Tips** helps them get a feel for what a company might be like to work for.

These steps are just the beginning. As you become accustomed to reading listings, you will think of more ways to mine this book for your potential clients. Some of our readers tell us they peruse listings to find the speed at which a magazine pays its freelancers. In publishing, it's often a long wait until an edition or book is actually published, but if you are paid "on acceptance," you'll get a check soon after you complete the assignment and it is approved by the art director.

When looking for galleries, savvy artists often check to see how many square feet of space are available and what hours the gallery is open. These details all factor in when narrowing down your search for target markets.

Pay Attention to Copyright Information

It's also important to consider what rights companies buy. It is preferable to work with companies that buy first or one-time rights. If you see a listing that buys "all rights," be aware you may be giving up the right to sell that particular artwork in the future. See the "Copyright Basics" article in this section for more information.

Look for Specialties and Niche Markets

Read listings closely. Most describe their specialties, clients, and products within the first paragraph. If you hope to design restaurant menus, for example, target agencies that have restaurants for clients. If you prefer illustrating people, you might target ad agencies whose clients are hospitals or financial institutions. If you like to draw cars, look for agencies with clients in the automotive industry, and so on. Many book publishers specialize, too. Look for a publisher who specializes in children's books if that's the type of work you'd like to do. The Niche Marketing Index lists possible opportunities for specialization.

Read Listings for Ideas

You'd be surprised how many artists found new niches they hadn't thought of by browsing the listings. One greeting card artist read about a company that produces mugs. Inspiration struck. Now this artist has added mugs to her repertoire, along with paper plates, figurines, and rubber stamps—all because she browsed the listings for ideas!

Sending Samples

Once you narrow down some target markets, the next step is sending them samples of your work. As you create your samples and submission packets, be aware that your package or postcard has to look professional. It must be up to the standards art directors and gallery dealers expect. There are examples throughout this book of some great samples sent out by other artists. Make sure your samples rise to that standard of professionalism.

See You Next Year

Use this book for one year. Highlight listings, make notes in the margins, fill it with Post-it notes. In November of 2016, our next edition—the *2017 Artist's & Graphic Designer's Market*—starts arriving in bookstores. By then, we'll have collected hundreds of new listings and changes in contact information. It is a career investment to buy the new edition every year. (And it's deductible! See the "How to Stay on Track & Get Paid" article in this section for information on tax deductions.)

COMPLAINT PROCEDURE

If you feel you have not been treated fairly by a company listed in *Artist's & Graphic Designer's Market*, we advise you to take the following steps:

- First, try to contact the company. Sometimes one e-mail or letter can quickly clear up the matter.
- Document all your correspondence with the company. If you write to us with a complaint, provide the details of your submission, the date of your first contact with the company, and the nature of your subsequent correspondence.
- We will enter your complaint into our files.
- The number and severity of complaints will be considered in our decision whether to delete the listing from the next edition.
- We reserve the right to not list any company for any reason.

Join a Professional Organization

Artists who have the most success using this book are those who take the time to read the articles to learn about the bigger picture. In our interviews, you'll learn what has worked for other artists and what kind of work impresses art directors and gallery dealers.

You'll find out how joining professional organizations such as the Graphic Artists Guild (www.gag.org) or the Society of Illustrators (www.societyillustrators.org) can jump-start your career. You'll find out the importance of reading trade magazines such as *HOW* (www.howdesign.com), *PRINT* (www.printmag.com) and *Greetings etc.* (www. greetingsmagazine.com) to learn more about the industries you hope to approach. You'll learn about trade shows, art reps, shipping, billing, working with vendors, networking, self-promotion, and hundreds of other details it would take years to find out about on your own. Perhaps most importantly, you'll read about how successful artists overcame rejection through persistence.

Hang In There!

Being professional doesn't happen overnight. It's a gradual process. It may take two or three years to gain enough information and experience to be a true professional in your field. So if you really want to be a professional artist, hang in there. Before long, you'll feel that heady feeling that comes from selling your work or seeing your illustrations on greeting cards or in magazines. If you really want it and you're willing to work for it, it *will* happen.

HOW TO STAY ON TRACK & GET PAID

As you launch your artistic career, be aware that you are actually starting a small business. It is crucial that you keep track of the details, or your business will not last very long. The most important rule of all is to find a system to keep your business organized and stick with it.

YOUR DAILY RECORD-KEEPING SYSTEM

Every artist needs to keep a daily record of art-making and marketing activities. Before you do anything else, visit an office supply store and pick out the items listed below (or your own variations of these items). Keep it simple so you can remember your system and use it on automatic pilot whenever you make a business transaction.

What You'll Need:

- A packet of colorful file folders or a basic Personal Information Manager on your smartphone, tablet, or computer.
- A notebook or legal pad to serve as a log or journal to keep track of your daily art-making and art-marketing activities.
- A small pocket notebook to keep in your car to track mileage and gas expenses.

How to Start Your System

Designate a permanent location in your studio or home office for two file folders and your notebook. Label one red file folder "Expenses." Label one green file folder "Income." Write in your daily log book each and every day.

Every time you purchase anything for your business, such as envelopes or art supplies, place the receipt in your red Expenses folder. When you receive payment for an assignment or painting, photocopy the check or place the receipt in your green Income folder.

Keep Track of Assignments

Whether you're an illustrator or fine artist, you should devise a system for keeping track of assignments and artworks. Most illustrators assign a job number to each assignment they receive and create a file folder for each job. Some arrange these folders by client name; others keep them in numerical order. The important thing is to keep all correspondence for each assignment in a spot where you can easily find it.

Pricing Illustration and Design

One of the hardest things to master is what to charge for your work. It's difficult to make blanket statements on this topic. Every slice of the market is somewhat different. Nevertheless, there is one recurring pattern: Hourly rates are generally paid only to designers working in-house on a client's equipment. Freelance illustrators working out of their own studios are almost always paid a flat fee or an advance against royalties.

If you don't know what to charge, begin by devising an hourly rate, taking into consideration the cost of materials and overhead as well as what you think your time is worth. If you're a designer, determine what the average salary would be for a full-time employee doing the same job. Then estimate how many hours the job will take and quote a flat fee based on these calculations.

There is a distinct difference between giving the client a job estimate and a job quote. An estimate is a ballpark figure of what the job will cost but is subject to change. A quote is a set fee which, once agreed upon, is pretty much carved in stone. Make sure the client understands which you are negotiating. Estimates are often used as a preliminary step in itemizing costs for a combination of design services such as concepting, typesetting, and printing. Flat quotes are generally used by illustrators, as there are fewer factors involved in arriving at fees.

For recommended fees for different services, refer to the *Graphic Artists Guild Handbook of Pricing & Ethical Guidelines* (www.gag.org). Many artists' organizations have standard pay rates listed on their websites.

As you set fees, certain stipulations call for higher rates. Consider these bargaining points:

- **Usage (rights).** The more rights purchased, the more you can charge. For example, if the client asks for a "buyout" (to buy all rights), you can charge more, because by relinquishing all rights to future use of your work, you will be losing out on resale potential.

PRICING YOUR FINE ART

There are no hard-and-fast rules for pricing your fine artwork. Most artists and galleries base prices on market value—what the buying public is currently paying for similar work. Learn the market value by visiting galleries and checking prices of works similar to yours. When you're starting out, don't compare your prices to established artists but to emerging talent in your region. Consider these factors when determining price:

- **Medium.** Oils and acrylics cost more than watercolors by the same artist. Price paintings higher than drawings.
- **Expense of materials.** Charge more for work done on expensive paper than for work of a similar size on a lesser grade paper.
- **Size.** Though a large work isn't necessarily better than a small one, as a rule of thumb you can charge more for the larger work.
- **Scarcity.** Charge more for one-of-a-kind works like paintings and drawings than for limited editions such as lithographs and woodcuts.
- **Status of artist.** Established artists can charge more than lesser-known artists.
- **Status of gallery.** Prestigious galleries can charge higher prices.
- **Region.** Works usually sell for more in larger cities like New York and Chicago.
- **Gallery commission.** The gallery will charge from 30 to 50 percent commission. Your cut must cover the cost of materials, studio space, taxes, and perhaps shipping and insurance, as well as enough extra to make a profit. If materials for a painting cost $25, matting and framing cost $37, and you spent five hours working on it, make sure you get at least the cost of material and labor back before the gallery takes its share. Once you set your price, stick to the same price structure wherever you show your work. A $500 painting by you should cost $500 whether it is bought in a gallery or directly from you. To do otherwise is not fair to the gallery and devalues your work.

As you establish a reputation, begin to raise your prices—but do so cautiously. Each time you graduate to a new price level, it will be that much harder to revert to former prices.

- **Turnaround time.** If you are asked to turn the job around quickly, charge more.
- **Budget.** Don't be afraid to ask about a project's budget before offering a quote. You won't want to charge $500 for a print ad illustration if the ad agency has a budget of $40,000 for that ad. If the budget is that big, ask for higher payment.
- **Reputation.** The more well known you are, the more you can charge. As you become established, periodically raise your rates (in small steps) and see what happens.

What Goes in a Contract?

Contracts are simply business tools used to make sure everyone agrees on the terms of a project. Ask for one any time you enter into a business agreement. Be sure to arrange for the specifics in writing or provide your own. A letter stating the terms of agreement signed by both parties can serve as an informal contract. Several excellent books, such as *Legal Guide for the Visual Artist* and *Business and Legal Forms for Illustrators*, both by Tad Crawford (Allworth Press), contain negotiation checklists and tear-out forms, and provide sample contracts you can copy. The sample contracts in these books cover practically any situation you might encounter.

The items specified in your contract will vary according to the market you're dealing with and the complexity of the project. Nevertheless, here are some basic points you'll want to cover:

Commercial Contracts

- **A description** of the service(s) you're providing.
- **Deadlines** for finished work.
- **Rights sold. Your fee.** Hourly rate, flat fee, or royalty.
- **Kill fee.** Compensatory payment received by you if the project is canceled.
- **Changes fees.** Penalty fees to be paid by the client for last-minute changes.
- **Advances.** Any funds paid to you before you begin working on the project.
- **Payment schedule.** When and how often you will be paid for the assignment.
- **Statement regarding return of original art.** Unless you're doing work for hire, your artwork should always be returned to you.

Gallery Contracts

- **Terms of acquisition or representation.** Will the work be handled on consignment? What is the gallery's commission?
- **Nature of the show(s).** Will the work be exhibited in group or solo shows or both?
- **Timeframes.** If a work is sold, when will you be paid? At what point will the gallery return unsold works to you? When will the contract cease to be in effect?
- **Promotion.** Who will coordinate and pay for promotion? What does promotion entail? Who pays for printing and mailing of invitations? If costs are shared, what is the breakdown?
- **Insurance.** Will the gallery insure the work while it is being exhibited and/or while it is being shipped to or from the gallery?
- **Shipping.** Who will pay for shipping costs to and from the gallery?

- **Geographic restrictions.** If you sign with this gallery, will you relinquish the rights to show your work elsewhere in a specified area? If so, what are the boundaries of this area?

How to Send Invoices

If you're a designer or illustrator, you will be responsible for sending invoices for your services. Clients generally will not issue checks without them, so mail or fax an invoice as soon as you've completed the assignment. Illustrators are generally paid in full either upon receipt of illustration or upon publication. Most graphic designers arrange to be paid in thirds, billing the first third before starting the project, the second after the client approves the initial roughs, and the third upon completion of the project.

Standard invoice forms allow you to itemize your services. The more you spell out the charges, the easier it will be for your clients to understand what they're paying for. Most freelancers charge extra for changes made after approval of the initial layout. Keep a separate form for change orders and attach it to your invoice.

If you're an illustrator, your invoice can be much simpler, as you'll generally be charging a flat fee. It's helpful, in determining your quoted fee, to itemize charges according to time, materials, and expenses. (The client need not see this itemization; it is for your own purposes.) Most businesses require your Social Security number or tax ID number before they can cut a check, so include this information in your bill. Be sure to put a due date on each invoice; include the phrase "payable within 30 days" (or other preferred time frame) directly on your invoice. Most freelancers ask for payment within ten to thirty days. Sample invoices are featured in *Business and Legal Forms for Illustrators* and *Business and Legal Forms for Graphic Designers*, both by Tad Crawford (Allworth Press).

If you're working with a gallery, you will not need to send invoices. The gallery should send you a check (generally within thirty days) each time one of your pieces is sold.

To ensure that you are paid in a timely manner, call the gallery periodically to touch base. Let the director or business manager know that you are keeping an eye on your work. When selling work independently of a gallery, give receipts to buyers and keep copies for your records.

Take Advantage of Tax Deductions

You have the right to deduct legitimate business expenses from your taxable income. Art supplies, studio rent, printing costs, and other business expenses are deductible against your gross art-related income. It is imperative to seek the help of an accountant or tax preparation service in filing your return. In the event your deductions exceed profits, the loss will lower your taxable income from other sources.

To guard against taxpayers fraudulently claiming hobby expenses as business losses, the IRS requires taxpayers to demonstrate a "profit motive." As a general rule, you must show a profit for three out of five years to retain a business status. If you are audited, the burden of proof will be on you to validate your work as a business and not a hobby. The nine criteria the IRS uses to distinguish a business from a hobby are:

- the manner in which you conduct your business
- expertise
- amount of time and effort put into your work
- expectation of future profits
- success in similar ventures
- history of profit and losses
- amount of occasional profits
- financial status
- element of personal pleasure or recreation

If the IRS rules that you paint for pure enjoyment rather than profit, they will consider you a hobbyist. Complete and accurate records will demonstrate to the IRS that you take your business seriously.

Even if you are a hobbyist, you can deduct expenses such as supplies on Schedule A, but you can only take art-related deductions equal to art-related income. If you sold two $500 paintings, you can deduct expenses such as art supplies, art books, and seminars only up to $1,000. Itemize deductions only if your total itemized deductions exceed your standard deduction. You will not be allowed to deduct a loss from other sources of income.

Figuring Deductions

To deduct business expenses, you or your accountant will fill out a 1040 tax form (not 1040EZ) and prepare a Schedule C, which is a separate form used to calculate profit or loss from your business. The income (or loss) from Schedule C is then reported on the 1040 form. In regard to business expenses, the standard deduction does not come into play as it would for a hobbyist. The total of your business expenses need not exceed the standard deduction.

There is a shorter form called Schedule C-EZ for self-employed people in service industries. It can be applicable to illustrators and designers who have receipts of $25,000 or less and deductible expenses of $2,000 or less. Check with your accountant to see if you qualify.

Deductible expenses include advertising costs, brochures, business cards, professional group dues, subscriptions to trade journals and arts magazines, legal and professional services, leased office equipment, office supplies, business travel expenses, etc. Your accountant can give you a list of all 100-percent and 50-percent deductible expenses. Don't forget to deduct the cost of this book!

CAN I DEDUCT MY HOME STUDIO?

If you freelance full time from your home and devote a separate area to your business, you may qualify for a home office deduction. If eligible, you can deduct a percentage of your rent or mortgage as well as utilities and expenses like office supplies and business-related telephone calls.

The IRS does not allow deductions if the space is used for purposes other than business. A studio or office in your home must meet three criteria:

- The space must be used exclusively for your business.
- The space must be used regularly as a place of business.
- The space must be your principle place of business.

The IRS might question a home office deduction if you are employed full time elsewhere and freelance from home. If you do claim a home office, the area must be clearly divided from your living area. A desk in your bedroom will not qualify. To figure out the percentage of your home used for business, divide the total square footage of your home by the total square footage of your office. This will give you a percentage to work with when figuring deductions. If the home office is 10 percent of the square footage of your home, deduct 10 percent of expenses such as rent, heat, and air conditioning.

The total home office deduction cannot exceed the gross income you derive from its business use. You cannot take a net business loss resulting from a home office deduction. Your business must be profitable three out of five years; otherwise, you will be classified as a hobbyist and will not be entitled to this deduction.

Consult a tax advisor before attempting to take this deduction, as its interpretations frequently change.

For additional information, refer to IRS Publication 587, Business Use of Your Home, which can be downloaded at www.irs.gov or ordered by calling (800)829-3676.

As a self-employed "sole proprietor," there is no employer regularly taking tax out of your paycheck. Your accountant will help you put money away to meet your tax obligations and may advise you to estimate your tax and file quarterly returns.

Your accountant also will be knowledgeable about another annual tax called the Social Security Self-Employment tax. You must pay this tax if your net freelance income is $400 or more.

The fees of tax professionals are relatively low, and they are deductible. To find a good accountant, ask colleagues for recommendations, look for advertisements in trade publications, or ask your local Small Business Association.

Whenever Possible, Retain Your Independent Contractor Status

Some clients automatically classify freelancers as employees and require them to file Form W-4. If you are placed on employee status, you may be entitled to certain benefits, but a portion of your earnings will be withheld by the client until the end of the tax year and you could forfeit certain deductions. In short, you may end up taking home less than you would if you were classified as an independent contractor.

The IRS uses a list of twenty factors to determine whether a person should be classified as an independent contractor or an employee. This list can be found in IRS Publication 937. Note, however, that your client will be the first to decide how you'll be classified.

Report All Income to Uncle Sam

Don't be tempted to sell artwork without reporting it on your income tax. You may think this saves money, but it can do real damage to your career and credibility—even if you are never audited by the IRS. Unless you report your income, the IRS will not categorize you as a professional, and you won't be able to deduct expenses. And don't think you won't get caught if you neglect to report income. If you bill any client in excess of $600, the IRS requires the client to provide you with a Form 1099 at the end of the year. Your client must send one copy to the IRS and a copy to you to attach to your income tax return. Likewise, if you pay a freelancer over $600, you must issue a 1099 form. This procedure is one way the IRS cuts down on unreported income.

Register With the State Sales Tax Department

Most states require a 2–7 percent sales tax on artwork you sell directly from your studio or at art fairs, or on work created for a client. You must register with the state sales tax department, which will issue you a sales permit or a resale number and send you appropriate forms and instructions for collecting the tax. Getting a sales permit usually involves filling out a form and paying a small fee. Reporting sales tax is a relatively simple procedure. Record all sales taxes on invoices and in your sales journal. Every three months, total the taxes collected and send it to the state sales tax department.

In most states, if you sell to a customer outside of your sales tax area, you do not have to collect sales tax. However, this may not hold true for your state. You may also need a business license or permit. Call your state tax office to find out what is required.

Save Money on Art Supplies

As long as you have the above sales permit number, you can buy art supplies without paying sales tax. You will probably have to fill out a tax-exempt form with your permit number at the sales desk where you buy materials. The reason you do not have to pay sales tax on art supplies is that sales tax is only charged on the final product. However, you must then add the cost of materials into the cost of your finished painting or the final artwork for your client. Keep all receipts in case of a tax audit. If the state discovers that you have not collected sales tax, you will be liable for tax and penalties.

If you sell all your work through galleries, they will charge sales tax, but you still need a sales permit number to get a tax exemption on supplies.

Some states claim "creativity" is a nontaxable service, while others view it as a product and therefore taxable. Be certain you understand the sales tax laws to avoid being held liable for uncollected money at tax time. Contact your state auditor for sales tax information.

Save Money on Postage

When you send out postcard samples or invitations to openings, you can save big bucks by mailing in bulk. Fine artists should send submissions via first-class mail for quicker service and better handling. Package flat work between heavy cardboard or foam core, or roll it in a cardboard tube. Include your business card or a label with your name and address on the outside of the packaging material in case the outer wrapper becomes separated from the inner packing in transit.

Protect larger works—particularly those that are matted or framed—with a strong outer surface, such as laminated cardboard, Masonite, or light plywood. Wrap the work in polyfoam, heavy cloth, or bubble wrap, and cushion it against the outer container with spacers to keep it from moving. Whenever possible, ship work before it is glassed. If the glass breaks en route, it may destroy your original image. If shipping large framed work, contact a museum in your area for more suggestions on packaging.

The US Postal Service will not automatically insure your work, but you can purchase up to $5,000 worth of coverage. Artworks exceeding this value should be sent by registered mail, which can be insured for up to $25,000. Certified packages travel a little slower but are easier to track.

Consider special services offered by the post office, such as Priority Mail, Express Mail Next Day Service, and Special Delivery. For overnight delivery, check to see which air freight services are available in your area. Federal Express automatically insures packages for $100 and will ship art valued up to $500. Their 24-hour computer tracking system enables you to locate your package at any time.

The United Parcel Service automatically insures work for $100, but you can purchase additional insurance for work valued as high as $25,000 for items shipped by air (there is no limit for items sent on the ground). UPS cannot guarantee arrival dates but will track lost packages. It also offers Two-Day Blue Label Air Service within the US and Next Day Service in specific ZIP code zones.

Before sending any original work, make sure you have a copy (digital, photocopy, slide, or transparency) in your files. Always make a quick address check by phone before putting your package in the mail.

Send Us Your Business Tips

If you've used a business strategy we haven't covered, please e-mail us at art.design@fwmedia. com. We may feature you and your work in a future edition.

COPYRIGHT BASICS

As creator of your artwork, you have certain inherent rights over your work and can control how each one of your works is used until you sell your rights to someone else. The legal term for these rights is called *copyright*. Technically, any original artwork you produce is automatically copyrighted as soon as you put it in tangible form.

To be automatically copyrighted, your artwork must fall within these guidelines:

- **It must be your original creation.** It cannot be a *copy* of somebody else's work.
- **It must be "pictorial, graphic, or sculptural."** Utilitarian objects, such as lamps or toasters, are not covered, although you can copyright an illustration featured on a lamp or toaster.
- **It must be fixed in "any tangible medium, now known or later developed."** Your work, or at least a representation of a planned work, must be created in or on a medium you can see or touch, such as paper, canvas, clay, a sketch pad, or even a website. It can't just be an idea in your head. An idea cannot be copyrighted.

Copyright Lasts for Your Lifetime Plus Seventy Years

Copyright is *exclusive*. When you create a work, the rights automatically belong to you and nobody else but you until those rights are sold to someone else.

Works of art created on or after January 1978 are protected for your lifetime plus seventy years.

The Artist's Bundle of Rights

One of the most important things you need to know about copyright is that it is not just a *singular* right. It is a *bundle* of rights you enjoy as creator of your artwork:

- **Reproduction right.** You have the right to make copies of the original work.
- **Modification right.** You have the right to create derivative works based on the original work.
- **Distribution rights.** You have the right to sell, rent, or lease copies of your work.
- **Public performance right.** You have the right to play, recite, or otherwise perform a work. (This right is more applicable to written or musical art forms than to visual art.)
- **Public display right.** You have the right to display your work in a public place. This bundle of rights can be divided up in a number of ways so that you can sell all or part of any of those exclusive rights to one or more parties. The system of selling parts of your copyright bundle is sometimes referred to as *divisible copyright*. Just as a land owner can divide up his property and sell it to many different people, the artist can divide up his rights to an artwork and sell portions of those rights to different buyers.

Divisible Copyright: Divide and Conquer

Why is divisible copyright so important? Because dividing up your bundle and selling parts of it to different buyers will help you get the most payment for each of your artworks. For any one of your artworks, you can sell your entire bundle of rights at one time (not advisable!) or divide each bundle pertaining to that work into smaller portions and make more money as a result. You can grant one party the right to use your work on a greeting card and sell another party the right to print that same work on T-shirts.

Divisible Copyright Terms

Clients tend to use legal jargon to specify the rights they want to buy. The terms below are commonly used in contracts to indicate portions of your bundle of rights. Some terms are vague or general, such as "all rights." Other terms are more specific, such as "first North American rights." Make sure you know what each term means before signing a contract.

- **One-time rights.** Your client buys the right to use or publish your artwork or illustration on a one-time basis. One fee is paid for one use. Most magazine and book cover assignments fall under this category.
- **First rights.** This is almost the same as one-time rights, except that the buyer is also paying for the privilege of being the first to use your image. He may use it only once unless the other rights are negotiated. Sometimes first rights can be further broken down geographically. The buyer might ask to buy **first North American rights**, meaning he would have the right to be the first to publish the work in North America.

- **Exclusive rights.** This guarantees the buyer's exclusive right to use the artwork in his particular market or for a particular product. Exclusive rights are frequently negotiated by greeting card and gift companies. One company might purchase the exclusive right to use your work as a greeting card, leaving you free to sell the exclusive rights to produce the image on a mug to another company.
- **Promotional rights.** These rights allow a publisher to use an artwork for promotion of a publication in which the artwork appears. For example, if *The New Yorker* bought promotional rights to your cartoon, they could also use it in a direct mail promotion.
- **Electronic rights.** These rights allow a buyer to place your work on electronic media such as websites. Often these rights are requested with print rights.
- **Work for hire.** Under the Copyright Act of 1976, section 101, a "work for hire" is defined as "(1) a work prepared by an employee within the scope of his or her employment; or (2) a work specially ordered or commissioned for use as a contribution to a collective work, as part of a motion picture or other audiovisual work . . . if the parties expressly agree in a written instrument signed by them that the work shall be considered a work made for hire." When the agreement is "work for hire," you surrender all rights to the image and can never resell that particular image again. If you agree to the terms, make sure the money you receive makes it well worth the arrangement.
- **All rights.** Again, be aware that this phrase means you will relinquish your entire copyright to a specific artwork. Before agreeing to the terms, make sure this is an arrangement you can live with. At the very least, arrange for the contract to expire after a specified date. Terms for all rights—including time period for usage and compensation—should be confirmed in a written agreement with the client.

Since legally your artwork is your property, when you create an illustration for a magazine you are, in effect, temporarily "leasing" your work to the client for publication.

Chances are you'll never hear an art director ask to lease or license your illustration, and he may not even realize he is leasing, not buying, your work. But most art directors know that once the magazine is published, the art director has no further claims to your work, and the rights revert back to you. If the art director wants to use your work a second or third time, he must ask permission and negotiate with you to determine any additional fees you want to charge. You are free to take that same artwork and sell it to another buyer.

However, if the art director buys "all rights," you cannot legally offer that same image to another client. If you agree to create the artwork as "work for hire," you relinquish your rights entirely.

What Licensing Agents Know

The practice of leasing parts or groups of an artist's bundle of rights is often referred to as *licensing*, because (legally) the artist is granting someone a "license" to use his work for a limited time for a specific reason. As licensing agents have come to realize, it is the exclusivity of the rights and the ability to divide and sell them that make them valuable. Knowing exactly what rights you own, which you can sell, and in what combinations, will help you negotiate with your clients.

Don't Sell Conflicting Rights to Different Clients

You also have to make sure the rights you sell to one client don't conflict with any of the rights sold to other clients. For example, you can't sell the exclusive right to use your image on greeting cards to two separate greeting card companies. You can sell the exclusive greeting card rights to one card company and the exclusive rights to use your artwork on mugs to a separate gift company. You should always get such agreements in writing and let both companies know your work will appear on other products.

When to Use the Copyright © and Credit Lines

A copyright notice consists of the word "Copyright" or its symbol ©, the year the work was created or first published, and the full name of the copyright owner. It should be placed where it can easily be seen, on the front or back of an illustration or artwork. It's also common to print your copyright notice on the back of reproductions or photographs of your artwork.

Under today's laws, placing the copyright symbol on your work isn't absolutely necessary to claim copyright infringement and take a plagiarist to court if he steals your work. If you browse through magazines, you will often see the illustrator's name in small print near the illustration, *without* the Copyright ©. This is common practice in the magazine industry. Even though the © is not printed, the illustrator still owns the copyright unless the magazine purchased all rights to the work. Just make sure the art director gives you a credit line near the illustration.

Usually you will not see the artist's name or credit line next to advertisements for products. Advertising agencies often purchase all rights to the work for a specified time. They usually pay the artist generously for this privilege and spell out the terms clearly in the artist's contract.

How to Register a Copyright

The process of registering your work is simple. Visit the United States Copyright Office website at www.copyright.gov to file electronically. You can still register with paper forms, but this method requires a higher filing fee. To request paper forms, call (202)707-9100 or write to the Library of Congress, Copyright Office-COPUBS, 101 Independence Ave. SE, Washington, DC 20559-6304, Attn: Information Publications, Section LM0455 and ask for package 115 and circulars 40 and 40A. Cartoonists should ask for package 111 and circular 44. They will send you a package containing Form VA (for visual artists).

You can register an entire collection of your work rather than one work at a time. That way you will have to pay only one fee for an unlimited number of works. For example, if you have created a hundred works between 2014 and 2016, you can complete a copyright form to register "the collected works of Jane Smith, 2014–2016." But you will have to upload digital files or send either slides or photocopies of each of those works.

Why Register?

It seems like a lot of time and trouble to complete the forms to register copyrights for all your artworks. It may not be necessary or worth it to you to register every artwork you create. After all, a work is copyrighted the moment it's created anyway, right? The benefits of registering are basically to give you additional clout in case an infringement occurs and you decide to take the offender to court. Without a copyright registration, it probably wouldn't be economically feasible to file suit, because you'd be entitled to only your damages and the infringer's profits, which might not equal the cost of litigating the case. If the works are registered with the US Copyright Office, it will be easier to prove your case and get reimbursed for your court costs.

Likewise, the big advantage of using the Copyright © also comes when and if you ever have to take an infringer to court. Since the Copyright © is the most clear warning to potential plagiarizers, it is easier to collect damages if the © is in plain sight.

Register with the US Copyright Office those works you fear are likely to be plagiarized before or shortly after they have been exhibited or published. That way, if anyone uses your work without permission, you can take action.

Deal Swiftly With Plagiarists

If you suspect your work has been plagiarized and you have not already registered it with the Copyright Office, register it immediately. You have to wait until it is registered before you can take legal action against the infringer.

Before taking the matter to court, however, your first course of action might be a well-phrased letter from your lawyer telling the offender to "cease and desist" using your work, because you have a registered copyright. Such a warning (especially if printed on your lawyer's letterhead) is often enough to get the offender to stop using your work.

Don't Sell Your Rights Too Cheaply

Recently a controversy has been raging about whether or not artists should sell the rights to their works to stock illustration agencies. Many illustrators strongly believe selling rights to stock agencies hurts the illustration profession. They say artists who deal with stock agencies, especially those who sell royalty-free art, are giving up the rights to their work too cheaply.

Another pressing copyright concern is the issue of electronic rights. As technology makes it easier to download images, it is more important than ever for artists to protect their work against infringement.

Log on to www.theispot.com and discuss copyright issues with your fellow artists. Join organizations that crusade for artists' rights, such as the Graphic Artists Guild (www.gag.org) or The American Institute of Graphic Arts (www.aiga.org). Volunteer Lawyers for the Arts (www.vlany.org) is a national network of lawyers who volunteer free legal services to artists who can't afford legal advice. A quick Internet search will help you locate a branch in your state. Most branches offer workshops and consultations.

PROMOTING YOUR WORK

So, you're ready to launch your freelance art or gallery career. How do you let people know about your talent? One way is by introducing yourself to them by sending promotional samples. Samples are your most important sales tool, so put a lot of thought into what you send. Your ultimate success depends largely on the impression they make.

We divided this article into three sections, so whether you're a fine artist, illustrator, or designer, check the appropriate heading for guidelines. Read individual listings and section introductions thoroughly for more specific instructions. As you read the listings, you'll see the term SASE, short for self-addressed, stamped envelope. Enclose an SASE with your submissions if you want your material returned. If you send postcards or tearsheets, no return envelope is necessary. Many art directors want only nonreturnable samples, because they are too busy to return materials, even with SASEs. So read listings carefully and save stamps.

ILLUSTRATORS & CARTOONISTS

You will have several choices when submitting to magazines, book publishers, and other illustration and cartoon markets. Many freelancers send a cover letter and one or two samples in initial mailings. Others prefer a simple postcard showing their illustrations. Here are a few of your options:

Postcard. Choose one (or more) of your illustrations or cartoons that represent your style, then have the image(s) printed on postcards. Have your name, address, phone number, e-mail, and website printed on the front of the postcard or in the return address corner. Somewhere on the card should be printed the word "Illustrator" or "Cartoonist." If you use one or two colors, you can keep the cost below $200. Art directors like postcards because they are easy to file or tack on a bulletin board. If the art director likes what she sees, she can always call you for more samples.

Promotional sheet. If you want to show more of your work, you can opt for an 8½×11 color or black-and-white printed image or photocopy of your work. No matter what size sample you send, never fold the page. It is more professional to send flat sheets, in a 9×12 envelope along with a typed query letter, preferably on your own professional stationery.

Tearsheets. After you complete assignments, acquire copies of any printed pages on which your illustrations appear. Tearsheets impress art directors because they are proof that you are experienced and have met deadlines on previous projects.

Photographs. Some illustrators have been successful sending photographs, but printed samples are preferred by most art directors.

Query or cover letter. A query letter is a nice way to introduce yourself to an art director for the first time. One or two paragraphs stating your desire and availability for freelance work is all you need. Include your phone number and e-mail address.

E-mail submissions. E-mail is a great way to introduce your work to potential clients. When sending e-mails, provide a link to your website or JPEGs of your best work.

DESIGNERS & DIGITAL ARTISTS

Plan and create your submission package as if it were a paying assignment from a client. Your submission piece should show your skill as a designer. Include one or both of the following:

Cover letter. This is your opportunity to show you can design a beautiful, simple logo or letterhead for your own business card, stationery, and envelopes. Have these all-important pieces printed on excellent-quality bond paper. Then write a simple cover letter stating your experience and skills.

Sample. Your sample can be a copy of an assignment you've completed for another client or a clever self-promotional piece. Design a great piece to show off your capabilities.

Stand Out From the Crowd

You may have only a few seconds to grab art directors' attention as they make their way through the "slush pile" (an industry term for unsolicited submissions). Make yourself stand out in simple, effective ways:

Tie in your cover letter with your sample. When sending an initial mailing to a potential client, include a cover letter of introduction with your sample. Type it on a great-looking letterhead of your own design. Make your sample tie in with your cover letter by repeating a design element from your sample onto your letterhead. List some of your past clients within your letter.

Send artful invoices. After you complete assignments, a well-designed invoice (with one of your illustrations or designs strategically placed on it, of course) will make you look

PRINT AND MAIL THROUGH THE USPS

If you're looking for a convenient, time-saving, and versatile service for printing and mailing promotional postcards, consider the US Postal Service. USPS offers a postcard service through several partner sites. You can have promotional postcards printed in a variety of sizes and buy as many or as few as you need.

One drawback of going through the USPS and its partner sites is that you can't order extra postcards to keep on hand—cards must be addressed online and are mailed out for you automatically. But you can essentially create a personal database and simply click on an address and mail a promo card whenever needed. You can upload different images and create postcards that are geared to specific companies. (When you visit the site, click on "Create Greeting Cards & Postcards!" in the Shipping & Mailing section.)

professional and help art directors remember you—and hopefully think of you for another assignment.

Follow up with seasonal promotions. Many illustrators regularly send out holiday-themed promo cards. Holiday promotions build relationships while reminding past and potential clients of your services. It's a good idea to get out your calendar at the beginning of each year and plan some special promos for the year's holidays.

Are Portfolios Necessary?

You do not need to send a portfolio when you first contact a market. But after buyers see your samples they may want to see more, so have a portfolio ready to show. Many successful illustrators started their careers by making appointments to show their portfolios. But it is often enough for art directors to see your samples. Some markets in this book have drop-off policies, accepting portfolios one or two days a week. You will not be present for the review and can pick up the work a few days later, after they've had a chance to look at it. Since things can get lost, include only duplicates that can be insured at a reasonable cost. Only show originals when you can be present for the review. Label your portfolio with your name, address, and phone number.

Portfolio Pointers

The overall appearance of your portfolio affects your professional presentation. It need not be made of high-grade leather to leave a good impression. Neatness and careful organization are essential whether you're using a three-ring binder or a leather case. The most popular portfolios are simulated leather with puncture-proof sides that allow the inclusion of loose samples. Choose a size that can be handled easily. Avoid the large "student-size" books, which are too big to fit easily on an art director's desk. Most artists choose 11×14 or 18×24.

If you're a fine artist and your work is too large for a portfolio, bring a digital portfolio on a smartphone or tablet or a few small samples.

- **Don't include everything you've done in your portfolio.** Select only your best work, and choose pieces relevant to the company you are approaching. If you're showing your book to an ad agency, for example, don't include greeting card illustrations.
- **Show progressives.** In reviewing portfolios, art directors look for consistency of style and skill. They sometimes like to see work in different stages (roughs, comps, and finished pieces) to examine the progression of ideas and how you handle certain problems.
- **Your work should speak for itself.** It's best to keep explanations to a minimum and be available for questions if asked. Prepare for the review by taking along notes on each piece. If the buyer asks a question, take the opportunity to talk a little bit about the piece in question. Mention the budget, time frame, and any problems you faced and solved. If you're a fine artist, talk about how the piece fits into the evolution of a concept and how it relates to other pieces you've shown.
- **Leave a business card.** Don't ever walk out of a portfolio review without leaving the buyer a sample to remember you by. A few weeks after your review, follow up by sending a small promo postcard or other sample as a reminder.

FINE ARTISTS

Send a 9×12 envelope containing whatever materials galleries request in their submission guidelines. Usually that means a query letter, images, and résumé, but check each listing for specifics. Some galleries like to see more. Here's an overview of the various components you can include:

- **Digital images or slides.** Send eight to twelve digital images (JPEGs on a disk) or slides of similar work in a plastic slide sleeve (available at art supply stores). Slide submissions are less common these days, but, if you do submit slides, protect them by inserting slide sheets between two pieces of cardboard. Ideally, images should be taken by a professional photographer, but if you want to photograph them yourself, refer to *The Quick & Easy Guide to Photographing Your Artwork* by Roger Saddington (North Light Books). Label each image with your name, the title of the work, the medium, and the dimensions of the work. For slides, also include an arrow indicating the top of the slide. Include a list of titles and suggested prices gallery directors can refer to as they review the disk or slides. Make sure the list is in the same order as the images on the disk or the slides. Type your name, address, phone number, e-mail, and website at the top of the list. Don't send a variety of unrelated work. Send work that shows one style or direction.

- **Query letter or cover letter.** Type one or two paragraphs expressing your interest in showing at the gallery, and include a date and time when you will follow up.
- **Résumé or bio.** Your résumé should concentrate on your art-related experience. List any shows your work has been included in, with dates. A bio is a paragraph describing where you were born, your education, the work you do, and where you have shown in the past. (See "Building an Art Résumé" in the Articles & Interviews section for more information.)
- **Artist's statement.** Some galleries require a short statement about your work and the themes you're exploring. Your statement should show you have a sense of vision. It should also explain what you hope to convey in your work.
- **Portfolios.** Gallery directors sometimes ask to see your portfolio, but they can usually judge from your JPEGs or slides whether your work would be appropriate for their galleries. Never visit a gallery to show your portfolio without first setting up an appointment.
- **SASE.** If you need material returned to you, don't forget to include a SASE.

ART OF BUSINESS

Work Your Art

....

by Jen Cushman

There's a rampant stereotype that artists make poor business people. The archetype of the starving artist is so entrenched in our culture; it's one of the most popular recurring themes in literature and filmmaking. It may be romantic to watch a movie about a tortured, sensitive artist, but it's not so pleasant to see in real life. It's also a cop-out. It's easier to perpetuate this myth than it is to do the hard work it takes to create a successful art-based business.

What separates the aesthetics of art from the business of art is money. While business and passion make great bedfellows, money and emotions often run at odds. As artists, we use our emotions as fuel to birth our imagery. Because we pour so much of ourselves into our work, it's difficult to separate the process of making art from the end product—the piece itself—and to see that piece as a commodity to be sold.

It's much easier to throw in the towel and let someone else handle the dirty money stuff than it is to buck up and learn viable business and marketing skills. But your ability to make a living from your art is in your hands, no one else's. Yes, you can get an agent or sales rep or a marketing guru, but good people can be costly. You first have to make money to spend money, and you *can* do it. You. All by yourself.

You may have to spend more time reading business and marketing advice books than you do making art. You may feel stressed as weeks fly by while you're designing business cards or creating a mailing list, writing a blog, or setting up a website. It's all good. Every time you feel stressed, remind yourself that you're working to bust the myth of the starving artist. You're showing yourself and the world that being a creative professional also means having business savvy. The world needs artists and makers, and we need to remind the world that being an artist is a viable profession.

Your ability to make a living off your art is in your hands, no one else's.

Q: I'm successful at selling my work at craft fairs and festivals. I travel across the country and do lots of shows. It seems like at every show there are always one or two customers who like my work and really want to own a particular piece, but they always want to haggle on the price. Everything about these people screams that they have the cash to pay for it, but they just want a deal. What would you do?

A: Ahh, the deal seekers. These are the people who have money because they have the confidence to ask for what they want. But deal seekers are different from bargain hunters. Bargain hunters will choose Painting A over Painting B because of the $10 difference in the price tag, and are willing to settle for any painting of yours instead of *the* piece. Deal seekers are people who want Painting A, but want it for the same price as Painting B. They know that if you put a range of prices on your work to sell them—a smart marketing move on your part, by the way—everything you sell is potentially up for negotiation. Also, don't forget there are people in this world who truly enjoy the art of negotiation.

Here are a couple of helpful business tips: First, figure out if this potential customer is really a bargain hunter or a deal seeker. If you've got a bargain hunter, start talking about your work in a general way, and lead them to pieces in a lower price range. Feel flattered that your work is appreciated, and, depending on the level of enthusiasm, you will most likely make a sale. If this potential customer is a deal seeker, then your encounter can be as much about how you play the game as the value of the piece itself. Start talking about the piece and why it's one of your favorites, too. Ask the person what he sees in it, and what draws him to it. Is it the story? The color? Does it trigger a good memory? Once you engage in conversation, your intuition will kick in and you'll be able to decide if the deal hunter truly feels a connection with your piece, and could potentially be a repeat customer. Then you'll know whether to cut

Jewelry and photos by Jen Cushman.

a slight deal, or hold firm on your price. Whatever you decide, own it. Don't second-guess yourself. It's your work and you decide its market value.

Q: I teach classes in my home studio, so teaching is part of my DNA. How do I begin teaching at retreats or conferences?

A: There are good artists and then there are good teachers, but they do not always go hand-in-hand. In my experience, the best teachers are the ones who deep down want their students to be successful, and feel as though it's part of their calling to see them thrive. It's terrific that you want to inspire others to succeed.

Building a successful teaching career is not as simple as hopping a plane to your next gig. Think of it more long term, like ripples on a pond.

If you're teaching in your home studio, how about branching out into your community? Approach a local art store or gallery and talk to the owners or managers. Be respectful of their time and ask for an appointment, rather than ambushing them with your portfolio. Show up to the appointment as if it were a job interview (because it is) and be ready to discuss your ideas. Approach it as a collaboration; they want to offer services to their customers, and you want to be of service.

In the end, successful classes are all about an exchange of positive energy and new ideas. Build your confidence and clientele first in your community and you'll soon find opportunities coming your way for bigger gigs. I'm a believer in being a big fish in your small pond first before jumping too soon to another pond where you might wind up feeling like bait.

Jen Cushman is a former journalist who found mixed-media art 14 years ago and never looked back. She's the author of *Making Metal Jewelry; How to Stamp, Forge, Fold and Form Metal Jewelry Designs* and *Explore, Create, Resinate: Mixed Media Techniques Using ICE Resin*. Jen writes the Mixed-Media Metalsmith column for *Cloth Paper Scissors* and teaches at CREATE Mixed-Media Retreats and at other national and international venues. She's also Vice President/Partner of Susan Lenart Kazmer LLC/ICE Resin. jencushman.com and jencushman.wordpress.com.

Excerpted from the winter 2015 issue of *Artists & Makers*. Used with the kind permission of *Artist's & Makers*, a publication of F+W, a Content + eCommerce Company.

THE SOCIAL LIFE

Working the Network

....

by Grace Dobush

The business of handmade has changed immensely in the last decade. Along with the amazing e-commerce options available, it's easier than ever for makers to reach their audiences. A well-crafted social media presence has the potential to reach customers around the world and blow up your sales. But using social media for sales or networking is quite different from personal pursuits. Not fluent in Facebook, trending on Twitter, or #instafamous on Instagram yet where your business is concerned? With these do's and don'ts, you can be.

Be Authentic

Although platforms such as Facebook have been around for years, I still get questions from creative entrepreneurs about how to share aspects of their lives on social media. Makers put themselves into every product they create, so by default we are our own brands. It's generally a good idea to keep your professional accounts separate from your personal accounts, but you still want to let your personality shine in everything you post. When promoting your handmade business on social media, the rule of thumb is to present your best self, keeping posts positive and attractive. But I also believe in keeping it real. You totally dropped that wet painting you just finished? Instagram it.

Don't Just Sell

The most common mistake I see newbies make is using social media networks as the T-shirt cannons of shop promos. While you certainly should tell your fans about new items and hot sales, those pure marketing posts aren't what create loyalty and inspire repeat customers. Your fans want to see your personality, what inspires you, and what you're working on. Follow other artists and makers you admire—the list of people you follow should reflect your taste. Get into conversations on the artistic life, like Oh My Handmade Goodness's perpetual #omhg Twitter chat. You'll likely get questions and feedback on any social network you have an account with, and customers expect you to respond promptly. Remember always: The social conversation is a two-way street.

Do Let Photos Do the Talking

If a picture is worth a thousand words, a well-done Instagram post is definitely worth at least 140 characters. Most humans are visual creatures; when it comes down to it, we just want to look at appealing things. So, if writing isn't your strength, this is great news: You could show off time-lapsed videos of works in progress, sneak peeks at new projects, a studio tour of your workspace, or a #shamestagram of your crazy craft supply closet.

Use social media to show off your latest projects.

Don't Market Just to Other Creatives

Unless your whole jam is selling to creative types, you need to reach beyond a realm like the Etsy bubble for your marketing efforts to get real results. You need to know who your customers and biggest fans are to know how to reach them. (For more on this, I highly recommend using my Profiling Your Most Valuable Customers worksheet from my book, *The Crafty Superstar Ultimate Craft Business Guide*.)

Do Focus on the Networks Where Your Fans Are

Whenever someone asks me which social networks are the best for artists and makers to be on, my answer is always this: wherever your target market is. For someone who peddles geeky plush, that could be Reddit. For a fashion-forward accessories maker, it'd be Instagram for sure. Creating accounts on Twitter and Facebook is generally a given, but if your audience prefers one over the other, focus on that one. When a new social network starts up, I like to join and preemptively reserve my standard username, just in case it becomes the next big thing.

Your fans want to see your personality, what inspires you, and what you're working on.

Don't Let Your Accounts Languish

How frequently you should post is determined by many factors: how many fans you have, what platforms they're using, what kind of work you do, and how much time you have. But generally speaking, you shouldn't let a week go by without a new post to each network you're on. One well-crafted post per day on a Facebook brand page might be enough for your needs, but on Twitter it makes more sense to post messages and replies throughout the day.

Do Work Smarter, Not Harder

Many tools exist to make managing your business's social media accounts easier. My personal favorite is Hootsuite (hootsuite.com), which lets you schedule posts, set up custom searches, and manage multiple accounts. Buffer (bufferapp.com) is another good one: You write the posts and Buffer sends them out at intervals you specify. You could set up a week's worth of social posts in just an hour or two every Sunday evening, with daily checks on the networks to see what's happening and reserving time to reply to new posts.

Use analytics in Hootsuite, Google, WordPress, or Etsy to gauge the results of your efforts, and give yourself a hand for a job well done.

Grace Dobush is the author of The Crafty Superstar craft business books and organizes Cincinnati's Crafty Supermarket. She has written for publications including *Wired*, *Print*, *HOW*, and *Cincinnati Magazine*.

Excerpted from the winter 2015 issue of *Artists & Makers*. Used with the kind permission of *Artist's & Makers*, a publication of F+W, a Content + eCommerce Company.

SELLING WITHOUT BEGGING

by David C. Baker

Forget cold-calling—reel in the clients you really want with these six practical techniques.

The problem is clear: You need more business. Not because you aren't busy, but because then you could be choosier about which clients you work with. But if there's one thing firm owners and entrepreneurs hate, it has to be selling themselves to prospects. Selling feels uncomfortable, needy, and it also seems like something we probably shouldn't have to do, right? If our work is great, shouldn't it sell itself?

I want to help you by explaining some ways to attract more business without begging for it. First, I'm going to assume that you're really talented. That's an important assumption. Unless you're an expert in something where there aren't a lot of other experts, clients will find you interchangeable, and when they have a lot of choices, they'll dive down to the cheapest option. Second, you need work, but you don't want to harm your carefully earned position as an expert. That means you need thoughtfully chosen and very effective methods of finding new clients. Here are six ways to reach prospects while keeping your expert status.

1. Send a Letter by Express Mail.

In the past, any letter you sent blended into all the other letters that a prospective client received, and so you had to resort to flashy and expensive brochures instead. But now, nobody gets letters, so they stand out. They're also quick and cheap, which makes them an even better choice.

Sit down and write a really good one, highlighting what helps you stand out from the crowd. Make it punchy (i.e., confident), but keep it short. About two-thirds of a page is ideal.

Next, find about fifty prospects to send it to. You might start with clients who work at a competitor to a client you just lost because those are the ones most likely to be intrigued by the chance to hire you. Then, concentrate on the companies where you know someone or have something that you could mention in the letter. Or maybe think of a place with a mission or work that ignites so much passion in you that the prospect will be drawn to that enthusiasm.

Now here's the trick: Send it by FedEx Express Saver or USPS Priority Mail to fifty contacts. First, no one throws a letter away that's delivered by an express service. Second, it's easier to get past a gatekeeper if you can say that you're calling to follow up on an express shipment. "May I ask what this is about, please?" now has a good answer: "I'm calling to follow up on a FedEx that I sent to her last week." Expect at least one nice project from this technique.

2. Put Paid Advertising on LinkedIn.

LinkedIn has become the digital water cooler among the next generation of decision-makers, and it's surprisingly easy to post messages on the bulletin board hanging above that water cooler. This often underutilized tool is a breeding ground for professionals looking to connect with practitioners who possess the skills they need for a particular project.

Once your profile is established, you need to promote your services and skills. Under your profile picture, use the pull-down menu to manage your "Advertising." Then select "Create New Campaign." From there, you can choose to create an ad or sponsor your content. If you've written a blog post that you think might get some traction with just a little help, choose that route. The content you've written that's most likely to help you get work is the kind that has a clear point of view. So don't aim to softly inform your readers, but rather aim to take a stand on something so that your prospect is almost required to agree or disagree with you. (Not everyone agrees with experts.)

Either way, target your promotion using these rules of thumb. Set aside about $25/week, and agree to pay $1–$2/click. LinkedIn will push you to pay more, but resist—you'll get plenty of clicks without dishing out more cash.

Think about how succinctly you can word your ad, because you get only 75 characters. Use an image (like your logo or a piece of compelling work you've done) to create a visual hook. Be sure to "collect leads"—it doesn't cost any more—so that prospects can request more information right then and there, delivering the request to your inbox.

Target the ad to your specific industry, and narrow your audience further by selecting an age range, seniority ranking (such as a job title) and geography. And here's the kicker: You can make the ad appear only to those who work for the specific companies you're targeting. Think about correlating this campaign with the express mail strategy, so prospects will receive your letter and then see your ad on LinkedIn and request more information. You'll get ten to twenty leads per week with this method, and you can expect to have a conversation with at least one of them.

3. Host a Webinar.

Online education webinars are very effective tools because they don't require travel, they can be watched on demand and there's none of the financial risk that comes from holding a seminar. Mostly, there's no risk of failure. Let's dive into this last point a bit more, as it's the secret sauce to this tool.

Contrast a webinar with a speaking engagement. For the latter, you'll spend months landing one and preparing for it. That big day will come—but what if you end up with three people in attendance? First of all, those numbers don't work. Most important, it looks like you've failed. The few people there look around and then wonder how much of an expert you really are. But now think of a webinar, where you can choose to hide the list of attendees from your prospects. Unless you tell them otherwise, they'll assume that there are dozens of others who are listening and learning.

I'd recommend you use GoToWebinar for this and keep it short: about 40 minutes long, using the rest of the hour for a question-and-answer session, in which attendees will type their questions into a box within the program. Have someone help you as a "guest presenter," pitching the questions to you: "John, we have a question from Lucy, who wants to know what elements are most interesting to teenage buyers these days." Write a few questions out for yourself in case the audience is slow to ask them. That will help you avoid awkward pauses.

GoToWebinar also allows you to record your presentation, syncing the slides with your voice. When you finish the webinar, it'll convert the recording into a file you can post. That will be even more content for your website, and it will give prospects a way to learn more about how you think. You can even transcribe your presentation at sites like www.rev.com and then post it as a downloadable PDF.

Practice, practice, practice, though, because talking to a "nonexistent audience"—which is what it feels like—can be very disorienting at first. One key is to over-deliver enthusiasm while you work hard to picture one very engaged attendee. Slow down, too, because there's something about doing a webinar that will tempt you to speak rapidly. Who do you invite? Round people up through your letter, your ad or a list—which is what we'll cover next.

4. Buy a List.

If you already have a subscriber list with at least 8,000 names of people who have opted-in to receive your e-mails, that should do it. Any quantity below that should grow on a net basis from e-mailing to e-mailing, but reaching a critical mass of that size organically will take too long if you need some quick hits, and that's when you buy a list. Keep in mind that the more data fields that come with each record, the better, but what matters most is getting a current e-mail address.

There are three places to look for good e-mail addresses for your own marketing purposes, and you want to do a search in this order. First, check with any associations that might gather your prospects. The Encyclopedia of Associations is a good place to double-check your knowledge and see if you've overlooked any. That source will also indicate how many members each association has and whether or not they make their list available for purchase.

The second place to check is www.thelistinc.com, a professional research service in Atlanta that does the hard work for you, verifying each name on the lists they sell every four months. Call them up and see if they can help. The third place is www.data.com, a more generalized list broker where you can buy from scratch, or just have them fill in any missing data for partial records you already have.

Once you get a list, set up your own marketing automation platform, ideally using software or a service such as Pardot, HubSpot or Act-On. But you can keep it simpler and cheaper with an e-mail marketing provider. My favorite is Campaign Monitor or MailChimp, but there are many viable platforms. There are no issues with the legality of this approach, either. The CAN-SPAM Act merely requires that there be a reasonable expectation that the recipient would be interested in what you send them and that there is a simple means to unsubscribe. From a best practices standpoint, avoid selling and give the recipient value instead. That means avoiding anything that might be construed as a newsletter. Prospects don't care about case studies or seeing work you're doing. Talk about what interests them and leave yourself out of the conversation.

When it comes to getting along with your e-mail marketing provider, remember to avoid doing things that will make them hate you. For example, when you do things that blacklist their e-mail servers, it affects their entire client base. And they won't hesitate to dump you on the street, regardless of whether your action violates any law.

Once your list has significant mass, and if you're doing this right, expect an unsubscribe rate of less than 0.5% per mailing, no more than one spam complaint per 4,000 records addressed, a soft bounce rate of less than 4% and an open rate of at least 30%.

5. Be Interviewed as an Expert.

Scour the free Help a Reporter Out website (www.helpareporter.com) and make yourself available for expert interviews. The signal-to-noise ratio is a little distracting, though, and you might be better off spending a little money and subscribing to the ProfNet service. It's Help a Reporter Out on steroids. It's curated, simpler, and collects more serious journalists.

If you have a good profile and your answers are well-written, you can expect one interview per month, based on about four times that many responses. Each day you'll receive 150–300 interview requests through several e-mails. Quickly eliminate the ones that don't apply to your focus and isolate one or two that might be worth contacting. Don't spend any more than 30 minutes in total every week. Prospects will learn about you in a respected, peer-reviewed manner, and some of them will reach out for help to this expert they've just learned about.

6. Write a Short E-Book.

Apple has a product called QuickReads, and Amazon has matched it with their Kindle Singles. The two products are nearly identical: 5,000–30,000 words, with a mandated low price. It's a wonderful tool in selling your services because it gives you a reason to contact a prospect by including a gift certificate to the book. Regardless of whether or not they read it, they'll be left with a suitable impression.

The topic should be something you'd expect from an expert, and not poorly disguised self-promotion. (However, the cover can be an opportunity to showcase your design skills.) Give away great thinking that isn't personalized for the prospect, and then charge big fees when you do apply your experience to a specific client. If you're starting from scratch, you should be able to write 5,000 words in one week. Chances are, though, you already have that much content in the can and it just needs some skillful editing.

There you have it. You need new clients, you need them quick, and you don't want to beg. So, pick two or three of these six suggestions and get busy. I bet you're pretty good at landing work once you get a chance to talk to a prospect, right? You just need more opportunity, and this list is designed to give you just that.

David C. Baker has been an author, speaker and adviser to the creative community for 20 years, and has worked closely with nearly 800 firms. His blog is read by 20,000 designers. www.recourses.com

Excerpted from the November 2014 issue of *HOW* magazine. Used with the kind permission of *HOW* magazine, a publication of F+W, a Content + eCommerce Company. Visit www.howdesign.com to subscribe.

MICRO FUNDING FOR MACRO DREAMS

by Sean J. Miller

Micro grants and grass-roots funding programs are helping artists and makers achieve success.

Amy Peterson and Diana Russell walked into the Jam Handy building in Detroit, Michigan, last summer ready to pitch an idea to potential investors. The friends wanted to start a jewelry business called Rebel Nell, and employ women transitioning from homelessness. "We wanted the jewelry to be teachable," Peterson says, "and we wanted to have complete creative input from the women so they could be really, truly the designers."

As more artists look for ways to turn their passions into profit, they're also looking for viable ways to finance their dreams. Today, getting a business loan or seed money to launch something like a small artisan jewelry company isn't as difficult as it used to be, thanks to a growing cultural shift toward appreciation of local and small over global and corporate. That appreciation isn't just happening among consumers, but among lenders and investors as well.

But a small creative enterprise is a different animal when it comes to capital, says Stephen Marotta, a researcher at Portland State University in Oregon. "It isn't like in the past when you drew up a business plan, went into a bank, and either came out with a smile on your face or pounded your fists in the sand."

Sure, you can fund your business by building a Kickstarter campaign or dipping into your 401(k), or begging mom and dad for a loan. Among other options now available are programs such as the partnership of ArtHome and Project Enterprise in New York City. This innovative setup offers business training and a peer-lending program for local, low-income artists, with loans ranging from $1,500 to $12,000.

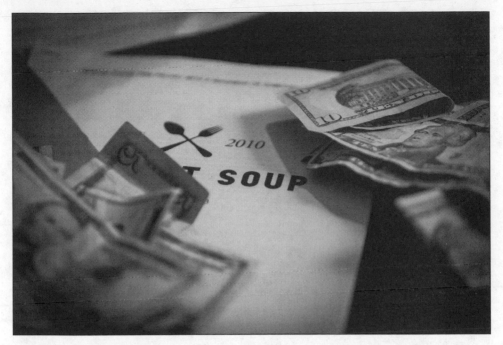

"It's not just about getting access to capital, it's also about getting a plan for a sustainable business," says Esther Robinson, founder of ArtHome. Photo by David Lewinski.

In the case of Peterson and Russell, without a small business track record the pair wasn't able to approach traditional funding sources like banks, foundations, or government agencies. Detroit, though, is one of the cities at the forefront of a shift away from the traditional funding model for artisans, artists, and social entrepreneurs.

Detroit SOUP, for example, offers micro grants for local creative and community projects. The money comes from fundraising dinners that Detroit SOUP hosts. But there's no high ticket price here—for just five dollars guests can judge presenters and award a grant. Peterson and Russell pitched their company at a July 2013 dinner, keeping their presentation light and making people laugh. When it came time to vote on the awardee, Rebel Nell received almost $1,500.

Peterson and Russell used the money to buy silver—the base metal for their jewelry— and then sold their first pieces for a $6,500 profit at a local market. "That money is really what we credit for being the catalyst for starting Rebel Nell," Peterson says.

Amy Kaherl, Detroit SOUP's director, said the group has awarded more than $75,000 to artists, craftspeople, and social entrepreneurs since it was founded five years ago. The micro grants range from $700 to $3,000, depending on the attendance at the dinner.

At Detroit SOUP, a pitch is attended by potential investors. Photo by David Lewinski.

"This is for people who have ideas but need some initial funding," says Kaherl. "There are only two rules: [The business] has to be within the city, and you cannot use technology to present."

The concept for Detroit SOUP originated in Chicago and is now spreading around the country and internationally. Kaherl says she's helped similar organizations get off the ground in cities such as Columbus, Ohio; Dublin, Ireland; and London, England.

Women work on jewelry designs at Rebel Nell. Photo by Sebastian Sullen.

Marotta, the researcher who has been exploring funding sources in Portland's artisan economy, says he's beginning to see artists and makers benefit from the kind of angel investors that launched Silicon Valley start-ups. He recently attended a small gathering of artisans to which an angel investor also came. "It's kind of like a loan officer going out into the community," he says.

As the artisan economy offers options to corporate-driven consumerism, it's also driving the creation of alternatives to traditional banking practices. Crowd funding lenders such as Kiva Zip put lenders and borrowers in direct contact. Moreover, loans are interest free up to $5,000.

To be sure, money may solve some of an artist's problems, but not all. In many cases they need the financial literacy and industrial acumen necessary to grow and expand an enterprise.

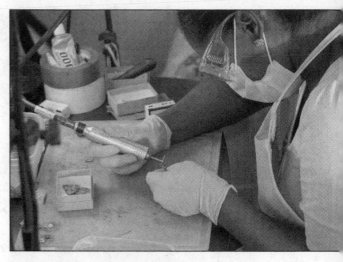

Photo by Sebastian Sullen.

"You really do need a business plan that has research and thought behind it," says Esther Robinson, founder of ArtHome, an entrepreneurial non-profit that works with artists and artisans.

ArtHome runs a program that matches the personal savings of low-income artists up to $2,000, but requires participants to take business classes. "It's not just about getting access to capital, it's also about getting a plan for a sustainable business," she says. For many participants there are "translation issues" when it comes to turning art into commerce. "There's somewhat of a disconnect with the language of commerce," she says.

A savings program is meant to help artists and artisans overcome one of the greatest challenges their businesses may face: variable income. "You need to learn how to save if your work is seasonal," Robinson says.

ArtHome founder Esther Robinson leads a personal finance bootcamp. Photo by Michelle Proffit.

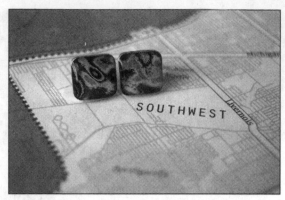

The jewelry Rebel Nell produces is made from repurposed graffiti. Photos by Amy Peterson.

Don't be surprised, Marotta says, if larger corporations start moving in on the micro financing trend, especially since it doesn't take much to fund an artisanal start up. "We've done some preliminary research on a maker's collective in East Portland, Oregon. A good chunk of them [operate] below $20,000," he says. "But there's collective power in these small numbers."

Back in Detroit, Peterson and Russell are ready for a busy holiday season. They plan to hire two more women by the end of the year to add to their three-person team of creative designers. "In the big scheme of loans and grants it's not that much," Peterson says of the $1,500 they received from SOUP. "But to us, that was the most important money we received, because at the time we were just an idea. It was a wonderful confirmation."

Sean J. Miller is a journalist and playwright based in Los Angeles, CA.

Excerpted from the winter 2015 issue of *Artists & Makers*. Used with the kind permission of *Artists & Makers*, a publication of F+W, a Content + eCommerce Company.

KICK START YOUR DREAM

Turn Your Goal of Publishing a Book Into a Reality

by Deborah Secor

A few years ago, you may never have even heard of the term *crowdfunding*; now the word seems almost ubiquitous. The concept of crowdfunding is quite simple:

A *crowd* of people *fund* your project. And, when executed thoughtfully, it can work. In a truly democratic manner, online-fundraising websites provide the means for an entrepreneur to engage with people from all over the world. Open to all kinds of ventures, this approach to financing especially may appeal to a creative mind-set. However, like any innovative endeavor, success comes only with careful thought and planning, and an investment of time, rather than a seat-of-the-pants approach.

Kickstarter, Indiegogo, GoFundMe and other crowdfunding websites provide a platform through which an artist may present a project idea to the world. These sites offer guidelines and campaign approval, and typically deduct a single-digit percentage from the total funds collected, but individuals set their own financial goals. The results depend on how much the project appeals to people who view the campaign page and pledge to support the plan.

On some crowdfunding sites, projects are required to reach the funding goal to receive the money, while other sites allow the entrepreneur to receive any money raised, regardless of whether the funding goal is met. To attract sponsors, the campaign can offer rewards; for an art project, for example, it might be anything from a $1 bookmark to an original painting worth thousands. Both artist and backer benefit.

Funding Her Dream

For years Tijeras, New Mexico, pastelist Nance McManus had hoped to produce a limited, signed edition of a book containing her paintings and charcoal drawings of birds. "I always wanted the credibility of publishing a monograph representing my work," she says, but due to the up-front investment needed, she put off the idea.

Intrigued with the possibility of crowdfunding the cost, McManus decided in 2012 to try a Kickstarter campaign. "I did three months of research before I actually started," she explains. "I think one of the biggest misconceptions people have is that crowdfunding means 'free money.' They have no idea how hard it is to pull off. This kind of project takes hard work, organization and follow-through. For about five months, it absorbed a lot of my time."

McManus' Kickstarter campaign officially lasted 17 days, and the response from her collectors, friends and people from around the world stunned her. "It only took 22 hours to reach my original $4,000 goal, which was mind-boggling. I was impressed with how well it paid off," she says, noting that she received pledges for a total of $5,176 from forty-seven backers.

Project Management

As in any fundraising effort, the planning is fundamental. The first step for McManus' Kickstarter venture was locating a publisher for the book and determining her costs. "I wanted a United States printer who could do a hardbound book with proper binding, using a spine, not staples." She decided on Bookmasters in Ashland, Ohio, and determined she could do her own design with layout and proofreading assistance from two friends. She asked a good friend, Stephen Bodio, to write the foreword.

Another vital campaign element was the written description that would introduce the concept, set her funding goal and offer incentive rewards to prospective backers. "I soaked up everything that Kickstarter had to offer in the way of advice and guidance, and looked at many projects that had failed as well as those that succeeded, to get ideas of funding levels and rewards," McManus says. "It was hard to figure out how much money I needed, in part because it's an international platform. I had to add some cushion that would cover the cost of possibly sending two hundred books to Europe, for instance."

To decide on the timeline, McManus had to consider countless time-consuming details. "I figured out the length of time I thought it would take and added a month to my shipping estimate," she says. "You have to build in extra time. It had taken me three weeks just to find the right shipping boxes for the book, posters and prints, and to locate archival bags for the book. Even things like driving to the post office could end up taking half a day and had to be included."

To attract maximum attention to her project, McManus made a video that visually presented the book and its contents to viewers on her campaign page. She kept things simple, showing herself painting at the easel with a live bird as her subject, as well as presenting a mockup of the 6×9-inch book, with a voice-over explaining the concept. "I knew that I had no more than nine seconds to get people interested," she says. Her husband served as videographer, filming over her shoulder as she turned pages. "I thought that would give people

Snowy Egret (20x20) is one of the paintings Nance McManus published in her crowdfunded book, *Pastel Passion: Birds*

a feel for the relative size of the book. I think a lot of people watched the video without investing, which was also good promotion."

Connecting With Backers

As a first-level reward for backers, McManus chose to offer anyone donating $25 a copy of the book with their names included on a thank-you page. There were several other reward levels that included posters and gicleé prints of various bird paintings. "I also offered three tiers of $1,000 each that included original paintings," McManus says. "That was less than the paintings sold for in galleries, so my collectors jumped on them, which helped lend credibility to the project."

Although she completed a good portion of the research before committing to the campaign, the bulk of the work came afterward. The job of updating backers on the progress of the campaign, as things unfolded, demanded a lot of time. She explains that many of the books sold to people who wanted to give a gift with a friend's name included on the contributors' page. "A woman from Denmark kept ordering more books and adding her friends' names," says McManus. "The book itself was ready, but I couldn't print it until I had all the names. That added about three weeks to the lead time."

Posters and prints were ready to ship before the book was printed. "I sent them out immediately, even without the book, which assured people that things were moving along," she says. "There's a way to update all your backers simultaneously at Kickstarter, which I used twice, but I e-mailed or called most of them personally." Even with setbacks, the book and other rewards were all shipped to her supporters within a month of the original deadline.

Enthused about the idea of the book from the beginning, McManus says the fact that she had actually succeeded in self-publishing a book finally sunk in one day as she signed the inside front cover of book one hundred. "This turned out to be just about the hardest thing I've ever done in my life," she says with a smile, "but if you're prepared to give it 110 percent and understand the need for commitment and organization, I highly recommend the process. It was very rewarding to use crowdfunding, and it's even more rewarding to have the book in my hand."

Deborah Secor (www.deborahsecor.com) is a columnist for *Pastel Journal*.

Excerpted from the February 2014 issue of *Pastel Journal*. Used with the kind permission of *Pastel Journal*, a publication of F+W, a Content + eCommerce Company.

PAYMENT OPTIONS

How to Accept Payment for Your Work

....

by Daniel Grant

At Sam's Club, members have a range of options to pay for their purchases, from cash and checks to credit and debit cards and even food stamps. Wal-Mart adds PayPal to the mix, and the California Department of Motor Vehicles notes its willingness to accept money orders and e-checks. A buyer comes into your studio or booth ready to make a purchase: What are you willing to accept?

Perhaps, the best answer is most of the above. "You want to make it as easy as possible for people to pay you," said Dr. William Osgood, director of the Knowledge Institute in Exeter, New Hampshire, which provides counseling for small business development. Let's consider the advantages and disadvantages of some of the payment options available.

Cash

Cash has obvious advantages. Unlike checks and credit card payments, it doesn't need any time to "clear," and there is no 2–4 percent service charge for the vendor to pay to a middle-man, as exist with credit cards and PayPal. In fact, vendors might have reason to encourage prospective buyers to pay in cash by offering a small discount. Still, as a practical matter, most people do not carry large amounts of cash on them for the same reason that vendors might be reluctant to be paid with large amounts of cash—they make themselves a potential target for thieves.

Money orders and certified checks are as close to actual cash as one may get, and some people use them to pay for purchases through the mail. A benefit of these types of payment for the buyer is that they do not contain any personal information (home address or telephone number). For the vendor, the benefit is a type of check that cannot bounce. Both money orders and certified checks are available through post offices and banks, and the principal

Cash may be king, but you and your customers may not want to keep large sums on hand.

difference between them is that money orders are written for specific amounts—say, $200 or $1,000—while certified checks may be for any amount (e.g., $126.27). There have been rare instances of counterfeit postal money orders, and they may not be accepted if damaged in the mail (e.g., if the routing number on the bottom of the money order cannot be read by a processing machine). The process of getting the bank or post office to issue a replacement is neither quick nor assured. In any case, it is very unlikely that someone entering your booth or studio will pay for anything by this method.

Personal Checks

Personal checks continue to be an option, although a declining number of people pay for their purchases this way these days, due to the ubiquity of credit cards. The benefit of a personal check is that, just like cash, they do not require the vendor to concede some percent of the payment to a middleman. Hanging over a check, however, is the potential that the buyer's bank account has insufficient funds, which would be discovered only after the purchased object has been taken and the check has been returned (five to ten business days later). A number of craftspeople in Minnesota had this experience when an elderly woman attended a number of crafts fairs, purchasing items with checks that did not clear. As one jeweler wrote on the ArtFairInsiders forum page, "I live in Florida and, after spending considerably more time on it than the amount was worth, have found that I can't attempt to collect on it without returning to Minnesota and taking her to conciliation court, where the filing fee is far higher than the amount of the check." Her comment named the individual, recommending that others not accept checks from her.

Publicly outing someone who writes bad checks may help the next person who interacts with her or make you feel slightly avenged, or it may open you up to a charge of defamation and the likely loss of this person as a future customer. Perhaps there was no scam intended, since the elderly woman might be suffering from dementia or her direct-deposit Social Security check was late.

There are other recourses for artists and craftspeople, including requiring those wishing to pay with a check to provide a telephone number (if it isn't preprinted on the check) and present a driver's license (write down the license number on the back of the check) in order to confirm his or her address and identity. If the check is returned, you will have a means of contacting the buyer to explain the problem and get it resolved amicably. If a telephone call doesn't work, artists might send a certified letter that restates what was requested over the phone, or contact the customer's bank to see if his or her account now has sufficient funds to cover the check—the bank may agree to collect the amount from that person's account following the next deposit, transferring the money to you. Another option is taking the individual to court or hiring a collection agency. Two final options include not delivering the purchased item until the check has cleared or not taking checks at all.

Debit Cards and E-Checks

Debit cards tend to be accepted at most of the same places that take credit cards, and the main difference between them and credit cards is where the money comes from. Using a credit card is a form of borrowing money, while debit cards draw directly from the purchaser's bank account. Vendors who receive authorization to accept debit cards can find out immediately if the buyer has the money to pay for the purchase, and the bank would put a hold on that amount of money in the account. Presumably, that should protect buyers and sellers, since no one would be able to spend money he or she doesn't have in the bank. The only problem in the system is that the process of transferring money from one bank account to the other may take a few days, during which time the "hold" has elapsed and the buyer may no longer have sufficient funds to cover the purchase. That doesn't happen often, but it has occurred.

E-checks are a paperless form of payment made online or over the telephone and are becoming more popular among people who don't have credit cards or are reluctant to use them. Similar to a debit card, the e-check taps one's checking account directly. Buyers supply the name of their bank, the name on their account, the account number and routing number, as well as the amount of the purchase. And the advantage for vendors is that payment is assured (otherwise, the check bounces immediately). The only drawback for vendors is that, similar to accepting credit cards, they must apply to and be accepted by an e-check processing service, paying an initial set-up fee ($100 is standard), monthly user fees ($20) and transaction fees, and there may be other optional or required fees, such as fraud detection and a chargeback fund. Vendors also may be required to purchase special payment processors.

Credit Cards

There are many different types of credit cards, including MasterCard and Visa, that are bank-issued and underwritten by these companies. Discover and Capital One as well as Diner's Club and American Express are charge cards. Too accept charge cards as payment, vendors must obtain a merchant services account,

Visa and MasterCard are credit cards, while Discover and American Express are charge cards.

which involves a range of set-up fees, the acquisition of a credit card terminal, transaction fees (the percentage of the purchase price that the company takes, plus a flat per-purchase cost), authorization fees (a charge for each time the company authorizes a transaction), statement fees, annual or monthly fees (the cost of having an account), monthly minimum fees (an additional cost if the amount of charges does not reach a certain amount) and charge-back fees (for reimbursing the buyer if there is a return).

American Express and Discover tend to be accepted by fewer businesses than MasterCard and Visa because the transaction fees are higher, sometimes as much as 4 percent as compared to the 1–2.5 percent that the bank-issued cards generally charge, which cuts down on a vendor's profits. Those merchants simply have to hope that the buyer has more than one type of card or some other way of paying.

Online Payments

PayPal (and other, similar companies) is quickly becoming a preferred way for consumers to make purchases online, though, just as with every other option, there are benefits and drawbacks. The largest benefit is that it is easy for buyers to use, paying for items with their credit cards or e-checks, and setting up a PayPal payment option on a vendor's website (with buttons for single purchases or a shopping cart) is quick and uncomplicated. What's more, customers may be familiar with PayPal already through purchases from eBay or Amazon, which adds to their comfort level.

There are no set-up fees for vendors setting up merchant accounts with PayPal, but it takes four business days for funds to be deposited into one's account, which is a bit slow. Vendors still may find the costs of being a PayPal merchant to be high, with monthly fees of up to $30 and transaction fees of 2.9 percent in addition to 30 cents for debit and credit card purchases. Even more costly are returns with chargeback fees of $20 (and PayPal will still retain its 2.9 percent transaction fee). As with many other online services, contacting an actual person at PayPal's customer service department about problems you may be experiencing is not easy.

Bitcoin is now accepted at a variety of online retailers including Etsy and Overstock.com.

With both e-checks and PayPal, the monthly costs of being able to use these payment systems may begin to bite if buyers don't want to make purchases in this way, or they do so rarely. Spending hundreds of dollars per year to enable just a few small sales may make the convenience unprofitable.

Bitcoin

In its short history of existence, the nontangible Internet currency bitcoin has earned an uneven reputation, but increasingly this "cryptocurrency" has gained legitimacy and is being used in a variety of online stores, such as at Etsy and Overstock.com. Will artwork and other collectibles be next? Perhaps. Burning Man, the nonprofit summer arts festival based in California, began accepting bitcoin donations in late 2014, and a number of online exhibition sites (cointemporary.com, btcartgallery.com, bitdazzle.com/art, art4bitcoin.net and bitpremier.com/4-fine-art-antiques) accept this form of currency.

So far, artists who have had their work displayed on bitcoin-accepting online galleries have not been disappointed at the experience, even if nothing has sold. "I like the idea of trading in bitcoins as it has parallels with the speculative nature of the art market," said Marita Fraser, a Viennese artist who showed a 2014 painting titled O.T. (priced at 3.5 bitcoin) on Cointemporary. She concluded, "I see trading art in bitcoins as an interesting experiment, and an art project within itself, which calls into question the value of things in the world and different kinds of exchange." On the other hand, British sketch artist Oli Witcomb claimed that he has sold two drawings on art4bitcoin.net, and "I've had a few donations."

Bitcoin, which was first created in 2009, is referred to as a "cryptocurrency," a form of money based not on the value of gold or other currencies but on computer code that controls the creation of new units and their transfer from one computer user to another. Banks and governments are not involved in the production or movement of new bitcoin (the U.S. Treasury refers to bitcoin as a "decentralized currency"), and "payments are processed almost instantly, with close to zero fees," according to Valentin Ruhry, one of Cointemporary's directors. Online exchange agencies convert bitcoin to dollars or other currencies on the basis of the current exchange rate, which has ranged from $160 to $1,200 per bitcoin.

The volatility in the exchange rate and the fact that banks have declined deposits of bitcoin into accounts has been discouraging for Orlando, Florida, painter Alex Vera whose payment for a single sale is "still stored in my digital wallet." However, he noted that "bitcoin could make huge gains again in value and would pay off once it is accepted everywhere."

The mainstream art selling businesses have tended to shy away from bitcoin. However, the tech world has become more comfortable with bitcoin's legitimacy. In December 2014, Microsoft began to accept bitcoin for buyers of Windows Phone, Xbox Music, Xbox Video, apps, games and other company products, following a similar move by both Apple and Dell in June 2014. The King's College, a liberal arts Christian college in Manhattan's financial district, began accepting bitcoin as tuition in 2013.

The subject of money often makes artists uneasy. How much should they charge for their work? Should they offer or agree to discounts? And then, when the sale is about to take place, comes the issue of what kind of money to accept. Every form of currency brings with it some form of anxiety, and artists need to select from this smorgasbord of options what makes them feel most secure and satisfies their buyers.

Daniel Grant is the author of several books including *The Business of Being an Artist* and *The Fine Artist's Career Guide* (Skyhorse Publishing).

SLOW DOWN TO GO FAST

by Peleg Top

Tackling everything at lightning speed can actually stifle a designer's most valuable asset: her creativity. Learn how going slower will help you achieve a clear mind and put you on the path to true productivity.

I suspect that at the start of your day, the first thing you do is reach for your phone. You might even do this before you get out of bed. From the moment your eyes open, the input begins. E-mail, Facebook, Twitter, texting, newsfeed—all pouring in like an electronic fire-hose aimed at your brain. From daybreak to sunset, it's a nonstop, get-it-done overload. It started in the 1980s when FedEx changed everything by introducing overnight delivery. Soon thereafter, fax machines came along, followed by e-mail and now smartphones. We've been spoiled. We're used to immediate results and, in return, we've lost our patience. We don't like waiting and when we have to, it causes anxiety and stress.

While technology brought convenience to our lives, it also brought a whole new set of expectations that soon became the status quo. Our world has become addicted to speed and impatience. Clients expect projects completed in ridiculous time frames and demand creative people to generate ideas instantaneously. Our over-connectivity has led to an avalanche of information that requires us to absorb far more than we ever did before. We've become a nation of anxious people who are always worried about what's next—so much so that we forget to look at what's in front of us.

And for creative people, it's even harder not to get distracted. We have many interests and options to choose from. Slowing down to actually experience life in its depth becomes the biggest challenge we face. Besides, "slow" in our society often means "lazy," "slacker" or plain "dumb"—and those are the last things we want to be known as. We keep cramming things into our lives, always searching for the combination that will provide us the most pleasure, and we distract ourselves from the tough questions (the slow questions) about what's really important: our values, beliefs, big-picture plans, goals and how to achieve them. Not to mention how this pace stifles creativity.

The No. 1 question I hear from creative business leaders isn't "Why are we running so fast?" It's "How do we keep up and stay ahead in this fast-paced world?" The answer is simple. We think that moving fast will help us keep up. But this only works when we do it with precision and purpose. And in order to so do, we have to slow down.

To move quickly with precision and purpose, however, slowing down is precisely what we need to do. Instead of running at full speed in all directions, we need to pause, think, focus, and then run in the right direction.

Stop Multitasking

At first glance, "slow down to go fast" doesn't seem to make much sense. Our brains tell us that if we pause even for a moment, we'll fall further behind. So we go at it with more grit than ever. In order to move quickly with precision and purpose, however, slowing down is precisely what we need to do. Instead of running at full speed in all directions, we need to pause, think, focus, and then run in the right direction.

But most creatives (and, really, most people) don't take the time to discern the "right" direction for themselves. We just start running. We say "yes" to too many things, fearing we'll miss out on whatever surprise is waiting around the corner. We mistake being busy for being productive. We pretend to be masterful multitaskers, thinking we'll get more done in less time if we do it all at once.

The truth is, multitasking is only slowing us down further—and not in a good way. Multitasking, as most people understand it, is a myth that makes overly scheduled and stressed-out people feel efficient. The lie is that you can actually do two or more tasks at the same time with full focus and attention, but in reality, what you're doing is serial tasking. You're shifting from one task to another to another in rapid succession. You think you're doing these tasks simultaneously. But you're not. Are you actually savoring that microwave dinner while you're reading e-mail? Not really.

Doing everything at once is neither effective nor efficient. You're expending more brain power switching from one thing to another, which only adds to feeling rushed and incomplete. It can't be done. Choose a single task, and slow down. Start one project and stay present with it until you complete it, and watch how much faster you'll get your to-do list done.

Be Mindful in Order to Be Present

If your creativity seems to suffer and you're having difficulty coming up with new ideas, then slow down. Don't panic and step on the gas; ease up instead. Slowing down can be a tremendous source of creativity, which exists in the present moment. You can't find it anywhere else. Taking our time ultimately helps us become more mindful. When we're mindful, we're able to create our best.

Here's an example of how putting this into practice helped me. Seven years ago, I spent a year in cooking school learning to be a chef. It was a creative experiment. I had no intention of starting a culinary career but rather wanted to awaken my creative spirit, which had become dormant and was missing from my life. I learned to chop and bake and broil, but the most important lesson I learned was about pacing myself.

On our first day of class, we were immediately shown the location of the first-aid kit. "Each of you will most likely have a serious kitchen accident during the course of the year," said the head chef, "unless you learn to slow down and be present."

And the head chef was right. As the year progressed, nearly every student experienced serious knife cuts, burns, slips and falls. Moving too fast led to first aid time-outs or, worse, no chance of getting the day's dish finished on time.

But safety concerns aside, in order for me to connect to my creativity in cooking school, I had to learn to be present and focused. I became more aware of how I handled myself. If I used my knife carefully, I'd avoid accidents. Not to mention, my dishes would turn out well, and I'd managed to get everything done ahead of the deadline, with enough time for dishwashing.

Practice a Slower Pace

The way I initially showed up in the kitchen was a reflection of how I was showing up in the rest of my life. I was distracted and not present. Now, I'm able to see that same malaise everywhere. Nearly everyone I know is suffering in this age of distraction, never catching up and always feeling like they're falling behind. It doesn't have to be that way. We've come to accept distractions as a way of life. But life isn't the problem; we are. We're simply moving too fast.

Slowing down allows us to create in an intentional way and not react from fear, which is generally the root cause of our speed. Slowing down takes practice and mindfulness. It's

BENEFITS OF SLOWING DOWN

There are lots of reasons to slow down. Here's just a few to give you an idea of why it's important to live a slower lifestyle:

1. **Better focus.** When you slow down, you focus better. Give yourself the time to complete just one task. With just one thing you have to do, you are less likely to procrastinate by doing other, less important tasks.

2. **Deeper insight.** Rushing produces shallowness, because you never have time to dig beneath the surface. Slow down and dive into deeper waters.

3. **Better appreciation.** When you slow down you notice more and pay attention to things you normally pass by. You can appreciate what you have, what you're doing and who you're with.

4. **Better communication.** Slowing down will help you choose your words carefully. Your written and oral communication will be more intentional and present and not come from a reactive place.

5. **Less stress.** Rushing produces anxiety and higher stress levels. You run the risk of becoming physically and emotionally exhausted, which causes high levels of anxiety and stress. Slowing down can help you manage and release stress as well as calm your body.

6. **Better creativity.** If your mind is constantly bombarded with new information it will be hard to find room for creative thinking. Our creative mind flows when we are relaxed, centered and open.

a way of being that requires focus, attention and work. To start this mindful pace, consider these tips for creating a slower life:

Disconnect. Set aside time to turn off your devices and e-mail alerts. Schedule a break where you don't take or make phone calls, when you're just creating, connecting with a friend, reading a book or simply taking a walk. And if you're brave, go an entire weekend disconnected. I promise, you'll be OK.

Practice mindfulness. Learn to live in the present rather than thinking so much about the future or the past. When you eat, fully appreciate your food. If you're with someone, be with them entirely. When you're walking, appreciate your surroundings, no matter where you are.

Eliminate commitments. Say "no" more often to non-essential commitments. Every "yes" is taking up space in your life, so slow down and reflect on every commitment and invitation you receive. Before you say "yes," make sure it isn't taking you away from your more important commitments.

Do less. Rename your to-do list as the much more gentle "All that I have to do today is …" list. Design a less stressful day that allows you to work in a natural, easy-going manner.

Single task. This is the opposite of multitasking. Focus on one thing at a time. When you feel the urge to switch to other tasks, pause, breathe and pull yourself back.

Slowing down can be a liberating experience for you, your business, your creativity and even your personal life. For example, Matt Steel, principal at Grain in St. Louis, put this advice into practice. After getting to a point of near-complete exhaustion and burnout, slowing down turned his life around. "The quality and variety of our design work has grown," Steel says. "We spend more time with our families. We have lives. We close the shop at 2 p.m. on Fridays and still manage to get things done on time. Our business is growing at a sustainable pace. We're far from perfect, but I wouldn't change a thing."

Take a close look at how you function throughout your day. Are you rushing around everywhere without ample time to do anything because you "don't have enough hours in the day"? Become the master of your own time, and watch your life change. Your days will start feeling longer and more satisfying, as you'll live a more intentional and present life. You'll begin to enjoy every moment of every day because you'll be present to witness them. And, surprise, you'll even get more done and find your creativity flowing.

Peleg Top is a leadership development coach and a business mentor to creative entrepreneurs worldwide. He teaches business owners how to create a profitable company while living an artistic, well-balanced life. www.PelegTop.com

DAVID MACAULAY

Artist at Play

....

by Will Hillenbrand

MacArthur fellow David Macaulay was born in England in 1946; his family moved to New Jersey in 1957. He studied at the Rhode Island School of Design (RISD), spending his fifth year in Rome. He then earned a degree in architecture. The book that inaugurated his brilliant series on architecture and engineering was the 1973 *Cathedral* (revisited twenty-five years later). Macaulay's many awards include the Caldecott Medal and Honor Awards; the Boston Globe–Horn Book Award; the Christopher Award; and the Washington Post/Children's Book Guild Nonfiction Award. Will Hillenbrand, himself a renowned illustrator, visited Macaulay in his studio in Vermont.

Q: I'd like to take you back to the things you saw when you were a child, in your kitchen, the only heated room in the house. What was life like for you as a child?

A: I had the advantage of growing up in the north of England. We lived in a row house and there were only two rooms on the first floor. One was the living room, which was kept clean for company that never arrived, and the other room was where we lived.

My childhood sort of ended when we left England and moved to the United States, even though I was only ten. In England, because we lived in one room, childhood was time spent outside, playing in the woods. And we were lucky. There were thousands of brick row houses, but we were at the edge of them, at the bottom of the street where there were trees and a stream. That was my way to school. I walked to school in the morning; I walked back to have lunch at home, which was the big meal of the day, then back to school, and then home again around four o'clock, so I made four trips through those woods every day. Occasionally, I'd find dead animals, like a mouse skeleton. I was always looking for things and looking at things, trying to pull frogs out of the pond, which was behind a fence, which made it difficult, and watching tadpoles turn into frogs. The link to nature was a part of my life.

When I wasn't in school, Saturday or Sunday, I was in the woods. I was Robin Hood. I was the Cisco Kid. I was anybody I wanted to be. I was running and galloping, completely lost in my imagination. I usually played by myself, but occasionally I'd meet up with some pals and we'd run through the woods together and throw rocks at each other. On a few occasions, we built things like forts out of wreaths.

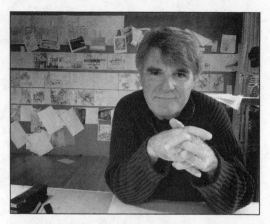

David Macaulay finds the origins of *Cathedral, Mosque, The Way Things Work*, etc., in walking and watching in the woods of England and Wales—and in the line drawings of Maurice Sendak.

Q: From the cemetery!

A: From the cemetery for St. Peter's Church. All the old wreaths were taken off the graves and dumped along the edge, and we built forts and that was pretty terrific, too.

In the summer we went to Wales for one week, because that's when the mills closed so my father was at home; that was our holiday. We were supposed to be sitting on the beach but it always rained, so we went places. We climbed a mountain where there was a big slate quarry on one side, and we drove to the castles, and we climbed all over them. It was a terrific time but really compact; it was literally five days, given the driving at either end. I was being introduced to the history of architecture, but not as such. It was the rock garden or the park itself that I found most enjoyable.

Q: The other day, when I called you to set up a time for this meeting, you answered the phone and you weren't there, because you had to come back from another century.

A: That's right! What was I doing? Was I on a ship—I was reading something about ironwork in the nineteenth century. I have to concentrate because the information comes from a history of technology. You put yourself back into these places and times and you try to absorb and then extract from yourself what you've learned, when you're trying to tell a story.

Q: You have to make that journey so we, as readers, can follow the path.

A: Which is why I can't think of anything more important than finding ways to develop your imagination when you're young. Play is my favorite way and I still play; I feel I'm

"What I wanted to do was not choose a style, not choose a technique," says Macaulay. Instead his approach arises from the content. In this spread from *The New Way Things Work*, he draws and demonstrates the working parts of radio and space telescopes.
The New Way Things Work, written and illustrated by David Macaulay (HMH Books for Young Readers, 1998)

playing even when the deadline is looming. I guess it's what keeps me coming back to the studio—I still feel that this is primarily an act of play. If it's going to work, it means I've played successfully.

Q: It's the sandbox in your backyard. What's the sandbox? Your imagination?

A: The sandbox reminds me of scale. As a child, I thought something was huge, and now I see a picture of it, and it was quite tiny. It's like time. There was this vast sort of space of opportunity, which turned out to be quite a small sandbox.

Q: We were smaller; things were bigger.

A: My favorite places as a kid, even when we got to the United States, when I was trying to catch up with my older-seeming New Jersey buddies, were along the railroad tracks because of all the untouched vegetation, the brambles: here were places to hide. You could be really close to the trains but not in danger. You'd watch the wheels go by, those big Erie Lackawanna diesel engines with their massive shaking. One of my favorite places in Bolton, England, was the bridge that crossed the railway track because you could see what track was going to have a train under the bridge. You'd race down the bridge to stand over the train, and you'd be completely engulfed in this wonderful-smelling smoke. One of the great smells is the smell of smoke from a coal-fired steam engine. It takes me back!

Q: I want to touch on your big award back in 1956, when you were ten and won the national handwriting prize!

A: It was the end of the day at an assembly in this huge hall. I knew they were going to call my name and they did. I got an award for actually concentrating on handwriting, which I'd never done before. When I wrote, it was sloppy and illegible, so it was a bit surprising to my parents. I just wasn't interested in words or writing. I loved pictures. I loved being read to. But the other stuff was hard work, and I didn't want to do that. I wanted to be out having fun.

Q: But you did discover the power of your concentration and also probably your ability to control line.

A: I don't know whether it sank in. The only other experience I had was the fire engine painting. The kids were working away at their tables. The two teachers in the room came along and saw the fire engine and basically removed it from the table before I could destroy it. It was still wet. And they said, "You're done." They took it and put it on the wall. I remember feeling so proud because it was the first time something had been recognized as having some merit that I did not perhaps see. And, having been a teacher, I now understand that there are those moments when you look at somebody's work and you want to say, "Stop. You're there."

Q: When we're really creating our own art, we have to decide: "How many lines does it take?"

A: And you have to learn that. The nice thing about being able to look at lots of people's work, thanks to its being produced in books, is that you can see who needed the most lines, who needed the fewest lines. And when I say who needed the most lines, if it still works, it

This three-part rendition shows the foundation, the columns, and the roof of wooden trusses of the Temple of Jupiter, Juno, and Minerva, which lies at the far side of the Forum in Rome. Macaulay's drawings for *City* are in pen and ink.
City: A Story of Roman Planning and Construction, written and illustrated by David Macaulay (Boston: Houghton Mifflin, 1974)

This pen- and-ink illustration from *Cathedral* shows how workmen hoisted the voussoirs, the cut stones of the ribs, and finally, the keystone of the arch, before mortaring voussoirs and keystone in place.
Cathedral: The Story of Its Construction, written and illustrated by David Macaulay (Houghton Mifflin Company,1973)

still works; that's fine; use tons of lines! The difference between Edward Ardizzone (English, 1900–79) and Ernest H. Shepard (English, 1879–1976) is a case in point. Ardizzone is a guy who cross-hatched the back spaces to create depth and push something forward. For the most part, when I think of Shepard's drawings (for instance, in *Winnie-the-Pooh* or *The Wind in the Willows*), I think of a spare line with just the right pressure on the nib to make the line swell and become thin again. What I can't believe is that Shepard did such a lot of sketches. He didn't draw anything until he was ready; he worked over it and over it, and in the end, traced it probably. You would think with a process like that, you'd drive every bit of vitality out of the finished image, but there's a character, a life in that line.

Q: I want to talk about your passage to America.

A: I looked forward to the Manhattan skyline because of my *Golden Book Encyclopedia* for children. One of the spreads was "the highest, the biggest, the fastest," and so on. And on that spread was a picture of the Empire State Building and what Harry McNaught, the illustrator, did to emphasize the Empire State Building was he lifted it off the skyline and faded the surroundings out, as if a little cloud bank had surrounded the base of the building. It was his way of legitimately separating the building from its surroundings and making it massive, because the illustration was about the building, not about the Manhattan skyline. But as a ten-year-old, I just assumed that the Empire State Building was that huge with a cloud bank surrounding the base. Getting on that ship, I was told by my mother that we were going to the United States. I thought: the Empire State Building!

I expected to be able to see it immediately, once we were in the water near Ireland. I thought, "Well, we're going to at least be able to see the top of it; it does go to the sky." And after four and a half days of a fairly boring trip, we finally pulled into New York Harbor, and I couldn't find the building! How could I miss it! Was this the right New York?

We got to the Hudson River finally, and we saw the Empire State Building, sort of floating, isolated in midtown. It wasn't huge; it didn't touch the sky. I recognized the shape of it, but I was disappointed.

Once we settled into our new home in New Jersey, I walked to school. As I crossed the railroad tracks on Orchard Street, I looked down the track and there at the end was the Empire State Building. And I had this wonderful feeling: OK, it let me down the day we arrived, but it's still here.

It was the connection that I needed between our new place and that encyclopedia back in Lancashire. And at night, for instance, after Boy Scouts, it was even better, because as I wandered back across the tracks on Orchard Street, heading home, there were the lights called freedom lights, four large revolving beams on the ninetieth floor. They would spin, so they would flash and then go dark, flash and go dark, and I remember standing there thinking, "That's my building."

Years later, I come back to do *Unbuilding*, in which I dismantled the Empire State Building. The fact is, it was a connection; it was an anchor between England and New Jersey.

After documenting the construction of a castle on the coast of Wales, Macaulay concludes by showing it as a ruin. He drew the pictures for *Castle* with fountain pen, colored pencil, or regular pencil and then used felt-tip markers or colored pencils to inject color.
Built to Last, written and illustrated by David Macaulay (HMH Books For Young Readers, 2010)

Q: C.S. Lewis felt the same way about walking. In Narnia, there are great spaces between one place and the next.

A: There's formal education at one end of this journey every day, and then there's the kind of informal education, the stuff you learn through observation, by surprise, which intermingles with your imagination and kind of sets you up. Then you sit down in class and do your times tables and so forth.

Q: I remember reading about one of your lessons, when you taught at RISD: an assignment to draw jet lag, which was not like any illustration project I'd had when I was in school.

A: Well, let's face it, you could draw a picture of people sitting in chairs in rows and every one of them could be jet-lagged, but there would be no indication necessarily of what was going on inside their heads and bodies. The task was to define jet lag to yourself, and then you had to think about a means of communication that would suggest a kind of hazy, foggy tiredness. I would suggest to the students—they didn't always do it—"Just write words down that come into your mind to start with," because some of those words might trigger a visual response from you.

This illustration from Macaulay's first book shows how plasterers covered the underside of the cathedral vaults while masons laid stone slabs for the floor in a maze pattern that mimicked the journey of a pilgrim toward a shrine.
Cathedral: The Story of Its Construction, written and illustrated by David Macaulay (Houghton Mifflin, 1973)

If you want to place the illustration in the airport, you don't start in the airport and stop in the airport. You go through a process of figuring out ways in which you can suggest that dizziness and confusion that would link the feelings to the airport and would convey that this isn't just exhaustion because you ran a marathon; this is exhaustion because you just got off a plane after 12 hours.

I would only give them half an hour; then we would put the sketches up. This was a class in "Think now; draw later." I felt there were too many students who were going to settle on the first idea and spend 28 minutes of their half hour trying to make it look as beautiful as possible.

The point was we only have half an hour and I want to see your best idea. Don't finish it. You'll never finish it. There are no finished drawings in this classroom, which frustrated many of them, but I stuck to my guns and I still hear from the members of that class.

Q: There is so much pressure when you come into a class like that. The imperative is to get to the finish, get to the last chapter.

A: There's this overwhelming demand: I've got to have a portfolio! That's where they're focused, and what I was trying to do was to work them toward that portfolio but with substance. You can illustrate meaningless things and illustrate them beautifully and have a wonderful surface and prove yourself to be a fine craftsman, but if you have nothing to say, it's empty. Particularly if you're talking about illustration, you're not talking about an object that stands by itself. The function of the illustration is to connect with a person—to engage with him, to bring him into your world. And you can't do that in a superficial way. You have to understand what you're trying to say before you choose the tools that will best accomplish that, whatever it is.

My students had a tendency to want to choose too quickly. They'd say, "This is my style, this is how I work." Your style? You're only a sophomore in illustration, for goodness sake! You're eighteen years old and you have a style? I want you to communicate something of substance to me; your style will come and go. I could choose a problem for you that would be exactly right for your "style," but what good would that be? You have to be willing to take on anything as an illustrator.

This illustration from *Castle* shows the castle's embrasures (where the soldier stands on the right), merlons (the stone segment that contains an arrow loop), and finials (vertical stone spikes on the very top)—drawn in fountain pen, colored pencil, and felt-tip markers.
Built to Last, written and illustrated by David Macaulay (HMH Books for Young Readers, 2010)

Q: You have a jukebox in your portfolio and you end up doing jukeboxes for the rest of your life. It won't give you an expansive world.

A: And you won't learn anything from it. This whole process is about learning. If, as an illustrator and an author, you reach a point you really feel you're not growing at all, you're not asking any questions of consequence, it's over, sadly. Do something else.

Q: That's the point. That's why I absolutely love your work and love you as a person.

A: I don't know how to do it any other way. There's no easy way out. The project I'm working on at the moment, whatever it is, isn't necessarily fun-filled, but the rewards of a successful day can't be quantified. You get to the end of the day and you think, I solved that one today; I figured out how to communicate that complicated piece of information that is important to the overall story, and I did it because I relaxed. I remembered that I'm also supposed to be playing.

I use the sketchbook a lot, of course, but I also use the wall in my studio, because I build these books piece by piece. I'll put up sixty-four pieces of white paper, or eighty or ninety-six, and then I start pasting things or pinning things to the white paper. You piece this thing together and every point of focus is an opportunity for discovery, for trying something new, or actually rediscovering something you did years ago that worked well then and would work well here, so it's not as if you're inventing new stuff; you just want to approach the questions with freshness even if the answer you end up choosing is actually quite familiar and comfortable. If you approached the question with a kind of openness, you know it's still the right choice even if it's not new to you.

Q: It's new for the reader, and it allows the reader to go from looking at something to understanding something.

A: It's the same actor but in a completely different play. I was lucky to start with *Cathedral*, because it was something I felt I could do, having studied architecture for five years. I understood the importance of the order. You don't start with the spires; you start digging holes in the ground to create a foundation. The nice thing about describing a building of any kind, even a garage, is that it's sort of self-explanatory. Start with the foundation; build the walls; put the roof on; finish the inside. It's a natural, though man-made, process, but choose a cathedral and not a garage and you have this fantastic thing to deal with.

Q: I want to take a step back to your fifth year at RISD when you were chosen for a European Honors program. That may have been the origin of *Cathedral: The Story of Its Construction*.

A: It was an incredible year for me. It was my first time away from home—that cannot be underrated. As a sophomore at RISD, I had Xeroxes of the Roman forum on the wall on my bedroom; I was surrounded by Rome and details of classical architecture. That was my goal: to do well enough in school that I would be selected for the European Honors program, and it all worked out, thank goodness. It was really the first opportunity I had to sort of figure out who I was a little bit and I mean "a little bit," because I wasn't very good at it.

I don't speak Italian well enough to have a conversation of any depth about anything of consequence, but when I wander the streets of Rome, I'm at home. I'm behind that bush next to railway tracks, in the fort near Bolton as an eight-year-old. I'm in a perfectly safe, welcoming place filled with surprises and the possibility of surprise. Where is home? Home is where you feel comfortable, and I feel most comfortable when I am in the presence of unusual connections, juxtapositions between strange things, old and new; the sense of the past; a kind of surprising beauty; the way light makes things work in particular ways; the scale of stone buildings versus brick buildings and steel and glass buildings. I admire aspects of all architecture but where I am really home is in those places (as in Europe) that have a sense of another time.

Q: Let's go to *Cathedral*. You're bringing in a book idea to Houghton Mifflin and it's about gargoyles coming to life.

A: For the annual beauty pageant! This young boy falls asleep while his father is cutting stone. The boy wakes up and Dad has gone home. The boy is surrounded by these stone creatures that have come to life and they tell him, "This is the night of our beauty pageant ... ." I laid it out and showed Walter Lorraine and Melanie Krupa at Houghton Mifflin, and I think it was Walter who said, "Well, we don't really need another book about gargoyles; we're pretty much done with gargoyles for a while." Of course there's always another opportunity for a book about gargoyles! But he looked at my drawing of the cathedral, and Walter said, "Why don't you just tell us about the cathedral?" So two months later, I was back with the layout of another story that simply started in the ground. I just followed the common sense behind the construction, discovering along the way these extraordinary proportions; the notion of piling stone on top of stone; the idea of tying these 100-foot high walls together with timber triangles and trusses.

The success of *Cathedral* was terrific but there was a pattern established and an expectation developed from that success. I was going to be the guy who did these architecture books, and I did five of them—this was what I was talking about a little while ago. I could have done fifty books on architecture and I would have been bored out of my mind. I needed to do something completely different.

Q: For *Cathedral* you have text, layout, and art— three pieces that have to dovetail together. So you're writing, you're creating—at one point you're thinking maybe the cathedral will be bombed in WWII, because you're making this up; it's not a literal cathedral we can go visit.

A: I was really representing the kind of pageant of the construction of this extraordinary architecture, and the star of the book was the cathedral. And then there were these ants (workmen) that moved things around and got things done. So I'm starting with a lot of white space and the text floats, and then as I turn the pages I realize I actually have less space to work with to simply convey the size of this growing thing—as if I were blowing air into it.

Q: You're showing us that the walls are going up; we're hovering above.

A: Drawing is the way to get behind things. A photograph is a crude representation; it might contain detail, but it won't help me or the reader understand the subject matter.

Twenty-five years later, I asked Walter Lorraine, "Can I revisit that first book, and he said, 'Why not?'" I'd shown slides of *Cathedral* for years, and I would think, "That white space isn't doing anything," etc., so I went back and cropped and threw things out and redrew them. I had a chance to make a book about the building of the book that also told the story of the building of the cathedral (*Building the Book Cathedral*, Houghton Mifflin, 1999).

Q: You chose to use line, drawing in pen and ink, though you could have done it with twentieth-century technology. And you made the right choice!

A: I did! And I chose the line because I was inspired by Maurice Sendak (1928–2012), especially by *Higglety Pigglety Pop*. I only got remotely close to drawing like that in 1984 in the *The Amazing Brain* where I used the crow quill pen. Sendak's lines got me going. As I began to draw the lines of stone in *Cathedral* I needed precision. I was building this building almost in a literal way; the pen and ink line was appropriate for all the architecture books.

Cathedral is crude from a pen and ink point of view. I simply chose a subject matter and played with perspective. I was competent enough with pen and ink to make it all work, but each book is a total package, much bigger than the lines.

Q: You also write the text. You have to assimilate a vast amount of information and then you have to distill it, because everything you know can't be put in each book.

A: I get so immersed in the context that I lose my objectivity. When I come into the studio in the morning I pull up a chair and look at the wall. I see things I didn't notice the day before. I see connections, I see possible links. I can draw straight for a half an hour; then I get up and wander downstairs to the refrigerator, and when I get back to the work place, I've broken that kind of mesmerizing connection to the thing I'm working on enough to be, for a moment, objective. I look at the drawing and say, "This is terrible! The perspective is way off," at which point I start again. That has happened and will continue to happen.

It's not like working on a canvas where I'd back up to see and make adjustments. I'm sitting in a seat at the same distance from this thing the whole time. I have to force myself to get up, which is why pinning on the wall is important. Having a wall with nothing on it is as important as having a drawing table, maybe more so. It's in that refreshed perspective that you discover possibilities you weren't allowing in, as the manufacturing process was going on.

Will Hillenbrand has written for *The Artist's Magazine* and has illustrated more than fifty children's books. His latest book is *Down by the Barn* (Amazon Children's Publishing, 2014). Visit his website at www.willhillenbrand.com.

Excerpted from the July/August 2014 issue of *The Artist's Magazine*. Used with the kind permission of *The Artist's Magazine*, a publication of F+W, a Content + eCommerce Company. Visit www.artistsnetwork.com to subscribe.

RICHARD MCLAUGHLIN

Fugu World Tour and Beyond

....

by Kenneth Smith

Richard McLaughlin is a man for all seasons: writer, poet, potter, ceramic sculptor, musician, educator, and artist. "At first glance," he says, "music, poetry, pottery, sculpture, and painting may not seem interrelated, yet for me they are." Indeed, his art is informed by all of these disciplines enabling him to express a broad range of content, style, and even whimsy.

As a result, his rich, warm artistic expression embraces a variety of categories, which McLaughlin is extremely comfortable defining and excited to talk about. He does not find the categories limiting. His art is continually evolving through his exploration of color and his consistent use of social media, designed to initiate dialogue about art in general and his art specifically with people throughout the world. His website may function importantly as a business card, but his No. 1 pri-

Music, poetry, sculpture, and painting are interrelated for artist Richard McLaughlin.

ority is his desire to have the site serve more to stimulate conversation and receive feedback to inform and enrich his evolving outlook and expression.

A survey of McLaughlin's website reveals the marvelous array of styles and subject matter, which are categorized into three major groupings: Fugu and Friends, Trees and Landscapes, and Abstracts and Dazzlers. To the casual observer, it might appear to be the work

The ocean and McLaughlin's formative years in Massachusetts are significant influences in his work. *Plum Island Light* (pastel on pastel board, 30x42, collection of James and Christy Pritchard)

of three different artists! McLaughlin laughs and is quick to inform, "I usually have several paintings going on at the same time. The style and subject matter and even the color palettes may all differ. But this is comfortable for me."

It may be comfortable for him, and certainly unusual, but the fusion of these various fields of creative expression took time to develop and evolve before he could express his innate gifts as consummately as he does.

"Creativity is something that is inside of you, and it's got to come out, one way or another," McLaughlin says. He remembers receiving a box of Crayola crayons when he was five years old. To this day, he remembers the sense of awe evoked by the myriad colors in the box. He experienced the initial stirrings of creativity, the desire to explore color and express himself through them. It was a transformational experience that continues to influence his life these many years later, keeping the little boy's wonder very much alive within the competent adult.

Early Influence of the Sea

The Dazzler series was developed through McLaughlin's desire to express his relationship with the sea.
Water Lilies (acrylic on canvas, 20×24)

McLaughlin grew up in the seacoast town of Newburyport, Massachusetts, a major center to the once thriving whaling industry and birthplace of the U.S. Coastguard. He spent summers living on Plum Island, a nearby barrier island. Even as a young lad he became enamored with the seeming mystical modulations of light, shadow, and color of the Great Marsh, the stalwart quietude of the glistening dunes, and the delight of the undulating sea. He learned to fear the ocean of storm hurtling unabated upon the berm, imprinting its violent power indelibly in his memory. And he learned to love the river, the mighty Merrimack, shimmering and churning in light and ever-changing color where it met the sea by the northern tip of the island. His best memories of childhood center on Plum Island, and it came to be a place of healing for him. Not surprisingly, these images of his youth were imprinted in his mind, and even living amid the rolling bluegrass fields of Kentucky, he can call them forth from memory.

Although he was not painting during his formative years, McLaughlin was always drawing with pen and ink. He was probably more consumed by his love of music which he pursued passionately, purchasing vinyl in all genres, learning the groups, the artists that comprised them, and paying close attention to the rhythms, and "licks." He took up playing the harmonica, teaching himself to play and emulate the blues greats.

It is important to note that McLaughlin is, for the most part, self-taught. No doubt, the lack of money while growing up contributed to this strategy, but his ability to succeed at such a competent level speaks to his innate capability, initiative, and creative drive.

Building a Meaningful Life Through Poetry

After high school and a three-year stint in the Navy, McLaughlin returned to Newburyport and attended the local community college. He recalls, "I got into a lot of trouble in the Navy and knew I had to get in touch with myself if I was going to build a new and meaningful life. I was dealing with intense emotion, and I directed my creative energies to writing to get in touch with myself and accomplish what I needed." Fortunately, he was challenged by an English professor, his most influential teacher, to "show and not tell." As a result, he used "visual, descriptive language" to convey his feelings. He explains, "I would be looking at my poems as if they were little movies. I see poetry that way, as almost another visual art 'inner vision,' as Stevie Wonder would say."

McLaughlin's poetry has been published by several presses in Massachusetts and Kentucky. His prose is contained primarily in personal and travel journals, some of which is appropriate for publication. Interestingly, the pages are replete with pen-and-ink drawings.

Turning to Ceramics in Greece

Travelling in the Greek Islands in the early 1970s, McLaughlin kept a journal for writing and drawing. He recalls, "I loved doing intricate pen-and-ink drawings of driftwood, fossils, and bone. You can find lots of bleached out pieces of bone on the beaches of Crete. I began drawing on them in India ink. Then I got the idea that it would be fun to make the shapes to draw on, so I determined to study ceramics."

When he returned from his lengthy trip he committed to ceramics and took a course in glaze chemistry at Mudflat Pottery School in Cambridge, Massachusetts.

Bright colors and detailed brushwork are hallmarks of McLaughlin's paintings.
Organic Abstraction (acrylic on canvas, 10×8, collection of Henry Li)

McLaughlin explains, "At first, I thought I would just use prepared glazes and paint on the clay with them. But I realized the potential for color that glazes afforded. I became fascinated with creating my own glazes, my own colors made up of elements that produce vastly different color results under different firing conditions. This experience and other explorations in the world of clay helped me to develop a keen appreciation for the subtle variations in color available, even within a limited palette." It was at Mudflat that McLaughlin met his wife, Verna Richards McLaughlin, also an accomplished artist. They married and started a family.

After moving to Kentucky, McLaughlin missed the ocean and began painting seascapes in pastel. *Plum Island Surf* (pastel on pastel board, 6×8)

Pursuing an Artist's Life in Massachusetts

They settled in the Newburyport area and for a time even lived on his beloved Plum Island. With a degree in English from the University of Massachusetts, McLaughlin began teaching at the local community college in an inventive program for non-traditional students, who responded eagerly to his devotion to learning, his commitment to exploration and personal growth, and his firm belief in their ability to achieve. Evenings would find him with his wife pursuing ceramics, writing poetry, or attending the local ale house, The Grog, famous for outstanding jazz and blues where he both listened as an avid fan and participated as a welcomed colleague.

It was during this time that his poetry was first published in several publications, and he was often found participating in local poetry readings. He and his wife were also invited to display their ceramics at the local college, public library, and group shows in Newburyport, gaining notoriety for their innovative creations.

Painting the Ocean in Kentucky

It was not until they moved to Elizabethtown, Kentucky, to care for his wife's parents that McLaughlin began to immerse himself in painting. "I found myself missing the ocean," he said, "so I began painting the images that were emblazoned into my memory. I didn't have

McLaughlin continued to paint beautiful sunsets and seascapes after transitioning from pastels to oil paints and then eventually to acrylics.
Plum Island Sunset (oil on canvas, 22×28)

a studio, and I had only short intervals of time to devote to art, so I began using dry pastels because they are easy to set out and clean up. I would spread out on the dining room table doing postcard-sized paintings. The pastels offered rich pigmentation, deep color, and the experience was like going back for a visit."

"I love pastels," McLaughlin asserts. "I worked with them for ten years. As Wolf Kahn once said, 'It's like painting with the dust from butterfly wings.'" McLaughlin painted deep, rich colors displaying the expansive, ethereal quality of sunsets and sunrises across the mutable marsh or from the inconstant seashore and riverbanks. His mother-in-law looked at one of his sunset vistas and said, "I get it, Dick. Don't fence me in." "I think she had something there," he muses. "It gave me a sense of freedom to be painting those seascapes."

As the canvases became larger, the dust from the process became problematic and, reluctantly, McLaughlin had to move away from the media for health reasons. He explains, "I moved into oil painting and devoted myself to painting the same subject matter—sunsets from Plum Island and at the Plum Island basin—blending the wet oil paint much like I blended the dry pastels, replicating the atmospheric look and feel that I had achieved with

McLaughlin's abstract works incorporate drips, impressions made by common household items, and detailed brushwork.
Desert Abstract (acrylic on canvas, 8×10, collection of Roland Egerton and Ellen Parrish)

the pastels." The experience made him mindful of Monet and his haystack series, exploring the nuances of color and light depending upon the time of day, the season, and the weather.

McLaughlin worked in oil exclusively for five years before switching to acrylic paint. "It was a trade-off," he says. "I found the color of the pigments to be richer with oil paint, but the cleanup took too much time. I was still working full-time at the University of Louisville, recruiting students for the joint program with United Parcel Services, which required a lot of travel. I had to make more efficient use of my creative time. Acrylic paint afforded shorter cleanup time and less toxic chemicals."

Turning to Social Media and New Styles

McLaughlin had his first one-man shows about this time, working with a local gallery owner in Elizabethtown. While he was satisfied with the commercial success of the show and the conversations engendered, he was forced to acknowledge the limited exposure afforded in rural Kentucky, and the prodigious amount of time and expense required to put on a show. McLaughlin had earned a graduate degree in media at Boston University, prior to moving

McLaughlin's tree paintings are influenced by pastel artist Wolf Kahn and Chinese brush painting. *Winter Woods* (acrylic on canvas, 24×48, collection of Neely McLaughlin and Cornelius Anderson)

to Kentucky, so his expertise and inclination in this direction was already present in his outlook. The use of social media as a means of creating enhanced exposure for his work and to stimulate a wider ranging dialogue began to percolate.

At the same time, McLaughlin's exploration into wider ranging challenges began. He explains, "I began exploring my way into abstract impressionism, action painting, and especially landscapes and trees heavily influenced by Wolf Kahn. I had long admired his use of color and the strength and freedom of his brushwork. I was very fortunate to have been invited to his seventy-fifth birthday celebration at the Jerald Melberg gallery in Charlotte, North Carolina, where I asked him lots of questions about his work. He was very generous with his time, and I was blessed to have spoken with him. He has had a huge influence on my tree paintings." McLaughlin adds, "Interestingly, I had studied for a while with a Chinese brush painter in the early 1970s and learned a lot about combining simple elements to make complex paintings. My trees and landscapes are greatly informed by the teaching of these two individuals."

Finding Fugu in Japan

It was shortly thereafter that McLaughlin travelled to Japan. He recalls, "The Fugu series came about as a result of my trip to Japan. I was drawn to the brightly colored images on restaurant signage, especially seafood restaurants. The original fugu sign was on a sidewalk in Tokyo and I thought the image was endearing. The bright colors and intensity of Tokyo opened a new world to me, strengthened my palette, and stimulated me to try something completely different. I began the Fugu series right after my return."

After traveling to New Mexico, McLaughlin began to incorporate southwestern iconography into his Japan-inspired fugu paintings.
Desert Fugu (acrylic on canvas, 30×40, collection of Henry Li)

McLaughlin explains, "Fugu and Friends paintings are fun for me. They are light-hearted, whimsical, and exploratory. They provide an opportunity to integrate new experiences and new ways of seeing things into my art." He continues, "After a trip to Santa Fe and Taos, New Mexico, I combined elements of southwestern art with my fugu paintings, calling them *Desert Fugu*." In that way, his cultural experiences continually influence his creative exploration.

Developing Abstracts and Dazzlers

His abstract series evolved similarly. "My abstract series came about by my being frugal and not wanting to waste paint," he says unapologetically. "I would just lay down color with leftover paint, and I would keep adding elements until I felt I had achieved a satisfying composition."

What McLaughlin calls his "Dazzlers" evolved differently. Profoundly motivated by his desire to express his relationship with the sea, McLaughlin calls these paintings "colorist textural paintings informed by light reflected on rippling water surfaces." The Dazzler

McLaughlin's Dazzler series is inspired by the space between objects in Monet's water lily series. *Water Music* (detail, oil on canvas, 24×48)

paintings are inspired by Impressionist and Postimpressionist artists. In studying Monet, for example, McLaughlin focused on the space between objects. He studied the composition of the water and how it reflected the environment above its surface and the world beneath. He studied light in rippling water or in stillness at different times of day. He notes, "Some people look at my Dazzlers and ask me how I can be so patient because the paintings are composed of layers and layers of little strokes. Actually, painting in this manner is like meditation for me and beneficial for my mental and emotional health.

"There are also many musical elements in my painting," he adds. "I always have music in the background, and its rhythm is translated into patterning, especially in these paintings." One friend suggested that his Dazzlers were examples of chromesthesia, where heard sounds automatically and involuntarily evoke an experience of color.

Sharing and Selling Through Social Media

Throughout this period of time, McLaughlin held several more one-man shows and participated in shows around the country, but he has adopted social media as the primary means of presenting his art, building a following, and maintaining ongoing dialogues. He ex-

McLaughlin's iconic fugu has inspired a world tour, with fans taking fugu t-shirts to far-off places from Ethiopia to Ecuador.
Fugu With Lemon Drop Fish (detail, oil on canvas, 30×40)

plains, "Facebook has worked well for me. I get to show and share my work with people all over the world and get feedback." His success with Facebook encouraged him to open a conversational style blog to engage people and keep the conversation going. He has recently added a website to display his work with images updated regularly. It is a lot of work to maintain all of these venues, but having retired from his position at the university, he now has the necessary time.

Fugu World Tour

McLaughlin's Fugu World Tour enterprise is perhaps his most interesting accomplishment. He explains, "Fugu World Tour actually came about in response to my desire to have art openings in distant places. I would love to have had shows in Geneva or the French Alps or Japan, but it is costly to underwrite such shows. I therefore determined to create a kind of worldwide artistic 'happening,' and Fugu World Tour was born." He had a series of fugu T-shirts silk screened, which people could purchase online or in person, and he encouraged fans to photograph the shirts on their travels and post the pictures on his Fugu World Tour Facebook page. McLaughlin believes that there are in excess of four hundred T-shirts in circulation with photographs having been posted from such interesting and disparate places as Machu Picchu, Bali, Ethiopia, Jakarta, Costa Rica, Ecuador, Brazil,

Friends and fans have posted pictures of themselves wearing McLaughlin's fugu shirts in exotic locations on the Fugu World Tour Facebook page.

MORE FROM RICHARD MCLAUGHLIN

Learn more and connect with Richard McLaughlin and the Fugu World Tour:

www.richardcmclaughlin.com

www.facebook.com/pages/Fugu-World-Tour/133915206622519

Paris, Iraq, Ireland, Wales, Graceland, Pikes Peak, Niagara Falls, and Plum Island, to name but a few!

Moving forward, McLaughlin intends to continue his journey exploring color and stretching his creative expression. Negotiating the process of selling art promises to occupy more of his time and become an ongoing learning experience. He notes, "Many of my artist colleagues refer to this process as building a 'tribe' or following for one's art. I see myself using more of my media experience to accomplish this. I have built a following of media friends, new acquaintances, and have been successful selling my art in this manner. My next project will be a multi-media show documenting the Fugu World Tour photos, and I have planned painting demonstrations and studio tours to stimulate more discussion." This man for all seasons will continue to express his poetry in the visual arts, keeping the little boy's wonder very much alive in the competent adult.

Kenneth Smith is an educator, businessman, and writer living on Plum Island in Newbury, Massachusetts.

MELISSA SWEET

Playing With Pieces

....

by Will Hillenbrand

The nearly one hundred fiction and nonfiction books illustrated by Melissa Sweet have won every possible award—the Caldecott Honor, the NCTE Notable, the New York Times Best Illustrated, the Parents' Choice, etc. Sweet's collages and paintings have appeared in the *New York Times*, *Martha Stewart Living*, and *Madison Park Greetings*; and on Smilebox.com and eeBoo Toys, which were honored with the Oppenheim and Parents' Choice awards. She has written three books, including *Balloons Over Broadway: The True Story of the Puppeteer of Macy's Parade*, which won the 2012 Sibert Medal, the NCTE Orbis Pictus Award, Flora Stieglitz Straus Award, and the Cook Prize, in addition to being named an ALA Notable Book. Will Hillenbrand talked to her in her studio in Rockport, Maine.

Q: You've done many books that I love and that children love. There are many places to begin, but I'm going to start with something very basic, and that is color. When I say color, it's a loaded term because when I say red, I know for you there are at least forty variations of red. You always bring complexity and playfulness to color.

Acclaimed children's book illustrator Melissa Sweet talks to another acclaimed illustrator, Will Hillenbrand, about combining watercolor with pieces of collage in the serious play of making picture books.

The illustrations in *The Boy Who Drew Birds*, a story of John James Audubon, are in mixed media on Twinrocker paper, including elements of collage (an actual bird's nest, eggs, feathers, seeds, bark). *The Boy Who Drew Birds* by Jacqueline Davies, illustrated by Melissa Sweet (New York: Houghton Mifflin Company, 2004)

A: In each book, I use every color on the color wheel, and I'm very big on complementary colors. So when you see me using a lot of red, you'll see me using a lot of green at the same time. And that kind of tension brings punch to the paintings.

Q: When did you study color theory?

A: I had two years of art school, a mix of liberal arts and art school, and after that I went on my own. I knew I wanted to study calligraphy, so I found a calligraphy teacher. I thought I wanted to do children's books and greeting cards, so I took adult education classes in those things. At that time, I did take a color theory class, one on one, from a watercolor artist who taught me his theory of mixing colors. He said, "I use the same palette as Winslow Homer; there are about thirteen colors here, and if it was good enough for Winslow Homer, it's good enough for me." I had every color in the book, every tube of paint you can imagine—and I didn't know how to mix them, so I used them right out of the tube. He got rid of 90 percent of my art supplies. He gave me this limited palette and showed me how to mix colors. I was off and running. I still am figuring it out, but basically I use that palette every day and I teach it whenever I can.

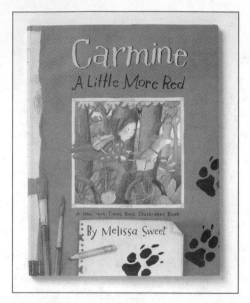

The cover of *Carmine: A Little More Red* shows one of Sweet's favorite motifs—a girl on a bike. Like Little Red Riding Hood, Carmine wanders off the path and into danger. A painter, she is searching for another shade of red, which she finds in a field of poppies.
Carmine: A Little More Red, written and illustrated by Melissa Sweet (New York, Houghton Mifflin, 2005)

Because I love red in all its iterations, I also add orange-red, carmine, opera gouache—to name a few.

Q: Books like *Mrs. Harkness and the Panda* or *The Boy Who Drew Birds* are based on historical characters, but in a book like *Carmine: A Little More Red*, you can make everything up.

A: Drawing William Carlos Williams (*A River of Words*) or John James Audubon (*The Boy Who Drew Birds*)—those are big, big shoes to fill, and I needed to honor who they were. I don't consider what I do cartooning or caricature, so I take some artistic license but not 100 percent license. The nonfictional characters are recognizable, but getting there takes a long time to craft that person so that I'm able to put him in every situation that the book needs. I liken it to making a movie: you show a character far away and close up—and the emotion is huge because that's what draws people into the book; they relate to the characters emotionally.

I always want the reader to fall in love with the characters; I've fallen in love with them! There's a lot of whimsy and fun and play, but it's serious play, because we (illustrators) have got to get it right. I can work a month or two drawing the characters over and over until I say, "Oh, that's what I want that character to look like!"

As for the setting, it's either something I have to make up or have to research. For *The Boy Who Drew Birds*, I went to see where John James Audubon lived. I got the context as authentic as I could within my own style. There are all those elements that come together and they're all brought forward slowly—then all of a sudden you've got what you need and you can begin. But you know, from doing what you do, too, that the practice goes on our whole lives, every day, every morning.

Q: It does, and the lessons that we've had inform those decisions we make every day. It's really critical to have your sea legs underneath you, so you can say to yourself, "I'm confident about this; I know how I'm going to go forward." It's

In this spread from *Tupelo Rides the Rails*, the story of a dog that finds comfort in the company of a fellow (but human) hobo, Sweet conveys a shimmering landscape in watercolor.
Tupelo Rides the Rails by Melissa Sweet (Boston: Houghton Mifflin, 2008)

not going to be "I have a beautiful drawing but I'm afraid to change it into color; making that transition could be disastrous." We make those transitions; it's not something we're afraid of.

A: I'm not afraid, but I have to confess, with every project that lands on my plate, I think, "I can't believe I'm going to do this! They've got the wrong person!" You have to muster that moment of beginning, doing it badly at first.

Q: But you don't get stuck, do you?

A: I don't get stuck because I don't have the privilege of being stuck. I don't have the privilege of saying, "I don't feel like it. I'm going to find something easier to do." The projects are the projects, and you have to call forth something that's bigger than yourself to get the project done. So yes, I wake up in the middle of the night thinking, "I don't know how to resolve this." It still happens.

Q: It happens to me, too! I think of the picture book as a really big canvas, and part of what you hinted at before was the many disciplines that come into it. We're taking our reader through time; we're using the reader's memory to take her from this page to the next page ... and we're also working with predictive qualities so she can imagine what's coming next.

Doing a single piece of art is incredibly challenging, and museums are full of completed pieces that satisfy that expectation, but in a picture book, we're doing something different. We're doing something that's going to incorporate time and words—or, if it's wordless, it's a narrative of pictures. Oftentimes, when I meet a person who wants to get into children's books and he asks me what he needs to know, I tell him it requires design. The book has a topography; it has shape and color and character and costuming.

A: Exactly. When people approach me about how to get started, I always send them to SCBWI (the Society of Children's Book Writers and Illustrators, www.scbwi.org). I try to let them figure out if illustration is the place they need to be, because it requires incredible discipline.

It's not about the book's publication. The book comes out and that's an amazing moment when you get it in the mail and you're thrilled and there's all that marketing end of things we do now that we didn't have to do so much before. But it's really the studio where it's happening, and if working in the studio isn't a thrill for you, if that doesn't get you up in the morning, it's maybe not the profession for you.

Q: We don't have the office with its buzz of people. We have a studio that we populate with our characters: our bears, our dogs, our pigs that come out of the woodwork.

A: Yes, yes, you stay in the chair, and you work through it. You keep working through it. The books I've written have a very layered feeling to them. Try as I may to simplify things, the layers still show. *Carmine: A Little More Red*, for instance, is a Little Red Riding Hood story; she's also an artist and there's an alphabet component to it. And all those layers have to work together. So I'm looking at ways to give the reader information without spelling everything out for him. A timeline or a map or a chart gives a different kind of information to think about; it gives the book a depth that's useful. Because if it isn't useful, there's no point to putting it in there.

I look for ways of collapsing a lot of information in a small space to get it across. It wasn't 100 percent necessary to put a timeline, which shows silly signposts in the history of dogs, at the beginning of *Tupelo Rides the Rails*, or end papers that map the constellations in the night sky, but I thought it was fun, since the hobo dogs in this book had their own sort of society, to think back to their legacy and their ancestors going all the way back. Why the heck was there a dog star? Canis Major and Canis Minor go back aeons. But there you have it! And what were the famous dogs through history? The timeline on the end papers inserts humor, too. I always think the end papers are incredibly valuable space in the book to further the story—either to get you into it or to lead you out in a way that closes the book on an upbeat note. For me the end papers are another visual field.

A Splash of Red: The Life and Art of Horace Pippin shows how Pippin, having been injured during World War I, learned to draw with his paralyzed hand. Sweet used watercolor, as well as pen and ink, gouache, and mixed media to create the illustrations.
A Splash of Red: The Life and Art of Horace Pippin, written by Jen Bryant and illustrated by Melissa Sweet (New York: Alfred A. Knopf, 2013)

Q: Your books have a rhythm that I think you often accomplish with collage. You create transitions so that a reader will be coming from a big page and then have something invite him or her to a smaller space—maybe to allow time for feeling emotion. Collage makes your work unique; it's your thumbprint. Would you talk about that collage aspect and how you make it work?

A: Watercolor is my favorite medium; whatever I do, watercolor is there. Years ago I wanted to fall in love with collage, but there was something about all those little pieces and that glue I didn't like. It was messy, and I wasn't used to being messy. So it took me a while to segue into it and understand the right glues and papers. And what I found was that the collage materials I would choose were very specific to the manuscript, to the era, and to the place. I think I can speak about it from the vantage of *The Boy Who Drew Birds* because that was about Audubon, and I started to collect stamps, ephemera, and old ledger books that I thought would be fun to use. I used them sparingly, but that was the key: it didn't have to be a massive amount of collage. The thing about one piece of paper on top of a painting is that it's different—and that difference is noticeable, so that's the place where your eye is drawn. You can use that to your advantage when you're designing a page. Maybe that's the place you lay type or maybe you paint on top of it, so my using collage elements started to show up slowly but surely.

And the beauty of collage is that it takes away the preciousness. If you don't like it, tear it off; put something else on. If you don't like part of the painting, put a piece of collage over it. And even in my paintings that I want to discard (though I don't discard a lot), sometimes there are elements that are really beautiful, so now I cut them out and use them as collage pieces.

Q: Even if you're only adding a layer of watercolor paper, all of sudden space is part of it. I'm thinking about *Balloons Over Broadway* and the puppetry and the textures and the marionettes that you created expressly for that book.

Before you started working with three-dimensional objects like puppets, you were sending pieces of watercolor paper that could be drum scanned, but now an assemblage has to be photographed. You create it on your desk, but you're going to be lighting it for reproduction.

A: When the art is done and it goes to the publisher, we're only about halfway there, because the production of the book is a huge part of making the art merge with the typography and text. *Balloons Over Broadway* is a true story of Tony Sarg, who was the puppeteer for the first Macy's Thanksgiving parades. I researched him for a number of years before I started. His work was so three-dimensional—the puppets and the balloons; this was in the 1920s, so he had only simple materials. When I set out to do the book, I started making puppets and toys in the same manner he did, with the same materials, to try to get a feel for what he'd been doing. And when I did that, I knew I'd hit on how the book would look.

Those objects—like finger puppets and marionettes—were extremely important to convey who he was. A normal watercolor just didn't do it. And he had such a multifaceted career: he was also a brilliant illustrator, but I couldn't tell the story of the Macy's parade through his illustrations.

I always work 100 percent to scale. For *Balloons Over Broadway* I made a dummy, then created the art—the paintings, collages, and assemblages. I packed everything up and drove from here in Maine to my publisher's office in Boston.

They photographed the art—that wasn't really my forte—so the production, in this case, was an amazing team effort between the art director at Houghton Mifflin, the production team, and me. They were talking about the depth of the shadows and getting the lighting just so. They had to merge those photographs with the flat art of the paintings. They did it so brilliantly. It would not be the book it is without that production team.

Q: A collaborative effort means that you can't be a control freak.

A: Yes, but I guess I'm old enough to know there are some things I'm good at and some things I'm not. And I wouldn't have known exactly what to ask the photographer for.

To illustrate *Balloons Over Broadway: The True Story of the Puppeteer of the Macy's Parade*, Sweet made actual puppets from the kind of materials Tony Sarg would have used.
Balloons Over Broadway: The True Story of the Puppeteer of the Macy's Parade written and illustrated by Melissa Sweet (New York: Houghton Mifflin, 2011)

I could say, "Not that!" (after the fact). But you're right. You have to give up some control—and the same thing with the typography. I take the fonts I use very seriously. The art director had to merge my hand lettering with the fonts. She was a genius.

Q: Bikes are everywhere in your work, and you have a number of trail and vintage bikes. In one book you describe the perfect day as riding your bike to the library. I have to ask why you love bicycles so much!

A: Probably because, while we were growing up in New Jersey in a very suburban neighborhood, that was our vehicle of choice. We were like a pack of wild kids, going to the corner store to get penny candy and having a pick-up kick-the-can game. We had a lot of freedom and bikes gave us that freedom.

I have two brothers and we're all bikeaholics, so to speak. I'm pretty sure it's the pace of a bicycle; riding a bike is the perfect way to see something. It's a little faster than walking, but you can take it all in.

Q: Learning to ride a bike—do you remember that?

A: I do! I remember the moment I got it. I had training wheels. I don't know if my father took them off or just raised them, but I remember that initial shove. And you got it and you never looked back. You just kept going down the street.

Q: It's that same sense of freedom and independence and going places with books.

A: That's a great way to look at it. You go at your own pace.

Q: Learning to read is the same as learning to ride a bicycle.

A: All of a sudden, you're getting it. There are all different methods to learning to read, but there's that moment you can do it.

Q: You can do your artwork for any audience, but you've chosen to do it for children. Can you tell me why?

A: I wasn't one of those kids who curled up with a book readily; it was a last resort! I would much rather have been making something or doing something with my hands. Or out on a bike. But when I thought about being an illustrator, I remembered, clear as a bell, Maurice Sendak's Little Bear series by Else Holmelund Minarik. I don't know how to describe this exactly, but I had the feeling I think I could do that. I think I could use pen and ink and make a drawing. It wasn't bravado; it was a comfort level. Those illustrations were just so appealing that I thought maybe my style at that time would be good for kids' books.

I love everything about illustrating children's books. I give it everything I've got and let the chips fall where they may—knowing that some kid is going to notice all the little details and that this story will be for her or him.

Q: We wouldn't know Wilbur or Charlotte unless E.B. White had been crazed enough to think he could do a story about a pig and a spider and get you engaged emotionally. What were the books in your childhood that stood out?

A: Definitely Maurice Sendak's. We had all the Dr. Seuss books, too. And there was one book whose illustrations I loved: *Miss Flora McFlimsey's Easter Bonnet* (by Mariana with illustrations by Caroline Walton Howe). This little girl makes Easter bonnets for all her dolls. Very spare illustrations, but my five-year-old imagination could see all the buttons and ribbons and trims coming out of that little hatbox when there wasn't that much detail in the illustrations. It didn't matter: it was all there for me. That was one I remember most.

I ran into a woman at a conference and she was describing the novels she was reading to her eleven- and thirteen-year-old kids, and I thought, "Who doesn't love to be read to? Who doesn't love a good story?" I think that reading to children as long as they'll let you read to them is as great as their learning to read on their own. I have no fear of the picture book's not being alive and well tomorrow, because a screen is never going to replace that.

Charles Demuth was studying painting at the same time William Carlos Williams was studying medicine. In this spread Sweet conveys, with watercolor and collage, Williams's poem, "The Great Figure," which was inspired by Demuth's *I Saw the Figure 5 in Gold*.
A River of Words: The Story of William Carlos Williams, written by Jen Bryant and illustrated by Melissa Sweet (Grand Rapids, Michigan: Eerdmans Books for Young Readers, 2008)

Q: You're between projects right now. You just sent one out. Can you tell us a little about it or what you're going to be looking forward to?

A: I just sent off a book called *Little Red Writing*, a very funny take on Little Red Riding Hood. She's a pencil—all the characters are pencils. She's a little red pencil, and she discovers an electric pencil sharpener in her school—that's the wolf. Those books are tricky, because there's a lot of humor involved, but it has to be somewhat plausible. Again, it's about characters and setting and timing.

And my most recent book is about the artist Horace Pippin. It's called *A Splash of Red* and it's by Jen Bryant who also wrote *A River of Words*, which was about William Carlos Williams. *A Splash of Red* has quite a bit of collage in it. It was an honor and a privilege to investigate Horace Pippin's life and bring forth this self-taught master with sensitivity and grace. He was such an amazing man. It's tricky being an illustrator and portraying an artist. Now I've done it twice. It's one of the hardest things to do—to find your voice within another artist's story.

Q: I remember that Horace was in the war and he did a lot of war pictures. Were you able to include any of those pictures?

A: Definitely. That was a huge part. Horace loved to draw as a kid. Of course, he knew he couldn't make his living that way. He went off to World War I where his shoulder was

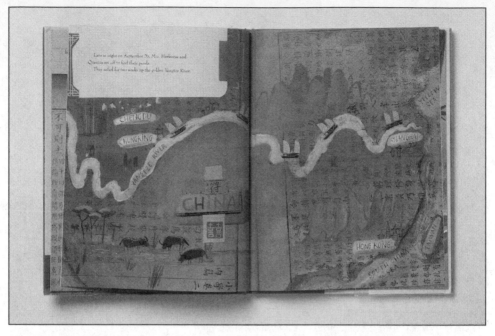

Mrs. Harkness and the Panda tells the story of the first American to travel to China in order to bring a panda to the United States. Sweet here combines layers of watercolor and gouache with collage elements.
Mrs. Harkness and the Panda, written by Alicia Potter and illustrated by Melissa Sweet (New York: Knopf Borzoi Books, 2012)

injured, so when he came back from the war he couldn't use his right hand the same way. It's a big part of the book—his relearning how to draw. And what was so moving to me, as an artist, was that Horace Pippin could not not paint or not draw, so he scrounged for materials. He made it happen, despite the pain, despite the war memories. He worked out a lot of what he was thinking about through those paintings. And I totally understood that. As an artist, whether it's deliberate or not, we're always working through our childhood or things that we love, like color, whatever—we're always bringing forth those things that are meaningful to us on paper.

Q: I can say flat out I'm so tickled I'm walking the earth with you! We both care deeply for children, for the child reader that's inside us, for the way the art world opened up to us through the pages of books, and for how it continues to do that. We want to invite another generation to this rich field of experience. And you've created an incredible body of work.

The final thing is something that I often find that children have and we have but sometimes goes missing in illustrators' work—but you have it—and that is a really wonderful, wry sense of humor. I mention this because writing humor for children is hard because we make all kinds of mistakes by making jokes that are inappropriate for kids. A big red line goes through it (the joke) and that goes deep! But children love humor.

A: It's such an amazing art form. When you watch stand-up comics or you watch Jon Stewart or *Saturday Night Live*, it's so much about timing and the right word. Growing up we had a big book of *New Yorker* cartoons. It was yellow. I remember it: the years 1925 to 1950 or something. We poured over that book! Those are cartoons that rely on timing and deadpan humor.

When I bring humor in, it's kind of inadvertent because I'm not really thinking I want to be funny. I just think, "Oh my goodness, wouldn't it be funny if the dogs were thinking this."

I look at other illustrators and how they do it, and sometimes I find the writing can be very funny, but the characters have a deadpan reaction that can be hilarious—or vice versa, the writing can be completely deadpan, and the characters are out-of-their-minds hilarious. So it's tricky. If I had advice, I'd say go one way or another. Be very funny in your language but keep your characters deadpan so they're not in on the joke. They're the straight guy.

Q: It's been a delight to have this opportunity to spend this time with you.

A: I want to say one last thing: We have a very solitary life, we illustrators, so I often think when I bump into someone like you, Will, these are the moments to live for. It's such a privilege and honor to be with someone who is in your field, whom you never get to see because you never take the time, so it's my honor.

Will Hillenbrand has illustrated over fifty books for children. Visit his website at willhillenbrand.com.

Excerpted from the January/February 2014 issue of *The Artist's Magazine*. Used with the kind permission of *The Artist's Magazine*, a publication of F+W, a Content + eCommerce Company. Visit www.artistsnetwork.com to subscribe.

MARK CRILLEY

Artist, Author, and YouTube "Dad"

by Neely McLaughlin

Mark Crilley, known for such hits as *Akiko*, *Mikki Falls*, and *Brody's Ghost*, is tremendously popular online, with about two million YouTube subscribers and a strong presence in other platforms. "My theory of online stuff is that you have to go where the people are rather than run around trying to lure people to your little ivory-tower website or blog off in some corner of the Internet," he explains. He has gone where the people are, and the people have gone to him.

Crilley, a self-described YouTube "dad-like guy," is an author, illustrator, and online presence.

"I'd guess people regard me as a kind of 'dad-like' guy on YouTube, making goofy jokes and not attempting to be particularly hip," he says. As he puts it, he starts with simply being there and does not emphasize sales: "I'm here, I'm putting up new videos, [and] I've got a book coming out next month." Crilley's first priorities are being present online and being himself. With an authentic persona established, he creates strong, high-quality content. Self-promotion, crucial as that is for a creative entrepreneur, comes last. It is Crilley's approachable yet professional—and perhaps above all authentic—web presence and focus on interactivity that has made him so successful.

The banner for Crilley's YouTube channel codifies his video-creating work as part of his identity.

Beginnings: YouTube Success

While his encouraging, honest, engaged online style is crucial to his success, Crilley also believes that his timing was particularly lucky. His YouTube channel tagline identifies him as "Author / Illustrator / Video Creator." His embrace of the "Video Creator" part of his identity as an artist and entrepreneur is closely tied to the rise of YouTube itself. Crilley does not see it as a coincidence that his involvement with the site came at a time when YouTube was young.

YouTube, a site that popularized online video sharing, saw its cultural prominence grow quite quickly and Crilley was able to grow with it. YouTube's first clip was posted in 2005, and in 2007, Crilley began to post instructional video clips. By 2008, YouTube was significant enough that U.S. presidential candidates used it, and the site has remained prominent. When Crilley started posting clips, the site had less participation than it does today. "I was lucky to get into YouTube early in 2007, when the number of people there was comparatively small," he says. Crilley believes that in that context, he, as an established illustrator, got attention fairly easily. "There was a bit of a big fish, small pond thing there," he says. At the time, he goes on, "[I was] one of very few professional illustrators doing how-to-draw videos." In his years of posting on YouTube, Crilley has honed his style and developed his friendly, engaged persona. He sees his audience awareness and his persistence as crucial to his success. In a 2009 realistic drawing instructional video, for instance, he asks viewers to let him know if they are interested in more videos on realistic drawing. "By keeping at it and paying close attention to what proved popular with viewers, I was rewarded with a fast-growing audience," he explains. Being an illustrator with high standards for his online content who was willing to engage directly and enthusiastically with those eager to learn his techniques brought Crilley a steady following. His current "new video every Friday" commitment keeps people coming back.

We've all seen drawings that almost look like real manga.

The problem with them is they are based on the belief that all you need to do is give a character big, shiny eyes and that will be close enough.

Well, it's not. There's a delicate balance between the lines of a real manga illustration.

Crilley encourages attention to detail by showing the contrast between a "close-enough" manga-like drawing and a carefully done "real manga" illustration.

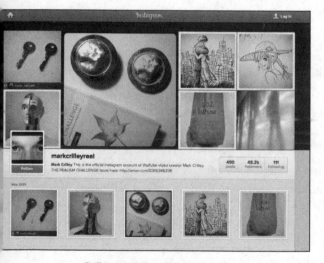

Crilley is active on Instagram.

Interactivity Across Platforms

Crilley engages with his audience regularly to promote interaction. "YouTube remains the core," he says, and in fact, his Instagram account is identified as "the official Instagram account of YouTube video creator Mark Crilley." But Instagram and other sites matter, too. "I do think it's also important to have a presence on other key social media sites," he says. "For me, it's Facebook, Twitter, Instagram, and DeviantArt." He pays attention to the way his audience engages on these sites. He recommends Instagram, in particular: "I found that Instagram grew particularly quickly and often gets more engagement from followers than Facebook, so I'd say any artist out there who's decided to skip that one should reconsider."

Questions, high quality comments, consistent engagement, and quick responses maintain Crilley's web presence. He sees his early YouTube audience as "people who'd maybe always wanted drawing tips from a pro but had never been able to get them." He analyzes his audience constantly, working from the starting point that he will be reaching out to an artistic fan base. "I assume that anyone following me on Facebook or Twitter is interested in drawing or in creative matters in general," he says, adding, "I go to these places like Twitter and Instagram and I try to build something there, providing content and engagement with people on a daily basis." The conversational quality of the comments on his YouTube videos highlights Crilley's commitment to continued interaction. He helps people find other videos, directing them by posting links when they ask about specific techniques or products. That personal touch contributes to a supportive and vibrant online community, promoting plenty of audience participation.

Crilley's connection to his audience is also evident in his videos and the conversations surrounding them. One of his most popular YouTube uploads, "How to Draw a Realistic Eye," an approximately ten minute clip from September 2009, has over twenty million views and remains popular over five years later. This clip continues to receive views and comments, and Crilley continues to respond to the comment thread in a way that is both typical of YouTube and evidence of his "YouTube Dad" style: When Sarah, a viewer in the Spring of 2015, writes "Dear markcrilley, You are amazing" and shares that Crilley is her inspiration, he replies right away with "Thank you Sarah! :)." This alert, friendly, emoticon-using comment brings in commenter "roma" who writes, "mark to see you comment 36 minutes ago means so much to me." The warmth of this exchange illustrates the kind of community Crilley is able to foster through his interactivity. The fact that this exchange takes place in the comment thread of a YouTube video years after its initial upload shows one way he keeps his older material alive for new viewers.

Crilley's interest in authenticity is evident in his promotion of a range of body images in his manga instructional materials, including the tutorial for this fuller-figured girl.

Although Crilley has not found Facebook to be the best virtual venue for facilitating viewer engagement, he regularly asks questions that receive many responses. "I like using

The introduction section of *Mastering Manga with Mark Crilley* emphasizes the importance of high quality work, a hallmark of his instructional materials.

Facebook as a way of posing questions and seeing what people think," he says. For instance, on March 30, 2015, he asked, "If someone is better at drawing than you, does that mean you aren't 'qualified' to criticize their work? Or are the two matters unrelated?" The interactivity facilitated by questions like this one keeps Crilley aware of the perspectives of his audience members. "My answer to this particular question is, 'No, absolutely you don't have to be good at something to criticize someone else's efforts.' I've never made a Hollywood movie but I don't hesitate to tear apart the one I've just seen if it did nothing for me as an audience member," he notes. Crilley's questions are motivated by genuine interest. He explains, "For me this is a way of starting a sort of virtual conversation with my viewers about art, and as I read through the answers they give, I'm often surprised by the huge variety in responses."

Sales and Professionalism

Crilley is not only personally engaged but consistently both professional and easy to relate to. He prioritizes a high level of professionalism in the face of the negativity and carelessness that can easily come to dominate virtual environments, going out of his way to be positive and helpful. He seeks out useful ways to engage. For example, when a commenter writes, "hey not trying to be rude but this isnt that realistic (and yes to all the people i can draw a better eye ever since i went to an actually realistic drawing of an eye) but still good drawing," Crilley responds by simply posting a link to another video with the comment, "This one is more the kind of realism you're looking for." The tone of this response is professional and respectful, allowing Crilley to promote his artistic range and his site even in response to a comment that could be viewed as annoying and condescending. "A lot of YouTubers swear and make edgy comments and so forth, and I have never gone into that territory," Crilley says.

High standards mean hard work, but Crilley encourages new artists not to be perfectionists when it causes them to want to give up.

Crilley keeps the tone in his instructional materials upbeat and encouraging, making comments like, "You can draw almost anything so long as you're willing to commit the time to it." He avoids the edgy tone common to many users and often associated with being genuine, but he clearly exhibits the authenticity many social media users value and require. "I'm really just being myself as I shoot these videos," he says. "If anyone were to meet me in real life they wouldn't find that I'm secretly some other person or anything." While Crilley may not have consciously developed an online brand, he is consistent, and an encouraging persona appropriate for all ages has emerged: "When I started uploading videos years ago, I never imagined I'd become someone with an online persona. But over time one has evolved, no question."

Crilley avoids being what he sees as too sales-oriented. "At least 90 percent of what you're sending out there should be fun con-

Crilley encourages his readers to pay attention to photographs as they learn to draw larger characters in order to foster respectful professionalism.

Together, words and images tell a story.

tent that's making people's feeds interesting," he says. "Then you can get away with the 10 percent of stuff that's more directly encouraging people to buy something or do something on your behalf." He believes that staying active on the Web gives him the opportunity to keep reminding people of his presence, while not focusing overtly on sales pitches: "I try to stay away from repeated obnoxious sales stuff. You can't be constantly tweeting the Amazon link to your books."

Artistic Range and the Joy of Comics

Crilley's subject matter is varied. His YouTube channel highlights this range: "My channel features how-to-draw videos on almost every topic you can imagine, from manga and anime styles to highly detailed photorealism," reads the channel description in part. Crilley is a writer as well as a visual artist, and it is bringing those skills and ways of thinking together that he finds most inspiring: "I've written prose fiction novels and enjoyed the experience, but when I do a graphic novel I feel I'm really firing on all cylinders, bringing my writing and drawing skills together to give readers everything I've got."

Bringing together different strands of expression has been part of Crilley's work since the beginning. "My first job as a published illustrator was in the comics industry back in

1995," he says. "So right from the start I've been engaged in this constant interaction between words and drawings, with one influencing the other in every single panel." Crilley sees this kind of work as particularly compelling for audiences. "The act of reading a comic book story really engages the human brain in a wonderful way, because you're processing the words one way and the images another: your brain is dancing between the two activities on a second-to-second basis."

The complexity of the audience experience excites Crilley. He believes that such an audience experience is almost unique: "A children's picture book is the only other form that comes close." Comics also provide a lot of artistic freedom. "Comics allow you to pick and choose what you present by way of text and what you supply only in the art. I really missed that aspect when I wrote prose fiction," he says. He particularly likes the way comics are able to present dialogue. "I love the way dialogue scenes work," he explains. "They are probably my favorite example of text and art serving a common purpose." These scenes engage the reader's imagination particularly well, while at the same time giving the reader a rich visual that helps to shape that imaginative experience. "The reader is given a bit of speech and asked to imagine the voice of the character, but the art is there to convey a facial expression or bit of body language

Setting is an important part of storytelling and something Crilley feels is best done through images rather than words.

Crilley emphasizes the importance of storytelling in his second manga instruction book.

that adds a lot to the scene." This is a part of the artistic process that Crilley dedicates time and energy to: "I love fine-tuning the dialogue and the art, and getting them to work together in perfect harmony."

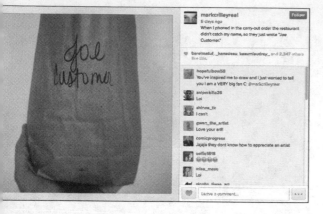

Crilley posts amusing photos and captions for his Instagram followers, including this paper bag photo, with the caption, "When I phoned in the carry-out order the restaurant didn't catch my name, so they just wrote 'Joe Customer.'"

One aspect of storytelling that Crilley particularly likes to do through image is establishing location. Doing that through text alone is "quite a challenge." He worries that readers will disengage when faced with long descriptions. "If I'm writing a novel and the characters come to a giant palace, I know I'll lose the readers if I spend three paragraphs describing the look of the building." Setting is important, but he has to get it done quickly to keep readers' attention, whereas in comics, that descriptive function is replaced by images and can be given attention in the background without alienating readers. "In comics I can just draw the setting in a huge establishing shot and continue to explore it in the backgrounds of each panel that follows," he says.

Dedication

As a reader, Crilley appreciates the authenticity he values in his own online work. One of his favorite comics is Raina Telgemeier's *Smile*. "I think it's an important book in the history of comics," he explains. "For years American comics have been mostly about superheroes and fantasy, but Raina uses the form to present an honest, real story in an approachable cartooning style that's completely true to who she is." He hopes that this kind of work will be influential. As much as he appreciates the comic form, he finds himself turning to non-fiction for his

Crilley's tone is encouraging and he stays approachable in his instructional materials.

recreational reading. "When I read for pleasure it's mostly non-fiction books, not graphic novels," he admits. "I can't think of anything more pleasant than curling up with a Bill Bryson travel book, for example." Perhaps it is easier to relax into the enjoyment of something unlike his own work. "I'm pretty sure I read them the way anyone else does: imagin

MORE FROM MARK CRILLEY

For more inspiration, check out these titles by Mark Crilley:

Mastering Manga With Mark Crilley: 30 Drawing Lessons From the Creator of Akiko (IMPACT Books, 2012)

Mastering Manga 2: Level Up With Mark Crilley (IMPACT Books, 2013)

ing the scenes to some degree, but mostly just admiring his prose and periodically busting my gut laughing."

For his regular audience, it is as easy to imagine Crilley laughing over Bryson's amusing take on a place as it is to picture him refining a drawing, dreaming up another installment of one of his hits, creating a new YouTube video, or posting something amusing or inspiring on Instagram, such as a photograph of a carry-out bag with "Joe Customer" from a restaurant that did not catch Crilley's name.

Crilley uses his various media outlets to build genuine connections with his audience, but he does not embrace the short-term thinking and speed that often dominate online media. "Basically I'm a 'long haul' kind of guy: Every day I'm chipping away at some big project, and the main thing is to maintain patience so that all the work is consistent in quality," he says. That dedication is as evident in his media presence as it is in his careful drawings.

Neely McLaughlin is a writer and assistant professor of English at the University of Cincinnati, Blue Ash, in Cincinnati, Ohio.

RAMI NIEMI

International Illustrator

....

by Luke McLaughlin

Rami Niemi has illustrated countless articles for a laundry list of internationally recognized publications. He has provided illustrations for Google and the US and UK versions of the technology magazine *Wired*. His work has been featured in the magazine *Men's Health* as well as the *New York Times*. He has provided his own brand of colorful, nostalgic comic book inspired images with a smooth, modern, computer-produced vector finish for all of these and countless more publications around the world.

Niemi is Finnish but lives in rural Sweden and spent several years working in Paris after university. Thanks to the digital nature of illustration work these days he is able to complete assignments for American magazines, often taking advantage of the fact that he is working in a time zone that is usually six or seven hours before the work day begins on the American east coast.

Details

Niemi uses bold color palettes that are familiar and recognizable without being repetitive and a halftone raster technique of tiny, repeated polka dots to create shading and texture in a way that echoes the print media

Niemi uses small details to create characters and stories in a single image. He uses negative space effectively to show space and height and allow his characters to breathe in the limited space of a single panel illustration.

of previous eras. Though he has worked for countless magazines, his images maintain a boyish enthusiasm. He loves to add more and more details, each of which adds to the visual story without cluttering up the illustrations.

Niemi says that it would be really hard to pick his favorite illustration job, but he says that the "'mags' slightly on the 'boyish' side have been really satisfying." He notes that he prefers jobs where he has "been given relatively free hands to garnish my illustrations with the geeky details I love and 'obsess' over." Niemi

Niemi shows television adventurer Dan Wildman, violinist virtuoso Joshua Bell, and tennis ace Andy Roddick with their favorite travel equipment for the magazine *Men's Health*. Their faces are simple facial icons, but they are immediately recognizable by their uniforms, hairstyles, and accessories.

loves to draw the paraphernalia of rock music, sports, and whole costumes of clothes. He uses the details of clothing and the objects in an illustration to add depth to the characters in his illustrations, which are usually pared down visually to an almost iconographic simplicity. "I like to think my 'wittiness' is in the details," Niemi explains. He says he thinks his works have matured over the last five years are so, but his work still retains an almost childlike freshness and optimism. He seems to be able to put his imagination straight onto the paper.

Characters

The faces on Niemi's characters can be as simple as two dots and a curve for a smile, although he often decorates them with moustaches or beards. He has a deft touch for hairstyles, too. He captures the personality of a person's hair with a few simple curves or shapes, a trick used by comic book artists and animators to create recognizable characters such as Bart Simpson and Tintin. This style of drawing has a universal appeal. It is recognizable across cultures and age groups and works well both in digital and print media.

In this illustration for a *Bloomberg View* article about American college entrepreneurship programs, Niemi sets the scene with the care and attention to detail of a set dresser. The books, posters, and general mess show the dorm room setting, but the student's accessories are jumbled with the top hat and cigar of a business tycoon.

This monochrome illustration for the *New York Times* shows a diverse classroom in action. It is composed of simple shapes and recognizable symbols. A basketball has more shading detail than any of the children's faces, but Niemi gives them each a unique character with their clothes, haircuts, and accessories.

Clothing is another strong suit for Niemi. He pays careful attention to shoes. In an illustration where three characters have exactly the same face, they will have three completely different styles of shoes with different heights, heels, materials, colors, gloss, and even different styles of shoelaces. He turns the characters wardrobes into recognizable uniforms that show who they are.

Niemi loves drawing subcultures. Though he doesn't feel like he belongs to them, he enjoys drawing rock, skater, and graffiti subculture figures as well as their accessories. In illustrations with groups of people you can tell he has created just enough background detail about the personality of each character to make them believable. What he draws might look simple, but it is a carefully drawn and designed simplicity. He uses his design and advertising agency experience to pare down his drawings to that which conveys the most information while keeping them fun, exciting, and recognizably his own.

A Classic Era

In Finland, Niemi studied graphic design at UIAH (now known as Aalto University), the University of Art and Design in Helsinki from 1999 to 2002. There he learned to use computer illustration, which was a revelation for him. He then moved to France for three formative years, which he describes as a "classic era." He recalls, "I went 'Erasmus generation,' moved to Paris and worked with various people for three years, for example, doing illustration and graphic design for Kuntzel+Deygas for two years." After returning to Finland from his years abroad he joined three friends to work for their "crew," a collaboration called Vänskap.

Living in the capitals of Finland and France exposed him to the myriad different types of people and characters that fill his illustrations. Though he now lives in rural Sweden, his illustrations have a cosmopolitan quality and feel at home in the cities where his illustrations feature in the publications that line the newsstands.

Among other projects, they created a television series that ran for ten episodes on Music Television Nordic. The series was called *We Could Be Heroes*. It didn't turn out the big break it

Niemi credits his success to hard work and determination to finish his assignments. He says that a lot of his magazine assignments are fun and even easy, but it is a lot of work to make a living as an illustrator.

might have been. Though he enjoyed working on the project, it didn't result in a career creating television. "This lasted for a year and a half, and was fun as hell but difficult," Niemi says.

Unfortunately, the series was largely unnoticed by the public and after his time with Vänskap, Niemi worked for an advertising agency again. He describes working for an ad agency as "toil," and it wasn't long before he decided to start working for himself. In 2007 he got an agent and set himself up as an illustrator.

Starting Up

Niemi says that when you are starting out you need to get a great portfolio together. It has to be original and says it should be "the stuff you know like your pockets, the stuff that

Niemi loves drawing sports like running and climbing. He enjoys drawing the details of the technical gear that athletes wear and the stripes fitted elements. Here he uses motion lines, stars, and bursts to convey the action of running on a treadmill in the manner of a vintage comic strip.

inspires you, and the stuff that you love." He explains that it is far better to stick with and master one style instead of showing people all of the different styles that you could do. Niemi says that eventually getting an agent will help you land good jobs, and he credits his agency, Agent Pekka, for helping him get work. But the first step is to put together a portfolio that stands out. You have to be prepared to work a lot in order to make it worthwhile and to make a living out of it.

Agents and Agencies

Niemi has been focusing on illustration since 2007, when he started working with an agent. He recalls, "Before that I was doing graphic odd jobs and working a bit at advertising agencies." He has loved to draw since he was a child. He says he never really had to think much about what to do for a living because of his love of drawing. He thinks that getting an agent is a really important step for a beginning illustrator and it seems that having an agent was a big part of the difference in getting really good illustration jobs. In order to get a good agent, however, you have to have a polished portfolio of good illustrations. Once you are established, it is your work that makes your reputation and in a way advertises itself. His agent's website features full page images of his illustrations.

Digital Workflow

Niemi usually works with a simple digital workflow. "I open a blank document and draw and see where it goes," he explains. He writes down some keywords for details and says that this method works for most jobs. Sometimes, however, he gets stuck and has to start from scratch. "Then I start over again, or maybe even sketch a bit with pen and paper. If push comes to shove, I'll just grind my teeth together and get the thing finished by deadline somehow," Niemi says. His ability to finish his work doesn't rely on fancy tricks, but on drawing skills built up in a lifetime of loving to draw and years of hard work drawing, designing, and illustrating.

In this illustration, Niemi has simplified the mass of noodles into an amorphous blob. Their identity is only revealed by the strand of noodle being slurped up in the previous bite. He simplifies the toppings into fun shapes that spill out over the sides of the bowl.

Niemi says that schedules for illustration jobs are often tight, but they do vary from "by tomorrow" to a month or more. He likes to do them if he has the time. He says that because he lives in Sweden and does a lot of illustrations for American magazines he gets a few extra hours to work on projects because of the time difference. He uses this extra time to add that extra bit of polish and detail that makes his work stand out.

Raster Master

A signature feature in most of Niemi's illustration is half-tone polka dots. These are recognizable from early pulp fiction covers, comic book, and other vintage printing techniques. "Back in the '90s, as a teen, I had that kind of sticker raster sheets I used in order to make shadows in my drawings," he recalls. He would cut a piece of a sticker covered in polka dots into the right shape with scissors and put it in the right place to painstakingly add the detail he wanted to his drawings. It wasn't until 1999 that he started making them digitally. He says that the polka dots are nostalgic to him: "They look sweet and out-of-date," he explains.

Niemi's illustrations are composed of smooth vector lines and simple shapes. Texture, shadow, and detail are usually implied rather than illustrated. In this image, simple dots represent the stars on the American flag, seeds on the bun, the texture of the hamburger, and the bumps on the outside of a pickle.

He has always related to the identity of a geeky '90s comic book guy, but in the end he just likes the life and shading that the raster polka dots add to an illustration.

Color Mixer

Niemi almost always starts out with a five-color palette: a skin color, a red, blue, green, and a yellow. From there he might add a few colors or even remove some to simplify the color scheme. He says that he doesn't have a go-to palette but comes up with a unique set of colors for each illustration. He judges the shades of color by eye. He uses the Adobe Illustrator color mixer to make the color palettes for each illustration, usually aiming for a slightly vintage flavor, with pastel colors he describes as "broken." He explains, "I mix them again every time. I stare at the screen to judge the shade of the color."

Niemi thinks that his playful, "naughty-but-not-too-naughty" illustrations make people smile. He tries to make lighthearted and fun illustrations. He thinks that people find his pop culture references endearing, and his fun colors and fluid vector lines suit many different purposes. He says that because he became an adult before the Internet was prominent and because he is a luddite when it comes to social media that he is a bit of an anachronism in the illustration scene. "Maybe my world is a bit askew, maybe the references I have aren't very hip," he admits. He wishes that he came from a skateboarding, graffiti, or hip-hop background, all of which he finds conceptually interesting.

Niemi's work features fields of block colors. He seldom uses color gradations. Although he sometimes uses bright primary colors, his color schemes are usually more pastel. His work seems to span the gap between retro and modern, and the color palettes reflect that. Niemi's recreation of the color palette is similar to the technique of color mixing that many traditional artists, especially painters, believe is fundamental. Because each color palette is different, the colors never seem stale and samey. They set the mood for the image, whether it is a late-night cool blue or a red technological glow.

Sometimes half of Niemi's image will be negative space, while other times every inch is filled with detail. He has an eye for details and is also aware that sometimes the absence of an object is more noticeable than the object itself. His use of space enables his illustrations to not feel constrained by the space that they inhabit.

"I'm not sure what's the secret ingredient, possibly just working hard and getting stuff done," Niemi says. "Come to think of it, I suppose colors count, too—I get compliments for my colors, and it's nice, as I haven't considered myself as 'the guy who's good with colors.'" But he is good with colors. Art classes often have students create color palettes for assignments. Ad agents certainly pay a lot of attention to colors. His pastel palettes hearken back to the golden age of animation and comic books, his polka-dot shading and textures echo the pop-art movement, and his smooth vector lines and the sleek simplicity of his work mean that his work continues to feature alongside articles far from his home in rural Sweden.

Luke McLaughlin is an American writer based in Oxford, England. Find out more about what he is working on at lucasmclaughlin.com.

GALLERIES

Most artists dream of seeing their work in a gallery. It's the equivalent of "making it" in the art world. That dream can be closer than you realize. The majority of galleries are actually quite approachable and open to new artists. Though there will always be a few austere establishments manned by snooty clerks, most are friendly places where people come to browse and chat with the gallery staff.

So don't let galleries intimidate you. The majority of gallery curators will be happy to take a look at your work if you make an appointment or e-mail JPEGs to them. If they feel your artwork doesn't fit their gallery, most will steer you toward a more appropriate one.

A Few Guidelines

- **Never walk into a gallery without an appointment** expecting to show your work to the director. When we ask gallery directors about their pet peeves, they always mention the talented newcomer walking into the gallery with paintings in hand. Most galleries prefer or even require electronic submissions. (Refer to the listings for more specific information on each gallery's preferred submission method.) Following the gallery's guidelines, send a polished package of about eight to twelve images, either by e-mail or on disk. If you prefer to work with slides and the gallery will accept them, send neatly labeled, mounted duplicate slides of your work in plastic slide sheets. Do not send original slides, as you will need them to reproduce later. Send a SASE, but realize your packet may not be returned.
- **Seek out galleries that show the type of work you create.** Most galleries have a specific "slant" or mission. A gallery that shows only abstract works will not be interested in your realistic portraits.

TYPES OF GALLERIES

As you search for the perfect gallery, it's important to understand the different types of spaces and how they operate. The route you choose depends on your needs, the type of work you do, your long-term goals, and the audience you're trying to reach.

- **Retail or commercial galleries.** The goal of the retail gallery is to sell and promote the work of artists while turning a profit. Retail galleries take a commission of 40 to 50 percent of all sales.
- **Co-op galleries.** Co-ops exist to sell and promote artists' work, but they are run by artists. Members exhibit their own work in exchange for a fee, which covers the gallery's overhead. Some co-ops also take a small commission of 20 to 30 percent to cover expenses. Members share the responsibilities of gallery-sitting, sales, housekeeping, and maintenance.
- **Rental galleries.** The rental gallery makes its profit primarily through renting space to artists and therefore may not take a commission on sales (or will take only a very small commission). Some rental spaces provide publicity for artists, while others do not. Showing in this type of gallery is risky. Rental galleries are sometimes thought of as "vanity galleries" and, consequently, do not have the credibility other galleries enjoy.
- **Nonprofit galleries.** Nonprofit spaces will provide you with an opportunity to sell your work and gain publicity, but will not market your work aggressively because their goals are not necessarily sales-oriented. Nonprofits generally take a small commission of 20 to 30 percent.
- **Museums.** Though major museums primarily show work by established artists, many small museums are open to emerging artists.
- **Art consultancies.** Consultants act as liaisons between fine artists and buyers. Most take a commission on sales (as would a gallery). Some maintain small gallery spaces and show work to clients by appointment.

- **Visit as many galleries as you can.** Browse for a while and see what type of work they sell. Do you like the work? Is it similar to yours in quality and style? What about the staff? Are they friendly and professional? Do they seem to know about the artists the gallery represents? Do they have convenient hours? If you're interested in a gallery outside your city and you can't manage a personal visit before you submit, read the listing carefully to make sure you understand what type of work is shown there. Check out the gallery's website to get a feel for what the space is like, or ask a friend or relative who lives in that city to check out the gallery for you.

- **Attend openings.** You'll have a chance to network and observe how the best galleries promote their artists. Sign each gallery's guest book or ask to be placed on galleries' mailing lists. That's also a good way to make sure the gallery sends out professional mailings to prospective collectors.

Showing in Multiple Galleries

Most successful artists show in several galleries. Once you've achieved representation on a local level, you might be ready to broaden your scope by querying galleries in other cities. You may decide to be a "regional" artist and concentrate on galleries in surrounding states. Some artists like to have East Coast and West Coast representation.

If you plan to sell work from your studio or from a website or other galleries, be up front with each gallery that shows your work. Negotiate commission arrangements that will be fair to you and all involved.

Pricing Your Fine Art

A common question of beginning artists is "What do I charge for my paintings?" There are no hard and fast rules. The better known you become, the more collectors will pay for your work. Though you should never underprice your work, you must take into consideration what people are willing to pay. Also keep in mind that you must charge the same amount for a painting sold in a gallery as you would for work sold from your studio.

Juried Shows, Competitions, and Other Outlets

It may take months, maybe years, before you find a gallery to represent you. But don't worry; there are plenty of other venues in which to show your work. Get involved with your local art community. Attend openings and read the arts section of your local paper. You'll see there are hundreds of opportunities.

Enter group shows and competitions every chance you get. Go to the art department of your local library and check out the bulletin board, then ask the librarian to direct you to magazines that list "calls to artists" and other opportunities to exhibit your work. Subscribe to the Art Deadlines List, available online (www.artdeadlineslist.com). Join a co-op gallery and show your work in a space run by artists for artists.

Another opportunity to show your work is through local restaurants and retail shops that exhibit the work of local artists. Ask the managers how you can get your art on their walls. Become an active member in an arts group. It's important to get to know your fellow artists. And since art groups often mount exhibitions of their members' work, you'll have a way to show your work until you find a gallery to represent you.

5+5 GALLERY

620 Fort Washington Ave., Suite 3N, New York NY 10040. (718)624-6048. **E-mail:** gallery1@fodde.com. **Website:** www.5plus5gallery.com. **Contact:** Raphael Foddé, director. Online gallery only. No exhibitions. Overall price range: $300-15,000; most work sold at $1,200.

MEDIA Exhibits paper, pastel, pen & ink, watercolor.

TERMS Artwork is accepted on consignment (50% commission).

SUBMISSIONS E-mail attachments only. Finds artists through submissions.

TIPS "Submit a very simple, short and to-the-point artist's statement and CV."

440 GALLERY

440 Sixth Ave., Brooklyn NY 11215. (718)499-3844. **E-mail:** gallery440@verizon.net. **Website:** www.440gallery.com. **Contact:** Nancy Lunsford, co-founder and director. Estab. 2005. 440 is a Cooperative gallery. We maintain our membership at approximately 14 artists and occasionally seek a new member when an individual moves or leaves the collective. There is a co-op membership fee plus a donation of time. All prospective members must submit a portfolio and be interviewed. In addition to members' solo exhibitions, we host 2 national juried exhibitions each year, in the summer and winter, with an outside curator making selections. Located in Park Slope (Brooklyn), the gallery is approximately 400 sq. ft. with 2 exhibition areas (the solo gallery in the front and Project Space in the back). Open Tuesday-Friday, 4-7; weekends, 11-7. Patrons are primarily from the New York City regions, especially Brooklyn. "Due to our proximity to popular Brooklyn destinations, we are visited often by tourists interested in culture and art." Overall price range: $100-12,000 with prices set by the artist. Average length of an exhibition is 5 weeks.

MEDIA Our artists most frequently exhibit painting, collage/assemblage, photography and sculpture.

TERMS Artwork is accepted on consignment and there is a 20% commission on sales for members and 30-40% on juried shows. Gallery provides promotion.

SUBMISSIONS "For consideration as a member, please e-mail a query including a link to your website, which should include a résumé. For an application to our juried shows, visit our website and find the 'Call for Entry' link."

ACADEMY GALLERY

8949 Wilshire Blvd., Beverly Hills CA 90211. (310)247-3000. **Fax:** (310)859-9619. **E-mail:** Via online contact form. **Website:** www.oscars.org. **Contact:** Moray Greenfield, theater operations. Estab. 1992. Exhibitions focus on all aspects of the film industry and the filmmaking process. Sponsors 3-5 exhibitions/year. Average display time: 3 months. Open all year; Tuesday–Friday, 10-5; weekends, 12-6. Gallery begins in building's Grand Lobby and continues on the 4th floor. Total square footage is approximately 8,000. Clients include students, senior citizens, film aficionados and tourists.

SUBMISSIONS Call or write to arrange a personal interview to show portfolio of photographs, slides and transparencies. Must be film process or history related.

ACA GALLERIES

529 W. 20th St., 5th Floor, New York NY 10011. (212)206-8080. **E-mail:** info@acagalleries.com. **Website:** www.acagalleries.com. Estab. 1932. For-profit gallery. The area of specialty is American, European and Contemporary art (ACA = American Contemporary Artists). "Founded in 1932, the American Contemporary Art Galleries are dedicated to representing and exhibiting prominent Contemporary and Modern artists. We exhibit traditional art forms such as painting, drawing and sculpture. We do not show photography, installation, video or new media. We handle established, mid-career artists that have had solo museum exhibitions and have major books or catalogs written about them that are not self-published." Exhibited artists include Faith Ringgold (painting, drawing, soft sculpture) and Anita Huffington (sculpture), Herb Alpert, Hyman Bloom Estate, Ilya Bolowsky, Alan Davie, Edgar Jerins, Richard Mayhew and more. Sponsors 6-8 exhibits/year. Average display time: 6-8 weeks. Open Tuesday-Saturday, 10:30-6. Clients include local community, international collectors, curators, upscale. 25% of sales are to corporate collectors. Overall price range: $1,000-6 million.

MEDIA Most frequently exhibits acrylic, ceramics, collage, drawing, fiber, mixed media, oil, paper, pastel, pen & ink, sculpture, watercolor.

STYLE Considers all styles, all genres. Most frequently exhibits color field, expressionism, impressionism, postmodernism, surrealism.

TERMS Artwork is accepted on consignment (10-50% commission). Retail price set by both artist and gallery. Gallery provides insurance, promotion, contract. Accepted work should be framed. Requires exclusive representation locally.

SUBMISSIONS Submission guidelines available online. "If you fit the above criteria, you may submit your artwork for consideration during the months of June and July. It will take approximately 6-8 weeks to review your submission and any work received after July 31 will not be reviewed. Please do not call the gallery to follow up on your submission, to set up an appointment for a studio visit, or ask us to recommend alternate galleries. We will contact you if we are interested."

ADIRONDACK LAKES CENTER FOR THE ARTS

3446 St. Rt. 28, Blue Mountain Lake NY 12812. (518)752-7715; (518)352-7715. **Fax:** (518)352-7333. **E-mail:** office@adirondackarts.org. **Website:** www.adirondackarts.org. **Contact:** Stephen Svodoba, executive director. Estab. 1967. Nonprofit galleries in multi-arts center. Represents 107 emerging, mid-career and established artists/year. Sponsors 6-8 shows/year. Average display time: 4-8 weeks. Open Thursday-Saturday, 10-4; July and August, daily. Located on Main Street next to post office; 176 sq. ft.; "pedestals and walls are white, some wood and very versatile." Clients include tourists, summer owners and year-round residents. 90% of sales are to private collectors, 10% corporate collectors. Overall price range: $100-10,000; most work sold at $100-1,000. Accepts work on consignment (30% commission). Retail price set by the artist. Gallery provides insurance, contract; shares promotion. Prefers artwork framed. Finds artists through word of mouth, art publications and artists' submissions.

MEDIA Considers all media and all types of prints. Most frequently exhibits paintings, sculpture, wood and fiber arts.

STYLE Exhibits all styles. Genres include landscapes, Americana, wildlife and portraits.

SUBMISSIONS Send query letter with slides or photos and bio. Annual submission deadline early November; selections complete by February 1. Files "slides, photos and bios on artists we're interested in." Reviews submissions once/year.

TIPS "We love to feature artists who can also teach a class in their media for us. It increases interest in both the exhibit and the class."

AGORA GALLERY

530 W. 25th St., New York NY 10001. (212)226-4151. **E-mail:** info@agora-gallery.com. **Website:** www.agora-gallery.com. **Contact:** Angela Di Bello, director. Estab. 1984. For-profit gallery. Represents emerging, mid-career and established artists. Sponsors 19 exhibits/year. Average display time: 3 weeks. Open Tuesday–Saturday, 11-6. Closed national holidays. Located in the heart of New York City's Chelsea art district, with expansive gallery space on 1st and 2nd floors on an exclusive gallery block. Clients include local, tourists, upscale collectors.

MEDIA Acrylic, collage, digital, drawing, mixed media, oil, pastel, photography, sculpture, watercolor.

STYLE Considers all styles.

TERMS There is a representation fee. There is a 30% commission to the gallery; 70% to the artist. Retail price set by the gallery and the artist. Gallery provides insurance and 18 months of promotion services.

SUBMISSIONS Guidelines available online (www.agora-gallery.com/artistinfo/GalleryRepresentation.aspx). Portfolio submitted through website and must include 5 images with titles, medium, and dimensions, biography, and artist statement.

AKRON ART MUSEUM

1 S. High St., Akron OH 44308. (330)376-9185. **Fax:** (330)376-1180. **E-mail:** mail@akronartmuseum.org. **Website:** www.akronartmuseum.org. Located on the corner of East Market and South High Streets in the heart of downtown Akron. Open Wednesday–Sunday, 11-5; Thursday, 11-9. Closed Monday and Tuesday. Closed holidays.

TERMS "Please submit a brief letter of interest, résumé, and 20-25 representative images (slides, snapshots, JPEGs on CD, DVDs or website links). Do not send original artworks. If you would like your material returned, please include a SASE." Allow 2-3 months for review.

SUBMISSIONS "Send professional-looking materials with high-quality images, a résumé and an artist's statement. Never send original prints."

ALASKA STATE MUSEUM

395 Whittier St., Juneau AK 99801-1718. (907)465-2901. Fax: (907)465-2151. **E-mail:** jackie.manning@alaska.gov. **Website:** www.museums.alaska.gov.

Contact: Jackie Manning, curator of exhibitions. Estab. 1900. Approached by 80 artists/year; exhibits 6 emerging, mid-career and established artists. The museum sponsors 10 exhibits/year. Average display time: 6-10 weeks. Downtown location exhibiting temporary and permanent exhibitions in a new building.

MEDIA Considers all media. Most frequently exhibits painting, photography, sculpture, new media and mixed media. Considers engravings, etchings, linocuts, lithographs, mezzotints, serigraphs and woodcuts.

STYLE Considers all styles.

SUBMISSIONS Finds Alaskan artists through submissions and portfolio reviews every 2 years. Register for e-mail notification at: http://list.state.ak.us/soal ists/Museum_Exhibits_Events_Calendar.

JEAN ALBANO GALLERY

215 W. Superior, Chicago IL 60654. (312)440-0770. **Fax:** (312)440-3103. **E-mail:** jeanalbano@aol.com; info@jeanalbanogallery.com. **Website:** www.jeanal banogallery.com. **Contact:** Jean Albano Broday, director. Estab. 1985. Represents 24 mid-career artists. Somewhat interested in seeing the work of emerging artists. Exhibited artists include Martin Facey and Jim Waid. Average display time: 5 weeks. Open Tuesday–Friday, 10-5; Saturday, 11-5; and by appointment. Located downtown in River North gallery district; 1,600 sq. ft.; 60% of space for special exhibitions; 40% of space for gallery artists. Clientele 80% private collectors, 20% corporate collectors. Overall price range: $1,000-20,000; most work sold at $2,500-6,000.

MEDIA Considers oil, acrylic, sculpture and mixed media. Most frequently exhibits mixed media, oil and acrylic. Prefers nonrepresentational, nonfigurative and abstract styles.

TERMS Accepts artwork on consignment (50% commission). Retail price set by gallery and artist; shipping costs are shared.

SUBMISSIONS Send query letter with résumé, bio, SASE and well-labeled slides (size, name, title, medium, top, etc.). Write for appointment to show portfolio. Responds in 6 weeks. If interested, gallery will file bio, résumé and selected slides.

TIPS "We look for artists whose work has a special dimension in whatever medium. We are interested in unusual materials and unique techniques."

ALBUQUERQUE MUSEUM

2000 Mountain Rd., NW, Albuquerque NM 87104. (505)243-7255. **Website:** www.cabq.gov/museum. Glenn Fye, photo archivist. **Contact:** Andrew Connors, curator of art. Estab. 1967. Nonprofit municipal museum. Located in Old Town, west of downtown.

STYLE Mission is to collect, promote, and showcase art and artifacts from Albuquerque, the state of New Mexico, and the Southwest and influences on art of the Southwest. Rarely hosts single-artist exhibitions, focusing instead on thematic or group shows and work from the permanent collection.

SUBMISSIONS Artists may send portfolio for exhibition consideration: slides, photos, disk, artist statement, résumé, SASE.

ALEX GALLERY

2106 R St. NW, Washington DC 20008. (202)667-2599. **E-mail:** alexgallerydc@gmail.com; info@alex galleries.com. **Website:** www.alexgalleries.com. Estab. 1985. Retail gallery and art consultancy. Represents 20 emerging and mid-career artists. Exhibited artists include Willem de Looper, Gunter Grass and Olivier Debre. Sponsors 8 shows/year. Average display time: 1 month. Open Tuesday–Saturday, 11-5; and by appointment. Located in the heart of a gallery neighborhood; 2 floors of beautiful turn-of-the-century townhouse; a lot of exhibit space. Clientele: diverse; international and local. 50% private collectors; 50% corporate collectors. Overall price range: $1,500-60,000.

MEDIA Considers oil, acrylic, watercolor, pastel, mixed media, collage, sculpture, photography, original handpulled prints, lithographs, linocuts and etchings. Most frequently exhibits painting, sculpture and works on paper.

STYLE Exhibits expressionism, abstraction, color field, impressionism and realism; all genres. Prefers abstract and figurative work.

TERMS Accepts artwork on consignment. Retail price set by gallery and artist. Gallery provides insurance, promotion and contract; shipping costs are shared.

SUBMISSIONS Send query letter with résumé, slides, bio, SASE and artist's statement. Write for appointment to show portfolio, which should include slides and transparencies. Responds in 2 months.

⊛ CHARLES ALLIS ART MUSEUM

1801 N. Prospect Ave., Milwaukee WI 53202. (414)278-8295. **E-mail:** jsterr@cavtmuseums.org.

Website: www.charlesallis.org. **Contact:** John Sterr, executive director. Estab. 1947. The Charles Allis Art Museum exhibits emerging, mid-career and established artists that have lived or studied in Wisconsin. Exhibited artists include Anne Miotke (watercolor); Evelyn Patricia Terry (pastel, acrylic, multi-media). Sponsors 3 exhibits/year. Average display time: 3 months. Open all year; Wednesday–Sunday, 1-5. Located in an urban area, historical home, 3 galleries. Clients include local community, students and tourists. 10% of sales are to corporate collectors. Overall price range: $200-6,000.

MEDIA Considers acrylic, collage, drawing, installation, mixed media, oil, pastel, pen & ink, sculpture, watercolor and photography. Print types include engravings, etchings, linocuts, lithographs, serigraphs and woodcuts.

TERMS Artwork can be purchased during run of an exhibition; a 30% commission fee applies. Retail price set by the artist. Museum provides insurance, promotion and contract. Accepted work should be framed. Does not require exclusive representation locally. Accepts only artists from or with a connection to Wisconsin.

SUBMISSIONS Finds artists through submissions to Request for Proposals which can be found at www.charlesallis.org/news.html.

AMERICAN PRINT ALLIANCE

302 Larkspur Turn, Peachtree City GA 30269-2210. **E-mail:** director@printalliance.org. **Website:** www.printalliance.org. **Contact:** Carol Pulin, director. Estab. 1992. Nonprofit arts organization with online gallery and exhibitions, travelling exhibitions, and journal publication; Print Bin: a place on website that is like the unframed, shrink-wrapped prints in a bricks-and-mortar gallery's "print bin." Approached by hundreds of artists/year; represents dozens of artists/year. "We only exhibit original prints, artists' books and paperworks." Usually sponsors 2 travelling exhibits/year—all prints, paperworks and artists' books. Most exhibits travel for 2 years. Hours depend on the host gallery/museum/arts center. "We travel exhibits throughout the US and occasionally to Canada." Overall price range for Print Bin: $150-3,200; most work sold at $300-500.

MEDIA Considers and exhibits original prints, paperworks, artists' books. Also all original prints includ-

ing any combination of printmaking techniques; no reproductions/posters.

STYLE Considers all styles, genres and subjects; the decisions are made on quality of work.

TERMS Individual subscription: $32-39. Print Bin is free with subscription. "Subscribers eligible to enter juried traveling exhibitions but must pay for framing and shipping to and from our office." Gallery provides promotion.

SUBMISSIONS Subscribe to journal, *Contemporary Impressions* (www.printalliance.org/alliance/al_sub form.html). Send one slide and signed permission form (www.printalliance.org/gallery/printbin_info.html). Returns slide if requested with SASE. Usually does not respond to queries from nonsubscribers. Files slides and permission forms. Finds artists through submissions to the gallery or Print Bin, and especially portfolio reviews at printmakers conferences. "Unfortunately, we don't have the staff for individual portfolio reviews, though we may—and often do—request additional images after seeing one work, often for journal articles. Generally about 100 images are reproduced per year in the journal."

TIPS "See the Standard Forms area of our website (www.printalliance.org/library/li_forms.html) for correct labels on slides and much, much more about professional presentation."

AMERICAN SOCIETY OF ARTISTS

P.O. Box 1326, Palatine IL 60078. (847)991-4748 or (312)751-2500. **E-mail:** asoaartists@aol.com. **Website:** www.americansocietyofartists.org. **Contact:** Helen Del Valle, membership chairman. "Our members range from internationally known artists to unknown artists—quality of work is the important factor."

TERMS Responds in 2 weeks.

SUBMISSIONS Submit 4 images of your work (résumé/show listing helpful), or send SASE and 4 slides/photographs that represent your work; request membership information and application.

TIPS Accepted work should be framed, mounted or matted. Accepted members may participate in lecture and demonstration service.

THE ANN ARBOR ART CENTER GALLERY SHOP

117 W. Liberty St., Ann Arbor MI 48104. (734)994-8004. **Fax:** (734)994-3610. **E-mail:** nrice@annarbor artcenter.org; sbingham@annarborartcenter.org. **Website:** www.annarborartcenter.org. **Contact:** Na-

than Rice, gallery curator; Samantha Bingham, gallery curator. Estab. 1909. Represents over 350 artists, primarily Michigan and regional. Gallery shop purchases support the Art Center's community outreach programs. "We are the only organization in Ann Arbor that offers hands-on art education, art appreciation programs and exhibitions all in one facility." Open Monday–Friday, 10-7; Saturday, 10-6; Sunday, 12-5.

○ The Ann Arbor Art Center also has exhibition opportunities for Michigan artists in its exhibition gallery and art consulting program.

MEDIA Considers original work in virtually all 2D and 3D media, including jewelry, prints and etchings, ceramics, glass, fiber, wood, photography and painting.

STYLE The gallery specializes in well-crafted and accessible artwork. Many different styles are represented, including innovative contemporary.

TERMS Submission guidelines available online. Accepts work on consignment. Retail price set by artist. Offers member discounts and payment by installments. Exclusive area representation not required. Gallery provides contract; artist pays for shipping.

SUBMISSIONS "The Art Center seeks out artists through the exhibition visitation, wholesale and retail craft shows, networking with graduate and undergraduate schools, word of mouth, in addition to artist referral and submissions."

ANTON ART CENTER

125 Macomb Place, Mount Clemens MI 48043. (586)469-8666. **Fax:** (586)469-4529. **E-mail:** information@theartcenter.org; sszmiot@theartcenter.org. **Website:** www.theartcenter.org. "Connect with us on Facebook and Twitter!" **Contact:** Stephanie Szmiot, exhibition and education manager. Estab. 1969. Nonprofit art center. Represents emerging, mid-career and established artists. Over 400 members. Sponsors 10-14 shows/year. Average display time: 1 month. Open Tuesday–Thursday & Saturday, 10-5; Friday, 10-6; Sunday, 12-4. Closed Mondays and holidays. Located in downtown Mount Clemens; 10,000 sq. ft. The Anton Art Center is housed in the historic Carnegie Library Building, listed in the State of Michigan Historical Register. A 2006 addition created new classroom and exhibit space as well as a gift shop featuring handmade items. Overall price range: $5-1,000; most work sold at $50-200.

MEDIA Main Gallery Space & Community Art Gallery. Open to all media.

STYLE Exhibits all styles, all genres.

TERMS The Anton Art Center receives a 40% commission on sales of original works.

SUBMISSIONS Send résumé, artist statement, image list, 10 images (JPEG on disk) and SASE if you want materials returned. Finds artists through word of mouth, membership and in response to open calls publicized through e-mail, social media and website. Submission guidelines available by mail and online.

TIPS "Visit our website to sign up for our e-mail list; all calls for artists are publicized via e-mail. General artist portfolio submissions and exhibition proposals are accepted year-round. All materials reviewed by exhibition committee."

ARC GALLERY & EDUCATIONAL FOUNDATION

2156 N. Damen Ave., Chicago IL 60647. (773)252-2232. **E-mail:** info@arcgallery.org. **Website:** www.arcgallery.org. **Contact:** Iris Goldstein, President. Estab. 1973. Nonprofit gallery. Exhibits emerging, mid-career and established artists. 21 members review work for solo and group shows on an ongoing basis. Visit website for prospectus. Exhibited artists include Miriam Schapiro. Average display time: 1 month. Located in the West Town neighborhood; 1,600 sq. ft. Clientele: 80% private collectors, 20% corporate collectors. Overall price range: $50-40,000; most work sold at $200-4,000.

MEDIA Considers all media. Most frequently exhibits painting, sculpture (installation) and photography.

STYLE Exhibits all styles and genres. Prefers postmodern and contemporary work.

TERMS There is a rental fee for space. Rental fee covers 1 month. No commission taken on sales. Gallery provides promotion; artist pays shipping costs. Prefers framed artwork.

SUBMISSIONS See website (www.arcgallery.org/call-for-entries.aspx) for info or send e-mail query. Reviews are ongoing. Call for deadlines. Digital images are accepted.

ARIZONA STATE UNIVERSITY ART MUSEUM

P.O. Box 872911, Tenth St. and Mill Ave., Tempe AZ 85287-2911. (480)965-2787. **Fax:** (480)965-5254. **Website:** asuartmuseum.asu.edu. **Contact:** Gordon Knox, director. Estab. 1950. Has 3 facilities and approximately 8 galleries of 2,500 square feet each; mounts approximately 15 exhibitions/year. Average display time 3-4 months.

MEDIA Considers all media. Greatest interests are contemporary art, crafts, video, and work by Latin American and Latino artists.

SUBMISSIONS "Interested artists should submit slides to the director or curators."

THE ARKANSAS ARTS CENTER

501 E. Ninth St., Little Rock AR 72202. (501)372-4000. **Fax:** (501)375-8053. **E-mail:** contact@arkarts.com; info@arkansasartscenter.org. **Website:** www.arkan sasartscenter.org. **Contact:** Brian Lang, chief curator. Museum art school, children's theater and traveling exhibition service. Estab. 1930s. Exhibits the work of emerging, mid-career and established artists. Sponsors 25 shows/year. Average display time: 12 weeks. Open Tuesday–Saturday, 10-5; Sunday, 11-5. Located downtown; 10,000 sq. ft.; 60% of space for special exhibitions.

MEDIA Most frequently exhibits drawings and crafts.

STYLE Exhibits all styles and all genres.

TERMS "Work in the competitive exhibitions (open to artists in Arkansas and 6 surrounding states) is for sale; we usually charge 10% commission."

SUBMISSIONS Send query letter with samples, such as photos or slides.

TIPS "Write for information about exhibitions for emerging and regional artists, and various themed exhibitions."

ARNOLD ART

210 Thames St., Newport RI 02840. (401)847-2273; (800)352-2234. **Fax:** (401)848-0156. **E-mail:** info@ar noldart.com. **Website:** www.arnoldart.com. **Contact:** William Rommel, owner. Estab. 1870. Retail gallery. Represents 40 emerging, mid-career and established artists. Exhibited artists include John Mecray, Willard Bond. Sponsors 4 exhibits/year. Average display time: 1 month. Open Monday-Saturday, 9:30-5:30; Sunday, 12-5. Clientele: local community, students, tourists and Newport collectors. 1% of sales are to corporate clients. Overall price range: $100-35,000; most work sold at $600.

MEDIA Considers oil, acrylic, watercolor, pastel, pen & ink, drawings, mixed media. Most frequently exhibits oil and watercolor.

STYLE Genres include marine sailing, classic yachts, America's cup, yachting/sailing.

TERMS Accepts work on consignment (40% commission). Retail price set by artist. Exclusive area representation not required. Gallery provides promotion.

SUBMISSIONS Send e-mail. Call or e-mail for appointment to show portfolio of originals. Returns materials with SASE.

TIPS To make your submissions professional you must "frame them well."

THE ARSENAL GALLERY

The Arsenal Bldg., Room 20, Central Park, 830 Fifth Ave., New York NY 10065. (212)360-8163. **Fax:** (212)360-1329. **E-mail:** artandantiquities@parks. nyc.gov; jennifer.lantzas@parks.nyc.gov. **Website:** www.nycgovparks.org/art. Jennifer Lantzas, public art coordinator. Estab. 1971. Nonprofit gallery. Approached by 100 artists/year. Exhibits 6 emerging, mid-career and established artists. Average display time: 6-7 weeks. Open all year; Monday-Friday, 9-5. Closed holidays and weekends. 100 linear feet of wall space on the 3rd floor of the Administrative Headquarters of the Parks Department located in Central Park. Clients include local community, students, tourists and upscale. Overall price range: $100-30,000.

MEDIA Considers all media except 3D work.

STYLE Considers all styles.

TERMS Retail price set by the artist. Does not require exclusive representation locally.

SUBMISSIONS Files résumé and photocopies.

● ART@NET INTERNATIONAL GALLERY

E-mail: artnetg@yahoo.com. **Website:** www.artnet. com. **Contact:** Yavor Shopov-Bulgari, director. Estab. 1998. For-profit online gallery. Approached by 150 artists/year. Represents 20 emerging, mid-career and established artists. Exhibited artists include Nicolas Roerich (paintings) and Yavor Shopov (photography). Sponsors 15 exhibits/year. Average display time: permanent. Open all year; Monday-Sunday, 24 hours. "Online galleries like ours have a number of unbelievable advantages over physical galleries and work far more efficiently, so they are expanding extremely rapidly and taking over many markets held by conventional galleries for many years. Our gallery exists only online, giving us a number of advantages both for our clients and artists. Our expenses are reduced to the absolute minimum, so we charge our artists lowest commission in the branch (only 10%) and offer to our clients lowest prices for the same quality of work. Unlike physical galleries, we have over 100 million potential online clients worldwide and are able to sell in over 150 countries without need to support offices or representatives everywhere. We mount cohesive shows of our artists, which are unlimited in size and may be permanent. Each artist has individual 'exhibition space' divided to separate thematic exhibitions along with bio and statement. We are just hosted in the Internet space, otherwise our organization is the same as of a traditional gallery." Clients include collectors and business offices worldwide; 30% corporate collectors. Overall price range: $150-50,000.

MEDIA Considers ceramics, crafts, drawing, oil, pastel, pen & ink, sculpture and watercolor. Most frequently exhibits photos, oil and drawing. Considers all types of prints.

STYLE Considers expressionism, geometric abstraction, impressionism and surrealism. Most frequently exhibits impressionism, expressionism and surrealism. Also considers Americana, figurative work, florals, landscapes and wildlife.

TERMS Artwork is accepted on consignment, and there is a 10% commission and a rental fee for space of $1/image per month or $5/image per year (first 6 images are displayed free of rental fee). Retail price set by the gallery or the artist. Gallery provides promotion. Accepted work should be matted. Does not require exclusive representation locally. "Every exhibited image will contain your name and copyright as watermark and cannot be printed or illegally used, sold or distributed anywhere."

SUBMISSIONS E-mail portfolio for review. E-mail attached scans of 900×1200 pixels (300 dpi for prints or 900 dpi for 36mm slides) as JPEG files for IBM computers. "We accept only computer scans; no slides, please." E-mail artist's statement, bio, résumé, and scans of the work. Cannot return material. Responds in 6 weeks. Finds artists through submissions, portfolio reviews, art exhibits, art fairs, and referrals by other artists.

TIPS "E-mail us a tightly edited selection of less than 20 scans of your best work. All work must be very appealing and interesting, and must force any person to look over it again and again. Main usage of all works exhibited in our gallery is for limited edition (photos) or original (paintings) wall decoration of offices and homes. Photos must have the quality of paintings. We like to see strong artistic sense of mood, composition, light and color, and strong graphic impact or expression of emotions. We exhibit only artistically perfect work in which value will last for decades. We would like to see any quality work facing these requirements on any media, subject or style. No distractive subjects. For us only quality of work is important, so new artists are welcome. Before you send us your work, ask yourself, 'Who and why will someone buy this work? Is it appropriate and good enough for this purpose?' During the exhibition, all photos must be available in signed limited edition museum quality 8×10 or larger matted prints."

ART 3 GALLERY

44 W. Brook St., Manchester NH 03101. (603)668-6650; (800)668-9983. **Fax:** (603)668-5136. **E-mail:** info@art3gallery.com. **Website:** www.art3gallery.com. **Contact:** Joni Taube, owner. Estab. 1980. For-profit gallery and art consultancy. Exhibits emerging, mid-career, and established artists. Approached by 50+ artists a year; represents of exhibits 180+ artists. Exhibited artists include James Aponorich (oil paitning) and Stan Moeller (oil painting). Sponsors 4 exhibits/year. Average display time: 2-3 months. Open Monday-Friday, 9-4. Located in downtown Manchester in a 2-story, 2,000-sq.-ft. exhibit space. Clients include local community, tourists, and upscale clients. Overall price range: $150-20,000. Most work sold at $1,000.

MEDIA Considers acrylic, ceramics, collage, drawing, fiber, glass, mixed media, oil, paper, pastel, pen & ink, sculpture, and watercolor. Most frequently exhibits oil, acrylic, and sculpture. Considers the following prints: etchings, linocuts, lithographs, serigraphs, and woodcuts.

STYLE Considers all styles and genres.

TERMS Artwork is accepted on consignment and there is a 50% commission. Retail price set by the gallery and artist. Gallery provides insurance, promotion, and contract. Accepted artwork should be framed, mounted, and matted. Does not require exlcusive local representation.

SUBMISSIONS E-mail query letter with link to artist's website or JPEG samples at 72 dpi. Materials returned with SASE. Responds if interested in 4 weeks. Finds artists through word of mouth, submissions, art exhibits, art fairs, and referrals by other artists.

ART CENTER OF BATTLE CREEK

265 E. Emmett St., Battle Creek MI 49017. (269)962-9511. Fax: (269)969-3838. **E-mail:** artcenterofbc@yahoo.com. **Website:** www.artcenterofbattlecreek.org.

Estab. 1948. Represents 150 emerging, mid-career and established artists. 90% private collectors, 10% corporate clients. Exhibition program offered in galleries, usually 3-4 solo shows each year, 2 artists' competitions, and a number of theme shows. Also offers Michigan Artworks Shop featuring work for sale or rent. Average display time: 1-2 months. Three galleries, converted from church—handsome high-vaulted ceiling, arches lead into galleries on either side. Welcoming, open atmosphere. Overall price range: $20-1,000; most work sold at $20-300. Open Tuesday–Friday, 10-5; Saturday, 11-3; closed Sunday, Monday and major holidays.

MEDIA Considers oil, acrylic, watercolor, pastel, pen & ink, drawings, mixed media, collage, works on paper, sculpture, ceramic, craft, fiber, glass, photography and original handpulled prints.

STYLE Exhibits painterly abstraction, minimalism, impressionism, photorealism, expressionism, neo-expressionism and realism. Genres include landscapes, florals, Americana, portraits and figurative work. Prefers Michigan artists.

TERMS Accepts work on consignment (40% commission). Retail price set by artist. Exclusive area representation not required. Gallery provides insurance, promotion and contract; artist pays for shipping.

SUBMISSIONS Michigan artists receive preference. Send query letter, résumé, brochure, slides and SASE. Slides returned; all other material is filed.

TIPS "Contact us before mailing materials. We are working on several theme shows with groupings of artists."

ART CENTER/SOUTH FLORIDA

924 Lincoln Rd., Suite 205, Miami Beach FL 33139. (305)674-8278. **Fax:** (305)674-8772. **E-mail:** email@artcentersf.org. **Website:** www.artcentersf.org. **Contact:** Cherese Crockett, exhibitions and artist relations manager. Estab. 1984. Nonprofit gallery. "The ACSF has one of the most rigorous nonprofit exhibition schedules in South Florida. A monthly exhibition schedule allows for comprehensive programming and assures that the ACSF can react to current trends. Curatorial initiatives from outside sources are the make-up of the majority of exhibits. Our exhibitions primarily focus on contemporary media, current aesthetic issues, contextual linkages and community awareness." Exhibits group shows by emerging artists. Average display time: 1 month. Open Monday–Thursday, 12-9; Friday-Saturday, 11-10; Sunday, 11-9. Clients include local community, students, tourists and upscale. Overall price range: $500-5,000. Office hours: 9:30-5:30.

MEDIA Considers all media except craft. Most frequently exhibits painting, sculpture, drawings and installation.

STYLE Exhibits themed group shows, which challenge and advance the knowledge and practice of contemporary arts.

TERMS Retail price set by the artist. Gallery provides insurance and promotion. Gallery receives 10% commission from sales. Accepted work should be ready to install. Does not require exclusive representation locally.

SUBMISSIONS Send query letter with SASE. Returns material with SASE. Artists apply with a proposal for an exhibition. It is then reviewed by a panel. See website for more details.

ART ENCOUNTER

5720 S. Arville Street, Suite 119, Las Vegas NV 89118. (702)227-0220; (800)395-2996. **Fax:** (702)227-3353. **E-mail:** scottf@artencounter.com. **Website:** www.artencounter.com. Estab. 1992. Retail gallery. "We have become one of the most popular destinations for locals as well as tourists. Conveniently located a short distance from the strip, we sell distinct works of art that utilize several styles and media. We also offer award-winning custom framing and our certified on staff appraiser (seen on History Channel's *Pawn Stars*)." Open Monday-Friday, 8:30-5. Clients include upscale tourists, locals, designers and casino purchasing agents.

ART GUILD OF BURLINGTON/THE ARTS FOR LIVING CENTER

301 Jefferson St., Burlington IA 52601. (319)754-8069. **Fax:** (319)754-4731. **E-mail:** artsforliving@artcenterofburlington.com. **Website:** www.artcenterofburlington.com. Estab. 1974. Exhibits the work of mid-career and established artists. May consider emerging artists. Sponsors 10 shows/year. Average display time: 3 weeks. Open Monday-Friday, 10–5; Saturday, 10-4. 15,000 sq. ft. total space; 4,500 sq. ft. for exhibitions. Overall price range: $25-1,000; most work sold at $75-500.

MEDIA Considers all visual media. Most frequently exhibits two dimensional work.

STYLE Exhibits all styles.

TERMS Accepts work on consignment (25% commission). Retail price set by artist. Gallery provides promotion and contract; artist pays for shipping. Prefers artwork framed.

SUBMISSIONS Send query letter with résumé, slides, bio, brochure, photographs, SASE and reviews.

ARTISTS' COOPERATIVE GALLERY

405 S. 11th St., Omaha NE 68102. (402)342-9617. **E-mail:** artistscoopgallery@gmail.com. **Website:** www.artistsco-opgallery.com. Estab. 1974. Sponsors 12 exhibits/year. Average display time: 1 month. Gallery sponsors all-member exhibits and outreach exhibits; individual artists sponsor their own small group exhibits throughout the year. Overall price range: $100-5,000. Open Tuesday–Thursday, 11-5; Friday-Saturday, 11-10; Sunday, 12-6. Thursdays during holiday season and summer hours until 10 p.m.

MEDIA Considers oil, acrylic, watercolor, pastel, drawings, mixed media, collage, paper, sculpture, ceramic, fiber, glass, photography, woodcuts, serigraphs. Most frequently exhibits sculpture, acrylic, oil and ceramic.

STYLE Exhibits all styles and genres.

TERMS Charges no commission. Reviews transparencies. Accepted work should be framed work only. "Artist must be willing to work 13 days per year at the gallery. We are a member-owned-and-operated cooperative. Artist must also serve on one committee."

SUBMISSIONS Send query letter with résumé, SASE. Responds in 2 months.

TIPS "Write for membership application. Membership committee screens applicants August 1-15 each year. Responds by September 1. New membership year begins October 1. Members must pay annual fee of $400. Our community outreach exhibits include local high school photographers and art from local elementary schools."

ARTISTS' GALLERY

Emerson Cultural Center, 111 S. Grand Ave., #106, Bozeman MT 59715. (406)587-2127. **E-mail:** surrattmarci@gmail.com. **Website:** www.artistsgalleryboze man.com. **Contact:** Marci Surratt. Estab. 1992. Retail and cooperative gallery. Represents the work of 20 local emerging and mid-career artists, 20 members. Sponsors 12 shows/year. Average display time 3 months. We are open Monday–Saturday, 10-5; some evenings until 8. Located near downtown; 900 sq. ft.; located in Emerson Cultural Center with other gal-

leries, studios, etc. Clients include tourists, upscale and local community.

MEDIA Considers oil, acrylic, watercolor, pastel, pen & ink, drawing, mixed media, collage, paper, sculpture, ceramics and glass, woodcuts, engravings, linocuts and etchings. Most frequently exhibits oil, watercolor and ceramics.

STYLE Exhibits painterly abstraction, impressionism, photorealism and realism. Exhibits all genres. Prefers realism, impressionism and western.

TERMS Co-op membership fee plus donation of time (20% commission). Rental fee for space; covers 1 month. Retail price set by the artist. Gallery provides promotion. Prefers artwork framed.

SUBMISSIONS "We take local artists who are able to share sitting in the gallery. We occasionally take consigners for 3D items." Application is available on website. Call or write for appointment to show actual work.

THE ART LEAGUE, INC.

105 N. Union St., Alexandria VA 22314. (703)683-1780. **Fax:** (703)683-5786. **E-mail:** gallery@theartleague. org. **Website:** www.theartleague.org. Estab. 1954. "Our engaging exhibition schedule makes the Art League Gallery an intriguing art space for gallery visitors in the D.C. metropolitan area to view original art of all media by talented artists from throughout Washington and the Mid-Atlantic region." Interested in emerging, mid-career and established artists. 1,200-1,400 members. Sponsors 7-8 solo and 14 group shows/year. Average display time: 1 month. Located in the Torpedo Factory Art Center. Accepts artists from metropolitan Washington area, northern Virginia and Maryland. 75% of sales are to private collectors, 25% corporate clients. Overall price range: $50-4,000; most work sold at $150-500.

MEDIA Considers all media. Most frequently exhibits watercolor, oil and photographs. Considers all types of prints.

STYLE Exhibits all styles and genres. Prefers impressionism, painted abstraction and realism. "The Art League is a membership organization open to anyone interested."

TERMS Accepts work by jury on consignment (40% commission) and co-op membership fee plus donation of time. Retail price set by artist. Offers customer discounts (designers only) and payment by installments (if requested on long term). Exclusive area representation not required.

SUBMISSIONS Work juried monthly for each new show from actual work (not slides). Work received for jurying on first Monday evening/Tuesday morning of each month; pick-up nonselected work throughout rest of week.

TIPS "Artists find us and join/exhibit as they wish within framework of our selections jurying process. It is more important that work is of artistic merit rather than salable."

⊙ ART LEAGUE OF HOUSTON

1953 Montrose Blvd., Houston TX 77006. (713)523-9530. **Fax:** (713)523-4053. **E-mail:** jennifer@artleaguehouston.org; alh@artleaguehouston.org. **Website:** www.artleaguehouston.org. **Contact:** Jennifer Ash. Estab. 1948. Nonprofit gallery. Represents emerging and mid-career artists. Sponsors 12 individual and group shows/year. Each season, ALH presents contemporary art in a variety of media in its 2 gallery spaces. Average display time 3-4 weeks. Located in a contemporary metal building; 1,300 sq. ft., specially lighted with a smaller inner gallery/video room. Open Tuesday–Friday, 9-5; Saturday, 12-5. Clientele: general, artists and collectors. Overall price range: $100-5,000; most artwork sold at $100-2,500.

MEDIA Considers all media.

STYLE Exhibits contemporary avant-garde, socially aware work. Features "high-quality artwork reflecting serious aesthetic investigation and innovation. Additionally the work should have a sense of personal vision."

TERMS 30% commission. Retail price set by artist. Exclusive area representation not required. Gallery provides insurance, promotion and contract; artist pays for shipping.

SUBMISSIONS Must be a Houston-area resident. Send query letter, résumé and slides that accurately portray the work. Portfolio review not required. Submissions reviewed once a year in mid-June, and exhibition agenda determined for upcoming year.

⊙ ART MUSEUM OF GREATER LAFAYETTE

102 S. Tenth St., Lafayette IN 47905. (765)742-1128. **Fax:** (765)742-1120. **E-mail:** glenda@artlafayette.org. **Website:** www.artlafayette.org. **Contact:** Glenda McClatchey, administrative assistant. Estab. 1909. Museum. Temporary exhibits of American and Indiana art, work by emerging, mid-career and established artists from Indiana and the midwest. 1,340 members. Sponsors 16-18 shows/year. Average display time: 10 weeks. Located 6 blocks from city center; 3,318 sq. ft.; 5 galleries. Open every day, 11-4. Clientele includes Purdue University faculty, students and residents of Lafayette/West Lafayette and 14 county area.

STYLE Exhibits all styles. Genres include landscapes, still life, portraits, abstracts, nonobjective and figurative work.

TERMS Accepts art from local artists for consignment in gift shop (30% mark-up).

SUBMISSIONS Send query letter with résumé, digital portfolio, artist's statement and letter of intent.

TIPS "Indiana artists specifically encouraged to apply."

ARTPROJECTA

P.O. Box 597, Ketchum ID 883340. (208)726-3036; (208)841-9200. **E-mail:** info@artprojecta.com; barbi@annereedgallery.com. **Website:** www.artprojecta.com. **Contact:** Barbi Reed. Estab. 1912. Represents emerging talent and established artists. Fonder, Barbi Reed, owner Anne Reed Gallery. Exhibited artists include: Kirk Anderson, Gary Mankus, Owen Mortensen, Andrew Romanoff, Andrew Saftel, Ruth Silverman, Bob Smith, Larry Stephenson, Maggie Hasbrouck, Lisa Holley, among others. All art retails from $65-4500. Clientele: 70% private collectors, 30% corporate collectors, art consultants, designers.

STYLE Most frequently exhibits photographs, paintings, fine art prints. Exhibits expressionism, abstraction, conceptualism, photorealism, realism, landscape. Prefers contemporary. Established to provide carefully curated fine art at affordable prices. Independent consulting available to achieve the most exciting, appropriate and tasteful art to complement and enhance residential, commercial, institutional settings.

TERMS Retail price set by gallery and artist. Sometimes we offer client discounts. Gallery provides promotion, networking on artist's behalf, shipping costs to clients. ARTprojectA is not responsible for materials sent that are unsolicited.

SUBMISSIONS E-mail your work and include your artist website's URL. Make sure the latest work and an updated résumé are on your site.

TIPS Spend time on our website www.artprojecta.com prior to contacting us.

ARTQUOTE INTERNATIONAL, LLC

4653 Chelsea Lane, Bloomfield Hills MI 48301. (248)470-5912. **Fax:** (248)851-6090. **E-mail:** artquote@comcast.net. **Contact:** M. Burnstein. Art consultancy; for-profit, wholesale gallery; corporate art and identity programs. Estab. 1985. Exhibits established artists. Exhibited artists include Andy Warhol (screenprints) and Bill Mack (sculpture). Clients include local community. Most sales are to corporate collectors. Does not sell art at retail prices. Supplier to Fortune 100 corporations (global).

SUBMISSIONS Depends on corporate client. Finds artists through "established network of channels."

THE ARTS CENTER

P.O. Box 363, 115 Second St. SW, Jamestown ND 58401. (701)251-2496. **Fax:** (701)251-1749. **E-mail:** sj eppson@jamestownarts.com. **Website:** www.james townarts.com. **Contact:** Sally Jepson, gallery manager. Estab. 1981. Nonprofit gallery. Sponsors 8 solo and 4 group shows/year. Average display time 6 weeks. Interested in emerging artists. Overall price range: $50-600; most work sold at $50-350.

STYLE Exhibits contemporary, abstraction, impressionism, primitivism, photorealism and realism. Genres include Americana, figurative and 3D work.

TERMS 20% commission on sales from regularly scheduled exhibitions. Retail price set by artist. Gallery provides insurance, promotion and contract; shipping costs are shared.

SUBMISSIONS Send query letter, résumé, brochure, slides, photograph and SASE. Write for appointment to show portfolio. Invitation to have an exhibition is extended by Arts Center gallery manager.

TIPS "We are interested in work of at least 20-30 pieces, depending on the size."

THE ARTS COMPANY

215 Fifth Ave., Nashville TN 37219. (615)254-2040; (877)694-2040. **Fax:** (615)254-9289. **E-mail:** art@ theartscompany.com. **Website:** www.theartscompa ny.com. **Contact:** Anne Brown, owner. Estab. 1996. Art consultancy, for-profit gallery. Estab. 1996. Over 6,000 sq. ft. of gallery space on 2 floors. Overall price range: $10-35,000; most work sold at $300-3,000.

We are not accepting artist submissions at this time.

MEDIA Considers all media. Most frequently exhibits painting, photography and sculpture.

STYLE Exhibits all styles and genres. Frequently exhibits contemporary outsider art.

TERMS Artwork is accepted on consignment. Gallery provides insurance and contract. Accepted work should be framed. Requires exclusive representation locally.

SUBMISSIONS "We prefer an initial info packet via e-mail." Send query letter with artist's statement, bio, brochure, business card, photocopies, résumé, reviews, SASE, CD. Returns material with SASE. Finds artists through word of mouth, art fairs/exhibits, submissions, referrals by other artists.

TIPS "Provide professional images on a CD along with a professional bio, résumé."

ARTS ON DOUGLAS

123 Douglas St., New Smyrna Beach FL 32168. (386)428-1133. **Fax:** (386)428-5008. **E-mail:** mmar tin@artsondouglas.net. **Website:** www.artsondoug las.net. **Contact:** Meghan Martin, gallery director. Estab. 1996. Represents 50 professional Florida artists and exhibits 8 established artists/year. Average display time: 1 month. Open all year; Tuesday-Friday, 10-5; Saturday, 11-3. 5,000 sq. ft. of exhibition space. Clients include local community, tourists and upscale. Accepts only professional artists from Florida. Returns material with SASE. Send a query letter and include a CD with 6 current images, bio, CV and artist's statement.

MEDIA Considers all media except installation.

STYLE Considers all styles and genres.

TERMS Overall price range varies. Artwork is accepted on consignment (50% commission). Retail price set by the artist. Gallery provides insurance and promotion. Accepted work should be framed.

SUBMISSIONS Artists may want to call gallery prior to sending submission package—not always accepting new artists.

ART SOURCE L.A., INC.

2801 Ocean Park Blvd., #7, Santa Monica CA 90405. (310)452-4411; (800)721-8477. **Fax:** (310)452-0300. **E-mail:** info@artsourcela.com. **Website:** www.artsour cela.com. **Contact:** Francine Ellman, president. Estab. 1980. Artwork is accepted on consignment (50% commission). No geographic restrictions. Finds artists through art fairs/exhibitions, submissions, referrals by other artists, portfolio reviews and word of mouth.

MEDIA Considers fine art in all media, including works on paper/canvas, sculpture, giclée and a broad array of accessories handmade by American artists. Considers all types of prints.

TERMS "Send minimum of 20 slides or photographs (laser copies are not acceptable) clearly labeled with your name, title and date of work, size and medium. Catalogs and brochures of your work are welcome. Also include a résumé, price list and SASE. We will not respond without a return envelope." Also accepts e-mail submissions. Responds in 30 days if interested.

SUBMISSIONS Submission guidelines available on website.

TIPS "Be professional when submitting visuals. Remember, first impressions can be critical! Submit a body of work that is consistent and of the highest quality. Work should be in excellent condition and already photographed for your records. Framing does not enhance presentation to the client."

ARTSPACE

0 E. Fourth St., Richmond VA 23224. (804)232-6464. **E-mail:** artspaceorg@gmail.com. **Website:** www.artspacegallery.org. Nonprofit gallery. Estab. 1988. Approached by 100 artists/year. Represents about 50 emerging, mid-career artists. Sponsors approximately 2 exhibits/year. Average display time: 1 month. Open all year; Tuesday-Sunday, 12-4. Located in the newly designated Arts District in Manchester, in Richmond VA. Brand new gallery facilities; 4 exhibition spaces; 3,000 sq. ft. Clients include local community, students, tourists and upscale. 2% of sales are to corporate collectors. Overall price range: $100-800; most work sold at $450.

MEDIA Considers all media and all types of prints. Most frequently exhibits photography, painting and sculpture.

STYLE Considers all styles and genres.

TERMS There are exhibition fees; 33% commission. Retail price set by the artist. Gallery provides insurance and contract. Accepted work should be framed, mounted and matted. Pedestals available for sculpture. Does not require exclusive representation locally.

SUBMISSIONS Send query letter with artist's statement, bio, résumé, SASE, and proposal form. Images should be sent digitally, either by e-mail or CD. Returns material with SASE. Responds to queries in 3 weeks. If accepted, all materials submitted are filed. Finds artists through referrals by other artists, submissions and word of mouth.

ARTSPACE/LIMA

65-67 Town Square, Lima OH 45801. (419)222-1721. **E-mail:** artspacelima@woh.rr.com. **Website:** www.artspacelima.com. **Contact:** operations manager. Nonprofit gallery. Exhibits 50-70 emerging and mid-career artists/year. Interested in seeing the work of emerging artists. Sponsors 8-10 shows/year. Average display time: 6-8 weeks. Open Tuesday–Friday, 10-5; Saturday, 10-2. Located downtown; 286 running ft. 100% of space for special exhibitions. Clientele local community. 80% private collectors, 5% corporate collectors. Overall price range: $300-6,000; most work sold at $500-1,000.

○ Most shows are thematic and geared toward education.

MEDIA Considers all media and all types of prints. Most frequently exhibits painting, sculpture, drawing.

STYLE Exhibits all styles of contemporary and traditional work.

TERMS Accepts work on consignment (40% commission). Retail price set by the artist. Gallery provides insurance, promotion and contract. Artwork must be ready to hang.

SUBMISSIONS Send query letter with résumé, slides, artist's statement and SASE. Portfolio should include slides. Responds only if interested within 6 weeks. Files résumé.

THE ART STORE

233 Hale St., Charleston WV 25301. (304)345-1038. **Fax:** (304)345-1858. **E-mail:** gallery@theartstorewv.com. **Website:** www.theartstorewv.com. "The Art Store is dedicated to showing original 20th-century and contemporary American art by leading local, regional and nationally recognized artists. Professional integrity, commitment and vision are the criteria for artist selection, with many artists having a history of exhibitions and museum placement. Painting, sculpture, photography, fine art prints and ceramics are among the disciplines presented. A diverse series of solo, group and invitational shows are exhibited throughout the year in the gallery." Retail gallery. Represents 50 mid-career and established artists. Sponsors 11 shows/year. Average display time: 4 weeks. Open Tuesday–Friday, 10-5:30; Saturday, 10-5; anytime by appointment. Located in a upscale shopping area; 2,000 sq. ft.; 50% of space for special exhibitions. Clientele: professionals, executives, deco-

rators. 80% private collectors, 20% corporate collectors. Overall price range: $200-8,000; most work sold at $2,000.

MEDIA Considers oil, acrylic, watercolor, pastel, mixed media, works on paper, ceramics, wood and metal.

STYLE Exhibits expressionism, painterly abstraction, color field and impressionism.

TERMS Accepts artwork on consignment (50% commission). Retail price set by gallery and artist. Gallery provides insurance, promotion and shipping costs from gallery. Prefers artwork unframed.

SUBMISSIONS Send query e-mail.

ART WITHOUT WALLS, INC.

P.O. Box 341, Sayville NY 11782. (631)567-9418. **Fax:** (631)567-9418. **E-mail:** artwithoutwalls@outlook. com. **Contact:** Sharon Lippman, executive director. Estab. 1985. Nonprofit gallery. Approached by 300 artists/year. Represents 100 emerging, mid-career and established artists. Sponsors 10 exhibits/year. Average display time: 1 month. Open daily, 9-5. Closed December 22-January 5 and Easter week. Overall price range: $1,000-25,000; most work sold a0t $3,000-5,000. "Sponsoring the upcoming Museum Without Walls, an award-winning fine art exhibition that allows both the profesional and emerging artist the opportunity to connect with the viewer in a public space. Artwork is accepted on consignment (20% commission). Retail price set by the artist. Gallery provides promotion and contract. Accepted work should be framed, mounted and matted. Finds artists through submissions, portfolio reviews and art exhibits." Annual show every year 2nd week of June in Central Park. Interested artists should e-mail or call for more information. Also accepting volunteers for website design and maintenance for non-profit.

MEDIA "Considers all media and all types of prints. Most frequently exhibits painting, sculpture and drawing."

STYLE Considers all styles and genres. Most frequently exhibits impressionism, expressionism, post-modernism.

SUBMISSIONS Mail portfolio for review. Send query letter with artist's statement, brochure, photographs, résumé, reviews, SASE and slides. Returns material with SASE. Responds in 1 month. Files artist résumé, slides, photos and artist's statement.

TIPS Work should be properly framed with name, year, medium, title and size.

THE ASHBY-HODGE GALLERY OF AMERICAN ART

Central Methodist University, 411 Central Methodist Square, Fayette MO 65248. (660)248-6324 (gallery) or (660)248-6304 (office). **Fax:** (660)248-2622. **E-mail:** dgebhard@centralmethodist.edu. **Website:** www. centralmethodist.edu/ashbyhodge/index.php. **Contact:** Denise Gebhardt, curator. Estab. 1993. Nonprofit gallery. "The Ashby Collection of oil paintings, lithographs, drawings, and acrylics, mainly represents the work of American Regionalist artists. Although the Ashby Collection is the principal focus of the gallery, special exhibits are scheduled throughout the year." Exhibits the work of 50 artists in permanent collection. Exhibited artists include Robert MacDonald Graham, Jr. and Birger Sandzen. Sponsors 5 shows/year. Average display time: 2 months. Open Sunday, Tuesday, Thursday, 1:30-4:30 and by appointment. Summer hours: Tuesday–Thursday, 1:30-4:30 and by appointment. 1,400 sq. ft.; on lower level of campus library. 100% of gallery artists for special exhibitions. Clientele local community and surrounding areas of Mid-America. Physically impaired accessible. Tours by reservation.

MEDIA Considers all media. Most frequently exhibits acrylic, lithographs, oil and fibers.

STYLE Exhibits Midwestern regionalists. Genres include portraits and landscapes. Prefers realism.

TERMS Accepts work on consignment (30% commission). Retail price set by the gallery. Gallery provides insurance and promotion; shipping costs are shared. Prefers artwork framed.

SUBMISSIONS Accepts primarily Midwestern artists. Send query letter with résumé, slides, photographs and bio. Call for appointment to show portfolio of photographs, transparencies and slides. Finds artists through recommendations and submissions.

ASIAN AMERICAN ARTS CENTRE

111 Norfolk St., New York NY 10002. **Fax:** (360)283-2154. **E-mail:** aaacinfo@artspiral.org. **Website:** www. artspiral.org. Estab. 1974. "Our mission is to promote the preservation and creative vitality of Asian American cultural growth through the arts, and its historical and aesthetic linkage to other communities." Exhibits should be Asian American or significantly influenced by Asian culture and should be entered into

the archive—a historical record of the presence of Asia in the US. Interested in "creative art pieces." Average display time: 6 weeks. Open Monday–Friday, 12:30-6:30 (by appointment).

TERMS 30% "donation" on works sold. Sometimes buys photos outright.

SUBMISSIONS Send dupes of slides, résumé, artist's statement, bio and online form to be entered into the archive. These will be kept for users of archive to review. Recent entries are reviewed once/year for the art centre's annual exhibition.

ATELIER GALLERY

153 King St., Charleston SC 29401. **E-mail:** gabrielle@theateliergalleries.com. **Website:** www.theateliergalleries.com. **Contact:** Gabrielle Egan, curator and owner. Estab. 2008. Fine art gallery. Exhibits mid-career, and established artists. Represents or exhibits 60 artists. For exhibited artists, see website. Open Monday-Friday, 10-6; Sundays, by chance. Closed Holidays. Clients include local community, students, tourists, upscale, and artists and designers. Overall price range: $50-15,000. Most work sold in the $2,500-5,000 range.

MEDIA Accepts acrylic, ceramics, collage, drawing, fiber, glass, mixed media, oil, paper, pastel, pen & ink, sculpture, and watercolor.

STYLE Exhibits expressionism, geometric abstraction, hyper realism, minimalism, pattern painting and painterly abstraction. Interested in figurative work and florals.

TERMS Artwork is accepted on consignment with a 50% comission. Retail price set by the gallery and artist. Gallery provides insurance, promotion, and contract. Atelier requires exclusive representation within 250 miles of the gallery in downtown Charleston SC.

SUBMISSIONS E-mail query letter along with 6 images of the most current body of work. Please include medium, dimensions, framing specifications, pricing. Also provide all artist contact information to include website, e-mail and telephone number. Atelier Gallery will contact each artist via e-mail once the submission has been reviewed. If more information is needed, the gallery will request it directly.

ATHENAEUM MUSIC AND ARTS LIBRARY

1008 Wall St., La Jolla CA 92037. (858)454-5872. **E-mail:** press@ljathenaeum.org; stutone@ljathenaeum.org. **Website:** www.ljathenaeum.org. **Contact:** Erika Torri, director. Estab. 1899. Nonprofit gallery. Represents/exhibits emerging, mid-career and established artists. "The Athenaeum Music & Arts Library, located in the heart of La Jolla, in San Diego County, is one of only 16 nonprofit membership libraries in the US. This rare cultural institution, an important one to the greater San Diego area, offers a depth and accessibility of resources and programs found nowhere else in the region." Exhibited artists include Ming Mur-Ray, Italo Scanga and Mauro Staccioli. Sponsors 8 exhibitions/year. Average display time: 2 months. Open Tuesday, Thursday–Saturday, 10-5:30; Wednesday, 10-8:30. Located downtown La Jolla. An original 1921 building designed by architect William Templeton Johnson 12-foot high wood beam ceilings, casement windows, Spanish-Italianate architecture. 100% of space for special exhibitions. Clientele tourists, upscale, local community, students and Athenaeum members. 100% private collectors. Overall price range: $100-1,000; most work sold at $100-500.

MEDIA Considers all media, all types of prints. Most frequently exhibits painting, multi-media and book art.

STYLE Exhibits all styles. Genres include florals, portraits, landscapes and figurative work.

TERMS Artwork is accepted on consignment, and there is a 25% commission. Retail price set by the artist. Gallery provides insurance and promotion; shipping costs are shared. Prefers artwork framed.

SUBMISSIONS Artists must be considered and accepted by the art committee. Send query letter with slides, bio, SASE and reviews. Write for appointment to show portfolio of photographs, slides and transparencies. Responds in 2 months. Files slide and bio only if there is initial interest in artist's work.

TIPS Finds artists through word of mouth and referrals.

ATLANTIC CENTER FOR THE ARTS, INC.

1414 Arts Center Ave., New Smyrna Beach FL 32168. (386)427-6975. **Fax:** (386)427-5669. **E-mail:** nconroy@atlanticcenterforthearts.org; mmartin@atlanticcenterforthearts.org. **Website:** www.atlanticcenterforthearts.org. **Contact:** Meghan Martin, gallery director; Nick Conroy, residency director. Estab. 1977. Nonprofit interdisciplinary, international artists-in-residence program. Sponsors 5-6 residencies/year. Located on secluded bayfront 3½ miles from downtown. This location accepts applications for residencies only, but they also run Harris House of Atlantic Center for the Arts, which accepts Florida artists only for exhibition opportunities. Harris House is located at 214 S. Riverside Dr., New Smyrna Beach FL 32168. (386)423-1753.

MEDIA Most frequently exhibits paintings, drawings, prints, video installations, sculpture, photographs.

STYLE Contemporary.

TERMS Call Harris House for more information.

SUBMISSIONS Call Harris House for more information.

ATLANTIC GALLERY

548 W. 28th St., Suite 540, New York NY 10001. (212)219-3183. **E-mail:** info@atlanticgallery.org. **Website:** www.atlanticgallery.org. **Contact:** Jeff Miller, president. Estab. 1974. Cooperative gallery. There is a co-op membership plus a donation of time required. Approached by 50 artists/year; represents 24 emerging, mid-career and established artists. Exhibited artists include Ragnar Naess (sculptor), Sally Brody (oil, acrylic), and Whitney Hansen (oil). Average display time: 4 weeks. Gallery open Tuesday, Wednesday, Friday, Saturday, 12-6; Thursday, 12-9. Closed August. Located in Chelsea. Has kitchenette. Clients include local community, tourists and upscale clients. 2% of sales are to corporate collectors. Overall price range: $100-13,000. Most work sold at $1,500-5,000. Finds artists through word of mouth, submissions, art exhibits, referrals by other artists.

MEDIA Considers all media. Considers all types of prints. Most frequently exhibits watercolor, acrylic and oil.

STYLE Considers all styles and genres. Most frequently exhibits impressionism, realism, imagism.

TERMS Artwork is accepted on consignment, and there is a 20% commission. There is a 10% commission. Rental fee for space covers 4 weeks. Retail price set by the artist. Gallery provides promotion and contract. Accepted work should be framed. Does not require exclusive representation locally. Currently accepting artists.

SUBMISSIONS Call or write to arrange a personal interview to show CD and artwork. Send query letter with artist's statement, bio, brochure, SASE and CD or slides. Returns material with SASE. Responds in 2 weeks. Files only accepted work.

ATLAS GALLERIES, INC.

535 N. Michigan Ave., Chicago IL 60611. (312)329-9330; (312)649-0999. **E-mail:** Via online contact form.

Website: www.atlasgalleries.com. Estab. 1967. For-profit gallery. Exhibits established artists. Sponsors 14 exhibits/year. Average display time: 2 days solo/ then permanently with collection. Two locations on Michigan Avenue's Magnificent Mile. See website for hours of both locations. Clients include local community, tourists, upscale. 5% of sales are to corporate collectors. Overall price range: $200-100,000; most work sold at $2,000.

MEDIA Considers acrylic, ceramics, collage, drawing, glass, mixed media, oil, paper, pastel, pen & ink, sculpture and watercolor. Most frequently exhibits oil, acrylic and sculpture. Considers prints of engravings, etchings, linocuts, lithographs, serigraphs, woodcuts and giclée.

STYLE Considers all styles and genres. Most frequently exhibits impressionism, surrealism/post modern. Exhibits all genres.

TERMS Artwork is accepted on consignment or bought outright. Retail price set by the gallery. Gallery provides insurance, promotion and contract. Requires exclusive representation locally.

SUBMISSIONS Send query letter with artist's statement, bio, photocopies, photographs and slides. Returns material with SASE. Responds to queries if interested within 3 months. Does not file materials unless we are interested in artist. Finds artists through art exhibits, portfolio reviews, referrals by other artists, submissions and word of mouth.

AUROBORA PRESS

340 Walnut Ave., Ketchum ID 83340. (415)546-7880. **E-mail:** monotype@aurobora.com. **Website:** www.aurobora.com. **Contact:** Michael Liener, founder/director. Estab. 1993. Retail gallery and fine arts press. Invitational Press dedicated to the monoprint and monotype medium. Represents/exhibits emerging, mid-career and established artists. Exhibited artists include William T. Wiley, David Ireland, Stephan De Staebler, Tony Delap. Sponsors 10 shows/year. Average display time: 6-8 weeks. Open Tuesday–Saturday, 10-5; and by appointment. Located Sun Valley ID; 1,500 sq. ft.; Clientele includes collectors, individuals, and art consultants. Overall price range: $1,200-30,000; most work sold at $1,500-4,000.

○ Aurobora Press invites artists each year to spend a period of time in residency working with Master Printers.

MEDIA Publishes monotypes and other unique works on paper.

TERMS Retail price set by gallery and artist. Gallery provides promotion.

SUBMISSIONS By invitation only.

AUSTIN MUSEUM OF ART

700 Congress Ave., Austin TX 78701. (512)453-5312 (downtown) or (512)458-8191 (Laguna Gloria). E-mail: info@amoa.org; curatorial@thecontemporary austin.org. **Website:** www.amoa.org. Estab. 1961. Downtown and Laguna Gloria locations. Interested in emerging, mid-career and established artists. Sponsors 2-3 solo and 6 group shows/year. Average display time: 1½ months. Clientele includes tourists and Austin and central Texas citizens.

MEDIA Currently exhibits 20th- and 21st-century art of the Americas and the Caribbean with an emphasis on 2D and 3D contemporary artwork to include experimental video, mixed media and outdoor site-specific installations.

STYLE Exhibits all styles and genres. No commercial cliquéd art.

TERMS Retail price set by artist. Gallery provides insurance and contract; shipping costs to be determined. Exhibitions booked 2 years in advance. "We are not a commercial gallery."

SUBMISSIONS Send query letter with résumé, slides and SASE attn: Artist Submission. Responds only if interested within 3 months. Files slides, résumé and bio. Material returned only when accompanied by SASE. Common mistakes artists make are "not enough information, poor slide quality, too much work covering too many changes in their development."

ALAN AVERY ART COMPANY

315 E. Paces Ferry Rd., Atlanta GA 30305. (404)237-0370. **E-mail:** info@alanaveryartcompany.com. **Website:** www.alanaveryartcompany.com. **Contact:** Alan Avery, owner. Estab. 1983. Retail gallery and corporate sales consultants. Represents/exhibits over 60 artists, from emerging to Modern Masters. Exhibited artists include Roy Lichtenstein, Jim Dine, Robert Rauschenberg, Andy Warhol, Caio Fonseca, Larry Gray, Robert Kipniss, Lynn Davison and Russell Whiting. Sponsors 6-8 shows/year. Average display time: 6-8 weeks. Open all year; Tuesday–Saturday, 11-5; Saturday, 11-5 and by appointment. Located: Buckhead; 6,700 sq. ft.; 25-year-old converted restaurant. 50-60% of space for

special exhibitions; 40-50% of space for gallery artists. Clientele: upscale, local, regional, national and international. 70% private collectors, 30% corporate collectors. Overall price range: $1,500-150,000.

MEDIA Considers all media. Most frequently exhibits painting, sculpture and works on paper.

STYLE Exhibits expressionism, conceptualism, color field, painterly abstraction, postmodern works and realism. Genres include landscapes, Americana and figurative work. Prefers realism, abstract and figurative.

TERMS Artwork is accepted on consignment (negotiable commission). Retail price set by gallery. Gallery pays promotion and contract. Shipping costs are shared. Prefers framed artwork.

SUBMISSIONS Currently not accepting artist submissions. When open, submission guidelines will be available online. Send query letter with résumé, at least 20 images, bio, prices, medium, sizes and SASE. Reviews every 6 weeks. Finds artists through submissions, word of mouth, research and referrals by other artists. Submission guidelines available online.

TIPS "Be as complete and professional as possible in presentation. We provide submittal process sheets, listing all items needed for review. Following these sheets is important."

SARAH BAIN GALLERY

110 W. Birch St., Suite 1, Brea CA 92821. (714)990-0500. **E-mail:** info@sarahbaingallery.com. **Website:** www.sarahbaingallery.com. For-profit gallery. A commercial art gallery located in downtown Anaheim. Exhibits emerging and mid-career artists. Approached by 200 artists/year; represents or exhibits 24 artists. Sponsors 12 total exhibits/year. Average display time: 1 month. Open Wednesday–Thursday, 11-6; Friday and Saturday, 11-9; Sunday, 11-6; or by appointment. Clients include local community, students, tourists and upscale. Overall price range: $700-15,000; most work sold at $4,000.

MEDIA Considers acrylic, drawing, mixed media, oil. Most frequently exhibits drawing, mixed media, paintings in representational or figurative style.

STYLE Exhibits representational or figurative.

TERMS Artwork is accepted on consignment. Retail price set by the gallery. Gallery provides promotion. Accepted work should be framed and mounted. Prefers only representational or figurative art.

SUBMISSIONS Submission guidelines available online. Mail portfolio for review. Send query letter with slides. Returns material with SASE. Responds to queries in 1 month.

TIPS "Show a consistent, comprehensive body of work as if it were its own show ready to be hung."

BAKEHOUSE ART COMPLEX

561 NW 32nd St., Miami FL 33127. (305)576-2828. **Fax:** (305)576-0316. **E-mail:** ademello@baclf.org. **Website:** www.bacfl.org. **Contact:** Ananda DeMello, director of exhibitions. Estab. 1986. A not-for-profit organization dedicated to attracting emerging and mid-career artists in South Florida to a workplace that provides affordable studios, exhibition galleries and professional development opportunities. Represents more than 100 emerging and mid-career artists. 65 tenants, more than 50 associate artists. Sponsors numerous shows and cultural events annually. Average display time: 3-5 weeks. Gallery open daily, 12-5. Located in Wynwood Art District; 3,200 sq. ft. gallery; 33,000 sq. ft. retro-fitted commercial bakery, 17 ft. ceilings. Clientel: 80% private collectors, 20% corporate collectors. Overall price range: $500-10,000.

MEDIA Considers all media.

STYLE Exhibits all styles, all genres.

TERMS Co-op membership fee plus donation of time. Rental fee for studio space. Retail price of art set by the artist.

SUBMISSIONS Submission guidelines available online. Accepts artists to juried membership. Send query letter for application or download online.

TIPS "Don't stop painting, sculpting, etc., while you are seeking representation. Daily work (works-in-progress, studies) evidences a commitment to the profession. Speaking to someone about your work while you are working brings an energy and an urgency that moves the art and the gallery representation relationship forward."

BAKER ARTS CENTER

624 N. Pershing Ave., Liberal KS 67901. (620)624-2810. **Fax:** (620)624-7726. **E-mail:** dianemarsh@bakerartscenter.org. **Website:** www.bakerartscenter.org. **Contact:** Diane Marsh, art director. Estab. 1986. Nonprofit gallery. Exhibits emerging, mid-career, and established artists. Approached by 6-10 artists a year. Represents of exhibits 6-10 artists. Exhibited artists include J. McDonald (glass) and J. Gustafson (assorted). Sponsors 5 total exhibits/year. 1 photography exhibit/year. Model and property release are preferred. Average display time: 40-50 days. Open Tuesday-Fri-

day, 9-5; Saturdays, 2-5. Closed Christmas, Thanksgiving and New Year's Eve. Clients include local community, students, and tourists. Overall price range: $10-1,000. Most work sold at $400.

MEDIA Considers all media. Most frequently exhibits glass, mixed media, and acrylic. Considers engravings, etchings, linocuts, lithographs, and woodcuts.

STYLE Considers all stlyes and genres

TERMS Artwork is accepted on consignment and there is a 30% commission fee. Retail price set by the artist. Gallery provides insurance, promotion, and contract. Accepted work should be framed, mounted, and matted.

SUBMISSIONS Write to arrange personal interview to show portfolio or e-mail query letter with link to artist's website or JPEG samples at 72 dpi. Returns material with SASE. Responds in 2-4 weeks. Finds artists through word of mouth, submissions, art exhibits, and referrals by other artists.

BALZEKAS MUSEUM OF LITHUANIAN CULTURE ART GALLERY

6500 S. Pulaski Rd., Chicago IL 60629. (773)582-6500. **Fax:** (773)582-5133. **E-mail:** info@balzekasmuseum. org. **Website:** www.balzekasmuseum.org. **Contact:** Stanley Balzekas, Jr., president. Estab. 1996. Museum, museum retail shop, nonprofit gallery, rental gallery. Approached by 20 artists/year. Sponsors 2 photography exhibits/year. Average display time: 6 weeks. Open daily, 10-4. Closed Christmas, Easter and New Year's Day. Overall price range: $150-6,000. Most work sold at $545.

MEDIA Considers all media and all types of prints.

STYLE Considers all styles and genres.

TERMS Artwork is accepted on consignment and there is a 33⅓% commission. Retail price set by the gallery. Gallery provides promotion. Accepted work should be framed.

SUBMISSIONS Write to arrange a personal interview to show portfolio. Cannot return material. Responds in 2 months. Finds artists through word of mouth, art exhibits, and referrals by other artists.

BANNISTER GALLERY

Rhode Island College, Roberts Hall, 124, 600 Mt. Pleasant Ave., Providence RI 02908-1991. (401)456-9765. **Fax:** (401)456-9718. **E-mail:** bannistergallery@ ric.edu; jmontford@ric.edu. **Website:** www.ric.edu/ bannister. **Contact:** James Montford, gallery director. Estab. 1978. Nonprofit gallery. Represents emerging, mid-career and established artists. Sponsors 9 shows/year. Average display time: 3 weeks. Open Tuesday–Friday, 12-8 (during academic year). Located on college campus; 1,600 sq. ft.; features spacious, well-lit gallery space with off-white walls, gloss black tile floor; 2 sections with 9-foot and 12-foot ceilings. 100% of space for special exhibitions. Clientele: students and public.

MEDIA Considers all media and all types of original prints. Most frequently exhibits painting, photography and sculpture.

STYLE Exhibits all styles.

TERMS Artwork is exhibited for educational purposes—gallery takes no commission. Retail price set by artist. Gallery provides insurance, promotion and limited shipping costs from gallery. Prefers artwork framed.

SUBMISSIONS Send query letter with résumé, slides, bio, brochure, SASE and reviews. Files addresses, catalogs and résumés.

KENISE BARNES FINE ART

1947 Palmer Ave., Larchmont NY 10538. (914)834-8077. **E-mail:** kenise@kbfa.com. **Website:** www.kenisebarnesfineart.com. **Contact:** Kenise Barnes, director. Estab. 1994. Fine art gallery. Works with 300 artists/year; exhibits 30 emerging and mid-career artists/year. See website for artists. Sponsors 12 exhibits/year. Average display time: 5-6 weeks. Open Tuesday–Saturday, 10-5:30 and by appointment. Clients include residential, hospitality and corporate collectors nationwide. 20% of sales are to corporate collectors. Overall price range: $1,000-15,000; most work sold at $5-8,000.

STYLE Exhibits abstract and representational art.

TERMS Gallery provides insurance and promotion. Requires exclusive representation locally.

SUBMISSIONS "Although we are not currently looking for new artists, the director does review work on a rolling basis. See gallery website for artist submission policies. If we would like to make a studio visit, we will contact you."

DAVID BARNETT GALLERY

1024 E. State St., Milwaukee WI 53202. (414)271-5058. **Fax:** (414)271-9132. **E-mail:** inquiries@david barnettgallery.com. **Website:** www.davidbarnettgallery.com. Estab. 1966. Retail and rental gallery and art consultancy. "From Picasso to Rembrandt, from Old Masters to emerging Wisconsin artists, we provide a spectacular selection of art. With over 5,000 works of art in our current inventory, the gallery presents a vast variety of mediums and styles in every price range. Our gallery also brings an array of quality services that meet your art needs." Represents 300-400 emerging, mid-career and established artists. Exhibited artists include Claude Weisbuch and Carol Summers. Sponsors 12 shows/year. Average display time: 1 month. Open Tuesday–Friday, 11-5:30; Saturday, 11-5. Located downtown at the corner of State and Prospect; 6,500 sq. ft.; Victorian-Italianate mansion built in 1875, 3 floors of artwork displayed. 25% of space for special exhibitions. Clientele: retail, corporations, interior decorators, private collectors, consultants, museums and architects. 20% private collectors, 10% corporate collectors. Overall price range: $50-375,000; most work sold at $1,000-50,000.

MEDIA Considers oil, acrylic, watercolor, pastel, pen & ink, drawings, mixed media, collage, sculpture, ceramic, fiber, glass, photography, bronzes, marble, woodcuts, engravings, lithographs, wood engravings, serigraphs, linocuts, etchings and posters. Most frequently exhibits prints, drawings and oils.

STYLE Exhibits expressionism, neo-expressionism, primitivism, painterly abstraction, surrealism, imagism, conceptualism, minimalism, postmodern works, impressionism, realism and photorealism. Genres include landscapes, florals, Southwestern, Western, wildlife, portraits and figurative work. Prefers old master graphics, contemporary and impressionistic.

TERMS Accepts artwork on consignment (50% commission). Retail price set by gallery and artist. Sometimes offers customer discounts and payment by installment. Gallery provides insurance and promotion; artist pays for shipping. Prefers artwork framed.

SUBMISSIONS Send query letter with slides, bio, brochure and SASE. "We return everything if we decide not to carry the artwork." Finds artists through agents, word of mouth, various art publications, sourcebooks, submissions and self-promotions.

BARRON ARTS CENTER

582 Rahway Ave., Woodbridge NJ 07095. (732)634-0413. **E-mail:** barronarts@twp.woodbridge.nj.us. **Website:** www.twp.woodbridge.nj.us/Departments/BarronArtsCenter/tabid/251/Default.aspx. **Contact:** Cynthia Knight, director. Estab. 1977. Nonprofit gallery. Interested in emerging, mid-career and established artists. Sponsors several solo and group shows/

year. Average display time: 1 month. Clients include culturally minded individuals mainly from the central New Jersey region. 80% of sales are to private collectors, 20% corporate clients. Overall price range: $200-5,000. Gallery hours during exhibits: Monday-Friday, 11-4; Sunday, 2-4; Closed holidays.

MEDIA Considers oil, acrylic, watercolor, pastel, pen & ink, drawings, mixed media, collage, works on paper, sculpture, ceramic, craft, fiber, glass, installation, photography, performance and original handpulled prints. Most frequently exhibits watercolor, oils, photography and mixed media.

STYLE Exhibits painterly abstraction, impressionism, photorealism, realism and surrealism. Genres include landscapes and figurative work. Prefers painterly abstraction, photorealism and realism.

TERMS Accepts work on consignment. Retail price set by artist. Exclusive area representation not required. Gallery provides insurance, promotion and contract; artist pays for shipping.

SUBMISSIONS Send query letter, résumé and slides. Call for appointment to show portfolio. Résumés and slides are filed.

TIPS Most common mistakes artists make in presenting their work are improper matting and framing and poor quality slides.

BATON ROUGE GALLERY, INC.

1515 Dalrymple Dr., Baton Rouge LA 70808. (225)383-1470. **E-mail:** jandreasen@batonrougegallery.org. **Website:** batonrougegallery.org. **Contact:** Jason Andreasen, executive director. Estab. 1966. Nonprofit contemporary art gallery. One of the oldest professional artist cooperative galleries in the US. Exhibits the work of over 50 professional artists. 300 community members. Presents 12 exhibitions annually. Monthly exhibitions at the gallery feature the work of current artist members including photographers, painters, sculptors, stained-glass artists, printmakers, ceramists, multi-media, and installation artists. The opening receptions are held for each exhibition on the first Wednesday of every month from 7-9 and are free and open to the public. Average display time: 1 month. Open Tuesday–Sunday, 12-6. Located in BREC's historic City Park Pavilion. Overall price range: $100-10,000; most work sold at $200-2,000.

○ The gallery presents monthly exhibitions, primarily focusing on professional contemporary artists who have strong ties to Louisi-

ana. Opening receptions are held on the first Wednesday of each month (excluding January and November). Many cultural programs are also offered year-round.

MEDIA All media considered. Most frequently exhibits 2D works including painting, photography and drawing, in addition to sculpture works.

STYLE Exhibits all cotemporary styles and genres.

TERMS Co-op membership fee plus donation of time. Gallery takes 40% commission on work sold.

SUBMISSIONS Membership and guest exhibitions are selected by a screening committee selected from artist members. The screening committee reviews applications in October of each year. Artist requirements and application for submissions are available online.

SETH JASON BEITLER FINE ARTS

250 NW 23rd St., Suite 202, Miami FL 33127. (305)438-0218. **Fax:** (800)952-7026. **E-mail:** info@sethjason.com. **Website:** www.sethjason.com. **Contact:** Seth Beitler, owner. Estab. 2000. For-profit gallery, art consultancy. Approached by 300 artists/year. Represents 40 mid-career, established artists. Exhibited artists include Florimond Dufoor, oil paintings; Terje Lundaas, glass sculpture. Sponsors 5 exhibits/year. Average display time: 2-3 months. Open Tuesday-Saturday, 12-5, and by appointment. Clients include local community and upscale. 5-10% of sales are to corporate collectors. Overall price range: $2,000-300,000; most work sold at $5,000.

MEDIA Considers acrylic, glass, mixed media, sculpture, drawing, oil. Most frequently exhibits sculpture, painting, photography. Considers etchings, linocuts, lithographs.

STYLE Exhibits color field, geometric abstraction and painterly abstraction. Most frequently exhibits geometric sculpture, abstract painting, photography. Genres include figurative work and landscapes.

TERMS Artwork is accepted on consignment (50% commission). Retail price set by the gallery. Gallery provides insurance, promotion and contract. Accepted work should be mounted.

SUBMISSIONS Write to arrange personal interview to show portfolio of photographs, slides, transparencies. Send query letter with artist's statement, bio, photographs, résumé, SASE. Returns material with SASE. Responds to queries in 2 months. Files photos, slides, transparencies. Finds artists through art fairs, portfolio reviews, referrals by other artists and word of mouth.

TIPS "Send easy-to-see photographs. E-mail submissions for quicker response."

CECELIA COKER BELL GALLERY

Coker College Art Dept., 300 E. College Ave., Hartsville SC 29550. (843)383-8150. **E-mail:** artgallery@coker.edu. **Website:** www.ceceliacokerbellgallery.com. **Contact:** Jean Grosser, gallery director & department chair. "A campus-located teaching gallery that exhibits a variety of media and styles to expose students and the community to the breadth of possibility for expression in art. Exhibits include regional, national and international artists with an emphasis on quality and originality. Shows include work from emerging, mid, and late career artists." Sponsors 5 solo shows/year, with a 4-week run for each show. Open Monday–Friday, 10-4 (when classes are in session).

MEDIA Considers all media including installation and graphic design. Most frequently exhibits painting, photography, sculpture/installation and mixed media.

STYLE Considers all styles. Not interested in conservative/commercial art.

TERMS Retail price set by artist (sales are not common). Exclusive area representation not required. Gallery provides insurance, promotion and contract; shipping costs are shared.

SUBMISSIONS Send résumé, 15-20 JPEG files on CD (or upload them to a Dropbox account) with a list of images, statement, résumé, and SASE. Reviews, web pages, and catalogues are welcome, though not required. If you would like response, but not your submission items returned, simply include an e-mail address. Visits by artists are welcome; however, the exhibition committee will review and select all shows from the JPEGs submitted by the artists.

BENNETT GALLERIES AND COMPANY

5308 Kingston Pike, Knoxville TN 37919. (865)584-6791. **Fax:** (865)588-6130. **E-mail:** info@bennettgalleries.com. **Website:** www.bennettgalleries.com. Estab. 1985. Retail gallery. Represents emerging and established artists. "Rick Bennett has spent years traveling the world, establishing relationships with artists, craftsmen and small family-owned furniture makers, bringing to Bennett Galleries one-of-a-kind pieces for your home. Whether traveling in Italy, France or throughout the US, the Bennetts are constantly on the lookout for people who still do hand-made work. Every piece is unique, each with its own story. This search for unusual, top-quality merchandise has filled the gallery with unique works of art, fine furnishings, distinctive jewelry and crafts." Exhibited artists include Richard Jolley, Carl Sublett, Scott Duce, Andrew Saftel, Akira Blount, Scott Hill, Marga Hayes McBride, Grace Ann Warn, Timothy Berry and Cheryl Warrick. Sponsors 10 shows/year. Average display time: 1 month. Open all year; Monday–Thursday, 10-6; Friday–Saturday, 10-5:30. Located in West Knoxville. Clientele: 80% private collectors, 20% corporate collectors. Overall price range: $200-20,000; most work sold at $2,000-8,000.

MEDIA Considers oil, acrylic, watercolor, pastel, drawing, mixed media, works on paper, sculpture, ceramic, craft, photography, glass, original handpulled prints. Most frequently exhibits painting, ceramic/clay, wood, glass and sculpture.

STYLE Exhibits contemporary works in abstraction, figurative, narrative, realism, contemporary landscape and still life.

TERMS Accepts artwork on consignment (50% commission). Retail price set by the gallery and the artist. Sometimes offers customer discounts and payment by installments. Gallery provides insurance on works at the gallery, promotion and contract. Prefers artwork framed. Shipping to gallery to be paid by the artist.

SUBMISSIONS Accepts artwork on consignment (50% commission). Retail price set by the gallery and the artist. Sometimes offers customer discounts and payment by installments. Gallery provides insurance on works at the gallery, promotion and contract. Prefers artwork framed. Shipping to gallery to be paid by the artist.

MONA BERMAN FINE ARTS

78 Lyon St., New Haven CT 06511. (203)562-4720. **E-mail:** info@monabermanfinearts.com. **Website:** www.monabermanfinearts.com. **Contact:** Mona Berman, director. Estab. 1979. Located near downtown; 1,400 sq. ft. Sells most styles, except figurative and large scale sculpture. Prefers abstract, landscape and transitional. 50% commission; net 30 days. Retail price is set by gallery and artist. Retail prices must be consistent regardless of venue. Customer discounts and payment by installment are available. Dealer provides insurance; artist pays for shipping. Prefers artwork unframed. Finds artists through word of

mouth, art publications and sourcebooks, submissions and self-promotions, and other professionals' recommendations. "We will not carry artists who do not maintain consistent retail pricing. We are not a gallery; please do not submit if you are looking for an exhibition venue. We are primarily art consultants. We continue to be busy selling high-quality art and related services to the corporate, architectural, design and private sectors."

TERMS Accepts e-mail submissions or links to website only. Must include retail prices to be considered. Portfolios are reviewed only after images have been reviewed. Responds in 1 month. No phone calls please. Contact by e-mail only.

BERTONI GALLERY

1392 Kings Hwy., Sugar Loaf NY 10981. (845)469-0993. **Fax:** (845)469-6808. **E-mail:** bertoni@optonline.net. **Website:** www.bertonigallery.com. **Contact:** Rachel Bertoni, owner. For-profit gallery, rental gallery, art consultancy. Custom picture framing services available. Estab. 2000. Exhibits emerging, mid-career and established artists. Approached by 15 artists/year; represents 5 artists/year. Exhibited artists include Mae Bertoni (award winning master watercolorist); Marylyn Vanderpool (watercolors); and Mike Jarosko (oil). Sponsors 5 exhibits/year. Average display time: 2 months. Open Thursday-Sunday, 11-6. Clients include local community, tourists. 10% of sales are to corporate collectors. Overall price range: $100-1,500; most work sold at $400.

MEDIA Considers all media. Most frequently exhibits watercolor, oil, mixed media. Considers all types of prints.

STYLE Exhibits all styles and genres.

TERMS Artwork is accepted on consignment (40% commission); or artwork is bought outright for 50% of retail price. The space can be rented, commission fees would change; rental fee covers 2 months. Retail price set by the artist. Accepted work should be professionally framed, mounted, matted.

SUBMISSIONS Send query letter with artist's statement, résumé and photographs. Returns material with SASE. Responds to queries in 2 weeks. Finds artists through word of mouth and referrals by other artists.

TIPS "Submit materials via e-mail or in a neat manner with SASE for easy return."

TOM BINDER FINE ARTS

825 Wilshire Blvd., #708, Santa Monica CA 90401. (800)332-4278. **Fax:** (800)370-3770. **E-mail:** info@art-man.net. **Website:** www.artman.net. **Contact:** Tom Binder, owner. For-profit gallery. Exhibits established artists. Clients include local community, tourists and upscale. Overall price range: $200-5,000.

See additional listing in the Posters & Prints section.

MEDIA Considers all media; types of prints include etchings, lithographs, posters and serigraphs.

STYLE Considers all styles and genres.

TERMS Artwork is accepted on consignment or bought outright. Retail price set by the gallery. Gallery provides insurance. Accepted work should be mounted. Write to arrange a personal interview to show portfolio. Returns material with SASE. Responds in 2 weeks.

BIRMINGHAM BLOOMFIELD ART CENTER

1516 S. Cranbrook Rd., Birmingham MI 48009. (248)644-0866. **E-mail:** annievangelderen@bbartcenter.org. **Website:** www.bbartcenter.org. **Contact:** Annie VanGelderen, president and CEO. Estab. 1962. Nonprofit gallery shop and gallery exhibit space. Represents emerging, mid-career and established artists. Presents ongoing exhibitions in 4 galleries. Open all year; Monday-Thursday, 9-6; Friday-Saturday, 9-5; second Sundays, 1-4. Suburban location. 70% of space for gallery artists. Clientele upscale, local. 100% private collectors. Overall price range: $50-25,000.

MEDIA Considers 2D and 3D fine art in all media. Most frequently exhibits 3D work: jewelry, glass, ceramics, fiber, mixed-media sculpture; and 2D work: painting, printmaking, drawing, mixed media and video.

STYLE Exhibits all styles.

SUBMISSIONS Send query letter with résumé, website address, digital images (preferred), photographs, review, artist's statement and bio.

TIPS "We consider conceptual content, technique, media, presentation and condition of work as well as professionalism of the artist."

BLACKFISH GALLERY

420 NW Ninth Ave., Portland OR 97209. (503)224-2634. **E-mail:** director@blackfish.com. **Website:** www.blackfish.com. **Contact:** Damara Bartlett, director. Estab. 1979. Retail cooperative gallery. Represents 30 emerging and mid-career artists. Exhibited

artists include Michael Knutson (oil paintings). Sponsors 12 shows/year. Open all year; Tuesday–Saturday, 11-5 and by appointment. Located downtown, in the Northwest Pearl District; 2,500 sq. ft.; street-level, garage-type overhead wide door, long, open space (100' deep). Typically 70% of space for feature exhibits by 1 or 2 member artists, and 30% for member artists or invited guests. 80% of sales are to private collectors, 20% corporate clients. Overall price range: $250-12,000; most artwork sold at $500-2,000.

MEDIA Considers oil, acrylic, watercolor, pastel, pen & ink, drawings, mixed media, collage, sculpture, ceramic, photography, woodcuts, wood engravings, linocuts, engravings, mezzotints, etchings, lithographs, pochoir and serigraphs. Most frequently exhibits paintings, sculpture and prints.

STYLE Exhibits expressionism, neo-expressionism, painterly abstraction, surrealism, conceptualism, minimalism, color field, postmodern works, impressionism and realism.

TERMS Accepts work on consignment from invited artists (50% commission); co-op membership includes monthly dues plus donation of time (40% commission on sales). Retail price set by artist with assistance from gallery on request. Customer discounts and payment by installment are available. Gallery provides insurance, promotion and contract, and shipping costs from gallery. Prefers artwork framed.

SUBMISSIONS Accepts only artists from northwest Oregon and southwest Washington ("unique exceptions possible"); "must be willing to be an active cooperative member; write for details." Send query letter with résumé, slides, SASE, reviews and statement of intent. Write for appointment to show portfolio of photographs and slides. Reviews throughout the year. Responds in 1 month. Files material only if exhibit invitation extended. Finds artists through agents, visiting exhibitions, word of mouth, various art publications and sourcebooks, submissions/self-promotions and art collectors' referrals.

TIPS "Understand particularities of cooperative gallery membership. Call or write for an information packet. Do not bring work or slides to us without first having contacted us by phone, mail, or e-mail."

BLACKWELL ST. CENTER FOR THE ARTS

P.O. Box 808, Denville NJ 07834-0808, (201)337-2143. **E-mail:** wblakeart2004@yahoo.com. **Website:** www. blackwell-st-artists.org. **Contact:** Wanda Blake. Estab.

1983. Nonprofit group. Exhibits the work of approximately 15 or more emerging and established artists. Sponsors 3-4 group shows/year. Average display time: 1 month. Overall price range: $100-5,000; most work sold at $150-350.

MEDIA Considers oil, acrylic, watercolor, pastel, pen & ink, drawings, mixed media, collage, paper, sculpture, ceramics, photography, egg tempera, woodcuts, wood engravings, linocuts, engravings, mezzotints, etchings, lithographs and serigraphs. Most frequently exhibits oil, photography and pastel.

STYLE Exhibits all styles and genres. Prefers painterly abstraction, realism and photorealism.

TERMS Membership fee plus donation of time; 20% commission. Retail price set by artist. Sometimes offers payment by installments. Exclusive area representation not required. Artist pays for shipping. Prefers artwork framed.

SUBMISSIONS Send query letter with résumé, brochure, slides, photographs, bio and SASE. Call or write for appointment to show portfolio of originals and slides. Responds in 1 month. Files slides of accepted artists. All material returned if not accepted or under consideration.

TIPS "Show one style of work and pick the best. Less is more. Slides and/or photos should be current work. Enthusiasm and organization are big pluses!"

BLOUNT-BRIDGERS HOUSE/HOBSON PITTMAN MEMORIAL GALLERY

130 Bridgers St., Tarboro NC 27886. (252)823-4159. **E-mail:** edgecombearts@embarqmail.com. **Website:** www.edgecombearts.org. Estab. 1982. Museum. Approached by 20 artists/year. Exhibits 6 emerging, mid-career and established artists. Sponsors 8 exhibits/year. Average display time: 6 weeks. Open Tuesday-Friday, 10-4; closed weekends December-April; open weekends, 2-4, by appointment only May-December. Closed major holidays. Located in historic house in residential area of small town; gallery on 2nd floor is accessible by passenger elevator. Room is approximately 48×20 sq. ft. Clients include local community, students and tourists. Overall price range: $250-5,000; most work sold at $500.

MEDIA Considers acrylic, ceramics, collage, craft, drawing, fiber, glass, mixed media, oil, paper, pastel, pen & ink and watercolor. Most frequently exhibits oil, watercolor and ceramic. Considers all types of prints.

STYLE Considers all styles and genres.

TERMS Artwork is accepted on consignment and there is a 30% commission. Retail price set by the artist. Gallery provides insurance and limited promotion. Accepted work should be framed. Does not require exclusive representation locally. Accepts artists from southeast and Pennsylvania.

SUBMISSIONS Send portfolio of photographs, slides or transparencies. Send query letter with artist's statement, bio, SASE and slides. Returns material with SASE. Responds in 3 months. Finds artists through word of mouth, submissions, art exhibits and referrals by other artists.

BLUE GALLERY

118 Southwest Blvd., Kansas City MO 64108. (816)527-0823. **E-mail:** kellyk@bluegalleryonline.com. **Website:** www.bluegalleryonline.com. **Contact:** Kelly Kuhn, owner/director. Estab. 2000. A for-profit gallery. Exhibits emerging, mid-career, and established artists. Approached by hundreds of artists a year; represents or exhibits 45 artists a year. Sponsors 12 total exhibits/year. Average display time: 30 days. Open Tuesday-Saturday, 10-5:30 or by appointment. Clients include local community, tourists, and upscale establishments among others. A large percentage is sold to corporate collectors. Overall price range: $50-80,000. Finds artists through word of mouth, submissions, portfolio reviews, art exhibits, art fairs, and referrals by other artists.

MEDIA Acylic, ceramics, collage, craft, drawing, fiber, glass, installation, mixed media, oil, paper, pastel, pen & ink, sculpture, and watercolor. Considers all media, but most frequently exhibits paintings.

STYLE Considers all styles but prefers contemporary. Exhibits Americana, figurative work, florals, landscapes, portraits and Southwestern pieces among others.

TERMS Artwork is accepted on consignment. Retail price set by the artist. Gallery provides insurance, promotion, and contract. Accepted work should be framed. Requires exclusive representation locally.

SUBMISSIONS E-mail query letter with link to artist's website and JPEG samples at 72 dpi. Mail portfolio for review. Send query letter with artist's statement, bio, brochure, business card, photocopies, résumé, reviews, and SASE. Returns material with SASE. Responds in 3 months.

BLUE MOUNTAIN GALLERY

530 W. 25th St., 4th Floor, New York NY 10001. (646)486-4730. **Fax:** (646)486-4345. **E-mail:** info@bluemountaingallery.org. **Website:** www.bluemountaingallery.org. Estab. 1980. Artist-run cooperative gallery. Exhibits 32 mid-career artists. Sponsors 13 solo and 1 group shows/year. Display time is 3 weeks. "We are located on the 4th floor of a building in Chelsea. We share our floor with 2 other well-established cooperative galleries. Each space has white partitioning walls and an individual floor-plan." Clients include art lovers, collectors and artists. 90% of sales are to private collectors, 10% corporate clients. Open Tuesday–Saturday, 11-6. Overall price range: $100-8,000; most work sold at $100-4,000.

MEDIA Considers painting, drawing and sculpture.

STYLE "The base of the gallery is figurative but we show work that shows individuality, commitment and involvement with the medium."

TERMS Co-op membership fee plus donation of time. Retail price set by artist. Exclusive area representation not required. Gallery provides insurance, some promotion and contract; artist pays for shipping.

SUBMISSIONS Send name and address with intent of interest and sheet of 20 good slides. "We cannot be responsible for material return without SASE." Finds artists through artists' submissions and referrals.

TIPS "This is a cooperative gallery, so it is important to represent artists who can contribute actively to the gallery. We look at artists who can be termed local or in-town more than out-of-town artists and would choose the former over the latter. The work should present a consistent point of view that shows individuality. Expressive use of the medium used is important also."

⬙ BLUE SPIRAL 1

38 Biltmore Ave., Asheville NC 28801. (828)251-0202. **Fax:** (828)251-0884. **E-mail:** jsours@bluespiral1.com. **Website:** www.bluespiral1.com. Estab. 1991. Retail gallery. "Blue Spiral 1 presents work by exceptional Southern artists and object makers in a beautifully renovated building in the heart of downtown Asheville. The light-filled, 15,000-sq.-ft. gallery spans 3 floors connected by an open stairway. This spacious setting allows Blue Spiral 1 to offer considerable diversity, affording accessibility to various tastes and aesthetics." Represents emerging, mid-career and established artists living in the Southeast. Over 100

exhibited artists including Julyan Davis, John Nickerson, Suzanne Stryk, Greg Decker and Will Henry Stephens. Sponsors 15-20 shows/year. Average display time: 6-8 weeks. Open Monday–Saturday, 10-6; Sunday, 12-5. Located downtown 2 blocks south of Pack Square next to the Fine Arts Theatre; historic building. 50% of space for special exhibitions; 50% of space for gallery artists. Clientele: "across the range;" 90% private collectors, 10% corporate collectors. Overall price range: less than $100-50,000; most work sold at $100-2,500.

MEDIA Considers all media. Most frequently exhibits painting, clay, sculpture and glass.

STYLE Exhibits all styles, all genres.

TERMS Accepts work on consignment (50% commission). Retail price set by the artist. Gallery provides insurance, promotion and contract; artist pays shipping costs to and from gallery. Prefers framed artwork.

SUBMISSIONS Accepts only artists from Southeast. Send query letter with résumé, slides, prices, statement and SASE. Responds in 3 months. Incude SASE for items to be returned. Finds artists through word of mouth, referrals and travel. Submission guidelines available online.

TIPS "Work must be technically well executed and properly presented."

BOCA RATON MUSEUM OF ART

501 Plaza Real, Minzer Park, Boca Raton FL 33432. (561)392-2500. **Fax:** (561)391-6410. **E-mail:** info@ bocamuseum.org. **Website:** www.bocamuseum.org. Estab. 1950. Represents established artists. 5,500 members. Exhibits change every 2-3 months. Open all year; Tuesday, Wednesday, Friday, 10-5; Thursday, 10-8; Saturday and Sunday, 12-5. Located one mile east of I-95 in Mizner Park; 44,000 sq. ft.; national and international temporary exhibitions and impressive second-floor permanent collection. Three galleries—1 shows permanent collection, 2 are for changing exhibitions. 66% of space for special exhibitions.

MEDIA Considers all media. Exhibits modern masters including Braque, Degas, Demuth, Glackens, Klee, Matisse, Picasso and Seurat; 19th- and 20th-century photographers; pre-Columbian and African art; contemporary sculpture.

SUBMISSIONS "Contact executive director in writing."

TIPS "Photographs of work of art should be professionally done if possible. Before approaching museums, an artist should be well-represented in solo exhibitions and museum collections. Their acceptance into a particular museum collection, however, still depends on how well their work fits into that collection's narrative and how well it fits with the goals and collecting policies of that museum."

BOEHM GALLERY

Palomar College, 1140 W. Mission Rd., San Marcos CA 92069-1487. (760)744-1150 ext. 2304. **Website:** www.palomar.edu/art/BoehmGallery.html. Estab. 1966. Nonprofit gallery. Represents/exhibits mid-career artists. May be interested in seeing the work of emerging artists in the future. Generally exhibits 30 or more artists/year in solo and group exhibitions, supplemented with faculty, student work. Exhibited artists include top illustrators, crafts people, painters and sculptors. Sponsors 6 shows/year. Average display time: 4-5 weeks. Open fall and spring semester; Monday and Thursday, 10-4; Tuesday, 11-8; Wednesday, 2-8; Friday, 10-2; closed Saturday, Sunday, Monday and school holidays. Located on the Palomar College campus in San Marcos; 2,000 sq. ft.; 100% of space for special exhibitions. Clientele regional community, artists, collectors and students. "Prices range dramatically depending on exhibition type and artist; $25 for student works to $10,000 for paintings, drawings, oils and installational sculptural works."

MEDIA Considers all media; all types of prints. Most frequently exhibits installation art, painting, sculpture, glass, illustration, quilts, ceramics, furniture design and photography.

STYLE Exhibits all styles. Styles vary. Exhibits primarily group exhibits based on either a medium or theme or genre.

TERMS If artwork is sold, gallery retains 10% gallery "donation." Gallery provides insurance and promotion.

SUBMISSIONS Accepts primarily artists from Southern California. Send query letter with résumé, slides, reviews and bio. Call or write for appointment to show portfolio of photographs and slides. Responds in 2-3 months. Files artist bio and résumé. Finds artists through "artist network, other reviewed galleries, or university visits or following regional exhibitions, and referrals from other professional artists and crafts people."

TIPS Advises artists to show "clear focus for art exhibition and good slides. Lucid, direct artist statement.

Be willing to take part in group exhibits—we have very few strictly 'solo' shows and then only for very prominent artists. Be professional in your contacts and presentations and prompt in meeting deadlines. Have a unified body of work which is identifiable as your expression."

BRADBURY GALLERY

P.O. Box 2339, Fowler Center, 201 Olympic Dr., State University AR 72467-1920. (870)972-3471. **Fax:** (870)972-3748. **E-mail:** dnspe@astate.edu. **Website:** www.bradburygallery.com. Estab. 2001. "The Bradbury Gallery was established in January 2001 by a generous endowment in honor of Charlotte (Chucki) Bradbury, an alumna of Arkansas State University who later became a member of the ASU Board of Trustees. The Bradbury Gallery features changing exhibitions of contemporary art in all mediums and programs that promote the understanding of art and its significance to society. Regionally, nationally and internationally recognized artists are represented to inform viewers of cultural developments across the US and around the world. The Bradbury Gallery is also the site of the Delta National Small Prints Exhibition, an annually held, nationally recognized juried print show. Founded in 1996 by Arkansas State professor Evan Lindquist, the Delta National Exhibition has received great acclaim as it has grown to be one of the country's foremost annual competitions for prints. Open during academic school year; Tuesday-Saturday, 12-5; Sunday, 2-5. Located on university campus in the Fowler Center (201 Olympic Dr.); 5,400 sq. ft. All exhibitions are admission free and open to the public. Clientele: students/university faculty and staff/community.

SUBMISSIONS Send query letter with résumé, CD/DVD and SASE or submit all materials via e-mail. Responds only if interested within 2 months. Files résumé.

RENA BRANSTEN GALLERY

1639 Market St., San Francisco CA 94103. (415)982-3292. **Fax:** (415)982-1807. **E-mail:** info@renabranstengallery.com; calvert@renabranstengallery.com; rena@renabranstengallery.com. **Website:** www.renabranstengallery.com. **Contact:** Rena Bransten, owner. Estab. 1974. For-profit gallery. Approached by 200 artists/year; represents or exhibits 12-15 artists. Average display time: 4-5 weeks. Open Tuesday–Friday, 10:30-5:30; Saturday, 11-5. Usually closed the last week of August and the first week of September. Retail price(s) set by the gallery and the artist.

MEDIA Considers all media and all styles of contemporary art; exhibits prints (etchings, lithographs, silk screens) if included in one of our artists' inventory. Highly unlikely to take on a dedicated printmaker as it is not our main area of focus.

STYLE Considers all styles of contemporary art. Retail price set by the gallery and the artist.

TERMS Send material via JPEGs at 72 dpi or website link via e-mail, rather than snail mail submissions.

TIPS Finds artists through word of mouth, art fairs and exhibits, submissions, portfolio reviews and referrals by other artists.

BRENAU UNIVERSITY GALLERIES

500 Washington St. SE, Gainesville GA 30501. (770)534-6263. **Website:** www.brenau.edu/about/brenau-university-galleries/. **Contact:** Nichole Rawlings, gallery director; Allison Lauricella, gallery manager. Estab. 1980s. Nonprofit gallery. Exhibits emerging, mid-career and established artists. Sponsors 7-9 shows/year. Average display time: 6-8 weeks. Open all year; Monday-Thursday, 10-4; Sunday, 2-5 during exhibit dates. "Please call for summer hours." Located near downtown; 3,958 sq. ft., 3 galleries—the main one in a renovated 1914 neoclassical building, another in an adjacent renovated Victorian building dating from the 1890s, the third in the center for performing arts. 100% of space for special exhibitions. Clientele: tourists, upscale, local community, students. "Although sales do occur as a result of our exhibits, we do not currently take any percentage, except in our invitational exhibitions. Our purpose is primarily educational."

MEDIA Considers all media.

STYLE Exhibits wide range of styles. "We intentionally try to plan a balanced variety of media and styles."

TERMS Retail price set by the artist. Gallery provides insurance and promotion; shipping costs are shared, depending on funding for exhibits. Prefers artwork framed. "Artwork must be framed or otherwise ready to exhibit."

SUBMISSIONS Send query letter with résumé, 10-20 slides, photographs and bio. Write for appointment to show portfolio of slides and transparencies. Responds within months if possible. Artist should call to follow up. Files 1 or 2 slides or photos with a short résumé or bio if interested. Remaining material returned. Finds artists through referrals, direct viewing of work and inquiries.

TIPS "Be persistent, keep working, be organized and patient. Take good slides and develop a body of work. Galleries are limited by a variety of constraints—time, budgets, location, taste—and rejection does not mean your work may not be good; it may not fit for other reasons at the time of your inquiry."

BROADHURST GALLERY

2212 Midland Rd., Pinehurst NC 28374. (910)295-4817. **E-mail:** judy@broadhurstgallery.com. **Website:** broadhurstgallery.com. Estab. 1990. Retail gallery. "Original art is displayed using 4500 sq. ft. of display area inside and outside sculpture in the garden." Represents/exhibits 25 established artists/year. Sponsors about 4 large shows and lunch and Artist Gallery Talks on most Fridays. Average display time: 1-3 months. Open all year; Monday, Tuesday, Thursday and Friday, 11-5; Saturday, 1-4; and by appointment. Art placement and interior design services available. Located on the main road between Pinehurst and Southern Pines; 3,000 sq. ft.; lots of space, ample light, large outdoor sculpture garden. 50% of space for special exhibitions; 50% of space for gallery artists. Clientele: people building homes and remodeling, also collectors. 80% private collectors, 20% corporate collectors. Overall price range: $5,000-40,000; most work sold at $5,000 and up.

MEDIA Considers oil, acrylic, watercolor, pastel, mixed media and collage. Most frequently exhibits oil and sculpture (stone and bronze).

STYLE Exhibits all styles, all genres.

TERMS Retail price set by the artist. Gallery provides insurance, promotion and contract; shipping costs are shared. Prefers artwork framed.

SUBMISSIONS Send query letter with résumé, slides or photographs, and bio. Write for appointment to show portfolio of originals and slides. Responds only if interested within 3 weeks. Files résumé, bio, slides or photographs. Finds artists through agents, exhibitions, word of mouth, various art publications and sourcebooks and artists' submissions.

TIPS "Talent is always the most important factor, but professionalism is very helpful."

BROOKFIELD CRAFT CENTER

286 Whisconier Rd., P.O. Box 122, Brookfield CT 06804-0122. (203)775-4526. **Fax:** (203)740-7815. **E-mail:** director@brookfieldcraft.org; info@brookfield

craft.org. **Website:** www.brookfieldcraft.org. **Contact:** Howard Lasser, executive director. Estab. 1954. Exhibits emerging, mid-career and established craft artists. Approached by 100 artists/year; represents 400+ craft artists.

MEDIA Considers functional and sculptural ceramics, fiber arts, jewelry and fine metals, forged metals, glass, mixed media and wood. Most frequently exhibits clay, metal, wood, fiber.

STYLE Original, handmade work by American artisans, one-of-a-kind items.

TERMS Work is accepted on consignment (50% commission); net 30 days. Retail price of the art set by the artist. Gallery provides insurance, promotion and contract.

SUBMISSIONS E-mail photographs or website links, or send query letter with brochure. Returns material with SASE. Responds to queries in 2 weeks to 1 month. Finds artists through art fairs/exhibits, portfolio reviews, referrals by other artists, submissions and word of mouth.

BROOKLYN BOTANIC GARDEN—STEINHARDT CONSERVATORY GALLERY

1000 Washington Ave., Brooklyn NY 11225. (718)623-7200. **E-mail:** steinhardt@bbg.org. **Website:** www.bbg.org/steinhardt_conservatory_gallery. Estab. 1988. Nonprofit botanic garden gallery. Represents emerging, mid-career and established artists. 20,000 members. Sponsors 10-12 shows/year. Average display time: 4-6 weeks. Open all year; Tuesday–Friday, 8-6, Saturday and Sunday, 10-6. Located near Prospect Park and Brooklyn Museum; 1,200 sq. ft.; part of a botanic garden, gallery adjacent to the tropical, desert and temperate houses. Clients include BBG members, tourists, collectors. 100% of sales are to private collectors. Overall price range: $75-7,500; most work sold at $75-500.

MEDIA Considers all media and all types of prints. Most frequently exhibits watercolor, oil and photography.

STYLE Exhibits all styles. Genres include landscapes, florals and wildlife.

TERMS Accepts work on consignment (20% commission). Retail price set by the artist. Gallery provides insurance, promotion and contract; artist pays shipping costs to and from gallery. Artwork must be framed or ready to display unless otherwise arranged. Artists hang and remove their own shows.

SUBMISSIONS Work must reflect the natural world. Send query letter with curriculum vitae, 8 to 10 visuals indicating title, date, materials used, and dimensions of the work (if sending JPEGs of the work, please use a resolution of 300 dpi or higher), and a description of the exhibit stating why BBG is an appropriate venue. Further guidelines available online.

TIPS "Artists' groups contact me by submitting résumé and slides of artists in their group. We favor seasonal art which echoes the natural events going on in the garden. Large format, colorful works show best in our multi-use space."

BRUNNER GALLERY

215 N. Columbia St., Covington LA 70433. (985)893-0444. **Fax:** (985)893-4332. **E-mail:** sbrunner@brunnergallery.com; curator@brunnergallery.com. **Website:** www.brunnergallery.com. **Contact:** Susan Brunner, owner/director. Estab. 1997. For-profit gallery. "Over the years, Brunner Gallery has grown to be one of the most popular and recognized contemporary art galleries in the South. Located in Historic Downtown Covington on New Orleans' Northshore, and rotates exhibitions in Downtown Baton Rouge at the Hilton Baton Rouge Capitol Center." Approached by 400 artists/year. Exhibits 45 emerging, mid-career and established artists. Sponsors 10-12 exhibits/year. Average display time: 1 month. Open by appointment. Located 45 minutes from metropolitan New Orleans, 1 hour from capital of Baton Rouge and Gulf Coast; 2,500 sq. ft. Building designed by Rick Brunner, artist and sculptor, and Susan Brunner, designer. Clients include local community, tourists, upscale and professionals. 20% of sales are to corporate collectors. Overall price range: $200-10,000; most work sold at $1,500-3,000.

MEDIA Considers all media. Types of prints include etchings and monoprints.

STYLE Considers all styles and genres. Most frequently exhibits abstraction, expressionism and conceptualism.

TERMS Artwork is accepted on consignment (50% commission) or bought outright for 90-100% of retail price (net 30 days). Retail price set by the gallery and the artist. Gallery provides insurance, promotion and contract. Accepted work should be framed. Requires exclusive representation locally.

SUBMISSIONS "We welcome submissions according to certain guidelines (found online). Please read them carefully. We are not able to critique your work because of time constraints; however, we are interested in seeing the newest work from Louisiana and across the US. We will send a response when your submission has been reviewed. Should we wish to consider your work for a second review, we will contact you by telephone or e-mail."

TIPS "In order for us to offer representation to an artist, it is necessary for us to consider whether the artist will be a good fit for the private and corporate collectors who make up our client base. We request that each image include not only the title, dimensions and medium, but also the retail price range."

BRYAN MEMORIAL GALLERY

180 Main St., P.O. Box 340, Jeffersonville VT 05464. (802)644-5100. **Fax:** (802)644-8342. **E-mail:** info@bryangallery.org. **Website:** www.bryangallery.org. Estab. 1984. Exhibits over 200 artists throughout the year in a schedule of revolving exhibitions. Artist membership fee required. "There is at least one juried exhibit and one open exhibit for members each year." Open Thursday–Sunday, 11-4 (spring and fall); daily, 11-5 (summer); by appointment at any time.

TERMS Membership is available online. Contact the gallery through e-mail after reviewing the website. Include artist's information, such as URL and small samples if possible.

CADEAUX DU MONDE

P.O. Box 212, Newport RI 02840. (401)935-8591. **E-mail:** info@cadeauxdumonde.com. **Website:** www.cadeaux-du-monde.myshopify.com. **Contact:** Katie Dyer, owner. **Owner:** Katie Dyer. Retail gallery. Estab. 1987. Represents emerging, mid-career and established artists. Exhibited artists include John Lyimo and A.K. Paulin. Clients include tourists, upscale, local community and students. 95% of sales are to private collectors, 5% corporate collectors. Overall price range: $20-5,000; most work sold at $100-300. Finds artists through submissions, word of mouth, referrals by other artists, visiting art fairs and exhibitions.

MEDIA Considers all media suitable for display in a stairway setting for special exhibitions. No prints.

STYLE Exhibits folk art. "Style is unimportant; quality of work is deciding factor. We look for unusual, offbeat and eclectic."

SUBMISSIONS Send query letter with résumé, 10 slides, bio, photographs and business card. Call for appointment to show portfolio of photographs or slides. Responds only if interested. Finds artists through submissions, word of mouth, referrals by other artists, visiting art fairs and exhibitions.

TIPS Artists who want gallery representation should "present themselves professionally; treat their art and the showing of it like a small business; arrive on time and be prepared; and meet deadlines promptly."

THE CAROLE CALO GALLERY

320 Washington St., Easton MA 02357. **Contact:** Candice Smith Corby, gallery director. Nonprofit, college gallery. Approached by 4-8 artists/year, represents/exhibits 10-20 artists/year. Closed during the summer when school is not in session. Clients include local community and students.

MEDIA Considers all media. Most frequently exhibits paintings, drawings and sculpture. Considers all types of prints.

STYLE Considers all styles and genres.

TERMS Proceeds of sales go to the artist, sales are not common. Price set by the artist. Gallery provides insurance and promotion. Accepted work should be framed and mounted.

SUBMISSIONS Mail portfolio for review. Include artist's statement, bio, résumé, SASE and CD. Returns material with SASE. Responds in 6 months. Files "interesting" materials. Finds artists through word of mouth, submissions, art exhibits and referrals by other artists.

WILLIAM CAMPBELL CONTEMPORARY ART

4935 Byers Ave., Ft. Worth TX 76107. (817)737-9566. **Fax:** (817)737-5466. **E-mail:** wcca@flash.net. **Website:** www.williamcampbellcontemporaryart.com. **Contact:** William Campbell, owner/director. Estab. 1974. Sponsors 8-10 exhibits/year. Average display time: 5 weeks. Sponsors openings; provides announcements, press releases, installation of work, insurance, cost of exhibition. Overall price range: $500-20,000.

TERMS Charges 50% commission. Reviews transparencies. Accepted work should be mounted. Requires exclusive representation within metropolitan area.

SUBMISSIONS Send CD (preferred) and résumé by mail with SASE. Responds in 1 month.

THE CANTON MUSEUM OF ART

1001 Market Ave. N., Canton OH 44702. (330)453-7666. **Fax:** (330)453-1034. **Website:** www.cantonart. org. Nonprofit gallery. Represents emerging, mid-career and established artists. Although primarily dedicated to large-format touring and original exhibitions, the CMA occasionally sponsors solo shows by local and original artists, and 1 group show every 2 years featuring its own "Artists League." Average display time: 6 weeks. Overall price range: $50-3,000; few sales above $300-500.

MEDIA Considers all media. Most frequently exhibits oil, watercolor and photography.

STYLE Considers all styles. Most frequently exhibits painterly abstraction, postmodernism and realism.

TERMS "While every effort is made to publicize and promote works, we cannot guarantee sales, although from time to time sales are made, at which time a 25% charge is applied." One of the most common mistakes in presenting portfolios is "sending too many materials. Send only a few slides or photos, a brief bio and a SASE."

TIPS "There seems to be a move back to realism, conservatism and support of regional artists."

CANTRELL GALLERY

8206 Cantrell Rd., Little Rock AR 72227. (501)224-1335. **E-mail:** cantrellgallery@sbcglobal.net. **Website:** www.cantrellgallery.com. **Contact:** Helen Scott or Cindy Scott-Huisman. Estab. 1970. Wholesale/retail gallery. "Cantrell Gallery is family owned and operated. In the beginning we were in a tiny storefront downtown, and our name was Art Fair. Today our business has grown to over 5,000 sq. ft. of showroom and production space. We get to know our clients and form a lasting relationship with them." Represents/exhibits 120 emerging, mid-career and established artists/year. Exhibited artists include Boulanger, Dali, G. Harvey, Warren Criswell, N. Scott and Robin Morris. Sponsors 8-12 shows/year. Average display time: 1 month. Open all year; Monday–Saturday, 10-5; or by appointment. Located in the strip center; "we have several rooms and different exhibits going at one time." Clientele: collectors, retail, decorators, museums. Overall price range: $100-10,000; most work sold at $250-3,000.

MEDIA Considers oil, acrylic, watercolor, pastel, pen & ink, drawing, mixed media, collage, paper, sculpture, woodcut, engraving, lithograph, wood engraving, mezzotint, serigraphs, linocut, etching. Most frequently exhibits etchings, watercolor, mixed media, oils and acrylics. Looking for outsider art.

STYLE Exhibits eclectic work, all genres.

TERMS Gallery provides insurance and promotion; shipping costs are shared. Prefers artwork unframed.

SUBMISSIONS Send query letter with résumé, 5 photos and bio. Write for appointment to show portfolio of originals. Responds in 2 months. Files all material. Finds artists through agents, by visiting exhibitions, word of mouth, art publications and sourcebooks, artists' submissions.

TIPS "Be professional. Be honest. Place a retail price on each piece, rather than only knowing what 'you need to get' for the piece. Don't spread yourself too thin in any particular area—only show in one gallery in any area."

CARNEGIE ARTS CENTER

204 W. Fourth St., Alliance NE 69301. (308)762-4571. **Fax:** (308)762-4571. **E-mail:** carnegieartscenter@bbc. net. **Website:** www.carnegieartscenter.com. **Contact:** Rose Pancost, gallery director. Estab. 1933. Visual art gallery. Represents 300 emerging, mid-career and established artists/year. 350 members. Exhibited artists include Liz Enyeart (functional pottery) and Silas Kern (handblown glass). Sponsors 12 shows/year. Average display time: 6 weeks. Open all year; Tuesday-Saturday, 10-4; Memorial Day, Labor Day, Sunday, 1-4. Located downtown; 2,346 sq. ft.; renovated Carnegie library built in 1911. Clients include tourists, upscale, local community and students. 90% of sales are to private collectors; 10% corporate collectors. Overall price range: $10-2,000; most work sold at $10-300.

MEDIA Considers all media and all types of prints. Most frequently exhibits pottery, blown glass, 2D, acrylics, bronze sculpture, watercolor, oil and silver jewelry.

STYLE Exhibits all styles and genres. Most frequently exhibits realism, modern realism, geometric, abstraction.

TERMS Accepts work on consignment (35% commission). Retail price set by the artist. Gallery provides promotion. Shipping costs negotiated. Prefers framed artwork.

SUBMISSIONS Accepts only quality work. Send query. Write for appointment to show portfolio of photographs, slides or transparencies. Responds within 1 month, only if interested. Files résumé and contracts. Finds artists through submissions, word of mouth, referrals by other artists, visiting art fairs and exhibitions.

TIPS "Presentations must be clean, 'new' quality— that is, ready to meet the public. Two-dimensional artwork must be nicely framed with wire attached for hanging. Unframed prints need protective wrapping in place."

CEDARHURST CENTER FOR THE ARTS

2600 Richview Rd., P.O. Box 923, Mt. Vernon IL 62864. (618)242-1236. **Fax:** (618)242-9530. **Website:** www.cedarhurst.org. **Contact:** Rusty Freeman, director of visual arts. Estab. 1973. Museum. Exhibits emerging, mid-career and established artists. Average display time: 6 weeks. Open all year; Tuesday–Saturday, 10-5; Sunday, 1-5; closed Mondays and federal holidays.

SUBMISSIONS Call or send query letter with artist's statement, bio, résumé, and digital images.

CENTER FOR DIVERSIFIED ART

P.O. Box 641062, Beverly Hills FL 34465. **E-mail:** diversifiedart101@gmail.com. **Website:** www.diversifiedart.org. **Contact:** Anita Walker, founder and director. Estab. 2010. Nonprofit gallery. Exhibits emerging, mid-career and established artists. Approached by 12 artists/year; represents or exhibits about 24 artists currently. Exhibited artists include David Kontra (acrylics) and Linda Litteral (sculptor). "We specialize in visual art that has a social and/or environmental theme that raises awareness. Sponsors 1 exhibit/year, photography is included in our annual exhibit. One piece from each of our artists is shown indefinitely in our online gallery and publications. We are a web-based gallery and sponsor 1 brick-and-mortar exhibition a year. We also use visual art to go with educational material that we produce and publish. Many of our artists have a strong commitment to raising awareness. Clients include the local community and students." Price range: $150-4,000.

MEDIA Considers all media and all types of prints (prints must be a limited edition and include a certificate of authenticity).

STYLE Considers all styles that have a social and/or environmental theme that raises awareness.

TERMS Artwork is accepted on consignment and there is a 20% commission. Retail price set by the artist. Gallery provides promotion. Accepted work should be framed.

SUBMISSIONS Please make sure your work has a social and/or environmental theme that raises awareness before submitting. E-mail query letter with link to artist's website, 3 JPEG samples at 72 dpi, résumé and how your work relates to raising awareness on social and/or environmental issues. Responds only if interested within 1 month. Finds artists through word of mouth, art exhibits, submissions, portfolio reviews and referrals by other artists.

TIPS Follow the directions above.

CENTRAL MICHIGAN UNIVERSITY ART GALLERY

Wightman 132, Central Michigan University, Mt. Pleasant MI 48859. (989)774-3800. **E-mail:** gochelas@cmich.edu. **Website:** www.uag.cmich.edu. **Contact:** Anne Gochenour, gallery director. Estab. 1970. Nonprofit academic gallery. Exhibits emerging, mid-career and established contemporary artists. Past artists include Sandy Skoglund, Michael Ferris, Blake Williams, John Richardson, Valerie Allen, Randal Crawford, Jane Gilmor, Denise Whitebread Fanning, Alynn Guerra, Dylan Miner. Sponsors 14 exhibits/year (2-4 curated). Average display time: 1 month. Open August-May while exhibits are present; Tuesday–Friday, 11-6; Saturday, 11-3. Clients include local community, students and tourists.

MEDIA Considers all media and all types of prints. Most frequently exhibits sculpture, prints, ceramics, painting and photography.

STYLE Considers all styles.

TERMS Buyers are referred to the artist. Gallery provides insurance, promotion and contract. Accepted work should be framed. Does not require exclusive representation locally.

SUBMISSIONS Send query letter with artist's statement, bio, résumé, reviews, and images on CD. Responds within 2 months, only if interested. Finds artists through word of mouth, submissions, portfolio reviews, art exhibits, and referrals by other artists.

CHABOT FINE ART GALLERY

P.O. Box 623, Greenville RI 02828. (401)432-7783. **Fax:** (401)432-7783. **E-mail:** chris@chabotgallery.com. **Website:** www.chabotgallery.com. **Contact:** Chris Chabot, director. Estab. 2007. Rental gallery. Approached by 50 artists/year; represents 30 emerging, mid-career and established artists. Exhibited artists include Lee Chabot (owner of the gallery). Sponsors 12 total exhibits/year; 1 photography exhibit/year. Average display time: 30 days. Open Tuesday-Saturday, 12-6, or by appointment or chance. The gallery is located on Historic Federal Hill in Providence. It has over 1,000 sq. ft of exhibition space and a sculpture courtyard garden that is open in the warmer months.

Clients include local community, tourists, upscale. 10% corporate collectors. Overall price range: $1,200-10,000. Most work sold at $3,500.

MEDIA Considers all media except craft. Most frequently exhibits oil, acrylics and watercolor.

STYLE Considers all styles and genres. Most frequently exhibits abstract, impressionism, abstract expressionism.

TERMS Artwork is accepted on consignment with a 50% commission. Retail price is set by the gallery and artist. Gallery provides insurance, promotion, and contract. Accepted work should be framed, mounted, and matted.

SUBMISSIONS Mail portfolio for review. Send query letter with artist's statement, bio, résumé, CD with images, and SASE. Returns material with SASE. Responds in 1 month. Files all submitted material. Finds artist through word of mouth, submissions, portfolio reviews, art exhibits, and referrals by other artists.

TIPS Be professional in your presentation, have good images in your portfolio, and submit all necessary information.

THE CHAIT GALLERIES DOWNTOWN

218 E. Washington St., Iowa City IA 52240. (319)338-4442. **Fax:** (319)338-3380. **E-mail:** attendant@thegalleriesdowntown.com; terri@thegalleriesdowntown.com; bpchait@aol.com. **Website:** www.chaitgalleries.com. **Contact:** Benjamin Chait, director. Estab. 2003. For-profit gallery. Approached by 100 artists/year. Represents 150 emerging, mid-career and established artists. Exhibited artists include Benjamin Chait (giclée), Corrine Smith (mixed media), Mary Merkel-Hess (fiber sculpture), Tam Bodkin Bryk (oil on canvas), Young Joo Yoo (gold and sterling silver jewelry), Nancy Lindsay (landscape paintings) and Ulfert Wilke (ink on paper). Sponsors 12 exhibits/year. Average display time: 90 days. Open all year; Monday–Friday, 11-6; Saturday, 10-5; Sunday, 12-4. Located in a downtown building restored to its original look (circa 1883), with 14-ft. molded ceiling and original 9-ft. front door. Professional museum lighting and scamozzi-capped columns complete the elegant gallery. Clients include local community, students, tourists, upscale. Overall price range: $50-10,000; most work sold at $250-1,000.

MEDIA Considers all media, all types of prints, all styles and all genres.

STYLE Considers all styles.

TERMS Call; mail portfolio for review. Returns material with SASE. Responds to queries in 2 weeks. Or, stop in anytime during normal business hours with a couple samples. Finds artists through art fairs, exhibits, portfolio reviews and referrals by other artists.
SUBMISSIONS Artwork is accepted on consignment, and there is a 50% commission. Retail price set by the gallery and the artist. Gallery provides insurance, promotion and contract. Accepted work should be framed. Requires exclusive representation locally.

CHAPMAN FRIEDMAN GALLERY

1835 Hampden Court, Louisville KY 40205. (502)584-7954. **E-mail:** friedman@imagesol.com. **Website:** www.imagesol.com. **Contact:** Julius Friedman, owner. Estab. 1992. For-profit gallery. Approached by 100 or more artists/year. Represents or exhibits 25 artists. Sponsors 7 exhibits/year. Average display time: 1 month. Open by appointment only. Located downtown; approximately 3,500 sq. ft. with 15-ft. ceilings and white walls. Clients include local community and tourists. 5% of sales are to corporate collectors. Overall price range: $75-10,000; most work sold at more than $1,000.
MEDIA Considers all media except craft. Types of prints include engravings, etchings, lithographs, posters, serigraphs and woodcuts. Most frequently exhibits painting, ceramics and photography. Exhibits color field, geometric abstraction, primitivism realism, painterly abstraction. Most frequently exhibits abstract, primitive and color field. Artwork is accepted on consignment (50% commission). Retail price set by the artist. Gallery provides insurance, promotion and contract. Accepted work should be framed.
TERMS Send query letter with artist's statement, bio, brochure, photographs, résumé, slides and SASE. Returns material with SASE. Responds to queries in 1 month. Finds artists through portfolio reviews and referrals by other artists.

CINCINNATI ART MUSEUM

953 Eden Park Dr., Cincinnati OH 45202. (513)639-2941. **E-mail:** information@cincyart.org. **Website:** www.cincinnatiartmuseum.org. Estab. 1881. Exhibits 6-10 emerging, mid-career and established artists/year. Sponsors 20 exhibits/year. Average display time: 3 months. Open Tuesday–Sunday, 11-5. Closed Mondays, Thanksgiving, Christmas, New Year's Day, Martin Luther King, Jr. Day, Presidents Day, Memorial Day, Fourth of July and Labor Day. General art museum with a collection spanning 6,000 years of world art. Over 100,000 objects in the collection with exhibitions on view annually. Clients include local community, students, tourists and upscale.
MEDIA Considers all media and all types of prints. Most frequently exhibits paper, mixed media and oil.
STYLE Considers all styles and genres.
SUBMISSIONS Send query letter with artist's statement, photographs, reviews, SASE and slides.

ⓦ CITYARTS, INC.

525 Broadway, Suite 602, New York NY 10012. (212)966-0377. **Fax:** (212)966-0551. **E-mail:** info@cityarts.org. **Website:** www.cityarts.org. Estab. 1968. CITYarts brings young people and professional artists together to create public art. Through this creative process, CITYarts empowers youth and connects children locally and around the world to become active participants in transforming communities. Funded by foundations, corporations, government and friends, CITYarts is a nonprofit public art organization involved in arts education and community development. Open all year; Monday–Friday, 9:30-5:30. Office located in Soho; however, "the city is our gallery." We have 300 murals located throughout all 5 of New York City's boroughs. As well as our Young Minds Build Bridges Program, which works to connect youth globally to engage in the conversation for peace. Through this program we have brought CITYarts projects to 65 countries and created 5 global mosaic Peace Walls. We represent emerging, mid-career and established artists and typically produce 4-8 projects/year.
MEDIA Our murals are a permanent testament to our youth and their positive contribution to their communities.
SUBMISSIONS If you are interested in becoming involved with CITYarts, sign up to volunteer on our website, or send an email inquiry.

CLAMPART

531 W. 25th St., Ground Floor, New York NY 10001. (646)230-0020. **E-mail:** info@clampart.com; portfolioreview@clampart.com. **Website:** www.clampart.com. **Contact:** Brian Paul Clamp, director. Estab. 2000. Sponsors 8-12 exhibits/year. Average display time: 5 weeks. Open Tuesday–Saturday, 11-6; closed the last 2 weeks of August. Located on the ground floor on Main Street in Chelsea. Medium-sized exhibition space.

MEDIA Considers acrylic, collage, drawing, mixed media, oil, paper, pastel, pen & ink and watercolor. Considers all types of prints. Most frequently exhibits photo, oil and paper.

STYLE Exhibits conceptualism, geometric abstraction, minimalism and postmodernism. Considers genres including figurative work, florals, landscapes and portraits. Most frequently exhibits postmodernism, conceptualism and minimalism.

TERMS E-mail query letter with artist's statement, bio and JPEGs. Cannot return material. Responds to queries in 2 weeks. Clients include local community, tourists and upscale. 5% of sales are to corporate collectors. Overall price range: $300-50,000; most work sold at $2,000. Artwork is accepted on consignment (50% commission). Retail price set by the gallery. Gallery provides insurance, promotion and contract. Does not require exclusive representation locally.

SUBMISSIONS "Include a bio and well-written artist statement. Do not submit work to a gallery that does not handle the general kind of work you produce." Accepted work should be framed, mounted and matted. Finds artists through portfolio reviews, referrals by other artists and submissions.

CATHARINE CLARK GALLERY

248 Utah St., San Francisco CA 94103. (415)399-1439. **Fax:** (415)543-1338. **E-mail:** info@cclarkgallery.com. **Website:** www.cclarkgallery.com. **Contact:** Catherine Clark, owner/director. Estab. 1991. Retail gallery. Represents 25+ emerging and mid-career artists. Curates 8-12 shows/year. Average display time: 4-6 weeks. Open all year. Located downtown San Francisco; 3,000 sq. ft., including video project room. 90% of space for special exhibitions. Clientele: 95% private collectors, 5% corporate collectors. Overall price range: $200-$300,000; most work sold at $2,000-$5,000.

MEDIA Considers painting, sculpture, installation, photography, printmaking, video and new genres. Most frequently exhibits painting, sculpture, installation and new genres.

STYLE Exhibits all styles and genres.

TERMS Accepts work on consignment (50% commission). Retail price set by gallery and artist. Offers customer payment by installments. Gallery provides insurance, promotion and contract; shipping costs are shared. Prefers artwork framed.

SUBMISSIONS Submission review is limited. Send query e-mail before sending submissions. Submissions will not be returned without SASE.

CLAY CENTER'S AVAMPATO DISCOVERY MUSEUM

1 Clay Square, Charleston WV 25301. (304)561-3570. **E-mail:** lferguson@theclaycenter.org; info@theclaycenter.org. **Website:** www.theclaycenter.org. **Contact:** R. Lewis Ferguson. Estab. 1974. Museum gallery. Represents emerging, mid-career and established artists. Sponsors 6 shows/year. Average display time: 2-3 months. Open all year; Wednesday-Saturday, 10-5; Sunday, 12-5. Located inside the Clay Center for the Arts & Sciences.

MEDIA Considers oil, acrylic, watercolor, pastel, pen & ink, drawings, mixed media, collage, works on paper, sculpture, installations, photography and prints.

STYLE Considers all styles and genres.

TERMS Retail price set by artist. Gallery pays shipping costs. Prefers framed artwork.

SUBMISSIONS Send query letter with bio, résumé, brochure, slides, photographs, reviews and SASE. Write for appointment to show portfolio of slides. Responds within 2 weeks, only if interested. Files everything or returns in SASE.

THE CLAY PLACE

One Walnut St., Carnegie PA 15106. (412)489-5240. **E-mail:** info@clayplacestandard.com. **Website:** www.clayplaceatstandard.com. Estab. 1973. Retail gallery. Represents 50 emerging, mid-career and established artists. Exhibited artists include Jack Troy and Kirk Mangus. Sponsors 7 shows/year. Open Monday–Friday, 9-4:30. Located in small shopping area; 1,200 sq. ft. 50% of space for special exhibitions. Overall price range: $10-2,000; most work sold at $40-100.

MEDIA Considers ceramic, sculpture, glass and pottery. Most frequently exhibits clay, glass and enamel.

TERMS Accepts artwork on consignment (50% commission) or buys outright for 50% of retail price (net 30 days). Retail price set by artist. Sometimes offers customer discounts and payment by installments. Gallery provides insurance, promotion and shipping costs from gallery. We also sell books, tools, equipment and supplies.

SUBMISSIONS Prefers only clay, some glass and enamel. Send query letter with résumé, slides, photographs, bio and SASE. Write for appointment to show portfolio. Portfolio should include actual work rather than slides. Responds in 1 month. Does not reply when busy. Files résumé. Does not return slides. Finds artists through visiting exhibitions and art collectors' referrals.

TIPS "Functional pottery sells well. Emphasis on form, surface decoration. Some clay artists have lowered quality in order to lower prices. Clientele look for quality, not price."

CLEVELAND STATE UNIVERSITY ART GALLERY

1307 Euclid Ave., Cleveland OH 44115-2214. (216)687-2103. **Fax:** (216)687-9394. **E-mail:** t.knapp@csuohio. edu. **Website:** www.csuohio.edu/artgallery/. **Contact:** Tim Knapp, assistant director. Exhibits 50 emerging, mid-career and established artists. Exhibited artists include Joel Peter Witkin and Buzz Spector. Sponsors 6 shows/year. Average display time: 6 weeks. Open Wednesday and Thursday, 10-5; Friday, 10-8; Saturday, 12-8. Open Monday and Tuesday by appointment only. Call for summer hours. Located downtown 4,500 sq. ft. (250 running ft. of wall space). 100% of space for special exhibitions. Clientele: students, faculty, general public. 85% private collectors, 15% corporate collectors. Overall price range: $250-50,000; most work sold at $300-1,000.

MEDIA Considers all media.

STYLE Exhibits all styles and genres. Prefers contemporary. Looks for challenging work.

TERMS 25% commission. Sales are not a priority. Gallery provides insurance, promotion, shipping costs to and from gallery; artists handle crating. Prefers artwork framed.

SUBMISSIONS By invitation. Unsolicited inquiries may not be reviewed.

TIPS "Submissions recommended by galleries or institutions are preferred."

◎ COAST GALLERIES

P.O. Box 223519, Carmel CA 93922. (831)625-8688. **E-mail:** gary@coastgalleries.com. **Website:** www. coastgalleries.com. **Contact:** Gary Koeppel, president/CEO. Estab. 1958. Retail galleries. Represents 300 emerging, mid-career and established artists and craftsmen. Sponsors 3-4 shows/year. Open daily, all year. Locations in Big Sur and Hana HI (Maui). Each gallery was designed specifically for its location and clientele. The Hana Coast Gallery features Hawaiiana; the Big Sur Coast Gallery features American Master Crafts and contemporary fine arts. The Big Sur Gallery is constructed from recycled municipal redwood water tanks and is one of the largest galleries of American crafts in the US. Big Sur has 7,500 sq. ft. of retail space and Hana has 2,500 sq. ft. Clientele: 90% private collectors, 10% corporate collectors. Overall price range: $25-60,000; most work sold at $400-4,000. See websites for hours and details on each gallery: www. coastgalleries.com and www.hanacoastgallery.com.

MEDIA Considers all media; paintings, prints, posters, sculpture, art glass.

STYLE Exhibits impressionism and realism. Genres include landscape, marine, abstract and wildlife.

TERMS Accepts fine art and master crafts on consignment and buys some master crafts outright (net 30 days). Retail price set by gallery. Gallery provides insurance, promotion and contract; artist pays for shipping. Requires framed artwork.

SUBMISSIONS Accepts only artists from Hawaii for Hana gallery; coastal and wildlife imagery and American crafts for Big Sur gallery. Send query letter with bio, brochure, images, and contact info; SASE mandatory if materials are to be returned. Write or e-mail info@coastgalleries.com for appointment. Owner responds to all inquiries.

COLEMAN FINE ART

79 Church St., Charleston SC 29401. (843)853-7000. **E-mail:** info@colemanfineart.com. **Website:** www.colemanfineart.com. Estab. 1974. Retail gallery; gilding, frame making and restoration. Exclusive representatives for watercolor artist Mary Whyte, b. 1953. Open all year; Tuesday–Saturday, 10-6; Sunday and Monday, by chance. "Both a fine art gallery and restoration studio, Coleman Fine Art has been representing regional and national artists for over 30 years. Located on the corner of Church and Tradd streets, the gallery reinvigorates one of the country's oldest art studios." Clientele: tourists, upscale and locals. 95-98% private collectors, 2-5% corporate collectors. Overall price range: $3,000-80,000.

MEDIA Considers oil, watercolor, pastel, pen & ink, drawing, sculpture. Most frequently exhibits watercolor, oil and sculpture.

STYLE Exhibits impressionism and realism. Genres include portraits, landscapes, still lifes and figurative work.

TERMS Accepts work on consignment (45% commission); net 30 days. Retail price set by the gallery and the artist. Gallery provides promotion and contract. Shipping costs are shared. Prefers artwork framed. **SUBMISSIONS** Send query letter with digital CD of most recent work, reviews and biography. E-mail for appointment to show portfolio. Finds artists through submissions.

COMPLEMENTS ART GALLERY

2131 Providence Pike, North Smithfield RI 02896. (401)766-6800. **Fax:** (401)766-6868. **E-mail:** teri@complementsartgallery.com. **Website:** www.complementsartgallery.com. Estab. 1986. Retail gallery. Represents hundreds of international and New England emerging, mid-career and established artists. Exhibited artists include Fairchild and Hatfield. Sponsors 6 shows/year. Average display time: 2-3 weeks. Open all year; Monday–Friday, 9-5; Saturday, 9-4. 3,500 sq. ft. "We have a piano and beautiful hardwood floors, also a great fireplace." 20% of space for special exhibitions; 60% of space for gallery artists. Clientele: upscale. 40% private collectors, 15% corporate collectors. Overall price range: $25-$10,000; most work sold at $600-2,000.
MEDIA Considers all media except offset prints. Types of prints include engravings, lithographs, wood engravings, mezzotints, serigraphs and etchings. Most frequently exhibits serigraphs, oils.
STYLE Exhibits expressionism, painterly abstraction, impressionism, photorealism, realism and imagism. Genres include florals, portraits and landscapes. Prefers realism, impressionism and abstract.
TERMS Accepts work on consignment (30% commission) or bought outright for 50% of retail price (90 days). Retail price set by the gallery. Gallery provides insurance, promotion and contract. Shipping costs are shared. Prefers artwork unframed.
SUBMISSIONS Size limitation due to wall space. Paintings no larger than 40×60, sculpture not heavier than 150 pounds. Send query letter with résumé, bio, 6 slides or photographs. Call for appointment to show portfolio of photographs and slides. Responds in 1 month. Files all materials from artists. Finds artists through word of mouth, referrals by other artists, visiting art fairs and all exhibitions and artist's submissions.
TIPS "Artists need to have an idea of the price range of their work and provide interesting information about themselves."

CONE EDITIONS

17 Powder Spring Rd., East Topsham VT 05076. (802)439-5751. **Fax:** (802)439-6501. **E-mail:** cathy@cone-editions.com. **Website:** www.cone-editions.com. **Contact:** Cathy Cone. Printmakers, publishers and distributors of computer and digitally made works of art. Estab. 1980. Represents/exhibits 12 emerging, mid-career and established artists/year. Exhibited artists include Norman Bluhm and Wolf Kahn. Sponsors 4 shows/year. Average display time: 3 months. Open all year; Monday-Friday, 9-5. Located downtown; 1,000 sq. ft.; post and beam, high ceilings, natural light. 50% of space for special exhibitions; 50% of space for gallery artists. Clientele: private, corporate. 40% private collectors, 60% corporate collectors. Overall price range: $300-5,000; most work sold at $500-1,500.
MEDIA Considers computer and digital art and computer prints. Most frequently exhibits iris ink jet print, digitial monoprint and digital gravure.
STYLE Exhibits expressionism, minimalism, color field, painterly abstraction and imagism.
TERMS Artwork is accepted on consignment (50% commission). Retail price set by the artist. Gallery provides promotion; shipping costs are shared. Prefers artwork unframed.
SUBMISSIONS Prefers computer and digital art. Contact through e-mail. Call for appointment to show portfolio on CD. Responds in 1-3 weeks. Files slides and CD.
TIPS "We find most of the artists we represent by referrals of our other artists."

CONTEMPORARY ART MUSEUM ST. LOUIS

3750 Washington Blvd., St. Louis MO 63108. (314)535-4660. **Fax:** (314)535-1226. **E-mail:** info@camstl.org. **Website:** www.camstl.org. Estab. 1980. Nonprofit museum. "A noncollecting museum dedicated to exhibiting contemporary art from international, national and local established and emerging artists." Open Wednesday, 10-5; Thursday-Friday, 10-8; and Saturday-Sunday, 10-5. Located mid-town, Grand Center; 27,200 sq. ft. building designed by Brad Cloepfil, Allied Works.

CONTEMPORARY ARTS CENTER (LAS VEGAS)

CAC @ Emergency Arts, 6th and Fremont, Suite 154, P.O. Box 582, Las Vegas NV 89125. (702)496-0569. **E-mail:** info@lasvegascac.org. **Website:** www.lasve

gascac.org. Estab. 1989. Nonprofit gallery. Sponsors more than 9 exhibits/year. Average display time: 1 month. Gallery open Thursday-Friday, 3-7; Saturday-Sunday, 2-7, and by appointment. Closed Thanksgiving, Christmas, New Year's Day. 1,200 sq. ft. Clients include tourists, local community and students. 75% of sales are to private collectors, 25% corporate collectors. Overall price range: $200-4,000. Most work sold at $400. Artwork is accepted through annual call for proposals of self-curated group shows. Gallery provides insurance, promotion, contract.

MEDIA Considers all media and all types of prints. Exhibits conceptualism, group shows of contemporary fine art. Genres include all contemporary art/all media.

CONTEMPORARY ARTS CENTER (NEW ORLEANS)

900 Camp St., New Orleans LA 70130. (504)528-3805. **Fax:** (504)528-3828. **E-mail:** jfrancino@cacno.org; info@cacno.org. **Website:** www.cacno.org. **Contact:** Jennifer Francino, visual arts manager. Estab. 1976. Alternative space, nonprofit gallery. Exhibits emerging, mid-career and established artists. Open all year; Wednesday-Monday, 11-5. Closed holidays. Located in Arts District of New Orleans; renovated/converted warehouse. Clients include local community, students, tourists and upscale.

MEDIA Considers all media and all types of prints. Most frequently exhibits painting, sculpture, installation and photography.

STYLE Considers all styles. Exhibits anything contemporary.

TERMS Artwork is accepted on loan for curated exhibitions. Retail price set by the artist. CAC provides insurance and promotion. Accepted work should be framed. Does not require exclusive representation locally. CAC is not a sales venue, but will refer inquiries. CAC receives 20% on items sold as a result of an exhibition.

SUBMISSIONS Send query letter with bio, SASE and slides or CDs. Responds in 4 months. Files letter and bio—slides when appropriate. Finds artists through word of mouth, submissions, art exhibits, art fairs, referrals by other artists, professional contacts and periodicals.

TIPS "Use only one slide sheet with proper labels (title, date, medium and dimensions)."

CONTRACT ART INTERNATIONAL, INC.

P.O. Box 629, Old Lyme CT 06371. (860)434-9799. **Fax:** (860)434-6240. **E-mail:** info@contractartinternational.com. **Website:** www.contractartinternational.com. In business approximately 40 years. "We contract artwork for hospitality, blue-chip, and specialized businesses." Collaborates with emerging, mid-career and established artists. Assigns site-specific commissions to artists based on project design needs, theme and client preferences. Studio is open all year to corporate art directors, architects, designers, and faculty directors. 1,600 sq. ft. studio. Clientele: 98% commercial. Overall price range: $500-500,000.

MEDIA Places all types of art mediums.

TERMS Pays for design by the project, negotiable; 50% up front. Rights purchased vary according to project.

SUBMISSIONS Send letter of introduction with résumé, slides, bio, brochure, photographs, DVD/video and SASE. If local, write for appointment to present portfolio; otherwise, mail appropriate materials, which should include slides and photographs. "Show us a good range of your talent. Also, we recommend you keep us updated if you've changed styles or media." Responds in 1 week. Files all samples and information in registry library.

TIPS "We exist mainly to art direct commissioned artwork for specific projects."

COOS ART MUSEUM

235 Anderson Ave., Coos Bay OR 97420. (541)267-3901. **E-mail:** info@coosart.org. **Website:** www.coosart.org; www.facebook.com/coosartmuseum. Estab. 1950. Not-for-profit corporation; 3rd-oldest art museum in Oregon. Mounts 4 juried group exhibitions/year of 85-150 artists; 20 curated single/solo exhibits/year of established artists; and 6 exhibits/year from the permanent collection. 5 galleries allow for multiple exhibits mounted simultaneously, averaging 6 openings/year. Average display time: 6-9 weeks. Open Tuesday–Friday, 10-4; Saturday, 1-4. Closed Sunday, Monday and all major holidays. Free admission during evening of the 1st Friday of the month (Wine Walk), 5-8. Clients include local community, students, tourists and upscale.

MEDIA For curated exhibition, considers all media including print, engraving, litho, serigraph. Posters and giclées not considered. Most frequently exhibits paintings (oil, acrylic, watercolor, pastel), sculpture (glass, metal, ceramic), drawings, etchings and prints.

STYLE Considers all styles and genres. Most frequently exhibits primitivism, realism, postmodernism and expressionism.

TERMS Gallery floor sales are accepted. Retail price set by the artist. Museum provides insurance, promotion and contract. Accepted work should be framed, mounted and matted. Accepts only artists from Oregon or Western United States.

SUBMISSIONS Send query letter with artist's statement, bio, résumé, SASE, digital files on CD or links to website. Responds to queries in 6 months. Never send originals of slides, résumés or portfolios. Exhibition committee reviews 2 times/year—schedule exhibits 2 years in advance. Files proposals. Finds artists through portfolio reviews and submissions.

TIPS "Have complete files electronically on a website or CD. Have a written positioning statement and proposal of show as well as letter(s) of recommendation from a producer/curator/gallery of a previous curated exhibit. Do not expect us to produce or create the exhibition. You should have all costs figured ahead of time and submit only when you have work completed and ready. We do not develop artists. You must be professional."

CORE NEW ART SPACE

900 Sante Fe Dr., Denver CO 80204. (303)297-8428. **E-mail:** corenewartspace@gmail.com. **Website:** www.corenewartspace.com. Estab. 1981. Cooperative, alternative and nonprofit gallery. Exhibits 24 emerging and mid-career artists. Sponsors 10 solo and 6 group shows/year. Average display time: 3 weeks. Open Thursday, 12-6; Friday, 12-9; Saturday, 12-6; Sunday, 1-4. Located Santa Fe Arts district. Accepts mostly artists from front range Colorado. Clientele: 97% private collectors; 3% corporate clients. Overall price range: $75-3,000; most work sold at $100-600.

MEDIA Considers all media. Specializes in cutting edge work. Prefers quality rather than marketability.

STYLE Exhibits expressionism, neo-expressionism, painterly abstraction, conceptualism; considers all styles and genres, but especially contemporary and alternative (nontraditional media and approach), including installations.

TERMS Co-op membership fee plus donation of time. Retail price set by artist. Exclusive area representation not required. Also rents annex space to nonmembers for $125-275/3 week run.

SUBMISSIONS Send query letter with SASE. Quarterly auditions to show portfolio of originals, slides and photographs. Request membership application. "Our gallery gives an opportunity for emerging artists in the metro-Denver area to show their work. We run 6 open juried shows a year. There is an entry fee charged, and a 25% commission is taken on any work sold. The member artists exhibit in a 2-person show once a year. Member artists generally work in more avant-garde formats, and the gallery encourages experimentation. Members are chosen by slide review and personal interviews. Due to time commitments we require that they live and work in the area." Finds artists through invitations, word of mouth, art publications.

TIPS "We want to see challenging art. If your intention is to manufacture coffee-table and over-the-couch art for suburbia, we are not a good place to start."

CORNERHOUSE GALLERY AND FRAME

3318 First Ave. NE, Suite A, Cedar Rapids IA 52402. (319)365-4348. **E-mail:** info@cornerhousegallery.com. **Website:** www.cornerhousegallery.com. Estab. 1976. For-profit gallery. "Innovation and creativity by experienced professionals. Features primarily local and Midwestern artists, as well as a few national and international artists." Exhibits emerging, mid-career and established artists. Approached by 75 artists/year. Sponsors 4 or more exhibits/year. Open Monday–Friday, 10-5:30; Saturday, 10-4. Located on main street through Cedar Rapids in the Kenwood Plaza. Clients include local community, students, tourists, upscale, and corporate. Overall price range: $200-20,000; most work sold at $1,000.

MEDIA Considers all media. Most frequently exhibits glass, oil and sculpture. Considers all prints except posters.

STYLE Considers all styles. Genres include figurative work, florals and landscapes.

TERMS Artwork is accepted on consignment and there is a 50% commission. Retail price is set by the artist.

SUBMISSIONS Call, e-mail or write to arrange personal interview to show portfolio of photographs, slides, transparencies or CDs, résumés and reviews with SASE. Returns material with SASE.

TIPS "Good photos of work, websites with enough work to get a feel for the overall depth and quality."

COURTHOUSE GALLERY, LAKE GEORGE ARTS PROJECT

1 Amherst St., Lake George NY 12845. (518)668-2616. **E-mail:** mail@lakegeorgearts.org. **Website:** www.lakegeorgearts.org. **Contact:** Laura Von Rosk, gallery director. Estab. 1986. Nonprofit gallery. Approached by 200 artists/year. Exhibits 10-15 emerging, mid-career and established artists. Sponsors 6 exhibits/year. Average display time: 5-6 weeks. Open all year; Tuesday-Friday, 12-5; Saturday, 12-4. Closed mid-December to mid-January. Clients include local community, tourists and upscale. Overall price range: $100-5,000; most work sold at $500.

MEDIA Considers all media and all types of prints. Most frequently exhibits painting, mixed media and sculpture.

STYLE Considers all styles and genres.

TERMS Artwork is accepted on consignment and there is a 25% commission. Retail price set by the artist. Gallery provides insurance, promotion and contract. Accepted work should be framed, mounted and matted.

SUBMISSIONS Mail portfolio for review. Deadline: January 31. Send query letter with artist's statement, bio, résumé, SASE and slides. Returns material with SASE. Finds artists through word of mouth, submissions, portfolio reviews, art exhibits, art fairs and referrals by other artists.

JAMES COX GALLERY AT WOODSTOCK

4666 Rt. 212, Willow NY 12495. (845)679-7608. **Fax:** (845)679-7627. **E-mail:** info@jamescoxgallery.com. **Website:** www.jamescoxgallery.com. Estab. 1990. Retail gallery. Represents 10 mid-career and established artists. Exhibited artists include Leslie Bender, Bruce North, Paola Bari and Mary Anna Goetz. Represents estates of 5 artists including James Chapin, Margery Ryerson, Joseph Garlock and Elaine Wesley. Sponsors 5 shows/year. Average display time: 1 month. Open all year; Tuesday–Sunday, 10-5, winter hours: Tuesday–Friday, 10-5, or by appointment. Elegantly restored Dutch barn. 50% of space for special exhibitions. Clients include New York City residents (within 50-mile radius) and tourists. 65% of sales are to private collectors. Overall price range: $500-50,000; most work sold at $1,000-10,000.

MEDIA Considers oil, watercolor, pastel, drawing, ceramics and sculpture. Considers "historic Woodstock, art." Most frequently exhibits oil paintings, watercolors, sculpture.

STYLE Exhibits impressionism, realism. Genres include landscapes and figurative work. Prefers expressive or evocative realism, painterly landscapes and stylized figurative work.

TERMS Accepts work on consignment (50% commission). Retail price set by the artist. Gallery provides promotion; artist pays shipping costs to and from gallery. Prefers artwork framed.

SUBMISSIONS Prefer submissions by e-mail. Prefers only artists from New York region. Send query letter with résumé, bio, brochure, photographs, CD, SASE and business card. Responds in 3 months. Files material on some artists for special, theme or group shows.

TIPS "Be sure to enclose SASE and be patient for response. Also, please include information on present pricing structure."

MILDRED COX GALLERY AT WILLIAM WOODS UNIVERSITY

One University Ave., Fulton MO 65251. (573)592-4244; (800)995-3159 ext. 4244. **E-mail:** nicole.petrescu@williamwoods.edu. **Website:** www.williamwoods.edu. **Contact:** Nicole Petrescu, gallery coordinator. Estab. 1970. Nonprofit gallery. Approached by 20 artist/year; exhibits 8 emerging, mid-career and established artists/year. Exhibited artists include Elizabeth Ginsberg and Frank Stack. Average display time: 1 month. Open Monday–Friday, 9-6; Saturday–Sunday, 1-4, while class is in session. Located in the Gladys Woods Kemper Center for the Arts; within large movable walls; 300 running feet. Clients include local community, students, upscale and foreign visitors. Overall price range: $800-10,000; most work sold at $800-1,000. Gallery takes no commission. "Our mission is education."

MEDIA Considers all media. Most frequently exhibits drawing, painting and sculpture. Considers all prints except commercial off-set.

STYLE Exhibits expressionism, geometric abstraction, impressionism, surrealism, painterly abstraction and realism. Most frequently exhibits figurative and academic. Genres include Americana, figurative work, florals, landscapes and portraits.

TERMS Artists work directly with person interested in purchase. Retail price of the art set by the artist. Gallery provides insurance and contract. Accepted work should be framed and matted. Does not require exclusive representation locally. Artists are selected by a committee from JPEG files or original presentation to faculty committee.

SUBMISSIONS Write to arrange a personal interview to show portfolio or send query letter with artist's statement, résumé and JPEGs to gallery director via e-mail. Does not reply to queries. Artist should call or e-mail. Files slides, statement and résumé until exhibit concludes. Finds artists through word of mouth.

COYOTE WOMAN GALLERY

160 E. Main St., Harbor Springs MI 49740. **E-mail:** office@coyotewomangallery.com; submissions@coyotewomangallery.com. **Website:** www.coyotewoman gallery.com. Estab. 1992. For-profit gallery. Exhibits emerging and established artists. Represents or exhibits 50+ artists such as Daniel Roache (sculpture). Clients include local community, tourists, and upscale clientele. Overall price range: $25-4,000.

MEDIA Considers acrylic, ceramics, drawing, fiber, glass, mixed media, oil, pastel, sculpture and watercolor, among others. Displays etchings, lithographs, serigraphs, woodcuts and other forms of prints.

STYLE Considers geometric abstraction, impressionism and painterly abstraction. Considers all genres.

TERMS Artowrk is accepte don consignment and there is a 50% commission. Gallery provides insurance and promotion. Accpeted work should be framed. Requires exclusive representation locally. Only represents American artists.

SUBMISSIONS Send query letter with artist's statement, bio, photoraphs, and résumé. Materials returned with SASE. Responds in 4 weeks. Finds artists throughs ubmissions, art exhibits, art fairs and referrals by other artists.

CRAFT & FOLK ART MUSEUM (CAFAM)

5814 Wilshire Blvd., Los Angeles CA 90036. (323)937-4230. **E-mail:** info@cafam.org. **Website:** www.cafam.org. Estab. 1973. "Located on Los Angeles' prestigious Museum Row, CAFAM is the city's only institution exclusively dedicated to celebrating craft, design and folk act. CAFAM's dynamic exhibitions feature established and emerging artists whose work is rooted in both traditional and contemporary craft and design. Through its exhibitions and programs, CAFAM challenges established ideas about craft and folk art." Sponsors 6 shows/year. Average display time: 2-3 months. Open Tuesday–Friday, 11-5; Saturday–Sunday, 12-6. Located on Miracle Mile; features design, contemporary crafts, international folk art.

MEDIA Considers all media; most frequently exhibits contemporary use of ceramics, found objects, wood, fiber, glass, textiles and paper.

STYLE Exhibits all styles, all genres.

SUBMISSIONS Submission details online.

CRAFT ALLIANCE GALLERY

6640 Delmar Blvd., St. Louis MO 63130. (314)725-1177 ext. 322. **Fax:** (314)725-2068. **E-mail:** gallery@craftalliance.org. **Website:** www.craftalliance.org. Nonprofit arts center with exhibition and retail galleries. Estab. 1964. Represents approximately 500 emerging, mid-career and established artists. Exhibition spaces sponsor 10-12 exhibits/year. Open Tuesday-Thursday, 10-5; Friday-Saturday, 10-6; Sunday, 11-5. Located in University City in the Delmar Loop Shopping District. Clients include local community, students, tourists and upscale. Retail gallery price range $20 and up. Most work sold at $100.

MEDIA Considers ceramics, metal, fiber and glass. Most frequently exhibits jewelry, glass and clay. Doesn't consider prints.

STYLE Exhibits contemporary craft.

TERMS Exhibition artwork is sold on consignment and there is a 50% commission. Artwork is bought outright. Retail price set by the gallery and the artist. Gallery provides insurance and promotion. Requires exclusive representation locally.

SUBMISSIONS Call or write to arrange a personal interview to show portfolio of slides or call first, then send slides or photographs. Returns material with SASE.

TIPS "Call and talk. Have professional slides and attitude."

CREATIVE GROWTH ART CENTER GALLERY

355 24th St., Oakland CA 94612. (510)836-2340, ext.15. **E-mail:** info@creativegrowth.org. **Website:** www.creativegrowth.org. Estab. 1978. Nonprofit gallery. Represents 100 emerging and established artists; 100 adults with disabilities work in our adjacent studio. Exhibited artists include Dwight Mackintosh, Nelson Tygart. Sponsors 10 shows/year. Average display time: 5 weeks. Open Monday–Friday, 10-4:30; Saturday 10-3. Located downtown; 1,200 sq. ft.; classic large white room with movable walls, track lights; visible from the street. 25% of space for special exhibitions; 75% of space for gallery artists. Clientele: private and corporate collectors. 90% private collectors, 10%

corporate collectors. Overall price range: $50-4,000; most work sold at $100-250.

○ This gallery concentrates mainly on the artists who work in an adjacent studio, but work from other regional or national artists may be considered for group shows. Only outsider and brut art are shown. Most of the artists have not formally studied art, but have a raw talent that is honest and real with a strong narrative quality.

MEDIA Considers oil, acrylic, watercolor, pastel, pen & ink, drawing, mixed media, collage, paper, sculpture, ceramics, fiber, woodcuts, engravings, lithographs, wood engravings, mezzotints, serigraphs, linocuts and etchings. Most frequently exhibits (2D) drawing and painting; (3D) sculpture, hooked rug/tapestries.

STYLE Exhibits expressionism, primitivism, color field, naive, folk art, brut. Genres include landscapes, florals and figurative work. Prefers brut/outsider, contemporary, expressionistic.

TERMS Accepts work on consignment (40% commission). Retail price set by the gallery. Gallery provides insurance, promotion and contract; artist pays shipping costs to and from gallery. Prefers artwork framed.

SUBMISSIONS Prefers only brut, naive, outsider; works by adult artists with disabilities. Send query letter with résumé, slides, bio. Write for appointment to show portfolio of photographs and slides. Responds only if interested. Files slides and printed material. Finds artists through agents, by visiting exhibitions, word of mouth, various art publications and sourcebooks, submissions and networking.

TIPS "Peruse publications that feature brut and expressionistic art (example *Raw Vision*)."

D5 PROJECTS

2525 Michigan Ave., Suite B7, Santa Monica CA 90404. (310)315-1937. **Fax:** (310)315-9688. **E-mail:** info@robertbermangallery.com. **Website:** www.robertbermangallery.com. **Contact:** Robert Berman, owner. For profit gallery. Approached by 200 artists/year; exhibits 25 mid-career artists. Sponsors 12 exhibits/year. Average display time: 1 month. Open Tuesday-Saturday, 11-6. Closed December 24-January 1 and last 2 weeks of August. Located in Bergamot Station Art Center in Santa Monica. Clients include local

community, students, tourists and upscale. Overall price range: $600-30,000; most work sold at $4,000.

MEDIA Considers all media. Most frequently exhibits oil on canvas.

STYLE Considers contemporary.

SUBMISSIONS "We currently accept submissions via e-mail *only* as URL address or no more than 3 images sent as attachments, JPEG or GIF. All 3 not to exceed 1.5 MB total. Images exceeding 1.5 MB will not be considered. If we receive slide submissions without a SASE, they will not be considered."

○ DALES GALLERY

537 Fisgard St., Victoria British Columbia V8W 1R3, Canada. (250)383-1552. **E-mail:** dalesgallery@shaw.ca. **Website:** www.dalesgallery.ca. **Contact:** Alison Trembath. Estab. 1976. Art gallery and framing studio. Approached by 200 artists/year, Sponsors 10 exhibits/year. Average display time: 4 weeks. Open all year; Monday-Friday, 10-5; Saturday, 11-4. Gallery situated in Chinatown (Old Town); approximately 650 sq. ft. of space—warm and inviting with brick wall and large white display wall. Clients include local community, students, tourists and upscale. Overall price range: $100-4000; most work sold at $800.

MEDIA Considers all media including photography. Most frequently exhibits oils, photography and sculpture.

STYLE Exhibits both solo and group artists.

TERMS Accepts work on consignment (40% commission). Retail price set by both gallery and artist. Accepted work should be framed by professional picture framers. Does not require exclusive representation locally.

SUBMISSIONS Please e-mail images. Portfolio should include contact number and prices. Responds within 2 months, only if interested. Finds artists through word of mouth, art exhibits, submissions, art fairs, portfolio reviews and referral by other artists.

DALLAS MUSEUM OF ART

1717 N. Harwood St., Dallas TX 75201. (214)922-1200. **Fax:** (214)922-1350. **Website:** www.dma.org. Estab. 1903. Museum. Exhibits emerging, mid-career and established artists. Average display time: 3 months. Open Tuesday—Sunday, 11-5; Thursday, 11-9; Late Night Fridays (3rd Friday of the month, excluding December) the museum is open until midnight. General admission is free. Clients include local community, students, tourists and upscale.

MEDIA Exhibits all media and all types of prints.
STYLE Exhibits all styles and genres.
SUBMISSIONS Does not accept unsolicited submissions. Call to request information.

DAVIDSON GALLERIES

313 Occidental Ave. S., Seattle WA 98104. (206)624-7684. **E-mail:** sam@davidsongalleries.com. **Website:** www.davidsongalleries.com. **Contact:** Sam Davidson, owner. Retail gallery. Estab. 1973. Represents 150 emerging, mid-career and established artists. Sponsors 36 shows/year. Average display time: 5 weeks. Open all year; Tuesday-Saturday, 10-5:30. Located in old, restored part of downtown; 3,200 sq. ft.; "beautiful antique space with columns and high ceilings built in 1890." 50% of space for special antique and modern works on paper; 50% of space for contemporary works on paper. Clientele: 90% private collectors, 10% corporate collectors. Overall price range: $50-70,000; most work sold at $250-5,000.
MEDIA Considers works on paper only: drawing (all types), watercolor, mixed media, pastel, woodcuts, wood engravings, linocuts, engravings, mezzotints, etchings, lithographs, **limited interest** in photography, digital manipulation or collage.
STYLE Exhibits expressionism, neo-expressionism, primitivism, painterly abstraction, postmodern works, realism, surrealism, impressionism.
TERMS Accepts work on consignment (50% commission). Retail price set by gallery and artist. Gallery provides insurance, promotion and contract; shipping costs are one way.
SUBMISSIONS Send query letter, e-mail a reference to a website or send a disc with appropriate descriptions and SASE. Responds in 6 weeks.
TIPS "Impressed by a simple straight-forward presentation."

THE DAYTON ART INSTITUTE

456 Belmonte Park N., Dayton OH 45405-4700. (937)223-5277. **Fax:** (937)223-3140. **E-mail:** info@daytonart.org. **Website:** www.daytonartinstitute.org. Estab. 1919. Museum. Galleries open Tuesday-Friday, 11-8; Saturday, 10-5; Sunday, 12-5.
STYLE Interested in fine art.

DELAWARE CENTER FOR THE CONTEMPORARY ARTS

200 S. Madison St., Wilmington DE 19801. (302)656-6466. **E-mail:** alaszczkowska@thedcca.org. **Website:** www.thedcca.org. **Contact:** Annette Laszczkowska, curatorial assistant. Alternative space, museum retail shop, nonprofit gallery. Approached by more than 800 artists/year; exhibits 50 artists. Sponsors 30 total exhibits/year. Average display time 6 weeks. Gallery open Tuesday, Thursday–Saturday, 10-5; Wednesday and Sunday, 12-5. Closed on Monday and major holidays. Seven galleries located along rejuvenated Wilmington riverfront.
MEDIA Considers all media, including contemporary crafts.
STYLE Exhibits contemporary, abstract, figurative, conceptual, representational and nonrepresentational, painting, sculpture, installation and contemporary crafts.
TERMS Accepts work on consignment (35% commission). Retail price is set by the gallery and the artist. Gallery provides insurance and promotion; shipping costs are shared. Prefers contemporary art.
SUBMISSIONS Send query letter with artist's statement, bio, SASE, 10 slides. Returns material with SASE. Responds within 6 months. Finds artists through word of mouth, submissions, portfolio reviews, art exhibits, referrals by other artists.

DEL MANO GALLERY

3051 Via Maderas, Altadena CA 91001. (818)421-2133. **E-mail:** gallery@delmano.com. **Website:** www.delmano.com. Estab. 1973. Online retail gallery representing more than 300 emerging, mid-career and established artists. Interested in seeing the work of emerging artists working in wood, glass, ceramics, fiber and metal. Gallery deals heavily in turned and sculpted wood, showing works by David Ellsworth, William Hunter and Ron Kent. Gallery hosts approximately 12 "online" exhibitions per year. Past exhibitions remain accessible on the website and there is a special section ("Artist Gallery") for individual artists to present available work. Work in this section is changed on a regular basis. Clients include professionals and affluent collectors. Overall price range: $300-30,000. Most work sold in the $500-5,000 range.
MEDIA Considers contemporary art in craft media: ceramics, glass, wood, fiber. No prints. Most frequently exhibits wood, ceramics, jewelry.
STYLE Exhibits all styles and genres.
TERMS Artist retains the work until sold. Gallery pays for shipping and pays artist prior to shipping. Retail price set by gallery and artist. Customer discounts and payment by installment are available. 10-

mile exclusive area representation required. Gallery provides insurance, promotion and shipping costs from gallery. Prefers artwork framed.

SUBMISSIONS E-mail images for review to Ray Leier (rayl@delmano.com) along with résumé, piece information and prices.

⊕ DETROIT ARTISTS MARKET

4719 Woodward Ave., Detroit MI 48201. (313)832-8540. **Fax:** (313)832-8543. **E-mail:** info@detroitartistsmarket.org. **Website:** www.detroitartistsmarket.org. Estab. 1932. Nonprofit gallery. Exhibits the work of emerging, mid-career and established artists; 1,000 members. Sponsors 8-10 shows/year. Average display time: 6 weeks. Open Tuesday–Saturday, 11-6. Located in midtown Detroit; 2,600 sq. ft.; 85% for special exhibitions. Clientele: "extremely diverse client base, varies from individuals to the Detroit Institute of Arts." 95% private collectors; 5% corporate collectors. Overall price range: $200-75,000; most work sold at $100-500.

MEDIA Considers all media. No posters. Most frequently exhibits paintings, glass and multimedia.

STYLE All contemporary styles and genres.

TERMS Prefers artists from the metro Detroit region. Accepts artwork on consignment (33% commission). Retail price set by artist. Gallery provides insurance. Artist pays all shipping costs.

SUBMISSIONS "Artists and artwork shown is selected by a jury (from submitted call-for-entry applications), exhibition curator or by invitation from DAM (for the Elements gallery—our regular sales gallery which we have in addition to the main exhibition gallery)."

TIPS "Detroit Artists Market educates the Detroit metropolitan community about the work of emerging and established Detroit and Michigan artists through exhibitions, sales and related programs."

DINNERWARE ARTSPACE

101 W. Sixth St., Tucson AZ 85701. (520)869-3166. **E-mail:** dinnerwareartspace@gmail.com. **Website:** dinnerwareartspace.org. **Contact:** David Aguirre, director. Estab. 1979. Considers all media. Most frequently exhibits painting and sculpture. Considers all types of prints.

STYLE Most frequently exhibits group theme exhibitions in all media including art installations, video, performance art, and spoken word. Dinnerware organizes workshops in silk screen, etching press, kids arts, ceramics, fiber arts and more.

TERMS Varied.

SUBMISSIONS E-mail query with résumé, images, website or Facebook link.

TIPS Subscribe to e-mail list to get updates on upcoming exhibition opportunities. Check Dinnerware's Facebook page for updates.

DISTRICT OF COLUMBIA ARTS CENTER (DCAC)

2438 18th St. NW, Washington DC 20009. (202)462-7833. **E-mail:** info@dcartscenter.org. **Website:** dcartscenter.org. **Contact:** Michael Matason, gallery manager. Estab. 1989. Nonprofit gallery and performance space. Exhibits emerging and mid-career artists. Sponsors 7-8 shows/year. Average display time: 1-2 months. Open Wednesday–Sunday, 2-7; later when there is a theater performance. Located "in Adams Morgan, a downtown neighborhood; 132 running exhibition feet in exhibition space and a 52-seat theater." Clientele: all types. Overall price range: $200-10,000; most work sold at $600-1,400.

MEDIA Considers all media including fine and plastic art. "No crafts." Most frequently exhibits painting, sculpture and photography.

STYLE Exhibits all styles. Prefers "innovative, mature and challenging styles."

TERMS Accepts artwork on consignment (30% commission). Artwork only represented while on exhibit. Retail price set by the gallery and artist. Offers payment by installments. Gallery provides promotion and contract; artist pays for shipping. Prefers artwork framed.

SUBMISSIONS Send query letter with résumé, slides, bio and SASE. Portfolio review not required. Responds in 4 months. More details are available on website.

TIPS "We strongly suggest the artist be familiar with the gallery's exhibitions and the kind of work we show strong, challenging pieces that demonstrate technical expertise and exceptional vision. Include SASE if requesting reply and return of slides!"

DOLPHIN GALLERIES

230 Hana Hwy., Suite 12, Kahului HI 96732. (800)669-5051. **Fax:** (808)873-0820. **E-mail:** christianadams@dolphingalleries.com; info@dolphingalleries.com. **Website:** www.dolphingalleries.com. **Contact:** Christian Adams, director of sales and artist development.

Estab. 1976. For-profit galleries. Exhibits emerging, mid-career and established artists. Exhibited artists include Alexei Butirskiy, Craig Alan and Dr. Seuss. Sponsors numerous exhibitions/year, "running at all times through 4 separate fine art or fine jewelry galleries." Average display time "varies from 1-night events to a 30-day run." Open 7 days/week, 9 a.m. to 10 p.m. Located in luxury resort, high-traffic tourist locations throughout Hawaii. Gallery locations on Maui are at Whalers Village in Kaanapali and in Wailea at the Shops at Wailea. On the Big Island of Hawaii, Dolphin Galleries is located at the Kings Shops at Waikoloa. Clients include local community and upscale tourists. Overall price range: $100-100,000; most work sold at $1,000-5,000.

○ The above address is for Dolphin Galleries' corporate offices. Dolphin Galleries has 4 locations throughout the Hawaiian islands—see website for details.

MEDIA Considers all media. Most frequently exhibits oil and acrylic paintings and limited edition works of art. Considers all types of mediums.

STYLE Most frequently exhibits impressionism, figurative art and sculpture. Considers American contemporary landscapes, portraits and florals.

TERMS Artwork is accepted on consignment with promotion and contract. Retail price set by the gallery. Gallery provides insurance, promotion and contract. Gallery happy to work with artist on a variety of terms. Requires exclusive representation locally.

SUBMISSIONS Submit via e-mail. Finds artists mainly through referrals by other artists, exhibitions, artist and agent submissions, portfolio reviews and word of mouth.

M.A. DORAN GALLERY

3509 S. Peoria Ave., Tulsa OK 74105. (918)748-8700. **E-mail:** maryann@madorangallery.com. **Website:** www.madorangallery.com. Estab. 1979. Retail gallery. Represents 45 emerging, mid-career and established artists/year. Exhibited artists include P.S. Gordon and Otto Duecker. Sponsors 10 shows/year. Average display time: 1 month. Open all year; Tuesday–Saturday, 10:30-6. Located central retail Tulsa; 2,000 sq. ft.; up and downstairs, Soho-like interior. 50% of space for special exhibitions; 50% of space for gallery artists. Clients include upscale. 65% of sales are to private collectors; 35% corporate collectors. Overall price range: $500-40,000; most work sold at $5,000.

MEDIA Considers all media except pen & ink, paper, fiber and installation; types of prints include woodcuts, engravings, lithographs, wood engravings, mezzotints, serigraphs, linocuts and etchings. Most frequently exhibits oil paintings, watercolor and crafts.

STYLE Exhibits painterly abstraction, impressionism, photorealism, realism and imagism. Exhibits all genres. Prefers landscapes, still life and fine American crafts.

TERMS Accepts work on consignment (50% commission). Retail price set by the gallery and artist. Gallery provides insurance and promotion; shipping costs are shared. Prefers artwork framed.

SUBMISSIONS "Please submit a CD with 20 current images. Include a typed sheet with corresponding information. If submitting slides/photos, clearly label (title, year, medium, size). Please include a résumé—education, solo exhibitions distinct from group shows, awards, publications, etc., an artist statement—further explanation about your technique(s), concept, vision, etc. Please include an SASE. We appreciate your effort and a response will be sent within 30 days."

DOT FIFTYONE GALLERY

187 NW 27th St., Miami FL 33127. (305)573-9994, ext. 450. **E-mail:** info@dotfiftyone.com; dot@dotfiftyone.com. **Website:** www.dotfiftyone.com. Estab. 2003. Sponsors 12 exhibits per year. Average display time: 30 days. Clients include the local community, tourists, and upscale corporate collectors. Art sold for $1,000-20,000 (avg. $5,000) with a 50% commission. Prices are set by the gallery and the artist. Gallery provides insurance, promotion, and contract. Work should be framed, mounted and matted.

TERMS E-mail 5 JPEG samples at 72 dpi.

DUCK CLUB GALLERY

2333 N. College, Fayetteville AR 72703. (479)443-7262. **Website:** www.duckclubgallery.com. Estab. 1980. Retail gallery. Represents mid-career and established artists. May be interested in seeing the work of emerging artists in the future. Exhibited artists include Terry Redlin, Jane Garrison and Linda Cullers. Displays work "until it sells." Open all year; Monday-Friday, 10-5:30; Saturday, 10-2. Located midtown; 1,200 sq. ft. 100% of space for gallery artists. Clientele: tourists, local community, students; "we are a university community." 80% private collectors, 20%

corporate collectors. Overall price range: $50-400; most work sold at $50-200.

MEDIA Considers all media including wood carved decoys. Considers engravings, lithographs, serigraphs, etchings, posters. Most frequently exhibits limited edition and open edition prints and poster art.

STYLE Exhibits all styles and genres. Prefers wildlife, local art and landscapes.

TERMS Buys outright for 50% of retail price (net 30 days). Retail price set by the artist. Gallery provides insurance and promotion; artist pays for shipping. Prefers artwork unframed.

SUBMISSIONS Send query letter with brochure, photographs and business card. Write for appointment to show portfolio. Finds artists through word of mouth, referrals by other artists, visiting art fairs and exhibitions, submissions, referrals from customers.

TIPS "Please call for an appointment. Don't just stop in. For a period of time, give exclusively to the gallery representing you. Permit a gallery to purchase 1 or 2 items, not large minimums."

DUCKTRAP BAY TRADING COMPANY

20 Main St., Camden ME 04843. (207)236-9568; (800)560-9568. **E-mail:** info@ducktrapbay.com. **Website:** www.ducktrapbay.com. **Contact:** Tim and Joyce Lawrence, owners. Estab. 1983. Retail gallery. "Our marine and wildlife art gallery features over 200 artists whose work spans from carving to painting, sculpture, scrimshaw, jewelry, ship models and much more!" Represents 200 emerging, mid-career and established artists/year. Exhibited artists include Sandy Scott, Stefane Bougie, Yvonne Davis, Beki Killorin, Jim O'Reilly and Gary Eigenberger. Open daily 10-5. Located downtown waterfront; 2 floors, 3,000 sq. ft. 100% of space for gallery artists. Clientele: tourists, upscale. 70% private collectors, 30% corporate collectors. Overall price range: $250-120,000; most work sold at $250-2,500.

MEDIA Considers watercolors, oil, acrylic, pastel, pen & ink, drawing, paper, sculpture, bronze and carvings. Types of prints include lithographs. Most frequently exhibits woodcarvings, watercolor, acrylic and bronze.

STYLE Exhibits realism. Genres include nautical, wildlife and landscapes. Prefers marine and wildlife.

TERMS Accepts work on consignment (40% commission) or buys outright for 50% of the retail price (net 30 days). Retail price set by the artist. Gallery pro-

vides insurance and minimal promotion; artist pays for shipping. Prefers artwork framed.

SUBMISSIONS Send query letter with 10-20 slides or photographs. Call or write for appointment to show portfolio of photographs. Files all material. Finds artists through word of mouth, referrals by other artists and submissions.

TIPS "Find the right gallery and location for your subject matter. Have at least 8-10 pieces or carvings or 3-4 bronzes."

DURHAM ART GUILD

120 Morris St., Durham NC 27701. (919)560-2713. **E-mail:** gallerycoordinator@durhamartguild.org. **Website:** www.durhamartguild.org. **Contact:** Katie Seiz, gallery director. Estab. 1948. Nonprofit gallery. Represents/exhibits 500 emerging, mid-career and established artists/year. Sponsors more than 20 shows/year, including an annual juried art exhibit. Average display time: 6 weeks. Open all year; Monday-Saturday, 9-9; Sunday, 1-6. Free and open to the public. Located in center of downtown Durham in the Arts Council Building; 3,600 sq. ft.; large, open, movable walls. 100% of space for special exhibitions. Clientele: general public; 80% private collectors, 20% corporate collectors. Overall price range: $100-14,000; most work sold at $200-1,200.

MEDIA Considers all media. Most frequently exhibits painting, sculpture and photography.

STYLE Exhibits all styles, all genres.

TERMS Artwork is accepted on consignment (30-40% commission). Retail price set by the artist. Gallery provides insurance and promotion. Artist installs show. Prefers artwork framed.

SUBMISSIONS Artists must be 18 years or older. Send query letter with résumé, slides and SASE. "We accept slides for review by February 1 for consideration of a solo exhibit or special projects group show." Finds artists through word of mouth, referral by other artists, call for slides.

TIPS "Before submitting slides for consideration, be familiar with the exhibition space to make sure it can accommodate any special needs your work may require."

⊕ EAST END ARTS

133 E. Main St., Riverhead NY 11901. (631)727-0900. **Fax:** (631)727-0966. **E-mail:** info@eastendarts.org. **Website:** www.eastendarts.org. **Contact:** Patricia Snyder, executive director. Estab. 1972. Nonprofit gallery

and arts center. Located in the historic Davis-Corwin House (circa 1840). Exhibits the juried work of artists of all media. Presents 8 shows annually most of which are juried group exhibitions. Exhibits include approximately 300 artists/year, ranging from emerging to mid-career to professional exhibitors of all ages. Average display time: 4-6 weeks. Prefers regional artists. Clientele small business and private collectors. Overall price range: $100-7,500; most work sold at $100-500. Open Tuesday–Saturday, 10-4.

MEDIA Considers all media including sculptures and installations. Considers matted but not framed giclees and serigraphs for gift shop but not shows.

STYLE Exhibits contemporary, abstract, naive, nonrepresentational, photorealism, realism, postpop works, projected installations and assemblages. "Being an organization relying strongly on community support, we aim to serve the artistic needs of our constituency and also expose them to current innovative trends within the art world. Therefore, there is not a particular genre bias; we are open to all art media."

TERMS Accepts work on consignment (30% commission). Retail price for art sold through our juried exhibits is set by the artist. Exclusive area representation not required.

SUBMISSIONS Submission guidelines available online.

TIPS "Visit, become a member ($50/year individual) and you'll be sent all the mailings that inform you of shows, lectures, workshops, grants and more! All work must be framed with clean mats and glass/plexi and wired for hanging. Artwork with clean gallery edge (no staples) is also accepted. Presentation of artwork is considered when selecting work for shows."

EASTERN SHORE ART CENTER

401 Oak St., Fairhope AL 36532. (251)928-2228. E-mail: kate@esartcenter.com. **Website:** www.esartcenter.com. **Contact:** Kate Fisher, executive director. Estab. 1957. Museum. Exhibits emerging, mid-career and established artists. Average display time: 1 month. Open Tuesday-Friday, 10-4; Saturday, 10-2. Open all year. Located downtown; 8,000 sq. ft. of galleries.

Artists applying to Eastern Shore should expect to wait at least a year for exhibits.

MEDIA Considers all media and prints.

STYLE Exhibits all styles and genres.

TERMS Accepts works on consignment (25% commission). Retail price set by artist. Gallery provides insurance, promotion and contract. Prefers artwork framed.

SUBMISSIONS Send query letter with résumé and slides. Write for appointment to show portfolio of originals and slides.

TIPS "Conservative, realistic art is appreciated more and sells better."

E BRACKNELL GALLERY; MANSION SPACES

South Hill Park Arts Centre, Ringmead, Bracknell, Berkshire RG12 7PA, United Kingdom. (44)(0)1344-484-123. **Website:** www.southhillpark.org.uk. **Contact:** Ron McAllister, chief executive and programming. Estab. 1991. Alternative space/nonprofit gallery. Approached by at least 50 artists/year; exhibits several shows of emerging, mid-career and established artists. "Very many artists approach us for the Mansion Spaces; all applications are looked at." Exhibited artists include Billy Childish (painting), Simon Roberts (photography) and Ed Piebn (digital installation/mixed media). Average display time: 2 months. Open all year; call or check website for hours. Located "within a large arts centre that includes theatre, cinema, studios, workshops and a restaurant; one large room and one smaller with high ceilings, plus more exhibiting spaces around the centre." Clients include local community and students.

MEDIA Considers all media. Most frequently exhibits painting, sculpture, live art, installations, group shows, video-digital works, craftwork (ceramics, glasswork, jewelery). Considers all types of prints.

STYLE Considers all styles and genres.

TERMS Artwork is accepted on consignment, and there is a 25% commission. Retail price set by the artist. Gallery provides insurance, promotion and contract.

SUBMISSIONS Send query letter with artist's statement, bio and photographs. Returns material with SASE. Responds to queries only if interested. Files all material "unless return of photos is requested." Finds artists through invitations, art exhibits, referrals by other artists, submissions and word of mouth.

TIPS "We have a great number of applications for exhibitions in the Mansion Spaces. Make yours stand out! Exhibitions at the Bracknell Gallery are planned 2-3 years in advance."

PETER ELLER GALLERY & APPRAISERS

(505)268-7437. **E-mail:** peter@peterellerart.com. **Website:** www.peterellerart.com. **Contact:** Peter Eller. Estab. 1981. Private dealer buys, sells, and does fee appraisals. Specializing in Albuquerque artists and minor New Mexico masters, 1925-1985. Overall price range $1,000-75,000.

MEDIA Considers acrylic, ceramics, drawing, mixed media, oil, pastel, pen & ink, sculpture, watercolor, engravings, etchings, linocuts, lithographs, mezzotints, serigraphs and woodcuts. Most frequently exhibits oil, sculpture and acrylic.

STYLE Considers all styles and genres. Most frequently exhibits Southwestern realism and geometric abstraction.

TERMS Primarily accepts consignments of resale works. Holds shows for contemporary artists occasionally.

SUBMISSIONS Call or write to arrange a personal interview to show portfolio or photographs. Finds artists through word of mouth and art exhibits.

EMEDIALOFT.ORG

744 Washington St., #A-629, New York NY 10014-2035. (646)368-5623. **Website:** www.emedialoft.org. **Contact:** CT Rhodes, director. Estab. 1982. Alternative space. Exhibits highly original mid-career artists. Sponsors 4-6 exhibits/year. Average display time: 2 months. Open during announced shows; or by appointment. Located in the Highline/Meatpacking/West Village neighborhood of Manhattan in New York City. Overall price range: $5-50,000; most work sold at $500-2,000. Two artists studios for artists-in-residence and archives/library.

MEDIA Contemporary art, photography, mixed media, oil, watercolor, collage, prints. Frequently exhibits new media, performance, readings, sound-art video, artists' books, artist's objects, image/text and conceptual art. Most all are editions or sequences.

STYLE Themes relate to art from the subconscious, even if it looks recognizable or figurative, including landscapes or objects. No political art, no abstraction. "Art so original, it's hard to categorize."

SUBMISSIONS E-mail 250 words and 5 JPEGs (72 dpi max, 300 pixels on longest side). Or send query letter with "anything you like, but no SASE—sorry, we can't return anything. We may keep you on file, but please do not call." Responds to queries only if interested.

THOMAS ERBEN GALLERY

526 W. 26th St., Floor 4, New York NY 10001. (212)645-8701. **Fax:** (212)645-9630. **E-mail:** info@thomaserben.com. **Website:** www.thomaserben.com. Estab. 1996. For-profit gallery. Approached by 100 artists/year. Represents 15 emerging, mid-career and established artists. Exhibited artists include Preston Scott Cohen (architecture) and Tom Wood (photography). Average display time 5-6 weeks. Open all year; Tuesday-Saturday, 10-6 (Monday–Friday in July). Closed Christmas/New Year's and August. Clients include local community, tourists and upscale.

MEDIA Considers all media. Most frequently exhibits photography, paintings and installation.

STYLE Exhibits contemporary art.

SUBMISSIONS Mail portfolio for review. Returns material with SASE. Responds in 1 month.

ETHERTON GALLERY

135 S. Sixth Ave., Tucson AZ 85701. (520)624-7370. **Fax:** (520)792-4569. **E-mail:** info@ethertongallery.com. **Website:** www.ethertongallery.com. **Contact:** Terry Etherton. Estab. 1981. Retail gallery and art consultancy. Specializes in vintage, modern and contemporary photography. Represents 50+ emerging, mid-career and established artists. Exhibited artists include Kate Breakey, Harry Callahan, Jack Dykinga, Elliott Erwitt, Mark Klett, Danny Lyon, Rodrigo Moya, Luis Gonzalez Palma, Lisa M. Robinson, Frederick Sommer, Joel-Peter Witkin and Alex Webb. Sponsors 3-5 shows/year. Average display time: 8 weeks. Open year round. Located in downtown Tucson; 3,000-sq.-ft. gallery in historic building with wood floors and 16-ft. ceilings. Clientele: 50% private collectors, 25% corporate collectors, 25% museums. Overall price range: $800-50,000; most work sold at $2,000-5,000. Media: Considers all types of photography, painting, works on paper. Etherton Gallery purchases 19th-century, vintage, and classic photography; occasionally purchases contemporary photography and artwork. Interested in seeing work that is "well-crafted, cutting-edge, contemporary, issue-oriented."

MEDIA Considers all types of photography, oil, acrylic, drawing, mixed media, collage, original hand pulled prints, woodcuts, wood engravings, linocuts, engravings, mezzotints, etchings and lithographs. Most frequently exhibits photography, painting and mixed media.

STYLE Exhibits expressionism, neo-expressionism, primitivism, postmodern works. Genres include landscapes, portraits and figurative work. Prefers expressionism, primitive/folk and postmodern. Interested in seeing work that is "cutting-edge, contemporary, issue-oriented. No decorator art."

TERMS Accepts work on consignment (50% commission). Buys outright for 50% of retail price (net 30 days). Retail price set by gallery and artist. Gallery provides insurance and promotion; shipping costs are shared. Prefers framed artwork.

SUBMISSIONS A maximum of 10-20 images JPEGs, résumé, artist statement, bio, reviews. Materials not returned. Responds in 6 weeks if interested.

EVERHART MUSEUM

1901 Mulberry St., Scranton PA 18510-2390. (570)346-7186. **Fax:** (570)346-0652. **E-mail:** curator@everhart-museum.org. **Website:** www.everhart-museum.org. **Contact:** Curatorial department. Estab. 1908. "The Everhart Museum is one of the oldest museums in the state and part of the early 20th-century regional museum movement." Exhibits established artists. 2,400 members. 15 gallery spaces providing display area for permanent and temporary exhibitions. Open Monday, Thursday, Friday, 12-4; Saturday, 10-5; Sunday, 12-5; closed in January for routine maintenance; closed on Easter, July 4th, Thanksgiving and Christmas. Located in urban park; 300 linear feet. 20% of space for special exhibitions.

MEDIA Considers all media.

STYLE Prefers regional, Pennsylvania artists but also national and international artists that feature science and culture in their work.

TERMS Museum provides insurance, promotion and shipping costs. 2D artwork must be framed.

SUBMISSIONS "Exhibition proposals are reviewed on an on-going basis by the curatorial department. Use the Exhibit Proposal form in order to have your proposal considered for display. If you are including work samples, slides, CDs, or other materials, please include a SASE if you would like your materials returned. Digital submissions and web portfolios also considered. Please do not send original material as the Everhart Museum accepts no responsibility for materials lost or damaged. Please note that the Everhart Museum receives many exhibition proposals each year so we would encourage you to contact a number of venues for your proposed exhibition. For additional information, or should you have difficulty downloading the online Exhibit Proposal form, please contact the curatorial department."

EVERSON MUSEUM OF ART

401 Harrison St., Syracuse NY 13202. (315)474-6064. **Fax:** (315)474-6943. **E-mail:** everson@everson.org; smassett@everson.org. **Website:** www.everson.org. **Contact:** Sarah Massett, assistant director. Estab. 1897. Museum. "In fitting with the works it houses, the Everson Museum building is a sculptural work of art in its own right. Designed by renowned architect I.M. Pei, the building itself is internationally acclaimed for its uniqueness. Within its walls, Everson houses roughly 11,000 pieces of art; American paintings, sculpture, drawings, graphics and one of the largest holdings of American ceramics in the nation." Open all year; Wednesday, Friday and Sunday, noon-5; Thursday, noon-8; Saturday, 10-5; closed Monday and Tuesday. Located in a distinctive I.M. Pie-designed building in downtown Syracuse NY. The museum features 4 large galleries with 24-ft. ceilings, back lighting and oak hardwood, a sculpture court, Art Zone for children, a ceramic study center and 5 smaller gallery spaces.

EVOLVE THE GALLERY

P.O. Box 5944, Sacramento CA 95817. **E-mail:** info@evolvethegallery.com. **Website:** www.evolvethegallery.com. **Contact:** A. Michelle Blakeley, co-owner. Estab. 2010. For-profit and art consultancy gallery. Approached by 250+ artists/year. Represents emerging, mid-career and established artists. Exhibited artists include Richard Mayhew (master fine artist, watercolor), Corinne Whitaker (pioneer digital painter), Ben F. Jones (prominent international artist). Sponsors 12+ exhibits/year. Model and property release required. Average display time: 1 month. Open Thursday-Saturday, by appointment. Clients include local community, students, tourists, upscale. 1% of sales are to corporate collectors. Overall price range: $1-10,000. Most work sold at $3,000.

MEDIA Considers all media (except craft).

STYLE Exhibits conceptualism, geometric abstraction, neo-expressionism, postmodernism and painterly abstraction.

TERMS Artwork is accepted on consignment and there is a 50% commission. Retail price of the art set by the artist; reviewed by the gallery. Gallery provides insurance, promotion, contract. Accepted work should be framed, mounted.

SUBMISSIONS E-mail with link to artist's website, JPEG samples at 72 dpi. Must include artist statement and CV. Materials returned with SASE. Responds only if interested (within weeks). Finds artists through word of mouth, submissions, portfolio reviews, art exhibits, art fairs, referrals by other artists.

☺ FALKIRK CULTURAL CENTER

1408 Mission Ave. at E St., San Rafael CA 94901. (415)485-3328. **E-mail:** Beth.Goldberg@cityofsan rafael.org. **Website:** www.falkirkculturalcenter.org. **Contact:** Beth Goldberg, curator. Estab. 1974. Nonprofit gallery. Approached by 500 artists/year. Exhibits 350 emerging, mid-career and established artists. Sponsors 8 exhibits/year. Average display time 2 months. Open Tuesday–Friday, 1-5; Saturday, 10-1; by appointment. Three galleries located on second floor with lots of natural light (UV filtered). National historic place (1888 Victorian) converted to multi-use cultural center. Clients include local community, students, tourists and upscale.

MEDIA Considers all media and all types of prints. Most frequently exhibits painting, sculpture and works on paper.

SUBMISSIONS Marin County and San Francisco Bay Area artists only. Send artist's statement, bio, résumé and slides. Returns material with SASE. Responds within 3 months.

FARMINGTON VALLEY ARTS CENTER'S FISHER GALLERY

25 Arts Center Lane, Avon CT 06001. (860)678-1867. **Fax:** (860)674-1877. **E-mail:** info@artsfvac.org; jim. brunelle@artsfvac.org. **Website:** www.artsfvac.org. **Contact:** Jim Brunelle. Estab. 1972. Nonprofit gallery. Exhibits the work of 100 emerging, mid-career and established artists. Open all year; Wednesday-Saturday, 12-4; or by appointment. Located in Avon Park North just off Route 44; 850 sq. ft.; "in a beautiful 19th-century brownstone factory building once used for manufacturing." Clientele: upscale contemporary art craft buyers. Overall price range: $35-500; most work sold at $50-100.

MEDIA Considers "primarily crafts," also some mixed media, works on paper, ceramic, fiber, glass and small prints. Most frequently exhibits jewelry, ceramics and fiber.

STYLE Exhibits contemporary, handmade craft.

TERMS Accepts artwork on consignment (50% commission). Retail price set by the artist. Gallery provides promotion and contract; shipping costs are shared. Requires artwork framed where applicable.

SUBMISSIONS Send query letter with résumé, bio, digital images, SASE. Responds only if interested.

FAR WEST GALLERY

2817 Montana Ave., Billings MT 59101. (800)793-7296. **E-mail:** farwest@180com.net. **Website:** www.farwest gallery.com. **Contact:** Sondra Daly, manager. Estab. 1994. Retail gallery. Represents emerging, mid-career and established artists. Exhibited artists include Joe Beeler, Dave Powell, Kevin Red Star and Stan Natchez. Sponsors 4 shows/year. Average display time: 6-12 months. Open all year, Monday-Saturday, 9-6. Located in downtown historic district in a building built in 1910. Clientele: tourists. Overall price range: $1-9,500; most work sold at $300-700.

MEDIA Considers all media and all types of prints. Most frequently exhibits Native American beadwork, oil and craft/handbuilt furniture.

STYLE Exhibits all styles. Genres include Western and Americana. Prefers Native American beadwork, Western bits, spurs, memorabilia, oil, watercolor and pen & ink.

TERMS Buys outright for 50% of retail price. Retail price set by the gallery and the artist. Gallery provides insurance and promotion.

FAYETTE ART MUSEUM

530 Temple Ave., Fayette AL 35555. (205)932-8727. **E-mail:** fayetteartmuseum@yahoo.com. **Website:** fay etteartmuseum.vpweb.com. Estab. 1969. Exhibits the work of emerging, mid-career and established artists. Located in downtown Fayette Civic Center; 16,500 sq. ft. "Over 4,000 pieces in the permanent art collection with over 500 running feet of display space on the main floor of the Civic Center and 6 folk art galleries downstairs, as well as a gallery used for the director/ curators office. Artists include internationally known and Fayette native Jimmy Lee Sudduth; Rev. Benjamin F. Perkins; Mr. Fred Webster of Berry; Sybil Gibson of Jasper; Jessi LaVon of central Alabama; Wanda Teel of north Alabama; Lois Wilson of Fayette; Moses T and Doug Odom of south Alabama; and Margarette Scruggs of Walker County." Open all year; Monday–Friday, 9-12 and 1-4; and by appointment for group tours.

MEDIA Considers all media and all types of prints. Most frequently exhibits oil, watercolor and mixed media.
STYLE Exhibits expressionism, primitivism, painterly abstraction, minimalism, postmodern works, impressionism, realism and hard-edge geometric abstraction. Genres include landscapes, florals, Americana, wildlife, portraits and figurative work.
TERMS Shipping costs negotiable. Prefers artwork framed.
SUBMISSIONS Send query letter with résumé, brochure and photographs. Write for appointment to show portfolio of photographs. Files possible exhibit material.
TIPS "Do not send expensive mailings (slides, etc.) before calling to find out if we are interested. We want to expand collection. Top priority is folk art from established artists."

FINE ARTS CENTER GALLERY

P.O. Box 1920, Jonesboro AR 72467. (870)972-3050. **Fax:** (870)972-3932. **Website:** www.astate.edu/college/fine-arts/art. Estab. 1968. Represents/exhibits 3-4 emerging, mid-career and established artists/year. Sponsors 3-4 shows/year. Average display time: 1 month. Open fall, winter and spring, Monday-Friday 10-5. Located on Arkansas State University campus; 1,868 sq. ft.; 60% of time devoted to special exhibitions, 40% to student work. Clientele include students and community.
MEDIA Considers all media and prints. Most frequently exhibits painting, sculpture and photography.
STYLE Exhibits conceptualism, photorealism, neo-expressionism, minimalism, hard-edge geometric abstraction, painterly abstraction, postmodern works, realism, impressionism and pop. "No preference except quality and creativity."
TERMS Exhibition space only, artist responsible for sales. Retail price set by the artist. Gallery provides promotion and contract; shipping costs are shared. Prefers artwork framed.
SUBMISSIONS Send query letter with résumé, CD/DVD and SASE to: FAC Gallery Director, c/o Department of Art, Arkansas State University, P.O. Box 1920, State University AR 72467. Portfolio should be submitted on CD/DVD only. Responds only if interested within 2 months. Files résumé. Finds artists through call for artists published in regional and national art journals.

TIPS Show us 20 digital images of your best work. Don't overload us with lots of collateral materials (reprints of reviews, articles, etc.). Make your vita as clear as possible.

FLEISHER/OLLMAN GALLERY

1216 Arch St., 5A, Philadelphia PA 19107. (215)545-7562. **Fax:** (215)545-6140. **E-mail:** info@fleisher-ollmangallery.com. **Website:** www.fleisher-ollmangallery.com. **Contact:** John Ollman, owner. Estab. 1952. Retail gallery. "In addition to our modern and contemporary interests (among them Joseph Cornell, H.C. Westermann, Ed Ruscha, and Alfred Jensen), the gallery continues to showcase the most significant American vernacular artists of the 20th-century, including the exclusive representation of Felipe Jesus Consalvos and the Philadelphia Wireman." Represents 12 emerging and established artists. Exhibited artists include James Castle and Bill Traylor. Sponsors 10 shows/year. Average display time: 5 weeks. Open Tuesday–Friday, 10:30-5:30; Saturday, 12-5; closed Saturdays, June–July; August, generally open during regular hours, but call first. Located downtown; 4,500 sq. ft. 75% of space for special exhibitions. Clientele primarily art collectors. 90% private collectors, 10% corporate collectors. Overall price range: $2,500-100,000; most work sold at $2,500-30,000.
MEDIA Considers oil, acrylic, watercolor, pastel, pen & ink, drawing, mixed media and collage. Most frequently exhibits drawing, painting and sculpture.
STYLE Exhibits self-taught and contemporary works.
TERMS Accepts artwork on consignment (commission) or buys outright. Retail price set by the gallery. Gallery provides insurance and promotion; shipping costs are shared. Prefers artwork framed.
SUBMISSIONS Artists wishing to submit portfolios for review should include a CD with images, a bio or CV, and SASE if you would like your materials returned. "Due to the volume of e-mail we receive, we cannot respond to all unsolicited electronic submissions."
TIPS "Be familiar with our exhibitions and the artists we exhibit."

FLORIDA STATE UNIVERSITY MUSEUM OF FINE ARTS

530 W. Call St., Room 250, Fine Arts Bldg., Tallahassee FL 32306-1140. (850)644-6836. **Fax:** (850)644-7229. **E-mail:** apalladinocraig@fsu.edu. **Website:** www.mofa.fsu.edu. Estab. 1970. Shows work by over

100 artists/year; emerging, mid-career and established. Sponsors 12-22 shows/year. Average display time 3-4 weeks. Located on the university campus; 16,000 sq. ft. 50% for special exhibitions.

MEDIA Considers all media, including electronic imaging and performance art. Most frequently exhibits painting, sculpture and photography.

STYLE Exhibits all styles. Prefers contemporary figurative and nonobjective painting, sculpture, printmaking, photography.

TERMS "Interested collectors are placed into direct contact with the artists; the museum takes no commission." Retail price set by the artist. Museum provides promotion and shipping costs to and from the museum for invited artists.

TIPS "The museum offers a yearly international competition and catalog: The Tallahassee International. Visit website for more information."

THE FLYING PIG, LLC

N6975 State Hwy. 42, Algoma WI 54201. (920)487-9902. **Fax:** (920)487-9904. **E-mail:** info@theflying pig.biz. **Website:** www.theflyingpig.biz. **Contact:** Susan Connor, owner/member. Estab. 2002. For-profit gallery. Located along Lake Michigan in Kewaunee County. Exhibits approximately 150 regional, national and international artists. Open daily, 10-5 (May-October); Friday-Sunday, 10-5 (November-January). Clients include local community, tourists and upscale. Overall price range: $5-2,000; most work sold at $300.

MEDIA Considers all media.

STYLE Exhibits impressionism, minimalism, painterly abstraction and primitivism realism. Most frequently exhibits primitivism realism, impressionism and minimalism. Genres include outsider and visionary.

TERMS Artwork is accepted on consignment (50% commission) or bought outright for 50% of retail price, net 15 days. Retail price set by the artist. Gallery provides insurance, promotion and contract. Accepted work should be framed. Does require exclusive representation locally.

SUBMISSIONS Send query letter with artist's statement, bio and photographs. Returns material with SASE. Responds to queries in 3 weeks. Files artist's statement, bio and photographs if interested. Finds artist's through art fairs and exhibitions, referrals by other artists, submissions, word of mouth and online.

FOCAL POINT GALLERY

321 City Island Ave., City Island NY 10464. (718)885-1403. **E-mail:** ronterner@gmail.com. **Website:** www.focalpointgallery.net. **Contact:** Ron Terner, photographer/director. Estab. 1974. Retail gallery and alternative space. Interested in emerging and mid-career artists. Sponsors 12 group shows/year. Average display time: 3-4 weeks. Clients include locals and tourists. Overall price range: $175-750; most work sold at $300-500.

MEDIA Considers all media. Most frequently exhibits photography, watercolor, oil. Also considers etchings, giclée, color prints, silver prints.

STYLE Exhibits all styles. Most frequently exhibits painterly abstraction, conceptualism, expressionism. Genres include figurative work, florals, landscapes, portraits. Open to any use of photography.

TERMS Accepts work on consignment. Exclusive area representation required. Customer discounts and payment by installment are available. Gallery provides promotion. Artwork must be framed. There is a $20 hanging fee for each piece. Takes 30% commission.

SUBMISSIONS "Please call for submission information. Do not include résumés. The work should stand by itself. Slides should be of high quality."

TIPS "Care about your work."

TORY FOLLIARD GALLERY

233 N. Milwaukee St., Milwaukee WI 53202. (414)273-7311. **Fax:** (414)273-7313. **E-mail:** info@toryfolliard.com. **Website:** www.toryfolliard.com. Estab. 1988. Retail gallery. Represents emerging and established artists. Exhibited artists include Tom Uttech, Fred Stonehouse, TL Solien, Eric Aho, and John Wilde. Sponsors 8-9 shows/year. Average display time: 4-5 weeks. Open all year; Tuesday-Friday, 11-5; Saturday, 11-4. Located downtown in historic Third Ward; 4,000 sq. ft.

STYLE Exhibits expressionism, abstraction, realism and surrealism.

GANNON & ELSA FORDE GALLERIES

1500 Edwards Ave., Bismarck ND 58501. (701)224-5520. **Fax:** (701)224-5400. **E-mail:** michelle_lindb lom@bsc.nodak.com. **Website:** www.bismarckstate.com. **Contact:** Michelle Lindblom, gallery director. College gallery. Represents emerging, mid-career and established art exhibitions. Sponsors 6 shows/year. Average display time: 6 weeks. Open all year; Monday-

Thursday, 7-9; Friday, 7:30-4; Sunday, 3-7. Summer exhibit is college student work (May-August). Located on Bismarck State College campus; high traffic areas on campus. Clientele all. 80% private collectors, 20% corporate collectors. Overall price range: $50-10,000; most work sold at $50-3,000.

MEDIA Considers oil, acrylic, watercolor, pastel, drawing, mixed media, collage, paper, sculpture, ceramics, fiber, photography, woodcut, engraving, lithograph, wood engraving, mezzotint, serigraphs, linocut and etching. Most frequently exhibits painting media (all), mixed media and sculpture.

STYLE Exhibits expressionism, neo-expressionism, painterly abstraction, surrealism, impressionism, photorealism, hard-edge geometric abstraction and realism, all genres.

TERMS Accepts work on consignment (20% commission). Retail price set by the artist. Gallery provides insurance on premises, promotion, contract and shipping costs from gallery; artist pays shipping costs to gallery. Prefers artwork framed.

SUBMISSIONS Send query letter with résumé, slides, bio and SASE. Call or write for appointment to show portfolio of photographs and slides. Responds in 2 months. Files résumé, bio, photos if sent. Finds artists through word of mouth, art publications, artists' submissions, visiting exhibitions.

TIPS "Because our gallery is a university gallery, the main focus is to expose the public to art of all genres. However, we do sell work, occasionally."

FOSTER/WHITE GALLERY

220 Third Ave. S., Seattle WA 98104. (206)622-2833. **Fax:** (206)622-7606. **E-mail:** seattle@fosterwhite.com; artistsubmissions.fosterwhite@gmail.com. **Website:** www.fosterwhite.com. **Contact:** Phen Huang, owner/director. Retail gallery. Estab. 1973. Represents 45 emerging, mid-career and established artists. Interested in seeing the work of local emerging artists. Exhibited artists include Alden Mason, Bobbie Burgers, Will Robinson, Guy Laramee, and the Northwest Masters. Average display time: 1 month. Open all year; Tuesday-Saturday, 10-6; closed Sunday. Located in historic Pioneer Square; 7,500 sq. ft. Clientele private, corporate and public collectors. Overall price range: $300-35,000; most work sold at $2,000-8,000.

MEDIA Considers oil, acrylic, watercolor, pastel, pen & ink, drawing, mixed media, collage, paper, sculpture, ceramics, craft, fiber, glass and installation.

TERMS Gallery provides insurance, promotion and contract.

SUBMISSIONS E-mail submissions are prefered. Guidelines available online. Responds in 1-2 month.

⊙ FOUNDRY GALLERY

1314 18th St. NW, 1st Floor, Washington DC 20036. (202)463-0203. **E-mail:** info@foundrygallery.org. **Website:** www.foundrygallery.org. **Contact:** Fran Abrams, president. Estab. 1971. Cooperative gallery and alternative space. "Founded to encourage and promote Washington area artists and to foster friendship with artists and arts groups outside the Washington area. The Foundry Gallery is known in the Washington area for its promotion of contemporary works of art." Interested in established and emerging artists. Sponsors 12 solo and 12 group shows by members (solo shows occur approximately every 1½ to 2 years. Average display time: 1 month. Open Wednesday-Sunday, 12-6. Clientele: 80% private collectors; 20% corporate clients. Overall price range: $200-2,500; most work sold at $200-1,400.

MEDIA Considers oil, acrylic, watercolor, pastel, pen & ink, drawings, mixed media, collage, paper, sculpture, ceramic, fiber, glass, installation, photography, woodcuts, engravings, mezzotints, etchings, pochoir and serigraphs. Most frequently exhibits painting, sculpture, paper and photography.

STYLE Exhibits "serious artists in all mediums and styles." Prefers nonobjective, expressionism abstract and figurative.

TERMS Co-op membership fee plus initiation fee at time required; 30% commission. Retail price set by artist. Offers customer discounts. Exclusive area representation not required. Gallery provides promotion, contract and website presence. Gallery does not provide insurance.

SUBMISSIONS See website for membership application. Send query e-mail with 5 or more large JPEG attachements to membership@foundrygallery.org or a letter with JPEGs on a CD. Portfolios reviewed at monthly meeting and succeed upon ⅔ vote of members. Finds artists through submissions. Members are primarily local artists who pool their resources to support the gallery. A few exhibition opportunities are available for artists residing outside the Washington area and Foundry keeps a list of interested "guest artists."

TIPS "Have a coherent body of work, professionally presented. Show your very best, strongest work. Looking for fresh, accomplished, distinctive work. Visit gallery to ascertain whether the work fits in."

FREEPORT ART MUSEUM

121 N. Harlem Ave., Freeport IL 61032. (815)235-9755. **Fax:** (815)235-6015. **E-mail:** info@freeportartmuseum.org. **Website:** www.freeportartmuseum.org. **Contact:** Jessica J. Modica, director. Interested in emerging, mid-career and established artists. Sponsors primarily group shows. Clientele: 30% tourists; 60% local; 10% students. Average display time 8 weeks.
MEDIA Considers all media and prints.
STYLE Exhibits all styles and genres.
TERMS Gallery provides insurance while on display and promotional postcards and e-mails; artist pays shipping costs. Artwork must be ready to hang; frames are strongly encouraged. Visit FAM's website for directions on sending exhibition proposal materials.

GALERIE BONHEUR

2534 Seagrass Dr., Palm City FL 34990. (314)409-6057. **E-mail:** gbonheur@aol.com. **Website:** www.galeriebonheur.com. **Owner:** Laurie Carmody Ahner. Private retail and wholesale gallery. Focus is on international folk art. Estab. 1980. Represents 60 emerging, mid-career and established artists/year. Exhibited artists include Milton Bond and Justin McCarthy. Sponsors 6 shows/year. Average display time: 1 year. Open all year; by appointment. Located in Ladue (a suburb of St. Louis); 3,000 sq. ft.; art is displayed all over very large private home. 75% of sales to private collectors. Overall price range: $25-25,000; most work sold at $50-1,000.
MEDIA Considers oil, acrylic, watercolor, pastel, pen & ink, drawing, mixed media, collage, paper, sculpture, ceramics and craft. Most frequently exhibits oil, acrylic and metal sculpture.
STYLE Exhibits expressionism, primitivism, impressionism, folk art, self-taught, outsider art. Genres include landscapes, florals, Americana and figurative work. Prefers genre scenes and figurative.
TERMS Accepts work on consignment (50% commission). Retail price set by the gallery and the artist. Gallery provides promotion; artist pays shipping costs to and from gallery. Prefers artwork framed.
SUBMISSIONS Prefers only self-taught artists. Send query letter with bio, photographs and business card.

Write for appointment to show portfolio of photographs. Responds within 6 weeks, only if interested. Finds artists through agents, visiting exhibitions, word of mouth, art publications, sourcebooks and submissions.
TIPS "Be true to your inspirations. Create from the heart and soul. Don't be influenced by what others are doing; do art that you believe in and love and are proud to say is an expression of yourself. Don't copy; don't get too sophisticated or you will lose your individuality!"

GALLERY 72

1806 Vinton St., Omaha NE 68108. (402)496-4797. **E-mail:** info@gallery72.com. **Website:** www.gallery72.com. **Contact:** John A. Rogers, owner. Estab. 1972. Represents or exhibits 20 artists. Sponsors 6 solo and 4 group shows/year. Average display time: 4-5 weeks. Gallery open Wednesday-Saturday, 10-6; by appointment and for special events. 1,800 sq. ft. of gallery space, 160 ft. of wall space.
MEDIA Considers oil, acrylic, digital, watercolor, pastel, pen & ink, drawings, mixed media, collage, sculpture, ceramic, installation, photography, original handpulled prints and posters. Most frequently exhibits paintings, prints and sculpture.
STYLE Exhibits hard-edge geometric abstraction, color field, minimalism, impressionism and realism. Genres include landscapes and figurative work. Most frequently exhibits color field/geometric, impressionism and realism.
TERMS Artwork is accepted on consignment (50% commission). Gallery provides insurance, promotion. Requires exclusive representation locally. "No Western art."
SUBMISSIONS Call, e-mail or write to arrange personal interview to show portfolio. Send query letter with artist's statement, brochure, photocopies, résumé. Accepts digital images. Finds artists through word of mouth, submissions, art exhibits.

GALLERY 110 COLLECTIVE

110 Third Ave. S., Seattle WA 98104. (206)624-9336. **E-mail:** director@gallery110.com. **Website:** www.gallery110.com. **Contact:** Paula Maratea Fuld, director. Estab. 2002. "Gallery 110 presents contemporary art in a wide variety of media in Seattle's premiere gallery district, historic Pioneer Square. Our artists are emerging and established professionals, actively engaged in their artistic careers. We aspire to present

fresh exhibitions of the highest professional caliber. The exhibitions change monthly and consist of solo, group and/or thematic shows." Open Wednesday-Saturday, 12-5; hosts receptions every first Thursday of the month, 6-8. Overall price range: $125-3,000; most work sold at $500-800.

SUBMISSIONS "Please follow directions on our website if you are interested in becoming an artist member. New members considered on a space available basis. Some membership duties apply."

TIPS "We want to know that the artist has researched us. We want to see original and creative works that shows the artist is aware of both contemporary art and art history. We seek artists who intend to actively contribute and participate as a gallery member."

GALLERY 218

207 E. Buffalo St., Suite 218, Milwaukee WI 53202. (414)643-1732. **E-mail:** director@gallery218.com. **Website:** www.gallery218.com. **Contact:** Judith Hooks, president/director. Estab. 1990. Nonprofit gallery, cooperative gallery, alternative space. "Gallery 218 is committed to providing exhibition opportunities to area artists. 218 sponsors exhibits, poetry readings, performances, recitals and other cultural events. 'The audience is the juror.'" Represents emerging, mid-career and established artists/year. Exhibited artists include Judith Hooks, Bernie Newman, Jared Plock, Daniel Fleming, Kathryn Kmet, Jean Marc Richel. Sponsors 12 shows a year. Average display time 1 month. Open all year; Thursday–Friday, 12-5; Saturday. Located just south of downtown; 1,500 sq. ft.; warehouse-type space, wooden floor, halogen lights; includes information area. 100% of space for gallery artists. 75% private collectors, 25% corporate collectors. Overall price range $200-5,000; most work sold at $200-600.

◯ Gallery 218 has a "brick-and-mortar" gallery as well as a great website, which provides lots of links to helpful art resources.

MEDIA Considers all media except crafts. Considers linocuts, monotypes, woodcuts, mezzotints, etchings, lithographs and serigraphs. Most frequently exhibits paintings/acrylic, photography, mixed media.

STYLE Exhibits expressionism, conceptualism, photorealism, neo-expressionism, minimalism, hard-edge geometric abstraction, painterly abstraction, postmodern works, realism, and surrealism. Prefers abrtract expressionism, fine art photography, personal visions.

TERMS There is a yearly co-op membership fee plus a monthly fee, and donation of time (25% commission.) Membership good for 1 year. There is a rental fee for space; covers 1 month. Group shows at least 8 times a year (small entry fee). Retail price set by the artist. Gallery provides promotion; artist pays for shipping. Prefers artwork framed.

SUBMISSIONS Prefers only adults (21 years plus), no students (grad students OK), serious artists pursuing their careers. E-mail query letter with résumé, business card, slides, photographs, bio, SASE or request for application with SASE. E-mail for appointment to show portfolio of photographs, slides, résumé, bio. Responds in 1 month. Files all. Finds artists through referrals, visiting art fairs, submissions. "We advertise for new members on a regular basis."

TIPS "Don't wait to be 'discovered.' Get your work out there not just once, but over and over again. Don't get distracted by material things, like houses, cars and real jobs. Be prepared to accept suggestions and/or criticism. Read entry forms carefully."

GALLERY 400

University of Illinois, Chicago, 400 S. Peoria St. (MC 034), Chicago IL 60607. (312)996-6114. **Fax:** (312)355-3444. **Website:** gallery400.uic.edu. **Contact:** Lorelei Stewart, director. Estab. 1983. Nonprofit gallery. Approached by 500 artists/year; exhibits 80 artists. Sponsors 8 exhibits/year. Average display time: 6 weeks. Open Tuesday–Friday, 10-6; Saturday, 12-6. Clients include local community, students, tourists and upscale.

MEDIA Considers drawing, installation, painting, photography, design, architecture, mixed media and sculpture.

STYLE Exhibits conceptualism, minimalism and postmodernism. Most frequently exhibits contemporary conceptually based artwork.

TERMS Gallery provides insurance and promotion.

SUBMISSIONS Interact, propose an exhibition. Check info section of website for guidelines (gallery400.uic.edu/interact-page/propose-an-exhibition--2). Responds in 4 months. Finds artists through word of mouth, art exhibits, referrals by other artists.

TIPS "Follow the proposal guidelines on the website. We do not respond to e-mail submissions that do not follow the guidelines."

GALLERY 825

Los Angeles Art Association, 825 N. La Cienega Blvd., Los Angeles CA 90069. (310)652-8272. **E-mail:** peter@laaa.org. **Website:** www.laaa.org. **Contact:** Peter Mays, executive director. Estab. 1925. Holds approximately 1 exhibition/month. Average display time 4-5 weeks. Fine art only. Exhibits all media.

MEDIA Considers all media and original handpulled prints. "Fine art only. No crafts." Most frequently exhibits mixed media, oil/acrylic and watercolor.

STYLE Exhibits all styles.

TERMS Retail price set by artist. Gallery provides promotion.

SUBMISSIONS Submit 2 pieces created during the last 3 years, 3 8×10 digital printouts of additional artwork, artist statement, membership application (available online) and nonrefundable $35 application fee. See website for more details. Membership screenings are held 3 times a year, at the beginning and middle of each calendar year. Dates will be posted 3 months prior to screening. If accepted there is a $250 annual member fee.

TIPS "Bring work produced in the last 3 years. No commercial work (e.g., portraits/advertisements)."

GALLERY 1988

Gallery 1988 (West), 7308 Melrose Ave., Los Angeles CA 90046. (323)937-7088. **E-mail:** gallery1988west@gmail.com; gallery1988east@gmail.com. **Website:** www.gallery1988.com. Estab. 2004. Exhibits emerging artists. Approached by 300 artists/year; represents or exhibits 100 artists. Sponsors 15 exhibits/year. Average display time: 3 weeks. Open Wednesday-Sunday, 11-6; closed Monday, Tuesday, and national holidays. Located in the heart of Hollywood; 1,250 sq. ft. with 20-ft.-high walls. Clients include local community, students, upscale. Overall price range: $75-15,000; most work sold at $750.

○ Second location: Gallery 1988 (East) 7021 Melrose Ave., Los Angeles, CA 90038.

MEDIA Considers acrylic, drawing, oil, paper, pen & ink. Most frequently exhibits acrylic, oil, pen & ink. Types of prints include limited edition giclées and limited edition screenprints.

STYLE Exhibits surrealism and illustrative work. Prefers character-based works.

TERMS Artwork is accepted on consignment. Retail price set by both the artist and gallery. Gallery provides insurance, promotion, contract. Accepted work should be framed.

SUBMISSIONS "If you are interested in submitting your work for review, please send an e-mail with 'submission' in the subject line. You can include a website link or several JPEGs of your work. Also include medium, dimensions and retail prices. If we feel your work would be a good fit for a future show at the gallery, we will contact you. Unfortunately, we cannot respond to all submissions due to the high volume we receive."

TIPS "Keep your e-mail professional and include prices. Stay away from trying to be funny, which you'd be surprised to know happens a *lot*. We are most interested in the art."

☉ THE GALLERY AT PETERS VALLEY SCHOOL OF CRAFT

19 Kuhn Rd., Layton NJ 07851. (973)948-5202. **Fax:** (973)948-0011. **E-mail:** gallery@petersvalley.org. **Website:** www.petersvalley.org. **Contact:** Brienne Rosner, gallery manager. Estab. 1977. "National Delaware Water Gap Recreation Area in the Historic Village of Bevans, Peters Valley School of Craft hosts a large variety of workshops in the spring and summer. The Gallery is located in an old general store; first floor retail space and second floor rotating exhibition gallery."

TERMS E-mail query with link to website and JPEG samples.

GALLERY FIFTY SIX

2231 Central Ave., Memphis TN 38104. (901)276-1251. **E-mail:** rollin@galleryfiftysix.com. **Website:** www.galleryfiftysix.com. Blog: www.galleryfiftysix.blogspot.com. **Contact:** Rollin Kocsis, director. Estab. 2008. For-profit gallery. Approached by 35 artists/year; represents or exhibits 24 emerging, mid-career and established artists. Exhibited artists include John Armistead (oil on canvas), Bryan Blankenship (painting and ceramics), Terry Kenney and Joseph Morzuch (painting). Sponsors 12 exhibits/year. Model and property release are preferred. Average display time: 1 month. Open Monday-Saturday, 10-5. Contains 1 large room with 1 level. Clients include local community, students, tourists and upscale. Overall price range: $200-3,000. Most work sold at $750.

MEDIA Considers acrylic, ceramics, collage, drawing, fiber, glass, mixed media, oil, pastel, pen & ink, sculpture, watercolor. Most frequently exhibits oil on canvas, acrylic on canvas, assemblages. Considers engravings, etchings, linocuts, serigraphs, woodcuts.

STYLE Considers color field, expressionism, geometric abstraction, imagism, impressionism, pattern painting, postmodernism, primitivism realism, surrealism, painterly abstraction. Most frequently exhibits realism, abstract, expressionism. Considers all genres. No nudes.

TERMS Artwork is accepted on consignment and there is a 50% commission. Gallery provides promotion and contract. Accepted work should be gallery wrapped or frames with black or natural wood finish. Requires exclusive representation locally.

SUBMISSIONS E-mail 8-12 JPEGs. Write to arrange personal interview to show portfolio of photographs, e-mail JPEG samples at 72 dpi or send query letter with artist's statement, bio, brochure, business card, photographs, résumé, reviews and SASE. Material returned with SASE. Responds in 2 weeks. Files JPEGs, CDs, photos. Finds artists through word of mouth, submissions, portfolio reviews, art exhibits and referrals by other artists.

TIPS "Send good quality photos, by e-mail, with all important information included. Not interested in installations or subject matter that is offensive, political, sexual or religious."

GALLERY JOE

302 Arch St., Philadelphia PA 19106. (215)592-7752. **Fax:** (215)238-6923. **E-mail:** mail@galleryjoe.com. **Website:** galleryjoe.com. Retail and commercial exhibition gallery. Represents/exhibits 15-20 emerging, mid-career and established artists. Exhibited artists include Astrid Bowlby and Rob Matthews. Sponsors 6 shows/year. Average display time: 6 weeks. Open Wednesday–Saturday, 12-5:30; or by appointment. Located in Old City; 1,400 sq. ft. 100% of space for gallery artists. 80% private collectors, 20% corporate collectors. Overall price range: $1,000-25,000; most work sold at $2,000-10,000.

MEDIA Only exhibits sculpture and drawing.

STYLE Exhibits representational/abstract.

TERMS Artwork is accepted on consignment (50% commission). Retail price set by the gallery and the artist. Gallery provides insurance and promotion. Artist pays for shipping costs. Prefers artwork framed.

SUBMISSIONS Send query letter with résumé, slides, reviews and SASE. Responds within 6 months. Finds

artists by visiting galleries and through referrals. Not currently reviewing portfolios.

GALLERY M

180 Cook St., Suite 101, Denver CO 80206. (303)331-8400. **Website:** www.gallerym.com. Estab. 1996. For-profit gallery. "Gallery M brings to Denver contemporary fine art, photography, sculpture and new media that is the quality and diversity found in New York, Los Angeles, San Francisco and Europe. Features the work of more than 30 national and international artists." Average display time: 6-12 weeks. Open Monday–Saturday, 10-6. Overall price range: $1,000-75,000.

MEDIA Considers acrylic, collage, drawing, glass, installation, mixed media, oil, paper, pastel, pen & ink, watercolor, engravings, etchings, linocuts, lithographs, mezzotints, serigraphs, woodcuts, photography and sculpture.

STYLE Exhibits color field, expressionism, geometric abstraction, neo-expressionism, postmodernism, primitivism, realism and surrealism. Considers all genres.

TERMS Retail price set by the gallery and the artist. Gallery provides insurance and promotion. Requires exclusive local and regional representation.

SUBMISSIONS "Artists interested in showing at the gallery should visit the Artist Submissions section of our website (under Site Resources). The gallery provides additional services for both collectors and artists, including our quarterly newsletter, *The Art Quarterly*."

ⓦ GALLERY NAGA

67 Newbury St., Boston MA 02116. (617)267-9060. **Fax:** (617)267-9040. **E-mail:** mail@gallerynaga.com. **Website:** www.gallerynaga.com. Estab. 1977. Retail gallery. "Our primary focus is painting and we represent many of the most highly regarded painters working in Boston and New England. In addition, exceptional contemporary photographers, printmakers, and sculptors exhibit with us." Represents 30 emerging, mid-career and established artists. Sponsors 9 shows/year. Average display time: 1 month. Open Tuesday–Saturday, 10-5 (September-June). Located in the neo-Gothic church building (Church of the Covenant) at the corner of Berkeley and Newbury Streets. Clientele: 90% private collectors, 10% corporate collectors. Overall price range: $500-60,000; most work sold at $2,000-10,000.

MEDIA Considers oil, acrylic, mixed media, photography, studio furniture. Most frequently exhibits painting and furniture.

STYLE Exhibits expressionism, painterly abstraction, postmodern works and realism. Genres include landscapes, portraits and figurative work. Prefers expressionism, painterly abstraction and realism.

TERMS Accepts work on consignment (50% commission). Retail price set by gallery and artist. Gallery provides insurance and promotion; artist pays for shipping. Prefers artwork framed.

SUBMISSIONS "We review unsolicited material 3 times a year on a rolling schedule. We accept a maximum of 20 images (slide, hard copy, MAC-formatted JPEG), a bio and, if applicable, a SASE. If you would like to e-mail JPEGs of 3 images (include the works' sizes and materials), we'll quickly suggest whether or not we think a complete presentation is warranted."

TIPS "We focus on Boston and New England artists. We exhibit the most significant studio furniture makers in the country. Become familiar with any gallery to see if your work is appropriate before you make contact."

GALLERY NORTH

90 N. Country Rd., Setauket NY 11733. (631)751-2676. **E-mail:** info@gallerynorth.org. **Website:** www.gallerynorth.org. **Contact:** Judith Levy, director. Regional arts center. "Our mission is to present exhibitions of exceptional contemporary artists and artisans, especially those from Long Island and the nearby regions; to assist and encourage artists by bringing their work to the attention of the public; and to stimulate interest in the arts by presenting innovative educational programs. Exhibits the work of emerging, mid-career and established artists from Long Island and throughout the Northeast. The Gallery North community involves regional and local artists, collectors, art dealers, corporate sponsors, art consultants, businesses and schools, ranging from local elementary students to the faculty and staff at Long Island's many colleges and universities including our neighbor, Stony Brook University and the Stony Brook Medical Center. With our proximity to New York City and the East End, our region attracts a wealth of talent and interest in the arts." Located in the Historic District of Setauket, Long Island, NY, in an 1840s farm house, 1 mile from the State University at Stony Brook. Open

year-round; Tuesday–Saturday, 10-5; Sunday, 12-5; closed Monday.

STYLE "Works to be exhibited are selected by our director, Judith Levy, with input from our Artist Advisory Board. We encourage artist dialogue and participation in gallery events and community activities and many artists associated with our gallery offer ArTrips and ArTalks, as well as teaching in our education programs. Along with monthly exhibitions in our 1,000-sq.-ft. space, our Gallery Shop strives to present the finest handmade jewelry and craft by local and nationally recognized artisans."

SUBMISSIONS To present work to the gallery, send an e-mail with 2-5 medium-sized images, price list (indicating title, size, medium, and date), artist's statement, biography and link to website. "We encourage artists to visit the gallery and interact with our exhibitions." Visit the website for more information.

THE FANNY GARVER GALLERY

230 State St., Madison WI 53703. (608)256-6755. **E-mail:** art@fannygarvergallery.com. **Website:** www.fannygarvergallery.com. Estab. 1972. Retail gallery. "Whether your taste is traditional or contemporary, there's something for everyone. Every month we feature a show of new artwork. One month it might be an invitational art glass show, the next it may be a watercolor show." Represents 100 emerging, mid-career and established artists/year. Exhibited artists include Lee Weiss, Jaline Pol. Sponsors 11 shows/year. Average display time: 1 month. Open Monday–Saturday, 10-5; or by appointment. Located downtown; 3,000 sq. ft.; older refurbished building in unique downtown setting. 33% of space for special exhibitions; 95% of space for gallery artists. Clientele: private collectors, gift-givers, tourists. 40% private collectors, 10% corporate collectors. Overall price range: $100-10,000; most work sold at $100-1,000.

MEDIA Considers oil, pen & ink, paper, fiber, acrylic, drawing, sculpture, glass, watercolor, mixed media, ceramics, pastel, collage, craft, woodcuts, wood engravings, linocuts, engravings, mezzotints, etchings, lithographs and serigraphs. Most frequently exhibits watercolor, oil and glass.

STYLE Exhibits all styles. Prefers landscapes, still lifes and abstraction.

TERMS Accepts work on consignment (50% commission) or buys outright for 50% of retail price (net 30 days). Retail price set by gallery. Gallery provides promotion and contract, artist pays shipping costs both ways. Prefers artwork framed.

SUBMISSIONS Send query letter with résumé, 8 photographs, bio, brochure, photographs and SASE. Write for appointment to show portfolio, which should include originals, photographs and slides. Responds within 1 month, only if interested. Files announcements and brochures.

TIPS "Don't take it personally if your work is not accepted in a gallery. Not all work is suitable for all venues. Send us an e-mail and we'll be happy to put you on our mailing list."

DAVID GARY LTD. FINE ART

277 Main St., Millburn NJ 07041. (973)467-9240. E-mail: davidgaryfineart@aol.com. **Website:** www.davidgaryfineart.com. Estab. 1971. Retail and wholesale gallery. Represents 17-20 mid-career and established artists. Exhibited artists include John Talbot and Theo Raucher. Sponsors 3 shows/year. Average display time: 3 weeks. Open all year. Located in the suburbs; 2,000 sq. ft.; high ceilings with sky lights. Clients include "upper income." 70% of sales are to private collectors, 30% corporate collectors. Overall price range: $250-25,000; most work sold at $1,000-15,000.

MEDIA Considers oil, acrylic, watercolor, drawings, sculpture, pastel, woodcuts, engravings, lithographs, wood engravings, mezzotints, linocuts, etchings and serigraphs. Most frequently exhibits oil, original graphics and sculpture.

STYLE Exhibits primitivism, painterly abstraction, surrealism, impressionism, realism and collage. All genres. Prefers impressionism, painterly abstraction and realism.

TERMS Accepts artwork on consignment (50% commission). Retail price set by gallery and artist. Gallery services vary; artist pays for shipping. Prefers artwork unframed.

SUBMISSIONS Send query letter with résumé, photographs and reviews. Call for appointment to show portfolio of originals, photographs and transparencies. Responds in 2 weeks. Files "what is interesting to gallery."

TIPS "Have a basic knowledge of how a gallery works, and understand that the gallery is a business."

SANDRA GERING, INC.

14 E. 64th St., New York NY 10065. (646)336-7183. E-mail: info@geringlopez.com; laura@geringlopez.com. **Website:** www.geringlopez.com. **Contact:** Laura Bloom, director. Estab. 1991. For-profit gallery. Exhibits emerging, mid-career and established artists. Gallery open Tuesday–Friday, 10-6; Saturday, 11-5. Located in the historic Crown Building.

MEDIA Considers mixed media, oil, sculpture and digital. Most frequently exhibits computer-based work, electric (light) sculpture and video/DVD.

STYLE Exhibits geometric abstraction. Most frequently exhibits cutting edge.

TERMS Artwork is accepted on consignment.

SUBMISSIONS Send e-mail query with link to website and JPEGs. Cannot return material. Responds within 6 months, only if interested. Finds artists through word of mouth, art fairs/exhibits, and referrals by other artists.

GIACOBBE-FRITZ FINE ART

702 Canyon Rd., Santa Fe NM 87501. (505)986-1156. **Fax:** (505)986-1158. **E-mail:** art@giacobbefritz.com. **Website:** www.giacobbefritz.com. **Contact:** Deborah Fritz, art consultant. Estab. 2000. For-profit gallery. Approached by 300+ artists/year. Represents 16 emerging, mid-career and established artists. Exhibits paintings, sculpture and graphics by outstanding emerging and established artists. Sponsors 12-20 exhibits/year. Average display time: 2 weeks. Open all year; Monday-Sunday, 10-5. Located on historic Canyon Road, Santa Fe's famous street of galleries. Classic 1890 adobe with 5 exhibit rooms. Clients include local community, tourists and upscale.

MEDIA Considers acrylic, collage, mixed media, oil, pastel, sculpture, watercolor and etchings. Prints include etchings and mezzotints. Most frequently exhibits oil, sculpture and acrylic.

STYLE Exhibits impressionism, abstract and realism. Considers all styles including expressionism, impressionism, surrealism and patinerly abstraction. Genres include figurative work, landscapes and figures.

TERMS Artwork is accepted on consignment and there is a 50% commission. Retail price set by the gallery. Gallery provides insurance, promotion and contract. Accepted work should be framed. Requires exclusive representation locally. No agents.

SUBMISSIONS Call, write, or e-mail to arrange a personal interview to show portfolio of photographs, transparencies and slides. Prefers to receive e-mailed portfolios. Send query letter with artist's statement, bio, photocopies, photographs, SASE, slides and CD. Returns material with SASE only. Responds to queries in 2 weeks. Finds artists through art fairs, art exhibits, portfolio reviews, referrals by other artists, submissions, word of mouth.

TIPS "Enclose SASE, brief query letter, and a few samples of your best work."

GLOUCESTER ARTS ON MAIN

6580-B Main St., Gloucester VA 23061. (804)824-9464. **Fax:** (804)824-9469. **E-mail:** curator@gloucesterarts.org. **Website:** www.gloucesterarts.org. **Contact:** Kay Van Dyke, curator. Estab. 2010. Nonprofit, rental gallery. Alternative space. Exhibits emerging, mid-career and established artists. Approached by 15 artists/year; represents or exhibits 60 artists currently. Exhibited artists include Harriett McGee (repoussee and mixed media) and Victoria Watson (animal drawings). Sponsors 12 exhibits/year, 1-2 photography exhibits/year. There are always photos on exhibit. Average display is one month or length of rental contract. Open Tuesday-Saturday, 12-6; weekend events, 6-9. Located on walkable Main Street near restaurants and other shops, small town near major cities in Eastern Virginia. Very flexible gallery space with 120+ ft. of perimeter exhibition space and 96 ft. of movable walls. 4,000 sq. ft. total exhibition space. Clients include the local community, students, tourists and upscale clients. 10% of sales are to corporate collectors. Price range: $20-7,500. Most work sold at $300.

MEDIA Considers all media. Most frequently exhibits paintings (oil, acrylic and watercolor), 2D and 3D metal work, and photography. Considers all types of prints except posters.

STYLE Considers all styles. Most frequently exhibits painterly abstraction, impressionism and realism. Considers all genres.

TERMS Artwork is accepted on consignment and there is a 30% commission with a rental fee for wall or shelf space. The fee covers 6 months and there is a 30% commission. Retail price set by the artist. Gallery provides promotion and contract. Accepted work should be framed, matted and mounted. Prefers to represent artists from Eastern Virginia.

SUBMISSIONS E-mail query letter with link to artist's website, JPEG samples at 72 dpi, résumé, artist's statement and bio; or call for appointment to show portfolio. Jury system responds within 2 weeks. Finds artists through word of mouth, art exhibits, submissions, portfolio reviews and referrals by other artists.

TIPS Work should be presented for jury ready to exhibit, i.e., framed or mounted appropriately. Digital images presented for review should be clear, cropped and professional in appearance at high resolution.

GOLD/SMITH GALLERY

8 McKown St., Boothbay Harbor ME 04538. (207)633-6252. **E-mail:** vandor_art@myfairpoint.net. **Website:** goldsmithgallery.net. Estab. 1974. Retail gallery. Represents 30 emerging, mid-career and established artists. Exhibited artists include John Vander and John Wissemann. Sponsors 6 shows/year. Average display time: 6 weeks. Open May-October; Monday-Saturday, 10-5. Located downtown across from the harbor. 1,500 sq. ft.; traditional 19th century house converted to contemporary gallery. 75% of space for special exhibitions; 25% of space for gallery artists. Clientele residents and visitors. 90% private collectors, 10% corporate collectors. Overall price range: $350-5,000; most work sold at $1,000-2,500.

◯ One of 2 Gold/Smith Galleries. The other is in Sugar Loaf; the 2 are not affiliated with each other. Artists creating traditional and representational work should try another gallery. The work shown here is strong, self-assured and abstract.

MEDIA Considers oil, acrylic, watercolor, pastel, pen & ink, drawing, mixed media, collage, paper, sculpture, photography, woodcuts, engravings, wood engravings and etchings. Most frequently exhibits acrylic and watercolor.

STYLE Exhibits expressionism, painterly abstraction "emphasis on nontraditional work." Prefers expressionist and abstract landscape.

TERMS Commission 50%. Retail price set by the artist. Gallery provides insurance and promotion; artist pays shipping costs to and from gallery. Prefers artwork framed.

SUBMISSIONS No restrictions—emphasis on artists from Maine. Send query letter with slides, bio, photographs, SASE, reviews and retail price. Write for appointment to show portfolio of originals. Responds in 2 weeks. Artist should write the gallery.

TIPS "Present a consistent body of mature work. We need 12 to 20 works of moderate size. The sureness of the hand and the maturity interest of the vision are most important."

GRAND RAPIDS ART MUSEUM

101 Monroe Center St. NW, Grand Rapids MI 49503. (616)831-1000. **E-mail:** rplatt@artmuseumgr.org. **Website:** www.artmuseumgr.org. Estab. 1910. Exhibits established artists. Sponsors 3 exhibits/year. Average display time 4 months. Open all year; Tuesday-Thursday, 10-5; Friday, 10-9; Sunday, 12-5. Closed Mondays and major holidays. Located in the heart of downtown Grand Rapids, the Grand Rapids Art Museum presents exhibitions of national caliber and regional distinction. The museum collection spans Renaissance to modern art, with particular strength in 19th- and 20th-century paintings, prints and drawings. Clients include local community, students, tourists.

MEDIA Considers all media and all types of prints. Most frequently exhibits paintings, prints and drawings.

STYLE Considers all styles and genres. Most frequently exhibits impressionist, modern and Renaissance.

THE GRAPHIC EYE GALLERY OF LONG ISLAND

402 Main St., Port Washington NY 11050. (516)883-9668. **Website:** www.graphiceyegallery.com. Estab. 1974. Represents 25 artists. Sponsors solo, 2-3 person and 4 group shows/year. Average display time: 1 month. Interested in emerging and established artists. Overall price range: $35-7,500; most artwork sold at $500-800. Open Thursday-Sunday, 12-5.

MEDIA Considers mixed media, collage, works on paper, pastels, photography, paint on paper, woodcuts, wood engravings, linocuts, engravings, mezzotints, etchings, lithographs, serigraphs, and monoprints.

STYLE Exhibits impressionism, expressionism, realism, primitivism and painterly abstraction. Considers all genres.

TERMS Co-op membership fee plus donation of time. Retail price set by artist. Offers payment by installments. Exclusive area representation not required. Prefers framed artwork.

SUBMISSIONS Send query letter with résumé, SASE, slides and bio. Portfolio should include originals and slides. "When submitting a portfolio, the artist should have a body of work, not a 'little of this, little of that.' Finds artists through visiting exhibitions, word of mouth, artist's submissions and self-promotions.

TIPS "Artists must produce their *own* work and be actively involved. We have a competitive juried art exhibit annually. Open to all artists who work on paper."

ⓖ GREENHUT GALLERIES

146 Middle St., Portland ME 04101. (207)772-2693; (888)772-2693. **E-mail:** greenhut@maine.com. **Website:** www.greenhutgalleries.com. **Contact:** Peggy Greenhut Golden, owner. Estab. 1977. Retail gallery. Represents/exhibits 20 emerging and mid-career artists/year. Sponsors 12 shows/year. Exhibited artists include Connie Hayes (oil/canvas), Sarah Knock (oil/canvas). Average display time: 3 weeks. Open all year; Monday–Friday, 10-5:30; Saturday, 10-5. Located in downtown, Old Port; 3,000 sq. ft. with neon accents in interior space. 60% of space for special exhibitions. Clientele tourists and upscale. 55% private collectors, 10% corporate collectors. Overall price range: $500-12,000; most work sold at $600-3,000.

MEDIA Considers acrylic, paper, pastel, sculpture, drawing, oil, watercolor. Most frequently exhibits oil, watercolor, pastel.

STYLE Considers all styles; etchings, lithographs, mezzotints. Genres include figurative work, landscapes, still life, seascape. Prefers landscape, seascape and abstract.

TERMS Artwork is accepted on consignment (50% commission). Retail price set by the gallery and artist. Gallery provides insurance and promotion. Artists pays for shipping costs. Prefers artwork framed (museum quality framing).

SUBMISSIONS Accepts only artists from Maine or New England area with Maine connection. Send query letter with slides, reviews, bio and SASE. Call for appointment to show portfolio of slides. Responds in 1 month. Finds artists through word of mouth, referrals by other artists, visiting art shows and exhibitions, and submissions.

TIPS "Visit the gallery and see if you feel your work fits in."

GREMILLION & CO. FINE ART, INC.

2501 Sunset Blvd., Houston TX 77005. (713)522-2701. **Fax:** (713)522-3712. **E-mail:** fineart@gremillion.com. **Website:** www.gremillion.com. Estab. 1980. Retail gallery. Represents more than 80 mid-career and established artists. May be interested in seeing the work of emerging artists in the future. Exhibited artists include John Pavlicek and Robert Rector. Sponsors 12 shows/year. Average display time: 4-6 weeks. Open

Tuesday–Saturday, 10-5; and by appointment. Located in "West University" area; 12,000 sq. ft. 50% of space for special exhibitions. 60% private collectors; 40% corporate collectors. Overall price range: $500-300,000; most work sold at $3,000-10,000.

○ Additional gallery located in Dallas. See website for more information.

MEDIA Considers oil, acrylic, watercolor, pastel, pen & ink, drawing, mixed media, collage, works on paper, sculpture, original handpulled prints, woodcuts, engravings, lithographs, wood engravings, mezzotints, linocuts, etchings and serigraphs.

STYLE Exhibits painterly abstraction, minimalism, color field and realism. Genres include landscapes and figurative work. Prefers abstraction, realism and color field.

TERMS Accepts artwork on consignment (varying commission). Retail price set by the gallery and artist. Gallery provides insurance and promotion; shipping costs are shared. Prefers artwork unframed.

SUBMISSIONS Call for appointment to show portfolio of slides, photographs and transparencies. Responds only if interested within 3 weeks. Finds artists through submissions and word of mouth.

CARRIE HADDAD GALLERY

622 Warren St., Hudson NY 12534. (518)828-1915. **Fax:** (518)828-3341. **E-mail:** carrie.haddad@carriehaddadgallery.com. **Website:** www.carriehaddadgallery.com. **Contact:** Carrie Haddad, owner. Estab. 1990. Art consultancy, for-profit gallery. Hailed as the premier gallery of the Hudson Valley, the Carrie Haddad Gallery presents 8 large exhibits/year and includes all types of painting, both large and small sculpture, works on paper and a variety of techniques in photography." Approached by 50 artists/year; represents or exhibits 60 artists. Open daily, 11-5; closed Wednesday.

MEDIA Considered: paintings, work on paper, no posters or reproductions.

STYLE Exhibits expressionism, impressionism and postmodernism. Genres include figurative work, landscapes and abstract.

TERMS Artwork is accepted on consignment and there is a 50% commission. Retail price set by the artist. Gallery provides insurance and promotion. Requires exclusive representation locally.

SUBMISSIONS The gallery is not looking to add new artists to the gallery, but artists may submit websites or CDs of their work by sending the information to the gallery.

JUDITH HALE GALLERY

1693 Copenhagen Dr., Solvang CA 93463. (805)688-1222. **E-mail:** info@judithhalegallery.com. **Website:** www.judithhalegallery.com. **Contact:** Judith Hale, owner. Estab. 1987. Retail gallery. Represents 70 mid-career and established artists. Exhibited artists include Dirk Foslien, Howard Carr, Kelly Donovan and Mehl Lawson. Sponsors 4 shows/year. Average display time: 6 months. Open daily 10-6. Located downtown; 2,100 sq. ft.; "the gallery is eclectic and inviting, an old building with 6 rooms." 20% of space for special exhibitions which are regularly rotated and rehung. Clientele: homeowners, tourists, decorators, collectors. Overall price range: $500-15,000; most work sold at $500-5,000.

○ Representing nationally recognized artists, including Ted Goerschner, Marilyn Simandle, Dave DeMatteo, Dick Heichberger, this old building once housed the blacksmith's shop.

MEDIA Considers oil, acrylic, watercolor, pastel, sculpture, engravings and etchings. Most frequently exhibits watercolor, oil, acrylic and sculpture.

STYLE Exhibits impressionism and realism. Genres include landscapes, florals, western and figurative work. Prefers figurative work, western, florals, landscapes, structure. No abstract or expressionistic.

TERMS Accepts work on consignment (40% commission). Retail price set by artist. Offers payment by installments. Gallery arranges reception and promotion; artist pays for shipping. Prefers artwork framed.

SUBMISSIONS "Call ahead, or e-mail a link to your website, or a couple of representative images. This saves the mailing of slides, etc., and I don't have to return them. Send query letter with 10-12 slides, bio, brochure, photographs, business card and reviews. Call for an appointment to show portfolio of photographs. Responds in 2 weeks. Files bio, brochure and business card."

TIPS "Create a nice portfolio. See if your work is comparable to what the gallery exhibits. Do not plan your visit when a show is on; make an appointment for a future time. I like genuine people who present quality work with fair pricing. Rotate artwork in a reasonable time, if unsold. Bring in your best work, not the 'seconds' after the show circuit."

HALLWALLS CONTEMPORARY ARTS CENTER

341 Delaware Ave., Buffalo NY 14202. (716)854-1694. **Fax:** (716)854-1696. **E-mail:** john@hallwalls.org; carolyn@hallwalls.org. **Website:** www.hallwalls.org. **Contact:** John Massier, visual arts curator; Carolyn Tennant, media arts director. Estab. 1974. Nonprofit multimedia organization. "Our mission is to bring the newest and most challenging work in the contemporary arts to the interested public, whether in painting and sculpture, conceptual art, experimental film, video art and activism, documentary film, performance, fiction, jazz, new music, or any number of other art forms that make up our eclectic programming mix." Sponsors 10 exhibits/year. Average display time: 6 weeks. Open Tuesday–Friday, 11-6; Saturday, 11-2.

MEDIA Considers all media including film, video, sound, multimedia, and web-based work.

STYLE Exhibits all styles and genres. "Contemporary cutting edge work which challenges traditional cultural and aesthetic boundaries."

TERMS Retail price set by artist. "Sales are not our focus. If a work does sell, we suggest a donation of 15% of the purchase price." Gallery provides insurance.

SUBMISSIONS Send material by mail for consideration. Work not returned within 3 months will be kept for up to a year for further review.

HAMPTON III GALLERY, LTD.

3110 Wade Hampton Blvd., Taylors SC 29687. (864)268-2771. **E-mail:** sandy@hamptoniiigallery. com. **Website:** www.hamptoniiigallery.com. **Contact:** Sandra Rupp, director. Estab. 1970. Approached by 20 artists/year; exhibits 25 mid-career and established artists/year. Exhibited artists include Carl Blair (oil paintings) and Darell Koons (acrylic paintings). Sponsors 8 exhibits/year. Artists are chosen by director and shows are produced for artists who are part of the gallery roster. Average display time: 4-6 weeks. Open all year: Tuesday–Friday, 1-5; Saturday 10-5. Located 3 miles outside of downtown Greenville SC; 1 large exhibition room in center with 7 exhibition rooms around center gallery. Clients include local community and upscale. 5% of sales are to corporate collectors. Overall price range: $200-15,000; most work sold at $2,500.

MEDIA Considers acrylic, ceramics, collage, drawing, mixed media, oil, paper, pastel, pen & ink, sculpture and watercolor. Most frequently exhibits oil and watercolor. Also considers engravings, etchings, linocuts, lithographs, mezzotints, serigraphs and woodcuts.

STYLE Exhibits color field, expressionism, geometric abstraction, imagism, impressionism and painterly abstraction. Most frequently exhibits painterly abstraction and realism. Considers all genres.

TERMS Artwork is accepted on consignment (40% commission). Retail price of the art set by the artist. Gallery provides insurance, promotion and contract. Accepted work should be framed. Requires exclusive representation locally.

SUBMISSIONS Send query letter with artist's statement, bio, reviews, SASE and slides. Returns material with SASE. Responds to queries in 3 months. Finds artists through art exhibits, referrals by other artists and word of mouth.

HAMPTON UNIVERSITY MUSEUM

Hampton University, 100 E. Queen St., Hampton VA 23668. (757)727-5308. **Fax:** (757)727-5170. **E-mail:** museum@hamptonu.edu. **Website:** museum.hamptonu.edu. **Contact:** Dr. Vanessa Thaxton-Ward, curator of collections. Estab. 1868. Exhibits established artists. Exhibited artists include Elizabeth Catlett and Jacob Lawrence. Exhibits 2-3 changing exhibitions/year. Average display time: 12-18 weeks. Open Monday–Friday, 8-5; Saturday, 12-4; closed on Sunday, major and campus holidays. Located on the campus of Hampton University. Presents a bi-annual exhibition, *New Power Generation: A National Juried Exhibition* featuring contemporary art by people of African descent.

MEDIA Considers all media and all types of prints. Most frequently exhibits oil or acrylic paintings, ceramics and mixed media.

STYLE Permanent exhibits include African-American, African and Native American art.

SUBMISSIONS For more information about New Power Generation please forward your mailing address and e-mail to vanessa.thaxton-ward@hamptonu.edu.

◎ HANA COAST GALLERY

5031 Hana Hwy., Hana HI 96713. (808)248-8636. **Fax:** (808)248-7332. **E-mail:** info@hanacoast.com. **Website:** www.hanacoast.com. Estab. 1990. Retail gallery and art consultancy. Represents 78 established artists. Sponsors 12 group shows/year. Average display time: 1 month. Open 7 days a week, 9-5. Open all year. Located in the Hotel Hana-Maui at Hana Ranch; 3,000 sq. ft.; "an elegant ocean-view setting in one of the top small luxury resorts in the world." 20% of space for special exhibitions. Clientele ranges from very upscale to highway traffic walk-ins. 85% private collectors, 15% corporate collectors. Overall price range: $150-50,000; most work sold at $1,000-6,500.

MEDIA Considers oil, acrylic, watercolor, pastel, mixed media, collage, works on paper, sculpture, ceramic, craft, fiber, glass, photography, original handpulled prints, engravings, lithographs, pochoir, wood engravings, mezzotints, serigraphs and etchings. Most frequently exhibits oil, watercolor and original prints.

STYLE Exhibits expressionism, primitivism, impressionism and realism. Genres include landscapes, florals, portraits, figurative work and Hawaiiana. Prefers landscapes, florals and figurative work. "We also display decorative art and master-level craftwork, particularly turned-wood bowls, blown glass, fiber, bronze sculpture and studio furniture.

TERMS Accepts artwork on consignment (60% commission). Retail price set by gallery and artist. Gallery provides insurance, promotion and shipping costs from gallery. Framed artwork only.

SUBMISSIONS *Accepts only full-time Hawaii resident artists.* Send query letter with résumé, slides, bio, brochure, photographs, SASE and reviews. Write for appointment to show portfolio after query and samples submitted. Portfolio should include originals, photographs, slides and reviews. Responds only if interested within 1 week. If not accepted at time of submission, all materials will be returned.

TIPS "Know the quality and price level of artwork in our gallery and know that your own art would be companionable with what's being currently shown. Be able to substantiate the prices you ask for your work. We do not offer discounts, so the mutually agreed upon price/value must stand the test of the market."

JOEL AND LILA HARNETT MUSEUM OF ART AND PRINT STUDY CENTER

University of Richmond Museums, 28 Westhampton Way, Richmond VA 23173. (804)289-8276. **Fax:** (804)287-1894. **E-mail:** rwaller@richmond.edu; museums@richmond.edu. **Website:** museums.richmond.edu. **Contact:** Richard Waller, executive director. Estab. 1968. Represents emerging, mid-career and established artists. Sponsors 6 exhibitions/year. Average display time 6 weeks. Open academic year; with limited summer hours May-August. Located on university campus; 5,000 sq. ft. 100% of space for special exhibitions.

MEDIA Considers all media and all types of prints. Most frequently exhibits painting, sculpture, prints, photography and drawing.

STYLE Exhibits all styles and genres.

TERMS Work accepted on loan for duration of special exhibition. Retail price set by the artist. Museum provides insurance, promotion, contract and shipping costs. Prefers artwork framed.

SUBMISSIONS Send query letter with résumé, 8-12 images on CD, brochure, SASE, reviews and printed material if available. Write for appointment to show portfolio of "whatever is appropriate to understanding the artist's work." Responds in 1 month. Files résumé and other materials the artist does not want returned (printed material, CD, reviews, etc.).

JANE HASLEM GALLERY

2025 Hillyer Place NW, Washington DC 20009. (202)232-4644. **E-mail:** haslem@mac.com. **Website:** www.janehaslemgallery.com. Estab. 1960. For-profit gallery. Exhibits American artists, 4-5 exhibits per year. Gallery open Wednesday-Saturday, 12-5 and by appointment. Located at DuPont Circle across from Phillips Museum; 2 floors of 1886 building; 3,000 sq. ft. Clients include local community, students, upscale and collectors worldwide. Overall price range: $30-30,000; most work sold at $500-2,000.

MEDIA Art/graphic design exhibits prints and works on paper and paintings. Considers engravings, etchings, linocuts, lithographs, mezzotints, serigraphs, woodcuts and digital images.

STYLE Exhibits expressionism, geometric abstraction, neo-expressionism, pattern painting, painterly abstraction, postmodernism, surrealism. Most frequently exhibits abstraction, realism and geometric. Genres include figurative work, florals and landscapes.

TERMS Artwork is accepted on consignment and there is a 50% commission. Retail price set by the artist and the gallery. Gallery provides promotion and contract. Accepts only artists from the US. Prefers only prints, works on paper and paintings.

SUBMISSIONS Artists should contact via e-mail.

TIPS "100% of our sales are Internet generated. We prefer all submissions initially by e-mail."

◉ WILLIAM HAVU GALLERY

1040 Cherokee St., Denver CO 80204. (303)893-2360. **Fax:** (303)893-2813. **E-mail:** info@williamhavugallery.com. **Website:** www.williamhavugallery.com. **Contact:** Bill Havu, owner and director; Nick Ryan, gallery administrator. For-profit gallery. "Engaged in an ongoing dialogue through its 7 exhibitions a year with regionalism as it affects and is affected by both national and international trends in realism and abstraction. Strong emphasis on mid-career and established artists." Approached by 120 artists/year; represents or exhibits 50 artists. Sponsors 1 photography exhibit/year. Average display time 6-8 weeks. Open Tuesday–Friday, 10-6; Saturday, 11-5; 1st Friday of each month, 10-8; Sundays and Mondays by appointment. Closed Christmas and New Year's Day. Overall price range $250-15,000. Most work sold at $1,000-4,000.

MEDIA Considers acrylic, ceramics, collage, drawing, mixed media, oil, paper, pastel, pen & ink, sculpture and watercolor. Most frequently exhibits painting, prints. Considers etchings, linocuts, lithographs, mezzotints, woodcuts, monotypes, monoprints and silkscreens.

STYLE Exhibits expressionism, geometric abstraction, impressionism, minimalism, postmodernism, surrealism and painterly abstraction. Most frequently exhibits painterly abstraction and expressionism.

TERMS Artwork is accepted on consignment (50% commission). Retail price set by the gallery and the artist. Gallery provides insurance, promotion and contract. Accepted work should be framed. Primarily accepts only artists from Rocky Mountain/Southwestern region.

SUBMISSIONS "Please submit a representative sampling of your current body of work. We prefer to receive digital printouts, printed cards and invitations, or other easily reviewed formats. If you prefer, you may submit CDs, e-mail a link to your website or include these materials in an e-mail. Mailed materials will only be returned if you have provided an SASE. Please also include: A current résumé listing your contact information, education, exhibition history, collections, and awards. An artist statement. Any other supporting materials (reviews, articles, etc.). An SASE for the return of your materials. (If you do not provide an SASE, your materials will not be returned to you.) We ask that you please not contact the gallery regarding the status of your portfolio review. Portfo-lios are reviewed only periodically, so it may be many months before the gallery reviews your materials. If, after evaluating your materials, we have an interest, we will be in touch with you to discuss next steps."

TIPS "Always mail a portfolio packet. We do not accept walk-ins or phone calls to review work. Explore our website or visit gallery to make sure work would fit with the gallery's objective. Archival-quality materials play a major role in selling fine art to collectors. We only frame work with archival-quality materials and feel its inclusion in work can 'make' the sale."

◉ HAYLEY GALLERY

270 E. Main St., New Albany OH 43054. (614)855-4856. **E-mail:** hayley@hayleygallery.com. **Website:** hayleygallery.com. Matthew Sutherland, gallery manager. **Contact:** Hayley Deeter, owner. Estab. 2007. For-profit gallery. Exhibits emerging, mid-career, and established local Ohio artists. Approached by hundreds of artists a year; represents or exhibits 60 artists. Exhibited artists include Todd Buschur (painting) and Laurie Clements (painting). Sponsors 10 total exhibits/year. Average display time: depends on artist. Open Tuesday-Thursday, 12-8; Friday-Saturday, 1-9; closed Sunday-Monday (open Sundays in December only from 1-4). Always available by appointment at 614-580-3596. Clients include the local community, interior designers and upscale clients. 5% of sales are to corporate collectors. Overall price range: $75-5,000; most work sold at $1,000.

MEDIA Considers acrylic, jewelry, ceramics, fiber, glass, wood, mixed media, oil, paper, and sculpture. Does not consider photography.

TERMS Artwork is accepted on consignment with a 50% commission. Retail price set by the gallery and the artist. Gallery provides insurance, promotion, and contract. Accepted work should be wired, framed or gallery wrapped. Only accepts artists from Ohio.

SUBMISSIONS E-mail query letter with link to artists website or JPEG samples at 72 dpi to hayley@hayleygallery.com or mail disc, artist's statement, and bio for review. Does not return materials. Responds in 1 week. Finds artists through word of mouth, submissions, art exhibits, art fairs and referrals by other artists.

TIPS "Artists seen by appointment only."

◉ MARIA HENLE STUDIO

55 Company St., Christiansted, St. Croix 00820, Virgin Islands. (340)718-0372. **E-mail:** henletina@gmail.

com. **Website:** www.mariahenlestudio.com. Estab. 1993. For-profit gallery. Exhibits mid-career and established artists. Approached by 4 artists/year; represents or exhibits 7 artists. Sponsors 4 exhibits/year. Average display time: 1 month. Hours vary, call for details. Located in an 18th-century loft space in historical Danish West Indian town; 750 sq. ft. Clients include local community, tourists, upscale. 10% of sales are to corporate collectors. Overall price range: $600-6,000; most work sold at $600.

MEDIA Considers all media. Most frequently exhibits painting, photography, printmaking. Types of prints include etchings, mezzotints.

STYLE Considers all styles. Most frequently exhibits realism, primitive realism, impressionism. Genres include figurative work, landscapes, Caribbean.

TERMS Artwork is accepted on consignment (40% commission). Retail price set by the artist. Gallery provides promotion. Accepted work should be matted. Requires exclusive representation locally.

SUBMISSIONS Send query letter with artist's statement, bio, brochure. Returns material with SASE. Responds in 4 weeks. Files promo cards, brochures, catalogues. Finds artists through art exhibits, referrals by other artists, submissions.

TIPS "Present good slides or photos neatly presented with a clear, concise bio."

MARTHA HENRY, INC. FINE ART

400 E. 57th St., Suite 7L, New York NY 10022. (212)308-2759. **E-mail:** mh@marthahenry.com. **Website:** www.marthahenry.com. **Contact:** Martha Henry, president. Estab. 1987. Art consultancy and appraisals. Specialist in American art from the 19th century to the present, including: African American, American, contemporary and emerging, figurative expressionism (1950s–'60s), School of Hans Hofmann, self-taught and folk. Exhibits emerging, mid-career and established artists, specializing in art by African-Americans. Approached by over 200 artists/year; exhibits 1-4 artists/year. Exhibited artists include Jan Muller (oil paintings), Mr. Imagination (sculpture), JAMA (acrylic paintings) and Bob Thompson (oil paintings, drawings). Sponsors 2 exhibits/year. Average display time: 4–6 weeks. Open all year; by appointment only. Located in a private gallery in an apartment building. 5% of sales are to corporate collectors. Overall price range: $5,000-200,000; most work sold under $50,000.

TERMS Considers all artists, with emphasis on African-American artists and secondary market works.

SUBMISSIONS E-mail portfolio for review or send website link. Responds in 3 months. Finds artists through art fairs and exhibits, portfolio reviews, referrals by other artists, submissions, word of mouth, and press.

HENRY ART GALLERY

University of Washington, 15th Ave. NE and NE 41st St., Seattle WA 98195. (206)543-2280. **Fax:** (206)685-3123. **E-mail:** press@henryart.org. **Website:** www.henryart.org. **Contact:** Luis Croquer, deputy director of exhibitions, collections and programs. Estab. 1927. Contemporary Art Museum. Exhibits emerging, mid-career, and established domestic and international artists. Presents approx. 20 exhibitions/year. Open Wednesday, Saturday, Sunday 11-4; Thursday-Friday, 11-9. Located on the University of Washington campus. Visitors include local community, students, and tourists.

MEDIA Considers all media. Most frequently exhibits photography, video, and installation work. Exhibits all types of prints.

STYLE Exhibits contemporary art.

TERMS Does not require exclusive representation locally.

SUBMISSIONS Send query letter with artist statement, résumé, SASE, 10-15 images. Returns material with SASE. Finds artists through art exhibitions, exhibition announcements, individualized research, periodicals, portfolio reviews, referrals by other artists, submissions, and word of mouth.

HENRY STREET SETTLEMENT/ABRONS ART CENTER

466 Grand St., New York NY 10002. (212)598-0400; (212)766-9200. **E-mail:** info@henrystreet.org; jdurham@henrystreet.org. **Website:** www.abronsartcenter.org. **Contact:** Jonathan Durham, director of exhibitions and AIRspace. Alternative space, nonprofit gallery, community center. "The Abrons Art Center brings innovative artistic excellence to Manhattan's Lower East Side through diverse performances, exhibitions, residencires, classes and workshops for all ages and arts-in-education programming at public schools. Holds 9 solo photography exhibits/year. Open Tuesday–Friday, 10-10; Saturday, 9-10; Sunday, 11-6. Closed major holidays.

MEDIA Considers all media and all types of prints. Most frequently exhibits mixed media, sculpture and painting.

STYLE Considers all styles and genres.

TERMS Artwork is accepted on consignment (20% commission). Gallery provides insurance and contract.

SUBMISSIONS Send query letter with artist's statement, résumé and SASE. Returns material with SASE. Files résumés. Finds artists through word of mouth, submissions and referrals by other artists.

HERA EDUCATIONAL FOUNDATION AND ART GALLERY

P.O. Box 336, Wakefield RI 02880. (401)789-1488. **E-mail:** info@heragallery.org. **Website:** www.hera gallery.org. Estab. 1974. Cooperative gallery. "Hera Gallery/Hera Educational Foundation was a pioneer in the development of alternative exhibition spaces across the U.S. in the 1970s and one of the earliest women's cooperative galleries. Although many of these galleries no longer exist, Hera is proud to have not only continued, but also expanded our programs, exhibitions and events." The number of photo exhibits varies each year. Average display time: 6 weeks. Open Wednesday–Friday, 1-5; Saturday, 10-4; or by appointment. Closed during the month of January. Sponsors openings; provides refreshments and entertainment or lectures, demonstrations and symposia for some exhibits. Call for information on exhibitions. Overall price range: $100-10,000.

MEDIA Considers all media and original handpulled prints.

STYLE Exhibits installations, conceptual art, expressionism, neo-expressionism, painterly abstraction, surrealism, conceptualism, postmodern works, realism and photorealism, basically all styles. "We are interested in innovative, conceptually strong, contemporary works that employ a wide range of styles, materials and techniques. Prefers a culturally diverse range of subject matter that explores contemporary social and artistic issues important to us all."

TERMS Co-op membership. Gallery charges 25% commission. Retail price set by artist. Sometimes offers customer discount and payment by installments. Gallery provides promotion; artist pays for shipping and shares expenses such as printing and postage for announcements. Works must fit inside a 6'6"×2'6" door.

SUBMISSIONS Inquire about membership and shows. Responds in 6 weeks. Membership guidelines and application available on website or mailed on request. Finds artists through word of mouth, advertising in art publications, and referrals from members.

TIPS "Hera exhibits a culturally diverse range of visual and emerging artists. Please follow the application procedure listed in the membership guidelines. Applications are welcome at any time of the year."

GERTRUDE HERBERT INSTITUTE OF ART

506 Telfair St., Augusta GA 30901-2310. (706)722-5495. **Fax:** (706)722-3670. **E-mail:** ghia@ghia.org. **Website:** www.ghia.org. **Contact:** Rebekah Henry, executive director. Estab. 1937. Nonprofit gallery. Exhibits 40 emerging, mid-career and established artists in 5 solo/group shows annually. Exhibited artists include John Kingerlee, Luis Cruz Azaceta, Tom Nakashima. Sponsors 5 exhibits/year. Average display time: 6-8 weeks. Open Monday-Friday, 10-5; Saturdays by advance appointment only; closed first week in August, December 15-31. Located in historic 1818 Ware's Folly mansion. Clients include local community, tourists and upscale. Approx. 5% of sales are to corporate collectors. Overall price range: $100-5,000; most work sold at $500.

MEDIA Considers all media except craft. Considers all types of prints.

STYLE Exhibits all styles.

TERMS Artwork is accepted on consignment (35% commission). Retail price set by the artist. Gallery provides insurance and promotion. Accepted works on paper must be framed and under Plexiglas. Does not require exclusive representation locally.

SUBMISSIONS Send query letter with artist statement, bio, brochure, résumé, reviews, SASE, slides or CD of current work. Returns material with SASE. Responds to queries quarterly after expeditions review committee meets. Finds artists through art exhibits, referrals by other artists and submissions.

THE HIGH MUSEUM OF ART

1280 Peachtree St. NE, Atlanta GA 30309. (404)733-4400. **E-mail:** highmuseum@woodruffcenter. org. **Website:** www.high.org. Estab. 1905. Exhibits emerging, mid-career and established artists. Has over 11,000 works of art in its permanent collection. The museum has an extensive anthology of 19th- and 20th-century American art; significant holdings of European paintings and decorative art; a growing collection of African-American art; and burgeoning collections of modern and contemporary art, photography and African art. Open Tuesday–Thursday, Saturday, 10-5; Friday, 10-9; Sunday, 12-5; closed Mondays and national holidays. Located in midtown Atlanta. "The museum's building, designed by noted architect Richard Meier, opened to worldwide acclaim in 1983 and has received many design awards, including 1991 citation from the American Institute of Architects as one of the 'ten best works of American architecture of the 1980s.' Meier's 135,000-sq.-ft. facility tripled the museum's space, enabling the institution to mount more comprehensive displays of its collections. In 2003, to celebrate the 20th anniversary of the building, the High unveiled enhancements to its galleries and interior, and a new chronological installation of its permanent collection. Three new buildings, designed by Italian architect Renzo Piano, more than double the museum's size to 312,000 sq. ft. This allows the High to display more of its growing collection, increase educational and exhibition programs, and offer new visitor amenities to address the needs of larger and more diverse audiences. The expansion strengthens the High's role as the premier art museum in the Southeast and allows the museum to better serve its growing audiences in Atlanta and from around the world." Clients include local community, students, tourists and upscale.

MEDIA Considers all media and prints.

STYLE Considers all styles and genres.

TERMS Retail price is set by the gallery and the artist. Gallery provides insurance, promotion and contract.

SUBMISSIONS Call, e-mail or write to arrange a personal interview to show portfolio of slides, artist's statement, bio, résumé and reviews. Returns materials with SASE.

⊕ HOCKADAY MUSEUM OF ART

302 Second Ave. E., Kalispell MT 59901. (406)755-5268. **E-mail:** director@hockadaymuseum.org. **Website:** www.hockadaymuseum.org. **Contact:** Elizabeth Moss, executive director. Estab. 1968. Located in the historic downtown, 2,650 sq. ft., 1906 Carnegie Library. Permanent collection includes Jogn Fery, Russell Chatham, Charles Marion Russell, Ace Powell, O.C. Seltzer, David Shaner, Rudy Autio and more. Seeking artists for exhibition including emerging, mid-career and established artists. Artists interested in exhibiting can access all information under the artist opportunities section on the the website.

STYLE Will consider all media, styles and genres.

TERMS Gallery provides contract, insurance, promotion and shipping one way. Submissions are reviewed twice a year in September and January.

HOOSIER SALON PATRONS ASSOCIATION & GALLERY

711 E. 65th St., Indianapolis IN 46220. (317)669-6051. **E-mail:** info@hoosiersalon.org; ddole@hoosiersalon.org. **Website:** www.hoosiersalon.org. Estab. 1925. Nonprofit fine art gallery. Membership of 500 emerging, mid-career and established artists. Sponsors 7 exhibits/year (6 in gallery, 1 juried show each year at the Indiana Historical Society). Average display time: 5-6 weeks. Open Thursday-Sunday, 1-4. Closed over Christmas week. Gallery is in the Carmel Arts District as part of a business building. Gallery occupies about 2,200 sq. ft. Clients include local community and tourists. 20% of sales are to corporate collectors. Overall price range $50-5,000; most work sold at $1,000.

◐ This gallery opened a new location in 2001 at 507 Church St., New Harmony IN 47631; (812)682-3970.

MEDIA Considers acrylic, ceramics, collage, drawing, fiber, mixed media, oil, paper, pastel, pen & ink, sculpture, watercolor and hand-pulled prints. Most frequently exhibits oil, watercolor and pastel.

STYLE Exhibits traditional impressionism to abstract. Considers all genres.

TERMS Artwork is accepted on consignment and there is a 60% commission. Retail price set by the artist. Gallery provides insurance and contract. Accepted work must be exhibit ready. Requires membership. Criteria for membership is 1 year's residence in Indiana. Accepts only artists from Indiana (1 year residency). Gallery only shows artists who have been in one annual exhibit (show of approx. 200 artists each year).

SUBMISSIONS Call or e-mail for membership and Annual Exhibition information. Responds ASAP. We do not keep artists' materials unless they are members. Finds artists through word of mouth, art exhibits and art fairs.

TIPS While not required, all mats, glass, etc., need to be archival-quality. Because the association is widely regarded as exhibiting quality art, artists are generally careful to present their work in the most professional way possible.

EDWARD HOPPER HOUSE ART CENTER

82 N. Broadway, Nyack NY 10960. (845)358-0774.
E-mail: info@hopperhouse.org; caroleperry@ed
wardhopperhouse.org. **Website:** www.edwardhop
perhouse.org. **Contact:** Carole Perry, director. Estab.
1971. Nonprofit gallery, historic house. Approached
by 200 artists/year. Exhibits 100 emerging, mid-career
and established artists. Sponsors 9 exhibits/year. Average display time 5 weeks. Open Thursday–Sunday,
1-5; or by appointment. The house was built in 1858.
There are 4 gallery rooms on the first floor. Clients
include local community, students, tourists, upscale.
Overall price range $100-12,000; most work sold at
$750.

MEDIA Considers all media and all types of prints
except posters. Most frequently exhibits watercolor,
photography, oil.

STYLE Considers all styles and genres. Most frequently exhibits realism, abstraction, expressionism.

TERMS Artwork is accepted on consignment and
there is a 35% commission. Retail price set by the
artist. Gallery provides insurance, promotion and
contract. Accepted work should be framed, mounted
and matted. Does not require exclusive representation locally.

SUBMISSIONS Call or check website for submission
guidelines. Send query letter with artist's statement,
bio, brochure, business card, photocopies, photographs, résumé, reviews, SASE and slides. Returns
material with SASE. Files all materials unless return
specified and paid. Finds artists through art fairs, art
exhibits, portfolio reviews, referrals by other artists,
submissions and word of mouth.

TIPS "When shooting slides, don't have your artwork at an angle and don't have a chair or hands in
the frame. Make sure the slides look professional and
are an accurate representation of your work."

HUDSON GALLERY

5645 N. Main St., Sylvania OH 43560. (419)885-
8381. **Fax:** (419)885-8381. **E-mail:** info@hudsongal
lery.net. **Website:** www.hudsongallery.net. **Contact:**
Scott Hudson, director. Estab. 2003. For-profit gallery. Approached by 30 artists a year; represents or
exhibits 90 emerging, mid-career and established artists. Sponsors 10 exhibits/year. Average display time
1 month. Open Tuesday-Friday, 10-6; Saturday, 10-3.
This street-level gallery has over 2,000 sq. ft. of primary exhibition space. Clients include local community, tourists and upscale. 5% of sales are to corporate
collectors. Overall price range $50-10,000.

MEDIA Considers acrylic, ceramics, collage, drawing, fiber, glass, mixed media, oil, paper, pastel, sculpture, watercolor, engravings, etchings, linocuts, lithographs, mezzotints, serigraphs, woodcuts. Most frequently exhibits acrylic, oil, ceramics.

STYLE Considers all styles and genres.

TERMS Artwork is accepted on consignment and
there is a 40% commission. Retail price of the art set
by the gallery and artist. Gallery provides insurance,
promotion and contract.

SUBMISSIONS Call, e-mail, write or send query letter with artist's statement, bio, JPEGs; include SASE.
Material returned with SASE. Responds within 4
months. Finds artists through word of mouth, submissions, portfolio reviews and referrals by other
artists.

TIPS Follow guidelines on our website.

HUDSON GUILD GALLERY

441 W. 26th St., New York NY 10001. (212)760-9837.
Fax: (212)760-9801. **E-mail:** info@hudsonguild.org;
jfurlong@hudsonguild.org. **Website:** www.hudson
guild.org. **Contact:** Jim Furlong, director. Estab. Hudson Guild Gallery, 1948; Guild Gallery II, 2001. Represents emerging, mid-career, community-based and
established artists. Sponsors 12 shows/year. Average
display time: 8 weeks. Open all year. Located in West
Chelsea; 1,200 sq. ft.; community center galleries in a
New York City neighborhood. 100% of space for special exhibitions. 100% of sales are to private collectors.

○   Additional gallery: Guild Gallery II, 119 Ninth
Ave., New York NY 10011.

MEDIA Considers oil, acrylic, watercolor, pastel, pen
& ink, drawings, mixed media, collage, paper, sculpture, original handpulled prints, woodcuts, wood engravings, linocuts, engravings, mezzotints, etchings,
lithographs, pochoir and serigraphs. Most frequently
exhibits paintings, sculpture and graphics. Looking
for artist to do an environmental installation.

STYLE Exhibits all styles and genres.

TERMS Accepts work on consignment (20% commission). Retail price set by artist. Gallery provides insurance; artist pays for shipping. Prefers artwork framed.

SUBMISSIONS Send query letter, résumé, JPEGs by
e-mail, or photos with SASE. Responds in 1 month.
Finds artists through visiting exhibitions, word of
mouth, various art publications and sourcebooks,

artists' submissions/self-promotions, art collectors' referrals.

TIPS "Medium or small works by emerging artists are more likely to be shown in group shows than large work."

⊕ HYDE PARK ART CENTER

5020 S. Cornell Ave., Chicago IL 60615. (773)324-5520. **Fax:** (773)324-6641. **E-mail:** generalinfo@hydeparkart.org; aquinn@hydeparkart.org. **Website:** hydeparkart.org. **Contact:** Allison Peters Quinn, director of exhibition & residency programs. Estab. 1939. Nonprofit gallery & art school. Exhibits primarily Chicago-based artists. Sponsors approximately 15 exhibitions/year. Average display time: 3 months. Office hours Monday–Friday, 9-5. Gallery open Monday–Thursday, 10-8; Friday-Saturday, 10-5; Sunday, 12-5. "Primary focus on Chicago area artists at all levels of their career." Clientele: general public. Overall price range: $100-10,000.

MEDIA Considers all media. Interested in seeing "innovative work by emerging artists; also interested in proposals from curators and individual proposals from artists for new projects."

TERMS Accepts work "for exhibition only." Retail price set by artist. Sometimes offers payment by installment. Exclusive area representation not required. Gallery provides insurance and contract.

SUBMISSIONS Send cover letter, résumé, CD with 10-15 images, artist's statement of 250-400 words, and SASE attn: Allison Peters Quinn, director of exhibitions.

TIPS "Do not bring work in person."

ICEBOX QUALITY FRAMING & GALLERY

1500 Jackson St. NE, Suite #443, Minneapolis MN 55413. (612)788-1790. **E-mail:** icebox@bitstream. net. **Website:** www.iceboxminnesota.com. Estab. 1988. Exhibition, promotion and sales gallery. Represents photographers and fine artists in all media, predominantly photography. "A sole proprietorship gallery, Icebox sponsors installations and exhibits in the gallery's 2,200-sq.-ft. space in the Minneapolis Arts District." Overall price range: $200-2,500; most work sold at $200-800.

MEDIA Considers mostly photography, with the door open for other fine art with some size and content limitations.

STYLE Exhibits photos of multicultural, environmental, landscapes/scenics, rural, adventure, travel and fine art photographs from artists with serious, thought-provoking work. Interested in alternative process, documentary, erotic, historical/vintage.

TERMS Charges 50% commission.

SUBMISSIONS "Send letter of interest telling why and what you would like to exhibit at Icebox. Include only materials that can be kept at the gallery and updated as needed. Check website for more details about entry and gallery history."

TIPS "Be more interested in the quality and meaning of your artwork than in a way to make money. Unique thought provoking artwork of high quality is more likely suited." Not interested in wall decor art.

ILLINOIS ARTISANS PROGRAM

James R. Thompson Center, 100 W. Randolph St., Suite 2-200, Chicago IL 60601. (312)814-5321. **E-mail:** illinoisartisans@museum.state.il.us. **Website:** www.museum.state.il.us/programs/illinois-artisans. Estab. 1985. "The Illinois Artisans Program was created in 1985 by Governor James R. Thompson to sustain and encourage local contemporary craft made in Illinois. The primary mission of the program is to draw national and statewide attention to the rich tradition of craft in the state and to provide venues to the display and sales of work by juried artists. Three not-for-profit venues operate under statutory authority of the Illinois State Museum Society to display and sell Illinois Artisans work in a range of media in curated gallery stores, art sprees, craft festivals, exhibitions and other events held at our 3 locations: Illinois Artisans, Chicago; The Museum Store, Illinois State Museum, 502 S. Spring St., Springfield IL 62706; and Southern Illinois Art & Artisans Center, 14967 Gun Creek Trail, Whittington IL 62897-1000."

MEDIA "The Illinois Artisans Program is continually looking for talented new artists to join the program." All areas of arts and crafts, including folk, traditional, contemporary, and ethnic, as well as fine art forms are eligible. Over 1,800 artists have been jury selected into the IAP. Once selected, their work can be shown at 1 or more Illinois Artisans locations.

STYLE Exhibits all styles. "Seeks contemporary, traditional, folk and ethnic arts from all regions of Illinois."

TERMS Accepts work on consignment (50% commission). Retail price set by gallery and artist. Sometimes offers customer discounts. Exclusive area representation not required.

SUBMISSIONS Applications are due twice a year (March 28 and October 12) and reviewed by a jury panel. Artists should submit 8 images, artist statement and information about each image on a CD. Cost per application is $30. Artists are required to live and work within Illinois and work must be handmade and original. Criteria can be reviewed and the application downloaded on the website: www.museum.state.il.us/artisans.

TIPS "Great work can be rejected because of poor or blurry photographs. Work is judged on quality, excellence of concept, and/or adherence to traditional design."

ILLINOIS STATE MUSEUM CHICAGO GALLERY

100 W. Randolph, Suite 2-100, Chicago IL 60601. (312)814-5322. **E-mail:** jstevens@museum.state.il.us. **Website:** www.museum.state.il.us./ismsites/chicago/exhibitions.html. **Contact:** Jane Stevens, gallery administrator. Estab. 1985. Museum. Exhibits emerging, mid-career and established artists. Sponsors 2-3 shows/year. Average display time: 5 months. Open all year. Located "in the Chicago loop, in the James R. Thompson Center designed by Helmut Jahn." 100% of space for special exhibitions.

MEDIA All media considered, including installations.

STYLE Exhibits all styles and genres, including contemporary and historical work.

TERMS "We exhibit work but do not handle sales." Gallery provides insurance and promotion; artist pays for shipping. Prefers artwork framed.

SUBMISSIONS Accepts only artists from Illinois. Send résumé, 12-20 JPEGs on a CD, bio and SASE.

IMPACT ARTIST GALLERY, INC.

Tri-Main Center, Suite 545, 2495 Main St., Buffalo NY 14214. (716)833-3110. **E-mail:** impactartistgallery@gmail.com. **Website:** www.impactartistgallery.org. Estab. 1993. "A cooperative members' gallery for women artists, one of a few in the nation. We mount 10 or more exhibitions of visual art each year, including 2-4 national juried shows, a members-only show, and several community service exhibits." Approached by 500 artists/year. Represents 310 emerging, mid-career and established artists. Open all year; Wednesday–Saturday, 11-4; most Saturdays, 1-4. Clients include local community, tourists and upscale.

MEDIA Considers all media except glass, installation and craft. Considers engravings, etchings, lithographs, serigraphs and woodcuts.

STYLE Considers all styles. Most frequently exhibits expressionism, painterly abstraction, surrealism. Considers all genres.

TERMS Artwork is accepted on consignment and there is a 25% commission. Retail price set by the artist. Gallery provides promotion. Accepted work should be framed, matted and ready for hanging. Does not require exclusive representation locally. Women's art except for Fall National Show and Summer Statewide Show.

SUBMISSIONS Write to arrange a personal interview to show portfolio of slides. Mail portfolio for review. Send query letter with SASE and slides. Responds in 2 months. Files artist statement and résumé.

INDIANAPOLIS ART CENTER

820 E. 67th St., Indianapolis IN 46220. (317)255-2464. **E-mail:** kyleh@indplsartcenter.org. **Website:** www.indplsartcenter.org. **Contact:** Kyle Herrington, director of exhibitions. Estab. 1934. "The Indianapolis Art Center is one of the largest community art facilities in the United States not connected with a university, welcoming more than 250,000 visitors a year. The mission of the Indianapolis Art Center is to engage, enlighten and inspire our community by providing interactive art education, outreach to underserved audiences, support of artists and exposure to the visual arts. The Art Center's campus includes the Marilyn K. Glick School of Art, a 40,000-sq.-ft. facility designed by renowned architect Michael Graves. The building houses 11 state-of-the-art studios, 5 public art galleries, a 224-seat auditorium and a library. It also features ArtsPark, a 9-acre outdoor creativity and sculpture garden that includes public art and is located in one of Indianapolis' most popular and diverse neighborhoods. The park is connected to one of the city's most utilized greenway trail systems, the Monan Trail."

TERMS "The Indianapolis Art Center Exhibitions Department accepts proposals for gallery and ArtsPark exhibits from June–December each year. Generally we are looking for exhibits to book 2 years out or more. Proposals will be accepted starting June 1–December 31. All works insured while on site and a stipend may be available in curated exhibitions. For further information about the gallery sizes and contract terms, please contact us."

SUBMISSIONS "Any artist may submit a proposal to be considered for a solo or group exhibition by sending a complete artist's packet to: Indianapolis Art Center, ATTN: Exhibits Department, 820 E. 67th St., Indianapolis IN 46220. Your proposal should include the following items on a CD or DVD: an artist statement, not to exceed 1 page; a résumé or biography, not to exceed 3 pages; 12-15 images of individual works (details may be included); a list with title, medium, size, and year completed for each image. Videos may also be submitted, as well as videos of interactive and/or performance work. NOTE: your proposal materials WILL NOT be returned to you. While all proposals will be given equal consideration, artists living or working within 250 miles of Indianapolis are especially encouraged to apply. All proposals collected during the year will be reviewed on a rolling basis. Proposals may be kept for upwards of 3 years by the exhibitions department for future consideration."

INDIAN UPRISING GALLERY

P.O. Box 1582, Bozeman MT 59771. (406)586-5831. **E-mail:** info@indianuprisinggallery.com. **Website:** www.indianuprisinggallery.com. "Dedicated exclusively to American Indian contemporary art featuring the unique beauty and spirit of the Plains Indians." The gallery specializes in ledger drawings, painted hides, jewelry. Artists include Linda Haukaas, Donald Montileaux, Dwayne Wilcox, Pauls Szabo, Jackie Bread. Conducts business by private appointment and e-commerce only.

MEDIA Considers all media. Most frequently exhibits contemporary works by gallery artists.

TERMS Buys outright at wholesale price. On occasion takes consignments.

SUBMISSIONS Accepts only Native American artists of the Plains region. Send résumé, slides, bio and artist's statement. Write for appointment to show portfolio of photographs. Responds in 2 weeks. Finds artists through visiting museums and juried art shows.

INDIVIDUAL ARTISTS OF OKLAHOMA

P.O. Box 60824, Oklahoma City OK 73146. (405)232-6060. **Fax:** (405)232-6061. **E-mail:** kbrown@iaogallery.org. **Website:** www.iaogallery.org. **Contact:** Kendall Brown. Estab. 1979. Alternative space. "IAO creates opportunities for Oklahoma artists by curating and developing socially relevant exhibitions in one of the finest gallery spaces in the region." Approached by 60 artists/year; represents or exhibits 30 artists.

Sponsors 10 photography exhibits/year. Average display time: 3-4 weeks. Open Tuesday–Saturday, 12-6. Gallery is located in downtown art district, 2,300 sq. ft. with 10 ft. ceilings and track lighting. Overall price range: $100-2,000; most work sold at $400.

MEDIA Considers all media. Most frequently exhibits photography, painting, installation.

STYLE Considers all styles. Most frequently exhibits "bodies of work with cohesive style and expressed in a contemporary viewpoint." Considers all genres.

SUBMISSIONS Mail portfolio for review. Send artist's statement, bio, photocopies or slides, résumé and SASE. Returns material with SASE. Responds in 3 months. Finds artists through word of mouth, art exhibits and referrals by other artists.

TIPS "IAO is committed to sustaining and encouraging emerging and established artists in all media who are intellectually and aesthetically provocative or experimental in subject matter or technique."

INTERSECTION FOR THE ARTS

925 Mission St., Suite 109, San Francisco CA 94103. (415)626-2787. **Website:** www.theintersection.org. **Contact:** Randy Rollison, executive director. Estab. 1965. Alternative space and nonprofit gallery. Exhibits the work of 10 emerging and mid-career artists/year. Sponsors 8 shows/year. Average display time: 6 weeks. Gallery open Tuesday-Saturday, 12-6; open all year. Located in the Mission District of San Francisco; 1,000 sq. ft.; gallery has windows at one end and cement pillars betwen exhibition panels. 100% of space for special exhibitions. Clientele: 100% private collectors.

This gallery supports emerging and mid-career artists who explore experimental ideas and processes. Interdisciplinary, new genre, video performance and installation are encouraged.

MEDIA Considers oil, pen & ink, acrylic, drawings, watercolor, mixed media, installation, collage, photography, site-specific installation, video installation, original handpulled prints, woodcuts, lithographs, posters, wood engravings, mezzotints, linocuts and etchings.

STYLE Exhibits all styles and genres.

TERMS Retail price set by artist. Customer discounts and payment by installment are available. Gallery provides promotion; shipping costs are shared.

SUBMISSIONS Submission guidelines available online.

TIPS "Create proposals which consider the unique circumstances of this location, utilizing the availability of the theater and literary program/resources/audience."

IVANFFY-UHLER GALLERY

(760)730-9166. **E-mail:** info@ivanffyuhler.com. **Website:** www.ivanffyuhler.com. **Contact:** Paul Uhler, director. Estab. 1990. Online gallery. Represents 20 mid-career and established artists/year. Clientele: upscale, local community, tourists. 85% private collectors, 15% corporate collectors. Overall price range: $1,000-20,000; most work sold at $1,500-4,000.

MEDIA Considers oil, acrylic, watercolor, pastel, pen & ink, drawing, mixed media, collage, paper, sculpture, woodcuts, engravings, lithographs, wood engravings, mezzotints, serigraphs, linocuts and etchings. Most frequently exhibits oils, mixed media, sculpture.

STYLE Exhibits neo-expressionism, painterly abstraction, surrealism, postmodern works, impressionism, hard-edge geometric abstraction, postmodern European school. Genres include florals, landscapes, figurative work.

TERMS Shipping costs are shared.

SUBMISSIONS Currently not accepting submissions.

JAILHOUSE GALLERY

310 North Center Ave., Hardin MT 59034. (406)665-3239. **E-mail:** jhghardin@hotmail.com. **Website:** www.jailhousegallery.org. Estab. 1978. Nonprofit gallery. Represents 25 emerging, mid-career and established artists/year. Exhibited artists include Gale Running Wolf, Sr. and Mary Blain. Sponsors 9 shows/year. Average display time 6 weeks. Open all year; Tuesday-Friday, 9:30-5:30; Saturday 9:30-3:30 (January-April); Tuesday-Saturday, 9:30-5:30 (May-December). Located downtown; 1,440 sq. ft. 75% space for special exhibitions; 25% of space for gallery artists. Clientele: all types. 95% private collectors, 5% corporate collectors. Overall price range $20-2,000; most work sold at $20-500.

MEDIA Considers all media and all types of prints. Most frequently exhibits mixed media, watercolor and pen & ink.

STYLE Exhibits all styles and all genres. Prefers western, Native American and landscapes.

TERMS Accepts work on consignment (30% commission). Retail price set by the gallery. Gallery provides insurance, promotion and contract. Artist pays shipping costs.

SUBMISSIONS Send query letter with résumé, business card, artist's statement and bio. Call for appointment to show portfolio of photographs. Responds in 3 weeks. Finds artists through word of mouth, referrals by other artists, visiting art fairs and exhibitions and artists' submissions.

ALICE AND WILLIAM JENKINS GALLERY

600 St. Andrews Blvd., Winter Park FL 32792. (407)671-1886. **Fax:** (407)671-0311. **E-mail:** btiffany2000@yahoo.com. **Website:** www.crealde.org. **Contact:** Barbara Tiffany, director of painting and drawing department. Estab. 1980. The Jenkins Gallery mission is to exhibit the work of noted and established Florida artists, as well as to introduce national and international artists to the Central Florida region. Each of the 4-6 annual exhibitions are professionally curated by a member of the Crealdé Gallery Committee or a guest curator.

JESSEL GALLERY

1019 Atlas Peak Rd., Napa CA 94558. (707)257-2350. **Fax:** (707)257-2396. **E-mail:** jessel@napanet.net. **Website:** www.jesselgallery.com. **Contact:** Jessel Miller, owner. Retail gallery. Represents 5 major artists. Exhibited artists include Clark Mitchell, Timothy Dixon and Jessel Miller. Sponsors 2-6 shows/year. Average display time: 1 month. Open all year; 7 days/week, 10-5. Located 1 mile out of town; 9,000 sq. ft. 20% of space for special exhibitions; 50% of space for gallery artists. Clientele: upper income collectors. 95% private collectors, 5% corporate collectors. Overall price range: $25-10,000; most work sold at $2,000-3,500.

MEDIA Considers oil, acrylic, watercolor, pastel, collage, sculpture, ceramic and craft. Most frequently exhibits acrylic, watercolor and pastel.

STYLE Exhibits painterly abstraction, photorealism, realism and traditional. Genres include landscapes, florals and figurative work. Prefers figurative, landscape and abstract.

TERMS Accepts work on consignment (50% commission). Retail price set by gallery. Gallery provides promotion; artist pays for shipping costs. Prefers artwork framed.

SUBMISSIONS Send query letter with résumé, slides, bio, SASE and reviews. Call (after sending slides and background info) for appointment to show portfolio of photographs or slides. Responds in 1 month.

STELLA JONES GALLERY

201 St. Charles Ave., New Orleans LA 70170. (504)568-9050. **E-mail:** stellajonesgallery.manalia@gmail.com. **Website:** www.stellajonesgallery.com. **Contact:** Stella Jones. Estab. 1996. For-profit gallery. "The gallery provides a venue for artists of the African diaspora to exhibit superior works of art. The gallery fulfills its educational goals through lectures, panel discussions, intimate gallery talks and exhibitions with artists in attendance." Approached by 40 artists/year; represents or exhibits 45 artists. Sponsors 1 photography exhibit/year. Average display time 6-8 weeks. Open Monday–Saturday, 12-5. Located on 1st floor of corporate 53-story office building downtown, 1 block from French Quarter. Overall price range $500-150,000. Most work sold at $5,000.

MEDIA Considers all media. Most frequently exhibits oil and acrylic. Considers all types of prints except posters.

STYLE Considers all styles. Most frequently exhibits postmodernism and geometric abstraction. Exhibits all genres.

TERMS Artwork is accepted on consignment (50% commission). Retail price set by the artist. Gallery provides insurance, promotion and contract. Accepted work should be framed. Requires exclusive representation locally.

SUBMISSIONS To show portfolio of photographs, slides and transparencies, mail for review. Send query letter with artist's statement, bio, brochure, business card, photocopies, photographs, résumé, reviews, SASE and slides. Returns material with SASE. Responds in 1 month. Finds artists through word of mouth, submissions, portfolio reviews, art exhibits, and referrals by other artists.

TIPS "Send organized, good visuals."

JRB ART AT THE ELMS

2810 North Walker, Oklahoma City OK 73103. (405)528-6336. **Fax:** (405)528-6337. **E-mail:** jreedbelt@jrbartgallery.com. **Website:** www.jrbartgallery.com. **Contact:** Joy Reed Belt, director. Estab. 2003. JRB Art at the Elms presents a diverse roster of emerging, established and internationally-exhibited artists who create in a wide range of media, including paintings, drawings, sculpture, ceramics, glass, fine crafts, functional objects, fiber art, fine art prints and photographs. This award-winning gallery in Oklahoma City's Paseo Arts District, with its historic 8,000 sq. ft. exhibition space, changes its exhibits monthly in a gracious environment that fosters a dialogue between the arts and the larger community while providing quality art for first-time buyers as well as individual, corporate and museum collections.

JVA ART GROUP

4151 Taylor St., San Diego CA 92110. (619)299-3232. **Fax:** (619)299-8709. **E-mail:** Via the online contact form. **Website:** www.jvaartgroup.com. Estab. 1972. Retail gallery and art consultancy. Represents emerging, mid-career and established artists. Exhibited artists include Susan Singleton and Reed Cardwell. Average display time: 1 month. Open Monday–Thursday, 8-5; Friday, 8:30-1. 1,000 sq. ft.; 100% of space for gallery artists. Clientele: upscale, business, decorators, health facilities, hotels, resorts, liturgical and residential artwork with interior designers, architects, landscape architects, developers and space planners. 50% private collectors, 50% corporate collectors. Overall price range: $175-10,000; most work sold at $450-1,000. Other services include giclée printing, online artist resource (slide collection), custom commission work available and beginning to do governmental work.

MEDIA Considers all media and all types of prints. Most frequently exhibits paintings, sculpture, monoprints.

STYLE Exhibits all styles. Genres include all genres, especially florals, landscapes and figurative work. Prefers abstract, semirealistic and realistic.

TERMS Artwork is accepted on consignment and there is a 50% commission. Retail price set by the artist. Gallery provides insurance. Gallery pays for shipping from gallery. Artist pays for shipping to gallery. Prefers artwork unframed.

SUBMISSIONS Send query letter with résumé and slides. Call for appointment to show portfolio of slides. Responds in 2 weeks. Files slides, biographies, information about artist's work. Finds artists through artist's submissions and referrals.

HAL KATZEN GALLERY

459 Washington St., Suite 2, New York NY 10013. (212)925-9777. **E-mail:** hkatzen916@aol.com. **Website:** www.artnet.com/galleries/hal-katzen-gallery. For-profit gallery. Estab. 1984. Exhibits established artists. Open Monday-Friday, 10-6; closed August.

Clients include local community, tourists and upscale. 10-20% of sales are to corporate collectors. Overall price range: $2,000-20,000; most work sold at $5,000.

MEDIA Considers acrylic, collage, drawing, oil, paper, pen & ink, sculpture and watercolor. Most frequently exhibits paintings, works on paper and sculpture. Considers all types of prints.

STYLE Considers all styles and genres.

TERMS Artwork is accepted on consignment or is bought outright. Accepts only established artists.

KAVANAUGH ART GALLERY

131 Fifth St. W. Des Moines IA 50265. (515)279-8682. **Fax:** (515)279-7609. **E-mail:** info@kagwdm.com. **Website:** www.kavanaughgallery.com. **Contact:** Carole Kavanaugh, director. Estab. 1990. Retail gallery. Represents 100 mid-career and established artists/year. May be interested in seeing the work of emerging artists in the future. Exhibited artists include Kati Roberts, Don Hatfield, Dana Brown, Gregory Steele, August Holland, Ming Feng and Larry Guterson. Sponsors 3-4 shows/year. Average display time: 3 months. Open all year; Monday–Saturday, 10-5. Located in Valley Junction shopping area; 10,000 sq. ft. 70% private collectors, 30% corporate collectors. Overall price range: $300-20,000; most work sold at $800-3,000.

MEDIA Considers all media and all types of prints. Most frequently exhibits oil, acrylic and pastel.

STYLE Exhibits color field, impressionism, realism, florals, portraits, western, wildlife, southwestern, landscapes, Americana and figurative work. Prefers landscapes, florals and Western.

TERMS Accepts work on consignment (50% commission). Retail price set by the artist. Gallery provides insurance, promotion and contract. Shipping costs are shared. Prefers artwork unframed.

SUBMISSIONS Send query letter with résumé, bio and photographs. Portfolio should include photographs. Responds in 3 weeks. Files bio and photos. Finds artists through word of mouth, referrals by other artists, visiting art fairs and exhibitions, artist's submissions.

TIPS "Get a realistic understanding of the gallery/artist relationship by visiting with directors. Be professional and persistent."

THE KENTUCK ART CENTER

503 Main Ave., Northport AL 35476. (205)758-1257. **Fax:** (205)758-1258. **E-mail:** kentuck@kentuck.org.

Website: www.kentuck.org. **Contact:** Amy Echols, executive director. Estab. 1980. Nonprofit gallery. "The Kentuck Art Center presents monthly exhibitions, showcasing the work of both established artists and of up-and-comers. Sometimes traditional, sometimes visionary, always authentic, Kentuck brings art to the community and builds community with art. The annual Kentuck Festival of Art began in 1971." Approached by 400 artists/year. Represents 100 artists/year. Sponsors 24 exhibits/year. Average display time: 1 month. Open Tuesday–Friday, 9-5; Saturday, 10-4:30; closed major holidays. Clients include local community. Overall price range: $150-10,000.

MEDIA Considers all media. Most frequently exhibits mixed media, natural materials, painting, pottery, and outsider art.

STYLE Considers all styles.

TERMS Artwork is accepted on consignment and there is a 40% commission on shop sales; 30% on exhibition sales. Retail price set by the artist. Gallery provides insurance, promotion and contract. For insurance purposes, artist must provide inventory manifest with photos of works, description, and value (even for not-for-sale items). Accepted work should be mounted.

SUBMISSIONS Submission instructions available online. Finds artists through word of mouth, submissions, portfolio reviews, art exhibits and referrals by other artists.

ANGELA KING GALLERY

241 Royal St., New Orleans LA 70130. (504)524-8211. **Fax:** (504)566-1944. **E-mail:** angela@angelaking gallery.com. **Website:** www.angelakinggallery.com. **Contact:** Angela King, gallery director. Estab. 1977. Formerly Hanson Gallery. For profit gallery. Represents 22 emerging, mid-career and established artists. Exhibited artists include Frederick Hart (sculptor) and Leroy Neiman (all mediums). Sponsors 6 exhibits/year. Average display time: ongoing to 3 weeks. Open Monday–Saturday, 10-5; Sundays and holidays, 11-5. Clients include local community, tourists and upscale. Overall price range: $650-100,000; most work sold at $4,000.

MEDIA Considers acrylic, drawing, oil, pastel, sculpture and watercolor. Most frequently exhibits oil, pastel and acrylic. Considers etchings, lithographs and serigraphs.

STYLE Exhibits impressionism, neo-expressionism and surrealism. Considers all styles. Genres include figurative work and landscapes.

TERMS Retail price set by the gallery and the artist. Gallery provides insurance. Requires exclusive representation locally.

SUBMISSIONS Write to arrange a personal interview to show portfolio of photographs and slides. Mail portfolio for review. Send query letter with artist's statement, bio, brochure, photographs, résumé, reviews, SASE and slides. Responds in 6 weeks. Finds artists through word of mouth, submissions, art exhibits and art fairs.

TIPS "Archival-quality materials play a major role in selling fine art to collectors."

KINGSTON GALLERY

450 Harrison Ave., #43, Boston MA 02118. (617)423-4113. **E-mail:** gallerydirector@kingstongallery.com. **Website:** www.kingstongallery.com. Estab. 1982. Cooperative gallery. Exhibits the work of 24 emerging, mid-career and established artists. Sponsors 12+ shows/year. Average display time: 1 month. Open Wednesday-Sunday, 12-5. Located in downtown Boston (South End); 1,300 sq. ft.; large, open room with 12 ft. ceiling and smaller center gallery—can accommodate large installation. Overall price range: $100-7,000; most work sold at $600-3,000.

MEDIA Considers all media. 20% of space for special exhibitions.

STYLE Exhibits all styles.

TERMS Co-op membership requires dues plus donation of time. Artist must fulfill monthly co-op responsibilities. 25% commission charged on sales by members. Retail price set by the artist. Sometimes offers payment by installments. Gallery provides insurance, some promotion and contract. Rental of center gallery by arrangement.

SUBMISSIONS Accepts only artists from the greater Boston area for membership. Send query letter with résumé, slides, SASE and "any pertinent information. Slides are reviewed every other month. Gallery will contact artist within 1 month." Does not file material but may ask artist to re-apply in future.

TIPS "Please include thorough, specific information on slides—size, price, etc."

KIRSTEN GALLERY, INC.

5320 Roosevelt Way NE, Seattle WA 98105. (206)522-2011. **E-mail:** kirstengallery@qwestoffice.net. **Web**-site: www.kirstengallery.com. **Contact:** Richard Kirsten, president. Estab. 1974. Retail gallery. Represents 60 emerging, mid-career and established artists. Exhibited artists include Birdsall and Daiensai. Sponsors 4 shows/year. Average display time: 1 month. Open Wednesday–Sunday, 11-5. 3,500 sq. ft.; outdoor sculpture garden. 40% of space for special exhibitions; 60% of space for gallery artists. 90% private collectors, 10% corporate collectors. Overall price range: $75-15,000; most work sold at $75-2,000.

MEDIA Considers oil, acrylic, watercolor, mixed media, sculpture, glass and offset reproductions. Most frequently exhibits oil, watercolor and glass.

STYLE Exhibits surrealism, photorealism and realism. Genres include landscapes, florals, Americana. Prefers realism.

TERMS Accepts work on consignment (50% commission). Retail price set by artist. Offers payment by installments. Gallery provides promotion; artist pays shipping costs. "No insurance; artist responsible for own work."

SUBMISSIONS Send query letter with résumé, slides and bio. Write for appointment to show portfolio of photographs. Responds in 2 weeks. Files bio and résumé. Finds artists through visiting exhibitions and word of mouth.

TIPS "Keep prices down. Be prepared to pay shipping costs both ways. Work is not insured (send at your own risk). Send the best work—not just what you did not sell in your hometown. Do not show up without an appointment."

🌀 🎧 MARIA ELENA KRAVETZ ART GALLERY

Peatonal 25 De Mayo 240, X5000 ELF Cordoba, Argentina. (54) 351 4239451. **Fax:** (54) 351 4271776. **E-mail:** mek@mariaelenakravetzgallery.com. **Website:** www.mariaelenakravetzgallery.com. **Contact:** Maria Elena Kravetz, director. Estab. 1998. For-profit gallery. Approached by 30 artists/year; exhibits 16 emerging and mid-career artists/year. Exhibited artists include Marina Gazulla and Tania Abrile (paintings); Anna Mazzoni (fiber arts); Edgardo de Bortoli (glass art); Noel Loeschbor (fiber art) and Marcelo Marques (paintings). Average display time: 60 days. Located in the main downtown of Cordoba city. Overall price range: $500-10,000; most work sold at $1,500-5,000.

MEDIA Considers all media. Most frequently exhibits glass sculpture and mixed media. Considers etchings, linocuts, lithographs and woodcuts.

STYLE Considers all styles. Most frequently exhibits new-expressionism and painterly abstraction. Considers all genres.

TERMS Artwork is accepted on consignment (30% commission). Retail price set by the artist. Requires exclusive representation locally. Prefers only artists from South America and emphasizes sculptors.

SUBMISSIONS Mail portfolio for review. Cannot return material. Responds to queries in 1 month. Finds artists through art fairs and exhibits, portfolio reviews, referrals by other artists, submissions and word of mouth.

TIPS Artists "must indicate a website to make the first review of their works, then give an e-mail address to contact them if we are interested in their work."

LA ARTISTS GALLERY

6650 Franklin Ave., Hollywood CA 90028. (323)461-0047. **Fax:** (323)960-3357. **E-mail:** susan100art@yahoo.com. **Website:** www.laartists.com. **Director:** Susan Anderson. Alternative space. Estab. 2000. Approached by 25 artists/year. Represents 25 mid-career artists. Exhibited artists include Dan Shupe, Esau Andrade. Gallery not open to walk-ins. Open by appointment. Clients include upscale dealers, designers, private clients. 10% of sales are to corporate collectors. Overall price range: $1,500-5,000.

MEDIA Considers collage, oil, sculpture, watercolor. Most frequently exhibits oil on canvas. Considers all types of prints.

STYLE Exhibits neo-expressionism, postmodernism, figurative, contemporary, folk. Most frequently exhibits figurative/contemporary.

TERMS Artwork is accepted on consignment (10-50% commission). Retail price set by the artist.

SUBMISSIONS Write to arrange personal interview to show portfolio of photographs. Mail portfolio for review. Returns material with SASE. Does not reply to queries.

TIPS "Keep submissions really short and enclose photographs, not slides."

THE LAB

2948 16th St., San Francisco CA 94103. (415)864-8855. **E-mail:** thelabs@thelab.org. **Website:** www.thelab.org. Estab. 1983. Nonprofit gallery and alternative space. Exhibits numerous emerging, mid-career artists/year. Interested in seeing the work of emerging artists. Sponsors 5-7 shows/year. Average display time: 1 month. Open all year; Thursday–Saturday, 1-6 (during exhibitions). 40×55 ft.; 17 ft. height; 2,200 sq. ft.; white walls. Doubles as a performance and gallery space. Clientele: artists and Bay Area communities.

The LAB often curates panel discussions, performances or other special events in conjunction with exhibitions. They also sponsor an annual conference and exhibition on feminist activism and art.

MEDIA Considers all media with emphasis on interdisciplinary and experimental art. Most frequently exhibits installation art, interdisciplinary art, media art and group exhibitions.

TERMS Artists receive honorarium from the art space. Work can be sold, but that is not the emphasis.

SUBMISSIONS Submission guidelines online. Finds artists through word of mouth, submissions, calls for proposals.

TIPS Ask to be put on their mailing list to get a sense of the LAB's curatorial approach and interests.

LAKE GEORGE ARTS PROJECT/ COURTHOUSE GALLERY

Old County Courthouse, 1 Amherst St., Lake George NY 12845. (518)668-2616. **E-mail:** mail@lakegeorgearts.org. **Website:** www.lakegeorgearts.org. Estab. 1986. Alternative space; nonprofit gallery. "Presents 5-7 exhibitions yearly of regional and national contemporary visual artists in all media." Approached by 200 artists/year; exhibits 8-15 artists/year. Average display time: 5 weeks. Open Tuesday–Friday, 12-5; Saturday, 12-4 (during exhibitions); all other times by request.

MEDIA Exhibits all media.

STYLE Considers all styles.

TERMS Artwork is accepted on consignment (25% commission). Retail price set by the artist. Gallery provides insurance, promotion, contract.

SUBMISSIONS Annual deadline for open call is January 31. Send artist's statement, résumé, 10-12 images (slides or CD), image script and SASE. Guidelines available online. Returns material with SASE. Finds artists through art exhibits, portfolio reviews, referrals by other artists, submissions, word of mouth.

TIPS "Do not send e-mail submissions or links to website. Do not send original art. Review guidelines on website."

LANCASTER MUSEUM OF ART

135 N. Lime St., Lancaster PA 17602. **E-mail:** info@lmapa.org. **Website:** www.lmapa.org. Estab. 1965. Nonprofit organization. "The Lancaster Museum of Art is recognized as one of the largest cultural organizations in the region responsible for an extensive collection of works by contemporary regional artists." Represents over 100 emerging, mid-career and established artists/year. 900+ members. Open Tuesday-Saturday, 10-4; Sunday, 12-4. Located downtown Lancaster; 4,000 sq. ft.; neoclassical architecture. 100% of space for special exhibitions. 100% of space for gallery artists. Overall price range: $100-25,000; most work sold at $100-10,000.

MEDIA Considers all media.

TERMS Accepts work on consignment. Retail price set by the artist. Gallery provides insurance; shipping costs are shared. Artwork must be ready for presentation.

SUBMISSIONS Send query letter with résumé, slides, photographs or CDs, SASE, and artist's statement for review by exhibitions committee. Annual deadline February 1.

TIPS Advises artists to submit quality slides and well-presented proposal. "No phone calls."

LANDING GALLERY

8 Elm St., Rockland ME 04841. (207)594-4544. **E-mail:** landinggallery@gmail.com. **Website:** www.landingart.com. **Contact:** Bruce Busko, president. Estab. 1985. For-profit gallery. Approached by 40 artists/year. Exhibits 35 emerging, mid-career and established artists. Exhibited artists include Bruce Busko (oil/mixed media), Irma Cerese (acrylic), Dorothy Simpsom Krause (mixed media), Roberta (photography), Michael Kahn (photography), Maria Nevelson (assemblage), Diana Godfrey (acrylic), and Bjorn Rundquist (oil). Sponsors 6 exhibits/year. Average display time: 1 month. Open 6 months, May through October; Monday-Saturday, 10-5; Sunday, 12-5; closed Tuesdays all year, Sundays in summer. Located in mid-coast Maine next to the Farnsworth Art Museum and part of a 25 member gallery community. 2,600 sq. ft. on 2 floors with skylights, granite floors and 24-ft. ceilings. The gallery building and Landing Gallery Garden Courtyard are in the center of town. Clients include local community, tourists and upscale. 5% of sales are to corporate collectors. Overall price range: $100-12,000; most work sold at $400-1,500.

MEDIA Considers all media. Most frequently exhibits paintings, photographs and sculpture. Considers engravings, etchings, lithographs, mezzotints and serigraphs.

STYLE Considers all styles. Most frequently exhibits realism, abstract and impressionism. Considers figurative work, florals and landscapes.

TERMS Artwork is accepted on consignment (50% commission). Retail price set by the gallery. Gallery provides insurance, promotion and contract. Accepted work should be framed. Requires exclusive representation in a 100-mile radius.

SUBMISSIONS E-mail or call to arrange a personal interview to show portfolio of photographs, slides and transparencies. Mail portfolio for review. Send query letter with artist's statement, bio, brochure, business card, photocopies, photographs, résumé, reviews, SASE and slides. Returns material with SASE. Responds in 2 weeks. Files photos, slides, photocopies and information. Finds artists through word of mouth, submissions, portfolio reviews, art exhibits, art fairs and referrals by other artists.

TIPS "Permanence denotes quality and professionalism."

ROBERT LANGE STUDIOS

2 Queen St., Charleston SC 29401. (843)805-8052. **E-mail:** info@robertlangstudios.com. **Website:** www.robertlangestudios.com. Estab. 2005. For-profit gallery. Approached by 100+ artists/year. Exhibits mid-career artists. Exhibited artists include Robert Lange, Amy Lind and Nathan Durfee. Sponsors 12 exhibits/year. Average display time: 6 months. Open Monday–Sunday, 11-5. Gallery located in an historic area; 3000+ sq. feet. Clients include: local community, tourists, upscale. Overall price range: $200-20,000. Most work sold at $2,000.

MEDIA Considers acrylic, collage, installation, pen & ink, mixed media, sculpture, drawing, oil. Most frequently exhibits oil.

STYLE Considers all styles. Most frequently exhibits surrealism, conceptualism. Considers all genres. Most frequently exhibits figurative work, landscapes and portraits.

TERMS Artwork accepted on consignment with a 50% commission. Retail price set by the artist. Gallery provides insurance, promotion, contract. Accepted work should be framed. Requires exclusive representation locally.

SUBMISSIONS Artists should e-mail query letter with link to website and 8 JPEG samples at 72 dpi. Responds in 1 week. Files images and contact info. Finds artists through submissions and referrals by other artists.

TIPS Have a nice website!

LATINO ARTS, INC.

1028 S. Ninth St., Milwaukee WI 53204. (414)384-3100. **Website:** www.latinoartsinc.org. Nonprofit gallery. Represents emerging, mid-career and established artists. Sponsors up to 5 individual and group exhibitions/year. Average display time 2 months. Open all year; Monday-Friday, 9-8. Latino Arts, Inc. is located in the United Community center on the near southeast side of Milwaukee (gallery is in the main building on the UCC campus); 1,200 sq. ft.; one-time church. Clientele: the general Hispanic community. Overall price range: $100-2,000.

MEDIA Considers all media, all types of prints. Most frequently exhibits original 2D and 3D works and photo exhibitions.

STYLE Exhibits all styles, all genres. Prefers artifacts of Hispanic cultural and educational interests.

TERMS "Our function is to promote cultural awareness (not to be a sales gallery)." Retail price set by the artist. Artist is encouraged to donate 15% of sales to help with operating costs. Gallery provides insurance, promotion, contract, shipping costs to gallery; artist pays shipping costs from gallery. Prefers artwork framed.

SUBMISSIONS Send query letter with résumé, slides, bio, business card and reviews. Call or write for appointment to show portfolio of photographs and slides. Responds in 2 weeks. Finds artists through recruiting, networking, advertising and word of mouth.

⊕ LAWNDALE ART CENTER

4912 Main St., Houston TX 77002. (713)528-5858. **Fax:** (713)528-4140. **E-mail:** askus@lawndaleartcenter.org. **Website:** www.lawndaleartcenter.org. **Contact:** Dennis Nance, exhibitions & programming director. Estab. 1979. Nonprofit gallery, museum, alternative space. Exhibits emerging, mid-career and established artists. Approached by 1,200 artists/year. Exhibits 150 artists. Sponsors 25 exhibits/year; approx. 5 photography exhibits/year. Model/property release preferred. Average display time: 5 weeks. Open Monday–Friday, 10–5; Saturday, 12–5; closed Sunday, Christmas Eve until New Year's Day, Presidents' Day, Memorial Day, Independence Day, Labor Day, Columbus Day and Thanksgiving. "Located at the edge of downtown in the Museum District, Lawndale includes 4 museum-quality galleries, 3 artist studios, an outdoor sculpture garden and annual rotating mural wall." Clients include: local community, students, tourists, upscale, artists, collectors, art enthusiasts, volunteers, young professionals.

MEDIA Considers all media. Gallery provides insurance, promotion, contract. Prefers artists from Houston TX and surrounding area.

TERMS "Visit the proposal section of our website: www.lawndaleartcenter.org/exhibitions/proposals.shtml." Does not accept mailed proposals. All proposals must be made online. Finds artists through word of mouth, submissions, referrals by other artists.

SUBMISSIONS Finds artists through word of mouth, submissions, referrals by other artists.

TIPS "Please visit us or our website to learn about what type of work we exhibit and how we accept submissions to artists before contacting."

SHERRY LEEDY CONTEMPORARY ART

2004 Baltimore Ave., Kansas City MO 64108. (816)221-2626. **Fax:** (816)221-8689. **E-mail:** sherryleedy@sherryleedy.com. **Website:** www.sherryleedy.com. **Contact:** Sherry Leedy, director. Estab. 1985. Retail gallery. Represents 50 mid-career and established artists. Exhibited artists include Jun Kaneko, Mike Schultz, Vera Mercer, and more. Sponsors 6 shows/year. Average display time: 6 weeks. Open Tuesday–Saturday, 11-5, and by appointment. 5,000 sq. ft. of exhibit area in 3 galleries. Clients include established and beginning collectors. 50% of sales are to private collectors, 50% corporate clients. Overall price range: $50-100,000; most work sold at $3,500-35,000.

MEDIA Considers all media and one-of-a-kind or limited-edition prints; no posters. Most frequently exhibits painting, photography, ceramic sculpture and glass.

STYLE Considers all styles.

TERMS Accepts work on consignment (50% commission). Retail price set by gallery in counsultation with the artist. Sometimes offers customer discounts and payment by installment. Exclusive area representation required. Gallery provides insurance, promotion; shipping costs are shared. Prefers artwork framed.

SUBMISSIONS E-mail query letter, résumé, artist's statement, and digital images or link to website. No work will be reviewed in person without a prior appointment.

TIPS "Please allow 3 months for gallery to review submissions."

LEEPA-RATTNER MUSEUM OF ART

P.O. Box 1545, Tarpon Springs FL 34688. (727)712-5762. **E-mail:** lrma@spcollege.edu. **Website:** www.spcollege.edu/museum. **Contact:** R. Lynn Whitelaw, curator. The museum's 20th century collection is made up of art from Abraham Rattner's estate, donated by Allen and Isabelle Leepa, and a large donation made by the Tampa Museum of Art. The museum is filled with Rattner's retrospective works: lithographs, tapestries, sculptures, paintings and stained glass." Open Tuesday, Wednesday, Saturday, 10-5; Thursday, 10-8; Friday, 10-4, Sunday, 1-5. Closed Mondays and national holidays. Located on the Tarpon Springs campus of St. Petersburg College.

MEDIA Considers all types of media and prints. Mostly exhibits 20th-century artwork.

STYLE Considers all genres.

LEGION ARTS

1103 Third St. SE, Cedar Rapids IA 52401-2305. (319)364-1580. **Fax:** (319)362-9156. **E-mail:** info@legionarts.org. **Website:** www.legionarts.org. **Contact:** Mel Andringa, producing director. Estab. 1991. Alternative space, nonprofit gallery. Approached by 50 artists/year. Exhibits 15 emerging artists. Exhibited artists include Bill Jordan (photographs), Paco Rosic (spray can murals). Sponsors 15 exhibits/year. Average display time 2 months. Open Wednesday–Sunday, 11-6. Closed July and August. Located in south end Cedar Rapids; old Czech meeting hall, 2 large galleries and off-site exhibits; track lights, carpet, ornamental tin ceilings. 65 events a year. Clients include local community. Overall price range $50-500; most work sold at $200.

MEDIA Considers all media and all types of prints. Most frequently exhibits painting, mixed media and installation.

STYLE Considers all styles. Most frequently exhibits postmodernism, conceptualism and surrealism.

TERMS Artwork is accepted on consignment and there is a 30% commission. Retail price set by the artist. Gallery provides insurance and promotion. Accepted work should be framed. Requires exclusive representation locally.

SUBMISSIONS Send query letter with artist's statement, bio, SASE and slides. Responds in 6 months. Files résumé, sample slide and statement. Finds artists through word of mouth, art exhibits and art trade magazines.

LEHIGH UNIVERSITY ART GALLERIES

420 E. Packer Ave., Bethlehem PA 18015. (610)758-3619; (610)758-3615. **Fax:** (610)758-4580. **E-mail:** rv02@lehigh.edu. **Website:** www.luag.org. **Contact:** Ricardo Viera, director/curator. Sponsors 5-8 exhibits/year. Average display time 6-12 weeks. Sponsors openings. Exhibits fine art/multicultural, Latin American. Interested in all types of works.

TERMS Arrange a personal interview to show portfolio. Send query letter with SASE. Responds in 1 month.

SUBMISSIONS "Don't send more than 10 slides or a CD."

LE MUR VIVANT FINE ART

Website: www.corporart.co.uk/exhibitions. **Contact:** Caro Lyle Skyrme. Estab. 1996. Sponsors 10 exhibits/year. Average display time 3 weeks. Collaboration considered with new artists. By appointment only. Gallery space is 2 connected rooms each approximately 12×15. Space: 30' long. Offices in central London, Westminster. High ceilings, Victorian shop. Clientele: local community, tourists, upscale media and theater people. 20% corporate collectors. Overall price range $1,000-20,000; most work sold at $5,000- 20,000 (£2,500-10,000).

MEDIA Considers all media. Most frequently exhibits oil on canvas or board, watercolor, mixed media.

STYLE Exhibits color field, expressionism, imagism, impressionism, neo-expressionism, painterly abstraction, postmodernism and surrealism. Most frequently exhibits abstract expressionism, impressionism, magic realism and surrealism. Considers all genres including Northern Romantic and photo-realism.

TERMS "We work on flexible percentages depending on standing of artist and potential following. We take smaller percentage from already established artists with excellent C.V. and good client list as we can rely on many sales. Retail price set with collaboration of the artist. Gallery provides contract. Accepted work should be framed or mounted by artist as agreed. Requires exclusive representation locally. Prefers only fully professional artists with excellent curriculum vitae.

SUBMISSIONS Write to arrange a personal interview to show portfolio of photographs, PowerPoint slides, transparencies. Send query letter with artist's statement, bio, photographs, résumé and SASE. Portfolio should include good photos or slides etc. Full curriculum vitae detailing college and professional experience. Returns material with SAE. Replies only if interested within 1 month. Finds artists through word of mouth, submissions, portfolio reviews, art exhibits, referrals by other artists, from college graduate shows, Royal Academy exhibitions, public shows and magazines.

TIPS "Send neatly presented details of past work/exhibitions/galleries, good quality transparencies, photos and/or slides. Do not expect to walk in and have your work looked at by a staff member in the middle of a business day!"

DAVID LEONARDIS GALLERY

1346 N. Paulina St., Chicago IL 60622. (312)863-9045. **E-mail:** david@dlg-gallery.com. **Website:** www.dlg-gallery.com. **Contact:** David Leonardis, owner. Estab. 1992. For-profit gallery. Approached by 100 artists/year. Represents 12 emerging, mid-career and established artists. Exhibited artists include Kristen Thiele and Christopher Makos. Average display time: 30 days. Open by appointment. Clients include local community, tourists, upscale. 10% of sales are to corporate collectors. Overall price range: $50-5,000; most work sold at $500.

MEDIA Most frequently exhibits painting, photography and lithography. Considers lithographs and serigraphs.

STYLE Exhibits pop. Most frequently exhibits contemporary, pop, folk, photo. Genres include figurative work and portraits.

TERMS Artwork is accepted on consignment, and there is a 50% commission. Retail price set by the gallery and the artist. Gallery provides promotion. Accepted work should be framed. Does not require local representation. Prefers artists who are professional and easy to deal with.

SUBMISSIONS E-mail. Responds only if interested. E-mails and JPEGs are filed. Finds artists through word of mouth, art exhibits, and referrals by other artists.

⊕ LEOPOLD GALLERY

324 W. 63rd St., Kansas City MO 64113. (816)333-3111. **Fax:** (816)333-3616. **E-mail:** email@leopoldgallery.com. **Website:** www.leopoldgallery.com. **Contact:** Paula Busser, assistant director. Estab. 1991.

MEDIA Considers all media. Most frequently exhibits oils, acrylics, blown glass, ceramic, stainless steel. Some works on paper.

STYLE Considers all styles and genres. Most frequently exhibits abstraction, impressionism, conceptual.

SUBMISSIONS E-mail query letter with JPEG samples or link to website. Mail query letter with résumé, printed images, reviews, SASE and disk with images. Returns material with SASE. Responds to queries in 2 months. Finds artists through submissions, portfolio reviews, referrals by clients and artists.

RICHARD LEVY GALLERY

514 Central Ave., SW, Albuquerque NM 87102. (505)766-9888. **Fax:** (505)242-4279. **E-mail:** info@levygallery.com. **Website:** www.levygallery.com. Estab. 1991. "Comprised of contemporary art of all mediums by emerging and established regional, national and international artists. The gallery shows 6-8 exhibitions/year and participates in selected art fairs." Open Tuesday–Saturday, 11-4; closed during art fairs (always noted on voice message). Located on Central Ave. between 5th and 6th. Clients include upscale.

MEDIA Considers all media. Most frequently exhibits paintings, prints and photography.

STYLE Contemporary art.

SUBMISSIONS Submissions by e-mail preferred. "Please include images and any other pertinent information (artist's statment, bio, etc.). When sending submissions by post, please include slides or photographs and SASE for return of materials."

TIPS "Portfolios are reviewed at the gallery by invitation or appointment only."

LIBERTY VILLAGE ARTS CENTER

410 Main St., Chester MT 59522. (406)759-5652. **E-mail:** lvac@mtintouch.net. **Website:** www.centralmomtana.com/listings. Estab. 1976. Nonprofit gallery. Represents 12-20 emerging, mid-career and established artists/year. Sponsors 6-12 shows/year. Average display time: 6-8 weeks. Open all year; Tuesday–Friday, 12:30-4:30. Located near a school; 1,000 sq. ft.; former Catholic Church. Clients include tourists and local community. 100% of sales are to private collectors. Overall price range: $100-2,500; most work sold at $250-500.

MEDIA Considers all media; types of prints include woodcuts, lithographs, mezzotints, serigraphs, linocuts and pottery. Most frequently exhibits paintings in oil, water, acrylic, b&w photos and sculpture assemblages.

STYLE Considers all styles. Prefers contemporary and historic.

TERMS Accepts work on consignment (30% commission) or buys outright for 40% of retail price. Retail price set by the gallery. Gallery provides insurance and promotion; shipping costs are shared. Prefers artwork framed or unframed.

SUBMISSIONS Send query letter with slides, bio and brochure. Portfolio should include slides. Responds only if interested within 1 year. "Artists should cross us off their list." Files everything. Finds artists through word of mouth and seeing work at shows.

TIPS "Artists make the mistake of not giving us enough information and permission to pass information on to other galleries."

LIMITED EDITIONS & COLLECTIBLES

697 Haddon Ave., Collingswood NJ 08108. (856)869-5228. **Fax:** (856)869-5228. **E-mail:** jdl697ltd@juno.com. **Website:** www.ltdeditions.net. **Contact:** John Daniel Lynch, Sr., owner. Estab. 1997. For-profit gallery. Approached by 24 artists/year. Exhibited artists include Richard Montmurro, James Allen Flood and Gino Hollander. Open all year. Located in downtown Collingswood; 700 sq. ft. Overall price range: $190-20,000; most work sold at $450.

MEDIA Considers all media and all types of prints. Most frequently exhibits acrylic, watercolors and oil.

STYLE Considers all styles and genres.

TERMS Artwork is accepted on consignment, and there is a 30% commission. Retail price set by the artist. Gallery provides insurance, promotion and contract. Accepted work should be framed, mounted and matted. Does not require exclusive representation locally.

SUBMISSIONS Call or write to arrange a personal interview to show portfolio. Send query letter with bio, business card and résumé. Responds in 1 month. Finds artists through word of mouth, portfolio reviews, art exhibits and referrals by other artists.

LIMNER GALLERY

123 Warren St., Hudson NY 12534. (518)828-2343. **E-mail:** thelimner@aol.com. **Website:** www.slowart.com. **Contact:** Tim Slowinski, director. Estab. 1987. Artist-owned alternative retail (consignment) gallery. Represents emerging and mid-career artists. Hosts periodic thematic exhibitions of emerging artists selected by competition, cash awards up to $1,000. Entry available for SASE or from website. Sponsors 6-8 shows/year. Average display time: 1 month. Open Thursday-Saturday, 12-5; Sunday, 12-4. Located in storefront 400 sq. ft. 60-80% of space for special exhibitions; 20-40% of space for gallery artists. Clients include lawyers, real estate developers, doctors, architects. 95% of sales are to private collectors, 5% corporate collectors. Overall price range: $300-10,000.

MEDIA Considers all media, all types of prints except posters. Most frequently exhibits painting, sculpture and works on paper.

STYLE Exhibits primitivism, surrealism, political commentary, satire, all styles, postmodern works, all genres. "Gallery exhibits all styles but emphasis is on nontraditional figurative work."

TERMS Accepts work on consignment (50% commission). Retail price set by the gallery and the artist. Gallery provides promotion and contract; artist pays shipping costs to and from gallery. Prefers artwork framed.

SUBMISSIONS Send query letter with résumé, slides, bio and SASE. Call for appointment to show portfolio of originals, photographs, slides and transparencies. Responds in 3 weeks. Files slides, résumé. Finds artists through word of mouth, art publications and sourcebooks, submissions.

LIZARDI/HARP GALLERY

P.O. Box 91895, Pasadena CA 91109. (626)791-8123. **Fax:** (626)791-8887. **E-mail:** lizardiharp@earthlink.net. **Contact:** Grady Harp, director. Estab. 1981. Retail gallery and art consultancy. Represents 15 emerging, mid-career and established artists/year. Exhibited artists include Wes Hempel, Gerard Huber and José Parra. Sponsors 4 shows/year. Average display time: 2 months. Open all year; Tuesday-Saturday, by appointment only. 80% private collectors, 20% corporate collectors. Overall price range: $900-80,000; most work sold at $2,000-15,000.

MEDIA Considers oil, acrylic, watercolor, pastel, pen & ink, drawing, mixed media, sculpture, installation, photography, lithographs and etchings. Most frequently exhibits works on paper and canvas, sculpture, photography.

STYLE Exhibits representational art. Genres include landscapes, figurative work (both portraiture and narrative) and still life. Prefers figurative, landscapes and experimental.

TERMS Accepts work on consignment (50% commission). Retail price set by the gallery and the artist. Gallery provides insurance, promotion, contract; artist pays shipping costs.

SUBMISSIONS Send query letter with artist's statement, résumé, 20 slides, bio, photographs, SASE and reviews. Write for appointment to show portfolio of photographs, slides and transparencies. Responds in 1 month. Files "all interesting applications." Finds artists through studio visits, group shows, submissions.

TIPS "Timelessness of message (rather than trendy) is a plus. Our emphasis is on quality or craftsmanship, evidence of originality and maturity of business relationship concept." Artists are encouraged to send an artist's statement with application and at least 10-20 JPEGs.

ANNE LLOYD GALLERY

125 N. Water St., Decatur IL 62523-1025. **E-mail:** sue@decaturarts.org. **Website:** www.decaturarts.org. **Contact:** Sue Powell, gallery director. Estab. 2004. Nonprofit gallery. Approached by 10 artists/year. Represents 20 artists. Exhibits emerging, mid-career and established artists. Exhibited artists include Seth Casteel (photographer) and Rob O'Dell (watercolor). Sponsors 8 exhibits/year, 1 photography exhibit. Average display time: 1 month. Open Monday–Friday, 8:30-4:30; Saturday, 10-2. Closed major holidays. Located within the Madden Arts Center (community arts center owned/operated by Decatur Area Arts Council) in downtown Decatur IL. Approx. 1,500 sq. ft. space with 113 linear feet wall space; 14 ft. ceilings; 10 ft. high gallery cloth walls. Excellent track/grid lighting. Clients include local community, students and tourists. 1% of sales are to corporate collectors. Overall price range: $100-5,000. Most work sold at $100-500.

MEDIA Considers all media except installation. Considers all types of prints. Considers all styles. Most frequently exhibits acrylic, oil, and watercolor.

STYLE Considers all styles and genres. Most frequently exhibits abstract representational, conceptual.

TERMS Artwork is accepted on consignment and there is a 35% commission. Retail price set by the artist. Museum provides insurance, promotion, and contract. Accepted work should be framed or mounted.

Does not require exclusive representation locally. Art must be appropriate for a family-type venue.

SUBMISSIONS Call; e-mail query letter with link to website and JPEG samples at 72 dpi; or send query letter with artist's statement, bio, CD with images. Can also mail portfolio for review. Material is returned with SASE. Responds in 4 weeks. Files bio, statement, images, contact info. Finds artists through art exhibits, referrals by other artists, portfolio reviews, art fairs, research online, submissions, and word of mouth.

TIPS "Please include 6-10 images on a CD. This is important."

LOCUST PROJECTS

3852 N. Miami Ave., Miami FL 33127. (305)576-8570. **E-mail:** info@locustprojects.org. **Website:** www.locustprojects.org. **Contact:** Submissions. Estab. 1998. Alternative space and nonprofit gallery. 5,000 sq. ft. Exhibited artists include Theaster Gates (sculpture/installation), Francesca DiMattio (mural/installation) and Ruben Ochoa (sculpture/installation). Sponsors 6+ exhibits/year. Average display time: 4-6 weeks. Open Tuesday–Saturday, 10-5; and by appointment.

MEDIA Most frequently exhibits site-specific installation.

STYLE Exhibits contemporary work.

TERMS Gallery provides promotion. Does not require exclusive representation locally.

SUBMISSIONS Submission details available online.

LONG BEACH ARTS GALLERY

5372 Long Beach Blvd., Long Beach CA 90805. (562)423-9689. **E-mail:** lba@longbeachart.org. **Website:** www.longbeachart.org. Estab. 1924. Since 1924, Long Beach Arts has been a nonprofit art organization and an on-going collaborative venture between local artists and the community. The gallery hosts a wide variety of juried, group exhibitions in most media. Open Wednesday–Sunday, 12-4 (during open exhibitions only).

STYLE Color field, conceptualism, expressionism, impressionism, minimalism, neo-expressionism, primitive realism, surrealism and painterly abstraction. Considers all genres.

TERMS Artwork is accepted on consignment with a 30% commission. Call or e-mail for further information.

LONGVIEW MUSEUM OF FINE ARTS

215 E. Tyler St., Longview TX 756016. (903)753-8103. **Fax:** (903)753-8217. **E-mail:** fineart@lmfa.org. **Website:** www.lmfa.org. **Contact:** Renee Hawkins, director. Estab. 1958. Contemporary regional art museum representing approximately 12 artists per year plus high school invitational. 840 members. Open all year except Thanksgiving weekend and 2 weeks at year's end; Tuesday–Friday, 10-4; Saturday, 10-2. Located downtown. 35% of space for special exhibitions. Clientele: members, visitors (local and out-of-town) and private collectors. Over 450 objects in private collection. Offers 10% discount to museum members.

MEDIA Most frequently exhibits painting, photography, sculpture, pottery and glass.

TERMS Gallery exhibitors are provided insurance and promotion.

SUBMISSIONS Send website or CD with vitae. Finds artists through art publications and shows in other areas.

LOS ANGELES MUNICIPAL ART GALLERY

4800 Hollywood Blvd., Los Angeles CA 90027. **Website:** www.lamag.org. **Contact:** Scott Canty, curator. Estab. gallery 1971; support group LAMAGA 1954. City-run, municipally-owned gallery. Exhibits emerging, mid-career, and established artists. Sponsors 8 total exhibits/year. Average display time is 8 weeks. Open Thursday-Sunday, 12-5. A 10,000-sq.-ft. city-run facility located in Barnsdall Park in Hollywood CA. Clients include local community, students, tourists, and upscale clientele.

MEDIA Accepts all media.

TERMS Gallery provides insurance and promotion.

SUBMISSIONS "Visit our website at lamag.org for upcoming show opportunities." Files artists and proposals of interests. Finds artists through word of mouth, submissions, portfolio review, art exhibits, art fairs, referrals by other artists and the DCA Slide Registry.

LOYOLA UNIVERSITY CHICAGO

101 W. Loyola, Suite 200, Chicago IL 60626. **Website:** www.luc.edu/dfpa. Crown Center Gallery, 6525 N. Sheridan Rd., Chicago IL 60626. (773)508-3811. **Fax:** (773)508-2282. **Contact:** Fine Arts Department. Nonprofit gallery. Estab. 1983. Approached by more than 100 artists/year. Sponsors 6 exhibits/year. Open all year; Monday-Friday, 10-3. Located on Chicago lakefront adjacent to glass wall overlooking lake and Michigan. Gallery is 85×19 with large lobby and auditorium. Clients include local community, students and upscale.

MEDIA Considers all media except performance art.

STYLE Considers all styles and genres.

TERMS We are nonprofit. Pass sales on to artists. Retail price set by the artist. Gallery provides insurance, promotion and contract. Accepted work should be framed, mounted and matted. Does not require exclusive representation locally. Prefer midwest and international artists.

SUBMISSIONS Send query letter with artist's statement, bio, SASE and slides. Returns material with SASE. Responds in 3 months. Finds artists through word of mouth and portfolio reviews.

MAIN STREET GALLERY

330 Main St., Ketchikan AK 99901. (907)225-2211. **E-mail:** info@ketchikanarts.org. **Website:** www.ketchikanarts.org. **Contact:** Marni Rickelmann, program director. Estab. 1953. Nonprofit gallery. Exhibits emerging, mid-career and established artists. Number of artists represented or exhibited varies based on applications. Applications annually accepted for March 1 deadline. Sponsors 11 total exhibits/year. Model and property release are preferred. Average display time 20 days-1 month. Open Monday-Friday, 9-5; Saturday 11-3. Closed last 2 weeks of December. Located in downtown Ketchikan, housed in renovated church. 800 sq. ft. Clients include local community, students, tourists, upscale. Overall price range of work sold $20-4,000. Most work sold at $150.

MEDIA Considers all media, most frequently exhibits acrylic, mixed media and oil. Considers all types of prints.

STYLE Considers all styles.

TERMS There is a membership fee plus a donation of time. There is a 25% commission. Retail price set by the artist. Gallery provides insurance, promotion and contract. Accepted work should be framed and mounted.

SUBMISSIONS E-mail query letter with link to artist's website, 10 JPEG samples at 72 dpi or résumé and proposal. March 1 gallery exhibit deadline for September-August season. Returns material with SASE. Responds in 2 months from March 1 deadline. Files all application materials. Finds artists through word of mouth, submissions, art exhibits and referrals from other artists.

TIPS Respond clearly to application.

MALTON GALLERY

3804 Edwards Rd., Cincinnati OH 45209. (513)321-8614. **E-mail:** srombis@maltonartgallery.com. **Website:** www.maltonartgallery.com. **Contact:** Sylvia Rombis, director. Estab. 1974. Retail gallery. Represents about 100 emerging, mid-career and established artists. Exhibits 20 artists/year. Exhibited artists include Alexa McNeill, Mark Chatterley, Terri Hallman and Dan Miller. Sponsors 7 shows/year (2-person shows alternate with display of gallery artists). Average display time: 1 month. Open all year; Tuesday-Saturday, 11-5; or by appointment. Located in high-income neighborhood shopping district; 2,500 sq. ft. Clientele: private and corporate. Overall price range: $250-10,000; most work sold at $1,000-8,000.

MEDIA Considers oil, acrylic, drawing, sculpture, watercolor, mixed media, pastel, collage and original handpulled prints.

STYLE Exhibits all styles. Genres include contemporary landscapes, figurative and narrative and abstractions work.

TERMS Accepts work on consignment only (50% commission). Retail price set by artist (sometimes in consultation with gallery). Gallery provides insurance, promotion and contract; artist pays shipping costs to gallery. Prefers unframed works for canvas; unframed works for paper.

SUBMISSIONS E-mail query letter with résumé, pictures, reviews, bio and SASE. Responds in 4 months. Files résumé, review or any printed material.

TIPS "Never drop in without an appointment. Be prepared and professional in presentation. This is a business."

BEN MALTZ GALLERY

Otis College of Art & Design, Ground Floor, Bronya and Andy Galef Center for Fine Arts, 9045 Lincoln Blvd., Los Angeles CA 90045. (310)665-6905. **E-mail:** galleryinfo@otis.edu. **Website:** www.otis.edu/ben maltzgallery. Estab. 1957. Nonprofit gallery. Exhibits local, national and international emerging, mid-career and established artists. Sponsors 4-6 exhibits/year. Average display time: 1-2 months. Open Tuesday, Wednesday, Friday, 10-5; Thursday, 10-9; Saturday-Sunday 12-4; closed Mondays and major holidays. Located near Los Angeles International Airport (LAX); approximately 3,520 sq. ft.; 14-ft. walls. Clients include students, Otis community, local and city community, regional art community, artists, collectors and tourists.

MEDIA Fine art/design. Considers all media, most frequently exhibits paintings, drawings, mixed media, sculpture and video.

SUBMISSIONS Submission guidelines available online. Submissions via Internet only. Do not send other materials unless requested by the gallery after your initial submission has been reviewed.

TIPS "Follow submission guidelines and be patient. Attend opening receptions when possible to familiarize yourself with the gallery, director, curators and artists."

MANITOU ART CENTER

513 Manitou Ave., Manitou Springs CO 80829. (719)685-1861. **E-mail:** director@thebac.org. **Website:** www.thebac.org. Estab. 1988. The MAC is a nonprofit gallery situated in 2 renovated landmark buildings in the Manitou Springs National Historic District located at 513 and 515 Manitou Ave. Art studios for rent and often include equipment. The Manitou Art Center sponsors 16 exhibits/year in 5 galleries. Average display time: 6 weeks-2 months. Gallery open most days, 8-8; closed Tuesday. Overall price range: $50-3,000. Most work sold at $300.

MEDIA Photos of environmental, landscapes/scenics, wildlife, gardening, rural, adventure, health/fitness, performing arts, travel. Interested in alternative process, avant garde, documentary, fashion/glamour, fine art.

TERMS "Artwork is accepted for our open submission and shows and there is a 30% commission." The gallery provides insurance, promotion and a basic contract. Accepted work should be framed and ready to hang.

SUBMISSIONS Write to arrange a personal interview to show portfolio. "We often find artists through word of mouth, submissions, art exhibits and referrals by other artists."

MARIN MUSEUM OF CONTEMPORARY ART

500 Palm Dr., Novato CA 94949. (415)506-0137. **Fax:** (415)506-0139. **E-mail:** info@marinmoca.org. **Website:** www.marinmoca.org. **Contact:** Heidi LaGrasta, executive director. Estab. 2007. Nonprofit gallery. Exhibits emerging, mid-career and established artists. Sponsors 15+ exhibits/year. Model and property release is preferred. Average display time: 5 weeks. Open Wednesday-Sunday, 11-4; closed Thanksgiving,

Christmas, New Year's Day. MarinMOCA is located in historic Hamilton Field, a former Army Air Base. The Spanish-inspired architecture makes for a unique and inviting exterior and interior space. Houses 2 exhibition spaces—the Main Gallery (1,633 sq. ft.) and the Ron Collins Gallery (750 sq. ft.). Part of the Novato Arts Center, which also contains approximately 50 artist studios and a classroom (offers adult classes and a summer camp for children). Clients include local community, students, tourists, upscale. Overall price range: $200-20,000; most work sold at $500-1,000.

MEDIA Considers all media except video. Most frequently exhibits acrylic, oil, sculpture/installation.

STYLE Considers all prints, styles and genres.

TERMS Artwork is accepted on consignment and there is a 40% commission. Retail price of the art set by the artist. Gallery provides insurance, promotion (for single exhibition only, not representation), contract (for consignment only, not representation). Accepted work should be framed (canvas can be unframed, but prints/collage/photos should be framed). "We do not have exclusive contracts with, nor do we represent artists."

SUBMISSIONS "We are currently not accepting portfolio submissions at this time. Please visit our website for updates. If you are interested in gallery rental, please contact Heidi LaGrasta." Finds artists through word of mouth and portfolio reviews.

TIPS "Keep everything clean and concise. Avoid lengthy, flowery language and choose clear explanations instead. Submit only what is requested and shoot for a confident, yet humble tone. Make sure images are good quality (300 dpi) and easily identifiable regarding title, size, medium."

MARIN-PRICE GALLERIES

7022 Wisconsin Ave., Chevy Chase MD 20815. (301)718-0622. **E-mail:** fmp@marin-price.com. **Website:** www.marin-price.com. Estab. 1992. Retail/wholesale gallery. Represents/exhibits 25 established painters and 4 sculptors/year. Exhibited artists include Joseph Sheppard, March Avery, William Woodward, Jeremiah Stermer, Jenness Cortez and others. Sponsors 24 shows/year. Average display time: 3 weeks. Open Monday–Saturday, 10:30-7; Sunday, 12-5. 1,500 sq. ft. 50% of space for special exhibitions. Clientele: upscale. 90% private collectors, 10% corporate collectors. Overall price range: $5,000-75,000; most work sold at $6,000-18,000.

MEDIA Considers oil, drawing, watercolor and pastel. Most frequently exhibits oil, watercolor and pastels.

STYLE Exhibits expressionism, photorealism, neo-expressionism, primitivism, realism and impressionism. Genres include landscapes, florals, Americana and figurative work.

TERMS Retail price set by the gallery and the artist. Gallery provides insurance, promotion and contract. Artist pays for shipping costs to and from the artist. Prefers artwork framed.

SUBMISSIONS Prefers only oils. Send query letter with résumé, photo prints, bio and SASE. Responds in 6 weeks. Will not respond to electronic submissions.

⊙ MARKEIM ARTS CENTER

104 Walnut St., Haddonfield NJ 08033. (856)429-8585. **E-mail:** markeim@verizon.net. **Website:** www.markeimartcenter.org. **Contact:** Elizabeth H. Madden, executive director. Estab. 1956. Nonprofit gallery. Sponsors 10-11 exhibits/year. Average display time: 4 weeks. Overall price range: $75-1,000; most work sold at $350.

MEDIA Considers all media. Must be original. Most frequently exhibits paintings, photography and sculpture.

STYLE Exhibits all styles and genres.

TERMS Charges 30% commission. Accepted work should be framed, mounted or unmounted, matted or unmatted. Artists from New Jersey and Delaware Valley region are preferred. Work must be professional and high quality.

SUBMISSIONS Send slides by mail for consideration. Include SASE, résumé and letter of intent. Responds in 1 month.

TIPS "Be patient and flexible with scheduling. Look not only for one-time shows, but for opportunities to develop working relationships with a gallery. Establish yourself locally and market yourself outward."

MARLBORO GALLERY

Prince George's Community College, 301 Largo Rd., Largo MD 20477. (301)322-0965. **E-mail:** beraulta@pgcc.edu. **Website:** academic.pgcc.edu/art/gallery. **Contact:** Tom Berault, curator-director. Estab. 1976. Interested in emerging, mid-career and established artists. Sponsors 3 solo and 3 group shows/year. Average display time: 5 weeks. Seasons for exhibition: August-April. 2, 100 sq. ft. with 10-ft. ceilings and 25-ft. clear story over 50% of space track lighting (incandescent) and daylight. Clientele: 100% private collectors. Overall price range: $50-4,000; most work sold at $300-2,500. "We are open to all serious artists and all media. We will consider all proposals without prejudice." Retail price set by artist. Exclusive area representation not required. Gallery provides insurance. Artist pays for shipping. Artwork must be ready for display.

MEDIA Considers all media. Most frequently exhibits acrylics, oils, photographs, watercolors and sculpture.

STYLE Exhibits mainly expressionism, neo-expressionism, realism, photorealism, minimalism, primitivism, painterly abstraction, conceptualism and imagism. Exhibits all genres.

TERMS Send cover letter with résumé, CD or digital media, SASE, photographs, artist's statement and bio.

SUBMISSIONS Responds every 6 months. Finds artists through word of mouth, visiting exhibitions and submissions. Impressed by originality. "Indicate if you prefer solo shows or will accept inclusion in group show chosen by gallery."

ASHOK JAIN GALLERY

58 Hester St., New York NY 10002. (212)969-9660. **Fax:** (212)969-9715. **E-mail:** info@ashokjaingallery.com. **Website:** www.ajaingallery.com. Estab. 1991. Retail gallery. Represents 30 emerging artists. Exhibited artists include Fernando Pomalaza and Pauline Gagnon. Open all year; Tuesday–Saturday, 11-5; or by appointment. Located in New York Gallery Bldg. 100% of space for special exhibitions. Clients include corporate and designer. 50% of sales are to private collectors, 50% corporate collectors. Overall price range: $1,000-20,000; most work sold at $5,000-10,000.

MEDIA Considers oil, acrylic and mixed media. Most frequently exhibits oil, acrylic and collage.

STYLE Exhibits painterly abstraction. Prefers abstract and landscapes.

TERMS Accepts work on consignment (50% commission). Retail price set by artist. Offers customer discount. Gallery provides contract; artist pays for shipping costs. Prefers artwork framed.

SUBMISSIONS "If you are interested in submitting materials to our gallery, please mail a current résumé as well as a representative set of images (maximum of 20) along with a SASE if you wish to have your materials returned. You may e-mail your materials or mail them to our gallery for consideration."

MATHIAS FINE ART

10 Mathias Dr., Trevett ME 04571. (207)633-7404. **Website:** www.mathiasfineart.com. **Contact:** Cordula Mathias, president. Estab. 1991. For profit gallery. Approached by 20-30 artists/year. Represents 15-20 emerging, mid-career and established artists. Exhibited artists include Brenda Bettinson and John Lorence. Sponsors 6 exhibits/year. Average display time: 2 months. Open all year, by appointment. Located in mid-coast area of Maine; 400 sq. ft. combination of natural and artificial lighting. Clients include local community, tourists and upscale. Percentage of sales to corporate collectors varies. Overall price range: $50-25,000; most work sold at $1,200.

MEDIA Considers acrylic, collage, drawing, original prints, mixed media, oil, paper and pen & ink. Most frequently exhibits painting, drawing and photography. Considers all types of prints except posters.

STYLE Considers all styles and genres.

TERMS Artwork is accepted on consignment and there is a 50% commission. Retail price set by the gallery and the artist. Gallery provides promotion and contract. Accepted work should be framed and matted. Requires exclusive representation locally. Prefers paintings or works on paper. Prefers artists who can deliver and pick up.

SUBMISSIONS Send query letter with bio, photographs, résumé, reviews and photographs. Returns material with SASE. Responds in 6 weeks. Files CV, artist's statement, visuals if of interest within 6-18 months. Finds artists through word of mouth, submissions, portfolio reviews, art exhibits, and referrals by other artists.

TIPS "Send clearly labeled photographs, well organized vita and an informative artist's statement. Archival-quality materials are 100% essential in selling fine art to collectors."

NEDRA MATTEUCCI GALLERIES

1075 Paseo De Peralta, Santa Fe NM 87501. (505)982-4631. **Fax:** (505)984-0199. **E-mail:** pr@matteucci.com. **Website:** www.matteucci.com. Estab. 1972. For-profit gallery. Main focus of gallery is on deceased artists of Taos, Santa Fe and the West. Approached by hundreds of artists/year. Represents approx. 35 established artists. Exhibited artists include Dan Ostermiller and Glenna Goodacre. Sponsors 3-5 exhibits/year. Average display time: 1 month. Open all year; Monday–Saturday, 9-5. Clients are upscale.

MEDIA Considers drawing, oil, pen & ink, sculpture and watercolor. Most frequently exhibits oil, watercolor and bronze sculpture.

STYLE Exhibits impressionism. Most frequently exhibits impressionism, modernism and realism. Genres include Americana, figurative work, landscapes, portraits, Southwestern, Western and wildlife.

TERMS Artwork is accepted on consignment. Retail price set by the gallery and the artist.

SUBMISSIONS Write to arrange a personal interview to show portfolio. Send query letter with bio, photographs, résumé and SASE.

MAUI HANDS

P.O. Box 974, Makawao, HI 96768 (808)573-2021. **Fax:** (808)573-2022. **E-mail:** panna@mauihands. com. **Website:** www.mauihands.com. **Contact:** Panna Cappelli, owner. Estab. 1992. For-profit gallery. Approached by 50-60 artists/year. Continuously exhibits 300 emerging, mid-career and established artists. Exhibited artists include Linda Whittemore (abstract monotypes) and Steven Smeltzer (ceramic sculpture). Sponsors 15-20 exhibits/year; 2 photography exhibits/year. Average display time: 1 month. Open Monday-Sunday, 10-7; weekends 10-6; closed on Christmas and Thanksgiving. Three spaces: #1 on Main Highway, 1,200 sq. ft. gallery, 165 sq. ft. exhibition; #2 on Main Highway, 1,000 sq. ft. gallery, 80 sq. ft. exhibition; #3 in resort, 900 sq. ft. gallery, 50 sq. ft. exhibition. Clients include local community, tourists and upscale. 3% of sales are to corporate collectors. Overall price range: $10-7,000. Most work sold at $350.

MEDIA Considers all media. Most frequently exhibits oils, pastels, and mixed media. Considers engravings, etchings, linocuts, lithographs, and serigraphs.

STYLE Considers painterly abstraction, impressionism and primitivism realism. Most frequently exhibits impressionism and painterly abstraction. Genres include figurative work, florals, landscapes and portraits.

TERMS Artwork accepted on consignment with a 55% commission. Retail price of the art set by the gallery and artist. Gallery provides insurance and promotion. Artwork should be framed, mounted and matted, as applicable. Only accepts artists from Hawaii.

SUBMISSIONS Artists should call, write to arrange personal interview to show portfolio of original pieces, e-mail query letter with link to artist's website (JPEG samples at 72 dpi,) or send query letter with artist's statement, bio, brochure, photographs, résumé, business cards and reviews. Responds in days. All materials filed. Finds artists through word of mouth, submissions, portfolio reviews, art exhibits, art fairs and referrals by other artists.

TIPS "Best to submit your work via e-mail."

ERNESTO MAYANS GALLERY

601 Canyon Rd., Santa Fe NM 87501. (505)983-8068. **E-mail:** arte2@aol.com. **Website:** ernestomayansgallery.com. **Contact:** Ernesto Mayans, director. Estab. 1977. Publishers, retail gallery and art consulancy. Publishes books, catalogs and portfolios. Overall price range: $200-$5,000. Considers oil, acrylic, watercolor, pastel, pen & ink, drawings, mixed media, sculpture, photography, and original, handpulled prints. Most frequently exhibits oil, photography and lithographs. Exhibits 20th-century American and Latin American art. Genres include landscapes and figurative work. "We exhibit Digital Chromogenic prints on Metallic Paper by Sibylle Szaggars-Redford, Photogravures by Unai San Martin; Pigment prints by Pablo Mayans, Digital prints by Eric Olson, Silver Gelatin prints by Richard Faller (Vintage Southwest Works) and Johanna Saretzki and Sean McGann (Nudes)."

TERMS Accepts work on consignment (50% commission). Retail price set by gallery and artist. Requires exclusive representation within area. "Please call before submitting." Arrange a personal interview to show portfolio. Send query by mail with SASE for consideration. Size limited to 11×20 maximum. Responds in 2 weeks.

MCGOWAN FINE ART, INC.

10 Hills Ave., Concord NH 03301. (603)225-2515. **Fax:** (603)225-7791. **E-mail:** art@mcgowanfineart.com. **Website:** www.mcgowanfineart.com. **Contact:** Sarah Chaffee, owner/art consultant. Estab. 1980. Retail gallery and art consultancy. Represents emerging, mid-career and established artists. Sponsors 8 shows/year. Average display time: 1 month. Located just off Main Street. 50% of space for special exhibitions. Clients include residential and corporate. Most work sold at $125-9,000. Open Tuesday–Friday, 10-6 (though frequently in store on Mondays); Saturday, 10-2; or by appointment; closed Memorial and Labor Day weekends, Christmas (and Dec. 26), New Year's Day.

MEDIA Considers oil, acrylic, watercolor, pastel, mixed media, collage, works on paper, sculpture, woodcuts, wood engravings, linocuts, engravings, mezzotints, etchings, lithographs and serigraphs. Most frequently exhibits sculpture, watercolor and oil/acrylic.

STYLE Exhibits painterly abstraction, landscapes, etc.
TERMS Accepts work on consignment (50% commission). Retail price set by artist. Gallery provides insurance and promotion; negotiates payment of shipping costs. Prefers artwork unframed.
SUBMISSIONS Send query letter with résumé, 5-10 slides and bio. Responds in 1 month. Files materials.
TIPS "I am interested in the number of years you have been devoted to art. Are you committed? Do you show growth in your work?"

MCLEAN PROJECT FOR THE ARTS

McLean Community Center, 1234 Ingleside Ave., McLean VA 22101. (703)790-1953. **E-mail:** info@mpaart.org. **Website:** www.mpaart.org. Nonprofit visual arts center; alternative space. Estab. 1962. Represents emerging, mid-career and established artists from the mid-Atlantic region. Exhibited artists include Yuriko Yamaguchi and Christopher French. Sponsors 12-15 shows/year. Average display time: 5-6 weeks. Open Tuesday–Friday, 10-4; Saturday, 11-5. Luminous "white cube" type of gallery, with moveable walls; 3,000 sq. ft. 85% of space for special exhibitions. Clientele: local community, students, artists' families. 100% private collectors. Overall price range: $200-15,000; most work sold at $800-1,800.

MEDIA Considers all media except graphic design and traditional crafts; all types of prints except posters. Most frequently exhibits painting, sculpture and installation.
STYLE Exhibits all styles, all genres.
TERMS Artwork is accepted on consignment (25% commission). Retail price set by the artist. Gallery provides insurance and promotion. Artist pays for shipping costs. Prefers framed artwork (if on paper).
SUBMISSIONS Accepts only artists from Maryland, District of Columbia, Virginia and some regional mid-Atlantic. Send query letter with résumé, slides, reviews and SASE. Responds within 4 months. Artists' bios, slides and written material kept on file for 2 years. Finds artists through referrals by other artists and curators, and by visiting exhibitions and studios.
TIPS "Visit the gallery several times before submitting proposals, so that the work you submit fits the framework of art presented."

MCMURTREY GALLERY

3508 Lake St., Houston TX 77098. (713)523-8238. **E-mail:** info@mcmurtreygallery.com. **Website:** www.mcmurtreygallery.com. Estab. 1983. Retail gallery. Primarily represents contemporary regional artists. "The gallery's emphasis is on painting by both early and mid-career artists, many of whom are included in museum collections and are recognized and exhibited nationally. The gallery also represents a select group of internationally known photographers." Represents 20 emerging and mid-career artists. Exhibited artists include Robert Jessup and Jean Wetta. Sponsors 10 shows/year. Average display time: 1 month. Open Tuesday–Friday, 10:30-5; Saturday, 11-5. Located near downtown; 2,600 sq. ft. Clients include corporations. 75% of sales are to private collectors, 25% corporate collectors. Overall price range: $400-17,000; most work sold at $1,800-6,000.

MEDIA Considers oil, acrylic, pastel, drawings, mixed media, collage, works on paper, photography and sculpture. Most frequently exhibits mixed media, acrylic and oil.
STYLE Exhibits figurative, narrative, painterly abstraction and realism.
TERMS Accepts work on consignment (50% commission). Retail price set by gallery and artist. Prefers artwork framed.
SUBMISSIONS Send query letter with résumé, images and SASE. Call for appointment to show portfolio of originals and slides.
TIPS "Be aware of the work the gallery exhibits and act accordingly. Please make an appointment."

MERIDIAN MUSEUM OF ART

628 25th Ave., P.O. Box 5773, Meridian MS 39302. (601)693-1501. **E-mail:** meridianmuseum@bellsouth.net. **Website:** www.meridianmuseum.org. Estab. 1970. Represents emerging, mid-career and established artists. Interested in seeing the work of emerging artists. Open Wednesday-Saturday, 11-5. Located downtown; 3,060 sq. ft. These figures refers to exhibit spaces only. The entire museum is about 6,000 sq. ft.; housed in renovated Carnegie Library building, originally constructed 1912-13. 50% of space for special exhibitions. Clientele: general public. Overall price range: $150-2,500; most work sold at $300-1,000.

MEDIA Considers all media.
STYLE Exhibits all styles, all genres.

TERMS Work available for sale during exhibitions. Retail price set by the artist. Gallery provides insurance and promotion; shipping costs are shared. Prefers framed artwork.

SUBMISSIONS Prefers artists from Mississippi, Alabama and the Southeast. Send query letter with résumé, digital images, bio and SASE. Responds in 3 months. Finds artists through submissions, referrals, work included in competitions and visiting exhibitions.

MESA CONTEMPORARY ARTS AT MESA ARTS CENTER

P.O. Box 1466, Mesa AZ 85211. (480)644-6561; (480)644-6567. **E-mail:** patty.haberman@mesa artscenter.com. **Website:** www.mesaartscenter.com. **Contact:** Patty Haberman, curator. Estab. 1980.

MEDIA Considers all media including sculpture, painting, printmaking, photography, fibers, glass, wood, metal, video, ceramics, installation and mixed.

STYLE Exhibits all styles and genres. Interested in seeing contemporary work.

TERMS Charges 25% commission. Retail price set by artist. Gallery provides insurance, promotion and contract; pays for shipping costs from gallery. Requires framed artwork.

SUBMISSIONS Send a query letter or postcard with a request for a prospectus. After you have reviewed prospectus, send slides of up to 4 works (may include details if appropriate). "We do not offer portfolio review. Artwork is selected through national juried exhibitions." Files slides and résumés. Finds artists through gallery's placement of classified ads in various art publications, mailing news releases and word of mouth.

TIPS "Scout galleries to determine their preferences before you approach them. Have professional quality slides. Present only your very best work in a professional manner."

R. MICHELSON GALLERIES

132 Main St., Northampton MA 01060. (413)586-3964. **Fax:** (413)587-9811. **E-mail:** RM@rmichelson. com. **Website:** www.rmichelson.com. **Contact:** Richard Michelson, owner and president. Estab. 1976. Retail gallery. Represents 100 emerging, mid-career and established artists/year. Exhibited artists include Barry Moser and Leonard Baskin. Sponsors 12 shows/year. Average display time 1 month. Open all year; Monday-Wednesday, 10-6; Thursday-Saturday, 10-9; Sunday, 12-5. Located downtown; Northampton gallery has 5,500 sq. ft.; 50% of space for special exhibitions. Clientele 80% private collectors, 20% corporate collectors. Overall price range $100-75,000; most artwork sold at $1,000-125,000.

MEDIA Considers all media and all types of prints. Most frequently exhibits oil, egg tempera, watercolor and lithography.

STYLE Exhibits illustration, realism, expressionism and photorealism.

TERMS Accepts work on consignment (commission varies). Retail price set by gallery and artist. Payment by installment is available. Gallery provides promotion; shipping costs are shared.

SUBMISSIONS Prefers Pioneer Valley artists. Not taking on new artists at this time.

MILL BROOK GALLERY & SCULPTURE GARDEN

236 Hopkinton Rd., Concord NH 03301. (603)226-2046. **E-mail:** artsculpt@mindspring.com. **Website:** www.themillbrookgallery.com. Estab. 1996. Exhibits 70 artists. Sponsors 1 photography exhibit/year. Average display time 6 weeks. Gallery open Tuesday–Sunday, 11-5, April 1–December 24; and by appointment. Outdoor juried sculpture exhibit. Three rooms inside for exhibitions, 1,800 sq. ft. Overall price range $8-30,000. Most work sold at $500-1,000.

MEDIA Considers acrylic, ceramics, collage, drawing, glass, mixed media, oil, pastel, sculpture, watercolor, etchings, mezzotints, serigraphs and woodcuts. Most frequently exhibits oil, acrylic and pastel.

STYLE Considers all styles. Most frequently exhibits color field/conceptualism, expressionism. Genres include landscapes. Prefers more contemporary art.

TERMS Artwork is accepted on consignment (50% commission). Retail price set by the artist. Gallery provides insurance, promotion and contract. Accepted work should be framed and matted.

SUBMISSIONS Provides insurance, promotion and contract. Accepted work should be framed and matted. Write to arrange a personal interview to show portfolio of photographs, slides. Send query letter with artist's statement, bio, photocopies, photographs, résumé, slides, SASE. Submission of artwork: Accept CDs, websites, slides, and digital images. Responds to all artists within month, only if interested. Finds artists through word of mouth, submissions, art exhibits, referrals by other artists.

MILLS POND HOUSE GALLERY

Smithtown Township Arts Council, 660 Rt. 25 A, St. James NY 11780. **E-mail:** gallery@stacarts.org. **Website:** www.stacarts.org. **Contact:** Gallery coordinator. Nonprofit gallery. Sponsors 9 exhibits/year (1-2 photography). Average display time: 4 weeks. Open Monday–Friday, 10-5; weekends, 12-4. Considers all types of prints, media and styles. Digital entries. Prices set by the artist. Gallery provides insurance and promotion. Work should be framed. Clients: local and national community.

HAROLD J. MIOSSI ART GALLERY

1504 Colusa Ave., San Luis Obispo CA 93405. (805)546-3201 (Fine Arts Dept.). **Website:** www.cuesta.edu. Estab. 1965. Formerly Cuesta College Art Gallery. Exhibits the work of emerging, mid-career and established artists. Exhibited artists include Italo Scanga and JoAnn Callis. Sponsors 8 shows/year. Average display time: 4½ weeks. Open all year. 1,300 sq. ft.; 100% for special exhibitions. Overall price range: $250-5,000; most work sold at $400-1,200.

MEDIA Considers all media and all types of prints. Most frequently exhibits painting, sculpture and photography.

STYLE Exhibits all styles, mostly contemporary.

TERMS Accepts work on consignment (20% commission). Retail price set by artist. Customer payment by installment available. Gallery provides insurance, promotion and contract; shipping costs are shared. Prefers artwork framed.

SUBMISSIONS Gallery currently not accepting applications. Send query letter with artist statement, slides, bio, brochure, SASE and reviews. Call for appointment to show portfolio. Responds in 6 months. Finds artists mostly by reputation and referrals, sometimes through slides.

TIPS "We have a medium budget, thus cannot pay for extensive installations or shipping. Present your work legibly and simply. Include reviews or a coherent statement about the work. Don't be too slick or too sloppy."

MOBILE MUSEUM OF ART

4850 Museum Dr., Mobile AL 36608-1917. (251)208-5200; (251)208-5221. **E-mail:** dklooz@mobilemuseumofart.com. **Website:** www.mobilemuseumofart.com. **Contact:** Donan Klooz, curator of exhibitions. Clientele tourists and general public. Sponsors 6 solo and 12 group shows/year. Average display time: 6-8 weeks. Interested in emerging, mid-career and established artists. Overall price range: $100-5,000; most artwork sold at $100-500.

MEDIA Considers all media and all types of visual art.

STYLE Exhibits all styles and genres. "We are a general fine arts museum seeking a variety of styles, media and time periods." Looking for "historical significance."

TERMS Accepts work on consignment (20% commission). Retail price set by artist. Exclusive area representation not required. Gallery provides insurance, promotion, contract; shipping costs are shared. Prefers framed artwork.

SUBMISSIONS Send query letter with résumé, brochure, business card, slides, photographs, bio and SASE. Write to schedule an appointment to show a portfolio, which should include slides, transparencies and photographs. Replies only if interested within 3 months. Files résumés and slides. All material is returned with SASE if not accepted or under consideration.

TIPS "Be persistent but friendly!"

MONTEREY MUSEUM OF ART—LA MIRADA

720 Via Mirada, Monterey CA 93940. (831)372-3689. **Fax:** (831)372-5680. **E-mail:** info@montereyart.org. **Website:** www.montereyart.org. **Contact:** curatorial department. Estab. 1959. Nonprofit museum. Exhibits the work of emerging, mid-career and established artists. Average display time: 3-4 months.

MEDIA Considers all media.

STYLE Exhibits contemporary, abstract, impressionistic, figurative, landscape, primitive, nonrepresentational, photorealistic, Western, realist, neo-expressionistic and postpop works.

TERMS No sales. Museum provides insurance, promotion and contract; shipping costs are shared.

SUBMISSIONS Send query letter, résumé, 20 slides and SASE. Portfolio review not required. Résumé and cover letters are filed. Finds artists through agents, visiting exhibitions, word of mouth, various art publications and sourcebooks, artists' submissions/self promotions, art collectors' referrals.

THE MUNSON GALLERY

1455 Main St., Chatham MA 02633. (508)237-5038. **E-mail:** art@munsongallery.net. **Website:** www.munsongallery.com. Estab. 1860. Art consultancy. "One of America's oldest art galleries." Approached by 400 artists/year; exhibits 50 emerging, mid-career and established artists/year. Exhibited artists include Elmer Schooley (oils on canvas) and Richard Segalman (oils, watercolors and monoprints). Sponsors 9 shows/year. Average display time: 3 weeks. Open all year; Monday-Friday, 9:30-5; weekends, 10-5. Located in a complex that houses about 10 contemporary art galleries. 100% of space for gallery artists. Clientele upscale locals and tourists. Overall price range: $450-150,000; most work sold at $2,000.

MEDIA Considers all media. Considers engravings, etchings, linocuts, lithographs, monotypes, woodcuts and aquatints. Most frequently exhibits oils watercolor, pastel.

STYLE Exhibits "contemporary representational, not too much abstract, except in sculpture." Genres include florals, southwestern, landscapes.

TERMS Accepts work on consignment (50% commission). Retail price set by the artist. Gallery provides promotion. Accepted work should be framed.

SUBMISSIONS Send query letter with artist's statement, bio, photographs, résumé, SASE and slides. Call or write for appointment to show portfolio of photographs, slides and transparencies. Responds as soon as possible. Finds artists through portfolio reviews, referrals by other artists, submissions and word of mouth. Files bios occasionally, announcements.

TIPS "At the moment, the gallery is not taking on any new artists, though portfolios will be reviewed. We will not actually be adding any new artists to our roster for at least a year. Submissions welcome, but with the understanding that this is the case."

THE CATHERINE G. MURPHY GALLERY

Visual Arts Bldg., St. Catherine University, 2004 Randolph Ave., St. Paul MN 55105. (651)690-6637. **E-mail:** kmdaniels@stkate.edu. **Website:** www.stkate.edu/gallery. **Contact:** Kathy Daniels, director. Estab. 1973. Nonprofit gallery. "The Catherine G. Murphy Gallery presents 6-7 exhibitions during each academic calendar year (September–May). These exhibitions are selected a year to a year and a half in advance of the actual show. Five-six of the venues are exhibitions selected from outside proposals representing local, national and international artists. The fifth exhibition, April-May, is set aside for the annual Senior Art Student Juried Show." Represents emerging, mid-career and nationally and regionally established artists. Open Monday–Friday, 8-8; Saturday and Sunday, 12-6

(see website for a list of university holidays and gallery closings). Located in the Visual Arts Building on the campus of St. Catherine University; 1,480 sq. ft.

○ Gallery shows 75% women's art since it is part of an all-women's undergraduate program.

MEDIA Considers a wide range of media for exhibition.

STYLE Considers a wide range of styles.

TERMS Artwork is loaned for the period of the exhibition. Gallery provides insurance. Shipping costs are shared. Prefers artwork framed.

SUBMISSIONS Send query letter with résumé, bio, artist's statement, CDs, checklist of images (title, size, medium, etc.) and color reproductions of 2-3 images. Include SASE for return of materials. Responds in 6 weeks. Files résumé and cover letters. Serious consideration is given to artists who do group proposals under one inclusive theme. Complete submission guidelines available online.

MICHAEL MURPHY GALLERY M

2701 S. MacDill Ave., Tampa FL 33629. (813)902-1414. **Fax:** (813)835-5526. **Website:** www.michaelmurphygallery.com. **Contact:** Michael Murphy. Estab. 1988. (Formerly Michael Murphy Gallery, Inc.) For-profit gallery. Approached by 100 artists/year; exhibits 35 artists. Sponsors 1 photography exhibit/year. Average display time: 1 month. See website for current gallery hours. Overall price range: $500-15,000; most work sold at less than $1,000. "We provide elegant, timeless artwork for our clients' home and office environment as well as unique and classic framing design. We strongly believe in the preservation of art through the latest technology in archival framing."

MEDIA Considers all media. Most frequently exhibits acrylic, oil and watercolor. Considers all types of prints.

STYLE Considers all styles. Most frequently exhibits color field, impressionism and painterly abstraction. Considers all genres.

TERMS Artwork is accepted on consignment and there is a 50% commission. Retail price set by the gallery. Accepted work should be framed. Requires exclusive representation locally.

SUBMISSIONS Send query with artist's statement, bio, brochure, business card, photocopies, photographs, résumé, reviews, SASE and slides. Cannot return material. Responds to queries only if interested in 1 month. Files all materials. Finds artists through art fairs and exhibits, portfolio reviews, referrals by other artists, submissions and word of mouth.

MUSEO ITALOAMERICANO

Fort Mason Center, Bldg. C, San Francisco CA 94123. (415)673-2200. **Fax:** (415)673-2292. **E-mail:** sfmuseo@sbcglobal.net. **Website:** www.museoitalo americano.org. Estab. 1978. Museum. Approached by 80 artists/year. Exhibits 15 emerging, mid-career and established artists/year. Exhibited artists include Sam Provenzano. Sponsors 7 exhibits/year. Average display time: 3-4 months. Open all year; Tuesday-Sunday, 12-4; closed major holidays. Located in the San Francisco Marina District with beautiful view of the Golden Gate Bridge; 3,500 sq. ft. of exhibition space. Clients include local community, students, tourists, upscale and members. Free admission.

MEDIA Considers all media and all types of prints. Most frequently exhibits mixed media, paper, photography, oil, sculpture and glass.

STYLE Considers all styles and genres. Most frequently exhibits primitivism realism, geometric abstraction, figurative and conceptualism; 20th-century and contemporary art.

TERMS "The museum sells pieces in agreement with the artist; and if it does, it takes 25% of the sale." Gallery provides insurance and promotion. Accepted work should be framed, mounted and matted. Accepts only Italian or Italian-American artists.

SUBMISSIONS Submissions accepted with artist's statement, bio, brochure, photography, résumé, reviews, SASE and slides or CDs. Returns material with SASE. Responds in 2 months. Files 2 slides, bio and artist's statement for each artist. Finds artists through word of mouth and submissions.

TIPS Looks for "good-quality slides and clarity in statements and résumés. Be concise."

MUSEUM OF ART—DELAND, FLORIDA, INC.

600 N. Woodland Blvd., DeLand FL 32720. (386)734-4371. **E-mail:** fithian@moartdeland.org. **Website:** www.moartdeland.org. **Contact:** David Fithian, curator of art and exhibitions. Estab. 1951. Exhibits the work of established artists. "The mission of the Museum shall be to promote and showcase Florida art, and emerging and established Florida artists, by providing a wide range of exceptional cultural experiences, exhibitions, and educational and interpretive programming made available to a diverse statewide audience of all ages." Sponsors 8-10 shows/year. Open Tuesday–Saturday, 10-4; Sunday, 1-4. Located near downtown; 5,300 sq. ft.; in the Cultural Arts Center; 18 ft. carpeted walls, 2 gallery areas, including a modern space. Clientele: 85% private collectors, 15% corporate collectors. Overall price range: $100-30,000; most work sold at $300-5,000.

MEDIA Considers oil, acrylic, watercolor, pastel, works on paper, sculpture, ceramic, woodcuts, wood engravings, engravings and lithographs. Most frequently exhibits painting, sculpture, photographs and prints.

STYLE Exhibits contemporary art, the work of Florida artists, expressionism, surrealism, impressionism, realism and photorealism; all genres. Interested in seeing work that is finely crafted and expertly composed, with innovative concepts and professional execution and presentation. Looks for "quality, content, concept at the foundation—any style or content meeting these requirements considered."

TERMS Accepts work on consignment for exhibition period only. Retail price set by artist. Gallery provides insurance, promotion and contract; shipping costs may be shared.

SUBMISSIONS Send résumé, slides, bio, brochure, SASE and reviews. Files slides and résumé. Reviews slides twice a year.

TIPS "Artists should have a developed body of artwork and an exhibition history that reflects the artist's commitment to the fine arts. Museum contracts 2-3 years in advance. Label each slide with name, medium, size and date of execution."

M.G. NELSON FAMILY GALLERY AT THE SAA

700 N. Fourth St., Springfield IL 62702. (217)523-2631. **Fax:** (217)523-3866. **E-mail:** director@springfieldart. org. **Website:** www.springfieldart.org. **Contact:** Betsy Dollar, executive director. Estab. 1913. Nonprofit gallery. Exhibits emerging, mid-career and established artists. Sponsors 13 total exhibits/year, including theme-based shows 2-3 times/year. Average display time: 1 month. Open Monday-Friday, 9-5; Saturday, 10-3. Closed Sundays and Christmas-New Year's Day. Located at the Springfield Art Association, campus includes a historic house, museum and community art school. Clients include local community, students, tourists and upscale clients. 5% of sales are to corporate collectors. Overall price range: $10-5,000; most work sold under $100.

MEDIA Considers all media. Most frequently exhibits paintings (pastel, acrylic, watercolor, oil), mixed media and sculpture. Considers engravings, etchings, linocuts, lithographs, mezzotints, serigraphs, woodcuts and alternative forms.

STYLE Considers all styles and genres.

TERMS Artwork is accepted on consignment and there is a 30% commission. Retail price set by the artist. Gallery provides insurance, promotion and contract. Accepted work should be framed, mounted and matted—ready to hang.

SUBMISSIONS Call or e-mail query letter with link to artist's website or JPEG samples at 72 dpi. Responds in 2 weeks. Will return material with SASE. Files CV, résumé, printed samples and business cards. Find artists through word of mouth, submissions, portfolio reviews, art exhibits, art fairs and referrals by other artists.

TIPS "Good quality images with artist's name included in file name."

NEVADA MUSEUM OF ART

160 W. Liberty St., Reno NV 89501. (775)329-3333. **Fax:** (775)329-1541. **Website:** www.nevadaart.org. **Contact:** Ann Wolfe, senior curator and deputy director. Estab. 1931. Sponsors 12-15 exhibits/year. Average display time: 2-3 months.

MEDIA Considers all media.

STYLE Exhibits all styles and genres.

TERMS Acquires art "by committee following strict acquisition guidelines per the mission of the institution."

SUBMISSIONS Send query letter with slides. Write to schedule an appointment to show a portfolio. "No phone calls and no e-mails, please."

TIPS "We are a museum of ideas. While building upon our founding collections and values, we cultivate meaningful art and societal experiences, and foster new knowledge in the visual arts by encouraging interdisciplinary investigation. The Nevada Museum of Art serves as a cultural and educational resource for everyone."

NEW HARMONY GALLERY OF CONTEMPORARY ART

506 Main St., New Harmony IN 47631. (812)682-3156. **E-mail:** gholstein@usi.edu. **Website:** www.nhgallery. com. **Contact:** Gary Holstein, director. Estab. 1975. Nonprofit gallery. Provides an exhibition space for current Midwestern artists to promote discourse about and access to contemporary art in the southern Indiana region. Approached by 25 artists/year. Represents 8 emerging and mid-career artists. Exhibited artists include Patrick Dougherty, sculpture/installation. Sponsors 8 exhibits/year. Average display time: 6 weeks. Open Tuesday–Saturday, 10-5; Sundays, 12-4 (April-December). Clients include local community, students, tourists and upscale.

MEDIA Considers all media and all types of prints. Most frequently exhibits sculpture and installation.

STYLE Considers all styles including contemporary. No genre specified.

TERMS Artwork is accepted on consignment and there is a 35% commission. Gallery provides insurance, promotion and contract. Accepted work should be framed, mounted and matted. Does not require exclusive representation locally. Prefers midwestern artists.

SUBMISSIONS Send query letter with artist's statement, bio, résumé, SASE and slides. Returns material with SASE. Finds artists through art fairs, art exhibits, portfolio reviews and submissions.

NEW VISIONS GALLERY, INC.

1000 N. Oak Ave., Marshfield WI 54449. (715)387-5562. **E-mail:** newvisions.gallery@frontier.com. **Website:** www.newvisionsgallery.org. Estab. 1975. Nonprofit educational gallery. Represents emerging, mid-career and established artists. Located in the lobby of Marshfield Clinic with additional office space and support on the lower level. The facilities are donated to the community program by Marshfield Clinic. "New Visions organizes a dynamic series of changing exhibitions which are displayed in a 1,600-sq.-ft. secure, climate-controlled gallery. Exhibits change every 6-8 weeks and feature a variety of art forms, including national traveling exhibitions, significant works on loan from private and public collections and quality regional art." Does not represent artists on a continuing basis but does accept exhibition proposals. Average display time: 6 weeks. Open all year; Monday–Friday, 9-5:30. Includes a small gift shop with original jewelry, notecards and crafts at $10-100. "We do not show country crafts."

MEDIA Considers all media.

STYLE Exhibits all styles and genres.

TERMS Accepts work on consignment (35% commission). Retail price set by artist. Gallery provides insurance and promotion. Prefers artwork framed.

SUBMISSIONS Send query letter with artist's statement, résumé, SASE, image list, and a CD with 8-10 images in JPEG format. "Images should be at 72 dpi and should not exceed 250 KB. Image files should be labeled with your last name, first initial and number corresponding to the number on your image list (ex. doej-01.jpg)." The image list should include the image file name, artwork title, size of artwork and art medium.

NEXUS/FOUNDATION FOR TODAY'S ART

1400 N. American St., Philadelphia PA 19122. **E-mail:** info@nexusphiladelphia.org. **Website:** www.nexus philadelphia.org. Estab. 1975. Alternative space; co-operative, nonprofit gallery. Approached by 40 artists/year; represents or exhibits 20 artists. Sponsors 2 photography exhibits/year. Average display time 1 month. Open Wednesday–Sunday, 12-6; closed July and August. Located in Fishtown, Philadelphia; 2 gallery spaces, approximately 750 sq. ft. each. Overall price range: $75-1,200. Most work sold at $200-400.
MEDIA Considers acrylic, ceramics, collage, craft, drawing, fiber, glass, installation, mixed media, oil, paper, pen & ink and sculpture. Most frequently exhibits installation and mixed media.
STYLE Exhibits conceptualism, expressionism, neo-expressionism, postmodernism and surrealism. Most frequently exhibits conceptualism, expressionism and postmodernism.
TERMS There is no commission for artwork sold by member artists; 30% commission on sales by artists outside of the organization.
SUBMISSIONS Membership reviews are held twice a year in September and February. Artists may submit an applicaton at any time throughout the year. Incomplete applications will not be considered for review. Notification of results will be made within one week of the scheduled review. Applicants cannot be presently enrolled in school and must live within a 50-mile radius of Philadelphia. Go to www.nexusphiladelphia.org/images/memberapp.pdf for an application form.
TIPS "Get great slides made by someone who knows how to take professional slides. Learn how to write a cohesive and understandable artist statement."

NICOLAYSEN ART MUSEUM

400 E. Collins St., Casper WY 82601. (307)235-5247. **E-mail:** info@thenic.org. **Website:** www.thenic.org. **Contact:** Brooks Joyner, executive director. Estab. 1967. Regional contemporary art museum. Average display time: 3-4 months. Interested in emerging, mid-career and established artists. Sponsors 10 solo and 10 group shows/year. Open all year. Clientele 90% private collectors, 10% corporate clients.
MEDIA Considers all media with special attention to regional art.
STYLE Exhibits all subjects.
TERMS Accepts work on consignment (40% commission). Retail price set by artist. Exclusive area representation not required. Gallery provides insurance, promotion and shipping costs from gallery.
SUBMISSIONS Send résumé, statement and biography as well as images in digital format. "Due to the volume of crrespondence we receive, we may not be able to respond directly to each and every submission and we cannot assume responsibility for or guarantee the return of any materials that are submitted."

NICOLET COLLEGE ART GALLERY

5355 College Dr., P.O. Box 518, Rhinelander WI 54501. (715)365-4556. **E-mail:** kralph@nicoletcollege.edu. **Website:** www.nicoletcollege.edu/about/creative-arts-series/art-gallery/index.html. **Contact:** Katy Ralph, gallery director. Exhibits 9-11 different shows each year including the Northern National Art Competition. The deadline for the annual competition is in May. For a prospectus, or more information, contact gallery director, Katy Ralph.
TERMS Call or e-mail for further information.

NKU GALLERY

Northern Kentucky University, Nunn Dr., Highland Heights KY 41099. (859)572-5148. **Fax:** (859)572-6501. **E-mail:** knight@nku.edu. **Website:** artscience.nku.edu/departments/art/galleries.html. **Contact:** David Knight, director of collections and exhibitions. Estab. 1970. University galleries. Represents emerging, mid-career and established artists. Sponsors 10 shows/year. Average display time: 1 month. Open Monday-Friday, 9-9, or by appointment; closed major holidays and between Christmas and New Year's. Located 8 miles from downtown Cincinnati; 3,000 sq. ft.; 2 galleries—1 small and 1 large space with movable walls. 100% of space for special exhibitions. 90% private collectors, 10% corporate collectors. Overall price range: $25-3,000; most work sold at $500.
MEDIA Considers all media and all types of prints. Most frequently exhibits painting, printmaking and photography.
STYLE Exhibits all styles, all genres.

TERMS Retail price set by the artist. Gallery provides insurance, promotion and contract; shipping costs are shared. Prefers framed artwork, "but we are flexible." Commission rate is 20%.

SUBMISSIONS "Proposals from artists must go through our art faculty to be considered." Unsolicited submissions/proposals from outside the NKU Department of Visual Arts are not accepted. Unsolicited submissions will be returned to sender.

NO MAN'S LAND MUSEUM

214 E Ave., Goodwell OK 73939. (580)349-2670. E-mail: nmlhs@ptsi.net. **Website:** nmlhs.org. Estab. 1934. Represents emerging, mid-career and established artists. Sponsors 12 shows/year. Average display time: 1 month. Open Tuesday–Saturday, 10-4 (June-August); Tuesday–Friday, 10-12 and 1-3; Saturday, 10-4 (September-May); other times by appointment. Located adjacent to university campus. 10% of space for special exhibitions. Clientele general, tourist. 100% private collectors. Overall price range: $20-1,500; most work sold at $20-500.

MEDIA Considers all media and all types of prints. Most frequently exhibits oils, watercolors and pastels.

STYLE Exhibits primitivism, impressionism, photorealism and realism. Genres include landscapes, florals, Americana, Southwestern, Western and wildlife. Prefers realist, primitive and impressionist.

TERMS "Sales are between artist and buyer; museum does not act as middleman." Retail price set by the artist. Gallery provides promotion and shipping costs to and from gallery. Prefers artwork framed.

SUBMISSIONS Send query letter with résumé, brochure, photographs and reviews. Call or write for appointment to show portfolio of photographs. Responds only if interested within 3 weeks. Files all material. Finds artists through art publications, exhibitions, news items, word of mouth.

NORMANDALE COLLEGE CENTER GALLERY

9700 France Ave. S., Bloomington MN 55431. (952)481-8121. **Website:** www.normandale.edu/community/fine-arts-gallery. **Contact:** Kristoffer Holmgren. Estab. 1975. Exhibits 6 emerging, mid-career and established artists/year. Sponsors 6 shows/year. Average display time: 2 months. Open all year. Suburban location; 30 running feet of exhibition space. 100% of space for special exhibitions. Clientele students, staff and community. Overall price range: $25-750; most artwork sold at $100-200.

MEDIA Considers all media and all types of prints. Most frequently exhibits watercolor, photography and prints.

STYLE Exhibits all styles and genres.

TERMS "We collect 10% as donation to our foundation." Retail price set by artist. Gallery provides insurance, promotion and contract; artist pays for shipping. Prefers framed artwork.

SUBMISSIONS "Send query letter; we will send application and info." Portfolio should include slides. Responds in 2 months. Files application/résumé.

◗ NORTHCOTE GALLERY

110 Northcote Rd., London SW11 6QP, United Kingdom. **E-mail:** info@northcotegallery.com. **Website:** www.northcotegallery.com. Estab. 1992. Art consultancy, wholesale gallery. Approached by 100 artists/year. Represents 30 emerging, mid-career and established artists. Exhibited artists include Daisy Cook and Robert McKellar. Sponsors 16 exhibits/year. Average display time: 3-4 weeks. Open all year; Tuesday-Friday, 11-7; Saturday, 11-6. Located in southwest London. 1 large exhibition space, 1 smaller space; average of 35 paintings exhibited/time. Clientele local community and upscale. 50% corporate collectors. Overall price range: $400-12,000; most work sold at $1,500.

MEDIA Considers acrylic, ceramics, drawing, glass, mixed media, oil, paper, photography, sculpture, watercolor, engravings, etchings and lithographs.

STYLE Exhibits conceptualism, expressionism, impressionism, painterly abstraction and postmodernism. Considers all genres.

TERMS Artwork is accepted on consignment (45% commission). Retail price set by the gallery. Gallery provides promotion. Accepted work should be framed.

SUBMISSIONS Send query letter with artist's statement, bio, brochure, photograph, résumé, reviews and SASE. Returns material with SASE. Responds in 4-6 weeks. Finds artists through word of mouth, submissions, portfolio reviews and referrals by other artists.

NORTHWEST ART CENTER

Minot State University, 500 University Ave. W., Minot ND 58707. (701)858-3264. **Fax:** (701)858-3894. **E-mail:** nac@minotstateu.edu. **Website:** www.minotstateu.edu/nac. Estab. 1969.

MEDIA Considers all media. Special interest in printmaking, works on paper, contemporary art and drawings.

STYLE Exhibits all styles, all genres.

TERMS Accepted work should be framed and mounted. Artwork is accepted on consignment with a 30% commission. Retail price set by the artist. Gallery provides insurance, promotion and contract.

SUBMISSIONS Send query letter with artist's statement, photocopies bio, résumé and reviews. Returns material with SASE. Responds, if interested, within 3 months. Finds artists through art exhibits, submissions, referrals by other artists and entries in our juried competitions.

NOYES ART GALLERY

119 S. Ninth St., Lincoln NE 68508. (402)475-1061. **E-mail:** julianoyes@aol.com. **Website:** www.noyesart gallery.com. **Contact:** Julia Noyes, owner. Estab. 1992. For-profit gallery. "The Noyes Gallery is a co-op type art gallery, featuring approximately 24 artist members, showing their work and volunteering their time to help operate the business. The gallery features a variety of original painting, photos, pottery and jewelry. We have recently expanded the gallery adding a classroom and additional display space to our facility." Average display time: 1 month minimum. ("If mutually agreeable, this may be extended or work exchanged.") Open Monday–Saturday, 10-5. Located downtown, near historic Haymarket District; 3,093 sq. ft.; renovated 128-year-old building. 25% of space for special exhibitions. Clientele: private collectors, interior designers and decorators. 90% private collectors, 10% corporate collectors. Overall price range: $100-5,000; most work sold at $200-750.

MEDIA Considers oil, acrylic, watercolor, pastel, pen & ink, drawings, mixed media, collage, paper, sculpture, ceramic, fiber, glass and photography; original handpulled prints, woodcuts, wood engravings, linocuts, engravings, mezzotints, etchings, lithographs and serigraphs. Most frequently exhibits oil, watercolor and mixed media.

STYLE Exhibits expressionism, neo-expressionism, impressionism, realism, photorealism. Genres include landscapes, florals, Americana, wildlife, figurative work. Prefers realism, expressionism, photorealism.

TERMS Accepts work on consignment (10-35% commission). Retail price set by artist (sometimes in conference with director). Gallery provides promotion and contract; artist pays for shipping. Prefers artwork framed.

SUBMISSIONS Send query letter with résumé, slides, bio, SASE; label slides concerning size, medium, price, top, etc. Submit at least 6-8 slides. Reviews submissions monthly. Responds in 1 month. Files résumé, bio and slides of work by accepted artists (unless artist requests return of slides).

NUANCE GALLERIES

804 S. Dale Mabry, Tampa FL 33609. (813)875-0511. **E-mail:** nuancegalleries@earthlink.net. **Website:** www. nuancegalleries.com. **Contact:** Robert Rowen, owner. Estab. 1981. Retail gallery. Represents 70 emerging, mid-career and established artists. Sponsors 3 shows/year. Open all year; Monday-Friday, 10-5; Saturday, 10-4. 3,000 sq. ft. "We've reduced the size of our gallery to give the client a more personal touch. We have a large extensive front window area."

MEDIA Specializing in watercolor, original mediums and oils.

STYLE "The majority of the work we like to see are realistic landscapes, escapism pieces, bold images, bright colors and semitropical subject matter. Our gallery handles quite a selection, and it's hard to put us into any one class."

TERMS Accepts work on consignment (50% commission). Retail price set by gallery and artist. Offers customer discounts and payment by installments. Gallery provides insurance and contract; shipping costs are shared.

SUBMISSIONS Send query letter with slides and bio, SASE if you want slides/photos returned. Portfolio review requested if interested in artist's work.

TIPS "Be professional; set prices (retail) and stick with them. There are still some artists out there that are not using conservation methods of framing. As far as submissions, we would like local artists to come by to see our gallery and get the idea of what we represent. Tampa has a healthy growing art scene, and the work has been getting better and better. But as this town gets more educated, it is going to be much harder for up-and-coming artists to emerge."

OPENING NIGHT GALLERY

2836 Lyndale Ave. S., Minneapolis MN 55408-2108. (612)872-2325. **Fax:** (612)872-2385. **E-mail:** deen@ onframe-art.com; info@onframe-art.com. **Website:** www.onframe-art.com. **Contact:** Deen Braathen. Estab. 1975. Rental gallery. Approached by 40 artists/year; represents or exhibits 15 artists. Sponsors 1 photography exhibit/year. Average display time 6-10 weeks. Gallery open Monday–Friday, 8:30-5; Saturday, 10:30-4. Overall price range $300-12,000. Most work sold at $2,500.

MEDIA Considers acrylic, ceramics, collage, drawing, fiber, glass, oil, paper, sculpture and watercolor.

STYLE Exhibits local and regional art.

TERMS Artwork is accepted on consignment, and there is a 50% commission. Retail price set by the gallery. Gallery provides insurance, promotion and contract.

SUBMISSIONS "E-mail Deen with cover letter, artist statement, and visuals."

⌂ ORANGE COUNTY CENTER FOR CONTEMPORARY ART

117 N. Sycamore St., Santa Ana CA 92701. (714)667-1517. **E-mail:** info.occca@gmail.com. **Website:** www.occca.org. Cooperative, nonprofit gallery. Exhibits emerging and mid-career artists. 18 members. Sponsors 8-10 shows/year. Average display time: 1 month. Open all year; Thursday—Sunday, 12-5; closed major holidays. Opening receptions first Saturday of every month, 6-10 p.m. Gallery space: 5,500 sq. ft. 25% of time for gallery artists exhibitions; 75% of time for collaboration, calls for art and curatorial exhibitions. Membership fee: $30/month.

MEDIA Considers all media-contemporary work.

TERMS Co-op membership fee plus a donation of time. Retail price set by artist.

SUBMISSIONS Accepts artists generally in and within 50 miles of Orange County. E-mail 3 images of current work format the items with "your_name_title. jpeg;" include a brief description of your work, an exhibition résumé, and a website link to your work. Subject line of e-mail should read "New membership submission (your name, date)." Responds in 1 week. More information about the membership process is available online.

TIPS "This is an artist-run nonprofit. Send SASE for application prospectus. Membership involves 10 hours per month of volunteer work at the gallery or gallery-related projects."

OXFORD GALLERY

267 Oxford St., Rochester NY 14607. (585)271-5885. **E-mail:** info@oxfordgallery.com. **Website:** www.oxfordgallery.com. Estab. 1961. Retail gallery. Represents 60 emerging, mid-career and established art-

ists. Sponsors 6 shows/year. Average display time: 5 weeks. Open all year; Tuesday-Friday, 12-5; Saturday, 10-5; and by appointment. Located "on the edge of downtown; 1,000 sq. ft.; large gallery in a beautiful 1924 building." Overall price range: $100-30,000; most work sold at $1,000-2,000.

MEDIA Considers oil, acrylic, watercolor, pastel, pen & ink, drawings, mixed media, collage, paper, sculpture, ceramic, fiber, original handpulled prints, woodcuts, engravings, lithographs, wood engravings, mezzotints, serigraphs, linocuts and etchings.

STYLE All styles.

TERMS Accepts artwork on consignment (50% commission). Retail price set by gallery and artist. Gallery provides promotion and contract.

SUBMISSIONS Send query letter or e-mail with résumé, digital images, bio and SASE. Responds in 3 months.

TIPS "Have good photos done of your artwork. Have a professional résumé and portfolio. Do not show up unannounced and expect to show your work. Either send in your information or call to make an appointment. An artist should have enough work to have a solo show (20-30 pieces). This allows an artist to be able to supply more than one gallery at a time, if necessary. It is important to maintain a strong body of available work."

PAINTERS ART GALLERY

30517 St. Rt. 706 E., Ashford WA 98304. **E-mail:** mtwoman2@centurytel.net. **Website:** www.painterartbeads.com. **Contact:** Joan Painter, owner. Retail gallery. Represents 3 emerging, mid-career and established artists. Open all year. Hours are chaotic, please call ahead to be sure you will not be wasting a trip. Located 5 miles from the entrance to Mt. Rainier National Park; 1,200 sq. ft. 70% of space for work of gallery artists. Clientele collectors and tourists. Overall price range: $10-7,500; most work sold at $300-2,500. ◯ It is a very informal, outdoors atmosphere.

MEDIA Considers oil, acrylic, watercolor, pastel, mixed media. "I am seriously looking for totem poles and outdoor carvings." Most frequently exhibits oil, pastel and acrylic.

STYLE Exhibits primitivism, surrealism, imagism, impressionism, realism and photorealism. All genres. Prefers Mt. Rainier themes and wildlife. "Indians and mountain men are a strong sell."

TERMS Accepts artwork on consignment (30% commission). Retail price set by gallery and artist. Gallery provides promotion; artist pays for shipping. Prefers artwork framed.

SUBMISSIONS Send query letter or call. "I can usually tell over the phone if artwork will fit in here." Portfolio review requested if interested in artist's work. Does not file materials.

TIPS "Sell paintings and retail price items for the same price at mall and outdoor shows that you price them in galleries. I have seen artists underprice the same paintings/items, etc., when they sell at shows. Do not copy the style of other artists. To stand out, have your own style."

PAINTER'S CHAIR FINE ART GALLERY

223 Sherman Ave., Coeur d'Alene ID 83814. (208)667-3606. **E-mail:** info@painterschairfineart.com. **Website:** www.painterschairfineart.com.

MEDIA Considers all media.

STYLE Exhibits all styles from realism and impressionism to contemporary and abstract. Genres include, but are not limited to, landscapes, floral, still life, Western, and wildlife.

TERMS Accepts artwork on consignment. Retail price set by gallery and artist. Gallery provides promotion and contract; artist pays for shipping. Prefers artwork framed.

SUBMISSIONS Submit portfolio with introduction letter, bio, photographs/slides, SASE (for return of materials if desired), website and other useful information. Gallery prefers portfolio and/or website submissions via e-mail. Files all material for 6-12 months. See website for further details.

TIPS "Devin Galleries now has a complete custom frame shop with 23 years experience in framing."

PARADISE CENTER FOR THE ARTS

321 Central Ave., Faribault MN 55021. (507)332-7372. **E-mail:** info@paradisecenterforthearts.org. **Website:** www.paradisecenterforthearts.org. **Contact:** Executive director. Formerly Faribault Art Center, Inc. Nonprofit gallery. Represents 26-30 emerging and mid-career artists/year. 650 members. Sponsors 8 theatre shows/year. Auditorium features regular events including comedy, live music and special events. Average display time: 1 month. Open all year; Tuesday–Saturday, 12-5; Thursday, 12-8 and 1 hour before all events. Education classes in all mediums. Located downtown; 1,600 sq. ft. 50% of space for special exhibitions; 50% of space for gallery artists. Clientele: local and tourists. 90% private collectors.

MEDIA Considers all media and all types of prints.

STYLE Open.

TERMS Accepts work on consignment (30% commission for members). Retail price set by the artist. Artist pays for shipping. Prefers artwork framed.

SUBMISSIONS Accepts local and regional artists. Send query letter with CD with 6-10 JPEG images, artist résumé, and artist's statement. Call or write for appointment to show portfolio of photographs. Artists are to follow "The Call for Artists" on the Paradise website. Finds artists through word of mouth, referrals by other artists, visiting art fairs and exhibitions and submissions.

TIPS "Artists should respond quickly upon receiving reply."

PARK WALK GALLERY

20 Park Walk, London SW10 0AQ, United Kingdom. 44(0) 207-351-0410. **E-mail:** mail@jonathancooper.co.uk. **Website:** www.jonathancooper.co.uk. **Contact:** Jonathan Cooper, gallery owner. Estab. 1988. Approached by 5 artists/year. Gallery represents 30 artists. Approached 60 artists/year. Exhibited artists include Kate Nessler. Sponsors 8 exhibits/year. Average display time: 3 weeks. Open all year; Monday-Saturday, 10-6:30; Sunday, 11-4. Located in Park Walk, which runs between Fulham Road to Kings Road. Clientele: upscale. 10% corporate collectors. Most work sold at £2,000-20,000.

MEDIA Considers drawing, mixed media, oil, paper, pastel, pen & ink, photography, sculpture, watercolor. Most frequently exhibits watercolor, oil and sculpture.

STYLE Exhibits conceptualism, impressionism. Genres include florals, landscapes, wildlife, equestrian.

TERMS Artwork is accepted on consignment (50% commission). Retail price set by the gallery. Gallery provides promotion. Requires exclusive representation locally.

SUBMISSIONS Call to arrange a personal interview to show portfolio. Returns material with SASE. Responds in 1 week. Finds artists through submissions, portfolio reviews, art exhibits, art fairs, referrals by other artists.

TIPS "Include full curriculum vitae and photographs of work."

THE PARTHENON

2500 West End Ave., Nashville TN 37203. (615)862-8431. **Fax:** (615)880-2265. **E-mail:** info@parthenon.org. **Website:** www.parthenon.org. Estab. 1931. Nonprofit gallery in a full-size replica of the Greek Parthenon. Exhibits the work of emerging to mid-career artists. Sponsors 3-4 shows/year. Average display time: 3-4 months. Clientele: general public, tourists. Overall price range: $300-2,000. "We also house a permanent collection of American paintings (1765-1923)."

MEDIA Considers "nearly all" media.

STYLE "Interested in both objective and nonobjective work. Professional presentation is important."

TERMS "Sales request a 20% donation." Retail price set by artist. Gallery provides a contract and limited promotion. The Parthenon does not represent artists on a continuing basis.

SUBMISSIONS Send images via CD, résumé and artist's statement addressed to curator.

TIPS "We plan our gallery calendar at least one year in advance." Find us on Facebook: "The Parthenon in Nashville."

PENTIMENTI GALLERY

145 N. Second St., Philadelphia PA 19106. **Website:** www.pentimenti.com. **Contact:** Christine Pfister, director. Estab. 1992. Commercial gallery. Represents 20-30 emerging, mid-career and established artists. Sponsors 7-9 exhibits/year. Average display time: 4-6 weeks. Open all year; Tuesday by appointment; Wednesday-Friday, 11-5; Saturday, 12-5; closed Sundays, August, Christmas and New Years. Located in the heart of Old City cultural district in Philadelphia.

MEDIA Considers all media. Most frequently exhibits paintings of all media.

STYLE Exhibits conceptualism, minimalism, postmodernism, painterly abstraction, and representational works. Most frequently exhibits postmodernism, minimalism and conceptualism.

TERMS Artwork is accepted on consignment. Retail price set by the gallery and the artist. Gallery provides insurance and promotion. Requires exclusive representation locally.

SUBMISSIONS Please review our guidelines in our website.

PETERS VALLEY SCHOOL OF CRAFT

19 Kuhn Rd., Layton NJ 07851. (973)948-5202. **Fax:** (973)948-0011. **E-mail:** store@petersvalley.org. **Website:** www.petersvalley.org. **Contact:** Brienne Rosner, gallery manager. Estab. 1970. Nonprofit gallery and store. Approached by about 100 artists/year. Represents about 350 artists. Exhibited artists include William Abranowitz and Clyed Butcher. Average display time vaires for store items. Gallery exhibitions approx. 1 month duration. Open year round, call for hours. Located in northwestern New Jersey in Delaware Water Gap National Recreation Area; 2 floors; approximately 3,000 sq. ft. Clients include local community, students, tourists and upscale. 5% of sales are to corporate collectors. Overall price range $5-3,000; most work sold at $100-300.

MEDIA "Focuses its programs on fine contemporary crafts in mediums such as ceramics, metals (both fine and forged), glass, wood, photography, fibers (surface design and structural), print." Considers all media and all types of prints. Also exhibits nonreferential, mixed media, collage and sculpture.

TERMS Artwork is accepted on consignment and there is a 60% commission. Retail price set by the gallery in conjunction with artist. Gallery provides insurance and promotion. Accepted work should be framed, mounted and matted.

SUBMISSIONS Submissions reviewed on an ongoing basis. Send e-mail with artist's statement, bio, résumé and images. Responds in 2 months. Finds artists through submissions, art exhibits, art fairs, and referrals by other artists. "Submissions must be neat and well-organized throughout."

⊙ PHILLIPS GALLERY

444 E. 200 S., Salt Lake City UT 84111. (801)364-8284. **Fax:** (801)364-8293. **Website:** www.phillips-gallery.com. **Contact:** Meri DeCaria, director/curator. Estab. 1965. Retail gallery, art consultancy, rental gallery. Represents 80 emerging, mid-career and established artists/year. Exhibited artists include Denis Phillips, Connie Borup, Hyunmee Lee, Cordell Taylor. Sponsors 10 shows/year. Average display time: 1 month. Open all year; Tuesday-Friday, 11-6; Saturday, 11-4; closed December 25-January 1. Located downtown; has 3 floors at 2,000 sq. ft. and a 2,400 sq. ft. sculpture deck on the roof. 40% private collectors, 60% corporate collectors. Overall price range: $100-18,000; most work sold at $200-4,000.

MEDIA Considers all media, woodcuts, engravings, lithographs, wood engravings, linocuts, etchings. Most frequently exhibits oil, acrylic, sculpture/steel.

STYLE Exhibits expressionism, conceptualism, neo-expressionism, minimalism, pattern painting, primitivism, color field, hard-edge geometric abstraction, painterly abstraction, postmodern works, realism, surrealism, impressionism. Genres include Western, Southwestern, landscapes, figurative work, contemporary. Prefers abstract, neo-expressionism, conceptualism.

TERMS Accepts work on consignment (50% commission). Gallery does not provide insurance and promotion; shipping costs are shared. Prefers artwork framed.

SUBMISSIONS Accepts only artists from western region/Utah. Accepts digital submissions only. Finds artists through word of mouth, referrals.

PHOENIX GALLERY

825 Massachusetts, Lawrence KS 66044. (785)843-0080. **E-mail:** info@phoenixgalleryart.com. **Website:** www.phoenixgalleryart.com. Estab. 1990. Retail gallery. Represents 60 emerging, mid-career and established artists/year. Exhibited artists include Dave Archer, Louis Copt, Nagel, Phil Starke, Robert Berkeley Green and Raymond Eastwood. Sponsors 6 shows/year. Average display time: 6 weeks-3 months. Clientele: upscale. 75% private collectors, 25% corporate collectors. Overall price range: $500-20,000.

MEDIA Considers all media and engravings, lithographs, woodcuts, mezzotints, serigraphs, linocuts, etchings and collage. Most frequently exhibits oil, watercolor, ceramic and artglass.

STYLE Exhibits expressionism and impressionism, all genres. Prefers regional, abstract and 3D type ceramic; national glass artists. "We find there is increased interest in original work and regional themes."

TERMS Terms negotiable. Retail price set by the gallery and the artist. Prefers artwork framed.

SUBMISSIONS Call for appointment to show portfolio of originals, photographs and slides.

PIERRO GALLERY OF SOUTH ORANGE

Baird Center, 5 Mead St., South Orange NJ 07079. (973)378-7754. **Fax:** (973)378-7833. **E-mail:** pierrogallery@southorange.org; smartiny@southorange.org. **Website:** www.pierrogallery.org. **Contact:** Sandy Martiny, gallery director. Estab. 1994. Nonprofit gallery. Approached by 75-185 artists/year; represents or exhibits 25-50 artists. Average display time: 5 weeks. Open Wednesday–Thursday, 2-7; Friday, 1-4; Saturday, 1-4 and by appointment; closed July-August. Overall price range: $100-10,000; most work sold at $800.

TERMS Artwork is accepted on consignment, and there is a 15% commission. Gallery provides insurance, promotion, contract. Accepted work should be framed.

SUBMISSIONS Mail portfolio for review. Send cover letter, biography and/or résumé, brief artist statement, up to 3 reviews/press clippings, representation of work in either CD or DVD format; no more than 10 labeled representative images. Responds in 2 months from review date. Finds artists through word of mouth, submissions, portfolio reviews, referrals by other artists.

POCATELLO ART CENTER GALLERY & SCHOOL

444 N. Main St., Pocatello ID 83204. (208)232-0970. **E-mail:** pocartctr@ida.net. **Website:** www.pocatelloartctr.org. Estab. 1970. Nonprofit gallery featuring work of artist/members. Represents approximately 60 emerging, mid-career and established artists/year. Approximately 150 members. Exhibited artists include Barbara Ruffridge, Jerry Younkin, Onita Asbury and Barbara Swanson. Sponsors 10-12 shows/year. Average display time: 2 months. Open all year; Monday-Friday, 10-4 (varies occasionally). Located downtown in "Old Town." "We sponsor the 'Sagebrush Arts Fest each year, usually in September, on the Idaho State University campus." We hold classes, feature all levels of artists and are a gathering place for artists. Clientele tourists, local community, students and artists. 100% private collectors. Overall price range: $25-1,000; most work sold at $25-300.

MEDIA Considers oil, acrylic, watercolor, pastel, pen & ink, drawing, mixed media, collage, paper, sculpture, ceramics, high-end craft, fiber, glass and photography; types of prints include woodcuts, engravings, wood engravings, serigraphs, linocuts and etchings. Most frequently exhibits watercolor, oil and pastel.

STYLE Exhibits expressionism, neo-expressionism, primitivism, painterly abstraction, surrealism, minimalism, impressionism, photorealism, hard-edge geometric abstraction, realism and imagism. Exhibits all genres. Prefers impressionism, realism and painterly abstraction.

TERMS Co-op membership fee plus donation of time. Donations-monetary. Retail price set by the artist. Gallery provides promotion; hand delivered works only. Prefers artwork framed.

SUBMISSIONS Accepts only artists from Southeast Idaho. Memberships open to all artists and persons interested in the visual arts. Send query letter or visit gallery. Finds artists through word of mouth, referrals by other artists, visiting art fairs and exhibitions. **TIPS** "Have work ready to hang."

POLK MUSEUM OF ART

800 E. Palmetto St., Lakeland FL 33801-5529. (863)688-7743, ext. 241 or 289. **Fax:** (863)688-2611. **E-mail:** kpope@polkmuseumofart.org. **Website:** www.polkmuseumofart.org. **Contact:** Kalisa Pope, curatorial assistant. Estab. 1966. Approached by 75 artists/year; represents or exhibits 3 artists. Sponsors 15 exhibits/year. Open Tuesday-Saturday, 10-5; Sunday, 1-5; closed Mondays and major holidays; reduced hours June-August. Four different galleries of various sizes and configurations. "Because we are a small institution, we do not regularly review submissions. Our curator will be happy to look at your slides, but he may not be able to respond immediately."
MEDIA Considers all media. Most frequently exhibits prints, photos and paintings. Considers all types of prints except posters.
STYLE Considers all styles and genres, provided the artistic quality is very high.
TERMS Gallery provides insurance, promotion and contract. Accepted work should be framed.
SUBMISSIONS Mail portfolio for review. Send query letter with artist's statement, bio, résumé and SASE. Returns material with SASE. Reviews 2-3 times/year and responds shortly after each review. Files slides or CDs and résumé.

PORTFOLIO ART GALLERY

2007 Devine St., Columbia SC 29205. (803)256-2434. **E-mail:** portfolioartgal@gmail.com. **Website:** www.portfolioartgal.com. **Contact:** Judith Roberts, gallery director. Estab. 1980. Retail gallery and art consultancy. Represents 40-50 emerging, mid-career and established artists. Exhibited artists include Junko Ono Rothwell, Sigmund Abeles, Holle Black and Shannon Bueker. Sponsors 3 shows/year. Average display time: 3 months. Open Monday–Friday, 11-6; Saturday, 10-6. Located in a 1930s shopping village, 1 mile from downtown; 2,000 sq. ft.; features 12-ft. ceilings. 100% of space for work of gallery artists. "A unique feature is glass shelves where matted and small to medium pieces can be displayed without hanging on the wall."

Clientele: professionals and collectors. Overall price range: $150-5,000; most work sold at $600-3,000.

◔ Gallery director Judith Roberts has a fine arts degree with an intensive in printmaking and is a former art teacher. Also named "A Top 100 Retailer of American Crafts."

MEDIA Considers oil, acrylic, watercolor, pastel, mixed media, collage, works on paper, sculpture, ceramic, glass, original handpulled prints, woodcuts, wood engravings, linocuts, engravings, mezzotints, etchings, lithographs and serigraphs. Most frequently exhibits oils, acrylics, ceramics and sculpture, and original jewelry.
STYLE Exhibits neo-expressionism, painterly abstraction, imagism, minimalism, color field, impressionism, and realism. Genres include landscapes and figurative work. Prefers landscapes/seascapes, painterly abstraction and figurative work. "I especially like mixed-media pieces, original prints and oil paintings. Pastel medium and watercolors are also favorites, as well as kinetic sculpture and whimsical clay pieces."
TERMS Accepts work on consignment (40% commission). Retail price set by gallery and artist. Offers payment by installments. Gallery provides insurance, promotion and contract; artist pays for shipping. Artwork may be framed or unframed.
SUBMISSIONS Send query letter with bio and images via e-mail, CD or slides. Write for appointment to show portfolio of originals, slides, photographs and transparencies. Responds within 1 month, only if interested. Files tearsheets, brochures and slides. Finds artists through visiting exhibitions and referrals.
TIPS "The most common mistake beginning artists make is showing all the work they have ever done. I want to see only examples of recent best work—unframed, originals (no copies)—at portfolio reviews."

PORT WASHINGTON PUBLIC LIBRARY

One Library Dr., Port Washington NY 11050. (516)883-4400. **E-mail:** library@pwpl.org. **Website:** www.pwpl.org/artgallery. Estab. 1970. Nonprofit gallery. Represents 10-12 emerging, mid-career and established artists/year. 23 members. Exhibited artists include Frank Stella, Robert Dash. Sponsors 10-12 shows/year. Average display time: 1 month. Open all year; Monday, Tuesday, Thursday, Friday, 9-9; Wednesday, 11-9; Saturday, 9-5; Sunday, 1-5 (except in the summer). See website for holiday closings. 972 sq. ft. Overall price range: up to $100,000.

MEDIA Considers all media and all types of prints.
STYLE Exhibits all styles.
TERMS Price set by the artist. Gallery provides insurance and promotion.
SUBMISSIONS Send query letter with résumé, slides, bio, SASE. Or contact via online submission form. Responds in 1 month. Artist should call library. Finds artists through word of mouth, referrals by other artists, visiting art fairs and exhibitions and submissions.

POSNER FINE ART

1212 S. Point View St., Los Angeles CA 90035. (323)933-3664. **Fax:** (323)933-3417. **E-mail:** info@posnerfineart.com. **Website:** www.posnerfineart.com. **Contact:** Wendy Posner, director. Estab. 1960. Private fine art dealer and art publisher. Represents 200 emerging, mid-career and established artists. By appointment only. Clientele: upscale and collectors; 50% private collectors, 50% corporate collectors. Overall price range: $25-50,000; most work sold at $500-10,000.

⊙ See additional listing in the Posters & Prints section.

MEDIA Considers oil, acrylic, watercolor, pastel, mixed media, collage, works on paper, sculpture, ceramics, original hand-pulled prints, engravings, etchings, lithographs, posters and serigraphs. Most frequently exhibits paintings, sculpture and original prints.
STYLE Exhibits painterly abstraction, minimalism, impressionism, realism, photorealism, pattern painting and hard-edge geometric abstraction. Genres include florals and landscapes. Prefers abstract, trompe l'oeil, realistic.
TERMS Accepts work on consignment (50% commission). Retail price set by the gallery. Gallery provides insurance and promotion; shipping costs are shared. Prefers unframed artwork.
SUBMISSIONS E-mail query letter with résumé and images. Responds in 2 weeks, only if interested. Finds artists through submissions and art collectors' referrals.
TIPS Looking for artists for corporate collections.

THE PRINT CENTER

1614 Latimer St., Philadelphia PA 19103. (215)735-6090. **Fax:** (215)735-5511. **E-mail:** info@printcenter.org. **Website:** www.printcenter.org. Estab. 1915. Exhibits emerging, mid-career and established artists. Approached by 500 artists/year. Sponsors 11 exhibits/year. Average display time: 2 months. Open all year Tuesday-Saturday, 11-6; closed Christmas Eve to New Year's Day. Gallery houses 3 exhibit spaces as well as a separate Gallery Store. Located in historic Rittenhouse area of Philadelphia. Clients include local community, students, tourists and collectors. 30% of sales are to corporate collectors. Overall price range: $15-15,000; most work sold at $200.
MEDIA Considers all forms of printmaking and photography. Accepts original artwork only—no reproductions.
STYLE Considers all styles and genres.
TERMS Accepts artwork on consignment (50%). Retail price set by the artist. Gallery provides insurance, promotion and contract. Accepted work should be ready to hang for exhibitions; unframed for gallery store. Does not require exclusive representation locally. Only accepts prints and photos.
SUBMISSIONS Must be member to submit work—member's work is reviewed by curator and gallery store manager. See website for membership application. Finds artists through submissions, art exhibits and membership.

THE PROPOSITION

2 Extra Place, New York NY 10003. (212)242-0035. **E-mail:** info@theproposition.com. **Website:** www.theproposition.com. Estab. 2002. For-profit gallery. Exhibits emerging and mid-career artists. Represents or exhibits 20+ artists/year. Currently not accepting unsolicited submissions. Exhibited artists include: Balint Zsako (drawing, collage, works on paper); Dane Patterson (drawing, painting, works on paper); Megan Burns (painting); Jason Gringler (mixed media, painting, work on paper); Mike Park (painting, video); Tim Evans (painting, video, works on paper); Huang Yan (sculpture); Mickalene Thomas (paintings, photos); Shinique Smith (multimedia, works on paper, installation, video, conceptual); Kyung Jeon (drawing, painting); Alfredo Martinez (sculpture, drawing, painting, performance). Average display time: 1 month. Overall price range: $0-20,000; most works on paper sold at $3,000; most paintings sold at $6,000.

PUCKER GALLERY, INC.

240 Newbury St., 3rd Floor, Boston MA 02116. (617)267-9473. **Fax:** (617)424-9759. **E-mail:** contact us@puckergallery.com; destiny@puckergallery.com. **Website:** www.puckergallery.com. **Contact:** Bernard H. Pucker, owner/director; Destiny M. Barletta, direc-

tor. Estab. 1967. Retail gallery. Represents 50 emerging, mid-career and established artists. Exhibited artists include modern masters such as Picasso, Chagall, Braque, and Samuel Bak and Brother Thomas. Sponsors 10 shows/year. Average display time: 4-5 weeks. Open all year. Located in the downtown retail district. 20% of space for special exhibitions. Clientele: private clients from Boston, all over the US. and Canada. 90% private collectors, 10% corporate clients. Overall price range: $20-200,000; most artwork sold at $5,000-20,000.

MEDIA Considers all media. Most frequently exhibits paintings, prints and ceramics.

STYLE Exhibits all styles.

TERMS Terms of representation vary by artist, "usually it is consignment." Retail price set by gallery. Gallery provides promotion; artist pays shipping. Prefers artwork unframed.

SUBMISSIONS Send query letter with résumé, slides, bio and SASE. Write for appointment to show portfolio of originals and slides. Responds in 3 weeks. Files résumés.

PUMP HOUSE CENTER FOR THE ARTS

P.O. Box 1613, Chillicothe OH 45601. **E-mail:** pumphouseartgallery@aol.com. **Website:** www.pumphouseartgallery.com. **Contact:** Priscilla V. Smith, director. Estab. 1991. Nonprofit gallery. Approached by 6 artists/year; represents or exhibits more than 50 artists. Sponsors 8 exhibits/year. Average display time: 6 weeks. Open Tuesay-Saturday, 11-4; Sunday, 1-4. Overall price range: $150-600; most work sold at $300. Facility is also available for rent (business meetings, reunions, weddings, receptions or rehearsals, etc.).

MEDIA Considers all media and all types of prints. Most frequently exhibits oil, acrylic and watercolor.

STYLE Considers all styles and genres.

TERMS Artwork is accepted on consignment (30% commission). Gallery provides insurance and promotion. Accepted work should be framed, matted and wired for hanging. The Pump House reserves the right to reject any artwork deemed inappropriate.

SUBMISSIONS Call or stop in to show portfolio of photographs, slides, originals or prints. Send query letter with bio, photographs, SASE and slides. Returns material with SASE. Responds in 1 month. Finds artists through word of mouth, submissions, portfolio reviews, art fairs/exhibits, and referrals by other artists.

TIPS "All artwork must be original designs, framed, ready to hang (wired—no sawtooth hangers)."

QUEENS COLLEGE ART CENTER

Benjamin S. Rosenthal Library, Flushing NY 11367. (718)997-3770. **Fax:** (718)997-3753. **E-mail:** tara. mathison@qc.cuny.edu; artcenter@qc.cuny.edu. **Website:** www.queenscollegeartcenter.org. **Contact:** Tara Tye Mathison, director and curator. Estab. 1955. Average display time: 6-8 weeks. Overall price range: $100-3,000.

MEDIA Considers all media.

STYLE Open to all styles and genres; decisive factors are originality and quality.

TERMS Charges 40% commission. Accepted work can be framed or unframed, mounted or unmounted, matted or unmatted. Sponsors openings.

SUBMISSIONS Online preferred or send query letter with résumé, samples and SASE. Responds in 1-2 months.

◎ MARCIA RAFELMAN FINE ARTS

10 Clarendon Ave., Toronto Ontario M4V 1H9, Canada. (416)920-4468. **Fax:** (416)968-6715. **E-mail:** info@ mrfinearts.com. **Website:** www.mrfinearts.com. **Contact:** Marcia Rafelman, president; Meghan Richardson, gallery director. Estab. 1984. Semiprivate gallery. Average display time: 1 month. Gallery is centrally located in Toronto; 2,000 sq. ft. on 2 floors. Clients include local community, tourists and upscale. 40% of sales are to corporate collectors. Overall price range: $800-25,000; the average selling price is now $2,500.

MEDIA Considers all media. Most frequently exhibits photography, painting and graphics. Considers all types of prints.

STYLE Exhibits geometric abstraction, minimalism, neo-expressionism, primitivism and painterly abstraction. Most frequently exhibits high realism paintings. Considers all genres except Southwestern, Western and wildlife.

TERMS Artwork is accepted on consignment (50% commission); net 30 days. Retail price set by the gallery and the artist. Gallery provides insurance, promotion and contract. Requires exclusive representation locally.

SUBMISSIONS Mail or e-mail portfolio for review; include bio, photographs, reviews. Responds within 2 weeks, only if interested. Finds artists through word of mouth, submissions, art fairs, referrals by other artists.

RAHR-WEST ART MUSEUM

610 N. Eighth St., Manitowoc WI 54220. (920)686-3090. **E-mail:** rahrwest@manitowoc.org. **Website:** www.rahrwestartmuseum.org. Estab. 1950. Five thematic exhibits, preferably groups of mid-career and established artists. Sponsors 8-10 shows/year. Average display time: 6-8 weeks. Open all year; Tuesday-Friday, 10-4; Saturday and Sunday, 11-4. Closed Mondays and major holidays. Clients include local community and tourists. Overall price range: $50-2,200; most work sold at $150-200.

MEDIA Considers all media and all types of original prints except posters or glicée prints. Most frequently exhibits painting, pastel and original prints.

STYLE Considers all styles. Most frequently exhibits impressionism, realism and various abstraction. Genres include figurative work, florals, landscapes and portraits.

TERMS Artwork is accepted on consignment and there is a 30% commission. Retail price set by the artist. Gallery provides insurance. Accepted work should be framed with hanging devices attached.

SUBMISSIONS Send query letter with artist's statement, bio, SASE and slides. Returns material only if requested with SASE if not considered. Otherwise slides are filed with contact info and bio. Responds only if interested.

RAIFORD GALLERY

1169 Canton St., Roswell GA 30075. (770)645-2050. **Fax:** (770)992-6197. **E-mail:** raifordgallery@mindspring.com. **Website:** www.raifordgallery.com. Estab. 1996. For-profit gallery. Approached by many artists/year. Represents 400 mid-career and established artists. Exhibited artists include Marianne van der Haar (paintings), Dale Rayburn (monotypes), and Richard Jacobus (metal). Open Tuesday–Saturday, 10-5. Located in historic district of Roswell; 4,500 sq. ft. in an open 2-story timber-frame space. Clients include local community, tourists and upscale. Overall price range: $10-2,000; most work sold at $200-300.

MEDIA Considers all media except installation. Most frequently exhibits painting, glass and turned wood.

STYLE Exhibits contemporary American art and craft.

TERMS Artwork is accepted on consignment, and there is a 50% commission. Retail price set by the artist. Gallery provides insurance, promotion and contract. Accepted work should be framed and/or ready for hanging. Requires exclusive representation locally.

SUBMISSIONS Call or write to show to review board original work, portfolio of photographs. Send query e-mail with artist's statement, website, bio, photo attachements. Finds artists through submissions, portfolio reviews, art exhibits and art fairs.

REHOBOTH ART LEAGUE, INC.

12 Dodds Lane, Rehoboth Beach DE 19971. (302)227-8408. **Fax:** (302)227-4121. **E-mail:** jay@rehobothartleague.org. **Website:** www.rehobothartleague.org. **Contact:** Jay Pastore, exhibitions director. Estab. 1938. Nonprofit gallery; offers education in visual arts. Exhibits the work of 1,000 emerging, mid-career and established artists. Sponsors 10-12 shows/year. Average display time: 4-5 weeks. Open January through December. Located in a residential area near the beach; "3½ acres, rustic gardens, built in 1743; listed in the National Register of Historic Places; excellent exhibition and studio space. Regional setting attracts artists and arts advocates." 100% of space for special exhibitions. Clientele: members, artists (all media), arts advocates.

MEDIA Considers all media and all types of prints.

STYLE Exhibits all styles and all genres.

TERMS Accepts artwork on consignment (30% commission) from members. Retail price set by the artist. Gallery provides insurance and promotion. Artist pays for shipping. Prefers artwork framed for exhibition, unframed for browser sales.

SUBMISSIONS Send query letter with résumé, slides and bio. Write to schedule an appointment to show a portfolio, which should include appropriate samples. Responds in 6 weeks. Files bios and slides in Member's Artist Registry.

ELLA WALTON RICHARDSON FINE ART

58 Broad St., Charleston SC 29401. (843)722-3660. **Fax:** (843)722-4330. **E-mail:** ella@ellarichardson.com. **Website:** www.ellarichardson.com. **Contact:** Ella Richardson, owner. Estab. 2001. For-profit gallery. Exhibits established artists. Approached by 100s of artists a year; represents or exhibits 28 artists. Exhibited artists include Aleksander and Lyuba Titovets, Lindsay Goodwin, the Baranovs, Jeff Jamison, and Michael Coleman. Model and property release are required. Open Monday-Saturday 10-5. Located in historic downtown Charleston, the gallery has 3 rooms of artwork. The gallery is in the heart of the gallery dis-

trict. It is an elegant and inviting space with hardwood floors, granite counters, and dual fireplaces. Clients included local community, students, tourists, and upscale. 5% of sales are to corporate collectors. Overall price range: $500-16,000.

MEDIA Coniders most media. But most frequently exhibits oil, acrylic, and bronze sculptures.

STYLE Exhibits impressionism and painterly abstraction.

TERMS Artwork is accepted on consignment and there is a 50% commission. Retail price set by the gallery and artist. gallery provides insurance and promotion. Accepted artwork should be framed. Requires exclusive representation locally.

SUBMISSIONS Mail or e-mail query letter with link to artist's website, JPEG samples at 72 dpi. Include artist's statement, bio, brochure, business card, photocopies, photographs, résumé, and reviews. Materials returned with SASE.

TIPS "Address the gallery individually. Sound knowledgeable about our space and artists. Organization, and preparation."

RIVER GALLERY

400 E. Second St., Chattanooga TN 37403. (423)265-5033, ext. 5. **E-mail:** art@river-gallery.com; details@river-gallery.com. **Website:** www.river-gallery.com. **Contact:** Mary R. Portera, owner/director. Estab. 1992. Retail gallery. Represents 100 emerging, mid-career and established artists/year. Exhibited artists include Michael Kessler and Scott E. Hill. Sponsors 12 shows/year. Open Monday–Saturday, 10-5; Sunday, 1-5; and by appointment. Located in Bluff View Art District in downtown area; 2,500 sq. ft.; restored early New Orleans-style 1900s home; arched openings into rooms. 20% of space for special exhibitions; 80% of space for gallery artists. Clients include upscale tourists, local community. 95% of sales are to private collectors, 5% corporate collectors. Overall price range $5-10,000; most work sold at $200-2,000.

MEDIA Considers all media. Most frequently exhibits oil, original prints, photography, watercolor, mixed media, fiber, clay, jewelry, wood, glass and sculpture.

STYLE Exhibits all styles and genres. Prefers painterly abstraction, impressionism, photorealism.

TERMS Accepts work on consignment (50% commission). Retail price set by the gallery. Gallery provides free gift wrap, insurance, promotion and contract; shipping costs are shared. Prefers artwork framed.

SUBMISSIONS Send query letter with résumé, slides, bio, photographs, SASE, reviews and artist's statement. Call or e-mail for appointment to show portfolio of photographs and slides. Files all material unless we are not interested then we return all information. Can also submit via form on website. Finds artists through word of mouth, referrals by other artists, visiting art fairs and exhibitions, submissions, ads in art publications.

ROCKPORT CENTER FOR THE ARTS

902 Navigation Circle, Rockport TX 78382. (361)729-5519. **Fax:** (361)729-3551. **E-mail:** info@rockportart center.com. **Website:** www.rockportartcenter.com. Estab. 1969. "Rockport Center for the Arts is a hub of creative activity on the Texas Gulf Coast. Two parlor galleries are dedicated entirely to the works of its member artists, while the main gallery allows the center to host local, regional, national, and internationally acclaimed artists in both solo and group exhibitions. In 2000, the Garden Gallery was added, allowing the center for the first time to simultaneously feature 3 distinct exhibitions, at times displaying over 100 original works of art. Today, the building also houses 2 visual arts classrooms and an outdoor sculpture garden featuring works by internationally acclaimed artists. A well-furnished pottery studio is always active, and includes a kiln room which hosts daily firings. Visitors enjoy the exhibitions, education programs and gift shop, as well as the Annual Rockport Art Festival every July 4th weekend." Gallery hours vary. Call, e-mail or visit website for more information.

ROGUE GALLERY & ART CENTER

40 S. Bartlett, Medford OR 97501. (541)772-8118. **E-mail:** info@roguegallery.org; kim@roguegallery. org. **Website:** www.roguegallery.org. **Contact:** Kim Hearon, executive director. Estab. 1961. Nonprofit sales rental gallery. Represents emerging, mid-career and established artists. Sponsors 8 shows/year. Average display time: 6 weeks. Open all year; Tuesday–Friday, 10-5; Saturday, 11-3. Located downtown Medford; main gallery 240 running ft. (2,000 sq. ft.); rental/sales and gallery shop, 1,800 sq. ft.; classroom facility, 1,700 sq. ft. "This is the only gallery/art center/exhibit space of its kind in the region, excellent facility, good lighting." 33% of space for special exhibitions; 33% of space for gallery artists. 95% of sales to private collectors.

Overall price range: $100-5,000; most work sold at $400-1,000.

MEDIA Considers all media and all types of prints. Most frequently exhibits mixed media, drawing, installation, painting, sculpture, watercolor.

STYLE Exhibits all styles and genres.

TERMS Accepts work on consignment (40% gallery; 60% artist). Retail price set by the artist. Gallery provides insurance, promotion and contract; in the case of main gallery exhibit.

SUBMISSIONS Accepts submissions for main gallery once a year. See our website www.roguegallery.org/calls_to_artists.html for dates and instructions.

ALICE C. SABATINI GALLERY

Topeka & Shawnee County Public Library, 1515 SW Tenth Ave., Topeka KS 66604-1374. (785)580-4515. **Website:** www.tscpl.org. **Contact:** Zan Popp, exhibit curator. Estab. 1976. Nonprofit gallery. Exhibits emerging, mid-career and established artists. Sponsors 6-8 shows/year. Average display time: 6 weeks. Open all year; Monday-Friday, 9-9; Saturday, 9-6; Sunday, 12-9. Located 1 mile west of downtown; 2,500 sq. ft.; security, track lighting, plex top cases; 5 moveable walls. 100% of space for special exhibitions and permanent collections. Overall price range: $150-5,000.

MEDIA Considers any media meeting educational mission. "We help people 'get' art. Emphasis currently on group and topical exhibits with educational potential."

STYLE Exhibits realism, abstraction, neo-expressionism, modern and postmodern arts, functional and fine art ceramic and crafts.

TERMS Retail price set by artist. Gallery provides insurance; artist pays for shipping costs. Prefers artwork framed. Does not handle sales, also does not take commission.

SUBMISSIONS Usually accepts regional artists. Send query letter with résumé and 12-24 images and description of educational goals. Call or write for appointment to show portfolio. Responds iannually. Files résumé. Finds artists through visiting exhibitions, word of mouth and submissions.

TIPS "Research galleries to find out if your work is a good match. Send good quality images to best represent your work. Include information about yourself (bio, artist's statement), and also describe what projects you have going on. We plan 1-2 years in advance, and we look for originality."

SAMEK ART MUSEUM OF BUCKNELL UNIVERSITY

Elaine Langone Center, Lewisburg PA 17837. (570)577-3792. **Fax:** (570)577-3215. **E-mail:** gas019@bucknell.edu. **Website:** www.bucknell.edu/samek. **Contact:** Greg Stuart. Estab. 1983. Nonprofit gallery. Exhibits emerging, mid-career and established international and national artists. Sponsors 6 shows/year. Average display time: 6 weeks. Open all year; Tuesday-Sunday, 12-5; Thursday, 11-8; Saturday-Sunday, 1-4. Located on campus; 3,500 sq. ft. including main gallery, project room and Kress Study Collection Gallery.

MEDIA Considers all media, traditional and emerging media. Most frequently exhibits painting, sculpture, works on paper and video.

STYLE Exhibits all styles, genres and periods.

TERMS Retail price set by the artist. Gallery provides insurance, promotion (local) and contract; artist pays shipping costs to and from gallery. Prefers artwork framed or prepared for exhibition.

SUBMISSIONS Send query letter with résumé, slides and bio. Write for appointment to show portfolio of originals. Responds in 12 months. Files bio, résumé, slides. Finds artists through museum and gallery exhibits, and through studio visits.

TIPS "Most exhibitions are curated by the director or by a guest curator."

SAN DIEGO ART INSTITUTE

1439 El Prado, San Diego CA 92101. (619)236-0011. **Fax:** (619)236-1974. **E-mail:** director@sandiego-art.org; admin@sandiego-art.org. **Website:** www.sandiego-art.org. **Contact:** Ginger Shulick Porcella, executive director. Estab. 1941. Nonprofit gallery. Represents 600 emerging and mid-career member/artists. 2,400 artworks juried into shows each year. Sponsors 11 all-media exhibits/year. Average display time: 4-6 weeks. Open Tuesday–Saturday, 10-4; Sunday 12-4. Closed major holidays and all Mondays. 10,000 sq. ft., located in the heart of Balboa Park. Clients include local community, students and tourists. 10% of sales are to corporate collectors. Overall price range: $100-4,000; most work sold at $800.

MEDIA Considers all media and all types of prints. Most frequently exhibits oil, mixed media, pastel, digital.

STYLE Considers all styles and genres. No craft or installations.

SUBMISSIONS Request membership packet and information about juried shows. Membership not required for submission in monthly juried shows, but fee required. Returns material with SASE. Finds artists through word of mouth and referrals by other artists. Submission guidelines available online.

TIPS "All work submitted must go through jury process for each monthly exhibition. Work required to be framed in professional manner."

SANGRE DE CRISTO ARTS CENTER AND BUELL CHILDREN'S MUSEUM

210 N. Santa Fe Ave., Pueblo CO 81003. (719)295-7200. **E-mail:** mail@sdc-arts.org. **Website:** sdc-arts.org. Estab. 1972. Nonprofit gallery and museum. Exhibits emerging, mid-career and established artists. Sponsors 20 shows/year. Average display time: 10 weeks. Open Tuesday–Thursday, 11-5; Friday, 11-7; Saturday–Sunday 12-5. Admission $8 adults; $6 children, military and seniors 65+. Located "downtown, right off 98B from Interstate I-25;" 16,000-sq.-ft.; 7 galleries, 1 showing a permanent collection of Western art; changing exhibits in the other 6. Also a new 12,000 sq. ft. children's museum with changing, interactive exhibits. Clientele: "We serve a 19-county region and attract 200,000 visitors yearly." Overall price range: $50-100,000; most work sold at $50-2,500.

MEDIA Considers all media.

STYLE Exhibits all styles. Genres include Southwestern, regional and contemporary.

TERMS Accepts work on consignment (40% commission). Retail price set by artist. Gallery provides insurance, promotion, contract and shipping costs. Prefers artwork framed.

SUBMISSIONS Send query letter with portfolio of slides. Responds in 2 months.

SAPER GALLERIES

433 Albert Ave., East Lansing MI 48823. (517)351-0815. **E-mail:** roy@sapergalleries.com. **Website:** www.sapergalleries.com. **Contact:** Roy C. Saper, director. Estab. 1978; new addition built in 1986. Displays the work of 150 artists, mostly mid-career, and artists of significant national prominence. Exhibited artists include Picasso, Peter Max, Rembrandt. Sponsors 2 shows/year. Average display time: 2 months. Open all year. Located downtown; 5,700 sq. ft. 50% of space for special exhibitions. Clients include students, professionals, experienced and new collectors. 80% of sales are to private collectors, 20% corporate collectors. Overall price range: $100-100,000; most work sold at $1,000.

MEDIA Considers oil, acrylic, watercolor, pastel, drawings, mixed media, collage, paper, sculpture, ceramic, craft, glass and original handpulled prints. Considers all types of prints except offset reproductions. Most frequently exhibits intaglio, serigraphy and sculpture. "Must be of highest professional quality."

STYLE Exhibits expressionism, painterly abstraction, surrealism, postmodern works, impressionism, realism, photorealism and hard-edge geometric abstraction. Genres include landscapes, florals, southwestern and figurative work. Prefers abstract, landscapes and figurative. Seeking extraordinarily talented, outstanding artists who will continue to produce exceptional work.

TERMS Accepts work on consignment (negotiable commission); or buys outright for negotiated percentage of retail price. Retail price set by the artist. Offers payment by installments. Gallery provides insurance, promotion and contract; shipping costs are shared. Prefers artwork unframed (gallery frames). Best way to present your work is through website link or online portfolio.

SUBMISSIONS Prefers digital pictures e-mailed to roy@sapergalleries.com. Call for appointment to show portfolio of originals or photos of any type. Responds in 1 week. Files any material the artist does not need returned. Finds artists mostly through New York Art Expo.

TIPS "Present your very best work to galleries that display works of similar style, quality and media. Must be outstanding, professional quality. Student quality doesn't cut it. Must be great. Be sure to include prices."

◯ SAW GALLERY INC.

67 Nicholas St., Ottawa Ontario K1N 7B9, Canada. (613)236-6181. **Fax:** (613)238-4617. **E-mail:** sawgallery@artengine.ca. **Website:** www.galeriesawgallery.com. **Contact:** Tam-Ca Vo-Van, director. Estab. 1973. Alternative space. Approached by 100 artists/year. Represents 8-30 emerging and mid-career artists. Average display time: 4-5 weeks. Open all year; Tuesday–Saturday, 11-6. Clients include local community, students, tourists and other members. Sales conducted with artist directly.

MEDIA Considers all media. Most frequently exhibits installation, mixed media, media arts (video/film/computer). Considers all types of prints.

STYLE Exhibits cutting edge contemporary art. Most frequently exhibits art attuned to contemporary issues. Considers critical and contemporary (avant-garde art).

TERMS All sales arranged between interested buyer and artist directly. Retail price set by the artist. Gallery provides insurance, promotion and contract. Does not require exclusive representation locally. Accepts only art attuned to contemporary issues.

SUBMISSIONS Send artist's statement, bio, résumé, reviews (if applicable), SASE, 10 slides. Returns material with SASE. Responds in 1-6 months. Proposals are reviewed in June and December. Files curriculum vitae. Finds artists through word of mouth, submissions, referrals by other artists, calls for proposals, advertising in Canadian art magazines.

TIPS "Have another artist offer an opinion of the proposal and build on the suggestions before submitting."

SCHERER GALLERY

3700 South Westport Ave., #1806, Sioux Falls SD 57106. (800)957-2673. **E-mail:** scherergallery@sedona.net. **Website:** www.scherergallery.com. **Contact:** Tess and Marty Scherer, owners. Estab. 1968. Online gallery. Represents over 30 mid-career and established artists. Interested in seeing the work of emerging artists. Exhibited artists include Tamayo, Hundertwasser, Friedlaender, Delaunay, Calder and Barnet.

MEDIA Considers nonfunctional glass sculpture; paintings and other works on paper including handpulled prints in all mediums; and kaleidoscopes.

STYLE Exhibits color field, minimalism, surrealism, expressionism, modern and post modern works. Looking for artists "with a vision. Work that shows creative handling of the medium(s) and uniqueness to the style." Specializes in handpulled graphics, artglass and kaleidoscopes.

TERMS Accepts work on consignment (50% commission). Retail price set by artist. Exclusive area representation required. Gallery provides insurance, promotion and contract; shipping costs are shared.

SUBMISSIONS Send query letter, résumé, bio, at least 12 slides (no more than 30), photographs and SASE. Follow up with a call for appointment to show portfolio. Responds in 1 month.

TIPS "Persevere! Don't give up!" Considers "originality and quality of the work."

WILLIAM & FLORENCE SCHMIDT ART CENTER

Southwestern Illinois College, 2500 Carlyle Ave., Belleville IL 62221. (618)222-5278. **Website:** www.swic.edu/sac. Estab. 2002. Nonprofit gallery. Exhibits emerging, mid-career and established artists. Sponsors 10-12 exhibits/year. Average display time: 6-8 weeks. Open Monday–Wednesday, 9-4; Thursday, 9-7; Friday, 10-4; Saturday, 11-4; closed during college holidays. Clients include local community, students and tourists.

MEDIA Considers all media.

STYLE Considers all styles.

SUBMISSIONS Mail portfolio for review. Send query letter with artist's statement, bio and digital images. Returns material with SASE. Finds artists through art fairs and exhibits, portfolio reviews, referrals by other artists, submissions and word of mouth.

SCOTTSDALE MUSEUM OF CONTEMPORARY ART

7374 E. Second St., Scottsdale AZ 85251. (480)874-4639. **E-mail:** smoca@sccarts.org. **Website:** www.smoca.org. **Contact:** Tim Rogers, director. Approached by 30-50 artists/year. "Arizona's only museum devoted to the art, architecture and design of our time." Sponsors 12 exhibits/year. Average display time: 10 weeks. See website for summer and fall/winter hours. Located in downtown Scottsdale; more than 20,000 sq. ft. of exhibition space. Clients include local community, students and tourists.

MEDIA Considers all media.

STYLE Considers works of contemporary art, architecture and design.

SUBMISSIONS Send query letter with artist's statement, bio, images, résumé and reviews via the submissions process on smoca.org/opportunities.

SCULPTURECENTER

44-19 Purves St., Long Island City NY 11101. (718)361-1750. **E-mail:** hstanton@sculpture-center.org. **Website:** www.sculpture-center.org. **Contact:** Holly Stanton, exhibition and program manager. Estab. 1928. Alternative space, nonprofit gallery. Exhibits emerging and mid-career artists. Sponsors 8-10 shows/year. Average display time: 2-4 months. Open all year; Thursday–Monday, 11-6. Does not actively sell work.

MEDIA Considers drawing, mixed media, sculpture and installation. Most frequently exhibits sculpture, installations and video installations.

TERMS Not for profit museum. Does not sell work.

SUBMISSIONS "SculptureCenter is able to view work from artists with whom we are not familiar during our annual In Practice open call. If you'd like to be notified by e-mail when the next call is opened, please sign up for our e-mail list. You don't need to sign up a second time if you're already on our list. Artist materials submitted outside of the In Practice open call will be reviewed, but due to the volume of requests we receive every day, we regret that we are not able to reply to submissions. If your work appears both appropriate and timely for us to consider, we will contact you for a more formal review. Before sending materials, we ask that you first familiarize yourself with SculptureCenter by reviewing our past exhibitions and mission. We are unable to return submitted materials. We do not accept e-mail submissions."

SCULPTURESITE GALLERY

Jack London Village, 14301 Arnold Dr., Suite 8, Glen Ellen CA 95442. (707)933-1300. **E-mail:** info@sculpturesite.com. **Website:** www.sculpturesite.com. Estab. 1990. Retail gallery. Represents 70 emerging, mid-career and established artists. Sponsors 5 sculpture shows/year. Average display time: 3-4 months. Open daily, 10-5. Clients include local community, nationwide, worldwide, upscale. Overall price range: $1,000-100,000; most work sold at $5,000-20,000.

MEDIA Considers sculpture, mixed media, ceramic and glass. Most frequently exhibits sculpture. No crafts. "No paintings or works on paper, please."

STYLE Exhibits only contemporary abstract and abstract figurative.

TERMS Accepts artwork on consignment. Retail price set by artist in cooperation with gallery. Gallery provides insurance. Exclusive area representation required.

SUBMISSIONS Digital images are best; or send e-mail link to your website for review. Responds 2-3 times per year.

TIPS "We suggest artists visit us if possible; and, in any case, check website before submitting."

SELECT ART

1025 Levee St., Dallas TX 75207. (214)521-6833. **Fax:** (214)760-9722. **E-mail:** selart@swbell.net. **Website:** selectartusa.com. **Contact:** Paul Adelson, owner. Es-

tab. 1986. Private art gallery. Represents 25 emerging, mid-career and established artists. Open all year; Monday–Friday, 9-5 by appointment only. Located in the art/design district. 4,000 sq. ft. Provides art for major public spaces—corporate and health care. Overall price range: $500-15,000.

MEDIA Considers oil, fiber, acrylic, sculpture, glass, watercolor, mixed media, ceramic, pastel, collage, photography, woodcuts, linocuts, engravings, etchings and lithographs. Prefers monoprints and paintings on paper.

STYLE No photography at this time. No impressionism or realism. Prefers abstraction and outdoor sculpture in all mediums.

TERMS Accepts work on consignment (50% commission). Retail price set by consultant and artist. Sometimes offers customer discounts. Provides contract (if the artist requests one). Consultant pays shipping costs from gallery; artist pays shipping to gallery. Prefers artwork unframed.

SUBMISSIONS "No florals or wildlife." Send query letter with résumé, bio and SASE. Responds within 1 month, only if interested. Files bio, price list. Finds artists through word of mouth and referrals from other artists.

TIPS "Be timely when you say you are going to send artwork, etc."

SILVERMINE GUILD GALLERY

1037 Silvermine Rd., New Canaan CT 06840. (203)966-9700. **Website:** www.silvermineart.org. **Contact:** Jeffrey Mueller, gallery director. Estab. 1922. Nonprofit gallery. Represents 300 emerging, mid-career and established artists/year. Sponsors 24 shows/year. Average display time: 1 month. Open Wednesday–Saturday, 12-5; Sunday, 1-5. 5,000 sq. ft. 95% of space for gallery artists. Clientele: private collectors, corporate collectors. Overall price range: $250-10,000; most work sold at $1,000-2,000.

MEDIA Considers all media and all types of prints. Most frequently exhibits paintings, sculpture and ceramics.

STYLE Exhibits all styles.

TERMS Accepts guild member work on consignment (50% commission). Co-op membership fee plus donation of time (50% commission.) Retail price set by the gallery and the artist. Gallery provides insurance, promotion and contract. Prefers artwork framed.

SUBMISSIONS Send query letter.

SIOUX CITY ART CENTER

225 Nebraska St., Sioux City IA 51101-1712. (712)279-6272. **Fax:** (712)255-2921. **E-mail:** siouxcityartcenter@sioux-city.org. **Website:** www.siouxcityartcenter.org. **Contact:** Todd Behrens, curator. Estab. 1938. Museum. Exhibits emerging, mid-career and established artists. Approached by 50 artists/year; represents or exhibits 2-3 artists. Sponsors 15 total exhibits/year. Average display time: 10-12 weeks. Gallery open Tuesday, Wednesday, Friday, Saturday, 10-4; Thursday 10-9; Sunday 1-4; closed on Mondays and municipal holidays. Located in downtown Sioux City; 2 galleries, each 40×80 ft. Clients include local community, students and tourists.

MEDIA Considers all media and types of prints. Most frequently exhibits paintings, sculpture and mixed media.

STYLE Considers all styles and genres.

TERMS Artwork is accepted on consignment with a 30% commission. "However, the purpose of our exhibitions is not sales." Retail price of the art set by the artist. Gallery provides insurance, promotion and contract.

SUBMISSIONS Artwork should be framed. Only accepts artwork from upper-Midwestern states. E-mail query letter with link to artist's website; JPEG samples at 72 dpi. Or send query letter with artist's statement, résumé and digital images. Returns materials if SASE is enclosed. Responds, only if interested, within 6 months. Files résumé, statement and images if artist is suitable. Finds artists through word of mouth, art exhibits, submissions, art fairs, portfolio reviews and referrals by other artists.

SNYDERMAN-WORKS GALLERY

303 Cherry St., Philadelphia PA 19106. (215)238-9576. **E-mail:** jen@snyderman-works.com. **Website:** www.snyderman-works.com. **Contact:** Jen Brown. Estab. 1965. Retail gallery. Represents 200 emerging, mid-career and established artists. Exhibited artists include Eileen Sutton, Larry Spaid, Ron Meyers, Gary Magakis, Doug Herren, Graceann Warn, Yvonne Bobrowicz. Sponsors 10 shows/year. Average display time: 2 months. Open all year; Tuesday–Saturday, 10-6; openings 1st Friday of every month 5:30-8:30. Exhibitions usually change on a monthly basis except through the summer. Located downtown ("Old City"); 3,000 sq. ft. 65% of space for special exhibitions. Clientele designers, lawyers, businessmen and women, students. 90% private collectors, 10% corporate collectors. Overall price range: $50-10,000; most work sold at $200-600.

MEDIA Considers ceramic, fiber, glass, photography and metal jewelry. Most frequently exhibits jewelry, ceramic and fiber.

STYLE Exhibits all styles.

TERMS Accepts artwork on consignment (50% commission); some work is bought outright. Gallery provides insurance, promotion and contract; shipping costs are shared.

SUBMISSIONS Send query letter with résumé, 5-10 photos and SASE. Files résumé and slides, if interested.

TIPS "Most work shown is one-of-a-kind. We change the gallery totally for our exhibitions. In our gallery, someone has to have a track record so that we can see the consistency of the work. We would not be pleased to see work of one quality once and have the quality differ in subsequent orders, unless it improved. Always submit slides with descriptions and prices instead of walking in cold. Enclose a SASE. Follow up with a phone call. Try to have a sense of what the gallery's focus is so your work is not out of place. It would save everyone some time."

SOHN FINE ART—GALLERY & GICLÉE PRINTING

69 Church St., Lenox MA 01240. (413)551-7353. **E-mail:** info@sohnfineart.com. **Website:** www.sohnfineart.com. **Contact:** Cassandra Sohn, owner. Estab. 2011. Alternative space and for-profit gallery. Approached by 25-50 artists/year; represents or exhibits 12-20 emerging, mid-career and established artists. Exhibited artists include Greg Gorman, Matchuska, Fran Forman, John Atchley, Seth Resnick, Savannah Spirit, Burce Checefsky, Cassandra Sohn, etc. Average display time: 1-3 months. Open Thursday-Monday, 10-5. Located in the Berkshires of Western Massachusetts. The area is known for arts and culture and full of tourists. 80% of the population are 2nd home owners from New York and Boston. Clients include local community, tourists and upscale. Overall price range: $300-6,000. Most work sold for $300-2,500.

MEDIA Considers photography and sculpture.

STYLE Considers all styles and genres.

TERMS Artwork is accepted on consignment and there is a 50% commission. Retail price of the art set by the artist. Gallery provides insurance, promotion and contract. Accepted work should be framed, mounted and matted. Requires exclusive representation locally.

SUBMISSIONS E-mail query letter with link to artist's website and JPEG samples at 72 dpi. Material cannot be returned. Responds only if interested. Finds artists through word of mouth, art exhibits, submissions, art fairs, portfolio reviews and referrals by other artists.

SOUTH ARKANSAS ARTS CENTER

110 E. Fifth St., El Dorado AR 71730. (870)862-5474. **E-mail:** info@saac-arts.org. **Website:** www.saac-arts. org. Estab. 1963. Nonprofit gallery. Exhibits the work of 30 emerging, mid-career and established artists. Hosts 15-20 shows/year including a national juried art competition each summer. Average display time: 1 month. 3,600 sq. ft. of exhibit space in 3 galleries attached to a larger community arts center in the middle of town. Open Monday–Friday, 9-5; appointments scheduled by special arrangement on weekends; closed on major holidays (see website for details). Overall price range: $50-1,500; most work sold at $200-600.

MEDIA Considers all fine art, mixed media, 3D work and prints. Most frequently exhibits watercolor, pastels and mixed media.

STYLE Exhibits all styles.

TERMS Accepts work on consignment (35% commission). Retail price set by the artist. Gallery provides insurance and promotion; contract and shipping may be negotiated. All work must be gallery display ready, framed prefered.

SUBMISSIONS Send exhibit query by e-mail or by mail to SAAC office. Include images of artist work and information about the artist or an artist statement. Materials sent will not be returned to artist.

TIPS "We exhibit a wide variety of works by local, regional and national artists. With 3 gallery spaces, we have space to display works of all types, including a large gallery that is excellent for 3D works and large pieces."

SOUTH DAKOTA ART MUSEUM

South Dakota State University, Medary Ave. and Harvey Dunn St., P.O. Box 2250, Brookings SD 57007. (605)688-5423. **Fax:** (605)688-4445. **Website:** www. southdakotaartmuseum.com. Sponsors 15 exhibits/ year. Average display time: 4 months. Open Monday-Friday, 10-5; Saturday, 10-4; Sunday, 12-4; closed state holidays and Sundays, January–March. Seven galleries offer 26,000 sq. ft. of exhibition space.

MEDIA Considers all media and all types of prints. Most frequently exhibits painting, sculpture and fiber.

STYLE Considers all styles.

TERMS Please visit website for additional details.

SPACES

2220 Superior Viaduct, Cleveland OH 44113. (216)621-2314. **E-mail:** msimmons@spacesgallery. org. **Website:** www.spacesgallery.org. **Contact:** Marilyn Ladd-Simmons, gallery manager. Estab. 1978. "SPACES is is a presenting contemporary art venue dedicated to artists who explore and experiment. Located on the west side of downtown Cleveland, SPACES currently operates 3 programs to feature the excellent works of our curated artists: R&D (Research & Development), SWAP (SPACES World Artists Program), and the Vault. Public projects feature artists who push boundaries by experimenting with new forms of expression and innovative uses of media, presenting work of emerging artists and established artists with new ideas. The SPACES World Artist Program is a residency program that gives national, international, and regional artists the opportunity to create new work and interact with the Northeast Ohio community. The R&D program invites artists curators and other cultural group, solo, or event-oriented. The Vault functions as a media flat file—a converted walk-in safe where audiences can experience a variety of video and audio art." Sponsors 8-12 shows/year. Average display time: 8 weeks. Open Tuesday–Wednesday, Friday–Sunday, 12-5; Thursday, 12-8. Located in Cleveland; 5,000 sq. ft.; "warehouse space with row of columns."

MEDIA Considers all media. Most frequently exhibits installation, painting, video and experimental.

STYLE "Style not relevant; presenting challenging new ideas is essential."

TERMS Artists are provided honoraria, and 25% commission is taken on work sold. Gallery provides insurance, promotion and contract.

SUBMISSIONS Contact SPACES for deadline and application.

SPAIGHTWOOD GALLERIES, INC.

P.O. Box 1193, Upton MA 01568-6193. (508)529-2511. **E-mail:** sptwd@verizon.net. **Website:** www.spaight woodgalleries.com. **Contact:** Sonja Hansard-Weiner, president; Andy Weiner, director. Estab. 1980. Exhibits mostly established artists. Presents 3-4 exhibits/year. Average display time: 3 months. Open Saturday-Sunday, 12-6 and by appointment. Located in a renovated former Unitarian Church; basic space is 90×46 ft; ceilings are 25 ft. high at center, 13 ft. at walls. See website for views of the gallery. "Clients include mostly Internet and visitors drawn by Internet; we are currently trying to attract visitors from Boston and vicinity via advertising and press releases." 2% of sales are to corporate collectors. Overall price range: $175-500,000; most work sold at $1,000-4,000.

MEDIA Considers all media except installations, photography, glass, craft, fiber. Most frequently exhibits original prints, drawings and ceramic sculpture, occasionally paintings.

STYLE Exhibits Old Masters to contemporary; most frequently Old Master prints and drawings, modern, contemporary, impressionist and postimpressionist. "Work shown is part of our inventory; we buy mostly at auction. In the case of some artists, we buy directly from the artist or the publisher; in a few cases we have works on consignment."

TERMS Retail price set by both artist and gallery. Accepted work should be unmatted and unframed. Requires exclusive representation locally.

SUBMISSIONS Prefers link to website with bio, exhibition history and images. Returns material with SASE. Responds to queries only if interested. Finds artists through art exhibits (particularly museum shows), referrals by other artists, books.

TIPS "Make high-quality art."

B.J. SPOKE GALLERY

299 Main St., Huntington NY 11743. (631)549-5106. **E-mail:** manager@bjspokegallery.com. **Website:** www.bjspokegallery.com. **Contact:** Marilyn Lavi, gallery manager. Estab. 1978. Cooperative and nonprofit gallery exhibiting artists on Long Island. Artists showing at the gallery are well represented in numerous public and private collections. "Our artworks are for sale in the gallery and through this online exhibit space." Exhibits the work of 26 emerging, mid-career and established artists. Sponsors 2-3 invitationals and juried shows/year. Average display time: 1 month. Open all year. Open Tuesday–Thursday, Saturday–Sunday, 11-5; Friday, 11-9. "Located in center of town; 1,400 sq. ft.; flexible use of space; 3 separate gallery spaces." 66% of space for special exhibitions. Overall price range: $300-2,500; most work sold at $900-1,600. Artist is eligible for a 2-person show every 2 years. Entire membership has ability to exhibit work 11 months of the year.

○ Sponsors annual international/national juried show. Deadline: early November (see website for more details). Fee: $35. Checks made payable to b.j. spoke gallery. Send SASE for prospectives. Application is online. Send to EXPO 30 with SASE. Images are to be submitted on CD, JPEG only. File size should be between 500K and 1 MB. They will be viewed on a PC computer. Filenames should read: lastname firstname-1, lastnamefirstname-2, lastname firstname-3, etc. (no spaces).

MEDIA Considers all media except crafts, all types of printmaking. Most frequently exhibits paintings, prints and sculpture. Craft sold separately.

STYLE Exhibits all styles and genres. Prefers painterly abstraction, realism and expressionism.

TERMS Co-op membership fee plus donation of time . Monthly fee covers rent, other gallery expenses. Retail price set by artist. Payment by installment is available. Gallery provides promotion and publicity; artists pay for shipping. Prefers artwork framed; large format artwork can be tacked.

SUBMISSIONS For membership, send query letter with résumé, high-quality slides, bio, SASE and reviews. For national juried show send SASE for prospectus and deadline. Judge: Maura Lynch, assistant curator of drawings, Museum of Modern Art. Award: Exhibition of selected works, March 2011. Eligibility: Artists living in USA may submit up to 6 flat or 3 3D works. Media: All fine arts media are acceptable. No crafts. Sculpture should not exceed 8 feet in any dimension.

TIPS "Call or write for appointment to show portfolio of originals and slides. Files résumés; may retain slides for awhile if needed for upcoming exhibition. Send slides that represent depth and breadth in the exploration of a theme, subject or concept. They should represent a cohesive body of work."

THE STATE MUSEUM OF PENNSYLVANIA

300 North St., Harrisburg PA 17120. (717)787-4980. **E-mail:** bhager@state.pa.us. **Website:** www.state museumpa.org. Offers visitors 4 floors representing Pennsylvania's story, from Earth's beginning to the present. Features archaeological artifacts, minerals, paintings, decorative arts, animal dioramas, in-

dustrial and technological innovations and military objects representing the Commonwealth's heritage. Number of exhibits varies. Average display time: 2 months. Open Wednesday–Saturday, 9-5; Sunday, 12-5. Overall price range: $50-3,000.

MEDIA Considers all media and all types of prints.

STYLE Exhibits all styles and genres.

TERMS Work is sold in gallery, but not actively. Connects artists with interested buyers. No commission. Accepted work should be framed. Art must be created by a native or resident of Pennsylvania, or contain subject matter relevant to Pennsylvania.

SUBMISSIONS Send material by mail for consideration; include SASE. Responds in 1 month.

TIPS "Have the best visuals possible. Make appointments. Remember most curators are also overworked, underpaid and on tight schedules."

STATE OF THE ART GALLERY

120 W. State St., Ithaca NY 14850. (607)277-1626. **E-mail:** gallery@soag.org. **Website:** www.soag.org. Estab. 1989. Cooperative gallery. Sponsors 12 exhibits/year. Average display time: 1 month. Open Wednesday-Friday, 12-6; weekends, 12-5. Located in downtown Ithaca; 2 rooms; about 1,100 sq. ft. Overall price range: $100-6,000; most work sold at $200-500.

MEDIA Considers all media and all types of prints. Most frequently exhibits sculpture, paintings, mixed media.

STYLE Considers all styles and genres.

TERMS There is a co-op membership fee plus a donation of time. There is a 10% commission for members, 30% for nonmembers. Retail price set by the artist. Gallery provides promotion and contract. Accepted work must be ready to hang.

SUBMISSIONS Write for membership application. Finds artists through word of mouth, submissions, portfolio reviews, art exhibits, referrals by other artists.

STATE STREET GALLERY

1804 State St., La Crosse WI 54601. (608)782-0101. **Contact:** Ellen Kallies, president. Estab. 2000. Retail gallery. Approached by 15 artists/year. Represents 40 emerging, mid-career and established artists. Exhibited artists include Diane French, Jerry Riness, Kathie Wheeler, Sara Lubinski, among others. Sponsors 6 exhibits/year. Average display time: 4-6 months. Open Tuesday, Thursday and Friday, 10-4; Wednesday 11:15-5:15; Saturday 10-2; other times by chance or appointment; closed Saturdays in July. Located across from the University of Wisconsin/La Crosse on one of the main east/west streets. "We are next to a design studio; parking behind gallery." Clients include local community, tourists, upscale. 40% of sales are to corporate collectors, 60% to private collectors. Overall price range: $150-25,000; most work sold at $500-5,000.

MEDIA Considers acrylic, collage, drawing, glass, mixed media, oil, pastel, sculpture, watercolor and photography. Most frequently exhibits oil, dry pigment, drawing, watercolor and mixed media collage. Considers all types of prints.

STYLE Considers all styles and genres. Most frequently exhibits contemporary representational, realistic watercolor, collage.

TERMS Artwork is accepted on consignment (40% commission). Retail price set by the gallery and the artist. Gallery provides insurance, promotion, contract. Accepted work should be framed and matted.

SUBMISSIONS Call to arrange a personal interview or mail portfolio for review. Send query letter with artist's statement, photographs or slides. Returns material with SASE. Responds in 1 month. Finds artists through word of mouth, art exhibits, art fairs, and referrals by other artists.

TIPS "Be organized; be professional in presentation; be flexible! Most collectors today are savvy enough to want recent works on archival-quality papers/boards, mattes, etc. Have a strong and consistant body of work to present."

PHILIP J. STEELE GALLERY AT ROCKY MOUNTAIN COLLEGE OF ART + DESIGN

1600 Pierce St., Denver CO 80214. (303)225-8575. **E-mail:** cstell@rmcad.edu. **Website:** www.rmcad.edu. **Contact:** Cortney Stell, gallery director. Estab. 1962. For-profit college gallery. Represents emerging, mid-career and established artists. Sponsors 10-12 shows/year. Exhibited artists include Christo, Herbert Bayer, Andy Warhol and others. Average display time: 1 month. Open all year; Monday–Friday, 11-4. Located in the Mary Harris Auditorium building on the southeast corner of the quad. Clientele: local community, students, faculty.

MEDIA Considers all media and all types of prints.

STYLE Exhibits all styles.

TERMS Artists sell directly to buyer; gallery takes no commission. Retail price set by the artist. Gallery provides insurance and promotion; artist pays shipping costs to and from gallery.

SUBMISSIONS Submission guidelines available online.

TIPS Impressed by "professional presentation of materials, good-quality slides or catalog."

STEVENSON UNIVERSITY ART GALLERY

1525 Greenspring Valley Rd., Stevenson MD 21153. (443)352-4491. **Fax:** (410)352-4500. **E-mail:** exhibitions@stevenson.edu. **Website:** www.stevenson.edu/stuarteffects. **Contact:** Matt Laumann, cultural programs manager. Estab. 1997. Sponsors 10 exhibits/year across 3 museum quality gallery spaces, University Art Gallery, St. Paul Companies Pavilion, and the new School of Design Galery. Average display time: 6 weeks. Gallery open Monday–Wednesday, Friday, 11-5; Thursday, 11-8; Saturday, 1-4. "Since its 1997 inaugural season, the Stevenson University Art Gallery has presented a dynamic series of substantive exhibitions in diverse media and has achieved the reputation as a significant venue for regional artists and collectors. The museum quality space was designed to support the Baltimore arts community, provide greater opportunities for artists, and be integral to the educational experience of Stevenson students."

MEDIA Considers all media. Most frequently exhibits painting, sculpture, photography and works on paper, installation and new media.

STYLE Considers all styles and genres. "We are looking for artwork of substance by artists from the mid-Atlantic region."

TERMS "We facilitate inquiries directly to the artist." Gallery provides insurance. *Accepts artists from mid-Atlantic states only; emphasis on Baltimore artists.*

SUBMISSIONS Write to show portfolio. Send artist's statement, bio, résumé, reviews, portfolio link or CD. Responds in 3 months. Finds artists through word of mouth, submissions, portfolio reviews, referrals by other artists.

TIPS "Be clear, concise. Have good representatation of your images."

STILL POINT ART GALLERY

193 Hillside Rd., Brunswick ME 04011. (207)837-5760. **Website:** www.stillpointartgallery.com. **Contact:** Christine Cote, owner/director. Estab. 2009. For-profit online gallery. Exhibits emerging, mid-career and established artists. Approached by 300 artists/year. Represents 25 artists. Sponsors 4 juried shows/year. Distinguished artists earn representation and publication in gallery's art journal, *Still Point Arts Quarterly.* Model and property release preferred. Average display time: 14 months. Overall price range: $200-5,000.

MEDIA Considers all media. Most frequently exhibits painting and photography. Considers engravings, etchings, serigraphs, linocuts, woodcuts, lithographs and mezzotints.

STYLE Considers all styles and genres.

TERMS Retail price set by the artist. Gallery takes no commission from sales. Gallery provides promotion. Respond to calls for artists posted on website.

TIPS "Follow the instructions posted on our website."

STUDIO GALLERY

2108 R St. NW, Washington DC 20008. (202)232-8734. **E-mail:** info@studiogallerydc.com. **Website:** www.studiogallerydc.com. Estab. 1964. Cooperative and nonprofit gallery. Exhibits the work of 30 emerging, mid-career and established local artists. Sponsors 11 shows/year. Average display time: 1 month. Gallery for rent the last of August. Open Wednesday-Friday, 1-7; Saturday, 1-6. Located downtown in the Dupont Circle area; 700 sq. ft.; "gallery backs onto a courtyard, which is a good display space for exterior sculpture and gives the gallery an open feeling." Clientele: private collectors, art consultants and corporations. 85% private collectors; 8% corporate collectors. Overall price range: $300-10,000; most work sold at $500-3,000.

MEDIA Considers glass, oil, acrylic, watercolor, pastel, pen & ink, drawings, mixed media, collage, works on paper, sculpture, ceramic, fiber, original hand-pulled prints, woodcuts, lithographs, monotypes, linocuts and etchings. Most frequently exhibits oil, acrylic and paper.

STYLE Considers all styles. Most frequently exhibits abstract and figurative paintings, landscapes, indoor and outdoor sculpture and mixed media.

TERMS Co-op membership fee plus a donation of time (65% commission).

SUBMISSIONS Send query letter with SASE. Artists must be local or willing to drive to Washington for monthly meetings and receptions. Artist is informed as to when there is a membership opening and a selection review. Files artist's name, address, telephone.

TIPS "This is a cooperative gallery. Membership is decided by the gallery membership. Ask when the next review for membership is scheduled. An appointment for a portfolio review with the director is required before the jurying process, however. Dupont Circle is an exciting gallery scene with a variety of galleries. First Fridays from 6-8 for all galleries of Dupont Circle."

⦿ STUDIO SEVEN ARTS

400 Main St., Pleasanton CA 94566. (925)846-4322. **E-mail:** info@studiosevenarts.com. **Website:** www. studiosevenarts.com. Estab. 1981. Retail gallery. Represents/exhibits established artists. Sponsors 10 shows/year. Average display time: 3 weeks. Open Sunday–Thursday, 10-7; Friday-Saturday, 10-9. Located in historic downtown Pleasanton; 2,500 sq. ft.; excellent lighting from natural and halogen sources. 30% of space for special exhibitions; 70% of space for gallery artists. Clientele "wonderful, return customers." 99% private collectors, 1% corporate designer collectors. Overall price range: $100-80,000; most work sold at under $2,000-3,000.

MEDIA Considers oil, acrylic, watercolor, pastel, drawing, mixed media, collage, paper, sculpture, ceramics, fine craft, glass, woodcuts, engravings, lithographs, mezzotints, serigraphs and etchings. Most frequently exhibits oil, acrylic, etching, watercolor, handblown glass, jewelry and sculpture.

STYLE Exhibits painterly abstraction and impressionism. Genres include landscapes and figurative work. Prefers landscapes, figurative and abstract.

TERMS Work only on consignment. Retail price set by the artist. Gallery provides promotion and contract and shares in shipping costs.

SUBMISSIONS Prefers artists from the Bay Area. Send query e-mail with several examples of work representing current style. Call for appointment to show portfolio of originals. Responds only if interested within 1 month. Finds artists through word of mouth and "my own canvassing."

TIPS "Be prepared! Please come to your appointment with an artist statement, an inventory listing including prices, a résumé, and artwork that is ready for display."

SUMNER MCKNIGHT CROSBY, JR. GALLERY

Arts Council of Greater New Haven, 70 Audubon St., 2nd Floor, New Haven CT 06510. (203)772-2788. **Fax:** (203)772-2262. **E-mail:** info@newhavenarts.org. **Website:** www.newhavenarts.org. Estab. 1985. Formerly Small Space Gallery. Alternative space. Interested in emerging artists. Sponsors 10 group shows/year. Average display time: 1-2 months. Open to Arts Council members only.

MEDIA Considers all media.

STYLE Exhibits all styles and genres. "The Gallery was established to provide our artist members with an opportunity to show their work. Particularly those who were just starting their careers. We're not a traditional gallery, but an alternative art space." Shows are promoted through *The Arts Paper*, the Arts Council's coprehensive arts and entertainment paper, as well as on our website; announcements are also posted on a variety of online calendars.

TERMS Arts Council requests 10% donation on sale of each piece. Retail price set by artist. Exclusive area representation not required. Gallery provides insurance (up to $10,000) and promotion.

SUBMISSIONS Send images, résumé and bio, attn: Debbie Hesse (dhesse@newhavenarts.org). Call (203)772-2788, ext. 17 to inquire about becoming an artist member.

SWOPE ART MUSEUM

25 S. Seventh St., Terre Haute IN 47807. (812)238-1676. **E-mail:** info@swope.org. **Website:** www.swope.org. **Contact:** Marianne Richter, executive director. Estab. 1942. Nonprofit museum. Approached by approximately 10 artists/year. Represents 1-3 mid-career and established America artists. Average display time: 6 and 12 weeks. Open all year; Tuesday–Friday, 10-5; Saturday, 12-5; closed national holidays. Located in downtown Terre Haute, Indiana, in an Italian Renaissance-revival building with art deco interior.

MEDIA Considers all media. Most frequently exhibits paintings, sculpture, and works on paper. Considers all types of prints except posters.

STYLE Exhibits American art of all genres. Exhibits permanent collection with a focus on mid-20th-century regionalism and Indiana artists but includes American art from all 50 states from 1800s to today.

TERMS Focuses on local and regional artists (size and weight of works are limited because we do not have a freight elevator).

SUBMISSIONS Send query letter with artist's statement, brochure, CD or slides, résumé and SASE (if need items returned). Returns material with SASE. Responds in 5 months. Files only what fits the mission statement of the museum for special exhibitions.

Finds artists through word of mouth, and annual juried exhibition at the museum.

TIPS The Swope has physical limitations due to its historic interior but is willing to consider newer media, unconventional media and installations.

☮ SWORDS INTO PLOWSHARES PEACE CENTER AND GALLERY

33 E. Adams Ave., Detroit MI 48226. (313)963-7575. **E-mail:** swordsintoplowshares313@gmail.com. **Website:** www.swordsintoplowsharesdetroit.org. Estab. 1985. Nonprofit peace center and gallery. Presents 3-4 major shows/year. Open Tuesday, Thursday- Saturday, 12- 6. Located in downtown Detroit in the Theater District; 2,881 sq. ft.; 1 large gallery, 3 small galleries. 100% of space for special exhibitions. Clients include walk-in, church, school and community groups. 100% of sales are to private collectors. Overall price range: $75-6,000; most work sold at $75-700.

MEDIA Considers all media and all types of prints.

TERMS Retail price set by the artist. Gallery provides insurance and promotion.

SUBMISSIONS Accepts artists primarily from Michigan and Ontario. Send query letter with statement on how work relates to theme. Responds in 2 months. Finds artists through lists from Michigan Council of the Arts and Windsor Council of the Arts.

SYNCHRONICITY FINE ARTS

106 W. 13th St., New York NY 10011. (646)230-8199. **E-mail:** jsa@synchroncityspace.com; contact@synchroncityspace.com. **Website:** www.synchroncityspace.com. **Contact:** John Amato, director. Estab. 1989. Nonprofit gallery. Approached by several hundred artists/year. Average display time: 1 month. Open Tuesday-Saturday, 12-6. Closed for 2 weeks in August. Clients include local community, students, tourists and upscale. 20% of sales are to corporate collectors. Overall price range: $1,500-10,000; most work sold at $3,000-5,000.

MEDIA Considers acrylic, collage, drawing, mixed media, oil, paper, pastel, pen & ink, sculpture, watercolor, engravings, etchings, mezzotints and woodcuts. Most frequently exhibits oil, sculpture and photography.

STYLE Exhibits color field, expressionism, impressionism, postmodernism and painterly abstraction. Most frequently exhibits semiabstract and semirepresentational abstract. Genres include figurative work, landscapes and portraits.

TERMS Retail price set by the gallery. Gallery provides insurance, promotion and contract. Accepted work should be framed, mounted and matted.

SUBMISSIONS Write or call to arrange a personal interview to show portfolio of photographs, slides and transparencies. Send query letter with photocopies, photographs, résumé, SASE and slides. Returns material with SASE. Files materials unless artist requests return. Finds artists through submissions, portfolio reviews, art exhibits and referrals by other artists.

LILLIAN & COLEMAN TAUBE MUSEUM OF ART

2 N. Main St., Minot ND 58703. (701)838-4445. **E-mail:** taube@srt.com. **Website:** www.taubemuseum.org. **Contact:** Nancy Walter, executive director. Estab. 1970. Established nonprofit organization. Sponsors 1-2 photography exhibits/year. Average display time: 4-6 weeks. Located in a renovated historic landmark building with room to show 2 exhibits simultaneously. Overall price range: $15-225. Most work sold at $40-100.

MEDIA Considers oil, acrylic, watercolor, pastel, pen & ink, drawings, mixed media, collage, works on paper, sculpture, ceramic, fiber, glass, photograph, woodcuts, engravings, lithographs, serigraphs, linocuts and etchings. Most frequently exhibits watercolor, acrylic and mixed media.

STYLE Exhibits all styles and genres. Prefers figurative, Americana and landscapes. No "commercial-style work (unless a graphic art display)." Interested in all media.

TERMS Accepts work on consignment (30% commission, members; 40% nonmembers). Retail price set by artist. Offers discounts to gallery members and sometimes payment by installments. Gallery provides insurance, promotion and contract; pays shipping costs from gallery or shipping costs are shared. Requires artwork framed.

SUBMISSIONS Send query letter with résumé and slides. Write for appointment to show portfolio of good quality photographs and slides. "Show variety in your work." Files material interested in. Finds artists through visiting exhibitions, word of mouth, submissions of slides and members' referrals.

TIPS "We will take in a small show to fill in an exhibit. Show your best. When shipping show, be uniform on sizes and frames. Have flat backs to pieces so work does not gouge walls. Be uniform on wire placement. Avoid sawtooth hangers."

TEW GALLERIES, INC.

425 Peachtree Hills Ave., #24, Atlanta GA 30305. (404)869-0511. **Fax:** (404)869-0512. **E-mail:** jules@tewgalleries.com; info@tewgalleries.com. **Website:** www.tewgalleries.com. **Contact:** Jules Bekker, director. Estab. 1987. For-profit gallery. "TEW Galleries is recognized as a leading contemporary fine art institution in Atlanta. The gallery has an established reputation for its representation of national and international artists and presents a broad spectrum of works in styles ranging from traditional to contemporary, including abstract, landscape, and figurative art. The gallery also focuses on the best of the next generation of emerging talent and regularly features young artists who have a defined direction alongside established contemporaries." Exhibits selected emerging and mid-career artists. Approached by over 200 artists/year; represents or exhibits 10-20 artists/year in solo and group exhibitions. Exhibited artists include Brian Rutenberg (oil), Deedra Ludwig (encaustic, mixed media, oil, pastel painting) and Kimo Minton (polychrome woodcut panels and sculpture). Sponsors 7 exhibits/year. Average display time: 28 days. Open Monday–Friday, 10-5; Saturday, 11-5. Located in a prestigious arts and antiques complex. Total of 3,600 sq. ft. divided over 3 floors. Clients include upscale and corporate. 15% of sales are to corporate collectors. Overall price range: $1,800-40,000; most work sold at $8,500 or less. Consignment only.

MEDIA Fine art: paintings, sculpture and drawings. Considers all media except craft and photography. Most frequently exhibits oil on canvas, works on paper and small to medium scale sculptures.

STYLE Considers all styles.

TERMS Artwork is accepted on consignment and there is a 50% commission. Retail price set by the gallery and the artist. Requires exclusive representation locally.

SUBMISSIONS Reviews artist submissions on an ongoing basis. Artists may send a submission by e-mail, with a maximum of 8 digital images. Links to websites are also welcome. Please be aware that we *do not* accept submissions by postal mail. With all submissions, please include a biographical history, résumé, and other material that supports your work.

TIPS "We kindly ask that artists not show up at the gallery and ask us to review their artwork. We do review everything sent to us and appreciate your attention to our submissions policy."

NATALIE AND JAMES THOMPSON ART GALLERY

Department of Art & Art History, San Jose State University, San Jose CA 95192-0089. (408)924-4723. **Fax:** (408)924-4326. **E-mail:** thompsongallery@sjsu.edu. **Website:** www.sjsu.edu. **Contact:** Jo Farb Hernandez, director. Nonprofit gallery. Approached by 100 artists/year. Sponsors 6 exhibits/year of emerging, mid-career and established artists. Average display time: 1 month. Open during academic year; Tuesday, 10-4, 6-7:30; Monday, Wednesday-Friday, 10-4; closed semester breaks, summer and weekends. Clients include local community, students and upscale.

MEDIA Considers all media and all types of prints.

STYLE Considers all styles and genres.

TERMS Retail price set by the artist. Gallery provides insurance, transportation and promotion. Accepted work should be framed or ready to display. Does not require exclusive representation locally.

SUBMISSIONS Send query letter with artist's statement, bio, résumé, reviews, SASE and slides. Returns material with SASE.

THORNE-SAGENDORPH ART GALLERY

Keene State College, 229 Main St., Keene NH 03435-3501. (603)358-2720. **E-mail:** thorne@keene.edu. **Website:** www.keene.edu/tsag. **Contact:** Brian Wallace, director. Estab. 1965. Nonprofit gallery. In addition to exhibitions of national and international art, the Thorne shows local artist as well as KSC faculty and student work. 600 members. Exhibited artists include Jules Olitski and Fritz Scholder. Sponsors 5 shows/year. Average display time: 4-6 weeks. Open Saturday-Wednesday, 12-5; Thursday and Friday evenings till 7; summer: Wednesday-Sunday, 12-5; closed Monday and Tuesday. Follows academic schedule. Located on campus; 4,000 sq. ft.; climate control, security. 50% of space for special exhibitions. Clients include local community and students.

MEDIA Considers all media and all types of prints.

STYLE Exhibits Considers all styles.

TERMS Gallery takes 40% commission on sales. Retail price set by the artist. Gallery provides insurance, promotion and contract; shipping costs are shared. Artwork must be framed.

SUBMISSIONS Artist's portfolio should include photographs and transparencies. Responds only if interested within 2 months. Returns all material.

THROCKMORTON FINE ART

145 E. 57th St., 3rd Floor, New York NY 10022. (212)223-1059. **Fax:** (212)223-1937. **E-mail:** info@throckmorton-nyc.com. **Website:** www.throckmorton-nyc.com. **Contact:** Spencer Throckmorton, owner; Norberto Rivera, photography. Estab. 1993. For-profit gallery. A New York-based gallery specializing in vintage and contemporary photography of the Americas for over 25 years. Its primary focus is Latin American photographers. The gallery also specializes in Chinese jades and antiquities, as well as pre-Columbian art. Located in the Hammacher Schlemmer Building; 4,000 sq. ft.; 1,000 sq. ft. exhibition space. Clients include local community and upscale. Approached by 50 artists/year; represents or exhibits 20 artists. Sponsors 5 photography exhibits/year. Average display time: 2 months. Open Tuesday–Saturday, 11-5. Overall price range: $1,000-10,000; most work sold at $2,500.

MEDIA Most frequently exhibits photography, antiquities. Also considers gelatin, platinum and albumen prints.

STYLE Exhibits expressionism. Genres include Latin American.

TERMS Retail price of the art set by the gallery. Gallery provides insurance and promotion. Requires exclusive representation locally. Accepts only artists from Latin America. Prefers only b&w and color photography.

SUBMISSIONS Call or write to arrange personal interview to show portfolio of photographs. Returns material with SASE. Responds to queries only if interested within 2 weeks. Files bios and résumés. Finds artists through portfolio reviews, referrals by other artists and submissions.

TIBOR DE NAGY GALLERY

724 Fifth Ave., New York NY 10019. (212)262-5050. **Fax:** (212)262-1841. **E-mail:** info@tibordenagy.com. **Website:** www.tibordenagy.com. **Contact:** Andrew Arnot and Eric Brown, owners. Estab. 1949. Retail gallery. The gallery focus is on painting within the New York School traditions, and photography. Represents emerging and mid-career artists. Sponsors 12 shows/year. Average display time: 1 month. Open Tuesday–Saturday, 10-5:30; summer hours: Monday–Friday, 10-5:30; closed December 24–January 3. Located midtown; 3,500 sq. ft. 100% of space for work of gallery artists. 60% private collectors, 40% corporate collec-

tors. Overall price range: $1,000-100,000; most work sold at $5,000-20,000.

MEDIA Considers oil, pen & ink, paper, acrylic, drawings, sculpture, watercolor, mixed media, pastel, collage, etchings, and lithographs. Most frequently exhibits oil/acrylic, watercolor and sculpture.

STYLE Exhibits representational work as well as abstract painting and sculpture. Genres include landscapes and figurative work. Prefers abstract, painterly realism and realism.

SUBMISSIONS Gallery is not looking for submissions at this time.

TILT GALLERY

7077 E. Main St., Suite 14, Scottsdale AZ 85251. (602)716-5667. **E-mail:** info@tiltgallery.com. **E-mail:** melanie@tiltgallery.com. **Website:** www.tiltgallery.com. **Contact:** Melanie Craven, gallery owner. Estab. 2005. For-profit gallery. "A contemporary fine art gallery specializing in hand applied photographic processes and mixed media projects." Represents or exhibits 30 emerging and established artists. Exhibited artists include France Scully Osterman and Mark Osterman, Aline Smithson, Jill Enfield, Anna Strickland. Sponsors 8 exhibits/year; 7 photography exhibits/year. Average display time: 1 month. Open Tuesday-Saturday, 10:30-5:30; Thursday (night art walk), 7-9; and by appointment.

TMCC ART GALLERIES

Truckee Meadows Community College, 7000 Dandini Blvd., RDMT 321, Reno NV 89503-4304. (775)674-7698. **Fax:** (775)674-4853. **Website:** www.tmcc.edu/artgalleries. Estab. 1991. "Truckee Meadows Community College (TMCC) provides the opportunity for visual artists working with a diversity of socio/cultural themes, a variety of styles, and different genres, to exhibit their works in the college's art galleries. The goals of the art galleries are to promote dialogue between artists and the public, and to specifically provide an educational arts forum dedicated to innovative programming and artistic excellence for Washoe County and the TMCC campus community. The exhibitions in the TMCC art galleries also serve as a great educational resource for our art history, studio art and art appreciation classes who write papers about the work as well as reaching out to other departments whom utilize visual vocabulary in their curriculum. TMCC Art Galleries are open during regular school hours." TMCC operates 7 galleries: TMCC Main Gallery,

Erik Lauritzen Gallery, Red Mountain Gallery, Red Mountain Student Gallery, Atrium Gallery, Meadowwood Center Galleries and Veterans Upward Bound Gallery.

J. TODD GALLERIES

572 Washington St. (Rt. 16), Wellesley MA 02482. (781)237-3434. **E-mail:** fineart@jtodd.com. **Website:** www.jtodd.com. **Contact:** Jay Todd, owner. Estab. 1980. Retail gallery. "Thousands of works by living US and European artists." Represents 55 emerging, mid-career and established artists. Sponsors 2-3 shows/year. Average display time: 1 month. Open Tuesday–Saturday, 10:30-5:30; Sunday (October 17-April 10), 1-5; closed Sunday, May through mid-October; open other times by appointment. Located 15 miles west of Boston; 4,000 sq. ft.; vast inventory, professionally displayed; 6 showrooms. 30% of space for special exhibitions; 70% of space for gallery artists. Clientele: residential and corporate; 75% private collectors, 25% corporate collectors. Overall price range: $500-40,000; most work sold at $1,000-15,000.

MEDIA Considers oil, acrylic, watercolor, pen & ink, drawing, mixed media, woodcuts, engravings, lithographs, wood engravings, mezzotints, serigraphs, linocuts and etchings. Most frequently exhibits oils, woodcuts and etchings. "We do not accept pastels, giclées or sculpture."

STYLE Exhibits primitivism, modern, contemporary, postmodern works, impressionism and realism. Genres include landscape, seascape, nautical, urban scenes, abstracts, interiors, florals, figurative work and still life. Prefers landscapes, abstracts, figures and still lifes.

TERMS Accepts work on consignment (negotiable commission). Retail price set by the artist. Gallery provides promotion. Prefers unframed artwork.

SUBMISSIONS Submit via e-mail. "We are mostly interested in oils on canvas. We will consider acrylics and watercolor only if you have a proven track record in the $1,000 and above price range. We are *not* currently accepting pastel, graphics or sculpture. Please allow 3 weeks to get a response." See website for complete submission instructions.

TOUCHSTONE GALLERY

901 New York Ave. NW, Washington DC 20001-2217. (202)347-2787. **E-mail:** info@touchstonegallery.com. **Website:** www.touchstonegallery.com. Estab. 1976. Cooperative member gallery. Representing 50 artists in various media uses exhibiting a new show monthly. "Our newly renovated contemporary space is available for event rental. Located near the heart of the bustling Penn Quarter district in downtown Washington DC, our large beautifully lit gallery can be found at street level and is easily accessible. Open Wednesday and Thursday, 11-6; Friday, 11-8; Saturday and Sunday, 12-5; closed Christmas–New Year's Day. Overall price range: $400-7,000. As a functioning co-op gallery, there is a monthly membership fee, plus a donation of time. A 40% commission is taken from sold works. To become a member, visit the website for further information, or contact the gallery directly.

UAB VISUAL ARTS GALLERY

Abroms-Engel Institute for the Visual Arts, 1221 10th Ave. S, Birmingham AL 35205. (205)975-6436. **Fax:** (205)975-2836. **E-mail:** aeiva@uab.edu. **Website:** www.uab.edu/cas/aeiva. Nonprofit university gallery. Represents emerging, mid-career and established artists. Sponsors 10-12 exhibits/year. Average display time: 3-4 weeks. Open Monday-Thursday, 11-6; Friday, 11-5; Saturday, 1-5; closed Sundays and holidays. Located on 1st floor of Humanities Building, a classroom and office building, 2 rooms with a total of 2,000 sq. ft. and 222 running ft. Clients include local community, students and tourists.

MEDIA Considers all media except craft. Considers all types of prints.

STYLE Considers all styles and genres.

SUBMISSIONS Write to arrange a personal interview to show portfolio of slides. Send query letter with artist's statement, bio, brochure, photographs, résumé, reviews, SASE and slides. Returns material with SASE. The gallery does not consider unsolicited exhibition proposals.

ULRICH MUSEUM OF ART

Wichita State University, 1845 Fairmount St., Wichita KS 67260-0046. (316)978-3664. **Fax:** (316)978-3898. **E-mail:** ulrich@wichita.edu. **Website:** www.ulrich.wichita.edu; www.facebook.com/ulrichmuseum; www.twitter.com/ulrichmuseum. **Contact:** Bob Workman, director. Estab. 1974. Wichita's premier venue for modern and contemporary art. Presents 6 shows/year with emerging, mid-career and established artists. Open Tuesday-Friday, 11-5; Saturday–Sunday, 1-5; closed Mondays and major/university holidays. Located in the southwest section of the

Wichita State University campus. Gallery admission, parking, and guided, group tours are free.
MEDIA "Exhibition program includes all range of media."
STYLE "Style and content of exhibitions aligns with leading contemporary trends."

UPSTREAM PEOPLE GALLERY

5607 Howard St., Omaha NE 68106-1257. (402)991-4741. **E-mail:** shows@upstreampeoplegallery.com. **Website:** www.upstreampeoplegallery.com. **Contact:** Laurence Bradshaw, curator. Estab. 1998. Exclusive online virtual gallery with over 40 international exhibitions in the archives section of the website. Represents mid-career and established artists. Approached by approximately 1,500 artists/year; represents or exhibits 20,000 artists. Sponsors 12 total exhibits/year and 7 photography exhibits/year. Average display time: 12 months to 4 years. Overall price range: $100-60,000; most work sold at $300. 15% of sales are to corporate collectors.
MEDIA Considers all media except video and film. Most frequently exhibits oil, acrylic and ceramics.
STYLE Considers all prints, styles and genres. Most frequently exhibits neo-expressionism, realism and surrealism.
TERMS Artwork is accepted on consignment; there is no commission if the artists sells, but a 20% commission if the gallery sells. Retail price set by the artist. Gallery provides promotion and contract.
SUBMISSIONS Accepted work should be photographed. Call or write to arrange personal interview to show portfolio, e-mail query letter with link to website and JPEG samples at 72 dpi or send query letter with artist's statement and CD/DVD. Returns material with SASE. Responds to queries within 1 week. Files résumés. Finds artists through art exhibits, referrals and online and magazine advertising.
TIPS "Make sure all photographs of works are in focus."

URBAN INSTITUTE FOR CONTEMPORARY ARTS

2 W. Fulton St., Grand Rapids MI 49503. (616)454-7000. **E-mail:** curator@uica.org. **Website:** www.uica.org. Estab. 1977. Alternative space and nonprofit gallery. Approached by 250 artists/year; represents or exhibits 20 artists. Sponsors 3-4 photography exhibits/year. Average display time: 6 weeks. Gallery open

Tuesday-Thursday, 5-9; Friday-Saturday, 12-9; Sunday, 12-7.
MEDIA Considers all media. Most frequently exhibits mixed media, avant garde and nontraditional.
STYLE Exhibits conceptualism and postmodernism.
TERMS Gallery provides insurance, promotion and contract.
SUBMISSIONS Check website for gallery descriptions and how to apply. Send query letter with artist's statement, bio, résumé, reviews, SASE, application fee, and slides. Returns material with SASE. Does not reply. Artist should see website, inquire about specific calls for submissions. Finds artists through submissions.
TIPS "Get submission requirements before sending materials."

VALE CRAFT GALLERY

230 W. Superior St., Chicago IL 60654. (312)337-3525. **Fax:** (312)337-3530. **E-mail:** valecraft@sbcglobal.net. **Website:** www.valecraftgallery.com. **Contact:** Peter Vale, owner. Estab. 1992. Retail gallery. "Vale Craft Gallery exhibits and sells contemporary American fine craft and sculpture including works in clay, fiber, metal, glass, wood and mixed media. Vale Craft Gallery features colorful textiles, beautiful glass objects, handcrafted furniture, innovative ceramics, whimsical sculpture, and unique jewelry." Represents 100 emerging, mid-career artists/year. Exhibited artists include Tana Acton, Mark Brown, Tina Fung Holder, John Neering and Kathyanne White. Sponsors 4 shows/year. Average display time: 3 months. Open all year; Tuesday–Friday, 10:30-5:30; Saturday, 11-5. Located in River North gallery district near downtown; 2,100 sq. ft.; lower level of prominent gallery building; corner location with street-level windows provides great visibility. Clientele: private collectors, tourists, people looking for gifts, interior designers and art consultants. Overall price range: $50-2,000; most work sold at $100-500.
MEDIA Considers paper, sculpture, ceramics, craft, fiber, glass, metal, wood and jewelry. Most frequently exhibits fiber wall pieces, jewelry, glass, ceramic sculpture and mixed media.
STYLE Exhibits contemporary craft. Prefers decorative, sculptural, colorful, whimsical, figurative, and natural or organic.
TERMS Accepts work on consignment (50% commission). Retail price set by the artist. Gallery provides in-

surance, promotion, contract and shipping costs from gallery; artist pays shipping costs to gallery.

SUBMISSIONS Accepts only craft media. No paintings, prints, or photographs. By mail: send query letter with résumé, bio or artist's statement, reviews if available, 10-20 slides, CD of images (in JPEG format) or photographs (including detail shots if possible), price list, record of previous sales, and SASE if you would like materials returned to you. By e-mail: include a link to your website or send JPEG images, as well as any additional information listed above. Call for appointment to show portfolio of originals and photographs. Responds in 2 months. Files résumé (if interested). Finds artists through submissions, art and craft fairs, publishing a call for entries, artists' slide registry and word of mouth.

TIPS "Call ahead to find out if the gallery is interested in showing the particular type of work that you make. Try to visit the gallery ahead of time or check out the gallery's website to find out if your work fits into the gallery's focus. I would suggest you have at least 20 pieces in a body of work before approaching galleries."

VIRIDIAN ARTISTS, INC.

548 W. 28th St., Suite 632, New York NY 10001. (212)414-4040. **Website:** www.viridianartists.com. **Contact:** Vernita Nemec, director. Estab. 1968. Artist-owned gallery. Approached by 200 artists/year. Exhibits 25-30 emerging, mid-career and established artists/year. Sponsors 15 total exhibits/year; 2-4 photography exhibits/year. Average display time: 3 weeks. Open Tuesday–Saturday, 12-6; closed in August. "Classic gallery space with 3 columns, hardwood floor, white walls and track lights, approximately 1,100 sq. ft. The gallery is located in Chelsea, the prime area of contemporary art galleries in New York City." Clients include: local community, students, tourists, upscale and artists. 15% of sales are to corporate collectors. Overall price range: $100-8,000; most work sold at $1,500.

MEDIA Considers all media except craft, traditional glass and ceramic, unless it is sculpture. Most frequently exhibits paintings, photography and sculpture. Considers engravings, etchings, linocuts, lithographs, mezzotints, serigraphs, woodcuts and monoprints/limited edition digital prints.

STYLE Mostly contemporary, but considers all styles. Most frequently exhibits paintingly abstraction, imagism and neo-expressionism. "We are not interested in particular styles, but in professionally conceived and professionally executed contemporary art. Eclecticism is our policy. The only unifying factor is quality. Work must be of the highest technical and aesthetic standards."

TERMS Artwork accepted on consignment with a 30% commission. There is a co-op membership fee plus a donation of time with a 30% commission. Retail price of the art is set by the gallery and artist. Gallery provides promotion and contract. "Viridian is an artist-owned gallery with a director and gallery assistant. Artists pay gallery expenses through monthly dues, but the staff takes care of running the gallery and selling the art. The director writes the press releases, helps install exhibits and advises artists on all aspects of their career. We try to take care of everything but making the art and framing it." Prefers artists who are familiar with the NYC art world and are working professionally in a contemporary mode which can range from realistic to abstract to conceptual and anything in between.

SUBMISSIONS Submitting art for consideration is a 2-step process: first through website or JPEGs, then if accepted at that level, by seeing 4-6 samples of the actual art. Artists should call, e-mail query letter with link to artist's website or JPEG samples at 72 dpi (include image list) or send query letter with artist's statement, bio, reviews, CD with images and SASE. Materials returned with SASE. Responds in 2-4 weeks. Files materials of artists who become members. Finds artists through word of mouth, submissions, art exhibits, portfolio reviews or referrals by other artists.

TIPS "Present current art completed within the last 2 years. Our submission procedure is in 2 stages: first we look at websites, JPEGs that have been e-mailed, or CDs that have been mailed to the gallery. When e-mailing JPEGs, include an image list with title, date of execution, size, media. Also, include a bio and artist's statement. Reviews about your work are helpful if you have them, but not necessary. If you make it through the first level, then you will be asked to submit 4-6 actual artworks. These should be framed or matted, and similar to the work you want to show. Realize it is important to present a consistency in your vision. If you do more than one kind of art, select what you feel best represents you, for the art you show will be a reflection of who you are."

VISUAL ARTS CENTER, WASHINGTON PAVILION OF ARTS & SCIENCE

301 S. Main, Sioux Falls SD 57104. (605)367-6000. E-mail: info@washingtonpavilion.org. **Website:** washingtonpavilion.org. Estab. 1961. Nonprofit museum. "The Visual Arts Center brings the visual arts to children and adults through exhibitions, education, collections and special events, and is devoted to building, preserving and conserving its collections for South Dakotans and worldwide audiences. Produces approximately 16 exhibitions a year. Includes the Raven Children's Studio and the Palidino-Holms Sculpture Garden." Open Monday–Thursday, Saturday, 10-5; Friday, 10-8; Sunday, 12-5.

⊙ VOLCANO ART CENTER GALLERY

Crater Rim Dr., Hawai'i Volcanoes National Park, (808)967-7565. **E-mail:** gallery@volcanoartcenter. org. **Website:** www.volcanoartcenter.org. Estab. 1974. Nonprofit gallery to benefit arts education; nonprofit organization. Represents 300 emerging, mid-career and established artists/year. 1,000 member organization. Exhibited artists include Dietrich Varez, Marian Berger, Michael & Misato Mortara and Brad Lewis. Sponsors 8 shows/year. Average display time: 6 weeks. Open Monday-Sunday, 9-5. Located in Hawaii Volcanoes National Park; 3,000 sq. ft.; in the historic 1877 Volcano House Hotel. 15% of space for special exhibitions; 85% of space for gallery artists. Clientele affluent travelers from all over the world. 95% private collectors, 5% corporate collectors. Overall price range: $20-12,000; most work sold at $50-400.

MEDIA Considers all media, all types of prints. Most frequently exhibits wood, ceramics, glass and 2D.

STYLE Prefers traditional Hawaiian, contemporary Hawaiian and contemporary fine crafts.

TERMS Accepts work on consignment (50% commission). 10% discount to VAC members. Retail price set by the gallery. Gallery provides promotion and contract; artist pays shipping costs to gallery. Exhibited artists must be Volcano Art Center members. Submission guidelines available online.

SUBMISSIONS Prefers work relating to the area and by Hawaii resident artists. Call for appointment to show portfolio. Responds if interested within 2 months. Files information on represented artists.

THE VON LIEBIG ART CENTER

585 Park St., Naples FL 34102. (239)262-6517. **Website:** www.naplesart.org. **Contact:** Jack O'Brien, curator.

Estab. 1954. The Von Liebig Art Center is operated by the Naples Art Association, a nonprofit 501(c)3 organization located in downtown Naples and presents changing exhibitions of contemporary art by regionally, nationally and internationally recognized artists at the Von Liebig Art Center and around Naples. Its education program offers professional studio art courses and workshops in painting, printmaking, drawing, photography, ceramics, sculpture and applied arts. A lecture series features visiting speakers who cover dynamic and stimulating topics in art. Five major outdoor art festivals are held annually and Art in the Park, an NAA members' outdoor art festival, is held the first Saturday of each month, November-April. Over 14 exhibitions are installed each year including *Camera USA: National Photography Award* held each summer, *National Art Encounter*, the non-juried *Show of Shows Exhibition* and many juried exhibitions. The Naples Art Association holds a collection of approximately 200 works of art created after 1950 by accomplished artists who have lived in or had a connection to Florida. Artwork is selected by a committee and accessioned through donations.

MEDIA Considers artwork in all media.

STYLE Considers all styles. Festivals feature both fine art and fine craft.

TERMS 30% commission on artwork sold during exhibitions. Artists participating in exhibitions may wish to acquire insurance to cover loss or damage.

SUBMISSIONS For more information on current exhibition and festival opportunities visit www.naplesart.org. For more information on the major outdoor art festivals, visit www.juriedartservices.com. For more information on Art in the Park, and to apply, visit www.naplesart.org/content/art-park.

TIPS Membership in the Naples Art Association offers many benefits. For more information, and to become a member, visit www.naplesart.org.

WAILOA CENTER

200 Piopio St., Hilo HI 96720. (808)933-0416. **E-mail:** wailoa@yahoo.com. **Contact:** Codie M. King, director. Nonprofit gallery and museum. Focus is on propagation of the culture and arts of the Hawaiian Islands and their many ethnic backgrounds. Estab. 1968. Represents/exhibits 300 emerging, mid-career and established artists. Interested in seeing work of emerging artists. Sponsors 36 shows/year. Average display time: 1 month. Open all year; Monday–Tuesday, Thursday–

Friday, 8:30-4:30; Wednesday, 12-4:30; closed weekends and state holidays. Located downtown; 10,000 sq. ft.; 4 exhibition areas. Clientele: tourists, upscale, local community and students. Overall price range: $25-25,000; most work sold at $1,500.

MEDIA Considers all media and most types of prints. No giclée prints; original artwork only. Most frequently exhibits mixed media.

STYLE Exhibits all styles.

TERMS "We cannot sell, but will refer buyer to artist." Gallery provides some promotion. Artist pays for shipping, invitation, and reception costs. Artwork must be framed.

SUBMISSIONS Send query letter with résumé, slides, photographs and reviews. Call for appointment to show portfolio of photographs and slides. Responds in 3 weeks. Finds artists through word of mouth, referrals by other artists, visiting art fairs and exhibitions, submissions.

TIPS "We welcome all artists, and try to place them in the best location for the type of art they create. Drop in and let us review what you have."

WALKER'S POINT CENTER FOR THE ARTS

839 S. Fifth St., Milwaukee WI 53204. (414)672-2787. **Fax:** (414)755-1960. **E-mail:** gary@wpca-milwaukee. org; staff@wpca-milwaukee.org. **Website:** www.wpca-milwaukee.org. **Contact:** Gary Tuma, executive director. Estab. 1987. Alternative space and nonprofit gallery. Represents emerging and established artists; 200+ members. Exhibited artists include Colin Dickson, Chris Silva, Josie Osborne and Shane Walsh. Sponsors 6-8 shows/year. Average display time: 2 months. Open Tuesday–Saturday, 12-5. Located in the heart of the historic Walker's Point neighborhood; 6,000-sq.-ft. brick building.

MEDIA Considers all media. Prefers installation, sculpture and video.

STYLE Considers all styles. Our gallery often presents work with Latino themes.

TERMS We are nonprofit and do not provide honoria. Gallery assumes a 30% commission. Retail prices set by the artist. Gallery provides insurance, contract and shipping costs. Prefers artwork framed.

SUBMISSIONS Send query letter, or e-mail, with résumé, images, bio, artist statement, SASE and reviews.

TIPS "WPCA is an alternative space, showing work for which there are not many venues. Experimental work is encouraged."

WASHINGTON COUNTY MUSEUM OF FINE ARTS

401 Museum Dr., Hagerstown MD 21741. (301)739-5727. **Fax:** (301)745-3741. **E-mail:** info@wcmfa.org; kpalmateer@wcmfa.org. **Website:** www.wcmfa.org. **Contact:** Kay Palmateer, manager of collections & exhibitions. Estab. 1929. Open Tuesday-Friday, 9-5; Saturday, 9-4; Sunday, 1-5; closed Mondays and major holidays.

MEDIA Considers all media except installation and craft. Most frequently exhibits oil, watercolor and ceramics. Considers all types of prints except posters.

STYLE Exhibits all genres including florals, landscapes, portraits and wildlife.

TERMS Museum is a non-profit and does not provide honoraria. Retail prices set by the artist. If applicable, museum handles sale of works, with 40% commission.

SUBMISSIONS Write or e-mail to initiate submission process. Mail portfolio for review. Usually responds within 3 months. Finds artists through word of mouth, portfolio reviews, art exhibits, referrals by other artists.

WASHINGTON PRINTMAKERS GALLERY

1641 Wisconsin Ave. NW, Washington DC 20007. (202)669-1497. **E-mail:** info@washingtonprintmakers.com. **Website:** www.washingtonprintmakers.com. Estab. 1985. Cooperative gallery. Exhibits 40 emerging and mid-career artists/year. Exhibited artists include Lee Newman, Max-Karl Winkler, Trudi Y. Ludwig and Margaret Adams Parker. Sponsors 12 exhibitions/year. Average display time: 1 month. Open Wednesday-Sunday, 12-5; closed on New Year's Day, Easter, 4th of July, Thanksgiving, Christmas. Located just outside DC proper on the Red Line Metro. 100% of space for gallery artists. Clientele: varied. 90% private collectors, 10% corporate collectors. Overall price range: $65-1,500; most work sold at $200-400.

MEDIA Considers all types of original prints, hand pulled by artist. No posters. Most frequently exhibits etchings, lithographs, serigraphs, relief prints.

STYLE Considers all styles and genres.

TERMS Co-op membership fee plus donation of time (40% commission). Retail price set by artist. Gallery provides promotion. Purchaser pays shipping costs of work sold.

SUBMISSIONS Send query letter. Call for appointment to show portfolio of original prints. Responds in 1 month.

TIPS "There is a monthly jury for prospective members. Call to find out how to present work. We are especially interested in artists who exhibit a strong propensity for not only the traditional conservative approaches to printmaking, but also the looser, more daring and innovative experimentation in technique."

WASHINGTON PROJECT FOR THE ARTS

10 I St. SW, Washington DC 20024. (202)234-7103. **Fax:** (202)234-7106. **E-mail:** info@wpadc.org. **Website:** www.wpadc.org. **Contact:** Christopher Cunetto, membership manager. Estab. 1975. Alternative space that exhibits emerging, mid-career and established artists. Approached by 1,500 artists/year, exhibits 800 artists. Sponsors 12 exhibits/year. Average display time of 4 weeks. WPA is located in the Capitol Skyline Hotel. We exhibit throughout the hotel and in various museums and venues throughout the region. Clients include local community, students, tourists and upscale. 5% of sales are to corporate collectors. Overall price range of works sold $100-5,000. Most work sold at $500-1,000.

MEDIA Considers all media. Most frequently exhibits performance, painting, drawing and photography. Considers all types of prints.

STYLE Considers all styles, most frequently exhibits contemporary works.

TERMS Artwork is accepted on consignment and there is a 50% commission. Retail price set by the artist. Gallery provides insurance, promotion and contract. Accepted work should be framed.

SUBMISSIONS E-mail query letter with link to artist's website. Responds in 2 months. Finds artists through word of mouth, submissions, portfolio reviews, art exhibits and referrals by other artists.

TIPS Use correct spelling, make sure packages/submissions are tidy.

⊙ WEST END GALLERY

5425 Blossom St., Houston TX 77007. (713)861-9544. **E-mail:** kpackl1346@aol.com. **Contact:** Kathleen Packlick. Estab. 1991. Retail gallery. Exhibits emerging and mid-career artists. Open all year. Located 5 minutes from downtown Houston; 800 sq. ft. "The gallery shares the building (but not the space) with West End Bicycles." 75% of space for special exhibitions; 25% of space for gallery artists. Clientele: 100% private collectors. Overall price range: $30-2,200; most work sold at $300-600.

MEDIA Considers oil, pen & ink, acrylic, drawings, watercolor, mixed media, pastel and collage. woodcuts, wood engravings, linocuts, engravings, mezzotints, etchings, lithographs and serigraphs. Prefers collage, oil and mixed media.

STYLE Genres include landscapes, florals, wildlife, portraits and figurative work.

TERMS Accepts work on consignment (40% commission). Retail price set by artist. Prefers framed artwork.

SUBMISSIONS Accepts only artists from Houston area. Send query letter and SASE. Portfolio review requested if interested in artist's work.

WALTER WICKISER GALLERY

210 11th Ave., Suite 303, New York NY 10001. (212)941-1817. **Fax:** (212)625-0601. **E-mail:** wwickiserg@aol.com. **Website:** www.walterwickisergallery.com. Estab. 1992. For-profit gallery. Specializing in contemporary American and Asian painting. Located in the prestigious fine art building in Chelsea. Shows only established artists. The Wickiser Gallery has received numerous reviews in *ARTnews, Art in America* and many other internationally recognized publications. Work by many of the gallery's artists have been exhibited at American museums including the Metropolitan Museum of Art, the Whitney Museum of American Art, the High Museum of Art in Georgia, the Dallas Museum of Art in Texas, and the New Britain Museum of American Art in Connecticut. Open Tuesday–Saturday, 11-6.

PHILIP WILLIAMS POSTERS

122 Chambers St., New York NY 10007. (212)513-0313. **E-mail:** philipwilliamsposters@gmail.com. **Website:** www.postermuseum.com. **Contact:** Philip Williams. Estab. 1973. Retail and wholesale gallery. Represents/exhibits vintage posters 1870-present. "The largest vintage poster gallery in the world, with more than 12,600 sq. ft. to display the largest collection of original posters for sale. We also sell advertising ephemera, maitre de l'affiche, poster books and other types of art, including a collection of more than 2,000 American Folk Art paintings and sculpture. Open all year; Monday–Saturday, 11-7.

TERMS Prefers artwork unframed.

SUBMISSIONS Prefers vintage posters and outsider artist. Send query letter with photographs.

WOMEN & THEIR WORK ART SPACE

1710 Lavaca St., Austin TX 78701. (512)477-1064. **Fax:** (512)477-1090. **Website:** www.womenandtheirwork. org. **Contact:** Chris Cowden, executive director. Estab. 1978. Alternative space, nonprofit gallery. Approached by more than 200 artists/year; sponsors 6 solo shows of emerging and mid-career women artists. Average display time: 6 weeks. Open Monday–Friday, 10-6; Saturday, 12-5; closed December 24–January 2, and other major holidays. Clients include Austinites, students, tourists and upscale. Exhibition space is 2,000 sq. ft. Overall price range: $500-5,000; most work sold at $800-2,000. 10% of sales are to corporate collectors.

MEDIA Considers all media. Most frequently exhibits photography, sculpture, installation and painting.

STYLE Exhibits contemporary works of art.

TERMS Selects artists through an artist advisory panel and curatorial/jury process. Pays artists to exhibit. Takes 25% commission if something is sold. Retail price set by the gallery and the artist. Gallery provides insurance, promotion and contract. Accepts Texas women in solo shows as well as out-of-state in one solo show. See website for more information.

SUBMISSIONS See website for current call for entries. Entries are now online. Online slide registry on website for members. Finds artists through submissions and annual juried process.

WOODWARD GALLERY

133 Eldridge St., Ground Floor, New York NY 10002. (212)966-3411. **Fax:** (212)966-3491. **E-mail:** art@woodwardgallery.net. **Website:** www.woodwardgallery.net. Estab. 1994.

MEDIA Considers acrylic, collage, drawing, mixed media, oil, paper, pastel, pen ink, sculpture, watercolor. Most frequently exhibits canvas, paper and sculpture. Considers all types of prints.

STYLE Most frequently exhibits realism/surrealism, pop, abstract and landscapes, graffiti. Genres include figurative work, florals, landscapes and portraits.

TERMS Artwork is bought outright (net 30 days) or consigned. Retail price set by the gallery.

SUBMISSIONS "Call before sending anything! Send query letter with artist's statement, bio, brochure, photocopies, photographs, reviews and SASE. Returns material with SASE. Finds artists through referrals or submissions. Policy posted on website—please adhere carefully to directions for artist review criteria."

WORCESTER CENTER FOR CRAFTS GALLERIES

25 Sagamore Rd., Worcester MA 01605. (508)753-8183. **E-mail:** ccasey4@worcester.edu. **Website:** www.worcestercraftcenter.org. **Contact:** Candace Casey, gallery director. Estab. 1856. Nonprofit rental gallery. Dedicated to promoting artisans and American crafts. Has several exhibits throughout the year, including 1 juried, catalogue show and 2 juried craft fairs in May and November. Exhibits student, faculty, visiting artists, regional, national and international artists. Open all year; Monday-Saturday, 10-5. Located at edge of downtown; 2,205 sq. ft. (main gallery); track lighting, security. Overall price range: $20-400; most work sold at $65-100.

MEDIA Considers all media except paintings and drawings. Most frequently exhibits wood, metal, fiber, ceramics, glass and photography.

STYLE Exhibits all styles.

TERMS Artwork is accepted on consignment (40% commission). Retail price set by the artist. Gallery provides insurance, promotion and contract. Shipping costs are shared.

SUBMISSIONS Call for appointment to show portfolio of photographs and slides. Responds in 1 month.

WORLD FINE ART GALLERY

179 E. Third St., Suite 16, New York NY 10009-7705. (646)539-9622. **Fax:** (646)478-9361. **E-mail:** info@worldfineart.com. **Website:** www.worldfineart.com. **Contact:** O'Delle Abney, director. Estab. 1992. Online gallery since 2010. Services include online websites (www.worldfineart.com/join.html) and personal marketing. Group exhibitions around the New York City area.

TERMS Responds to queries in 1 week. Nonexclusive agent to 12 current portfolio artists. Finds artists online.

TIPS "Have website available or send JPEG images for review."

RIVA YARES GALLERY

3625 Bishop Lane, Scottsdale AZ 85251. (480)947-3251 (Scottsdale). **Fax:** (480)947-4251 (Scottsdale). **E-mail:** art@rivayaresgallery.com. **Website:** www.rivayaresgallery.com. Estab. 1963. Retail gallery. Represents 30-40 emerging, mid-career and established artists/year. Exhibited artists include Rodolfo Morales and Esteban Vicente. Sponsors 12-16 shows/year. Average display time: 3-6 weeks. Call for the hours of each gallery. Scottsdale gallery located in downtown area; 8,000 sq. ft.; national design award architecture; international artists. 50% of space for special exhibitions; 50% of space for gallery artists. Clientele: collectors. 90% private collectors; 10% corporate collectors. Overall price range: $1,000-1 million; most work sold at $20,000-50,000.

MEDIA Considers all media except craft and fiber and all types of prints. Most frequently exhibits paintings (all media), sculpture and drawings.

STYLE Exhibits expressionism, photorealism, neo-expressionism, minimalism, pattern painting, color field, hard-edge geometric abstraction, painterly abstraction, realism, surrealism and imagism. Prefers abstract expressionistic painting and sculpture, surrealistic sculpture and modern schools' painting and sculpture.

TERMS Accepts work on consignment (50% commission). Retail price set by the artist. Gallery provides insurance, promotion and contract; gallery pays for shipping from gallery; artist pays for shipping to gallery. Prefers artwork framed.

SUBMISSIONS Not accepting new artists at this time.

TIPS "Few artists take the time to understand the nature of a gallery and if their work even applies."

YEISER ART CENTER INC.

200 Broadway St., Paducah KY 42001. (270)442-2453. **E-mail:** jewhite@theyeiser.org. **Website:** www.theyeiser.org. **Contact:** Joshua E. White, director. Estab. 1957. Nonprofit gallery. Exhibits emerging, mid-career and established artists. 450 members. Sponsors 7-8 shows/year. Average display time: 6-8 weeks. Open Tuesday–Saturday, 10-5. Located downtown; 1,800 sq. ft.; "in historic building that was farmer's market." 90% of space for special exhibitions. Clientele: professionals and collectors. 90% private collectors. Overall price range: $200-8,000; most artwork sold at $200-1,000.

MEDIA Considers all media. Prints considered include original handpulled prints, woodcuts, wood engravings, linocuts, mezzotints, etchings, lithographs and serigraphs.

STYLE Exhibits all styles and genres.

TERMS Gallery takes 40% commission on all sales (60/40 split). Expenses are negotiated.

SUBMISSIONS Send résumé, slides, bio, SASE and reviews. Responds in 3 months.

TIPS "Do not call. Give complete information about the work—media, size, date, title, price. Have good-quality slides of work, indicate availability, and include artist statement. Presentation of material is important."

YELLOWSTONE GALLERY

P.O. Box 472, Gardiner MT 59030. (406)848-7306. **E-mail:** info@yellowstonegallery.com. **Website:** www.yellowstonegallery.com. Estab. 1983. Retail gallery. Represents 20 emerging and mid-career artists/year. Exhibited artists include Mary Blain and Nancy Glazier. Sponsors 2 shows/year. Average display time: 2 months. Located downtown; 3,000 sq. ft. 25% of space for special exhibitions; 50% of space for gallery artists. Clientele: tourist and regional. 90% private collectors, 10% corporate collectors. Overall price range: $25-8,000; most work sold at $75-600.

MEDIA Considers oil, acrylic, watercolor, ceramics, craft and photography; types of prints include wood engravings, serigraphs, etchings and posters. Most frequently exhibits watercolors, oils and limited edition, signed and numbered reproductions.

STYLE Exhibits impressionism, photorealism and realism. Genres include Western, wildlife and landscapes. Prefers wildlife realism, Western and watercolor impressionism.

TERMS Accepts work on consignment (45% commission). Retail price set by the artist. Gallery provides contract; artist pays for shipping. Prefers artwork framed.

SUBMISSIONS Send query letter with brochure or 10 slides. Write for appointment to show portfolio of photographs. Responds in 1 month. Files brochure and biography. Finds artists through word of mouth, regional fairs and exhibits, mail and periodicals.

TIPS "Don't show up unannounced without an appointment."

LEE YOUNGMAN GALLERIES

1316 Lincoln Ave., Calistoga CA 94515. (707)942-0585; (800)551-0585. **E-mail:** leeyg@comcast.net. **Website:** www.leeyoungmangalleries.com. **Contact:** Ms. Lee Love Youngman, owner. Estab. 1985. Retail gallery. "We feature a broad selection of work by important national and regional artists." Represents 40 established artists. Exhibited artists include Ralph Love and Paul Youngman. Sponsors 3 shows/year. Average display time: 1 month. Open Monday–Saturday, 10-5; Sunday, 11-4. Located downtown; 3,000 sq. ft.; "contemporary décor." Clientele 100% private collectors. Overall price range: $500-24,000; most artwork sold at $1,000-3,500.

MEDIA Considers oil, acrylic, watercolor and sculpture. Most frequently exhibits oils, bronzes and alabaster.

STYLE Exhibits impressionism and realism. Genres include landscapes, Figurative and still life. Interested in seeing American realism.

TERMS Accepts work on consignment (50% commission). Retail price set by gallery. Customer discounts and payment by installment are available. Gallery provides insurance and promotion. Artist pays for shipping to and from gallery. Prefers framed artwork.

SUBMISSIONS "No unsolicited portfolios." Portfolio review requested if interested in artist's work. "The most common mistake artists make is coming on weekends, the busiest time, and expecting full attention." Finds artists through publication, submissions and owner's knowledge.

TIPS "Don't just drop in—make an appointment. No agents. While quality and eye appeal are paramount, we also select with an eye towards investment and potential appreciation for our collectors."

ZENITH GALLERY

1429 Iris St. NW, Washington DC 20012. (202)783-2963. **Fax:** (202)783-0050. **E-mail:** margery@zenith gallery.com; art@zenithgallery.com. **Website:** www.zenithgallery.com. **Contact:** Margery E. Goldberg, founder/owner/director. Estab. 1978. For-profit gallery. Exhibits emerging, mid-career and established artists. Open Friday and Saturday, 12-6 and by appointment. Three rooms; 2,400 sq. ft. of exhibition space. Clients include local community, tourists and upscale. 50% of sales are to corporate collectors. Overall price range: $5,000-15,000.

MEDIA Considers all media.

TERMS Requires exclusive representation locally for solo exhibitions.

SUBMISSIONS Send query e-mail or letter with artist's statement, bio, résumé, reviews, brochures, images on CD, SASE. Returns material with SASE. Responds to most queries if interested. Finds artists through art fairs/exhibits, portfolio reviews, referrals by other artists, submissions and word of mouth.

TIPS "The review process can take anywhere from one month to one year. Please be patient and do not call the gallery for acceptance information." Visit website for detailed submission guidelines before sending any materials.

MAGAZINES

Magazines are a major market for freelance illustrators. The best proof of this fact is as close as your nearest newsstand. The colorful publications competing for your attention are chock-full of interesting illustrations, cartoons, and caricatures. Since magazines are generally published on a monthly or bimonthly basis, art directors look for dependable artists who can deliver on deadline and produce quality artwork with a particular style and focus.

Art that illustrates a story in a magazine or newspaper is called "editorial illustration." Art directors look for the best visual element to hook the reader into the story. In some cases this is a photograph, but often, especially in stories dealing with abstract ideas or difficult concepts, an illustration makes the story more compelling. A whimsical illustration can set the tone for a humorous article, or an edgy caricature of movie stars in boxing gloves might work for an article describing conflicts within a film's cast. Flip through a dozen magazines in your local drugstore, and you will quickly see that each illustration conveys the tone and content of articles while fitting in with the magazine's "personality." The key to success in the magazine arena is matching your style to appropriate publications.

Target Your Markets

Read each listing carefully. Knowing how many artists approach each magazine will help you understand how stiff your competition is. (At first, you might do better submitting to art directors who aren't swamped with submissions.) Look at the preferred subject matter to make sure your artwork fits the magazine's needs. Note the submission requirements and develop a mailing list of markets you want to approach.

Visit newsstands and bookstores. Check the cover and interior; if illustrations are used, flip to the masthead (usually a box in one of the beginning pages), and note the art direc-

- A great source for new magazine leads is in the business section of your local library. Ask the librarian to point out the business and consumer editions of the *Standard Rate and Data Service (SRDS)* and *Bacon's Newspaper and Magazine Directory*. These huge directories list thousands of magazines and will give you an idea of the magnitude of magazines published today. Another good source is a yearly directory called *Samir Husni's Guide to New Magazines*, also available in the business section of the public library and online at www.mrmagazine.com. *Folio* magazine provides information about new magazine launches and redesigns.

- Each year the Society of Publication Designers sponsors a juried competition, the winners of which are featured in a prestigious exhibition. For information about the annual competition, contact the Society of Publication Designers at (212)223-3332 or visit their website at www.spd.org.

- Networking with fellow artists and art directors will help you find additional success strategies. The Graphic Artists Guild (www.gag.org), The American Institute of Graphic Artists (www.aiga.org), your city's Art Directors Club (www.adcglobal.org) or branch of the Society of Illustrators (www.societyillustrators.org) hold lectures and networking functions. Attend one event sponsored by each organization in your city to find a group you are comfortable with, then join and become an active member.

tor's name. The circulation figure is also relevant; the higher the circulation, the higher the art director's budget (generally). When art directors have a good budget, they tend to hire more illustrators and pay higher fees.

Look at the credit lines next to each illustration. Notice which illustrators are used often in the publications you wish to work with. You will see that each illustrator has a very definite style. After you have studied dozens of magazines, you will understand what types of illustrations are marketable.

Although many magazines can be found at a newsstand or library, some of your best markets may not be readily available. If you can't find a magazine, check the listing in *Artist's & Graphic Designer's Market* to see if sample copies are available. Keep in mind that many magazines also provide artists' guidelines on their websites.

Create a Promo Sample

Focus on one or two consistent styles to present to art directors in sample mailings. See if you can come up with a style that is different from every other illustrator's style, if only slightly. No matter how versatile you may be, limit the styles you market to one or two. That way, you'll be more memorable to art directors. Choose a style or two that you enjoy and can work in relatively quickly. Art directors don't like surprises. If your sample shows a line drawing, they expect you to work in that style when they give you an assignment. It's fairly standard practice to mail nonreturnable samples: either postcard-size reproductions of your work, photocopies, or whatever is requested in the listing. Some art directors like to see a résumé, while others do not.

More Marketing Tips

- **Don't overlook trade magazines and regional publications.** While they may not be as glamorous as national consumer magazines, some trade and regional publications are just as lavishly produced. Most pay fairly well, and the competition is not as fierce. Until you can get some of the higher-circulation magazines to notice you, take assignments from smaller magazines. Alternative weeklies are great markets as well. Despite their modest payment, there are many advantages to working with them. You develop your signature style and learn how to communicate with art directors and to work quickly to meet deadlines. Once the assignments are done, the tearsheets become valuable samples to send to other magazines.

- **Develop a spot illustration style in addition to your regular style.** "Spots"—illustrations that are half-page or smaller—are used in magazine layouts as interesting visual cues to lead readers through large articles or to make filler articles more appealing. Though the fee for one spot is less than for a full layout, art directors often assign five or six spots within the same issue to the same artist. Because spots are small in size, they must be all the more compelling. So send art directors a sample showing a few powerful small pieces along with your regular style.

- **Be prepared to share your work electronically.** Art directors often require illustrators to fax or e-mail sketched or preliminary illustrations so layouts can be reviewed and suggestions can be offered. Invest in a scanner if you aren't already working digitally.

- **Get your work into competition annuals and sourcebooks.** The term "sourcebook" refers to the creative directories published annually to showcase the work of freelancers. Art directors consult these publications when looking for new styles. Many listings mention if an art director uses sourcebooks. Some directories such as *The Black Book*, *American Showcase*, and *RSVP* carry paid advertisements costing several thousand dollars per page. Other annuals, like the *PRINT Regional Design Annual* or *Communication Arts Illustration Annual*, feature award winners of various competitions.

- **Consider working with a rep.** If after working successfully on several assignments, you decide to make magazine illustration your career, consider contracting with an artists' representative to market your work for you. (See the Artists' Representatives section.)

A&U MAGAZINE

25 Monroe St., Suite 205, Albany NY 12210. (518)426-9010. **Fax:** (518)436-5354. **E-mail:** mailbox@aumag.org. **Website:** www.aumag.org. **Contact:** Chael Needle, managing editor. Estab. 1991. Circ. 180,000. Monthly 4-color literary magazine. "*A&U* is an AIDS publication. Our audience is everyone affected by the AIDS crisis." Art guidelines are free for #10 SASE with first-class postage.

CARTOONS Approached by 10 cartoonists/year. Buys 1 cartoon/year. Prefers work relating to HIV/AIDS disease. Prefers single panel, double panel or multiple panel humorous, b&w washes, color washes or line drawings.

ILLUSTRATION Approached by 15 illustrators/year. Buys 5 illustrations/issue. Features humorous illustration, realistic illustrations, charts & graphs, informational graphics, medical illustration, spot illustrations and computer illustration of all subjects affected by HIV/AIDS. Prefers all styles and media. Assigns 50% of illustrations to well-known or "name" illustrators; 25% to experienced, but not well-known illustrators; 25% to new and emerging illustrators. 50% of freelance illustration demands knowledge of Adobe Illustrator or Photoshop.

FIRST CONTACT & TERMS Submission guidelines available online.

TIPS "We would like to get cutting-edge and unique illustrations or cartoons about the HIV/AIDS crisis, they can be humorous or nonhumorous."

AD ASTRA

National Space Society, 1155 15th St. NW, Suite 500, Washington DC 20005. (202)429-1600. **Fax:** (202)530-0659. **E-mail:** adastra@nss.org. **Website:** www.nss.org/adastra. **Contact:** Gary Barnhard, editor-in-chief. Estab. 1989. Circ. 25,000. Quarterly feature magazine popularizing and advancing space exploration and development for the general public interested in all aspects of the space program.

ILLUSTRATION Illustrators: Send postcard sample or slides. "Color slides are best."

DESIGN Designers: Send query letter with brochure and photographs. Samples not filed are returned by SASE. Responds in 6 weeks. Pays $100-300 color cover; $25-100 color inside. "We do commission original art from time to time." Fees are for one-time reproduction of existing artwork. Considers rights purchased when establishing payment. Pays designers by the project.

FIRST CONTACT & TERMS Needs freelancers for multimedia design. Works with 40 freelancers/year. Uses freelancers for magazine illustration. Buys 10 illustrations/year. "We are looking for original artwork on space themes, either conceptual or representing specific designs, events, etc." Prefers acrylics, then oils and collage. "Show a set of slides showing planetary art, spacecraft and people working in space. I do not want to see 'science-fiction' art. Label each slide with name and phone number. Understand the freelance assignments are usually made far in advance of magazine deadline."

ADVENTURE CYCLIST

Adventure Cycling Association, Box 8308, Missoula MT 59807. (406)721-1776, ext. 222. **Fax:** (406)721-8754. **E-mail:** magazine@adventurecycling.org. **Website:** www.adventurecycling.org/adventure-cyclist. **Contact:** Greg Siple, art director; Michael Deme, editor. Estab. 1975. Circ. 45,500. Journal of adventure travel by bicycle, published 9 times/year.

ILLUSTRATION Send digital samples. Samples are filed. Buys 1 illustration/issue. Has featured illustrations by Margie Fullmer, Ludmilla Tomova, Ed Jenne, and Anita Dufalla. Works on assignment only.

FIRST CONTACT & TERMS Will contact artist for portfolio review if interested. Pays on publication, $75-500. Buys one-time rights. Originals returned at job's completion.

AFRICAN PILOT

Wavelengths 10 (Pty) Ltd., 6 Barbeque Heights, 9 Dytchley Rd., Barbeque Downs, Midrand 1684 South Africa. +27 11 466-8524. **Fax:** +27 11 466 8496. **E-mail:** editor@africanpilot.co.za. **Website:** www.africanpilot.co.za. **Contact:** Athol Franz, editor. Estab. 2001. Circ. 7,000+ online; 6,600+ print. "*African Pilot* is southern Africa's premier monthly aviation magazine. It publishes a high-quality magazine that is well known and respected within the aviation community of southern Africa. The magazine offers a number of benefits to readers and advertisers, including a weekly e-mail Aviation News, annual service guide, aviation training supplement, executive wall calendar and an extensive website. The monthly aviation magazine is also available online as an exact replica of the paper edition, but where all major advertising pages are hyperlinked to the advertisers website. The magazine offers clean layouts with outstanding photography and reflects editorial professionalism as well as a responsible approach to journalism. The magazine offers a complete and tailored promotional solution for all aviation businesses operating in the African region."

FIRST CONTACT & TERMS Send e-mail with samples. Samples are kept on file. Portfolio not required. Credit line given.

TIPS "*African Pilot* is an African aviation specific publication and therefore preference is given to articles, illustrations and photographs that have an African theme. The entire magazine is online in exactly the same format as the printed copy for the viewing of our style and quality. Contact me for specific details on our publishing requirements for work to be submitted. Articles together with a selection of about ten thumbnail pictures to be submitted so that a decision can be made on the relevance of the article and what pictures are available to be used to illustrate the article. If we decide to go ahead with the article, we will request high-res images from the portfolio already submitted as thumbnails."

ALARM

Alarm Press, 900 N. Franklin St., Suite 300, Chicago IL 60610. (312)341-1290. **E-mail:** info@alarmpress. com. **Website:** www.alarmpress.com/alarm-magazine. *ALARM*, published 6 times/year, "does one thing, and it does it very well: it publishes the best new music and art in *ALARM* Magazine and alarmpress. com. From our headquarters in a small Chicago office, along with a cast of contributing writers spread across the country, we listen to thousands of CDs, view hundreds of gallery openings, and attend lectures and live concerts in order to present inspirational artists who are fueled by an honest and contagious obsession with their art."

○ Art event listings should be e-mailed to artlistings@alarmpress.com.

FIRST CONTACT & TERMS Submit by e-mail with the subject line "ALARM Magazine Submissions." "Please send your work as part of the body of an e-mail; we cannot accept attachments." Alternatively, submissions may be sent by regular mail to Submissions Dept. "*ALARM* is not responsible for the return, loss of, or damage to unsolicited manuscripts, unsolicited artwork, or any other unsolicited materials. Those submitting manuscripts, artwork, or any other materials should not send originals."

ALASKA

301 Arctic Slope Ave., Suite 300, Anchorage AK 99518-3035. **E-mail:** editor@alaskamagazine.com. **Website:** www.alaskamagazine.com. **Contact:** Michelle Theall, editor; Corrynn Cochran, photo editor. Estab. 1935. Circ. 180,000. Monthly 4-color regional consumer magazine featuring Alaskan issues, stories and profiles exclusively.

ILLUSTRATION Approached by 200 illustrators/year. Buys 1-4 illustrations/issue. Has featured illustrations by Bob Crofut, Chris Ware, Victor Juhaz, and Bob Parsons. Features humorous and realistic illustrations. Works on assignment only. Assigns 50% to new and emerging illustrators. 50% of freelance illustration demands knowledge of Illustrator, Photoshop, and QuarkXPress.

FIRST CONTACT & TERMS Send postcard or other nonreturnable samples. Accepts Mac-compatible disk submissions. Samples are not returned. Responds only if interested. Will contact artist for portfolio review if interested. Buys first North American serial rights and electronic rights; rights purchased vary according to project. Pays on publication. Pays illustrators $125-300 for color inside; $400-600 for 2-page spreads; $125 for spots.

TIPS "We work with illustrators who grasp the visual in a story quickly and can create quality pieces on tight deadlines."

ALASKA BUSINESS MONTHLY

Alaska Business Publishing, 501 W. Northern Lights Blvd., Suite 100, Anchorage AK 99503-2577. (907)276-4373; (800)770-4373. **Fax:** (907)279-2900. **E-mail:** editor@akbizmag.com. **Website:** www.akbizmag.com. **Contact:** Susan Harrington, managing editor; David Geiger, art director. Estab. 1985. Circ. 12,000-15,000. *Alaska Business Monthly*, produced in Alaska for Alaskans and other US and international audiences interested in business affairs of the 49th state. Aims to provide a thorough and objective analysis of issues and trends of interest to the Alaska business community. Featuring stories about individuals, organizations and companies shaping the Alaskan economy, *Alaska Business Monthly* emphasizes the importance of enterprise and strives for statewide business coverage.

TIPS "We usually use local photographers for photos and employees for illustrations. Read the magazine before submitting anything."

ALFRED HITCHCOCK MYSTERY MAGAZINE

Dell Magazines, 44 Wall Street, Suite 904, New York NY 10005-2401. (212)686-7188. **E-mail:** alfredhitch cockmm@dellmagazines.com or via online contact form. **Website:** www.themysteryplace.com/ahmm. **Contact:** associate art director. Estab. 1956. Circ. 202,470. Monthly b&w magazine with 4-color cover emphasizing mystery fiction. Accepts previously published artwork. Original artwork returned at job's completion. Art guidelines available with #10 SASE and first-class postage.

ILLUSTRATION Approached by 300 illustrators/year. Buys 2-3 illustrations/issue. Prefers semirealistic, realistic style. Works on assignment only. Considers pen & ink. Send query letter with printed samples, photocopies or tearsheets and SASE.

FIRST CONTACT & TERMS Guidelines at: www. themysteryplace.com/ahmm/guidelines. Illustrators: Send follow-up postcard sample every 3 months. Samples are filed or returned by SASE. Responds only if interested. "No phone calls." Portfolios may be dropped off every Tuesday and should include b&w and color tearsheets. "No original art please." Rights purchased vary according to project. **Pays on acceptance**; $1,000-1,200 for color cover; $100 for b&w inside; $35-50 for spots. Finds artists through submissions drop-offs, RSVP.

TIPS "No close-up or montages. Show characters within a background environment."

ALL ANIMALS MAGAZINE

2100 L St. NW, Washington DC 20037. **Fax:** (301)721-6468. **E-mail:** jcork@humanesociety.org. **Website:** www.humanesociety.org. **Contact:** Jennifer Cork, creative director. Estab. 1954. Circ. 550,000. Bimonthly 4-color membership magazine focusing on the Humane Society of the United States news and animal protection issues.

FIRST CONTACT & TERMS Features realistic, conceptual and spot illustration. Work by assignment only. themes vary by story. E-mail link to portfolio website or mail samples to above address. **Pays on acceptance**; $700 for 2-page spreads; $100-300 for spots.

ALTERNATIVE THERAPIES IN HEALTH AND MEDICINE

3140 Neil Armstrong Blvd., Suite 307, Eagan MN 55121. (877)904-7951. **Fax:** (651)344-0774. **E-mail:** rpalmer@innovisionhm.com; cgustafson@innovi sionhm.com. **Website:** www.alternative-therapies. com. **Contact:** Randy Palmer, creative director; Craig Gustafson managing editor. Estab. 1995. Circ. 25,000. Bimonthly trade journal. "*Alternative Therapies* is a peer-reviewed medical journal established to promote integration between alternative and cross-cultural medicine with conventional medical traditions." Sample copies available.

ILLUSTRATION Buys 6 paintings/year. Purchases fine art for the covers, not graphic art or cartoons.

FIRST CONTACT & TERMS Send e-mail with samples or link to website. Responds within 10 days. Will contact artist if interested. Samples should include subject matter consistent with impressionism, expressionism and surrealism. Buys one-time and reprint rights. Pays on publication; negotiable. Accepts previously published artwork. Originals returned at job's completion. Finds artists through websites, galleries and word of mouth.

AMERICAN FITNESS

15250 Ventura Blvd., Suite 200, Sherman Oaks CA 91403. (800)446-2322, ext. 200. **E-mail:** americanfit ness@afaa.com. **Website:** www.afaa.com. **Contact:** Meg Jordan, editor. Estab. 1983. Circ. 42,900. Bimonthly magazine for fitness and health professionals. Official publication of the Aerobics and Fitness Association of America, the world's largest fitness educator. Send postcard promotional sample. Acquires one-time rights. Accepts previously published material. Original artwork returned after publication. Approached by 12 illustrators/month. Assigns 2 illustrations/issue. Works on assignment only.

ILLUSTRATION Prefers "very sophisticated" 4-color or line drawings. Subjects include fitness, exercise, wellness, sports nutrition, innovations and trends in sports, anatomy and physiology, body composition. "Excellent source for never-before-published illustrators who are eager to supply full-page lead artwork."

THE AMERICAN LEGION MAGAZINE

P.O. Box 1055, Indianapolis IN 46206-1055. (317)630-1253; (317) 630-1298. **Fax:** (317)630-1280. **E-mail:** magazine@legion.org; mgrills@legion.org; hsoria@ legion.org. **Website:** www.legion.org. **Contact:** Matt Grills, cartoon editor; Holly Soria, art director. Estab. 1919. Circ. 2,550,000. Emphasizes the development of the world at present and milestones of history; 4-color general-interest magazine for veterans and their families. Monthly. Original artwork not returned after publication.

CARTOONS Uses 3 freelance cartoons/issue. Receives 150 freelance submissions/month. "Experience level does not matter and does not enter into selection process." Especially needs general humor in good taste. "Generally interested in cartoons with broad appeal. Those that attract the reader and lead us to read the caption rate the highest attention. Because of tight space, we're not in the market for spread or multipanel cartoons but use both vertical and horizontal single-panel cartoons. Themes should be home life, business, sports and everyday Americana. Cartoons that pertain only to one branch of the service may be too restricted for this magazine. Service-type gags should be recognized and appreciated by any ex-service man or woman. Cartoons that may offend the reader are not accepted. Liquor, sex, religion and racial differences are taboo."

FIRST CONTACT & TERMS Cartoonists: "No roughs. Send final product for consideration." Usually responds within 1 month. Buys first rights. **Pays on acceptance**; $150.

TIPS "Artists should submit their work as we are always seeking new slant and more timely humor. Black & white submissions are acceptable, but we purchase only color cartoons. Want good, clean humor—something that might wind up on the refrigerator door. Consider the audience!"

AMERICAN LIBRARIES

50 E. Huron St., Chicago IL 60611. (800)545-2433. **Fax:** (312)440-0901. **Website:** www.americanlibrariesmagazine.org. **Contact:** Amy Carlton, senior editor. Estab. 1907. Circ. 51,000. Bimonthly professional 4-color journal of the American Library Association for its members, providing independent coverage of news and major developments in and related to the library field. Sample copy $6. Art guidelines available with SASE and first-class postage.

CARTOONS Approached by 15 cartoonists/year. Buys no more than 1 cartoon/issue. Themes related to libraries only. Average payment $50.

ILLUSTRATION Approached by 20 illustrators/year. Buys 1-2 illustrations/issue. Assigns 25% of illustrations to new and emerging illustrators. Works on assignment only.

FIRST CONTACT & TERMS Cartoonists: Send query letter with brochure and finished cartoons. Illustrators: Send query letter with brochure, tearsheets and résumé. Samples are filed. Does not respond to submissions. To show a portfolio, mail tearsheets, photographs and photocopies. Portfolio should include broad sampling of typical work with tearsheets of both b&w and color. Buys first rights. **Pays on acceptance.**

TIPS "I suggest inquirer go to a library and take a look at the magazine first." Sees trend toward "more contemporary look, simpler, more classical, returning to fewer elements."

AMERICAN LITERARY REVIEW

University of North Texas, P.O. Box 311307, Denton TX 76203-1307. (940)565-2755. **E-mail:** americanliteraryreview@gmail.com. **Website:** www.americanliteraryreview.com. **Contact:** Bonnie Friedman, editor in chief. Estab. 1990.

"Send up to 5 original photographs in a standard web-readable format (we prefer JPEG). Each photograph should have a title. We are looking for work that exhibits technical skill and artistic merit to incorporate into our online journal."

AMERICAN MUSIC TEACHER

1 W. 4th St., Suite 1550, Cincinnati OH 45202-3004. (513)421-1420; (888)512-5278. **Fax:** (513)421-2503. **E-mail:** bpieper@mtna.org. **Website:** www.mtna.org. **Contact:** Brian Pieper, graphic designer. Estab. 1951. Circ. 26,424. Bimonthly 4-color trade journal emphasizing music teaching. Features historical and how-to articles. "*AMT* promotes excellence in music teaching and keeps music teachers informed. It is the official journal of the Music Teachers National Association, an organization which includes concert artists, independent music teachers and faculty members of educational institutions." Accepts previously published material. Sample copies available.

ILLUSTRATION Buys 1 illustration/issue. Uses freelancers mainly for diagrams and illustrations. Prefers musical theme. "No interest in cartoon illustration."

FIRST CONTACT & TERMS Accepts digital submissions only. Buys one-time rights. Pays on publication; $50-150 for b&w and color, cover and inside.

AMERICAN SCHOOL BOARD JOURNAL

1680 Duke St., Alexandria VA 22314. (703) 838-6739. **Fax:** (703)549-6719. **E-mail:** editorial@asbj.com. **Website:** www.asbj.com. **Contact:** Kathleen Vail, managing editor. Estab. 1891. Circ. 36,000. National monthly magazine for school board members and school administrators. Sample copies available.

ILLUSTRATION Buys 40-50 illustrations/year. Considers all media. Send postcard sample.

FIRST CONTACT & TERMS Illustrators: Send follow-up postcard sample every 3 months. Will not accept samples as e-mail attachment. Please send URL. Responds only if interested. Art director will contact artist for portfolio review of tearsheets if interested. Buys one-time rights. **Pays on acceptance.** Pays $1,200 maximum for color cover; $250-350 for b&w, $300-600 for color inside. Finds illustrators through agents, sourcebooks, online services, magazines, word of mouth and artist's submissions.

TIPS "We're looking for new ways of seeing old subjects—children, education, management. We also write a great deal about technology and love high-tech, very sophisticated mediums. We prefer concept over narrative styles."

ANALOG

Dell Magazines, 44 Wall St., Suite 904, New York NY 10005-2401. (212)686-7188; (203)866-6688. **E-mail:** analog@dellmagazines.com. **Website:** www.analogsf. com. **Contact:** Victoria Green, senior art director; Trevor Quachri, editor. Estab. 1930. Circ. 80,000. Monthly consumer magazine. Art guidelines free for #10 SASE with first-class postage or free online.

CARTOONS Prefers single panel cartoons.

ILLUSTRATION Buys 4 illustrations/issue. Prefers science fiction, hardware, robots, aliens and creatures. Considers all media.

FIRST CONTACT & TERMS Cartoonists: Send query letter with photocopies or tearsheets and SASE. Samples are not filed and are returned by SASE. Illustrators: Send query letter with printed samples or tearsheets and SASE. Send follow-up postcard sample every 4 months. Accepts disk submissions compatible with QuarkXPress 7.5/version 3.3. Send EPS files. Files samples of interest, others are returned by SASE. Responds only if interested. "No phone calls." Portfolios may be dropped off every Tuesday and should include b&w and color tearsheets and transparencies. "No original art please, especially oversized." Buys one-time rights. **Pays on acceptance.** Pays cartoonists $35 minimum for b&w cartoons. Pays illustrators $1,200 for color cover; $125 minimum for b&w inside; $35-50 for spots. Finds illustrators through *Black Book*, *LA Workbook*, *American Showcase* and other reference books.

ANALOG SCIENCE FICTION & FACT

Dell Magazines, 44 Wall St., Suite 904, New York NY 10005-2401. **E-mail:** analog@dellmagazines. com. **Website:** www.analogsf.com. **Contact:** Trevor Quachri, editor. Estab. 1930. Circ. 50,000. Monthly magazine for general future-minded audience. "We are interested in professional-level, mostly realistic work. Photographs are not normally used, but artists illustrating for us have worked with photos, using surrealistic effects. The illustration must be able to visually interpret the story in such a way that it accurately represents the story, hooks the reader into reading it, and doesn't give away the ending. The subject matter of the stories usually contain a wide range of things that you must be able to draw. We would like to see an ability to illustrate an entire scene; one that not only has a character or characters but also has a detailed background. You must know anatomy, perspective, balance, and figure proportions. We are not a comic book company, so please don't send samples of comics pages."

ILLUSTRATION Payment $125 for b&w interiors; $1,200 for color cover.

FIRST CONTACT & TERMS Send 4-6 samples of best work; do not send originals. Reviews photocopies, stats, slides, transparencies, tearsheets. Include SASE.

ARTHRITIS TODAY

Arthritis Foundation, 1330 W. Peachtree St., Suite 100, Atlanta GA 30309. (404)872-7100. **Website:** www.arthritistoday.org. Estab. 1987. Circ. 650,000. Bimonthly consumer magazine. "*Arthritis Today* is the official magazine of the Arthritis Foundation. The award-winning publication is more than the most comprehensive and reliable source of information about arthritis research, care and treatment. It is a magazine for the whole person—from their lifestyles to their relationships. It is written both for people with arthritis and those who care about them." Originals returned at job's completion. Sample copies available. 20% of freelance work demands knowledge of Illustrator, QuarkXPress or Photoshop.

ILLUSTRATION Approached by over 100 illustrators/year. Buys 5-10 illustrations/issue. Works on assignment only; stock images used in addition to original art.

FIRST CONTACT & TERMS Illustrators: Send query letter with brochure, tearsheets, photostats, slides (optional) and transparencies (optional). Samples are filed. Publication will contact artist for portfolio review if interested. Portfolio should include color tearsheets, photostats, photocopies, final art and photographs. Buys first-time North American serial rights. Other usage negotiated. **Pays on acceptance.** Finds artists through sourcebooks, Internet, other publications, word of mouth, submissions.

TIPS "No limits on areas of the magazine open to freelancers. Two to 3 departments in each issue use spot illustrations. Submit tearsheets for consideration. No cartoons."

THE ARTIST'S MAGAZINE

F+W, a Content + eCommerce Company, 10151 Carver Rd., Blue Ash OH 45242. (513)531-2690, ext. 11731. **Fax:** (513)891-7153. **Website:** www.artistsmagazine. com. **Contact:** Maureen Bloomfield, editor-in-chief; Brian Roeth, senior art director. Circ. 100,000. Emphasizes the techniques of working artists for the serious beginning, amateur and professional artist. Published 10 times/year. Sample copy available for $5.99 US, $8.99 Canadian or international; remit in US funds. Sponsors 3 annual contests. Send SASE for more information. Pays illustrators $350-1,000 for color inside, $100-500 for spots. Occasionally accepts previously published material. Returns original artwork after publication. Must be related to art and artists.

CARTOONS Cartoonists: Contact cartoon editor, senior art director, Brian Roeth. Send query letter with brochure, photocopies, photographs and tearsheets to be kept on file. Prefers photostats or tearsheets as samples. Samples not filed are returned by SASE. Buys 4-6 cartoons/year. Buys first rights. **Pays on acceptance.** Pays cartoonists $65.

ILLUSTRATION Buys 2-3 illustrations/year. Has featured illustrations by Penelope Dullaghan, A. Richard Allen, Robert Carter, Chris Sharp and Brucie Rosch. Features concept-driven illustration. Works on assignment only.

ASIAN ENTERPRISE MAGAZINE

Asian Business Ventures, Inc., P.O. Box 1126, Walnut CA 91788. (909)896-2865; (909)319-2306. **E-mail:** willyb@asianenterprise.com; alma.asianent@gmail.com; almag@asianenterprise.com. **Website:** www.asian enterprise.com. Estab. 1993. Circ. 100,000. Monthly trade publication. "The largest Asian small business focus magazine in the US."

CARTOONS Buys 12 cartoons/year. Prefers business-humorous, single-panel, political, b&w line drawings.

ILLUSTRATION Buys 12 illustrations/issue. Features cariatures of politicians, humorous illustration and spot illustrations of business subjects. 100% of freelance illustrations demands knowledge of Photoshop, PageMaker and QuarkXPress.

FIRST CONTACT & TERMS Cartoonists: Send query letter with samples. Illustrators: Send query letter with tearsheets. Accepts disk submissions. Send TIFF files. Samples are filed. Responds only if interested. Portfolio review not required. Buys one-time rights. Negotiates rights purchased. Pays on publication. Pays cartoonists $25-50 for b&w, $25-50 for comic strips. Pays illustrators $25-50 for b&w, $200 maximum for color cover; $25-50 for b&w inside. Finds illustrators through promo samples and word of mouth.

ASIMOV'S SCIENCE FICTION

Dell Magazines, 44 Wall St., Suite 904, New York NY 10005. **E-mail:** asimovs@dellmagazines.com. **Website:** www.asimovs.com. **Contact:** Sheila Williams, editor; Victoria Green, senior art director. Estab. 1977. Circ. 50,000. Monthly b&w with 4-color cover magazine of science fiction and fantasy. Art guidelines available for #10 SASE with first-class postage.

CARTOONS Prefers single-panel, b&w washes or line drawings with or without gagline. "No comic book artists. Realistic work only, with science fiction/fantasy themes. Show characters with a background environment." Pays cartoonists $35 minimum. Pays illustrators $600-1,200 for color cover. Accepts previously published artwork. Original artwork returned at job's completion. Approached by 20 cartoonists/year. Buys 10 cartoons/year. Address cartoons to Brian Bieniowski.

ILLUSTRATION Accepts illustrations done with Illustrator and Photoshop. No longer buys interior illustration.

FIRST CONTACT & TERMS Now accepts submissions online. Portfolios may be dropped off every Tuesday and should include b&w and color tearsheets. Cartoonists: Send query letter with printed samples, photocopies and/or tearsheets, and SASE. Accepts disk submissions compatible with QuarkXPress version 3.3. Send EPS files. Samples are filed or returned by SASE. Responds only if interested. Buys one-time and reprint rights. **Pays on acceptance.** Commissions

2 covers/year; the rest are second-time rights or stock images.

ASPEN MAGAZINE

P.O. Box 4577, Aspen CO 81611. (970)300-3071. E-mail: aklein@modernluxury.com. **Website:** www.aspenmagazine.com; www.modernluxury.com/aspen. **Contact:** Alan Klein. Circ. 18,300. Bimonthly 4-color city magazine with the emphasis on Aspen and the valley. Accepts previously published artwork. Original artwork returned at job's completion. Sample copies and art guidelines available.

ILLUSTRATION Approached by 15 illustrators/year. Buys 2 illustrations/issue. Themes and styles should be appropriate for editorial content. Considers all media. Send query letter with tearsheets, photostats, photographs, slides, photocopies and transparencies. Samples are filed. Responds only if interested. Call for appointment to show a portfolio, which should include thumbnails, roughs, tearsheets, slides and photographs. Buys first, one-time or reprint rights. Pays on publication.

ASSOCIATION OF COLLEGE UNIONS INTERNATIONAL

One City Centre, 120 W. Seventh St., Suite 200, Bloomington IN 47404-3925. (812)245-2284. **Fax:** (812)245-6710. **E-mail:** acui@acui.org; alangeve@acui.org. **Website:** www.acui.org. **Contact:** Andrea Langeveld, marketing designer. Estab. 1914. Professional higher education association magazine covering "multicultural issues, creating community on campus, union and activities programming, managing staff, union operation, professional development and student development."

○ Also publishes hardcover and trade paperback originals. See listing in the Book Publishers section for more information.

ILLUSTRATION Works on assignment only. Considers all kinds of illustration.

DESIGN Needs designers for production.

FIRST CONTACT & TERMS Illustrators: Send query letter with résumé, photocopies, tearsheets, photographs, websites or color transparencies of college student union activities. Designers: Send query letter with résumé and samples. Samples are filed. Responds only if interested. Negotiates rights purchased. Pays by project.

TIPS "We are a volunteer-driven association. Most people submit work on that basis. We are on a limited budget."

ASTRONOMY

Kalmbach Publishing, 21027 Crossroads Circle, P.O. Box 1612, Waukesha WI 53187-1612. (800)533-6644. **Fax:** (262)798-6468. **Website:** www.astronomy.com. **Contact:** David J. Eicher, editor; LuAnn Williams Belter, art director (for art and photography). Estab. 1973. Circ. 108,000. Monthly consumer magazine emphasizing the study and hobby of astronomy. Published by Kalmbach Publishing. Also see listings for *Classic Toy Trains, Finescale Modeler, Model Railroader, Model Retailer, Bead and Button* and *Trains*.

ILLUSTRATION Send query letter. "If you are submitting digital images, please send TIFF or JPEG files to us via our FTP site. Send duplicate images by mail for consideration." Samples are filed and not returned. Buys one-time rights. Finds illustrators through word of mouth and submissions. Approached by 20 illustrators/year. Buys 2 illustrations/issue. Has featured illustrations by James Yang, Gary Baseman. Considers all media. 10% of freelance illustration demands knowledge of Photoshop, Illustrator, InDesign.

FIRST CONTACT & TERMS Illustrators: Send query letter. "If you are submitting digital images, please send TIFF or JPEG files to us via our FTP site. Send duplicate images by mail for consideration." Samples are filed and not returned. Buys one-time rights. Finds illustrators through word of mouth and submissions.

A.T. JOURNEYS

Appalachian Trail Conservancy Headquarters, 799 Washington St., P.O. Box 807, Harpers Ferry WV 25425-0807. (304)535-6331. **Fax:** (304)535-2667. **E-mail:** editor@appalachiantrail.org; journeys@appalachiantrail.org. **Website:** www.appalachiantrail.org. **Contact:** Editor. Circ. 50,000. Membership publication focuses on the stories of people who experience and support the Appalachian Trail, as well as conservation-oriented stories related to the Appalachian Mountain region. Published 6 times/year. Sometimes accepts previously published material. Returns original artwork after publication. Sample copy and art guidelines available for legitimate queries.

ILLUSTRATION Buys 8-12 illustrations/issue. Accepts all styles and media; computer generated (identified as such) or manual. Original artwork should be directly related to the Appalachian Trail.

FIRST CONTACT & TERMS Illustrators: Send query letter with samples to be kept on file. Prefers non-returnable postcards, photocopies or tearsheets as samples. Samples not filed are returned by SASE. Responds in 2 months. Negotiates rights purchased. **Pays on acceptance**; $25-$250 for b&w, color. Finds most artists through references, word of mouth and samples received through the mail.

ATLANTA MAGAZINE

260 Peachtree St., Suite 300, Atlanta GA 30303. (404)527-5500. **Fax:** (404)527-5575. **E-mail:** sfennessy@atlantamagazine.com. **Website:** www.atlantamagazine.com. **Contact:** Steve Fennessy, editor. Estab. 1961. Circ. 66,000. Monthly 4-color consumer magazine.

ILLUSTRATION Buys 3 illustrations/issue. Has featured illustrations by Fred Harper, Harry Campbell, Jane Sanders, various illustrators repped by Wanda Nowak, various illustrators repped by Gerald & Cullen Rapp, Inc. Features caricatures of celebrities, fashion illustration, humorous illustration and spot illustrations. Prefers a wide variety of subjects. Style and media depend on the story. Assigns 60% of illustrations to well-known or "name" illustrators; 30% to experienced but not well-known illustrators; 10% to new and emerging illustrators.

FIRST CONTACT & TERMS Illustrators: Send non-returnable postcard sample. Samples are filed. Will contact artist for portfolio review if interested. Buys first rights. **Pays on acceptance.** Finds freelancers through promotional samples, artists' reps, *The Alternative Pick.*

AUTHORSHIP

National Writers Association, 10940 S. Parker Rd., #508, Parker CO 80134. (303)841-0246. **E-mail:** natlwritersassn@hotmail.com. **Website:** www.nationalwriters.com. Estab. 1950s. Circ. 4,000. Quarterly magazine. "Our publication is for our 3,000 members and is cover-to-cover about writing."

FIRST CONTACT & TERMS Cartoonists: Samples are returned. Responds in 4 months. Buys first North American serial and reprint rights. **Pays on acceptance.** Pays cartoonists $25 minimum for b&w. Illustrators: Accepts disk submissions. Send TIFF or JPEG files.

TIPS "We only take cartoons slanted to writers."

AUTOMOBILE MAGAZINE

831 S. Douglas St., El Segundo CA 90245. **Website:** www.automobilemag.com. **Contact:** art director. Estab. 1986. Circ. 650,000. Monthly 4-color automobile magazine for upscale lifestyles. Art guidelines are specific for each project.

ILLUSTRATION Buys illustrations mainly for spots and feature spreads. Works with 5-10 illustrators/year. Buys 2-5 illustrations/issue. Works on assignment only. Considers airbrush, mixed media, colored pencil, watercolor, acrylic, oil, pastel and collage. Needs editorial and technical illustrations.

FIRST CONTACT & TERMS Send query letter with brochure showing art style, résumé, tearsheets, slides, photographs or transparencies. Show automobiles in various styles and media. "This is a full-color magazine; illustrations of cars and people must be accurate." Samples are returned only if requested. "I would like to keep something in my file." Responds to queries/submissions only if interested. Buys first rights and one-time rights. Pays $200 and up for color inside. Pays $2,000 maximum depending on size of illustration. Finds artists through mailed samples.

TIPS "Send samples that show cars drawn accurately with a unique style and imaginative use of medium."

AUTO RESTORER

BowTie, Inc., 3 Burroughs, Irvine CA 92618. (213)385-2222. **Fax:** (213)385-8565. **E-mail:** tkade@i5publishing.com. **Website:** www.autorestorermagazine.com. **Contact:** Ted Kade, editor. Estab. 1989. Circ. 60,000. Monthly b&w consumer magazine with focus on collecting, restoring and enjoying classic cars and trucks. Originals returned at job's completion. Sample copies available for $7.

ILLUSTRATION Technical drawings that illustrate articles in black ink are welcome. Approached by 5-10 illustrators/year. Buys 1 illustration/issue. Prefers technical illustrations and cutaways of classic/collectible automobiles through 1979. Considers pen & ink, watercolor, airbrush, acrylic, marker, colored pencil, oil, charcoal, mixed media, and pastel.

FIRST CONTACT & TERMS Illustrators: Send query letter with SASE, slides, photographs, and photocopies. Samples are filed or returned by SASE if requested by artist. Responds to the artist only if interested. Buys one-time rights. Pays on publication; technical illustrations negotiable. Finds artists through submissions.

TIPS Areas most open to freelance work are technical illustrations for feature articles and renderings of classic cars for various sections.

BABYBUG

Cricket Magazine Group, 70 East Lake St., Suite 800, Chicago IL 60601. **E-mail:** babybug@babybugmag kids.com. **Website:** www.cricketmag.com/babybug; www.babybugmagkids.com. **Contact:** submissions editor. Estab. 1994. Circ. 45,000. *Babybug* is a look-and-listen magazine for babies and toddlers ages 6 months-3 years. Publishes 9 issues per year. Art by assignment only. See submission guidelines for details about submitting portfolio samples (submittable. cricketmag.com; www.cricketmag.com/submissions). **FIRST CONTACT & TERMS** No advance list of themes. Do not query. Include exact word count. Prefers onilne submissions. Please allow 3-6 months response time.

BACKPACKER MAGAZINE

Cruz Bay Publishing, Inc., Active Interest Media Co., 5720 Flatiron Pkwy., Boulder CO 80301. **E-mail:** gful lerton@backpacker.com (senior associate photo editor). **Website:** www.backpacker.com. Dennis Lewon, editor-in-chief (features & people), dlcwon@back packer.com; Rachel Zurer, senior editor, (destinations & heroes), rzurer@backpacker.com; Casey Lyons, senior editor (skills & survival), caseylyons@aimme dia.com; Maren Kasselik, assistant editor (destinations), mkasselik@aimmedia.com; Kristin Hostetter, gear editor, khostetter1@gmail.com. Estab. 1973. Circ. 340,000. Approached by 200-300 illustrators/year. Buys 10 illustrations/issue. *Backpacker* does not buy cartoons. 60% of freelance illustration demands knowledge of FreeHand, Photoshop, Illustrator, QuarkXPress.

TIPS "Know the subject matter, and know *Backpacker Magazine*."

BALTIMORE JEWISH TIMES

11459 Cronhill Dr., Suite A, Owings Mills MD 21117. (410)902-2300. **Fax:** (410)902-2338. **E-mail:** artdirec tor@jewishtimes.com; mjaffe@jewishtimes.com; ed itor@jewishtimes.com. **Website:** www.jewishtimes. com. **Contact:** Maayan Jaffe, managing editor; Lindsey Bridwell, art director. Circ. 10,000. Weekly b&w tabloid with 4-color cover. Emphasizes special interests to the Jewish community for largely local readership. Sample copies available.

Alter Communications also publishes *Style*, a Baltimore lifestyle magazine. See www.altery ourview.com for more information on these publications.

ILLUSTRATION Approached by 50 illustrators/year. Buys 4-6 illustrations/year. Works on assignment only. Prefers high-contrast, b&w illustrations.

FIRST CONTACT & TERMS Illustrators: Send query letter with brochure showing art style or tearsheets and photocopies. Samples not filed are returned by SASE. Responds if interested. To show a portfolio, mail appropriate materials or write/call to schedule an appointment. Portfolio should include original/final art, final reproduction/product and color tearsheets and photostats. Buys first rights. Pays on publication: $500 for b&w or color cover; $50-100 for b&w inside. Accepts previously published artwork. Returns original artwork after publication, if requested.

TIPS Finds artists through word of mouth, self-promotion and sourcebooks. Sees trend toward "more freedom of design integrating visual and verbal."

BALTIMORE MAGAZINE

1000 Lancaster St., Suite 400, Baltimore MD 21202. (443)873-3900. **E-mail:** wmax@baltimoremagazine. net; mjane@baltimoremagazine.net; ghilary@balti moremagazine.net; ikcn@baltimoremagazine.net; cron@baltimoremagazine.net; wlydia@baltimore magazine.net. **Website:** www.baltimoremagazine. net. **Contact:** Send correspondence to the appropriate editor: Max Weiss (lifestyle, film, pop culture, general inquiries); Jane Marion (food, travel); Hilary Geisbert (style, home, beauty, wellness); Ken Iglehart (business, special editions); Ron Cassie (politics, environment, health, sports); Lydia Woolever (calendar, events, party pages). Estab. 1907. Circ. 70,000. Monthly city magazine featuring news, profiles, and service articles. Sample copies available for $4.99. Considers all media, depending on assignment. 10% of freelance work demands knowledge of InDesign, FreeHand, Illustrator, or Photoshop, or any other program that is saved as a TIFF or PICT file. All art is freelance-humorous front pieces, feature illustrations, etc.

CARTOONS Does not use cartoons.

ILLUSTRATION Samples are filed. Will contact for portfolio review if interested. Originals returned at job's completion. Buys one-time rights. Pays on publication: $200-1,500 for color inside; 60 days after invoice. Finds artists through sourcebooks, pub-

lications, word of mouth, submissions. Approached by 1,000 illustrators/year. Buys 4 illustrations/issue. Works on assignment only.
FIRST CONTACT & TERMS Send postcard sample. Accepts disk submissions.

BARTENDER MAGAZINE

Foley Publishing, P.O. Box 158, Liberty Corner NJ 07938. (908)766-6006. **Fax:** (908)766-6607. **E-mail:** barmag@aol.com. **Website:** www.bartender.com. **Contact:** Jackie Foley, editor. Estab. 1979. Circ. 150,000. Quarterly 4-color trade journal emphasizing restaurants, taverns, bars, bartenders, bar managers, owners, etc. Prefers bar themes; single-panel. Works on assignment only.

CARTOONS Send query letter with finished cartoons. Buys first rights. Approached by 10 cartoonists/year. Buys 3 cartoons/issue. Pays cartoonists $50 for b&w and $100 for color inside.

ILLUSTRATION Send query letter with brochure. Samples are filed. Negotiates rights purchased. Pays on publication. Approached by 5 illustrators/year. Buys 1 illustration/issue. Pays illustrators $500 for color cover.

DESIGN Considers any media.

TIPS Prefers bar themes.

BAY WINDOWS

28 Damrell St., Suite 204, Boston MA 02127. (617)464-7280. **Fax:** (617)464-7286. **E-mail:** letters.baywindows@gmail.com. **Website:** www.baywindows.com. **Contact:** editorial design manager. Estab. 1983. Circ. 60,000. Weekly newspaper "targeted to politically-aware lesbians, gay men and other political allies publishing noneROTIC news and features"; b&w with 2-color cover. Sample copies available.

CARTOONS Approached by 25 cartoonists/year. Buys 1-2 cartoons/issue. Buys 50 cartoons/year. Preferred themes include politics and lifestyles. Prefers double and multiple panel, political and editorial cartoons with gagline; b&w line drawings.

ILLUSTRATION Approached by 60 illustrators/year. Buys 1 illustration/issue. Buys 50 illustrations/year. Works on assignment only. Preferred themes include politics; "humor is a plus." Considers pen & ink and marker drawings. Needs computer illustrators familiar with Illustrator or FreeHand.

FIRST CONTACT & TERMS Cartoonists: Send query letter with roughs. Samples are returned by SASE if requested by artist. Illustrators: Send query letter with photostats and SASE. Samples are filed. Responds in 6 weeks, only if interested. Portfolio review not required. Rights purchased vary according to project. Pays on publication. Accepts previously published artwork. Original artwork returned after publication.

⊙ Ⓝ BC OUTDOORS HUNTING AND SHOOTING

Outdoor Group Media, 7261 River Place, 201a, Mission British Columbia V4S 0A2, Canada. (604)820-3400. **Fax:** (604)820-3477. **E-mail:** info@outdoorgroupmedia.com; mmitchell@outdoorgroupmedia.com; production@outdoorgroupmedia.com. **Website:** www.bcoutdoorsmagazine.com. **Contact:** Mike Mitchell, editor. Estab. 1945. Circ. 30,000. Biannual 4-color magazine, emphasizing fishing, hunting, camping, wildlife/conservation in British Columbia. Original artwork returned after publication unless bought outright. Works on assignment only. Samples returned by SASE (nonresidents include IRC). Reports back on future assignment possibilities. Subject matter and the art's quality must fit with publication. Buys first North American serial rights or all rights on a work-for-hire basis. Interested in outdoors, wildlife (British Columbia species only) and activities as stories require.

⊙ "Send us material on fishing and hunting. We generally just send back nonrelated work."

ILLUSTRATION Approached by more than 10 illustrators/year. Buys 4-6 illustrations/year. Format b&w line drawings and washes for inside and color washes for inside. Has featured illustrations by Ian Forbes, Brad Nickason and Michael McKinell. Prefers local artists. Pays on publication; $40 minimum for spots.

FIRST CONTACT & TERMS Arrange personal appointment to show portfolio or send samples of style.

THE BEAR DELUXE MAGAZINE

Orlo, 240 N. Broadway, #112, Portland OR 97227. **E-mail:** bear@orlo.org. **Website:** www.orlo.org. **Contact:** Tom Webb, editor-in-chief; Kristin Rogers Brown, art director. Estab. 1993. Circ. 19,000. "*The Bear Deluxe Magazine* is a national independent environmental arts magazine publishing significant works of reporting, creative nonfiction, literature, visual art, and design. Based in the Pacific Northwest, it reaches across cultural and political divides to engage readers on vital issues effecting the environment. Published twice per year, *The Bear Deluxe* includes a wider array and a higher percentage of visual artwork and design than many other publications. Artwork is included both as editorial support and as standalone or independent art. It has included nationally recognized artists as well as emerging artists. As with any publication, artists are encouraged to review a sample copy for a clearer understanding of the magazine's approach. Unsolicited submissions and samples are accepted and encouraged. *The Bear Deluxe* has been recognized for both its editorial and design excellence."

CARTOONS Approached by 50 cartoonists/year. Buys 5 cartoons/issue. Prefers work related to environmental, outdoor, media, arts. Prefers single-panel, political, humorous, b&w line drawings. Buys first rights. Pays on publication. Cartoonists should continue to send us their latest and greatest, not just samples.

ILLUSTRATION Pays illustrators $200 for b&w or color cover; $15-75 for b&w or color inside; $15-75 for 2-page spreads; $20 for spots.

FIRST CONTACT & TERMS Send postcard sample and nonreturnable samples. Accepts Mac-compatible disk submissions. Send EPS, TIFF, or JPEG files. Samples are filed or returned by SASE. Responds only if interested. Portfolios may be dropped off by appointment. "If you submit via e-mail, send PDF format files only, or a URL address for us to visit. (Note on e-mail submissions and URL suggestions, we still prefer hard-copy work samples but will consider electronic submissions and links. We cannot, however, guarantee a response to electronic submissions.) Always include an appropriately stamped SASE for the return of materials. No faxes. *The Bear Deluxe* assumes no liability for submitted work samples."

TIPS "Most of our work (besides cartoons) is assigned out as editorial illustration or independent art. Indicate whether an assignment is possible for you. Indicate your fastest turn-around time. We sometimes need people who can work with 2- to 3-week turnaround or faster."

BIRD WATCHER'S DIGEST

P.O. Box 110, Marietta OH 45750. (740)373-5285; (800)879-2473. **E-mail:** editor@birdwatchersdigest. com; submissions@birdwatchersdigest.com. **Website:** www.birdwatchersdigest.com. **Contact:** Bill Thompson III, editor. Estab. 1978. Circ. 42,000. *BWD* is a nontechnical magazine interpreting ornithological material for amateur observers, including the knowledgeable birder, the serious novice and the backyard bird watcher; strives to provide good reading and good ornithology. Rarely buys rights for art/graphic design.

FIRST CONTACT & TERMS Accepts high-res (300 dpi) digital images via Dropbox or HighTail. See guidelines online.

BIRMINGHAM PARENT

Evans Publishing LLC, 3590-B Hwy 31S. #289, Pelham AL 35124. (205)987-7700. **Fax:** (205)987-7600. **E-mail:** carol@biringhamparent.com. **Website:** www.birminghamparent.com. **Contact:** Carol Evans, publisher/editor. Estab. 2004. Circ. 30,000. Monthly magazine serving parents of families in Central Alabama/Birmingham with news pertinent to them. Art guidelines free with SASE or on website.

CARTOONS Approached by 12-20 cartoonists/year. Buys 1-2 cartoons/year. Prefers fun, humorous, parenting issues, nothing controversial. Format: single panel. Media: color washes.

ILLUSTRATION Approached by 2 illustrators/year. Assigns 5% of illustrations to new and emerging illustrators. 95% of freelance work demands computer skills. Freelancers should be familiar with InDesign, QuarkXPress, Photoshop.

FIRST CONTACT & TERMS E-mail submissions accepted with link to website. Portfolio not required. Pays cartoonists $0-25 for b&w or color cartoons. Pays on publication. Buys electronic rights, first North American serial rights. Magazine is completely online, so permission must be granted for use in the magazine.

TIPS "We do very little freelance artwork. We are still a small publication and don't have space or funds for it. Our art director provides the bulk of our needs. It would have to be outstanding for us to consider purchasing right now."

BITCH: A FEMINIST RESPONSE TO POP CULTURE

Bitch Media, 4930 NE 29th Ave., Portland OR 97211-7034. (503)282-5699. **E-mail:** bitch@bitchmagazine. com. **Website:** www.bitchmedia.com. **Contact:** Art director. Estab. 1996. Circ. 80,000. Quarterly 2-color magazine "devoted to incisive commentary on our media-driven world. We examine popular culture in all its forms for women and feminists of all ages."

ILLUSTRATION Approached by 300 illustrators/year. Buys 3-7 illustrations/issue. Features conceptual, fashion, and humorous illustration, some portraits and hand lettering. Work on assignment only. Prefers b&w ink drawings and photo collage, or selective use of color. Assigns 85% of illustrations to experienced but not well-known illustrators; 12% to new and emerging illustrators; 3% to well-known or "name" illustrators.

FIRST CONTACT & TERMS Send postcard sample, nonreturnable samples. Samples are filed and are not returned. Will contact artist for portfolio review if interested. Finds illustrators through magazines and word of mouth.

TIPS "We have a few illustrators we work with regularly, but we are open to others. Our circulation has been doubling annually, and we are distributed internationally. Read our magazine and send something we might like. Please review our contributors guidelines online for more specifics, at bitchmagazine.org/writers-guidelines#illustratorsguidelines. No stock submissions."

BIZTIMES MILWAUKEE

BizTimes Media, 126 N. Jefferson St., Suite 403, Milwaukee WI 53202-6120. (414)277-8181. **Fax:** (414)277-8191. **E-mail:** shelly.tabor@biztimes.com. **Website:** www.biztimes.com. **Contact:** Shelly Tabor, art director. Estab. 1994. Circ. 13,500. Biweekly business news magazine covering southeastern Wisconsin region.

ILLUSTRATION Uses 1-2 illustrations/year. Features business concepts, charts & graphs, computer, humorous illustration, information graphics and realistic illustrations. Prefers business subjects in simpler styles that reproduce well on thin, glossy paper. Assigns 75% of work to new and emerging illustrators.

FIRST CONTACT & TERMS Illustrators: Send postcard sample and follow-up postcard every year. Will contact artist for portfolio review if interested. Buys one-time rights for print and online usage. Pays illustrators $200-400 for color cover; $80-100 for inside. **Pays on acceptance.**

TIPS "Conceptual work wanted! Audience is business men and women in southeast Wisconsin. Need ideas relative to today's business issues/concerns (insurance, law, banking, commercial real estate, health care, manufacturing, finance, education, technology, retirement). One- to 2-week turnaround."

BLACK ENTERPRISE

260 Madison Ave., 11th Floor, New York NY 10016. (212)242-8000; (312) 664-8667; (310) 552-6900. **E-mail:** beeditors@blackenterprise.com. **Website:** www.blackenterprise.com. Estab. 1970. Circ. 450,000. Monthly 4-color consumer magazine targeting African Americans and emphasizing personal finance, careers and entrepreneurship.

ILLUSTRATION Approached by over 100 illustrators/year. Buys 10 illustrations/issue. Has featured illustrations by Ray Alma, Cecil G. Rice, Peter Fasolino. Features humorous and spot illustrations, charts & graphs, computer illustration on business subjects. Assigns 10% of illustrations to new and emerging illustrators. 50% of freelance illustration demands knowledge of Illustrator and Photoshop.

FIRST CONTACT & TERMS Illustrators: Send postcard sample. Samples are filed. After introductory mailing, send follow-up postcard every 3 months. Responds only if interested. Portfolios may be dropped off Monday-Friday and should include color finished, original art and tearsheets. Buys first rights. **Pays on acceptance**; $200-800 for color inside; $800-1,000 for 2-page spreads. Finds illustrators through agents, artist's submissions and *Directory of Illustration.*

BLOOMBERG MARKETS MAGAZINE

731 Lexington Ave., New York NY 10022-1331. (212)318-2000. **E-mail:** bloombergmag@bloomberg.net. **Website:** www.bloomberg.com. **Contact:** art director. Circ. 300,000. Monthly financial/business magazine.

ILLUSTRATION Has featured Doug Ross, Steven Biver and Lisa Ferlic.

FIRST CONTACT & TERMS Illustrators: Send nonreturnable postcard sample. After introductory mailing, send follow-up postcard sample every 6 months. Responds only if interested. Pays illustrators $450 for color inside. Buys one-time rights. Find freelancers through artists' submissions.

BLUELINE

120 Morey Hall, Dept. of English and Communication, Postdam NY 13676. (315)267-2044. **E-mail:** blueline@potsdam.edu. **Website:** bluelinemagadk.com. **Contact:** Donald McNutt, editor; Caroline Downing, art editor; Donald McNutt, nonfiction editor; Stephanie Coyne-Deghett, fiction editor; Rebecca Lehmann, poetry editor. Estab. 1979. Circ. 400. Open to all artists. Editors are interested in art in all media suitable for 2D b&w or color reproduction that addresses in some way the concerns and experiences of the Adirondacks and regions of similar spirit. There is no entry fee. The editors review all submissions from July

1-November 30. Editorial decisions are made by mid-February. Accepted work will be retained until the publication of the journal (in May/June). Work not accepted will be returned by mid-February. *Blueline* reserves one-time publishing rights. All other rights are the property of the artist. Payment in copies.

FIRST CONTACT & TERMS Do not send original art. Submission is by .jpg files only.

BOYS' QUEST

P.O. Box 227, Bluffton OH 45817-0227. (419)358-4610, ext. 101. **Fax:** (419)358-8020. **Website:** www.funforkidzmagazines.com. **Contact:** Marilyn Edwards, editor. Estab. 1995. Circ. 10,000. Bimonthly consumer magazine "geared for elementary boys." Sample copies $6 each, Canada is $8 (includes postage) other countries is $10.50 (includes 4.50 airmail); art guidelines for SASE with first-class postage. Prefers wholesome children themes. Prefers single or double panel, humorous, b&w line drawings with gagline. Approached by 100 illustrators/year. Buys 6 illustrations/issue. Has featured illustrations by Chris Sabatino, Gail Roth and Pamela Harden. "Read our magazine. Send in a few samples of work in pen and ink. Everything revolves around a theme; the theme list is available with SASE."

CARTOONS Send finished cartoons. Illustrators: Send query letter with printed samples. Samples are filed or returned by SASE. Responds in 2 months. Buys first rights. Pays on publication. Pays cartoonists $5-25 for b&w. Buys 1-3 cartoons/issue.

ILLUSTRATION Features humorous illustration; realistic and spot illustration. Assigns 40% of illustrations to new and emerging illustrators. Prefers childhood themes. Considers all media. Pays illustrators $200-250 for color cover; $25-35 for b&w inside; $50-70 for 2-page spreads; $10-25 for spots. Finds illustrators through artist's submissions.

FIRST CONTACT & TERMS To arrange portfolio review of b&w work, artist should follow up with call or letter after initial query.

TIPS "Most art will be by assignment, in support of features used. The magazine is anxious to find artists capable of illustrating stories and features and welcomes copies of sample work, which will remain on file. Our work inside is pen and ink. We pay $35 for a full page and $25 for a partial page."

⌂ BREWERS ASSOCIATION

P.O. Box 1679, Boulder CO 80306. (303)447-0816; (888)822-6273. **E-mail:** allison@brewersassociation.org. **Website:** www.brewersassociation.org. **Contact:** Jill Redding, editor; Kristi Switzer, publisher; Allison Seymour, art director. Estab. 1978. "Our nonprofit organization hires illustrators for 2 magazines, *Zymurgy* and *The New Brewer*, each published bimonthly. *Zymurgy* is the journal of the American Homebrewers Association. The goal of the AHA division is to promote public awareness and appreciation of the quality and variety of beer through education, research and the collection and dissemination of information." Circ. 25,000. "*The New Brewer* is the journal of the Brewers Association. It offers practical insights and advice for breweries that range in size from less than 500 barrels per year to more than 800,000. Features articles on brewing technology and problem solving, pub and restaurant management, and packaged beer sales and distribution, as well as important industry news and industry sales and market share performance." Circ. 10,000.

ILLUSTRATION Approached by 50 illustrators/year. Buys 3-6 illustrations/year. Prefers beer and homebrewing themes. Considers all media.

DESIGN Prefers local design freelancers with experience in Photoshop, QuarkXPress, Illustrator.

FIRST CONTACT & TERMS Illustrators: Send postcard sample or query letter with printed samples, photocopies, tearsheets; follow-up sample every 3 months. Accepts disk submissions with EPS, TIFF or JPEG files. "We prefer samples we can keep." No originals accepted; samples are filed. Responds only if interested. Art director will contact artist for portfolio review if interested. Buys one-time rights. Pays 60 days net on acceptance. Pays illustrators $700-800 for color cover; $200-300 for b&w inside; $200-400 for color inside. Pays $150-300 for spots. Finds artists through agents, sourcebooks and magazines (Society of Illustrators, *Graphis*, *PRINT*, *Colorado Creative*), word of mouth, submissions. Designers: Send query letter with printed samples, photocopies, tearsheets.

TIPS "Keep sending promotional material for our files. Anything beer-related for subject matter is a plus. We look at all styles."

BRIDE'S MAGAZINE

Condé Nast, 4 Times Square, New York NY 10036. **Website:** www.brides.com. Estab. 1934. Circ. 336,598.

Bimonthly 4-color; "classic, clean, sophisticated design style." Original artwork is returned after publication.

ILLUSTRATION Buys illustrations mainly for spots and feature spreads. Buys 5-10 illustrations/issue. Works on assignment only. Considers pen & ink, airbrush, mixed media, colored pencil, watercolor, acrylic, collage and calligraphy. Needs editorial illustrations.

FIRST CONTACT & TERMS Illustrators: Send postcard sample. In samples or portfolio, looks for "graphic quality, conceptual skill, good 'people' style; lively, young but sophisticated work." Samples are filed. Will contact for portfolio review if interested. Portfolios may be dropped off every Monday-Thursday and should include color and b&w final art, tearsheets, photographs and transparencies. Buys one-time rights or negotiates rights purchased. Pays on publication; $250-350 for b&w or color inside; $250 minimum for spots. Finds artists through word of mouth, magazines, submissions/self-promotions, sourcebooks, artists' agents and reps, attending art exhibitions.

BUSINESS & COMMERCIAL AVIATION

The McGraw-Hill Companies, PMB 327, 54 Danbury Rd., Ridgefield CT 06877-4019. (800)525-5003. **Fax:** (888)385-1428. **Website:** www.aviationweek.com. **Contact:** William Garvey, editor-in-chief. Circ. 55,000. Monthly technical publication for corporate pilots and owners of business aircraft. 4-color; "contemporary design."

ILLUSTRATION Works with 12 illustrators/year. Buys 12 editorial and technical illustrations/year. Uses artists mainly for editorials and some covers. Especially needs full-page and spot art of a business-aviation nature. "We generally only use artists with a fairly realistic style. This is a serious business publication and graphically conservative. Need artists who can work on short deadline time." 70% of freelance work demands knowledge of Photoshop, Illustrator, QuarkXPress and FreeHand.

FIRST CONTACT & TERMS Illustrators: Query with samples and SASE. Responds in 1 month. Photocopies OK. Buys all rights, but may reassign rights to artist after publication. Negotiates payment. **Pays on acceptance.**

BUSINESS LONDON

P.O. Box 7400, London Ontario N5Y 4X3, Canada. (519)471-2907. **Fax:** (519)473-7859. **E-mail:** gord. delamont@sunmedia.ca. **Website:** www.business london.ca. **Contact:** Gord Delamont, publisher and editor. Circ. 14,000. Monthly magazine "covering London and area businesses, entrepreneurs, building better businesses." Sample copies not available; art guidelines not available.

CARTOONS Approached by 2 cartoonists/year. Buys 1 cartoon/issue. Prefers business-related line art. Prefers single panel, humorous b&w washes and line drawings without gagline.

ILLUSTRATION Approached by 5 illustrators/year. Buys 2 illustrations/issue. Has featured illustrations by Nigel Lewis and Scott Finch. Features humorous and realistic illustration; informational graphics and spot illustration. Assigns 50% of illustrations to experienced but not well-known illustrators; 50% to new and emerging illustrators. Prefers business issues. Considers all media. 10% of freelance illustration demands knowledge of Photoshop 3, Illustrator 5.5, QuarkXPress 3.2.

FIRST CONTACT & TERMS Send query letter with roughs and printed samples. Accepts disk submissions compatible with QuarkXPress 7/version 3.3, Illustrator 5.5, Photoshop 3, TIFFs or EPS files. Samples are filed and are not returned. Responds only if interested. Art director will contact artist for portfolio review of b&w, color, final art, photographs, slides and thumbnails if interested. Pays on publication. Buys first rights. Finds illustrators through artist's submissions.

TIPS "Arrange personal meetings, provide vibrant, interesting samples, start out cheap! Quick turnaround is a must."

BUSINESS TRAVEL NEWS

116 W. 32nd St., 14th Floor, New York NY 10001. (646)380-6248. **E-mail:** jchan@thebtngroup.com. **Website:** www.businesstravelnews.com. **Contact:** Jonathan Chan, art director. Estab. 1984. Circ. 50,000. Monthly 4-color trade publication focusing on business and corporate travel news/management.

ILLUSTRATION Approached by 300 illustrators/year. Buys 4-8 illustrations/month. Features charts & graphs, computer illustration, conceptual art, informational graphics and spot illustrations. Preferred subjects: business concepts, electronic business and travel. Assigns 30% of illustrations to well-known, experienced and emerging illustrators.

FIRST CONTACT & TERMS Illustrators: Send postcard or other nonreturnable samples. Samples are filed. Buys first rights. **Pays on acceptance.** Finds illustrators through artists' promotional material and sourcebooks.

TIPS "Send your best samples. We look for interesting concepts and print a variety of styles. Please note we serve a business market."

BUSINESSWEEK

1221 Ave. of the Americans, 3rd Floor, New York NY 10020-1001. (212)318-2000; (212)512-2511. **Fax:** (212)512-4938. **E-mail:** malcom_frouman@businessweek.com. **Website:** www.businessweek.com. **Contact:** Diane Daley; Malcolm Frouman, art director. Weekly business magazine to keep readers informed on important news that affects the business community in the U.S. and abroad. Circ. 985,025.

ILLUSTRATION Approached by hundreds of illustrators/year. Buys 50 illustrations/year. Has featured illustrations by Steven Brodner. Features caricatures of politicians, charts & graphs, humorous, informational and spot illustrations of business. Assigns 5% to new and emerging illustrators. 10% of freelance illustration demands knowledge of Illustrator and QuarkXPress.

FIRST CONTACT & TERMS Illustrators: Send postcard sample with URL. After introductory mailing, send follow-up postcard sample every 3 months. Samples are filed. Responds only if interested. Portfolio not required. Pays illustrators $1,000-2,000 for color cover; $450-1,000 for color inside. Pays on publication. Negotiates rights purchased. Finds freelancers through artists' submissions and sourcebooks.

◉ CALIFORNIA HOME & DESIGN

680 Second St., San Francisco CA 94107. (888)260-4269; (818)487-2080. **Fax:** (818)487-4550. **Website:** www.californiahomedesign.com. Estab. 1994. Circ. 52,500. Bimonthly magazine of Northern California lifestyle. Sample copy free with 9×10 SASE and first-class postage.

ILLUSTRATION Approached by 100 illustrators/year. Buys 6 illustrations/year. Prefers financial, fashion. Considers all media. 50% of freelance illustration demands knowledge of Photoshop, Illustrator, QuarkXPress.

DESIGN Needs freelancers for design and production. Prefers local design freelancers. 100% of freelance work demands knowledge of Photoshop, Illustrator, QuarkXPress.

FIRST CONTACT & TERMS Illustrators: Send postcard sample or query letter with printed samples. Accepts disk submissions compatible with QuarkXPress (EPS files). Designers: Send printed samples. Samples are filed. Responds only if interested. Buys one-time rights. Pays on publication. Pays illustrators $100-250 for spots. Finds illustrators through submissions.

TIPS "Read our magazine."

CALYX

P.O. Box B, Corvallis OR 97339. (541)753-9384. **Fax:** (541)753-0515. **E-mail:** info@calyxpress.org; editor@calyxpress.org. **Website:** www.calyxpress.org. **Contact:** Brenna Crotty, senior editor. Estab. 1976. Circ. 6,000. "CALYX exists to publish fine literature and art by women and is committed to publishing the work of all women, including women of color, older women, working class women and other voices that need to be heard. We are committed to discovering and nurturing developing writers."

◐ "We publish color art inside *CALYX* now. Separate guidelines for electronic art are available."

FIRST CONTACT & TERMS Visual art should be submitted (1) electronically via CD or e-mail; or (2) 5×7 or 8×10 glossy photographs; or (3) 35mm slides. Limit of 6 images/photos/slides. All art media are considered. Please include list of all images/photos/slides with your name, titles, media, dimensions. Also mark the top of the work. Make sure all the proper information is included when sending art electronically. Include a 50-word biographical statement and a separate 50-word statement about your artwork. Submit art separately from prose and poetry.

◔ CANADIAN BUSINESS

Rogers Media, 1 Mount Pleasant Rd., 11th Floor, Toronto Ontario M4Y 2Y5, Canada. (416)764-2000. **E-mail:** letters@canadianbusiness.com. **Website:** www.canadianbusiness.com. Circ. 85,000. Biweekly 4-color business magazine focusing on Canadian management and entrepreneurs.

ILLUSTRATION Approached by 200 illustrators/year. Buys 5-10 illustrations/issue. Has featured illustrations by Gerard Dubois, Joe Morse, Seth, Gary Taxali, Dan Page. Features conceptual illustrations, portraits, caricatures and infographics of business subjects. Assigns 70% of illustrations to well-known or "name" illustrators; 30% to new and emerging illustrators. 50% of freelance illustration demands knowledge of Illustrator and Photoshop.

FIRST CONTACT & TERMS Illustrators: Send postcard sample, printed samples and photocopies. Accepts Mac-compatible disk submissions. Responds only if interested. Will contact artist for portfolio review if interested. **Pays on acceptance**; $1,000-2,000 for color cover; $300-1,500 for color inside; $300 for spots. Finds illustrators through magazines, word of mouth and samples.

◎ CANADIAN GARDENING

Transcontinental Media G.P., TVA Publications, 1010 Sérigny St., Longueuil Quebec J4k 5G7, Canada. (416)733-7600; (514) 848-7000. **E-mail:** online form. **Website:** www.canadiangardening.com. Estab. 1990. Circ. 152,000. Special interest magazine published 8 times/year. "A down-to-earth, indispensable magazine for Canadians who love to garden."

ILLUSTRATION Approached by 50 illustrators/year. Prefers using Canadian artists. Buys 2 illustrations/ issue. Considers all media. 50% of freelance illustration demands knowledge of Photoshop, Illustrator and InDesign.

FIRST CONTACT & TERMS Illustrators: Send query letter with tearsheets. Accepts disk submissions compatible with Slide Show, InDesign, Illustrator or Photoshop (Mac). Samples are filed and are not returned. Responds only if interested. Buys first rights. Pays within 45 days, $50-250 (CDN) for spots.

CATALINA

(212)851-3427. **Fax:** (212)202-7608. **E-mail:** cat@ catalinamagazine.com; cathy@catalinamagazine. com. **Website:** www.catalinamagazine.com. Estab. 2001. Bimonthly consumer magazine for Hispanic women between 24 and 54 focusing on careers, beauty, food, parenting, relationships, health and travel.

ILLUSTRATION Approached by 100 illustrators/year. Buys 10 illustrations/year. Preferred subjects: families, Hispanic women, fashion, health, career.

FIRST CONTACT & TERMS Illustrators: Send postcard sample. After introductory mailing, send followup postcard sample every 6 months. Responds only if interested. Buys one-time rights.

CAVE WALL

P.O. Box 29546, Greensboro NC 27429. **E-mail:** editor@cavewallpress.com. **Website:** www.cavewall press.com. Biannual magazine dedicated to publishing the best in contemporary poetry. "Visit our website to see a few images of work we have published or purchase a sample copy. We are looking for fine art in b&w. Follow the submission guidelines on our website." Sample copy $5.

◯ "At the moment we are accepting art submissions year-round. This issue is subject to change. Refer to our website for updates. We publish graphic works and drawings in b&w with no gray values. We do not publish photography or other work with gray tones. Response time can take up to 4 months. Cave Wall acquires one-time publication rights for artwork."

ILLUSTRATION Illustrators paid $3,000-$4,500. 12-15 freelance illustrators/year.

FIRST CONTACT & TERMS Send postcard sample or e-mail with URL and samples. Send 5-10 8½×11 reproductions (photocopies accepted) to the address above. Include artist, title of work, medium, and date on the back of each print. If the work has been published before, please let us know where. Include SASE for response. Please do not send originals or other materials that need to be returned. If your work is accepted for publication, we will send you the specifications for submitting each piece as a digital file. Follow up every 6-12 months. Samples kept on file for possible future assignments. Samples are not returned. Buys all rights. Send query letter with b&w photocopies. Samples not kept on file, returned only by SASE. Responds in 1-3 months. Guidelines free with SASE, available on website or via e-mail request.

CED (COMMUNICATIONS, ENGINEERING & DESIGN)

Advantage Business Media, 100 Enterprize Dr., Suite 600, Rockaway NJ 07866. **E-mail:** brian.santo@ad vantagemedia.com. **Website:** www.cedmagazine. com. **Contact:** Brian Santo, editor. Estab. 1978. Circ. 25,000. Monthly trade journal; "the premier magazine of broadband technology." Sample copies and art guidelines available.

ILLUSTRATION Works on assignment only. Features caricatures of celebrities, realistic illustration, charts and graphs, informational graphics and computer illustrations. Prefers cable TV industry themes. Considers watercolor, airbrush, acrylic, colored pencil, oil, charcoal, mixed media, pastel, computer disk formatted in Photoshop, Illustrator or FreeHand.

FIRST CONTACT & TERMS Contact only through artist rep. Samples are filed. Portfolio should include final art, b&w/color tearsheets, photostats, photographs and slides. Rights purchased vary according to project. **Pays on acceptance.** Most illustration done in-house. Pays illustrators $400-800 for color cover; $125-400 for b&w and color inside; $250-500 for 2-page spreads; $75-175 for spots. Accepts previously published work. Original artwork not returned at job's completion.

TIPS "Be willing to change in mid course; be willing to have finished work rejected. Make sure you can draw and work fast."

CHARISMA

600 Rinehart Rd., Lake Mary FL 32746. (407)333-0600. **Fax:** (407)333-7100. **E-mail:** charisma@charismamedia.com; sean.roberts@charismamedia.com. **Website:** www.charismamedia.com. **Contact:** Joe Deleon, magazine design director. Circ. 200,000. Publishes religious magazines and books for general readership. Illustrations used for text illustrations, promotional materials, book covers, children and gift books, dust jackets. Illustration guidelines free with SASE.

FIRST CONTACT & TERMS Illustrators: Send nonreturnable promotional postcard, tearsheets, color copies or other appropriate promotional material. Accepts digital submissions. Send query letter with samples. Provide résumé, business card, brochure, flyer or tearsheets to be kept on file for possible future assignments. Works with freelancers on assignment only. Keeps samples on file. Simultaneous submissions and previously published work OK. Pays $5-75 for b&w; $50-550 for color spots; $100-550 for color covers. Payment negotiable. Pays on publication. Credit line given. Buys one-time, first-time, book, electronic and all rights; negotiable.

CHARLESTON MAGAZINE/CHARLESTON HOME/CHARLESTON WEDDINGS

P.O. Box 1794, Mt. Pleasant SC 29465-1794. (843)971-9811 or (888)242-7624. **E-mail:** mmonk@charlestonmag.com. **Website:** www.charlestonmag.com. **Contact:** Melinda Smith-Monk, art director. Estab. 1974. Circ. 20,000. Monthly 4-color consumer magazine. *Charleston Home* is quarterly, *Charleston Weddings* is 2 times/year with a more regional and national distribution. "Indispensible resource for information about modern-day Charleston SC, addresses issues of relevance and appeals to both visitors and residents." Art guidelines are free with #10 SASE and first-class postage.

ILLUSTRATION Approached by 35 illustrators/year. Buys 1 illustration/issue. Features realistic illustra-

tions, informational graphics, spot illustrations, computer illustration. Prefers business subjects, children, families, men, pets, women and teens. 35% of freelance illustration demands knowledge of Illustrator, Photoshop, FreeHand, PageMaker, QuarkXPress.

FIRST CONTACT & TERMS Illustrators: Send postcard sample and follow-up postcard every month or send query letter with printed samples. Accepts Mac-compatible disk submissions. Samples are filed or returned by SASE. Responds only if interested. Rights purchased vary according to project. Finds illustrators through sourcebooks, artists' promo samples, word of mouth.

TIPS "Our magazine has won several design awards and is a good place for artists to showcase their talent in print. We welcome letters of interest from artists interested in semester-long, unpaid internships-at-large. If selected, artists would provide 4-5 illustrations for publication in return for masthead recognition and sample tearsheets. Staff internships (unpaid) also available on-site in Charleston SC. Send letter of interest and samples of work to art director."

CHARLOTTE MAGAZINE

Morris Visitor Publications, 214 W. Tremont Ave., Suite 303, Charlotte NC 28203. (704)335-7181. **Fax:** (704)335-3757. **E-mail:** richard.thurmond@charlottemagazine.com. **Website:** www.charlottemagazine.com. **Contact:** Richard Thurmond, publisher. Circ. 40,000. Monthly 4-color city-based consumer magazine for Charlotte and surrounding areas. Sample copy for $6.

ILLUSTRATION Approached by many illustrators/year. Buys 1-5 illustrations/issue. Features caricatures of celebrities and politicians; computer illustration; humorous illustration; natural history, realistic and spot illustration. Prefers wide range of media/conceptual styles. Assigns 20% of illustrations to new and emerging illustrators.

FIRST CONTACT & TERMS Illustrators: Send postcard sample and follow-up postcard every 6 months. Send nonreturnable samples. Accepts e-mail submissions. Send EPS or TIFF files. Samples are filed. Responds only if interested. Portfolio review not required. Finds illustrators through promotional samples and sourcebooks.

TIPS "We are looking for diverse and unique approaches to illustration. Highly creative and conceptual styles are greatly needed. If you are trying to get your name out there, we are a great avenue for you."

CHEF

704 N. Wells St., 2nd Floor, Chicago IL 60654. (312)849-2220. **Fax:** (312)849-2174. **E-mail:** bwujcik@talcott.com. **Website:** www.chefmagazine.com. **Contact:** Barbara Wujcik, editor. Circ. 42,000. Trade publication for chefs who manage commercial and non-commercial kitchens, catering firms, restaurants, hotels/resorts/casinos, culinary schools, country clubs, universities, health care facilities. Reports on latest food service tools, food safety issues, and profiles on chefs.

CARTOONS Approached by 50 cartoonists/year. Buys 2 cartoons/year. Prefers cooking/chef related themes. Prefers single panel and humorous.

ILLUSTRATION Approached by 100 illustrators/year. Buys 5 illustrations/year. Features cooking, catering and cafeterias. Assigns 50% to new and emerging illustrators.

FIRST CONTACT & TERMS Cartoonists: Send 2-3 photocopies with link to website. Illustrators: Send postcard sample. After introductory mailing, send follow-up postcard every 6 months. Responds only if interested. At this time, no payment offered for cartoons or illustrations. Finds freelancers through artists' submissions.

TIPS "Only interested in work related to cooking, kitchens, chefs and catering."

CHEMICAL WEEK

IHS, 2 Grand Central Tower, 140 E. 45th St., 40th Floor, New York NY 10017. (212)884-9528. **Fax:** (212)884-9514. **Website:** www.chemweek.com. **Contact:** Nanette Santiago, global advertising sales. Estab. 1908. Circ. 23,000. Bimonthly, 4-color trade publication emphasizing commercial developments in specialty chemical markets.

ILLUSTRATION Features charts and graphs, computer illustration, informational graphics, natural history illustration, realistic illustrations, medical illustration of business subjects. Prefers bright colors and clean look. Assigns 100% of illustrations to experienced but not well-known illustrators. 100% of freelance illustration demands knowledge of Illustrator, Photoshop, QuarkXPress.

FIRST CONTACT & TERMS Illustrators: Send nonreturnable postcard sample and follow-up postcard every 6 months. Accepts Mac-compatible disk submis-

sions. Send EPS or TIFF files. Samples are filed and are not returned. Responds only if interested. Portfolio review not required. Rights purchased vary according to project. Pays on publication; $500-800 for color.

TIPS "Freelancers should be reliable and produce quality work. Promptness and the ability to meet deadlines are most important."

CHESAPEAKE BAY MAGAZINE

1819 Bay Ridge Ave., Annapolis MD 21403. (410)263-2662, ext. 32. **Fax:** (410)267-6924. **E-mail:** editor@chesapeakeboating.net. **Website:** www.chesapeakeboating.net. **Contact:** Ann Levelle, managing editor; T.F. Sayles, editor. Estab. 1972. Circ. 46,000. Monthly 4-color magazine focusing on the boating environment of the Chesapeake Bay, including its history, people, places, events, environmental issues and ecology. Original artwork returned after publication upon request. Sample copies free for SASE with first-class postage. Art guidelines available.

ILLUSTRATION Pays illustrators $75-200 for quarter-page or spot illustrations; up to $500-800 for spreads—4-color inside. Approached by 12 illustrators/year. Buys 2-3 technical and editorial illustrations/issue. Has featured illustrations by Jim Paterson, Kim Harroll, Jan Adkins, Tamzin B. Smith, Marcy Ramsey, Peter Bono, Stephanie Carter and James Yang. Assigns 50% of illustrations to new and emerging illustrators. Considers pen & ink, watercolor, collage, acrylic, marker, colored pencil, oil, charcoal, mixed media and pastel. Also digital. Usually prefers watercolor or acrylic for 4-color editorial illustration. "Style and tone are determined by the artist after he/she reads the story."

DESIGN "Our magazine design is relaxed, fun, and oriented toward people who enjoy recreation on the water. Boating interests remain the same. But for the Chesapeake Bay boater, water quality and the environment are more important now than in the past. Colors brighter. We like to see samples that show the artist can draw boats and understands our market environment. Send tearsheets or send website information. We're always looking. Artist should have some familiarity with the appearance of different types of boats, boating gear and equipment."

FIRST CONTACT & TERMS Illustrators: Send query letter with résumé, tearsheets and photographs. Samples are filed. Make sure to include contact information on each sample. Responds only if interested. Pub-

lication will contact artist for portfolio review if interested. Portfolio should include "anything you've got." No b&w photocopies. Buys one-time rights.
TIPS "Price decided when contracted."

CHESS LIFE

P.O. Box 3967, Crossville TN 38557. (931)787-1234. **Fax:** (931)787-1200. **E-mail:** dlucas@uschess.org; fbutler@uschess.org. **Website:** www.uschess.org. **Contact:** Daniel Lucas, editor; Francesca "Frankie" Butler, art director. Estab. 1939. Circ. 85,000. Official publication of the United States Chess Federation. Contains news of major chess events with special emphasis on American players, plus columns of instruction, general features, historical articles, personality profiles, tournament reports, cartoons, quizzes, humor and short stories. Monthly b&w with 4-color cover. Design is "heavy with chess games." Accepts previously published material and simultaneous submissions. Sample copy for SASE with 6 first-class stamps; art guidelines for SASE with first-class postage. *Chess Life* commissioned cover rate $400; inside full page $100; half page $50; quarter page $25. Works on assignment, but will also consider unsolicited work.
CARTOONS Approached by 5-10 cartoonists/year. Buys 0-12 cartoons/year. All cartoons must be chess related. Prefers single panel with gagline; b&w line drawings.
ILLUSTRATION Approached by 30-50 illustrators/year. Works with 4-5 illustrators/year from freelancers. Buys 4-5 illustrations/year. Uses artists mainly for cartoons and covers.
FIRST CONTACT & TERMS Send query letter with samples or e-mail Frankie Butler at fbutler@uschess.org. Responds in 2 months. Negotiates rights purchased. Pays on publication.

CICADA MAGAZINE

Cricket Magazine Group, 70 E. Lake St., Suite 800, Chicago IL 60601. **E-mail:** cicada@cicadamag.com. **Website:** www.cricketmag.com/cicada. **Contact:** submissions editor. Estab. 1998. Circ. 6,000. *Cicada* publishes comics, zines, visual poems, and any other work in image and/or text.
FIRST CONTACT & TERMS No advance list of themes. Do not query. Include exact word count. Prefers online submissions (submittable.cricketmag.com; www.cricketmag.com/submissions). Please allow 3-6 months response time. E-mail comics to cicada@cicadamag.com, subject line COMIC SUBMISSIONS.

CINCINNATI CITYBEAT

811 Race St., 5th Floor, Cincinnati OH 45202. (513)665-4700. **Fax:** (513)665-4368. **E-mail:** rsylvester@citybeat.com. **Website:** www.citybeat.com. Estab. 1994. Circ. under 50,000. Weekly alternative newspaper emphasizing Cincinnati issues, arts and events.
ILLUSTRATION Buys 6-12 illustrations/year. Assigns 90% of illustrations to local artists.
FIRST CONTACT & TERMS Illustrators: Submit PDF samples of work via e-mail, will respond only if interested. Please do not send paper samples. Buys one-time rights. Pays on publication.
TIPS "Please research alternative weeklies before contacting the art director. She reports receiving far too many inappropriate submissions."

CITY & SHORE MAGAZINE

500 E. Broward Blvd., 9th Floor, Ft. Lauderdale FL 33394-3019. (954)356-4686. **E-mail:** mgauert@sunsentinel.com. **Website:** www.cityandshore.com. **Contact:** Mark Gauert, editor and publisher. Estab. 2000. Circ. 42,000. Bimonthly "luxury lifestyle magazine published for readers in South Florida." Sample copies available for $4.95.
ILLUSTRATION "We rarely use illustrations, but when we do, we prefer sophisticated, colorful styles, with lifestyle-oriented subject matter. We don't use illustration whose style is dark or very edgy."
FIRST CONTACT & TERMS Accepts e-mail submissions with image file.

CITY LIMITS

Community Service Society of New York, 31 E. 32nd St., 3rd Floor, New York NY 10016. (212)481-8484, ext. 313. **E-mail:** editor@citylimits.org. **Website:** www. citylimits.org. **Contact:** Jarrett Murphy, executive editor and publisher. Estab. 1976. Monthly urban affairs magazine covering issues important to New York City's low- and moderate-income neighborhoods, including housing, community development, the urban environment, crime, public health and labor. Originals returned at job's completion. Sample copies for 9×12 SAE and 4 first-class stamps. "Our production schedule is tight, so publication is generally within 2 weeks of acceptance, as is payment."
CARTOONS Send query letter with finished cartoons and tearsheets. Buys 5 cartoons/year. Prefers N.Y.C. urban affairs—social policy, health care, environment and economic development. Prefers political cartoons; single, double or multiple panel b&w washes

and line drawings without gaglines. Buys first rights and reprint rights. Pays cartoonists $50 for b&w.

ILLUSTRATION Send postcard sample or query letter with tearsheets, photocopies, photographs and SASE. Buys 2-3 illustrations/issue. Has featured illustrations by Noah Scalin. Must address urban affairs and social policy issues, affecting low- and moderate-income neighborhoods, primarily in New York City. Considers pen & ink, watercolor, collage, airbrush, mixed media and anything that works in b&w. Samples are filed. Responds in 1 month. Request portfolio review in original query. Buys first rights. Pays $50-100 for b&w cover; $50 for b&w inside; $25-50 for spots. Pays on publication.

TIPS Finds artists through other publications, word of mouth and submissions. "Our niche is fairly specific. Freelancers are welcome to call and talk."

CKI MAGAZINE

Circle K International, 3636 Woodview Trace, Indianapolis IN 46268. (317)217-6174. **Fax:** (317)879-0204. **E-mail:** ckimagazine@kiwanis.org. **Website:** www.circlek.org. Estab. 1968. Circ. 12,000. Digital magazine published 1-4 times/year for college-age students, emphasizing service, leadership, etc. Free sample copy with SASE and 3 first-class postage stamps.

○ Kiwanis International also publishes *Kiwanis* and *Key Club* magazines.

ILLUSTRATION Approached by more than 30 illustrators/year. Buys 1-2 illustrations/issue. Works on assignment only. Needs editorial illustration. "We look for variety."

FIRST CONTACT & TERMS Send query letter with photocopies, photographs, tearsheets and SASE. Samples are filed. Will contact for portfolio review if interested. Portfolio should include tearsheets and slides. Originals and sample copies returned to artist at job's completion. **Pays on acceptance:** $100 for b&w cover; $250 for color cover; $50 for b&w inside; $150 for color inside.

CLARETIAN PUBLICATIONS

205 W. Monroe, Chicago IL 60606. (312)236-7782. **Fax:** (312)236-8207. **E-mail:** coxa@claretians.org. **Website:** www.claretianpubs.org. **Contact:** Angela Cox, design/production editor. Estab. 1960. Circ. 40,000. Monthly magazine "covering the Catholic family experience and social justice." Sample copies and art guidelines available.

ILLUSTRATION Approached by 20 illustrators/year. Buys 4 illustrations/issue. Considers all media.

FIRST CONTACT & TERMS Illustrators: Send postcard sample and query letter with printed samples and photocopies or e-mail with an attached website to visit. Accepts disk submissions compatible with EPS or TIFF. Samples are filed. Responds only if interested. Art director will contact artist for portfolio review if interested. Negotiates rights purchased. **Pays on acceptance.** $100-400 for color inside.

TIPS "We like to employ humor in our illustrations and often use clichés with a twist and appreciate getting art in digital form."

CLEVELAND MAGAZINE

City Magazines, Inc., 1422 Euclid Ave., Suite 730, Cleveland OH 44115. (216)771-2833. **Fax:** (216)781-6318. **E-mail:** gleydura@clevelandmagazine.com; miller@clevelandmagazine.com. **Website:** www.clevelandmagazine.com. **Contact:** Kristen Miller, design director; Steve Gleydura, editor. Estab. 1972. Circ. 50,000. Monthly city magazine, with 4-color cover, emphasizing local news and information.

CARTOONS "We do not publish gag cartoons, but do print editorial illustrations with a humorous twist."

ILLUSTRATION Approached by 100 illustrators/year. Buys 3-4 editorial illustrations/issue on assigned themes. Sometimes uses humorous illustrations. 40% of freelance work demands knowledge of InDesign, Illustrator or Photoshop. "Full-page editorial illustrations usually deal with local politics, personalities and stories of general interest. Generally, we are seeing more intelligent solutions to illustration problems and better techniques."

FIRST CONTACT & TERMS Please provide self-promotions, JPEG samples or tearsheets via e-mail or mail to be kept on file for possible future assignments. Responds if interested. Illustrators: Send postcard sample with brochure or tearsheets.

TIPS "Artists are used on the basis of talent. We use many talented college graduates just starting out in the field. The economy has drastically affected our budgets; we pick up existing work as well as commissioning illustrations."

CLOUD RODEO

E-mail: editors@cloudrodeo.org; submit@cloudrodeo.org. **Website:** cloudrodeo.org. "We want your problems deploying a term liek nonelen. We want your isolated photographs of immense locomotives slogged down by the delirium of drunken yet pristine jungles. We want the one eye you caught on fire doing alchemy. The world you collapsed playing architect. We want what you think is too. We want you to anesthetize this aesthetic. Your Enfer, your Ciel, your Qu'importe. We want all your to to sound out."

ILLUSTRATION "If you are sending us art, photography, audio, or any other medium, attach your work as a .JPEG, TIFF, PDF, RTF, WPF, GIF, PNG, or MP3/MP4A file. If somehow your work can't be transmitted or be best represented by these file types, shoot us an e-mail at editors@cloudrodeo.org, and we'll do our best to accommodate."

FIRST CONTACT & TERMS "Simultaneous submissions are encouraged provided you notify us if your work has found another cloud to call rodeo. Please send these notification e-mails as responses to your original submission. Please provide a little cover letter in the body of your e-mail even if it's just to say hi. We want to be able to say hi back. Please limit your submissions to 1 prose piece, 5 pieces of art, or 5 poems at a time. Should we publish your work, all we ask is for first electronic publishing rights. After that the rights will revert to you, although your work will be archived on the site where it will be available for you to spam your friends with, which we encourage wholeheartedly."

TIPS "Let's get weird."

COBBLESTONE

Cobblestone Publishing, 30 Grove St., Suite C, Peterborough NH 03458. **Website:** www.cobblestonepub.com. **Contact:** Meg Chorlian. Circ. 15,000. "Our magazine emphasizes American history; features nonfiction, supplemental nonfiction, fiction, biographies, plays, activities, and poetry for children ages 8-14." Accepts previously published material and simultaneous submissions. Sample copy $6.95 plus $2 s&h; art guidelines on website. Material must relate to theme of issue; subjects and topics published in guidelines for SASE. Freelance work demands knowledge of Illustrator, Photoshop, and QuarkXPress. Other magazines published by Cobblestone include *Calliope* (world history), *Dig* (archaeology for kids), *Faces* (cultural anthropology), *Odyssey* (science), all for kids ages 8-15, and *AppleSeeds* (social studies), for ages 7-9.

ILLUSTRATION Buys all rights. Pays on publication; $20-125 for b&w inside; $40-225 for color inside. Artists should request illustration guidelines. Buys 2-5 illustrations/issue. Prefers historical theme as it pertains to a specific feature. Works on assignment only. Has featured illustrations by Annette Cate, Beth Stover, David Kooharian. Features caricatures of celebrities and politicians, humorous, realistic illustration, informational graphics, computer and spot illustration. Assigns 15% of illustrations to new and emerging illustrators.

FIRST CONTACT & TERMS Send query letter with brochure, résumé, business card, and b&w photocopies or tearsheets to be kept on file or returned by SASE. Write for appointment to show portfolio.

TIPS "Study issues of the magazine for style used. Send update samples once or twice a year to help keep your name and work fresh in our minds. Send nonreturnable samples we can keep on file; we're always interested in widening our horizons."

COMMONWEAL

Commonweal Foundation, 475 Riverside Dr., Room 405, New York NY 10115. (212)662-4200. **Fax:** (212)662-4183. **E-mail:** editors@commonwealmagazine.org. **Website:** www.commonwealmagazine.org. **Contact:** Paul Baumann, editor; Tiina Aleman, production editor. Estab. 1924. Circ. 20,000. Journal of opinion edited by Catholic laypeople concerning public affairs, religion, literature and the arts, full color. Biweekly. See website to order complimentary copies and for submission guidelines. Become familiar with publication before mailing submissions.

CARTOONS Send query letter with finished cartoons. Approached by 20+ cartoonists/year. Buys 1-2 cartoons/issue from freelancers. Prefers simple lines and high-contrast styles. Prefers single panel, with or without gagline. Has featured cartoons by Baloo.

ILLUSTRATION Approached by 20+ illustrators/year. Buys 1-2 illustrations/issue from freelancers. Prefers high-contrast illustrations that speak for themselves. First contact: Send query letter with tearsheets, photographs. Send SASE and photocopies to Tiina Aleman, production editor. Samples are filed or returned by SASE if requested by artist. Responds in 4 weeks. To show a portfolio, mail tearsheets, photographs and photocopies. Buys nonexclusive rights.

TIPS Pays cartoonists $15. Pays illustrators $15. Pays on publication.

CONVERGENCE: AN ONLINE JOURNAL OF POETRY AND ART

E-mail: clinville@csus.edu. **Website:** www.conver gence-journal.com. **Contact:** Cynthia Linville, managing editor. Estab. 2003. "We look for well-crafted work with fresh images and a strong voice. Work from a series or with a common theme has a greater chance of being accepted. Seasonally-themed work is appreciated (spring and summer for the January deadline, fall and winter for the June deadline). Please include a 75-word bio with your work (bios may be edited for length and clarity). A cover letter is not needed. Absolutely no simultaneous or previously published submissions."

FIRST CONTACT & TERMS Submit up to 6 JPEGs of your work, no larger than 4MB each.

DAVID C. COOK

4050 Lee Vance View, Colorado Springs CO 80918. (719)536-0100; (800)708-5550. **Website:** www.da vidccook.com. Publisher of teaching booklets, books, take-home papers for Christian market, "all age groups." Art guidelines available for SASE with first-class postage only.

ILLUSTRATION Buys about 10 full-color illustrations/month. Has featured illustrations by Richard Williams, Chuck Hamrick and Ron Diciani. Assigns 5% of illustrations to new and emerging illustrators. Features realistic illustration, Bible illustration, computer and spot illustration. Works on assignment only.

FIRST CONTACT & TERMS Illustrators: Send tearsheets, color photocopies of previously published work; include self-promo pieces. No samples returned unless requested and accompanied by SASE. **Pays on acceptance;** $400-700 for color cover; $250-400 for color inside; $150-250 for b&w inside; $500-800 for 2-page spreads; $50-75 for spots. Considers complexity of project, skill and experience of artist, and turnaround time when establishing payment. Buys all rights.

TIPS "We do not buy illustrations or cartoons on speculation. Do *not* send book proposals. We welcome those just beginning their careers, but it helps if the samples are presented in a neat and professional manner. Our deadlines are generous but must be met. Fresh, dynamic, the highest of quality is our goal; art that appeals to everyone from preschoolers to senior citizens; realistic to humorous, all media."

COPING WITH CANCER

P.O. Box 682268, Franklin TN 37068-2268. (615)790-2400. **Fax:** (615)794-0179. **E-mail:** editor@copingmag. com; info@copingmag.com. **Website:** www.coping mag.com/cwc. Estab. 1987. Circ. 90,000. "*Coping With Cancer* is a bimonthly, nationally-distributed consumer magazine dedicated to providing the latest oncology news and information of greatest interest and use to its readers. Readers are cancer survivors, their loved ones, support group leaders, oncologists, oncology nurses and other allied health professionals. The style is very conversational and, considering its sometimes technical subject matter, quite comprehensive to the layman. The tone is upbeat and generally positive, clever and even humorous when appropriate, and very credible." Sample copy available for $3. Art guidelines for SASE with first-class postage. Guidelines are available on the website.

COSMOPOLITAN

Hearst Corp., 300 W. 57th St., New York NY 10019-3791. (212)649-2000. **E-mail:** cosmo@hearst.com; youtellcosmo@hearst.com. **Website:** www.cosmo politan.com. Estab. 1886. Circ. 3 million. Monthly 4-color consumer magazine for contemporary women covering a broad range of topics including beauty, health, fitness, fashion, relationships and careers.

ILLUSTRATION Approached by 300 illustrators/year. Buys 10-12 illustrations/issue. Features beauty, humorous and spot illustration. Preferred subjects include women and couples. Prefers trendy fashion palette. Assigns 5% of illustrations to new and emerging illustrators.

FIRST CONTACT & TERMS Send postcard sample and follow-up postcard every 4 months. Samples are filed. Responds only if interested. Buys first North American serial rights. Pays on acceptance. Finds illustrators through sourcebooks and artists' promotional samples.

CRICKET

Cricket Magazine Group, 70 E. Lake St., Suite 800, Chicago IL 60601. **Website:** www.cricketmag.com/ckt-cricket-magazine-for-kids-ages-9-14; www. cricketmagkids.com. **Contact:** Submissions editor. Estab. 1973. Circ. 73,000. Monthly literary magazine for young readers, ages 9-14. Art is commisssioned separately from text. Accepts illustrations in various media: pencil, ink, watercolor, acrylic, oil, pastels, scratchboard and woodcut. Guidelines available online at submittable.cricketmag.com or www.cricket-mag.com/submissions.

FIRST CONTACT & TERMS Send tearsheets or photocopies, each clearly labled with name, address and phone number. No advance list of themes. Do not query. Include exact word count. Prefers online submissions. Please allow 3-6 months response time.

TIPS "*Cricket* would like to reach as many children's illustrators and authors as possible for original contributions, but our standards are very high, and we will accept only top-quality material. Art should be realistic and humorous, but not caricatures or 'cartoony.'"

DAIRYBUSINESS

DairyBusiness Communications, 6437 Collamer Road, East Syracuse NY 13057. (315) 703-7979 ext: 229. **Website:** www.dairybusiness.com. Estab. 1922. Circ. 10,051. Monthly trade journals, *DairyBusiness West* and *DairyBusiness East*, with audience comprised of "Western-based milk producers, herd size 100 and larger, all breeds of cows, covering the 17 Western states." Accepts previously published artwork. Samples copies and art guidelines available. Not currently accepting freelance work for stories or photographs.

ILLUSTRATION Approached by 5 illustrators/year. Buys 1-4 illustrations/issue. Works on assignment only. Preferred themes "depend on editorial need." Considers 3D and computer illustration.

FIRST CONTACT & TERMS Send query letter with brochure, tearsheets and résumé. Samples are filed or are returned by SASE if requested by artist. Responds in 2 weeks. Write for appointment to show portfolio of thumbnails, tearsheets and photographs. Buys all rights. Pays on publication; $100 for b&w, $200 for color cover; $50 for b&w, $100 for color inside.

TIPS "We have a small staff. Be patient if we don't get back immediately. A follow-up letter helps. Being familiar with dairies doesn't hurt. Quick turnaround will put you on the 'A' list."

DAKOTA COUNTRY

P.O. Box 2714, Bismarck ND 58502. (701)255-3031. **Fax:** (701)255-5038. **E-mail:** dcmag@orbitcom.biz. **Website:** www.dakotacountrymagazine.com. **Contact:** Bill Mitzel, editor. Estab. 1979. Circ. 14,200. Monthly hunting and fishing magazine with readership in North and South Dakota. Features stories on hunting/fishing/conservation. Basic 3-column format, 2 and 4 columns accepted, glossy full-color

throughout magazine, 4-color cover, feature layout. Accepts previously published artwork. Original artwork is returned after publication. Sample copies for $4; art guidelines with SASE and first-class postage.

CARTOONS Likes to buy cartoons in volume. Prefers outdoor themes, hunting and fishing. Prefers multiple or single panel cartoon with gagline; b&w line drawings.

ILLUSTRATION Features humorous and realistic illustration of the outdoors. Portfolio review not required.

FIRST CONTACT & TERMS Send query letter with samples of style. Samples not filed are returned by SASE. Responds to queries/submissions within 2 weeks. Negotiates rights purchased. **Pays on acceptance.** Pays cartoonists $15 per cartoon, b&w. Pays illustrators $20-25 for b&w inside; $12-30 for spots.

TIPS "Always need good-quality hunting and fishing line art and cartoons."

DELAWARE TODAY MAGAZINE

3301 Lancaster Pike, Suite 5C, Wilmington DE 19805. (302)656-1809. **E-mail:** dostroski@delaware today.com. **Website:** www.delawaretoday.com. **Contact:** Drew Ostroski, managing editor. Circ. 25,000. Monthly 4-color magazine emphasizing regional interest in and around Delaware. Features general interest, historical, humorous, interview/profile, personal experience and travel articles. "The stories we have are about people and happenings in and around Delaware. Our audience is middle-aged (40-45) people with incomes around $79,000, mostly educated. We try to be trendy in a conservative state." Needs computer-literate freelancers for illustration.

ILLUSTRATION Buys approximately 1-2 illustrations/issue. Has featured illustrations by Nancy Harrison, Tom Deja, Wendi Koontz, Craig LaRontonda and Jacqui Oakley. "I'm looking for different styles and techniques of editorial illustration!" Works on assignment only. Open to all styles.

FIRST CONTACT & TERMS Send postcard sample. "Will accept work compatible with QuarkXPress 7.5/version 4.0. Send EPS or TIFF files (RGB)." Send printed color promos. Samples are filed. Responds only if interested. Publication will contact artist for portfolio review if interested. Portfolio should include printed samples, color or b&w tearsheets and final reproduction/product. Pays on publication; $200-400 for cover; $100-150 for inside. Buys first rights or one-time rights. Finds artists through submissions and self-promotions.

TIPS "Be conceptual, consistent and flexible."

DERMASCOPE MAGAZINE

Aesthetics International Association, 310 E. Interstate 30, Suite B107, Garland TX 75043. (469)429-9300. **Fax:** (469)429-9301. **E-mail:** amanda@dermascope.com. **Website:** www.dermascope.com. **Contact:** Amanda Strunk-Miller, managing editor. Estab. 1978. Circ. 16,000. Monthly magazine/trade journal, 128 pages, for aestheticians, plastic surgeons, and stylists. Articles should include quality images, graphs, or charts when available. Sample copies and art guidelines available.

ILLUSTRATION Approached by 5 illustrators/year. Prefers illustrations of "how-to" demonstrations. Considers digital media. 100% of freelance illustration demands knowledge of Photoshop, Illustrator, InDesign, Fractil Painter.

DUCTS

E-mail: vents@ducts.org. **Website:** www.ducts.org. **Contact:** Jonathan Kravetz, editor-in-chief. Estab. 1999. Circ. 12,000. Semiannual. *DUCTS* is a webzine of personal stories, fiction, essays, memoirs, poetry, humor, profiles, reviews and art. "*DUCTS* was founded in 1999 with the intent of giving emerging writers a venue to regularly publish their compelling, personal stories. The site has been expanded to include art and creative works of all genres. We believe that these genres must and do overlap. *DUCTS* publishes the best, most compelling stories and we hope to attract readers who are drawn to work that rises above."

FIRST CONTACT & TERMS Submission period is January 1 through August 31. Accepts submissions by e-mail to art@ducts.org. Guidelines on website.

THE EAST BAY MONTHLY

The Berkeley Monthly, Inc., 1305 Franklin St., Suite 501, Oakland CA 94612. (510)238-9101. **Fax:** (510)238-9163. **Website:** www.themonthly.com. Estab. 1970. Circ. 62,000. Monthly consumer tabloid; 4-color. Editorial features are general interests (art, entertainment, business owner profiles) for an upscale audience. Sample copy and guidelines available for SASE with 5-ounce first-class postage.

CARTOONS Approached by 75-100 cartoonists/year. Buys 3 cartoons/issue. Prefers single-panel, b&w line drawings; "any style, extreme humor."

ILLUSTRATION Approached by 150-200 illustrators/year. Buys 0-1 illustrations/issue. Prefers pen & ink, watercolor, acrylic, colored pencil, oil, charcoal, mixed media and pastel. No nature or architectural illustrations.

DESIGN Occasionally needs freelancers for design and production. 100% of freelance design requires knowledge of Adobe CS.

FIRST CONTACT & TERMS Cartoonists: Send query letter with finished cartoons, or e-mail kartoons@themonthly.com. Illustrators: Send postcard sample or query letter with tearsheets and photocopies, or e-mail artdirector@themonthly.com. Designers: Send query letter with résumé, photocopies, or tearsheets. Accepts submissions on CD, Mac-compatible with Adobe CS. Samples are filed or returned by SASE. Responds only if interested. Write for appointment to show portfolio of thumbnails, roughs, b&w tearsheets, and slides, or e-mail to artdirector@themonthly.com. Buys one-time rights. Pays 15 days after publication. Pays cartoonists $35 for b&w. Pays illustrators $100-200 for b&w inside; $25-50 for spots. Pays for design by project. Accepts previously published artwork. Originals returned at job's completion.

ELECTRICAL APPARATUS

Barks Publications, Inc., Suite 901, 500 N. Michigan Ave., Chicago IL 60611. (312)321-9440. **Fax:** (312)321-1288. **E-mail:** eamagazine@barks.com. **Website:** www.barks.com/eacurr.html. **Contact:** Elizabeth Van Ness, publisher; Kevin N. Jones, senior editor. Estab. 1967. Circ. 16,000. Monthly 4-color magazine emphasizing industrial electrical/mechanical maintenance. Original artwork not returned at job's completion. Sample copy $5.

CARTOONS Buys 3-4 cartoons/issue. Has featured illustrations by Joe Buresch, Martin Filchock, James Estes, John Paine, Bernie White and Mark Ziemann. Prefers themes relevant to magazine content; with gagline. "Captions are edited in our style."

ILLUSTRATION "We have staff artists, so there is little opportunity for freelance illustrators, but we are always glad to hear from anyone who believes he or she has something relevant to contribute."

FIRST CONTACT & TERMS Cartoonists: Send query letter. Responds in 3 weeks. Buys all rights. Pays $125-125 for b&w and color single panels and strips.

TIPS "We prefer single-panel cartoons that portray an industrial setting, ideally with an electrical bent.

We also use cartoons with more generic settings and tailor the gaglines to our needs."

ELECTRONIC MUSICIAN

NewBay Media, LLC., 28 E. 28th St., 12th Floor, New York NY 10016. (212)378-0400. **E-mail:** sjones@musicplayer.com; asavona@nbmedia.com. **Website:** www.emusician.com. **Contact:** Sarah Jones, editor; Tony Savona, vice president/content director. Estab. 1986. Circ. 30,000. Monthly consumer magazine for music how-to. Sample copies and art guidelines available on request.

CARTOONS Approached by 100 cartoonist/year. Buys 12 cartoons/year. Prefers humorous.

ILLUSTRATION Approached by 500 illustrators/year. Buys 12 illustrations/year. Has featured Colin Johnson, Kitty Meek. Prefers computer and realistic illustrations of music. Assigns 80% to new and emerging illustrators. 50% of freelance illustrations demands knowledge of whatever software they do best.

FIRST CONTACT & TERMS Cartoonists/Illustrators: Send postcard sample with samples and tearsheets. After introducing mailing, send follow-up postcard sampled every 6 months. Accepts e-mail submissions with link to website. Prefers Mac-compatible, JPEG files. Samples are filed. Company will contact artist for portfolio review if interested. Portfolio should include finished art. Pays cartoonists $100-400 for b&w. Pays illustrators $800-1,200 for color cover. Pays on publication. Buys one-time rights. Finds freelancers through artists' submissions.

ELLERY QUEEN'S MYSTERY MAGAZINE

Dell Magazines, 267 Broadway, 4th Floor, New York NY 10017. (212)686-7188. **Fax:** (212)686-7414. **E-mail:** elleryqueenmm@dellmagazines.com. **Website:** www.themysteryplace.com/eqmm. **Contact:** Jackie Sherbow, assistant editor. Estab. 1941. Circ. 100,000. Emphasizes mystery stories and reviews of mystery books. Art guidelines available online.

Also publishes *Alfred Hitchcock Mystery Magazine, Analog,* and *Asimov's Science Fiction.*

CARTOONS "We are looking for cartoons with an emphasis on mystery, crime, and suspense."

ILLUSTRATION Prefers line drawings. All other artwork is done in house.

FIRST CONTACT & TERMS Now accepting online submissions. Cartoons should be addressed to Jackie Sherbow, assistant editor. Illustrators: Accepts disk submissions. Responds in 3 months. **Pays on accep**tance; $1,200 for color covers; $125 for b&w interior art. Considers all media in b&w and halftones. Accepts finished art on disk.

TIPS "Please see our magazine before submitting samples."

EMERGENCY MEDICINE

7 Century Dr., Suite 302, Parsippany NJ 07054-4609. **E-mail:** mdales@frontlinemedcom.com; imnews@frontlinemedcom.com. **Website:** www.emedmag.com. **Contact:** Mary Jo Dales, editorial director. Estab. 1969. Circ. 80,000. Emphasizes emergency medicine for emergency physicians, emergency room personnel, medical students. Monthly. Returns original artwork after publication. Art guidelines not available.

ILLUSTRATION Works with 10 illustrators/year. Buys 1-2 illustrations/issue. Has featured illustrations by Scott Bodell, Craig Zuckerman and Steve Oh. Features realistic, medical and spot illustration. Assigns 70% of illustrations to well-known or "name" illustrators; 30% to experienced, but not well-known illustrators. Works on assignment only.

FIRST CONTACT & TERMS Send postcard sample or query letter with brochure, photocopies, photographs, tearsheets to be kept on file. Samples not filed are not returned. Accepts disk submissions. To show a portfolio, mail appropriate materials. Responds only if interested. Buys first rights. Pays $1,200-1,700 for color cover; $200-500 for b&w inside; $500-800 for color inside; $250-600 for spots.

ESQUIRE

300 W. 57th St., 21st Floor, New York NY 10019. (212)649-4020. **Website:** www.esquire.com. Estab. 1933. Circ. 720,000. Contemporary culture magazine for men ages 28-40 focusing on current events, living trends, career, politics, and the media.

FIRST CONTACT & TERMS Illustrators: Send postcard mailers. Drop off portfolio on Wednesdays for review.

EVENT

Douglas College, P.O. Box 2503, New Westminster British Columbia V3L 5B2, Canada. (604)527-5293. **Fax:** (604)527-5095. **E-mail:** event@douglascollege.ca. **Website:** www.eventmags.com. Estab. 1971. Circ. 1,000. For "those interested in literature and writing" b&w with 4-color cover. Published 3 times/year. Art guidelines available on website.

CARTOONS No cartoons or illustrations.

ILLUSTRATION Buys approximately 3 photographs/year. Has featured photographs by Mark Mushet, Lee Hutzulak and Anne de Haas. Assigns 50% of photographs to new and emerging photographers. Uses freelancers mainly for covers. "We look for art that is adaptable to a cover, particularly images that are self-sufficient and don't lead the reader to expect further artwork within the journal. Please send photography/artwork (no more than 10 images) to *EVENT*, along with SASE (Canadian postage, or IRCs, or USD $1) for return of your work. We also accept e-mail submissions of cover art. We recommend that you send low-res versions of your photography/art as small JPEG or PDF attachments. If we are interested, we will request high-res files. We do not buy the actual piece of art; we only pay for the use of the image." Pays $150 on publication. Credit line given. Buys one-time rights.

TIPS "On the cover of each issue we present the work of a notable or up-and-coming Canadian visual artist. It is our goal to support and encourage a thriving literary community in Canada while maintaining our international reputation for excellence."

FAMILY CIRCLE

Meredith Corp., 805 Third Ave., 24th Floor, New York NY 10022. **Website:** www.familycircle.com. Lisa Kelsey, art director. **Contact:** Cassie Kreitner, editorial assistant; Lisa Kelsey, art director. Estab. 1932. Circ. 4.2 million. Supermarket-distributed publication for women/homemakers covering areas of food, home, beauty, health, child care and careers. 17 issues/year. Submissions should focus on families with children ages 8-16. Does not accept previously published material. Original artwork returned after publication.

ILLUSTRATION Buys 2-3 illustrations/issue. Works on assignment only.

FIRST CONTACT & TERMS Provide query letter with nonreturnable samples or postcard sample to be kept on file for future assignments. Do not send original work. Prefers transparencies, postcards or tearsheets as samples. Responds only if interested. Prefers to see finished art in portfolio. Submit portfolio by appointment. All art is commissioned for specific magazine articles. Negotiates rights. **Pays on acceptance.**

FAST COMPANY

7 World Trade Center, New York NY 10007-2195. (212) 389-5300. **Fax:** (212) 389-5496. **E-mail:** pr@fastcompany.com. **Website:** www.fastcompany.com. **Contact:** Lori Hoffman, managing editor. Estab. 1996. Circ. 750,000. Monthly cutting edge business publication supplying readers with tools and strategies for business today.

ILLUSTRATION Approached by "tons" of illustrators/year. Buys approximately 20 illustrations/issue. Has used illustrations by Bill Mayer, Ward Sutton and David Cowles. Considers all media.

FIRST CONTACT & TERMS Illustrators: Send postcard sample or printed samples, photocopies. Accepts disk submissions compatible with QuarkXPress for Mac. Send EPS files. Send all samples to the attention of Julia Moburg. Samples are filed and not returned. Responds only if interested. Rights purchased vary according to project. **Pays on acceptance**: $300-1,000 for color inside; $300-500 for spots. Finds illustrators through submissions, illustration annuals, *Workbook* and *Alternative Pick*.

FAULTLINE JOURNAL OF ART & LITERATURE

University of California, Irvine, Dept. of English, 435 Humanities Instructional Bldg., Irvine CA 92697-2650. (949)824-1573. **E-mail:** faultline@uci.edu. **Website:** faultline.sites.uci.edu. Pushcart prize-winning journal. "We publish new poetry, fiction, translations, and artwork in an annual spring issue, and feature the work of emerging and established writers from the US and abroad."

"Even though this is not a paying market, this high-quality literary magazine would be an excellent place for fine artists to gain exposure. Postcard samples with a website address are the best way to show us your work."

FIRST CONTACT & TERMS Submit up to 5 8×10 color or b&w prints for consideration. Slides might be required if accepted.

FEDERAL COMPUTER WEEK

1105 Media, Inc., 8609 Westwood Center Dr., Suite 500, Vienna VA 22182. (703)876-5100; (703) 876-5096. **E-mail:** tschneider@fcw.com. **Website:** www. fcw.com. **Contact:** Troy Schneider, editor-in-chief. Estab. 1987. Circ. 120,000. Trade publication for federal, state and local government information technology professionals.

ILLUSTRATION Approached by 50-75 illustrators/year. Buys 5-6 illustrations/month. Features charts & graphs, computer illustrations, informational graphics, spot illustrations of business subjects. Assigns 5%

of illustrations to well-known or "name" illustrators; 85% to experienced but not well-known illustrators; 10% to new and emerging illustrators.

FIRST CONTACT & TERMS Send postcard or other nonreturnable samples. Accepts Mac-compatible disk submissions. Samples are filed. Will contact artist for portfolio review if interested. Rights purchased vary according to project. Pays $800-1,200 for color cover; $600-800 for color inside; $200 for spots. Finds illustrators through samples and sourcebooks.

TIPS "We look for people who understand 'concept' covers and inside art, and very often have them talk directly to writers and editors."

FLORIDA REALTOR

7025 Augusta National Dr., Orlando FL 32822-5017. (407)438-1400. **Fax:** (407)438-1411. **E-mail:** magazine@floridarealtors.org. **Website:** www.floridarealtors.org/magazine. Estab. 1925. Circ. 104,562. Monthly trade publication covers news and issues of the Florida real estate industry, including sales practices, brokerage management, market trends, legislation and legal matters.

FIRST CONTACT & TERMS Approached by 100 illustrators/year. Buys 10 illustrations/year. Features real estate professionals at work. Send postcard samples with URL. After introductory mailing, send follow-up postcard sample every 6 months. Pays illustrators $100 for color inside. Pays on publication. Buys one-time rights. Finds freelancers through artists' submissions.

FOCUS ON THE FAMILY

8605 Explorer Dr., Colorado Springs CO 80920. (719)531-5181. **Fax:** (719)531-3424. **E-mail:** help@focusonthefamily.com. **Website:** www.family.org. Estab. 1977. Circ. 2.7 million. Publishes magazines. Specializes in religious-Christian. Publishes 12 titles/year.

FIRST CONTACT & TERMS Send query letter with photocopies, printed samples, résumé, SASE and tearsheets portraying family themes. Send follow-up postcard every year. Samples are filed. Responds in 2 weeks. Will contact artist for portfolio review of photocopies of artwork portraying family themes if interested. Buys first, one-time or reprint rights. Finds freelancers through agents, sourcebooks and submissions.

FOGGED CLARITY

(231)670-7033. **E-mail:** editor@foggedclarity.com; submissions@foggedclarity.com. **Website:** www.foggedclarity.com. **Contact:** Editors. Estab. 2008. Circ. between 15,000 and 22,000 visitors per month. *Fogged Clarity* is an arts review that accepts submissions of poetry, fiction, nonfiction, music, visual art, and reviews of work in all mediums. We seek art that is stabbingly eloquent. Our print edition is released once every year, while new issues of our online journal come out at the beginning of every month. Artists maintain the copyrights to their work until they are monetarily compensated for said work. If your work is selected for our print edition and you consent to its publication, you will be compensated."

FIRST CONTACT & TERMS Reviews GIF, JPEG, PNG, TIFF, PSD, AI, and PDF files, at least 700 pixels.

FOLIATE OAK LITERARY MAGAZINE

University of Arkansas-Monticello, P.O. Box 3460, Monticello AR 71656. (870)460-1247. **E-mail:** foliateoak@uamont.edu. **Website:** www.foliateoak.com. **Contact:** Online submission manager. Estab. 1973. Circ. 500. "We are a university general literary magazine publishing new and established artists." Has featured Terry Wright, Brett Svelik, Lucita Peek, David Swartz and Fariel Shafee.

FIRST CONTACT & TERMS Online submission manager must be used to submit all artwork.

TIPS "We are unable to pay our contributors but we love to support freelancers. We solicit work for our online magazine and our annual print anthology. Read submission guidelines online."

FOLIO:

10 Norden Place, Norwalk CT 06855. (203)854-6730; (203) 899-8433; (203) 899-8427. **Fax:** (203)854-6735. **E-mail:** bmickey@accessintel.com. **Website:** www.foliomag.com. **Contact:** Bill Mickey, editor. Circ. 9,380. Trade magazine covering the magazine publishing industry. Sample copies with SASE and first-class postage.

ILLUSTRATION Approached by 200 illustrators/year. Buys 150-200 illustrations/year. Works on assignment only. Artists' online galleries welcome in lieu of portfolio.

FIRST CONTACT & TERMS Illustrators: Send postcard samples or photocopies or other appropriate samples. No originals. Samples are filed and returned by SASE if requested by artist. Responds only if interested. Call for appointment to show portfolio of tearsheets, slides, final art, photographs and transparencies. Buys one-time rights. Pays by the project. **TIPS** "Art director likes to see printed 4-color and b&w sample illustrations. Do not send originals unless requested. Computer-generated illustrations are used but not always necessary. Charts and graphs must be Mac-generated."

● FOLIO

10 Gate St., Lincoln's Inn Fields, London WCZA 3HP, United Kingdom. +44 0207 242 9562. **Fax:** +44 0207 242 1816. **E-mail:** info@folioart.co.uk. **Website:** www. folioart.co.uk. "Folio is an illustration agency based in London. We pride ourselves on representing illustrators and artists of a particularly high quality and versatility." Exclusive representation required. Finds new talent through submissions and recommendations. **FIRST CONTACT & TERMS** "Send a query letter, bio, résumé and digital images. Will respond if interested. Portfolio should include b&w, roughs, finished art and digital images."

◑ FOODSERVICE AND HOSPITALITY

Kostuch Media, Ltd., 23 Lesmill Rd., #101, Toronto Ontario M3B 3P6, Canada. (416)447-0888. **Fax:** (416)447-5333. **E-mail:** web@kostuchmedia.com. **Website:** www.foodserviceworld.com. **Contact:** Margaret Moore, art director. Estab. 1973. Circ. 25,000. Monthly business magazine for foodservice industry/operators. Sample copies available. Art guidelines available.
◯ Also publishes *Hotelier Magazine*.
ILLUSTRATION Approached by 30 illustrators/year. Buys 1 illustration/issue. Prefers serious/businessy/stylized art for *Hotelier Magazine*; casual free and fun style for *Foodservice and Hospitality*. Considers all media.
FIRST CONTACT & TERMS Illustrators: Send query letter with printed samples and tearsheets or postcards. Samples are filed. Responds only if interested. Art director will contact artist for portfolio review of final art and tearsheets if interested. Portfolios may be dropped off every Monday and Tuesday. Buys one-time rights. Pays on publication; $500 minimum for color cover; $300 minimum for color inside. Finds illustrators through sourcebooks, word of mouth, artist's submissions.

FORBES MAGAZINE

499 Washington Blvd., Jersey City NJ 07310. (800)295-0893; (212) 620-1887. **E-mail:** readers@forbes.com. **Website:** www.forbes.com. **Contact:** art director or editors. Estab. 1917. Circ. 950,000. Biweekly business magazine read by company executives and those who are interested in business and investing. Art guidelines not available.
ILLUSTRATION Assigns 20% of illustrations to new and emerging illustrators.
FIRST CONTACT & TERMS "Assignments are made by one of 5 art directors. We do not use, nor are we liable for, ideas or work that a *Forbes* art director didn't assign. We prefer contemporary illustrations that are lucid and convey an unmistakable idea with wit and intelligence. No cartoons please. Illustration art must be rendered on a material and size that can be separated on a drum scanner or submitted digitally. We are prepared to receive art on ZIP, Scitex, CD, floppy disk, or downloaded via e-mail. Discuss the specifications and the fee before you accept the assignment. **Pays on acceptance** whether reproduced or not. Pays up to $3,000 for a cover assignment and an average of $450 to $700 for an inside illustration depending on complexity, time and the printed space rate. Dropping a portfolio off is encouraged. Deliver portfolios by 11 a.m. and plan to leave your portfolio for a few hours or overnight. Call first to make sure an art director is available. Address the label to the attention of the Forbes Art Department and the individual you want to reach. Attach your name and local phone number to the outside of the portfolio. Include a note stating when you need it. Robin Regensberg, the art traffic coordinator, will make every effort to call you to arrange for your pickup. Samples: Do not mail original artwork. Send printed samples, scanned samples or photocopies of samples. Include enough samples as you can spare in a portfolio for each person on our staff. If interested, we'll file them. Otherwise they are discarded. Samples are returned only if requested."
TIPS "Look at the magazine to determine if your style and thinking are suitable. The art director and associate art directors are listed on the masthead, located within the first ten pages of an issue. The art directors make assignments for illustration. We get a large number of requests for portfolio reviews and many mailed promotions daily. This may explain why, when you follow up with a call, we may not be able to acknowledge receipt of your samples. If the work is

memorable and we think we can use your style, we'll file samples for future consideration."

GAME & FISH

3330 Chastain Meadows Pkwy. NW, Suite 200, Kennesaw GA 30144. (770)953-9222. **Fax:** (678)279-7512. **E-mail:** ken.dunwoody@imoutdoors.com. **Website:** www.gameandfishmag.com. **Contact:** Ken Dunwoody, editorial director; Ron Sinfelt, photo editor; Allen Hansen, graphic artist. Estab. 1975. Circ. 570,000 for 28 state-specific magazines. Publishes 29 different monthly outdoor magazines, each covering the fishing and hunting opportunities in a particular state or region (see individual titles to contact editors). Original artwork is returned after publication. Sample copies available.

ILLUSTRATION Approached by 50 illustrators/year. Buys illustrations mainly for spots and feature spreads. Buys 1-5 illustrations/issue. Considers pen & ink, watercolor, acrylic, and oil.

FIRST CONTACT & TERMS Illustrators: Send query letter with photocopies. "We look for an artist's ability to realistically depict North American game animals and game fish or hunting and fishing scenes." Samples are filed or returned only if requested. Responds only if interested. Portfolio review not required. Buys first rights. Pays 2½ months prior to publication; $25 minimum for b&w inside; $75-100 for color inside.

TIPS "We do not publish cartoons, but we do use some cartoonlike illustrations which we assign to artists to accompany specific humor stories. Send us some samples of your work, showing as broad a range as possible, and let us hold on to them for future reference. Being willing to complete an assigned illustration in a 4-6 week period and providing what we request will make you a candidate for working with us."

⍟ GEORGIA MAGAZINE

Georgia Electric Membership Corp., P.O. Box 1707, Tucker GA 30085. (770)270-6500. **Fax:** (770)270-6995. **E-mail:** ann.orowski@georgiaemc.com. **Website:** www.georgiamagazine.org. **Contact:** Ann Orowski, editor. Estab. 1945. Circ. 516,000. Monthly consumer magazine promoting electric co-ops. "*GEORGIA Magazine* is the most widely read magazine for and about Georgians. Each issue celebrates the Georgia lifestyle in word and photo, revealing the spirit of its people and the flavor of its past in a friendly, conversational tone. Feature articles and departments focus on what's in it for the reader, bringing home the story in a useful, personal way that touches their lives directly. Copies are mailed each month to members of Georgia's electric co-ops."

CARTOONS Approached by 20 cartoonists/year. Buys 2 cartoons/year. Prefers electric industry theme. Prefers single-panel, humorous, 4-color or b&w washes and line drawings.

ILLUSTRATION Approached by 20 illustrators/year. Prefers electric industry theme. Considers all media. 50% of freelance illustration demands knowledge of Illustrator, InDesign and QuarkXPress.

DESIGN Uses freelancers for design and production. Prefers local designers with magazine experience. 80% of design demands knowledge of Photoshop, Illustrator, QuarkXPress and InDesign.

FIRST CONTACT & TERMS Cartoonists: Send query letter with photocopies. Samples are filed and not returned. Illustrators: Send postcard sample or query letter with photocopies. Designers: Send query letter with printed samples and photocopies. Accepts disk submissions compatible with QuarkXPress and InDesign. Samples are filed or returned by SASE. Responds in 3 months if interested. Rights purchased vary according to project. **Pays on acceptance.** Pays cartoonists $50 for b&w, $50-100 for color. Pays illustrators $50-100 for b&w, $50-200 for color. Finds illustrators through word of mouth and submissions.

GLAMOUR

Conde Nast Publications, Inc., 4 Times Square, 16th Floor, New York NY 10036. (212)286-2860. **Fax:** (212)286-8336. **Website:** www.glamour.com. **Contact:** Cynthia Leive, editor-in-chief. Estab. 1939. Circ. 2,374,170. Monthly. Covers fashion and issues concerning working women (ages 20-35). Originals returned at job's completion. Sample copies available on request. 5% of freelance work demands knowledge of Illustrator, QuarkXPress, Photoshop and FreeHand.

CARTOONS Buys 1 cartoon/issue.

ILLUSTRATION Buys 1 illustration/issue. Works on assignment only. Considers all media.

FIRST CONTACT & TERMS Illustrators: Send postcard-size sample. Samples are filed and not returned. Publication will contact artist for portfolio review if interested. Rights purchased vary according to project. Pays on publication.

GLAMOUR LATINOAMERICA

Conde Nast, 4 Times Square, New York NY 10036. (212)286-2860. **E-mail:** miguelgarcia@condenast.

com. **Website:** www.glamour.mx. **Contact:** art director. Estab. 1998. Circ. 406,760. Monthly consumer magazine for the contemporary Hispanic woman. Covers the latest trends in fashion and beauty, health, relationships, careers and entertainment.

ILLUSTRATION Approached by 100 illustrators/year. Buys 40 illustrations/year. Features fashion caricatures of celebrities, fashion illustration and spot illustrations. Assigns 10% to new and emerging illustrators. Illustrators: Send postcard sample with link to website. After introductory mailing, send follow-up postcard sample every 6 months. Responds only if interested.

FIRST CONTACT & TERMS Illustrators: $150-400 for color inside. Buys one-time rights. Finds freelancers through submissions.

THE GOLFER

59 E. 72nd St., New York NY 10021. (212)867-7070. **Fax:** (212)867-8550. **E-mail:** info@thegolferinc.com. **Website:** www.thegolferinc.com. Estab. 1994. Circ. 253,000. Bimonthly "sophisticated golf magazine with an emphasis on travel and lifestyle."

ILLUSTRATION Approached by 200 illustrators/year. Buys 6 illustrations/issue. Considers all media.

FIRST CONTACT & TERMS Send postcard sample. "We will accept work compatible with QuarkXPress 3.3. Send EPS files." Samples are not filed and are not returned. Responds only if interested. Rights purchased vary according to project. Pays on publication. Payment to be negotiated.

TIPS "I like sophisticated, edgy, imaginative work. We're looking for people to interpret sport, not draw a picture of someone hitting a ball."

GOLF TIPS MAGAZINE

Werner Publishing Corp., 12121 Wilshire Blvd., 12th Floor, Los Angeles CA 90025-1176. (310)820-1500. **Fax:** (310)820-5008. **E-mail:** editors@golftipsmag. com. **Website:** www.golftipsmag.com. Estab. 1986. Circ. 300,000. Monthly 4-color consumer magazine featuring golf instruction articles.

ILLUSTRATION Approached by 100 illustrators/year. Buys 3 illustrations/issue. Has featured illustrations by Phil Franke, Scott Matthews, Ed Wexler. Features charts and graphs, humorous illustration, informational graphics, realistic and medical illustration. Preferred subjects men and women. Prefers realism or expressive, painterly editorial style or graphic humorous style. Assigns 30% of illustrations to well-known or

"name" illustrators; 50% to experienced but not well-known illustrators; 20% to new and emerging illustrators. 15% of freelance illustration demands knowledge of Illustrator, Photoshop and FreeHand.

FIRST CONTACT & TERMS Submission guidelines available online at www.golftipsmag.com/submissions.html. Illustrators: Send postcard or other nonreturnable samples. Accepts Mac-compatible disk submissions. Send EPS or TIFF files. Samples are filed. Will contact artist for portfolio review if interested. Rights purchased vary according to project. Pays on publication; $500-700 for color cover; $100-200 for b&w inside; $250-500 for color inside; $500-700 for 2-page spreads. Finds illustrators through *LA Workbook*, *Creative Black Book* and promotional samples.

TIPS "Look at our magazine and you will see straightforward, realistic illustration, but I am also open to semi-abstract, graphic humorous illustration, gritty, painterly, editorial style, or loose pen & ink and watercolor humorous style."

⌂ GRAND RAPIDS MAGAZINE

Gemini Publications, 549 Ottawa Ave. NW, Suite 201, Grand Rapids MI 49503. (616)459-4545. **Fax:** (616)459-4800. **E-mail:** cvalade@geminipub.com. **Website:** www.grmag.com. Estab. 1964. Circ. 20,000. Monthly general interest life and style magazine designed for those who live in the Grand Rapids metropolitan area or desire to maintain contact with the community. Original artwork returned after publication. Local artists only.

CARTOONS Buys 2-3 cartoons/issue. Prefers Michigan, Western Michigan, Lake Michigan, city, issue, consumer/household, fashion, lifestyle, fitness and travel themes.

ILLUSTRATION Buys 2-3 illustrations/issue. Prefers Michigan, Western Michigan, Lake Michigan, city, issue, consumer/household, fashion, lifestyle, fitness and travel themes.

FIRST CONTACT & TERMS Cartoonists/illustrators: Send query letter with samples. Samples not filed are returned by SASE. Responds in 1 month. To show a portfolio, mail printed samples and final reproduction/product or call for an appointment. Buys all rights. Pays on publication. Pays cartoonists $35-50 for b&w. Pays illustrators $200 minimum for color cover; $40 minimum for b&w inside; $40 minimum for color inside.

TIPS "Particular interest in those who are able to capture the urban lifestyle."

GREENPRINTS

P.O. Box 1355, Fairview NC 28730. (828)628-1902. **E-mail:** pat@greenprints.com. **Website:** www.greenprints.com. **Contact:** Pat Stone, managing editor. Estab. 1990. Circ. 11,000. Quarterly magazine "that covers the personal, not the how-to, side of gardening." Sample copy for $5; art guidelines available on website or free with #10 SASE and first-class postage.

ILLUSTRATION Approached by 46 illustrators/year. Works with 15 illustrators/issue. Has featured illustrations by Claudia McGehee, P. Savage, Marilynne Roach and Jean Jenkins. Assigns 30% of illustrations to emerging and 5% to new illustrators. Prefers plants and people. Considers b&w only.

TIPS "Read our magazine and study the style of art we use. Can you do both plants and people? Can you interpret as well as illustrate a story?"

GUERNICA MAGAZINE

112 W. 27th St., Suite 600, New York NY 10001. **E-mail:** editors@guernicamag.com; art@guernicamag.com; publisher@guernicamag.com. **Website:** www.guernicamag.com. **Contact:** See masthead online for specific editors. Estab. 2005. "*Guernica*, published bi-weekly, is one of the web's most acclaimed new magazines. 2009: *Guernica* is called a 'great online literary magazine' by *Esquire*. *Guernica* contributors come from dozens of countries and write in nearly as many languages."

FIRST CONTACT & TERMS Submit via online submissions manager.

GUITAR PLAYER

NewBay Media, LLC, c/o Guitar World, 28 E. 28th St., 12th Floor, New York NY 10016. (212) 378-0400. **E-mail:** asavona@nbmedia.com. **Website:** www.guitarplayer.com. **Contact:** Tony Savona, vice president/corporate director. Estab. 1975. Circ. 150,000. Monthly 4-color magazine focusing on technique, artist interviews, etc.

ILLUSTRATION Approached by 15-20 illustrators/week. Buys 5 illustrations/year. Works on assignment only. Features caricatures of celebrities; realistic, computer and spot illustration. Assigns 33% of illustrations to new and emerging illustrators. Prefers conceptual, "outside, not safe" themes and styles. Considers pen & ink, watercolor, collage, airbrush, digital, acrylic, mixed media and pastel.

FIRST CONTACT & TERMS Send query letter with brochure, tearsheets, photographs, photocopies, photostats, slides and transparencies. Accepts Mac-compatible disk submissions. Samples are filed. Responds only if interested. Will contact artist for portfolio review if interested. Buys first rights. Pays on publication.

HADASSAH MAGAZINE

50 W. 58th St., New York NY 10019. (212)688-0227. **Fax:** (212)446-9521. **E-mail:** magazine@hadassah.org. **Website:** www.hadassah.org/magazine. **Contact:** Elizabeth Barnea. Circ. 255,000. Bimonthly consumer magazine chiefly of and for Jewish interests—both in the US and in Israel.

ILLUSTRATION Approached by 50 freelance illustrators/year. Works on assignment only. Features humorous, realistic, computer and spot illustration. Prefers themes of news, Jewish/family, Israeli issues, holidays.

FIRST CONTACT & TERMS Samples are filed or are returned by SASE. Write for appointment to show portfolio of original/final art, tearsheets and slides. Buys first rights. Pays on publication. Payment depends on size and usage.

HARPER'S MAGAZINE

666 Broadway, 11th Floor, New York NY 10012. (212)420-5720. **Fax:** (212)228-5889. **E-mail:** readings@harpers.org; scg@harpers.org. **Website:** www.harpers.org. **Contact:** Ellen Rosenbush, editor. Estab. 1850. Circ. 230,000. Monthly 4-color literary magazine. "The nation's oldest continually published magazine providing fiction, satire, political criticism, social criticism, essays." *Harper's Magazine* encourages national discussion on current and significant issues in a format that offers arresting facts and intelligent opinions.

ILLUSTRATION Approached by 250 illustrators/year. Buys 5-10 illustrations/issue. Has featured illustrations by Ray Bartkus, Steve Brodner, Istvan Banyai, Andrea Ventura, Hadley Hooper, Ralph Steadman, Raymond Verdaguer, Andrew Zbihlyj, Danijel Zezelj. Features intelligent concept-oriented illustration. Preferred subjects: literary, artistic, social, fiction-related. Prefers intelligent, original thought and imagery in any media. Assigns 25% of illustrations to new and emerging illustrators.

TIPS "Intelligence, originality, and beauty in execution are what we seek. A wide range of styles is appropriate; what counts most is content."

HEARTLAND BOATING

The Waterways Journal, Inc., 319 N. Fourth St., Suite 650, St. Louis MO 63102. (314)241-4310. **Fax:** (314)241-4207. **E-mail:** brad@heartlandboating.com. **Website:** www.heartlandboating.com. **Contact:** Brad Kovach, editor. Estab. 1989. Circ. 10,000. "*Heartland Boating's* content is both informative and inspirational—describing boating life as the heartland boater knows it. The content reflects the challenge, joy, and excitement of our way of life afloat. We are devoted to both power and sailboating enthusiasts throughout middle America; houseboats are included. The focus is on the freshwater inland rivers and lakes of the heartland, primarily the waters of the Arkansas, Tennessee, Cumberland, Ohio, Missouri, Illinois, and Mississippi rivers, the Tennessee-Tombigbee Waterway, the Gulf Intracoastal Waterway, and the lakes along these waterways." Samples kept on file. Portfolio not required. Credit line given.

FIRST CONTACT & TERMS Send query letter with samples or postcard sample. No follow-ups.

TIPS "Please read the magazine first. Our rates are low, but we do our best to take care of and promote our contributors. Remember to include your contact info, all of it! Please make it easy to find you."

HIGH COUNTRY NEWS

119 Grand Ave., P.O. Box 1090, Paonia CO 81428. (970)527-4898. **E-mail:** editor@hcn.org; cindy@hcn.org. **Website:** www.hcn.org. **Contact:** Cindy Wehling, art director. Estab. 1970. Circ. 25,000. Biweekly nonprofit newspaper. Covers environmental, public lands and community issues in the 10 western states.

CARTOONS Buys 1 editorial cartoon/issue. Only issues affecting Western environment. Prefers single panel, political, humorous on topics currently being covered in the paper. Color or b&w. Professional quality only.

ILLUSTRATION Considers all media if reproducible.

FIRST CONTACT & TERMS Cartoonists: Send query letter with finished cartoons and photocopies. Illustrators: Send query letter with printed samples and photocopies. Accepts e-mail and disk submissions compatible with QuarkXPress and Photoshop. Samples are filed or returned by SASE. Responds only if interested. Rights purchsed vary according to project. Pays on publication. Pays cartoonists $50-125 depending on size used. Pays illustrators $100-200 for color cover; $35-100 for inside. Finds illustrators through magazines, newspapers and artist's submissions. Mail photos to the attention of Cindy Wehling, art director, or via e-mail at cindy@hcn.org.

HIGHLIGHTS FOR CHILDREN

803 Church St., Honesdale PA 18431. (570)253-1080. **Fax:** (570)251-7847. **Website:** www.highlights.com. **Contact:** Christine French Cully, editor-in-chief. Estab. 1946. Circ. approximately 1.5 million. Monthly 4-color magazine for children ages 6-12. Art guidelines available on Highlights.com.

CARTOONS Interested in upbeat, positive cartoons involving children, family life or animals; single or multiple panel. "One flaw in many submissions is that the concept or vocabulary is too adult, or that the experience necessary for its appreciation is beyond our readers. Frequently, a wordless self-explanatory cartoon is best."

ILLUSTRATION Buys 30 illustrations/issue. Works on assignment only. Prefers "realistic and stylized work; upbeat, fun, more graphic than cartoon." Pen & ink, colored pencil, watercolor, marker, cut paper and mixed media are all acceptable. Discourages work in fluorescent colors.

FIRST CONTACT & TERMS Cartoonists: Send roughs or finished cartoons and SASE. Illustrators: Send query letter with photocopies, SASE and tearsheets. Samples are kept on file. Buys all rights on a work-for-hire basis. **Pays on acceptance.** Pays cartoonists $20-40 for line drawings. Pays illustrators $50-$700 for color inside. "We are always looking for good hidden pictures. We require a picture that is interesting in itself and has the objects well-hidden. Usually an artist submits pencil sketches. In no case do we pay for any preliminaries to the final hidden pictures. Hidden pictures should be submitted to Juanita Galuska."

TIPS "We have a wide variety of needs, so I would prefer to see a representative sample of an illustrator's style."

HOME BUSINESS MAGAZINE

20711 Holt Ave., #807, Lakeville MN 55044. **E-mail:** editor@homebusinessmag.com. **Website:** www.homebusinessmag.com. Estab. 1993. Circ. 105,000. Bimonthly consumer magazine. "*Home Business Magazine* covers every angle of the home-based business market including: cutting edge editorial by well-known authorities on sales and marketing, business operations, the home office, franchising, business opportunities, network marketing, mail order and other subjects to help readers choose, manage and prosper in a home-based business; display advertising, classified ads and a directory of home-based businesses; technology, the Internet, computers and the future of home-based business; home-office editorial including management advice, office set-up, and product descriptions; business opportunities, franchising and work-from-home success stories." Sample copies free for 10×13 SASE and $2.53 in first-class postage.

ILLUSTRATION Approached by 100 illustrators/year. Buys several illustrations/issue. Features natural history illustration, realistic illustrations, charts & graphs, informational graphics, spot illustrations and computer illustration of business subjects, families, men and women. Prefers pastel and bright colors. Assigns 40% of illustrations to well-known or "name" illustrators; 40% to experienced but not well-known illustrators; 20% to new and emerging illustrators. 100% of freelance illustration demands knowledge of Illustrator and QuarkXPress.

FIRST CONTACT & TERMS Illustrators: Send query letter with printed samples, photocopies and SASE. Send electronically as JPEG files. Responds only if interested. Will contact artist for portfolio review if interested. Buys reprint rights. Negotiates rights purchased. Pays on publication. Finds illustrators through magazines, word of mouth or via Internet.

HOME EDUCATION MAGAZINE

P.O. Box 1083, Tonasket WA 98855. (800)236-3278; (509)486-1351. **Fax:** (509)486-2753. **E-mail:** articles@homeedmag.com. **Website:** www.homeedmag.com. **Contact:** Jeanne Faulconer, articles editor. Estab. 1983. Circ. 120,000. "We publish one of the largest magazines available for homeschooling families." Desktop bimonthly published in full color; 4-color glossy cover. Original artwork is returned after publication upon request. Sample copy $6.50. Guidelines available via e-mail.

CARTOONS Approached by 15-20 cartoonists/year. Buys 1-2/year. Style preferred is open, but theme must relate to home schooling. Prefers single, double or multiple panel b&w line drawings and washes with or without gagline.

FIRST CONTACT & TERMS Cartoonists: Send query letter with samples of style, roughs and finished cartoons, "any format is fine with us." Accepts disk submissions. "We're looking for originality, clarity, warmth. Children, families and parent-child situations are what we need." Samples are filed or are returned by SASE. Responds in 3 weeks. Will contact for portfolio review if interested. Buys one-time rights, reprint rights or negotiates rights purchased. **Pays on acceptance.** Pays cartoonists $10-20 for b&w. Finds artists primarily through submissions and self-promotions.

TIPS "Most of our artwork is produced by staff artists. We receive very few good cartoons. Study what we've done in the past, suggest how we might update or improve it."

HONOLULU MAGAZINE

PacificBasin Communications, 1000 Bishop St., Suite 405, Honolulu HI 96813. (808)537-9500. **Fax:** (808)537-6455. **E-mail:** kristinl@honolulumagazine.com. **Website:** www.honolulumagazine.com. **Contact:** Kristin Lipman, senior art director; Michael Keany, managing editor. Estab. 1888. Circ. 30,000. Monthly 4-color city/regional magazine reporting on current affairs and issues, people profiles, lifestyle. Readership is generally upper income (based on subscription). Contemporary, clean, colorful and reader-friendly design. Original artwork is returned after publication. Sample copies for SASE with first-class postage. Art guidelines available free for SASE.

ILLUSTRATION Buys illustrations mainly for spots and feature spreads. Buys 2-6 illustrations/issue. Has featured illustrations by Rob Barber, Dean Hayashi and Charlie Pedrina. Assigns 10% of illustrations to new and emerging illustrators. Works on assignment only. Considers any media but not pencil work.

FIRST CONTACT & TERMS Illustrators: Send postcard or published sample showing art style. Looks for local subjects, conceptual abilities for abstract subjects (editorial approach) likes a variety of techniques. Knowledge of Hawaii a must. Samples are filed or are returned only if requested with a SASE. Responds only if interested. Write to schedule an appointment to show a portfolio which should include original/final art and color and b&w tearsheets. Buys first rights or one-time rights. Pays 60 days after publication; $300-500 for cover; $100-350 for inside; $75-

150 for spots. Finds artists through word of mouth, magazines, submissions, attending art exhibitions.

TIPS "Needs both feature and department illustration—best way to break in is with small spot illustration. Prefers art on ZIP disk or e-mail. Friendly and professional attitude is a must. Be a very good conceptual artist, professional, fast, and, of course, a sense of humor."

HORSE ILLUSTRATED

I-5 Publishing, P.O. Box 12106, Lexington KY 40580. (800)546-7730. **E-mail:** horseillustrated@i5pub lishing.com. **Website:** www.horseillustrated.com. **Contact:** Elizabeth Moyer, editor. Estab. 1976. Circ. 160,660. Monthly consumer magazine providing "information for responsible horse owners." Art guidelines available on website.

○ "Readers are primarily adult horsewomen, ages 18-40, who ride and show mostly for pleasure, and who are very concerned about the well being of their horses."

HORTICULTURE

F+W, a Content + eCommerce Company, 10151 Carver Rd., Suite #200, Blue Ash OH 45242. (513)531-2690. **Fax:** (513)891-7153. **E-mail:** edit@hortmag.com. **Website:** www.hortmag.com. Circ. 160,000. Monthly magazine for all levels of gardeners (beginners, intermediate, highly skilled). "*Horticulture Magazine* strives to inspire and instruct avid gardeners of every level." Art guidelines available.

ILLUSTRATION Approached by 75 freelance illustrators/year. Buys up to 3 illustrations/issue. Works on assignment only. Features realistic illustration; informational graphics; spot illustration. Assigns 20% of illustrations to new and emerging illustrators. Prefers tight botanicals; garden scenes with a natural sense to the clustering of plants; people; hands and "how-to" illustrations. Considers all media.

FIRST CONTACT & TERMS Send query letter with brochure, résumé, SASE, tearsheets, slides. Samples are filed or returned by SASE. Art director will contact artist for portfolio review if interested. Buys one-time rights. Pays 1 month after project completed. Payment depends on complexity of piece; $800-1,200 for 2-page spreads; $150-250 for spots. Finds artists through word of mouth, magazines, submissions/self-promotions, sourcebooks, agents/reps, art exhibits.

HOW MAGAZINE

F+W, a Content + eCommerce Company, 10151 Carver Rd., Suite 200, Blue Ash OH 45242. (513)531-2690. **E-mail:** bridgid.mccarren@fwcommunity.com; edito rial@howdesign.com. **Website:** www.howdesign.com. **Contact:** Bridgid McCarren, community content director. Estab. 1985. Circ. 40,000. Bimonthly trade journal covering creativity, business and technology for graphic designers. Sample copy available for $8.50.

○ Sponsors 2 annual conferences for graphic artists, as well as annual Promotion, International, Interactive and In-House Design competitions. See website for more information.

ILLUSTRATION Approached by 100 illustrators/year. Buys 4-8 illustrations/issue. Works on assignment only. Considers all media, including photography and computer illustration.

FIRST CONTACT & TERMS Illustrators: Send nonreturnable samples. Accepts disk submissions. Responds only if interested. Buys first rights or reprint rights. Pays on publication: $350-1,000 for color inside. Original artwork returned at job's completion.

TIPS "Send good samples that reflect the style and content of illustration commonly featured in the magazine. Be patient; art directors get a lot of samples."

IEEE SPECTRUM

3 Park Ave., 17th Floor, New York NY 10016. (212)419-7555. **E-mail:** m.montgomery@ieee.org; b.palacio@ieee.org; e.vrielink@ieee.org. **Website:** www.spec trum.ieee.org. **Contact:** Mark Montgomery, senior art director; Brandon Palacio, deputy art director; Erik Vrielink, associate art director. Estab. 1964. Circ. 400,000. Monthly nonprofit technology magazine serving electrical and electronics engineers worldwide.

ILLUSTRATION Buys 5-7 illustrations/issue. Features editorial illustrations and informational graphics. Preferred subjects include technology and science. Assigns 30% to new and emerging illustrators.

FIRST CONTACT & TERMS Illustrators: Send samples in print or digital formats, or URL to online portfolio. Samples are filed and are not returned. Responds only if interested. Art director will contact artist for portfolio review if interested. Purchases print edition first rights and permanent rights for website and future digital editions. **Pays on acceptance.** Finds illustrators through *American Showcase, Workbook.*

TIPS "Our primary needs are artists who can interpret complex technical information into compelling editorial concepts and information graphics."

⊕ IMAGE BY DESIGN LICENSING

Suite 3, 107 Bancroft, Hitchin, Herts SG4 1NB, United Kingdom. 44(0) 1462 422244. **E-mail:** lucy@ibd-licensing.co.uk. **Website:** www.ibd-licensing.co.uk. **Contact:** Lucy Brenham. Agency specializing in art licensing. Serves fine artists, illustrators, and photographers. Interested in reviewing fine art, design, and photography.

FIRST CONTACT & TERMS Send a link to a website with résumé, bio, brochure of work, photocopies or digital images in low-res JPEG format.

TIPS "Be aware of current trends."

⊕ THE INDEPENDENT WEEKLY

P.O. Box 1772, Durham NC 27702. (919)286-1972. **Fax:** (919)286-4274. **E-mail:** mmills@indyweek.com. **Website:** www.indyweek.com. **Contact:** Maxine Mills, art director. Circ. 50,000. Weekly 4-color cover tabloid; general interest alternative.

ILLUSTRATION Buys 5-10 illustrations/year. Prefers local (North Carolina) illustrators. Has featured illustrations by Tyler Bergholz, Keith Norvel, V. Cullum Rogers, Nathan Golub. Works on assignment only. Considers pen and ink; b&w, computer generated art and color.

FIRST CONTACT & TERMS Samples are filed or are returned by SASE if requested. Responds only if interested. Pays on publication; $150 for cover illustrations; $25-50 for inside illustrations.

TIPS "Have a political and alternative point of view. Understand the peculiarities of newsprint. Be easy to work with. No prima donnas."

INDUSTRYWEEK

The Penton Media Bldg., 1300 E. Ninth St., Cleveland OH 44114. (216)696-7000. **E-mail:** Bill.Szilagyi@penton.com. **Website:** www.industryweek.com. **Contact:** Bill Szilagyi, art director. Estab. 1882. Circ. 200,000+. Weekly business magazine written for industry executives and key decision makers looking for insight into the latest business developments in the manufacturing world.

ILLUSTRATION Approached by 150 illustrators/year. Buys 75 illustrations/year. Has featured illustrations by Patrick Corrigan, Dave Joly, Vala Kondo. Features humorous, informational and spot illustrations of business. Assigns 10% to new and emerging illustra-tors. 10% of freelance illustration demands knowledge of Illustrator.

FIRST CONTACT & TERMS Illustrators: Send query letter with URL. After introductory mailing, send follow-up postcard sample every 2-3 months. Accepts e-mail submissions with link to website. Prefers JPEG files. Samples are filed. Responds only if interested. Art director will contact artist for portfolio review if interested. Pays illustrators $250-700 for color inside. Pays on publication. Buys one-time rights. Finds freelancers through artists' submissions.

IN THE FRAY

113 Schumacher Dr., New Hyde Park NY 11040-3644. (347)850-3935. **E-mail:** art@inthefray.org. **Website:** www.inthefray.org. **Contact:** Benjamin Gottlieb, art director. Estab. 2001. Biweekly, online publication. In the Fray publishes personal stories on global issues, with the goal of understanding other people and encouraging empathy and tolerance.

CARTOONS Approached by 1-2 cartoonists. Does not currently purchase cartoons, but has in the past.

ILLUSTRATION Approached by 20 freelance illustrators each year. Does not currently purchase illustrations, but has in the past. Feature realistic illustration, informational graphics, computer illustration, spot illustrations, humorous and caricatures of celebrities/politicians. Preferred subjects include children, families, men, women, teens and politics. Gives 100% of assignments to new and emerging illustrators.

FIRST CONTACT & TERMS Send e-mail with JPEG samples at 72 dpi. Keeps samples on file, please provide business card to be kept on file for possible future assignments. Responds only if interested, send non-returnable samples. Company will contact artist for portfolio review if interested.

ISLANDS

460 N. Orlando Ave., Suite 200, Winter Park FL 32789. (407)628-4802. **E-mail:** editor@islands.com. **Website:** www.islands.com. **Contact:** Audrey St. Clair, managing editor. Estab. 1981. Circ. 500,000. 4-color travel magazine "exclusively about islands," published 8 times/year. Internships available for graphic artist students, photography, etc. Latest print issue has apps.

ILLUSTRATION Buys 0-1 illustrations/issue. Needs editorial illustration. Considers all media.

FIRST CONTACT & TERMS Illustrators: Send query letter with tearsheets. Samples are filed. Responds only if interested. Buys first rights or one-time rights.

Pays on acceptance; $100-400 per image inside. Original artwork returned after publication.

JEWISH ACTION

Orthodox Union, 11 Broadway, New York NY 10004. (212)613-8146. **Fax:** (212)613-0646. **E-mail:** ja@ou.org. **Website:** www.ou.org/jewish_action. **Contact:** Nechama Carmel, editor; Rashel Zywica, assistant editor. Estab. 1986. Circ. 40,000. Quarterly magazine "published by Orthodox Union for members and subscribers. Orthodox Jewish contemporary issues." Sample copies can be seen on website.

CARTOONS Approached by 2 cartoonists/year. Prefers themes relevant to Jewish issues. Prefers single, double or multiple panel, political, humorous b&w washes and line drawings with or without gaglines.

ILLUSTRATION Approached by 4-5 illustrators. Considers all media. Assigns 50% of illustrations to experienced but not well-known illustrators; 50% to new and emerging illustrators. Knowledge of Photoshop, Illustrator and QuarkXPress "not absolutely necessary, but preferred."

DESIGN Needs freelancers for design and production. Prefers local design freelancers only.

FIRST CONTACT & TERMS Send query letter with photocopies and SASE. Accepts disk submissions. Prefer QuarkXPress TIFF or EPS files. Can send ZIP disk. Samples are not filed and are not returned. Responds only if interested. Art director will contact artist for portfolio review of photographs if interested. Buys one-time rights. Pays within 6 weeks of publication. Pays cartoonists $20-50 for b&w. Pays illustrators $25-75 for b&w, $50-300 for color cover; $50-200 for b&w, $25-150 for color inside. Finds illustrators through submissions.

TIPS Looking for "sensitivity to Orthodox Jewish traditions and symbols. Be aware that models must be clothed in keeping with Orthodox laws of modesty. Make sure to include identifying details. Don't send work depicting religion in general. We are specifically Orthodox Jewish."

JOURNAL OF ACCOUNTANCY

AICPA, 220 Leigh Farm Rd., Durham NC 27707. (919)402-4500. **Fax:** (919)402-4505. **E-mail:** mjohnstone@aicpa.org. **Website:** www.aicpa.org; www.journalofaccountancy.com. **Contact:** Michael Schad Johnstone, art director. Circ. 400,000. Monthly 4-color magazine of the American Institute of Certified Public Accountants that focuses on the latest news and developments related to the field of accounting for CPAs; corporate/business format.

ILLUSTRATION Approached by 200 illustrators/year. Buys 2-6 illustrations/issue. Prefers business, finance and law themes. Accepts mixed media, pen & ink, airbrush, colored pencil, watercolor, acrylic, oil, pastel and digital. Works on assignment only. 35% of freelance work demands knowledge of Illustrator, QuarkXPress and FreeHand.

FIRST CONTACT & TERMS Send query letter with brochure showing art style. Samples not filed are returned by SASE. Portfolio should include printed samples and tearsheets. Buys first rights. Pays on publication: $1,200 for color cover; $200-600 for color inside. Accepts previously published artwork. Original artwork returned after publication. Finds artists through submissions/self-promotions, sourcebooks and magazines.

TIPS "We look for indications that an artist can turn the ordinary into something extraordinary, whether it be through concept or style. In addition to illustrators, I also hire freelancers to do charts and graphs. In portfolios, I like to see tearsheets showing how the art and editorial worked together."

KALEIDOSCOPE

701 S. Main St., Akron OH 44311-1019. (330)762-9755. **Fax:** (330)762-0912. **E-mail:** kaleidoscope@udsakron.org. **Website:** www.kaleidoscopeonline.org. **Contact:** Gail Willmott, editor-in-chief. Estab. 1979. Art of all media, from watercolor and charcoals to collage, sculpture, and photography; 5-10 works maximum.

FIRST CONTACT & TERMS Art must be submitted at 72 dpi, RGB, JPEG files. The photos should have neutral background with the art as the main focus. Include caption information including title, dimensions, and medium. All rights revert to artist upon publication.

KASHRUS MAGAZINE

The Kashrus Institute, P.O. Box 204, Brooklyn NY 11204. (718)336-8544. **E-mail:** editorial@kashrusmagazine.com. **Website:** www.kashrusmagazine.com. **Contact:** Rabbi Wikler, editor. Estab. 1981. Circ. 10,000. "The periodical for the kosher consumer. We feature updates including mislabeled kosher products and recalls. Important for vegetarians, lactose intolerant and others with allergies."

CARTOONS Prefers food, dining, or Jewish humor cartoons.

FIRST CONTACT & TERMS Send query letter with photographs, call for follow-up. Byline given. Pays on publication. Submit seasonal materials 2 months in advance. Responds in 2 weeks.

◎ KC MAGAZINE

Anthem Publishing, 4303 W. 119th St., Leawood KS 66209. (913)894-6923. **Website:** www.kcmag.com. Estab. 1994. Circ. 31,000. Monthly lifestyle-oriented magazine, celebrating living in Kansas City. "Life's Better in KC" including: dining, shopping, home décor, and local personalities." Sample copies available with SASE and first-class postage, or online.

ILLUSTRATION Approached by 100-200 illustrators/year. Buys 3-5 illustrations/issue. Works on assignment only. Prefers conceptual editorial style. Considers all media. 25% of freelance illustration demands knowledge of Illustrator and Photoshop. Prefers local freelancers only.

DESIGN Does not need freelancers for design and production. Prefers local freelancers only. 100% of freelance work demands knowledge of Photoshop, Illustrator, and QuarkXPress.

FIRST CONTACT & TERMS Illustrators: Send postcard-size sample or query letter with tearsheets, photocopies, and printed samples. Accepts disk submissions compatible with Mac files (EPS, TIFF, Photoshop, etc.). Samples are filed. Will contact artist for portfolio review if interested. **Pays on acceptance;** rates vary by project.

TIPS "We have a high-quality, clean, cultural, creative format. Look at magazine before you submit."

KENTUCKY LIVING

Kentucky Association of Electric Co-Ops, P.O. Box 32170, Louisville KY 40232. (800)595-4846. **Fax:** (502)459-1611. **E-mail:** e-mail@kentuckyliving.com. **Website:** www.kentuckyliving.com. **Contact:** Paul Wesslund, editor; Anita Travis Richter, managing editor. Estab. 1948. Circ. 500,000. Monthly 4-color magazine emphasizing Kentucky-related and general feature material for Kentuckians living outside metropolitan areas.

CARTOONS Approached by 10-12 cartoonists/year.

ILLUSTRATION Buys occasional illustrations. Works on assignment only. Prefers b&w line art.

FIRST CONTACT & TERMS Illustrators: Send query letter with résumé and samples. Samples not filed are returned only if requested. Buys one-time rights. **Pays on acceptance.** Pays cartoonists $30 for b&w. Pays illustrators $50 for b&w inside. Accepts previously published material. Original artwork returned after publication if requested.

KEY CLUB MAGAZINE

Kiwanis International, 3636 Woodview Trace, Indianapolis IN 46268. (317)875-8755. **E-mail:** keyclub@kiwanis.org; memberservices@kiwanis.org. **Website:** www.keyclub.org. Circ. 275,000. One printed/digital and one digital-only annual magazine with "contemporary design for mature teenage audience." Free sample copy for SASE with 3 first-class postage stamps.

◎ Kiwanis International also publishes *Circle K* and *Kiwanis* magazines; see separate listings in this section.

ILLUSTRATION Buys 3 editorial illustrations/issue. Works on assignment only.

FIRST CONTACT & TERMS Include SASE. Responds in 2 weeks. Simultaneous submissions OK. Original artwork is returned after publication by request. Buys first rights. Pays on receipt of invoice: $50 for b&w inside and $150 for color inside.

KIPLINGER'S PERSONAL FINANCE

1100 13th St. NW, Washington DC 20005. (202)887-6400; (646) 695-7046. **E-mail:** jbodnar@kiplinger.com; alex@rosengrouppr.com. **Website:** www.kiplinger.com. **Contact:** Janet Bodnar, editor; Stacie Harrison, art director; Alex Kutler, account executive. Estab. 1947. Circ. 800,000. Monthly 4-color magazine covering personal finance issues such as investing, saving, housing, cars, health, retirement, taxes and insurance.

ILLUSTRATION Approached by 350 illustrators/year. Buys 4-6 illustrations/issue. Works on assignment only. Has featured illustrations by Alison Sieffer, Harry Campbell, Dan Page, Mark Smith, A. Richard Allen and James O'Brien. Features computer, conceptual editorial and spot illustration. Assigns 5% of illustrations to new and emerging illustrators. Interested in editorial illustration in new styles, including computer illustration.

FIRST CONTACT & TERMS Illustration: Send postcard or e-mail samples. Accepts Mac-compatible CD submissions. Samples are filed or returned by SASE if requested by artist. Will contact artist for portfolio review if interested. Buys one-time rights. Pays on publication; $400-1,200 for color inside; $250-500 for spots. Finds illustrators through reps, online, magazines, *Workbook* and award books. Originals are returned at job's completion.

LADYBUG

Cricket Magazine Group, 700 E. Lake St., Suite 800, Chicago IL 60601. **Website:** www.cricketmag.com/ladybug; ladybugmagkids.com. **Contact:** submissions editor. Estab. 1990. Circ. 125,000. Monthly 4-color magazine emphasizing literature and activities for children ages 3-6. Art by assignment only (see submission guidelines for details about submitting portfolio samples). Guidelines available online at submittable.cricketmag.com or www.cricketmag.com/submissions.

FIRST CONTACT & TERMS "When reviewing submissions, the editors look for clear and beautiful language, a sense of joy and wonder, and a genuinely childlike point of view." No advance list of themes. Do not query. Include exact word count. Prefers online submissions. Please allow 3-6 months response time.

LATINA

Latina Media Ventures, LLC, 625 Madison Ave, 3rd Floor, New York NY 10022. (212)642-0200. **Fax:** (212)575-3088. **E-mail:** editor@latina.com; info@latina.com. **Website:** www.latina.com. Estab. 1996. Circ. 397,447. Monthly consumer magazine for Hispanic women living in the United States who have strong ties to their Latin roots. Features articles on successful Latina women, health, careers, family life, fitness, parenting, fashion, beauty and entertainment.

ILLUSTRATION Approached by 100 illustrators/year. Buys 10-15 illustrations/year. Features caricatures of Hispanic celebrities, humorous illustration and spot illustrations of families and women. Assigns 25% to new and emerging illustrators.

FIRST CONTACT & TERMS Send postcard sample with URL. After introductory mailing, send follow-up postcard sample every 4-6 months. Responds only if interested. Pays $100-400 for color inside. Buys one-time rights. Find freelancers through submissions.

LOG HOME LIVING

Home Buyer Publications, Inc., 4125 Lafayette Center Dr., Suite 100, Chantilly VA 20151. (703)222-9411; (800)826-3893. **Fax:** (703)222-3209. **E-mail:** editor@timberhomeliving.com. **Website:** www.loghome.com. Estab. 1989. Circ. 132,000. Monthly 4-color magazine "dealing with the aspects of buying, building and living in a log home. We emphasize upscale living (decorating, furniture, etc)." Accepts previously published

artwork. Sample copies not available. Art guidelines with SASE with first-class postage. 20% of freelance work demands knowledge of QuarkXPress, Illustrator and Photoshop.

ILLUSTRATION Buys 2-4 illustrations/issue. Works on assignment only. Prefers editoral illustration with "a strong style—ability to show creative flair with not-so-creative a subject." Considers watercolor, airbrush, colored pencil, pastel and digital illustration.

DESIGN Needs freelancers for design and production occasionally. 100% of freelance work demands knowledge of Photoshop, Illustrator, QuarkXPress and InDesign.

FIRST CONTACT & TERMS Illustrators: Send postcard sample. Designers: Send query letter with brochure, résumé, and samples. Accepts disk submissions compatible with Illustrator, Photoshop and QuarkXPress. Samples are filed. Publication will contact artist for portfolio review if interested. Portfolio should include thumbnails, roughs, printed samples or color tearsheets. Buys all rights. **Pays on acceptance.** Pays illustrators $100-200 for b&w inside; $250-800 for color inside; $100-250 for spots. Pays designers by the project. Finds artists through submissions/self-promotions, sourcebooks.

THE LOOKOUT

Standard Publishing, 8805 Governor's Hill Dr., Suite 400, Cincinnati OH 45249. (513)931-4050. **Fax:** (513)931-0950. **E-mail:** lookout@standardpub.com. **Website:** www.lookoutmag.com. **Contact:** Kelly Carr, editor. Estab. 1894. Circ. 35,000. Weekly 4-color magazine for conservative Christian adults and young adults. Sample copy available for $1.

ILLUSTRATION "We no longer publish cartoons."

TIPS "Do not send e-mail submissions, unless we ask to see them on speculation; we publish strictly by theme list."

ⓦ LOS ANGELES MAGAZINE

5900 Wilshire Blvd., 10th Floor, Los Angeles CA 90036. (323)801-0100. **Fax:** (323)801-0105. **E-mail:** lamagedit@lamag.com. **Website:** www.losangelesmagazine.com. Circ. 170,000. Monthly 4-color magazine with a contemporary, modern design, emphasizing lifestyles, cultural attractions, pleasures, problems and personalities of Los Angeles and the surrounding area. Especially needs very localized contributors—custom projects needing person-to-person concepting and implementation. Previously published work

OK. 10% of freelance work demands knowledge of QuarkXPress, Illustrator and Photoshop.

ILLUSTRATION Buys 10 illustrations/issue on assigned themes. Prefers general interest/lifestyle illustrations with urbane and contemporary tone. To show a portfolio, send or drop off samples showing art style (tearsheets, photostats, photocopies and dupe slides).

FIRST CONTACT & TERMS Pays on publication; negotiable.

TIPS "Show work similar to that used in the magazine. Study a particular publication's content, style and format. Then proceed accordingly in submitting sample work. We initiate contact of new people per *Showcase* reference books or promo flyers sent to us. Portfolio viewing is all local."

LUCKY

Conde Nast Publications, 4 Times Square, 6th Floor, New York NY 10036. (212)286-2860. **Fax:** (212)286-4654. **E-mail:** feedback@luckymag.com; lucky-community@tid.al. **Website:** www.luckymag.com. Estab. 2002. Circ. 1,161,200. Monthly consumer magazine focusing on shopping, fashion, beauty and lifestyles for women. Provides upbeat, practical tips on shopping, latest fashion accessories and new items.

ILLUSTRATION Approached by hundreds of illustrators/year. Buys 35 illustrations/year. Features fashion illustration, humorous illustration and spot illustrations of women.

FIRST CONTACT & TERMS Illustrators: Send postcard sample or e-mail with link to website. After introductory mailing, send follow-up postcard sample every 3-6 months. Samples are filed. Responds only if interested. Pays illustrators $200-500 for color inside. Buys one-time rights. Finds freelancers through sourcebooks.

LULLWATER REVIEW

P.O. Box 122036, Atlanta GA 30322. **E-mail:** emorylullwaterreview@gmail.com. **Website:** www.lullwaterreview.wordpress.com. **Contact:** Aneyn M. O'Grady, editor-in-chief; Gabriel Unger, managing editor. Estab. 1990. Circ. 2,000. "We're a small, student-run literary magazine published out of Emory University in Atlanta GA with 2 issues yearly—once in the fall and once in the spring. You can find us in the *Index of American Periodical Verse*, the *American Humanities Index* and as a member of the Council of Literary Magazines and Presses. We welcome work that brings a fresh perspective, whether through language or the visual arts."

FIRST CONTACT & TERMS Send an e-mail with photos. Samples kept on file. Portfolio should include b&w, color, photos and finished, original art. Credit line given when appropriate.

TIPS "Read our magazine. We welcome work of all different types, and we encourage submissions that bring a fresh or alternative perspective. Submit at least 5 works. We frequently accept 3-5 pieces from a single artist and like to see a selection."

THE MACGUFFIN

18600 Haggerty Rd., Livonia MI 48152. (734)462-4400, ext 5327. **E-mail:** macguffin@schoolcraft.edu. **Website:** www.macguffin.org. **Contact:** Steven A. Dolgin, editor; Gordon Krupsky, managing editor;. Estab. 1984. Magazine covering the best new work in contemporary poetry, prose and visual art. "Our purpose is to encourage, support and enhance the literary arts in the Schoolcraft College community, the region, the state, and the nation. We also sponsor annual literary events and give voice to deserving new writers as well as established writers."

FIRST CONTACT & TERMS Send an e-mail with samples. "Please submit name and contact information with your work, along with captions." Portfolio not required. Credit line given.

MAD MAGAZINE

DC Entertainment, 1700 Broadway, New York NY 10019. (212)506-4850. **E-mail:** submissions@madmagazine.com. **Website:** www.madmag.com. Estab. 1952. Monthly magazine always on the lookout for new ways to spoof and to poke fun at hot trends.

ILLUSTRATION Approached by 300 illustrators/year. Works with 50 illustrators/year. Has featured illustrations by Mort Drucker, Al Jaffee, Sergio Aragonès, Peter Kuper, Drew Friedman, Tom Richmond and Hermann Mejia. Features humor, realism, caricature.

DESIGN Uses local freelancers for design infrequently. 100% of freelance design demands knowledge of Illustrator, Photoshop and QuarkXPress.

FIRST CONTACT & TERMS Illustrators: Send query letter with tearsheets and SASE. Samples are filed. Buys all rights. Pays $2,000 for color cover; $300-500 for inside. Finds illustrators through direct mail, sourcebooks (all).

TIPS "Know what we do! *MAD* is very specific. Everyone wants to work for *MAD*, but few are right for what *MAD* needs! Understand reproduction process, as well as give-and-take between artist and client."

MARKETING MAGAZINE

One Mount Pleasant Rd., 7th Floor, Toronto Ontario M4Y 2Y5, Canada. (416)764-1563; (416) 764-1212. **E-mail:** Glenn.Taylor@marketingmag.rogers.com. **Website:** www.marketingmag.ca. **Contact:** Glenn Taylor, art director. Estab. 1980. Circ. 13,000. Weekly trade publication featuring news, commentary and articles on advertising, promotion, direct marketing, public relations and digital marketing in Canada. Sample copies available on request. Art guidelines available on website.

ILLUSTRATION Approached by 150 illustrators/year. Buys 10 illustrations/year. Features humorous illustration and spot illustrations of business.

FIRST CONTACT & TERMS Illustrators: Send postcard sample with tearsheets. Responds only if interested. Buys one-time rights.

MARKETWATCH

Dow Jones & Co., 1211 Avenue of the Americas, New York NY 10036. **Website:** www.marketwatch.com. Estab. 1992. *MarketWatch*, published by Dow Jones & Co., tracks the pulse of markets for engaged investors with more than 16 million visitors per month. The site is a leading innovator in the business news, personal finance information, real-time commentary and investment tools and data, with dedicated journalists generating hundreds of headlines, stories, videos and market briefs a day from 10 bureaus in the US, Europe and Asia.

ILLUSTRATION Approached by 200-300 illustrators/year. Buys 10 illustrations/issue. Works on assignment only. Considers pen & ink, airbrush, colored pencil, mixed media, collage, charcoal, watercolor, acrylic, oil, pastel and digital.

FIRST CONTACT & TERMS Illustrators: Send postcard-size sample. Samples are filed. Publication will contact artist for portfolio review if interested. Portfolio should include tearsheets and photocopies. Buys first and one-time rights. Pays 30 days from invoice; $1,500 for color cover; $400-700 for spots. Finds artists through sourcebooks and submissions.

MEN'S HEALTH

Rodale, Inc., 400 S. 10th St., Emmaus PA 18098. (212)697-2040. **E-mail:** mhletters@rodale.com. **Website:** www.menshealth.com. **Contact:** Kevin Donahue, senior managing editor. Estab. 1987. Circ.

1,918,387. Men's fitness/lifestyle magazine. Art guidelines not available.

CARTOONS Buys 10 cartoons/year.

ILLUSTRATION Buys 100 illustrations/year. Has featured illustrations by Daniel Adel, Gary Taxali, Eboy, Mirkoilic, Jonathon Carlson. Features caricatures of celebrities/politicians, realistic illustration, charts & graphs, humorous illustration, medical illustration, computer illustration, informational graphics, spot illustrations. Prefer subjects about men. 100% of freelance work demands computer skills. Freelancers should be familiar with InDesign, Illustrator, Photoshop. E-mail submissions accepted with link to website. Samples are not filed and are not returned. Portfolio not required.

MICHIGAN OUT-OF-DOORS

P.O. Box 30235, Lansing MI 48912. (517)371-1041. **Fax:** (517)371-1505. **E-mail:** thansen@mucc.org; magazine@mucc.org. **Website:** www.michiganoutofdoors.com. **Contact:** Tony Hansen, editor. Estab. 1947. Circ. 40,000. Four-color magazine emphasizing hunting and fishing. Six print issues/year with 4 additional digital-only issues.

ILLUSTRATION "Following the various hunting and fishing seasons, we have a limited need for illustration material; we consider submissions 6-8 months in advance." Has featured illustrations by Ed Sutton and Nick Van Frankenhuyzen. Assigns 10% of illustrations to new and emerging illustrators.

FIRST CONTACT & TERMS Responds as soon as possible. **Pays on acceptance**; $30 for pen & ink illustrations in a vertical treatment.

MID-AMERICAN REVIEW

Bowling Green State University, Dept. of English, Bowling Green OH 43403. (419)372-2725. **E-mail:** mar@bgsu.edu; marsubmissions.bgsu.edu. **Website:** www.bgsu.edu/midamericanreview. **Contact:** Abigail Cloud, editor in chief; Laura Walter, fiction editor. Estab. 1981. Circ. 1,500. Semiannual literary magazine publishing "the best contemporary poetry, fiction, essays, and work in translation we can find. Each issue includes poems in their original language and in English." Reads all year. Originals are returned at job's completion. Sample copies available for $9.

ILLUSTRATION Approached by 10-20 illustrators/year. Uses 1 artwork per issue for the cover.

FIRST CONTACT & TERMS Send query letter with brochure, SASE, tearsheets, photographs, or photocopies. Samples are filed or are returned by SASE if requested. Buys first rights. Pays $50 when funding permits.

TIPS "*MAR* only publishes artwork on its cover. We like to use the same artist for 1 volume (2 issues). We are looking for full-color artwork for a front-to-back, full bleed effect. Visit our website!"

THE MILITARY OFFICER

201 N. Washington St., Alexandria VA 22314. (703)549-2311; (800)234-6622. **E-mail:** editor@ moaa.org; msc@moaa.org. **Website:** www.moaa.org. Estab. 1945. 4-color magazine for retired and active duty military officers of the uniformed services; concerns current military/political affairs; recent military history, especially Vietnam, Korea and Iraq; holiday anecdotes; travel; human interest; humor; hobbies; second-career job opportunities and military family lifestyle.

ILLUSTRATION Works with 9-10 illustrators/year. Buys 15-20 illustrations/year. Buys illustrations on assigned themes. Uses freelancers mainly for features and covers.

FIRST CONTACT & TERMS Send samples.

TIPS "We look for artists who can take a concept and amplify it editorially."

THE MISFIT JOURNAL

E-mail: matt@misfit-inc.com. **Website:** misfit-inc. com/quarterly. **Contact:** Matt Owen, general editor. Estab. 2012. "*The Misfit Journal* is a multimedia arts journal. A textual-visual manifesto. A celebration-in-print. It is a 'literary journal' without the pretentious overtones, and with more pictures. The Misfits ethos, at its core, is about freedom. We don't mean that in a vague campaign trail sort of way; we're talking about genuine, freedom-from-the-shackles of an unchosen life, personal emancipation. A Misfit is someone who is driven—however challenging it might be, however unsteady—to live their life in the way they want to. By their own rules, but also by their own loves, their own cares, their own desires, and even their own dreams. It is about independence. It is about the life you want; the life you need; the life you will fight for. And we want everything. Short stories, novel excerpts, essays, memoir, creative nonfiction, poetry, artwork, photography. Seriously, everything. We're not sticklers for medium, form or genre. As long as it reflects that Misfit ethos, we want it. Whether it's social realism or Dadaism, watercolor or fractals—we want it."

ILLUSTRATION Accepts digital format only. Send via e-mail as TIFF, BMP, GIF, or JPEG.

FIRST CONTACT & TERMS Submit via website. Responds in 2 days for queries, 1 month for submissions. Accepts simultaneous submissions. Credit line given.

MODEL RAILROADER

Kalmbach Publishing Co., 21027 Crossroads Circle, P.O. Box 1612, Waukesha WI 53187-1612. **Website:** www.modelrailroader.com; mrr.trains.com. Circ. 230,000. Monthly magazine for hobbyists, rail fans. Sample copies available with 9×12 SASE and first-class postage. Art guidelines available.

⦿ Published by Kalmbach Publishing. Also publishes *Classic Toy Trains, Astronomy, Finescale Modeler, Model Retailer, Nutshell News* and *Trains*.

CARTOONS Prefers railroading themes. Prefers b&w line drawings with gagline.

ILLUSTRATION Prefers railroading, construction, how-to. Considers all media. 90% of freelance illustration demands knowledge of Photoshop 3.0, Illustrator 6.0, FreeHand 3.0, QuarkXPress 3.31 and Fractal Painter.

FIRST CONTACT & TERMS Submission guidelines available online.

⦿ MONTANA MAGAZINE

Lee Enterprises, P.O. Box 8689, Missoula MT 59807. **E-mail:** editor@montanamagazine.com. **Website:** www.montanamagazine.com. Estab. 1970. Circ. 20,000. Bimonthly. Covers Montana recreation, history, people, wildlife. Geared to Montanans.

ILLUSTRATION Approached by 15-20 illustrators/year. Buys 1-2 illustrations/year. Prefers outdoors. Considers all media. Knowledge of InDesign, Photoshop, Illustrator helpful but not required. Send query letter via e-mail to editor@montanamagazine.com.

FIRST CONTACT & TERMS Submission guidelines available online.

TIPS "We work with local artists usually because of convenience and turnaround." No cartoons.

MORE

Meredith Corp., 125 Park Ave., New York NY 10017. **E-mail:** more@meredith.com. **Website:** www.more. com. **Contact:** Ila Stanger, managing editor. Estab. 1998. Circ. 1.8 million. Monthly publication focusing on the smart and sophisticated women, addressing real-life concerns, such as changing role of women

in society, with advice on self-improvement, health, fashion, and style. Art guidelines available on website.
ILLUSTRATION Buys 20 illustrations/year. Features fashion and humorous illustration of men and women, health, relationships, office, politics, and the sophisticated look.
FIRST CONTACT & TERMS Illustrators: Send postcard sample. After introductory mailing, send follow-up postcard sample every 6 months. Accepts e-mail submission with link to website. Samples are filed. Responds only if interested. Company will contact artist for portfolio review if interested. Pays illustrators $200 for spot illustrations. Finds freelancers through artists' submissions and sourcebooks.

THE MORGAN HORSE—OFFICIAL BREED JOURNAL

American Morgan Horse Association, 4066 Shelburne Rd., Suite 5, Shelburne VT 05482-6908. (802)985-4944. **Fax:** (802)985-8897. **Website:** www.morgan horse.com. **Contact:** Publications department. Circ. 4,500-7,000 (numerous copies distributed at equine events). Emphasizes all aspects of the Morgan horse breed including educating Morgan owners, trainers and enthusiasts. Published monthly. Accepts previously published materials, simultaneous submissions. Original artwork returned after publication. Sample copy $5.
FIRST CONTACT & TERMS Illustrators: Send query letter with samples and tearsheets to editorial director: stephen@morganhorse.com. Buys all rights and negotiates rights purchased. **Pays on acceptance.**

MORPHEUS TALES

E-mail: morpheustales@blueyonder.co.uk. **Website:** www.morpheustales.com. **Contact:** Adam Bradley, publisher. Estab. 2008. Circ. 1,000. Publishes experimental fiction, fantasy, horror, and science fiction. Publishes 4-6 titles/year.
ILLUSTRATION "Look at magazine and website for style." Portfolio should include b&w, color, finished, and original art.
FIRST CONTACT & TERMS Responds within 30 days. Model and property release are required. Publisher buys first rights, electronic rights, which may vary according to the project.

MOTHER JONES

Foundation for National Progress, 222 Sutter St., Suite 600, San Francisco CA 94108. (415)321-1700. **E-mail:** mmurrmann@motherjones.com; query@mother jones.com. **Website:** www.motherjones.com. **Contact:** Mark Murrmann, photo editor; Ivylise Simones, creative director; Monika Bauerlein and Clara Jeffery, editors. Estab. 1976. Circ. 240,000. Bimonthly magazine covering politics, investigative reporting, social issues, and pop culture. Accepts previously published artwork. Originals returned at job's completion. Sample copies available.

○ "*Mother Jones* is a 'progressive' magazine—but the core of its editorial well is reporting (i.e., fact-based). No slant required. MotherJones. com is an online sister publication."

CARTOONS Approached by 25 cartoonists/year. Prints one cartoon/issue (6/year). Prefers full page, multiple-frame color drawings. Works on assignment only.
ILLUSTRATION "Approached by hundreds of illustrators/year. *Mother Jones* sees powerful, smart illustration as an essential part of serious journalism. Artists who have appeared in *Mother Jones* include Barry Blitt, Steve Brodner, Tomer Hanuka, Yuko Shimizu, and Ralph Steadman; and work from our pages has appeared in top illustration showcases from *American Illustration* to *Juxtapoz*. If this is where you're headed, we'd like to hear from you. It's best to give us a URL for a portfolio website. Or you can mail non-returnable samples or disks to: Carolyn Perot, art director. Please do not submit original artwork or any samples that will need to be returned. Assigns 90% of illustrations to well-known or 'name' illustrators; 5% to experienced but not well-known illustrators; 5% to new and emerging illustrators. Works on assignment only. Considers all media."
FIRST CONTACT & TERMS Cartoonists: Send query letter with postcard-size sample or finished cartoons. Illustrators: Send postcard-size sample or query letter with samples. Samples are filed or returned by SASE. Responds to the artist only if interested. Portfolio should include photographs, slides and tearsheets. Buys first rights. Pays on publication; payment varies widely. Finds artists through illustration books, other magazines, word of mouth.

MUSHING MAGAZINE

P.O. Box 1195, Willow AK 99688. (907)495-2468. **E-mail:** editor@mushing.com. **Website:** www.mushing. com. **Contact:** Greg Sellentin, publisher and executive editor. Estab. 1987. Circ. 10,000. Bimonthly "year-round, international magazine for all dog-powered sports, from sledding to skijoring to weight pulling to carting to packing. We seek to educate and entertain." Photo/art originals are returned at job's completion. Sample copies available for $5. Art guidelines available upon request.

CARTOONS Approached by 20 cartoonists/year. Buys up to 1 cartoon/issue. Prefers humorous cartoons; single panel b&w line drawings with gagline.

ILLUSTRATION Approached by 20 illustrators/year. Buys 0-1 illustrations/issue. Prefers simple; healthy, happy sled dogs; some silhouettes. Considers pen & ink and charcoal. Send query letter with SASE and photocopies. Accepts disk submissions if Mac compatible.

FIRST CONTACT & TERMS Cartoonists: Send query letter with roughs. Illustrators: Send EPS or TIFF files with hardcopy. Samples are returned by SASE if requested by artist. Prefers to keep copies of possibilities on file and use as needed. Responds in 6 months. Portfolio review not required. Buys first rights and reprint rights. Pays on publication. Pays cartoonists $25 for b&w and color. Pays illustrators $150 for color cover; $25 for b&w and color inside; $25 for spots. Finds artists through submissions.

TIPS "Be familiar with sled dogs and sled dog sports. We're most open to using freelance illustrations with articles on dog behavior, adventure stories, health and nutrition. Illustrations should be faithful and/or accurate to the sport. Cartoons should be faithful and tasteful (e.g., not inhumane to dogs)."

MUZZLE MAGAZINE

312 N. Geneva St., #5, Ithaca NY 14850. **E-mail:** muzzlemagazine@gmail.com. **Website:** www.muzzlemagazine.com. **Contact:** Stevie Edwards. editor-in-chief. Estab. 2010. Circ. About 300 unique viewers on average. Quarterly literary magazine. *Muzzle Magazine* aims to bring together the voices of poets from a diverse array of backgrounds, playing special homage to those from communities that are historically underrepresented in literary magazines. Muzzle takes submissions year round for poetry, art, interviews, poetry book reviews and poetry performance reviews. Sample copies available online. Art and photo submission guidelines available on website or via mail with SASE.

NA'AMAT WOMAN

505 Eighth Ave., Suite 1204, New York NY 10018. (212)563-5222. **E-mail:** naamat@naamat.org; judith@naamat.org. **Website:** www.naamat.org. **Contact:** Judith Sokoloff, editor. Estab. 1926. Circ. 12,000. Quarterly magazine for Jewish women, covering a wide variety of topics that are of interest to the Jewish community. Affiliated with NA'AMAT USA (a nonprofit organization). Sample copies available for $2 each or look online.

ILLUSTRATION Approached by 30 illustrators/year. Buys 2-3 illustrations/issue. We publish in 4-color through out the issue. Has featured illustrations by Julie Delton, Ilene Winn-Lederer, Avi Katz, Marilyn Rose and Yevgenia Nayberg.

FIRST CONTACT & TERMS Illustrators: Send query letter with tearsheets, or by e-mail. Samples are filed or are returned by SASE if requested by artist. Responds only if interested. Will contact artist for portfolio review if interested. Portfolio should include tearsheets and final art. Rights purchased vary according to project. Pays on publication. Pays illustrators $250 maximum for cover; $75-100 for inside. Finds artists through sourcebooks, publications, word of mouth, submissions. Originals are returned at job's completion.

TIPS "Give us a try! We're small, but nice."

⚙ NAILPRO

Creative Age Publications, 7628 Densmore Ave., Van Nuys CA 91406. (800)442-5667; (818)782-7328. **Fax:** (818)782-7450. **E-mail:** nailpro@creativeage.com. **Website:** www.nailpro.com. **Contact:** Stephanie Yaggy, executive editor. Estab. 1989. Circ. 65,000. Monthly trade magazine for the nail and beauty industry audience nail technicians. Sample copies available.

CARTOONS Prefers subject matter related to nail industry. Prefers humorous color washes and b&w line drawings with or without gagline.

ILLUSTRATION Approached by tons of illustrators. Buys 3-4 illustrations/issue. Has featured illustrations by Kelley Kennedy, Nick Bruel and Kathryn Adams. Assigns 20% of illustrations to well-known or "name" illustrators; 70% to experienced but not well-known illustrators; 10% to new and emerging illustrators. Prefers whimsical computer illustrations. Considers all media. 85% of freelance illustration demands knowledge of Photoshop 5.5, Illustrator 8.0 and QuarkXPress 4.04.

DESIGN Needs freelancers for design, production and multimedia projects. Prefers local design freelancers only. 100% of freelance work demands knowledge of Photoshop 5.5, Illustrator 8.0 and QuarkX-Press 4.04.

FIRST CONTACT & TERMS Cartoonists: Send query letter with samples. Responds only if interested. Rights purchased vary according to project. Illustrators: Send postcard sample. Designers: Send query letter with printed samples and tearsheets. Accepts disk submissions compatible with QuarkXPress 4.04, TIFFs, EPS files submitted on ZIP, JAZ or CD (Mac format only). Send samples to Attn: Art director. Samples are filed. Responds only if interested. Art director will contact artist for portfolio review of b&w, color, final art and tearsheets if interested. Buys first rights. Payment to cartoonists varies with projects. Pays on publication. Pays illustrators $350-400 for 2-page, full-color feature spread; $300 for 1-page; $250 for ½ page. Pays $50 for spots. Finds illustrators through *Workbook*, samples sent in the mail, magazines.

NAILS MAGAZINE

Bobit Business Media, 3520 Challenger St., Torrance CA 90503. (310)533-2400 (main); (310)533-2537 (art director). **Fax:** (310)533-2507. **E-mail:** danielle.parisi@bobit.com. **Website:** www.nailsmag.com. **Contact:** Danielle Parisi, art director. Estab. 1982. Circ. 60,000. Monthly 4-color trade journal; "seeks to educate readers on new techniques and products, nail anatomy and health, customer relations, chemical safety, salon sanitation and business." Originals can be returned at job's completion. Sample copies available. Art guidelines vary. Needs computer-literate freelancers for design, illustration and production. 100% of freelance work demands knowledge of QuarkXPress, Illustrator or Photoshop.

ILLUSTRATION Buys 3 illustrations/issue. Works on assignment only. Needs editorial and technical illustration; charts and story art. Prefers "fashion-oriented styles." Interested in all media.

FIRST CONTACT & TERMS Illustrators: Send query letter with brochure and tearsheets. Samples are filed. Responds in 1 month or artist should follow up with call. Call for an appointment to show a portfolio of tearsheets and transparencies. Buys all rights. **Pays on acceptance.** Finds artists through self-promotion and word of mouth.

THE NATION

33 Irving Place, 8th Floor, New York NY 10003. **E-mail:** submissions@thenation.com. **Website:** www.thenation.com. Steven Brower, art director. **Contact:**

Roane Carey, managing editory; Ange Mlinko, poetry editor. Estab. 1865. Circ. 100,000. Weekly journal of "left/liberal political opinion, covering national and international affairs, literature and culture." Sample copies available.

○ *The Nation*'s art director works out of his design studio at Steven Brower Design. You can send samples to *The Nation* and they will be forwarded.

ILLUSTRATION Approached by 50 illustrators/year. Buys 1-3 illustrations/issue. Works with 15 illustrators/year. Has featured illustrations by Peter O. Zierlien, Ryan Inzana, Tim Robinson and Karen Caldecott. Buys illustrations mainly for spots and feature spreads. Works on assignment only. Considers all media.

FIRST CONTACT & TERMS "Queries can be sent using our online form or sent by regular mail (the form is preferred). If sending by regular mail, please double-space and include a SASE. Our standard payment for a comment is $150; for an article $350-$500 depending on length. Payment for arts pieces is dependent on length; generally $225 and up. Samples are filed or are returned by SASE." Responds only if interested. Buys first rights. Pays $135 for color inside. Originals are returned after publication upon request.

TIPS "On top of a defined style, artist must have a strong and original political sensibility."

NATIONAL ENQUIRER

4950 Communication Ave., Boca Raton FL 33431. (561)997-7733. **Website:** www.nationalenquirer.com. Circ. 2 million (readership 14 million). A weekly tabloid. Originals are returned at job's completion.

CARTOONS "We get 1,000-1,500 cartoons weekly." Buys 200 cartoons/year. Has featured cartoons by Norm Rockwell, Glenn Bernhardt, Earl Engelman, George Crenshaw, Mark Parisi, Marty Bucella and Vahan Shirvanian. Prefers animal, family, husband/wife and general themes. Nothing political or off-color. Prefers single panel b&w line drawings and washes with or without gagline. Computer-generated cartoons are not accepted. Prefers to do own coloration.

FIRST CONTACT & TERMS Cartoonists: Send query letter with good, clean, clear copies of finished cartoons. Samples are not returned. Buys first and one-time rights. Pays $200 for b&w plus $20 each additional panel. Editor will notify if cartoon is accepted.

TIPS "Study several issues to get a solid grasp of what we buy. Gear your work accordingly."

NATIONAL GEOGRAPHIC

P.O. Box 98199, Washington DC 20090-8199. **Fax:** (202)828-5460. **E-mail:** ngsforum@nationalgeo graphic.com. **Website:** www.nationalgeographic.com. **Contact:** Chris Johns, editor-in-chief. Estab. 1888. Circ. 9 million. *National Geographic* receives up to 30 inquiries a day from freelancers, most of which are not appropriate to their needs. Please make sure you have studied several issues before you submit. They have a roster of artists they work with on a regular basis, and it's difficult to break in, but if they like your samples they will file them for consideration for future assignments.

ILLUSTRATION Works with 20 illustrators/year. Contracts 50 illustrations/year. Interested in "full-color renderings of historical and scientific subjects. Nothing that can be photographed is illustrated by artwork. No decorative, design material. We want scientific geological cut-aways, maps, historical paintings, prehistoric scenes." Works on assignment only.

FIRST CONTACT & TERMS Send color copies, postcards, tearsheets, proofs or other appropriate samples. Art director will contact for portfolio review if interested. Samples are returned by SASE. **Pays on acceptance**; varies according to project.

TIPS "Do your homework before submitting to any magazine. We only use historical and scientific illustrations—ones that are very informative and very accurate. No decorative, abstract or portraits."

THE NATIONAL NOTARY

9350 De Soto Ave., Chatsworth CA 91311-4926. 800-876-6827. **E-mail:** publications@nationalnotary.org. **Website:** www.nationalnotary.org. Circ. 300,000. Bimonthly. Emphasizes "notaries public and notarization—goal is to impart knowledge, understanding and unity among notaries nationwide and internationally." Readers are notaries of varying primary occupations (legal, government, real estate and financial), as well as state and federal officials and foreign notaries. Original artwork not returned after publication. Sample copy $5.

Also publishes *Notary Bulletin*.

CARTOONS Approached by 5-8 cartoonists/year. Cartoons "must have a notarial angle"; single or multiple panel with gagline, b&w line drawings.

ILLUSTRATION Approached by 3-4 illustrators/year. Uses about 3 illustrations/issue; buys all from local freelancers. Works on assignment only. Themes vary, depending on subjects of articles. 100% of freelance work demands knowledge of Illustrator, QuarkXPress or FreeHand.

FIRST CONTACT & TERMS Cartoonists: Send samples of style. Illustrators: Send business card, samples and tearsheets to be kept on file. Samples not returned. Responds in 6 weeks. Call for appointment. Buys all rights. Negotiates pay.

TIPS "We are very interested in experimenting with various styles of art in illustrating the magazine. We generally work with Southern California artists, as we prefer face-to-face dealings."

NATIONAL REVIEW

215 Lexington Ave., New York NY 10016. (212)679-7330. **E-mail:** letters@nationalreview.com. **Website:** www.nationalreview.com. **Contact:** Luba Myts, art director. Circ. 150,000+. Emphasizes world events from a conservative viewpoint; bimonthly color publication, design is "straight forward—the creativity comes out in the illustrations used." Originals are returned after publication. Uses freelancers mainly for illustrations of articles and covers.

CARTOONS Buys 6 cartoons/issue. Interested in "light political, social commentary on the conservative side."

ILLUSTRATION Buys 3-4 illustrations/issue. Especially needs portraits of political figures and conceptual editorial art. "I look for a strong graphic style; well-developed ideas and well-executed drawings." Style of Tim Bower, Jennifer Lawson, Janet Hamlin, Alan Nahigian. Works on assignment only.

FIRST CONTACT & TERMS Cartoonists: Send appropriate samples and SASE. Responds in 2 weeks. Illustrators: Send query letter with brochure showing art style or tearsheets and photocopies plus digital submissions. No samples returned. Responds to future assignment possibilities. Call for an appointment to show portfolio of final art. Include SASE. Buys first North American serial rights. Pays on publication. Pays cartoonists $50 for b&w. Pays illustrators $450 for color inside; $1,000 for color cover.

TIPS "Tearsheets and mailers are helpful in remembering an artist's work. Artists ought to make sure their work is professional in quality, idea and execution. Recent printed samples alongside originals help.

Changes in art and design in our field include fine art influence and use of more halftone illustration." A common mistake freelancers make in presenting their work is "not having a distinct style, i.e., they have a cross sample of too many different approaches to rendering their work. This leaves me questioning what kind of artwork I am going to get when I assign a piece."

NATION'S RESTAURANT NEWS

1166 Avenue of the Americas, 10th Floor, New York NY 10036. (212)204-4200; (212)204-4385. **E-mail:** joe. anderson@penton.com or via online contact form. **Website:** www.nrn.com. **Contact:** Joe Anderson, art director. Estab. 1967. Circ. 100,000. Weekly 4-color trade publication/tabloid.

ILLUSTRATION Buys 2-3 illustrations/year. Features illustrations of business subjects in the food service industry. Prefers pastel and bright colors. Assigns 5% of illustrations to well-known or "name" illustrators; 70% to experienced but not well-known illustrators; 25% to new and emerging illustrators. 20% of freelance illustration demands knowledge of Illustrator or Photoshop.

FIRST CONTACT & TERMS Illustrators: Send postcard sample or other nonreturnable samples, such as tearsheets. Accepts Mac-compatible disk submissions. Send EPS files. Samples are filed. Will contact artist for portfolio review if interested. Buys one-time rights. Pays on publication. Finds illustrators through *Creative Black Book* and *LA Work Book*, *Directory of Illustration* and *Contact USA*.

◑ NEO-OPSIS SCIENCE FICTION MAGAZINE

4129 Carey Rd., Victoria British Columbia V8Z4G5, Canada. (250)881-8893. **E-mail:** neoopsis@shaw.ca. **Website:** www.neo-opsis.ca. Buys first North American serial rights, electronic rights (for the issue). Only accepts fiction.

FIRST CONTACT & TERMS Send an e-mail with URL and JPEG samples at 72 dpi. Samples kept on file, not returned (Returned only by SASE). Responds only if interested. Pays on publication.

TIPS "Check the guidelines (on website) and the paid rate; if your work fits the genre and the rate is acceptable, then and only then, submit your work for consideration. It would also be nice if artists all had some examples of their work online so it is easy to see."

NEW HAMPSHIRE MAGAZINE

150 Dow St., Manchester NH 03103. (603)624-1442, ext. 128. **E-mail:** callen@nhmagazine.com. **Website:** www.nhmagazine.com. Estab. 1990. Circ. 26,000. Monthly 4-color magazine emphasizing New Hampshire lifestyle and related content.

ILLUSTRATION Approached by 300 illustrators/year. Has featured illustrations by Brian Hubble and Stephen Sauer. Features lifestyle illustration, charts & graphs and spot illustration. Prefers conceptual illustrations to accompany articles. Assigns 50% to experienced but not well-known illustrators; 50% to new and emerging illustrators.

FIRST CONTACT & TERMS Send postcard sample and follow-up postcard every 3 months. Samples are filed. Portfolio review not required. Negotiates rights purchased. Pays on publication. Pays $75-250 for color inside; $150-500 for 2-page spreads; $125 for spots.

TIPS "Lifestyle magazines want 'uplifting' lifestyle messages, not dark or disturbing images."

NEW JERSEY MONTHLY

55 Park Place, P.O. Box 920, Morristown NJ 07963-0920. (973)539-8230. **Fax:** (973)538-2953. **E-mail:** dcarter@njmonthly.com. **Website:** www.njmonthly.com. **Contact:** Deborah Carter, managing editor. Estab. 1976. Circ. 92,000. Monthly city magazine focuses on topics related to the New Jersey regions, especially the New Jersey business community, political issues and human interest articles.

ILLUSTRATION Features New Jersey caricatures of business leaders, celebrities/politicians and humorous illustration of business, families, pets, cooking and health. Assigns 50% to new and emerging illustrators.

FIRST CONTACT & TERMS Illustrators: Send postcard sample. After introductory mailing, send follow-up postcard sample every 3-6 months. Samples are filed. Responds only if interested. Pays illustrators $100 for color inside. Buys one-time rights.

TIPS "Be familiar with New Jersey personalities and topics. Have a consistent style and professional presentation. Follow through with assignments. Be willing to take directions from art director."

NEW MEXICO MAGAZINE

Lew Wallace Bldg., 495 Old Santa Fe Trail, Santa Fe NM 87501-2750. (505)827-7447. **E-mail:** artdirector@nmmagazine.com. **Website:** www.nmmagazine.com. Estab. 1923. Circ. 100,000. Monthly regional magazine for residents and tourists to the state of New Mexico.

○ Covers areas throughout the state. "We want to publish a lively editorial mix, covering both the down-home (like a diner in Tucumcari) and the upscale (a new bistro in world-class Santa Fe)." Explore the gamut of the Old West and the New Age.

ILLUSTRATION Buys 10 illustrations/year. Features spot illustrations. Assigns 5% to new and emerging illustrators.

FIRST CONTACT & TERMS Illustrators: Send post-card sample with URL. Responds only if interested. Pays illustrators $100 for color inside. Buys one-time rights. Find freelancers through artists' submissions.

NEW MOON GIRLS

New Moon Girl Media, P.O. Box 161287, Duluth MN 55816. (218)728-5507; (800) 381-4743. **E-mail:** submissions@newmoon.org. **Website:** www.newmoon.org. Estab. 1992. Circ. 30,000. Bimonthly 4-color cover, 4-color inside consumer magazine. Sample copies are $7.00.

ILLUSTRATION Buys 3-4 illustrations/issue. Has featured illustrations by Andrea Good, Liza Ferneyhough, Liza Wright. Features realistic illustrations, informational graphics and spot illustrations of children, women and girls. Prefers colored work. Assigns 30% of illustrations to new and emerging illustrators.

FIRST CONTACT & TERMS Submission guidelines available online.

TIPS "Be very familiar with the magazine and our mission. We are a magazine for girls ages 8-14 and look for illustrators who portray people of all different shapes, sizes and ethnicities in their work. Women and girl artists preferred. See cover art guidelines at www.newmoon.org."

THE NEW REPUBLIC

525 Ninth St. NW, Suite 600, Washington DC 20004. (202)508-4444. **E-mail:** letters@tnr.com. **Website:** www.tnr.com. (646) 404-4981. **Contact:** media. Estab. 1914. Circ. 50,000. Weekly political/literary magazine; political journalism, current events in the front section, book reviews and literary essays in the back; b&w with 4-color cover. Original artwork returned after publication. Sample copy for $4.94. 100% of freelance work demands computer skills.

CARTOONS Possible, not regular.

ILLUSTRATION Approached by 400 illustrators/year. Buys up to 5 or more illustrations/issue. Uses freelancers or photographers for cover art. Works on assignment only stand alone submissions also accepted. Prefers caricatures, portraits, and smart concepts 4-color.

FIRST CONTACT & TERMS Portfolio should include color photocopies. First-reproduction rights including web for duration of publication date unless otherwise negotiated. Pays on commission, kill fees may apply. Up to $1,200 for cover; $300-700 for b&w and color inside depending on space.

THE NEW YORKER

1 World Trade Center, New York NY 10007. **Website:** www.newyorker.com. **Contact:** David Remnick, editor in chief. Estab. 1925. Circ. 938,600. A quality weekly magazine of distinct news stories, articles, essays, and poems for a literate audience. Emphasizes news analysis and lifestyle features.

CARTOONS Buys b&w cartoons. Receives 3,000 cartoons/week.

FIRST CONTACT & TERMS Cartoonists: Accepts unsolicited submissions by e-mail (as PDF attachment) by mail. Reviews unsolicited submissions every 1-2 weeks. Photocopies only. Strict standards regarding style, technique, plausibility of drawing. Especially looks for originality. Pays $575 minimum for cartoons. Contact cartoon editor. Illustrators: Mail samples, no originals. "Because of volume of submissions we are unable to respond to all submissions." No calls please. Emphasis on portraiture. Contact illustration department.

TIPS "Familiarize yourself with *The New Yorker*."

NITE-WRITER'S INTERNATIONAL LITERARY ARTS JOURNAL

158 Spencer Ave., Suite 100, Pittsburgh PA 15227. (412)668-0691. **E-mail:** nitewritersliteraryarts@gmail.com. **Website:** nitewritersinternational.webs.com. **Contact:** John Thompson. Estab. 1994. *Nite-Writer's International Literary Arts Journal* is an online literary arts journal. "We are 'dedicated to the emotional intellectual' with a creative perception of life."

FIRST CONTACT & TERMS Send as .jpg and at 800 pixels (please include title of work).

NORTH AMERICAN HUNTER

12301 Whitewater Dr., #260, Minnetonka MN 55343-4103. (952)936-9333. **E-mail:** editors@huntingclub.com; ads@scout.com; editors@scout.com. **Website:**

www.huntingclub.com. Estab. 1978. Circ. 700,000. Bimonthly consumer magazines. *North American Hunter* is the official publication of the North American Hunting Club. Accepts previously published artwork. Originals are returned at job's completion. Sample copies available. Art guidelines for SASE with first-class postage. Needs computer-literate freelancers for illustration. 20% of freelance work demands computer knowledge of Illustrator, QuarkXPress, Photoshop or FreeHand.

○ This publisher also publishes *Cooking Pleasures* (circ. 300,000), *Handy* (circ. 900,000), *PGA Partners* (circ. 600,000), *Health & Wellness* (circ. 300,000), *Creative Home Arts* (circ. 300,000), *History* (circ. 300,000), *Street Thunder* (circ. 200,000) and *Gardening How-To* (circ. 500,000).

CARTOONS Approached by 20 cartoonists/year. Buys 3 cartoons/issue. Prefers humorous work portraying outdoorsmen in positive image; single panel b&w washes and line drawings with or without gagline.

ILLUSTRATION Approached by 40 illustrators/year. Buys 3 illustrations/issue. Prefers illustrations that portray wildlife and hunting and fishing in an accurate and positive manner. Considers pen & ink, watercolor, airbrush, acrylic, colored pencil, oil, charcoal, mixed media, pastel and electronic renderings.

FIRST CONTACT & TERMS Cartoonists: Send query letter with brochure. Illustrators: Send query letter with brochure, tearsheets, résumé, photographs and slides. Samples are filed. Portfolio review not required. Rights purchased vary according to project. **Pays on acceptance.**

◯ NORTH CAROLINA LITERARY REVIEW

East Carolina University, Mailstop 555 English, Greenville NC 27858-4353. (252)328-1537. **Fax:** (252)328-4889. **E-mail:** nclrsubmissions@ecu.edu. **Website:** www.nclr.ecu.edu. **Contact:** Margaret Bauer. Estab. 1992. Circ. 750. Annual literary magazine with North Carolina focus. *NCLR* publishes poetry, fiction and nonfiction by and interviews with NC writers, and articles and essays about NC literature, literary history and culture. Sample copy available for $15.

FIRST CONTACT & TERMS Send query letter with website address to show sample of work. If selected, art acquisitions editor will be in touch.

NOTRE DAME MAGAZINE

University of Notre Dame, 500 Grace Hall, Notre Dame IN 46556-5612. (574)631-5335. **E-mail:** ndmag@nd.edu. **Website:** magazine.nd.edu. **Contact:** Kerry Temple, editor; Kerry Prugh, art director. Estab. 1972. Circ. 150,000. "We are a university magazine with a scope as broad as that found at a university, but we place our discussion in a moral, ethical, and spiritual context reflecting our Catholic heritage."

ILLUSTRATION Buys 5-8 illustrations/issue. Has featured illustrations by Raymond Verdaguer, Vivienne Fleshner, Cap Pannell and Stephanie Dalton Cowan. Works on assignment only.

FIRST CONTACT & TERMS "Don't send submissions—only tearsheets or samples." Tearsheets, photographs, brochures and photocopies OK for samples. Samples are returned by SASE if requested. Buys first rights.

TIPS "Create images that can communicate ideas. Looking for noncommercial style editorial art by accomplished, experienced editorial artists. Conceptual imagery that reflects the artist's awareness of fine art ideas and methods is the kind of thing we use. Sports action illustrations not used. Cartoons not used."

◯ NURSEWEEK

1721 Moon Lake Blvd., Suite 540, Hoffman Estates IL 60169. (847)839-1700; (888) 206-3791. **Website:** www.nurse.com. Circ. over 1 million. "*Nurseweek* is a biweekly 4-color letter-size magazine mailed free to registered nurses nationwide. *Nurseweek* provides readers with nursing-related news and features that encourage and enable them to excel in their work and that enhance the profession's image by highlighting the many diverse contributions nurses make. In order to provide a complete and useful package, the publication's article mix includes late-breaking news stories, news features with analysis (including in-depth bimonthly special reports), interviews with industry leaders and achievers, continuing education articles, career option pieces and reader dialogue (Letters, Commentary, First Person)." Sample copy $3. Art guidelines not available. Needs computer-literate freelancers for production. 90% of freelance work demands knowledge of QuarkXPress, Photoshop, Illustrator, Adobe Acrobat.

ILLUSTRATION Approached by 10 illustrators/year. Buys 1 illustration/year. Prefers pen ink, watercolor, airbrush, marker, colored pencil, mixed media and pastel. Needs medical illustration.

DESIGN Needs freelancers for design. 60% of design demands knowledge of Photoshop CS2, QuarkXPress 6.1, InDesign. Prefers local freelancers. Send query letter with brochure, résumé, SASE and tearsheets. Photographs: Stock photographs used 80%.

NUTRITION HEALTH REVIEW

P.O. Box #406, Haverford PA 19041. (610)896-1853. **Fax:** (610)896-1857. **Contact:** A. Rifkin, publisher. Estab. 1975. Circ. 285,000. Quarterly newspaper covering nutrition, health and medical information for the consumer. Sample copies available for $3. Art guidelines available.

CARTOONS Prefers single panel, humorous, b&w drawings.

ILLUSTRATION Features b&w humorous, medical and spot illustrations pertaining to health.

FIRST CONTACT & TERMS Cartoonists/illustrators: Send query letter with b&w photocopies. After introductory mailing, send follow-up postcard every 3-6 months. Samples are filed or returned by SASE. Responds in 6 months. Company will contact artist for portfolio review if interested. Pays cartoonists $20 maximum for b&w. Pays illustrators $200 maximum for b&w cover; $30 maximum for b&w inside. **Pays on acceptance.** Buys first rights, one-time rights, reprint rights. Finds freelancers through agents, artists' submissions, sourcebooks.

O&A MARKETING NEWS

KAL Publications, Inc., 559 S. Harbor Blvd., Suite A, Anaheim CA 92805-4525. (714)563-9300. **Fax:** (714)563-9310. **E-mail:** kathy@kalpub.com. **Website:** www.kalpub.com. Estab. 1966. Circ. 7,500. Bimonthly trade publication about the service station/petroleum marketing industry.

CARTOONS Approached by 10 cartoonists/year. Buys 1-2 cartoons/issue. Prefers humor that relates to service station industry. Prefers single panel, humorous, b&w line drawings.

FIRST CONTACT & TERMS Cartoonists: Send b&w photocopies, roughs, or samples and SASE. Samples are returned by SASE. Responds in 1 month. Buys one-time rights. Pays on acceptance; $10 for b&w.

TIPS "We run a cartoon (at least 1) in each issue of our trade magazine. We're looking for a humorous take on business—specifically the service station/pe-troleum marketing/carwash/quick lube industry that we cover."

OFFICEPRO

IAAP, 10502 N. Ambassador Dr., Suite 100, Kansas City MO 64153. (816)891-6600. **E-mail:** eallen@iaap-hq.org. **Website:** www.iaap-hq.org. **Contact:** Emily Allen, managing editor. Estab. 1945. Circ. 40,000. Trade journal published 8 times/year. Official publication of the International Association of Administrative Professionals. Emphasizes workplace issues, trends and technology. Sample copies available; contact subscription office at (816)891-6600, ext. 2236.

ILLUSTRATION Approached by 50 illustrators/year. Buys 20 or fewer illustrations/year. Works on assignment and purchases stock art. Prefers communication, travel, meetings and international business themes. Considers pen & ink, airbrush, colored pencil, mixed media, collage, charcoal, watercolor, acrylic, oil, pastel, marker and computer.

FIRST CONTACT & TERMS Illustrators: Send postcard-size sample or send query letter with brochure, tearsheets and photocopies. Samples are filed. Responds only if interested. Will contact artist for portfolio review if interested. Portfolio should include final art and tearsheets. Accepts previously published artwork. Originals returned at job's completion upon request only. Usually buys one-time rights, but rights purchased vary according to project. Pays $500-600 for color cover; $200-400 for color inside; $60-150 for b&w inside; $60 for b&w spots. Finds artists through word of mouth and artists' samples.

OFF THE COAST

Resolute Bear Press, P.O. Box 14, Robbinston ME 04671. (207)454-8026. **E-mail:** poetrylane2@gmail.com. **Website:** www.off-the-coast.com. **Contact:** Valerie Lawson, editor/publisher. Estab. 1994. "The mission of *Off the Coast* is to become recognized around the world as Maine's international poetry journal, a publication that prizes quality, diversity and honesty in its publications and in its dealings with poets. *Off the Coast*, a quarterly journal, publishes poetry, artwork and reviews. Arranged much like an anthology, each issue bears a title drawn from a line or phrase from one of its poems."

FIRST CONTACT & TERMS "We accept b&w graphics and photos to grace the pages of *Off the Coast*, and color or b&w for the cover. Send 3-6 images in TIFF, PNG or JPEG format, minimum 300 dpi resolution.

Please use submission manager: www.offthecoast.submittable.com/submit to send artwork."

OHIO MAGAZINE

Great Lakes Publishing Co., 1422 Euclid Ave., Suite 730, Cleveland OH 44115. (216)771-2833. **E-mail:** vpospisil@ohiomagazine.com. **Website:** www.ohiomagazine.com. **Contact:** Vivian Pospisil, executive editor. Estab. 1978. Circ. 40,000.

ILLUSTRATION Approached by 100+ illustrators/year. Uses as needed. Assignment and stock illustrations used. Has featured illustrations by A.G. Ford, Neal Aspinall, Ellyn Lusis, Doug Boehm, D. Brent Campbell, Jeff Suntala, and Daniel Vasconcellos. Considers pen, ink, watercolor, acrylic, colored pencil, and oil.

DESIGN Freelance work demands knowledge of InDesign, Photoshop, and Illustrator CS4 or higher. Freelancers from Ohio or bordering states preferred.

TIPS "Please have a knowledge of the magazine and audience before submitting. Freelancers should send all queries electronically or through the mail. Telephone inquiries are strongly discouraged."

⊙ OKLAHOMA TODAY

P.O. Box 1468, Oklahoma City OK 73101-1468. (405)230-8450. **Fax:** (405)230-8650. **E-mail:** megan.rossman@travelok.com. **Website:** www.oklahomaday.com. **Contact:** Nathan Gunter managing editor; Megan Rossman, photography editor. Estab. 1956. Circ. 45,000. Bimonthly regional, upscale consumer magazine focusing on all things that define Oklahoma and interest Oklahomans. Accepts previously published artwork. Originals are returned at job's completion. Sample copies available with SASE.

ILLUSTRATION Approached by 24 illustrators/year. Buys 5-10 illustrations/year. Has featured illustrations by Rob Silvers, Tim Jessel, Steven Walker and Deby Kaspari. Features caricatures of celebrities; natural history; realistic and spot illustration. Assigns 10% of illustrations to new and emerging illustrators. Considers pen & ink, watercolor, collage, airbrush, acrylic, marker, colored pencil, oil, charcoal and pastel. 20% of freelance work demands knowledge of PageMaker, Illustrator and Photoshop.

FIRST CONTACT & TERMS Illustrators: Send query letter with brochure, résumé, SASE, tearsheets and slides. Samples are filed. Responds in days if interested; months if not. Portfolio review required if interested in artist's work. Portfolio should include b&w and color thumbnails, tearsheets and slides. Buys one-time rights. Finds artists through sourcebooks, other publications, word of mouth, submissions and artist reps.

TIPS Illustrations to accompany short stories and features are most open to freelancers. "Read the magazine. Be willing to accept low fees at the beginning. We enjoy working with local artists or those with Oklahoma connections."

ON EARTH

Natural Resources Defense Council, 40 W. 20th St., New York NY 10011. (212)727-4412. **E-mail:** onearth@nrdc.org. **Website:** www.onearth.org. **Contact:** Gail Ghezzi, art director. Estab. 1979. Circ. 140,000. Quarterly "award-winning environmental magazine exploring politics, nature, wildlife, science and solutions to problems."

ILLUSTRATION Buys 4 illustrations/issue.

FIRST CONTACT & TERMS Illustrators: Send postcard sample. "We will accept work compatible with InDesign CS4, QuarkXPress, Illustrator 8.0, Photoshop 5.5 and below." Responds only if interested. Buys one-time rights. Also may ask for electronic rights. Pays $100-300 for b&w inside. Payment for spots varies. Finds artists through sourcebooks and submissions.

TIPS "We prefer 4-color. Our illustrations are often conceptual, thought-provoking, challenging. We enjoy thinking artists, and we encourage ideas and exchange."

THE OPTIMIST

4494 Lindell Blvd., St. Louis MO 63108. (314)371-6000. **Fax:** (314)371-6006. **E-mail:** magazine@optimist.org. **Website:** www.optimist.org. Circ. 100,000. Quarterly 4-color magazine with 4-color cover that emphasizes activities relating to Optimist clubs in US and Canada (civic-service clubs). "Magazine is mailed to all members of Optimist clubs. Average age is 42; most are management level with some college education." Sample copy available with SASE.

CARTOONS Buys 2 cartoons/issue. Has featured cartoons by Joe Engesser, Randy Glasbergen and Tim Oliphant. Prefers themes of general interest family-orientation, sports, kids, civic clubs. Prefers color, single-panel, with gagline. No washes.

FIRST CONTACT & TERMS Send query letter with samples. Send art on a Mac-compatible disk, if possible. Submissions returned by SASE. Buys one-time rights. **Pays on publication.**

TIPS "Send clear cartoon submissions, not poorly photocopied copies."

ORACLE MAGAZINE

Oracle Corp., 500 Oracle Pkwy., Redwood Shores CA 94065. (650)506-7000; (650)506-6859; (800) 392-2999. **E-mail:** opubedit_us@oracle.com; richard.merchan@ oracle.com. **Website:** www.oracle.com/technetwork/ oramag/magazine. **Contact:** Richard Merchan, art director. Estab. 2000. Circ. 524,000. Bimonthly trade publication for information managers, database administrators and Oracle users.

ILLUSTRATION Approached by 200 illustrators/year. Buys 50 illustrations/year. Features informational graphics and spot illustrations of business and computers. Assigns 10% to new and emerging illustrators.

FIRST CONTACT & TERMS Illustrators: Send postcard sample with URL. After introductory mailing, send follow-up postcard sample every 3 months. Responds only if interested. Pays illustrators $250-1,000 for color inside. Pays on publication. Buys one-time rights. Finds freelancers through agents, artists' submissions, sourcebooks and word-of-mouth.

ORANGE COAST MAGAZINE

Orange Coast Kommunications, Inc., 3701 Birch St., Suite 100, Newport Beach CA 92660. (949)862-1133. **Fax:** (949)862-0133. **E-mail:** editorial@orangecoast. com. **Website:** www.orangecoast.com. **Contact:** Martin J. Smith, editor-in-chief. Estab. 1974. Circ. 52,000. Monthly 4-color local consumer magazine with celebrity covers.

ILLUSTRATION Approached by 100 illustrators/year. Has featured illustrations by Cathi Mingus, Gweyn Wong, Scott Laumann, Santiago Veeda, John Westmark, Robert Rose, Nancy Harrison. Features computer, fashion and editorial illustrations featuring children and families. Prefers serious subjects; some humorous subjects. Assigns 10% of illustrations to well-known or "name" illustrators; 40% to experienced but not well-known illustrators; 50% to new and emerging illustrators. 40% of freelance illustration demands knowledge of Illustrator or Photoshop.

FIRST CONTACT & TERMS Send postcard or other nonreturnable samples. Accepts Mac-compatible disk submissions. Send EPS files. Samples are filed. Responds in 1 month. Will contact artist for portfolio review if interested. **Pays on acceptance:** $175 for

b&w or color inside; $75 for spots. Finds illustrators through artists' promotional samples.

TIPS "Looking for fresh and unique styles. We feature approximately 4 illustrators per publication. I've developed great relationships with all of them."

OREGON QUARTERLY

5228 University of Oregon, Eugene OR 97403. (541)346-5046; (541) 346-5047. **E-mail:** quarterly@ uoregon.edu. **Website:** www.oregonquarterly.com. Estab. 1919. Circ. 100,000. Quarterly 4-color alumni magazine. Emphasizes regional (Northwest) issues and events as addressed by University of Oregon faculty members and alumni. Sample copies available for SASE with first-class postage.

ILLUSTRATION Approached by 25 illustrators/year. Buys 1-2 illustrations/issue, nearly always from artists previously purchased from.

FIRST CONTACT & TERMS Illustrators: E-mail query and link to website or portfolio. Responds only if interested. Portfolio review not required. Buys one-time rights for print and electronic versions. **Pays on acceptance**; rates negotiable. Accepts previously published artwork.

ORGANIC GARDENING

Rodale, 400 S. 10th St., Emmaus PA 18098-0099. **E-mail:** og@rodale.com. **Website:** www.organicgarden ing.com. **Contact:** Jim Oseland, editor in chief. Estab. 1942. Circ. 300,000. Magazine emphasizing gardening; 4-color; uncluttered design. "*Organic Gardening* is for gardeners who enjoy gardening as an integral part of a healthy lifestyle. Editorial shows readers how to grow flowers, edibles, and herbs, as well as information on ecological landscaping. Also covers organic topics including soil building and pest control." Published 6 times/year.

ILLUSTRATION Buys 10 illustrations/issue. Works on assignment only.

FIRST CONTACT & TERMS Illustrators: Send tearsheets. Samples are filed or are returned by SASE only. Occasionally needs technical illustration. Buys first rights or one-time rights. Sample copies available only with SASE.

TIPS "Our emphasis is 'how-to' gardening; therefore illustrators with experience in the field will have a greater chance of being published. Detailed and fine rendering quality is essential."

ORLANDO MAGAZINE

801 N. Magnolia Ave., Suite 201, Orlando FL 32803. (407)423-0618. **Fax:** (407)237-6258. **E-mail:** christine. dupont@orlandomagazine.com. **Website:** www.orlandomagazine.com. **Contact:** Christine Dupont, art director. Estab. 1946. Circ. 40,000. "We are a 4-color monthly city/regional magazine covering the Central Florida area—local issues, sports, home and garden, business, entertainment and dining." Accepts previously published artwork. Originals are returned at job's completion. Sample copies available.

ILLUSTRATION Buys 2-3 illustrations/issue. Has featured illustrations by T. Sirell, Rick Martin, Mike Wright, Jon Krause. Assigns 100% of illustrations to experienced, but not necessarily well-known illustrators. Works on assignment only. Needs editorial illustration.

DESIGN Needs freelancers for design and production.

FIRST CONTACT & TERMS Illustrators: Send postcard, brochure or tearsheets. Samples are filed and are not returned. Responds only if interested with a specific job. Portfolio review not required. Buys first rights, one-time rights or all rights (rarely). Pays for design by the project.

TIPS "Send appropriate samples. Most of my illustration hiring is via direct mail. The magazine field is still a great place for illustration. Have several ideas ready after reading editorial to add to or enhance our initial concept."

OUR STATE: DOWN HOME IN NORTH CAROLINA

P.O. Box 4552, Greensboro NC 27404. (336)286-0600; (800)948-1409. **Fax:** (336)286-0100. **E-mail:** art_director@ourstate.com; editorial@ourstate.com; marketing@ourstate.com. **Website:** www.ourstate.com. editorial@ourstate.com. Estab. 1933. Circ. 140,000. Monthly 4-color consumer magazine featuring travel, history and culture of North Carolina. Art guidelines free with #10 SASE and first-class postage.

ILLUSTRATION Approached by 6 illustrators/year. Buys 1-10 illustrations/issue. Features representations of towns in North Carolina in every issue, plus various illustrations for "down home" North Carolina stories. Prefers vintage/antique/literary look. Assigns 100% to new and emerging illustrators. 100% of freelance illustration demands knowledge of Illustrator.

FIRST CONTACT & TERMS Illustrators: Send e-mail with a link to work. Send postcard sample or nonreturnable samples. Samples are not filed and are not returned. Portfolio review not required. Buys one-time rights. Pays on publication: $400-600 for color cover; $75-350 for b&w inside; $75-350 for color inside; $350 for 2-page spreads. Finds illustrators through web searches, marketing mailings, resource books.

☉ OUTDOOR CANADA MAGAZINE

54 St. Patrick St., Toronto Ontario M5T 1V1, Canada. (416)599-2000. **E-mail:** editorial@outdoorcanada.ca. **Website:** www.outdoorcanada.ca. Estab. 1972. Circ. 90,000. 4-color magazine for Canadian anglers and hunters. Stories on fishing, hunting and conservation. Readers are 81% male. Publishes 6 regular issues/year. "We are looking for strong, attention-grabbing images that capture the love our readers have for hunting and fishing. We're interested in finding and cultivating new Canadian talent and appreciate submissions from new photographers and illustrators to add to our list."

ILLUSTRATION Approached by 12-15 illustrators/year. Buys approximately 10 drawings/issue. Has featured illustrations by Malcolm Cullen, Stephen MacEachren and Jerzy Kolatch. Features humorous, computer and spot illustration. Assigns 90% to experienced, but not well-known illustrators; 10% to new and emerging illustrators. Uses freelancers mainly for illustrating features and columns. Uses pen & ink, acrylic, oil and pastel.

DESIGN Needs freelancers for multimedia. 20% of freelance work demands knowledge of Photoshop, Illustrator and Adobe InDesign.

FIRST CONTACT & TERMS Illustrators: Send postcard sample or tearsheets. Designers: Send brochure, tearsheets and postcards. Accepts disk submissions compatible with Illustrator 7.0. Send EPS, TIFF and PICT files. Buys first rights. Fees negotiated. Pays designers by the project. Artists should show a representative sampling of their work. Finds most artists through references/word of mouth.

TIPS "Meet our deadlines and our budget. Know our product. Fishing and hunting knowledge an asset."

☉ OWL

10 Lower Spadina Ave., Suite #400, Toronto Ontario M5V 2Z2, Canada. (416)340-2700 x318. **Fax:** (416)340-9769. **E-mail:** owl@owlkids.com. **Website:** www.owlkids.com. **Contact:** Tracey Jacklin; Angela Colucci. Estab. 1979. Circ. 67,900 in North America.

10 issues/year. Children's discovery magazine. Also publishes *Chirp* for ages 3-6 and *chikaDEE* for ages 6-9. Each issue contains photos, illustrations, an easy-to-read animal story, a craft project, fiction, puzzles, a science experiment and a pull-out poster. Originals returned at job's completion. Sample copies available. Uses all types of conventional methods of illustration. Digital illustrators should be familiar with Illustrator or Photoshop.

○ The same company that publishes *chickaDEE* now also publishes *Chirp*, a science, nature and discovery magazine for preschoolers 2 to 6 years old, and *OWL*, a similar publication for children over 8 years old.

ILLUSTRATION Approached by 500-750 illustrators/year. Buys 3-7 illustrations/issue. Works on assignment only. Prefers animals, children, situations and fiction. All styles, loaded with humor but not cartoons. Realistic depictions of animals and nature. Considers all media and computer art. No b&w illustrations.

FIRST CONTACT & TERMS Illustrators: Send postcard sample, photocopies and tearsheets. Accepts disk submissions compatible with Illustrator 8.0. Send EPS files. Samples are filed or returned by SASE. Will contact for portfolio review if interested. Portfolio should include final art, tearsheets and photocopies. Buys all rights. Pays within 30 days of invoice. Finds artists through sourcebooks, word of mouth, submissions as well as looking in other magazines to see who's doing what.

TIPS "Please become familiar with the magazine before you submit. Ask yourself whether your style is appropriate before spending the money on your mailing. Magazines are ephemeral and topical. Ask yourself if your illustrations are editorial and contemporary. Some styles suit books or other forms better than magazines." Impress this art director by being "fantastic, enthusiastic and unique."

THE OXFORD AMERICAN

P.O. BOX 3235, Little Rock AR 72205. (501)374-0000. **Fax:** (501)374-0001. **E-mail:** editors@oxfordamerican.org. **Website:** www.oxfordamerican.org. **Contact:** Roger D. Hodge, editor; Eliza Bornè, managing editor. Circ. 55,000. Quarterly literary magazine. "The Southern magazine of good writing." Art guidelines on website.

○ This award-winning magazine suspended publication in July 2003, but it relaunched in the fall of 2004 as a not-for-profit publication allied with the University of Central Arkansas.

ILLUSTRATION Approached by many artists/year. Uses a varying number of illustrations/year. Considers all media.

FIRST CONTACT & TERMS Prefers digital submissions (attach JPEGs to e-mail) or include link to website. Also accepts printed tearsheets, photocopies or postcard sample of work. Samples are filed. Responds only if interested. To have materials returned, send SASE. Art director will contact artist for portfolio review of final art and roughs if interested. Buys one-time rights. Pays on publication. Finds artists through word of mouth and submissions.

TIPS "See the magazine."

OYEZ REVIEW

Roosevelt University, Dept. of Literature & Languages, 430 S. Michigan Ave., Chicago IL 60605. **E-mail:** oyezreview@roosevelt.edu. **Website:** oyezreview.wordpress.com. Estab. 1965. Circ. 600 with an e-book available. Annual magazine of the Creative Writing Program at Roosevelt University, publishing fiction, creative nonfiction, poetry, and art. There are no restrictions on style, theme, or subject matter. Each issue has 100 pages: 92 pages of text and an 8-page b&w or color spread of 1 artist's work (usually drawing, painting or photography). In addition to the 8-page spread, the front and back cover feature the artist's work as well, totaling 10 pieces.

CARTOONS Now accepting submissions through Submittable as well as regular mail. No longer accepting e-mail submissions.

ILLUSTRATION Features realistic illustrations.

DESIGN Be familiar with InDesign software.

PACIFIC PRESS PUBLISHING ASSOCIATION

1350 North Kings Rd., Nampa ID 83687. (208)465-2500. **Fax:** (208)465-2531. **Website:** www.pacificpress.com. Estab. 1875. Book and magazine publisher. Specializes in Christian lifestyles and Christian outreach.

○ This association publishes magazines and books. Also see *Signs of the Times* listing for needs.

◯ PACIFIC YACHTING

OP Publishing, Ltd., 1166 Alberni St., Suite 802, Vancouver British Columbia V6E 3Z3, Canada. (604)428-

0259. **Fax:** (604)620-0425. **E-mail:** editor@pacific yachting.com; ayates@oppublishing.com. **Website:** www.pacificyachting.com. **Contact:** Dale Miller, editor; Arran Yates, art director. Estab. 1968. Circ. 19,000. Monthly 4-color magazine focused on boating on the West Coast of Canada. Power/sail cruising only. Accepts previously published artwork. Original artwork returned at job's completion. Sample copies available for $6.95 cover price plus postage. Art guidelines not available.

CARTOONS Approached by 12-20 cartoonists/year. Buys 2-3 illustrations or cartoons/issue. Boating themes only; single panel b&w line drawings.

ILLUSTRATION Approached by 25 illustrators/year. Buys 10-20 illustrations/year. Has featured illustrations by Dave Alavoine, Roger Jackson and Tom Shardlow. Boating themes only. Considers pen & ink, watercolor, airbrush, acrylic, colored pencil, oil and charcoal.

FIRST CONTACT & TERMS Cartoonists and Illustrators: Send query letter with brochure and roughs. "Will keep on file and contact if interested." Illustrators: Call for appointment to show portfolio of appropriate samples related to boating on the West Coast. Buys one-time rights. Pays on publication. Pays cartoonists $25-50 for b&w. Pays illustrators $300 for color cover; $50-100 for color inside; $25-50 for spots.

TIPS "Know boats and how to draw them correctly. Know and love my magazine."

PAINT HORSE JOURNAL

American Paint Horse Association, P.O. Box 961023, Ft. Worth TX 76161-0023. (817)834-2742. **Fax:** (817)834-3152. **E-mail:** jhein@apha.com. **Website:** www.phj.apha.com. **Contact:** Jessica Hein, editor. Estab. 1966. Circ. 12,000. Monthly 4-color, official publication of breed registry of the American Paint Horse for people who raise, breed and show, or just appreciate Paints. Original artwork returned after publication if requested. Sample copy for $7 (includes shipping); artist's guidelines for SASE.

ILLUSTRATION Purchase a few illustrations each year.

FIRST CONTACT & TERMS Illustrators: Send business card and samples to be kept on file. Prefers snapshots of original art or photostats as samples. Samples returned by SASE if not filed. Responds in 1 month. Buys first rights but may wish to use small, filler art many times. Payment varies by project.

TIPS "No matter what style of art you use, you must include Paint Horse(s) with conformation acceptable (to the APHA). Horses of Arabian-type, Draft-type or Saddlebred-type conformation or with markings not appropriate for Paint Horses will not be considered. Please refer to our website to learn more about the breed and specifics at www.apha.com/breed."

PARABOLA MAGAZINE

20 W. 20th St., 2nd Floor, New York NY 10011. (212)822-8806; (510) 548-1680. **E-mail:** editorial@parabola.org; ads-promo@parabola.org; info@parabola.org. **Website:** www.parabola.org. Estab. 1974. Circ. 40,000. Quarterly magazine of world myth, religious traditions and arts/comparative religion. Sample copies available. Art guidelines on website.

ILLUSTRATION Approached by 20 illustrators/year. Buys 4-6 illustrations/issue. Prefers traditional b&w high contrast. Considers all media.

FIRST CONTACT & TERMS Illustrators: Send postcard or query letter with printed nonreturnable samples, photocopies and SASE. Accepts disk submissions. Samples are filed. Responds only if interested. Buys one-time rights. Pays on publication (kill fee given for commissioned artwork only); $300 maximum for cover; $150 maximum for b&w inside. Pays $50-100 for spots. Finds illustrators through sourcebooks, magazines, word of mouth and artist's submissions. "We rarely commission cover."

TIPS "Familiarity with religious traditions and symbolism a plus. Timeless or classic look is preferred over trendy."

PARADE MAGAZINE

711 Third Ave., New York NY 10017-4014. (212)450-7000; (615) 327-0747; (212) 478-1910; (312) 948-0310. **E-mail:** mediarelations@parade.com; or via the online contact form. **Website:** www.parade.com. partners@amgparade.com; sollinick@amgparade. Circ. 32 million. Weekly emphasizing general-interest subjects. Sample copies available. Art guidelines available with SASE and first-class postage.

ILLUSTRATION Works on assignment only.

DESIGN Needs freelancers for design. 100% of freelance work demands knowledge of Photoshop, Illustrator, InDesign and QuarkXPress. Prefers local freelancers.

FIRST CONTACT & TERMS Illustrators: Send query letter with brochure, résumé, business card, postcard or tearsheets to be kept on file. Designers: Send query letter with résumé. Call or write for appointment to show portfolio. Responds only if interested. Buys first rights, occasionally all rights. Pays for design by the project, by the day or by the hour depending on assignment.

TIPS "Provide a good balance of work."

PC MAGAZINE

28 E. 28th St., 11th Floor, New York NY 10016. (212)503-5216. **Website:** www.pcmag.com. **Contact:** Cynthia Passanante, creative director. Estab. 1983. Circ. 125,000. Monthly consumer magazine featuring comparative lab-based reviews of current PC hardware and software. Sample copies available.

ILLUSTRATION Approached by 100 illustrators/year. Buys 2-3 illustrations/issue. Considers all media.

FIRST CONTACT & TERMS Send postcard sample or printed samples, photocopies, tearsheets. Accepts CD or e-mail submissions. Samples are filed. Portfolios may be dropped off and should include tearsheets and transparencies; art department keeps for one week to review. **Pays on acceptance.** Payment negotiable for cover and inside; $350 for spots.

PENNSYLVANIA LAWYER

100 South St., Harrisburg PA 17101. (717)238-6715. **E-mail:** editor@pabar.org. **Website:** www.pabar.org. Circ. 30,000. Bimonthly association magazine "featuring nuts and bolts articles and features of interest to lawyers." Sample copies with #10 SASE and first-class postage.

PERSIMMON HILL

1700 NE 63rd St., Oklahoma City OK 73111. (405)478-2250, ext. 213. **Fax:** (405)478-4714. **E-mail:** editor@nationalcowboymuseum.org. **Website:** www.nationalcowboymuseum.org. **Contact:** Judy Hilovsky. Estab. 1970. Circ. 7,500. Biannual 4-color journal of western heritage "focusing on both historical and contemporary themes. It features nonfiction articles on notable persons connected with pioneering the American West; art, rodeo, cowboys, ranching, floral and animal life; or other phenomena of the West of today or yesterday. Lively articles, well written, for a popular audience. Contemporary design follows style of *Architectural Digest*, *European Travel* and *Life*. Accepts no reprints. Pays on publication. Query with clips. We do not accept multiple submissions. Allow a minimum of 6 weeks for a response from the editor and editorial staff. Sample copy for $11.

TIPS "We are a western museum publication. Most illustrations are used to accompany articles. Work with our writers, or suggest illustrations to the editor that can be the basis for a freelance article or a companion story. More interest in the West means we have to provide more contemporary photographs and articles about what people in the West are doing today. Study the magazine first—at least 4 issues."

PEST CONTROL

North Coast Media, 1360 E. Ninth St., Cleveland OH 44114. **Website:** www.mypmp.net. Circ. 21,298. Monthly trade publication for pest control specialists focusing on crawling and flying insect control, termite control, rodent and other pest control and public health issues.

CARTOONS Approached by 50 cartoonists/year. Buys 1-2 cartoons/year. Prefer pest control, single panel and humorous.

ILLUSTRATION Approached by 50 illustrators/year. Buys 3-5 illustrations/year. Prefers pest control. Assigns 50% to new and emerging illustrators.

FIRST CONTACT & TERMS Cartoonists/illustrators: Send postcard sample with URL. After introductory mailing, send follow-up postcard sample every 6 months. Samples are filed. Responds only if interested. Buys one-time rights. Finds freelancers through artists' submissions.

PHILADELPHIA WEEKLY

1617 JFK Blvd., Suite 1005, Philadelphia PA 19103. (215)563-7400. **E-mail:** abarbalios@philadelphiaweekly.com; editor@philadelphiaweekly.com. **Website:** www.philadelphiaweekly.com. **Contact:** Anastasia Barbalios, managing editor. Estab. 1971. Circ. 105,500. Alternative weekly, 4-color, tabloid focusing on news and opinion and arts and culture.

CARTOONS Approached by 25 cartoonists/year. Buys 0-1 cartoon/issue. Prefers single panel, multiple panel, political, humorous, b&w washes, b&w line drawings.

ILLUSTRATION Approached by scores of illustrators/year. Buys 3-5 illustrations/issue. Has featured illustrations by Brian Biggs, Jay Bevenour, James McHugh. Features caricatures of celebrities and politicians; humorous, realistic and spot illustrations. Considers a wide range of styles.

FIRST CONTACT & TERMS Cartoonists: Send query letter with b&w photocopies. Illustrators: Send postcard sample or query letter with printed samples and photocopies. Send nonreturnable samples. Samples are filed and are not returned. Responds only if interested. Buys one-time rights. Pays on publication. Finds illustrators through promotional samples.

PLANNING

American Planning Association, 205 N. Michigan Ave., Suite 1200, Chicago IL 60601. (312)431-9100. **Fax:** (312)786-6700. **E-mail:** slewis@planning.org. **Website:** www.planning.org. **Contact:** Sylvia Lewis, editor; Joan Cairney, art director. Estab. 1972. Circ. 44,000. Monthly magazine emphasizing urban planning for adult, college-educated readers who are regional and urban planners in city, state, or federal agencies or in private business, or university faculty or students.

FIRST CONTACT & TERMS Send query letter with samples; include SASE for return of material. Responds in 1 month. Previously published work OK. Pays on publication. Credit line given.

PLAYBOY MAGAZINE

9346 Civic Center Dr., #200, Beverly Hills CA 90210. (310)264-6600. **Fax:** (310)786-7440. **Website:** www. playboy.com. Estab. 1953. Monthly.

CARTOONS Playboy Enterprises, Inc., Cartoon Dept., 730 Fifth Ave., New York NY 10019.

ILLUSTRATION Approached by 700 illustrators/year. Prefers "uncommercial looking" artwork. Considers all media.

FIRST CONTACT & TERMS Illustrators: Send postcard sample or query letter with slides and photocopies or other appropriate sample. Does not accept originals. Samples are filed or returned. Responds in 2 weeks. Buys all rights. **Pays on acceptance.**

TIPS "No phone calls, only formal submissions of 5 pieces."

PLAYSTATION: THE OFFICIAL MAGAZINE

Future US, Inc., 4000 Shoreline Court, Suite 400, South San Francisco CA 94080. (650)872-1642. **Website:** www.futureus.com. **Contact:** art director. Estab. 1997. Circ. 400,000. Monthly 4-color consumer magazine focused on PlayStation video games for youth (preteens and older). Style is "comic booky." Free sample copies available.

CARTOONS Prefers multiple-panel, humorous b&w line drawings; manga/comic book style.

ILLUSTRATION Approached by 20-30 illustrators/year. Buys 24 illustrations/issue. Has featured illustrations by Joe Madureira, Art Adams, Adam War-

ren, Hajeme Soroyana, Royo, J. Scott Campbell and Travis Charest. Features comic-book style, computer, humorous, realistic and spot illustration. Preferred subject: video game characters. Assigns 80% of illustrations to well-known or "name" illustrators; 10% to experienced, but not well-known, illustrators; and 10% to new and emerging illustrators. 50% of freelance illustration demands knowledge of Illustrator and Photoshop.

FIRST CONTACT & TERMS Cartoonists: Send query letter with b&w and color photocopies and samples. Illustrators: Send postcard sample or nonreturnable samples; send query letter with printed samples, photocopies and tearsheets. Accepts Mac-compatible disk submissions. E-mail JPEG or web link (preferred method). Samples are filed. Responds only if interested. Will contact artist for portfolio review if interested. Buys all rights. Pays on publication. Finds illustrators through magazines and word of mouth.

TIPS "If you're an artist, confident that your vision is unique, your quality is the best, ever evolving, send us samples!"

PN

PVA Publications, 2111 E. Highland Ave., Suite 180, Phoenix AZ 85016-4702. (602)224-0500. **E-mail:** andy@pvamag.com; anngarvey@pvamag.com; chuck@pvamag.com. **Website:** www.pvamag.com. **Contact:** Andy Nemann (article/editorial, text and photo submissions); Ann Garvey and Chuck McKenzie (cartoons and photos). Estab. 1947. Formerly known as *Paraplegia News*. Circ. 30,000. Monthly 4-color magazine emphasizing wheelchair living for wheelchair users, rehabilitation specialists and caregivers. Accepts previously published artwork. Original artwork not returned after publication. Sample copy free with large-size SASE and $4 postage.

CARTOONS Buys cartoons according to need. Prefers b&w line drawings with or without gagline depicting wheelchair living with medical and/or financial topics as themes. Accepted file formats are InDesign, Photoshop or Illustrator.

FIRST CONTACT & TERMS Submission guidelines available online. Prefers digital images, but will accept prints, slides and transparencies.

POCKETS

The Upper Room, P.O. Box 340004, Nashville TN 37203. (615)340-7333. **E-mail:** pockets@upperroom. org. **Website:** pockets.upperroom.org. **Contact:** Lynn

W. Gilliam, editor. Estab. 1981. Magazine published 11 times/year. "*Pockets* is a Christian devotional magazine for children ages 6-12. All submissions should address the broad theme of the magazine. Each issue is built around one theme with material which can be used by children in a variety of ways. Scripture stories, fiction, poetry, prayers, art, graphics, puzzles, and activities are included. Submissions do not need to be overtly religious. They should help children experience a Christian lifestyle that is not always a neatly-wrapped moral package, but is open to the continuing revelation of God's will. Seasonal material, both secular and liturgical, is desired."

FIRST CONTACT & TERMS Send photos, contact sheets, prints, or digital images. Must be 300 dpi.

PORTLAND REVIEW

Portland State University, P.O. Box 751, Portland OR 97207. **Website:** portlandreview.org. **Contact:** Alex Dannemiller, editor-in-chief. Estab. 1956. Circ. 1,500. Triannual magazine covering short prose, poetry, photography, and art. Art guidelines available on website.

ILLUSTRATION Approached by 50 illustrators/year. We don't pay contributors. Features art illustrations and photography. Currently prefer Portland-based artists but international welcome.

FIRST CONTACT & TERMS Accepts submissions only through Submittable submission manager. Prefers Mac-compatible. Samples are not filed and not returned. Responds with acceptance in 2-4 months. Portfolio not required.

PRACTICELINK

415 2nd Ave., Hinton WV 25951. (502)272-3831, (800)776-8383 Ext. 834. **Website:** www.practicelink. com. **Contact:** Barbara Barry, creative director; Tammy Hager, director. Estab. 1991. Circ. 80,000. Formerly *Unique Opportunities*. Quarterly career magazine for physicians. Audience is 80,000 physicians who will soon be looking for a new practice. Editorial focus is on physician career topics. Prefers files in JPEG, TIFF, or PDF format.

ILLUSTRATION Buys 1 illustration/issue. Works on assignment or stock. Considers pen ink, mixed media, collage, pastel and computer illustration. Must supply in digital format.

FIRST CONTACT & TERMS Views online portfolios. E-mail digital files. Buys first or one-time rights. Pays 30 days after acceptance; $950 for color cover; $300 for spots. Finds artists through Internet only. Do not send samples in the mail.

PRAIRIE JOURNAL OF CANADIAN LITERATURE

28 Crowfoot Terrace, NW, P.O. Box 68073, Calgary Alberta T3G 3N8, Canada. **E-mail:** prairiejournal@ yahoo.com. **Website:** www.prairiejournal.org. Estab. 1983. Circ. 750. Biannual literary magazine. Sample copies available for $6 each; art guidelines and past cover art available for viewing online.

ILLUSTRATION Approached by 25 illustrators/year. Buys 6 illustrations/year. Has featured cover art by Amanda Rehagen and John Howard, illustrations by Hubert Lacey, Rita Diebolt and Lucie Chan. Considers artistic/experimental b&w line drawings or screened prints.

FIRST CONTACT & TERMS Illustrators: Send postcard sample or query letter with b&w photocopies. Samples are filed. Responds only if interested. Portfolio review not required. Acquires one-time rights. Pays $50 maximum (Canadian) for b&w cover and $25 maximum for inside drawings. Pays on publication. Finds freelancers through unsolicited submissions and queries.

TIPS "We are looking for b&w line drawings that are high-contrast and camera-ready copy. Never send originals through the mail."

PRAIRIE MESSENGER

Benedictine Monks of St. Peter's Abbey, P.O. Box 190, Muenster Saskatchewan S0K 2Y0, Canada. (306)682-1772. **Fax:** (306)682-5285. **E-mail:** pm.canadian@ stpeterspress.ca. **Website:** www.prairiemessenger. ca. **Contact:** Maureen Weber, associate editor. Estab. 1904. Circ. 5,000. Weekly Catholic publication published by the Benedictine Monks of St. Peter's Abbey in Muenster Saskatchewan, Canada. Has a strong focus on ecumenism, social justice, interfaith relations, aboriginal issues, arts and culture.

FIRST CONTACT & TERMS E-mail JPEG samples at 72dpi.

PREMONITIONS

13 Hazely Combe, Arrenton Isle of Wight PO30 3AJ, United Kingdom. **E-mail:** mail@pigasuspress.co.uk. **Website:** www.pigasuspress.co.uk. **Contact:** Tony Lee, editor.

FIRST CONTACT & TERMS Wants "quality color or b&w genre illustrations for A4 front and back covers. Also, talented artists wanted to produce sequential artwork for our unique 'graphic poems.'" Send photocopied samples of work, published or unpublished, to contribute.

◎ THE PRESBYTERIAN RECORD

50 Wynford Dr., Toronto Ontario M3C 1J7, Canada. (416)441-1111; (800)619-7301, (905) 833-6200 ex. 23. **Fax:** (416)441-2825. **E-mail:** record@presbyterianre cord.ca; online form. **Website:** www.presbyterianre cord.ca. Circ. 50,000. Published 11 times/year. Deals with family-oriented religious themes. Original artwork returned after publication. Simultaneous submissions and previously published work OK. Free sample copy and artists' guidelines for SASE with first-class postage.

CARTOONS Approached by 12 cartoonists/year. Buys 1-2 cartoons/issue. Interested in some theme or connection to religion.

ILLUSTRATION Approached by 6 illustrators/year. Buys 1 illustration/year on religion. Has featured illustrations by Ed Schnurr, Claudio Ghirardo and Chrissie Wysotski. Features humorous, realistic and spot illustration. Assigns 50% of illustrations to new and emerging illustrators. "We are interested in excellent color artwork for cover." Any line style acceptable—should reproduce well on newsprint. Works on assignment only.

FIRST CONTACT & TERMS Cartoonists: Send roughs and SAE (nonresidents include IRC). Illustrators: Send query letter with brochure showing art style or tearsheets, photocopies and photographs. Will accept computer illustrations compatible with Quark XPress 4.1, Illustrator 8.0, Photoshop 6.0. Samples returned by SAE (nonresidents include IRC). Responds in 1 month. To show a portfolio, mail final art and color and b&w tearsheets. Buys all rights on a work-for-hire basis. Pays on publication. Pays cartoonists $25-50 for b&w. Pays illustrators $50-100 for b&w cover; $100-300 for color cover; $25-80 for b&w inside; $25-60 for spots.

TIPS "We don't want any 'cute' samples (in cartoons). We prefer some theological insight in cartoons; some comment on religious trends and practices."

PRESBYTERIANS TODAY

Presbyterian Church (U.S.A.), 100 Witherspoon St., Louisville KY 40202-1396. (502)569-5627. **Fax:** (502)569-8887. **E-mail:** editor@pcusa.org. **Website:** www.pcusa.org/today. **Contact:** Patrick David Heery, editor. Estab. 1867. Circ. 40,000. Denominational magazine published 8 times/year covering religion, denominational activities, and public issues for members of the Presbyterian Church (U.S.A.). "The magazine's purpose is to increase understanding and appreciation of what the church and its members are doing to live out their Christian faith."

ILLUSTRATION Works on assignment only. Media varies according to need.

PREVENTION

E-mail: editor@prevention.com. **Website:** www.pre vention.com. Estab. 1950. Circ. 3,150,000. Monthly consumer magazine covering health and fitness for women. Art guidelines available.

ILLUSTRATION Approached by 500-750 illustrators/year. Buys 1-2 spot illustrations/issue. Considers all media.

FIRST CONTACT & TERMS Illustrators: Send postcard sample or query letter with photocopies, tearsheets, URL. Samples are filed. Responds only if interested. Art director will contact artist for portfolio review of b&w, color, photographs, tearsheets, transparencies if interested. Buys rights for all media. Finds illustrators through www.ispot.com, magazines, submissions.

PRICK OF THE SPINDLE

P.O. Box 17067, Birmingham AL 35217. **E-mail:** pse ditor@prickofthespindle.com. **Website:** www.prick ofthespindle.com. **Contact:** Cynthia Reeser, editor-in-chief. Estab. 2007. Circ. 6,200 hits/day. Literary magazine published quarterly online, biannually in print. We accept artwork that shows imagination and skill that covers a broad range of themes and subjects. Sample copy available for $10. Art/photo submission guidelines available on website.

ILLUSTRATION Approached by approximately 150 freelancers/year. Buys 10-15 illustrations from freelancers/year. Featured artists include Rose Mambert, Regina Valluzzi and Loren Kantor. Features realistic, abstract and interpretive illustrations of general artistic subjects. Prefers b&w line drawings (for print edition—cover art and interior illustrations). 75% of assignments given to new and emerging illustrators. 10% of work demands computer skills. Artists should be familiar with Illustrator and Photoshop. Accepts prints in various sizes in glossy, matte, color or b&w, as well as images in digital format.

FIRST CONTACT & TERMS Send query letter or e-mail with résumé, prints and SASE (regular mail) or

JPEG samples at 72 dpi. Keeps samples on file, provide résumé, business card or self-promotion piece to be kept on file for future assignments. Samples only return with SASE. Responds in 7 days. Will contact artist for portfolio review if interested. Portfolio should include b&w, color, finished art, original art, photographs. Considers simultaneous submissions and previously published work. Credit line given. Buys first North American rights. Willing to negotiate. Finds freelancers through submissions.

PRINT MAGAZINE

F+W, a Content + eCommerce Company, 10151 Carver Rd., Suite #200, Blue Ash OH 45242. (513)531-2690. **E-mail:** info@printmag.com. **Website:** www.print mag.com. **Contact:** Zachary Petit, editor. Estab. 1940. Circ. 55,000. Bimonthly professional magazine for "art directors, designers and anybody else interested in graphic design." Art guidelines available.

FIRST CONTACT & TERMS Illustrators/designers: Send postcard sample, printed samples and tearsheets. Samples are filed. Responds only if interested. Art director will contact artist for portfolio review if interested. Portfolios may be dropped off every Wednesday, and artists are responsible for retrieving them. Buys first rights. Pays on acceptance. Finds illustrators through agents, sourcebooks, word of mouth and submissions.

TIPS "Read the magazine: We showcase design, typography, illustration and photography. We're also interested in individual creative approaches to design problems. Note: We have themed issues; please ask to see our editorial calendar."

☺ PRISM INTERNATIONAL

Dept. of Creative Writing, Buch E462, 1866 Main Mall, University of British Columbia, Vancouver British Columbia V6T 1Z1, Canada. (604)822-2514. **Fax:** (604)822-3616. **E-mail:** prismcirculation@gmail.com. **Website:** www.prismmagazine.ca. Estab. 1959. Circ. 1,200. Quarterly literary magazine. "We use cover art for each issue." Sample copies available for $12 each; art guidelines free for SASE with first-class Canadian postage.

ILLUSTRATION Buys 1 cover illustration/issue. Has featured illustrations by Mark Ryden, Mark Mothersbaugh, Annette Allwood, the Clayton Brothers, Maria Capolongo, Mark Korn, Scott Bakal, Chris Woods, Kate Collie and Angela Grossman. Features representational and non-representational fine art.

Assigns 50% of illustrations to experienced but not well-known illustrators; 50% to new and emerging illustrators. "Most of our covers are full color artwork and sometimes photography; on occasion we feature a b&w cover."

FIRST CONTACT & TERMS Illustrators: Send postcard sample. Most samples are filed; those not filed are returned by SASE if requested by artist. Responds in 6 months. Portfolio review not required. Buys first rights. "Image may also be used for promotional purposes related to the magazine." Pays on publication: $300 Canadian and 2 copies of magazine. Original artwork is returned to the artist at job's completion. Finds artists through word of mouth and going to local exhibits.

TIPS "We are looking for fine art suitable for the cover of a literary magazine. Your work should be polished, confident, cohesive and original. Please send postcard samples of your work. As with our literary contest, we will choose work that is exciting and which reflects the contemporary nature of the magazine."

PROCEEDINGS

U.S. Naval Institute, 291 Wood Rd., Annapolis MD 21402-5034. (410)268-6110. **Fax:** (410)571-1703. **E-mail:** articlesubmissions@usni.org. **Website:** www. usni.org/magazines/proceedings. **Contact:** Paul M. Merzlak, editor-in-chief; Emily Martin, photo researcher. Estab. 1873. Circ. 60,000. Monthly 4-color magazine emphasizing naval and maritime subjects. "*Proceedings* is an independent forum for the sea services." Design is clean, uncluttered layout, "sophisticated." Accepts previously published material. Sample copies and art guidelines available.

CARTOONS Buys 23 cartoons/year from freelancers. Prefers cartoons assigned to tie in with editorial topics.

ILLUSTRATION Buys 1 illustration/issue. Works on assignment only. Has featured illustrations by Tom Freeman, R.G. Smith, and Eric Smith. Features humorous and realistic illustration; charts and graphs; informational graphics; computer and spot illustration. Needs editorial and technical illustration. "We like a variety of styles if possible. Do excellent illustrations and meet the requirement for military appeal." Prefers illustrations assigned to tie in with editorial topics.

FIRST CONTACT & TERMS Cartoonists: Send query letter with samples of style to be kept on file. Illustrators: Send query letter with printed samples, tearsheets, or photocopies. Accepts submissions on disk (call production manager for details). Samples are filed or are returned only if requested by artist. Responds only if interested. Publication will contact artist for portfolio review if interested. Negotiates rights purchased. Sometimes requests work on spec before assigning job. Pays cartoonists $25-50 for b&w, $50 for color. Pays illustrators $50 for b&w inside; $50-75 for color inside; $150-200 for color cover; $25 minimum for spots. "Contact us first to see what our needs are."

☼ ⬤ PROFIT

Rogers Media, 1 Mt. Pleasant Rd., 11th Floor, Toronto Ontario M4Y 2Y5, Canada. (416)764-1402. **Fax:** (416)764-1404. **E-mail:** profit@profit.rogers.com. **Website:** www.profitguide.com. Estab. 1982. Circ. 84,632. Illustrators: Send postcard or other nonreturnable samples. Accepts Mac-compatible disk submissions. Samples are not returned. Will contact artist for portfolio review if interested. Buys first rights. **Pays on acceptance**; $500-750 for color inside; $750-1,000 for 2-page spreads; $350 for spots. Pays in Canadian funds. Finds illustrators through promo pieces, other magazines.

ILLUSTRATION Buys 3-5 illustrations/issue. Has featured illustrations by Jerzy Kolacz, Jason Schneider, Ian Phillips. Features charts and graphs, computer, realistic and humorous illustration, informational graphics, and spot illustrations of business subjects. Assigns 50% of illustrations to well-known or "name" illustrations; 50% to experienced but not well-known illustrators.

THE PROGRESSIVE

409 E. Main St., Madison WI 53703. (608)257-4626. **Fax:** (608)257-3373. **E-mail:** editorial@progressive. org; mattr@progressive.org. **Website:** www.progressive.org. **Contact:** Matthew Rothschild, editor. Estab. 1909. Monthly b&w plus 4-color cover political magazine. "Grassroots publication from a left perspective, interested in foreign and domestic issues of peace and social justice." Originals returned at job's completion. Free sample copy and art guidelines.

ILLUSTRATION Works with 50 illustrators/year. Buys 10 b&w illustrations/issue. Features humorous and political illustration. Has featured illustrations by Luba Lukova, Alex Nabaum and Seymour Chwast. Assigns 30% of illustrations to new and emerging il-

lustrators. Needs editorial illustration that is "original, smart and bold." Works on assignment only.

FIRST CONTACT & TERMS Illustrators: Send query letter with tearsheets and/or photocopies. Samples returned by SASE. Responds in 6 weeks. Portfolio review not required. Pays $1,000 for b&w and color cover; $300 for b&w line or tone drawings/paintings/collage inside. Buys first rights. Do not send original art. Send samples, postcards or photocopies and appropriate postage for materials to be returned.

TIPS "Check out a copy of the magazine to see what kinds of art we've published in the past. A free sample copy is available by visiting our website."

PUBLIC CITIZEN NEWS

1600 20th St. NW, Washington DC 20009. (202)588-1000. **E-mail:** bblair@citizen.org. **Website:** www.citizen.org. **Contact:** Bridgette Blair, editorial and art director. Circ. 70,000. Bimonthly magazine emphasizing consumer issues for the membership of Public Citizen, a group founded by Ralph Nader in 1971. Accepts previously published material. Sample copy available with 9×12 SASE and first-class postage.

ILLUSTRATION Buys up to 2 illustrations/issue. Assigns 15% of illustrations to new and emerging illustrators. Prefers contemporary styles in pen & ink.

FIRST CONTACT & TERMS Illustrators: Send query letter with samples to be kept on file. Buys first rights or one-time rights. Pays on publication. Payment negotiable.

TIPS "Send several keepable samples that show a range of styles and the ability to conceptualize. We want cartoons that lampoon policies and politicians, as well as 4-color pen & ink or watercolor illustrations."

A PUBLIC SPACE

323 Dean St., Brooklyn NY 11217. (718)858-8067. **E-mail:** general@apublicspace.org. **Website:** www.apublicspace.org. **Contact:** Brigid Hughes, founding editor; Anne McPeak, managing editor.

○ *A Public Space*, published quarterly, "is an independent magazine of literature and culture. In an era that has relegated literature to the margins, we plan to make fiction and poetry the stars of a new conversation. We believe that stories are how we make sense of our lives and how we learn about other lives. We believe that stories matter." Single copy: $15; subscription: $36/year or $60/2 years.

FIRST CONTACT & TERMS Sample artwork, to be considered as story illustrations or as portfolios, can be sent to art@apublicspace.org. Please send no more than 4 low-res files. All artwork will be kept on file.

PUBLISHERS WEEKLY

71 W. 23rd St., #1608, New York NY 10010. (212)377-5500; (212) 377-5703. **E-mail:** cchiu@publishersweekly.com; dberchenko@publishersweekly.com. **Website:** www.publishersweekly.com. **Contact:** Clive Chiu, art director; Dan Berchenko, managing editor. Circ. 50,000. Weekly magazine emphasizing book publishing for "people involved in the creative or the technical side of publishing." Original artwork is returned to the artist after publication.

ILLUSTRATION Buys 75 illustrations/year. Works on assignment only. "Open to all styles."

FIRST CONTACT & TERMS Illustrators: Send postcard sample or query letter with brochure, tearsheets, photocopies. Samples are not returned. Responds only if interested. **Pays on acceptance.**

QUE ONDA!

P.O. Box 692150, Houston TX 77269-2150. (713)880-1133; (800)331-1374. **Fax:** (713)880-2322. **E-mail:** aida@queondamagazine.com; staff@queondamagazine.com. **Website:** www.queondamagazine.com. **Contact:** Aida Ulloa, art director; Oscar Guevara, assistant editor. Estab. 1993. Circ. 160,000. Biweekly bilingual magazine providing news and entertainment sources for Latino community in and around San Antonio and Houston areas. Focusing on local politics, area celebrities, health, sports and food.

ILLUSTRATION Approached by 20 illustrators/year. Buys 10 illustrations/year. Features caricatures of local celebrities/politicians, Latino community, sports, health and local politics. Assigns 50% to new and emerging illustrators.

FIRST CONTACT & TERMS Send postcard sample. After introductory mailing, send follow-up postcard sample every 6 months. Responds only if interested. Buys one-time rights.

○ QUILL & QUIRE

111 Queen St. E., Suite 320, Toronto Ontario M5C 1S2, Canada. (416)364-3333. **Fax:** (416)595-5415. **E-mail:** sjager@quillandquire.com. **Website:** www.quillandquire.com. **Contact:** Shannon Jager, art director. Estab. 1935. Monthly magazine of the Canadian book trade. Features book news and reviews for publishers, booksellers, librarians, writers, students and educators.

ILLUSTRATION Approached by 25 illustrators/year. Buys 3 visuals/issue. Assigns 1 to 2 illustrations per issue, 11 issues per year. 100% of illustrations to experienced but not necessarily well-known illustrators. Considers pen & ink and collage. 10% of freelance illustration requires knowledge of Photoshop, Illustrator, InDesign and QuarkXPress.

FIRST CONTACT & TERMS Send postcard sample. Accepts disk submissions. Samples are filed. Responds only if interested. Negotiates rights purchased. **Pays on acceptance.** Finds illustrators through word of mouth, submissions, and updated database.

RANGER RICK

1100 Wildlife Center Dr., Reston VA 20190. **E-mail:** Use online contact form. **Website:** www.nwf.org/kidsd. Estab. 1967. Monthly 4-color children's magazine focusing on wildlife and conservation.

ILLUSTRATION Approached by 100-200 illustrators/year. Buys 4-6 illustrations/issue. Has featured illustrations by Danielle Jones, Jack Desrocher, John Dawson and Dave Clegg. Features computer, humorous, natural science and realistic illustrations. Preferred subjects children, wildlife and natural world. Assigns 1% of illustrations to new and emerging illustrators. 50% of freelance illustration demands knowledge of Illustrator, Photoshop.

FIRST CONTACT & TERMS Accepts Mac-compatible disk submissions. Samples are filed or returned by SASE. Responds in 3 months. Will contact artist for portfolio review if interested. Buys one-time rights. Pays on publication. Pay depends on project; $200-$2,500.

TIPS "Looking for new artists to draw animals using Illustrator, Photoshop and other computer drawing programs. Please read our magazine before submitting."

REAL ESTATE

RISMedia, Inc., 69 East Ave., Norwalk CT 06851. (800)724-6000. **Fax:** (203)855-1234. **E-mail:** christy@rismedia.com. **Website:** www.rismedia.com. **Contact:** Christy LaSalle, art director. Circ. 42,100. Monthly trade publication for real estate and relocation professionals.

ILLUSTRATION Approached by 50 illustrators/year. Buys 10 illustrations/year. Features families, houses, real estate topics and relocation. Assigns 50% to new and emerging illustrators.

FIRST CONTACT & TERMS Cartoonists: Send 2-3 photocopies of cartoons of real estate topics. Illustrators: Send postcard sample. After introductory mailing, send follow-up postcard sample every 4-6 months. Samples are filed. Responds only if interested. Buys one-time rights. Finds freelancers through artists' submissions.

RELIX

104 W. 29th St., 11th Floor, New York NY 10001. (646)230-0100. **Fax:** (646)230-0200. **E-mail:** dean@relix.com. **Website:** www.relix.com. Estab. 1974. Circ. 100,000. Bimonthly consumer magazine emphasizing independent music and the jamband scene.

FIRST CONTACT & TERMS Cartoonists: Send query letter with finished cartoons. Illustrators: Send query letter with SASE and photocopies. Samples are not filed and are returned by SASE if requested by artist. Responds to the artist only if interested. Portfolio review not required. Buys first-time rights. Pays on publication. Finds artists through word of mouth.

TIPS "Not looking for any skeleton artwork."

REP.

1166 Avenue of the Americas, 10th Floor, New York NY 10036. (212)204-4260. **E-mail:** sean.barrow@penton.com. **Website:** www.wealthmanagement.com. **Contact:** Sean Barrow, art director. Estab. 1976. Circ. 100,000. Monthly trade publication provides stockbrokers and investment advisors with industry news and financial trends.

ILLUSTRATION Approached by 100 illustrators/year. Buys 15 illustrations/year. Features spot illustrations of business.

FIRST CONTACT & TERMS Illustrators: Send postcard sample. Send electronically or via CD as 300 dpi JPEG files. After introductory mailing, send follow-up postcard sample every 6 months. Responds only if interested. Company will contact artist for portfolio review if interested. Pays illustrators $500-1,500 for cover. Pays 30 days after publication. Buys one-time rights. Finds freelancers through artists' submissions.

TIPS "If you wish to contribute, please spend some time familiarizing yourself with REP's various sections and features."

RESTAURANT HOSPITALITY

Penton Media, 1300 E. Ninth St., Cleveland OH 44114. (216)931-9942. **Fax:** (216)696-0836. **E-mail:** chris.ro

berto@penton.com. **Website:** www.restaurant-hospitality.com. **Contact:** Chris Roberto, group creative director; Michael Sanson, editor-in-chief. Estab. 1919. Circ. 100,000. Monthly. Emphasizes "ideas for full-service restaurants" including business strategies and industry menu trends. Readers are restaurant owners/operators and chefs for full-service independent and chain concepts.

ILLUSTRATION Approached by 150 illustrators/year. Buys 3-5 illustrations per issue (combined assigned and stock). Prefers food- and business-related illustration in a variety of styles. Has featured illustrations by Mark Shaver, Paul Watson and Brian Raszka. Assigns 10% of illustrations to well-known or "name" illustrators; 60% to experienced but not well-known illustrators; and 30% to new and emerging illustrators. Welcomes stock submissions.

FIRST CONTACT & TERMS Illustrators: Postcard samples preferred. Follow-up card every 3-6 months. Buys one-time rights. **Pays on acceptance.** Payment range varies for full page or covers; $300-500 range for departments/features. Finished illustrations must be delivered as high-res digital. E-mail or FTP preferred.

TIPS "I am always open to new approaches—contemporary, modern visuals that explore various aspects of the restaurant industry and restaurant experience. Please include a web address on your sample so I can view an online portfolio."

THE ROANOKER

Leisure Publishing Co., 3424 Brambleton Ave., Roanoke VA 24018. (540)989-6138; (800)548-1672. **Fax:** (540)989-7603. **E-mail:** jwood@leisurepublishing.com; krheinheimer@leisurepublishing.com. **Website:** www.theroanoker.com. **Contact:** Kurt Rheinheimer, editor; Austin Clark, creative director; Patty Jackson, production director. Estab. 1974. Circ. 10,000. Bimonthly general interest magazine for the city of Roanoke, VA, and the Roanoke valley. Originals are returned. Art guidelines not available.

ILLUSTRATION Approached by 20-25 freelance illustrators/year. Buys 2-5 illustrations/year.

FIRST CONTACT & TERMS Illustrators: Send query letter with brochure, tearsheets and photocopies. Samples are filed. Responds only if interested. No portfolio reviews. Buys one-time rights. Pays on publication; $100 for b&w or color cover; $75 for b&w or color inside.

TIPS "Works primarily on assignment. Welcomes a great story idea pertaining to the Roanoke Valley. Please *do not* call or send any material that needs to be returned."

ROBB REPORT

CurtCo Robb Media, LLC, 29160 Heathercliff Rd., Suite #200, Malibu CA 90265. (310)589-7700. **Fax:** (310)589-7701. **E-mail:** editorial@robbreport.com. **Website:** www.robbreport.com. Estab. 1976. Circ. 104,000. Monthly 4-color consumer magazine "for the luxury lifestyle, featuring exotic cars, investment, entrepreneur, boats, etc." Accepts previously published artwork. Original artwork is returned at job's completion. Art guidelines for SASE with first-class postage.

ROLLING STONE

Wenner Media, 1290 Avenue of the Americas, New York NY 10104. (212)484-1616. **Fax:** (212)484-1664. **E-mail:** rseditors@rollingstone.com. **Website:** www. rollingstone.com. **Contact:** Caryn Ganz, editorial director. Circ. 1.46 million. Monthly. Originals returned at job's completion. 100% of freelance design work demands knowledge of Illustrator, QuarkXPress, and Photoshop. (Computer skills not necessary for illustrators.) Art guidelines available.

ILLUSTRATION Approached by "tons" of illustrators/year. Buys approximately 4 illustrations/issue. Works on assignment only. Considers all media.

FIRST CONTACT & TERMS Illustrators: Send postcard sample and/or query letter with tearsheets, photocopies or any appropriate sample. Samples are filed. Does not reply. Portfolios may be dropped off every Tuesday before 3 p.m. and should include final art and tearsheets. Portfolios may be picked back up on Thursday after 3 p.m. "Please make sure to include your name and address on the outside of your portfolio." Publication will contact artist for portfolio review if interested. Buys first and one-time rights. **Pays on acceptance**; payment for cover and inside illustration varies; pays $300-500 for spots. Finds artists through word of mouth, *American Illustration*, *Communication Arts*, mailed samples, and drop-offs.

♺ ROOM

P.O. Box 46160, Station D, Vancouver British Columbia V6J 5G5, Canada. **E-mail:** contactus@room magazine.com. **Website:** www.roommagazine.com. Estab. 1975. Circ. 1,000. Quarterly literary journal. Emphasizes feminist literature for women and librar-

ies. Original artwork returned after publication if requested. Sample copy for $13; art guidelines for SASE (nonresidents include 3 IRCs).

ILLUSTRATION Illustrators: Send photographs, slides, or original work as samples to be kept on file. Samples not kept on file are returned by SAE (nonresidents include IRC). Responds in 6 months. Buys first rights. Pays cartoonists $25 minimum for b&w and color. Pays illustrators $25-50, b&w, color. Pays on publication. Buys 3-5 illustrations/issue from freelancers. Prefers good realistic illustrations of women and b&w line drawings. Prefers pen & ink, then charcoal/pencil and collage.

RTOHQ: THE MAGAZINE

1504 Robin Hood Trail, Austin TX 78703. (800)204-2776. **Fax:** (512)794-0097. **E-mail:** nferguson@rtohq. org; bkeese@rtohq.org. **Website:** www.rtohq.org. **Contact:** Neil Ferguson, art director; Bill Keese, executive editor. Estab. 1980. Circ. 5,500. Bimonthly publication for members of the Association of Progressive Rental Organizations, the national association of the rental-purchase industry. Sample copy free for catalog-size SASE with first-class postage.

ILLUSTRATION Buys 2-3 illustrations/issue. Has featured illustrations by Barry Fitzgerald, Aletha St. Romain, A.J. Garces, Edd Patton and Jane Marinsky. Features conceptual illustration. Assigns 15% of illustrations to new and emerging illustrators. Prefers cutting edge; nothing realistic; strong editorial qualities. Considers all media. Accepts computer-based illustrations (Photoshop, Illustrator).

FIRST CONTACT & TERMS Illustrators: Send postcard sample, query letter with printed samples, photocopies, or tearsheets. Accepts disk submissions (must be Photoshop-accessible EPS high-res at 300 dpi or Illustrator file). Samples are filed or returned by SASE. Responds in 1 month if interested. Rights purchased vary according to project. Pays on publication: $300-450 for color cover; $250-350 for color inside. Finds illustrators mostly through artist's submissions, some from other magazines.

TIPS "Must have a strong conceptual ability—that is, they must be able to illustrate for editorial articles dealing with business/management issues. We are looking for cutting-edge styles and unique approaches to illustration. I am willing to work with new, lesser-known illustrators."

RUNNER'S WORLD

Rodale, 400 S. Tenth St., Emmaus PA 18098-0099. (610)967-8441. **Fax:** (610)967-8883. **E-mail:** rwedit@rodale.com. **Website:** www.runnersworld.com. **Contact:** David Willey, editor-in-chief; Suzanne Perrault, managing editor; Benjamen Purvis, design director. Estab. 1966. Circ. 500,000. Monthly 4-color with a "contemporary, clean" design emphasizing serious, recreational running. Accepts previously published artwork "if appropriate." Returns original artwork after publication. Art guidelines not available. Illustration Approached by hundreds of illustrators/year. Works with 50 illustrators/year. Buys average of 10 illustrations/issue. Has featured illustrations by Sam Hundley, Gil Eisner, Randall Enos and Katherine Adams. Features humorous and realistic illustration; charts & graphics; informational graphics; computer and spot illustration. Assigns 40% of illustrations to well-known or "name" illustrators; 40% to experienced but not well-known illustrators; 20% to new and emerging illustrators. Needs editorial, technical and medical illustrations. "Styles include tightly rendered human athletes, graphic and cerebral interpretations of running themes. Also, *RW* uses medical illustration for features on biomechanics." No special preference regarding media but appreciates electronic transmission. "No cartoons or originals larger than 11×14." Works on assignment only. 30% of freelance work demands knowledge of Illustrator, Photoshop or FreeHand.
FIRST CONTACT & TERMS Illustrators: Send postcard samples to be kept on file. Accepts submissions on disk compatible with Illustrator 5.0. Send EPS files. Publication will contact artist for portfolio review if interested. Buys one-time international rights. Pays $1,800 maximum for 2-page spreads; $400 maximum for spots. Finds artists through word of mouth, magazines, submissions/self-promotions, sourcebooks, artists' agents and reps and attending art exhibitions.
TIPS Portfolio should include "a maximum of 12 images. Show a clean presentation, lots of ideas and few samples. Don't show disorganized thinking. Portfolio samples should be uniform in size. Be patient!"

RURAL HERITAGE

P.O. Box 2067, Cedar Rapids IA 52406. (319)362-3027. **E-mail:** info@ruralheritage.com. **Website:** www.ruralheritage.com. **Contact:** Joe Mischka, editor. Estab. 1976. Circ. 9,500. Bimonthly farm magazine "published in support of modern-day farming and logging with draft animals (horses, mules, oxen)." Sample copy for $8 postpaid; art guidelines not available.
○ Editor stresses the importance of submitting cartoons that deal only with farming and logging using draft animals.
CARTOONS "Approached by not nearly enough cartoonists who understand our subject." Buys 2 or more cartoons/issue. Prefers bold, clean, minimalistic draft animals and their relationship with the teamster. "No unrelated cartoons!" Prefers single panel, humorous, b&w line drawings with or without gagline.
FIRST CONTACT & TERMS Cartoonists: Send query letter with finished cartoons and SASE. Samples accepted by US mail only. Samples are not filed (unless we plan to use them—then we keep them on file until used) and are returned by SASE. Responds in 2 months. Buys first North American serial rights or all rights rarely. Pays on publication; $10 for one-time rights; $20 for all rights.
TIPS "Know draft animals (horses, mules, oxen, etc.) well enough to recognize humorous situations intrinsic to their use or that arise in their relationship to the teamster. Our best contributors read *Rural Heritage* and get their ideas from the publication's content."

SALT HILL LITERARY JOURNAL

E-mail: salthillart@gmail.com. **Website:** www.salthilljournal.net. **Contact:** Art Editor. Circ. 1,000. *Salt Hill* seeks unpublished 2D art-drawings, paintings, photography, mixed media, documentation of 3D art, typographic art diagrams, maps, etc. for its semiannual publication. We offer all colors, shapes, and stripes.
FIRST CONTACT & TERMS See website for specifications.

SANDY RIVER REVIEW, THE

University of Maine at Farmington, 114 Prescott St., Farmington ME 04938. **E-mail:** srreview@gmail.com. **Website:** sandyriverreview.com. **Contact:** Nicole Byrne, editor. "*The Sandy River Review* seeks prose, poetry, and art submissions twice a year for our Spring and Fall issues."
FIRST CONTACT & TERMS Pays 3 contributor copies of the published issue. "Most of our art is published in b&w and must be submitted as 300-dpi quality, CMYK color mode, and saved as a TIFF file."

SANTA BARBARA MAGAZINE

2064 Alameda Padre Serra, Suite 120, Santa Barbara CA 93103. (805)965-5999. **Fax:** (805)965-7627. **E-mail:** alisa@sbmag.com. **Website:** www.sbmag.com. **Contact:** Alisa Baur, art director; Gina Tolleson, editor. Estab. 1975. Circ. 40,000. Bimonthly 4-color magazine with classic design emphasizing Santa Barbara culture and community. Original artwork returned after publication if requested.

ILLUSTRATION Approached by 20 illustrators/year. Works with 2-3 illustrators/year. Buys about 1-3 illustrations/year. Uses freelance artwork mainly for departments. Works on assignment only.

FIRST CONTACT & TERMS Send postcard, tearsheets or photocopies. To show a portfolio, mail b&w and color art, final reproduction/product and tearsheets; will contact if interested. Buys first rights. **Pays on acceptance**; approximately $275 for color cover; $175 for color inside. "Payment varies."

TIPS "Be familiar with our magazine."

SCIENTIFIC AMERICAN

75 Varick St., 9th Floor, New York NY 10013-1917. (212)451-8200. **E-mail:** editors@sciam.com. **Website:** www.sciam.com. **Contact:** Mariette DiChristina, editor-in-chief. Estab. 1845. Circ. 710,000. Monthly 4-color consumer magazine emphasizing scientific information for educated readers, covering geology, astronomy, medicine, technology and innovations.

ILLUSTRATION Approached by 100+ illustrators/year. Buys 15-30 illustrations/issue, mostly science-related, but there are oppurtunities for editorial art in all media. Assigns illustrations to specialized science illustrators, to well-known editorial illustrators, and to relative newcomers in both areas.

FIRST CONTACT & TERMS Illustrators: Send postcard sample or e-mail with link to website; followup in 6 months. Responds only if interested. Portfolio reviews done as time allows. **Pays on acceptance**; $750-2,000 for color inside; $350-750 for spots.

TIPS "We use all styles of illustration and you do not have to be an expert in science although some understanding certainly helps. The art directors at *Scientific American* are highly skilled at computer programs, have a broad-based knowledge of science, and closely guide the process. Editors are experts in their field and help with technical backup material. One caveat: content is heavily vetted here for accuracy, so a huge plus on the part of our illustrators is their ability to make changes and corrections cheerfully and in a timely fashion."

SCOUTING

Boy Scouts of America, 1325 W. Walnut Hill Lane, P.O. Box 152079, Irving TX 75015-2079. **Website:** www.scoutingmagazine.org. Estab. 1913. Circ. 1 million. Magazine published 6 times/year covering Scouting activities for adult leaders of the Boy Scouts, Cub Scouts, and Venturing. "We use about 4-6 cartoons in each issue. They are normally 1-panel, although we occasionally use a 1-column vertical 3-panel. Humor should be seen through the eyes of adults who are similar to our readers: volunteer leaders and/or parents of Cub Scouts or Boy Scouts. Avoid stereotypes such as dumb housewives, buxom blondes, lady drivers, lazy or dimwitted husbands, as well as common ethnic stereotypes. And especially avoid the stereotype of the fat Scoutmaster leading a brood of young Scouts through the woods. We emphasize more the self-reliance of the Scout and his patrol. Cartoons can feature uniformed Cub Scouts or Boy Scouts, but please be sure that you (1) know what the current uniform looks like, and (2) are familiar with the Scouting program. No smoking, hunting, or cruelty. New settings and situations are appreciated, as we get tired of deserted islands or thirsty men crawling throught the desert."

CARTOONS "Size: 8×10 or 5×7. Paper: White, any weight you are comfortable with. Finish: If you send pencil roughs and we like the idea, you will be contacted to do a finish. However, we prefer finished art in case we want to use a cartoon immediately." Pays $75 per cartoon for first rights. Pays on acceptance.

SCRAP

1615 L St. NW, Suite 600, Washington DC 20036-5664. (202)662-8547. **Fax:** (202)626-0947. **E-mail:** kentkiser@scrap.org. **Website:** www.scrap.org. **Contact:** Kent Kiser, publisher. Estab. 1987. Circ. 9,600. Bimonthly 4-color trade publication that covers all aspects of the scrap recycling industry.

CARTOONS "We occasionally run single-panel cartoons that focus on the recycling theme/business."

ILLUSTRATION Approached by 100 illustrators/year. Buys 0-2 illustrations/issue. Features realistic illustrations, business/industrial/corporate illustrations and international/financial illustrations. Prefered subjects business subjects. Assigns 10% of illustrations to new and emerging illustrators.

FIRST CONTACT & TERMS Illustrators: Send post-card sample. Samples are filed. Portfolio review not required. Buys first North American serial rights. **Pays on acceptance**; $1,200-2,000 for color cover; $300-1,000 for color inside. Finds illustrators through creative sourcebook, mailed submissions, referrals from other editors, and "direct calls to artists whose work I see and like."

TIPS "We're always open to new talent and different styles. Our main requirement is the ability and willingness to take direction and make changes if necessary. No prima donnas, please. Send a postcard to let us see what you can do."

SEA MAGAZINE

17782 Cowan, Suite C, Irvine CA 92614. (949)660-6150. **Fax:** (949)660-6172. **Website:** www.seamag.com. Estab. 1908. Circ. 55,000. Monthly 4-color magazine emphasizing recreational boating for owners or users of recreational powerboats, primarily for cruising and general recreation; some interest in boating competition; regionally oriented to 13 Western states. Accepts previously published artwork. Return of original artwork depends upon terms of purchase. Sample copy with SASE and first-class postage.

Also publishes *Go Boating* magazine.

ILLUSTRATION Approached by 20 illustators/year. Buys 10 illustrations/year mainly for editorial. Considers airbrush, watercolor, acrylic and calligraphy.

FIRST CONTACT & TERMS Illustrators: Send query letter with brochure showing art style. Samples are returned only if requested. Publication will contact artist for portfolio review if interested. Portfolio should include tearsheets and cover letter indicating price range. Negotiates rights purchased. Pays on publication; $50 for b&w, $250 for color inside (negotiable).

TIPS "We will accept students for portfolio review with an eye to obtaining quality art at a reasonable price. We will help start career for illustrators and hope that they will remain loyal to our publication."

SEATTLE WEEKLY

307 Third Ave. S., 2nd Floor, Seattle WA 98104. (206)623-0500. **Fax:** (206)467-4338. **E-mail:** editorial@seattleweekly.com; mbaumgarten@seattleweekly.com. **Website:** www.seattleweekly.com. **Contact:** Matt Baumgarten, editor-in-chief. Estab. 1976. Circ. 105,000. Weekly consumer magazine with emphasis on local and national issues and arts events. Accepts previously published artwork. Original artwork can

be returned at job's completion if requested, "but you can come and get them if you're local." Sample copies available for SASE with first-class postage. Art guidelines not available.

ILLUSTRATION Approached by 30-50 freelance illustrators/year. Buys 3 freelance illustrations/issue. Works on assignment only. Prefers "sophisticated themes and styles."

FIRST CONTACT & TERMS Illustrators: Send query letter with tearsheets and photocopies. Samples are filed and are not returned. Does not reply, in which case the artists should "revise work and try again." To show a portfolio, mail b&w and color photocopies; "always leave us something to file." Buys first rights. Pays on publication; $200-250 for color cover; $60-75 for b&w inside.

TIPS "Give us a sample we won't forget. A really beautiful mailer might even end up on our wall, and when we assign an illustration, you won't be forgotten. All artists used must sign contract. Feel free to e-mail for a copy."

SHEEP! MAGAZINE

Countryside Publications, Ltd., 145 Industrial Dr., Medford WI 54451. (715)785-7979; (800)551-5691. **Fax:** (715)785-7414. **E-mail:** sheepmag@tds.net; singersol@countrysidemag.com. **Website:** www.sheepmagazine.com. **Contact:** Nathan Griffith, editor. Estab. 1980. Circ. 11,000. Bimonthly publication covering sheep, wool, and woolcrafts. Accepts previously published work.

CARTOONS Approached by 30 cartoonists/year. Buys 5 cartoons/year. Considers all themes and styles. Prefers single panel with gagline.

ILLUSTRATION Approached by 10 illustrators/year. Buys 5 illustrations/year; no inside color. Considers pen & ink. Features charts & graphs, computer illustration, informational graphics, realistic, medical and spot illustrations. All art should be sheep related.

FIRST CONTACT & TERMS Cartoonists: Send query letter with brochure and finished cartoons. Illustrators: Send query letter with brochure, SASE and tearsheets. To show a portfolio, mail thumbnails and b&w tearsheets. Buys first rights or all rights. **Pays on acceptance.** Pays cartoonists $5-15 for b&w. Pays illustrators $75 minimum for b&w.

TIPS "Demonstrate creativity and quality work."

⊕ SHOW-ME PUBLISHING, INC.

2049 Wyandotte, Kansas City MO 64108. (816)842-9994. **Fax:** (816)474-1111. **Website:** www.ingrams.com. "We publish a regional business magazine (*Ingram's*) and several business-to-business publications and websites covering Kansas and Missouri. We require all freelancers to allow us full usage/copyright and resale of all work done for our publications and websites." Has occasional use for graphic designers and photographers. Prefers local talent.

FIRST CONTACT & TERMS Send cover letter, résumé, references, and samples of work to HR Department. Portfolios are not returned. Do not send original work; send digital files on CD. Pays $10-15/hour for Internet design and photography.

SKIING MAGAZINE

Bonnier Corp., 5720 Flatiron Pkwy., Boulder CO 80301. (303)253-6300. **Fax:** (303)448-7638. **E-mail:** editor@skiingmag.com. **Website:** www.skinet.com/skiing. Estab. 1936. Circ. 430,000. Online publication emphasizing instruction, resorts, equipment and personality profiles. For new, intermediate and expert skiers. Published online. Previously published work OK "if we're notified." Sponsors summer internships. The internship is roughly 12 weeks long in Boulder, CO. All internships are unpaid. "Duties include working directly with the art director, photo editor and editorial staff on the development of pages from inception to final output, designing and flowing type in a number of our column and regular-section pages, and other design and production-related duties. Our staff is small and candidates will get an intimate knowledge of the day-to-day cycle of publishing a national magazine. We work with the Adobe Creative Suite 3. InDesign, Photoshop and Illustrator are all used on a daily basis. Proficiency in InDesign is critical. A passion for the sport of skiing is helpful, but not critical." Please e-mail résumé, cover letter, and portfolio or link to online portfolio to: mark@skiingmag.com.

CARTOONS Illustrators: Mail art and SASE. Responds immediately. Buys one-time rights. **Pays on acceptance;** $1,200 for color cover; $150-500 for color inside.

ILLUSTRATION Approached by 30-40 freelance illustrators/year. Buys 25 illustrations/year.

TIPS "The best way to break in is an interview and a consistent style portfolio. Then, keep us on your mailing list."

SKILLSUSA CHAMPIONS

14001 SkillsUSA Way, Leesburg VA 20176. (703)777-8810. **E-mail:** thall@skillsusa.org. **Website:** www.skillsusa.org/champions. **Contact:** Tom Hall, editor. Estab. 1965. Circ. 300,000. Quarterly 4-color magazine. "*SkillsUSA Champions* is primarily a features magazine that provides motivational content by focusing on successful members. SkillsUSA is an organization of more than 300,000 students and teachers in technical, skilled and service careers. Sample copies available.

ILLUSTRATION Approached by 4 illustrators/year. Works on assignment only. Prefers positive, youthful, innovative, action-oriented images. Considers pen & ink, watercolor, collage, airbrush and acrylic.

DESIGN Needs freelancers for design. 100% of freelance work demands knowledge of Adobe CS.

FIRST CONTACT & TERMS Illustrators: Send postcard sample. Designers: Send query letter with brochure. Accepts disks compatible with Illustrator CS5, and InDesign CS53. Send Illustrator and EPS files. Portfolio should include printed samples, b&w and color tearsheets and photographs. Accepts previously published artwork. Originals returned at job's completion (if requested). Rights purchased vary according to project. **Pays on acceptance.** Pays illustrators $200-300 for color; $100-300 for spots. Pays designers by the project.

SKIPPING STONES: A MULTICULTURAL LITERARY MAGAZINE

P.O. Box 3939, Eugene OR 97403-0939. (541)342-4956. **E-mail:** editor@skippingstones.org. **Website:** www.skippingstones.org. **Contact:** Arun Toké, editor. Estab. 1988. Circ. 1,400 print, plus Web. "We promote multicultural awareness, international understanding, nature appreciation, and social responsibility. We suggest authors not make stereotypical generalizations in their articles. We like when authors include their own experiences, or base their articles on their personal immersion experiences in a culture or country." Has featured Lori Eslick, Xuan Thu Pham, Soma Han, Jon Bush, Zarouhie Abdalian, Paul Dix, Elizabeth Zunon and Najah Clemmons.

CARTOONS Humorous cartoons. Prefers multicultural, social issues, nature/ecology themes. Requests b&w washes and line drawings. Has featured cartoons by Lindy Wojcicki of Florida. Prefers cartoons by youth under age 19.

ILLUSTRATION Approached by 100 illustrators/year. Buys 10-20 illustrations/year. Has featured illustrations by Lori Eslick, Sarah Solie, Wisconsin; Alvina Kong, California; Elizabeth Wilkinson, Vermont; Inna Svjatova, Russia; Jon Bush, Massachusetts. Features humorous illustrations, informational graphics, natural history and realistic, authentic illustrations. Preferred subjects children and teens. Prefers pen & ink. Assigns 80% of work to new and emerging illustrators. Recent issues have featured multicultural artists—their life and works.

FIRST CONTACT & TERMS Send query letter or e-mail with photographs (digital JPEGs at 72 dpi). Cartoonists: Send b&w photocopies and SASE. Illustrators: Send nonreturnable photocopies and SASE. Samples are filed or returned by SASE. Responds in 3 months if interested. Portfolio review not required. Buys first rights, reprint rights. Pays on publication 1-4 copies. No financial reimbursement. Finds illustrators through word of mouth, artists' promo samples.

TIPS "We are a multicultural magazine for youth and teens. We consider your work as a labor of love that contributes to the education of youth. We publish photoessays on various cultures and countries/regions of the world in each issue of the magazine to promote international and intercultural (and nature) understanding. Tell us a little bit about yourself, your motivation, goals, and mission."

SMITHSONIAN MAGAZINE

Capital Gallery, Suite 6001, MRC 513, P.O. Box 37012, Washington DC 20013. (202)275-2000. **E-mail:** smithsonianmagazine@si.edu. **Website:** www.smithsonianmag.com. **Contact:** Molly Roberts, photo editor; Jeff Campagna, art services coordinator. Circ. 2.3 million. Monthly consumer magazine exploring lifestyles, cultures, environment, travel and the arts. Smithsonian.com expands on *Smithsonian* magazine's in-depth coverage of history, science, nature, the arts, travel, world culture and technology.

Submit proposals online: www.smithsonian-mag.com/contact-us.

ILLUSTRATION Approached by hundreds of illustrators/year. Buys 1-3 illustrations/issue. Illustrations are not the responsibility of authors, but it is helpful to know what photographic possibilities exist regarding your subject. Photographs published in the magazine are usually obtained through assign-

ments, stock agencies or specialized sources. Submission guidelines: www.smithsonianmag.com/contact-us/submission-guidelines.html. Features charts and graphs, informational graphics, humorous, natural history, realistic and spot illustration.

FIRST CONTACT & TERMS Samples are filed. Responds only if interested. Will contact artist for portfolio review if interested. Buys first rights. **Pays on acceptance;** $350-$1,200 for color inside. Finds illustrators through agents and word of mouth.

SOAP OPERA DIGEST

American Media, Inc., 4 New York Plaza, 2nd Floor, New York NY 10004. **E-mail:** sodask@soapoperadigest.com; sodsound@soapoperadigest.com. **Website:** www.soapdigest.com. Estab. 1976. Circ. 2 million. Emphasizes soap opera and prime-time drama synopses and news. Weekly. Accepts previously published material. Returns original artwork after publication upon request. Sample copy available for SASE.

TIPS "Review the magazine before submitting work."

SOLIDARITY MAGAZINE

UAW Solidarity House, 8000 E. Jefferson, Detroit MI 48214. (313)926-5000. **E-mail:** uawsolidarity@uaw.net. **Website:** www.uaw.org. Published by United Auto Workers. 4-color magazine for "1.3 million member trade union representing US, Canadian and Puerto Rican workers in auto, aerospace, agricultural-implement, public employment and other areas." Contemporary design.

CARTOONS Carries "labor/political" cartoons. Payment varies.

ILLUSTRATION Works with 10-12 illustrators/year for posters and magazine illustrations. Interested in graphic designs of publications, topical art for magazine covers with liberal-labor political slant. Looks for "ability to grasp our editorial slant."

FIRST CONTACT & TERMS Illustrators: Send postcard sample or tearsheets and SASE. Samples are filed. Pays $500-600 for color cover; $200-300 for b&w inside; $300-450 for color inside. Graphic Artists Guild members only.

SPIDER

70 E. Lake St., Suite 800, Chicago IL 60601. **E-mail:** spider@spidermagkids.com. **Website:** www.cricketmag.com/spider; www.spidermagkids.com. **Contact:** Submissions editor. Circ. 70,000. *SPIDER* is full-color, 8×10, 34 pages with a 4-page activity pullout for children ages 6-9. Features the world's best children's

authors. Art samples and photos considered. For submission guidelines, visit submittable.cricketmag.com or www.cricketmag.com/submissions.

FIRST CONTACT & TERMS "No advance list of themes. Do not query. Include exact word count. Prefers online submissions. Please allow 3-6 months response time."

SPITBALL: THE LITERARY BASEBALL MAGAZINE

5560 Fox Rd., Cincinnati OH 45239. **E-mail:** spitball5@hotmail.com. **Website:** www.spitballmag.com. **Contact:** Mike Shannon, editor-in-chief. Estab. 1981. Quarterly 2-color magazine emphasizing baseball, exclusively for "well-educated, literate baseball fans." *Spitball* has a regular column called "Brushes With Baseball" that features one artist and his/her work. Chooses artists for whom baseball is a major theme/subject. Prefers to buy at least one work from the artist to keep in its collection. Sometimes prints color material in b&w on cover. Returns original artwork after publication if the work is donated; does not return if purchased. Sample copy available for $6.

CARTOONS Prefers single-panel b&w line drawings with or without gagline. Prefers "old fashioned *Sport Magazine/New Yorker* type. Please, cartoonists, make them funny, or what's the point?"

ILLUSTRATION "We need 2 types of art illustration (for a story, essay or poem) and filler. All work must be baseball-related." Prefers pen & ink, airbrush, charcoal/pencil and collage. Interested artists should write to find out needs for specific illustration. Buys 3 or 4 illustrations/issue.

FIRST CONTACT & TERMS Cartoonists: Query with samples of style, roughs and finished cartoons. Illustrators: Send query letter with b&w illustrations or slides. Target samples to magazine's needs. Samples not filed are returned by SASE. Responds in 1 week. Negotiates rights purchased. **Pays on acceptance.** Pays cartoonists $10 minimum. Pays illustrators $20-40 for b&w inside.

TIPS "Usually artists contact us and if we hit it off, we form a long-lasting mutual admiration society. Please, you cartoonists out there, drag your bats up to the *Spitball* plate! We like to use a variety of artists."

SPORTS AFIELD

Field Sports Publishing, 15621 Chemical Lane, Huntington Beach CA 92649. (714)373-4910. **E-mail:** letters@sportsafield.com. **Website:** www.sportsafield.

com. **Contact:** Jerry Gutierrez, art director. Estab. 1887. Circ. 50,000. Bimonthly magazine. "*SA* is edited for hunting enthusiasts. We are the oldest outdoor magazine. We cater to the upscale hunting market, especially hunters who travel to exotic destinations like Alaska and Africa. We are not a deer hunting magazine, and we do not cover fishing."

ILLUSTRATION Hunting/wildlife themes only. Considers all media. Freelancers should be familiar with Photoshop, Illustrator, InDesign.

FIRST CONTACT & TERMS Illustrators: Send postcard sample or query letter with photocopies and tearsheets. Accepts disk submissions. Samples are filed. Responds only if interested. Will contact for portfolio of b&w or color photographs, slides, tearsheets and transparencies if interested. Buys first North American serial rights. Pays on publication; negotiable. Finds illustrators through *Black Book*, magazines, submissions.

STANFORD MAGAZINE

Frances C. Arrillaga Alumni Center, 326 Galvez St., Stanford CA 94305-6105. (650)725-0672. **E-mail:** gvirgili@stanford.edu; stanford.magazine@stanford.edu. **Website:** alumni.stanford.edu/get/page/magazine/home. **Contact:** Giorgia Virgili, art director. Estab. 1973. Circ. 105,000. Consumer magazine, "geared toward the alumni of Stanford University. Articles vary from photo essays to fiction to academic subjects." Accepts previously published artwork. Original artwork is returned at job's completion. Sample copies available.

ILLUSTRATION Approached by 200-300 illustrators/year. Buys 4-6 illustrations/issue. Works on assignment only. Interested in all styles.

FIRST CONTACT & TERMS Send samples only. Call for appointment to show portfolio. Buys one-time rights. **Pays on acceptance.**

TIPS "We're always looking for unique styles, as well as excellent traditional work. We like to give enough time for the artist to produce the piece."

STILL POINT ARTS QUARTERLY

193 Hillside Rd., Brunswick ME 04011. (207)837-5760. **Fax:** (207)725-4909. **E-mail:** info@stillpointartgallery.com. **Website:** www.stillpointartsquarterly.com. **Contact:** Christine Cote, editor. Estab. 2011. Circ. 2,000. Quarterly literary magazine and art journal focused on art, artists, artistry; for artists and art enthusiasts.

FIRST CONTACT & TERMS Send e-mail with URL and JPEG samples at 72 dpi. Samples are kept on file and not returned. Responds only if interested. Request portfolio review in original query. Portfolio should include photographs. Accepts images in digital format. Images may be submitted as JPEGs or ZIP at 300 dpi. Finds freelancers through submissions, word-of-mouth, magazines and internet.

TIPS "Read our magazine and our guidelines."

STONE SOUP

Children's Art Foundation, P.O. Box 83, Santa Cruz CA 95063-0083. (831)426-5557. **E-mail:** editor@ stonesoup.com. **Website:** http://stonesoup.com. **Contact:** Ms. Gerry Mandel, editor. Estab. 1973. Bi-monthly 4-color magazine with "simple and conservative design" emphasizing writing and art by children. Features adventure, ethnic, experimental, fantasy, humorous and science fiction articles. "We only publish writing and art by children through age 13. We look for artwork that reveals that the artist is closely observing his or her world." Sample copies available for $4 each. Art guidelines available online.

ILLUSTRATION Buys 12 illustrations/issue. Prefers complete and detailed scenes from real life. All art must be by children ages 8-13.

FIRST CONTACT & TERMS Illustrators: Send query letter with color copies. Samples are not returned. Responds in 1 month. Buys all rights. Pays on publication; $50 for color cover, $25 for color inside, $15 for spots.

STONE VOICES

193 Hillside Rd., Brunswick ME 04011. (207)837-5760. **Fax:** (207)725-4909. **E-mail:** info@stone-voices.com. **Website:** www.stone-voices.com. **Contact:** Christine Cote, editor. Estab. 2011. Circ. 2,000. Quarterly literary and art magazine. Emphasis on connecting art and spirit. For artists and art enthusiasts. "A beautiful publication."

FIRST CONTACT & TERMS Send e-mail with URL and JPEG samples at 72 dpi. Samples are kept on file and not returned. Responds only if interested. Request portfolio review in original query. The portfolios we publish are much like small gallery exhibitions. We encourage artists to submit images of a collection or series of works that are related in some way, rather than to submit images of completely random and disparate pieces of art. Accepts images in digital format. Images may be submitted as JPEGs or ZIP at 300 dpi. Finds freelancers through submissions, word-of-mouth, magazines and internet.

TIPS "Read our magazine and our guidelines."

STRATEGIC FINANCE

10 Paragon Dr., Montvale NJ 07645. (201)474-1558. **Fax:** (201)474-1603. **E-mail:** mzisk@imanet.org. **Website:** www.imanet.org; www.strategicfinancemag. com. **Contact:** Mary Zisk, art director. Estab. 1919. Circ. 58,000. Monthly 4-color emphasizing management accounting for corporate accountants, controllers, chief financial officers, and treasurers.

ILLUSTRATION Approached by 4 illustrators/day. Buys 3 illustrations/issue.

FIRST CONTACT & TERMS Illustrators: Send non-returnable postcard samples or e-mail link to online portfolio. Prefers financial and corporate themes. Looking for smart concepts and unique technique.

STUDENT LAWYER

ABA Publishing, Law Student Division, American Bar Association, 321 N. Clark St., Chicago IL 60654. (312)988-6049. **Fax:** (312)988-6365. **Website:** www. abanet.org/lsd/studentlawyer. **Contact:** Darhiana Mateo Téllez, editor. Estab. 1972. Circ. 32,000.

ILLUSTRATION Approached by 120 illustrators/year. Buys 8 illustrations/issue. Has featured illustrations by Sean Kane and Jim Starr. Features realistic, computer, and spot illustration. Assigns 50% of illustrations to experienced but not well-known illustrators; 50% to new and emerging illustrators. Needs editorial illustration with an "innovative, intelligent style." Works on assignment only. Needs computer-literate freelancers for illustration. No cartoons please.

FIRST CONTACT & TERMS Send postcard sample, brochure, tearsheets and printed sheet with a variety of art images (include name and phone number). Samples are filed. Call for appointment to show portfolio of final art and tearsheets. Buys 1-time rights. **Pays on acceptance.** $500-800 for color cover; $450-650 for color inside; $150-350 for spots.

TIPS "In your samples, show a variety of styles with an emphasis on editorial work."

SUN VALLEY MAGAZINE

Valley Publishing, LLC, 111 First Ave. N., #1M, Meriwether Bldg., Hailey ID 83333. (208)788-0770. **Fax:** (208)788-3881. **E-mail:** adam@sunvalleymag.com; julie@sunvalleymag.com. **Website:** www.sunvalleymag. com. **Contact:** Adam Tanous, editor; Julie Molema, art director. Estab. 1973. Circ. 17,000. Consumer magazine published 3 times/year, "highlighting the activities and lifestyles of people of the Wood River Valley." Sample copies available. Art guidelines free for #10 SASE with first-class postage.

ILLUSTRATION Approached by 10 illustrators/year. Buys 3 illustrations/issue. Prefers forward, cutting edge styles. Considers all media.

FIRST CONTACT & TERMS Illustrators: Send query letter with SASE. Accepts disk submissions compatible with Macintosh, and/or InDesign. Send EPS files. Samples are filed. Does not report back. Artist should call. Art director will contact artist for portfolio review of b&w, color, final art, photostats, roughs, slides, tearsheets and thumbnails if interested. Buys first rights. Pays on publication; $350 cover; $80-240 inside.

TIPS "Read our magazine. Send ideas for illustrations and examples."

T+D

1640 King St., Box 1443, Alexandria VA 22313-1443. (703)683-8100; (800) 628-2783. **Website:** www.astd. org/Publications/Magazines/TD. Estab. 1945. Circ. 40,000. Monthly trade journal magazine that covers training and development in all fields of business. Accepts previously published artwork. Original artwork is returned at job's completion. Art guidelines not available.

ILLUSTRATION Approached by 20 freelance illustrators/year. Buys a limited number of freelance illustrations per issue. Works on assignment only. Has featured illustrations by Alison Seiffer, James Yang and Riccardo Stampatori. Features humorous, realistic, computer and spot illustration. Assigns 10% of work to new and emerging illustrators. Prefers sophisticated business style. Considers collage, pen & ink, airbrush, acrylic, oil, mixed media, pastel.

FIRST CONTACT & TERMS Illustrators: Send postcard sample. Accepts disks compatible with Illustrator 9, FreeHand 5.0, Photoshop 5. Send EPS, JPEG or TIFF files. Use 4-color (process) settings only. Samples are filed. Responds to the artist only if interested. Write for appointment to show portfolio of tearsheets, slides. Buys one-time rights or reprint rights. Pays on publication; $700-1,200 for color cover; $350 for b&w inside; $350-800 for color inside; $800-1,000 for 2-page spreads; $100-300 for spots.

TIPS "Send more than one image if possible. Do not keep sending the same image. Try to tailor your samples to the art director's needs if possible."

TAMPA BAY MAGAZINE

2531 Landmark Dr., Suite 101, Clearwater FL 33761. (727)791-4800. **E-mail:** production@tampabaymagazine.com. **Website:** www.tampabaymagazine.com. Aaron Fodiman; Margaret Word Burnside. Estab. 1986. Circ. 40,000. Bimonthly local lifestyle magazine with upscale readership. Accepts previously published artwork. Sample copy available for $4.50. Submission guidelines available online.

CARTOONS Approached by 30 cartoonists/year. Buys 6 cartoons/issue. Prefers single-panel color washes with gagline.

ILLUSTRATION Approached by 100 illustrators/year. Buys 5 illustrations/issue. Prefers happy, stylish themes. Considers watercolor, collage, airbrush, acrylic, marker, colored pencil, oil and mixed media.

FIRST CONTACT & TERMS Cartoonists: Send query letter with finished cartoon samples. Illustrators: Send query letter with photographs and transparencies. Samples are not filed and are returned by SASE if requested. To show a portfolio, mail color tearsheets, slides, photocopies, finished samples and photographs. Buys one-time rights. Pays on publication. Pays cartoonists $15 for b&w, $20 for color. Pays illustrators $150 for color cover; $75 for color inside.

TECHNICAL ANALYSIS OF STOCKS & COMMODITIES

4757 California Ave. SW, Seattle WA 98116. (206)938-0570. **E-mail:** editor@traders.com. **Website:** www. traders.com. Estab. 1982. Circ. 60,000. Monthly traders' magazine for stocks, bonds, futures, commodities, options, mutual funds. Sample copy: $5. Art guidelines on website.

This magazine has received several awards, including the Step by Step Design Annual, American Illustration IX, XXIII, XIV, NY Society of Illustrators Annuals 40, 46, 48, 49. Separate listing for Technical Analysis, Inc., in the Book Publishers section.

CARTOONS Approached by 30 cartoonists/year. Buys 1-4 cartoons/issue. Prefers humorous cartoons, single-panel b&w line drawings with tagline related to industry.

ILLUSTRATION Approached by 100 illustrators/year. Buys 6 illustrations/issue. Works on assignment only.

Features humorous, realistic, computer (occasionally) and spot illustrations.

FIRST CONTACT & TERMS Cartoonists: Send query letter with finished cartoons (nonreturnable copies only) or e-mail. Illustrators: Send e-mail JPEGs, brochure, tearsheets, photographs, photocopies, photostats, slides. Accepts submissions compatible with any Adobe products (PDF, TIFF, or EPS files). Samples are filed and are not returned. E-mail portfolio for review if interested. Portfolio should include b&w and color art, slides, photostats, photocopies, final art and photographs. Buys one-time rights and reprint rights. Pays on publication. Pays cartoonists $35 for b&w. Pays illustrators $135-350 for color cover; $165-220 for color inside; $105-150 for b&w inside. Accepts previously published artwork.

TIPS "Looking for creative, imaginative, and conceptual types of illustration that relate to articles' concepts. Also interested in caricatures with market charts and computers."

TERRAIN.ORG: A JOURNAL OF THE BUILT & NATURAL ENVIRONMENTS

(520)241-7390. **E-mail:** contact2@terrain.org. **Website:** www.terrain.org. **Contact:** Simmons Buntin. editor-in-chief. Estab. 1997. Circ. 250,000 visits/year. Tri-annual online literary journal. Terrain.org publishes a mix of literary and technical work—editorials, poetry, essays, fiction, articles, reviews, interviews and unsprawl case studies; plus artwork (the ARTerrain gallery plus photo essays and the like; only online for free at www.terrain.org. Terrain has an international audience. Sample copies available online. Art and photo submission guidelines available on website or via mail with SASE. Very general guidelines, query first for artwork.

ILLUSTRATION Approached by 1-2 freelance illustrators/year. Generally do not purchase freelance illustrations. Terrain.org has featured the illustrations of Tom Low, Paul Hoffman and Suzanne Stryk. Features realistic illustrations, informational graphics, computer illustration, charts & graphs, scientific, natural history, architectural and fine art. Prefers architectural and environmental subjects. Design format not important, as long as it can be converted to online formats.

FIRST CONTACT & TERMS Send e-mail with link to artist's website or JPEGS at 72 dpi. Keeps samples on file, include self-promotion piece to be kept on file for possible future assignments. Responds in 4 weeks.

Considers simultaneous submissions and previously published work. Portfolio not required. "We do not pay for illustrations." Finds freelancers through submissions, word-of-mouth and Internet.

TIPS "Because Terrain.org is a self-funded, nonprofit endeavor, we currently do not pay for contributions, whether artwork, photographs or narrative. However, we truly value high-quality artwork and provide broad international exposure to work, particularly in each issue's ARTerrain gallery. We seek photo essays, hybrid forms and other work that takes advantage of our online medium (photo essays with audio, for example). Submit direct samples, or at least URLs to specific artwork. We unfortunately don't have time to investigate a full website or portfolio if all the artist sends is the home page link."

TEXAS MEDICINE

401 W. 15th St., Austin TX 78701. (800)880-1300, ext. 1385. **Fax:** (512)370-1300. **E-mail:** crystal.zuzek@texmed.org. **Website:** www.texmed.org. **Contact:** Crystal Zuzek, editorial contact. Circ. 35,000. Monthly trade journal published by Texas Medical Association for the statewide Texas medical profession. Sample copies and art guidelines available.

ILLUSTRATION Approached by 30-40 illustrators/year. Buys 4-6 illustrations/issue. Prefers medical themes. Considers all media.

FIRST CONTACT & TERMS Illustrators: Send postcard sample or query letter with photocopies. Accepts disk submissions of EPS or TIFF files for QuarkXPress 3.32. Samples are filed and are not returned. Responds only if interested. Art director will contact artist for portfolio review of b&w, color, final art, photographs, photostats, tearsheets or transparencies if interested. Rights purchased vary according to project. Pays on publication. Payment varies; $350 for spots. Finds artists through agents, magazines and submissions.

TEXAS MONTHLY

Emmis Publishing LP, P.O. Box 1569, Austin TX 78767. (512)320-6900. **Fax:** (512)476-9007. **E-mail:** lbaldwin@texasmonthly.com. **Website:** www.texasmonthly.com. **Contact:** Brian D. Sweany, editor; Leslie Baldwin, photo editor; Andi Beierman, deputy art director. Estab. 1973. Circ. 300,000. *Texas Monthly* is edited for the urban Texas audience and covers the state's politics, sports, business, culture and changing lifestyles. It contains lengthy feature articles, reviews and interviews, and presents critical analysis of popular books, movies and plays. Accepts previously published artwork. Originals are returned to artist at job's completion.

ILLUSTRATION Approached by hundreds of illustrators/year. Works on assignment only. Considers all media.

FIRST CONTACT & TERMS Art/graphic design illustrators: Send postcard sample of work or an e-mail with link to your website. Appropriate samples are filed or returned by SASE if requested by artist. Fees vary based on size and complexity of illustration.

TEXAS PARKS & WILDLIFE

4200 Smith School Rd., Bldg. D, Austin TX 78744. (800)937-9393. **Fax:** (512)389-8397. **E-mail:** magazine@tpwd.texas.gov. **Website:** www.tpwmagazine.com. Estab. 1942. Circ. 150,000.

ILLUSTRATION 10% of freelance illustration.

FIRST CONTACT & TERMS Illustrators: Send sample via PDF. Samples are not filed and are not returned. Responds only if interested. Buys one-time rights. Pays on publication; negotiable. Finds illustrators through magazines, word of mouth, artist's submissions.

TIPS "Read our magazine."

THRASHER

High Speed Productions, 1303 Underwood Ave., San Francisco CA 94124. (415)822-3083. **Fax:** (415)822-8359. **E-mail:** photos@thrashermagazine.com. **Website:** www.thrashermagazine.com. Estab. 1981. Circ. 200,000. Monthly 4-color magazine. "*Thrasher* is the dominant publication devoted to the latest in extreme youth lifestyle, focusing on skateboarding, snowboarding, new music, videogames, etc." Originals returned at job's completion. Sample copies for SASE with first-class postage. Art guidelines available online. Needs computer-literate freelancers for illustration. Freelancers should be familiar with Illustrator or Photoshop.

CARTOONS Approached by 100 cartoonists/year. Has featured illustrations by Mark Gonzales and Robert Williams. Prefers skateboard, snowboard, music, youth-oriented themes. Assigns 100% of illustrations to new and emerging illustrators.

ILLUSTRATION Approached by 100 illustrators/year. Prefers themes surrounding skateboarding/skateboarders, snowboard/music (rap, hip hop, metal) and characters and commentary of an extreme nature.

Prefers pen & ink, collage, airbrush, marker, charcoal, mixed media and computer media (Mac format).

FIRST CONTACT & TERMS Cartoonists: Send query letter with brochure and roughs. Illustrators: Send query letter with brochure, résumé, SASE, tearsheets, photographs and photocopies. Publication will contact artist for portfolio review if interested. Portfolio should include b&w and color tearsheets, photocopies and photographs. Rights purchased vary according to project. Negotiates payment for covers. Sometimes requests work on spec before assigning job. Pays on publication. Pays cartoonists $50 for b&w, $75 for color. Pays illustrators $75 for b&w, $100 for color inside.

TIPS "Send finished quality examples of relevant work with a bio/intro/résumé that we can keep on file and update contact info. Artists sometimes make the mistake of submitting examples of work inappropriate to the content of the magazine. Buy/borrow/steal an issue and do a little research. Read it. Desktop publishing is now sophisticated enough to replace all high-end prepress systems. Buy a Mac. Use it. Live it."

TIKKUN

2342 Shattuck Ave., Suite 1200, Berkeley CA 94704. (510)644-1200. **Fax:** (510)644-1255. **E-mail:** magazine@tikkun.org. **Website:** www.tikkun.org. **Contact:** managing editor. Estab. 1986. Circ. 41,000. Quarterly Jewish and interfaith critique of politics, culture and society; includes articles regarding Jewish and nonJewish issues, left-of-center politics. "Looks for art that evokes awe and wonder at the grandeur of the universe or art that portrays the depth of human understanding, wisdom, love and humanity."

ILLUSTRATION Approached by 50-100 illustrators/year. Buys 1-5 illustrations/issue. Features symbolic and figurative illustration and political cartoons in color and b&w. Assigns 50% of illustrations to experienced, but not well known illustrators; 50% to new and emerging illustrators. Prefers line drawings.

FIRST CONTACT & TERMS Prefers electronic submissions. E-mail web link or JPEGs. Do not send originals; unsolicited artwork will not be returned. Accepts previously published material. Often we hold onto line drawings for last-minute use. Pays on publication. Artists must agree to these terms: Nonexclusive worldwide publishing rights for use of the images in *Tikkun* is, in the whole or in part, distributed, displayed and archived, with no time restriction.

TIPS Prefers art with progressive religious and ethical themes. "We invite you to send us a sample of a *Tikkun* article we've printed, showing how you would have illustrated it."

TIME

1271 Avenue of the Americas, New York NY 10020. **E-mail:** letters@time.com. **Website:** www.time.com. **Contact:** Nancy Gibbs, managing editor. Estab. 1923. Circ. 4 million. Weekly magazine covering breaking news, national and world affairs, business news, societal and lifestyle issues, culture and entertainment.
ILLUSTRATION Considers all media.
FIRST CONTACT & TERMS Send postcard sample, printed samples, photocopies or other appropriate samples. Accepts disk submissions. Samples are filed. Responds only if interested. Buys first North American serial rights. Payment is negotiable. Finds artists through sourcebooks and illustration annuals.

THE TOASTMASTER

Toastmasters International, P.O. Box 9052, Mission Viejo CA 92690. (949)858-8255. **E-mail:** submissions@toastmasters.org. **Website:** www.toastmasters.org. **Contact:** Suzanne Frey, editor; Susan Campbell, graphic design manager. Estab. 1933. Circ. 235,000 in 11,700 clubs worldwide. Monthly trade journal for association members. "Language, public speaking, communication are our topics." Accepts previously published artwork. Originals returned at job's completion. Sample copies available.
ILLUSTRATION Buys 6 illustrations/issue. Works on assignment only. Prefers communications themes. Considers watercolor and collage.
FIRST CONTACT & TERMS Illustrators: Send postcard sample. Accepts disk submissions. Samples are filed or returned by SASE if requested by artist. Responds to the artist only if interested. Portfolio should include tearsheets and photocopies. Negotiates rights purchased. **Pays on acceptance;** $500 for color cover; $50-200 for b&w, $100-250 for color inside.

TODAY'S PARENT

Rogers Media, Inc., 1 Mt. Pleasant Rd., 8th Floor, Toronto Ontario M4Y 2Y5, Canada. (416)764-2883. **Fax:** (416)764-2894. **E-mail:** editors@todaysparent.com. **Website:** www.todaysparent.com; website@todaysparent.com. **Contact:** Alicia Kowalewski, art director. Circ. 2 million. Monthly parenting magazine. Sample copies available.

ILLUSTRATION Send query letter with printed samples, photocopies or tearsheets.
FIRST CONTACT & TERMS Illustrators: Send follow-up postcard sample every year. Accepts disk submissions. Art director will contact artist for portfolio review of b&w and color photographs, slides, tearsheets and transparencies if interested. Buys first rights. **Pays on acceptance;** $100-300 for b&w and $250-800 for color inside. Pays $400 for spots. Finds illustrators through magazines, submissions and word of mouth.
TIPS Looks for "good conceptual skills and skill at sketching children and parents."

TRAINING MAGAZINE

P.O. Box 247, Excelsior MN 55331. (516)524-3504. **E-mail:** lorri@trainingmag.com. **Website:** www.trainingmag.com. **Contact:** Lorri Freifeld, editor-in-chief. Estab. 1964. Circ. 45,000. 4-color trade journal published 6 times/year covering job-related training and education in business and industry, both theory and practice, for audience training directors, personnel managers, sales and data processing managers, general managers, etc. Sample copies available with SASE and first-class postage.
ILLUSTRATION Works on assignment only. Prefers themes that relate directly to business and training. Styles are varied. Considers pen & ink, airbrush, mixed media, watercolor, acrylic, oil, pastel and collage.
FIRST CONTACT & TERMS Send postcard sample, tearsheets or photocopies. Accepts digital submissions. Samples are filed. Responds only if interested. Buys first rights or one-time rights. **Pays on acceptance.** Pays illustrators $1,500 for color cover; $500 for color inside; $100 for spots.
TIPS "Show a wide variety of work in different media and with different subject matter."

TRAINS

Kalmbach Publishing Co., P.O. Box 1612, Waukesha WI 53187-1612. (262)796-8776. **Fax:** (262)796-1142. **E-mail:** editor@trainsmag.com; photoeditor@trainsmag.com. **Website:** www.trn.trains.com. **Contact:** Jim Wrinn, editor; Tom Danneman, art director. Estab. 1940. Circ. 92,419. Monthly magazine about trains, train companies, tourist RR, latest railroad news. Art guidelines available online.
Kalmbach Publishing also publishes *Classic Toy Trains, Astronomy, Finescale Modeler,*

Model Railroader, Classic Trains, Bead and Button, Birder's World.

ILLUSTRATION 100% of freelance illustration demands knowledge of Photoshop CS 5.0, Illustrator CS 8.0.

FIRST CONTACT & TERMS Illustrators: Send query letter with printed samples, photocopies and tearsheets. Accepts disk submissions (opticals) or CDs, using programs above. Samples are filed. Art director will contact artist for portfolio review of color tearsheets if interested. Buys one-time rights. Pays on publication.

TIPS "Quick turnaround and accurately built files are a must."

TRAVEL + LEISURE

1120 Avenue of the Americas, 9th Floor, New York NY 10036. (212)382-5600. **E-mail:** TLPhoto@aexp. com. **Website:** www.travelandleisure.com. Monthly magazine emphasizing travel, resorts, dining and entertainment. Original artwork returned after publication. Art guidelines with SASE.

ILLUSTRATION Approached by 250-350 illustrators/year. Buys 1-15 illustrations/issue. Interested in travel and leisure-related themes. "Illustrators are selected by excellence and relevance to the subject." Works on assignment only.

FIRST CONTACT & TERMS Provide samples and business card to be kept on file for future assignment. Responds only if interested. E-mail form for queries available online. In most cases these are responded to the quickest.

TIPS No cartoons.

TREASURY & RISK

475 Park Ave. S., Room 601, New York NY 10016-6901. **E-mail:** mwaters@summitpronets.com. **Website:** www.treasuryandrisk.com. **Contact:** Meg Waters, editor-in-chief. Circ. 50,000. Monthly trade publication for financial/CFO-treasurers. Sample copies available on request.

ILLUSTRATION Buys 45-55 illustrations/year. Features business computer illustration, humorous illustration and spot illustrations. Prefers electronic media. Assigns 25% of illustrations to new and emerging illustrators. Freelance artists should be familiar with Illustrator and Photoshop.

FIRST CONTACT & TERMS Send postcard sample. After introductory mailing, send follow-up postcard sample every 3 months. Accepts e-mail submissions

with link to website and image file. Prefers Mac-compatible JPEG files. Responds only if interested. Will contact artist for portfolio review if interested. Portfolio should include color and tearsheets. Pays illustrators $1,000-1,200 for color cover; $400 for spots; $500 for ½ page color inside; $650 for full page; $800 for spread. Buys first rights, one-time rights, reprint rights and all rights. Finds freelancers through agents, submissions, magazines and word of mouth.

TV GUIDE

11 W. 42nd St., 16th Floor, New York NY 10036. (212)852-7500. **Fax:** (212)852-7470. **Website:** www. tvguide.com. **Contact:** Debra Birnbaum, editor-in-chief. Estab. 1953. Circ. 9 million. Weekly consumer magazine for television viewers. Has featured illustrations by Mike Tofanelli and Toni Persiani.

🗨 Focuses on all aspects of network, cable, and pay television programming and how it affects and reflects audiences.

ILLUSTRATION Approached by 200 illustrators/year. Buys 50 illustrations/year. Considers all media.

FIRST CONTACT & TERMS Illustrators: Send postcard sample. Samples are filed. Art director will contact artist for portfolio review of color tearsheets if interested. Negotiates rights purchased. **Pays on acceptance;** $1,500-4,000 for color cover; $1,000-2,000 for full page color inside; $200-500 for spots. Finds artists through sourcebooks, magazines, word of mouth, submissions.

UBM ADVANSTAR

Advanstar Coomunications Inc., 2450 Colorado Ave., Suite 300 East, Santa Monica CA 90404. (310) 857-7500. **Fax:** (210) 857-7510. **Website:** www.advanstar. com; ubmadvanstar.com. Estab. 1909. Publishes 15 health-related publications and special products. Uses freelance artists for "most editorial illustration in the magazines."

CARTOONS Prefers general humor topics (workspace, family, seasonal); also medically related themes. Prefers single-panel b&w drawings and washes with gagline.

ILLUSTRATION Interested in all media, including 3D, electronic and traditional illustration. Needs editorial and medical illustration that varies "but is mostly on the conservative side." Works on assignment only.

FIRST CONTACT & TERMS Cartoonists: Send unpublished cartoons only with SASE group art director. Buys first world publication rights. Samples are filed. Responds only if interested. Write for portfolio review. Buys nonexclusive worldwide rights. Pays $1,000-1,500 for color cover; $250-800 for color inside; $200-600 for b&w. Accepts previously published material. Originals are returned at job's completion.

UROLOGY TIMES

125 W. First St., Duluth MN 55802. (440) 891-2758. **Fax:** (408)962-1125. **Website:** www.urologytimes. com. Estab. 1972. Circ. 10,000. Monthly trade publication. The leading news source for urgologists. Art guidelines available.

ILLUSTRATION Buys 6 illustrations/year. Has featured illustrations by DNA Illustrations, Inc. Assigns 25% of illustrations to new and emerging illustrators. 90% of freelance work demands computer skills. Freelancers should be familiar with Illustrator, Photoshop. E-mail submissions accepted with link to website. Prefers TIFF, JPEG, GIF, EPS. Samples are filed. Art director will contact artist for portfolio review if interested. Portfolio should include finished art and tearsheets. Pays on publication. Buys multiple rights. Finds freelancers through artists' submissions.

FIRST CONTACT & TERMS Illustrators: Send postcard sample with photocopies.

U.S. KIDS MAGAZINES

1100 Waterway Blvd., Indianapolis IN 46202. (317)634-1100; (800) 558-2376. **E-mail:** editor@satur dayeveningpost.com; jackandjill@emailcustomerser vice.com; humptydumpty@emailcustomerservice. com. **Website:** www.uskidsmags.com; www.turtle mag.org. Estab. 1979. Circ. 300,000. Emphasizes health, nutrition, exercise and safety for children 2-5 years. Published 6 times/year; 4-color. Original artwork not returned after publication. Sample copy for $1.75; art guidelines with SASE and first-class postage. Needs computer-literate freelancers familiar with Macromedia FreeHand and Photoshop for illustrations.

ILLUSTRATION Approached by 100 illustrators/year. Works with 20 illustrators/year. Buys 15-30 illustrations/issue. Interested in "stylized, humorous, realistic and cartooned themes; also nature and health." Works on assignment only.

FIRST CONTACT & TERMS Illustrators: Send query letter with good photocopies and tearsheets. Accepts disk submissions. Samples are filed or are returned by SASE. Responds only if interested. Portfolio re-

view not required. Buys all rights. Pays on publication: $275 for color cover, $35-90 for b&w inside, $70-155 for color inside, $35-70 for spots. Finds most artists through samples received in mail.

TIPS "Familiarize yourself with our magazine and other children's publications before you submit any samples. The samples you send should demonstrate your ability to support a story with illustration."

UTNE READER

1503 SW 42nd St, Topeka KS 66609. (785)274-4300; (800) 678-5779. **E-mail:** editor@utne.com. **Website:** www.utne.com. **Contact:** Carolyn Lang, art director. Estab. 1984. Circ. 250,000. Bimonthly digest featuring articles and reviews from the best of alternative media; independently published magazines, newsletters, books, journals and websites. Topics covered include national and international news, history, art, music, literature, science, education, economics and psychology.

○   *Utne Reader* seeks to present a lively diversity of illustration and photography "voices." We welcome artistic samples which exhibit a talent for interpreting editorial content.

FIRST CONTACT & TERMS "We are always on the lookout for skilled artists with a talent for interpreting editorial content, and welcome examples of your work for consideration. Because of our small staff, busy production schedule, and the volume of samples we receive, however, we ask that you read and keep in mind the following guidelines. We ask that you not call or e-mail seeking feedback, or to check if your package has arrived. We wish we could be more generous in this regard, but we simply don't have the staff or memory capacity to recall what has come in (SASEs and reply cards will be honored). Send samples that can be quickly viewed and tacked to a bulletin board. Single-sided postcards are preferred. Make sure to include a link to your online portfolio so we can easily view more samples of your work. DO NOT SEND cover letters, résumés, and gallery or exhibition lists. Be assured, if your art strikes us as a good fit for the magazine, we will keep you in mind for assignments. Clearly mark your full name, address, phone number, website address and e-mail address on everything you send. Please do not send original artwork or original photographs of any kind."

⚲ VALLUM: CONTEMPORARY POETRY

5038 Sherbrooke West, P.O. Box 23077, CP Vendome, Montreal Quebec H4A 1T0, Canada. (514)937-8946. **Fax:** (514)937-8946. **E-mail:** info@vallummag.com; editors@vallummag.com. **Website:** www.vallummag.com. **Contact:** Joshua Auerbach and Eleni Zisimatos, editors. Estab. 2000. Poetry/fine arts magazine published twice/year. Publishes exciting interplay of poets and artists. Content for magazine is selected according to themes listed on website.

FIRST CONTACT & TERMS Material is not filed but is returned upon request by SASE. E-mail response is preferred.

VEGETARIAN JOURNAL

P.O. Box 1463, Baltimore MD 21203-1463. (410)366-8343. **E-mail:** vrg@vrg.org. **Website:** www.vrg.org. **Contact:** Debra Wasserman, editor. Estab. 1982. Circ. 20,000. Accepts previously published artwork. Originals returned at job's completion upon request. Sample copies available for $4.

CARTOONS Approached by 4 cartoonists/year. Buys 2 cartoons/year. Prefers humorous cartoons with an obvious vegetarian theme; single panel b&w line drawings.

ILLUSTRATION Approached by 20 illustrators/year.

FIRST CONTACT & TERMS Cartoonists: Send query letter with roughs. Illustrators: Send query letter with photostats. Samples are not filed and are returned by SASE if requested by artist. Responds in 2 weeks. Portfolio review not required. Rights purchased vary according to project. **Pays on acceptance.** Pays cartoonists $25 for b&w. Pays illustrators $25-50 for b&w/color inside. Finds artists through word of mouth and job listings in art schools.

TIPS Areas most open to freelancers are recipe section and feature articles. "Review magazine first to learn our style. Send query letter with photocopy sample of line drawings of food."

⚲ VERSAL

E-mail: versal@versaljournal.org. **Website:** www.wordsinhere.com. **Contact:** Megan M. Garr and Robert Glick, editors; Daniel J. Cecil, managing editor. Estab. 2002. Circ. 650. "*Versal*, published each May by *wordsinhere*, is the only literary magazine of its kind in the Netherlands and publishes new poetry, prose and art from around the world. *Versal* and the writers behind it are also at the forefront of a growing translocal European literary scene, which includes exciting communities in Amsterdam, Paris and Berlin. *Versal* seeks work that is urgent, involved and unexpected."

FIRST CONTACT & TERMS Submission guidelines online. Samples not kept on file. Portfolio not required. Credit line is given. Work accepted by submission period (September–January).

TIPS "After reviewing the journal, if you are interested in what we're doing and would like to get involved, please send a query and CV to editor Megan Garr at Megan@wordsinhere.com. Artists submitting to *Versal* must follow our submission guidelines online and submit during our review period, September–January. Others interested in helping should always send an inquiry with a cover letter and CV. Please *do not* submit images of artwork via e-mail."

VIM & VIGOR

1010 E. Missouri Ave., Phoenix AZ 85014. (602)395-5850; (219) 836-0130. **Fax:** (602)395-5853. **Website:** www.comhs.org/vim_vigor/. Estab. 1985. Circ. 800,000. Quarterly consumer magazine focusing on health. Originals returned at job's completion. Sample copies available. Art guidelines available.

⚲ The company publishes many other titles as well.

ILLUSTRATION Approached by 100 illustrators/year. Buys 10 illustrations/issue. Works on assignment only. Considers mixed media, collage, charcoal, acrylic, oil, pastel and computer.

FIRST CONTACT & TERMS Illustrators: Send postcard sample with tearsheets and online portfolio/website information. Accepts disk submissions. Samples are filed. Rights purchased vary according to project. **Pays on acceptance.** Finds artists through agents, Web sourcebooks, word of mouth and submissions.

VIRGINIA TOWN & CITY

P.O. Box 12164, Richmond VA 23241. (804)649-8471. **Fax:** (804)343-3758. **E-mail:** dparsons@vml.org; e-mail@vml.org. **Website:** www.vml.org. **Contact:** David Parsons, editor. Estab. 1965.

CARTOONS "Currently none appear, but we would use cartoons focusing on local government problems and issues."

FIRST CONTACT & TERMS Publication will contact artist for portfolio review if interested. Rights purchased vary according to project. **Pays on acceptance.** Pays $25 for b&w. Pays illustrators $50-75 for b&w and $55 for color cover; $25-45 for b&w and $35 for color inside.

TIPS "We occasionally need illustrations of local government services. For example, police, firefighters, education, transportation, public works, utilities, cable TV, meetings, personnel management, taxes, etc. Usually b&w. Illustrators who can afford to work or sell for our low fees, and who can provide rapid turnaround should send samples of their style and information on how we can contact them."

VISUAL STUDIO MAGAZINE

1105 Media, 4 Venture, Suite 150, Ivine CA 92618. (949)265-1520. **E-mail:** privacy@1105media.com. **Website:** reddevnews.com. **Contact:** mdomingo@1105media.com; whernandez@1105media.com. Estab. 1990. Circ. 50,000. Twice-monthly 4-color trade publication for corporate software managers.

ILLUSTRATION Approached by 40 illustrators/year. Features charts & graphs, informational graphics, spot illustrations and computer illustration of business subjects. Has featured illustrations by Ryan Etter and Greg Mably. Assigns 50% of illustrations to experienced, but not well-known illustrators; 50% to new and emerging illustrators.

FIRST CONTACT & TERMS E-mail submissions or PDF files. Samples are filed. Responds in 1 month. Portfolio review not required. Pays $400 for spots.

TIPS "Illustrate technology concepts in a unique way."

VOGUE PATTERNS

120 Broadway, 34th Floor, New York NY 10271. E-mail: mailbox@voguepatterns.com or via online contact form. **Website:** voguepatterns.mccall.com. Manufacturer of clothing patterns with the *Vogue* label. Uses freelance artists mainly for fashion illustration for the *Vogue Patterns* catalog and editorial illustration for *Vogue Patterns* magazine. "The nature of catalog illustration is specialized; every button, every piece of top-stitching has to be accurately represented. Editorial illustration assigned for our magazine should have a looser editorial style. We are open to all media."

ILLUSTRATION Assigns 18 editorial illustration jobs and 100-150 fashion illustration jobs/year. Looking for "sophisticated modern fashion and intelligent creative and fresh editorial."

FIRST CONTACT & TERMS Illustrators: Send query letter with résumé, tearsheets, slides or photographs. Samples not filed are returned by SASE. Call or write for appointment to drop-off portfolio. Pays for design by the hour, illustration by the project.

TIPS "Drop off comprehensive portfolio with a current business card and sample. Make sure name is on outside of portfolio. When a job becomes available, we will call illustrator to view portfolio again."

WASHINGTON CITY PAPER

1400 Eye St. NW, Suite 900, Washington DC 20005. (202)332-2100. **Fax:** (202)332-8500. **E-mail:** mail@washingtoncitypaper.com; listings@washingtoncitypaper.com; contact@washingtoncitypaper.com; ccauterucci@washingtoncitypaper.com. **Website:** www.washingtoncitypaper.com. (202) 650-6962. **Contact:** Christina Cauterucci, arts editor. Estab. 1981. Circ. 95,000. Weekly tabloid "distributed free in DC and vicinity. We focus on investigative reportage, arts, and general interest stories with a local slant." Art guidelines not available.

CARTOONS Only accepts weekly features, no spots or op-ed style work.

ILLUSTRATION Approached by 100-200 illustrators/year. Buys 2-8 illustrations/issue. Has featured illustrations by Michael Kupperman, Peter Hoey, Greg Houston, Joe Rocco, Susie Ghahremani, and Robert Meganck. Features caricatures of politicians; humorous illustration; informational graphics; computer and spot illustration. Considers all media, if the results do well in b&w.

FIRST CONTACT & TERMS Illustrators: Send query letter with printed or e-mailed samples, photocopies or tearsheets. Art director will contact artist for more if interested. Buys first-rights. Pays on publication which is usually pretty quick. Pays cartoonists $25 minimum for b&w. Pays illustrators $110 minimum for b&w cover; $220 minimum for color cover; $85 minimum for inside. Finds illustrators mostly through submissions.

TIPS "We are a good place for freelance illustrators, we use a wide variety of styles, and we're willing to work with beginning illustrators. We like illustrators who are good on concept and can work fast if needed. We avoid cliché D.C. imagery such as the Capitol and monuments."

WASHINGTON FAMILY MAGAZINE

11260 Roger Bacon Dr., Suite 20, Reston VA 20190. (703)318-1385. **Fax:** (703)318-5509. **E-mail:** editor@thefamilymagazine.com. **Website:** www.washingtonfamily.com. Estab. 1992. Circ. 100,000. Monthly consumer parenting magazine. Art guidelines available by e-mail.

ILLUSTRATION Approached by 100 illustrators/year. Features computer illustration. Preferred subjects: children, families, women. Prefers bright colors with process colors of no more than 2 color mixes. Freelancers should be familiar with PageMaker, Illustrator, Photoshop. E-mail submissions not accepted. Prefers JPEG, high-res. Samples are filed. Portfolio not required. Pays illustrators 100 for color cover. Pays on publication. Buys one-time rights. Finds freelancers through artists' submissions.

FIRST CONTACT & TERMS Illustrators: Send postcard sample, brochure, samples.

WASHINGTONIAN MAGAZINE

1828 L St. NW, Suite 200, Washington DC 20036. (202)296-3600. **E-mail:** editorial@washingtonian.com. **Website:** www.washingtonian.com. Estab. 1965. Circ. 185,000. Monthly 4-color consumer lifestyle and service magazine.

ILLUSTRATION Approached by 200 illustrators/year. Buys 2-3 illustrations/issue. Has featured illustrations by Pat Oliphant, Chris Tayne and Richard Thompson. Features caricatures of celebrities, caricatures of politicians, humorous illustration, realistic illustrations, spot illustrations, computer illustrations and photo collage. Preferred subjects: men, women and creative humorous illustration. Assigns 20% of illustrations to new and emerging illustrators. 20% of freelance illustration demands knowledge of Photoshop.

FIRST CONTACT & TERMS Illustrators: Send postcard sample and follow-up postcard every 6 months. Send nonreturnable samples. Accepts Mac-compatible submissions. Send EPS or TIFF files. Responds only if interested. Will contact artist for portfolio review if interested. Buys first rights. **Pays on acceptance.** Finds illustrators through magazines, word of mouth, promotional samples, sourcebooks.

TIPS "We like caricatures that are fun, not mean and ugly. Want a well-developed sense of color, not just primaries."

WATERCOLOR ARTIST

F+W, a Content + eCommerce Company, 10151 Carver Rd., Suite 200, Blue Ash OH 45242. (513)531-2690. **Fax:** (513)891-7153. **Website:** www.watercolorartistmagazine.com. **Contact:** Jennifer Hoffman, art director; Kelly Kane, editor. Estab. 1984. Circ. 44,000. (Formerly *Watercolor Magic*.) Bimonthly 4-color consumer magazine for artists to explore and master watermedia. "*Watercolor Artist* is the definitive source of how-to instruction and creative inspiration for artists working in water-based media." Art guidelines free for #10 SASE with first-class postage.

FIRST CONTACT & TERMS Illustration: Pays on publication. Finds illustrators through word of mouth, visiting art exhibitions, unsolicited queries, reading books.

TIPS "We are looking for watermedia artists who are willing to teach special aspects of their work and their techniques to our readers."

WEEKLY READER

Scholastic/Weekly Reader, PO Box 7502, Jefferson City MO 65102-9733. (914)242-4000; (800) 446-3355. **Website:** www.weeklyreader.com. Estab. 1928. Publishes educational periodicals, posters and books. "*Weekly Reader* teaches the news to kids pre-K through high school age. The philosophy is to connect students to the world." Publications are 4-color. Sample copies are available.

ILLUSTRATION Needs editorial and technical illustration. Style should be "contemporary and age-level appropriate for the juvenile audience." Buys more than 50 illustrations/week. *Works on assignment only.* Uses computer and reflective art.

FIRST CONTACT & TERMS Illustrators: Send brochure, tearsheets, SASE and photocopies. Samples are filed or are returned by SASE if requested by artist. Accepts previously published artwork. Original artwork is returned at job's completion. Payment is usually made within 3 weeks of receiving the invoice. Finds artists through submissions/self-promotions, sourcebooks, agents and reps. Some periodicals need quick turnarounds.

TIPS "Our primary focus is the children's and young adult marketplace. Art should reflect creativity and knowledge of audience's needs. Our budgets are tight, and we have very little flexibility in our rates. We need artists who can work with our budgets. Avoid using fluorescent dyes. Use clear, bright colors. Work on flexible board."

WINDSURFING MAGAZINE

Bonnier Corporation, 460 N. Orlando Ave., Suite 200, Winter Park FL 32789. (407)628-4802; (212) 779-5000. **E-mail:** sarah.moore@bonniercorp.com; perri.dorset@bonniercorp.com. **Website:** windsurfingmag.com. **Contact:** Sarah Moore; Perri Dorset. Estab. 1981.

Circ. 75,000. Consumer magazine "for windsurfers and those interested in the sport. Audience is 30ish, mostly male and affluent." 8 issues/year. Original artwork returned if requested at job's completion. One sample copy available to the artist. Art guidelines not available.

ILLUSTRATION Approached by 1-2 illustrators/year. Buys 15-20 illustrations/year, mostly maps. Works on assignment only. Prefers "maps and a fun cartoon-like style." Considers airbrush, watercolor and collage.

FIRST CONTACT & TERMS Illustrators: Send query letter with SASE, "samples of various styles and short bio listing where published material has appeared." Samples are filed or are returned by SASE if requested by artist. Responds only if interested as need arises. "Please do not call." To show a portfolio, mail color tearsheets, photostats, photographs and photocopies. Rights purchased vary according to project. Pays on publication; $50-400 average for color inside.

TIPS "Send a good selection of styles for us to review."

WOODENBOAT MAGAZINE

WoodenBoat Publications, Inc., P.O. Box 78, Brookline ME 04616. (207)359-4651. **Website:** www.woodenboat.com. **Contact:** Matt Murphy, editor. Estab. 1974. Circ. 90,000. Bimonthly magazine for wooden boat owners, builders and designers. Previously published work OK. Sample copy for $6. Art guidelines free for SASE with first-class postage.

ILLUSTRATION Approached by 10-20 illustrators/year. Buys 2-10 illustrations/issue on wooden boats or related items. Uses some illustration, usually by several regularly appearing artists, but occasionally featuring others.

DESIGN Not currently using freelancers.

FIRST CONTACT & TERMS Illustrators: Send postcard sample or query letter with printed samples and tearsheets. Designers: Send query letter with tearsheets, résumé and slides. Samples are filed. Does not report back. Artist should follow up with call. Pays on publication. Pays illustrators $50-$400 for spots.

TIPS "We work with several professionals on an assignment basis, but most of the illustrative material that we use in the magazine is submitted with a feature article. When we need additional material, however, we will try to contact a good freelancer in the appropriate geographic area."

WORLD TRADE

2401 W. Big Beaver Rd., Suite 700, Troy MI 48084. (216)280-4467. **Fax:** (248)502-1060. **E-mail:** toscanoc@bnpmedia.com. **Website:** www.worldtradewt100.com. **Contact:** Cristina Toscano. Estab. 1988. Circ. 75,000. Monthly 4-color consumer journal; "read by upper management, presidents and CEOs of companies with international sales." Accepts previously published artwork. Original artwork is returned to artist at job's completion. Sample copies and art guidelines not available.

CARTOONS Prefers business/social issues.

ILLUSTRATION Approached by 15-20 illustrators/year. Buys 1-2 illustrations/issue. Works on assignment only. "We are open to all kinds of themes and styles." Considers pen & ink, colored pencil, mixed media and watercolor.

FIRST CONTACT & TERMS Illustrators: Send query letter with brochure and tearsheets to Mike Powell, art director, powellm@bnpmedia.com. Samples are filed. Responds only if interested. Portfolio review not required. Buys first rights or reprint rights. Pays on publication; $800 for color cover; $275 for color inside.

TIPS "Send an example of your work. We prefer previous work to be in business publications. Artists need to understand we work from a budget to produce the magazine, and budget controls and deadlines are closely watched."

BOOK PUBLISHERS

///

Walk into any bookstore and start counting the number of images you see on books and calendars. The illustrations you see on covers and within the pages of books are, for the most part, created by freelance artists. Publishers rarely have enough artists on staff to generate such a vast array of styles. If you like to read and work creatively to solve problems, the world of book publishing could be a great market for you.

The artwork appearing on a book cover must grab readers' attention and make them want to pick up the book. It must show at a glance what type of book it is and who it is meant to appeal to. In addition, the cover has to include basic information such as title, the author's name, the publisher's name, blurbs, and price.

Most assignments for freelance work are for jackets/covers. The illustration on the cover, combined with typography and the layout choices of the designer, announce to the prospective readers the style and content of a book. Suspenseful spy novels tend to feature stark, dramatic lettering and symbolic covers. Fantasy and science fiction novels, as well as murder mysteries and historical fiction, might show a scene from the story on their covers. Visit a bookstore and then decide which kinds of books interest you and would be best for your illustration style.

Book interiors are also important. The page layouts and illustrations direct readers through the text and complement the story, particularly in children's books and textbooks. Many publishing companies hire freelance designers with computer skills to design interiors on a contract basis. Look within each listing for the subheading Book Design to find the number of jobs assigned each year and how much is paid per project.

Finding Your Best Markets

The first paragraph of each listing describes the types of books each publisher specializes in. You should submit only to publishers who specialize in the types of books you want to illustrate or design. There's no use submitting to a publisher of literary fiction if you want to illustrate children's picture books.

The publishers in this section are just the tip of the iceberg. You can find additional publishers by visiting bookstores and libraries and looking at covers and interior art. When you find covers you admire, write down the name of the books' publishers in a notebook. If the publisher is not listed in *Artist's & Graphic Designer's Market*, go to your public library and ask to look at a copy of *Literary Market Place*, also called *LMP*, published annually by Information Today, Inc. The cost of this large directory is prohibitive to most freelancers, but you should become familiar with it if you plan to work in the book publishing industry. Though it won't tell you how to submit to each publisher, it does give art directors' names. Also be sure to visit publishers' websites—many offer artist's guidelines.

How to Submit

Send one to five nonreturnable samples along with a brief letter. Never send originals. Most art directors prefer samples that can fit in file drawers. Bulky submissions are considered a nuisance. After sending your initial introductory mailing, you should follow up with postcard samples every few months to keep your name in front of art directors. If you want to e-mail TIFF or JPEG files, check the publishers' preferences to see if they will accept submissions via e-mail.

Getting Paid

Payment for design and illustration varies depending on the size of the publisher, the type of project, and the rights purchased. Most publishers pay on a per-project basis, although some publishers of highly illustrated books (such as children's books) pay an advance plus royalties. Small, independent presses may pay only in copies.

Children's Book Illustration

Working in children's books requires a specific set of skills. You must be able to draw the same characters in a variety of poses and situations. Many publishers are expanding their product lines to include multimedia projects. While a number of children's book publishers are listed in this book, *Children's Writer's & Illustrator's Market*, published by Writer's Digest Books, is an invaluable resource if you enter this field. Visit www.writersdigestshop.com to order the most recent edition. You may also want to consider joining the Society of Children's Book Writers and Illustrators (www.scbwi.org), an international organization that offers support, information, networking opportunities, and conferences.

HARRY N. ABRAMS, INC.

115 W. 18th St., 6th Floor, New York NY 10011. (212)206-7715. **Fax:** (212)519-1210. **E-mail:** abrams@ abramsbooks.com. **Website:** www.abramsbooks.com. **Contact:** Managing Editor. Estab. 1951. Publishes hardcover originals, trade paperback originals and reprints. Types of books include fine art and illustrated books. Publishes 250 titles/year. 60% require freelance design. Visit website for art submission guidelines.

NEEDS Uses freelance designers to design complete books including jackets and sales materials. Uses illustrators mainly for maps and occasional text illustration. 100% of freelance design and 50% of illustration demands knowledge of Illustrator, InDesign or QuarkXPress and Photoshop. Works on assignment only.

FIRST CONTACT & TERMS Send query letter with résumé, tearsheets, photocopies. Accepts disk submissions or Web address. Samples are filed "if work is appropriate." Samples are returned by SASE if requested by artist. Portfolio should include printed samples, tearsheets and/or photocopies. Originals are returned at job's completion, with published product. Finds artists through word of mouth, submissions, attending art exhibitions and seeing published work.

DESIGN Assigns several freelance design jobs/year. Pays by the project.

⟲ ALLYN & BACON PUBLISHERS

445 Hutchinson Ave., Columbus OH 43235. **Website:** www.allynbaconmerrill.com. Find local rep to submit materials via online rep locator. Publishes more than 300 hardcover and paperback college textbooks/year. 60% require freelance cover designs. Our subject areas include education, psychology and sociology, political science, theater, music and public speaking.

NEEDS Designers must be strong in book cover design and contemporary type treatment. 50% of freelance work demands knowledge of Illustrator, Photoshop and FreeHand.

JACKETS/COVERS Assigns 100 design jobs and 2-3 illustration jobs/year. Pays for design by the project, $500-1,000. Pays for illustration by the project, $500-1,000. Prefers sophisticated, abstract style in pen & ink, airbrush, charcoal/pencil, watercolor, acrylic, oil, collage and calligraphy.

TIPS "Keep stylistically and technically up to date. Learn *not* to overdesign. Read instructions and ask questions. Introductory letter must state experience and include at least photocopies of your work. If I like what I see, and you can stay on budget, you'll probably get an assignment. Being pushy closes the door. We primarily use designers based in the Boston area."

THE AMERICAN BIBLE SOCIETY

1865 Broadway, New York NY 10023-7505. (212)408-1200. **Fax:** (212)408-1512. **E-mail:** info@american bible.org. **Website:** www.americanbible.org. Company publishes religious products including Bibles/ New Testaments, portions, leaflets, calendars and bookmarks. Additional products include religious children's books, posters, seasonal items, teaching aids, audio casettes, videos and CDs. Specializes in contemporary applications to the Bible. 90% requires freelance design. Book catalog on website.

NEEDS Approached by 50-100 freelancers/month. Works with 10 freelance illustrators and 20 designers/year. Uses freelancers for jacket/cover illustration and design, text illustration, book design and children's activity books. 90% of freelance work demands knowledge of Illustrator, QuarkXPress, Photoshop. Works on assignment only. 5% of titles require freelance art direction.

FIRST CONTACT & TERMS Send postcard samples of work or send query letter with brochure and tearsheets. Samples are filed or returned. *Please do not call.* Responds in 2 months. Product design department will contact artist for portfolio review if additional samples are needed. Portfolio should include final art and tearsheets. Buys all rights. Finds artists through artists' submissions, *The Workbook* (by Scott & Daughters Publishing) and *RSVP Illustrator.*

DESIGN Assigns 3-5 freelance interior book design jobs/year. Pays by the project.

JACKETS/COVERS Assigns 60-80 freelance design and 20 freelance illustration jobs/year. Pays by the project.

TEXT ILLUSTRATION Assigns several freelance illustration jobs/year. Pays by the project.

TIPS "Looking for contemporary, multicultural artwork/designs and good graphic designers familiar with commercial publishing standards and procedures. Have a polished and professional-looking portfolio or be prepared to show polished and professional-looking samples."

AMERICAN INSTITUTE OF CHEMICAL ENGINEERING

120 Wall St., Foor 23, New York NY 10005-4020. (800)242-4363. **Fax:** (203)775-5177. **E-mail:** kares@aiche.org. **Website:** www.aiche.org. **Contact:** Karen Simpson, sales administrator. Estab. 1925. Book and magazine publisher of hardcover originals and reprints, trade paperback originals and reprints and magazines. Specializes in chemical engineering.
NEEDS Approached by 30 freelancers/year. Works with 17-20 freelance illustrators/year. Prefers freelancers with experience in technical illustration. Macintosh experience a must. Uses freelancers for concept and technical illustration. Also for multimedia projects. 100% of design and 50% of illustration demand knowledge of all standard Mac programs.
FIRST CONTACT & TERMS Send query letter with tearsheets. Accepts disk submissions. Samples are filed. Responds only if interested. Call for appointment to show portfolio of color tearsheets and electronic media. Buys first rights or one-time rights. Originals are returned at job's completion.
JACKETS/COVERS Payment depends on experience, style.
TEXT ILLUSTRATION Assigns 250 jobs/year. Pays by the hour.

AMERICAN PSYCHIATRIC PRESS, INC.

1000 Wilson Blvd., Suite 1825, Arlington VA 22209. (703)907-7322 or (800)368-5777. **Fax:** (703)907-1091. **E-mail:** appi@psych.org; ngray@psych.org. **Website:** www.appi.org. **Contact:** Nicole Gray, editorial support services manager. Estab. 1981. Imprint of American Psychiatric Association. Company publishes hardcover originals and textbooks. Specializes in psychiatry and its subspecialties. Publishes 60 titles/year. 10% require freelance illustration; 10% require freelance design. Book catalog free by request.
NEEDS Uses freelancers for jacket/cover design and illustration. Needs computer-literate freelancers for design. 100% of freelance work demands knowledge of QuarkXPress, Illustrator 3.0, PageMaker 5.0. Works on assignment only.
FIRST CONTACT & TERMS Designers: Send query letter with brochure, photocopies, photographs or tearsheets. Illustrators: Send postcard sample. Samples are filed. Promotions coordinator will contact artist for portfolio review if interested. Portfolio should include final art, slides and tearsheets. Rights purchased vary according to project.
DESIGN Pays by the project.
JACKETS/COVERS Pays by the project.
TIPS Finds artists through sourcebooks. "Book covers are now being done in CorelDraw 5.0 but will work with Mac happily. Book covers are for professional books with clean designs. Type treatment design are done in-house."

AMHERST MEDIA, INC.

175 Rano St., Suite 200, Buffalo NY 14207. (716)874-4450. **Fax:** (716)874-4508. **E-mail:** submissions@amherstmedia.com. **Website:** www.amherstmedia.com. **Contact:** Craig Alesse, publisher. Estab. 1974. Company publishes trade paperback originals. Types of books include instructional and reference. Specializes in photography, how-to. Publishes 30 titles/year. Recent titles include: *Portrait Photographer's Handbook; Creating World Class Photography.* 20% require freelance illustration; 80% require freelance design.
NEEDS Approached by 12 freelancers/year. Works with 3 freelance illustrators and 3 designers/year. Uses freelance artists mainly for illustration and cover design. Also for jacket/cover illustration and design and book design. 80% of freelance work demands knowledge of InDesign or Photoshop. Works on assignment only.
FIRST CONTACT & TERMS Prefers digital submissions. Send brochure, résumé and photographs. Samples are filed. Responds only if interested. Art director will contact artist for portfolio review if interested. Rights purchased vary according to project. Originals are returned at job's completion. Finds artists through word of mouth.
DESIGN Assigns 12 freelance design jobs/year. Pays for design by the hour $25 minimum; by the project $2,000.
JACKETS/COVERS Assigns 12 freelance design and 4 illustration jobs/year. Pays $200-1200. Prefers computer illustration (InDesign/Photoshop).
TEXT ILLUSTRATION Assigns 12 freelance illustration jobs/year. Pays by the project. Only accepts computer illustration (InDesign).

ANDREWS MCMEEL PUBLISHING

100 Front St., Riverside NJ 08075. (816)581-8921; (800)851-8923. **Fax:** (816)932-6781; (816) 581-7486. **E-mail:** tlynch@amuniversal.com; marketing@amuniversal.com. **Website:** www.andrewsmcmeel.com. **Contact:**

Tim Lynch, executive art director. Estab. 1972. Publishes calendars: all formats, trade hardcover and paperback originals and reprints. Category of books include humor, gift, nonfiction, reference, puzzles and games, cookbooks. Specializes in calendars and comic strip collection books. Recent titles include *Knits for Nerds, My New Orleans Cookbook, America's Best BBQ, Dilbert 2.0 Cartoon Collection* and *Posh Puzzle* book series. Publishes 200 titles/year; 10% require freelance illustration; 80% require freelance design.

NEEDS Prefers freelancers experienced in book jacket design. Freelance designers must have working knowledge of Illustrator, Photoshop, QuarkXPress, or InDesign. Food photographers experienced in cook book photography.

FIRST CONTACT & TERMS Send sample sheets and web address or contact through artist's rep. Samples are filed and not returned. Responds only if interested. Portfolio review not required. Rights purchased vary according to project.

DESIGN Assigns 60 freelance design jobs and 20 illustration jobs/year.

TIPS "We want designers who can read a manuscript and design a concept for the best possible cover. Communicate well and be flexible with design." Designer portfolio review once a year in New York City.

ANTARCTIC PRESS

7272 Wurzbach, Suite 204, San Antonio TX 78240. (210)614-0396. **E-mail:** submissions@antarctic-press.com. **Website:** www.antarctic-press.com. **Contact:** David Hutchison. Estab. 1985. Publishes CDs, mass market paperback originals and reprints, trade paperback originals and reprints. Types of books include adventure, comic books, fantasy, humor, juvenile fiction. Specializes in comic books. Publishes 18 titles/year. Recent titles include: *Gold Digger, President Evil, The Last Zombie, Time Lincoln.* 50% requires freelance illustration. Submission guidelines on website.

"Antarctic Press is among the top 10 publishers of comics in the United States. However, the difference in market shares between the top 5 publishers and the next 5 publishers is dramatic. Most of the publishers ranked above us have a far greater share of the market place. That being the case, we are an independent publisher with a small staff, and many of our employees have multiple responsibilities. Bigger companies would spread these responsibilities out among a larger staff. Additionally, we don't have the same financial power as a larger company. We cannot afford to pay high page rates; instead, we work on an advance and royalty system which is determined by sales or potential sales of a particular book. We pride ourselves on being a company that gives new talent a chance to get published and take a shot at comic stardom."

NEEDS Approached by 60-80 illustrators/year. Works with 12 illustrators/year. Prefers local illustrators. 100% of freelance illustration demands knowledge of Photoshop.

FIRST CONTACT & TERMS Digital submissions should be sent to Submissions Editor or David Hutchison. Do not send originals. Send copies only. Accepts e-mail submissions from illustrators. Prefers TIFF or JPEG files. Samples are filed or returned by SASE. Portfolios may be dropped off every Monday-Friday. Portfolio should include b&w, color finished art. All submissions must include finished comic book art, 10 pages minimum. Buys first rights. Rights purchased vary according to project. Finds freelancers through anthologies published, artist's submissions, Internet, word of mouth. Payment is made on royalty basis after publication.

TEXT ILLUSTRATION Negotiated.

TIPS "You must love comics and be proficient in doing sequential art."

APPALACHIAN MOUNTAIN CLUB BOOKS

5 Joy St., Boston MA 02108. (617)523-0636. **Fax:** (617)523-0722. **E-mail:** amcbooks@outdoors.org. **Website:** www.outdoors.org. Estab. 1876. Publishes trade paperback originals and reprints. Types of books include adventure, instructional, nonfiction, travel and children's nature books. Specializes in hiking guidebooks. Publishes 7-10 titles/year. Recent titles include: *Best Day Hikes.* 5% requires freelance illustration; 100% requires freelance design. Book catalog free for #10 SASE.

NEEDS Typesetting work for 7-10 books per year. Prefers local freelancers experienced in book design. 100% of freelance design demands knowledge of InDesign.

FIRST CONTACT & TERMS Designers: Send link to web portfolio. Illustrators: Send link to web portfolio. Samples are not returned. Will contact artist for portfolio review of book dummy, photocopies, photographs, tearsheets, thumbnails if interested.

DESIGN Assigns 1-3 freelance design jobs/year. Pays for design by the project, $800-1,500.

JACKETS/COVERS Assigns 1-3 illustration jobs/year.

ATHENEUM BOOKS FOR YOUNG READERS

Simon & Schuster, 1230 Avenue of the Americas, New York NY 10020. **Website:** kids.simonandschuster.com. Estab. 1961. "Atheneum Books for Young Readers publishes books aimed at children, preschool through high school." Publishes hardcover originals, picture books for young kids, nonfiction for ages 8-12 and novels for middle-grade and young adults. Types of books include biography, historical fiction, history, nonfiction. Publishes 60 titles/year. 100% require freelance illustration. Book catalog free by request. Approached by hundreds of freelance artists/year.

NEEDS Approached by hundreds of freelance artists/year. Works with 40-50 illustrators/year. "We are interested in artists of varying media and are trying to cultivate those with a fresh look appropriate to each title." Send postcard sample of work or send query letter with tearsheets, résumé and photocopies. Samples are filed. Responds only if interested. Art director will contact artist for portfolio review if interested. Portfolio should include final art if appropriate, tearsheets, and folded and gathered sheets from any picture books you've had published. Rights purchased vary according to project. Originals are returned at job's completion. Finds artists through submissions, magazines ("I look for interesting editorial illustrators"), word of mouth.

TEXT ILLUSTRATION 100% of the books published require freelance illustration.

⊕ AUGSBURG FORTRESS PUBLISHERS

P.O. Box 1209, Minneapolis MN 55440-1209. (800)328-4648. **E-mail:** imagesub@augsburgfortress.org. **Website:** www.augsburgfortress.org. **Contact:** senior art director. Publishes hard cover and paperback Protestant/Lutheran books (90 titles/year), religious education materials, audiovisual resources, periodicals.

NEEDS Uses freelancers for marketing and product print design, illustration, video production, and web design. Freelancers should be familiar with Adobe Creative Cloud Suite. Freelancers work on contract. Bids for future assignment possibilities are sent out in conjunction with new product development, and schedules may vary. Please e-mail PDF samples or website portfolio links for review. Buys all rights on a work-fo-hire basis. Pay by project, and negotiates contracts for multi-project assignments.

FIRST CONTACT & TERMS "Please e-mail PDF samples or website portfolio links for review." Buys all rights on a work-fo-hire basis. Pay by project, and negotiates contracts for multi-project assignments.

TIPS "Be knowledgeable of company product and Christian market."

BAEN BOOKS

P.O. Box 1188, Wake Forest NC 27588. (919)570-1640. **E-mail:** info@baen.com. **Website:** www.baen.com. Estab. 1983. Publishes science fiction and fantasy. Publishes 60-70 titles/year; 90% require freelance illustration/design. Book catalog free on request.

NEEDS Approached by 500 freelancers/year. Works with 10 illustrators and 3 designers/year. 50% of work demands computer skills.

FIRST CONTACT & TERMS Designers: Send query letter with résumé, color photocopies, color tearsheets and SASE. Illustrators: Send query letter with color photocopies, slides, color tearsheets and SASE. Samples are filed. Originals are returned to artist at job's completion. Buys exclusive North American book rights.

JACKETS/COVERS Pays by the project. Pays designers $200 minimum; pays illustrators $1,000 minimum.

TIPS Wants to see samples within science fiction/fantasy genre only. "Do not send b&w illustrations or surreal art. Please do not waste our time and your postage with postcards. Serious submissions only."

BARBOUR PUBLISHING, INC.

1810 Barbour Dr., P.O. Box 719, Urichsville OH 44683. **E-mail:** editors@barbourbooks.com; aschrock@barbourbooks.com; fictionsubmit@barbourbooks.com. **Website:** www.barbourbooks.com. Estab. 1981. "Barbour Books publishes inspirational/devotional material that is nondenominational and evangelical in nature. We're a Christian evangelical publisher." Specializes in short, easy-to-read Christian bargain books. "Faithfulness to the Bible and Jesus Christ are the bedrock values behind every book Barbour's staff produces."

BEARMANOR MEDIA

P.O. Box 71426, Albany GA 31708. (800)755-4506. **Fax:** (814)690-1559. **E-mail:** books@benohmart.com. **Website:** www.bearmanormedia.com. **Contact:** Ben Ohmart, publisher. Estab. 2000. Publishes 60+ titles/year. Payment negotiable. Responds only if interested. Catalog available online or free with a 8×10 SASE submission.

TIPS "Potential freelancers should be familiar with our catalog and be computer savvy."

BECKER&MAYER!

11120 NE 33rd Place, Suite 101, Bellevue WA 98004. (425)827-7120. **Fax:** (425)828-9659. **E-mail:** infobm@beckermayer.com. **Website:** www.beckermayer.com. Estab. 1973. Publishes nonfiction biography, humor, history and coffee table books. Publishes 100+ titles/year. 10% require freelance design; 75% require freelance illustration. Book catalog available on website.

○   becker&mayer! is spelled in all lower case letters with an exclamation mark.

NEEDS Works with 6 designers and 20-30 illustrators/year. Freelance design work demands skills in InDesign, Illustrator, Photoshop. Freelance illustration demands skills in Illustrator, Photoshop.

FIRST CONTACT & TERMS Designers: Send query letter with résumé and tearsheets. Illustrators: Send query letter, nonreturnable postcard sample, résumé and tearsheets. Does not accept e-mail submissions. Samples are filed. Responds only if interested. Will request portfolio review of color finished art, roughs, thumbnails and tearsheets, only if interested. Rights purchased vary according to project.

TEXT ILLUSTRATION Assigns 30 freelance illustration jobs a year. Pays by the project.

TIPS "No phone calls!"

○ BLUE DOLPHIN PUBLISHING, INC.

P.O. Box 8, Nevada City CA 95959-0008. (530)477-1503. **Fax:** (530) 265-0603. **E-mail:** bdolphin@bluedolphinpublishing.com. **Website:** www.bluedolphinpublishing.com. **Contact:** Paul M. Clemens, president. Estab. 1985. Publishes hardcover and trade paperback originals. Types of books include biography, cookbooks, humor and self-help. Specializes in comparative spiritual traditions, lay psychology and health. Recent titles include *Vegan Inspiration*, *Consciousness Is All*, *Embracing the Miraculous*, *Mary's Message to the World*, *The Fifth Tarot* and *The Fifth Gospel*. Publishes 20 titles/year; 25% require freelance illustration; 30% require freelance design. Books are "high quality on good paper, with laminated dust jacket and color covers." Book catalog free upon request.

NEEDS Works with 5-6 freelance illustrators and designers/year. Uses freelancers mainly for book cover design; also for jacket/cover and text illustration. "More hardcovers and mixed media are requiring box design as well." 50% of freelance work demands knowledge of PageMaker, QuarkXPress, FreeHand, Illustrator, Photoshop, CorelDraw, InDesign and other IBM-compatible programs. Works on assignment only.

FIRST CONTACT & TERMS Send postcard sample or query letter with brochure and photocopies. Samples are filed or are returned by SASE if requested. Responds "whenever work needed matches portfolio." Originals are returned to artist at job's completion. Sometimes requests work on spec before assigning job. Considers project's budget when establishing payment. Negotiates rights purchased. Considers buying second rights (reprint rights) to previously published work.

DESIGN Assigns 3-5 jobs/year. Pays by the hour, $10-15; or by the project, $300-900.

JACKETS/COVERS Assigns 5-6 design and 5-6 illustration jobs/year. Pays by the hour, $10-15; or by the project, $300-900.

TEXT ILLUSTRATION Assigns 1-2 jobs/year. Pays by the hour, $10-15; or by the project, $300-900.

TIPS "Send query letter with brief sample of style of work. We usually use local people, but are always looking for something special. Learning good design is more important than designing on the computer, but we are very computer-oriented. Basically we look for original artwork of any kind that will fit the covers for the subjects we publish. Please see our online catalog of over 250 titles to see what we have selected so far."

○ BLUEWOOD BOOKS

242 Aragon Blvd., San Mateo CA 94402. (650)548-0754. **Fax:** (650)548-0654. **E-mail:** bluewoodb@aol.com. Estab. 1990. Publishes trade paperback originals. Types of books include biography, history, nonfiction and young adult. Publishes 4-10 titles/year. Titles include: *True Stories of Baseball's Hall of Famers*, *100 Scientists Who Shaped World History* and *American Politics in the 20th Century*. 100% require freelance

illustration; 75% require freelance design. Catalog not available.

NEEDS Works with 5 illustrators and 3 designers/year. Prefers local freelancers experienced in realistic, b&w line illustration and book design. Uses freelancers mainly for illustration and design. 80-100% of freelance design demands knowledge of Photoshop, Illustrator and QuarkXPress. 80-100% of freelance illustration demands knowledge of FreeHand, Photoshop, Illustrator and QuarkXPress.

FIRST CONTACT & TERMS Designers: Send query letter with brochure, photocopies, résumé, SASE and tearsheets. Illustrators: Send query letter with photocopies, résumé, SASE and tearsheets. Samples are filed. Responds only if interested. Will contact artist for portfolio review of photocopies, photographs, roughs, slides, tearsheets, thumbnails and transparencies if interested. Buys all rights.

DESIGN Assigns 4-10 freelance design jobs/year. Pays by the hour or project.

JACKETS/COVERS Pays by the project, $150-200 for color.

TEXT ILLUSTRATION Assigns 4-10 freelance illustration jobs/year. Pays $15-30 for each b&w illustration. Finds freelancers through submissions.

NICHOLAS BREALEY PUBLISHING

20 Park Plaza, Suite 610, Boston MA 02116. (617)523-3801. **Fax:** (617)523-3708. **Website:** www.nicholasbrealey.com. **Contact:** Aquisitions Editor. Estab. 1992. Publishes paperback and hardcover originals. Types of books include text and reference. Specializes in global business, popular psychology, travel memoir, and crossing cultures. Recent titles: *Co-Active Coaching*, 3rd ed. by Henry Kimsey-House, Karen Kimsey-House and Phillip Sandahl; *Around India in 80 Trains* by Monisha Rajesh; *Breakthrough Branding* by Catherine Kaputa. Publishes 20 titles/year. Book catalog free by request.

NEEDS Approached by 20 freelancers/year. Works with 2-3 freelance illustrators/year. Prefers freelancers with experience in trade books, multicultural field. Uses freelancers mainly for jacket/cover design and illustration. 100% of freelance work demands knowledge of Illustrator, Photoshop, InDesign and Quark.

FIRST CONTACT & TERMS Send query letter with brochure, tearsheets, résumé and photocopies. Samples are filed or are returned by SASE if requested by artist. Will contact artist for portfolio review if inter-

ested. Portfolio should include b&w final art. Buys all rights. Originals are not returned. Finds artists through submissions and word of mouth.

JACKETS/COVERS Assigns 6 freelance illustration jobs/year. Pays by the project, $300-500.

TIPS First-time assignments are usually book jackets only; book jackets with interiors (complete projects) are given to "proven" freelancers. "We look for artists who have flexibility with schedule and changes to artwork. We appreciate an artist who will provide artwork that doesn't need special attention by prepress in order for it to print properly."

BROOKS/COLE PUBLISHING COMPANY

Cengage Learning, 10650 Toebben Dr., Independence KY 41051. (800)354-9706. **Fax:** (800)487-8488. **Website:** www.brookscole.com; www.cengage.com. **Contact:** Art director. Estab. 1967. Specializes in hardcover and paperback college textbooks on mathematics, chemistry, earth sciences, physics, computer science, engineering and statistics. Publishes 100 titles/year. 85% requires freelance illustration. Books are bold, contemporary textbooks for college level.

NEEDS Works with 25 freelance illustrators and 25 freelance designers/year. Uses freelance artists mainly for interior illustration. Uses illustrators for technical line art and covers. Uses designers for cover and book design and text illustration. Also uses freelance artists for jacket/cover illustration and design. Works on assignment only.

FIRST CONTACT & TERMS Send query letter with brochure, résumé, tearsheets and photographs. Samples are filed or are returned by SASE. Art director will contact artist for portfolio review if interested. Portfolio should include roughs, tearsheets, final reproduction/product, photographs, slides and transparencies. Considers complexity of project, skill and experience of artist, project's budget and turnaround time in determining payment. Negotiates rights purchased. Not interested in second rights to previously published work unless first used in totally unrelated market. Finds illustrators and designers through word of mouth, magazines, submissions/self promotion, sourcebooks, and agents.

DESIGN Assigns 70 design and many illustration jobs/year. Pays by the project.

JACKETS/COVERS Assigns 90 design and many illustration jobs/year. Pays by the project.

TEXT ILLUSTRATION Assigns 85 freelance jobs/year. Prefers ink/Macintosh. Pays by the project.

TIPS "Provide excellent package in mailing of samples and cost estimates. Follow up with phone call. Don't be pushy. Would like to see abstract and applied photography/illustration; single strong, memorable bold images."

CANDLEWICK PRESS

99 Dover St., Somerville MA 02144. (617)661-3330. **Fax:** (617)661-0565. **E-mail:** bigbear@candlewick.com. **Website:** www.candlewick.com. Estab. 1991. Publishes hardcover, trade paperback children's books. Publishes 200 titles/year. 100% require freelance illustration. Book catalog not available. Works with approx. 170 illustrators/year.

FIRST CONTACT & TERMS "If you think your illustration style is well-suited to our list, you may contact our art coordination associate by e-mail at illustratorsubmissions@candlewick.com. No phone calls or office visits please! We prefer to receive a link to your website or online portfolio with a brief summary highlighting relevant professional and publishing experience in the covering e-mail. If you would like to include specific samples, please attach JPEGs to your e-mail and ensure your name is present in the file name. We will contact you if we have or anticipate a project that suits your particular talents."

TEXT ILLUSTRATION Finds illustrators through agents, word of mouth, submissions, art schools. "We generally use illustrators with prior trade book experience."

CANDY CANE PRESS

Guideposts Co., 2630 Elm Hill Pike, Suite 100, Nashville TN 37214. (615)333-0478. **Fax:** (615)781-1447. **E-mail:** idealsinfo@guideposts.org. **Website:** www.idealsbooks.com. **Contact:** Peggy Schaefer, publisher. Estab. 1996. Publishes hardcover and trade paperback originals. Types of books include board books, children's picture books, educational activity books, juvenile and preschool. Publishes 10 titles/year.

CAPSTONE PRESS

1710 Roe Crest Dr., North Mankato MN 56003. (800)747-4992. **Fax:** (888)262-0705. **E-mail:** nf.il.sub@capstonepub.com (nonfiction); il.sub@capstonepub.com (fiction). **Website:** www.capstonepress.com. **Contact:** Dede Barton, photo director. Estab. 1991. Publishes juvenile nonfiction and educational books. Subjects include animals, ethnic groups, vehicles, sports, history, scenics. Photos used for text illustrations, promotional materials, book covers. "To see examples of our products, please visit our website." Submission guidelines available online.

FIRST CONTACT & TERMS Send query letter with stock list. E-mail résumé, sample artwork, and a list of previous publishing credits if applicable. Accepts images in digital format for submissions as well as for use. Digital images must be at least 8×10 at 300 dpi for publishing quality (TIFF, EPS or original camera file format preferred). Keeps samples on file. Responds in 6 months. Simultaneous submissions and previously published work OK. Pays after publication. Credit line given. Looking to buy worldwide all language rights for print and digital rights. Producing online projects (interactive websites and books); printed books may be bound up into binders.

TIPS "Be flexible. Book publishing usually takes at least 6 months. Capstone does not pay holding fees. Be prompt. The first photos in are considered for covers first."

CENTERSTREAM PUBLICATION LLC

P.O. Box 17878, Anaheim CA 92807. (714)779-9390. **E-mail:** centerstrm@aol.com. **Website:** www.centerstream-usa.com. **Contact:** Ron Middlebrook, owner. Estab. 1982. "Centerstream is known for its unique publications for a variety of instruments. From instructional and reference books and biographies, to fun song collections and DVDs, our products are created by experts who offer insight and invaluable information to players and collectors." Publishes DVDs, audio tapes, and hardcover and softcover originals. Types of books include music reference, biography, music history and music instruction. Publishes 10-20 titles/year. Samples are not filed and are returned by SASE. Responds only if interested. Rights purchased vary according to project.

FIRST CONTACT & TERMS Accepts Mac-compatible submissions.

TEXT ILLUSTRATION 100% requires freelance illustration. Works with 3 illustrators/year. Approached by 12 illustrators/year.

CHURCH PUBLISHING INC.

19 E. 34th St., New York NY 10016. (800)223-6602. **Fax:** (212)779-3392. **E-mail:** nabryan@cpg.org. **Website:** www.churchpublishing.org. **Contact:** Nancy Bryan, editorial director. Estab. 1884. Company publishes trade paperback and hardcover originals

and reprints. Specializes in spirituality, Christianity/contemporary issues.

NEEDS Works with illustrators as needed.

FIRST CONTACT & TERMS Samples are filed. Usually buys one-time rights. Finds artists through freelance submissions and web.

CLARION BOOKS

Houghton Mifflin Co., 215 Park Ave. S., New York NY 10003. **Website:** www.hmhco.com. Estab. 1965. Imprint publishes hardcover originals and trade paperback reprints. Book catalog free with SASE. Approached by "countless" freelancers. Works with 48 freelance illustrators/year. Uses freelancers mainly for picture books and novel jackets. Also for jacket/cover and text illustration. Pays by the project. "Be familiar with the type of books we publish before submitting. Send a SASE for a catalog or look at our books in the bookstore."

NEEDS Picture books, chapter books, middle grade novels and nonfiction, including historical and animal behavior. Publishes 60 titles/year. 90% requires freelance illustration.

FIRST CONTACT & TERMS Send children's book-related samples. Send query letter with tearsheets and photocopies. Samples are filed "if suitable to our needs." Responds only if interested. Portfolios may be dropped off every Monday. Art director will contact artist for portfolio review if interested. Rights purchased vary according to project. Originals are returned at job's completion.

TEXT ILLUSTRATION Assigns 48 freelance illustration jobs/year.

CRC MINISTRY SUPPORT SERVICES

1700 28th St. SE, Grand Rapids MI 49508-1407. (616)224-0780. **Fax:** (616)224-0834. **E-mail:** dheet derks@crcna.org. **Website:** www.crcna.org. Estab. 1866. Publishes hardcover and trade paperback originals and magazines. Types of books include instructional, religious, young adult, reference, juvenile and preschool. Specializes in religious educational materials. Publishes 4-6 titles/year. 85% require freelance illustration. 5% require freelance art direction.

NEEDS Approached by 30-45 freelancers/year. Works with 12-16 freelance illustrators/year. Prefers freelancers with religious education, cross-cultural sensitivities. Uses freelancers for jacket/cover and text illustration. Works on assignment only.

FIRST CONTACT & TERMS Send query letter with brochure, résumé, tearsheets, photographs, photocopies. Submissions will not be returned. Buys one-time rights. Originals are returned at job's completion.

JACKETS/COVERS Assigns 2-3 freelance illustration jobs/year. Pays by the project, $300-1,000.

TIPS "Be absolutely professional. Know how people learn and be able to communicate a concept clearly in your art."

CYCLE PUBLICATIONS, INC.

Van der Plas Publications, 1282 Seventh Ave., San Francisco CA 94112. (415)665-8214. **Fax:** (415)753-8572. **E-mail:** rvdp@cyclepublishing.com. **Website:** www.cyclepublishing.com. Estab. 1985. Book publisher. Publishes trade paperback originals. Types of books include instructional and travel. Specializes in subjects relating to cycling and bicycles. Publishes 6 titles/year. 20% require freelance illustration. Book catalog for SASE with first-class postage.

NEEDS Approached by 5 freelance artists/year. Buys 100 freelance illustrations/year. Uses freelance artists mainly for technical (perspective) and instructions (anatomically correct hands, posture). Also uses freelance artists for text illustration; line drawings only. Also for design. 50% of freelance work demands knowledge of CorelDraw and FreeHand. Works on assignment only.

FIRST CONTACT & TERMS Send query letter with tearsheets. Accepts disk submissions. Please include print-out with EPS files. Samples are filed. Call "but only after we have responded to query." Portfolio should include photostats. Rights purchased vary according to project. Originals are not returned to the artist at the job's completion.

DESIGN Pays by the project.

TEXT ILLUSTRATION Assigns 5 freelance illustration jobs/year. Pays by the project.

TIPS "Show competence in line drawings of technical subjects and 2-color maps."

DA CAPO PRESS

Perseus Books Group, 44 Farnsworth St., 3rd Floor, Boston MA 02210. (617)252-5200. **Website:** www.dacapopress.com. Estab. 1975. Publishes hardcover originals, trade paperback originals, trade paperback reprints. Types of books include self-help, parenting, biography, memoir, coffee table books, history, travel, music, and film. Specializes in self-help, parenting, music and history (trade). Publishes 100 titles/year.

25% requires freelance design; 5% requires freelance illustration.

NEEDS Approached by 30+ designers and 30+ illustrators/year. Works with 10 designers and 1 illustrator/year.

FIRST CONTACT & TERMS Send query letter with résumé, URL, color prints/copies. Send follow-up postcard sample every 6 months. Prefers Mac-compatible, JPEG, and PDF files. Samples are filed. Responds only if interested. Portfolios may be dropped off every Wednesday, Thursday and Friday and should include finished, printed samples. Rights purchased vary according to project. Finds freelancers through art competitions, artist submissions, Internet and word of mouth.

JACKETS/COVERS Assigns 20 freelance cover illustration jobs/year.

TIPS "Visit our website to view work produced/assigned by Da Capo."

DARK HORSE

10956 SE Main St., Milwaukie OR 97222. (503)652-8815. **Fax:** (503)654-9440. **E-mail:** dhcomics@dark horse.com. **Website:** www.darkhorse.com. **Contact:** Submissions Dept. Estab. 1986. Publishes mass market and trade paperback originals. Types of books include comic books and graphic novels. Specializes in comic books. Book catalog available on website.

FIRST CONTACT & TERMS Send photocopies (clean, sharp, with name, address and phone number written clearly on each page). Do not submit via fax or e-mail. Samples are not filed and not returned. Responds only if interested. Company will contact artist for portfolio review if interested. Please see website for more detail guidelines.

TIPS "If you're looking for constructive criticism, show your work to industry professionals at conventions."

DAW BOOKS, INC.

Penguin Group (USA), 375 Hudson St., New York NY 10014-3658. (212)366-2096. **Fax:** (212)366-2090. **E-mail:** daw@us.penguingroup.com. **Website:** www.dawbooks.com. **Contact:** Peter Stampfel, submissions editor. Estab. 1971. Publishes hardcover and mass market paperback originals and reprints. Specializes in science fiction and fantasy. Publishes 72 titles/year. All require freelance illustration. Guidelines available on website.

NEEDS Works with numerous illustrators and 1 designer/year. Buys more than 36 illustrations/year. Works with illustrators for covers. Works on assignment only.

FIRST CONTACT & TERMS Send postcard sample or query letter with brochure, résumé, tearsheets, transparencies, photocopies, photographs and SASE. "Please don't send slides." Samples are filed or are returned by SASE only if requested. Responds in 3 days. Originals returned at job's completion. Call for appointment to show portfolio of original/final art, final reproduction/product and transparencies. Considers complexity of project, skill and experience of artist and project's budget when establishing payment. Buys first rights and reprint rights.

JACKETS/COVERS Pays by the project. "Our covers illustrate the story."

TIPS "We have a drop-off policy for portfolios. We accept them on Tuesdays, Wednesdays and Thursdays and report back within a day or so. Portfolios should contain science fiction and fantasy color illustrations *only*. We do not want to see anything else. Look at several dozen of our covers."

DC COMICS

1700 Broadway, 5th Floor, New York NY 10019-5905. (212)636-5400. **Website:** www.dccomics.com. Estab. 1948. Publishes hardcover originals and reprints, mass market paperback originals and reprints, trade paperback originals and reprints. Types of books include adventure, comic books, fantasy, horror, humor, juvenile, science fiction. Specializes in comic books. Publishes 1,000 titles/year.

DC Comics does not accept unsolicited submissions. During a convention visit, drop off photocopied samples of your work. If representatives like what they see, a time is schedule for you the following day to meet a representative personally and discuss your artistic interests and portfolio.

DIAL BOOKS FOR YOUNG READERS

Imprint of Penguin Group (USA), 345 Hudson St., New York NY 10014. (212)366-2000. **Website:** www.penguin.com/youngreaders. **Contact:** Lauri Hornik, president/publisher. Estab. 1961. Specializes in juvenile and young adult hardcover originals. Publishes 50 titles/year. 100% require freelance illustration. Books are "distinguished children's books."

NEEDS Approached by 400 freelancers/year. Works with 40 freelance illustrators/year. Prefers freelancers with some book experience. Works on assignment only.

FIRST CONTACT & TERMS Send query letter with photocopies, tearsheets and SASE. Samples are filed or returned by SASE. Responds only if interested. Considers complexity of project, skill and experience of artist and project's budget when establishing payment. Rights purchased vary.

JACKETS/COVERS Assigns 8 illustration jobs/year. Pays by the project.

TEXT ILLUSTRATION Assigns 40 freelance illustration jobs/year. Pays by the project.

TIPS "Never send original art. Never send art by e-mail, fax or CD. Please do not phone, fax or e-mail to inquire after your art submission."

◔ DUTTON CHILDREN'S BOOKS

Penguin Group (USA), 375 Hudson St., New York NY 10014. **E-mail:** duttonpublicity@us.penguingroup. com. **Website:** www.penguin.com. **Contact:** Julie Strauss-Gabel, vice president and publisher. Estab. 1852. Publishes hardcover, trade picture books and illustrated middle grade. Publishes 50-75 titles/year.

NEEDS Prefers local designers.

FIRST CONTACT & TERMS Send postcard sample, printed samples, tearsheets. Samples are filed or returned by SASE. Will contact artist for portfolio review if interested. Portfolios may be dropped off every Tuesday and picked up by end of the day. Do not send samples via e-mail.

JACKETS/COVERS Pays for illustration by the project $1,800-2,500.

◔ EDWARD ELGAR PUBLISHING, INC.

The William Pratt House, 9 Dewey Ct., Northampton MA 01060. (413)584-5551. **Fax:** (413)584-9933. **E-mail:** submissions@e-elgar.co.uk. **Website:** www.e-elgar.com. Estab. 1986. Publishes hardcover originals and textbooks. Types of books include instructional, nonfiction, reference, textbooks, academic monographs, references in economics and business and law. Publishes 200 titles/year.

◑   This publisher uses only freelance designers. Its academic books are produced in the United Kingdom. Direct marketing material is done in US. There is no call for illustration.

NEEDS Prefers local designers experienced in direct mail and academic publishing. 100% of freelance design demands knowledge of Photoshop, InDesign.

FIRST CONTACT & TERMS Send query letter with printed samples. Accepts Mac-compatible disk submissions. Samples are filed. Will contact artist for portfolio review if interested. Buys one-time rights or rights purchased vary according to project. Finds freelancers through word of mouth, local sources (i.e., phone book, newspaper, etc.).

FALCONGUIDES

246 Goose Lane, P.O. Box 480, Guilford CT 06437. (203)458-4500. **Website:** www.falcon.com; www. globepequot.com. Book publisher. The Falcon line specializes in outdoor recreation topics such as hiking, biking, climbing, surfing and other areas.

FIRST CONTACT & TERMS "We welcome solicited and unsolicited submissions from authors, agents and book packagers sent in hard copy by mail or other shipping carrier. We will not return any materials without a SASE containing sufficient postage. Never send original copies. We aren't responsible for the loss of any materials sent to us. No calls, please, unless you are a professional literary agent or have a book contract with GPP. Proposals should only be e-mailed to an editor by request." See website for complete proposal guidelines.

FANTAGRAPHICS BOOKS, INC.

7563 Lake City Way NE, Seattle WA 98115. (206)524-1967. **Fax:** (206)524-2104. **Website:** www.fantagraphics.com. **Contact:** Submissions Editor. Estab. 1976. Publishes hardcover and trade paperback originals and reprints. Types of books include contemporary, experimental, mainstream, historical, humor and erotic. "All our books are comic books or graphic stories." Publishes 100 titles/year. 10% require freelance illustration. Book catalog free by request. Art submission guidelines available on website.

◎   See additional listing in the Magazines section.

NEEDS Approached by 500 freelancers/year. Works with 25 freelance illustrators/year. Must be interested in and willing to do comics. Uses freelancers for comic book interiors and covers.

FIRST CONTACT & TERMS Send query letter addressed to Submissions Editor with résumé, SASE, photocopies and finished comics work. Samples are not filed and are returned by SASE. Responds only if interested. Call or write for appointment to show

portfolio of original/final art and b&w samples. Buys one-time rights or negotiates rights purchased. Originals are returned at job's completion. Pays royalties.
TIPS "We want to see completed comics stories. We don't make assignments, but instead look for interesting material to publish that is preexisting. We want cartoonists who have an individual style, who create stories that are personal expressions."

FARRAR, STRAUS & GIROUX FOR YOUNG READERS

Macmillan Children's Publishing Group, 175 Fifth Ave., New York NY 10010. (212)741-6900. **Fax:** (212)633-2427. **E-mail:** childrens.editorial@fsgbooks. com. **Website:** www.fsgkidsbooks.com. Estab. 1946. Book publisher. Publishes hardcover and trade paperback originals and trade paperback reprints. Publishes nonfiction and juvenile fiction. Publishes 200 titles/year. 20% require freelance illustration; 40% freelance design.
NEEDS Works with 12 freelance designers and 3-5 illustrators/year. Uses artists for jacket/cover and book design.
FIRST CONTACT & TERMS Submission guidelines available online.
DESIGN Assigns 40 freelance design jobs/year. Pays by the project.
JACKETS/COVERS Assigns 20 freelance design jobs/year and 10-15 freelance illustration jobs/year. Pays by the project.
TIPS The best way for a freelance illustrator to get an assignment is "to have a great portfolio."

FIRST BOOKS/INKWATER PRESS

6750 SW Franklin St., Suite A, Portland OR 97223. (503)968-6777. **Fax:** (503)968-6779. **E-mail:** design@ inkwaterpress.com. **Website:** www.inkwaterpress. com; www.inkwater.com. Estab. 1988. Publishes trade paperback originals. Publishes 100+ titles/year. 5% require freelance illustration.
NEEDS Works with 5 designers and 5 illustrators/year. Uses freelance designers not illustrators mainly for interiors and covers.
FIRST CONTACT & TERMS Designers: Send any samples you want to send and SASE but *no original art.* Illustrators: Send query letter with a few photocopies or slides. Samples are filed or returned by SASE. Rights purchased vary according to project.
DESIGN Payment varies per assignment.

TIPS "Small samples get looked at more than anything bulky and confusing. Little samples are better than large packets and binders. Postcards are easy. Save a tree!"

FLASHLIGHT PRESS

527 Empire Blvd., Brooklyn NY 11225. (718)288-8300. **Fax:** (718)972-6307. **E-mail:** editor@flashlightpress. com. **Website:** www.flashlightpress.com. **Contact:** Shari Dash Greenspan, editor. Estab. 2004. Publishes hardcover and trade paperback originals. Book catalog available online.
FIRST CONTACT & TERMS E-mail with URL or low-res digital images. Submission guidelines available at www.flashlightpress.com/submissionguidelines.html.

FRANKLIN WATTS

338 Euston Rd., London NW1 3BH, United Kingdom. (44)(20)7873-6000. **Fax:** (44)(20)7873-6024. **E-mail:** ad@hachettechildrens.co.uk. **Website:** www. franklinwatts.co.uk. Estab. 1942. Franklin Watts is well known for its high quality and attractive information books, which support the National Curriculum and stimulate children's enquiring minds. Reader Development is one of Franklin Watts' specialisations; the list offers titles on a wide array of subjects for beginner readers. It is also the proud publisher of many award-winning authors/illustrators, including Mick Manning and Brita Granstrom.
FIRST CONTACT & TERMS Submission guidelines available online.

FULCRUM PUBLISHING

4690 Table Mountain Dr., Suite 100, Golden CO 80403. **E-mail:** acquisitions@fulcrumbooks.com. **Website:** www.fulcrum-books.com. **Contact:** T. Baker, acquisitions editor. Estab. 1984. Publishes hardcover originals and trade paperback originals and reprints. Types of books include biography, Native American, reference, history, self help, children's, teacher resource books, travel, humor, gardening and nature. Specializes in history, nature, teacher resource books, travel, Native American, environmental and gardening. Publishes 30 titles/year. 15% requires freelance illustration; 15% requires freelance design. Book catalog free by request.
NEEDS Uses freelancers mainly for cover and interior illustrations for gardening books. Also for other jacket/covers, text illustration and book design. Works on assignment only.

FIRST CONTACT & TERMS Send query letter with tearsheets, photographs, photocopies and photostats. Samples are filed. Responds to artist only if interested. To show portfolio, mail b&w photostats. Buys one-time rights. Originals are returned at job's completion.

DESIGN Pays by the project.

JACKETS/COVERS Pays by the project.

TEXT ILLUSTRATION Pays by the project.

TIPS Previous book design experience a plus.

GALISON/MUDPUPPY PRESS

28 W. 44th St., Suite 1411, New York NY 10036. (800)670-7441. **Fax:** (212)391-4037. **E-mail:** juanita@galison.com. **Website:** www.galison.com. **Contact:** Juanita Dharmazi-Virani, art director. Publishes note cards, journals, stationery, children's products. Publishes 120 titles/year.

NEEDS Works with 20 illustrators. Some freelance design demands knowledge of Photoshop, Illustrator and QuarkXPress.

FIRST CONTACT & TERMS "To submit your artwork for consideration, please e-mail a letter and PDF files to juanita@galison.com. For Mudpuppy children's products, please submit artwork for consideration to cynthia@galison.com. We will contact you if a suitable project arises."

GALLAUDET UNIVERSITY PRESS

800 Florida Ave. NE, Washington DC 20002-3695. (202)651-5488. **Fax:** (202)651-5489. **E-mail:** gupress@gallaudet.edu. **Website:** gupress.gallaudet.edu. **Contact:** Ivey Pittle Wallace, assistant eirector (editorial). Estab. 1980. Publishes hardcover and trade paperback originals, hardcover and trade paperback reprints, DVDs, videotapes and textbooks. Types of books include reference, biography, coffee table books, history, instructional and textbook nonfiction. Specializes in books related to deafness. Publishes 12-15 new titles/year. 90% requires freelance design; 2% requires freelance illustration. Book catalog free on request.

NEEDS Approached by 10-20 designers and 30 illustrators/year. Works with 15 designers/year. 100% of freelance design work demands knowledge of Illustrator, PageMaker, Photoshop and QuarkXPress.

FIRST CONTACT & TERMS Send query letter with postcard sample with résumé, sample of work and URL. After introductory mailing, send follow-up postcard sample every 6 months. Accepts disk submissions. Prefers Windows-compatible, PDF files.

Samples are filed. Responds only if interested. Company will contact artist for portfolio review if interested. Portfolio should include color finished art. Rights purchased vary according to project. Finds freelancers through Internet and word of mouth.

TIPS "Do not call us."

GIBBS SMITH

P.O. Box 667, Layton UT 84041. (801)544-9800. **Fax:** (801)544-8853. **E-mail:** duribe@gibbs-smith.com. **Website:** www.gibbs-smith.com. **Contact:** Suzanne Taylor, associate publisher and creative director (children's activity books); Jennifer Grillone, art acquisitions. Estab. 1969. Imprints include Sierra Book Club for Children and Hill Street Press. Company publishes hardcover and trade paperback originals. Types of books include children's activity books, architecture and design books, cookbooks, humor, juvenile, western. Publishes 100 titles/year. 10% requires freelance illustration; 90% requires freelance design

NEEDS Approached by 250 freelance illustrators and 50 freelance designers/year. Works with 5 freelance illustrators and 15 designers/year. Designers may be located anywhere with broadband service. Uses freelancers mainly for cover design and book layout, cartoon illustration, children's book illustration. 100% of freelance design demands knowledge of QuarkXPress or InDesign. 70% of freelance illustration demands knowledge of Photoshop, Illustrator and FreeHand.

DESIGN Assigns 90 freelance design jobs/year. Pays by the project.

JACKETS/COVERS Assigns 90 freelance design jobs and 5 illustration jobs/year. Pays for design by the project. Pays for illustration by the project.

TEXT ILLUSTRATION Pays by the project.

GLENCOE

McGraw-Hill Education, P.O. Box 182605, Columbus OH 43218. (646) 766-2574; (800) 334-7344. **E-mail:** mhe_cust_service@mcgraw-hill.com. **Website:** www.glencoe.com; MHEonline.com. Estab. 1965. Publishes textbooks. Types of books include marketing and career education, art and music, health, computer technology. Specializes in most el-hi (grades 7-12) subject areas, as well as postsecondary career subjects. Publishes 350 titles/year.

🖸 Glencoe also has divisions in Peoria IL, and Columbus OH, with separate art departments.

NEEDS Approached by 50 freelancers/year. Works with 10-20 freelance illustrators and 10-20 designers/

year. Prefers experienced artists. Uses freelance artists mainly for illustration and production. Also for jacket/cover design and illustration, text illustration and book design. 100% of design and 50% of illustration demand knowledge of Adobe, InDesign, or Illustrator on Mac. Works on assignment only.

FIRST CONTACT & TERMS Send nonreturnable samples. Accepts disk submissions compatible with above program. Samples are filed. Sometimes requests work on spec before assigning a job. Negotiates rights purchased. Originals are not returned.

DESIGN Assigns 10-20 freelance design and many illustration jobs/year. Pays by the project.

JACKETS/COVERS Assigns 10-20 freelance design jobs/year. Pays by the project.

TEXT ILLUSTRATION Assigns 20-30 freelance design jobs/year. Pays by the project.

GLOBE PEQUOT PRESS

246 Goose Lane, P.O. Box 480, Guilford CT 06437. (203)458-4500. **Website:** www.globepequot.com. **Contact:** design department. Estab. 1947. Publishes hardcover and trade paperback originals and reprints. Types of books include (mostly) travel, kayak, outdoor, cookbooks, instruction, self-help and history. Specializes in regional subjects New England, Northwest, Southeast bed-and-board country inn guides. Publishes 600 titles/year. 20% require freelance illustration; 75% require freelance design. Design of books is "classic and traditional, but fun." Book catalog available.

NEEDS Works with 10-20 freelance illustrators and 15-20 designers/year. Uses freelancers mainly for cover and text design and production. Also for jacket/cover and text illustration and direct mail design. Needs computer-literate freelancers for production. 100% of design and 75% of illustration demand knowledge of QuarkXPress 3.32, Illustrator 7.0 or Photoshop 5. Works on assignment only.

FIRST CONTACT & TERMS Send query letter with résumé, photocopies and photographs. Accepts disk submissions compatible with QuarkXPress 3.32, Illustrator 7.0 or Photoshop 5. Samples are filed and not returned. Request portfolio review in original query. "Due to the volume of inquiries, we are unable to respond individually unless suitable work is available at that time." Art director will contact artist for portfolio review if interested. Portfolio should include roughs, original/final art, photostats, tearsheets and dum-

mies. Requests work on spec before assigning a job. Considers complexity of project, project's budget and turnaround time when establishing payment. Buys all rights. Originals are not returned. Finds artists through word of mouth, submissions, self promotion and sourcebooks.

DESIGN Pays by the hour or by the project for cover design.

JACKETS/COVERS Prefers realistic style. Pays by the hour or by the project.

TEXT ILLUSTRATION Pays by the project. Mostly b&w illustration, preferably computer-generated.

TIPS "Our books are being produced on Macintosh computers. We like designers who can use the Mac competently enough that their design looks as if it *hasn't* been done on the Mac."

GRAYWOLF PRESS

250 Third Ave. N., Suite 600, Minneapolis MN 55401. **E-mail:** wolves@graywolfpress.org. **Website:** www. graywolfpress.org. **Contact:** Lucia Cowles, editorial and administrative assistant. Estab. 1974. Publishes hardcover originals, trade paperback originals and reprints. Specializes in novels, nonfiction, memoir, poetry, essays and short stories. Publishes 30 titles/year. 100% require freelance cover design. Books use solid typography, strikingly beautiful and well-integrated artwork.

○ Graywolf is recognized as one of the finest small presses in the nation.

NEEDS Works with 7 designers/year. Buys 25 illustrations/year (existing art only). Uses freelancers mainly for cover design only. Works on assignment only.

FIRST CONTACT & TERMS Send query letter with résumé and photocopies. Samples are returned by SASE if requested by artist. Editorial director will contact artist for portfolio review if interested. Portfolio should include b&w, color photostats and tearsheets. Negotiates rights purchased. Originals are returned at job's completion. Pays by the project.

JACKETS/COVERS Assigns 25 design jobs/year. Pays by the project, $800-1,200.

TIPS "Have a strong portfolio of literary (fine press) design."

GREENWOOD PUBLISHING

ABC-CLIO, P.O. Box 1911, Santa Barbara CA 93116-1911. (805)968-1911. **E-mail:** editorial@abc-clio.com; ccasey@abc-clio.com. **Website:** www.greenwood.com. **Contact:** Cathleen Casey, acquisitions department/Greenwood. Estab. 1964. (Formerly Libraries Unlimited/Teacher Ideas Press.) Specializes in hardcover and paperback original reference books concerning library science and school media for librarians, educators and researchers. Also publishes in resource and activity books for teachers. Publishes more than 60 titles/year. Book catalog free by request.

NEEDS Works with 4-5 freelance artists/year.

FIRST CONTACT & TERMS Designers send query letter with résumé and photocopies. Illustrators send query letter with photocopies. Samples not filed are returned only if requested. Considers complexity of project, skill and experience of artist, and project's budget when establishing payment. Buys all rights. Originals not returned.

JACKETS/COVERS Assigns 4-6 design jobs/year. Pays by the project, $500 minimum.

TEXT ILLUSTRATION Assigns 2-4 illustration jobs/year. Pays by the project.

TIPS "We look for the ability to draw or illustrate without overly loud cartoon techniques. Freelancers should have the ability to use 2-color effectively, with screens and screen builds. We ignore anything sent to us that is in 4-color. We also need freelancers with a good feel for typefaces."

GROSSET & DUNLAP

Penguin Group Publishers, 375 Hudson St., New York NY 10014-3657. (212)366-2000. **Website:** us.penguingroup.com. Publishes hardcover, trade paperback and mass market paperback originals and board books for preschool and juvenile audience (ages 1-10). Specializes in "very young mass market children's books." Publishes more than 200 titles/year. 100% require freelance illustration; 10% require freelance design. Grosset & Dunlap publishes children's books that examine new ways of looking at the world of children. Many books by this publisher feature unique design components such as acetate overlays, 3D pop-up pages, or actual projects/toys that can be cut out of the book.

NEEDS Works with 100 freelance illustrators and 10 freelance designers/year. Buys 80 books' worth of illustrations/year. "Be sure your work is appropriate for our list." Uses freelance artists mainly for book illustration. Also for jacket/cover and text illustration and design. 100% of design and 50% of illustration demand knowledge of Illustrator 5.5, QuarkXPress 3.3, and Photoshop 2.5.

FIRST CONTACT & TERMS Designers: Send query letter with website address and tearsheets. Illustrators: Send postcard sample or query letter with résumé, photocopies, SASE, and tearsheets. Samples are filed. Responds to the artist only if interested. Call for appointment to show portfolio, or mail slides, color tearsheets, transparencies and dummies. Rights purchased vary according to project. Originals are returned at job's completion.

GROUNDWOOD BOOKS

110 Spadina Ave., Suite 801, Toronto Ontario M5V 2K4, Canada. (416)363-4343. **Fax:** (416)363-1017. **E-mail:** ssutherland@groundwoodbooks.com. **Website:** www.groundwoodbooks.com. Publishes 19 picture books/year; 2 young readers/year; 3 middle readers/year; 3 young adult titles/year, approximately 2 nonfiction titles/year. 10% of books by first-time authors.

GUERNICA EDITIONS

1569 Heritage Way, Oakville Ontario L6M 2Z7, Canada. (905)599-5304. **Fax:** (416)981-7606. **E-mail:** michaelmirolla@guernicaeditions.com. **Website:** www.guernicaeditions.com. **Contact:** Michael Mirolla, editor/publisher (poetry, nonfiction, short stories, novels). Estab. 1978. Types of books include contemporary and experimental fiction, biography and history. Specializes in ethnic/multicultural writing and translation of European and Quebecois writers into English. Recent titles: *Playing to Win* by F.G. Paci; and *The Stalinist's Wife* by France Theoret (trans. Luise von Flotow). Publishes 25-30 titles/year.

HARLEQUIN ENTERPRISES, LTD.

P.O. Box 5190, Buffalo NY 14240-5190. (888)432-4879. **E-mail:** customerservice@harlequin.com; public_relations@harlequin.ca. **Website:** www.harlequin.com. **Contact:** art director. Publishes mass-market paperbacks. Specializes in women's fiction. Publishes more than 100 titles/year. 15% require freelance design; 100% require freelance illustration. Book catalog not available.

NEEDS Approached by 1-3 designers and 20-50 illustrators/year. Works with 3 designers and 25 illustrators/year. 100% of freelance design work demands knowledge of Illustrator, Photoshop and InDesign.

FIRST CONTACT & TERMS Designers: Send postcard sample with brochure, photocopies, tearsheets and URL. Illustrators: Send postcard sample with brochure, photocopies, tearsheets and URL. After introductory mailing, send follow-up postcard sample every 6 months. Samples are filed and not returned. Does not reply. Company will contact artist for portfolio review if interested. Portfolio should include b&w and color tearsheets and color outputs. Buys all rights. Finds freelancers through art competitions, art exhibits/fairs, art reps, artist's submissions, competition/book credits, Internet, sourcebooks, word of mouth.

JACKETS/COVERS Assigns more than 50 freelance cover illustration jobs/year. Prefers variety of representational art—not just romance genre.

HARPERCOLLINS CHILDREN'S BOOKS/ HARPERCOLLINS PUBLISHERS

195 Broadway, New York NY 10007. (212)207-7000. **Website:** www.harpercollins.com. **Contact:** Katherine Tegen, vice president and publisher; Anica Mrose Rissi, executive editor; Claudia Gabel, executive editor; Kathleen Duncan, general design assistant; Erica Dechavez, picture book assistant designer. Publishes hardcover originals and reprints, trade paperback originals and reprints, mass market paperback originals and reprints, and audiobooks. 500 titles/year.

NEEDS Babies/children/teens, couples, multicultural, pets, food/drink, fashion, lifestyle. Send links to work. No attachments, please. "We are interested in seeing samples of map illustrations, chapter spots, full page pieces, etc. We are open to half-tone and line art illustrations for our interiors." Negotiates a flat payment fee upon acceptance. Will contact if interested. Catalog available online.

FIRST CONTACT & TERMS Art only, no mss. Only agented submissions to editorial departments. All unsolicited mss returned unopened.

TIPS "Be flexible and responsive to comments and corrections. Hold to scheduled due dates for work. Show work that reflects the kinds of projects you *want* to get, be focused on your best technique and showcase the strongest, most successful examples."

☉ HARPERCOLLINS PUBLISHERS LTD. (CANADA)

2 Bloor St. E., 20th Floor, Toronto Ontario M4W 1A8, Canada. (416)975-9334. **Website:** www.harpercollins.com. **Contact:** Neil Erickson, vice president production. Publishes hardcover, trade paperback and mass market paperback originals and reprints. Types of books include adventure, biography, coffee table books, fantasy, history, humor, juvenile, mainstream fiction, New Age, nonfiction, preschool, reference,

religious, self-help, travel, true crime, western and young adult. Publishes 200 titles/year. 10% require freelance illustration; 25% require freelance design.

NEEDS Prefers freelancers experienced in mixed media. Uses freelancers mainly for illustration, maps, cover design. 100% of freelance design demands knowledge of Photoshop and Illustrator.

FIRST CONTACT & TERMS Designers: Send query letter with photocopies, tearsheets. Illustrators: Send postcard sample or query letter with photocopies, tearsheets. Does not accept disk submissions compatible with QuarkXPress. Send EPS or TIFF files. Samples are filed. Will contact artist for portfolio review "only after review of samples if I have a project they might be right for." Portfolio should include book dummy, photocopies, photographs, tearsheets. Rights purchased vary according to project.

DESIGN Pays by the project.

HARVEST HOUSE PUBLISHERS

990 Owen Loop N., Eugene OR 97402. (541)343-0123. **Fax:** (541)302-0731. **Website:** www.harvesthousepublishers.com. Estab. 1974. Specializes in hardcover and paperback editions of Christian evangelical adult fiction and nonfiction, children's books, gift books and youth material. Publishes 100-125 titles/year. Books are of contemporary designs that compete with the current book market.

NEEDS Works with 1-2 freelance illustrators and 4-5 freelance designers/year. Uses freelance artists mainly for cover art. Also uses freelance artists for text illustration. Works on assignment only.

FIRST CONTACT & TERMS Send query letter with brochure, résumé, tearsheets and photographs. Art director will contact artist for portfolio review if interested. Requests work on spec before assigning a job. Originals may be returned at job's completion. Buys all rights. Finds artists through word of mouth and submissions/self-promotions.

DESIGN Pays by the project.

JACKETS/COVERS Assigns 100-125 design and less than 5 illustration jobs/year. Pays by the project.

TEXT ILLUSTRATION Assigns fewer than 5 jobs/ year. Pays by the project.

HAY HOUSE, INC.

P.O. Box 5100, Carlsbad CA 92018. (760)431-7695. **Fax:** (760)431-6948. **E-mail:** editorial@hayhouse.com. **Website:** www.hayhouse.com. Estab. 1985. Publishes hardcover originals and reprints, trade paperback originals and reprints, eBook/POD originals, CDs and DVDs. Types of books include self-help, mind-body-spirit, psychology, finance, health and fitness, nutrition, astrology and a limited amount of spiritual-themed fiction. Recent titles: *A Course in Weight Loss* by Marianne Williamson; *Getting Into the Vortex* by Esther and Jerry Hicks; *The Angel Therapy Handbook* by Doreen Virtue; *Power Up Your Brain* by David Perlmutter, M.D. and Alberto Villoldo, Ph.D. Publishes 75 titles/year; 40% require freelance illustration; 30% require freelance design.

NEEDS Approached by 50 illustrators and 5 designers/year. Works with 20 illustrators and 2-5 designers/year. Uses freelancers mainly for cover design and illustration. 80% of freelance design demands knowledge of Photoshop, Illustrator, InDesign and QuarkXPress. 20% of titles require freelance art direction.

FIRST CONTACT & TERMS Send e-mail or send nonreturnable samples to the address above. Art director will contact if interested. Buys all rights. Finds freelancers through word of mouth and submissions.

TIPS "We look for freelancers with experience in graphic design, desktop publishing, printing processes, production and illustrators with strong ability to conceptualize."

HEAVY METAL MEDIA, LLC

116 Pleasant St., Box 18, Easthampton MA 01027. (413)527-7481. **E-mail:** editor@heavymetal.com. **Website:** www.heavymetal.com. Estab. 1977. Publishes *Heavy Metal* magazine bi-monthly and monthly comic book series in the fantasy genres (specializing in science fiction, fantasy and horror). Submission guidelines available on website.

FIRST CONTACT & TERMS Responds within 1 week, but can take 3-12 months for a submission to be accepted for publication. Will begin publishing graphic novels in 2015.

TIPS "Please look over the kinds of work we publish carefully so you get a feel for what we are looking for."

⊙ HIPPOCRENE BOOKS, INC.

171 Madison Ave., New York NY 10016. (718)454-2366. **E-mail:** info@hippocrenebooks.com. **Website:** www.hippocrenebooks.com. Estab. 1971. Publishes hardcover originals and trade paperback reprints. Types of books include cookbooks, history, nonfiction, reference, travel, dictionaries, foreign language, bilingual. Specializes in dictionaries, cookbooks. Publishes 60 titles/year.

NEEDS Approached by 150 illustrators and 50 designers/year. Works with 2 illustrators and 3 designers/year. Prefers local freelancers experienced in line drawings.

FIRST CONTACT & TERMS Designers: Send query e-mail with small attachment or website link.

JACKETS/COVERS Assigns 4 freelance design and 2 freelance illustration jobs/year. Pays by the project.

TEXT ILLUSTRATION Assigns 4 freelance illustration jobs/year. Pays by the project.

TIPS "We prefer traditional illustrations appropriate for gift books and cookbooks."

HOLIDAY HOUSE

425 Madison Ave., New York NY 10017. (212)688-0085. **Fax:** (212)421-6134. **E-mail:** info@holidayhouse.com. **Website:** www.holidayhouse.com. **Contact:** Claire Counihan, director of art and design. Specializes in hardcover children's books. Recent titles: *Washington at Valley Forge* by Russell Freedman; *Tornadoes* by Gail Gibbons; *The Carbon Diaries* by Saci Lloyd. Publishes 70 titles/year. 75% require illustration. Art submission guidelines available on website.

NEEDS Accepts art suitable for children and young adults only. Works on assignment only.

FIRST CONTACT & TERMS Send cover letter with photocopies and SASE. Submissions are not returned. Request portfolio review in original query. Responds only if interested. Originals are returned at job's completion. Finds artists through submissions and agents.

JACKETS/COVERS Assigns 5-10 freelance illustration jobs/year. Pays by the project.

TEXT ILLUSTRATION Assigns 35 freelance jobs/year (picture books). Pays royalty.

HOMESTEAD PUBLISHING

1068 14th St., San Francisco CA 94114. (307)733-6248; 415.621.5039. **Website:** www.homesteadpublishing.net. **Contact:** art director. Estab. 1980. Publishes hardcover and paperback originals. Types of books include art, biography, history, guides, photography, nonfiction, natural history, and general books of interest. Publishes more than 6 print, 100 online titles/year. 75% require freelance illustration. Book catalog free for SASE with 4 first-class stamps.

NEEDS Works with 20 freelance illustrators and 10 designers/year. Prefers pen & ink, airbrush, pencil and watercolor. 25% of freelance work demands knowledge of PageMaker or FreeHand. Works on assignment only.

FIRST CONTACT & TERMS Submission guidelines available online.

DESIGN Assigns 6 freelance design jobs/year. Pays by the project.

JACKETS/COVERS Assigns 2 freelance design and 4 illustration jobs/year. Pays by the project.

TEXT ILLUSTRATION Assigns 50 freelance illustration jobs/year. Prefers technical pen illustration, maps (using airbrush, overlays, etc.), watercolor illustrations for children's books, calligraphy and lettering for titles and headings. Pays by the hour or by the project.

TIPS "We are using more graphic, contemporary designs and looking for exceptional quality."

HOUGHTON MIFFLIN HARCOURT COMPANY

222 Berkeley St., Boston MA 02116. (617)351-5000; 800.225.5425. **E-mail:** corporate.communications@ hmhpub.com. **Website:** www.hmhco.com. Estab. 1980. Company publishes hardcover originals. Types of books include juvenile, preschool and young adult. Publishes 60-70 titles/year. 100% requires freelance illustration; 10% requires freelance design.

Houghton Mifflin Harcourt now has a new imprint, Graphia, a high-end paperback book series for teens.

NEEDS Approached by 6-10 freelancers/year. Works with 50 freelance illustrators and 10 designers/year. Prefers artists with interest in or experience with children's books. Uses freelance illustrators mainly for jackets, picture books. Uses freelance designers primarily for photo essay books. 100% of freelance design work demands knowledge of QuarkXPress, Photoshop and Illustrator.

FIRST CONTACT & TERMS Please send samples through artist rep only. Finds artists through artist reps, sourcebooks, word of mouth.

DESIGN Assigns 10-20 freelance design jobs/year. Pays by the project.

JACKETS/COVERS Assigns 5-10 freelance illustration jobs/year. Pays by the project.

TEXT ILLUSTRATION Assigns up to 50 freelance illustration jobs/year. Pays by the project.

HOW BOOKS

F+W, a Content + eCommerce Company, 10151 Carver Rd., Suite 200, Blue Ash OH 45242. (513)531-2690. **E-mail:** scott.francis@fwmedia.com. **Website:** www. howdesign.com. **Contact:** Scott Francis, editor. Estab.

1985. "We look for material that reflects the cutting edge of trends, graphic design, and culture. Nearly all HOW Books are intensely visual, and authors must be able to create or supply art/illustration for their books."

FIRST CONTACT & TERMS Query via e-mail. Submit proposal package, outline, 1 sample chapter, sample art or sample design.

HUMANIX BOOKS

2200 NW Corporate Blvd., Suite 404, Boca Raton FL 33431. (855)371-7810; (561)459-5997. **Fax:** (561)241-6448; (855)371-7809. **E-mail:** info@humanixbooks. com. **Website:** www.humanixbooks.com. Estab. 1976. Publishes college textbooks, paperback trade, New Age and educational activity books. Publishes 30 titles/year. Trade paperbacks are 6×9 with 4-color covers. Book catalog for 9×12 SASE. Specify which imprint when requesting catalog. Learning or trade paperbacks.

No longer publishes children's fiction or picture books.

FIRST CONTACT & TERMS Send query letter with résumé, SASE and photocopies. Samples are filed or are returned by SASE if requested by artist. Rights purchased vary according to project.

DESIGN Pays by the project.

TIPS "Books on self-help and spirituality emphasized under current program. A new imprint on mysteries, started in 2008, is called Sleuth Hound Books."

IDEALS PUBLICATIONS, INC.

2630 Elm Hill Pike, Suite 100, Nashville TN 37214. (615)333-0478. **E-mail:** idealsinfo@guideposts.org. **Website:** www.idealsbooks.com. Estab. 1944. Company publishes hardcover originals and *Ideals* magazine. Specializes in nostalgia and holiday themes. Publishes 25-40 children's book titles and 2 magazine issues/ year. 50% require freelance illustration. Guidelines available online.

NEEDS Approached by 100 freelancers/year. Works with 10-12 freelance illustrators/year. Prefers freelancers with experience in illustrating people, nostalgia, botanical flowers. Uses freelancers mainly for flower borders (color), people and spot art. Also for text illustration, jacket/cover and book design. Works on assignment only.

FIRST CONTACT & TERMS Art submission guidelines available online. Send to Attn: Art department.

TEXT ILLUSTRATION Assigns 75 freelance illustration jobs/year. Pays by the project. Prefers watercolor or gouache.

TIPS "Looking for illustrations with unique perspectives, perhaps some humor, that not only tells the story but draws the reader into the artist's world. We accept all styles."

IDW PUBLISHING

5080 Santa Fe, San Diego CA 92109. **E-mail:** letters@idwpublishing.com. **Website:** www.idwpublishing.com. Estab. 1999. Publishes hardcover, mass market and trade paperback originals. Types of books include comic books, illustrated novel and art book nonfiction. Publishes 20 titles/year. Submission guidelines available on website.

FIRST CONTACT & TERMS Send proposal with cover letter, photocopies (5 fully inked and lettered 8½×11 pages showing story and art), 1-page synopsis of overall story. Samples are not returned. Responds only if interested.

TIPS "Do not send original art. Make sure photocopies are clean, sharp, and easy to read. Be sure that each page has your name, address and phone number written clearly on it. Do not call."

IGNATIUS PRESS

1348 Tenth Ave., San Francisco CA 94122. (415)387-2324. **Fax:** (415)387-0896. **E-mail:** info@ignatius.com. **Website:** www.ignatius.com/Default.aspx. **Contact:** Roxanne Lum, art director. Estab. 1978. Company publishes Catholic theology and devotional books for lay people, priests and religious readers. Publishes 30 titles/year.

NEEDS Works with 1-2 freelance illustrators/year. Works on assignment only.

FIRST CONTACT & TERMS Will send art guidelines "if we are interested in the artist's work." Accepts previously published material. Send brochure showing art style or résumé and photocopies. Samples not filed and not returned. Responds only if interested. To show a portfolio, mail appropriate materials; "we will contact you if interested." **Pays on acceptance.**

JACKETS/COVERS Buys cover art from freelance artists. Prefers Christian symbols/calligraphy and religious illustrations of Jesus, saints, etc. (used on cover or in text). "Simplicity, clarity, and elegance are the rule. We like calligraphy, occasionally incorporated with Christian symbols. We also do covers with type and photography." Pays by the project.

TEXT ILLUSTRATION Pays by the project.

TIPS "I do not want to see any schmaltzy religious art. Since we are a nonprofit Catholic press, we cannot always afford to pay the going rate for freelance art, so we are always appreciative when artists can give us a break on prices and work *ad maiorem Dei gloriam.*"

IMAGE COMICS

2001 Center St., 6th Floor, Berkeley CA 94704. **E-mail:** submissions@imagecomics.com. **Website:** www.imagecomics.com. **Contact:** Eric Stephenson, publisher. Estab. 1992. Publishes comic books, graphic novels. See this company's website for detailed guidelines.

NEEDS "We are looking for good, well-told stories and exceptional artwork that run the gamut in terms of both style and genre."

FIRST CONTACT & TERMS Send proposals only. See website for guidelines. No e-mail submissions. All comics are creator-owned. Image only wants proposals for comics, not "art submissions." Proposals/samples not returned. Do not include SASE. Responds as soon as possible.

TIPS "Please do not try to 'impress' us with all the deals you've lined up or testimonials from your Aunt Matilda. We are only interested in the comic."

IMMEDIUM

P.O. Box 31846, San Francisco CA 94131. (415)452-8546. **Fax:** (360)937-6272. **Website:** www.immedium.com. Estab. 2005. "*Immedium* focuses on publishing eye-catching children's picture books, Asian American topics, and contemporary arts, popular culture, and multicultural issues."

NEEDS Babies/children/teens, multicultural, families, parents, entertainment, lifestyle. Illustrations for text illustration, dust jackets, promotional materials and book covers.

FIRST CONTACT & TERMS Send query letter with résumé, samples and/or SASE.

TIPS "Look at our catalog, it's colorful and a little edgy. Tailor your submission to our catalog. We need responsive workers."

IMPACT BOOKS

F+W, a Content + eCommerce Company, 10151 Carver Rd., Suite 200, Blue Ash OH 45242. **Fax:** (513)531-2686. **E-mail:** mona.clough@fwcommunity.com. **Website:** www.northlightshop.com; www.impactbooks.com. **Contact:** Mona Clough, content director (art instruction for fantasy, comics, manga, anime, popular culture, graffiti, science fiction, cartooning and body art). Estab. 2004. Publishes trade paperback originals. Specializes in illustrated art instruction books. Recent titles: *Furries Furever, Mastering Manga 2 With Mark Crilley, Shojo Fashion Manga Art School Boys, Winged Fantasy*. Publishes 9 titles/year.

○ IMPACT Books publishes titles that emphasize illustrated how-to-draw manga, graffiti and fantasy art instruction. Currently emphasizing Japanese-style (manga and anime), science-fiction art and pop art. This market is for experienced artists who are willing to work with an IMPACT editor to produce a step-by-step how-to book about the artist's creative process.

NEEDS Approached by 30 author-artists/year. Works with 10 author-artists/year.

FIRST CONTACT & TERMS Send query letter via e-mail; digital art, tearsheets, photocopies; résumé and URL. Accepts Mac-compatible e-mail submissions (TIFF or JPEG). Samples may be filed but are not returned. Responds only if interested. Company will contact artist for portfolio review of color finished art, digital art, roughs, photographs, tearsheets if interested. Buys world rights with royalty usually. Finds freelancers through referrals, submissions, conventions, Internet and word of mouth. Give notice is submitting simultaneously.

TIPS Submission guidelines available online www.artistnetwork.com/contactus and impact-books.com. Does not use freelance illustration, but may use freelance design.

INNER TRADITIONS/BEAR & COMPANY

1 Park St., Rochester VT 05767. (802)767-3174. **Fax:** (802)767-3726. **E-mail:** peris@innertraditions.com. **Website:** www.innertraditions.com. **Contact:** Peri Ann Swan, art director. Estab. 1975. Publishes hardcover originals and trade paperback originals and reprints. Types of books include self-help, psychology, esoteric philosophy, alternative medicine, Eastern religion, and art books. Recent titles: *Mystery of the Crystal Skulls, Thai Yoga Massage* and *Science and the Akashic Field*. Publishes 65 titles/year; 10% require freelance illustration; 5% require freelance design. Book catalog free by request.

NEEDS Works with 3-4 freelance illustrators and 3-4 freelance designers/year. 100% of freelance design demands knowledge of QuarkXPress, InDesign or Photoshop. Buys 10 illustrations/year. Uses freelancers for jacket/cover illustration and design. Works on assignment only.

FIRST CONTACT & TERMS Send query letter with résumé, tearsheets, photocopies, photographs, slides and SASE. Accepts disk submissions. Samples are filed if interested; returned by SASE if requested by artist. Responds only if interested. To show portfolio, mail tearsheets, photographs, slides and transparencies. Rights purchased vary according to project. Originals returned at job's completion. Pays by the project.

JACKETS/COVERS Assigns approximately 10 design and illustration jobs/year. Pays by the project.

☺ INTERNATIONAL MARINE/RAGGED MOUNTAIN PRESS

90 Mechanic St., Camden ME 04843. **E-mail:** molly_mulhern@mcgraw-hill.com; Tania_loghmani@mcgraw-hill.com. **Website:** www.books.mcgraw-hill.com/im. Tania Loghmani, editing. **Contact:** Molly Mulhern, editing/design/production director. Estab. 1969. Imprint of McGraw-Hill. Specializes in hardcovers and paperbacks on marine (nautical) and outdoor recreation topics. Publishes 50 titles/year. 50% require freelance illustration. Book catalog free by request.

NEEDS Works with 20 freelance illustrators and 20 designers/year. Uses freelancers mainly for interior illustration. Prefers local freelancers. Works on assignment only.

FIRST CONTACT & TERMS Submission guidelines available online.

DESIGN Assigns 20 freelance design jobs/year. Pays by the project or by the hour.

JACKETS/COVERS Assigns 20 freelance design and 3 illustration jobs/year. Pays by the project or by the hour.

TEXT ILLUSTRATION Assigns 20 jobs/year. Prefers technical drawings. Pays by the hour or by the project.

TIPS "Do your research. See if your work fits with what we publish. Write with a résumé and sample; then follow with a call; then come by to visit."

JEWISH LIGHTS PUBLISHING

LongHill Partners, Inc., Sunset Farm Offices, Rt. 4, P.O. Box 237, Woodstock VT 05091. (802)457-4000. **Fax:** (802)457-4004. **Website:** www.jewishlights.com. **Contact:** Acquisitions Editor. Estab. 1990. Types of books include children's picture books, history, juvenile, nonfiction, reference, religious, self help, spirituality, life cycle, theology and philosophy, wellness.

Specializes in adult nonfiction and children's picture books. Publishes 50 titles/year. 10% requires freelance illustration; 50% requires freelance design. Book catalog free on request.

○ "People of all faiths and backgrounds yearn for books that attract, engage, educate and spiritually inspire. Our principal goal is to stimulate thought and help all people learn about who the Jewish people are, where they come from, and what the future can be made to hold."

NEEDS Approached by 75 illustrators and 20 designers/year. Prefers freelancers experienced in fine arts, children's book illustration, typesetting and design. 100% of freelance design demands knowledge of QuarkXPress. 50% of freelance design demands knowledge of Photoshop.

FIRST CONTACT & TERMS Designers: Send postcard sample, query letter with printed samples, tearsheets. Illustrators: Send postcard sample or other printed samples. Samples are filed and are not returned. Portfolio review not required. Buys all rights. Finds freelancers through submission packets, websites, searching local galleries and shows, Graphic Artists' Guild's *Directory of Illustrators* and *Picture Book*.

DESIGN Assigns 40 freelance design jobs/year. Pays for design by the project.

JACKETS/COVERS Assigns 30 freelance design jobs and 5 illustration jobs/year. Pays for design by the project.

TIPS "We prefer a painterly, fine-art approach to our children's book illustration to achieve a quality that would intrigue both kids and adults. We do not consider cartoonish, caricature art for our children's book illustration."

JONATHAN DAVID PUBLISHERS, INC.

68-22 Eliot Ave., Middle Village NY 11379. (718)456-8611. **Fax:** (718)894-2818. **Website:** www.jdbooks.com. **Contact:** David Kolatch, editorial director. Estab. 1948. Publishes hardcover and paperback originals. Types of books include biography, religious, young adult, reference, juvenile and cookbooks. Specializes in Judaica. Titles include: *Drawing a Crowd* and *The Presidents of the United States & the Jews*. Publishes 25 titles/year. 50% require freelance illustration; 75% require freelance design.

NEEDS Approached by numerous freelancers/year. Works with 5 freelance illustrators and 5 designers/year. Prefers freelancers with experience in book jacket design and jacket/cover illustration. 100% of design and 5% of illustration demand computer literacy. Works on assignment only.

FIRST CONTACT & TERMS Designers: Send query letter with résumé and photocopies. Illustrators: Send postcard sample and/or query letter with photocopies, résumé. Samples are filed. Production coordinator will contact artist for portfolio review if interested. Portfolio should include color final art and photographs. Buys all rights. Originals are not returned. Finds artists through submissions.

DESIGN Assigns 15-20 freelance design jobs/year. Pays by the project.

JACKETS/COVERS Assigns 15-20 freelance design and 4-5 illustration jobs/year. Pays by the project.

TIPS First-time assignments are usually book jackets, mechanicals and artwork.

KAEDEN BOOKS

P.O. Box 16190, Rocky River OH 44116. **Website:** www.kaeden.com. Estab. 1986. Publishes children's books. Types of books include picture books and early juvenile. Specializes in elementary educational content. Publishes 8-20 titles/year; 90% require freelance illustration. Book catalog available upon request.

NEEDS Approached by 100-200 illustrators/year. Works with 5-10 illustrators/year. Prefers freelancers experienced in juvenile/humorous illustration and children's picture books. Uses freelancers mainly for story illustration.

FIRST CONTACT & TERMS Designers: Send query letter with brochure and résumé. Illustrators: Send postcard sample or query letter with photocopies, photographs, printed samples or tearsheets, no larger than 8½×11. Samples are filed and not returned. Responds only if interested. Art director will contact artist for portfolio review if interested. Buys all rights.

TEXT ILLUSTRATION Assigns 8-20 jobs/year. Pays by the project. Looks for a variety of styles.

TIPS "We look for professional-level drawing and rendering skills, plus the ability to interpret a juvenile story. There is a tight correlation between text and visual in our books, plus a need for attention to detail. Drawings of children are especially needed. Please send only samples that pertain to our market."

KALMBACH PUBLISHING CO.

21027 Crossroads Circle, P.O. Box 1612, Waukesha WI 53187. (262)796-8776. **Fax:** (262)798-6468. **Website:**

www.kalmbach.com. Estab. 1934. Types of books include reference and how-to books for serious hobbyists in the railfan, model railroading, plastic modeling, and toy train collecting/operating hobbies. Also publishes books and booklets on jewelry-making, beading and general crafts. Publishes 50+ new titles/year.

NEEDS 10-20% require freelance illustration; 10-20% require freelance design. Book catalog free upon request. Approached by 25 freelancers/year. Prefers freelancers with experience in the hobby field. Uses freelance artists mainly for book layout/design and line art illustrations. Freelancers should have the most recent versions of Adobe InDesign, Photoshop and Illustrator. Projects by assignment only.

FIRST CONTACT & TERMS Send query letter with résumé, tearsheets and photocopies. No phone calls please. Samples are filed and will not be returned. Art director will contact artist for portfolio review. Finds artists through word of mouth, submissions. Assigns 10-12 freelance design jobs/year. Pays by the project. Assigns 3-5 freelance illustration jobs/year. Pays by the project.

TIPS First-time assignments are usually illustrations or book layouts. Complex projects (e.g., track plans, 100+ page books) are given to proven freelancers. Admires freelancers who present an organized and visually strong portfolio, who meet deadlines, and follow instructions carefully.

KAR-BEN PUBLISHING

Lerner Publishing Group, 241 First Ave. N, Minneapolis MN 55401. (612)215-6229. **Fax:** 612-332-7615. **E-mail:** Editorial@Karben.com. **Website:** www.karben.com. Estab. 1974. "Kar-Ben publishes 12-15 new titles on Jewish themes for young children and families each year." Publishes hardcover, trade paperback and electronic originals. 12-15 titles/year.

NEEDS Need children's text illustration, book covers and dust jackets.

FIRST CONTACT & TERMS Send postcard sample or e-mail with URL and samples. Follow up every 6-12 months. Samples kept on file for possible future assignments. Samples are not returned. Buys all rights. Illustrators paid $4,000-4,500. 12-15 freelance illustrators/year.

TIPS "Look at our catalog online for a sense of what we like—bright colors and lively composition."

KIRKBRIDE BIBLE CO., INC.

1102 Deloss St., Indianapolis IN 46203. (800)428-4385. **Fax:** (317)633-1444. **E-mail:** info@kirkbride.com. **Website:** www.kirkbride.com. Estab. 1915. Publishes Thompson Chain-Reference Bible hardcover originals and quality leather bindings styles and translations of the Bible. Types of books include reference and religious. Specializes in reference and study material. Publishes 6 main titles/year. Recent titles: *The Thompson Student Bible* and *The Thompson Chain-Reference Bible Centennial Edition.* 2% require freelance illustration; 10% require freelance design. Catalog available.

NEEDS Approached by 1-2 designers/year. Works with 1-2 designers/year. Prefers freelancers experienced in layout and cover design. Uses freelancers mainly for artwork and design. 100% of freelance design and most illustration demands knowledge of PageMaker, InDesign, Photoshop, Illustrator and QuarkXPress. 5-10% of titles require freelance art direction.

FIRST CONTACT & TERMS Designers: Send query letter with portfolio of recent works, printed samples and résumé. Illustrators: Send query letter with Photostats, printed samples and résumé. Accepts disk submissions compatible with QuarkXPress or Photoshop files 4.0 or 3.1. Samples are filed. Responds only if interested. Rights purchased vary according to project.

DESIGN Assigns 1 freelance design job/year. Pays by the hour $100 minimum.

JACKETS/COVERS Assigns 1-2 freelance design jobs and 1-2 illustration jobs/year. Pays for design by the project, $100-1,000. Pays for illustration by the project, $100-1,000. Prefers modern with traditional text.

TEXT ILLUSTRATION Assigns 1 freelance illustration/year. Pays by the project, $100-1,000. Prefers traditional. Finds freelancers through sourcebooks and references.

TIPS "Quality craftsmanship is our top concern, and it should be yours, too!"

KNOPF

Imprint of Random House, 1745 Broadway, New York NY 10019. **Fax:** (212)940-7390. **Website:** knopfdoubleday.com/imprint/knopf. **Contact:** editors. Estab. 1915. Publishes hardcover originals for adult trade. Specializes in history, fiction, art and cookbooks. Publishes 200 titles/year.

Random House, Inc. and its publishing entities are not accepting unsolicited submissions via e-mail at this time.

NEEDS Prefers artists with experience in b&w. Uses freelancers mainly for cookbooks and biographies. Also for text illustration and book design.

FIRST CONTACT & TERMS Send query letter with SASE. Request portfolio review in original query. Artist should follow up. Sometimes requests work on spec before assigning a job. Originals are returned at job's completion.

TEXT ILLUSTRATION Pays by the project, $100-5,000; $50-150/illustration; $300-800/maps.

TIPS Finds artists through submissions, agents and sourcebooks. "Freelancers should be aware that Macintosh/Quark is a must for design and becoming a must for maps and illustration."

LAREDO PUBLISHING CO./RENAISSANCE HOUSE

465 WestView, Englewood NJ 07631. (201)408-4048. **Fax:** (201)408-5011. **E-mail:** info@renaissancehouse. net ; laredo@renaissancehouse.net. **Website:** renaissancehouse.net. **Contact:** Sam Laredo, art director. Estab. 1991. Publishes children and juvenile books. Specializes in the development and management of educational and multicultural materials for young readers, Spanish and bilingual. Publishes biographies, legends and multicultural with a focus on the Hispanic market. Recent titles include *Un Hombre Sincero (Marti's biography)* (International Book Award, 2014; Best Latino Focused Bilingual Children's Picture Book, Best Children's Non Fiction Picture Book, Best First Book Children & Youth); *Postcard from Copenhagen* (Bilingual); *I Do Not Want This on My Plate* (Purple Dragonfly Book Award); *Super Jack* (Purple Dragonfly Book Award); *Mother Oak; But, Mama, How Come Grandpa Comes To?*. Publishes 35 titles/year.

NEEDS Approached by 25 illustrators/year. Works with 10 designers/year.

FIRST CONTACT & TERMS Designers/illustrators: E-mail samples responds only if interested.

DESIGN Assigns 5 freelance design jobs/year. Pays for design by the project.

JACKETS/COVERS Pays for illustration by the project, page.

TEXT ILLUSTRATION Pays by the project, page.

LEE & LOW BOOKS

95 Madison Ave., #1205, New York NY 10016. (212)779-4400. **E-mail:** general@leeandlow.com. **Website:** www.leeandlow.com. Jessica Echeverria, associate editor; Samantha Wolf, editorial assistant. **Contact:** Louise May, vice president/editorial director (multicultural children's fiction/nonfiction). Estab. 1991. Publishes hardcover originals for the juvenile market. Specializes in multicultural children's books. Publishes 12-15 titles/year. 100% require freelance illustration and design. Book catalog available.

NEEDS Approached by 100 freelancers/year. Works with 12-15 freelance illustrators and 4-5 designers/year. Uses freelancers mainly for illustration of children's picture books. 100% of design work demands computer skills. Works on assignment only.

FIRST CONTACT & TERMS Contact through artist rep or send query letter with brochure, résumé, SASE, tearsheets or photocopies. Samples of interest are filed. Art director will contact artist for portfolio review if interested. Portfolio should include color tearsheets and dummies. Rights purchased vary according to project. Originals are returned at job's completion.

DESIGN Pays by the project.

TEXT ILLUSTRATION Pays by the project.

TIPS "We want an artist who can tell a story through pictures and who is familiar with the children's book genre. We are now also developing materials for older children, ages 8-12, so we are interested in seeing work for this age group, too. Lee & Low Books makes a special effort to work with writers and artists of color and encourages new talent. We prefer filing samples that feature children, particularly from diverse backgrounds."

LEGACY PRESS

P.O. Box 261129, San Diego CA 92196. (858)277-1167. **E-mail:** john.gregory@rainbowpublishers.com. **Website:** www.rainbowpublishers.com. Estab. 1979. Publishes trade paperback originals. Types of books include religious books, reproducible Sunday School books for children ages 2-12, and Bible teaching books for children and adults. Recent titles include *Favorite Bible Families, Instant Bible Lessons, The Christian Girl's Guides, Bill the Warthog, Gotta Have God, God and Me*. Publishes 20 titles/year. Book catalog available for SASE with 2 first-class stamps.

NEEDS Approached by hundreds of illustrators and 50 designers/year. Works with 5-10 illustrators and 5-10 designers/year. 100% of freelance design and illustration demands knowledge of Illustrator, Photoshop and InDesign.

FIRST CONTACT & TERMS Send query letter with printed samples, SASE and tearsheets. Samples are filed or returned by SASE. Responds only if interested. Will contact artist for portfolio review if interested. Finds freelancers through samples sent and personal referrals. For submission directions, go to: www.RainbowPublishers.com/submissions.apsx.

DESIGN Assigns 25 freelance design jobs/year. Pays for design by the project, $350 minimum. Pays for art direction by the project, $350 minimum.

JACKETS/COVERS Assigns 25 freelance design jobs and 25 illustration jobs/year. "Prefers computer generated-high energy style with bright colors appealing to kids." Pays for design and illustration by the project, $350 minimum. "Prefers designers/illustrators with some Biblical knowledge."

TEXT ILLUSTRATION Assigns 20 freelance illustration jobs/year. Pays by the project, $350 minimum. "Prefers b&w line art, preferably computer generated with limited detail yet fun."

TIPS "We look for illustrators and designers who have some Biblical knowledge and excel in working with a fun, colorful, high-energy style that will appeal to kids and parents alike. Designers must be well versed in InDesign, Illustrator and Photoshop, know how to visually market to kids and have wonderful conceptual ideas!"

LERNER PUBLISHING GROUP

1251 Washington Ave. N., Minneapolis MN 55401. (800)452-7236; (612)332-3344. **Fax:** (612)337-7615. **E-mail:** editorial@karben.com. **Website:** www.karben.com; www.lernerbooks.com. Estab. 1957. Publishes educational books for young people. Subjects include animals, biography, history, geography, science and sports. Publishes 200 titles/year. 100% require freelance illustration. Book catalog free on request. Art submission guidelines available on website.

NEEDS Uses 10-12 freelance illustrators/year. Uses freelancers mainly for book illustration; also for jacket/cover design and illustration, book design and text illustration.

FIRST CONTACT & TERMS Submit samples that show skill specifically in children's book illustration.

Do not send original art. Submit slides, JPEG, or PDF files on disk, color photocopies of full-color artwork, photocopies of b&w linework, or tearsheets.

TIPS "Send samples showing active children, not animals or still life. Don't send original art. Look at our books to see what we do."

LIPPINCOTT WILLIAMS & WILKINS

351 W. Camden St., Baltimore MD 21201. (401)528-4000; (800)638-3030. **E-mail:** orders@lww.com. **Website:** www.lww.com. Estab. 1890. Publishes audio tapes, CDs, hardcover originals and reprints, textbooks, trade paperbook originals and reprints. Types of books include instructional and textbooks. Specializes in medical publishing. 100% requires freelance design.

See website for a listing of all locations.

NEEDS Approached by 20 illustrators and 20 designers/year. Works with 10 illustrators and 30 designers/year. Prefers freelancers experienced in medical publishing. 100% of freelance design demands knowledge of Illustrator, Photoshop, QuarkXPress.

FIRST CONTACT & TERMS Send query letter with printed samples and tearsheets. Accepts Mac-compatible disk submissions. Send EPS or TIFF files. Responds only if interested. Will contact artist for portfolio review if interested. Buys all rights. Finds freelancers through submission packets, word of mouth.

DESIGN Assigns 150 freelance design jobs/year. Pays by the project.

JACKETS/COVERS Assigns 150 freelance design jobs/year. Pays for design by the project. Prefers medical publishing experience.

TEXT ILLUSTRATION Assigns 150 freelance illustration jobs/year. Pays by the project. Prefers freelancers with medical publishing experience.

TIPS "We're looking for freelancers who are flexible and have extensive clinical and textbook medical publishing experience. Designers must be proficient in Quark, Illustrator and Photoshop and completely understand how design affects the printing (CMYK 4-color) process."

THE LYONS PRESS

The Globe Pequot Press, Inc., Box 480, 246 Goose Ln., Guilford CT 06437. (203)458-4500. **Fax:** (203)458-4668. **Website:** www.lyonspress.com. Estab. 1984 (Lyons & Burford), 1997 (The Lyons Press). Publishes hardcover and trade paperback originals and reprints. Types of books include adventure, humor, biography, memoir, coffee table books, cookbooks, history, military history, instructional, reference, self-help, sporting (also hunting and fishing), and travel. Publishes 180 titles/year. Book catalog available.

MADISON HOUSE PUBLISHERS

4501 Forbes Blvd., Suite 200, Lanham MD 20706. (301)459-3366. **Fax:** (301)429-5748. **E-mail:** custom ercare@rowman.com. **Website:** www.rowmanlittle field.com. Estab. 1984. Publishes hardcover and trade paperback originals. Specializes in biography, history and popular culture. Publishes 10 titles/year. 40% require freelance illustration; 100% require freelance jacket design. Book catalog free by request.

Madison House is just one imprint of Rowman & Littlefield Publishing Group, which has 8 imprints.

NEEDS Approached by 20 freelancers/year. Works with 4 freelance illustrators and 12 designers/year. Prefers freelancers with experience in book jacket design. Uses freelancers mainly for book jackets. Also for catalog design. 80% of freelance work demands knowledge of Illustrator, QuarkXPress, Photoshop or FreeHand. Works on assignment only.

FIRST CONTACT & TERMS Send query letter with tearsheets, photocopies and photostats. Samples are filed or are returned by SASE if requested by artist. Responds to the artist only if interested. Call for appointment to show portfolio of roughs, original/final art, tearsheets, photographs, slides and dummies. Buys all rights. Interested in buying second rights (reprint rights) to previously published work.

JACKETS/COVERS Assigns 16 freelance design and 2 illustration jobs/year. Pays by the project. Prefers typographic design, photography and line art.

TEXT ILLUSTRATION Pays by project.

TIPS "We are looking to produce trade-quality designs within a limited budget. Covers have large type, clean lines; they 'breathe.' If you have not designed jackets for a publishing house but want to break into that area, have at least 5 'fake' titles designed to show ability. I would like to see more Eastern European style incorporated into American design. It seems that typography on jackets is becoming more assertive, as it competes for attention on bookstore shelf. Also, trends are richer colors, use of metallics."

MAPEASY, INC.

P.O. Box 80, Wainscott NY 11975. (631)537-6213. **Fax:** (631)537-4541. **E-mail:** lbechert@mapeasy.com.

Website: www.mapeasy.com. Estab. 1990. Publishes maps. 100% requires freelance illustration; 25% requires freelance design. Book catalog not available.

NEEDS Approached by 15 illustrators and 10 designers/year. Prefers local freelancers. 100% of freelance design and illustration demands knowledge of Illustrator, Photoshop and InDesign.

FIRST CONTACT & TERMS Send query letter with photocopies. Accepts Mac-compatible disk submissions. Samples are filed. Responds only if interested. Will contact artist for portfolio review if interested. Portfolio should include photocopies. Finds freelancers through ads and referrals.

TEXT ILLUSTRATION Pays by the hour.

MCGRAW-HILL EDUCATION

P.O. Box 182605, Columbus OH 43218. (630)789-4000; (800) 338-3987. **E-mail:** customerservice@ mcgraw-hill.com. **Website:** www.mheducation.com. Estab. 1969. Independent book producer/packager of textbooks and reference books. Specializes in social studies, history, geography, vocational, math, science, etc. 80% require freelance design.

NEEDS Approached by 30 freelance artists/year. Works with 4-5 illustrators and 5-15 designers/year. Buys 5-10 illustrations/year. Prefers artists with experience in textbooks, especially health, medical, social studies. Works on assignment only.

FIRST CONTACT & TERMS Send query letter with tearsheets and résumé. Samples are filed. Responds to the artist only if interested. To show portfolio, mail roughs and tearsheets. Rights purchased vary according to project. Originals returned at job's completion.

DESIGN Assigns 5-15 jobs/year. Pays by the project.

JACKETS/COVERS Assigns 1-2 design jobs/year. Pays by the project.

TIPS "Designers, if you contact us with samples we will invite you to do a presentation and make assignments as suitable work arises. Graphic artists, when working assignments we review our files. Enclose typical rate structure with your samples."

MCGRAW-HILL HIGHER EDUCATION GROUP

P.O. Box 182605, Columbus OH 43218. (877)833-5524; (800) 338-3987. **Fax:** (614)759-3749; (614) 759-3644. **E-mail:** customer.service@mcgraw-hill.com. **Website:** www.mhhe.com; www.mcgraw-hill.com. Estab. 1944. Publishes hardbound and paperback college textbooks. Specializes in science, engineering and math. Produces more than 200 titles/year. 10% require freelance design; 70% require freelance illustration.

NEEDS Works with 15-25 freelance designers and 30-50 illustrators/year. Uses freelancers for advertising. 90% of freelance work demands knowledge of Page-Maker, Illustrator, QuarkXPress, Photoshop or Free-Hand. Works on assignment only.

FIRST CONTACT & TERMS Prefers color 35mm slides and color or b&w photocopies. Send query letter with brochure, résumé, slides and/or tearsheets. "Do not send samples that are not a true representation of your work quality." Responds in 1 month. Accepts disk submissions. Samples returned by SASE if requested. Responds on future assignment possibilities. Buys all rights. Pays half contract for unused assigned work.

DESIGN Assigns 100-140 freelance design jobs/year. Uses artists for all phases of process. Pays by the project. Payment varies widely according to complexity.

JACKETS/COVERS Assigns 100-140 freelance design jobs and 20-30 illustration jobs/year. Pays $1,700 for 4-color cover design and negotiates pay for special projects.

TEXT ILLUSTRATION Assigns 75-100 freelance jobs/year. Considers b&w and color work. Prefers computer-generated, continuous tone, some mechanical line drawings; ink preferred for b&w.

TIPS "In the McGraw-Hill field, there is more use of color. There is need for sophisticated color skills—the artist must be knowlegeable about the way color reproduces in the printing process. Be prepared to contribute to content as well as style. Tighter production schedules demand an awareness of overall schedules. *Must* be dependable."

MITCHELL LANE PUBLISHERS, INC.

P.O. Box 196, Hockessin DE 19707. (302)234-9426. **Fax:** (866)834-4164. **E-mail:** barbaramitchell@mitchelllane.com. **Website:** www.mitchelllane.com. **Contact:** Barbara Mitchell, publisher. Estab. 1993. Publishes library bound originals. Types of books include biography. Specializes in multicultural biography for young adults. Publishes 50 titles/year; none require freelance illustration; none require freelance design.

NEEDS Approached by 20 illustrators and 5 designers/year. Works with 2 illustrators/year. Prefers freelancers experienced in illustrations of people. Looks for cover designers and interior book designers.

FIRST CONTACT & TERMS Send query letter with printed samples, photocopies. Interesting samples are filed and are not returned. Will contact artist for portfolio review if interested. Buys all rights.

JACKETS/COVERS Prefers realistic portrayal of people.

MONDIAL

203 W. 107th St., Suite 6C, New York NY 10025. (212)851-3252. **Fax:** (208)361-2863. **E-mail:** contact@ mondialbooks.com. **Website:** www.mondialbooks. com; www.librejo.com. **Contact:** Andrew Moore, editor. Estab. 1996. Publishes mainstream fiction, romance, history and reference books. Specializes in linguistics. Payment on acceptance.

NEEDS Landscapes, travel and erotic. Printing rights are negotiated according to project. Illustrations are used for text illustration, promotional materials and book covers. Publishes 20 titles/year. Responds only if interested.

MORGAN KAUFMANN PUBLISHERS

Elsevier, 225 Wyman St., Waltham MA 02144. (781)663-5200. **Website:** www.mkp.com. Estab. 1984. Publishes computer science books for academic and professional audiences in paperback, hardback and book/CD-ROM packages. Publishes 60 titles/year. 75% require freelance interior illustration; 100% require freelance text and cover design; 15% require freelance design and production of 4-color inserts. Morgan Kaufmann is now part of Elsevier (www.elsevier.com).

NEEDS Approached by 150-200 freelancers/year. Works with 10-15 freelance illustrators and 10-15 designers/year. Uses freelancers for covers, text design and technical and editorial illustration, design and production of 4-color inserts. 100% of freelance work demands knowledge of at least one of the following Illustrator, QuarkXPress, Photoshop, Ventura, Framemaker, or laTEX (multiple software platform). Works on assignment only.

FIRST CONTACT & TERMS Send query letter with samples. Samples must be nonreturnable or with SASE. "No calls, please." Samples are filed. Production editor will contact artist for portfolio review if interested. Portfolio should include final printed pieces. Buys interior illustration on a work-for-hire basis. Buys first printing and reprint rights for text and cover design. Finds artists primarily through word of mouth and submissions.

DESIGN Pays by the project. Prefers Illustrator and Photoshop for interior illustration and QuarkXPress for 4-color inserts.

JACKETS/COVERS Pays by the project. Uses primarily stock photos. Prefers designers take cover design through production to film and MatchPrint. "We're interested in a look that is different from the typical technical publication." For covers, prefers modern, clean, spare design, with emphasis on typography and high-impact imagery.

TIPS "Although experience with book design is an advantage, sometimes artists from another field bring a fresh approach, especially to cover design."

MOUNTAIN PRESS PUBLISHING CO.

P.O. Box 2399, Missoula MT 59806. (406)728-1900 or (800)234-5308. **Fax:** (406)728-1635. **E-mail:** info@ mtnpress.com. **Website:** www.mountain-press.com. **Contact:** Jennifer Carey, editor. Estab. 1948. Company publishes trade paperback originals and reprints; some hardcover originals and reprints. Types of books include western history, geology, natural history/nature. Specializes in geology, natural history, history, horses, western topics. Publishes 20 titles/year. Book catalog free by request.

NEEDS Prefers artists with experience in book illustration and design, book cover illustration. Uses freelance artists for jacket/cover illustration, text illustration and maps. 100% of design work demands knowledge of InDesign, Photoshop, Illustrator. Works on assignment only.

FIRST CONTACT & TERMS Send query letter with résumé, SASE and any samples. Samples are filed or are returned by SASE. Responds only if interested. Project editor will contact artist for portfolio review if interested. Buys one-time rights or reprint rights depending on project. Originals are returned at job's completion. Finds artists through submissions, word of mouth, sourcebooks and other publications.

DESIGN Pays by the project.

JACKETS/COVERS Pays by the project.

TEXT ILLUSTRATION Pays by the project.

TIPS "First-time assignments are usually book cover/ jacket illustration or map drafting; text illustration projects are given to proven freelancers."

NBM PUBLISHING

160 Broadway, Suite 700, East Bldg., New York NY 10038. **E-mail:** nbmgn@nbmpub.com. **Website:** nbm pub.com. **Contact:** Terry Nantier, editor/art director.

Estab. 1976. Publishes graphic novels for an audience of adults. Types of books include fiction, mystery and social parodies. Not accepting submissions unless for graphic novels.

○ Publisher reports too many inappropriate submissions from artists who "don't pay attention." Check their website for instructions before submitting, so you're sure that your art is appropriate for them.

NEW ENGLAND COMICS (NEC PRESS)

732 Washington St., Norwood MA 02062. (508)857-3530. **Fax:** (508)588-4704. **E-mail:** necsupport@newenglandcomics.com. **Website:** www.newenglandcomics.com. Types of books include comic books and games. Book catalog available on website.

NEEDS Seeking pencillers and inkers.

FIRST CONTACT & TERMS Send SASE and 2 pages of pencil or ink drawings derived from the submissions script posted on website. Responds in 2 weeks (with SASE only).

TIPS Visit website for submissions script. Do not submit original characters or stories. Do not call.

NORTH LIGHT BOOKS

F+W, a Content + eCommerce Company, 10151 Carver Rd., Suite 200, Blue Ash OH 45242. **Fax:** (513)891-7153. **E-mail:** mona.clough@fwcommunity.com. **Website:** www.fwcommunity.com; www.artistsnetwork.com; www.createmixedmedia.com. **Contact:** Mona Clough, content director art and mixed media. "North Light Books publishes art and craft books, including watercolor, drawing, mixed media and decorative painting that emphasize illustrated how-to art instruction. Currently emphasizing drawing, acrylic, creativity and inspiration." "We do not use freelance illustration. We do use freelance designers occasionally." Recent titles: *The Urban Sketcher, Creating Abstract Art, Zen Doodle, Oil Painting With the Masters, No Excuses Art Journaling, Acrylic Illuminations.*

NEEDS Approached by 100 author-artists/year. Works with 50 artists/year.

FIRST CONTACT & TERMS Send query letter with photographs, digital images. Accepts e-mail submissions. Samples are not filed and are not returned. Responds only if interested. Company will contact artist for portfolio review if interested. Buys all rights; exclusive rights with royalty for authors. Finds freelancers through art competitions, art exhibits, submissions, Internet and word of mouth. "Please tell us if you are submitting to multiple publishers at once if you submit simultaneously."

TIPS "Visit www.artistsnetwork.com/contactus and scroll down to download submission guidelines."

OCP (OREGON CATHOLIC PRESS)

5536 NE Hassalo, Portland OR 97213. (800)548-8749. **Fax:** (800)462-7329. **E-mail:** liturgy@ocp.org; submissions@ocp.org. **Website:** www.ocp.org. **Contact:** Judy Urben, art director. Nonprofit publishing company, producing music and liturgical publications used in parishes throughout the U.S., Canada, England and Australia. 30% require freelance illustration. Catalog available with 9×12 SASE with first-class postage.

TIPS "I am always looking for appropriate art for our projects. We tend to use work already created on a one-time-use basis, as opposed to commissioned pieces. I look for tasteful, not overtly religious art."

ONSTAGE PUBLISHING

190 Lime Quarry Rd., Suite 106-J, Madison AL 35758-8962. (256)461-0661. **E-mail:** onstage123@knology.net. **Website:** www.onstagepublishing.com. **Contact:** Dianne Hamilton, senior editor. Estab. 1999. Small, independent publishing house specializing in children's literature. "We currently publish chapter books, middle-grade fiction and YA. At this time, we only produce fiction books for ages 8-18."

NEEDS "Our chapter books need inside b&w line illustrations. All books need full color cover illustrations. Sample illustrations need to have one sample in full color to show your style and one sample in b&w to show your skill. The main characters in our books are children. We need to see how you portray children, especially children in action."

FIRST CONTACT & TERMS Please remember to include a cover letter and a SASE large enough, with sufficient postage, to safely return your work if we do not put your work on file. Never send originals! The art director requests that you send your samples by mail. *Please do not send your work by e-mail or computer disk unless specifically requested.*

ORCHARD BOOKS

Hachette Children's Books, 50 Victoria Embankment, London EC4Y 0DZ , United Kingdom. +44 (0)20 3122 6000. **Fax:** +44 (0)20 7873 6024. **E-mail:** ad@hachettechildrens.co.uk. **Website:** www.orchardbooks.co.uk. Estab. 1987. Publishes children's books. Specializes in picture books and novels for children and young adults. 100% require freelance illustration.

NEEDS Works on assignment only.

FIRST CONTACT & TERMS Designers: Send PDFs of portfolio. Illustrators: Send copies or PDFs of samples. Samples are filed or are returned by SASE only if requested. Responds to queries/submissions only if interested. Originals returned to artist at job's completion. Considers complexity of project, skill and experience of artist and project's budget when establishing payment. See website.

RICHARD C. OWEN PUBLISHERS, INC.

P.O. Box 585, Katonah NY 10536. (914)232-3903 or (800)336-5588. **Fax:** (914)232-3977. **E-mail:** richardowen@rcowen.com. **Website:** www.rcowen.com. **Contact:** Richard Owen, publisher. Estab. 1982. Company publishes children's books, juvenile fiction and nonfiction for 5-, 6- and 7-year-olds. Publishes 15-20 titles/year. 100% require freelance illustration.

"Focusing on adding nonfiction for young children on subjects such as history, biography, social studies, science and technology; with human characters, buildings, structures, machines. Realistic but appealing to a child."

NEEDS Prefers freelancers with focus on children's books who can create consistency of character from page to page in an appealing setting. Uses freelancers for jacket/cover and text illustration. Works on assignment only.

FIRST CONTACT & TERMS Art director will contact artist if interested and has a suitable project available. Buys all rights. Original illustrations are returned at job's completion.

TIPS Be willing to work with the art director. All our books have a trade book look.

OXFORD UNIVERSITY PRESS

198 Madison Ave., New York NY 10016. (212)726-6000. **E-mail:** custserv.us@oup.com. **Website:** www.oup.com/us. Chartered by Oxford University. Specializes in fully illustrated, not-for-profit, contemporary textbooks emphasizing English as a second language for children and adults. Also produces wall charts, picture cards, CDs and cassettes.

NEEDS Approached by 1,000 freelance artists/year. Works with 100 illustrators and 8 designers/year. Uses freelancers mainly for interior illustrations of exercises. Also uses freelance artists for jacket/cover illustration and design. Some need for computer-literate freelancers for illustration. 20% of freelance work demands knowledge of QuarkXPress or Illustrator. Works on assignment only.

FIRST CONTACT & TERMS Send query letter with brochure, tearsheets, photostats, slides or photographs. Samples are filed. Art buyer will contact artist for portfolio review if interested. Artists work from detailed specs. Considers complexity of project, skill and experience of artist and project's budget when establishing payment. Artist retains copyright. Originals are returned at job's completion. Finds artists through submissions, artist catalogs such as *Showcase*, *Guild Book*, etc., occasionally from work seen in magazines and newspapers, other illustrators.

JACKETS/COVERS Pays by the project.

TEXT ILLUSTRATION Assigns 500 jobs/year. Uses black line, half-tone and 4-color work in styles ranging from cartoon to realistic. Greatest need is for natural, contemporary figures from all ethnic groups, in action and interaction. Pays for text illustration by the project, $45/spot, $2,500 maximum/full page.

TIPS "Please wait for us to call you. You may send new samples to update your file at any time. We would like to see more natural, contemporary, nonwhite people from freelance artists. Art needs to be fairly realistic and cheerful."

⌂ PARENTING PRESS, INC.

P.O. Box 75267, Seattle WA 98175. (206)364-2900 or (800)992-6657. **Fax:** (206)364-0702. **Website:** www. parentingpress.com. **Contact:** Carolyn Threadgill, publisher. Estab. 1979. Publishes trade paperback originals and hardcover originals. Types of books include nonfiction: instruction and parenting. Specializes in parenting and social skill building books for children. 100% requires freelance design; 100% requires freelance illustration. Book catalog online

NEEDS Approached by 10 designers/year and 100 illustrators/year. Works with 2 designers/year. Prefers local designers. 100% of freelance design work demands knowledge of Photoshop, QuarkXPress, and InDesign.

FIRST CONTACT & TERMS Send query letter with brochure, SASE, postcard sample with photocopies, photographs and tearsheets. After introductory mailing, send follow-up postcard sample every 6 months. Accepts e-mail submissions. Prefers Windows-compatible, TIFF, JPEG files. Samples returned by SASE if not filed. Responds only if interested. Company will contact artist for portfolio review if interested. Port-

folio should include b&w or color tearsheets. Rights purchased vary according to project.

JACKETS/COVERS Pays for illustration by the project. Prefers appealing human characters, realistic or moderately stylized.

TEXT ILLUSTRATION Pays by the project or shared royalty with author.

TIPS "Be willing to supply 2-4 roughs before finished art."

PAULINE BOOKS & MEDIA

50 St. Paul's Ave., Boston MA 02130. (617)522-8911. **Fax:** (617)541-9805. **E-mail:** design@paulinemedia. com; editorial@paulinemedia.com. **Website:** www. pauline.org. Estab. 1932. Publishes hardcover and trade paperback originals. Religious publishers; types of books include adult books on catholic spirituality, prayer, scriptural spirituality, adult and children's lives of saints, marian themes, adult faith formation, media literacy formation, themes on the theology of the body, family life, prayer books, teacher resources, children's prayer books, children's bible stories, children's catechetical and reference books, children's Christmas and easter stories, seasonal activity books, pastoral resources, supplemental faith formation materials, children's inspirational biographies, children's conceptual picture books, children's faith-oriented stories, children's faith-oriented tales and legends picture books. Publishes 30-40 titles/year.

NEEDS Approached by 50 freelancers/year. Works with 10-15 freelance illustrators/year. Knowledge and use of InDesign, Illustrator, Photoshop, etc., is valued.

FIRST CONTACT & TERMS Postcards, tearsheets, photocopies, include website address if you have one. Samples are filed or returned by SASE. Responds only if interested. Rights purchased; work for hire or exclusive rights.

TEXT ILLUSTRATION Assigns 6-10 freelance illustration jobs/year. Pays by the project.

PAULIST PRESS

997 MacArthur Blvd., Mahwah NJ 07430. (201)825-7300. **Fax:** (201)825-8345. **Website:** www.paulist press.com. **Contact:** Trace Murphy, editorial director. Estab. 1865. Publishes hardcover and trade paperback originals, textbooks. Types of books include religion, theology, and spirituality. Specializes in academic and pastoral theology. Publishes 70 titles/year; 5% require freelance design.

NEEDS Works on assignment only.

FIRST CONTACT & TERMS Send query letter with brochure, résumé and tearsheets. Samples are filed. Portfolio review not required. Royalties and advances are negotible. Illustrators sometimes receive a flat fee when all we need are spot illustrations.

JACKETS/COVERS Pays by the project.

PEACHTREE PUBLISHERS

1700 Chattahoochee Ave., Atlanta GA 30318-2112. (404)876-8761. **Fax:** (404)875-2578. **E-mail:** loraine@peachtree-online.com; hello@peachtree-online.com. **Website:** www.peachtree-online.com. Social media: Facebook, Twitter, Peachtreepub.blogspot.com. **Contact:** Helen Harriss, acquisitions editor; Nicki Carmack, creative director; Loraine Joyner, senior art director. Estab. 1978. Publishes hardcover and trade paperback originals. Types of books include children's picture books, young adult fiction, early reader fiction, middle reader fiction and nonfiction, parenting, regional. Specializes in children's and young adult titles. Publishes 24-30 titles/year. 95% require freelance illustration. Call for catalog.

NEEDS Approached by 750 illustrators/year. Works with 15-20 illustrators. "We normally do not use book designers. When possible, send samples that show your ability to depict subjects or characters in a consistent manner. See our website to view styles of artwork we utilize."

JACKETS/COVERS Assigns 18-20 illustration jobs/year. Prefers acrylic, oils, watercolor, or mixed media on flexible material for scanning, or digital files. Pays for illustration by the project.

TEXT ILLUSTRATION Assigns 4-6 freelance illustration jobs/year. Pays by the project.

TIPS "We are an independent, award-winning, high-quality house with a limited number of new titles per season; therefore, each book must be a jewel. We expect the illustrator to bring creative insights which expand the readers' understanding of the storyline through visual clues not necessarily expressed within the text itself."

PELICAN PUBLISHING COMPANY

1000 Burmaster St., Gretna LA 70053. (504)368-1175. **Fax:** (504)368-1195. **E-mail:** editorial@pelicanpub.com. **Website:** www.pelicanpub.com. Estab. 1926. Publishes hardcover and paperback originals and reprints. Publishes 70 titles/year. Types of books include cookbooks, business/motivational, architecture, history, art and children's books. Books have a "high-quality, conservative and detail-oriented" look. Recent titles include: *The Maxims of General Patton, The Art of Brazilian Cooking, The Discovery of Longitude.*

NEEDS Approached by 2,000 freelancers/year. Works with 20 freelance illustrators/year. Uses freelancers for illustration and photo projects. Works on assignment only. 100% of design and 50% of illustration demand knowledge of InDesign, Photoshop, Illustrator.

FIRST CONTACT & TERMS Designers: Send photocopies, photographs, SASE, slides and tearsheets. Illustrators: Send postcard sample or query letter with photocopies, SASE, slides and tearsheets. Samples are not returned. Responds on future assignment possibilities. Buys all rights. Originals are not returned.

DESIGN Pays by the project, $500 minimum.

JACKETS/COVERS Pays by the project, $150-500.

TEXT ILLUSTRATION Pays by the project, $50-250.

TIPS "Show your versatility. We want to see realistic detail and color samples."

PENGUIN GROUP (USA), INC.

375 Hudson St., New York NY 10014-3657. (212)366-2372. **Website:** www.penguinputnam.com. **Contact:** art director. Publishes hardcover and trade paperback originals.

NEEDS Works with 100-200 freelance illustrators and 100-200 freelance designers/year. Uses freelancers mainly for jackets, catalogs, etc.

FIRST CONTACT & TERMS Send query letter with tearsheets, photocopies and SASE. Rights purchased vary according to project.

DESIGN Pays by the project; amount varies.

JACKETS/COVERS Pays by the project; amount varies.

PENGUIN RANDOM HOUSE

1745 Broadway, New York NY 10019. (212)782-9000. **E-mail:** atrandompublicity@randomhouse.com. **Website:** www.randomhouse.com. **Contact:** art director. Imprint publishes hardcover, trade paperback and reprints, and trade paperback originals. Types of books include adventure, coffee table books, cookbooks, children's books, fantasy, historical fiction, history, horror, humor, instructional, mainstream fiction, New Age, nonfiction, reference, religious, romance, science fiction, self-help, travel and western. Specializes in contemporary authors' work. 80% requires freelance illustration; 50% requires freelance design.

NEEDS Uses freelancers mainly for jacket/cover illustration and design for fiction and romance titles. 100% of design and 50% of illustration demands knowledge of Illustrator, QuarkXPress, Photoshop and FreeHand. Works on assignment only.

FIRST CONTACT & TERMS Designers: Send résumé and tearsheets. Illustrators: Send postcard sample, brochure, résumé and tearsheets. Samples are filed. Request portfolio review in original query. Art director will contact artist for portfolio review if interested. Portfolio should include tearsheets. Buys first rights. Originals are returned at job's completion. Finds artists through *American Showcase*, *Workbook*, *The Creative Illustration Book*, artist's reps.

DESIGN Pays by the project.

JACKETS/COVERS Assigns 50 freelance design and 20 illustration jobs/year. Pays by the project.

TIPS "Study the product to make sure styles are similar to what we have done new, fresh, etc."

PENNY-FARTHING PRODUCTIONS

1 Sugar Creek Center Blvd., Suite 820, Sugar Land TX 77478. (713)780-0300 or (800)926-2669. **Fax:** (713)780-4004. **E-mail:** corp@pfpress.com. **Website:** www.pfpress.com. Estab. 1998. Publishes hardcover and trade paperback originals. Types of books include adventure, comic books, fantasy, science fiction. Specializes in comics and graphic novels. Book catalog and art guidelines available on website.

FIRST CONTACT & TERMS Pencillers: Send 3-5 penciled pages "showing story-telling skills and versatility. Do not include dialogue or narrative boxes." Inkers: Send at least 3-5 samples (full-sized and reduced to letter-sized) showing interior work. "Include copies of the pencils." Illustrators: Send color photocopies. "Please do not send oversized copies." Samples are returned by SASE only. Submissions in the form of URLs may be e-mailed to submissions@pfpress.com with PFP Art Submission as the subject line. See website for specific instructions. Responds in several months. Do not call to check on status of your submission.

TIPS "Do not send originals."

CLARKSON N. POTTER, INC.

Crown Publishers, a division of Random House, Inc., 1745 Broadway, New York NY 10019. (212)782-9000. **E-mail:** crownosm@penguinrandomhouse.com. **Website:** www.clarksonpotter.com. Publishes hardcover originals and reprints. Types of books include coffee table books, cookbooks, gardening, crafts, gift, style, decorating. Specializes in lifestyle (cookbooks, gardening, decorating). Publishes 50-60 titles/year. 20% requires freelance illustration; 25% requires freelance design.

NEEDS Works with 10-15 illustrators and 15 designers/year. Prefers freelancers experienced in illustrating food in traditional styles and mediums and designers with previous book design experience. 100% of freelance design demands knowledge of Illustrator, Photoshop, QuarkXPress, InDesign.

FIRST CONTACT & TERMS Send postcard sample or query letter with printed samples, photocopies, tearsheets. Samples are filed and are not returned. Will contact artist for portfolio review if interested or portfolios may be dropped off any day. Negotiates rights purchased. Finds freelancers through submission packets, promotional postcards, web sourcebooks, illustration annuals and previous books.

DESIGN Assigns 20 freelance design jobs/year.

JACKETS/COVERS Assigns 20 freelance design and 15 illustration jobs/year. Pays for design by the project. Jackets are designed by book designer, i.e., the whole book and jacket are viewed as a package.

TEXT ILLUSTRATION Assigns 15 freelance illustration jobs/year.

TIPS "We no longer have a juvenile books department. We do not publish books of cartoons or humor. We look at a wide variety of design styles. We look at mainly traditional illustration styles and mediums and are always looking for unique food and garden illustrations."

PRAKKEN PUBLICATIONS, INC.

P.O. Box 8623, Ann Arbor MI 48107. (734)975-2800. **Fax:** (734)975-2787. **E-mail:** pam@eddigest.com. **E-mail:** susanne@eddigest.com. **Contact:** Susanne Peckham, book editor; Sharon K. Miller, art/design/production manager. Estab. 1934. "We publish books for educators in career/vocational and technology education, as well as books for the machine trades and machinists' education. Currently emphasizing machine trades." Publishes 2 magazines: *The Education Digest* and *Tech Directions*; text and reference books for technology and career/technical education. Book catalog free by request.

NEEDS Rarely uses freelancers. 50% of freelance work demands knowledge of InDesign. Works on assignment only.

FIRST CONTACT & TERMS Send samples. Samples are filed or are returned by SASE if requested by artist. Responds only if interested. Art director will contact artist for portfolio review if interested. Portfolio should include b&w and color final art and tearsheets.

PRENTICE HALL COLLEGE DIVISION

Pearson Education, 200 Old Tappan Rd., Old Tappan NJ 07675. (201)236-7000. **Fax:** 201-767-5956. **E-mail:** communications@pearsoned.com; USAPermissions@pearsoned.com. **Website:** www.prenhall.com. Specializes in college textbooks in education and technology. Publishes 400 titles/year.

NEEDS Approached by 25-40 designers/freelancers/year. Works with 15 freelance designers/illustrators/year. Uses freelancers mainly for cover textbook design. 100% of freelance design and 70% of illustration demand knowledge of QuarkXPress 6.5, Illustrator and Photoshop CS.

FIRST CONTACT & TERMS Send query letter with résumé and tearsheets; sample text designs on CD in Mac format. Samples are filed and portfolios are returned. Responds if appropriate. Rights purchased vary according to project. Originals are returned at job's completion.

DESIGN Pays by the project.

TIPS "Send a style that works well with our particular disciplines."

PRO LINGUA ASSOCIATES

P.O. Box 1348, Brattleboro VT 05302-1348. (802)257-7779. **Fax:** (802)257-5117. **E-mail:** info@prolingua associates.com. **Website:** www.prolinguaassociates.com. **Contact:** Arthur A. Burrows, president. Estab. 1980. Publishes textbooks. Specializes in language textbooks. Recent titles: *Writing Strategies*, *Dictations for Discussion*. Publishes 3-8 titles/year. Some require freelance illustration. Book catalog free by request.

NEEDS Approached by 10 freelance artists/year. Works with up to 3 freelance illustrators/year. Uses freelance artists mainly for pedagogical illustrations of various kinds; also for jacket/cover and text illustration. Works on assignment only.

FIRST CONTACT & TERMS Send postcard sample or query letter with brochure, photocopies and photographs. Samples are filed. Responds in 1 month. Portfolio review not required. Buys all rights. Originals are returned at job's completion if requested. Finds artists through word of mouth and submissions.

TEXT ILLUSTRATION Assigns 1-3 freelance illustration jobs/year. Pays by the project, $200-1,200.

G.P. PUTNAM'S SONS, PENGUIN YOUNG READERS GROUP

345 Hudson St., 14th Floor, New York NY 10014. (212)366-2000. **Website:** us.penguingroup.com. **Contact:** Annie Ericsson, designer. Publishes hardcover juvenile books. Publishes 65 titles/year.

NEEDS Picture book illustration on assignment only.

FIRST CONTACT & TERMS Provide printed samples or color copies to be kept on file for possible future assignments. Samples are returned by SASE only. Do not send samples via e-mail, original art, or CDs. If you are interested in illustrating picture books, we will need to see at least 3-4 sequential scenes of the same children or animals interacting in different settings.

QUITE SPECIFIC MEDIA GROUP, LTD.

7373 Pyramid Place, Hollywood CA 90046. **E-mail:** info@quitespecificmedia.com. **Website:** www.quitespecificmedia.com. Estab. 1967. Publishes hardcover originals and reprints, trade paperback reprints and textbooks. Specializes in costume, fashion, theater and performing arts books. Recent titles: *Understanding Fashion History*; *The Medieval Tailor's Assistant*. Publishes 12 titles/year. 10% require freelance illustration; 60% require freelance design.

◯ Imprints of Quite Specific Media Group, Ltd. include Drama Publishers, Costume & Fashion Press, By Design Press, EntertainmentPro, and Jade Rabbit.

NEEDS Works with 2-3 freelance designers/year. Uses freelancers mainly for jackets/covers; also for book, direct mail and catalog design and text illustration. Works on assignment only.

FIRST CONTACT & TERMS Send query letter with brochure and tearsheets. Samples are filed. Responds only if interested. Rights purchased vary according to project. Originals not returned. Pays by the project.

RAINBOW BOOKS INC.

P.O. Box 430, Highland City FL 33846. (863)648-4420. **Fax:** (863)647-5951. **E-mail:** submissions@rainbow booksinc.com. **Website:** www.rainbowbooksinc.com. **Contact:** editorial department. Estab. 1978. Publishes hardcover and trade paperback originals. Types of books include instruction, adventure, biography, travel, self-help, mystery and reference. Specializes in nonfiction, self-help, mystery fiction, and how-to. Recent titles: *False as the Day Is Long: A Keegan Shaw*

Mystery; *Eavesdropping: As Real Women Talk About the Gifts and Challenges of Aging*; *Protecting Your Family's Assets in Florida: How to Legally Use Medicaid to Pay for Nursing Home and Assisted Living Care* (2nd edition). Publishes 10-15 titles/year.

NEEDS All in-house.

RAINBOW PUBLISHERS

P.O. Box 261129, San Diego CA 92196. (858)277-1167. **E-mail:** editor@rainbowpublishers.com. **Website:** www.rainbowpublishers.com; www.legacypresskids.com. Estab. 1979. Publishes trade paperback originals. Types of books include religious books, reproducible Sunday School books for children ages 2-12, and Bible teaching books for children and adults. Recent titles include *Favorite Bible Families, Instant Bible Lessons, The Christian Girl's Guides, Bill the Warthog, Time Crashers, Gotta Have God, God and Me*. Publishes 20 titles/year. Book catalog available for SASE with 2 first-class stamps.

NEEDS Approached by hundreds of illustrators and 50 designers/year. Works with 5-10 illustrators and 5-10 designers/year. 100% of freelance design and illustration demands knowledge of Illustrator, Photoshop and InDesign.

FIRST CONTACT & TERMS Send query letter with printed samples, SASE and tearsheets. Samples are filed or returned by SASE. Responds only if interested. Will contact artist for portfolio review if interested. Finds freelancers through samples sent and personal referrals. For submission directions, go to: www.rainbowpublishers.com/submissions.apsx.

DESIGN Assigns 25 freelance design jobs/year. Pays for design by the project, $350 minimum. Pays for art direction by the project, $350 minimum.

JACKETS/COVERS Assigns 25 freelance design jobs and 25 illustration jobs/year. "Prefers computer generated-high energy style with bright colors appealing to kids." Pays for design and illustration by the project, $350 minimum. "Prefers designers/illustrators with some Biblical knowledge."

TEXT ILLUSTRATION Assigns 20 freelance illustration jobs/year. Pays by the project, $500 minimum. "Prefers black & white line art, preferably computer generated with limited detail yet fun."

TIPS "We look for illustrators and designers who have some Biblical knowledge and excel in working with a fun, colorful, high-energy style that will appeal to kids and parents alike. Designers must be well versed in InDesign, Illustrator and Photoshop, know how to visually market to kids and have wonderful conceptual ideas!"

RANDOM HOUSE CHILDREN'S BOOKS

1745 Broadway, New York NY 10019. (212)782-9000. **Website:** www.randomhouse.com. Estab. 1925. Largest English-language children's trade book publisher. Specializes in books for preschool children through young adult readers, in all formats from board books to activity books to picture books and novels. Recent titles: *How Many Seeds in a Pumpkin?*; *How Not to Start Third Grade*; *Spells & Sleeping Bags*; *The Power of One*. Publishes 250 titles/year. 100% require freelance illustration.

○ The Random House publishing divisions hire their freelancers directly. To contact the appropriate person, send a cover letter and résumé to the department head at the publisher as follows: "Department Head" (e.g., Art Director, Production Director), "Publisher/Imprint" (e.g., Knopf, Doubleday, etc.), 1745 Broadway, New York NY 10019.

NEEDS Works with 100-150 freelancers/year. Works on assignment only.

FIRST CONTACT & TERMS Send query letter with résumé, tearsheets and printed samples; no originals. Samples are filed. Negotiates rights purchased.

DESIGN Assigns 5 freelance design jobs/year. Pays by the project.

TEXT ILLUSTRATION Assigns 150 illustration jobs/year. Pays by the project.

⊕ REGNERY PUBLISHING, INC.

Eagle Publishing, 300 New Jersey Ave. NW, Suite 500, Washington DC 20001-2253. (202)216-0600; (888)219-4747. **Fax:** (202)216-0612. **E-mail:** editorial@regnery.com; submissions@regnery.com. **Website:** www.regnery.com. **Contact:** Art Director. Estab. 1947. Publishes hardcover originals and reprints, trade paperback originals and reprints. Types of books include biography, history, nonfiction. Specializes in nonfiction. Publishes 30 titles/year. Recent titles include: *God, Guns and Rock & Roll* by Ted Nugent. 20-50% requires freelance design. Book catalog available for SASE.

NEEDS Approached by 20 illustrators and 20 designers/year. Works with 6 designers/year. Prefers local illustrators and designers. Prefers freelancers experienced in Mac, QuarkXPress and Photoshop. 100%

of freelance design demands knowledge of QuarkX-Press. 50% of freelance illustration demands knowledge of Photoshop, QuarkXPress.

FIRST CONTACT & TERMS "We will only accept proposals submitted by agents."

DESIGN Assigns 5-10 freelance design jobs/year. Pays for design by the project; negotiable.

JACKETS/COVERS Assigns 5-10 freelance design and 1-5 illustration jobs/year. Pays by the project; negotiable.

TIPS "We welcome designers with knowledge of Mac platforms and the ability to design 'bestsellers' under extremely tight guidelines and deadlines!"

RENAISSANCE HOUSE

465 Westview Ave., Englewood NJ 07631. (201)408-4048. **E-mail:** info@renaissancehouse.net. **Website:** www.renaissancehouse.net.

TIPS "We look for artists with quick turnaround. Submit artwork via e-mail through our website. Share with us any book project you might have written and illustrated yourself."

ROBERTS PRESS

False Bay Books, 685 Spring St., #PMB 161, 330 False Bay Dr., Harbor WA 98250. **E-mail:** submit-robertspress@falsebaybooks.com. **Website:** www.robertsbookpress.com. Estab. 2004. Publishes ebook originals and reprints, trade paperback originals and reprints, and audio books. Publishes fiction, including Christian fiction, fantasy, thrillers, mystery, women's fiction, family drama, juvenile fiction, mainstream fiction, science fiction, young adult and literary fiction, anthologies and multi-author collaborations. Recent titles include *The End of Law, Elemental, Drowning, Camouflage.*

SCHOLASTIC, INC.

557 Broadway, New York NY 10012. (212)343-6100. **Website:** www.scholastic.com. Scholastic Trade Books is an award-winning publisher of original children's books. Scholastic publishes more than 600 new hardcover, paperback and novelty books each year. The list includes the phenomenally successful publishing properties Harry Potter®, Goosebumps®, The 39 Clues™, I Spy™, and The Hunger Games; best-selling and award-winning authors and illustrators, including Blue Balliett, Jim Benton, Meg Cabot, Suzanne Collins, Christopher Paul Curtis, Ann M. Martin, Dav Pilkey, J.K. Rowling, Pam Muñoz Ryan, Brian Selznick, David Shannon, Mark Teague, and Walter

Wick, among others; as well as licensed properties such as Star Wars® and Rainbow Magic®.

SCHOOL GUIDE PUBLICATIONS

606 Halstead Ave., Mamaroneck NY 10543. (800)433-7771. **E-mail:** mridder@schoolguides.com; info@schoolguides.com. **Website:** www.schoolguides.com. **Contact:** Myles Ridder, publisher. Estab. 1935. Types of books include reference and educational directories. Specializes in college recruiting publications. 1% requires freelance illustration; 1% requires freelance design.

NEEDS Approached by 10 illustrators and 10 designers/year. Prefers local freelancers. Prefers freelancers experienced in book cover and brochure design. 100% of freelance design and illustration demands knowledge of Illustrator, Photoshop, QuarkXPress.

FIRST CONTACT & TERMS Send e-mail query with samples. Send EPS files. Samples are filed. Responds only if interested. Will contact artist for portfolio review if interested. Rights purchased vary according to project. Finds freelancers through word of mouth.

SIMON & SCHUSTER

1230 Avenue of the Americas, New York NY 10020. (212)698-7000. **Website:** www.simonandschuster.com. Imprints include Pocket Books and Archway. Company publishes hardcover, trade paperback and mass market paperback originals, reprints and textbooks. Types of books include juvenile, preschool, romance, self-help, young adult and many others. Specializes in young adult, romance and self-help. Publishes 125 titles/year. Recent titles include *Plan of Attack* by Bob Woodward; *The Price of Loyalty* by Ron Suskind. 95% require freelance illustration; 80% require freelance design.

NEEDS Works with 50 freelance illustrators and 5 designers/year. Prefers freelancers with experience working with models and taking direction well. Uses freelancers for hand lettering, jacket/cover illustration and design and book design. 100% of design and 75% of illustration demand knowledge of Illustrator and Photoshop. Works on assignment only.

FIRST CONTACT & TERMS Send query letter with tearsheets. Accepts disk submissions. Samples are filed and are not returned. Responds only if interested. Portfolios may be dropped off every Monday and Wednesday and should include tearsheets. Buys all rights. Originals are returned at job's completion.

TEXT ILLUSTRATION Assigns 50 freelance illustration jobs/year.

TECHNICAL ANALYSIS, INC.

4757 California Ave. SW, Seattle WA 98116-4499. (206)938-0570, (800)832-4642. **E-mail:** cmorrison@traders.com. **Website:** www.traders.com. **Contact:** Christine Morrison, art director. Estab. 1982. Publishes trade paperback reprints, magazines and software. Types of books include instruction, reference, self-help and financial. Specializes in stocks, options, futures and mutual funds. Publishes 3 titles/year. 100% require freelance illustration; 10% require freelance design.

NEEDS Approached by 100 freelance artists/year. Works with 20 freelance illustrators/year. Buys 70 freelance illustrations/year. Uses freelance artists for magazine illustration; also for text illustration and direct mail design. Works on assignment only. Art awards for illustration include AI NY, 3×3, SI NY, HOW, StepintoDesign, Spectrum, SI LA, etc.

FIRST CONTACT & TERMS Send e-mail/postcards with links to artwork on website to cmorrison@traders.com. Will contact for possible assignment if interested. Buys first rights or reprint rights.

DESIGN Assigns 5 freelance design, 70 freelance illustration jobs/year. Pays by project.

JACKETS/COVERS Assigns 1 freelance design, 15 freelance illustration jobs/year. Pays by project.

TEXT ILLUSTRATION Assigns 5 freelance design and 70 freelance illustration jobs/year. Pays by the hour or by the project.

◎ TIGHTROPE BOOKS

#207-2 College St., Toronto Ontario M5G 1K3, Canada. (416)928-6666. **E-mail:** tightropeasst@gmail.com. **Website:** www.tightropebooks.com. **Contact:** Jim Nason, publisher. Estab. 2005. Publishes hardcover and trade paperback originals.

NEEDS Publishes 12 titles/year. SASE returned. Responds only if interested. Catalog and guidelines free upon request and online.

FIRST CONTACT & TERMS Send an e-mail with résumé, digital images and artist's website, if available.

TILBURY HOUSE PUBLISHERS

WordSplice Studio, Inc., 12 Starr St., Thomaston ME 04861. (800)582-1899. **Fax:** (207)582-8772. **E-mail:** tilbury@tilburyhouse.com. **Website:** www.tilburyhouse.com. **Contact:** Audrey Maynard, children's book editor; Jonathan Eaton, publisher. Estab. 1990.

Publishes hardcover originals, trade paperback originals. 10 titles/year.

FIRST CONTACT & TERMS Send photocopies of photos/artwork.

TIMEWELL

Bandanna Books, 1212 Punta Gorda St., #13, Santa Barbara CA 93103. (805)899-2145. **E-mail:** bandanna@cox.net. **Website:** www.bandannabooks.com; www.bandannabooks.com/time; www.timewell.us. Estab. 2013. The theme of TimeWell is to intermingle classic literature excerpts with contemporary writing, poems, art/graphic design based on a monthly theme. Publishes short pieces, no pay. Free to subscribe; sign up at the magazine.

TORAH AURA PRODUCTIONS

2710 Supply Avenue, Los Angeles CA 90040. (800)238-6724; (800) 689-0793. **Fax:** (323)585-0327. **E-mail:** misrad@torahaura.com. **Website:** www.torahaura.com. **Contact:** Jane Golub, art director. Estab. 1981. Publishes Jewish educational textbooks. Specializes in textbooks for Jewish schools. Recent titles: *Experiencing the Jewish Holidays, Experiencing the Torah.* Publishes 3-4 titles/year. 5% require freelance illustration. Book catalog free for 9×12 SASE with 10 first-class stamps.

NEEDS Approached by 50 illustrators and 20 designers/year. Works with 1-2 illustrators/year.

FIRST CONTACT & TERMS Illustrators: Send postcard sample and follow-up postcard every 6 months, printed samples, photocopies. Accepts Windows-compatible disk submissions. Samples are filed. Will contact artist for portfolio review if interested. Rights purchased vary according to project. Finds freelancers through submission packets.

TREEHAUS COMMUNICATIONS, INC.

906 W. Loveland Ave., P.O. Box 249, Loveland OH 45140. (800)638-4287. **Fax:** (513)683-2882. **E-mail:** treehaus@treehaus1.com. **Website:** www.treehaus1.com. Estab. 1973. Publisher. Specializes in books, periodicals, texts, TV productions. Product specialties are social studies and religious education. Recent titles: *The Stray; Rosanna the Rainbow Angel* (for children ages 4-8).

NEEDS Approached by 12-24 freelancers/year. Works with 2 or 3 freelance illustrators/year. Prefers freelancers with experience in illustrations for children. Works on assignment only. Uses freelancers for all work. 5% of work is with print ads. Needs computer-literate freelancers for illustration.

FIRST CONTACT & TERMS Send query letter with résumé, transparencies, photocopies and SASE. Samples sometimes filed or returned by SASE if requested by artist. Responds in 1 month. Art director will contact artist for portfolio review if interested. Portfolio should include final art, tearsheets, slides, photostats and transparencies. Pays for design and illustration by the project. Rights purchased vary according to project. Finds artists through word of mouth, submissions and other publisher's materials.

TIPS "We are looking for original style that is developed and refined. Whimsy helps."

TRIUMPH BOOKS

814 N. Franklin St., Chicago IL 60610. (312)939-3330; (800)335-5323. **Fax:** (312)663-3557. **Website:** www. triumphbooks.com. Estab. 1990. Publishes hardcover originals and reprints, trade paperback originals and reprints. Types of books include biography, coffee table books, humor, instructional, reference, sports. Specializes in sports titles. Publishes 100 titles/year. 5% requires freelance illustration; 60% requires freelance design. Book catalog free for SASE.

NEEDS Approached by 5 illustrators and 5 designers/year. Works with 2 illustrators and 8 designers/year. Prefers freelancers experienced in book design. 100% of freelance design demands knowledge of Photoshop, InDesign, Illustrator, QuarkXPress.

FIRST CONTACT & TERMS Send query letter with printed samples, SASE. Accepts Mac-compatible disk submissions. Send TIFF files. Samples are filed or returned by SASE. Will contact artist for portfolio review if interested. Buys all rights. Finds freelancers through word of mouth, organizations (Chicago Women in Publishing), submission packets. "Because of the workload, phone calls will not be returned."

DESIGN Assigns 20 freelance design jobs/year. Pays for design by the project.

JACKETS/COVERS Assigns 30 freelance design and 2 illustration jobs/year. Pays for design by the project. Prefers simple, easy-to-read, in-your-face cover treatment.

TIPS "Most of our interior design requires a fast turnaround. We do mostly one-color work with occasional 2-color and 4-color jobs. We like a simple, professional design."

TYNDALE HOUSE PUBLISHERS, INC.

351 Executive Dr., Carol Stream IL 60188. (800)323-9400. **Fax:** (800)684-0247. **Website:** www.tyndale.com. **Contact:** Katara Washington Patton, acquisitions; Talinda Iverson, art acquisitions. Estab. 1962. Estab. 1962. Publishes hardcover and trade paperback originals. Specializes in children's books on "Christian beliefs and their effect on everyday life." Publishes 150 titles/year. 15% require freelance illustration.

NEEDS Approached by 200-250 freelance artists/year. Works with 5-7 illustrators.

FIRST CONTACT & TERMS Send query letter and tearsheets only. Samples are filed or are returned by SASE. Responds only if interested. Considers complexity of project, skill and experience of artist, project's budget and rights purchased when establishing payment. Negotiates rights purchased. Originals are returned at job's completion except for series logos.

JACKETS/COVERS Assigns 5-10 illustration jobs/year. Prefers progressive but friendly style. Pays by the project, no royalties.

TEXT ILLUSTRATION Assigns 1-5 jobs/year. Prefers progressive but friendly style. Pays by the project.

TIPS "Only show your best work. We are looking for illustrators who can tell a story with their work and who can draw the human figure in action when appropriate."

UNIVERSITY OF PENNSYLVANIA PRESS

3905 Spruce St., Philadelphia PA 19104. (215)898-6261. **Fax:** (215)898-0404. **Website:** www.pennpress.org. **Contact:** Peter Agree, editor-in-chief. Estab. 1890. Publishes hardcover originals. Types of books include biography, history, nonfiction, landscape architecture, art history, anthropology, literature and regional history. Publishes 80 titles/year. 10% requires freelance design.

NEEDS 100% of freelance work demands knowledge of Illustrator, Photoshop and QuarkXPress.

FIRST CONTACT & TERMS Designers: Send query letter with photocopies. Illustrators: Send postcard sample. Accepts Mac-compatible disk submissions. Samples are not filed or returned. Will contact artist for portfolio review if interested. Portfolio should include book dummy and photocopies. Rights purchased vary according to project. Finds freelancers through submission packets and word of mouth.

DESIGN Assigns 2 freelance design jobs/year. Pays by the project.

JACKETS/COVERS Assigns 6 freelance design jobs/year. Pays by the project.

VOYAGEUR PRESS

Quayside Publishing Group, 400 First Ave. N., Suite 400, Minneapolis MN 55401. (800)458-0454. **Fax:** (612)344-8691. **Website:** voyageurpress.com. Estab. 1972. Publishes hardcover originals and reprints. Subjects include regional history, nature, popular culture, travel, wildlife, Americana, collectibles, lighthouses, quilts, tractors, barns and farms. Specializes in natural history, travel and regional subjects. Publishes 50 titles/year. 10% require freelance illustration; 10% require freelance design. Book catalog free by request.

NEEDS Approached by 100 freelance artists/year. Works with 2-5 freelance illustrators and 2-5 freelance designers/year. Prefers artists with experience in maps and book and cover design. Uses freelance artists mainly for cover and book design; also for jacket/cover illustration and direct mail and catalog design. 100% of design requires computer skills. Works on assignment only.

FIRST CONTACT & TERMS Send postcard sample and query letter with brochure, photocopies, SASE and tearsheets, list of credits and nonreturnable samples of work that need not be returned. Samples are filed. Responds only if interested. "We do not review portfolios unless we have a specific project in mind. In that case, we'll contact artists for a portfolio review." Usually buys first rights. Originals returned at job's completion.

DESIGN Assigns 2-5 freelance design jobs and 2-5 freelance illustration jobs/year.

JACKETS/COVERS Assigns 2-5 freelance design and 2-5 freelance illustration jobs/year.

TEXT ILLUSTRATION Assigns 2-5 freelance design and 2-5 design illustration jobs/year.

TIPS "We use more book designers than artists or illustrators, since most of our books are illustrated with photographs."

WATERBROOK MULTNOMAH PUBLISHING GROUP

Random House, 12265 Oracle Blvd., Suite 200, Colorado Springs CO 80921. (719)590-4999. **Fax:** (719)590-8977. **E-mail:** info@waterbrookmultnomah.com. **Website:** www.waterbrookmultnomah.com. Estab. 1996. Publishes audio tapes, hardcover, mass market paperback and trade paperback originals. Types of books include romance, science fiction, western, young adult fiction; biography, coffee table books, religious, self-help nonfiction. Specializes in Christian titles. Publishes 60 titles/year. 30% requires freelance design; 10% requires freelance illustration. Book catalog free on request.

NEEDS Approached by 10 designers and 100 illustrators/year. 90% of freelance design work demands knowledge of Illustrator, QuarkXPress and Photoshop.

FIRST CONTACT & TERMS Designer/illustrators: Send postcard sample with brochure, tearsheets. After introductory mailing, send follow-up postcard sample every 3 months. Samples are filed and not returned. Portfolio not required. Buys one-time rights, first North American serial rights. Finds freelancers through artist's submissions, Internet.

JACKETS/COVERS Assigns 2 freelance cover illustration jobs/year. Pays for illustration by the project.

TEXT ILLUSTRATION Assigns 4 freelance illustration jobs/year. Pays by the project.

ALBERT WHITMAN & COMPANY

250 S. Northwest Hwy., Suite 320, Park Ridge IL 60068. (800)255-7675. **Fax:** (847)581-0039. **E-mail:** submissions@awhitmanco.com. **Website:** www.albertwhitman.com. Estab. 1919. Publishes hardcover originals. Specializes in picture books for young children. Publishes 40 titles/year; 100% require freelance illustration. Responds "if we have a project that seems right for the artist. We like to see evidence that an artist can show the same children and adults in a variety of moods, poses and environments."

NEEDS Prefers working with artists who have experience illustrating picture books. Works on assignment only. Illustrators: Send postcard sample and tearsheets. "One sample is not enough. We need at least 3. Do *not* send original art through the mail."

WILLIAMSON BOOKS

2630 Elm Hill Pike, Suite 100, Nashville TN 37214. **Website:** www.idealsbooks.com. Estab. 1983. Publishes trade paperback originals/casebound. Types of books include children's nonfiction (science, history, the arts), creative play, early learning, preschool and educational. Specializes in children's active hands-on learning. Publishes 8 titles/year. Book catalog free for 8½×11 SASE with 6 first-class stamps.

This publisher is an imprint of Ideals Publications, a division of Guideposts.

NEEDS Approached by 100 illustrators and 10 designers/year. 100% of freelance design demands Quark computer skills. "We especially need illustrators whose art communicates with kids and has a vibrant style, as well as a sense of humor and quirky characterizations evident in illustrations. We are not looking for traditional or picture book styles." All illustrations must be provided in scanned, electronic form.

FIRST CONTACT & TERMS "Please do not e-mail large files to us. We prefer receiving postcards with references to your website. We really will look if we are interested." Designers: Send query letter with with website or brochure, photocopies, résumé, SASE. Illustrators: Send postcard sample and/or query letter with website or photocopies, résumé and SASE. Samples are filed. Responds only if interested.

DESIGN Pays for design by the project.

TIPS "We are actively seeking freelance illustrators and book designers to support our growing team. We are looking for full color distinctive illustration, along with an 'energized' view of how-to illustrations (always drawn with personality as opposed to technical drawings). Go to the library and look up several of our books in our 4 series. You'll immediately see what we're all about. Then do a few samples for us. If we're excited about your work, you'll definitely hear from us. We always need designers who are interested in a nontraditional approach to kids' book design. Our books are award-winners, and design and illustration are key elements to our books' phenomenal success."

GREETING CARDS, GIFTS, & PRODUCTS

The companies listed in this section contain some great potential clients for you. Although greeting card publishers make up the bulk of the listings, you'll also find many businesses that need images for all kinds of other products. We've included manufacturers of everyday items such as paper plates, napkins, banners, shopping bags, T-shirts, school supplies, personal checks, and calendars, as well as companies looking for fine art for limited edition collectibles.

TIPS FOR GETTING STARTED

Use the following tips as you prepare your greeting card or product submissions:

1. Read the listings carefully to learn exactly what products each company makes and the specific styles and subject matter they use.

2. Browse store shelves to see what's out there. Take a notebook and jot down the types of cards and products you see. If you want to illustrate greeting cards, familiarize yourself with the various categories of cards and note which images tend to appear again and again in each category.

3. Pay attention to the larger trends in society, such as diversity, patriotism, and the need to feel connected to others. Fads such as reality TV and scrapbooking, as well as popular celebrities, often show up in images on cards and gifts. Trends can also be spotted in movies and on websites.

GUIDELINES FOR SUBMISSION

- Do *not* send originals. Companies want to see photographs, photocopies, printed samples, computer printouts, tearsheets, or slides. Many also accept digital files on disk or via e-mail.

GREETING CARD BASICS

- Approximately 7 billion greeting cards are purchased annually, generating more than $7.5 billion in retail sales.

- Women buy more than 80% of all greeting cards.

- Seasonal cards express greetings for more than twenty different holidays, including Christmas, Easter, and Valentine's Day. Christmas cards account for 60 percent of seasonal greeting card sales.

- Everyday cards express nonholiday sentiments. The everyday category includes get well cards, thank you cards, sympathy cards, and a growing number of person-to-person greetings. There are cards of encouragement that say "Hang in there!" and cards to congratulate couples on staying together, or even getting divorced! There are cards from "the gang at the office" and cards to beloved pets. Check store racks for possible everyday occasions.

- Categories are further broken down into the following areas: traditional, humorous, and alternative. Alternative cards feature quirky, sophisticated, or offbeat humor.

- There are more than 3,000 greeting card publishers in America, ranging from small family businesses to major corporations.

- Artwork should be upbeat, brightly colored, and appropriate to one of the major categories or niches popular in the industry.
- Make sure each sample is labeled with your name, address, phone number, e-mail address, and website.
- Send three to five appropriate samples of your work to the contact person named in the listing. Include a brief cover letter with your initial mailing.
- Enclose a self-addressed, stamped envelope (SASE) if you need your samples back.
- Within six months, follow up with another mailing to the same listings and additional card and gift companies you have researched.

Don't Overlook the Collectibles Market

Limited edition collectibles, such as ornaments, figurines, and collector plates, appeal to a wide audience and are a lucrative niche for artists. To do well in this field, you have to be flexible enough to take suggestions. Companies test-market products to find out which images will sell the best, so they will guide you in the creative process. For a collectible plate, for example, your work must fit into a circular format or you'll be asked to extend the painting out to the edge of the plate.

Popular themes for collectibles include animals (especially kittens and puppies), children, dolls, TV nostalgia, patriotic, Native American, wildlife, religious (including madonnas and angels), gardening, culinary, and sports images.

E-Cards

Electronic greeting cards are very popular. Many can be sent for free, but they drive people to websites and can, therefore, be a smart marketing tool. The most popular e-cards are animated, and there is an increasing need for artists who can animate their own designs for the Internet, using Flash animation. Search the Internet and visit sites such as www.hallmark.com, www.bluemountain.com, and www.americangreetings. com to get an idea of the variety of images that appear on e-cards. Companies often post their design needs on their websites.

PAYMENT AND ROYALTIES

Most card and product companies pay set fees or royalty rates for design and illustration. Card companies almost always purchase full rights to work, but some are willing to negotiate for other arrangements such as greeting card rights only. If the company has ancillary plans in mind for your work (calendars, stationery, party supplies, or toys), they will probably want to buy all rights. In such cases, you may be able to bargain for higher payment. For more tips, see Copyright Basics in the Business Basics section.

4WALLS

4700 Lakeside Ave., 3rd Floor, Cleveland OH 44114. (216)881-8888. **Fax:** (216)274-9308. **E-mail:** pat@4walls.com. **Website:** www.4walls.com. **Contact:** Pat Walker, vice president. Estab. 1984. Produces fabrics/peel and stick accents/wallpaper/borders. Specializes in wallcovering, border and mural design, self-adhesive accents, also ultra-wide "mural" borders.

NEEDS Approached by 40-80 freelancers/year. Works with 20-40 freelancers/year. Buys hundreds of freelance designs and illustrations/year. Art guidelines free for SASE with first-class postage. Works on assignment and some licensing. Uses freelancers mainly for designs, color work. Looking for traditional, country, floral, texture, woven, menswear, children's and novelty styles. 50% of freelance design work demands computer skills. Wallcovering CAD expcrience a plus. Produces material for everyday.

FIRST CONTACT & TERMS Illustrators: Send query letter with photocopies, examples of work, résumé and SASE. Accepts disk submissions compatible with Illustrator or Photoshop files (Mac), also accepts digital files on CD or DVD. Samples are filed or returned by SASE on request. Responds in 1 month. Request portfolio review of color photographs and slides in original query, follow-up with letter after initial query. Rights purchased vary according to project. Pays by the project, $500-1,500, "but it varies." Finds freelancers through agents and local ads, word of mouth.

TIPS "Send great samples, especially childrens and novelty patterns, and also modern, organic textures and bold conteporary graphic work and digital files are very helpful. Study the market closely; do very detailed artwork."

KURT S. ADLER, INC.

7 W. 34th St., New York NY 10001. (212)924-0900. **E-mail:** info@kurtadler.com. **Website:** www.kurtadler. com. **Contact:** Howard Adler, president. Estab. 1946. Manufacturer and importer of Christmas ornaments and giftware products. Produces collectible figurines, decorations, gifts, ornaments.

NEEDS Prefers freelancers with experience in giftware. Considers all media. Will consider all styles appropriate for Christmas ornaments and giftware. Produces material for Christmas, Halloween.

FIRST CONTACT & TERMS Send query letter with brochure, photocopies, photographs. Responds within 1 month. Will contact for portfolio review if interested. Payment negotiable.

TIPS "We rely on freelance designers to give our line a fresh, new approach and innovative new ideas."

⊙ ALEF JUDAICA, INC.

15020 S. Figueroa St., Gardena CA 90248. (310)630-0024; (800)262-2533. **Fax:** (310)808-0940. **E-mail:** sales@alefjudaica.com. **Website:** www.alefjudaica. com. Estab. 1979. Manufacturer and distributor of a full line of Judaica, including menorahs, Kiddush cups, greeting cards, giftwrap, tableware, etc.

NEEDS Approached by 15 freelancers/year. Works with 10 freelancers/year. Buys 75-100 freelance designs and illustrations/year. Prefers local freelancers with experience. Works on assignment only. Uses freelancers for new designs in Judaica gifts (menorahs, etc.) and ceramic Judaica. Also for calligraphy, pasteup and mechanicals. All designs should be upper scale Judaica.

FIRST CONTACT & TERMS Mail brochure, photographs of final art samples. Art director will contact artist for portfolio review if interested, or portfolios may be dropped off every Friday. Sometimes requests work on spec before assigning a job. Pays $300 for illustration/design; pays royalties of 10%. Considers buying second rights (reprint rights) to previously published work.

ALLPORT EDITIONS

716 NE Lawrence Ave., Portland OR 97232. (503)223-7268. **Fax:** (503)223-9182. **E-mail:** art@allport.com. **Website:** www.allport.com/artists_commitment. aspx. Estab. 1982. Produces greeting cards. Specializes in regional designs (specifically depicting American cities and states). Currently only working with hand-rendered art (pen & ink, watercolor, acrylic, etc.). Does not use any photography. Art guidelines available on website.

NEEDS Approached by 200 freelancers/year. Works with 2-3 freelancers/year. Licenses 60 freelance designs and illustrations/year. Prefers art scaleable to card size. Produces material for holidays, birthdays and everyday. Submit seasonal material 1 year in advance.

FIRST CONTACT & TERMS Send query letter with photocopies and SASE. Accepts submissions on disk compatible with PC-formatted TIFF or JPEG files. Samples are filed or returned by SASE. Responds in 4-5 months if response is requested. Rights purchased vary according to project. All contracts on royalty basis.

AMERICAN GREETINGS CORP.

1 American Rd., Cleveland OH 44144-2398. (216)252-7300. **Fax:** (216)252-6778. **Website:** www.corporate.americangreetings.com. Estab. 1906. Produces greeting cards, stationery, calendars, paper tableware products, giftwrap and ornaments. Also recruiting for AG Interactive.

NEEDS Prefers designers with experience in illustration, graphic design, surface design and calligraphy. Also looking for skills in motion graphics, Photoshop, animation and strong drawing skills. Usually works from a list of 100 active freelancers.

FIRST CONTACT & TERMS Apply online. Submission guidelines available online.

TIPS "Get a BFA in graphic design with a strong emphasis on typography."

AR-EN PARTY PRINTERS, INC.

3416 Oakton St., Skokie IL 60076. (847)673-7390. **Fax:** (847)673-7379. **E-mail:** customerservice@ar-en.net; artwork@ar-en.net. **Website:** www.ar-en.com. Estab. 1978. Produces stationery and paper tableware products. Makes personalized party accessories for weddings and all other affairs and special events.

NEEDS Works with 1-2 freelancers/year. Buys 10 freelance designs and illustrations/year. Works on assignment only. Uses freelancers mainly for new designs; also for calligraphy. Looking for contemporary and stylish designs, especially b&w line art (no grayscale) to use for hot stamping dyes. Prefers small (2×2) format.

FIRST CONTACT & TERMS Send query letter with brochure, résumé and SASE. Samples are filed or returned by SASE if requested by artist. Responds in 2 weeks. Will contact artist for portfolio review if interested. Rights purchased vary according to project.

TIPS "My best new ideas always evolve from something I see that turns me on. Do you have an idea/style that you love? Market it. Someone out there needs it."

ARTFUL GREETINGS

2104 Riddle Rd., Durham NC 27713. (919)598-7599. **Fax:** (919)598-1381. **E-mail:** myw@artfulgreetings.com. **Website:** www.artfulgreetings.com. Estab. 1990. Produces bookmarks, greeting cards, T-shirts and magnetic notepads. Specializes in multicultural subject matter, all ages.

NEEDS Approached by 200 freelancers/year. Works with 10 freelancers/year. Buys 20 freelance designs and illustrations/year. No b&w art. Uses freelancers mainly for cards. Considers bright color art, no photographs. Looking for art depicting people of all races. Prefers a multiple of 2 sizes: 5×7 and 5½×8. Produces material for Christmas, Mother's Day, Father's Day, graduation, Kwanzaa, Valentine's Day, birthdays, everyday, sympathy, get well, romantic, thank you, woman-to-woman and multicultural. Submit seasonal material 1 year in advance.

FIRST CONTACT & TERMS Designers: Send photocopies, SASE, slides, transparencies (call first). Illustrators: Send photocopies (call first). May send samples and queries by e-mail. Samples are filed. Artist should follow up with call or letter after initial query. Will contact for portfolio review of color slides and transparencies if interested. Negotiates rights purchased. Pays for illustration by the project, $50-100. Finds freelancers through word of mouth, NY Stationery Show.

ARTISTS TO WATCH

E-mail: submissions@artiststowatch.com. **Website:** www.artiststowatch.com. "Manufacturer of high-quality greeting cards featuring the work of contemporary national and international artists."

NEEDS Art submission guidelines available on the website. "We encourage illustrators, printmakers and photographers of all kind to submit. Please only 4-color images."

FIRST CONTACT & TERMS "E-mail small JPEG files or website URL. We will contact you if we'd like to see more. Use of artwork is compensated with royalty payments."

ART LICENSING

P.O. Box 2568, Manchester Center VT 05250. (802)362-3662. **Fax:** (802)549-8004. **E-mail:** jack@artlicensing.com. **Website:** www.artlicensing.com. Licenses art for wall decor, greeting cards, calendars, puzzles, rugs/floor mats, gift bags/gift wrap, T-shirts, fabric, iPhone/iPad cases, ornaments, figurines, rubber stamps, pillows, bedding, and other stationery products.

NEEDS Looking for variety of styles and subject matter. Art guidelines free for SASE with first-class postage. Considers all media and all styles. Produces material for all holidays.

FIRST CONTACT & TERMS Send color photocopies, photographs, tearsheets, CD or e-mail. Accepts disk submissions compatible with Mac. Samples are filed or returned by SASE only. Responds in 1 month. Will contact artist for portfolio review if interested.

ARTVISIONS: FINE ART LICENSING

12117 SE 26th St., Bellevue WA 98005-4118. **E-mail:** See website for contact form; nonospam0@gmail.com. **Website:** www.artvisions.com. **Contact:** Neil Miller, president. Estab. 1993. Licenses fine art and professional photography. Fine art and professional photography licensing only. Review guidelines on website. "Not currently seeking new talent. However, we are always willing to view the work of top-notch established artists. If you fit this category, please contact ArtVisions via the website contact form and include a link to a website where your art can be seen."

○ "To gain an idea of the type of art we license, please view our website. Artist MUST be able to provide high-res, professionally made digital files of artwork on DVD. We are firmly entrenched in the digital world, if you are not, then we cannot represent you."

FIRST CONTACT & TERMS Written contract provided.

TIPS "If you need advice about marketing your art, please visit: www.artistsconsult.com."

BARTON-COTTON, INC.

3030 Waterview Ave., Baltimore MD 21230. (800)348-1102. **Fax:** (410)565-5011. **E-mail:** info@bartoncotton.com; art.submission@bartoncotton.com. **Website:** www.bartoncotton.com. Produces religious greeting cards, commercial all-occasion, Christmas cards, wildlife designs and spring note cards. Licenses wildlife art, photography, traditional Christmas art for note cards, Christmas cards, calendars and all-occasion cards.

NEEDS Buys 150-200 freelance illustrations/year. Please submit no more then 15-20 pieces of your work in a neat and orderly format. When reviewing the artwork we are looking for concept, style, drawing skill, and color usage. Submit seasonal work any time. Free art guidelines for SASE with first-class postage and sample cards; specify area of interest (religious, Christmas, spring, etc.).

FIRST CONTACT & TERMS Send query letter with résumé, tearsheets, photocopies or slides. Submit full-color work only (watercolor, gouache, pastel, oil and acrylic). Previously published work and simultaneous submissions accepted. Responds in 1 month. Pays by the project. Pays on acceptance. "Please do not send original artwork at this time. Photos, color copies, digital files, slides or transparencies are great for initial review. Include your name, address, and phone number somewhere on each piece you provide."

TIPS "Spend some time studying current market trends in the greeting card industry. There is an increased need for creative ways to paint traditional Christmas scenes with up-to-date styles and techniques." See website for more guidelines.

BEISTLE CO.

1 Beistle Plaza, Shippensburg PA 17257-9623. (717)532-2131. **Fax:** (717)532-7789. **E-mail:** rlbuterbaugh@beistle.com. **Website:** www.beistle.com. **Contact:** Rick Buterbaugh, art director. Estab. 1900. Manufacturer of paper and plastic decorations, party goods, gift items, tableware and greeting cards. Targets general public, home consumers through point-of-purchase displays, specialty advertising, school market and other party good suppliers.

NEEDS Approached by 250-300 freelancers/year. Works with 50 freelancers/year. Prefers artists with experience in designer gouache illustration. Also needs digital art (Mac platform or compatible). Art guidelines available. Looks for full-color, camera-ready artwork for separation and offset reproduction. Works on assignment only. Uses freelance artists mainly for product rendering and brochure design and layout. Prefers digital art using various styles and techniques. 50% of freelance design and 50% of illustration demand knowledge of QuarkXPress, Illustrator, Photoshop or Painter.

FIRST CONTACT & TERMS Send query letter with résumé and color reproductions with SASE. Samples are filed or returned by SASE. Art director will contact artist for portfolio review if interested. Sometimes requests work on spec before assigning a job. Pays by the project. Considers buying second rights (reprint rights) to previously published work. Finds artists through word of mouth, magazines, submissions/self-promotions, sourcebooks, agents, visiting artists' exhibitions, art fairs and artists' reps.

TIPS "Our primary interest is in illustration; often we receive freelance propositions for graphic design brochures, logos, catalogs, etc. These are not of interest to us as we are manufacturers of printed decorations. Send color samples rather than b&w."

BELLAMUSE

71 Nassau St., 2nd Floor, New York NY 10038. (212)727-0102;. **Fax:** (212)727-2102. **E-mail:** info@bellamuse.com. **Website:** www.bellamuse.com. Estab. 2003. "BellaMuse was established in 2003 by artist and typographer Alicia Peck. Alicia's work draws upon a love of writing, whimsy, humor, and antique illustrations. Little luxuries from BellaMuse are sold in upscale home stores and boutiques throughout the US."
NEEDS Produces conventional, formal, counter humor, alternative and cute cards and gifts. Categories include: Mother's Day, Christmas, Thanksgiving, graduation, birthday, Father's Day, Easter, Halloween, Valentine's Day, congratulations, wedding/anniversary, get-well/sympathy and everyday. Artists should be familiar with Adobe Illustrator, InDesign and Photoshop. Could use freelance Web design; designers should be familiar with Dreamweaver, Flash, GoLive and HTML. Submitted samples are kept on file. Seasonal material should be submitted 10 months in advance.
FIRST CONTACT & TERMS Send a query letter, e-mail or postcard sample including artist's URL, résumé, tearsheets and photographs. Follow up every 3 months.

BERGQUIST IMPORTS, INC.

1412 Hwy. 33 S., Cloquet MN 55720. (800)328-0853. **Fax:** (218)879-0010. **E-mail:** info@bergquistimports.com. **Website:** www.bergquistimports.com. Estab. 1948. Produces paper napkins, mugs and tile. Wholesaler of mugs, decorator tile, plates and dinnerware.
NEEDS Approached by 25 freelancers/year. Works with 5 freelancers/year. Buys 50 designs and illustrations/year. Prefers freelancers with experience in Scandinavian designs. Works on assignment only. Also uses freelancers for calligraphy. Produces material for Christmas, Valentine's Day and everyday. Submit seasonal material 6-8 months in advance.
FIRST CONTACT & TERMS Send query letter with brochure, tearsheets and photographs. Samples are returned, not filed. Responds in 2 months. Request portfolio review in original query. Artist should follow up with a letter after initial query. Portfolio should include roughs, color tearsheets and photographs. Rights purchased vary according to project. Originals are returned at job's completion. Requests

work on spec before assigning a job. Pays by the project, $50-300; average flat fee of $100 for illustration/design; or royalties of 5%. Finds artists through word of mouth, submissions/self-promotions and art fairs.

BERWICK OFFRAY

2015 W. Front St., Berwick CA 18603. (800)237-9425; (570)752-5934. **Fax:** (570)752-5934. **E-mail:** pattijo.smith@berwickoffray.com. **Website:** offray.com. **Contact:** PattiJo Smith, director of creative and design. Estab. 1900. Produces ribbons, gift bags, wrapping paper, tissues and more. "We're mainly a ribbon company. For ribbon designs we look to the textile design studios and textile-oriented people; children's designs, craft motifs, fabric trend designs, floral designs, Christmas designs, bridal ideas, etc. Our range of needs is wide, so we need various looks."
NEEDS Looking for artists able to translate a trend or design idea into a 1½" to 2½" width ribbon. Produce ribbons for fall, Christmas, Valentine's Day, Easter, bridal and everyday.
FIRST CONTACT & TERMS Send postcard sample or query letter with résumé or call.

BLOOMIN' FLOWER CARDS

3080 Valmont Rd., Boulder CO 80301. (800)894-9185, ext. 2. **E-mail:** flowers@bloomin.com. **Website:** bloomin.com. Estab. 1995. Produces greeting cards, stationery and gift tags—all embedded with seeds.
NEEDS Approached by 100 freelancers/year. Works with 1-5 freelancers/year. Buys 1-5 freelance designs and illustrations/year. Art guidelines available. Uses freelancers mainly for card images. Considers all media. Looking for florals, garden scenes, holiday florals, birds, and butterflies—bright colors, no photography. Produces material for Christmas, Easter, Mother's Day, Father's Day, Valentine's Day, Earth Day, birthdays, everyday, get well, romantic and thank you. Submit seasonal material 8 months in advance.
FIRST CONTACT & TERMS Accepts digital submissions only—show us samples of your work. Responds if interested. Finds freelancers through word of mouth, submissions, and local artists' guild.
TIPS "All submissions *must* be relevant to flowers and gardening."

BLUE MOUNTAIN ARTS, INC.

P.O. Box 4549, Boulder CO 80306. (303)449-0536; (800)525-0642. **Fax:** (800)545-8573. **E-mail:** editorial@sps.com. **Website:** www.sps.com. Estab. 1970. Produces books, bookmarks, calendars, greeting cards, mugs and prints. Specializes in handmade-looking greeting cards, calendars and books with inspirational or whimsical messages accompanied by colorful hand-painted illustrations.

NEEDS Art guidelines via e-mail. Uses freelancers mainly for hand-painted illustrations. Considers all media. Product categories include alternative cards, alternative/humor, conventional, cute, inspirational and teen. Submit seasonal material 10 months in advance. Art size should be 5×7 vertical format for greeting cards.

FIRST CONTACT & TERMS Send query letter with photocopies, photographs, SASE and tearsheets. Send no more than 5 illustrations initially. Or e-mail with subject line "Greeting Card Submission." No phone calls or faxes. Samples are filed or are returned by SASE. Responds in 2 months. Portfolio not required. Buys all rights. Pays freelancers flat rate: $150-250/illustration if chosen. Finds freelancers through submissions and word of mouth.

TIPS "We are an innovative company, always looking for fresh and unique art styles to accompany our sensitive or whimsical messages. We also welcome illustrated cards accompanied with your own editorial content. We strive for a handmade look. We love color! We don't want photography! We don't want slick computer art! Do in-store research to get a feel for the look and content of our products. We want illustrations for printed cards, not e-cards! We want to see illustrations that fit with our existing looks, and we also want fresh, new and exciting styles and concepts. Remember that people buy cards for what they say. The illustration is a beautiful backdrop for the message."

☺ ◐ BLUE MOUNTAIN WALLCOVERINGS

15 Akron Rd., Toronto Ontario M8W 1T3, Canada. (800)219-2424; (866)563-9872. **Fax:** (800)741-2083. **E-mail:** info@blmtn.com. **Website:** www.blmtn.com. Produces wallpaper.

NEEDS Works with 20-50 freelancers/year. Prefers local designers/illustrators with experience in wallpaper. Art guidelines available. Product categories include conventional, country, juvenile and teen. 5% of freelance work demands knowledge of Photoshop.

FIRST CONTACT & TERMS Send brochure, photocopies and photographs. Samples are filed. Responds only if interested. Company will contact artist for portfolio review of color, finished art, original art, photographs, transparencies if interested. Buys

rights for wallpaper or all rights. Pays freelancers by the project. Finds freelancers through agents, artist submissions and word of mouth.

BON ART

66 Fort Point St., Norwalk CT 06855. (203)845-8888. **E-mail:** sales@bonartique.com. **Website:** www.bonartique.com. **Contact:** Brett Bonnist. Estab. 1980. Art publisher, poster company, licensing and design studio. Publishes/distributes fine art prints, canvas transfers, unlimited editions, offset reproductions and posters. Clients: Internet purveyors of art, picture frame manufacturers, catalog companies, distributors.

NEEDS Seeking decorative and fashionable art for the commercial and designer markets. Considers oil, acrylic, pastel, watercolor and mixed media. Artists represented include Eric Yang, Tom Butler, Mid Gordon, Martin Wiscombe, Julia Hawkins, Gloria Ericksen, Janet Stever, Louise Montillio, Maxwell Hutchinson, Bennie Diaz and Tina Chaden. Editions are created by collaborating with the artist or by working from an existing painting. Approached by 500 artists/year. Publishes/distributes the work of 30 emerging artists/year.

FIRST CONTACT & TERMS E-mail or send query letter with brochure, samples, photographs, URL. Accepts e-mail submissions with image files or link to website. Prefers JPEG or PDF files. Samples are kept on file or returned by SASE if requested. Responds only if interested. Will contact artist for portfolio review if interested. Portfolio should include b&w, color, finished art, roughs, photographs. Pays flat fee or royalties. Offers advance when appropriate. Rights purchased vary according to project; negotiated. Requires exclusive representation. Provides insurance while work is at firm, shipping from firm, promotion and written contract. Finds artists through agents/reps, submissions, portfolio reviews, art fairs/exhibits, word of mouth, referrals by other artists, magazines, sourcebooks, Internet.

TIPS "We welcome submissions from a wide range of international artists. As leaders in the field of fine art publishing for the past 30 years, we believe in sharing our knowledge of the trends, categories and styles with our artists. Although interested in working with veterans of our industry, we actively recruit and encourage all accomplished artists to submit their portfolios—preferably by e-mail with links to images."

ASHLEIGH BRILLIANT ENTERPRISES

117 W. Valerio St., Santa Barbara CA 93101. (805)682-0531. **E-mail:** ashleigh@west.net; ashleigh@ashleighbrilliant.com. **Website:** www.ashleighbrilliant.com. **Contact:** Ashleigh Brilliant, president. Publishes postcards.

○ Prefers single-panel. Maximum size of artwork: 5½×3½, horizontal only. Samples are returned by SASE if requested by artist. Responds in 2 weeks. **Pays on acceptance**; minimum flat fee of $60. Buys all rights. Syndicate owns original art. "Our product is so unusual that freelancers will be wasting their time and ours unless they first carefully study our catalog. Our product is so unusual that freelancers will be wasting their time and ours unless they first carefully study our catalog."

NEEDS Buys up to 300 designs/year. Freelancers may submit designs for word-and-picture postcards, illustrated with line drawings.

FIRST CONTACT & TERMS Submit 5½×3½ horizontal b&w line drawings and SASE. Responds in 2 weeks. Buys all rights. Pays $60 minimum.

BRISTOL GIFT CO., INC.

6 North St., P.O. Box 425, Washingtonville NY 10992. (845)496-2821; (800)225-8234. **E-mail:** bristol6@frontiernet.net. **Website:** www.bristolgift.net. Estab. 1988. Specializes in framed pictures for inspiration and religious markets. Art guidelines available for SASE.

NEEDS Approached by 5-10 freelancers/year. Works with 2 freelancers/year. Buys 15-30 freelance designs and illustrations/year. Works on assignment only. Uses freelancers mainly for design; also for calligraphy, P-O-P displays, Web design and mechanicals. Prefers 16×20 or smaller. 10% of design and 60% of illustration require knowledge of PageMaker or Illustrator. Produces material for Christmas, Mother's Day, Father's Day and graduation. Submit seasonal material 6 months in advance.

FIRST CONTACT & TERMS Send query letter with brochure and photocopies. Samples are filed or returned. Responds in 2 weeks. Will contact artist for portfolio review if interested. Portfolio should include roughs. Requests work on spec before assigning a job. Originals are not returned. Pays by the project, $30-50 or royalties of 5-10%. Rights purchased vary according to project. Interested in buying second rights (reprint rights) to previously published artwork.

BRUSH DANCE, INC.

3060 El Cerrito Plaza, Suite 400, San Rafael CA 94530. **E-mail:** art@brushdance.com. **Website:** www.brushdance.com. **Contact:** April Welches-Greenhill. Estab. 1989. Produces greeting cards, stationery, blank journals, illustrated journals, boxed notes, calendars, holiday cards and magnets. The line of Brush Dance products is inspired by the interplay of art and words. "We develop products that combine powerful and playful words and images that act as daily reminders to inspire, connect, challenge and support."

NEEDS Approached by 200 freelancers/year. Works with 3-5 freelancers/year. Uses freelancers for illustration, photography and calligraphy. Looking for nontraditional work conveying emotion or message. "We are also interested in artists who are using both images and original words in their work."

FIRST CONTACT & TERMS Submission guidelines available online. "You can send us 3 to 4 images to get the ball rolling. Tell us something about you, too—we love feeling the connection between the art and the artist." Please limit custom formats to no larger than 11×14. Please do not send original artwork as we are unable to return your submissions. "We're a small company doing really really big things and while we review art on a continual basis and do our best to respond quickly, that time is sometimes longer so that we can give consideration to all of the wonderful submissions we receive. (Submitting electronically makes this part of the process easier on us and will probably yield a faster response time for you, too.)"

TIPS *"Please* do your research, and look at our website to be sure your work will fit into our line of products."

CALYPSO CARDS

9 DamonMill Square, Suite 6B, Concord MA 01742. (978)287-5900. **Fax:** (978)287-5902. **E-mail:** nicky@calypsocards.com; info@calypsocards.com; submissions@calypsocards.com. **Website:** www.calypsocards.com. Estab. 2004. Produces greeting cards and fridge magnets. Specializes in greeting cards for all occasions and ages, with contemporary design.

NEEDS Works with 50-100 freelancers/year. Buys 200+ freelance design and illustrations/year. Art submission guidelines free on website. Product categories include alternative, counter humor, alternative/humor, inspirational, juvenile. Produces material for all holidays and seasons. Submit seasonal material one year in advance.

FIRST CONTACT & TERMS E-mail query letter. Samples kept on file or returned with SASE. Responds only if interested. Portfolio not required. Buys rights for cards. Freelancers paid royalties of 8%. Finds freelancers through agents/reps, submissions, word-of-mouth and online.

TIPS "Send examples of work via e-mail. We will contact you within 3-4 months if interested."

CANETTI DESIGN GROUP, INC.

P.O. Box 1848, New York NY 10156. (646)791-8242. **Fax:** (914)801-4080. **E-mail:** info@canettidesign group.com. **Website:** www.canettidesigngroup.com. Estab. 1982. Produces photo frames, writing instruments, kitchen accessories and product design.

NEEDS Approached by 50 freelancers/year. Works with 3-4 freelancers/year. Works on assignment only. Uses freelancers mainly for illustration/computer. Also for calligraphy and mechanicals. Considers all media. Looking for contemporary style. Needs computer-literate freelancers for illustration and production. 80% of freelance work demands knowledge of Illustrator, Photoshop.

FIRST CONTACT & TERMS Please send e-mail query. Samples are not filed. Portfolio review not required. Buys all rights. Originals are not returned. Pays by the hour. Finds artists through agents, sourcebooks, magazines, word of mouth and artists' submissions.

CAPE SHORE, INC.

86 Downeast Dr., Yarmouth ME 04096. (800)343-2424. **Fax:** (800)457-7087. **E-mail:** webmail@cape-shore.com. **Website:** www.cape-shore.com. **Contact:** creative director. Estab. 1947. "Cape Shore is concerned with seeking, manufacturing and distributing a quality line of gifts and stationery for the souvenir and gift market." Licenses art by noted illustrators with a track record for paper products and giftware. Guidelines available online.

NEEDS Approached by 100 freelancers/year. Works with 50 freelancers/year. Buys 400 freelance designs and illustrations/year. Prefers artists and product designers with experience in gift product, hanging ornament and stationery markets. Art guidelines available free for SASE. Uses freelance illustration for boxed note cards, Christmas cards, ornaments, home accessories, ceramics and other paper products. Considers all media. Looking for skilled wood carvers with a warm, endearing folk art style for holiday gift products.

FIRST CONTACT & TERMS "Do not call; no exceptions." Send query letter with color copies. Samples are filed or are returned by SASE. Art director will contact artist for portfolio review if interested. Portfolio should include finished samples, printed samples. Pays for design by the project, advance on royalties or negotiable flat fee. Buys varying rights according to project. "Please submit your art on a cd with a few representative color copies. If your art is appropriate for us we will keep your portfolio on file and call you when we are interested in licensing it or commissioning something similar. If you would like your submission returned, please enclose a SASE."

TIPS "Cape Shore is looking for realistic detail, good technique, and traditional themes or very high quality contemporary looks for coastal as well as inland markets. We will sometimes buy art for a full line of products, or we may buy art for a single note or gift item. Proven success in the giftware field a plus, but will consider new talent and exceptional unpublished illustrators."

CARDMAKERS

424 Fore St., Portland ME 04101. (207)761-4279. **E-mail:** info@cardmakers.com. **Website:** www.card makers.com. Estab. 1978. "We produce cards for special interests and greeting cards for businesses—primarily Christmas-themed. We also publish everyday cards for stockbrokers and boaters."

NEEDS Approached by more than 300 freelancers/year. Works with 5-10 freelancers/year. Buys approx. 10 designs and illustrations/year. Prefers professional-caliber artists. Art guidelines available on website only. "Please do not e-mail us for same." Works on assignment only. Uses freelancers mainly for greeting card design and calligraphy. Considers all media. "We market 5×7 cards designed to appeal to individual's specific interest-boating, building, cycling, stocks and bonds, etc." Prefers an upscale look. Submit seasonal ideas 6-9 months in advance.

FIRST CONTACT & TERMS Submit via online submission form. Artists may submit 6-8 JPEGs at 72 dpi.

TIPS "We like to see new work in the early part of the year. Getting published and gaining experience should be the main objective of freelancers entering the field. We favor fresh talent (but do also feature seasoned talent). PLEASE be patient waiting to hear from us! Make sure your work is equal to or better than that which is commonly found in use presently. Go to a large greeting card store. If you think you're as good or better than the artists there, continue!"

CENTRIC CORP.

6712 Melrose Ave., Los Angeles CA 90038. (323)936-2100. **Fax:** (323)936-2101. **E-mail:** centric@juno.com. **Website:** www.centriccorp.com. Estab. 1986. Produces products such as watches, pens, T-shirts, pillows, clocks, and mugs. Specializes in products that feature nostalgic, humorous, thought-provoking images or sayings on them and some classic licensed celebrities. **NEEDS** Looking for freelancers who know Photoshop, InDesign and Illustrator well.
FIRST CONTACT & TERMS Send examples of your work. Pays when project is completed.
TIPS "Research the demographics of buyers who purchase Elvis, Lucy, Marilyn Monroe, James Dean, Betty Boop and Bettie Page products to know how to 'communicate a message' to the buyer."

CITY MERCHANDISE, INC.

228 40th St., Brooklyn NY 11232. (718)832-2931. **Fax:** (718)832-2939. **E-mail:** city@citymerchandise.com. **Website:** www.citymerchandise.com. Produces calendars, collectible figurines, gifts, mugs, souvenirs of New York.
NEEDS Works with 6-10 freelancers/year. Buys 50-100 freelance designs and illustrations/year. "We buy sculptures for our casting business." Prefers freelancers with experience in graphic design. Works on assignment only. Uses freelancers for most projects. Considers all media. 50% of design and 80% of illustration demand knowledge of Photoshop, QuarkXPress, Illustrator. Does not produce holiday material.
FIRST CONTACT & TERMS Designers: Send query letter with brochure, photocopies, résumé. Illustrators or cartoonists: Send postcard sample of work only. Sculptors: Send résumé and slides, photos or photocopies of their work. Samples are filed. Include SASE for return of samples. Responds in 2 weeks. Portfolios required for sculptors only if interested in artist's work. Buys all rights. Pays by project.

COMSTOCK CARDS

1344 Disc Dr., #185, Sparks NV 89436. (800)326-7825. **Fax:** (888)266-2610. **E-mail:** production@cmpmarket. com. **Website:** www.comstockmarketplace.com. Estab. 1986. Produces greeting cards, giftbags and invi-

tations. Styles include alternative and adult humor, outrageous and shocking themes. Art guidelines available for SASE with first-class postage.
NEEDS Approached by 250-350 freelancers/year. Works with 30-35 freelancers/year. "Especially seeking artists able to produce outrageous adult-oriented cartoons." Uses freelancers mainly for cartoon greeting cards. No verse or prose. Gaglines must be brief. Prefers 5×7 final art. Produces material for all occasions. Submit holiday concepts 6 months in advance.
FIRST CONTACT & TERMS Send query letter with SASE, tearsheets or photocopies. Samples are not usually filed and are returned by SASE if requested. Responds only if interested. Portfolio review not required. Originals are not returned. Pays royalties of 5%. Pays by the project, $50-150 minimum; may negotiate other arrangements. Buys all rights.
TIPS "Submit with SASE if you want material returned."

COURAGE CARDS

Courage Kenny Cards, 1750 Tower Blvd., North Mankato MN 56003. (800)992-6872. **E-mail:** artsearch@couragecenter.org. **Website:** www.couragecards.org. Estab. 1958. "Courage Cards is a greeting card company that produces a holiday card collection to support the programs of Courage Kenny Rehabilitation Institute, a nonprofit rehabilitation and resource center advancing the lives of people with disabilities."
NEEDS Seeking colorful holiday artwork that is appropriate for greeting cards, including traditional Christmas, city scenes, winter landscape, peace, international and fall seasonal images. Courage Cards supports the works of artists with a disability, but all artists are encouraged to enter the annual Courage Card Art Search.
FIRST CONTACT & TERMS Submit online, or call or e-mail name and address to receive Art Search guidelines, which are mailed in September for the November 30 entry deadline. Do not send original artwork! Responds within 5 months. Submissions returned with an SASE. Courage Cards pays a licensing fee of $400 per selected image chosen, which secures reprint rights for Courage Cards for 5 years. Artist retains ownership of their artwork. Artists are recognized through a nationwide distribution of more than 900,000 catalogs and promotional pieces, Internet, radio, TV and print advertising.

CREATIF LICENSING

31 Old Town Crossing, Mt. Kisco NY 10549-4030. (914)241-6211. **E-mail:** info@creatifusa.com. **Website:** www.creatifusa.com. Estab. 1975. "Creatif is a licensing agency that represents artists and brands." Licensing art for commercial applications on consumer products in the gift, stationery and home furnishings industries.

NEEDS Looking for unique art styles or concepts that are applicable to multiple products and categories.

FIRST CONTACT & TERMS Send e-mail query or letter with photocopies, photographs, SASE or tearsheets. Accepts e-mail attachments and will review website links. Responds in 1 month. Samples are returned with SASE. Creatif will obtain licensing agreements on behalf of the artists, negotiate and manage the licensing programs and pay royalties. Artists are responsible for filing all copyright and trademark. Requires exclusive representation of artists. Also, the exclusivity is for "core" artists, meaning artists we work with day in day out. We will represent artists on a non-exclusive basis if their art has limited but specialized licensing application.

TIPS "We are looking to license talented and committed artists. It is important to understand current trends, and design with specific products in mind."

DALOIA DESIGN

100 Norwich E., West Palm Beach FL 33417-7910. (561)452-4150. **E-mail:** daloiades@aol.com. Estab. 1983. Produces art for stationery and gift products such as magnets, photo frames, coasters, bookmarks, home decor, etc.

NEEDS Approached by 20-30 freelancers/year. Uses freelancers for original and innovative product art. Freelancers must know software appropriate for project.

FIRST CONTACT & TERMS Send samples of your work to be filed and not returned. Responds only if interested. Payment "depends on project and use." Negotiates rights purchased.

TIPS "Keep an open mind, strive for excellence, push limitations."

DELJOU ART GROUP

1616 Huber St., Atlanta GA 30318. (404)350-7190 or (800)237-4638. **Fax:** (404)350-7195. **E-mail:** submit@deljouartgroup.com. **Website:** www.deljouartgroup.com. Estab. 1980. Art publisher, distributor and gallery of original work as well as limited editions, hand-pulled originals, monoprints/monotypes, sculpture, fine art photography, fine art prints and paintings on paper and canvas. Clients: galleries, designers, corporate buyers and architects. Previous and current clients include Coca-Cola, Xerox, Exxon, Marriott Hotels, General Electric, Charter Hospitals, AT&T and more than 3,000 galleries worldwide, "forming a strong network throughout the world."

NEEDS Seeking creative, fine and decorative art for the designer market and serious collectors. Considers oil, acrylic, pastel, sculpture, mixed media and photography. Artists represented include Craig Alan, Yunessi, T.L. Lange, Michael Emani, Vincent George, Nela Soloman, Alterra, Ivan Reyes, Mindeli, Sanford Wakeman, Niro Vessali, Lee White, Alexa Kelemen, Bika, Kamy, Roya Azim, Jian Chang, Elya DeChino, Antonio Dojer, Emanuel Mattini, Lun Tse, Martin Quen, Cecil K. Seika, Prescott, J. Kani, Say and Mia Stone. Editions are created by collaborating with the artist. Approached by 300 artists/year. Publishes the work of 10 emerging, 20 mid-career and 20 established artists/year.

FIRST CONTACT & TERMS "All submissions to be made via postal mail or e-mail. If sending hard copy material, it will be returned only if a self-addressed, postage-paid envelope is included. Send a minimum of 5 images from your portfolio. Images should be in JPG format, smaller than 5MB each. Please include the following for all artwork: Title, Medium, Dimensions, and Retail Pricing. Include all contact information including a biography, website, artist statement, exhibition history, email and phone number. Allow 4-6 weeks for the review process. If we select your work for further consideration we will contact you directly. Notifications are not sent for submissions which do not make it to the next phase of consideration. You may submit your work at a later date, please allow at least 2 months from your original submission date."

TIPS "We need landscape artists, 3D wall art (any media), strong figurative artists, sophisticated abstracts and soft-edge abstracts. We are also beginning to publish sculptures and are interested in seeing slides of such. We also have the largest gallery in the country. We have added an art consulting and hospitality division and need images in different categories for our print on demand collection."

DELTA CREATIVE, INC.

3225 Westech Dr., Norcross GA 30092. (800)842-4197. **E-mail:** advisor@deltacreative.com; general@plaidonlinemail.com. **Website:** www.deltacreative.com. Estab. 1978. Produces art and novelty rubber stamps, kits, glitter pens, ink pads, papers, stickers, scrapbooking products.

NEEDS Approached by 30 freelance artists/year. Works with 10-20 freelance artists/year. Buys 200-300 freelance designs and illustrations/year. Uses freelance artists for calligraphy, P-O-P displays, and original art for rubber stamps. Considers pen & ink. Looks for whimsical, feminine style and fashion trends. Produces seasonal material Christmas, Valentine's Day, Easter, Hanukkah, Thanskgiving, Halloween, birthdays and everyday (includes wedding, baby, travel, and other life events). Submit seasonal material 9 months in advance.

FIRST CONTACT & TERMS Send nonreturnable samples. Samples are filed. Responds only if interested. Rights purchased vary according to project. Originals are not returned.

DESIGN DESIGN, INC.

19 La Grave Ave., Grand Rapids MI 49503. (616)771-8319; (866)935-2648. **E-mail:** susan.birnbaum@designdesign.us; retailhelp@designdesign.us; tom.vituj@designdesign.us. **Website:** www.designdesign.us. Estab. 1986. Specializes in greeting cards and paper-related product development.

NEEDS Uses freelancers for all of the above products. Considers most media. Produces cards for everyday and all holidays. Submit seasonal material 1 year in advance.

FIRST CONTACT & TERMS Send query letter with appropriate samples and SASE. Samples are not filed and are returned by SASE if requested by artist. To show portfolio, send color copies, photographs or slides. Do not send originals. Pays various royalties per product development.

EMERY-BURTON FINE CARDS & GIFTS

P.O. Box 31130, Seattle WA 98103. (866)617-1259. **Fax:** (866)617-8424. **E-mail:** info@emery-burton.com. **Website:** www.emery-burton.com. Produces greeting cards.

NEEDS Product categories include conventional, counter humor and cute. Produces material for Mother's Day, Valentine's Day, Christmas, birthday, cards for pets, congratulations, baby congrats, woman-to-woman, wedding/anniversary, getwell/sympathy and everyday. Seasonal material should be submitted 6 months in advance. Final art should be 5×7. 100% of freelance work demands computer skills; artists should be familiar with Illustrator, Photoshop and InDesign. No need for freelance Web design.

FIRST CONTACT & TERMS Send query letter with SASE, or e-mail digital images (TIFF at 300 dpi). Samples not kept on file; returned by SASE.

ENESCO GROUP, INC.

225 Windsor Dr., Itasca IL 60143. (630)875-5300. **E-mail:** dbernar@enesco.com. **Website:** www.enesco.com. Producer and importer of fine gifts, home decor and collectibles, such as resin, porcelain bisque and earthenware figurines, plates, hanging ornaments, bells, picture frames, decorative housewares. Clients gift stores, card shops and department stores.

NEEDS Works with multiple freelance artists/year. Prefers artists with experience in gift product and packaging development. Uses freelancers for rendering, illustration and sculpture. 50% of freelance work demands knowledge of Photoshop, QuarkXPress or Illustrator.

FIRST CONTACT & TERMS Submit via "product idea and artist submissions" form on website. Accepts .bmp, .flv, .gif, .jpg, .mov, .mpeg, .mpg, .png, .ppt, .rm, .tif or .wmv formats.

TIPS "All will be reviewed by our senior creative director, executive vice president and licensing director. If your talent is a good match to Enesco's product development, we will contact you to discuss further arrangements. Please do not send slides. Have a well-thought-out concept that relates to gift products before mailing your submissions."

EPIC PRODUCTS, INC.

2801 S. Yale St., Santa Ana CA 92704. (800)548-9791. **Fax:** (714)641-8217. **E-mail:** info@epicproductsinc.com. **Website:** www.epicproductsinc.com. Estab. 1978. Produces paper tableware products and wine and spirits accessories. "We manufacture products for the gourmet/housewares market; specifically products that are wine-related. Many have a design printed on them."

NEEDS Approached by 50-75 freelance artists/year. Works with 10-15 freelancers/year. Buys 25-50 designs and illustrations/year. Prefers artists with experience in gourmet/housewares, wine and spirits, gift and stationery.

FIRST CONTACT & TERMS Send query letter with résumé and photocopies. Samples are filed. Write for appointment to show portfolio. Portfolio should include thumbnails, roughs, final art, b&w and color. Buys all rights. Originals are not returned. Pays by the project.

FENTON ART GLASS CO.

700 Elizabeth St., Williamstown WV 26187. (304)375-6122. **Fax:** (304)375-7833. **E-mail:** askfenton@fentonartglass.com. **Website:** www.fentonartglass.com. Estab. 1905. Produces collectible figurines, gifts. Largest manufacturer of handmade colored glass in the US.

○ Design director Nancy Fenton says this company rarely uses freelancers because they have their own staff of artisans. "Glass molds aren't very forgiving," says Fenton. Consequently it's a difficult medium to work with. There have been exceptions. "We were really taken with Linda Higdon's work," says Fenton, who worked with Higdon on a line of historical dresses.

NEEDS Uses freelancers mainly for sculpture and ceramic projects that can be translated into glass collectibles. Considers clay, ceramics, porcelain figurines. Looking for traditional artwork appealing to collectibles market.

FIRST CONTACT & TERMS Send query letter with brochure, photocopies, photographs, résumé and SASE. Samples are filed. Responds only if interested. Negotiates rights purchased. Pays for design by the project; negotiable.

FIDDLER'S ELBOW

101 Fiddler's Elbow Rd., Greenwich NY 12838. (518)692-9665. **Fax:** (518)692-9186. **E-mail:** john@fiddlerselbow.com; licensing@fiddlerselbow.com. **Website:** www.fiddlerselbow.com. Estab. 1974. Produces decorative doormats, pillows, totes, soft sculpture, kitchen textiles, mouse pads, mugs.

NEEDS Introduces 100+ new products/year. Currently uses freelance designs and illustrations. Looking for adult contemporary, traditional, dog, cat, horse, botanical, inspirational, humorous, nature and beach themes. Main images with supporting art helpful in producing collections.

FIRST CONTACT & TERMS Send digital or hardcopy submissions by mail. Samples are filed or returned by SASE. Responds generally within 4 months if interested. "Please, no phone calls."

TIPS "Please visit website first to see if art is applicable to current lines and products."

FISHER-PRICE

636 Girard Ave. E., Aurora NY 14052. (716)687-3000. **Fax:** (716)687-3636. **Website:** www.fisher-price.com. Estab. 1931. Manufacturer of toys and other children's products.

NEEDS Approached by 10-15 freelance artists/year. Works with 25-30 freelance illustrators and sculptors and 15-20 freelance graphic designers/year. Assigns 100-150 jobs to freelancers/year. Prefers artists with experience in children's style illustration and graphics. Works on assignment only. Uses freelancers mainly for product decoration (label art). Prefers all media and styles except loose watercolor. Also uses sculptors. 25% of work demands knowledge of FreeHand, Illustrator, Photoshop and FreeForm (sculptors).

FIRST CONTACT & TERMS Send query letter with nonreturnable samples showing art style or photographs. Samples are filed. Responds only if interested. Call to schedule an appointment to show a portfolio. Portfolio should include original, final art and color photographs and transparencies. Pays for design and illustration by the hour, $25-50. Buys all rights.

FOTOFOLIO, INC.

561 Broadway, New York NY 10012. (212)226-0923. **E-mail:** contact@fotofolio.com; submissions@fotofolio.com. **Website:** www.fotofolio.com. **Contact:** Submissions department. Estab. 1976. Publishes art and photographic postcards, greeting cards, notebooks, books, T-shirts and postcard books.

NEEDS Buys 60-120 freelance designs and illustrations/year. Reproduces existing works. Primarily interested in photography and contemporary art. Produces material for Christmas, Valentine's Day, birthday and everyday. Submit seasonal material 8 months in advance. Art guidelines with SASE with first-class postage.

FIRST CONTACT & TERMS "Fotofolio, Inc. reviews color and b&w photography for publication in postcard, notecard, poster and T-shirt formats. To submit your work, please make a well-edited selection of no more than 40 images, attn: Submissions. Fotofolio will accept photocopies, laser copies and promotional pieces only. Fotofolio will not accept digital images via e-mail to be downloaded or digital files submitted on disk. You may e-mail a website address where your work may be viewed. You'll be contacted if we are interested in seeing further work. Please note that Fotofolio, Inc. is not responsible for any lost or damaged submissions."

TIPS "When submitting materials, present a variety of your work (no more than 40 images) rather than one subject/genre."

THE FRANKLIN MINT

US Rt. 1, Franklin Center PA 19091-0001. (610)459-6000. **Website:** www.franklinmint.com. Estab. 1964. Franklin Center PA 19091-0001. (610)459-7975. **Fax:** (610)459-6463. **Website:** www.franklinmint.com. **Contact:** Cathy La Spada, art relations manager. Estab. 1964. Direct response marketing of high-quality collectibles. Produces collectible porcelain plates, prints, porcelain and coldcast sculpture, figurines, fashion and traditional jewelry, ornaments, precision diecast model cars, luxury board games, engineered products, heirloom dolls and plush, home decor items and unique gifts. Clients general public worldwide, proprietary houselist of 8 million collectors and 55 owned-and-operated retail stores. Markets products in countries worldwide, including US, Canada, UK and Japan.

NEEDS Approached by 3,000 freelance artists/year. Contracts 500 artists/sculptors per year to work on 7,000-8,000 projects. Uses freelancers mainly for illustration and sculpture. Considers all media. Considers all styles. 80% of freelance design and 50% of illustration demand knowledge of PageMaker, FreeHand, Photoshop, Illustrator, QuarkXPress and 3D Studio Eclipse (2D). Accepts work in SGI format. Produces material for Christmas and everyday.

FIRST CONTACT & TERMS Send query letter, résumé, SASE and samples (clear, professional full-color photographs, transparencies, slides, greeting cards and/or brochures and tearsheets). Sculptors send photographic portfolios. Do not send original artwork. Samples are filed or returned by SASE. Responds in 2 months. Portfolio review required for illustrators and sculptors. Company gives feedback on all portfolios submitted. Payment varies.

TIPS "In search of artists and sculptors capable of producing high quality work. Those willing to take art direction and to make revisions of their work are encouraged to submit their portfolios."

THE FUNNY APRON CO.

P.O. Box 1780, Lake Dallas TX 75065-1780. (940)498-3308. **Fax:** (940)498-1596. **E-mail:** info@funnyaprons.

com. **Website:** www.funnyaproncompany.com. **Contact:** Ellice Lovelady, creative director. Estab. 1992. "Our primary focus is now on our subdivision, The Funny Apron Co., that manufactures humorous culinary-themed aprons and T-shirts for the gourmet marketplace. Do not send greeting card submissions!"

NEEDS Works with 6 freelancers/year. Artists must be fax/e-mail accessible and able to work on fast turnaround. Check website to determine if your style fits our art direction. 100% of freelance work requires knowledge of Illustrator, CorelDraw, or programs with ability to electronically send vector-based artwork for screenprinting. Do not submit text or concepts. (Photoshop alone is not sufficient.) Currently not accepting text or concepts.

FIRST CONTACT & TERMS Send query letter with brochure, photographs, SASE and photocopies. E-mail inquiries must include a link to a website to view artwork. Do not send unsolicited attachments; they are automatically deleted. Samples are filed or returned by SASE if requested by artist. Company will contact artist if interested. Negotiates rights and payment terms. Finds artists via word of mouth from other freelancers or referrals from publishers.

GALISON/MUDPUPPY

28 W. 44th St., New York NY 10036. (212)354-8840. **E-mail:** sko@galison.com (Galison submissions); emily@galison.com (Mudpuppy submissions). **Website:** www.galison.com. Estab. 1978. Produces boxed greeting cards, stationery, puzzles, address books, specialty journals and fine paper gifts. Many projects are done in collaboration with museums around the world.

NEEDS Buys 100 designs and illustrations/year. Works on assignment only. Uses freelancers mainly for illustration. Considers all media. Also produces material for holidays (Christmas, Hanukkah and New Year). Submit seasonal material 1 year in advance. (Submit to above e-mails via PDF only.)

FIRST CONTACT & TERMS Send postcard sample, photocopies, résumé, tearsheets (no unsolicited original artwork) and SASE. Accepts submissions on disk compatible with Photoshop, Illustrator or QuarkXPress (but not preferred). Samples are filed. Responds only if interested. Request portfolio review in original query. Art director will contact artist for portfolio review if interested. Portfolio should include color photostats, slides, tearsheets and dummies. Originals are returned at job's completion. Pays by project. Rights purchased vary according to project. Finds artists through word of mouth, magazines and artists' reps.

TIPS "Looking for great presentation and artwork we think will sell and be competitive within the gift market. Please visit our website to see if your style is compatible with our design aesthetic."

GALLANT GREETINGS CORP.

(800)621-4279; (847)671-6500. **Fax:** (847)671-7500. **E-mail:** info@gallantgreetings.com; custserv@gallantgreetings.com. **Website:** www.gallantgreetings.com. Estab. 1966. "Creator and publisher of seasonal and everyday greeting cards. Send low-res JPEG files (no more than 12 at a time) to the attention of our Creative Department, using the subject line 'New Art Submission'. If you cannot send via e-mail we will accept color copies no larger than 8½×11. No original artwork, please! Include your name, address, phone number, e-mail address and date on each submission. Submissions will not be returned if we are not provided with a SASE. Please be patient! Our review committee receives many submissions, which we try to attend to in a timely manner. If we feel we have an immediate use for your work, we will notify you and discuss our process and compensation at that time."

FIRST CONTACT & TERMS Samples are filed or returned. Will respond within 3 weeks if interested. Do not send originals.

C.R. GIBSON

402 BNA Dr., Bldg. 100, Suite 600, Nashville TN 37217. (615)724-2900. **E-mail:** customerservice@crgibson.com. **Website:** www.crgibson.com. Producer of stationery and gift products, baby, kitchen and wedding collections. Specializes in baby, children, feminine, floral, wedding and kitchen-related subjects, as well as holiday designs. 80% require freelance illustration; 15% require freelance design. Gift catalog free by request.

NEEDS Approached by 200-300 freelance artists/year. Works with 30-50 illustrators and 10-30 designers/year. Assigns 30-50 design and 30-50 illustration jobs/year. Uses freelancers mainly for covers, borders and cards. 50% of freelance work demands knowledge of QuarkXPress, FreeHand and Illustrator. Works on assignment only.

FIRST CONTACT & TERMS Send query letter with brochure, résumé, tearsheets and photocopies. Samples are filed or are returned. Responds only if interested. Request portfolio review in original query.

Portfolio should include thumbnails, finished art samples, color tearsheets and photographs. Return of original artwork contingent on contract. Sometimes requests work on spec before assigning a job. Interested in buying second rights (reprint rights) to previously published work. "Payment varies due to complexity and deadlines." Finds artists through word of mouth, magazines, artists' submissions/self-promotion, sourcebooks, agents, visiting artist's exhibitions, art fairs and artists' reps.

TIPS "The majority of our mechanical art is executed on the computer with discs and laser runouts given to the engraver. Please give a professional presentation of your work."

GLITTERWRAP, INC.

11 Executive Ave., Edison NJ 08817. (732)662-6700; (800)654-6960. **E-mail:** info@designergreetings.com; submissions@designergreetings.com. **Website:** www.glitterwrap.com. Estab. 1987. Produces giftwrap, gift totes, allied accessories, photo albums, diaries and stationery items for all ages—party and special occasion market.

NEEDS Art/graphic designer submissions: Works with 10-15 artists/year. Buys 10-30 designs and illustrations/year. Art guidelines available online. Prefers artists with experience in textile design who are knowledgeable in repeat patterns or surface, or designers who have experience with the gift industry. Considers many styles and mediums. Style varies with season and year. Consider trends and designs already in line, as well as up-and-coming motifs in gift market. Produces material for baby, wedding and shower, florals, masculine, Christmas, graduation, birthdays, Valentine's Day, Hanukkah and everyday. Submit seasonal material 9 months in advance.

FIRST CONTACT & TERMS Send an e-mail with samples in JPEG format at 150 dpi. Responds only if interested. Does not accept submissions via mail. Rights purchased vary according to project. Freelancers paid $200/project.

GLM CONSULTING

366 Amsterdam Ave., #159, New York NY 10024. (212)683-5830. **Fax:** (212)779-8564. **E-mail:** george@glmconsultart.com. **Website:** www.glmconsultart.com. Estab. 1967. Sells reproduction rights of designs to manufacturers of multiple products around the world. Rep resents artists in 50 different countries. "Our clients specialize in greeting cards, giftware,

giftwrap, calendars, postcards, prints, posters, stationery, paper goods, food tins, playing cards, tabletop, bath and service ware and much more. "

NEEDS Approached by several hundred artists/year. Seeking creative decorative art in traditional and computer media (Photoshop and Illustrator work accepted). Prefers artwork previously made with few or no rights pending. Graphics, sports, occasions (e.g., Christmas, baby, birthday, wedding), humorous, "soft touch," romantic themes, animals. Accepts seasonal/holiday material any time. Prefers artists/designers experienced in greeting cards, paper products, tabletop and giftware.

FIRST CONTACT & TERMS Please submit via e-mail, a link to your website or a sampling of your work, consisting of 6-10 designs which represent your collection as a whole. The sampling should show all range of subject matter, technique, style, and medium that may exist in your collection. Digital files should be submitted as e-mail attachments and in low-res. Low-res (LR) image files are typically 5×7, 72 dpi, CMYK, JPERG/TIFF/PDF format and are under 100 KB. "Once your art is accepted, we require original color art—Photoshop files on disc (TIFF, 300 dpi). We will respond only if interested." Pays on publication. No credit line given. Offers advance when appropriate. Sells one-time rights and exclusive product rights. Simultaneous submissions and previously published work OK. "Please state reserved rights, if any."

TIPS Recommends the annual New York SURTEX and Licensing shows. In portfolio samples, wants to see "a neat presentation, thematic in arrangement, consisting of a series of interrelated images (at least 6). In addition to having good drawing/painting/designing skills, artists should be aware of market needs and trends."

GOES LITHOGRAPHING CO.

111 Hallberg St., Delavan WI 53115. (800)348-6700. **E-mail:** sales@goeslitho.com. **Website:** www.goeslitho.com. **Contact:** Eric Goes. Estab. 1879. Produces stationery/letterheads, custom calendars to sell to printers and office product stores.

NEEDS Approached by 5-10 freelance artists/year. Works with 2-3 freelance artists/year. Buys 4-30 freelance designs and illustrations/year. Art guidelines for SASE with first-class postage. Uses freelance artists mainly for designing holiday letterheads. Considers pen & ink, color, acrylic, watercolor. Prefers final art

17×22, CMYK color compatible. Produces material for Christmas, Halloween and Thanksgiving.

FIRST CONTACT & TERMS "Send nonreturnable examples for your ideas." Responds in 1-2 months if interested. Pays $100-200 on final acceptance. Buys first rights and reprint rights.

TIPS "Keep your art fresh and be aggressive with submissions."

GRAHAM & BROWN

239 Prospect Plains Rd., Suite D201, Monroe Township NJ 08831. (609)395-9200; (800)554-0887. **E-mail:** publicrelations@grahambrownusa.com. **Website:** www.grahambrown.com. Estab. 1946. Produces residential wall coverings and home decor products.

NEEDS Prefers freelancers for designs. Also for artwork. Produces material for everyday.

FIRST CONTACT & TERMS Designers: Send query letter with photographs. Illustrators: Send postcard sample of work. Samples are filed or returned. Responds only if interested. Buys all rights. For illustration pays a variable flat fee.

GREAT ARROW GRAPHICS

2495 Main St., Suite 457, Buffalo NY 14214. (716)836-0408. **E-mail:** design@greatarrow.com. **Website:** www.greatarrow.com. **Contact:** Denise Ryan. Estab. 1981. Produces greeting cards and stationery. "We produce silkscreened greeting cards—seasonal and everyday—to a high-end design-conscious market."

NEEDS Approached by 150 freelancers/year. Works with 75 freelancers/year. Buys 350-500 images/year. Prefers freelancers with experience in silkscreen printing process. Uses freelancers for greeting card design only. Considers all 2D media. Looking for sophisticated, classic, contemporary or cutting edge styles. Requires knowledge of Illustrator or Photoshop. Produces material for all holidays and seasons. Submit seasonal material 1 year in advance.

FIRST CONTACT & TERMS Please send digital submissions with link to portfolio or JPEGs at 72 dpi. Limit e-mail attachment size to 5 MB. Responds in 6 weeks if we are interested. Art director will contact artist for portfolio review if interested. Portfolio should include color roughs, final art, photographs and transparencies. Originals are returned at job's completion. Pays royalties of 5% of net sales. Rights purchased vary according to project.

TIPS "We are interested in artists familiar with the assets and limitations of screenprinting, but we are always looking for fun new ideas and are willing to give help and guidance in the silkscreen process. Be original, be complete with ideas. Don't be afraid to be different .. forget the trends .. do what you want. Make your work as complete as possible at first submission. The National Stationery Show in New York City is a great place to make contacts."

⊙ HAMPSHIRE PEWTER CO.

350 Rt. 108, Unit 201, Somersworth NII 03878. (603)569-4944. **E-mail:** gifts@hampshirepewter. com. **Website:** www.hampshirepewter.com. Estab. 1974. Manufacturer of handcast pewter tableware, accessories and Christmas ornaments. Clients jewelry stores, department stores, executive gift buyers, tabletop and pewter specialty stores, churches and private consumers.

NEEDS Works with 3-4 freelance artists/year. "Prefers New England or East Coast-based artists." Works on assignment only. Uses freelancers mainly for illustration and models. Also for brochure and catalog design, product design, illustration on product and model-making.

FIRST CONTACT & TERMS Please send e-mail with link to portfolio. Pays for design and sculpture by the hour or project. Considers complexity of project, client's budget and rights purchased when determining payment. Buys all rights.

TIPS "Inform us of your capabilities. For artists who are seeking a manufacturing source, we will be happy to bid on manufacturing of designs under private license to the artists, all of whose design rights are protected. If we commission a project, we intend to have exclusive rights to the designs by contract as defined in the Copyright Law, and we intend to protect those rights."

HARLAND CLARKE

15955 La Cantera Parkway, San Antonio TX 78256. (210)694-1473. **Website:** www.clarkeamerican.com. Estab. 1874. Produces checks and other products and services sold through financial institutions. "We're a national printer seeking original works for check series, consisting of 1, 3 or 5 scenes. Looking for a variety of themes, media and subjects for a wide market appeal."

NEEDS Uses freelancers mainly for illustration and design of personal checks. Considers all media and a range of styles. Prefers to see art at twice the size of a standard check.

FIRST CONTACT & TERMS Send postcard sample or query letter with résumé and brochure (or website if work is online). "Indicate whether the work is available; do not send original art." Samples are filed and are not returned. Responds only if interested. Rights purchased vary according to project. Payment for illustration varies by the project.

TIPS "Keep red and black in the illustration to a minimum for image processing."

MARIAN HEATH GREETING CARDS

9 Kendrick Rd., Wareham MA 02571. **E-mail:** dreposa@marianheath.com; submissions@marianheath. com. **Website:** www.marianheath.com. **Contact:** Diane Reposa, licensing agent. Publishes greeting cards.

NEEDS Model and property release preferred. Art guidelines available with SASE.

FIRST CONTACT & TERMS Send color copies via e-mail or on CD as JPEG files. Submission should be clearly labeled with artists name and identifying number or title if available. Approached by 100 freelancers/year. Works with 35-45 freelancers/year. Buys 500 freelance designs and illustrations/year. Prefers freelancers with experience in social expression. Art guidelines free for SASE with first-class postage or e-mail requesting guidelines. Uses freelancers mainly for greeting cards. Considers all media and styles. Generally 5¼×7¼ unless otherwise directed. Will accept various sizes due to digital production/manipulation. 30% of freelance design and illustration work demands knowledge of Photoshop, Illustrator, QuarkXPress. Produces material for all holidays and seasons and everyday. Submit seasonal material 1 year in advance. "If you wish samples to be returned, please indicate so and include postage-paid packaging."

HOFFMASTER GROUP, INC.

2920 N. Main St., Oshkosh WI 54901. (800)327-9774. **E-mail:** marketing@hoffmaster.com. **Website:** www. hoffmaster.com. Produces decorative disposable paper tableware including: placemats, plates, tablecloths and napkins for institutional and consumer markets. Printing includes offset, letterpress and up to 6 color flexographic napkin printing.

NEEDS Approached by 5-10 freelancers/year. Works with 3-4 freelancers/year. Prefers freelancers with experience in paper tableware products. Art guidelines and specific design needs based on current market are available from art managers. Looking for trends and traditional styles. Produces material for all holidays and seasons and everyday.

FIRST CONTACT & TERMS Send query letter with photocopies, résumé, appropriate samples by mail, fax or e-mail to marketing@hoffmaster.com. Ideas may be sent in a color rough sketch. Accepts submissions compatible with Adobe CS6. Samples are filed or returned by SASE if requested by artist. Responds in 90 days, only if interested. Creative manager will contact artist for portfolio review if interested. Prefers to buy artwork outright. Rights purchased vary according to project. Pays by the project. Amounts vary according to project. May work on a royalty arrangement for recognized properties. Finds freelancers through art fairs and artists' reps.

TIPS "Looking for new trends and designs appropriate for placemats, plates and napkins."

ⓘ IGPC

161 Helen St., South Plainfield NJ 07080. (908)548-8088. **Fax:** (908)822-7379. **E-mail:** frontdesk@igpc.com. **Website:** www.igpc.net. Agent to foreign governments. "We produce postage stamps and related items on behalf of 40 different foreign governments."

NEEDS Approximately 10 freelance graphic artists. Prefers artists within metropolitan New York or Tri-State area. Must have extremely sophisticated computer, design and composition and prepress skills, as well as keen research ability. Artwork must be focused and alive (4-color). Artist's pricing needs to be competitive. Works on assignment only. Uses artists for postage stamp art. Must have expert knowledge of Photoshop and Quark/InDesign. Illustrator a plus.

FIRST CONTACT & TERMS E-mail only. Send samples as PDFs or link to a web portfolio. Art Director will contact artist for portfolio review if interested. Portfolio should contain "4-color illustrations of realistic, flora, fauna, technical subjects, autos or ships." Sometimes requests work on spec before assigning a job. Pays by the project. Consider government allowance per project when establishing payment.

TIPS "Artists considering working with IGPC must have excellent drawing or rendering abilities in general or specific topics—e.g., flora, fauna, transport, famous people—typographical skills; the ability to create artwork with clarity and perfection. Familiarity with printing process and print call-outs a plus. Generally, the work we require is realistic art. In some cases, we supply the basic layout and reference material; however, we appreciate an artist who knows where to find references and can present new and interesting concepts. Initial contact should be made by appointment. "

INKADINKADO, INC.

1801 N. 12th St., Reading PA 19604. (610)939-9900 or (800)523-8452. **Fax:** (610)939-9666. **E-mail:** inkacustomerservice@eksuccess.com. **Website:** www.inkadinkado.com. **Contact:** Mark Nelson, licensing contact; Pamela Keller, designer relations coordinator. Estab. 1978. Creates artistic rubber stamps, craft kits, and craft accessories. Also offers licenses to illustrators depending upon number of designs interested in producing and range of style by artist. Distributes to craft, gift and toy stores and specialty catalogs.

NEEDS Works mainly with in house illustrators and designers. Uses freelancers mainly for illustration, lettering, line drawing, type design. Considers pen & ink. Themes include animals, education, holidays and nature. Prefers small; about 3×3. work demands knowledge of Photoshop, Illustrator and InDesign. Produces material for all holidays and seasons. Submit seasonal material 6-8 months in advance.

FIRST CONTACT & TERMS Designers and Illustrators: Send query letter with 6 non-returnable samples. Accepts submissions on disk. Samples are filed and not returned. Responds only if interested. Company will contact artist for portfolio review of b&w and final art if interested. Pays for illustration by the project, $100-250/piece. Rights purchased vary according to project. Stamps, pays $50-100/project.

TIPS "Work small. The average size of an artistic rubber stamp is 3×3. Line art without color stands the best chance of acceptance."

JILLSON & ROBERTS

3300 W. Castor St., Santa Ana CA 92704-3908. (714)424-0111. **Fax:** (714)424-0054. **E-mail:** sales@jillsonroberts.com. **Website:** www.jillsonroberts.com. **Contact:** Art Director. Estab. 1974. Specializes in gift wrap, totes, printed tissues and accessories using recycled/recyclable products. Art guidelines available on website.

NEEDS Works with 10 freelance artists/year. Prefers artists with experience in giftwrap design. Considers all media. "We are looking for colorful graphic designs as well as humorous, sophisticated, elegant or contemporary styles." Produces material for Christmas, Valentine's Day, Hanukkah, Halloween, graduation, birthdays, baby announcements and everyday. Submit 3-6 months before holiday.

FIRST CONTACT & TERMS Send color copies or photocopies. Samples are kept on file. Responds in up to 2 months. Simultaneous submissions to other companies is acceptable. "If your work is chosen, we will contact you to discuss final art preparation, procedures and payment."

TIPS "We are particularly interested in baby shower and wedding shower designs."

JODDS

P.O. Box 353, Bicester OX27 0GS, United Kingdom. +44 1869 278550. **E-mail:** joddscard@hotmail.co.uk. **Website:** www.joddscards.com. **Contact:** Jill Payne, art director. Estab. 1988. "Jodds produces innovative design-led birthday cards, occasion cards and stationery products. Our full product range includes gift wrap, gift bags, birthday calendars and party invites with matching thank you cards. We print on the highest quality board and use the very latest finishing techniques." Rights purchased vary according to the project.

NEEDS Works with 10 freelancers/year. Need freelancers for animation in counter humor, teen, cute, religious and juvenile themes. Also produce Mother's Day, Christmas, birthday, Father's Day, Valentine's Day, congratulations, wedding/anniversary, get well/sympathy and everyday cards. Seasonal materials should be submitted 9 months in advance. Artists should be familiar with Adobe Photoshop.

FIRST CONTACT & TERMS Send an e-mail with low-resolution JPEGs to: joddscard@hotmail.co.uk. Samples kept on file. Company will contact artist for portfolio review if interested.

KALAN LP

97 S. Union Ave., Lansdowne PA 19050. (610)623-1900; (800) 345-8138. **E-mail:** submissions@kalanlp.com. **Website:** www.kalanlp.com. **Contact:** Chris Wiemer, art director. Estab. 1973. Produces giftbags, greeting cards, school supplies, stationery and novelty items such as keyrings, mouse pads, shot glasses and magnets.

NEEDS Approached by 50-80 freelancers/year. Buys 100 freelance designs and illustrations/year. Art guidelines are available. Uses freelancers mainly for fresh ideas, illustration and design. Considers all media and styles. Some illustration demands knowledge of Photoshop 7.0 and Illustrator 10. Produces material for major holidays such as Christmas, Mother's Day, Valentine's Day; plus birthdays and everyday. Submit seasonal material 9-10 months in advance.

FIRST CONTACT & TERMS Designers: Send query letter with photocopies, photostats and résumé. Illustrators and cartoonists: Send query letter with photocopies and résumé. Accepts disk submissions compatible with Illustrator 10 or Photoshop 7.0. Send EPS files. Samples are filed. Responds in 1 month if interested in artist's work. Will contact artist for portfolio review of final art if interested. Buys first rights. Pays by the project, $75 and up. Finds freelancers through submissions and newspaper ads.

KENZIG KARDS, INC.

2300 Julia Goldbach Ave., Ronkonkoma NY 11779-6317. (631)737-1584. **Fax:** (631)737-8341. **Contact:** Jerry Kenzig, president. Estab. 1999. Produces greeting cards and stationery. Specializes in greeting cards (seasonal and everyday) for a high-end, design-conscious market (all ages).

NEEDS Approached by 75 freelancers/year. Works with 3 freelancers/year. Prefers local designers/illustrators, but will consider freelancers working anywhere in the US. Art guidelines free with SAE and first-class postage. Uses freelancers mainly for greeting cards/design and calligraphy. Considers watercolor, colored pencils and most other mediums. Product categories include alternative/humor, business and cute. Produces material for baby congrats, birthday, cards for pets, Christmas, congratulations, everyday, get well, sympathy, Valentine's Day and wedding/anniversary. Submit seasonal material 6 months in advance. Art size should be 5×7 or 5¾×5¾ square. 20% of freelance work demands knowledge of Illustrator, QuarkXPress and Photoshop.

FIRST CONTACT & TERMS Send query letter with brochure, résumé and tearsheets. After introductory mailing, send follow-up postcard sample every 6 months. Samples are filed. Responds in 2 weeks. Company will contact artist for portfolio review if interested. Portfolio should include color, original art, roughs and tearsheets. Buys one-time rights and reprint rights for cards. Negotiates rights purchased. Pays freelancers by the project, $150-350; royalties (subject to negotiation). Finds freelancers through industry contacts (Kenzig Kards, Inc., is a member of the Greeting Card Association), submissions and word of mouth.

KID STUFF MARKETING

1401 NW Moundview Dr., Suite C, Topeka KS 66618.
(785)862-3707. **E-mail:** michael@kidstuff.com. **Website:** www.kidstuff.com. **Contact:** Michael Oden, senior director of creative. Estab. 1982. Produces collectible figurines, toys, kids' meal sacks, edutainment activities and cartoons for restaurants and entertainment venues worldwide.

NEEDS Approached by 50 freelancers/year. Works with 10 freelancers/year. Buys 30-50 freelance designs and illustrations/year. Works on assignment only. Uses freelancers mainly for illustration, activity or game development and sculpting toys. Looking for humorous, child-related styles. Freelance illustrators should be familiar with Photoshop, Illustrator and InDesign. Produces material for all holidays and everyday themes.

FIRST CONTACT & TERMS Illustrators and Cartoonists: Send e-mail with JPEG or PDF files or link to website. "I DO REVIEW ALL SUBMISSIONS, but only respond if interested." Pays by the project, $250-5,000 for illustration or game activities. Kid Stuff Marketing owns all rights of art or designs after purchase.

THE LANG CO.

P.O. Box 1605, Waukesha WI 53187. (800)967-3399. **Fax:** (262)523-2888. **Website:** www.lang.com. Estab. 1982. Produces high-quality linen-embossed greeting cards, stationery, calendars, boxes and gift items. Art guidelines available for SASE.

NEEDS Approached by 300 freelance artists/year. Works with 40 freelance artists/year. Uses freelancers mainly for card and calendar illustrations. Considers all media and styles. Looking for traditional and nonabstract country-inspired, folk, contemporary and fine art styles. Produces material for Christmas, birthdays and everyday. Submit seasonal material 6 months in advance.

FIRST CONTACT & TERMS Send query letter with SASE and brochure, tearsheets, photostats, photographs, slides, photocopies or transparencies. Samples are returned by SASE if requested by artist. Responds in 6 weeks. Pays royalties based on net wholesale sales. Rights purchased vary according to project.

TIPS "Research the company and submit compatible art. Be patient awaiting a response."

⬙ LANTERN COURT, LLC

P.O. Box 61613, Irvine CA 92602. (800)454-4018; (714)798-2270. **Fax:** (714)798-2281. **E-mail:** art@lanterncourt.com; customerservice@lanterncourt.com. **Website:** www.lanterncourt.com. **Contact:** Seher Zaman, creative director. Estab. 2011. Lantern Court specializes in party supplies and paper goods for the Muslim community or anyone who appreciates Islamic art and design. Produces balloons, calendars, decorations, e-cards, giftbags, giftwrap/wrapping paper, greeting cards, paper tableware, and part supplies. Buys 10-30 freelance designs/illustrations each year. Prefers freelancers with experience in stationery design. Buys stock photos and offers assignments.

NEEDS Uses freelancers for font designs and new designs. Needs Islmaic themed and Muslim holiday related designs. Seasonal material should be submitted 10-12 months in advance. 100% of freelance work demands computer skills. Artists should be familiar with Illustrator, Photoshop, InDesign, and QuarkXPress.

FIRST CONTACT & TERMS Guidelines available free online. E-mail letter with digital images as JPEG or TIFF files at 300 dpi. Keeps samples on file; samples not returned. Responds only if interested. Company will contact artist for portfolio review if interested. Pays by the project. Buys one-time rights. Maximum payment $750.

TIPS "Please look at our website to be sure your work will fit into our line of products, or can be altered to fit in."

LEGACY PUBLISHING GROUP

75 Green St., Clinton MA 01510. (800)322-3866. **E-mail:** info@shoplegacy.com. **Website:** www.shoplegacy.com. **Contact:** art department. Produces bookmarks, calendars, gifts, Christmas and seasonal cards and stationery pads. Specializes in journals, note cards, address and recipe books, coasters, placemats, magnets, book marks, albums, calendars and grocery pads.

NEEDS Works with 8-10 freelancers/year. Buys 25-30 freelance designs and illustrations/year. Prefers traditional art. Art guidelines available for SASE. Works on assignment only. Uses freelancers mainly for original art for product line. Considers all color media. Looking for traditional, contemporary, garden themes and Christmas. Produces material for Christmas, everyday (note cards) and cards for teachers.

FIRST CONTACT & TERMS Illustrators: Send query letter with photocopies, photographs, résumé, tearsheets, SASE and any good reproduction or color copy. We accept work compatible with Adobe or QuarkXPress plus color copies. Samples are filed. Responds in 2 weeks. Company will contact artist for portfolio review if interested. Portfolio should include color photographs, slides, tearsheets and printed reproductions. Buys all rights. Pays by the project. Finds freelancers through word of mouth and artists' submissions.

TIPS "Get work out to as many potential buyers as possible. *Artist's & Graphic Designer's Market* is a good source. Initially, plan on spending 80% of your time on self-promotion."

◯ THE LEMON TREE STATIONERY CORP.

95 Mahan St., West Babylon NY 11704. (631)253-2840; (800)229-3710. **Fax:** (631)253-3369; (800)229-3709. **E-mail:** lucy@lemontreestationery.com. **Website:** www.lemontreestationery.com. **Contact:** Lucy Mleczko, president. Estab. 1969. Produces birth announcements, Bar Mitzvah and Bat Mitzvah invitations and wedding invitations.

NEEDS Buys 100-200 pieces of calligraphy/year. Prefers local designers. Works on assignment only. Uses Mac designers. Also for calligraphy, mechanicals, paste-up, P-O-P. Looking for traditional, contemporary work. 50% of freelance work demands knowledge of Photoshop, QuarkXPress, Illustrator.

FIRST CONTACT & TERMS Send query letter with résumé. Calligraphers send photocopies of work. Samples are not filed and are not returned. Responds only if interested. Company will contact artist for portfolio review of final art, photostats, thumbnails if interested. Pays for design by the project. Pays flat fee for calligraphy.

TIPS "Look around at competitors' work to get a feeling of the type of art they use."

LPG GREETINGS, INC.

813 Wisconsin St., Walworth WI 53184. (262)275-5600. **Fax:** (262)275-5609. **E-mail:** judy@lpgcards.com. **Website:** www.lpgcreative.com. **Contact:** Judy Cecchi, creative director. Estab. 1992. Specializes in boxed Christmas cards, everyday greeting cards, wall art, and other gift items.

NEEDS Approached by 50-100 freelancers/year. Works with 20 freelancers/year. Buys 70 freelance designs and illustrations/year. Uses freelancers mainly for original artwork for Christmas cards and wall art. Considers any media. Artwork can be vertical or horizontal; 5×7, 8×10 or 5.5×17. Submit seasonal material 1 year in advance.

FIRST CONTACT & TERMS Send e-mail with link to website samples. E-mail for art guidelines. Please do not send unsolicited samples via e-mail without prior contact; they will not be considered. Will contact artist for samples if interested. Rights purchased vary according to project. Pays for design by the project. For illustration: pays flat fee. Finds freelancers through word of mouth and artists' submissions.

MADISON PARK GREETINGS

The Madison Park Group, 800 S. Michigan St., Suite B, Seattle WA 98108. (206)324-5711; (800)638-9622. **Fax:** (206)324-5822. **E-mail:** info@madpark.com. **Website:** www.madisonparkgreetings.com. Estab. 1977. Produces greeting cards, stationery.

NEEDS Approached by 1,000 freelancers/year. Works with 20 freelancers/year. Buys 100 freelance designs and illustrations/year. Art guidelines available free for SASE. Works on assignment only. Uses freelancers mainly for greeting cards; also for calligraphy. Considers all paper-related media. Produces material for Christmas, Easter, Mother's Day, Father's Day, graduation, New Years, Valentine's Day, birthdays, everyday, sympathy, get well, anniversary, baby congratulations, wedding, thank you, expecting, friendship. Are interested in floral and whimsical imagery, as well as humor." Submit seasonal material 10 months in advance.

FIRST CONTACT & TERMS "We are interested in receiving art submissions that offer a fresh, unique design perspective and enhance our current product line." Does not respond to unsolicited submissions unless interested. Guidelines available online.

MCGAW GRAPHICS, INC.

(888)426-2429 ext. 206. **Website:** www.mcgawgraphics.com. **Contact:** Katy Daly. Estab. 1979. Clients: specialty retailers, museum shops, wholesale framers, e-tailers, poster shops, galleries, frame shops.

FIRST CONTACT & TERMS If your work is not accepted, please remember that we choose work for publication and licensing based on current market trends, and that our opinion only pertains to our market segment, not to the aesthetic value of your work. Send your portfolio to attn: Acquisitions Department.

TIPS "Form and palette are critical to our decision process. We have a tremendous need for decorative pieces, especially new abstracts, landscapes and florals. There are a lot of prints and posters being published these days. Market your best material! Review our website before submitting. Send your best work."

MEAD

4751 Hempstead Station Dr., Kettering OH 45429. (937)495-6323; (800)565-5396. **Website:** www.ata glance.com; www.meadwestvaco.com. Publishes calendars, note cards, Christmas cards and other stationery items and books. Markets to a broad distribution channel, including better gifts, books, department stores and larger chains throughout US. Some sales to Europe, Canada and Japan. "We look for illustration and design that can be used in many ways: calendars, note cards, address books and more, so we can develop a collection. We license art that appeals to a widely female audience."

NEEDS Prefers work in horizontal format. No gag humor or cartoons. Art guidelines available for SASE with first-class postage or online.

FIRST CONTACT & TERMS Send query letter with brochure, résumé, photographs, slides, tearsheets and transparencies. Include an SASE for return of material. Responds within 6 weeks. Will contact artist for portfolio review if interested. Pays for illustration by the project, advance against royalty.

TIPS "Research what is selling and what's not. Go to gift shows and visit lots of stationery stores. Read all the trade magazines. Talk to store owners."

NALPAC, LTD.

1111 E. Eight Mile Rd., Ferndale MI 48220. (248)541-1140. Estab. 1971. Produces coffee mugs gift bags, trendy gift and novelty items, and T-shirts for gift and mass merchandise markets. Licenses all kinds of artwork for T-shirts, mugs and gifts.

NEEDS Approached by 10-15 freelancers/year. Works with 2-3 freelancers/year. Buys 70 designs and illustrations/year. Works on assignment only. Considers all media. Needs computer-literate freelancers for design, illustration and production. 60% of freelance work demands computer skills.

FIRST CONTACT & TERMS Send query letter with brochure, résumé, SASE, photographs, photocopies, slides and transparencies. Samples are filed or are returned by SASE if requested by artist. Responds in 1 month. Call for appointment to show portfolio. Usu-

ally buys all rights, but rights purchased may vary according to project. Also needs package/product designers, pay rate varies. Pays for design and illustration by the hour $10-25; or by the project $40-500, or offers royalties of 4-10%.

⊙ NATIONAL DESIGN CORP.

12121 Scripps Summit Dr., San Diego CA 92131. (800)366-7367; (858)674-6040. **Fax:** (858)674-4166. **E-mail:** ccoats@pens.com. **Website:** www.nationalde sign.com. Estab. 1985. Produces gifts, writing instruments and stationery accoutrements. Markets include gift/souvenir and premium markets.

NEEDS Works with 3-4 freelancers/year. Buys 3 freelance designs and illustrations/year. Prefers local freelancers only. Works on assignment only. Uses freelancers mainly for design illustration. Considers computer renderings to mimic traditional medias. Prefers children's and contemporary styles. 100% of freelance work demands knowledge of Illustrator and Photoshop. Produces material for Christmas and everyday.

FIRST CONTACT & TERMS Prefer submissions via e-mail/web link. Company will contact artist for final art if interested. Rights purchased vary according to project. Payments depends on complexity, extent of project(s).

TIPS "Fresh ideas always of interest."

NOBLEWORKS CARDS

500 Paterson Plank Rd., Union City NJ 07087. (201)420-0095; (800) 346-6253. **E-mail:** info@no bleworksinc.com; support@nobleworkscards.com. **Website:** www.nobleworkscards.com. **Contact:** art department. Estab. 1981. "Lucky you. You found Noble Works Cards' online funny card store. Some might even say the world's funniest greeting cards. So what if those people also happen to work at NobleWorks? BTW we are also the publisher of just about all the cards here, and selling them wholesale is our main business. Publishing and wholesaling unique funny cards has been our main business for over 32 years. Irreverent, inappropriate humor, naughty cards, adult jokes and even mean, rude or sarcasm, are practially a religion, in fact, funny happy birthday wishes often make it into our prayers. Honest. Always pushing the envelope, our cards redefine the edge of sophisticated, sassy, and downright silly fun." Art guidelines available for SASE with first-class postage.

NEEDS Looking for humorous "off-the-wall" adult contemporary and editorial illustration. Produces

material for Christmas, Mother's Day, Father's Day, graduation, Halloween, Valentine's Day, birthdays, thank you, anniversary, get well, astrology, sympathy, etc. Submit seasonal material 18 months in advance.
FIRST CONTACT & TERMS Designers: Send query as an e-mail attachment. Illustrators and cartoonists: Send query as an e-mail attachment. Responds in 1 month. Buys reprint rights. Pays for design and illustration by the project. Finds freelancers through sourcebooks, illustration annuals, referrals.

☺ NORTHERN CARDS

5035 Timberlea Blvd., Unit #9, Mississauga Ontario L4W 2K9, Canada. (905)625-4083. **Website:** www.northerncards.com. Estab. 1992. Produces 3 brands of greeting cards.
NEEDS Approached by 200 freelancers/year. Works with 25 freelancers/year. Buys 75 freelance designs and illustrations/year. Uses freelancers for "camera-ready artwork and lettering." Art guidelines with SASE with first-class postage. Looking for traditional, sentimental, floral and humorous styles. Prefers 5½×7¾ or 5×7. Produces material for Christmas, Easter, Mother's Day, Father's Day, graduation, Valentine's Day, birthdays and everyday. Also sympathy, get well, someone special, thank you, friendship, new baby, good-bye and sorry. Submit seasonal material 6 months in advance.
FIRST CONTACT & TERMS Designers: Send query letter with brochure, photocopies, slides, résumé and SASE. Illustrators and Cartoonists: Send photocopies, tearsheets, résumé and SASE. Lettering artists send samples. Samples are filed or returned by SASE. Responds only if interested. Pays flat fee, $200 (CDN). Finds freelancers through newspaper ads, gallery shows and Internet.

THE NOTEWORTHY COMPANY

336 Forest Ave., Amsterdam NY 12010. (518)842-2660. **E-mail:** photo@noteworthy.com. **Website:** www.noteworthy.com. Estab. 1954. Produces bags and coloring books. Advertising specialty manufacturer selling to distributors with clients in the health, real estate, banking and retail fields.
NEEDS Buys 25 illustrations/year. Prefers freelancers with experience in designing for flexographic printing. Works on assignment only. Uses freelancers mainly for stock bag art and coloring book themes.

FIRST CONTACT & TERMS Send query letter with brochure, résumé, samples and SASE. Samples are filed. Pays $200 for bag design.

☺ NOVA MEDIA, INC.

1724 N. State St., Big Rapids MI 49307-9073. (231)796-4637. **E-mail:** trund@netonecom.net. **Website:** www.novamediainc.com. **Contact:** Thomas J. Rundquist, chairman. Estab. 1981. Specializes in CDs, CDs/cassettes, games, limited edition plates, posters, school supplies, T-shirts. Licenses e-prints.
NEEDS Seeking creative art for the serious collector. Considers oil, acrylic. Prefers expressionism, impressionism, abstract. Editions are created by collaborating with the artist or by working from an existing painting. Approached by 14 artists/year. Publishes/distributes the work of 2 emerging, 2 mid-career and 1 established artists/year. Also needs freelancers for design. Prefers local designers.
FIRST CONTACT & TERMS Send query letter with samples. Accepts e-mail submissions. Responds in 1 month. Keeps samples on file; does not return material. Simultaneous submissions and previously published work OK. Pays royalties of 10% or negotiates payment. No advance. Rights purchased vary according to project. Provides promotion.
TIPS "The most effective way to contact us is by e-mail or regular mail. Visit our website."

OATMEAL STUDIOS

P.O. Box 191, Rochester VT 05767. 1-800-628-6325. **Fax:** 413-663-3465. **E-mail:** dawn@oatmealstudios.com. **Website:** www.oatmealstudios.com. Publishes humorous greeting cards and notepads, creative ideas for everyday cards. Art guidelines available for SASE with first-class postage or on website.
NEEDS Approached by approximately 300 freelancers/year. Buys 100-150 freelance designs and illustrations/year. Considers all media.
FIRST CONTACT & TERMS Write for art guidelines; send query letter with SASE, roughs, printed pieces or brochure/flyer to be kept on file. "If brochure/flyer is not available, we ask to keep one sample printed piece; color or b&w photocopies also acceptable for our files." Samples are returned by SASE. Responds in 6 weeks.
TIPS "We are looking for fresh and fun-looking artwork in any media and style. Also, sophisticated, funky cartoony-type art (people and/or animals) with or without words. Color work is best, but we will look

at black and white. Overall, we're looking for exciting, innovative, clever, humorous, fun, and most important, original designs and ideas. All work is speculative, so put your greeting cards ideas in rough sketch form. Be sure to include printed samples or tearsheets. If possible, you can provide us with a sample which we can keep on file for future assignments. **Please indicate which ones we can keep.** You will also need to include an SASE large enough to accommodate the return of your artwork. Our creative department often has concepts that call for a particular style. So even if you don't have specific greeting card ideas of your own, send us some samples of your work. Perhaps your style and our ideas will work well together. The size of our cards is 5"×7" and all artwork designed for us must match these requirements either exactly or proportionately. The cards are usually vertical and can be with or without a border. And last but not least, payment. We negotiate payment with each artist depending on the complexity of the work. We look forward to reviewing your work!"

THE OCCASIONS GROUP

Fax: (507)625-3388. **E-mail:** dknutson@theoccasionsgroup.com. **Website:** theoccasionsgroup.com. **Contact:** Deb Knutson, creative director. Estab. 1967. Produces calendars, greeting cards, stationery, posters, memo pads, advertising specialties. Specializes in Christmas, everyday, dental, health care greeting cards and postcards, and calendars for businesses and professionals.

NEEDS Art guidelines available free for SASE. Works with 20-30 freelancers/year. Buys approximately 300 freelance designs and illustrations/year. Prefers freelancers with experience in greeting cards. Works on assignment only. Uses freelancers mainly for illustration, calligraphy, lettering, humorous writing, cartoons. Prefers traditional Christmas and contemporary and conservative cartoons. Some design work demands knowledge of Photoshop, Illustrator, QuarkXPress and InDesign. Produces material for Christmas, Thanksgiving, birthdays, everyday.

FIRST CONTACT & TERMS Designers: Send brochure, résumé, tearsheets. Illustrators and cartoonists: Send tearsheets. After introductory mailing, send follow-up postcard sample every 6 months. Calligraphers: Send photocopies of their work. Accepts Mac-compatible disk submissions. Samples are filed. Buys one-time or all rights. Pays for illustration by the

project, $250-500. Finds freelancers through agents, other professional contacts, submissions and recommendations.

OHIO WHOLESALE, INC./KENNEDY'S COUNTRY COLLECTION

286 W. Greenwich Rd., Seville OH 44273. (330)769-5050. **Fax:** (330)769-5566. **E-mail:** annes@ohiowholesale.com; AnneV@ohiowholesale.com. **Website:** www.ohiowholesale.com. **Contact:** Anne Secoy, vice president of product development. Estab. 1978. Home décor, giftware, seasonal. Produces home décor, wall art, canvas, tabletop, seasonal decorations, gifts, ornaments and textiles.

NEEDS Prefers freelancers with experiences in home decor and giftware. Works with 16 freelancers/year. Buys 100 freelance designs/illustrations per year. Will consider wood, glass, resin, tin, canvas, acrylic, metal, fabric and paper mediums in the areas of religion, counter humor or inspirational pieces. Also produce materials for Christmas, Thanksgiving, Easter, Halloween, Grandparent's Day, St. Patrick's Day, woman-to-woman and everyday gifts. Seasonal materials should be submitted 18 months in advance. Artists should be familiar with Adobe Illustrator, Photoshop and QuarkXPress.

FIRST CONTACT & TERMS Send an e-mail query with brochure, photographs and SASE. Samples not kept on file. Company will contact artist for portfolio if interested. Pays by the project. Rights negotiated.

TIPS "Be able to work independently with your own ideas—use your 'gift' and think outside the box. *Wow me!*"

PAPERLINK

356 Kennington Rd., London SE11 4LD, United Kingdom. 020 7582 8244. **Fax:** 020 7587 5212. **E-mail:** info@paperlink.co.uk; or via online contact form. **Website:** www.paperlink.co.uk. Estab. 1985. Produces contemporary art and humorous greeting cards.

NEEDS Product categories include alternative/humor, counter humor, cute, juvenile and teen. Produces material for Mother's Day, Father's Day, Christmas, Easter, Valentine's Day, graduation, congratulations, wedding/anniversary, birthday, baby congrats, get-well/sympathy, everyday and all holidays and seasons. No specific size needed for final art. 50% of freelance work demands computer skills. Artists should be familiar with Illustrator, Photoshop and QuarkXPress. No need for freelance design.

FIRST CONTACT & TERMS Submission guidelines available online.

PAPER MAGIC GROUP, INC.

54 Glenmaura National Blvd., Suite 200, Moosic PA 18507. (800)278-4085. **E-mail:** orders@papermagic. com. **Website:** www.papermagic.com. **Contact:** Creative Director. Estab. 1984. Produces greeting cards, stickers, vinyl wall decorations, 3D paper decorations. "We publish seasonal cards and decorations for the mass market. We use a wide variety of design styles." **NEEDS** Works with 60 freelance artists/year. Prefers artists with experience in greeting cards. Work is by assignment; or send submissions on spec. Designs products for Christmas and Valentine's Day. Also uses freelancers for lettering and art direction.

FIRST CONTACT & TERMS Send query letter with résumé, samples (color photocopies) and SASE, Attn: creative director. Samples are filed or are returned by SASE if requested by artist. Originals not returned. Pays by the project. Buys all rights.

TIPS "Please, experienced illustrators only."

PAPER PRODUCTS DESIGN

60 Galli Dr., Suite 1, Novato CA 94949. (800)370-9998; (415)883-1888. **Fax:** (415)883-1999. **E-mail:** carol@ ppd.co. **Website:** www.paperproductsdesign.com. **Contact:** Carol Florsheim. Estab. 1992. Produces paper napkins, plates, designer tissue, giftbags and giftwrap, porcelain accessories. Specializes in high-end design, fashionable designs.

NEEDS Approached by 50-100 freelancers/year. Buys multiple freelance designs and illustrations/year. Artists do not need to write for guidelines. They may send samples to the attention of Carol Florsheim at any time. Uses freelancers mainly for designer paper napkins. Looking for very stylized/clean designs and illustrations. Prefers 6½×6½. Produces seasonal and everyday material. Submit seasonal material 9 months in advance.

FIRST CONTACT & TERMS Designers: Send brochure, photocopies, photographs, tearsheets. Samples are not filed and are returned if requested with SASE. Responds in 6 weeks. Request portfolio review of color, final art, photostats in original query. Rights purchased vary according to project. Pays for design and illustration by the project in advances and royalties. Finds freelancers through agents, *Workbook*.

TIPS "Shop the stores, study decorative accessories, fashion clothing. Read European magazines. We are a design house."

PICKARD CHINA

782 Pickard Ave., Antioch IL 60002. (847)395-3800. **Fax:** (847)395-3827. **E-mail:** info@pickardchina.com. **Website:** www.pickardchina.com. Estab. 1893. Manufacturer of fine china dinnerware. Clients: Upscale specialty stores and department stores. Current clients include Gearys, Macy's and Gump's.

NEEDS Assigns 2-3 jobs to freelance designers/year. Prefers designers for china pattern development with experience in home furnishings. Tabletop experience is a plus but not required.

FIRST CONTACT & TERMS Send query letter with résumé and color photographs, tearsheets, slides or transparencies showing art styles. Samples are filed or are returned if requested. Art director will contact artist for portfolio review if interested. Negotiates rights purchased. May purchase designs outright, work on royalty basis (usually 2%) or negotiate nonrefundable advance against royalties.

THE POPCORN FACTORY

13970 W. Laurel Dr., Lake Forest IL 60045. (847)362-0028. **Fax:** (847)362-9680. **Website:** www.thepop cornfactory.com. Estab. 1979. Manufacturer of popcorn packed in exclusive designed cans and other gift items sold via e-commerce and catalog for Christmas, Halloween, Valentine's Day, Easter and year-round gift giving needs.

PORTERFIELD'S FINE ART LICENSING

4837 Tuttle Ave., Suite 410, Sarasota FL 34243. (800)660-8345 or (941)487-8581. **Fax:** (941)487-8582. **E-mail:** lance@porterfieldsfineart.com; art@porter fieldsfineart.com. **Website:** www.porterfieldsfineart. com. **Contact:** Lance J. Klass, president. Estab. 1994. Licenses representational, Christmas, holiday, seasonal, Americana, and many other subjects. "We're a major, internationally recognized full-service licensing agency and function as a full-service licensing representative for individual artists wishing to license their work into a wide range of consumer-oriented retail product categories. In addition to our top-rated art licensing portfolio site, we also run a major blog for artists on the business of art licensing at www. art-licensing.biz, where artists can learn the basics of how to go about licensing their work for commercial retail products. Stop by our site for more information about how to become a Porterfield's artist and have us represent you and your work for licenses in wall and home decor, home fabrics, stationery and all paper products, crafts, giftware and many other fields." Send sample JPEGs via e-mail or direct us to a site with your artwork, for fastest response. No mail submissions.

NEEDS Approached by as many as 1,000 artists/year. Licenses many designs and illustrations/year, but only takes 2-4 new artists each year. Prefers commercially oriented artists who can create beautiful pieces of art that people want to look at again and again, and that will help sell products to the core consumer, that is, "women over 30 who purchase 85% of all consumer goods in America." Art guidelines listed on website. Considers existing works first. Considers any media, oil, pastel, watercolor, acrylics, digital. "We are seeking artists who have exceptional artistic ability and commercial savvy, who study the market for trends and who would like to have their art and their talents introduced to the broad public. Artists must be willing to work hard to produce art for the market."

THE PRINTERY HOUSE

Conception Abbey, P.O. Box 12, 37112 State Hwy. V V, Conception MO 64433. (660)944-3110. **Fax:** (660)944-3116. **E-mail:** art@printeryhouse.org. **Website:** www.printeryhouse.org. **Contact:** Steve Hess, creative director. Estab. 1950. Publishes religious greeting cards. Licenses art for greeting cards and wall prints. Specializes in religious Christmas and all-occasion themes for people interested in religious, yet contemporary, expressions of faith. Card designs are meant to speak to the heart. They feature strong graphics, calligraphy and other appropriate styles.

NEEDS Approached by 100 freelancers/year. Works with 40 freelancers/year. Art guidelines and technical specifications available upon request. Uses freelancers for product illustration and lettering. Looking for dignified styles and solid religious themes. Has preference for high-quality, broad-edged pen lettering with simple backgrounds/illustrations. Produces seasonal material for Christmas and Easter as well as the religious birthday, get well, sympathy, thank you, etc. Digital work is accepted in Photoshop or Illustrator format.

FIRST CONTACT & TERMS Send query e-mail with résumé, JPEGs or PDFs with examples of work. Low-res samples may be submitted digitally in JPEG or PDF format to art@printeryhouse.org. Usually re-

sponds within 3-4 weeks. To show portfolio, e-mail appropriate materials only after query has been answered. "Generally, we continue to work with artists once we have accepted their work." Pays flat fee of $350-$650 for illustration/design, and $150-$250 for calligraphy. Usually buys exclusive reproduction rights for ink or paper use, but artist retains copyright for any other usage.

TIPS "Remember that our greeting cards need to have a definite Christian/religious dimension but not overly sentimental. Artwork must be appealing and of high quality. We sell mostly via mail-order catalogs and online, so artwork has to reduce well for those formats."

PRISMATIX, INC.

324 Railroad Ave., Hackensack NJ 07601. (800)222-9662. **Fax:** (201)525-2828. **E-mail:** info@prismatix.biz. **Website:** www.prismatixinc.com. **Contact:** Miriam Salomon, vice president. Estab. 1977. Produces novelty humor programs. "We manufacture screen-printed novelties to be sold in the retail market."

NEEDS Works with 3-4 freelancers/year. Buys 100 freelance designs and illustrations/year. Works on assignment only. 90% of freelance work demands computer skills.

FIRST CONTACT & TERMS Send query letter with brochure, résumé. Samples are filed. Responds only if interested. Portfolio should include color thumbnails, roughs, final art. Payment negotiable.

PRUDENT PUBLISHING

65 Challenger Rd., Ridgefield Park NJ 07660. (201)641-7900. **Fax:** (201)641-9356. **E-mail:** mfrancesco@prudentpublishing.com. **Website:** www.gallerycollection.com. Estab. 1928. Produces greeting cards. Specializes in business/corporate all-occasion and holiday cards. Art guidelines available.

NEEDS Buys calligraphy. Uses freelancers mainly for card design, illustrations and calligraphy. Considers traditional media. Prefers no cartoons or cute illustrations. Prefers 5½×7⅞ horizontal and vertical formats (or proportionate). Produces material for Christmas, Thanksgiving, birthdays, everyday, sympathy, get well and thank you.

FIRST CONTACT & TERMS Designers, illustrators and calligraphers: Send query letter with brochure, photostats, photocopies, tearsheets. Samples are filed or returned by SASE if requested. Responds ASAP. Portfolio review not required. Buys all rights. No roy alty or licensing arrangements. Payment is negotiable. Finds freelancers through submissions, magazines, sourcebooks, agents and word of mouth.

P.S. GREETINGS

5730 N. Tripp Ave., Chicago IL 60646. (773)267-6150; (800)621-8823. **Fax:** (773)267-6055. **E-mail:** artdirector@psgreetings.com. **Website:** www.psgreetings.com. Manufacturer of boxed greeting and counter cards. Artists' guidelines are posted on website, or send SASE.

NEEDS Receives submissions from 300-400 freelance artists/year. Works with 50-100 artists/year on greeting card designs. Publishes greeting cards for everyday and holidays. 70% of work demands knowledge of InDesign, Illustrator and Photoshop.

FIRST CONTACT & TERMS Send all submissions to the attention of Design Director. All requests as well as submissions must be accompanied by SASE. "Samples will *not* be returned without SASE!" Responds in 1 month. Pays flat fee. Buys exclusive worldwide rights for greeting cards and stationery. No phone calls, please.

TIPS "Our line includes a whole spectrum from everyday needs (florals, scenics, feminine, masculine, humorous, cute) to every major holiday (from New Year's to Thanksgiving) with a very extensive Christmas line. We continue to grow every year and are always looking for innovative talent."

🌀 REALLY GOOD

Old Mast House, The Square, Abingdon Oxon OX14 5AR, United Kingdom. +44 01235 537888. **Fax:** +44 01235 537779. **E-mail:** Online contact form. **Website:** www.reallygood.uk.com. **Contact:** David Hicks, managing director. Estab. 1987. Produces gifts, stationery, giftwrap, greeting cards. Works with several freelancers/year. Purchases 100+ designs/illustrations per year. Buys cards and stationery 3-5 year rights. Freelancers are paid royalites.

NEEDS Trendy, fun, graphic, modern designs. Seeks alternative, humor and trend designs. Produces material for Mother's Day, birthdays, Father's Day, Valentine's Day, congratulations, baby congratulations, woman-to-woman, wedding/anniversary, get-well/sympathy and everyday cards. Seasonal material should be submitted 12 months in advance.

FIRST CONTACT & TERMS E-mail letter with artist's URL and small JPEG/PDF samples. Samples not kept on file, returned by SASE. Company will contact if interested.

RECYCLED PAPER GREETINGS, INC.

111 N. Canal St., Suite 700, Chicago IL 60606-7206. (800)777-3331. **Website:** www.recycledpapergreetings.com. **Contact:** Art Director. Estab. 1971. "Since the beginning, we've always worked with independent artists because we value the power of true individual expression. Together, we create the most productive (and awesome) greeting cards out there. We take great pride in our family of independent artists, a family we are always looking to grow. Want to join our family?"

FIRST CONTACT & TERMS "Artwork should be designed to mimic a complete greeting card—message included (vertical 5×7). Please send up to 10 ideas Birthday ideas (labeled with your name, address and phone number). Please do not send holiday-specific cards, as we work far in advance of holidays. Do not send slides, disks, tearsheets, or original artwork. Recycled Paper Greetings is not responsible for any damage to artwork submitted. We suggest submitting color copies or photographs of your art. Do not send previously published cards. The review process can take up to 2 months. Simultaneous submissions to other companies are perfectly acceptable. If your work is chosen, we will contact you to discuss all of the details. If your work is not selected, we will return it to you. Thank you for your interest in Recycled Paper Greetings. Send submissions to the Art Department. E-mail low-res files (less than 2MB total) of formatted designs or links to your portfolio to: newartistsubs@prgreetings.com."

THE REGAL LINE/ACME GRAPHICS

P.O. Box 2052, Cedar Rapids IA 52406. (319)364-0233. **E-mail:** info@regalline.com. **Website:** www.regalline.com. **Contact:** Jeff Scherrman, president. Estab. 1913. Produces printed merchandise used by funeral directors, such as acknowledgments, register books and prayer cards. Floral subjects, religious subjects and scenes are their most popular products. Art guidelines free for SASE.

🗨 Acme Graphics manufactures a line of merchandise for funeral directors. Floral subjects, religious subjects and scenes are their most popular products.

NEEDS Approached by 30 freelancers/year. Considers pen & ink, watercolor and acrylic. "We will send a copy of our catalog to show the type of work we do."

Art guidelines available for SASE with first-class postage. Looking for religious, inspirational, church window, floral and nature art. Also uses freelancers for calligraphy and lettering.

FIRST CONTACT & TERMS Designers: Send query letter with résumé, photocopies, photographs, slides and transparencies. Illustrators: Send postcard sample or query letter with brochure, photocopies, photographs, slides and tearsheets. Accepts submissions on disk. Samples are not filed and are returned by SASE. Responds in 10 days. Call or write for appointment to show portfolio of roughs. Originals are returned. Requests work on spec before assigning a job. Pays by the project. Buys all rights.

TIPS "Send samples or prints of work from other companies. No modern art. Some designs are too expensive to print. Learn all you can about printing production. Please refer to website for examples of appropriate images!"

RIGHTS INTERNATIONAL GROUP, INC.

500 Paterson Plank Rd., Union City NJ 07087. (201)863-4500. **E-mail:** info@rightsinternational. com. **Website:** www.rightsinternational.com. Estab. 1996. Agency for cross licensing. Licenses images for manufacturers/publishers of giftware, stationery, posters and home furnishings.

NEEDS Approached by 50 freelancers/year. Uses freelancers mainly for creative, decorative art for the commercial and designer market; also for textile art. Considers oil, acrylic, watercolor, mixed media, pastels and photography.

FIRST CONTACT & TERMS Submission guidelines available online.

RITE LITE, LTD.

333 Stanley Ave., Brooklyn NY 11207. (718)498-1700. **Fax:** (718)498-1251. **E-mail:** info@ritelite.com. **Website:** www.ritelite.com. Estab. 1948. Manufacturer and distributor of a full range of Judaica. Clients include department stores, galleries, gift shops, museum shops and jewelry stores.

NEEDS Looking for new menorahs, mezuzahs, children's Judaica, Passover and matza plates. Works on assignment only. Must be familiar with Jewish ceremonial objects or design. Also uses artists for illustration, and product design. Most of freelance work requires knowledge of Illustrator and Photoshop. Produces material for Hanukkah, Passover and oth-

er Jewish holidays. Submit seasonal material 1 year in advance.

FIRST CONTACT & TERMS Designers: Send query letter with brochure or résumé and photographs. Illustrators: Send photocopies. Do not send originals. Samples are filed. Responds in 1 month, only if interested. Art director will contact for portfolio review if interested. Portfolio should include color tearsheets, photographs and slides. Pays flat fee per design. Buys all rights. Finds artists through word of mouth.

TIPS "Be open to the desires of the consumers. Don't force your preconceived notions on them through the manufacturers. Know that there is one retail price, one wholesale price and one distributor price."

ROMAN, INC.

472 Brighton Dr., Bloomingdale IL 60108. (800)729-7662. **Website:** www.roman.com. Estab. 1963. Produces collectible figurines, decorative housewares, decorations, gifts, limited edition plates, ornaments. Specializes in collectibles and giftware to celebrate special occasions.

NEEDS Approached by 25-30 freelancers/year. Works with 3-5 freelancers/year. Uses freelancers mainly for graphic packaging design, illustration. Considers variety of media. Looking for traditional-based design. Roman also has an inspirational niche. 80% of freelance design and illustration demands knowledge of Photoshop, QuarkXPress, Illustrator. Produces material for Christmas, Mother's Day, graduation, Thanksgiving, birthdays, everyday. Submit seasonal material 1 year in advance.

FIRST CONTACT & TERMS Send query letter with photocopies. Samples are filed or returned by SASE. Responds in 2 months if artist requests a reply. Portfolio review not required. Pays by the project. Finds freelancers through submissions and word of mouth. "All submissions are submitted at your own risk and Roman cannot guarantee return of materials. Please do not send original artwork or prototypes. Allow 6-8 weeks for review. Please no phone calls."

THE SARUT GROUP

P.O. Box 110495, Brooklyn NY 11211. (718)387-7484; (800) 345-6404. **E-mail:** sarut@thesarutgroup.com. **Website:** www.thesarutgroup.com. **Contact:** Frederic Rambaud, vice president-marketing. Estab. 1979. Produces museum-quality science and nature gifts. "Marketing firm with 20 employees. 36 trade shows a year. No reps. All products are exclusive. Medium- to high-end market."

NEEDS Approached by 4-5 freelancers/year. Works with 4 freelancers/year. Uses freelancers mainly for new products. Seeks contemporary designs. Produces material for all holidays and seasons.

FIRST CONTACT & TERMS Samples are returned. Responds in 2 weeks. Write for appointment to show portfolio. Rights purchased vary according to project.

TIPS "We are looking for concepts; products, not automatically graphics."

🌙 SECOND NATURE, LTD.

10 Malton Rd., London W10 5UP, United Kingdom. +44 (0)20 8960-0212. **Fax:** +44 (0)20 8960-8700. **E-mail:** via online contact form. **Website:** www.second nature.co.uk. Greeting card publisher specializing in unique 3D/handmade cards and special finishes.

NEEDS Prefers interesting new contemporary but commercial styles. Also calligraphy and web design. Art guidelines available. Produces material for Christmas, Valentine's Day, Mother's Day and Father's Day. Submit seasonal material 19 months in advance.

FIRST CONTACT & TERMS Send query letter with samples showing art style. Samples not filed are returned only if requested by artist. Responds in 2 months. Originals are not returned at job's completion. Pays flat fee.

TIPS "We are interested in all forms of paper engineering or anything fresh and innovative."

PAULA SKENE DESIGNS

1250 45th St., Suite 240, Emeryville CA 94608. (510)654-3510. **Fax:** (510)654-3496. **E-mail:** paula skene@aol.com. **Website:** www.paulaskenedesigns. com.

NEEDS Works with 1-2 freelancers/year. Works on assignment only. Produces material for all holidays and seasons, everyday.

FIRST CONTACT & TERMS "Designers, artists, and illustrators: send tearsheets and photocopies. *Do not send more than 2 examples!* Samples are returned. Responds in 1 week. Buys all rights. Pays for design and illustration by the project."

SMART ALEX, INC.

1800 W. Grace St., #322, Chicago IL 60613. **E-mail:** submissions@smartalexinc.com. **Website:** www. smartalexinc.com. Estab. 1980. "From graphic artwork to cartooning, we employ a wide variety of artistic styles in our greeting cards. We will pay $150

for one time payment to purchase exclusive rights." Works with 5 freelancers/year. Buys 50 freelance designs/year.

NEEDS We are always looking for funny lines, with a definite emphasis on humor for grown-ups. Our style of humor tends to be topical, witty, smart, ironic, or sexually suggestive. We will pay $100 for each submission we select to be published. Send an e-mail with copy/samples in e-mail format.

FIRST CONTACT & TERMS Graphic submissions should be sent as an e-mail attachment, in JPEG format and at a resolution of 72 dpi.

TIPS "We like our cards to be: surprising without being shocking; a bit dirty without being filthy; we like to poke fun without being insulting. We prefer no sexual themes on Christmas Holidays cards, just funny and humorous."

🌙 SOUL

Old Mast House, The Square, Oxford Oxfordshire OX14 SAR, United Kingdom. +44 1235 537816. **E-mail:** smile@souluk.com. **Website:** www.souluk. com. **Contact:** David Hicks, managing director. Estab. 1997. Produces giftware, greeting cards, notebooks, giftwrap, and other stationery items. Works with 5 freelancers/year. Purchases 100+ designs/illustrations per year. Buys 3-5 year license. Freelancers paid royalties.

NEEDS Contemporary, modern, trend greeting cards. Birthdays, Mother's Day, Father's Day, Easter, Valentine's Day, congratulations baby congratulations, woman-to-woman, wedding/anniversary, get-well/sympathy, everyday.

FIRST CONTACT & TERMS E-mail query letter with URL of artist's site or small JPEG/PDF samples of work. Samples not kept on file. Will contact if interested.

TIPS "Check our website first for style."

SPENCER'S

6826 Black Horse Pike, Egg Harbor Twp. NJ 08234-4197. **Website:** www.spencersonline.com. Estab. 1947. Retail gift chain located in approximately 850 stores in 43 states, including Hawaii and Canada. Includes 2 new retail chain stores named Spirit Halloween Superstores and ToyZam (toy chain).

⚲ Products offered by store chain include: posters, T-shirts, games, mugs, novelty items, cards, 14K jewelry, neon art, novelty stationery. Spencer's offers different product lines, such as custom lava lights and Halloween costumes and products. Visit a store if you can to get a sense of what they offer.

NEEDS Prefers artists with professional experience in advertising design. Uses artists for illustration (hard line art, fashion illustration, airbrush). Also needs product and fashion photography (primarily jewelry), as well as stock photography. Uses a lot of freelance computer art. 50% of freelance work demands knowledge of InDesign, Illustrator, Photoshop and QuarkXPress. Also uses production and packaging companies. "You don't necessarily have to be local for freelance production."

FIRST CONTACT & TERMS Send postcard sample or query letter with *nonreturnable* brochure, résumé and photocopies, including phone number where you can be reached during business hours. Accepts submissions on disk. Will contact artist for portfolio review if interested. Will contact only upon job need. Considers buying second rights (reprint rights) to previously published work. Finds artists through sourcebooks.

TIPS "Become proficient in as many computer programs as possible."

SUNSHINE ART STUDIOS, INC.

150 Kingswood Rd., P.O. Box 8465, Mankato MN 56002-8465. (800)873-7681. **Fax:** (800)232-3633. **E-mail:** cs@sunshinebusinessclass.com. **Website:** sunshinebusinessclass.com. Estab. 1921. Produces greeting cards, stationery and calendars that are sold in own catalog, appealing to all age groups.

NEEDS Works with 50 freelance artists/year. Buys 100 freelance designs and illustrations/year. Prefers artists with experience in greeting cards. Art guidelines available for SASE with first-class postage. Works on assignment only. Uses freelancers for greeting cards, stationery and gift items. Also for calligraphy. Considers all media. Looking for traditional or humorous look. Produces material for Christmas, birthdays and everyday. Submit seasonal material 6-8 months in advance.

FIRST CONTACT & TERMS Send query letter with brochure, résumé, SASE, tearsheets and slides. Samples are filed or are returned by SASE if requested by artist. Responds only if interested. Portfolio should include finished art samples and color tearsheets and slides. Originals not returned. Buys all rights.

SYRACUSE CULTURAL WORKERS

P.O. Box 6367, Syracuse NY 13217. (315)474-1132. **Fax:** (877)265-5399. **E-mail:** karenk@syracusecultural workers.com. **Website:** www.syracuseculturalworkers.com. **Contact:** Karen Kerney, art director. Estab. 1982. Produces posters, note cards, postcards, greeting cards, T-shirts and calendars that are feminist, progressive, radical, multicultural, lesbian/gay allied, racially inclusive and honoring of elders and children. Publishes and distributes peace and justice resources through their Tools For Change catalog.

NEEDS Approached by many freelancers/year. Considers all media. Art guidelines available on website or free for SASE with first-class postage. Specifically seeking artwork celebrating peace-making diverstiy, people's history and community building. "Our mission is to help sustain a culture that honors diversity and celebrates community; that inspires and nurtures justice, equality and freedom; that respects our fragile Earth and all its beings; that encourages and supports all forms of creative expression." Themes include environment, positive parenting, positive gay and lesbian images, multiculturalism and cross-cultural adoption.

FIRST CONTACT & TERMS Send query letter with sample of work and SASE. Samples are filed or returned by SASE. Responds in 1 month with SASE. Will contact for portfolio review if interested. Buys one-time rights. Pays flat fee, $70-450; royalties of 4-6% gross sales. Finds artists through submissions and word of mouth.

TIPS "Please do *not* send original art. Rather, send photocopies, printed samples or duplicate slides. Also, one postcard sample is not enough for us to judge whether your work is right for us. Include return postage if you would like your artwork/slides returned. December and January are major art selection months. Please visit our website to get a sense of what we've chosen to publish in the past at www.syracuseculturalworkers.com."

TALICOR, INC.

901 Lincoln Pkwy., Plainwell MI 49080. (269)685-2345; (800)433-GAME (4263). **Fax:** (269)685-6789. **E-mail:** orders@talicor.com; or via online form. **Website:** www.talicor.com. Estab. 1971. Manufacturer and distributor of educational and entertainment games and toys. Clients chain toy stores, department stores, specialty stores and Christian bookstores.

NEEDS Works with 4-6 freelance illustrators and designers/year. Prefers local freelancers. Works on assignment only. Uses freelancers mainly for game design. Also for advertising, brochure and catalog design, illustration and layout; product design; illustration on product; P-O-P displays; posters and magazine design.

FIRST CONTACT & TERMS Send query letter with tearsheets, samples or postcards. Samples are not filed and are returned only if requested. Responds only if interested. Call or write for appointment to show portfolio. Pays for design and illustration by the project. Negotiates rights purchased. Accepts digital submissions via e-mail.

VAGABOND CREATIONS, INC.

2560 Lance Dr., Dayton OH 45409. (937)298-1124. **Fax:** (800)738-7237. **E-mail:** sales@vagabondcreations.net. **Website:** www.vagabondcreations.net. Publishes stationery and greeting cards with contemporary humor; also a line of coloring books. 99% of artwork used is provided by staff artists.

NEEDS Works with 3 freelancers/year. Buys 6 finished illustrations/year. Seeking line drawings, washes and color separations. Material should fit in standard-size envelope.

FIRST CONTACT & TERMS Query. Samples are returned by SASE. Responds in 2 weeks. Submit Christmas, Valentine's Day, everyday and graduation material at any time. Originals are returned only upon request. Payment negotiated.

TIPS "Important! Currently we are *not* looking for additional freelance artists because we are very satisfied with the work submitted by those individuals working directly with us. Our current artists are very experienced and have been associated with us in some cases for over 30 years. We do not in any way wish to offer false hope to anyone, but it would be foolish on our part not to give consideration."

WANDA WALLACE ASSOCIATES

323 E. Plymouth, Suite 2, Inglewood CA 90302. (310)419-0376. **E-mail:** wandawallacefoundation@yahoo.com. **Website:** www.wandawallacefoundation.org. **Contact:** Wanda Wallace, president. Estab. 1980. Nonprofit organization produces greeting cards and posters for general public appeal. "We produce black art prints, posters, originals and other media."

○ This publisher is doing more educational programs, touring schools nationally with artists.

NEEDS Approached by 10-12 freelance artists/year. Works with varying number of freelance artists/year. Buys varying number of designs and illustrations/year from freelance artists. Prefers artists with experience in black/ethnic art subjects. Uses freelance artists mainly for production of originals and some guest appearances. Considers all media. Produces material for Christmas. Submit seasonal material 4-6 months in advance.

FIRST CONTACT & TERMS Send query letter with any visual aid. Some samples are filed. Policy varies regarding answering queries and submissions. Call or write to schedule an appointment to show a portfolio. Rights purchased vary according to project. Art education instruction is available. Pays by the project.

WARNER PRESS INC.

1201 E. Fifth St., Anderson IN 46012. (800)741-7721. **E-mail:** curtis@warnerpress.org. **Website:** www.warnerpress.org. **Contact:** Curtis Corzine, creative director. Estab. 1884. Warner Press produces church bulletins, church supplies, Christian Art boxed greeting cards, activity and coloring books, and ministry teaching resources. We produce products for the Christian marketplace. Our main markets are the Church and Christian bookstores. We provide products for all ages. Art submission guidelines available online. Works on assignment only. Warner Press uses freelancers for all products, as listed above. Considers media and photography. Work demands knowledge of Photoshop, Illustrator and InDesign.

NEEDS Approached by 50 freelancers/year. Works with 15-20 freelancers/year. Buys 200 freelance designs and illustrations/year. Works on assignment only. Uses freelancers for all products, including bulletins and coloring books. Considers all media and photography.

FIRST CONTACT & TERMS Send postcard or query letter with samples. Do not send originals. Creative director will contact artist for portfolio review if interested. Samples are filed for later review if necessary. Pays by the project. Buys all rights (occasionally varies).

TIPS "Subject matter must be appropriate for Christian market. Most of our art purchases are for children's materials."

ZITI CARDS

601 S. Sixth St., St. Charles MO 63301. (800)497-5908. **Fax:** (636)352-2146. **E-mail:** mail@ziticards.

com. **Website:** www.ziticards.com. **Contact:** Salvatore Ventura, owner. Estab. 2006. Produces greeting cards. Specializes in holiday cards for architects, construction businesses and medical professionals. Art guidelines available via e-mail.

NEEDS Architecture, cities/urban, construction trades and medical imagery. All styles/media considered. Submit seasonal work 2 months in advance. Pays $50 advance and 5% royalties at the end of the season or flat fee. Finds freelancers through submissions.

FIRST CONTACT & TERMS Accepts e-mail submissions with image files or link to website. "E-mail attachments are preferred, but anything that accurately shows the work is fine." After introductory mailing, send follow-up postcard sample every 6 months. Samples are filed or returned by sase if requested. Responds only if interested.

POSTERS & PRINTS

Have you ever noticed, perhaps at the opening of an exhibition or at an art fair, that though you have many paintings on display, everybody wants to buy the same one? Do friends, relatives, and co-workers ask you to paint duplicates of work you've already sold? Many artists turn to the print market because they find certain images have a wide appeal and will sell again and again. This section lists publishers and distributors who can produce and market your work as prints or posters. It is important to understand the difference between the terms "publisher" and "distributor" before you begin your research. Art publishers work with you to publish a piece of your work in print form. Art distributors assist you in marketing a preexisting poster or print. Some companies function as both publisher and distributor. Look in the first paragraph of each listing to determine if the company is a publisher, distributor, or both.

RESEARCH THE MARKET

Some listings in this section are fine art presses, and others are more commercial. Read the listings carefully to determine which companies create editions for the fine art market or for the decorative market. Visit galleries, frame shops, furniture stores, and other retail outlets that carry prints to see where your art fits in. You may also want to visit designer showrooms and interior decoration outlets.

To further research this market, check each company's website or send for their catalog. Some publishers will not send their catalogs because they are too expensive, but you may be able to see one at a local poster shop, print gallery, upscale furniture store, or frame shop. Examine the colors in the catalogs to make sure the quality is high.

YOUR PUBLISHING OPTIONS

1. Working with a commercial poster manufacturer or art publisher. If you don't mind creating commercial images and following current trends, the decorative market can be quite lucrative. On the other hand, if you work with a fine art publisher, you will have more control over the final image.

2. Working with a fine art press. Fine art presses differ from commercial presses in that press operators work side by side with you every step of the way, sharing their experience and knowledge of the printing process. You may be charged a fee for the time your work is on the press and for the expert advice of the printer.

3. Working at a co-op press. Instead of approaching an art publisher, you can learn to make your own hand-pulled original prints—such as lithographs, monoprints, etchings, or silk-screens. If there is a co-op press in your city, you can rent time on a press and create your own editions. It can be rewarding to learn printing skills and have the hands-on experience. You also gain total control of your work. The drawback is you have to market your images yourself by approaching galleries, distributors, and other clients.

4. Self-publishing. Several national printing companies advertise heavily in artists' magazines, encouraging artists to publish their own work. If you are a savvy marketer who understands the ins and outs of trade shows and direct marketing, this is a viable option. However, it takes a large investment up front, whether you work with a printing company or choose to do everything on your own. If you contract with a printer, you could end up with a thousand prints taking up space in your basement. On the other hand, if you are a good marketer, you could end up selling them all and making a much larger profit than if you had gone through an art publisher or poster company.

   Another option is to create the prints yourself from your computer, using a high-quality digital printer and archival paper. You can make the prints as needed, which will save money.

5. Marketing through distributors. If you choose the self-publishing route but don't have the resources to market your prints, distributors will market your work in exchange for a percentage of sales. Distributors have connections with all kinds of outlets like retail stores, print galleries, framers, college bookstores, and museum shops.

What to Send

To approach a publisher, send a brief query letter, a short bio, a list of galleries that represent your work, and five to ten JPEGs, TIFFs, or slides. (Check the listing or submission guidelines to see the type of samples they prefer.) It helps to send printed pieces or tearsheets as samples, as these show publishers that your work reproduces well and that you have some understanding of the publication process. Most publishers will accept digital submissions via e-mail or CD.

Signing and Numbering Your Editions

Before you enter the print arena, follow the standard method of signing and numbering your editions. You can observe how this is done by visiting galleries and museums and talking to fellow artists.

If you are creating a limited edition—with a specific, set number of prints—all prints should be numbered, such as 35/100. The larger number is the total number of prints in the edition; the smaller number is the sequential number of the actual print. Some artists hold out 10 percent as artist's proofs and number them separately with AP after the number (e.g., 5/100 AP). Many artists sign and number their prints in pencil.

Types of Prints

Original prints. Original prints may be woodcuts, engravings, linocuts, mezzotints, etchings, lithographs, or serigraphs (see Glossary for definitions). What distinguishes them is that they are produced by hand by the artist (and consequently often referred to as hand-pulled prints). In a true original print, the work is created specifically to be a print. Each print is considered an original because the artist creates the artwork directly on the plate, woodblock, etching stone, or screen. Original prints are sold through specialized print galleries, frame shops, high-end decorating outlets, and fine art galleries.

Offset reproductions and posters. Offset reproductions, also known as posters and image prints, are reproduced by photochemical means. Since plates used in offset reproductions do not wear out, there are no physical limits on the number of prints that can be made. Quantities, however, may still be limited by the publisher in order to add value to the edition.

Giclée prints. As color-copier technology matures, inkjet fine art prints, also called giclées, are gaining popularity. Iris prints, images that are scanned into a computer and output on oversized printers, are even showing up in museum collections.

Canvas transfers. Canvas transfers are becoming increasingly popular. Instead of, and often in addition to, printing an image on paper, the publisher transfers the image onto canvas so the work has the look and feel of a painting. Some publishers market limited editions of 750 prints on paper, along with a smaller edition of 100 of the same image on canvas. The edition on paper might sell for about half the price (or a little less) than the price of the canvas transfer.

Pricing Criteria for Limited Editions and Posters

Because original prints are always sold in limited editions, they command higher prices than posters, which are not numbered. Since plates for original prints are made by hand, and as a result can withstand only a certain amount of use, the number of prints pulled is limited by the number of impressions that can be made before the plate wears out. Some publishers impose their own limits on the number of impressions to increase a print's value. These limits may be set as high as 700 to 1,000 impressions, but some prints are limited to just 250 to 500, making them highly prized by collectors.

A few publishers buy work outright for a flat fee, but most pay on a royalty basis. Royalties for hand-pulled prints are usually based on retail price and range from 5 to 20 percent, while percentages for posters and offset reproductions are lower (from 2½ to 5 percent) and are based on the wholesale price. Be aware that some publishers may hold back royalties to cover promotion and production costs; this is not uncommon.

Prices for prints vary widely depending on the quantity available; the artist's reputation; the popularity of the image; the quality of the paper, ink, and printing process. Because prices for posters are lower than for original prints, publishers tend to select images with high-volume sales potential.

Negotiating Your Contract

As in other business transactions, ask for a contract and make sure you understand and agree to all the terms before you sign. Make sure you approve the size, printing method, paper, number of images to be produced, and royalty terms. Other things to watch for include insurance terms, marketing plans, and guarantees of a credit line or copyright notice.

Always retain ownership of your original work. Negotiate an arrangement in which you're selling publication rights only. You'll also want to sell rights for only a limited period of time. That way you can sell the image later as a reprint or license it for other use (e.g., as a calendar or note card). If you are a perfectionist about color, make sure your contract gives you final approval of your print. Stipulate that you'd like to inspect a press proof prior to the print run.

MORE INDUSTRY TIPS

Find a niche. Consider working within a specialized subject matter. Prints with Civil War themes, for example, are avidly collected by Civil War enthusiasts. But to appeal to Civil War buffs, every detail, from weapons and foliage in battlefields to uniform buttons, must be historically accurate. Signed limited editions are usually created in a print run of 950 or so and can average about $175–200; artists' proofs sell from between $195–250, with canvas transfers selling for $400–500. The original paintings from which images are taken often sell for thousands of dollars to avid collectors.

Sport art is another lucrative niche. There's a growing trend toward portraying sports figures from football, basketball, and racing (both sports car and horse racing) in prints that include both the artist's and the athlete's signatures. Movie stars and musicians from the 1950s (such as James Dean, Marilyn Monroe, and Elvis) are also cult favorites, but any specialized style (such as science fiction/fantasy or wildlife art) can be a marketable niche. See the Market Niche Index for more ideas.

Work in a series. It is easier to market a series of small prints exploring a single theme than to market single images. A series of similar prints works well in long hospital corridors, office meeting rooms, or restaurants. Paired images also are rather profitable. Hotels often purchase two similar prints for each of their rooms.

Study trends. If you hope to get published by a commercial art publisher or poster company, realize your work will have a greater chance of acceptance if you use popular colors and themes.

Attend trade shows. Many artists say it's the best way to research the market and make contacts. It's also a great way for self-published artists to market their work. DECOR Expo is held each year in four cities: Atlanta, New York, Orlando, and Los Angeles. For more information, call (888)608-5300 or visit www.decor-expo.com. Artexpo is held every spring in New York and now every fall in Las Vegas. The SOLO Independent Artists' Pavilion, a special section of Artexpo dedicated to showcasing the work of emerging artists, is the ultimate venue for artists to be discovered. See www.artexpos.com for more information.

ARNOLD ART STORE & GALLERY

210 Thames St., Newport RI 02840. (401)847-2273; (800)352-2234. **Fax:** (401)848-0156. **E-mail:** info@arnoldart.com. **Website:** www.arnoldart.com. **Contact:** Bill Rommel, owner. Estab. 1870. Poster company; art publisher/distributor; gallery specializing in marine art. Publishes/distributes limited and unlimited editions, fine art prints, offset reproductions and posters. **NEEDS** Seeking creative, fashionable, decorative art for the serious collector, commercial and designer markets. Considers oil, acrylic, watercolor, mixed media, pastel, pen & ink, sculpture. Prefers sailing images—America's Cup or other racing images. Artists represented include Kathy Bray, Thomas Buechner and James DeWitt. Editions are created by working from an existing painting. Approached by 100 artists/year. Publishes/distributes the work of 10-15 established artists/year.
CONTACT & TERMS Send query letter with 4-5 photographs. Samples are filed or returned by SASE. Call to arrange portfolio review. Pays flat fee, royalties or consignment. Negotiates rights purchased; rights purchased vary according to project. Provides advertising and promotion. Finds artists through word of mouth.

HERBERT ARNOT, INC.

250 W. 57th St., 10th Floor, Suite 1014, New York NY 10107. (212)245-8287; after-hours (917)570-7910. **E-mail:** arnotart@aol.com. **Website:** www.arnotart.com. **Contact:** Vicki Arnot, owner/partner with Peter Arnot. Art dealer of original paintings, color Kasimir Etching, and limited edition Luigi Rocca Giclées. Clients: art galleries, design firms and collectors.
NEEDS Seeking creative and decorative art for the serious collector and designer market. Considers oil and acrylic paintings in all styles. Considers sculpture. Has wide range of themes and styles "mostly traditional/impressionistic." Artists represented include Raymond Campbell, Claudio Simonetti, Guy Dessapt, MALVA, Estate of Christian Nesvadba, Gerhard Nesvadba, Claudia Fisher, Michael Minthorn, and many others. Distributes the work of 250 artists/year.
CONTACT & TERMS Send query letter with brochure, résumé, business card—photographs are discarded or returned by SASE. Responds in 1 month. Portfolios may be mailed, or by appointment. Provides promotion.
TIPS "Artist should be professional."

ART BROKERS OF COLORADO

7615 Jeffrey Lane, Colorado Springs CO 80919. (719)520-9177; (800)210-9177. **Fax:** (719)633-5747. **E-mail:** artbrokers@aol.com. **Website:** www.artbrokers.com. Estab. 1991. Art publisher. Publishes limited and unlimited editions, posters and offset reproductions. Clients: galleries, decorators, frame shops.
NEEDS Seeking decorative art by established artists for the serious collector. Prefers oil, watercolor and acrylic. Prefers western theme. Editions created by collaborating with the artist. Approached by 20-40 artists/year. Publishes the work of 1-2 established artists/year.
CONTACT & TERMS Send query letter with photographs. Samples are not filed and are returned by SASE. Responds in 4-6 weeks. Company will contact artist for portfolio review of final art if interested. Pays royalties. Rights purchased vary according to project. Provides insurance while work is at firm.
TIPS Advises artists to attend all the trade shows and to participate as often as possible.

ART DALLAS, INC.

2325 Valdina St., Dallas TX 75207. (214)688-0244. **Fax:** (214)688-7758. **E-mail:** info@artdallas.com. **Website:** www.artdallas.com. **Contact:** Judy Martin, president. Estab. 1988. Art distributor, gallery, framing and display company. Distributes handpulled originals, offset reproductions. Clients: designers, architects. "Art Dallas, Inc. provides art and framing services to the design trade. Our goal is to provide the best, most complete service at the best possible price. The Gallery at Art Dallas, Inc. is a recently renovated 8,000 ft. showroom in the Dallas Design District. It is a commercial, working gallery with lots of table space. This allows our designers to spread out, facilitating the design of more than one project at a time."
NEEDS Seeking creative art for the commercial and designer markets. Considers mixed media. Prefers abstract, landscapes.
CONTACT & TERMS Send query letter with résumé, photocopies, slides, photographs and transparencies. Samples are filed or are returned. Call for appointment to show portfolio of slides and photographs. Pays flat fee $50-5,000. Offers advance when appropriate. Negotiates rights purchased.

◯ ART SOURCE

1040 Ronsa Court, Mississauga Ontario L4W 3Y4, Canada. (905)475-8181. **Fax:** (905)479-4966. **E-mail:**

art@artsource.ca. **Website:** www.artsource.ca. **Contact:** Victoria Fenninger, art director. Estab. 1978. Poster company and distributor. Publishes/distributes hand-pulled originals, limited editions, unlimited editions, canvas transfers, fine art prints, monoprints, monotypes, offset reproductions and posters. Clients: galleries, decorators, frame shops, distributors, corporate curators, museum shops and gift shops.

NEEDS Seeking creative, fashionable and decorative art for the designer market. Considers oil, acrylic, watercolor, mixed media, pastel and pen & ink. Editions are created by collaborating with the artist and by working from an existing painting. Approached by 50 artists/year. Publishes the work of 2 emerging, 5 mid-career and 8 established artists/year. Distributes the work of 2 emerging, 5 mid-career and 8 established artists/year.

CONTACT & TERMS Send query letter with brochure, photocopies, photographs, photostats, résumé, SASE, slides, tearsheets and transparencies. Accepts submissions via e-mail. Company will contact artist for portfolio review if interested. Portfolios may be dropped off every Monday and Tuesday. Portfolio should include color photographs, photostats, roughs, slides, tearsheets, thumbnails and transparencies. Artist should follow up with letter after initial query. Pays royalties of 6-12%; flat fee is optional. Payment is negotiable. Offers advance when appropriate. Negotiates rights purchased. Rights purchased vary according to project. Sometimes requires exclusive representation of artist. Provides advertising, promotion and written contract.

TIPS "We are looking for more original art for our distribution."

THE BENJAMAN GALLERY

419 Elmwood Ave., Buffalo NY 14222. (716)886-0898. **Fax:** (716)886-0546. **E-mail:** info@thebenjamangallery.com. **Website:** www.benjamangallery.com. Estab. 1970. Art publisher, distributor, gallery, frame shop and appraiser. Publishes and distributes handpulled originals, limited and unlimited editions, posters, offset reproductions and sculpture. Clients include P&B International.

NEEDS Seeking decorative art for the serious collector. Considers oil, watercolor, acrylic and sculpture. Prefers art deco and florals. Artists represented include Peter Max, Robert Blair, Joan Miro, Charles Birchfield, J.C. Litz, Jason Barr and Eric Dates. Edi-

tions created by collaborating with the artist. Approached by 20-30 artists/year. Publishes and distributes the work of 4 emerging, 2 mid-career and 1 established artists/year.

CONTACT & TERMS Send query letter with SASE, slides, photocopies, résumé, transparencies, tearsheets or photographs. Samples are filed or returned. Responds in 2 weeks. Company will contact artist for portfolio review if interested. Pays on consignment basis. Firm receives 30-50% commission. Offers advance when appropriate. Rights purchased vary according to project. Does not require exclusive representation of artist. Provides advertising, promotion, shipping to and from firm, written contract and insurance while work is at firm.

TIPS "Keep trying to join a group of artists and try to develop a unique style."

THE BLACKMAR COLLECTION

P.O. Box 537, Chester CT 06412. (860)526-9303. **E-mail:** carser@mindspring.com. Art publisher. Publishes offset reproduction and giclée prints. Clients: individual buyers.

NEEDS "We are not actively recruiting at this time." Artists represented include DeLos Blackmar, Blair Hammond, Gladys Bates and Keith Murphey. Editions are created by working from an existing painting. Approached by 24 artists/year. Publishes the work of 3 established artists/year. Provides advertising, in-transit insurance, insurance while work is at firm. Finds artists through personal contact. All sales have a buy back guarantee.

JOE BUCKALEW

1825 Annwicks Dr., Marietta GA 30062. (800)971-9530. **Fax:** (770)971-6582. **E-mail:** art@joebuckalew.com; joesart@bellsouth.net. **Website:** www.joebuckalew.com. Estab. 1990. Distributor and publisher. Distributes limited editions, canvas transfers, fine art prints and posters. Clients: frame shops, galleries, interior designers, corporate accounts, financial institutions.

NEEDS Seeking creative, fashionable, decorative art for the serious collector. Considers oil, acrylic and watercolor. Prefers florals, landscapes, Civil War and sports. Approached by 25-30 artists/year. Distributes work of 10 emerging, 10 mid-career and 50 established artists/year. Art guidelines free with SASE and first-class postage.

CONTACT & TERMS Send sample prints. Accepts disk submissions. "Please call. Currently using a 460 commercial computer." Samples are filed or are returned. Does not reply. Artist should call. To show portfolio, artist should follow up with call after initial query. Portfolio should include sample prints. Pays on consignment basis. Firm receives 50% commission, paid net 30 days. Provides advertising on website, shipping from firm and company catalog. Finds artists through ABC shows, regional art & craft shows, frame shops, other artists.
TIPS "Paint your own style."

☺ CANADIAN ART PRINTS AND WINN DEVON ART GROUP INC.

Unit 110, 6311 Westminster Hwy., Richmond British Columbia V7C 4V4, Canada. **E-mail:** artsubmissions@capandwinndevon.com. **Website:** www.capandwinndevon.com. Estab. 1965. Art publisher/distributor. Publishes or distributes open edition and limited edition, canvas & poster prints, and art cards. Clients: galleries, various interior design and decorators (homes, hospitality & tourism), frame shops, distributors, corporate curators, museums, giftshops and home décor retailers. Licenses all subjects of open editions for wallpaper, writing paper, placemats, books, etc.
NEEDS Seeking fashionable and decorative art for the commercial and designer markets. Considers oil, acrylic, watercolor, mixed media, pastel paintings, photography, and digital art. Prefers representational/transitional and florals, landscapes, abstracts, marine, decorative and street scenes. Editions created by collaborating with the artist and working from an existing painting. Approached by 300-400 artists/year. Publishes/distributes the work of more than 150 artists/year.
CONTACT & TERMS Send e-mail with low-res JPEGs, website, address or send query letter with photographs, SASE, slides, tearsheets, transparencies. Samples are not filed and are returned by SASE. Will contact artist for portfolio review if interested. Normally takes 4-6 weeks to review submissions. Pays range of royalties. Obtains licensing rights to publish. Provides promotion and advertising, in-transit insurance, insurance while work is at firm, shipping and contract. Finds artists through art exhibitions, art fairs, word of mouth, art reps, Internet research and submissions.

TIPS "Keep up with trends by following decorating magazines."

CARPENTREE, INC.

2724 N. Sheridan, Tulsa OK 74115. (800)736-2787. **E-mail:** smorris@carpentree.com; jhobson@carpentree.com. **Website:** www.carpentree.com. **Contact:** Dan and Ginny Hobson, owners. Estab. 1976. Wholesale framed art manufacturer. Clients: decorators, frame shops, galleries, gift shops and museum shops.
NEEDS Seeking decorative art for the commercial market. Considers acrylic, mixed media, oil, pastel, pen & ink, sculpture, watercolor and photography. Prefers traditional, family-oriented, Biblical themes, landscapes. Editions created by collaborating with the artist and by working from an existing painting. Approached by 50 artists/year.
CONTACT & TERMS Send JPEG files only to smorris@carpentree.com. Prefers Windows compatible JPEG files. Do not send original art. Samples are not filed. Responds in 2-4 months. Portfolio not required. Negotiates payment. No advance. Negotiates rights purchased. Requires exclusive regional representation of artist. Provides advertising, promotion, and written contract. Finds artists through art exhibits/fairs and artist's submissions.

CHALK & VERMILION FINE ARTS

55 Old Post Rd., #2, Greenwich CT 06830. (203)869-9500. **Website:** www.chalk-vermilion.com. **Contact:** artist submission department. Estab. 1976. Art publisher. Publishes original paintings, hand-pulled serigraphs and lithographs, posters, limited editions and offset reproductions. Clients: 4,000 galleries worldwide.
NEEDS Publishes decorative art for the serious collector and the commercial market. Considers oil, mixed media, acrylic and sculpture. Editions created by collaboration. Approached by 350 artists/year.
CONTACT & TERMS Full submission guidelines available online. Send samples of your work (photos or slides), contact information, a resume and/or a biography and any other information you can share about yourself and your art.

CIRRUS EDITIONS

2011 S. Santa Fe Ave., Los Angeles CA 90021. (213)680-3473. **Fax:** (213)680-0930. **E-mail:** cirrus@cirrusgallery.com. **Website:** www.cirrusgallery.com. **Contact:** Jean R. Milant, director. Produces limited edition hand-pulled originals. Clients: museums, galleries and private collectors.

NEEDS Seeking fine art for the serious collector and museums. Prefers abstract, conceptual work. Publishes and distributes the work of 6 emerging, 2 mid-career and 1 established artists/year.

CONTACT & TERMS Prefers CD or low-res JPEGs. Samples are returned by SASE. No illustrators, graphic designers or commercial art submissions.

CLAY STREET PRESS, INC.

1312 Clay St., Cincinnati OH 45202. (513)241-3232. E-mail: mpginc@iac.net. **Website:** www.patsfallgraph ics.com. **Contact:** Mark Patsfall, owner. Estab. 1981. Art publisher and printer. Publishes fine art prints, hand-pulled original etchings, lithographs, woodcuts and silk screen prints in limited editions. Clients: architects, corporate curators, decorators, galleries and museum print curators.

NEEDS Works are conceptual/contemporary and are created by collaborating with the artist. Publishes the work of 2-3 emerging artists/year.

CONTACT & TERMS Contact through e-mail or phone.

COLOR CIRCLE ART PUBLISHING, INC.

791 Tremont St., Box A, Suite N104, Boston MA 02118. (800)254-1795. **Fax:** (617)437-9217. **E-mail:** colorcir cleart@gmail.com. **Website:** www.colorcircle.com. **Contact:** Bernice Robinson, co-founder/marketing and administration. Estab. 1991. Art publisher. Publishes limited editions, unlimited editions, fine art prints, offset reproductions, posters. Clients: galleries, art dealers, distributors, museum shops. Current clients include Deck the Walls, Things Graphics, Essence Art.

NEEDS Seeking creative, decorative art for the serious collector and the commercial market. Considers oil, acrylic, watercolor, mixed media, pastel, pen & ink. Prefers ethnic themes. Artists represented include Paul Goodnight. Editions created by collaborating with the artist or by working from an existing painting. Approached by 12-15 artists/year. Publishes the work of 2 emerging, 1 mid-career artists/year. Distributes the work of 4 emerging, 1 mid-career artists/year.

CONTACT & TERMS Send query letter with slides. Samples are filed or returned by SASE. Responds in 2 months. Negotiates payment. Rights purchased vary according to project. Provides advertising, insurance

while work is at firm, promotion, shipping from our firm and written contract. Finds artists through submissions, trade shows and word of mouth.

TIPS "We like to present at least 2 pieces by a new artist that are similar in theme, treatment or colors."

DARE TO MOVE

6621 83rd St. E., Puyallup WA 98371. (206)380-4378. **E-mail:** daretomove@aol.com. **Website:** www.dare tomove.com. **Contact:** Steve W. Sherman, president. Estab. 1987. Art publisher, distributor. Publishes/distributes limited editions, unlimited editions, canvas transfers, fine art prints, offset reproductions. Licenses aviation and marine art for puzzles, note cards, bookmarks, coasters, etc. Clients include art galleries, aviation museums, frame shops and interior decorators.

◯ This company has expanded from aviation-related artwork to work encompassing most civil service areas. Steve Sherman likes to work with artists who have been painting for 10-20 years. He usually starts off distributing self-published prints. If prints sell well, he will work with artists to publish new editions.

NEEDS Seeking naval, marine, firefighter, civil service and aviation-related art for the serious collector and commercial market. Considers oil and acrylic. Editions are created by collaborating with the artist or working from an existing painting. Approached by 15-20 artists/year.

CONTACT & TERMS Send query letter with photographs, slides, tearsheets and transparencies. Samples are filed or sometimes returned by SASE. Artist should follow up with a call. Portfolio should include color photographs, transparencies and final art. Pays royalties of 10% commission of wholesale price on limited editions; 5% commission of wholesale price on unlimited editions. Buys one-time or reprint rights. Provides advertising, in-transit insurance, insurance while work is at firm, promotion, shipping from firm, and written contract.

TIPS "Present your best work professionally."

EDITIONS LIMITED GALLERIES, INC.

4090 Halleck St., Emeryville CA 94608. (510)923-9770, ext. 6998; (800)228-0928. **Fax:** (510)923-9777. **E-mail:** submissions@editionslimited.com. **Website:** www.editionslimited.com. **Contact:** Todd Haile, poster publishing; Christy Carleton, original art. Art publisher and distributor of limited open edition prints and fine art posters. Clients: contract framers, galleries, framing stores, art consultants and interior designers.

NEEDS Seeking art for the original and designer markets. Considers oil, acrylic and watercolor painting, monoprint, monotype, photography and mixed media. Prefers landscape, floral and abstract imagery. Editions created by collaborating with the artist or by working from existing works.

CONTACT & TERMS Send query letter with résumé, slides and photographs or JPEG files (8 inch maximum at 72 dpi) via e-mail. Samples are filed or are returned by SASE. Responds in 2 months. Publisher/distributor will contact artist for portfolio review if interested. Payment method is negotiated. Negotiates rights purchased.

TIPS "We deal both nationally and internationally, so we need art with wide appeal. When sending slides or photos, send at least 6 so we can get an overview of your work. We publish artists, not just images."

ENCORE GRAPHICS & FINE ART

P.O. Box 32, Huntsville AL 35804. (256)509-7944. **E-mail:** encore@randenterprises.com; or by contact form. **Website:** www.egart.com. Estab. 1995. Poster company, art publisher, distributor. Publishes/distributes limited edition, unlimited edition, fine art prints, offset reproduction, posters. Clients: galleries, frame shops, distributors.

NEEDS Creative art for the serious collector. Considers all media. Prefers African-American and abstract. Art guidelines available on company's website. Artists represented include Greg Gamble, Tod Fredericks, Tim Hinton, Mario Robinson, Lori Goodwin, Wyndall Coleman, T.H. Waldman, John Will Davis, Burl Washington, Henry Battle, Cisco Davis, Delbert Iron-Cloud, Gary Thomas and John Moore. Also Buffalo Soldier Prints and historical military themes. Editions created by working from an existing painting. Approached by 15 artists/year. Publishes the work of 3 emerging artists, 1 mid-career artist/year. Distributes the work of 3 emerging, 2 mid-career and 3 established artists/year.

CONTACT & TERMS Send photocopies, photographs, résumé, tearsheets. Samples are filed. Responds only if interested. Company will contact artist for portfolio review of color, photographs, tearsheets if interested. Negotiates payment. Offers advance when appropriate. Requires exclusive representation

of artist. Provides advertising, in-transit insurance, insurance while work is at firm, promotion, shipping from firm, written contract. Finds artists through the Internet and art exhibits.

TIPS "Prints of African Americans with religious themes or children are popular now. Paint from the heart."

ELEANOR ETTINGER, INC.

24 W. 57th St., New York NY 10019. (212)925-7474 (57th St.); (212)925-7686 (Chelsea location). **Fax:** (212)925-7734. **E-mail:** eegallery@aol.com or via online contact form. **Website:** www.eegallery.com. **Contact:** Eleanor Ettinger, president. Estab. 1975. Art dealer of limited edition lithographs, limited edition sculpture and unique works (oil, watercolor, drawings, etc.).

NEEDS Seeks classically inspired realistic work involving figurative, landscapes and still lifes for the serious collector. Considers oil, acrylic, mixed media. Prefers American realism.

CONTACT & TERMS Send query letter with visuals (slides, photographs, etc.), a brief biography, résumé (including a list of exhibitions and collections) and SASE for return of the materials. Responds in 3-4 weeks.

FAIRFIELD ART PUBLISHING

87 35th St., 3rd Floor, Brooklyn NY 11232. (800)835-3539. **Fax:** (718)832-8432. **E-mail:** fairfieldart@gmail.com. **Contact:** Peter Lowenkron, vice president. Estab. 1996. Art publisher. Publishes posters, limited editions and offset reproductions. Clients: galleries, frame shops, museum shops, decorators, corporate curators, gift shops, manufacturers and contract framers.

NEEDS Decorative art for the designer and commercial markets. Considers photography, collage, oil, watercolor, pastel, pen & ink, acrylic. Artists represented include Daniel Pollera, Roger Vilarchao, Carol Saxe and Eve Turek.

CONTACT & TERMS Send query letter with slides and brochure. Samples are returned by SASE if requested by artist. Responds only if interested. Pays flat fee, or royalties of 7-15%. Offers advance when appropriate. Rights purchased vary according to project. Interested in buying second rights (reprint rights) to previously published artwork.

RUSSELL FINK GALLERY

P.O. Box 250, Lorton VA 22199. (703)550-9699. **Fax:** (703)339-6150. **E-mail:** info@russellfinkgallery.com. **Website:** russellfinkgallery.com. **Contact:** Russell A. Fink. Art publisher.

NEEDS Considers oil, acrylic and watercolor. Prefers wildlife and sporting themes. Prefers individual works of art; framed. "Submit photos or slides of at least near-professional quality. Include size, price, media and other pertinent data regarding the artwork. Also send personal résumé and be courteous enough to include SASE for return of any material sent to me." Artists represented include Ray Harris-Ching, Ken Carlson, John Loren Head, Robert Abbett, Rod Crossman, Manfred Schatz and Chet Reneson.

CONTACT & TERMS Send query letter with slides or photographs to be kept on file. Call or write for appointment to show portfolio. Samples returned if not kept on file.

TIPS "Looks for composition, style and technique in samples. Also how the artist views his own art. Mistakes artists make are arrogance, overpricing, explaining their art and underrating the role of the dealer."

FORTUNE FINE ART

7825 E. Redfield Rd., Suite 105, Scottsdale AZ 85260. (480)946-1055; (800)350-1030. **E-mail:** carolv@fortunefa.com; inquiry@fortunefa.com. **Website:** www.fortunefa.com. **Contact:** Carol J. Vidic, principal. Publishes fine art prints, hand-pulled serigraphs, giclées, originals, limited editions, offset reproductions, posters and unlimited editions. Clients: art galleries, dealers and designers.

NEEDS Seeking creative art for the serious collector. Considers oil on canvas, acrylic on canvas, mixed media on canvas and paper. Artists represented include John Powell, Daniel Gerhartz, Marilyn Simandle, Ming Feng, S. Burkett Kaiser and B. Nicole Klassen. Publishes and distributes the work of a varying number of emerging artists/year.

CONTACT & TERMS Send query letter with résumé, slides, photographs, biography and SASE or send digital images to carolv@fortunefa.com. Samples are not filed. Responds in 1 month. To show a portfolio, mail appropriate materials. Prefers exclusive representation of artist. Provides in-transit insurance, insurance while work is at firm, promotion and written contract.

TIPS "Establish a unique style, look or concept before looking to be published."

GALAXY OF GRAPHICS, LTD.

30 Murray Hill Pkwy., Suite 300, East Rutherford NJ 07073-2180. (888)464-7500. **E-mail:** clbuchweitz@gmail.com; susan.murphy@kapgog.com. **Website:** www.galaxyofgraphics.com. **Contact:** Colleen Buchweitz, art director. Estab. 1983. Art publisher and distributor of unlimited editions. Licensor of images for retail and home decor products such as kitchen textiles, bath accessories, stationery, etc. Licensing handled by Susan Murphy. Clients: distributors and picture frame manufacturers that sell to retail stores.

NEEDS Seeking landscape, floral, and decorative artists that are excited by home decor style trends. We are seeking artists that have a unique look and decorative approach to their work. Editions are created by collaborating with the artist or by working from an existing painting. Considers any media. "Any currently popular and generally accepted themes." Art guidelines free via e-mail request. Approached by several hundred artists/year. Publishes and distributes the work of 20 emerging and 20 mid-career and established artists/year.

CONTACT & TERMS "Please e-mail submissions or send color copies or a CD (in Mac-based files or JPEG format). Include a SASE if you would like your submission returned and write 'Artist Submission' above the address. We can take anywhere from 2-4 weeks to review your work so please be patient, as we carefully review each submission we receive."

TIPS "We sell images that coordinate with changing home decor trends in style and color. Consider this the 'fashion' market for 2D Artists."

GALLERY GRAPHICS, INC.

P.O. Box 631, 2210 S. Main St., Ft. Scott Kansas 66701. (620)223-5190 ext. 7014. **Fax:** (620)223-6955. **E-mail:** info@gallerygraphics.com; britegraphix@gmail.com. **Website:** www.gallerygraphics.com. Estab. 1979. Wholesale producer and distributor of prints, cards, sachets, stationery, calendars, framed art, stickers. Clients: frame shops, craft shops, florists, pharmacies and gift shops.

NEEDS Seeking art with nostalgic look, country, Victorian, children, angels, florals, landscapes, animals—nothing abstract or nonrepresentational. Considers oil, watercolor, mixed media, pastel and pen & ink.

10% of editions created by collaborating with artist. 90% created by working from an existing painting.

CONTACT & TERMS Send query letter with brochure showing art style and tearsheets. Designers send photographs, photocopies and tearsheets. Accepts disk submissions compatible with IBM or Mac. Samples are filed or returned by SASE. Responds in 2 months. To show portfolio, mail finished art samples, color tearsheets. Can buy all rights or pay royalties. Provides a written contract.

TIPS "Please submit artwork on different subjects and styles. Some artists do certain subjects particularly well, but you don't know if they can do other subjects. Don't concentrate on just one area. Don't limit yourself, or you could be missing out on some great opportunities."

GEME ART, INC.

209 W. Sixth St., Vancouver WA 98660. (360)693-7772 or (800)426-4424. **Fax:** (360)695-9795. **E-mail:** gemeart@hotmail.com. **Website:** www.gemeart.com. Estab. 1966. Art publisher. Publishes fine art prints and reproductions in unlimited and limited editions. Clients: galleries, frame shops, art museums, manufacturers, craft shops. Licenses designs.

NEEDS Considers oil, acrylic, watercolor and mixed media. "We use a variety of styles from realistic to whimsical, catering to 'mid-America art market.' Artists represented include Lois Thayer, Crystal Skelley, Steve Nelson.

CONTACT & TERMS Send color slides, photos or brochure. Include SASE. Publisher will contact artist for portfolio review if interested. Simultaneous submissions OK. Payment on a royalty basis. Purchases all rights. Provides promotion, shipping from publisher and contract.

GLEEDSVILLE ART PUBLISHERS

5 W. Loudoun St., Leesburg VA 20175. (703)771-8055 or (800)771-8055. **Fax:** (703)771-8055. **E-mail:** buy art@gleedsvilleart.com. **Website:** www.gleedsville gallery.com. **Contact:** Lawrence J. Thomas, president. Estab. 1999. Prints fine art prints, photography and graphic designs. Clients: art collectors, artists, photographers, decorators, distributors, frame shops and galleries.

NEEDS Seeking fine art and photography for the serious collector, commercial and designer markets. Considers all fine art mediums including photography and

digital design.Editions created by collaborating with the artist.

CONTACT & TERMS The preferred method of submission is e-mail with low resolution files or link to website. Company will contact artist for portfolio review if interested. Pays royalties and requires exclusive representation or artist.

HADDAD'S FINE ARTS, INC.

3855 E. Mira Loma Ave., Anaheim CA 92806. (714)996-2100; (800)942-3323. **Fax:** (714)996-4153. **E-mail:** artmail@haddadsfinearts.com. **Website:** www. haddadsfinearts.com. **Contact:** art director. Estab. 1953. Art publisher and distributor. Produces unlimited edition offset reproductions and posters. Clients: galleries, art stores, museum stores and manufacturers. Sells to the trade only—no retail.

NEEDS Seeking creative and decorative art for the commercial and designer markets. Seeks traditional/transitional scenes: landscapes, floral, decorative, abstract contemporary, and more—broad subject mix. Editions created by collaborating with the artist or by working from an existing painting. Approached by 200-300 artists/year. Publishes the work of 10-15 emerging artists/year. Also uses freelancers for design. 20% of projects require freelance design. Design demands knowledge of QuarkXPress and Illustrator.

CONTACT & TERMS Submission guidelines available online. "We would like to see slides, color copies, photographs or other representative examples of your artwork. Please do not send original art or transparencies as we do not want your irreplaceable items to be lost or damaged en route. We can also accept PC-readable CDs and e-mailed files, but mailed materials are preferred (attn: Art Director). We appreciate receiving a SASE for the return of your materials. We are not able to accept any posters or prints already in distribution."

HADLEY HOUSE PUBLISHING

4816 Nicollet Ave. S., Minneapolis MN 55419. (800)423-5390. **Fax:** (952)943-8098. **Website:** www. hadleyhouse.com. Estab. 1974. Art publisher, distributor. Publishes and distributes canvas transfers, fine art prints, giclées, limited and unlimited editions, offset reproductions and posters. Licenses all types of flat art. Clients: wholesale and retail.

NEEDS Seeking artwork with creative artistic expression and decorative appeal. Considers oil, watercolor, acrylic, pastel and mixed media. Prefers florals, landscapes, figurative and nostalgic Americana themes and styles. Art guidelines free for SASE with first-class postage. Artists represented include Nancy Howe, Steve Hamrick, Sueellen Ross, Collin Bogle, Lee Bogle and Bruce Miller. Editions are created by collaborating with artist and by working from an existing painting. Approached by 200-300 artists/year. Publishes the work of 3-4 emerging, 15 mid-career and 8 established artists/year. Distributes the work of 1 emerging and 4 mid-career artists/year.

CONTACT & TERMS Send query letter with brochure showing art style or résumé and tearsheets, slides, photographs and transparencies. Samples are filed or are returned. Responds in 2 months. Call for appointment to show portfolio of slides, original final art and transparencies. Pays royalties. Requires exclusive representation of artist or art. Provides insurance while work is at firm, promotion, shipping from firm, a written contract and advertising through dealer showcase.

TIPS "Build a market for your originals by affiliating with an art gallery or 2. Never give away your copyrights! When you can no longer satisfy the overwhelming demand for your originals, *that* is when you can hope for success in the reproduction market."

IMAGE CONNECTION

456 Penn St., Yeadon PA 19050. (610)626-7770. **Fax:** (610)626-2778. **E-mail:** sales@imageconnection.biz. **Website:** www.imageconnection.biz. **Contact:** Michael Markowicz, president. Estab. 1988. Publishes and distributes limited editions and posters. Represents several European publishers.

NEEDS Seeking fashionable and decorative art for the commercial market. Considers oil, pen & ink, watercolor, acrylic, pastel and mixed media. Prefers contemporary and popular themes, realistic and abstract art. Editions are created by collaborating with the artist and by working from an existing painting. Approached by 200 artists/year.

CONTACT & TERMS Send query letter with brochure showing art style or résumé, slides, photocopies, photographs, tearsheets and transparencies. Accepts e-mail submissions with link to website or Mac-compatible image file. Samples are not filed and are returned by SASE. Responds in 2 months. Will contact artist for portfolio review if interested. Portfolio should include b&w and color finished, original art, photographs, slides, tearsheets and transparen-

cies. Payment method is negotiated. Offers advance when appropriate. Negotiates rights purchased. Requires exclusive representation of artist for product. Finds artists through art competitions, exhibits/fairs, reps, submissions, Internet, sourcebooks and word of mouth.

IMAGE CONSCIOUS

147 Tenth St., San Francisco CA 94103. (415)626-1555 or (800)532-2333. **Fax:** (415)626-2481. **E-mail:** inquiries@imageconscious.com; jweiss@imageconscious.com. **Website:** www.imageconscious.com. **Contact:** Jan Weiss, art director. Estab. 1980. Art publisher and domestic and international distributor of offset and poster reproductions. Now licensing images as well. Clients: poster galleries, frame shops, department stores, design consultants, interior designers and gift stores.

NEEDS Seeking creative and decorative art for the designer market. Considers oil, acrylic, pastel, watercolor, tempera, mixed media and photography. Prefers individual works of art, pairs or unframed series. Editions created by collaborating with the artist and by working from an existing painting or photograph. Approached by hundreds of artists/year. Publishes the work of 4-6 emerging, 4-6 mid-career and 8-10 established artists/year. Distributes the work of 50 emerging, 200 mid-career and 700 established artists/year.

CONTACT & TERMS Send query letter with brochure, résumé, tearsheets, photographs, slides or transparencies. Samples are filed or returned by SASE. Accepts low-res e-mail submissions. Please limit initial submissions to 10 images. Responds in 1 month. Publisher/distributor will contact artist for portfolio review if interested. No original art. Payment method is negotiated. Negotiates rights purchased. Provides promotion, shipping from firm and a written contract.

TIPS "Research the type of product currently in poster shops. Note colors, sizes and subject matter trends."

IMAGE SOURCE INTERNATIONAL

320 Main St., Unit B, Buzzards Bay MA 02532. (774)302-4076. **Fax:** (774)302-4973. **E-mail:** pdownes@isiposters.com; jwaters@isiposters.com. **Website:** www.isiposters.com. **Contact:** Patrick Downes; Jobe Waters, art director. Poster company, art publisher/distributor. Publishes/distributes unlimited editions, fine art prints, fine art prints, canvas and offset reproductions, posters. Clients: direct to retail chain stores, galleries, decorators, frame shops, distribu-

tors, architects, corporate curators, museum shops, gift shops, foreign distributors (Germany, Holland, Asia, South America).

◯ Image Source International is one of America's fastest-growing publishers.

NEEDS Seeking fashionable, decorative art for the designer market. Considers oil, acrylic, pastel.

CONTACT & TERMS Send query letter with brochure, photocopies, photographs, résumé, slides, tearsheets, transparencies, postcards. Samples are filed and are not returned. Responds only if interested. Company will contact artist for portfolio review if interested. Pays flat fee or 10% royalty "that depends on artist and work and risk." Buys all rights for prints and posters. Does not require exclusive representation of artist.

TIPS Notes trends as sports art, neo-classical, nostalgic, oversize editions. "Think marketability. Watch the furniture market."

INSPIRATIONART & SCRIPTURE, INC.

P.O. Box 5550, Cedar Rapids IA 52406. (319)651-3419. **Fax:** (319)861-2103. **E-mail:** customerservice@inspirationart.com. **Website:** www.inspirationart.com. Estab. 1993. Produces Christian posters. "We create and produce jumbo-sized (24×36) posters targeted at preteens (10-14), teens (15-18) and young adults (18-30). A Christian message appears on every poster. Some are fine art and some are very commercial. We prefer contemporary images." Art guidelines available on website or for SASE with first-class postage.

NEEDS Approached by 150-200 freelance artists/year. Works with 10-15 freelancers/year. Buys 10-15 designs, photos, illustrations/year. Christian art only. Uses freelance artists for posters. Considers all media. Looking for "something contemporary or unusual that appeals to teens or young adults and communicates a Christian message."

CONTACT & TERMS Submission guidelines available online.

TIPS "The better the quality of the submission, the better we are able to determine if the work is suitable for our use (slides are best). The more complete the submission (i.e., design, art layout, scripture, copy), the more likely we are to see how it may fit into our poster line. We do accept traditional work but are looking for work that is more commercial and hip. A poster needs to contain a Christian message that is relevant to teen and young adult issues and beliefs.

Understand what we publish before submitting work. Visit our website to see what it is that we do. We are not simply looking for beautiful art, but rather we are looking for art that communicates a specific scriptural passage."

◑ ◯ INTERNATIONAL GRAPHICS

Walmsley GmbH, Junkersring 11, Eggenstein DE-76344, Germany. (49)(721)978-0620. **Fax:** (49)(721)978-0651. **E-mail:** LW@ig-team.de. **Website:** www.international-graphics.com. **Contact:** Lawrence Walmsley, president. Estab. 1981. Poster company, art publisher/distributor. Publishes/distributes limited editions, offset reproductions, posters, and silkscreens. Clients: galleries, framers, department stores, gift shops, card shops and distributors. Current clients include Art.com, Windsor Art, etc.

NEEDS "We are seeking creative, fashionable and decorative art for the commercial and designer markets. Also seeking Americana art for gallery clients." Considers oil, acrylic, watercolor, mixed media, pastel and photos. Prefers landscapes, florals, painted still lifes. Also photography is a big theme for us lately. Art guidelines are available with a SASE with first-class postage. Artists represented include Christian Choisy, Benevolenza, Thiry, Magis, Marthe, Zacher-Finet, Shirin Donia, Panasenko, Valverde, Terrible, Gery Luger, and many more. Editions are created by working from an existing painting. Approached by 100-150 artists/year. Publishes the work of 10-20 emerging artists/year. Distributes the work of 10-20 emerging artists/year.

CONTACT & TERMS Send query letter with brochure, photocopies, photographs, photostats, résumé, slides, tearsheets, or an e-mail. Accepts disk submissions for Mac or Windows. Samples are filed and returned. Responds in 2 months. Will contact artist for portfolio review if interested. Negotiates payment on basis of per-piece-sold arrangement or percentage for print-on-demand sales. Needs first rights. Provides advertising, promotion, shipping from firm, and contract. Also works with freelance designers. Prefers local designers. Finds artists through exhibitions, word of mouth, submissions.

TIPS "Black-and-white photography, landscapes and still-life pictures are good at the moment. Earthtones are popular—especially lighter shades. At the end of the day, we seek the unusual that has not yet been published."

☺ ISLAND ART PUBLISHERS

P.O. Box 952, Bragg Creek Alberta T0L 0K0, Canada. (403)949-7767. **Fax:** (403)949-3224. **E-mail:** submissions@islandart.com. **Website:** www.islandart.com. **Contact:** Graham Thomson, art director. Estab. 1985. Art publisher, distributor and printer. Publishes and distributes art cards, posters, open-edition prints, calenders, bookmarks, giclées and custom products. Clients: galleries, museums, Federal and local governments, major sporting events, department stores, distributors, gift shops, artists and photographers. Art guidelines available for SASE or on website.

NEEDS See website for current needs and requirements. Considers oil, watercolor and acrylic. Prefers themes related to the Pacific Northwest. Editions are created by working from an existing painting. Approached by 100 artists/year. Publishes the work of 2-4 emerging artists/year.

CONTACT & TERMS Send submissions to Attn: Art director. Submit résumé/CV, tearsheets, slides, photographs, transparencies or digital files on CD/DVD (must be TIFF, EPS, PSD or JPEG files compatible with Photoshop). Please DO NOT send originals. Samples are not filed and are returned only by SASE if requested by artist. Responds in 3-6 months. Will contact artist for portfolio review if interested. Pays royalties of 5-10%. Licenses reproduction rights. Requires exclusive representation of artist for selected products only. Provides promotion, insurance while work is at firm, shipping from firm, written contract, fair trade representation and Internet service. Finds artists through art fairs, submissions and referrals.

TIPS "Provide a body of work along a certain theme to show a fully developed style that can be built upon. We are influenced by our market demands. Please review our submission guidelines before sending work on spec."

☺ JADEI GRAPHICS, INC.

4943 McConnell Ave., Suite Y, Los Angeles CA 90066. (310)578-0082 or (800)717-1222. **Fax:** (310)823-4399. **E-mail:** info@jadeigraphics.com. **Website:** www.jadeigraphics.com. **Contact:** Art Director. Poster company that publishes limited edition, unlimited edition and posters. Clients: galleries, framers. Licenses calendars, puzzles, etc.

NEEDS Seeking creative, decorative art for the commercial market. Considers oil, acrylic, watercolor and photographs. Editions created by collaborating with the artist or by working from an existing painting. Approached by 100 artists/year. Publishes work of 3-5 emerging artists each year. Also needs freelancers for design. Prefers local designers only.

CONTACT & TERMS Materials submitted may include but are not limited to slides, photos, color copies or transparancies. Please do not send originals. Include a suitable SASE if you would like your materials returned. Up to 5 JPEG files of no more than 600k per file may be submitted electronically.

LOLA LTD. LT'EE

1817 Egret St. SW, Shallotte NC 28470-5433. (910)754-8002. **E-mail:** lolaltd@yahoo.com. **Contact:** Lola Jackson, owner. Distributor of limited editions, offset reproductions, unlimited editions, hand-pulled originals, antique prints and etchings. Clients: art galleries, architects, picture frame shops, interior designers, major furniture and department stores, industry and antique gallery dealers.

☺ This distributor also carries antique prints, etchings and original art on paper and is interested in buying/selling to trade.

NEEDS Seeking creative and decorative art for the commercial and designer markets. "Hand-pulled graphics are our main area." Considers oil, acrylic, pastel, watercolor, tempera or mixed media. Prefers unframed series, up to 30×40 maximum. Artists represented include Buffet, White, Brent, Jackson, Mohn, Baily, Carlson, Coleman. Approached by 100 artists/year. Distributes the work of 5 emerging, 5 mid-career and 5 established artists/year. Distributes the work of 40 emerging, 40 mid-career and 5 established artists/year.

CONTACT & TERMS Send query letter with samples. Samples are filed or are returned only if requested. Responds in 2 weeks. Payment method is negotiated. "Our standard commission is 50%, less 50% off retail." Offers an advance when appropriate. Provides insurance while work is at firm, shipping from firm and written contract.

TIPS "We find we cannot sell black and white only. Leave wide margins on prints. Send all published print samples before end of May each year as our main sales are targeted for summer. We do a lot of business with birds, botanicals, boats and shells—anything nautical."

MARCO FINE ARTS

4860 W. 147th St., Hawthorne CA 90250. (310)615-1818. **E-mail:** info@mfatalon.com. **Website:** www.mfatalon.com. Publishes/distributes limited edition, fine art prints and posters. Clients: galleries, decorators and frame shops.

NEEDS Seeking creative and decorative art for the serious collector and design market. Considers oil, acrylic and mixed media. Prefers landscapes, florals, figurative, Southwest, contemporary, impressionist, antique posters. Accepts outside serigraph and digital printing (giclée) production work. Editions created by collaborating with the artist or working from an existing painting. Approached by 80-100 artists/year. Publishes the work of 3 emerging, 3 mid-career and 3-5 established artists/year.

CONTACT & TERMS Send query letter with brochure, photocopies, photographs, photostats, résumé, SASE, slides, tearsheets and transparencies. Accepts disk submissions. Samples are filed and are returned by SASE. Responds only if interested. Company will contact artist for portfolio review or original artwork (show range of ability) if interested. Payment to be discussed. Requires exclusive representation of artist.

MCGAW GRAPHICS

(888)426-2429 ext. 206. **E-mail:** katy.daly@mcgawgraphics.com. **Website:** www.mcgawgraphics.com. **Contact:** Katy Daly. Art publisher. Publishes open edition prints and posters. Clients: e-tailers, specialty retailers, picture frame manufacturers, distributors, manufacturers, galleries and frame shops.

NEEDS Seeking creative, on-trend, and decorative art and photography for commercial and designer markets. Considers all media, including oil, watercolor, acrylic, pastel, digital illustration and mixed media.

CONTACT & TERMS Send a website link or at least 12-15 examples of your art in JPEG or PDF file-formats to katy.daly@mcgawgraphics.com. Choose a wide variety of images that you feel best represent your style and technique. Pays royalties. Usually requires exclusive representation of artist. Finds artists through submissions, sourcebooks, agents, art shows, galleries and word of mouth.

TIPS look for subjects with a universal appeal. Some subjects that would be appropriate are florals, still lifes, wildlife, landscapes and contemporary images/abstracts.

MILITARY GALLERY

821 E. Ojai Ave., Ojai CA 93023. (805)640-0057; (800)248-0317. **Fax:** (805)640-0059. **E-mail:** enquiries usa@militarygallery.com. **Website:** www.militarygallery.com. Estab. 1967. Art publisher and distributor. Publishes/distributes limited edition, unlimited edition, canvas transfers, fine art prints, offset reproduction and posters. Clients galleries and mail order.

NEEDS Seeking creative, fashionable and decorative art. Considers oil, acrylic, watercolor and pen & ink. Prefers aviation and maritime. Editions created by collaborating with the artist or by working from an existing painting. Approached by 10 artists/year. Publishes and distributes work of 1 emerging, 1 mid-career and 1 established artist/year.

CONTACT & TERMS Send query letter with photographs, slides, tearsheets and transparencies. Samples are not filed and are returned with SASE. Prefers high-res e-mail submissions. Responds in 1 month. Company will contact artist for portfolio review if interested. Portfolio should include photographs, tearsheets and transparencies. Payment negotiable. Buys all rights. Requires exclusive representation of artist. Provides advertising, promotion and written contract. Finds artists through word of mouth.

TIPS "Get to know us via our catalogs."

MUNSON GRAPHICS

7502 Mallard Way, Unit C, Santa Fe NM 87507. (888)686-7664. **Fax:** (505)424-6338. **E-mail:** sales@munsongraphics.com. **Website:** www.munsongraphics.com. Estab. 1997. Poster company, art publisher and distributor. Publishes/distributes limited edition, fine art prints and posters. Clients: galleries, museum shops, gift shops and frame shops.

NEEDS Seeking creative art for the serious collector and commercial market. Considers oil, acrylic, watercolor and pastel. Editions created by working from an existing painting. Approached by 75 artists/year. Publishes work of 3-5 emerging, 3-5 mid-career and 3-5 established artists/year. Distributes the work of 5-10 emerging, 5-10 mid-career and 5-10 established artists/year.

CONTACT & TERMS Send query letter with slides, SASE and transparencies. Samples are not filed and are returned by SASE. Responds in 1 month. Company will contact artist for portfolio review if interested. Negotiates payment. Offers advance. Rights purchased vary according to project. Provides written contract. Finds artists through art exhibitions, art fairs, word of mouth and artists' submissions.

MUSEUM MASTERS INTERNATIONAL

185 E. 85th St., Suite 27B, New York NY 10028. (212)360-7100. **Fax:** (212)360-7102. **E-mail:** MMI-Marilyn@aol.com; Marilyn.Goldberg@museummasters.com. **Website:** www.museummasters.com. **Contact:** Marilyn Goldberg, president. Licensing agent for international artists and art estates. Distributor of limited editions, posters, tapestry and sculpture for galleries, museums and gift boutiques.

NEEDS Seeking artwork with decorative appeal for the designer market. Considers oil, acrylic, pastel, watercolor and mixed media.

CONTACT & TERMS E-mail with sample download of artwork offered. Samples are filed or returned. Call or write for appointment to show portfolio or mail slides and transparencies. Payment method is negotiated. Offers advance when appropriate. Negotiates rights purchased. Exclusive representation is not required. Provides insurance while work is at firm, shipping to firm and a written contract.

NEW YORK GRAPHIC SOCIETY

130 Scott Rd., Waterbury CT 06705. **E-mail:** donna@nygs.com. **Website:** www.nygs.com. **Contact:** Donna LeVan, vice president of publishing (contact via e-mail only, no phone calls). Estab. 1925. Specializes in fine art reproductions, prints, posters, canvases. Merged with print company Artbeats Inc.

NEEDS Buys 150 images/year; 125 are supplied by freelancers. "Looking for a variety of images."

CONTACT & TERMS Send query letter with samples to Attn: Artist Submissions. Does not keep samples on file; include SASE for return of material. Responds in 3 months. Payment negotiable. Pays on usage. Credit line given. Buys exclusive product rights. No phone calls.

TIPS "Visit website to review artist submission guidelines and to see appropriate types of imagery for publication."

OLD WORLD PRINTS, LTD.

8080 Villa Park Dr., Richmond VA 23228. (804)213-0600, ext. 634. **Fax:** (804)213-0700. **E-mail:** orders@theworldartgroup.com; artists@theworldartgroup.com. **Website:** www.oldworldprintsltd.com. Estab. 1973. Art publisher and distributor of open-edition, hand-printed reproductions of antique engravings as well as all subject matter of color printed art. Clients: retail galleries, frame shops and manufacturers, hotels and fund raisers.

○ Old World Prints reports the top-selling art in their 10,000-piece collection includes botanical and decorative prints.

NEEDS Seeking traditional and decorative art for the commercial and designer markets. Specializes in handpainted prints. Considers "b&w (pen & ink or engraved) art which can stand by itself or be hand painted by our artists or originating artist." Prefers traditional, representational, decorative work. Editions created by collaborating with the artist. Distributes the work of more than 1,000 artists. "Also seeking golf, coffee, tea, and exotic floral images."

CONTACT & TERMS Send query letter with brochure showing art style or résumé and tearsheets and slides. Samples are filed. Responds in 6 weeks. Write for appointment to show portfolio of photographs, slides and transparencies. Pays flat fee of $100/piece and royalties of 10% of profit. Offers an advance when appropriate. Negotiates rights purchased. Provides in-transit insurance, insurance while work is at firm, promotion, shipping from firm and a written contract. Finds artists through word of mouth.

TIPS "We are a specialty art publisher, the largest of our kind in the world. We are actively seeking artists to publish and will consider all forms of art."

OUT OF THE BLUE LICENSING, LLC

P.O. Box 727, Nokomis FL 34274. (941)966-4042. **E-mail:** ootblicensing@gmail.com. **Website:** www.ootblicensing.com. **Contact:** Michael Woodward, president; Jane Mason, licensing manager. Estab. 1986. "We are looking for decorative art and photography that we can license for product categories such as mass market canvas, posters/print and high-quality giclées for the home décor market as well as images for greeting cards, calendars, stationery and gift products. We specialize particularly in the home decor canvas and framed art market." We also require very high quality landscapes and panoramas for large scale murals. Must be very large quality digital files.

NEEDS "We need series and collections of art or photography that have wide consumer appeal. E-mail presentations only. Keep files to 250K JPEGs and around 12×10 at 72 dpi."

CONTACT & TERMS Terms are 50/50 with no expense to artist. Artist/photographer needs to provide high-res digital files if we agree on representation.

Submission guidelines are available on website at www.ootblicensing.com/submissions.html.

TIPS "Pay attention to trends and color palettes. Artists need to consider actual products when creating new art. Look at products in retail outlets and get a feel for what is selling well. Get to know the markets you want to sell your work to."

PENNY LANE PUBLISHING, INC.

1791 Dalton Dr., New Carlisle OH 45344. (937)849-1101 or (800)273-5263. **Fax:** (937)849-9666. **E-mail:** info@pennylanepublishing.com. **Website:** www.pennylanepublishing.com. Estab. 1993. Art publisher. Publishes limited editions, unlimited editions, offset reproductions. Clients: galleries, frame shops, distributors, decorators.

NEEDS Seeking creative, decorative art for the commercial market. Considers oil, acrylic, watercolor, mixed media, pastel. Editions are created by collaborating with the artist or working from an existing painting. Approached by 100+ artists/year. Publishes the work of 20 emerging, 15 mid-career and 6 established artists/year.

CONTACT & TERMS Send query letter or e-mail with samples of artwork. Requirements for submissions via e-mail; send JPEG files @ 72 dpi; maximum file size 1 MB (not to exceed 10 MB per e-mail). "Please send a variety of images (at least 6-10 images) so we can get a good feel for the type of artwork you have available." Samples are filed or returned by SASE. Responds in 2-6 weeks. Will contact artist for portfolio review of color, final art, photographs, slides and tearsheets if interested. Pays royalties. Buys first rights. Requires exclusive representation of artist. Provides advertising, shipping from firm, promotion, written contract. Finds artists through art fairs and exhibitions, submissions, decorating magazines.

TIPS "Be aware of current color trends, and work in a series. Please review our website to see the style of artwork we publish."

PGM ART WORLD

Dieselstrasse 28, 85748 Garching, Germany. +49 (89)3 20 02-150. **Fax:** +49 (89)3 20 02-250. **E-mail:** info@pgm.de. **Website:** www.pgm.de. Estab. 1969. International fine art publisher, distributor, gallery. Publishes/distributes limited and unlimited editions, offset reproductions, art prints, giclées, art cards and originals. Worldwide supplier to galleries, framers, distributors, decorators.

PGM publishes around 180 images/year and distributes more than 6,000 images. The company also operates 3 galleries in Munich.

NEEDS Seeking creative, fashionable and decorative art for the commercial and designer markets. Considers oil, acrylic, watercolor, mixed media, pastel, pen & ink, photography and digital art. Considers any accomplished work of any theme or style. Editions are created by working from an existing painting or high-resolution digital data. Approached by more than 420 artists/year.

CONTACT & TERMS Send query letter with photographs, slides, color copies, color prints or work in digital format (JPEG) on CD/DVD. Sent documentation will be returned. Responds within 1 month. Will contact artist for portfolio review if interested. Pays royalties per copies sold; negotiable. Requires exclusive representation of artist. Provides promotion of prints in catalogs and promotional material, presentation of artists (biography & photo) on website.

TIPS "Get as much worldwide exposure as possible at art shows and with own website."

PORTER DESIGN

7 St. Andrews Terrace, Bath BA1 2QR, United Kingdom. (01144)1225 680628; 1-866-293-2079 (US office). **Fax:** (01144)1225 849156. **E-mail:** service@porter-design.com; pdny@porter-design.com (US office). **Website:** www.porter-design.com. **Contact:** Henry Porter and Mary Porter, partners. Estab. 1985. Publishes limited and unlimited editions and offset productions and hand-colored reproductions. Clients: international distributors, interior designers and hotel contract art suppliers. Current clients include Grand Image, Top Art, Harrods, hotels in the Caribbean and SE Asia.

NEEDS Seeking fashionable and decorative art for the designer market. Considers watercolor. Prefers 16th-19th century traditional styles. Artists represented include Victor Postolle, Joseph Hooker, Georg Ehret and Adrien Chancel. Editions are created by working from an existing painting. Approached by 10 artists/year. Publishes and distributes the work of 10-20 established artists/year.

CONTACT & TERMS Send query letter with brochure showing art style or résumé and photographs. Accepts disk submissions compatible with QuarkXPress on Mac. Samples are filed or are returned. Responds only if interested. To show portfolio, mail photographs. Pays flat fee or royalties. Offers an advance when appropriate. Negotiates rights purchased.

POSNER FINE ART

1212 S. Point View St., Los Angeles CA 90035. (323)933-3664. **Fax:** (323)933-3417. **E-mail:** info@posnerfineart.com. **Website:** www.posnerfineart.com. **Contact:** Wendy Posner, president. Estab. 1994. Art distributor and gallery. Distributes contemporary fine art prints, monoprints, sculpture and paintings. Clients: galleries, frame shops, distributors, architects, corporate curators, museum shops. Current clients include Renaissance Hollywood Hotel, Nuveen Investments, Fandango.

NEEDS Seeking creative art for the serious collector and commercial market. Considers oil, acrylic, watercolor, mixed media, sculpture. Prefers very contemporary style. Artists include David Shapiro, Chuck Arnoldi, Robert Cottingham, and Sam Francis. Editions are created by collaborating with the artist. Approached by hundreds of artists/year. Distributes the work of 5-10 emerging, 5 mid-career and 200 established artists/year. Art guidelines free with SASE (first-class postage).

CONTACT & TERMS E-mail submission. Responds in a few weeks. Pays on consignment basis; firm receives 50% commission. Buys one-time rights. Provides advertising, promotion, insurance while work is at firm. Finds artists through art fairs and exhibitions, word of mouth, submissions, art reps.

TIPS "Know color trends of design market. Look for dealer with same style in gallery. Send consistent work."

⊘ POSTERS INTERNATIONAL

1180 Caledonia Rd., Toronto Ontario M6A 2W5, Canada. (416)789-7156 or (800)363-2787. **Fax:** (416)789-7159. **E-mail:** info@picreativeart.com; art@picreativeart.com. **Website:** www.picreativeart.com. Estab. 1976. Poster company, art publisher. Publishes fine art posters and giclée prints. Licenses for gift and stationery markets. Clients: galleries, designers, art consultants, framing, manufacturers, distributors, hotels, restaurants, etc., around the world.

NEEDS Seeking creative, fashionable art for the commercial market. Considers oil, acrylic, watercolor, mixed media, b&w and color photography. Prefers landscapes, florals, abstracts, photography, vintage, collage and tropical imagery. Editions are created by

collaborating with the artist or by working from an existing painting. Approached by 100 artists/year.

CONTACT & TERMS Send query letter or e-mail with attachment, brochure, photographs. Responds in 2 months. Company will contact artist for portfolio review of photographs, tearsheets, thumbnails if interested. Pays flat fee or royalties of 10%. Rights purchased vary according to project. Provides advertising, promotion, shipping from firm, written contract. Finds artists through art fairs, art reps, submissions.

TIPS "Be aware of current home décor color trends and always work in a series of 2 or more per theme/subject. Visit home décor retailers in their wall décor area for inspiration and guidance before submitting artwork."

⊘ PROGRESSIVE EDITIONS

2586 Dunwin Dr., Unit 5A, Mississauga Ontario L5L 1J5, Canada. (416)860-0983 or (800)487-1273. **Fax:** (416)367-2724. **E-mail:** info@progressivefineart.com. **Website:** www.progressiveeditions.com. Estab. 1982. Art publisher. Publishes handpulled originals, limited edition fine art prints and monoprints. Clients: galleries, decorators, frame shops, distributors.

NEEDS Seeking creative and decorative art for the serious collector and designer market. Considers oil, acrylic, watercolor, mixed media, pastel. Prefers figurative, abstract, landscape and still lifes. Editions created by working from an existing painting. Approached by 100 artists/year. Publishes the work of 4 emerging artists/year. Distributes the work of 10 emerging artists/year.

CONTACT & TERMS Send query letter with photographs, slides. Samples are not filed and are returned. Responds in 1 month. Will contact artist for portfolio review if interested. Negotiates payment. Offers advance when appropriate. Negotiates rights purchased. Requires exclusive representation of artist. Provides advertising, in-transit insurance, insurance while work is at firm, promotion, shipping and contract. Finds artists through exhibition, art fairs, word of mouth, art reps, sourcebooks, submissions, competitions.

TIPS "Develop organizational skills."

◉ FELIX ROSENSTIEL'S WIDOW & SON, LTD.

33-35 Markham St., Chelsea Green London SW3 3NR, United Kingdom. (44)207-352-3551. **Fax:** (44)207-351-5300. **E-mail:** sales@felixr.com. **Website:** www.felixr.

com. Estab. 1880. Publishes art prints and posters, both limited and open editions. Licenses all subjects on any quality product. Art guidelines on website.

NEEDS Seeking decorative art for the serious collector and the commercial market. Considers oil, acrylic, watercolor, mixed media and pastel. Prefers art suitable for homes or offices. Editions are created by collaborating with the artist or by working from an existing painting. Approached by 200-500 artists/year.

CONTACT & TERMS Send query letter with photographs. Samples are not filed and are returned by SASE. Responds in 2 weeks. Company will contact artist for portfolio review of final art and transparencies if interested. Negotiates payment. Offers advance when appropriate. Rights purchased vary according to project.

TIPS "We publish decorative, attractive, contemporary art."

SAGEBRUSH FINE ART

3065 S. West Temple, Salt Lake City UT 84115. (801)466-5136; (800)643-7243. **Fax:** (801)466-5048. **E-mail:** submissions@sagebrushfineart.com. **Website:** www.sagebrushfineart.com. **Contact:** Pansy Winterburn, art review coordinator. Estab. 1991. Art publisher. Publishes and licenses fine art prints. Clients: frame shops, distributors, corporate curators and chain stores.

NEEDS Seeking decorative art for the commercial and designer markets. Considers all media. Open to all themes and styles. Current artists include Jennifer Pugh, Ninalee Irani, Stephanie Marrott, Susan Comish and Jo Moulton. Editions created by collaborating with the artist or by working from an existing painting. Markets and presents the work of new and emerging artists.

CONTACT & TERMS Submission guidelines available online. Send to the attention of Pansy Winterburn. "We see a lot of art and in order for art to be reviewed, we prefer an emailed PDF presentation of 20-35 pieces of your art along with any website information available. Once received, our art development team reviews submissions for print and licensing potential. It can take 4-6 weeks before we get back to you with a response."

SCHLUMBERGER GALLERY

P.O. Box 2864, Santa Rosa CA 95405. (707)544-8356. **E-mail:** sande@schlumberger.org. **Website:** www.schlumbergergallery.com. Estab. 1986. Private art dealer, art publisher, distributor and gallery. Publishes and distributes limited editions, posters, original paintings and sculpture. Specializes in decorative and museum-quality art and photographs. Clients: collectors, designers, distributors, museums, galleries, film and television set designers.

NEEDS Seeking decorative art for the serious collector and the designer market. Prefers trompe l'oeil, realist, architectural, figure, portrait. Editions created by collaborating with the artist or by working from an existing painting. Approached by 50 artists/year.

CONTACT & TERMS Send query letter with tearsheets and photographs. Samples are not filed and are returned by SASE if requested by artist. Publisher/distributor will contact artist for portfolio review if interested. Portfolio should include color photographs and transparencies. Negotiates payment. Offers advance when appropriate. Rights purchased vary according to project. Provides advertising, in-transit insurance, insurance while work is at firm, promotion, shipping to and from firm, written contract and shows. Finds artists through exhibits, referrals, submissions and "pure blind luck."

TIPS "Strive for quality, clarity, clean lines and light, even if the style is impressionistic. Bring spirit into your images. It translates!"

SEGAL FINE ART

11955 Teller St., Unit C, Broomfield CO 80020. (303)926-6800. **Fax:** (303)926-0340. **E-mail:** poppysegal@gmail.com. **Website:** www.segalfineart.com. **Contact:** Ron Segal. Estab. 1986. Art publisher. Publishes limited edition giclèes. Clients: bikers at motorcycle rallies. Artists represented include David Mann, and Michael Kneeper.

◉ SJATIN ART B.V.

P.O. Box 7201, 5980 AE Panningen, the Netherlands. (31)77-475-1998. **E-mail:** art@sjatin.nl. **Website:** www.sjatin.nl. Estab. 1977. (Formerly Sjatin Publishing & Licensing BV.) Art publisher. Publishes open editions, fine art prints. Licenses decorative art to appear on placemats, calendars, greeting cards, stationery, photo albums, embroidery, posters, canvas, textile, puzzles and gifts. Clients: picture framers, wholesalers, distributors of art print. Sjatin actively promotes worldwide distribution for artists they sign.

NEEDS Seeking decorative art for the commercial market. Considers oil, acrylic, watercolor, pastel. Prefers romantic themes, florals, landscapes/garden scenes, still lifes. Editions created by collaborating with the artist or by working from an existing painting. Approached by 50 artists/year. "We publish a very wide range of art prints and we sell copyrights over the whole world."

CONTACT & TERMS Submission guidelines available online.

TIPS "Follow the trends in interior decoration; look at the furniture and colors. I receive so many artworks that are beautiful and very artistic, but are not commercial enough for reproduction. I need designs which appeal to many many people, worldwide such as flowers, gardens, interiors and kitchen scenes. I do not wish to receive graphic art."

SOHN FINE ART—GALLERY & GICLÉE PRINTING

69 Church St., Lenox MA 01240. (413)551-7353. **E-mail:** info@sohnfineart.com. **Website:** www. sohnfineart.com. Art gallery and fine art archival giclée printing. Canvas, fine art prints, limited editions. Considers photography, mixed media and sculpture. **NEEDS** Decorative art, fashionable art, for the serious collector, commercial market, or designer market. **CONTACT & TERMS** Contact via query letter, postcard sample, or e-mail letter with digital images, photographs or transparencies. Work will not be returned.

SOMERSET FINE ART

29370 McKinnon Rd., Suite A, P.O. Box 869, Fulshear TX 77441. (800)444-2540. **Fax:** (866)742-2925; (281)346-8902. **E-mail:** jjenkins@somersethouse. com. **Website:** www.somersetfineart.com. **Contact:** J. Jenkins, art department. Estab. 1972. Leading publisher of fine art reproductions in limited and open editions; giclees on canvas and giclées on paper. Clients: independent galleries in the United States, Canada, Australia, Mexico, Brazil, and other countries. Artists represented: Bill Anton, Susan Blackwood, Rod Chase, Norm Clasen, Tim Cox, Kimerlee Curyl, Michael Dudash, June Dudley, Larry Dyke, Ragan Gennusa, Nancy Glazier, Bruce Green, Martin Grelle, George Hallmark, Jim Hansel, G. Harvey, Karen Kelley, David Mann, Denis Mayer, Chris Owen, Robert Peters, Phillip Philbeck, Kyle Polzin, Jim Rey, James Seward, Kyle Sims, Claude Steelman, Andy Thomas, Evan Wilson, Bob Wygant, and HongNian Zhang.

NEEDS Art is reproduced from original paintings or collaborating with the artist; considers oil, acrylic, watercolor, mixed media, pastel.

CONTACT & TERMS Send inquiry via e-mail or by letter to post office box; submissions by e-mail should include digital files in JPEG format or 10–12 slides or photos of work (include SASE) if by mail. Will review art on artist's website or submitted material; also include number/size/price of all paintings sold within last 24 months and gallery representation. Samples filed for future reference unless return is requested. Publisher will contact artist for portfolio review if interested. Pays royalties; artist retains painting and copyrights; written contract; company provides advertising, promotion, in-transit insurance for original art, and shipping.

JACQUES SOUSSANA GRAPHICS

37 Pierre Koenig St., Jerusalem 91041, Israel. (972)(2)6782678. **Fax:** (972)(2)6782426. **E-mail:** jsgraphics@soussanart.com. **Website:** www.soussanart.com. Estab. 1973. Art publisher. Publishes hand-pulled originals, limited editions, sculpture. Clients: galleries, decorators, frame shops, distributors, architects. **NEEDS** Seeking decorative art for the serious collector and designer market. Considers oil, watercolor and sculpture. Editions are created by collaborating with the artist. Approached by 20 artists/year. Publishes/distributes the work of 5 emerging artists/year.

CONTACT & TERMS Send query letter with brochure, slides. To show portfolio, artist should follow up with letter after initial query. Portfolio should include color photographs.

SULIER ART PUBLISHING

PMB 55, 3735 Palomar Centre, Suite 150, Lexington KY 40513. (859)621-5511. **Fax:** (859)296-0650. **E-mail:** info@NeilSulier.com; or via online contact form. **Website:** www.neilsulier.com. **Contact:** Neil Sulier, art director. Art publisher and distributor. Publishes and distributes handpulled originals, limited and unlimited editions, posters, offset reproductions and originals. Clients: designers.

NEEDS Seeking creative, fashionable and decorative art for the serious collector and the commercial and designer markets. Considers oil, watercolor, mixed media, pastel and acrylic. Prefers impressionist. Editions created by collaborating with the artist or by working from an existing painting. Approached by 20 artists/year. Publishes the work of 5 emerging, 30 mid-career and 6 established artists/year. Distributes the work of 5 emerging artists/year.

CONTACT & TERMS Send query letter with brochure, slides, photocopies, résumé, photostats, transparencies, tearsheets and photographs. Samples are filed or are returned. Responds only if interested. Request portfolio review in original query. Artist should follow up with call. Publisher will contact artist for portfolio review if interested. Portfolio should include slides, tearsheets, final art and photographs. Pays royalties of 10%, on consignment basis or negotiates payment. Offers advance when appropriate. Negotiates rights purchased (usually one-time or all rights). Provides in-transit insurance, promotion, shipping to and from firm, insurance while work is at firm and written contract.

SUN DANCE GRAPHICS & NORTHWEST PUBLISHING

9580 Delegates Dr., Building B, Orlando FL 32837. (407)240-1091; (800)617-5532. **Fax:** (407)240-1951. **E-mail:** info@northwestpublishing.com. **Website:** www.northwestpublishing.com. Estab. 1996. Publishers and printers of giclée prints, fine art prints, and posters. Sun Dance Graphics provides trend-forward images to customers that manufacture for upscale hospitality, retail, and home furnishings markets. Primarily looking for images in sets/pairs with compelling color palette, subject, and style. Northwest Publishing provides fine art prints and posters in the following categories: classics, traditional, inspirational, contemporary, home and hearth, photography, motivationals, wildlife, landscapes and ethnic art.

NEEDS Approached by 300 freelancers/year. Works with 50 freelancers/year. Buys 200 freelance designs and illustrations/year. Art guidelines free for SASE with first-class postage. Works on assignment only. Looking for high-end art. 20% of freelance design work demands knowledge of Photoshop, Illustrator and QuarkXPress.

CONTACT & TERMS Art submissions may be electronic (e-mail low-res image or website link) or via mail. Please do not send original art unless specifically requested. Artists will be contacted if there is interest in further review. All submissions are reviewed for potential inclusion in either line as well as for licensing potential, and are kept on file for up to 6 months. Art may be purchased or signed under royalty agreement. Royalty/licensing contracts will be signed before any images can be considered for inclusion in either line.

TIPS "Focus on style. We tend to carve our own path with unique, compelling and high-quality art, and as a result are not interested in 'me too' images."

JOHN SZOKE EDITIONS

24 W. 57th St., Suite 304, New York NY 10019. (212)219-8300. **E-mail:** info@johnszokeeditions.com. **Website:** www.johnszokeeditions.com. Estab. 1974. Located in Soho. Gallery hours: Tuesday-Saturday 10-5 or by appointment. Exhibits unique and limited edition works on paper, rare prints, limited-edition multiples. Modern Masters: Pablo Picasso and Henri Matisse. Clients: art dealers and collectors. 20% of sales to private collectors.

TAKU GRAPHICS

5763 Glacier Hwy., Juneau AK 99801. (907)780-6310; (800)ART-3291. **Fax:** (907)780-6314. **E-mail:** takugraphics@gmail.com; info@takugraphics.com. **Website:** www.takugraphics.com. **Contact:** Adele Hamey. Estab. 1991. Distributor. Distributes hand-pulled originals, limited edition, unlimited edition, fine art prints, offset reproduction, posters, paper cast, bead jewelry and note cards. Clients: galleries and gift shops.

NEEDS Seeking art from Alaska and the Pacific Northwest exclusively. Considers oil, acrylic, watercolor, mixed media, pastel and pen & ink. Prefers regional styles and themes. Artists represented include JoAnn George, Barbara Lavalle, Byron Birdsall, Brenda Schwartz and Barry Herem. Editions created by working from an existing painting. Approached by 30-50 artists/year. Distributes the work of 50 emerging, 20 mid-career and 6 established artists/year.

CONTACT & TERMS Submission guidelines available online.

BRUCE TELEKY, INC.

87 35th St., 3rd Floor, Brooklyn NY 11232. (718)965-9690 or (800)835-3539. **Fax:** (718)832-8432. **E-mail:** sales@teleky.com. **Website:** www.teleky.com. **Contact:** Bruce Teleky, president. Estab. 1975. Clients include galleries, manufacturers and other distributors.

NEEDS Works from existing art to create open edition posters or works with artist to create limited editions. Visit our website to view represented artists. Also likes coastal images, music themes and Latino images. Uses photographs. Likes to see artists who

can draw. Prefers depictions of African American and Carribean scenes or African themes.
CONTACT & TERMS Send query letter with digital files. Publisher will contact artist for portfolio review if interested. Payment negotiable.

VLADIMIR ARTS USA, INC.

2504 Sprinkle Rd., Kalamazoo MI 49001. (269)383-0032 or (800)678-8523. **E-mail:** vladimir@vladimirarts.com. **Website:** www.vladimirarts.com. Art publisher, distributor and gallery. Publishes/distributes handpulled originals, limited edition, unlimited edition, canvas transfers, fine art prints, monoprints, monotypes, offset reproduction, posters and giclée. Clients: galleries, decorators, frame shops, distributors, architects, corporate curators, museum shops, giftshops and West Point military market.
NEEDS Seeking creative, fashionable and decorative art for the serious collector, commercial market and designer market. Considers oil, acrylic, watercolor, mixed media, pastel, pen & ink and sculpture. Editions created by collaborating with the artist. Approached by 30 artists/year. Publishes work of 10 emerging, 10 mid-career and 10 established artists/year. Distributes work of 1-2 emerging, 1 mid-career and 1-2 established artists/year.
CONTACT & TERMS Send query letter with brochure, photocopies, photographs and tearsheets. Samples are filed or returned with SASE. Responds only if interested. Company will contact artist for portfolio review if interested. Portfolio should include b&w, color, fine art, photographs and roughs. Negotiates payment. No advance. Provides advertising, promotion and shipping from our firm. Finds artists through art exhibitions, art fairs, word of mouth, Internet, art reps, sourcebooks, artists' submissions and watching art competitions.
TIPS "The industry is growing in diversity of color. There are no limits."

WILD APPLE GRAPHICS, LTD.

2513 W. Woodstock Rd., Woodstock VT 05091. (800)756-8359. **Fax:** (800)411-2775. **E-mail:** artsubmissions@wildapple.com. **Website:** www.wildapple.com. Estab. 1990. "Wild Apple publishes, distributes and represents a diverse group of contemporary artists. Clients: manufacturers, galleries, designers, poster distributors (worldwide) and framers. Licensing: Acting as an artist's agent, we present your artwork to manufacturers for consideration."

NEEDS "We are always looking for fresh talent and varied images to show." Considers oil, watercolor, acrylic, pastel, mixed media and photography. Publishes 400+ new works each year.
CONTACT & TERMS Submission guidelines available online

WILD WINGS, LLC

2101 S. Hwy. 61, Lake City MN 55041. (800)445-4833. **Fax:** (651)345-2981. **E-mail:** info@wildwings.com; jgrippo@wildwings.com. **Website:** www.wildwings.com. **Contact:** Jackie Grippo, publishing & artist relations manager. Estab. 1968. Art publisher/distributor and gallery. Publishes and distributes limited editions and offset reproductions. Clients: retail and wholesale.
NEEDS Seeking artwork for the commercial market. Considers oil, watercolor, mixed media, pastel and acrylic. Prefers wildlife. Artists represented include David Maass, Lee Kromschroeder, Ron Van Gilder, Rosemary Millette, Michael Sieve and Persis Clayton Weirs. Editions are created by working from an existing painting. Approached by 300 artists/year. Publishes the work of 36 artists/year. Distributes the work of numerous emerging artists/year.
CONTACT & TERMS Send query letter with digital files or color printouts and résumé. Samples are filed and held for 6 months, then returned. Responds in 3 weeks if uninterested; 6 months if interested. Will contact artist for portfolio review if interested. Pays royalties for prints. Accepts original art on consignment and takes 40% commission. No advance. Requires exclusive representation of artist. Provides in-transit insurance, promotion, shipping to and from firm, insurance while work is at firm and a written contract. See website for further details.

◐ WINN DEVON ART GROUP

Cap & Winn Devon, Unit 110, 6311 Westminster Hwy., Richmond British Columbia V7C 4V4, Canada. (800)663-1166; (604)276-4551. **Fax:** (888)744-8275; (604)276-4552. **E-mail:** artsubmissions@encoreartgroup.com. **Website:** www.winndevon.com. Art publisher. Publishes open and limited editions, offset reproductions, giclées and serigraphs. Clients: mostly trade, designer, decorators, galleries, retail frame shops.
NEEDS Seeking decorative art for the designer market. Considers oil, watercolor, mixed media, pastel, pen & ink and acrylic. Editions are created by working from an existing painting. Approached by 300-

400 artists/year. Publishes and distributes the work of 0-3 emerging, 3-8 mid-career and 8-10 established artists/year.

CONTACT & TERMS Send query letter with brochure, slides, photocopies, résumé, photostats, transparencies, tearsheets or photographs. Samples are returned by SASE if requested by artist. Responds in 4-6 weeks. Publisher will contact artist for portfolio review if interested. Portfolio should include "whatever is appropriate to communicate the artist's talents." Payment is based on royalties. Copyright remains with artist. Provides written contract. Finds artists through art exhibitions, agents, sourcebooks, publications, submissions.

TIPS Advises artists to attend WCAF Las Vegas and DECOR Expo Atlanta. "Attend just to see what is selling and being shown, but keep in mind that this is not a good time to approach publishers/exhibitors with your artwork."

ADVERTISING, DESIGN, & RELATED MARKETS

This section offers a glimpse at one of the most lucrative markets for artists. Because of space constraints, the companies listed are just the tip of the proverbial iceberg. There are thousands of advertising agencies and public relations, design, and marketing firms across the country and around the world. All rely on freelancers. Look for additional firms in industry directories such as *The Black Book* and *Workbook*. Find local firms in the yellow pages and your city's business-to-business directory. You can also pick up leads by reading *Adweek*, *HOW*, *PRINT*, *Communication Arts*, and other design and marketing publications.

Find Your Best Clients

Read listings carefully to identify firms whose clients and specialties are in line with the type of work you create. (You'll find clients and specialties in the first paragraph of each listing.) For example, if you create charts and graphs, contact firms whose clients include financial institutions. Fashion illustrators should approach firms whose clients include department stores and catalog publishers. Sculptors and modelmakers might find opportunities with firms specializing in exhibition design.

Payment and Copyright

You will most likely be paid by the hour for work done on the firm's premises (in-house), and by the project if you take the assignment back to your studio. Most checks are issued 40–60 days after completion of assignments. Fees depend on the client's budget, but most companies are willing to negotiate, taking into consideration the experience of the freelancer, the lead time given, and the complexity of the project. Be prepared to offer an estimate for your services, and ask for a purchase order (P.O.) before you begin an assignment.

Some art directors will ask you to provide a preliminary sketch on speculation or "on spec," which, if approved by the client, can land you a plum assignment. If you are asked to create something "on spec" be aware that you may not receive payment beyond an hourly fee for your time if the project falls through. Be sure to ask up front about payment policy before you start an assignment.

If you're hoping to retain usage rights to your work, you'll want to discuss this up front, too. You can generally charge more if the client is requesting a buyout. If research and travel are required, make sure you find out ahead of time who will cover these expenses.

ADVANCED DESIGNS CORP.

1169 W. Second St., Bloomington IN 47403. (812)333-1922. **Fax:** (812)333-2030. **E-mail:** mmcgrath@doprad.com. **Website:** www.doprad.com. **Contact:** Matt McGrath, president. Estab. 1982. AV firm. Specializes in TV news broadcasts. Product specialties are the doppler radar and display systems.

NEEDS Prefers freelancers with experience. Works on assignment only. Uses freelancers mainly for TV/film (weather) and cartographic graphics. Needs computer-literate freelancers for production. 100% of freelance work demands skills in ADC Graphics.

FIRST CONTACT & TERMS Send query letter with résumé and SASE. Samples are not filed and are returned by SASE. Pays for design and illustration by the hour, $7 minimum. Will contact artist for portfolio review if interested. Rights purchased vary according to project. Finds artists through classifieds.

⊕ THE ADVERTISING CONSORTIUM

10536 Culver Blvd., Suite C, Culver City CA 90232. (310)287-2222. **Fax:** (310)287-2227. **E-mail:** theadco@pacbell.net. **Contact:** Kim Miyade. Estab. 1985. Ad agency. Full-service, multimedia firm. Specializes in print, collateral, direct mail, outdoor, broadcast, packaging, PR/Events.

NEEDS Works with 1 illustrator and 2 art directors/month. Prefers local artists only. Works on assignment only. Uses freelance artists and art directors for everything (none on staff), including brochure, catalog and print ad design and illustration and mechanicals and logos. 80% of work is with print ads. Also for multimedia projects. 100% of freelance work demands knowledge of PageMaker, QuarkXPress, FreeHand, Illustrator and Photoshop.

FIRST CONTACT & TERMS Send postcard sample or query letter with brochure, tearsheets, photocopies, photographs and anything that does not have to be returned. Samples are filed. Write for appointment to show portfolio. "No phone calls, please." Portfolio should include original/final art, b&w and color photostats, tearsheets, photographs, slides and transparencies. Pays for design by the hour, $60-75. Pays for illustration by the project, based on budget and scope.

TIPS Looks for "exceptional style."

AFA KRAUSE

45 West 10000 S., Suite #201, Sandy UT 84070. (801)486-7455. **Fax:** (801)486-7454. **Website:** www.afakrause.com. Formerly Alan Frank & Associates,

Inc. Serves clients in travel, fast food chains and retailing. Clients include KFC, A&W, Taco Bell and Tuffy Automotive.

NEEDS Uses freelancers for illustrations, animation and retouching for annual reports, billboards, ads, letterheads, TV and packaging.

FIRST CONTACT & TERMS Mail art with SASE. Responds in 2 weeks. Minimum payment $500, animation; $100, illustrations; $200, brochure layout.

⊕ ALLEN & GERRITSEN

300 N. Second St., Suite 1001, Harrisburg PA 17101. (717)232-5554. **Website:** www.a-g.com. Estab. 1978. Full-service ad agency specializing in print collateral and ad campaigns. Product specialties are health care, banks, retail and industry.

○   Second location: 1619 Walnut St., 4th Floor, Philadelphia PA 19103; (215)667-8719.

NEEDS Prefers local artists with experience in comps and roughs. Works on assignment only. Uses freelancers mainly for advertising illustration and comps. Also uses freelancers for brochure design, mechanicals, retouching, lettering and logos. 50% of work is with print ads. 3% of design and 1% of illustration demands knowledge of Illustrator and Photoshop.

FIRST CONTACT & TERMS Designers: Send query letter with résumé. Illustrators: Send postcard sample, query letter or tearsheets. Samples are filed. Will contact artist for portfolio review if interested. Portfolio should include color thumbnails, roughs, original/final art, photographs. Pays for design and illustration by the project. Finds artists through sourcebooks and workbooks.

TIPS "Try to get a potential client's attention with a novel concept. Never, ever, miss a deadline. Enjoy what you do."

ANDERSON STUDIO, INC.

2609 Grissom Dr., Nashville TN 37204. (615)255-4807. **Fax:** (615)255-4812. **E-mail:** sherry@andersonstudioinc.com. **Website:** andersonstudioinc.com. **Contact:** Sherry Anderson. Estab. 1976. Specializes in T-shirts (designing and printing of art on T-shirts for retail/wholesale promotional market). Clients business, corporate retail, gift and specialty stores.

NEEDS Approached by 20 freelancers/year. Works with 1-2 freelance illustrators and 1-2 designers/year. "We use freelancers with realistic (photorealistic) style. Works on assignment only. We need artists for automotive-themed art. Also motorcycle designs as seen in the current line of shirts produced for Orange County Choppers of the Discovery Channel. We're also in need of Hot Rod art and designs for T-shirts along with graphic work and logo designs of the same."

FIRST CONTACT & TERMS Send postcard sample or query letter with color copies, brochure, photocopies, photographs, SASE, slides, tearsheets and transparencies. Samples are filed and are returned by SASE if requested by artist. Portfolio should include slides, color tearsheets, transparencies and color copies. Sometimes requests work on spec before assigning a job. Pays for design and illustration by the project, $300-1,000 or in royalties per piece of printed art. Negotiates rights purchased. Considers buying second rights (reprint rights) to previously published work.

TIPS "Be flexible in financial/working arrangements. Most work is on a commission or flat buyout. We work on a tight budget until product is sold. Art-wise, the more professional, the better." Advises freelancers entering the field to "show as much work as you can. Even comps or ideas for problem solving. Let art directors see how you think. Don't send disks as they take too long to review. Most art directors like hard copy art."

⊘ ARIZONA CINE EQUIPMENT, INC.

2125 E. 20th St., Tucson AZ 85719. (520)623-8268. **Fax:** (520)623-1092. **E-mail:** Leejr@azcine.com. **Website:** www.azcine.com. Estab. 1967. Number of employees: 11. Approximate annual billing: $850,000. AV firm. Full-service, multimedia firm. Specializes in video. Product specialty is industrial.

NEEDS Approached by 5 freelancers/year. Works with 5 illustrators and 5 freelance designers/year. Prefers local artists. Uses freelancers mainly for graphic design. Also for brochure and slide illustration, catalog design and illustration, print ad design, storyboards, animation and retouching. 20% of work is with print ads. Also for multimedia projects. 70% of design and 80% of illustration demand knowledge of PageMaker, QuarkXPress, FreeHand, Illustrator or Photoshop.

FIRST CONTACT & TERMS Send query letter with brochure, résumé, photocopies, tearsheets, transparencies, photographs, slides and SASE. Samples are filed. Responds only if interested. Will contact artist for portfolio review if interested. Portfolio should include color thumbnails, final art, tearsheets, slides,

photostats, photographs and transparencies. Pays for design by the project, $100-5,000. Pays for illustration by the project, $25-5,000. Buys first rights or negotiates rights purchased.

ASHCRAFT DESIGN

821 N. Nash St., El Segundo CA 90245. (310)640-8330. **E-mail:** info@ashcraftdesign.com. **Website:** www.ashcraftdesign.com. Specializes in corporate identity, display and package design and signage. Client list available upon request.

NEEDS Approached by 2 freelance artists/year. Works with 1 freelance illustrator and 2 freelance designers/year. Works on assignment only. Uses freelance illustrators mainly for technical illustration. Uses freelance designers mainly for packaging and production. Also uses freelance artists for mechanicals and model making.

FIRST CONTACT & TERMS Send query letter with tearsheets, résumé and photographs. Samples are filed and are not returned. Responds only if interested. To show a portfolio, e-mail samples or mail color copies. Pays for design and illustration by the project. Rights purchased vary according to project.

⊘ ASHER AGENCY

535 W. Wayne St., Ft. Wayne IN 46802. (260)424-3373 (Ft. Wayne); (859)273-5530 (Lexington). **E-mail:** hello@asheragency.com. **Website:** www.asheragency.com. Estab. 1974. Approximate annual billing: $12 million. Full service ad agency and PR firm. Clients: automotive firms, financial/investment firms, area economic development agencies, health care providers, fast food companies, gaming companies and industrial.

NEEDS Works with 5-10 freelance artists/year. Assigns 25-50 freelance jobs/year. Prefers local artists. Works on assignment only. Uses freelance artists mainly for illustration; also for design, brochures, catalogs, consumer and trade magazines, retouching, billboards, posters, direct mail packages, logos and advertisements.

FIRST CONTACT & TERMS Send query letter with brochure showing art style or tearsheets and photocopies. Samples are filed or are returned by SASE. Responds only if interested. Will contact artist for portfolio review if interested. Portfolio should include roughs, original/final art, tearsheets and final reproduction/product. Pays for design by the hour, $40 minimum. Pays for illustration by the project,

$40 minimum. Finds artists usually through word of mouth.

A.T. ASSOCIATES

63 Old Rutherford Ave., Charlestown MA 02129. (617)242-6004. **Website:** www.atadesign.net. Estab. 1976. Specializes in annual reports, industrial, interior, product and graphic design, model making, corporate identity, signage, display and packaging. Clients nonprofit companies, high tech, medical, corporate clients, small businesses and ad agencies. Client list available upon request.

NEEDS Approached by 20-25 freelance artists/year. Works with 3-4 freelance illustrators and 2-3 freelance designers/year. Prefers local artists; some experience necessary. Uses artists for posters, model making, mechanicals, logos, brochures, P-O-P display, charts/graphs and design.

FIRST CONTACT & TERMS Send résumé and nonreturnable samples. Samples are filed or are returned by SASE if requested by artist. Responds only if interested. Call to schedule an appointment to show a portfolio, which should include a "cross section of your work." Pays for design and illustration by the hour or by the project. Rights purchased vary according to project.

AURELIO & FRIENDS, INC.

14971 SW 43 Terrace, Miami FL 33185. (305)225-2434. **Fax:** (305)225-2121. **E-mail:** info@aurelioandfriends. com. **Website:** aurelioandfriends.com. **Contact:** Aurelio Sica, president; Nancy Sica, vice president. Estab. 1973. Number of employees: 3. Specializes in corporate advertising and graphic design. Clients: corporations, retailers, large companies, hotels and resorts.

NEEDS Approached by 4-5 freelancers/year. Works with 1-2 freelance illustrators and 3-5 designers/year. Uses freelancers for ad design and illustration, brochure, catalog and direct mail design. 50% of freelance work demands knowledge of Adobe Ilustrator and Photoshop.

FIRST CONTACT & TERMS Send brochure and tearsheets. Samples are filed. Will contact artist for portfolio review if interested. Portfolio should include b&w and color final art, photographs, roughs. Pays for design and illustration by the project. Buys all rights.

THE BAILEY GROUP, INC.

200 W. Germantown Pike, Plymouth Meeting PA 19462. (610)940-9030. **E-mail:** info@baileygp.com. **Website:** www.baileygp.com. Estab. 1985. Number of employees: 38. Specializes in package design, brand and corporate identity, sales promotion materials, corporate communications and signage systems. Clients: corporations (food, drug, health and beauty aids). Current clients include Aetna, Johnson & Johnson Consumer Products Co., Wills Eye Hospital and Welch's. Professional affiliations: AIGA, PDC, APP, AMA, ADC.

NEEDS Approached by 10 freelancers/year. Works with 3-6 freelance illustrators and 3-6 designers/year. Uses illustrators mainly for editorial, technical and medical illustration and final art, charts and airbrushing. Uses designers mainly for freelance production (*not* design), or computer only. Also uses freelancers for mechanicals, brochure and catalog design and illustration, P-O-P illustration and model-making.

FIRST CONTACT & TERMS Send query letter with brochure, résumé, tearsheets and photographs. Samples are filed. Responds only if interested. Will contact for portfolio review if interested. Portfolio should include finished art samples, color tearsheets, transparencies and artist's choice of other materials. May pay for illustration by the hour, $10-15; by the project, $300-3,000. Rights purchased vary according to project.

TIPS Finds artists through word of mouth, self-promotions and sourcebooks.

BASIC-BEDELL ADVERTISING & PUBLISHING

255 Limoneria Ave. #B, Ventura CA 93003. (805)650-1565; (805)695-0079. **E-mail:** barriebedell@gmail. com. **Contact:** Barrie Bedell, president. Specializes in advertisements, direct mail, how-to books, direct response websites and manuals. Clients publishers, direct response marketers, retail stores, software developers, Web entrepreneurs, plus extensive self-promotion of proprietary advertising how-to manuals.

This company's president is seeing "a glut of 'graphic designers,' and an acute shortage of 'direct response' designers."

NEEDS Uses artists for publication and direct mail design, book covers and dust jackets, and direct response websites. Especially interested in hearing from professionals experienced in e-commerce and in converting printed training materials to electronic media, as well as designers of direct response websites.

FIRST CONTACT & TERMS Portfolio review not required. Pays for design by the project, $100-1,000 and up or royalties based on sales.

TIPS "There has been a substantial increase in the use of freelance talent and an increasing need for true professionals with exceptional skills and responsible performance (delivery as promised and 'on target'). It is very difficult to locate freelance talent with expertise in design of print publication and/or direct mail advertising, and websites with heavy use of type. E-mail query with website link or contact with personal letter and photocopy of one or more samples of work that needn't be returned."

BBDO NEW YORK

1285 Avenue of the Americas, New York NY 10019. (212)459-5000. **Website:** www.bbdo.com. Estab. 1891. Number of employees: 850. Approximate annual billing: $50 million. Ad agency; full-service multimedia firm. Specializes in business, consumer advertising, sports marketing and brand development. Clients include Lowe's, VW, FedEx, Pepsi, and Nike.

○ BBDO art director told our editors he is always open to new ideas and maintains an open drop-off policy. If you call and arrange to drop off your portfolio, he'll review it, and you can pick it up in a couple days.

◍ BEDA DESIGN

38663 Thorndale Place, Lake Villa IL 60046. (847)245-8939. **Fax:** (847)245 8939. **E-mail:** bedadesign@comcast.net. **Contact:** Lynn Beda, president. Estab. 1971. Design firm specializing in packaging, print material, publishing, film and video documentaries. Clients: business-to-business accounts, producers to writers, directors and artists. Approximate annual billing: $300,000.

NEEDS Web page builders in Mac platforms. Use skilled Mac freelancers for retouching, technical, illustration, production, Photoshop, QuarkXPress, Illustrator, Premiere, and Go Live. Use film and editorial writers and photographers.

FIRST CONTACT & TERMS Designers: Send query letter with brochure, photocopies and résumé. Illustrators: Send postcard samples and/or photocopies. Samples are filed and are not returned. Will contact for portfolio review if interested.

BARRY DAVID BERGER & ASSOCIATES, INC.

2 Eli Circle, East Hampton NY 11937. (631)324-4484. **Fax:** (631)329-5578. **E-mail:** bergerbarry@hotmail.com. **Website:** www.bergerdesign.com. Estab. 1977. Number of employees: 5. Approximate annual billing: $500,000. Specializes in brand and corporate identity, P-O-P displays, product and interior design, exhibits and shows, corporate capability brochures, advertising graphics, packaging, publications and signage. Clients: manufacturers and distributors of consumer products, office/stationery products, art materials, chemicals, health care, pharmaceuticals and cosmetics. Clients: Dennison, Timex, Sheaffer, Bausch & Lomb and Kodak. Professional affiliations: IDSA, AIGA, APDF.

NEEDS Approached by 12 freelancers/year. Works with 5 freelance illustrators and 7 designers/year. Uses artists for advertising, editorial, medical, technical and fashion illustration, mechanicals, retouching, direct mail and package design, model-making, charts/graphs, photography, AV presentations and lettering. Needs computer-literate freelancers for illustration and production. 50% of freelance work demands computer skills.

FIRST CONTACT & TERMS Send query letter, then call for appointment. Works on assignment only. Send "whatever samples are necessary to demonstrate competence" including multiple roughs for a few projects. Samples are filed or returned. Responds immediately. Provide brochure/flyer, résumé, business card, tearsheets and samples to be kept on file for possible future assignments. Pays for design by the project, $1,000-10,000. Pays for illustration by the project.

TIPS Looks for creativity and confidence.

BERSON, DEAN, STEVENS

P.O. Box 3997, Westlake Village CA 91359. (877)447-0134, ext. 111. **E-mail:** info@bersondeanstevens.com. **Website:** www.bersondeanstevens.com. **Contact:** Lori Berson, owner. Estab. 1981. Specializes in branding, website design and development, content marketing, e-mail marketing, social media marketing, video production, collateral, direct mail, exhibits, signage, promotions and packaging. Clients: manufacturers, professional and finance service firms, ad agencies, corporations and movie studios. Professional affiliation: L.A. Ad Club.

NEEDS Approached by 50 freelancers/year. Works with 10-20 illustrators and 10 designers/year. Works on assignment only. Uses illustrators mainly for brochures, packaging, and comps. Also for catalog, P-O-P, ad and poster illustration, lettering, logos and model-making. 90% of freelance work demands skills in Illustrator, InDesign, Photoshop, as well as web authoring, Dreamweaver, Flash/HTML, CGI, Java, etc. **FIRST CONTACT & TERMS** Send query letter with tearsheets and photocopies. Samples are filed. Will contact artist for portfolio review if interested. Pays for design and illustration by the project. Rights purchased vary according to project. Considers buying second rights (reprint rights) to previously published work. Finds artists through word of mouth, submissions/self-promotions, sourcebooks and agents.

BFL MARKETING COMMUNICATIONS

1399 Lear Industrial Pkwy., Avon OH 44011. (216)875-8860. **Fax:** (216)875-8870. **Website:** www.bflcom.com. Estab. 1955. Number of employees: 12. Approximate annual billing: $6.5 million. Marketing communications firm; full-service multimedia firm. Specializes in new product marketing, website design, interactive media. Product specialty is consumer home products. Client list available upon request. Professional affiliations: North American Advertising Agency Network, BPAA.

NEEDS Approached by 20 freelancers/year. Works with 5 freelance illustrators and 5 designers/year. Prefers freelancers with experience in advertising design. Uses freelancers mainly for graphic design, illustration; also for brochure and catalog design and illustration, lettering, logos, model making, posters, retouching, TV/film graphics. 80% of work is with print ads. Needs computer-literate freelancers for design, illustration, production and presentation. 50% of freelance work demands knowledge of FreeHand, Photoshop, QuarkXPress, Illustrator.

FIRST CONTACT & TERMS Send postcard-size sample of work or send query letter with brochure, photostats, tearsheets, photocopies, résumé, slides and photographs. Samples are filed or returned by SASE. Responds in 2 weeks. Artist should follow-up with call or letter after initial query. Will contact artist for portfolio review if interested. Portfolio should include b&w and color final art, photographs, photostats, roughs, slides and thumbnails. Pays by the project, $200 minimum.

TIPS Finds artists through *Creative Black Book*, *Illustration Annual*, *Communication Arts*, local interviews. "Seeking specialist in Internet design, CD computer presentations and interactive media."

BLOCK & DECORSO

3 Claridge Dr., Verona NJ 07044. (973)857-3900. **Fax:** (973)857-4041. **E-mail:** bdecorso@blockdecorso.com. **Website:** www.blockdecorso.com. Estab. 1939. Approximate annual billing: $12 million. Product specialties are food and beverage, education, finance, home fashion, giftware, health care and industrial manufacturing. Professional affiliations: Ad Club of North Jersey.

NEEDS Approached by 100 freelancers/year. Works with 25 freelance illustrators and 25 designers/year. Prefers to work with "freelancers with at least 3-5 years experience as Mac-compatible artists and 'on premises' work as Mac artists." Uses freelancers for "consumer friendly" technical illustration, layout, lettering, mechanicals and retouching for ads, annual reports, billboards, catalogs, letterhead, brochures and corporate identity. Needs computer-literate freelancers for design and presentation. 90% of freelance work demands knowledge of QuarkXPress, Illustrator, Type-Styler and Photoshop.

FIRST CONTACT & TERMS To show portfolio, mail appropriate samples and follow up with a phone call. Pays for design by the hour; illustration by the project.

TIPS "We are fortunately busy—we use 4-6 freelancers daily. Be familiar with the latest versions of QuarkXpress, Illustrator and Photoshop. We like to see sketches of the first round of ideas. Make yourself available occasionally to work on premises. Be flexible in usage rights!"

BOYDEN & YOUNGBLUTT ADVERTISING & MARKETING

120 W. Superior St., Ft. Wayne IN 46802. (260)422-4499. **E-mail:** talk@b-y.net; info@b-y.net. **Website:** www.b-y.net. **Contact:** Jerry Youngblutt. Estab. 1990. Number of employees: 24. Ad agency. Full-service, multimedia firm. Specializes in magazine ads, collateral, web, media, social media, app development and television.

NEEDS Approached by 10 freelancers/year. Works with 3-4 development types and 5-6 designers/year. Uses freelancers mainly for collateral layout and web. Also for annual reports, billboards, brochure design and illustration, logos and model-making. Ten percent of work is with print ads, 40% web, 15% media, and 35% TV. Needs computer-literate freelancers for design. 100% of freelance work demands knowledge of

FreeHand, Photoshop, Adobe Ilustrator, Web Weaver and InDesign.

FIRST CONTACT & TERMS Send query letter with web links and résumé. Inquires are filed. Will contact artist for portfolio review if interested. Portfolio should include b&w and color final art. Pays for design and illustration by the project. Buys all rights.

TIPS Finds talent through sourcebooks, word of mouth and submissions. "Send a precise résumé with what you feel are your 'best' samples—less is more."

BRAINWORKS DESIGN GROUP, INC.

177 Van Ess Way, Carmel Highlands CA 93923. (831)657-0650. **Fax:** (831)574-3037. **E-mail:** alfred@ brainwks.com. **Website:** www.brainwks.com. Estab. 1970. Brainworks specializes in emotional response communication. Number of employees: 8. Specializes in graphic design, corporate identity, direct mail and publication, website design, research and e blast campaigns. Clients: colleges, universities, nonprofit organizations; majority are colleges and universities.

Additional location: 221 W. 82nd St., Suite 8A, New York NY 10024; (201)240-5555.

NEEDS Prefers freelancers with experience in type, layout creative visual thinking. Works on assignment only. Uses freelancers mainly for web design; also for brochure, direct mail and poster design; lettering; and logos. 100% of design work demands knowledge of QuarkXPress, Illustrator, Photoshop and InDesign.

FIRST CONTACT & TERMS Send brochure or résumé, photocopies, photographs, tearsheets and transparencies. Samples are filed. Artist should follow up with call and/or letter after initial query. Will contact artist for portfolio review if interested. Portfolio should include thumbnails, roughs, final reproduction/product and b&w and color tearsheets, photostats, photographs and transparencies. Pays for design by the project, $100-1,000. Considers complexity of project and client's budget when establishing payment. Rights purchased vary according to project. Finds artists through sourcebooks and self-promotions.

TIPS "Creative thinking and a positive attitude are a plus." The most common mistake freelancers make in presenting samples or portfolios is that the "work does not match up to the samples they show."

BRAMSON + ASSOCIATES

7400 Beverly Blvd., Los Angeles CA 90036. (323)938-3595. **E-mail:** gene@bramson-associates.com. Web-

site: www.bramson-associates.com. **Contact:** Gene Bramson, principal. Estab. 1970. Number of employees 15. Approximate annual billing more than $4 million. Advertising agency. Specializes in corporate communications, branding, magazine branding ads, collateral, ID, signage, graphic design, imaging, campaigns. Product specialties are health care, consumer, business to business. Clients include Johnson & Johnson, Chiron Vision, Lawry's, Sumitomo Metal/ Mining, iScience Interventionals, Afgrow division of Hair Raising Personal Care Products, Inc.

NEEDS Approached by 150 freelancers/year. Works with 10 freelance illustrators, 2 animators and 5 designers/year. Prefers local freelancers but work internationally. Works on assignment only. Uses freelancers for brochure and print ad design; brochure, technical, medical and print ad illustration, storyboards, mechanicals, retouching, lettering, logos. 30% of work is with print ads. 50% of freelance work" knowledge of Illustrator, Photoshop, Freehand or 3-D Studio and InDesign.

FIRST CONTACT & TERMS Send query letter with brochure, photocopies, résumé, photographs, tearsheets, SASE. Samples are filed. Will contact artist for portfolio review if interested. Portfolio should include roughs, color tearsheets. Sometimes requests work on spec before assigning job. Pays for design by the hour, $20-75. Pays for illustration by the project, $250-2,000. Buys all rights or negotiates rights purchased. Finds artists through sourcebooks.

TIPS "We look for very unique talent only. Price and availability are also important."

LEO J. BRENNAN, INC.

1130 S. Lake Valley Dr., Fenton MI 48430. (248)362-3131. **Fax:** (248)362-2355. **E-mail:** lbrennan@ljbrennan.com; request@ljbrennan.com. **Website:** www.ljbrennan.com. **Contact:** Leo Brennan, president. Estab. 1969. Number of employees: 3. Ad, PR and marketing firm. Clients: industrial, electronics, robotics, automotive, chemical, tooling, B2B.

NEEDS Works with 2 illustrators and 2 designers/year. Prefers experienced artists. Uses freelancers for design, technical illustration, brochures, catalogs, retouching, lettering, keylining and typesetting; also for multimedia projects. 40% of work is with print ads. 100% of freelance work demands knowledge of non Mac software graphics programs.

FIRST CONTACT & TERMS Send query letter with résumé and samples. Samples not filed are returned only if requested. Responds only if interested. Call for appointment to show portfolio of thumbnails, roughs, original/final art, final reproduction/product, color tearsheets, and photographs. Payment for design and illustration varies. Buys all rights.

BRIGHT LIGHT PRODUCTIONS, INC.

602 Main St., Suite 810, Cincinnati OH 45202. (513)721-2574. **Fax:** (513)721-3329. **E-mail:** info@ brightlightusa.com. **Website:** www.brightlightusa. com. Estab. 1976. "We are a full-service film/video communications firm producing TV commercials and corporate communications."

NEEDS Works on assignment only. Uses artists for editorial, technical and medical illustration and brochure and print ad design, storyboards, slide illustration, animatics, animation, TV/film graphics and logos. Needs computer-literate freelancers for design and production. 50% of freelance work demands knowledge of Photoshop, Illustrator and After Effects.

FIRST CONTACT & TERMS Send query letter with brochure and résumé. Samples not filed are returned by SASE only if requested by artist. Request portfolio review in original query. Portfolio should include roughs and photographs. Pays for design and illustration by the project. Negotiates rights purchased. Finds artists through recommendations.

TIPS "Our need for freelance artists is growing."

BROADCAST CENTER STUDIOS

700 Millbridge Gardens, Clementon NJ 08021. (856)751-3500. **E-mail:** larry@broadcastcenterstudios.com. **Website:** www.broadcastcenterstudios. com. **Contact:** Larry Scott, president. Estab. 2007. Ad agency/AV firm. Full-service multimedia firm. Specializes in magazine, radio and television. Current clients include Hartcourt Books, WCAU 10, Philadelphia, Cardinal Freight and Transport.

NEEDS Works with 10 freelance illustrators and 5 designers/year. Prefers freelancers with experience in TV. Works on assignment only. Uses freelancers for storyboards, animatics, animation, TV/film graphics. Also for multimedia projects. 90% of freelance work demands knowledge of Adobe Creative Suite CS, Apple Final Cut Pro HD, including motion.

FIRST CONTACT & TERMS Mail query with DVD/CD as samples. Samples are filed or are returned by SASE. Accepts submissions on disk from all applica-

tions. Send EPS files. Responds only if interested. Pays for design and illustration by the project; rate varies. Buys first rights or all rights.

⊕ BROMLEY COMMUNICATIONS

401 E. Houston St., San Antonio TX 78205-2615. (210)244-2000. **E-mail:** Ron.Landreth@bromley.biz. **Website:** www.bromley.biz. **Contact:** Ron Landreth, vice president creative director. Number of employees: 80. Approximate annual billing: $80 million. Estab. 1986. Full-service, multimedia ad agency and PR firm. Specializes in TV, radio and magazine ads, etc. Specializes in consumer service firms and Hispanic markets. Current clients include BellSouth, Burger King, Continental Airlines, Nestlé, Procter & Gamble.

NEEDS Approached by 3 artists/month. Prefers local artists only. Works on assignment only. Uses freelancers for storyboards, slide illustration, new business presentations and TV/film graphics and logos. 35% of work is with print ads. 25% of freelance work demands knowledge of PageMaker, QuarkXPress and Illustrator.

FIRST CONTACT & TERMS Send query letter with brochure and résumé. Samples are not filed and are returned by SASE only if requested by artist. Responds only if interested. Write for appointment to show portfolio.

BROWNING ADVERTISING

1 Browning Place, Morgan UT 84050. (801)876-2711. **Website:** www.browning.com. **Contact:** art director. Estab. 1878. Distributor and marketer of outdoor sports products, particularly firearms. In-house agency for 2 main clients. In-house divisions include outdoor hunting products, firearms and accessories.

NEEDS View website for any upcoming freelance opportunites. Prefers freelancers with experience in outdoor sports hunting, shooting, fishing. Works on assignment only. Uses freelancers occasionally for design, illustration and production. Also for advertising and brochure layout, catalogs, product rendering and design, signage, P-O-P displays, and posters.

FIRST CONTACT & TERMS Send a digital query letter with résumé along with a link or a web address that can be accessed to view your work. Responds only if interested. Pays for design by the hour, $50-75. Pays for illustration by the project. Buys all rights or reprint rights.

CAHAN & ASSOCIATES

171 Second St., 5th Floor, San Francisco CA 94105. (415)621-0915. **E-mail:** info@cahanassociates.com; billc@cahanassociates.com. **Website:** www.cahanassociates.com. **Contact:** Bill Cahan, president. Estab. 1984. Specializes in annual reports, corporate identity, package design, signage, business and business collateral. Clients: public and private companies (real estate, finance and biotechnology). Client list available upon request.

NEEDS Approached by 50 freelance artists/year. Works with 5-10 freelance illustrators and 3-5 freelance designers/year. Works on assignment only. Uses freelance illustrators mainly for annual reports. Uses freelance designers mainly for overload cases. Also uses freelance artists for brochure design.

FIRST CONTACT & TERMS Send query letter with brochure, tearsheets, photostats, résumé, photographs, and photocopies. Samples are filed and are not returned. Responds only if interested. To show a portfolio, mail thumbnails, roughs, tearsheets, and transparencies. Pays for design or illustration by the hour or by the project. Negotiates rights purchased.

THE CALIBER GROUP

4007 E. Paradise Falls Dr., Suite 210, Tucson AZ 85712. (520)795-4500 (Tucson); (480)442-4505 (Tempe). **Fax:** (520)795-4565 (Tucson). **E-mail:** info@calibergroup.com; freelancing@calibergroup.com. **Website:** www.calibergroup.com. Estab. 1997. Specializes in annual reports, brand identity, corporate identity, display design, direct mail design, environmental graphics, package design, publication design and signage. Client list available upon request.

◯ The creative team has won over 500 international, national and local awards.

NEEDS Approached by 100 freelance artists/year. Works with 10 freelance illustrators and 5-10 freelance designers/year. Works on assignment only. Uses designers and illustrators for brochure, poster, catalog, P-O-P and ad illustration, mechanicals, retouching, airbrushing, charts/graphs and audiovisual materials.

FIRST CONTACT & TERMS Send query letter with PDF samples and résumé. Samples are filed. Responds only if interested. Call to schedule an appointment to show portfolio. Portfolio should include roughs, original/final art. Pays for design by the hour and by

the project. Pays for illustration by the project. Negotiates rights purchased.

TIPS When presenting samples or portfolios, designers and illustrators "sometimes mistake quantity for quality. Keep it short and show your best work."

CARNASE, INC.

300 E. Molino Rd., Palm Springs CA 92262. **E-mail:** carnase@carnase.com. **Website:** www.carnase.com. **Contact:** Tom Carnase, president. Estab. 1978. Specializes in annual reports, brand and corporate identity, display, package and publication design, signage and technical illustration. Clients: agencies, corporations, consultants, Brooks Brothers, *Fortune Magazine*, Calvin Klein, Saks Fifth Avenue (list too long to post).

NEEDS Approached by 60 freelance artists/year. Works with 2 illustrators and 1 designer/year. Prefers artists with 5 years experience. Works on assignment only. Uses artists for brochure, catalog, book, magazine and direct mail design and brochure and collateral illustration. Needs computer-literate freelancers. 50% of freelance work demands skills in QuarkXPress or Illustrator.

FIRST CONTACT & TERMS Send query letter with brochure, résumé and tearsheets. Samples are filed. Responds in 10 days. Will contact artist for portfolio review if interested. Portfolio should include digital prints and color tearsheets. Negotiates payment. Rights purchase vary according to project. Finds artists through word of mouth, magazines, submissions/self-promotions, sourcebooks and agents.

CGT MARKETING, LLC

275-B Dixon Ave., Amityville NY 11701. (631)842-4600. **Fax:** (631)842-6301. **E-mail:** info@cgtllc.net. **Website:** www.cgtmarketing.com. **Contact:** The Tobol Group, Mitch Tobol, president. Estab. 1981. Ad agency. Product specialties are business to business and business to consumer.

NEEDS Approached by 2 freelance artists/month. Works with 1 freelance illustrator and 4 designers/month. Works on assignment only. Uses freelancers for brochure, catalog and print ad design and technical illustration, retouching, billboards, posters, TV/film graphics, lettering and logos. 25% of work is with print ads. 75% of freelance work demands knowledge of QuarkXPress, Illustrator, Photoshop, GoLive or Dreamweaver.

FIRST CONTACT & TERMS Send query letter with SASE and tearsheets. Samples are filed or are returned by SASE. Responds in 1 month. Call for appointment to show portfolio or mail thumbnails, roughs, b&w and color tearsheets and transparencies. Pays for design by the hour. Pays for illustration by the project, $300-1,500 ($50 for spot illustrations). Negotiates rights purchased.

◎ CHAPPELLROBERTS

1600 E. Eighth Ave., Suite A-133, Tampa FL 33605. (813)281-0088. **E-mail:** info@chappellroberts.com. **Website:** www.chappellroberts.com. Estab. 1986. Number of employees: 20. Ad agency, PR firm, full-service multimedia firm. Specializes in integrated communications campaigns using multiple media and promotion. Professional affiliations: AIGA, PRSA, AAF, TBAF and AAAAS.

NEEDS Approached by 50 freelancers/year. Works with 15 freelance illustrators and designers/year. Prefers local artists with experience in conceptualization and production knowledge. Uses freelancers for billboards, brochure design and illustration, logos, mechanicals, posters, retouching and website production. 60% of work is with print ads. 80% of freelance work demands knowledge of Adobe Creative Suite 2, QuarkXPress 6.5.

FIRST CONTACT & TERMS E-mail query with samples in PDF files. Will contact artist for portfolio review if interested. Portfolio should include b&w and color final art, roughs and thumbnails. Pays for design by the hour, by the project, by the day. Pays for illustration by the project, negotiable. Refers to *Graphic Artists Guild Handbook* for fee structure. Rights purchased vary according to project. Finds artists through agents, sourcebooks, seeing actual work done for others, annuals (*Communication Arts, PRINT, One Show*, etc.).

TIPS Impressed by "work that demonstrates knowledge of product, willingness to work within budget, contributing to creative process, delivering on-time."

◎ CLIFF & ASSOCIATES

10061 Riverside Dr., #808, Toluca Lake CA 91602. (323)876-1180. **Fax:** (323)876-5484. **E-mail:** design@cliffassoc.com. **Website:** www.cliffassoc.com. **Contact:** Gregg Cliff, owner/creative director. Estab. 1984. Number of employees: 10. Approximate annual billing: $1 million. Specializes in annual reports, corporate identity, direct mail, publication design and signage. Clients: Fortune 500 corporations and performing arts companies. Current clients include BP, IXIA, WSPA, IABC, Capital Research and ING.

NEEDS Approached by 50 freelancers/year. Works with 30 illustrators and 10 designers/year. Prefers local freelancers and Art Center graduates. Uses freelancers mainly for brochures; also for technical, "fresh" editorial and medical illustration, mechanicals, lettering, logos, catalog/book/magazine design, P-O-P and poster design and illustration, and model making. Needs computer-literate freelancers for design and production. 90% of freelance work demands knowledge of QuarkXPress, FreeHand, Illustrator, Photoshop, etc.

FIRST CONTACT & TERMS Send query letter with résumé and a nonreturnable sample of work. Samples are filed. Will contact artist for portfolio review if interested. Portfolio should include thumbnails, b&w photostats and printed samples. Pays for design by the hour, $25-35. Pays for illustration by the project, $50-3,000. Buys one-time rights. Finds artists through sourcebooks.

COMMUNICATIONS ELECTRONICS, INC.

P.O. Box 1045, Ann Arbor MI 48106-1045. (734)996-8888. **E-mail:** ken.ascher@usascan.com. **Website:** www.usascan.com. **Contact:** Ken Ascher, editor. Estab. 1969.

NEEDS Approached by 300 freelancers/year. Works with 40 freelance illustrators and 40 designers/year. Uses freelancers for brochure and catalog design, illustration and layout, advertising, product design, illustration on product, P-O-P displays, posters and renderings. Needs editorial and technical illustration. Prefers pen & ink, airbrush, charcoal/pencil, watercolor, acrylic, marker and computer illustration. 60% of freelance work demands skills in PageMaker or InDesign.

FIRST CONTACT & TERMS Send query letter with brochure, résumé, business card, samples and tearsheets to be kept on file. Samples not filed are returned by SASE. Responds in 1 month. Will contact artist for portfolio review if interested. Pays for design and illustration by the hour, $10-120; by the project, $10-10,000; by the day, $40-500.

COMPASS MEDIA, INC.

175 Northshore Place, Gulf Shores AL 36542. (251)968-4600; (800)239-9880. **E-mail:** info@compassmedia.com. **Website:** www.compassmedia.com.

Estab. 1988. Number of employees: 25-30. Approximate annual billing: $4 million. Integrated marketing communications agency and publisher. Specializes in tourism products and programs. Product specialties are business and consumer tourism. Current clients include Alabama Bureau of Tourism and Alabama Gulf Coast CVB. Client list available upon request. **NEEDS** Approached by 5-20 designers/year. Works with 4-6 designers/year. Prefers freelancers with experience in digital and/or magazine work. Uses freelancers mainly for sales collateral, advertising collateral and illustration. 5% of work is with print ads. 100% of design demands skills in Photoshop and InDesign. **FIRST CONTACT & TERMS** Designers: Send query letter with photocopies, résumé and tearsheets. Samples are filed and are not returned. Responds in 1 month. Art director will contact artist for portfolio review of slides and tearsheets if interested. Pays by the project, $100 minimum. Rights purchased vary according to project. Finds artists through sourcebooks, networking and print.
TIPS "Be fast and flexible. Have digital and/or magazine experience."

⊕ CONCORD DIRECT

92 Old Turnpike Rd., Concord NH 03301-7305. (603)410-1205. **Fax:** (603)224-5503. **E-mail:** dchristiansen@concord-direct.com. **Website:** www.directconcord.com. **Contact:** Deidre Christiansen, art resource coordinator. Estab. 1958. Number of employees: 50. Integrated marketing communications, printer with in-house design department. Specializes in direct mail, greeting cards. Clients: non-profit.
NEEDS Approached by 20 illustrators/year. Work with 3 illustrators/year. Prefers illustrators with experience in watercolor, gouache, oil, acrylic. Buys stock photos. Pays $150-750. Works with beginning an established photographers. Uses photos for direct mail, greeting cards, calendars.
FIRST CONTACT & TERMS E-mail query letter with website and JPEG samples at 72 dpi. No Flickr or Facebook sites. Does not keep samples on file. Responds in 1 month. Illustration: pays by the project, $200-700. Licensing fee per project or term. Photography: Pays by the project, $150-700. Pays on receipt of invoice. Credit line given. Buys one time rights, reprint rights; rights purchased vary according to project. Finds illustrators/photographers through agents, internet and Surtex.

TIPS "Have a website withe keyword images and a search option. It's easier to forward to members of a design team, who need to quickly select from a variety of art styles. Use scans of artwork (never photographs) and have high resolution scans available when the image is licensed."

⊕ COUSINS DESIGN

330 E. 33rd St., New York NY 10016. (212)685-7190. **Fax:** (212)689-3369. **E-mail:** info@cousinsdesign.com. **Website:** www.cousinsdesign.com. **Contact:** Michael Cousins, president. Number of employees: 4. Specializes in packaging and product design. Clients: marketing and manufacturing companies. Professional affiliation: IDSA.
NEEDS Occassionally works with freelance designers. Prefers local designers. Works on assignment only.
FIRST CONTACT & TERMS Send nonreturnable postcard sample or e-mail website link. Samples are filed. Responds in 2 weeks only if interested. Write for appointment to show portfolio of roughs, final reproduction/product and photostats. Pays for design by the hour or flat fee. Considers skill and experience of artist when establishing payment. Buys all rights.
TIPS "Send great work that fits our direction."

⊕ CREATIVE COMPANY, INC.

726 NE Fourth St., McMinnville OR 97128. (866)363-4433. **Fax:** (503)883-6817. **E-mail:** jlmorrow@creativeco.com; optimize@creativeco.com. **Website:** www.creativeco.com. Specializes in branding, marketing-driven corporate identity, collateral, direct mail, packaging and ongoing marketing campaigns. Product specialties are food, financial services, colleges, manufacturing, pharmaceutical, medical, agricultural products.
NEEDS Works with 1-2 freelance designers and 1-2 illustrators/year. Prefers local artists. Works on assignment only. Uses freelancers for design, illustration, digital production (Mac), retouching and lettering. "Looking for clean, fresh designs!" 100% of design and 60% of illustration demand skills in InDesign, Illustrator and Photoshop.
FIRST CONTACT & TERMS Send query letter with brochure, résumé, online access to website, or PDF portfolio. Will contact for portfolio review if interested. "We require a portfolio review. Years of experience not important if portfolio is good. We prefer one-on-one review to discuss individual projects/

time/approach." Pays for design by the hour or project, $50-90. Pays for illustration by the project. Considers complexity of project and skill and experience of artist when establishing payment.

TIPS Common mistakes freelancers make in presenting samples or portfolios are: "1) poor presentation, samples not mounted or organized; 2) not knowing how long it took them to do a job to provide a budget figure; 3) not demonstrating an understanding of the audience, the problem or printing process and how their work will translate into print or online 4) just dropping in without an appointment; 5) not following up periodically to update information or a résumé that might be on file."

CREATIVE CONSULTANTS

17510 E. Montgomery Ave., Greenacres WA 99016-8541. (509)326-3604. **E-mail:** solutions@creative consultants.com. **Website:** www.creativeconsultants. com. **Contact:** Edmond A. Bruneau, president. Estab. 1980. Approximate annual billing: $5,000. Ad agency and design firm. Specializes in collateral, logos, ads, annual reports, radio and TV spots. Product specialties are business and consumer. Client list available upon request.

NEEDS Approached by 20 illustrators and 25 designers/year. Works with 1–2 illustrators and designers/year. Uses freelancers mainly for animation, brochure, catalog and technical illustration, model-making and TV/film graphics. 36% of work is with print ads. Designs and illustration demands skills in Photoshop, InDesign, and Illustrator.

FIRST CONTACT & TERMS Designers: Send query letter. Illustrators: Send postcard sample of work and e-mail. Accepts disk submissions if compatible with Photoshop, InDesign, and Illustrator. Responds only if interested. Pays by the project. Buys all rights. Finds artists through Internet, word of mouth, reference books and agents.

THE CRICKET CONTRAST

(602)390-4940. **E-mail:** cricket@thecricketcontrast. com. **Website:** www.thecricketcontrast.com. Estab. 1982. Specializes in providing solutions for branding, corporate identity, web page design, advertising, package and publication design, and traditional online printing. Clients: corporations. Professional affiliations: AIGA, Scottsdale Chamber of Commerce, Phoenix Society of Communicating Arts, Phoenix Art Museum, Phoenix Zoo.

NEEDS Approached by 25-50 freelancers/year. Works with 5 freelance illustrators and 5 designers/year. Uses freelancers for ad illustration, brochure design and illustration, lettering and logos. Needs computer-literate freelancers for design and production. 100% of freelance work demands knowledge of Illustrator, Photoshop, InDesign, and QuarkXPress.

FIRST CONTACT & TERMS Send photocopies, photographs and résumé via e-mail. Will contact artist for portfolio review if interested. Pays for design and illustration by the project. Negotiates rights purchased. Finds artists through self-promotions and sourcebooks.

TIPS "Beginning freelancers should send all info through e-mail."

CTCREATIVE

Valcourt Group, 214 W. River Rd., St. Charles IL 60174. (630)587-6000. **E-mail:** info@valcort.com. **Website:** www.ctcreative.com. Estab. 1989. Integrated marketing communications agency. Specializes in consulting, creative branding, collateral. Product specialties: health care, family. Current clients include Kidspeace, Cook Communications, Opportunity International.

NEEDS Works with 1-2 freelance illustrators and 2-3 designers/year. Needs freelancers for brochure design and illustration, logos, multimedia projects, posters, signage, storyboards, TV/film graphics. 20% of work is with print ads. 100% of freelance design demands skills in Illustrator and InDesign.

FIRST CONTACT & TERMS Designers: Send query letter with brochure and photocopies. Illustrators: Send postcard sample of work. Samples are filed. Responds only if interested. Portfolio review not required. Pays by the project. Buys all rights.

ⓦ JO CULBERTSON DESIGN, INC.

939 Pearl St., Denver CO 80203. (303)861-4303. **Contact:** Jo Culbertson, president. Estab. 1976. Number of employees: 1. Approximate annual billing: $75,000. Specializes in direct mail, packaging, publication and marketing design, annual reports, corporate identity, and signage. Clients: corporations, not-for-profit organizations. Current clients include Love Publishing Co., Gabby Krause Foundation, Jace Management Services, Vitamin Cottage, Sun Gard Insurance Systems. Client list available upon request.

NEEDS Approached by 2 freelancers/year. Works with 1 freelance illustrator/year. Prefers local freelancers only. Works on assignment only. Uses illustrators mainly for corporate collateral pieces, illustration and ad illustration. 50% of freelance work demands knowledge of QuarkXPress, Photoshop, CorelDraw. **FIRST CONTACT & TERMS** Send query letter or e-mail with résumé, tearsheets and photocopies. Samples are filed. Responds only if interested. Artist should follow up with call. Portfolio should include b&w and color thumbnails, roughs and final art. Pays for design by the project, $250 minimum. Pays for illustration by the project, $100 minimum. Finds artists through file of résumés, samples, interviews.

☺ DAIGLE DESIGN, INC.

6606 Eagle Harbor Dr., Bainbridge Island WA 98110. (206)842-5356. **Fax:** (206)331-4222. **E-mail:** can dace@daigle.com. **Website:** www.daigledesign.com. **Contact:** Candace Daigle, creative director. Estab. 1987. Number of employees: 3. Approximate annual billing: $250,000. Design firm. Specializes in brochures, catalogs, logos, magazine ads, trade show displays, and websites. Product specialties are agriculture, law, nutraceuticals, furniture, real estate development, aviation, yachts, restaurant equipment, and automotive.
NEEDS Approached by 10 illustrators and 20 designers/year. Works with 5 illustrators and 5 designers/year. Prefers local designers with experience in Photoshop, After Effects, 3D Studio Max, V-Ray, Rhino, Illustrator, Dreamweaver, CSS and InDesign. Uses freelancers mainly for concept and production. Also for brochure design and illustration, lettering, logos, multimedia projects, signage, technical illustration and web page design. 50% of work is with print, 50% of design demands skills in Photoshop, Illustrator and InDesign; 50% of illustration demands skills in Photoshop, Illustrator.
FIRST CONTACT & TERMS Designers: Send query letter with résumé. Illustrators: Send query letter with photocopies. Accepts PDF submissions. Send JPEG files. Samples are filed and are not returned. Responds only if interested. Will contact for portfolio review of b&w, color, final art, digital photos/illustrations and tearsheets if interested. Pays for design by the hour, $35; pays for illustration by the project, $150-1,500. Buys all rights. Finds artists through submissions, reps, temp agencies and word of mouth.

DEFOREST GROUP

300 W. Lake St., Elmhurst IL 60126. (630)834-7200. **Fax:** (630)279-8410. **E-mail:** info@deforestgroup. com. **Website:** www.deforestgroup.com. Number of employees: 15. Marketing solutions, graphic design and digital photography firm.
NEEDS Approached by 50 freelance artists/year. Works with 3-5 freelance designers/year. Prefers artists with experience in PhotoShop, Illustrator and InDesign, and photographers with expertise in PhaseOne camera systems and PhotoShop. Freelance web designers and programmers are also utilized.
FIRST CONTACT & TERMS Send query letter with résumé and samples. Physical samples are filed or returned by SASE if requested by artist. To arrange for portfolio review artist should fax or e-mail. Pays for production by the hour, $25-75. Finds designers through word of mouth and artists' submissions.
TIPS "Be hardworking, honest, and good at your craft."

DESIGN ASSOCIATES GROUP, INC.

1828 Asbury Ave., Evanston IL 60201-3504. (847)425-4800. **E-mail:** info@designassociatesinc.com. **Website:** www.designassociatesinc.com. Estab. 1986. Number of employees: 5. Specializes in text and trade book design, corporate marketing and communications: annual reports, corporate branding/identity, website development, eCommerce and online store development, content management systems, mobile app development. Clients: corporations, publishers and institutions. Client list available upon request.
NEEDS Approached by 10-20 freelancers/year. Works with 100 freelance illustrators and 2 designers/year. Uses freelancers for design and production. 100% of freelance work demands knowledge of Illustrator, Photoshop and InDesign.
FIRST CONTACT & TERMS Send query letter with samples that best represent work. Accepts disk submissions. Samples are filed. Will contact artist for portfolio review if interested. Portfolio should include b&w and color samples.

DESIGN RESOURCE CENTER

424 Fort Hill Dr., Suite 118, Naperville IL 60540. (630)357-6008. **Fax:** (630)357-6040. **E-mail:** info@ drcchicago.com. **Website:** www.drcchicago.com. Estab. 1990. "By leveraging consumer insights and smart design, we deliver strategic branding and package design with refreshing efficiency. Design Resource Cen-

ter has been delivering brand design solutions that delight our clients and motivate consumers since 1990."

NEEDS "We supplement our staff of designer and production artists, and purchase illustrations and custom typography based on project needs. In most cases, we prefer production artists and designers work on site in our Naperville, Illinois office and must be highly skilled in Illustrator and Photoshop."

FIRST CONTACT & TERMS "Design and production: Please feel free to contact us via e-mail and include your résumé and portfolio. We pay hourly based on negotiated rate. Illustration and typography: Please feel free to contact us via e-mail and include your portfolio. Negotiated fees include all buyouts."

DEVER DESIGNS

14203 Park Center Dr., Suite 308, Laurel MD 20707. (301)776-2812. **Fax:** (866)665-1196. **E-mail:** info@deverdesigns.com. **Website:** www.deverdesigns.com. **Contact:** Kay Rosburg. Estab. 1985. Number of employees: 7. Specializes in annual reports, corporate identity and publication design. Clients: associations, nonprofit organizations, educational institutions, museums, government agencies.

NEEDS Approached by 100 freelance illustrators/year. Works with 0-5 freelance illustrators/year. Prefers artists with experience in editorial illustration. Uses illustrators mainly for publications.

FIRST CONTACT & TERMS Send postcard, samples or query letter with résumé and website. Accepts PDFs and disk submissions compatible with Photoshop, Illustrator or InDesign, but prefers hard copy samples which are filed. Will contact artist for portfolio review if interested. Pays for illustration by the project. Rights purchased vary according to project. Finds artists through referrals and sourcebooks.

TIPS Impressed by consistent quality.

⊙ ANTHONY DI MARCO

301 Aris Ave., Metairie LA 70005. (504)833-3122. **Website:** www.anthonydimarcostudio.com. **Contact:** Anthony Di Marco, creative director. Estab. 1972. Number of employees: 1. Specializes in illustration, sculpture, costume design, art and photo restoration and retouching. Current clients include Audubon Institute, Louisiana Nature and Science Center, Fair Grounds Race Course. Client list available upon request. Professional affiliations: Art Directors Designers Association, Entergy Arts Council, Louisiana

Crafts Council, Louisiana Alliance for Conservation of Arts.

NEEDS Approached by 50 or more freelancers/year. Works with 5-10 freelance illustrators and 5-10 designers/year. Seeks "local freelancers with ambition. Freelancers should have substantial portfolios and an understanding of business requirements." Uses freelancers mainly for fill-in and finish design, illustration, mechanicals, retouching, airbrushing, posters, model-making, charts/graphs. Prefers highly polished, finished art in pen & ink, airbrush, charcoal/pencil, colored pencil, watercolor, acrylic, oil, pastel, collage and marker. 25% of freelance work demands computer skills.

FIRST CONTACT & TERMS Send query letter with résumé, business card, slides, brochure, photocopies, photographs, transparencies and tearsheets to be kept on file. Samples not filed are returned by SASE. Responds in 1 week if interested. Call or write for appointment to show portfolio. Pays for illustration by the hour or by the project, $100 minimum.

TIPS "Keep professionalism in mind at all times. Put forth your best effort. Apologizing for imperfect work is a common mistake freelancers make when presenting a portfolio. Include prices for completed works (avoid overpricing). 3D works comprise more of our total commissions than before."

CHARLES DUFF ADVERTISING

301 W. Osborn Rd., Suite 3600, Phoenix AZ 85013. (800)234-2269; (602)285-1660. **Website:** www.farnam.com. **Fax:** (602)207-2193. **E-mail:** bdawes@mail.farnam.com. **Contact:** Brian Dawes, executive art director. Estab. 1948. Number of employees 13. Approximate annual billing $1 million. Ad agency. Full-service multimedia firm. Specializes in agri-marketing promotional materials, literature, audio, video, trade literature. Specializes in animal health. Charles Duff Advertising is the in-house ad agency for Farnam Companies, a multimillion dollar company specializing in horse care and agricultural products.

NEEDS Approached by 50 freelancers/year. Works with 10 freelance illustrators and 10 designers/year. Prefers freelancers with experience in animal illustration: equine, pets and livestock. Uses freelancers mainly for brochure, catalog and print ad illustration and retouching, billboards and posters. 35% of work is with print ads. Needs computer-literate freelancers for design, illustration, production and presentation.

25% of freelance work demands knowledge of Photoshop, QuarkXPress and Illustrator.

FIRST CONTACT & TERMS Send query letter with brochure, photocopies, SASE, résumé, photographs, tearsheets, slides or transparencies. Samples are filed or are returned by SASE if requested by artist. Responds in 2 weeks. Reviews portfolios "only by our request." Pays by the project, $100-500 for design; $100-700 for illustration. Buys one-time rights.

DYKEMAN ASSOCIATES, INC.

4115 Rawlins St., Dallas TX 75219. (214)587-2995. **E-mail:** info@dykemanassociates.com. **Website:** www.dykemanassociates.com. Estab. 1974. PR/marketing firm. Specializes in business, hospitality, sports, environmental, energy, health.

NEEDS Works with 5 illustrators and designers/year. Local freelancers preferred. Uses freelancers for editorial and technical illustration, brochure design, exhibits, corporate identification, POS, signs, posters, ads and all design and finished artwork for websites and printed materials. PC or Mac.

FIRST CONTACT & TERMS Request portfolio review in original query. Pays by the project, $300-3,000. "Artist makes an estimate; we approve or negotiate."

TIPS "Be enthusiastic. Present an organized portfolio with a variety of work. Portfolio should reflect all that an artist can do. Don't include examples of projects for which you only did a small part of the creative work. Have a price structure but be willing to negotiate per project. We prefer to use artists/designers/illustrators who will work with barter (trade) dollars and join one of our trade exchanges. We see steady growth ahead."

EJW ASSOCIATES, INC.

1602 Abbey Court, Alpharetta GA 30004. (770)664-9322. **Fax:** (770)664-9324. **E-mail:** emilw@ejwassoc.com. **Website:** www.ejwassoc.com. **Contact:** Emil Walcek, president. Estab. 1982. Ad agency. Specializes in website design and development, eCommerce sites, adversting, corporate ID, brochures, and show graphics. Product specialty is business-to-business.

NEEDS Works with 1-2 freelance illustrators and designers/year. Prefers local freelancers with experience in open source coding (LAMP) for websites, and creatives with design/illustration and Photoshop expertise. Hires for assignment only. Uses freelancers to augment in-house capabilities when needed for brochure, website development, catalog and print ad design and illustration, editorial, technical illustra-

tion and logos. 50% of work is with print ads. 75% of freelance work demands skills in FreeHand, Photoshop, Web coding, Flash.

FIRST CONTACT & TERMS Send query letter containing brief résumé/bio information. Responds only if interested. Pays for design by the hour, $20-80; or by the project. Buys all rights.

TIPS "We prefer freelancers with experience in non-consumer, industrial or technology account work. Visit our website first, then e-mail or call. Do not send e-mail attachments."

THE EMERY GROUP

2707 Congress St., #2M, San Diego CA 92110. (619)299-0775 (San Diego); (915)532-3636 (El Paso). **E-mail:** tome@emerygroup.com. **Website:** www.emerygroup.com. Number of employees: 18. Ad agency. Specializes in automotive and retail firms, banks and restaurants. Clients: Texas National Bank and Horizon Co., Ltd.

Second location: 1519 Montana Ave., El Paso TX 79902.

NEEDS Approached by 3-4 freelancers/year. Works with 2-3 freelance illustrators and 4-5 designers/year. Uses freelancers mainly for design, illustration and production. Needs technical illustration and cartoons.

FIRST CONTACT & TERMS Works on assignment only. Send query letter with résumé and samples to be kept on file. Prefers tearsheets as samples. Samples not filed are returned by SASE. Will contact artist for portfolio review if interested. Sometimes requests work on spec before assigning a job. Pays for design by the hour, $15 minimum; by the project, $100 minimum; by the day, $300 minimum. Pays for illustration by the hour, $15 minimum; by the project, $100 minimum. Considers complexity of project, client's budget and turnaround time when establishing payment. Rights purchased vary according to project.

TIPS Especially looks for "consistency and dependability; high creativity; familiarity with retail, Southwestern and Southern California look."

ERICKSEN ADVERTISING & DESIGN, INC.

12 W. 37th St., 9th Floor, New York NY 10018. (212)239-3313. **Fax:** (212)239-3321. **E-mail:** bobe@eadcom.com. **Website:** www.eadcom.com. **Contact:** Robert P. Ericksen, creative director. Full-service ad agency providing all promotional materials and commercial services for clients. Product specialties are

promotional, commercial and advertising material. Current clients include BBC, *National Geographic*, CBSTV and Prudential.

NEEDS Works with several freelancers/year. Assigns several jobs/year. Works on assignment only. Uses freelancers mainly for advertising, packaging, brochures, catalogs, trade, P-O-P displays, posters, lettering and logos. Prefers composited and computer-generated artwork.

FIRST CONTACT & TERMS Contact through artist's agent or send query letter with brochure or tearsheets and slides. Samples are filed and are not returned unless requested with SASE; unsolicited samples are not returned. Responds in 1 week if interested or when artist is needed for a project. Does not respond to all unsolicited samples. "Only on request should a portfolio be sent." Pays for illustration by the project, up to $5,000. Buys all rights, and retains ownership of original in some situations. Finds artists through word of mouth, magazines, submissions and sourcebooks.

TIPS "Advertising artwork is becoming increasingly 'commercial' in response to very tightly targeted marketing. The artist has to respond to increased creative team input. Must be experienced in computer softwares; Quark, Photoshop, Acrobat, Illustrator, MS Office, Dreamweaver, and other design/web programs."

EVENTIV

10116 Blue Creek North, Whitehouse OH 43571. (419)877-5711. **E-mail:** jan@eventiv.com. **Website:** www.eventiv.com. **Contact:** Janice Robie, president/creative director. Agency specializing in graphics, promotions and tradeshow marketing.

NEEDS Assigns freelance jobs. Works with illustrators and designers on assignment only. Uses freelancers for brochures, P-O-P displays, AV presentations, posters and illustrations (technical or creative) electronic authoring, animation, web design. Requires computer skills.

FIRST CONTACT & TERMS E-mail samples. Responds only interested. Pays by the hour or by the project. Considers client's budget and skill and experience of artist when establishing payment. Retains rights purchased.

FLINT COMMUNICATIONS

101 Tenth St. N., Suite 300, Fargo ND 58102. (701)237-4850. **Fax:** (701)234-9680. **E-mail:** gerril@flintcom.com; dawnk@flintcom.com. **Website:** www.flintcom.com. **Contact:** Gerri Lien, creative director; Dawn Ko-

randa, creative director. Estab. 1946. Number of employees: 60. Approximate annual billing: $14 million. Ad agency; full-service multimedia firm. Product specialties are agriculture, manufacturing, health care, insurance, tourism and banking. Professional affiliations: AIGA, MN Ad Fed.

NEEDS Approached by 50 freelancers/year. Works with 6-10 freelance illustrators and 3-4 designers/year. Uses freelancers for annual reports, brochure design and illustration, lettering, logos and TV/film graphics. 40% of work is with print ads. 20% of freelance work demands knowledge of InDesign, Photoshop, QuarkXPress and Illustrator.

FIRST CONTACT & TERMS Send query letter and postcard-size or larger sample of work. Samples are filed. Will contact artist for portfolio review if interested. Pays for illustration by the project, $100-2,000. Rights purchased vary according to project.

FLINT GROUP ADVERTISING

101 10th St. North, Fargo ND 58201. (701)237-4850. **Fax:** (701)234-9680. **Website:** www.flint-group.com. Estab. 1947. Number of employees: 90. Approximate annual billing: $5.5 million. Ad agency. Specializes in magazine ads, collateral, documentaries, web design, etc. Product specialties are agriculture, gardening, fast food/restaurants, healthcare. Client list available upon request.

◯ A division of Flint Communications, Fargo ND, with 5 locations in North Dakota and Minnesota.

NEEDS Approached by 3-6 freelancers/year. Works with 3 freelance illustrators and 2 designers/year. Works on assignment only. Uses freelancers mainly for illustration. Also for brochure, catalog and print ad design and illustration; storyboards; billboards; and logos. 10% of work is with print ads. 10% of freelance work demands knowledge of QuarkXPress, Photoshop, Illustrator.

FIRST CONTACT & TERMS Send postcard, tearsheets or digital submission. Samples are filed or are returned. Will contact artist for portfolio review if interested. Portfolio should include color thumbnails, roughs, tearsheets, and photographs. Pays for design and illustration by the hour, by the project, or by the day. Rights purchased vary according to project.

FORDESIGN GROUP

5405 South 550 East, Ogden UT 84405. (801)479-4002. **E-mail:** steven@fordesign.net. **Website:** www.

fordesign.net. **Contact:** Steven Ford, owner. Estab. 1990. Specializes in brand and corporate identity, package and website design. Clients: corporations. Current clients include Sony, IBM, Cadbury Beverage, Carrs, MasterCard. Professional affiliations: AIGA, PDC.

NEEDS Approached by 100 freelancers/year. Works with 6-10 freelance illustrators and 4-6 designers/year. Uses illustrators mainly for brochures, ads. Uses designers mainly for corporate identity, packaging, collateral. Also uses freelancers for ad and brochure design and illustration, logos. Needs bright, conceptual designers and illustrators. 90% of freelance work demands skills in Illustrator, Photoshop, FreeHand and Dreamweaver.

FIRST CONTACT & TERMS Send postcard sample of work or send photostats, slides and transparencies. Samples are filed or returned by SASE if requested by artist. Will contact artist for portfolio review if interested. Portfolio should include b&w and color samples. Pays for design by the hour or by the project. Pays for illustration by the project.

TIPS "We review *Showcase, Workbook*, etc. We are impressed by great work, simply presented. Save money on promotional materials by partnering with printers. Create a joint project or tie-in."

FREEASSOCIATES

8117 W. Manchester Ave., Suite 417, Playa Del Rey CA 90293. (310)441-9950. **Fax:** (310)441-9949. **E-mail:** jfreeman@freeassoc.com. **Website:** www.freeassoc. com. **Contact:** Josh Freeman, president/creative director. Estab. 1993. Number of employees: 4. Design firm. Specializes in marketing materials for corporate clients. Client list available upon request. Professional affiliations: AIGA.

NEEDS Approached by 60 illustrators and 30 designers/year. Works with 3 illustrators and 3 designers/year. Prefers freelancers with experience in top level design and advertising. Uses freelancers mainly for design, production, illustration; also for airbrushing, brochure design and illustration, catalog design and illustration, lettering, logos, mechanicals, multimedia projects, posters, retouching, signage, storyboards, technical illustration and web page design. 30% of work is with print ads. 90% of design and 50% of illustration demand skills in Photoshop, InDesign CS, Illustrator.

FIRST CONTACT & TERMS Designers: E-mail query letter with PDFs or JPEGs of work, résumé, website link. Illustrators: E-mail sample of work. Accepts Mac-compatible disk submissions to view in current version of major software or self-running presentations—CD OK. Samples are filed or returned by SASE. Will contact for portfolio review if interested. Pays for design and illustration by the project; negotiable. Rights purchased vary according to project. Finds artists through iSpot.com and other online resources, *LA Workbook, CA, Print, Graphis*, submissions and samples.

TIPS "Designers should have their own computer and high speed Internet connection. Must have sensitivity to marketing requirements of projects they work on. Deadline commitments are critical."

G2 PARTNERS

(888)309-5818. **E-mail:** jamie@g2partners.com. **Website:** www.g2partners.com. **Contact:** Jamie Greenebaum. Estab. 1975. Ad agency. Specializes in business-to-business marketing communications (advertising, direct mail, branding and identity, Internet presence, corporate literature, investor relations) for a variety of regional, national and international clients, large and small.

NEEDS Uses freelancers mainly for advertising, direct mail and literature; also for brochure and print ad illustration.

FIRST CONTACT & TERMS Samples are filed or are returned by SASE if requested by artist. Responds only if interested. Pays for illustration by the project: $500-3,500. Finds artists through online sources.

GIRVIN STRATEGIC BRANDING

3131 Western Ave. #510, Seattle WA 98121. (206)674-7808. **Fax:** (206)674-7909. **E-mail:** info@girvin.com. **Website:** www.girvin.com. Estab. 1977. Design firm. Number of employees: 20. Specializes in corporate identity and brand strategy, naming, Internet strategy, graphic design, signage and packaging. Clients: Kerzner, Kraft, NaturoMedica, Nintendo, Paramount, Procter & Gamble, Simon Golub & Sons and Schwartz Brothers.

NEEDS Works with some freelance copy writers, photographers, web programmers, illustrators, production artists and designers/year.

FIRST CONTACT & TERMS Designers: Send query letter with appropriate samples. Illustrators: Send postcard sample or other nonreturnable samples. Will contact for portfolio review if interested. Payment negotiable.

GLOBAL FLUENCY

1494 Hamilton Ave., San Jose CA 95125. (408)677-5300. **Fax:** (408)677-5301. **Website:** www.globalfluency.com. Estab. 1986. Communications, integrated marketing and PR firm. Specializes in promotions, corporate identity, collateral design, annuals, graphic and ad design and web design. Product specialties are Internet, high-tech, computer systems and peripherals, medical and consumer packaged goods. Clients include NTT Group, Host Analytics, Courtyard by Marriott Palo Alto, Netline, among others.

NEEDS Approached by 20 freelance artists/month. Works with 2-3 freelance illustrators and 2-3 freelance designers/month. Prefers local artists with experience in all areas of manual and electronic art capabilities. Works on assignment only. Uses freelance artists mainly for brochure design and illustration, print ad illustration, infographics, presentations and videography. Needs freelancers for design, illustration, production and presentation.

FIRST CONTACT & TERMS Send query letter with "best work samples in the area you're best in or e-mail it with links to online portfolio and profile." Pays for design by the hour. Negotiates rights purchased.

GRAPHIC DESIGN CONCEPTS

15329 Yukon Ave., El Camino Village CA 90260-2452. (310)978-8922. **Contact:** C. Weinstein, president. Estab. 1980. Specializes in package, publication and industrial design, annual reports, corporate identity, displays and direct mail. Clients: Trust Financial Financial Services (marketing materials). Current projects include new product development for electronic, hardware, cosmetic, toy and novelty companies.

NEEDS Works with 15 illustrators and 25 designers/year. "Looking for highly creative idea people, all levels of experience." All styles considered. Uses illustrators mainly for commercial illustration. Uses designers mainly for product and graphic design. Also uses freelancers for brochure, P-O-P, poster and catalog design and illustration; book, magazine, direct mail and newspaper design; mechanicals; retouching; airbrushing; model-making; charts/graphs; lettering; logos. Also for multimedia design, program and content development. 50% of freelance work demands knowledge of PageMaker, Illustrator, QuarkXPress, Photoshop or FreeHand.

FIRST CONTACT & TERMS Send query letter with brochure, résumé, tearsheets, photostats, photocopies, slides, photographs or transparencies. Accepts disk submissions compatible with Windows. Samples are filed or returned if accompanied by SASE. Responds in 10 days with SASE. Portfolio should include thumbnails, roughs, original/final art, final reproduction/product, tearsheets, transparencies and references from employers. Pays by the hour, $15-50. Considers complexity of project, client's budget, skill and experience of artist, how work will be used, turnaround time, and rights purchased when establishing payment.

TIPS "Send a résumé, if available. Send samples of recent work or *high-quality* copies. Everything sent to us should have a professional look. After all, it is the first impression we will have of you. Selling artwork is a business. Conduct yourself in a professional manner."

GRETEMAN GROUP

1425 E. Douglas Ave., Wichita KS 67211. (316)263-1004. **E-mail:** info@gretemangroup.com. **Website:** www.gretemangroup.com. **Contact:** Sonia Greteman, owner. Estab. 1989. Number of employees: 19. Marketing communications. Specializes in corporate identity, advertising, annual reports, signage, website design, interactive media, brochures, collateral. Professional affiliations AIGA.

NEEDS Approached by 20 illustrators and 20 designers/year. Illustration demands computer skills in Photoshop and Illustrator.

FIRST CONTACT & TERMS Send query letter with brochure and résumé. Accepts disk submissions. Send EPS files. Samples are filed. Will contact for portfolio review of b&w and color final art and photostats if interested. Pays for illustration by the project. Rights purchased vary according to project.

GREY NEW YORK

200 Fifth Ave., New York NY 10010. (212)546-2000. **Fax:** (212)546-2001. **E-mail:** jim.heekin@grey.com; inquiries@grey.com. **Website:** www.grey.com. **Contact:** Jim Heekin, chairman and CEO. Professional affiliations 4A's Art Services Committee.

NEEDS Approached by hundreds of freelancers/year. Clients include Pantene, DDF, Diagio, and 3M. Works with about 300 freelancers/year. Freelancers are needed mostly for illustration and photography, but also for model-making, fashion styling and lettering.

FIRST CONTACT & TERMS Works on assignment only. E-mail query with website link for initial contact. No follow-up e-mails. Does not respond unless interested and an appropriate project arises. Pays by the project. Considers client's budget and rights purchased when establishing fees.

TIPS "Show your work in a neat and organized manner. Have sample leave-behinds or website link and do not expect to leave with a job."

GRIFFIN MARKETING SERVICES, INC.

7357 International Place, Suite 102, Sarasota FL 34240. 941-312-5350. **E-mail:** shannon@griffinmarketingservices.com. **Website:** www.griffinmarketingservices.com. **Contact:** Shannon Luther, vice president/creative director. Estab. 1974. Number of employees 20. Approximate annual billing $4 million. Integrated marketing firm. Specializes in collateral, direct mail, multimedia. Product specialty is industrial. Current clients include Hyatt, USX, McDonald's.

NEEDS Works with 20-30 freelance illustrators and 2-30 designers/year. Prefers artists with experience in computer graphics. Uses freelancers mainly for design and illustration. Also uses freelancers for animation, model making and TV/film graphics. 75% of work is with print ads. Needs computer-literate freelancers for design, illustration, production and presentation. 95% of freelance work demands knowledge of PageMaker, FreeHand, Photoshop, QuarkXPress and Illustrator.

FIRST CONTACT & TERMS Send query letter with SASE or e-mail. Samples are not filed and are returned by SASE if requested by artist. Responds in 1 month. Will contact artist for portfolio review if interested. Pays for design and illustration by the hour, $20-150; or by the project.

TIPS Finds artists through *Creative Black Book.*

HANSEN BELYEA

109 West Denny Way, Suite 312, Seattle WA 98119. (206)682-4895. **E-mail:** hello@hansenbelyea.com. **Website:** www.hansenbelyea.com. Estab. 1988. Creative agency specializes in branding, marketing and communication programs including corporate identity, websites and videos, marketing collateral. Clients: B2B and B2C-professional services, education, manufacturers. Current clients include PEMCO Insurance, University of Washington, Washington Global Health Alliance, Robbins Tunnel Boring Machines.

NEEDS Approached by 20-30 freelancers/year. Works with 1-3 freelance illustrators/photographers and no designers/year. Works on assignment only. Also uses freelancers for calligraphy.

FIRST CONTACT & TERMS Direct mail and electronic communication accepted. Responds only if interested. Pays for illustration by the project. Rights purchased vary according to project. Finds artists through submissions and referral by other professionals.

TIPS "Illustrators and photographers must deliver digital files. Illustrators must develop a style that makes them unique in the marketplace. When pursuing potential clients, send something distinctive. Follow up. Be persistent (it can take 1 or 2 years to get noticed) but not pesky."

HARMON GROUP

807 Third Ave. S., Nashville TN 37210. (615)256-3393. **E-mail:** contact@harmongrp.com. **Website:** www.harmongrp.com. Estab. 1988. Approximate annual billing $7.2 million. Specializes in luxury consumer products, brand identity, display and direct mail design and signage. Clients: consumer product companies, corporations, mid-size businesses.

NEEDS Approached by 20 freelancers/year. Uses illustrators mainly for P-O-P. Uses designers mainly for flyers and catalogs. Also uses freelancers for ad, brochure, catalog, poster and P-O-P design and illustration, logos, magazine design, mechanicals and retouching. 85% of freelance work demands skills in Illustrator, Photoshop and QuarkXPress.

FIRST CONTACT & TERMS Send photographs, résumé, slides and transparencies. Samples are filed. Will contact artist for portfolio review if interested. Portfolio should include color final art, roughs, slides and thumbnails. Pays for design and illustration by the project. Rights purchased vary according to project. Finds artists through sourcebooks and portfolio reviews.

HILL AND KNOWLTON, INC.

(212)885-0300. **Website:** www.hkstrategies.com. Estab. 1927. Number of employees: 1,800 (worldwide). PR firm; full-service multimedia firm. Specializes in corporate communications, marketing communications, public affairs, health care/pharmaceuticals, technology. Creative services include reports, collateral materials, corporate identity, presentation design, signage and advertisements.

NEEDS Works with 0-10 freelancers/month. Works on assignment only. Uses freelancers for editorial, technical and medical illustration; also for storyboards, slide illustration, animatics, mechanicals, presentation design, retouching. 10% of work is with print ads. Needs computer-literate freelancers for illustration. Freelancers should be familiar with Adobe Creative Suite: Photoshop, Illustrator, InDesign, and Microsoft PowerPoint.

FIRST CONTACT & TERMS Send query letter with promo and samples. Samples are filed. Does not respond, in which case the artist should "keep in touch by mail—do not call." Call and drop-off only for a portfolio review. Pays freelancers by the project, $250-5,000. Negotiates rights purchased.

TIPS Looks for "variety; unique but marketable styles are always appreciated."

HORNALL ANDERSON

710 Second Ave., Suite 1300, Seattle WA 98104. (206)467-5800. **E-mail:** us@hornallanderson.com. **Website:** www.hornallanderson.com. Estab. 1982. Specializes in full-range integrated brand and communications strategy, corporate identity, digital and interactive experience design, packaging, corporate literature, collateral, retail and environmental graphics. Clients: Holland America Line, Redhook Brewery, Microsoft, Madison Square Garden, Starbucks, Skydeck Chicago at Willis Tower, Empire State Building, Pepsico, and HTC. Professional affiliations: AIGA, Seattle Design Association, Art Directors Club.

○ This firm has received numerous awards and honors, including the International Mobius Awards, London International Advertising Awards, ADDY Awards, Communication Arts, AIGA, Clio Awards, Webby Awards, and Graphis Awards.

NEEDS Interested in all levels, from senior print and interactive design personnel to interns with design experience. Additional illustrators and freelancers are used on an as-needed basis in design and online media projects

FIRST CONTACT & TERMS Designers: Send query letter with photocopies and résumé or e-mail. Illustrators: Send résumé/cover letter and samples (URL link, PDF, JPEGS, If appropriate hard copies are accepted, but won't be returned. Samples are filed. Responds only if interested. Portfolios may be dropped off, but must be picked up by owner following review. Finds designers through word of mouth and submissions; illustrators through sourcebooks, reps and sub-

missions. No unsolcited third party recruiter résumé submissions.

HOWARD DESIGN GROUP

20 Nassau St., Suite 250W, Princeton NJ 08542. (609)924-1106. **Fax:** (609)924-1165. **E-mail:** diane@howarddesign.com. **Website:** www.howarddesign.com. **Contact:** Diane Savoy, vice president. Estab. 1980. Number of employees: 10. Specializes in marketing and design for packaging websites, corporate identity, college recruitment materials and publication design. Clients: corporations, wholesalers, schools and colleges.

NEEDS Approached by 20 freelancers/year. Works with 10 freelance illustrators and 5 designers/year. Uses freelancers mainly for publication design; also for brochure design and illustration; catalog, direct mail, magazine and poster design; logos. Needs computer-literate freelancers for design and production. 100% of freelance work demands knowlege of Illustrator, Photoshop, FreeHand and QuarkXPress.

FIRST CONTACT & TERMS Send résumé. Samples are filed. Will contact artist for portfolio review if interested. Portfolio should include color final art, roughs and thumbnails. Pays for design and illustration by the project. Buys one-time rights. Finds artists through *Showcase*.

TIPS Looks for "innovative design in portfolio."

HOWARD/FROST ADVERTISING COMMUNICATIONS

1420 NW Gilman Blvd. #2756, Issaquah WA 98027. (206)310-4878. **E-mail:** jack@hofro.com. **Website:** www.hofro.com. Estab. 1994. Number of full-time employees 4. Ad agency. Specializes in media advertising, collateral, web design, web advertising and direct mail. Client list is available upon request.

NEEDS Approached by 20-30 illustrators and 10-15 designers/year. Works with 10 illustrators and 2 designers/year. Works only with artist reps. Uses freelancers mainly for illustration, design overload. Also for airbrushing, animation, billboards, brochure, humorous and technical illustration, lettering, logos, multimedia projects, retouching, storyboards, web page design. 60% of work is with print ads. 60% of freelance design demands knowledge of PageMaker, FreeHand and Photoshop.

FIRST CONTACT & TERMS Designers: Send query letter with photocopies. Illustrators: Send postcard sample. Accepts disk submissions. Send files compatible with Acrobat, InDesign, Illustrator, Dreamweaver, Flash or Photoshop. Samples are filed and not returned. Responds only if interested. Art director will contact artist for portfolio review if interested. Pays for design and illustration by the project. Negotiates rights purchased.

TIPS "Be patient."

HOWARD/MERRELL

4800 Falls of Neuse Rd., Suite 300, Raleigh NC 27609. (919)848-2400. **Fax:** (919)845-9845. **E-mail:** sstyons@ howardmerrellgroup.com. **Website:** www.howard merrellgroup.com. Estab. 1993. Number of employees: 60. Approximate annual billing: $90 million. Ad agency. Full-service, multimedia firm. Specializes in ads, collateral, full service TV, broadcast. Product specialties are industrial and high-tech. Clients include Colonial Bank, Interton, Zilla.

NEEDS Approached by 25-50 freelancers/year. Works with 10-12 freelance illustrators and 20-30 designers/year. Uses freelancers for brochure design and illustration, catalog design, logos, posters, signage and P-O-P. 40% of work is with print ads. Needs computer-literate freelancers for design, illustration, production and presentation. 100% of freelance work demands knowledge of Photoshop, InDesign and Illustrator.

FIRST CONTACT & TERMS Send postcard sample of work or query letter with photocopies. Samples are filed. Request portfolio review in original query. Will contact artist for portfolio review if interested. Portfolio should include b&w and color final art. Pays for design by the hour, $25-65. Pays for design and illustrator by the hour or project.

HOWRY DESIGN ASSOCIATES

354 Pine St., Suite 600, San Francisco CA 94104. (415)433-2035. **Fax:** (415)433-0816. **E-mail:** hello@ howry.com. **Website:** www.howry.com. **Contact:** Jill Howry, principal/creative director. Estab. 1988. Full service design studio. Number of employees: 10. Specializes in annual reports, corporate identity, print, advertising and multimedia. Clients: startups to Fortune 100 companies. Current clients include Del Monte, Affymetrix, Geron Corp., McKesson Corp., First Republic Bank. Professional affiliation: AIGA.

NEEDS Works with 30 freelance illustrators, photographers and Internet and print designers/year. Works on assignment only. Uses illustrators for "anything that applies." Uses designers mainly for newsletters, brochures, corporate identity. Also uses freelancers for production, programming, retouching, photography/illustration, logos and charts/graphs. 100% of design work, 10% of illustration work demands knowledge of InDesign, Illustrator or Photoshop.

FIRST CONTACT & TERMS Samples are filed. Responds only if interested. Portfolios may be dropped off every Thursday. Pays for design/production by the hour, or by the job, $25-60. Pays for photography and illustration on a per-job basis. Rights purchased vary according to project.

TIPS Finds artists through sourcebooks, samples, representatives.

HUTCHINSON ASSOCIATES, INC.

822 Linden Ave., Suite 200, Oak Park IL 60302. (312)455-9191. **Fax:** (312)455-9190. **E-mail:** hutch@ hutchinson.com. **Website:** www.hutchinson.com. **Contact:** Jerry Hutchinson, president. Estab. 1988. Member of American Institute of Graphic Arts. Design firm. Number of employees: 3. Firm specializes in brand identity design, website design and development, annual reports, collateral, advertising, publication design, marketing brochures. Types of clients: industrial, financial, real estate, retail, publishing, nonprofit and medical. Recent client: Cardinal Growth.

Work from Hutchinson Associates has been published in the following design books: *Graphis Design* (Graphis Publications); *Revival of the Fittest: Digital Versions of Classic Typefaces* (North Light Books); *Simpson Paper Show Catalog* (Simpson Paper, San Francisco); *Working With Computer Type*, Vols. 1-3 (Rotovision); *Context One* (Sappi Papers); *Logo Lounge*, Vols. 1-3 (Rockport); *1,000 Invitations* (Rockport); *Publication Design Workbook* (Rockport); *Letterhead and Logo Design 9* (Rockport).

NEEDS Approached by 5-10 freelancers/year. Works with 3-4 freelance illustrators and 5-15 designers/year.

FIRST CONTACT & TERMS Send e-mail with link/postcard. Designers, please send letter, link and resume. Samples/links are filed/marked. Request portfolio review in original query. Artist should follow up with call. Will contact artist for portfolio review if interested. Pays by the project, $100-10,000. Rights purchased vary according to project. Finds artists through sourcebooks, submissions, websites and reps.

TIPS "Persistence pays off."

⊕ IDEA BANK MARKETING

701 W. Second St., Hastings NE 68901. (402)463-0588. **Fax:** (402)463-2187. **E-mail:** sherma@ideabankmarketing.com or via online contact form. **Website:** www.ideabankmarketing.com. **Contact:** Sherma Jones, creative director. Estab. 1982. Number of employees: 14. Approximate annual billing: $2.5 million. Ad agency. Specializes in print materials, direct mail. Product specialty is manufacturers. Client list available upon request. Professional affiliations: Advertising Federation of Lincoln, American Marketing Association.

NEEDS Approached by 2 illustrators/year. Works with 2 illustrators and 2 designers/year. Prefers local designers only. Uses freelancers mainly for illustration; also for airbrushing, catalog and humorous illustration, lettering. 30% of work is with print ads. 75% of design demands knowledge of Photoshop, Illustrator. 60% of illustration demands knowledge of Photoshop, Illustrator.

FIRST CONTACT & TERMS Designers/illustrators: Send query letter with brochure. Send follow-up postcard samples every 6 months. Accepts disk submissions compatible with original illustration files or Photoshop files. Samples are filed or returned by SASE. Responds only if interested. Will contact artist for portfolio review of b&w, color, final art, tearsheets if interested. Pays by the project. Rights purchased vary according to project and are negotiable. Finds artists through word of mouth.

IMAGE ASSOCIATES, INC.

5311 S. Miami Blvd., Suite G, Durham NC 27703. (919)876-6400. **Fax:** (919)876-6400. **E-mail:** info@imageassociates.com. **Website:** www.imageassociates.com. Estab. 1984. Marketing communications group offering advanced web-based solutions, multimedia and print. Visual communications firm specializing in computer graphics and AV, multi-image, interactive multimedia, Internet development, print and photographic applications.

NEEDS Prefers freelancers with experience in Web, CD and print. Works on assignment only. Uses freelancers mainly for web design and programming. Also for print ad design and illustration and animation. 90% of freelance work demands skills in Flash, HTML, DHTML, ASP, Photoshop and Macromind Director.

FIRST CONTACT & TERMS Send query letter with brochure, résumé and tearsheets. Samples are filed or are returned by SASE if requested by artist. Responds only if interested. To show portfolio, mail roughs, finished art samples, tearsheets, final reproduction/product and slides. Pays for assignments by the project. Considers complexity of project, client's budget and how work will be used when establishing payment. Rights purchased vary according to project.

⊕ IMAGINASIUM, INC.

110 S. Washington St., Green Bay WI 54301. (920)431-7872, ext. 101 or (800)820-4624. **E-mail:** info@imaginasium.com. **Website:** www.imaginasium.com. **Contact:** Denis Kreft. Estab. 1992. Approximate annual billing: $4 million. Strategic marketing communications firm. Specializes in brand development. Product specialties are business to business.

NEEDS Prefer local designers. Uses freelancers mainly for overflow. 100% of design and 75% of illustration demands skills in Photoshop, QuarkXPress and Illustrator.

FIRST CONTACT & TERMS Send query letter with work samples. Accepts Mac-compatible disk submissions. Samples are filed and are not returned. Will contact for portfolio review if interested. Pays for design by the hour; illustration by the project. Rights purchased vary according to project. Finds artists through submissions, word of mouth, Internet.

IMPACT COMMUNICATIONS GROUP

(714)963-6760. **Fax:** (714)963-0080. **E-mail:** web@impactgroup.com; via online contact form. **Website:** www.impactgroup.com. **Contact:** Brad Vinikow, creative director. Estab. 1983. Number of employees: 15. Marketing communications firm; full-service multimedia firm. Specializes in electronic media, business-to-business and print design. Current clients include Yamaha Corp., Prudential, Isuzu. Professional affiliations: IICS, NCCC and ITVA.

NEEDS Approached by 12 freelancers/year. Works with 12 freelance illustrators and 12 designers/year. Uses freelancers mainly for illustration, design and computer production; also for brochure and catalog design and illustration, multimedia and logos. 10% of work is with print ads. 90% of design and 50% of illustration demands knowledge of Photoshop, QuarkXPress, Illustrator and Macro Mind Director.

FIRST CONTACT & TERMS Designers: Send query letter with photocopies, photographs, résumé and tearsheets. Illustrators: Send postcard sample. Samples are filed and are not returned. Will contact artist for portfolio review if interested. Portfolio should include b&w and color final art, photographs, photostats, roughs, slides, tearsheets and thumbnails. Pays for design and illustration by the project, depending on budget. Rights purchased vary according to project. Finds artists through sourcebooks and self-promotion pieces received in mail.

TIPS "Be flexible."

ⓦ INNOVATIVE DESIGN & GRAPHICS

1327 Greenleaf St., Evanston IL 60202-1152. (847)475-7772. **E-mail:** sales@idgevanston.com. **Website:** idgevanston.com. Clients: corporate communication and marketing departments.

NEEDS Works with 1-2 freelance artists/year. Prefers local artists only. Uses artists for editorial and technical illustration and marketing, advertising and spot illustration. Illustrators should be knowledgeable in Adobe Illustrator and Photoshop.

FIRST CONTACT & TERMS Send query letter with résumé or brochure showing art style, tearsheets and photographs. Will contact artist for portfolio review if interested. Pays for illustration by the project, $200-1,000 average. Considers complexity of project, client's budget and turnaround time when establishing payment. Interested in buying second rights (reprint rights) to previously published work.

TIPS "Looking for people who can grasp complex ideas and turn them into high-quality illustrations. Ability to draw people well is a must. Do not call for an appointment to show your portfolio. Send nonreturnable tearsheets or self-promos; we will call you when we have an appropriate project for you."

ⓦ JUDE STUDIOS

8000 Research Forest, Suite 115-266, The Woodlands TX 77382. (281)364-9366. **E-mail:** frontdesk@judestudios.com. **Contact:** Judith Dollar, art director. Estab. 1994. Number of employees: 2. Design firm. Specializes in printed material, brochure, trade show, collateral, illustration, and logodesign. Product specialties are destination marketing, restaurant, homebuilder, financial, business to business, nonprofit, and event marketing materials.

NEEDS Uses freelancers mainly for illustration and lettering. Use of Adobe CS required.

FIRST CONTACT & TERMS Designers and illustrators can e-mail with link to webpage or blog (no attachments). Pays by the project; varies. Negotiates

rights purchased. Finds artists through directories or online.

TIPS Wants freelancers with good type usage who contribute to concept ideas. "We are open to designers and illustrators who are just starting out their careers."

ⓦ KETCHUM PLEON CHANGE

1285 Avenue of the Americas, New York NY 10019. (646)935-4300. **Website:** www.ketchum.com. **Contact:** Jon Abels. (Formerly Stromberg Consulting.) Specializes in direct marketing, internal and corporate communications. Clients: industrial and corporate. Produces multimedia presentations and print materials.

NEEDS Assigns 25-35 jobs/year. Prefers local designers only (Manhattan and its 5 burroughs) with experience in animation, computer graphics, multimedia and Macintosh. Uses freelancers for animation logos, posters, storyboards, training guides, Web Flash, application development, design catalogs, corporate brochures, presentations, annual reports, slide shows, layouts, mechanicals, illustrations, computer graphics and desktop publishing web development, application development.

FIRST CONTACT & TERMS "Send note on availability and previous work." Responds only if interested. Provide materials to be kept on file for future assignments. Originals are not returned. Pays hourly or by the project.

TIPS Finds designers through word of mouth and submissions.

KIZER INCORPORATED ADVERTISING & COMMUNICATIONS

13514 Vixen Ln., Suite B, Oklahoma City OK 73131. (405)708-4302. **E-mail:** mrkt@kizerincorporated.com. **Website:** www.kizerincorporated.com. Estab. 1998. Number of employees: 5. Creative shop specializing in campaign planning, creative development and production. 65% print, 20% web, 15% broadcast/other. 65% of work is print ads, brochures, annual reports, direct mail. InDesign is primary design software used. Professional affiliations: OKC Ad Club, AMA, AIGA.

NEEDS Approached by 30+ illustrators and designers/year. Works with varying number of illustrators and designers/year.

FIRST CONTACT & TERMS Direct mail or e-mail queries are both acceptable. For e-mail contacts, prefers link back to artist's portfolio to see samples. No large attachments, please. Responds if interested. Pays by the project. Rights purchased vary according to project. Finds artists through agents, sourcebooks, online services, magazines, word of mouth, artist's submissions.

ⓦ LEKASMILLER

1460 Maria Lane, Suite 260, Walnut Creek CA 94596. (925)934-3971. **Fax:** (925)934-3978. **E-mail:** tina@lekasmiller.com. **Website:** www.lekasmiller.com. Estab. 1979. Specializes in annual reports, corporate identity, advertising, direct mail and brochure design. Clients: corporate, higher education, and retail. Current clients include UC Berkeley, UCSF, Stanford and UCLA, Mills College, Sutter Health, Dignity Health, John Muir Health Foundation.

NEEDS Approached by 80 freelance artists/year. Works with 1-3 illustrators and 5-7 designers/year. Prefers local artists only with experience in design and production. Works on assignment only. Uses artists for brochure design and illustration, mechanicals, direct mail design, logos, ad design and illustration. 100% of freelance work demands knowledge of InDesign, Photoshop and Illustrator.

FIRST CONTACT & TERMS Designers/illustrators: E-mail PDF or résumé and portfolio. Responds only if interested. Considers skill and experience of artist when establishing payment. Negotiates rights purchased.

LISA LELEU STUDIOS, INC.

187 E. Court St., Doylestown PA 18901. (215)345-1233. **E-mail:** contact@lisaleleustudios.com. **Website:** www.lisaleleustudios.com. Estab. 1986. (Formerly Fullmoon Creations, Inc.) Number of employees: 10. Specializes in new product ideas, new product concept development, product name generations, brand development, product design, packaging design, packaging structure design, packaging descriptive copy writing. Clients: Fortune 500 corporations to middle companies. Current clients are top manufacturers involved in new product and packaging development including health, cosmetic, food, candy, product and service of any kind.

FIRST CONTACT & TERMS Freelance writers and illustrators are welcome to send postcards and/or e-mail to us for review.

LOHRE & ASSOCIATES, INC.

126A W. 14th St., 2nd Floor, Cincinnati OH 45202-7535. (513)961-1174. **Website:** www.lohre.com. **Contact:** Chuck Lohre, president. Number of employees: 6. Approximate annual billing: $1 million. Ad agency. Specializes in industrial firms. Professional affiliation: SMPS, U.S. Green Building Council, Cincinnati Regional Chapter.

NEEDS Approached by 24 freelancers/year. Works with 10 freelance illustrators and 10 designers/year. Works on assignment only. Uses freelance artists for trade magazines, direct mail, P-O-P displays, multimedia, brochures and catalogs. 100% of freelance work demands knowledge of InDesign, Photoshop and Illustrator.

FIRST CONTACT & TERMS Send postcard sample or e-mail. Accepts submissions on disk, any Mac application. Pays for design and illustration by the hour, $10 minimum.

TIPS Looks for artists who "have experience in chemical and mining industry, can read blueprints and have worked with metal fabrication." Also needs "Mac-literate artists who are willing to work at office, day or evenings."

ⓦ LORENC & YOO DESIGN, INC.

109 Vickery St., Roswell GA 30075-4926. (770)645-2828. **Fax:** (770)998-2452. **E-mail:** jan@lorencyoodesign.com. **Website:** www.lorencyoodesign.com; Blog: www.janondesign.com. **Contact:** Jan Lorenc, president. Celebrating over 35 years of practicing design for the world's finest brands in China, Korea, Japan, India, Europe, Middle East, Africa and the US. Specializes in architectural signage design; exhibit design for museums and trade shows. Clients: corporate, developers, product manufacturers, architects, real estate and institutions. Current clients include Delta Air Lines, Samsung, Sony, UPS, Georgia-Pacific, IBM, Simon Property Co., Mayo Clinic. Client list available upon request.

NEEDS Approached by 25 freelancers/year. Works with 2 illustrators and 5 designers/year. Local senior designers only. Uses freelancers for design, illustration, brochures, catalogs, books, P-O-P displays, mechanicals, retouching, airbrushing, posters, direct mail packages, model-making, charts/graphs, AV materials, lettering and logos. Needs editorial and technical illustration. Especially needs architectural signage and exhibit designers. 95% of freelance work demands knowledge of QuarkXPress, Illustrator and InDesign.

FIRST CONTACT & TERMS Send brochure, weblink, CD, résumé and samples to be kept on file. Prefers digital files as samples. Samples are filed or returned. Call or write for appointment to show portfolio of thumbnails, roughs, original/final art, final reproduction/product, color photostats and photographs. Pays for design by the hour, $40-100; by the project, $250-20,000; by the day, $80-400. Pays for illustration by the hour, $40-100; by the project, $100-2,000; by the day, $80-400. Considers complexity of project, client's budget, and skill and experience of artist when establishing payment.

TIPS "We utilize freelancers on specialized needs and project overload."

JODI LUBY & COMPANY, INC.

288 Twin Lakes Rd., Salisbury CT 06068. (860)824-7039. **E-mail:** jodiluby@gmail.com. **Website:** www.jodiluby.com; jodiluby.blogspot.com. **Contact:** Jodi Luby, president. Estab. 1983. Specializes in branding, direct marketing, packaging, and web design. Clients: major magazines, startup businesses and corporate clients.

NEEDS Uses freelancers for production and web production. 100% of freelance work demands computer skills.

FIRST CONTACT & TERMS Send e-mail samples only. Samples are not filed and are not returned. Will contact artist for portfolio review if interested.

⏣ JACK LUCEY/ART & DESIGN

84 Crestwood Dr., San Rafael CA 94901. (415)453-3172. **Contact:** Jack Lucey. Estab. 1960. Art agency. Specializes in annual reports, brand and corporate identity, publications, signage, technical illustration and illustrations/cover designs, courtroom art (trial drawing). Clients businesses, ad agencies and book publishers. Current clients include U.S. Air Force, California Museum of Art & Industry, ABC-TV, CBS-TV, NBC-TV, CNN, Associated Press. Client list available upon request. Professional affiliations Art Directors Club; College of Marin Alumni, Academy of Art Alumni, San Francisco.

NEEDS Approached by 20 freelancers/year. Works with 1-2 freelance illustrators/year. Uses mostly local freelancers. Uses freelancers mainly for type and airbrush. Also for lettering for newspaper work.

FIRST CONTACT & TERMS Query. Prefers photostats and published work as samples. Provide brochures, business card and resume to be kept on file. Portfolio review not required. Originals are not returned to artist at job's completion. Requests work on spec before assigning a job. Pays for design by the project.

TIPS "Show variety in your work. Many samples I see are too specialized in one subject, one technique, one style (such as air brush only, pen & ink only, etc.). Subjects are often all similar too."

TAYLOR MACK ADVERTISING

21 W. Mountain, Suite 227, Fayetteville AR 72701. (479)444-7770. **E-mail:** greg@taylormack.com. **Website:** www.taylormack.com. **Contact:** Greg Mack, managing director. Estab. 1990. Number of employees 16. Approximate annual billing $3 million. Ad agency. Specializes in collateral. Current clients include Cobb, Jose's, Rheem-Rudd and Bikes, Blues and BBQ. Client list available upon request.

NEEDS Approached by 12 illustrators and 20 designers/year. Works with 4 illustrators and 6 designers/year. Uses freelancers mainly for brochure, catalog and technical illustration, TV/film graphics and web page design. 30% of work is with print ads. 50% of design and illustration demands skills in Photoshop, Illustrator and InDesign.

FIRST CONTACT & TERMS Designers: E-mail website links or URLs. Samples are filed or are returned. Responds only if interested. Art director will contact artist for portfolio review of photographs if interested. Pays for design by the project or by the day; pays for illustration by the project, $10,000 maximum. Rights purchased vary according to project.

MAHAN GRAPHICS

4 Brickyard Way, Bowdoinham ME 04008. (207)666-1098. **E-mail:** ldelorme@mahangraphics.com. **Website:** www.mahangraphics.com. Estab. 1986. Number of employees: 5. Approximate annual billing $500,000. Design firm. Specializes in publication design—catalogs and direct mail. Product specialties are furniture, fine art and high tech. Clients: Bowdoin College, Bath Iron Works and Monhegan Museum. Professional affiliations G.A.G., AIGA and Art Director's Club-Portland ME.

NEEDS Approached by 5-10 illustrators and 10-20 designers/year. Works with 2 illustrators and 2 designers/year. Uses freelancers mainly for production.

Also for brochure, catalog and humorous illustration and lettering. 5% of work is with print ads. 100% of design demands skills in Photoshop, QuarkXPress and InDesign.

FIRST CONTACT & TERMS Designers: Send query letter with photocopies and résumé. Illustrators: Send query letter with photocopies. Accepts CD/DVD submissions. Samples are filed and are not returned. Responds only if interested. Art director will contact artist for portfolio review of final art roughs and thumbnails if interested. Pays for design by the hour, $15-40. Pays for illustration by the hour, $18-60. Rights purchased vary according to project. Finds artists through word of mouth and submissions.

MANGAN HOLCOMB PARTNERS

2300 Cottondale Lane, Suite 300, Little Rock AR 72202. (501)376-0321. **Fax:** (501)376-6127. **E-mail:** chip@manganholcomb.com; david@manganholcomb.com. **Website:** www.manganholcomb.com. **Contact:** Chip Culpepper, creative director. Number of employees: 12. Approximate annual billing: $3 million. Marketing, advertising and PR firm. Clients: recreation, financial, tourism, retail, agriculture. Current clients include Citizens Bank, Farmers Bank & Trust, The Wilcox Group.

NEEDS Approached by 50 freelancers/year. Works with 8 freelance illustrators and 20 designers/year. Uses freelancers for consumer magazines, stationery design, direct mail, brochures/flyers, trade magazines and newspapers. Needs computer-literate freelancers for production and presentation. 30% of freelance work demands skills in Mac-based page layout and illustration software.

FIRST CONTACT & TERMS Query with samples, flier and business card to be kept on file. Include SASE. Responds in 2 weeks. Call or write for appointment to show portfolio of final reproduction/product. Pays by the project, $250 minimum.

MARKEFXS

E-mail: mark@mfxs.com. **Website:** www.mfxs.com. **Contact:** Mark Tekushan, creative director. Estab. 1985. Full-service multimedia firm. Specializes in TV, video, advertising, design and production of promos, show openings and graphics. Current clients include ESPN and HBO.

○ Los Angeles office: (323)933-3673

NEEDS Prefers freelancers with experience in television or advertising production. Works on assignment only. Uses freelancers mainly for design production. Also for animation, TV/film graphics and logos. Needs computer-literate freelancers for design, production and presentation.

FIRST CONTACT & TERMS E-mail your website link or mail DVD/CD. Coordinating Producer will contact artist for portfolio review if interested. Pays for design by the hour, $25-50. Finds artists through word of mouth.

ⓦ MARKETAIDE SERVICES, INC.

P.O. Box 500, Salina KS 67402. (785)825-7161; (800)204-2433. **Fax:** (785)825-4697. **E-mail:** creative@marketaide.com. **Website:** www.marketaide.com. **Contact:** production manager. Estab. 1975. Full-service ad/marketing/direct mail firm. Clients: financial, industrial and educational.

NEEDS Prefers artists within one-state distance who possess professional expertise. Works on assignment only. Needs computer-literate freelancers for design, illustration and web design. 90% of freelance work demands knowledge of QuarkXPress, Illustrator and Photoshop.

FIRST CONTACT & TERMS Send query letter with résumé, business card and samples to be kept on file. Samples not filed are returned by SASE only if requested. Responds only if interested. Write for appointment to show portfolio. Pays for design by the hour, $15-75 average. "Because projects vary in size, we are forced to estimate according to each job's parameters." Pays for illustration by the project.

TIPS "Artists interested in working here should be highly polished in technical ability, have a good eye for design, and be able to meet all deadline commitments."

MARKETING BY DESIGN

2012 19th St., Suite 200, Sacramento CA 95818. (916)441-3050. **Fax:** (916)446-4641. **E-mail:** creative@mbdstudio.com. **Website:** www.mbdstudio.com. Estab. 1977. Specializes in corporate identity and brochure design, publications, direct mail, trade shows, signage, display and packaging. Clients: associations and corporations.

NEEDS Approached by 50 freelance artists/year. Works with 6-7 freelance illustrators and 1-3 freelance designers/year. Works on assignment only. Uses illustrators mainly for editorial; also for brochure and catalog design and illustration, mechanicals, retouching, lettering, ad design and charts/graphs.

FIRST CONTACT & TERMS Send query letter with brochure, résumé, tearsheets. Samples are filed and are not returned. Does not respond. Artist should follow up with call. Call for appointment to show portfolio of roughs, color tearsheets, transparencies and photographs. Rights purchased vary according to project. Finds designers through word of mouth; illustrators through sourcebooks.

SUDI MCCOLLUM DESIGN

(818)243-1345. **E-mail:** sudimccollum@earthlink. net. **Website:** www.sudimccollum.com. **Contact:** Sudi McCollum. Specializes in home fashion design, graphic design, web design and illustration. Clients: home furnishing and giftware manufacturers, advertising agencies, businesses and graphic design studios; majority of clients are medium- to large-size businesses in home fashion and graphic design industry.

NEEDS Uses freelance production people either on computer or with painting and product design skills. Potential to develop into full-time job.

FIRST CONTACT & TERMS "Send query letter with samples or e-mail with web link. Responds only if interested."

MEDIA ENTERPRISES

1440-4 S. State College Blvd., Suite J, Anaheim CA 92806. (714)778-5336. **Fax:** (714)778-6367. **E-mail:** john@media-enterprises.com. **Website:** www.media-enterprises.com. **Contact:** John Lemieux Rose. Estab. 1982. Number of employees: 10. Approximate annual billing: $22 million. Integrated marketing communications agency. Specializes in web, social network marketing, mobile applications, public relations, magazine publishing. Product specialty high-tech, medical, manufacturing, luxury goods, apparel, food. Client list available upon request. Professional affiliations Small Business Administration, Society of North American Goldsmiths, Software Council of Southern California, NCECA, CODA, IPCA.

NEEDS Approached by 30 freelance illustrators and 10 designers/year. Works with 8-10 freelance illustrators and 3 designers/year. Uses freelancers for animation, humorous illustration, lettering, logos, web design, video, trade show & display, packaging, POP. 20% of work is with print ads, 80% digital media. 100% of freelance work demands skills in 3D, video, Photoshop, InDesign, Illustrator.

FIRST CONTACT & TERMS E-mail digital samples or website; pays by project; negotiated. Buys all rights.

MEDIA LOGIC INC.

1 Park Place, Albany NY 12205. (518)456-3015. **Website:** www.mlinc.com. **Contact:** Carol Ainsburg, director of studio services. Estab. 1984. Number of employees: 75. Approximate annual billing: $50 million. Media Logic, a leader in marketing innovation, is ushering in a new era of conversation-centric marketing, putting social at the center of business to achieve better customer engagement, advocacy and revenue growth. Combining more than 25 years of experience with its breakthrough Zeitgeist & Coffee social management program, Media Logic is helping organizations harness the power of social media to drive marketing strategy and brand evolution. Prefers freelancers with experience on MAC platform. Uses freelancers for Multimedia/Rich Media full build (footage editing and element animation for video creation) using Adobe Flash (including Action Script 3.0), After Effects, Premiere, Apple Final Cut Pro, and Maxon Cinema 4D. Interactive design, and build using HTML, PHP, CSS, CMS (especially WordPress and Expression Engine). Also, high-end traditional print projects (DM, collateral, trade show panels, P-O-P) using Photoshop, InDesign, Illustrator, QuarkXPress. Candidates must be able to work on site. Compensation via hourly rate.

DONYA MELANSON ASSOCIATES

5 Bisson Lane, Merrimac MA 01860. (978)346-9240; (800)521-9172. **Fax:** (978)346-8345. **E-mail:** dmelanson@dmelanson.com. **Website:** www.dmelanson. com. **Contact:** Donya Melanson. Advertising agency. Number of employees: 1. Clients: government, education, associations, publishers, financial services and industries. Current clients include US Geological Survey, Mannesmann, Cambridge College, American Psychological Association, Ledakka Enterprises and US Department of Agriculture.

NEEDS Approached by 30 artists/year. Works with 2-3 illustrators/year. Most work is handled by staff, but may occasionally use freelance illustrators and designers. Uses artists for stationery design, direct mail, brochures/flyers, annual reports, charts/graphs and book illustration. Needs editorial and promotional illustration. Most freelance work demands skills in Adobe Illustrator, InDesign, Photoshop, or QuarkXPress.

FIRST CONTACT & TERMS Query with brochure, résumé, photocopies, tearsheets or CD. Provide mate-

ADVERTISING

rials (no originals) to be kept on file for future assignments. Originals returned to artist after use only when specified in advance. Call or write for appointment to show portfolio or mail nonoriginal, nonreturnable materials. Pays for design and illustration by the project, $100 minimum. Considers complexity of project, client's budget, skill and experience of artist and how work will be used when establishing payment. **TIPS** "Be sure your work reflects concept development."

THE M. GROUP

2512 E. Thomas Rd., Suite 12, Phoenix AZ 85016. (480)998-0600. **Fax:** (480)998-9833. **E-mail:** gary@themgroupinc.com. **Website:** www.themgroupinc.com. **Contact:** Gary Miller. Estab. 1987. Number of employees: 7. Approximate annual billing: $2.75 million. Strategic visual communications firm. Specializes in annual reports, corporate identity, direct mail, package design, advertising. Clients: corporations and small business. Current clients include American Cancer Society, BankOne, Dole Foods, Giant Industries, Motorola, Subway.

NEEDS Approached by 50 freelancers/year. Works with 5-10 freelance illustrators/year. Uses freelancers for ad, brochure, poster and P-O-P illustration. 95% of freelance work demands skills in Illustrator, Photoshop and QuarkXPress.

FIRST CONTACT & TERMS Send postcard sample or query letter with samples. Samples are filed or returned by SASE if requested by artist. Responds only if interested. Request portfolio review in original query. Artist should follow-up. Portfolio should include b&w and color final art, photographs and transparencies. Rights purchased vary according to project. Finds artists through publications (trade) and reps.

TIPS Impressed by "good work, persistence and professionalism."

MILICI VALENTI NG PACK

999 Bishop St., 24th Floor, Honolulu HI 96813. (808)536-0881. **E-mail:** ideas@mvnp.com. **Website:** www.mvnp.com. Estab. 1946. Approximate annual billing: $40 million. Ad agency. Clients: travel/tourism, food, finance, utilities, entertainment and public service. Current clients include First Hawaiian Bank, Aloha Airlines, Sheraton Hotels.

NEEDS Works with 2-3 freelance illustrators/month. Uses freelance artists mainly for illustration, retouching and lettering for newspapers, multimedia kits,

magazines, radio, TV and direct mail. Artists must be familiar with advertising demands; used to working long distance through the mail and over the Internet; and familiar with Hawaii.

FIRST CONTACT & TERMS Send brochure, flyer and tearsheets or PDFs to be kept on file for future assignments.

MONDERER DESIGN, INC.

2067 Massachusetts Ave., 3rd Floor, Cambridge MA 02140. (617)661-6125. **Fax:** (617)661-6126. **E-mail:** info@monderer.com. **Website:** www.monderer.com. stewart@monderer.com. **Contact:** Stewart Monderer, president. Estab. 1981. Specializes in corporate identity, branding, print collateral, website, event and interactive solutions. Clients: corporations (technology, education, consulting and life science). Current clients include Solidworks, Thermo Scientific, MIT Sloan, Northeastern University, Progress Software, Kronos, Greenlight Fund, Canaccord Genuity.

NEEDS Approached by 40 freelancers/year. Works with 10-12 illustrators and photographers/year. Works on assignment only.

FIRST CONTACT & TERMS Send query letter with brochure, tearsheets, photographs, photocopies or nonreturnable postcards, or links to website/HTML e-mails. Will look at links and PDF files. Samples are filed. Will contact artist for portfolio review if interested. Negotiates rights purchased. Finds artists through submissions, self-promotions and sourcebooks.

MRW COMMUNICATIONS

6 Barker Square Dr., Pembroke MA 02359. (781)924-5282. **Fax:** (781)926-0371. **E-mail:** jim@mrwinc.com. **Website:** www.mrwinc.com. **Contact:** Jim Watts, president. Estab. 2003. Ad agency. Specializes in branding, advertising, collateral, direct marketing, website development, online marketing. Product specialties are high tech, health care, business to business, financial services, and consumer. Client list available upon request.

NEEDS Approached by 40-50 freelance illustrators and 40-50 designers/year. Works with 5-10 freelance illustrators and 2-5 designers/year. Prefers freelancers with experience in a variety of techniques: brochure, medical and technical illustration, multimedia projects, retouching, storyboards, TV/film graphics and web page design. 50% of work is with print ads. 90% of design and 90% of illustration demands skills in Free-Hand, Photoshop, QuarkXPress, Illustrator.

FIRST CONTACT & TERMS Designers: Send query letter with photocopies, photographs, résumé. Illustrators: Send postcard sample and résumé, follow-up postcard every 6 months. Accepts disk submissions compatible with InDesign. Send EPS files. Samples are filed. Will contact for portfolio review of b&w, color final art if interested. Pays by the hour, by the project or by the day, depending on experience and ability. Rights purchased vary according to project. Finds artist through sourcebooks and word of mouth.

MYERS, MYERS & ADAMS ADVERTISING INC.

934 N. Victoria Park Road, Ft. Lauderdale FL 33304. (954)523-6262. **E-mail:** pete@mmanda.com. **Website:** www.mmanda.com. Estab. 1986. Number of employees 6. Approximate annual billing $2 million. Ad agency. Full-service, multimedia firm. Specializes in magazines and newspaper ads; radio and TV; brochures; and various collateral. Product specialties are consumer and business-to-business. Current clients include Harley-Davidson, Wendy's and Embassy Suites. Professional affiliation Advertising Federation.

NEEDS Approached by 10-15 freelancers/year. Works with 3-5 freelance illustrators and 3-5 designers/year. Uses freelancers mainly for overflow. Also for animation, brochure and catalog illustration, model-making, posters, retouching and TV/film graphics. 55% of work is with print ads. Needs computer-literate freelancers for illustration and production. 20% of freelance work demands knowledge of PageMaker, Photoshop, QuarkXPress and Illustrator.

FIRST CONTACT & TERMS Send postcard-size sample of work or send query letter with tearsheets. Samples are filed and are returned by SASE if requested by artist. Will contact artist for portfolio review if interested. Portfolio should include b&w and color final art, roughs, tearsheets and thumbnails. Pays for design and illustration by the project, $50-1,500. Buys all rights. Finds artists through *Creative Black Book*, *Workbook* and artists' submissions.

⚲ THE NAPOLEON GROUP

48 W. 25th St., 7th Floor, New York NY 10010. (212)692-9200. **Fax:** (212)692-0309. **E-mail:** jobs@ napoleongroup.com. **Website:** www.napoleongroup. com. Estab. 1985. Number of employees: 40. AV firm. Full-service, multimedia firm. Specializes in story-boards, comps, magazine ads, computer graphic art and animatics. Leading provider in the "TEST" market. Product specialty is consumer. Clients: "all major New York City ad agencies." Client list not available.

NEEDS Approached by 20 freelancers/year. Works with 15 freelance illustrators and 5 designers/year. Prefers local freelancers with experience in animation, computer graphics, film/video production and multimedia. Works on assignment only. Uses freelancers for storyboards, animation, direct mail, logos and retouching. Needs computer-literate freelancers for design, illustration, production and presentation. 80% of freelance work demands skills in Illustrator or Photoshop.

FIRST CONTACT & TERMS Send e-mail samples with attachments of current work, query letter with photocopies, tearsheets, DVD or CD. Samples are filed. Responds only if interested. Will contact artist for portfolio review if interested. Currently seeking cutting edge contemporary artists that can produce fast clean and realistic storyboard and animatic artwork. Computer coloring and drawing skills desired in applicants. Also seeking 3D animation artists, modelers and animators for consideration. Pays for design and illustration by the project. Rights purchased vary according to project. Finds artists through word of mouth and submissions.

THE OFFICE OF LOUIS NELSON

P.O. Box 995, New York NY 10025. (212)620-9191. **E-mail:** info@louisnelson.com. **Website:** www.louis nelson.com. **Contact:** Louis Nelson, president. Estab. 1980. Number of employees: 3-4. Approximate annual billing: $1.2 million. Specializes in environmental, interior and product design and brand and corporate identity, displays, packaging, publications, signage and wayfinding, exhibitions and marketing. Clients: nonprofit organizations, corporations, associations and governments. Current clients include Sutter Gold Mining, Wildflower Records, Port Authority of New York & New Jersey, MTA and NYC Transit, Massachusetts Port Authority. Professional affiliations: IDSA, AIGA, SEGD, APDF.

NEEDS Approached by 30-40 freelancers/year. Works with 30-40 designers/year. Works on assignment only. Uses freelancers mainly for specialty graphics and 3D design; also for design, photo-retouching, model-making and charts/graphs. 100% of design demands knowledge of PageMaker, QuarkXPress, Photoshop,

Velum, Autocad, Vectorworks, Alias, Solidworks or Illustrator. Needs editorial illustration. Needs design more than illustration or photography.

FIRST CONTACT & TERMS Send postcard sample or query letter with résumé. Accepts disk submissions compatible with Illustrator 10.0 or Photoshop 7.0. Send EPS/PDF files. Samples are returned only if requested. Responds in 2 weeks. Write for appointment to show portfolio of roughs, color final reproduction/product and photographs. Pays for design by the hour, $15-25; or by the project, negotiable.

TIPS "I want to see how the artist responded to the specific design problem and to see documentation of the process–the stages of development. The artist must be versatile and able to communicate a wide range of ideas. Mostly, I want to see the artist's integrity reflected in the work."

NICE, LTD.—NICOSIA CREATIVE EXPRESSO, LTD.

330 W. Fifth Ave., New York NY 10001. (212)515-6617. **E-mail:** andrew.j@niceltd.com. **Website:** www.niceltd.com. **Contact:** Andrew Jacobi, executive director of development. Estab. 1993. Number of employees: 100. Full-service multicultural creative agency. Specializes in brand strategy, holistic design, graphic design, corporate/brand identity, brochures, promotional material, packaging, fragrance bottles and 3D animations. Current clients include Albion, AmorePacific, Estée Lauder Companies, Procter & Gamble, Dunhill, Gillette, Montblanc, Old Spice and Pantene.

◔ Additional locations in Singapore, Tokyo, Phuket and Bangkok (see website for details).

NEEDS Approached by additional 80 freelancers/year. Works with10 illustrators and 12 designers/year. Works by assignment only. Uses photographers, illustrators, designers, 3D computer artists and computer artists familiar with Illustrator, Photoshop, After Effects, Premiere, Macromedia Director, Flash and Alias Wavefront.

FIRST CONTACT & TERMS Send query letter and résumé. Responds for portfolio review only if interested. Pays for design by the hour. Pays for illustration by the project. Rights purchased vary according to project.

TIPS Looks for "promising talent and the right attitude."

NOSTRADAMUS ADVERTISING

884 West End Ave., Suite #2, New York NY 10025. (212)581-1362. **E-mail:** nos@nostradamus.net. **Website:** www.nostradamus.net. **Contact:** B. Sher, creative director. Specializes in book design, Web design, fliers, advertising and direct mail. Clients book publishers, nonprofit organizations and politicians.

NEEDS Works with 3 artists/year. Needs computer-literate freelancers for design and production. Freelancers should know InDesign, Quark, Photoshop, Dreamweaver.

FIRST CONTACT & TERMS Send query letter with brochure, résumé, business card, samples and tearsheets. Do *not* send slides as samples; will accept "anything else that doesn't have to be returned." Samples not kept on file are not returned. Responds only if interested. Call for appointment to show portfolio. Pays for illustration by the project, $150 minimum. Considers skill and experience of artist when establishing payment.

NOTOVITZ COMMUNICATIONS

15 Cutter Mill Rd., Suite 212, Great Neck NY 11021. (516)467-4672. **E-mail:** joseph@notovitz.com. **Website:** www.notovitz.com. **Contact:** Joseph Notovitz, president. Number of employees: 4. Specializes in marketing communications (branding, annual reports, literature, publications, websites), corporate identity, exhibit signage, event design and writing. Clients: finance, real estate and industry. Professional affiliation: Specialty Graphic Imaging Association.

NEEDS Approached by 100 freelancers/year. Works with 10 freelance illustrators and 10 designers/year. Uses freelancers for brochure, poster, direct mail and booklet illustration; mechanicals; charts/graphs; and logo design. Needs computer-literate freelancers for design, illustration and production. 90% of freelance work demands expertise in InDesign, Illustrator and Photoshop. Needs pool of freelance Web developers with expertise in Flash, coding and design. Also collaborates on projects that writers and freelancers bring.

FIRST CONTACT & TERMS Send résumé and links to online examples of work. Responds "if there is fit and need." Pays for design and production work by the hour, $25-75. Pays for illustration by the project.

TIPS "Do a bit of research on the firm you are contacting. Send pieces that reflect the firm's style and needs. If we never produce book covers, book cover art does not interest us. Stress what you can do for the firm, not what the firm can do for you."

NOVUS VISUAL COMMUNICATIONS

59 Page Ave., Suite 300, Tower One, Yonkers NY 10704. (212)473-1377. **E-mail:** novuscom@aol.com. **Website:** www.novuscommunications.com. **Contact:** Robert Antonik, managing director. Estab. 1988. Number of employees: 2 + Freelance. Specializes in integrated marketing, interactive display design, multimedia, packaging, software developers, industrial, financial, retail, health care, entertainment and non-profits. Understanding all components of Adobe Creative Suite tools. "Don't give up on the fine art of what you can create."

NEEDS Considers oil, acrylic, watercolor, pastel, mixed media, collage, paper, sculpture, ceramics, craft, fiber, glass, photography, and all types of prints. Exhibits all styles. Genres include landscapes, abstracts, florals and figurative work. Prefers landscapes, abstract and figurative.

FIRST CONTACT & TERMS E-mail letter with a brief introduction. Do like to meet when possible to review a portfolio. Responds only if interested within 1 month. Files weblinks. Finds artists through credit lines, direct mail or e-mail, agents, visiting exhibitions, word of mouth, art publications and source-books, submissions.

TIPS "Update with current work via postcard directing them to a website or send an e-mail in the future. Direct mail works."

ⓦ OAKLEY DESIGN STUDIOS

Website: oakleydesign.com; oakleydesign.blogspot. com. **Contact:** Tim Oakley, creative director. Estab. 1992. Specializes in brand and corporate identity, display, package, feature film and television design, along with advertising. Clients: advertising agencies, record companies, motion picture studios, major television studios, surf apparel manufacturers, mid-size businesses. Current clients include NBC, Vineyard Horizons, Patrick Lamb Productions, Metro Computerworks, Tiki Nights Entertainment, Hui Nalu Brand Surf, Stona Winery, Mt. Hood Jazz Festival, Think AV, Audient Events and Portland Center for the Media Arts. Professional affiliations: GAG, AIGA, PAF, Type Directors Club, Society of Illustrators.

NEEDS Approached by 3-5 freelancers/year. Works with 3 freelance illustrators and 2 designers/year. Prefers local artists with experience in technical & free-hand illustration, airbrush. Uses illustrators mainly for advertising. Uses designers mainly for brand and corporate identity. Also uses freelancers for ad and P-O-P illustration, airbrushing, catalog illustration, lettering and retouching. 60% of design and 30% of illustration demands skills in CS2 Illustrator, CS2 Photoshop and CS2 InDesign.

FIRST CONTACT & TERMS Contact through artist rep or send query letter with brochure, photocopies, photographs, plus resume. Samples are filed or returned by SASE if requested by artist. Request portfolio review in original query. Will contact artist for portfolio review if interested. Portfolio should include b&w and color final art, photocopies, photostats, roughs and/or slides. Pays for design by the project, $200 minimum. Pays for illustration by the project. Rights purchased vary according to project. Finds artists through design workbooks.

TIPS "Just be yourself and bring coffee."

ODEN MARKETING & DESIGN

119 S. Main St., Suite 300, Memphis TN 38103. (901)578-8055; (800)371-6233. **Website:** www.oden. com. **Contact:** design director. Estab. 1971. Specializes in annual reports, brand and corporate identity, design and package design. Clients: corporations. Current clients include International Paper, Federal Express.

NEEDS Works with 5-8 freelance illustrators and photographers/year. Works on assignment only. Uses illustrators mainly for collateral. 50% of freelance work demands knowledge of QuarkXPress, InDesign, Illustrator, or Photoshop.

FIRST CONTACT & TERMS Send query letter with brochure, photographs, slides and transparencies. Samples are filed and are not returned. Responds only if interested. Portfolio review not required. Pays for illustration by the project. Rights purchased vary according to project.

TIPS Finds artists through sourcebooks.

OMNI PRODUCTIONS

P.O. Box 302, Carmel IN 46082-0302. (317)846-2345. **Fax:** (317)846-6664. **E-mail:** omni@omniproductions.com. **Website:** www.omniproductions.com. **Contact:** Winston Long, president. Estab. 1984. AV firm. Full-service, multimedia firm. Specializes in video, Intranet, CD and Internet. Current clients include "a variety of industrial clients, government and international agencies."

NEEDS Works on assignment only. Uses freelancers for brochure design and illustration, storyboards, slide illustration, animation, and TV/film graphics. Needs computer-literate freelancers for design, illustration and production. Most of freelance work demands computer skills.

FIRST CONTACT & TERMS Send résumé. Samples are filed and are not returned. Artist should followup with call or letter after initial query. Pays by the project. Finds artists through agents, word of mouth and submissions.

ORIGIN DESIGN

One Origin Center, 2600 Travis, Suite 200, Houston TX 77006. (877)520-9544. **E-mail:** hola@originaction. com. **Website:** www.originaction.com. Design and marketing firm.

○ Recent Origin projects have been recognized in *HOW Magazine*, the national Summit Awards, the Dallas Society of Visual Communicators Annual Show, and the regional Addys.

FIRST CONTACT & TERMS Send query letter with résumé and samples.

OUTSIDE THE BOX INTERACTIVE, LLC

150 Bay St., Suite 706, Jersey City NJ 07302. (201)610-0625. **E-mail:** theoffice@outboxin.com. **Website:** www.outboxin.com. Estab. 1995. Number of employees: 6. Interactive design and marketing firm. "For over a decade we have been providing strategic and integrated solutions for branding, advertising, and corporate communications. Our skills lie in creating active experiences versus passive messages. We focus on the strengths of each particular delivery platform, whether multimedia, web or print, to create unique solutions that meet our client's needs. Our strategies are as diverse as our clients, but our focus is the same: to maximize the full potential of integrated marketing, combining the best in new media and traditional assets. We offer a unique blend of creativity, technology, experience and commitment." Clients include Society of Illustrators, Dereckfor Shipyards, Educational Testing Service, Nature's Best.

NEEDS Approached by 5-10 illustrators and 5-10 designers/year. Works with 2-5 freelance illustrators and 4-6 designers/year. Freelancers must be digitally fluent. Uses freelancers for airbrushing, animation, brochure and humorous illustration, logos, model-making, multimedia projects, posters, retouching, storyboards, TV/film graphics, web page design. 90%

of design demands skills in Photoshop, QuarkXPress, Illustrator, Director HTML, Java Script and any 3D program. 60% of illustration demands skills in Photoshop, QuarkXPress, Illustrator, any animation and 3D program.

FIRST CONTACT & TERMS Send query letter with brochure, photocopies, photographs, résumé, SASE, slides, tearsheets, transparencies. Send follow-up postcard every 3 months. Accepts DVD/CD submissions. Samples are filed and are returned by SASE. Will contact if interested. Pays by the project. Rights purchased vary according to project.

⦿ OXFORD COMMUNICATIONS, INC.

11 Music Mountain Blvd., Lambertville NJ 08530. (609)397-4242. **Fax:** (609)397-5915. **E-mail:** solutions@oxfordcommunications.com. **Website:** www. oxfordcommunications.com. **Contact:** Chris Ledford. Estab. 1986. Ad agency. Full-service, integrated multimedia firm. Specializes in branding, strategic planning, integrated marketing. Product specialties are retail, real estate, health care, education, and destination marketing.

NEEDS Approached by 6 freelancers/month. Works with 3 designers every 6 months. Currently all design and production handled by staff. Prefers local freelancers with experience in Illustrator, InDesign and Photoshop. Uses freelancers mainly for production and interactive development. 50% of work is with print ads.

FIRST CONTACT & TERMS E-mail résumé and PDF samples. Samples are filed. Responds only if interested. Will contact artist for portfolio review if interested. Pays for design and illustration by the project, negotiable. Rights purchased vary according to project.

PAPAGALOS STRATEGIC COMMUNICATIONS

7330 N. 16th St., Suite B-102, Phoenix AZ 85020. (602)279-2933. **Website:** www.papagalos.com. **Contact:** Nicholas Papagalos, creative director. Specializes in advertising, brochures, annual corporate identity, displays, packaging, publications and signage. Clients major regional, consumer and business-to-business. Clients include Tutor Perini, McMillan Fiberglass Stocks, Schuff Steel, Walsh Group and Targas.

NEEDS Works with 6-20 freelance artists/year. Works on assignment only. Uses artists for illustration, retouching, design and production. Needs computer-literate freelancers, web programmers and Web designers for design, illustration and production. 100% of freelance work demands skills in Illustrator, InDesign or Photoshop.

FIRST CONTACT & TERMS Mail résumé and appropriate samples. Pays for design by the hour or by the project. Pays for illustration by the project. Considers complexity of project, client's budget, skill and experience of artist when establishing payment. Exclusive nonrecurring rights payment.

⬡ PHOENIX LEARNING GROUP, INC.

141 Millwell Dr., Suite A, St. Louis MO 63043. (314)569-0211; (800)221-1274. **Fax:** (314)569-2834. **E-mail:** info@phoenixlearninggroup.com. **Website:** phoenixlearninggroup.com. **Contact:** Erin Bryant, vice president of operations and management. Number of employees: 50. Produces and distributes educational films. Clients: libraries, museums, religious institutions, US government, schools, universities, film societies and businesses. Catalog available on website or by request.

NEEDS Works with 1-2 freelance illustrators and 2-3 designers/year. Prefers local freelancers only. Uses artists for motion picture catalog sheets, direct mail brochures, posters and study guides; also for multimedia projects. 85% of freelance work demands knowledge of PageMaker, QuarkXPress and Illustrator.

FIRST CONTACT & TERMS Send postcard sample and query letter with brochure (if applicable). Send recent samples of artwork and rates to director of promotions. "No telephone calls, please." Responds if need arises. Buys all rights. Keeps all original art "but will loan to artist for use as a sample." Pays for design and illustration by the hour or by the project. Rates negotiable.

⬡ PICCIRILLI DORSEY

502 Rock Spring Rd., Bel Air MD 21014. (410)879-6780. **Fax:** (410)879-6602. **E-mail:** hello@picdorsey. com. **Website:** www.picdorsey.com. **Contact:** Micah Piccirilli, creative director. Estab. 1974. Specializes in design and advertising; also annual reports, advertising campaigns, direct mail, brand and corporate identity, displays, packaging, publications and signage. Clients: recreational sport industries, fleet leasing companies, technical product manufacturers, commercial packaging corporations, direct mail advertising firms, realty companies, banks, publishers and software companies.

NEEDS Works with 4 freelance designers/year. Works on assignment only. Mainly uses freelancers for layout or production. Prefers local freelancers. 75% of design demands skills in Illustrator and QuarkXPress.

FIRST CONTACT & TERMS Send query letter with brochure, résumé and tearsheets; prefers originals as samples. Samples are returned by SASE. Responds on whether to expect possible future assignments. To show a portfolio, mail roughs and finished art samples or call for an appointment. Pays for design and illustration by the hour, $20-45. Considers complexity of project, client's budget, and skill and experience of artist when establishing payment. Buys one-time or reprint rights; rights purchased vary according to project.

TIPS "Portfolios should include work from previous assignments. The most common mistake freelancers make is not being professional with their presentations. Send a cover letter with photocopies of work."

⬡ POSNER ADVERTISING

71 Fifth Ave., 5th Floor, New York NY 10003. (212)727-4790. **Website:** www.posneradv.com. Estab. 1959. Number of employees: 35. Full-service multimedia firm. Specializes in digital, branding, ads, collaterals, packaging, outdoor. Product specialties are hospitality, health care, luxury real estate, consumer business to business, corporate.

NEEDS Approached by 25 freelance artists/month. Works with 1-3 illustrators and 5 designers/month. Prefers local artists only with experience in digital and print design. Uses freelancers mainly for web and print design. 40% of work is with print ads. Needs computer-fluent freelancers for web and print design. 90% of freelance work demands knowledge of Adobe Creative Cloud.

FIRST CONTACT & TERMS Send query letter with samples/website. Samples are filed. Responds only if interested. Pays for design by the hour ($15-35) or by the project ($300-2,000). Negotiates rights purchased.

TIPS Advises freelancers starting out in advertising field to offer to intern at agencies for minimum wage.

⬡ PRECISION ARTS ADVERTISING, INC.

57 Fitchburg Rd., Ashburnham MA 01430. (978)855-7648. **E-mail:** info@precisionarts.com. **Website:** www.precisionarts.com. **Contact:** Terri Adams, president. Estab. 1985. Number of employees: 2. Full-service Web/print ad agency. Specializes in Internet marketing strategy, website/print design, graphic design.

NEEDS Approached by 5 illustrators and 5 designers/year. Works with 1 freelance illustrator and 1 designer/year. Prefers local freelancers. website design is now 75% and print marketing is 25% of the business. Freelance Web skills required in Macintosh DreamWeaver and Photoshop; freelance print skills required in QuarkXPress, Photoshop, Illustrator and Pre-Press.

FIRST CONTACT & TERMS Send résumé with links to artwork and suggested hourly rate.

⚲ PRINCETON MARKETECH

2 Alice Rd., Princeton Junction NJ 08550. **E-mail:** bzyontz@princetonmarketech.com. **Website:** www.princetonmarketech.com. **Contact:** creative director. Estab. 1987. Ad agency. Specializes in direct mail, multimedia, websites. Product specialties are financial, computer, senior markets. Current clients include Citizens Bank, ING Direct, Diamond Tours. Client list available upon request.

NEEDS Approached by 12 freelance illustrators and 25 designers/year. Works with 2 freelance illustrators and 5 designers/year. Prefers local designers with Mac experience. Uses freelancers for airbrushing, animation, brochure design and illustration, multimedia projects, retouching, technical illustration, TV/film graphics. 10% of work is with print ads. 90% of design demands skills in Photoshop, QuarkXPress, Illustrator and Macromedia Director. 50% of illustration demands skills in Photoshop, Illustrator.

FIRST CONTACT & TERMS Send query letter with résumé, tearsheets, digital files or sample disk. Send follow-up postcard every 6 months. Accepts disk submissions compatible with QuarkXPress, Photoshop. Samples are filed. Responds only if interested. Pay negotiable. Rights purchased vary according to project.

PRO INK

200 NE First St., Suite 200, Gainesville FL 32605. (352)377-8973. **Fax:** (352)373-1175. **E-mail:** info@proink.com. **Website:** www.proink.com. **Contact:** Terry Bachmann, president. Estab. 1979. Number of employees: 2. Specializes in publications, marketing, health care, engineering, development and ads. Professional affiliations: Public Relations Society of America, Society of Professional Journalists, International Association of Business Communicators, Gainesville Advertising Federation, Florida Public Relations Association.

NEEDS Works with 3-5 freelancers/year. Works on assignment only. Uses freelancers for brochure/annu-al report illustration and lettering. 100% of freelance work demands knowledge of Illustrator, InDesign, or Photoshop. Needs editorial, medical and technical illustration.

FIRST CONTACT & TERMS Send résumé, samples, tearsheets, photostats, photocopies, slides and photography. Samples are filed or are returned if accompanied by SASE. Responds only if interested. Call or write for appointment to show portfolio of original/final art. Pays for design and illustration by the project, $50-500. Rights purchased vary according to project.

QUALLY & CO., INC.

(312)280-1898. **E-mail:** iva@quallycompany.com; michael@quallycompany.com. **Website:** www.quallycompany.com. **Contact:** Michael Iva, creative director. Estab. 1979. Specializes in integrated marketing/communication, new product launches, antidotes for propaganda. Clients: major corporations, high net worth individuals and think tanks.

NEEDS Works with 10-12 freelancers/year. "Freelancers must have talent and the right attitude." Works on assignment only. Uses freelancers for design, copywriting, illustration, retouching, and computer production.

FIRST CONTACT & TERMS Send query letter with résumé, business card and samples that we can keep on file. Call or write for appointment to show portfolio.

TIPS Looking for "people with ideas, talent, point of view, style, craftsmanship, depth and innovation." Sees "too many look-alikes, very little innovation."

QUARACORE

1 E. Wacker Dr., Suite 1900, Chicago IL 60601. (312)981-2500. **E-mail:** info@quaracore.com. **Website:** www.quaracore.com. Estab. 1982. Full-service product developer. Specializes in educational products. Clients: educational publishers.

NEEDS Approached by 400 freelancers/year. Works with 700-900 illustrators/year. Prefers freelancers with publishing experience. Uses freelancers for illustration, books, mechanicals, charts/graphs, lettering and production. Needs computer-literate freelancers for illustration. 50% of freelance illustration work demands skills in Illustrator, QuarkXPress, Photoshop or FreeHand. Needs editorial, technical, medical and scientific illustration.

FIRST CONTACT & TERMS Send query letter with brochure or résumé and samples to be circulated and kept on file. Prefers "anything that we can retain for our files–photocopies, color tearsheets, e-mail submissions, disks or dupe slides that do not have to be returned." Responds only if interested. Pays for illustration by the piece/project, $40-750 average. Considers complexity of project, client's budget, how work will be used and turnaround time when establishing payment.

TIPS Current job openings posted on website.

QUON DESIGN

543 River Rd., Fair Haven NJ 07704-3227. (732)212-9200. **E-mail:** studio@quondesign.com. **Website:** www.quondesign.com; www.quonart.com. **Contact:** Mike Quon, president/creative director. Specializes in corporate and brand identity, collateral, packaging, publications and web design. Clients: corporations (financial, healthcare, telecommunications), nonprofits (hospitals, museums), PR firms and ad agencies. Current clients include Pfizer, UNICEF, American Express, Hasbro, Verizon, AT&T. Professional affiliations: AIGA, Society of Illustrators, Graphic Artists Guild, Art Alliance, Guild of Creative Arts, MCAC.

FIRST CONTACT & TERMS E-mail résumé with website link or mail query letter with résumé and samples. Pays for illustration by the project, $100-500. Buys first rights.

GERALD & CULLEN RAPP

420 Lexington Ave., New York NY 10170. (212)889-3337. **Fax:** (212)889-3341. **E-mail:** info@rappart.com; nancy@rappart.com. **Website:** www.rappart.com. **Contact:** Nancy Moore. Estab. 1944. Clients: ad agencies, corporations and magazines. Client list not available. Professional affiliations: GAG, S.I.

NEEDS Approached by 500 freelance artists/year. Exclusive representations of freelance illustrators. Works on assignment only. Uses freelance illustrators for editorial advertising and corporate illustration.

FIRST CONTACT & TERMS E-mail query letter with samples or website link. Will contact artist for portfolio review if interested. Responds in 2 weeks. Pays for illustration by the project, $500-40,000. Negotiates fees and rights purchased with clients on per-project basis.

⊙ REALLY GOOD COPY CO.

(860)659-9487. **E-mail:** copyqueen@aol.com. **Website:** www.reallygoodcopy.com. **Contact:** Donna Donovan, president. Estab. 1982. Number of employees: 1. Ad agency; full-service multimedia firm. Special-izes in direct response, brochures, catalogs and collateral. Product specialties are medical/health care, business services, consumer products and services. Current clients include Eastern Connecticut Health Network, WSHU Public Radio, Wellspring, That's Amore Gelato Cafés, Buddy's Appliance and Furniture Retail, Avid Marketing, Glastonbury Chamber of Commerce. Professional affiliations: Connecticut Art Directors Club, New England Mail Order Association, Glastonbury Chamber of Commerce.

NEEDS Approached by 40-50 freelancers/year. Works with 1-2 freelance illustrators and 6-8 designers/year. Prefers local freelancers whenever possible. Works on assignment only. Uses freelancers for all projects. "There are no on-staff artists." 50% print, 50% Web. 100% of design and 50% of illustration demand knowledge of InDesign or QuarkXPress, Illustrator or Photoshop and HTML.

FIRST CONTACT & TERMS Designers: send query letter with résumé. Illustrators: send postcard samples. Accepts CD submissions, EPS or JPEG files only. Samples are filed or are returned by SASE, only if requested. Responds only if interested. Portfolio review not required, but portfolio should include roughs and original/final art. Pays for design by the hour, $50-125. Pays by the project or by the hour.

TIPS "Continue to depend upon word of mouth from other satisfied agencies and local talent. I'm fortunate to be in an area that's overflowing with good people. Send 2 or 3 good samples—not a bundle."

RH POWER AND ASSOCIATES, INC.

9621 Fourth St. NW, Albuquerque NM 87114-2128. (505)761-3150; (800)552-1993. **Fax:** (505)761-3153. **E-mail:** info@rhpower.com. **Website:** www.rhpower.com. Estab. 1989. Number of employees: 10. Ad agency. Full-service, multimedia firm. Specializes in TV, magazine, billboard, direct mail, marriage mail, newspaper, radio. Product specialties are recreational vehicles and automotive. Current clients include Albany RV, Ultra-Fab Products, Consolidated Solar Technologies, Bullyan RV, Holiday World. Client list available upon request.

NEEDS Approached by 10-50 freelancers/year. Works with 5-10 freelance illustrators and 5-10 designers/year. Prefers freelancers with experience in retail automotive layout and design. Uses freelancers mainly for work overload, special projects and illustrations. Also for annual reports, billboards, brochure and catalog design and illustration, logos, mechanicals, posters and TV/film graphics. 50% of work is with print ads.

FIRST CONTACT & TERMS Send query letter with photocopies or photographs and résumé. Accepts disk submissions in PC format compatible with Illustrator 10.0 or Adobe Acrobat (PDF). Send PC EPS files. Samples are filed and are not returned. Will contact artist for portfolio review if interested. Portfolio should include b&w and color final art, roughs and thumbnails. Pays for design and illustration by the hour, $25 minimum; by the project, $100 minimum. Buys all rights.

TIPS Impressed by work ethic and quality of finished product. "Deliver on time and within budget. Do it until it's right without charging for your own corrections."

RIPE CREATIVE

1543 W. Apollo Rd., Phoenix AZ 85041. (602)304-0703. **Fax:** (480)247-5339. **E-mail:** mark@ripecreative.com; info@ripecreative.com. **Website:** www.ripecreative.com. **Contact:** Mark Anthony Munoz, principal. Estab. 2005. Number of employees: 5. Approximate annual billing: $500,000. Design firm. Specializes in branding, advertising, strategic marketing, publication design, trade-show environments. Clients: American Bar Association, AonConsulting, Healthways, LifeLock, Superior Case Coding, PetSmart. Client list available upon request. Professional affiliations: American Advertising Federation, National Organization of Women Business Owners, Greater Phoenix Chamber of Commerce, Arizona Hispanic Chamber of Commerce.

NEEDS Approached by 100 illustrators and 10 designers/year. Works with 10 illustrators and 3 designers/year. Works on assignment only. Uses freelancers mainly for illustration, graphic design, website design. Also for animation, brochure design/illustration, direct mail, industrial/structural design, logos, posters, print ads, storyboards, catalog design and technical illustration. 15% of work is assigned with print ads. 100% of design work demands skills in InDesign, Illustrator and Photoshop. 100% of illustration work demands skills in Illustrator, Photoshop and traditional illustration media.

FIRST CONTACT & TERMS Designers: Send query letter with contact information, résumé, samples, and URL if applicable. Illustrators: Send tearsheets, URL. Samples are returned if requested and SASE is provided. Designers and illustrators should attach PDF files or URL. Samples are filed or returned by SASE. Responds in 2 weeks. Company will contact artist for portfolio review if interested. Portfolio should include color finished art, photographs and tearsheets. Pays for illustration. Set rate negotiated and agreed to between RIPE and talent. Pays for design by the hour, $25-100. Rights purchased vary according to project. Finds artists through submissions, word of mouth, *Workbook, The Black Book.*

TIPS "Calls are discouraged. When making first contact , the preferred method is via mail or electronically. If interested, RIPE will follow up with talent electronically or by telephone. When providing samples, please ensure talent/rep contact is listed on all samples."

○ RIVET

219 Dufferin St., Suite 200A, Liberty Village, Toronto Ontario M6K 3J1, Canada. (416)483-3624. **E-mail:** todd.henwood@rivetglobal.com. **Website:** www.rivetglobal.com. Number of employees: 235. Approximate annual billing: $30 million. Full service marketing agency. Specializes in branding, promotion, digital, advertising, social media, event, CRM, direct marketing. Also maintains electronic design division that designs, develops and manages client websites, develops client intranets, extranets and CDs, consults on web marketing strategies, competitive analysis, and domain name research. Product specialties are food and beverage. Current clients include McNeil, Microsoft, Levi's, Visa, Johnson & Johnson, Purina, Dreyer's, Exxon Mobil. Client list available on website.

○ Also has locations in St. Louis, New York, San Francisco and Toronto.

NEEDS Approached by 200 illustrators and 50 designers/year. Works with 35 illustrators/year. Uses freelancers mainly for P-O-P displays, brochures; also for brochure design and illustration, model-making, posters and web graphics.

FIRST CONTACT & TERMS Send query letter with brochure or photocopies and résumé. Send postcard sample of work with follow-up postcard samples every 3 months. Accepts disk submissions. Samples are filed. Pays by the project, $300-8,000. Negotiates rights purchased. Finds illustrators through *American Showcase, The Black Book, Directory of Illustration* and submissions.

❄ SAATCHI & SAATCHI ADVERTISING WORLDWIDE

375 Hudson St., New York NY 10014. (212)463-2000. **Fax:** (212)463-9856. **E-mail:** talentteam@saatchiny. com. **Website:** www.saatchiny.com. Full-service advertising agency. Clients: Delta Airlines, Eastman Kodak, General Mills and Procter & Gamble. This company has 153 offices in 83 countries. See website for specific details of each location.

NEEDS Approached by 50-100 freelancers/year. Works with 1-5 designers and 15-35 illustrators/year. Uses freelancers mainly for illustration and advertising graphics. Prefers freelancers with knowledge of electronic/digital delivery of images.

FIRST CONTACT & TERMS Send query letter and nonreturnable samples or postcard sample. Prefers illustrators' sample postcards or promotional pieces to show around a half a dozen illustrations, enough to help art buyer determine illustrator's style and visual vocabulary. Files interesting promo samples for possible future assignments. Pays for design and illustration by the project.

SAI COMMUNICATIONS

P.O. Box 743, Media PA 19063. (215)923-6466. **E-mail:** saicommun@aol.com. **Website:** www.saicommunications.com. Full-service multimedia firm.

NEEDS Approached by 5 freelance artists/month. Works with 3 freelance designers/month. Uses freelance artists mainly for computer-generated slides; also for brochure and print ad design, storyboards, slide illustration and logos. 1% of work is with print ads.

FIRST CONTACT & TERMS Send query letter with résumé. Samples are filed. Call to schedule an appointment to show a portfolio. Portfolio should include slides. Pays for design by the hour, $15-20. Pays for illustration by the project. Buys first rights.

⊕ JACK SCHECTERSON ASSOCIATES

27010 Grand Central Parkway, #32, Floral Park NY 11005. (718)225-3536. **Contact:** Jack Schecterson, principal. Estab. 1967. Ad agency. Specializes in 2D and 3D visual marketing; new product introduction; product; package; graphic and corporate design.

NEEDS Works direct and with artist reps. Prefers local freelancers. Works on assignment only. Uses freelancers for package, product, and corporate design; illustration, brochures, catalogs, logos. 100% of design

and 90% of graphic illustration demands skills in Illustrator, Photoshop and InDesign.

FIRST CONTACT & TERMS Send query letter with brochure, photocopies, tearsheets, résumé, photographs, slides, transparencies and SASE; "whatever best illustrates work." Samples not filed are returned by SASE only if requested by artist. Requests portfolio review in original query. Will contact artist for portfolio review if interested. Portfolio should include roughs, b&w and color—"whatever best illustrates creative abilities/work." Pays for design and illustration by the project; depends on budget. Buys all rights.

THOMAS SEBASTIAN COMPANIES

677 Evers Loop, Surfside Beach SC 29575. **E-mail:** sebastiancompanies@mac.com. **Website:** www.thomassebastiancompanies.com. **Contact:** Pete Secker, creative director; Thomas Sebastian, owner. Estab. 1996. Number of employees: 5. Integrated marketing communications agency and Internet service. Specializes in e-mail marketing and graphic design for print materials. Client list available upon request.

NEEDS Approached by 12 illustrators and 12 designers/year. Works with 2-3 illustrators and 1-2 designers/year. Uses freelancers mainly for design and computer illustration; also for humorous illustration, lettering, logos and web page design. 5% of work is with print ads. 90% of design and 70% of illustration demands knowledge of Adobe Creative Suite.

FIRST CONTACT & TERMS Send query via e-mail. Send follow-up postcard samples every 6 months. Accepts Mac-compatible submissions on CD or DVD. Samples are filed and are not returned. Responds only if interested. Will contact artist for portfolio review if interested. Pays by the project. Negotiates rights purchased. Finds freelancers through *The Black Book*, creative sourcebooks, Internet.

SELBERT-PERKINS DESIGN COLLABORATIVE

5 Water St., Arlington MA 02476. (781)574-6605 x138. **E-mail:** joberto@selbertperkins.com. **Website:** www.selbertperkins.com. Estab. 1980. Number of employees 25. Specializes in annual reports, brand identity design, displays, landscape architecture and urban design, direct mail, product and package design, exhibits, interactive media and CD-ROM design and print and environmental graphic design. Clients: airports, colleges, theme parks, corporations, hospitals, com-

puter companies, retailers, financial institutions, architects. Professional affiliations: AIGA, SEGD.

○ This company has several locations throughout the world. See website for a complete listing.

NEEDS Approached by "hundreds" of freelancers/year. Works with 10 freelance illustrators and 20 designers/year. Prefers artists with "experience in all types of design and computer experience." Uses freelance artists for brochures, mechanicals, logos, P-O-P, poster and direct mail. Also for multimedia projects. 100% of freelance work demands knowledge of Photoshop, Canvas, InDesign, Illustrator.

FIRST CONTACT & TERMS Send query letter with brochure, résumé, tearsheets, photographs, photocopies, slides and transparencies. Samples are filed. Responds only if interested. Portfolios may be dropped off every Monday-Friday. Artist should follow up with call or letter after initial query. Will contact artist for portfolio review if interested. Pays for design by the hour, or by the project. Pays for illustration by the project. Rights purchased vary according to project. Finds artists through word of mouth, magazines, submissions/self-promotions, sourcebooks and agents.

STEVEN SESSIONS, INC.

One Riverway, Suite 1700, Houston TX 77056. (713)850-8450. **E-mail:** info@sessionsgroup.com. **Website:** www.sessionsgroup.com. **Contact:** Steven Sessions, president/creative director. Estab. 1981. Number of employees: 8. Approximate annual billing: $2.5 million. Specializes in annual reports; brand and corporate identity; fashion, package and publication design. Clients corporations and ad agencies. Current clients are listed on website. Professional affiliations AIGA, Art Directors Club, American Ad Federation.

NEEDS Approached by 50 freelancers/year. Works with 10 illustrators and 2 designers/year. Uses freelancers for brochure, catalog and ad design and illustration; poster illustration; lettering; and logos. 100% of freelance work demands knowledge of Illustrator, InDesign, QuarkXPress, Photoshop. Needs editorial, technical and medical illustration.

FIRST CONTACT & TERMS Designers: Send query letter with brochure, tearsheets, CDs, PDF files and SASE. Illustrators: Send postcard sample or other nonreturnable samples. Samples are filed. Responds only if interested. To show portfolio, mail slides. Payment depends on project. Rights purchased vary according to project.

○ SIGNATURE DESIGN

949 West Marietta St. SW, Suite X-104, Atlanta GA 30318. (314)971-2869. **E-mail:** therese@thesignature design.com; info@thesignaturedesign.com. **Website:** www.thesignaturedesign.com. Estab. 1993. Signature Design seeks to convey the authentic story of ecological and manmade environments in a memorable and meaningful way. Specialists—Interpretive planning and design of exhibits and signage. Innovative—Design collaborative of diverse unique skills; designers, writers, illustrators interactive media producers/animators creating experiences that entertain, educate and engage visitors. Clients include Bureau of Land Management, Missouri Botanical Garden, US Post Office. Client list available upon request.

NEEDS Approached by 15 freelancers/year. Works with 1-2 illustrators and 4-6 designers/year. Prefers local freelancers. Works on assignment only. 90% of freelance work demands knowledge of InDesign, Flash animation, Illustrator or Photoshop. Helpful to have web and animation software skills.

FIRST CONTACT & TERMS Send query letter with résumé, tearsheets and photocopies. Samples are filed. Responds only if interested. Artist should follow up with letter after initial query. Portfolio should include "whatever best represents your work." Pays for design by the hour. Pays for illustration by the project.

○ SILVER FOX ADVERTISING

Silver Fox Studios, 117 Ann St., North Providence RI 02904. (401)725-2161. **Fax:** (401)726-8270. **Website:** www.silverfoxstudios.com. **Contact:** Lysa Marzocchi. Estab. 1979. Specializes in package and publication design, logo design, brand and corporate identity, display, technical illustration and annual reports. Clients: corporations, retail. Client list available upon request.

NEEDS Works only with artist reps. Prefers local artists. Uses illustrators mainly for cover designs. Also for multimedia projects. 50% of freelance work demands knowledge of Illustrator, Photoshop, PageMaker and QuarkXPress.

FIRST CONTACT & TERMS Send query letter with résumé and photocopies. Accepts disk submissions compatible with Photoshop, Illustrator. Samples are filed. Does not reply. Artist should follow up with call or letter after initial query. Portfolio should include final art, photographs, roughs and slides.

ⓦ SMITH & DRESS, LTD.

432 W. Main St., Huntington NY 11743. (631)427-9333. **Fax:** (631)427-9334. **E-mail:** dress2@att.net. **Website:** www.smithanddress.com. Full-service ad firm. Specializes in branding, publications, websites, trade shows, and signage.

NEEDS Works with 2-3 freelance artists/year. Prefers local artists only. Works on assignment only. Uses artists for illustration, retouching, and lettering.

FIRST CONTACT & TERMS Send query letter with brochure showing art style or tearsheets to be kept on file (except for works larger than 8½×11). Pays for illustration by the project on a work for hire basis. Considers client's budget and turnaround time when establishing payment.

J. GREG SMITH

14707 California St., Suite 6, Omaha NE 68154. (402)444-1600. **Fax:** (402)444-1610. **Website:** jgregsmith.com. **Contact:** Greg Smith, senior art director. Estab. 1974. Number of employees: 8. Approximate annual billing: $1.5 million. Ad agency. Clients: financial, banking, associations, agricultural, travel and tourism, insurance. Professional affiliation: AAAA.

NEEDS Approached by 1-10 freelancers/year. Works with 4-5 freelancers illustrators and 1-2 designers/year. Works on assignment only. Uses freelancers mainly for mailers, brochures and projects; also for consumer and trade magazines, catalogs and AV presentations. Needs illustrations of farming, nature, travel.

FIRST CONTACT & TERMS Send query letter with samples showing art style or photocopies. Responds only if interested. To show portfolio, mail final reproduction/product, color and b&w. Pays for design and illustration by the project: $500-5,000. Buys first, reprint or all rights.

SMITH DESIGN

P.O. Box 8278, 205 Thomas St., Glen Ridge NJ 07028. (973)429-2177. **Fax:** (973)429-7119. **E-mail:** info@smithdesign.com. **Website:** www.smithdesign.com. West Coast office: Carmel CA, 93922; (831)620-1198; Florida office: Ft. Lauderdale FL; (974)429-2177 ext. 2001. **Contact:** Laraine Blauvelt. Brand design firm. Specializes in strategy-based visual solutions for leading consumer brands. Clients: grocery, mass market consumer brands, electronics, construction, automotive, toy manufacturers. Current clients include

Popsicle, Hain, Pfizer, Sika. Client list available upon request.

NEEDS Approached by more than 100 freelancers/year. Works with 10-20 freelance illustrators and 3-4 designers/year. Requires experience, talent, quality work and reliability. Uses freelancers for package design, brochure design, print ads, illustration, POP display design, web programming. 90% of freelance work demands knowledge of Illustrator, Photoshop, 3D rendering programs. Design style must be current to trends. "Our work ranges from classic brands to cutting edge."

FIRST CONTACT & TERMS Send query letter with brochure/samples showing work, style and experience. Include contact information. Responds in 1 week. Call for appointment to show portfolio. Pays for design by the hour, $35-125; or by the project, $175-5,000. Pays for illustration by the project, $175-5,000. Considers complexity of project and client's budget when establishing payment. Buys all rights. (For illustration work, rights may be limited to a particular use TBD). Also buys rights for use of existing noncommissioned art. Finds artists through word of mouth, self-promotions/sourcebooks and agents.

TIPS "Know who you're presenting to (visit our website to see our needs). Show work which is relevant to our business at the level and quality we require. We use more freelance designers and illustrators for diversity of style and talent."

SOFTMIRAGE

201 E. Sandpointe Ave., Suite 125, South Coast Metro CA 92707. (714)546-7030. **Fax:** (714)546-7031. **E-mail:** contact@softmirage.com. **Website:** www.softmirage.com. **Contact:** Steve Pollack, design director. Estab. 1995. Number of employees: 28. Approximate annual billing: $3 million. Visual communications agency. Specializes in architecture, luxury, real estate. Needs people with strong spatial design skills, modeling and ability to work with computer graphics. Current clients include Four Seasons Hotels, Ford, Richard Meier & Partners and various real estate companies.

NEEDS Approached by 15 computer freelance illustrators and 5 designers/year. Works with 6 freelance 3D modelers, and 10 graphic designers/year. Prefers West coast designers with experience in architecture, engineering, technology. Uses freelancers mainly for concept, work in process computer modeling. Also for animation, brochure design, mechanicals, mul-

ADVERTISING

timedia projects, retouching, technical illustration, TV/film graphics. 50% of work is renderings. 100% of design and 30% of illustration demand skills in Photoshop, 3-D Studio Max, Flash and Director. Need Macromedia Flash developers.

FIRST CONTACT & TERMS Designers: Send e-mail query letter with samples. 3D modelers: Send e-mail query letter with photocopies or link to website. Accepts digital and video submissions. Samples are filed or returned by SASE. Will contact for portfolio review if interested. Pays for design by the hour, $15-85. Pays for modeling by the project, $100-2,500. Rights purchased vary according to project. Finds artists through Internet, AIGA and referrals.

TIPS "Be innovative, push the creativity, understand the business rationale and accept technology. Check our website, as we do not use traditional illustrators, all our work is now digital. Send information electronically, making sure work is progressive and emphasizing types of projects you can assist with."

SPECTRUM BOSTON CONSULTING, INC.

P.O. Box 689, Westwood MA 02090-0689. (508)660-1300. **Fax:** (508)660-1305. **E-mail:** gboesel@spectrumboston.com. **Website:** www.spectrumboston.com. **Contact:** George Boesel, president. Estab. 1985. Specializes in brand and corporate identity, display and package design and signage. Clients: consumer products manufacturers.

NEEDS Approached by 30 freelance artists/year. Works with 1 illustrator and 1 designers/year. All artists employed on work-for-hire basis. Works on assignment only. Uses illustrators mainly for package and brochure work.

FIRST CONTACT & TERMS Illustrators: Send query e-mail with images. Samples are filed. Responds only if interested.

⦾ SPIRIT CREATIVE SERVICES, INC.

3157 Rolling Rd., Edgewater MD 21037. (410)956-1117. **Fax:** (410)956-1118. **E-mail:** info@spiritcreativeservices.com. **Website:** www.spiritcreativeservices.com. Number of employees: 2. Approximate annual billing: $15,000. Specializes in publications, brochures, catalogs, signage, books, annual reports, brand and corporate identity, display, direct mail, packaging, website design, technical and general illustration, photography, copywriting, and marketing. Clients/associations: corporations, government.

NEEDS Approached by 10 freelancers/year. Works with local Mac-based designers only. Uses freelancers for ad, brochure, catalog, poster and P-O-P design, technical illustration, books, direct mail, magazine, charts/graphs, logos, multimedia and design projects. 100% of design and 10% of illustration demands knowledge of Illustrator, Photoshop, Type Manager, InDesign and IWeb.

FIRST CONTACT & TERMS Call before sending submissions. Does not accept e-mail submissions without prior contact via phone. Portfolio samples and résumé. Responds in 1-3 weeks if interested. Portfolio should include b&w and color samples of artwork. Pays by the design project, $50-6,000.

TIPS "Being responsive to all communications and due dates is vital with attention to details, with emphasis on creativity and intuition."

SPLANE DESIGN ASSOCIATES

30634 Persimmon Lane, Valley Center CA 92082. (760)749-6018. **Fax:** (760)749-6388. **E-mail:** splanedesign@gmail.com. **Website:** www.splanedesign.com. **Contact:** Robson Splane, president. Specializes in product design. Clients: small, medium and large companies. Current clients include Lockheed Aircraft, Western Airlines, Liz Claiborne, Max Factor, Sunkist, Universal studios. Client list available upon request.

NEEDS Approached by 25-30 freelancers/year. Works with 1-2 freelance illustrators and 6-12 designers/year. Works on assignment only. Uses illustrators mainly for logos, mailings to clients, renderings. Uses designers mainly for sourcing, drawings, prototyping, modeling; also for brochure design and illustration, ad design, mechanicals, retouching, airbrushing, model making, lettering and logos. 75% of freelance work demands skills in FreeHand, Ashlar Vellum, Solidworks and Excel.

FIRST CONTACT & TERMS Send query letter with résumé and photocopies. Samples are filed or are returned. Responds only if interested. Will contact artist for portfolio review if interested. Portfolio should include color roughs, final art, photostats, slides and photographs. Pays for design and illustration by the hour, $7-25. Rights purchased vary according to project. Finds artists through submissions and contacts.

STEVENS STRATEGIC COMMUNICATIONS, INC.

Gemini Towers, Suite 500, 1991 Crocker Rd., Westlake OH 44145. (440)617-0100; (877)900-3366. **Fax:** (440)614-0529. **E-mail:** estevens@stevensstrategic. com. **Website:** www.stevensstrategic.com. Estab. 1956. Ad agency. Specializes in public relations, advertising, corporate and crisis communications, integrated marketing, magazine ads and collateral. Product specialties are business-to-business, food, building products, technical products, industrial food service, health care, safety.

NEEDS Approached by 30-40 freelance artists/ month. Prefers artists with experience in food, healthcare and technical equipment. Works on assignment only. Uses freelance artists mainly for specialized projects; also for brochure, catalog and print ad illustration and retouching. Freelancers should be familiar with InDesign, Adobe Creative Suite Master Collection, QuarkXPress, Illustrator and Photoshop.

FIRST CONTACT & TERMS Send query letter with résumé and photocopies. Samples are filed and are not returned. Responds only if interested. "Artist should send only samples or copies that do not need to be returned." Will contact artist for portfolio review if interested. Portfolio should include final art and tearsheets. Pay for design depends on style. Pay for illustration depends on technique. Buys all rights. Finds artists through agents, sourcebooks, word of mouth and submissions.

STRONGTYPE

(973)919-4265. **E-mail:** richard@strongtype.com. **Website:** www.strongtype.com. **Contact:** Richard Puder. Estab. 1985. Approximate annual billing: $300,000. Specializes in marketing communications, direct mail and publication design, technical illustration. Client history includes Hewlett-Packard, Micron Electronics, R.R. Bowker, Scholastic, Simon & Schuster and Sony. Professional affiliation: Type Directors Club.

NEEDS Approached by 100 freelancers/year. Uses designers mainly for corporate, publishing clients; also for ad and brochure design and illustration, book, direct mail, magazine and poster design, charts/graphs, lettering, logos and retouching. 100% of freelance work demands skills in Illustrator, Photoshop, FreeHand, Acrobat, QuarkXPress, Director, Flash, Fireworks and Dreamweaver.

FIRST CONTACT & TERMS E-mail with links and follow up with call, or send postcard sample, résumé and tearsheets. Samples are filed. Will contact artist for portfolio review if interested. Pays for design and production by the hour, depending on skills, $10-100. Pays for illustration by the job. Buys first rights or rights purchased vary according to project. Finds artists through sourcebooks (e.g., *American Showcase* and *Workbook*) and by client referral.

TIPS Impressed by "listening, problem-solving, speed, technical competency and creativity."

STUDIO WILKS

2148-A Federal Ave., Los Angeles CA 90025. (310)478-4442. **Fax:** (310)477-7888. **E-mail:** info@studiowilks. com. **Website:** www.studiowilks.com. Estab. 1990.

NEEDS Works with 6-10 freelance illustrators and 10-20 designers/year. Uses illustrators mainly for packaging illustration. Also for brochures, print ads, collateral, direct mail and promotions.

FIRST CONTACT & TERMS Designers: Send query letter with brochure, résumé, photocopies and tearsheets. Illustrators: Send postcard sample or query letter with tearsheets. Samples are returned by SASE if requested by artist. Will contact artist for portfolio review if interested. Pays for design by the project. Buys all rights. Considers buying second rights (reprint rights) to previously published work. Finds artists through *The Workbook* and word of mouth.

TIPS Specializes in print, collateral, packaging, editorial and environmental work. Clients ad agencies, architects, corporations and small business owners. Current clients include Walt Disney Co., Target, Nokia, City of Cerritos, Major League Soccer and Yoga Works.

SWANSON RUSSELL ASSOCIATES

1222 P St., Lincoln NE 68508. (402)437-6427. **Fax:** (402)437-6401. **E-mail:** daveh@swansonrussell. com; brianb@swansonrussell.com. **Website:** www. swansonrussell.com. **Contact:** Tracy Stanko, executive vice president/managing director; Dave Hansen, partner/CEO. Estab. 1962. Number of employees: 150. Approximate annual billing: $100 million. Integrated marketing communications agency. Specializes in collateral, catalogs, print and digital advertising, interactive/web development and direct mail. Product specialties are health care, agriculture, green industry, outdoor recreation and construction. Professional affiliations: PRSA, AIGA, Ad Club.

ADVERTISING

○ Second location: 14301 FNB Pkwy., Suite 312, Omaha NE 68154. (402)393-4940. Fax: (402)393-6926.

NEEDS Approached by 12 illustrators and 3-4 designers/year. Works with 5 illustrators and 2 designers/year. Prefers freelancers with experience in agriculture, pharmaceuticals, human and animal health. Uses freelancers mainly for collateral, ads, direct mail, storyboards; also for brochure design and illustration, humorous and technical illustration, lettering, logos, mechanicals, posters, storyboards. 10% of work is with print ads. 90% of design demands knowledge of Photoshop 7.0, FreeHand 5.0. 30% of illustration demands knowledge of Photoshop, Illustrator, Free-Hand.

FIRST CONTACT & TERMS Designers: Send query letter with photocopies, photographs, photostats, SASE, slides, tearsheets, transparencies. Illustrators: Send query letter with SASE. Send follow-up postcard samples every 3 months. Accepts Mac-compatible disk submissions. Send self-expanding archives and player for multimedia, or JPEG, EPS and TIFFs. Software FreeHand or Adobe. Samples are filed or returned by SASE. Responds only if interested within 2 weeks. Art director will contact artist for portfolio review of final art, photographs, photostats, transparencies if interested. Pays for design by the hour; pays for illustration by the project. Rights purchased vary according to project. Finds artists through agents, submissions, word of mouth, *Laughing Stock*, *American Showcase*.

◐ TASTEFUL IDEAS, INC.

7638 Bell Dr., Shawnee KS 66217. (913)722-3769. **Fax:** (913)722-3967. **E-mail:** john@tastefulideas.com. **Website:** www.tastefulideas.com. **Contact:** John Thomsen, president. Estab. 1986. Number of employees: 4. Approximate annual billing: $500,000. Design firm. Specializes in consumer packaging. Product specialties are largely, but not limited to, food and food service.

NEEDS Approached by 15 illustrators and 15 designers/year. Works with 3 illustrators and 3 designers/year. Prefers local freelancers. Uses freelancers mainly for specialized graphics; also for airbrushing, animation, humorous and technical illustration. 10% of work is with print ads. 75% of design and illustration demand skills in Photoshop and Illustrator.

FIRST CONTACT & TERMS Designers: Send query letter with photocopies. Illustrators: Send nonre-turnable promotional sample. Accepts submissions compatible with Illustrator, Photoshop (Mac based). Samples are filed. Art director will contact artist for portfolio review of final art if interested. Pays by the project. Finds artists through submissions.

TGADESIGN

4649 Ponce De Leon Blvd., Suite 401, Coral Gables FL 33146. (305)669-2550. **Fax:** (305)669-2539. **E-mail:** info@tgadesign.com. **Website:** www.tgadesign.com. **Contact:** Tom Graboski, president. Estab. 1980. Also known as Tom Graboski Associates, Inc. Specializes in exterior/interior signage, environmental graphics, corporate identity, urban design and print graphics. Clients: corporations, cities, museums, a few ad agencies. Current clients include Universal Studios, Florida; Royal Caribbean Cruise Line; The Equity Group; Disney Development; Celebrity Cruises; Baptist Health So. Florida; City of Miami; City of Coral Gables.

NEEDS Approached by 20-30 freelance artists/year. Works with approximately 4-8 designers/draftspersons/year. Prefers artists with a background in signage and knowledge of architecture and industrial design. Freelance artists used in conjunction with signage projects, occasionally miscellaneous print graphics. 100% of design and 10% of illustration demand knowledge of Illustrator, Photoshop and QuarkXPress.

FIRST CONTACT & TERMS Send query letter with brochure and résumé. "We will contact designer/artist to arrange appointment for portfolio review. Portfolio should be representative of artist's work and skills; presentation should be in a standard portfolio format." Pays by the project. Payment varies by experience and project. Rights purchased vary by project.

TIPS "Look at what type of work the firm does. Tailor presentation to that type of work. For this firm, knowledge of environmental graphics and detailing is a plus."

J. WALTER THOMPSON CO.

3630 Peachtree Rd. NE, Suite 1200, Atlanta GA 30326. (404)365-7300. **Website:** www.jwt.com. Ad agency. Current clients include Domino's, Ford, HSBC, Kraft, Shell, Unilever.

○ JWT has offices all over the world. See website for details.

NEEDS Works on assignment only. Uses freelancers for billboards, consumer and trade magazines and newspapers. Needs computer-literate freelancers for design, production and presentation. 60% of freelance work demands skills in Illustrator, Photoshop, InDesign, Flash, and Dreamweaver.

FIRST CONTACT & TERMS *Deals with artist reps only.* Send slides, original work, stats. Samples returned by SASE. Responds only if interested. Originals not returned. Call for appointment to show portfolio.

TIPS Wants to see samples of work done for different clients. Likes to see work done in different mediums; variety and versatility. Freelancers interested in working here should "be *professional* and do top-grade work."

TOKYO DESIGN CENTER

1508 Fillmore St., Suite 300, San Francisco CA 94115-3597. (415)543-4886. **Fax:** (415)543-4956. **E-mail:** info@tokyodesign.com. **Website:** www.tokyodesign.com. Specializes in annual reports, brand identity, corporate identity, packaging and publications. Clients: consumer products, travel agencies and retailers.

NEEDS Uses artists for design and editorial illustration.

FIRST CONTACT & TERMS Send business card, slides, tearsheets and printed material to be kept on file. Samples not kept on file are returned by SASE, if requested. Will contact artist for portfolio review if interested. Pays for design and illustration by the project, $100-1,500 average. Sometimes requests work on spec before assigning job. Considers client's budget, skill and experience of artist, turnaround time and rights purchased when establishing payment. Interested in buying second rights (reprint rights) to previously published work. Finds artists through self-promotions and sourcebooks.

THE TOMBRAS GROUP

630 Concord St., Knoxville TN 37919. (865)524-5376. **Website:** www.tombras.com. Estab. 1946. Number of employees: 68. Approximate annual billing: $75 million. Ad agency. Full-service multimedia firm. Specializes in full media advertising, collateral, interactive. Clients: National Highway Traffic, Safety Administration, Fred's Stores, Bristol Motor Speedway, Lowe's Motor Speedway, Atlanta Motor Speedway, and Farm Bureau Insurance. Client list available upon request. Professional affiliations AAAA, Worldwide Partners, AMA.

NEEDS Approached by 20-25 freelancers/year. Works with 20-30 freelance illustrators and 10-15 designers/year. Uses freelancers mainly for illustration and photography. Also for brochure design and illustration, model-making and retouching. 60% of work is with print ads. Needs computer-literate freelancers for design and presentation. 25% of freelance work demands skills in InDesign, Photoshop and QuarkXPress.

FIRST CONTACT & TERMS Send query letter with photocopies and résumé. Samples are filed. Will contact artist for portfolio review if interested. Portfolio should include b&w and color samples. Pays for design by the hour, $25-75; by the project, $250-2,500. Pays for illustration by the project, $100-10,000. Rights purchased vary according to project.

TIPS "Stay in touch with quality promotion. 'Service me to death' when you get a job."

A. TOMLINSON/SIMS ADVERTISING

250 S. Poplar St., P.O. Box 2530, Florence AL 35630. (256)766-4222; (800)779-4222. **Fax:** (256)766-4106. **Website:** www.atsa-usa.com. **Contact:** Allen Tomlinson, president/managing partner. Estab. 1990. Number of employees: 9. Approximate annual billing: $5 million. Ad agency. Specializes in magazine, collateral, catalog, business-to-business. Product specialties are home building products. Client list available upon request.

NEEDS Approached by 20 illustrators and 20 designers/year. Works with 5 illustrators and 5 designers/year. Uses freelancers for airbrushing, billboards, brochure and catalog design and illustration, logos and retouching. 35% of work is with print ads. 85% of design and illustration demand skills in PageMaker, Photoshop, Illustrator and QuarkXPress.

FIRST CONTACT & TERMS Designers: Send query letter with brochure and photocopies. Illustrators: Send samples of work, photocopies and résumé. Samples are filed and are not returned. Does not reply; artist should call. Artist should also call to arrange for portfolio review of color photographs, thumbnails and transparencies. Pays by the project. Rights purchased vary according to project.

⊙ T-P DESIGN, INC.

7007 Eagle Watch Court, Stone Mountain GA 30087. (770)413-8276. **Fax:** (770)413-9856. **E-mail:** tpdesign@att.net. **Website:** www.tpdesigninc.com. **Contact:** creative director. Estab. 1991. Number of employees: 3. Approximate annual billing: $500,000.

ADVERTISING

Specializes in brand identity, display, package and publication design. Clients corporations. Current clients include Georgia Pacific, Cartoon Network, General Mills, KFC.

NEEDS Approached by 4 freelancers/year. Works with 2 freelance illustrators and 2 designers/year. Prefers local artists with Mac systems, traditional background. Uses illustrators and designers mainly for comps and illustration on Mac. Also uses freelancers for ad, brochure, poster and P-O-P design and illustration; book design, charts/graphs, lettering, logos, mechanicals (important) and page layout. Also for multimedia projects. 75% of freelance work demands skills in Illustrator, Photoshop, InDesign. "Knowledge of multimedia programs such as Director and Premier would also be desirable."

FIRST CONTACT & TERMS Send query letter or photocopies, résumé and tearsheets. Also accepts e-mail submissions. Samples are filed. Will contact artist for portfolio review if interested. Portfolio should include b&w and color final art, roughs (important) and thumbnails (important). Pays for design and illustration by the project. Rights purchased vary according to project. Finds artists through submissions and word of mouth. Desires freelancers with web design or web programming experience and skills.

TIPS "Be original, be creative and have a positive attitude. Need to show strength in illustration with a good design sense. A flair for typography would be desirable."

◍ TR PRODUCTIONS

2 13th St., Floor 3, Charleston MA 02129. (617)241-5500. **Website:** www.trprod.com. **Contact:** creative director. Estab. 1947. Number of employees: 12. AV firm; full-service multimedia firm. Specializes in Flash, collateral, multimedia, Web graphics and video.

NEEDS Approached by 15 freelancers/year. Works with 5 freelance illustrators and 5 designers/year. Prefers local freelancers with experience in slides, Web, multimedia, collateral and video graphics. Works on assignment only. Uses freelancers mainly for slides, Web, multimedia, collateral and video graphics; also for brochure and print ad design and illustration, slide illustration, animation and mechanicals. 25% of work is with print ads. Needs computer-literate freelancers for design, production and presentation. 95% of work demands skills in FreeHand, Photoshop, Pre-

mier, After Effects, Powerpoint, QuarkXPress, Illustrator, Flash.

FIRST CONTACT & TERMS Send query letter. Samples are filed. Does not reply. Artist should follow up with call. Will contact artist for portfolio review if interested. Rights purchased vary according to project.

TVN—THE VIDEO NETWORK

P.O. Box 270, Ashland MA 01721. (508)881-1800. **E-mail:** info@tvnvideo.com. **Website:** www.tvnvideo.com. Estab. 1986. AV firm. Full-service multimedia firm. Specializes in video production for business, broadcast and special events. Product specialties "cover a broad range of categories." Current clients include Marriott, Digital, IBM, VistaPrint, National Park Service.

NEEDS Approached by 1 freelancer/month. Works with 1 illustrator/month. Prefers freelancers with experience in Mac, 2D and 3D programs. Works on assignment only. Uses freelancers mainly for video production, technical illustration, flying logos and 3D work. Also for storyboards, animation, TV/film graphics and logos.

FIRST CONTACT & TERMS Send query e-mail and links. Will contact artist for portfolio review if interested. Pays for design by the hour, $50; by the project, $1,000-5,000; by the day, $250-500. Buys all rights. Finds artists through word of mouth, magazines and submissions.

TIPS Advises freelancers starting out in the field to find a company internship or mentor program.

ULTITECH, INC.

Foot of Broad St., Stratford CT 06497. (203)375-7300. **Fax:** (203)375-6699. **E-mail:** ultitech@meds.com. **Website:** www.meds.com. Estab. 1993. Number of employees: 3. Approximate annual billing: $1 million. Integrated marketing communications agency. Specializes in interactive multimedia, software, online services. Product specialties are medicine, science, technology. Current clients include large pharmaceutical companies.

NEEDS Approached by 10-20 freelance illustrators and 10-20 designers/year. Works with 2-3 freelance illustrators and 6-10 designers/year. Prefers freelancers with experience in interactive media design and online design. Uses freelancers mainly for design of websites and interactive CDs/DVDs. Also for animation, brochure design, medical illustration, multimedia projects, TV/film graphics. 10% of work is with print ads. 100% of freelance design demands skills in Photoshop, QuarkXPress, Illustrator, 3D packages.

FIRST CONTACT & TERMS E-mail submission is best. Include links to online portfolio. Responds only if interested. Pays for design by the project or by the day. Pays for illustration by the project. Buys all rights. Finds artists through sourcebooks, word of mouth, submissions.

TIPS "Learn design principles for interactive media."

UNICOM

9470 N. Broadmoor Rd., Bayside WI 53217. (414)352-5070. **Fax:** (414)352-4755. **E-mail:** keichenbaum@wi.rr.com. **Contact:** Ken Eichenbaum, senior partner. Estab. 1974. Specializes in annual reports, brand and corporate identity, display, direct, package and publication design and signage. Clients: corporations, business-to-business communications, and consumer goods. Client list available upon request.

NEEDS Approached by 5-10 freelancers/year. Works with 1-2 freelance illustrators/year. Works on assignment only. Uses freelancers for brochure, book and poster illustration, prepress composition. Systems used include QuarkXPress and InDesign.

FIRST CONTACT & TERMS Send query letter with brochure. Samples not filed or returned. Does not reply; send nonreturnable samples. Write for appointment to show portfolio of thumbnails, photostats, slides and tearsheets. Pays by the project, $200-3,000. Rights purchased vary according to project.

⊕ UNO BRANDING—A CROSS-CULTURAL DESIGN AGENCY

111 E. Franklin Ave., Suite 101, Minneapolis MN 55404. (612)874-1920. **Fax:** (612)874-1912. **E-mail:** luis@unobranding.com. **Website:** www.unobranding.com. **Contact:** Luis Fitch, creative director. Estab. 1990. Number of employees: 6. Approximate annual billing: $950,000. Specializes in brand and corporate identity, display, package and retail design and signage for the US Hispanic markets. Clients: Latin American corporations, retail. Current clients include MTV Latino, Target, Mervyn's, 3M, Univision, Wilson's. Client list available upon request. Professional affiliations AIGA, GAG.

NEEDS Approached by 33 freelancers/year. Works with 40 freelance illustrators and 20 designers/year. Works only with artists' reps. Prefers local artists with experience in retail design, graphics. Uses illustrators mainly for packaging. Uses designers mainly for retail

graphics. Also uses freelancers for ad and book design, brochure, catalog and P-O-P design and illustration, audiovisual materials, logos and model making. Also for multimedia projects (Interactive Kiosk, CD-Educational for Hispanic Market). 60% of design demands computer skills in Illustrator, Photoshop, FreeHand and QuarkXPress.

FIRST CONTACT & TERMS Designers: Send postcard sample, brochure, résumé, photographs, slides, or tearsheets. Illustrators: Send postcard sample, brochure, or tearsheets. Accepts disk submissions compatible with Illustrator, Photoshop, FreeHand. Send EPS files. Samples are filed. Will contact artist for portfolio review if interested. Portfolio should include color final art, photographs and slides. Pays for design by the project, $500-6,000. Pays for illustration by the project, $200-20,000. Rights purchased vary according to project. Finds artists through artist reps, *Creative Black Book* and *Workbook*.

TIPS "It helps to be bilingual and to have an understanding of Hispanic cultures."

UTOPIAN EMPIRE CREATIVEWORKS

P.O. Box 9, Traverse City MI 49865. (231)715-1614. **E-mail:** traverse_city@utopianempire.com. **Website:** www.utopianempire.com. Estab. 1970. Full-service multimedia firm. Specializes in corporate and industrial products, as well as TV and radio spots.

NEEDS Works on assignment. Uses freelance talent.

FIRST CONTACT & TERMS Send query letter with brochure, SASE, and tearsheets. Samples are filed to review for project relevancy or returned by SASE if requested by artist. Responds only if interested. To show portfolio, mail samples or CD/DVD media. Pays for design and illustration by the project, negotiated rate. Rights purchased vary according to project.

THE VAN NOY GROUP

3315 Westside Rd., Healdsburg CA 95448-9453. (707)433-3944. **Fax:** (707)433-0375. **E-mail:** vng@vannoygroup.com. **Website:** www.vannoygroup.com. **Contact:** Jim Van Noy. Estab. 1972. Specializes in brand and corporate identity, displays and package design. Clients: corporations, consumer product, beverage, health and beauty, lawn and garden and decorative hardware companies. Client list available upon request.

NEEDS Approached by 1-10 freelance artists/year. Works with 2 illustrators and 3 designers/year. Prefers artists with experience in Mac design. Works on assignment only. Uses freelancers for packaging design and illustration, Photoshop production and lettering. **FIRST CONTACT & TERMS** Send query letter with résumé and photographs. Samples are filed. Will contact artist for portfolio review if interested. If no reply, artist should follow up. Pays for design by the hour, $35-100. Pays for illustration by the hour or by the project at a TBD fee. Finds artists through sourcebooks, self-promotions and primarily agents. Also have permanent positions available.

TIPS "I think more and more clients will be setting up internal art departments and relying less and less on outside designers and talent. The computer has made design accessible to the user who is not design-trained."

VIDEO RESOURCES

1809 E. Dyer Rd., #307, Santa Ana CA 92705. (949)261-7266; (800)261-7266. **Fax:** (949)261-5908. **E-mail:** brad@videoresouces.com. **Website:** www.videore sources.com. **Contact:** Brad Hagen, producer. Number of employees: 15. Video and multimedia firm. Specializes in automotive, banks, restaurants, computer, health care, transportation and energy.

○ Additional location: 110 Campus Dr., Marlborough MA 01752; (508)485-8100.

NEEDS Approached by 10-20 freelancers/year. Works with 5-10 freelance illustrators and 5-10 designers/ year. Works on assignment only. Uses freelancers for graphics, multimedia, animation, etc.

FIRST CONTACT & TERMS Send query letter with brochure showing art style or résumé, business card, photostats and tearsheets to be kept on file. Samples not filed are returned by SASE. Considers complexity of the project and client's budget when establishing payment. Buys all rights.

VISUAL HORIZONS

180 Metro Park, Rochester NY 14623. (585)424-5300; (800)424-1011. **Fax:** (585)424-5313. **E-mail:** cs@visu alhorizons.com. **Website:** www.visualhorizons.com. Estab. 1971. AV firm; full-service multimedia firm. Specializes in presentation products, digital imaging of 35mm slides. Current: US government agencies, corporations and universities.

NEEDS Works on assignment only. Uses freelancers mainly for web design. 5% of work is with print ads. 100% of freelance work demands skills in Photoshop.

FIRST CONTACT & TERMS Send query letter with tearsheets. Samples are not filed and are not returned.

Responds if interested. Portfolio review not required. Pays for design and illustration by the hour or project, negotiated. Buys all rights.

VML

261 E. Kalamazoo Ave., Suite 300, Kalamazoo MI 49007-3990. (269)349-7711. **Website:** www.vml.com. Ad agency; full-service digital marketing agency. Specializes in traditional advertising (print, collateral, TV, radio, outdoor), branding, strategic planning, e-business development, and media planning and buying. Product specialties are consumer, business-to-business, marine and health care. Clients include Morningstar Farms, Pfizer, Kellogg Co., Zimmer, Beaner's Coffee, United Way.

NEEDS Approached by 10 artists/month. Works with 1-3 illustrators and designers/month. Works both with artist reps and directly with artist. Prefers artists with experience with client needs. Works on assignment only. Uses freelancers mainly for completion of projects needing specialties; also for brochure, catalog and print ad design and illustration, storyboards, mechanicals, retouching, billboards, posters, TV/film graphics, lettering and logos.

FIRST CONTACT & TERMS Send query letter with brochure, photocopies and résumé. Samples are filed. Responds only if interested. Call for appointment to show portfolio. Portfolio should include all samples the artist considers appropriate. Pays for design and illustration by the hour and by the project. Rights purchased vary according to project.

WALKER DESIGN GROUP

421 Central Ave., Great Falls MT 59401. (406)727-8115. **Fax:** (406)791-9655. **E-mail:** info@walk erdesigngroup.com. **Website:** www.walkerdesign group.com. **Contact:** Duane Walker, president. Number of employees: 6. Design firm. Specializes in annual reports and corporate identity. Professional affiliations: AIGA and Ad Federation.

NEEDS Uses freelancers for animation, annual reports, brochure, medical and technical illustration, catalog design, lettering, logos and TV/film graphics. 80% of design and 90% of illustration demand skills in PageMaker, Photoshop and Illustrator.

FIRST CONTACT & TERMS Send query letter with brochure, photocopies, postcards, résumé or tearsheets. Accepts digital submissions. Samples are filed and are not returned. Responds only if interested. To arrange portfolio review, artist should follow up with call or letter after initial query. Portfolio should include color photographs, photostats and tearsheets. Pays by the project; negotiable. Finds artists through *Workbook*.

TIPS "Stress customer service and be very aware of deadlines."

WARKULWIZ DESIGN ASSOCIATES, INC.

89 E. Wynnewood Rd., Merion Station PA 19066. (215)988-1777. **E-mail:** info@warkulwiz.com. **Website:** www.warkulwiz.com. **Contact:** Bob Warkulwiz, president. Estab. 1985. Number of employees: 6. Approximate annual billing: $1 million. Specializes in annual reports, publication design and corporate communications. Clients: corporations and universities. Client list available upon request. Professional affiliations: AIGA

NEEDS Approached by 100 freelancers/year. Works with 10 freelance illustrators and 5-10 photographers/year. Works on assignment only. Uses freelance illustrators mainly for editorial and corporate work; also for brochure and poster illustration and mechanicals. Freelancers should be familiar with most recent versions of QuarkXPress, Illustrator, Photoshop, FreeHand and Director.

FIRST CONTACT & TERMS Send query letter with tearsheets and photostats. Samples are filed. Responds only if interested. Call for appointment to show portfolio of "best edited work—published or unpublished." Pays for illustration by the project, "depends upon usage and complexity." Rights purchased vary according to project.

TIPS "Be creative and professional."

WAVE DESIGN WORKS

55 Elmgrove Ave., Providence RI 02906. (774)254-0946. **E-mail:** ideas@wavedesignworks.com. **Website:** www.wavedesignworks.com. **Contact:** John Buchholz, principal. Estab. 1986. Specializes in corporate identity and display, package and publication design. Clients corporations primarily biotech, medical and health care, B2B.

NEEDS Approached by 24 freelance graphic artists/year. Works with 1-5 freelance illustrators and 1-5 freelance designers/year. Works on assignment only. Uses freelancers for brochure, catalog, poster and ad illustration; lettering; and charts/graphs. 100% of design and 50% of illustration demand knowledge of QuarkXPress, InDesign, Illustrator or Photoshop.

FIRST CONTACT & TERMS Designers send query letter with brochure, résumé, photocopies, photographs and tearsheets. Illustrators send postcard promo. Samples are filed. Responds only if interested. Artist should follow up with call or letter after initial query. Portfolio should include b&w and color thumbnails and final art. Pays for illustration by the project. Rights purchased vary according to project. Finds artists through submissions and sourcebooks.

WEST CREATIVE, INC.

10780 S. Cedar Niles Circle, Overland Park KS 66210. (913)839-2181. **Fax:** (913)839-2176. **E-mail:** stan@westcreative.com. **Website:** www.westcreative.com. **Contact:** Stan Chrzanowski. Estab. 1974. Number of employees: 8. Approximate annual billing $600,000. Design firm and agency. Full-service multimedia firm. Client list available upon request. Professional affiliation AIGA.

◐ Additional locations in Dallas and Tucson.

NEEDS Approached by 50 freelancers/year. Works with 4-6 freelance illustrators and 1-2 designers/year. Uses freelancers mainly for illustration. Also for animation, lettering, mechanicals, model-making, retouching and TV/film graphics. 20% of work is with print ads. Needs computer-literate freelancers for design, illustration and production. 95% of freelance work demands knowledge of FreeHand, Photoshop, QuarkXPress and Illustrator. Full service web design capabilities.

FIRST CONTACT & TERMS Send postcard-size sample of work or query letter with brochure, photocopies, résumé, SASE, slides, tearsheets and transparencies. Samples are filed or returned by SASE if requested by artist. Responds only if interested. Portfolios may be dropped off Monday-Thursday. Portfolios should include color photographs, roughs, slides and tearsheets. Pays for illustration by the project; pays for design by the hour, $25-60. "Each project is bid." Rights purchased vary according to project. Finds artists through *Creative Black Book* and *Workbook*.

WEYMOUTH DESIGN, INC.

332 Congress St., Floor 6, Boston MA 02210. (617)542-2647. **Fax:** (617)451-6233. **E-mail:** info@weymouthdesign.com. **Website:** www.weymouthdesign.com. Estab. 1973. Number of employees: 16. Specializes in annual reports, corporate collateral, website design, CDs and multimedia. Clients: corporations and small businesses. Member of AIGA.

○ Second location: 600 Townsend St., San Francisco CA 94103. (415)487-7900. Fax: (415)431-7200.

NEEDS Works with 3-5 freelance illustrators or photographers. Needs editorial, medical and technical illustration mainly for annual reports and multimedia projects.

FIRST CONTACT & TERMS Send query letter with résumé or illustration samples/tearsheets. Samples are filed or are returned by SASE if requested by artist. Will contact artist for portfolio review if interested.

⌂ DANA WHITE PRODUCTIONS

2623 29th St., Santa Monica CA 90405-2915. (310)450-9101. **E-mail:** dwprods@aol.com. **Contact:** Dana C. White, president. AV firm. "We are a full-service audiovisual and print design and production company, providing video and audio presentations for training, marketing, awards, historical and public relations uses. We now offer design and development of full-color books, brochures and other printed material. We have complete in-house production resources, including computer multimedia, photo digitizing, image manipulation, program assembly, graphics, soundtrack production, photography and AV multi-image programming. We serve major industries such as US. Forest Services; medical, such as Whittier Hospital, Florida Hospital; schools, such as University of Southern California, Pepperdine University; publishers, such as McGraw-Hill, West Publishing; and public service efforts, including fundraising."

NEEDS Works with 8-10 freelancers/year. Prefers freelancers local to greater Los Angeles, "with timely turnaround, ability to keep elements in accurate registration, neatness, design quality, imagination and price." Uses freelancers for design, illustration, retouching, characterization/animation, lettering and charts. 50% of freelance work demands knowledge of Adobe InDesign, Illustrator, Photoshop, Quark and Premier.

FIRST CONTACT & TERMS Send query letter with brochure or tearsheets, photostats, photocopies, slides and photographs. Samples are filed or are returned only if requested. Responds in 2 weeks, only if interested. Call or write for appointment to show portfolio. Pays by the project. Payment negotiable by job.

TIPS "Be flexible. Negotiate. Your work should show that you have spirit, enjoy what you do, and that you can deliver high-quality work on time."

L.C. WILLIAMS & ASSOCIATES

150 N. Michigan Ave., 38th Floor, Chicago IL 60601. (312)565-3900; (800)837-7123. **E-mail:** info@lcwa. com. **Website:** www.lcwa.com. **Contact:** Monica McFadden, creative services manager. Estab. 2000. Number of employees: 28. Approximate annual billing: $3.5 million. PR firm. Specializes in marketing, communication, publicity, direct mail, brochures, newsletters, trade magazine ads, AV presentations. Product specialty is consumer home products. Current clients include Pergo, Ace Hardware, La-Z-Boy Inc. and Glidden. Professional affiliations: Chicago Direct Marketing Association, Sales & Marketing Executives of Chicago, Public Relations Society of America, Publicity Club of Chicago.

○ LCWA is among the top 15 public relations agencies in Chicago. It maintains a satellite office in New York.

NEEDS Approached by 50-100 freelancers/year. Works with 1-2 freelance illustrators and 2-5 designers/year. Works on assignment only. Uses freelancers mainly for brochures, ads, newsletters. Also for print ad design and illustration, editorial and technical illustration, mechanicals, retouching and logos. 90% of freelance work demands computer skills.

FIRST CONTACT & TERMS Send query letter with brochure and résumé. Samples are filed. Does not reply. Request portfolio review in original query. Artist should call within 1 week. Portfolio should include printed pieces. Pays for design and illustration by the project, fee varies. Rights purchased vary according to project. Finds artists through word of mouth and queries.

TIPS "Many new people are opening shop and you need to keep your name in front of your prospects."

THE WILLIAMS MCBRIDE GROUP

P.O. Box 910433, Lexington KY 40591-0433. (859)253-9319. **E-mail:** tsmith@williamsmcbride.com. **Website:** www.williamsmcbride.com. Estab. 1988. Number of employees: 12. Design firm specializing in brand management, corporate identity and business-to-business marketing.

NEEDS Approached by 10-20 freelance artists/year. Works with 4 illustrators and 3 designers/year. Prefers freelancers with experience in corporate design, branding. Works on assignment only. 100% of freelance design work demands knowledge of InDesign,

Photoshop and Illustrator. Will review résumés of web designers with knowledge of Director and Flash.

FIRST CONTACT & TERMS Designers: Send query letter with résumé. Will review online portfolios or hardcopy samples. Illustrators: Send website link or postcard sample of work. Samples are filed. Responds only if interested. Pays for design by the hour, $50-65. Pays for illustration by the project. Rights purchased vary according to project. Finds artists through submissions, word of mouth, *Creative Black Book*, *Workbook*, *American Showcase*, artist's representatives.

TIPS "Keep our company on your mailing list; remind us that you are out there."

WISNER CREATIVE

18200 NW Sauvie Island Rd., Portland OR 97231-1338. (503)282-3929. **Fax:** (503)282-0325. **E-mail:** wizbiz@wisnercreative.com. **Website:** www.wisnercreative.com. **Contact:** Linda Wisner, creative director. Estab. 1979. Number of employees: 1. Specializes in brand and corporate identity, book design, publications and exhibit design. Clients: small businesses, manufacturers, restaurants, service businesses and book publishers.

NEEDS Works with 3-5 freelance illustrators/year. Prefers experienced freelancers and "fast, accurate work." Works on assignment only. Uses freelancers for technical and fashion illustration and graphic production. Knowledge of QuarkXPress, InDesign, Photoshop, Illustrator, Dreamweaver, and other software required.

FIRST CONTACT & TERMS Send query e-mail with résumé and samples. Prefers electronic "examples of completed pieces that show the fullest abilities of the artist." Will contact artist for portfolio review if interested. Pays for illustration by the project, by bid. Pays for graphic production by the hour, $35-50 or by project, by bid.

⊙ MICHAEL WOLK DESIGN ASSOCIATES

31 NE 28th St., Miami FL 33137. (305)576-2898. **Fax:** (305)576-2899. **E-mail:** contact@wolkdesign.com. **Website:** www.wolkdesign.com. **Contact:** Michael Wolk, chairman/creative director. Estab. 1985. Specializes in corporate identity, displays, interior design and signage. Clients: corporate and private. Client list available on website.

NEEDS Approached by 10 freelancers/year. Works with 5 illustrators and 5 freelance designers/year. Prefers local artists only. Works on assignment only.

Needs editorial and technical illustration mainly for brochures. Uses designers mainly for interiors and graphics; also for brochure design, mechanicals, logos and catalog illustration. Prefers "progressive" illustration. Needs computer-literate freelancers for design, production and presentation. 75% of freelance work demands knowledge of PageMaker, QuarkXPress, FreeHand, Illustrator or other software.

FIRST CONTACT & TERMS Send query letter with slides. Samples are not filed and are returned by SASE. Responds only if interested. To show a portfolio, mail slides. Pays for design by the hour, $10-20. Rights purchased vary according to project.

ERIC WOO DESIGN, INC.

Pacific Guardian Center, 733 Bishop St., Suite 1280, Honolulu HI 96813. (808)545-7442. **Fax:** (808)545-7445. **E-mail:** eric@ericwoodesign.com. **Website:** www.ericwoodesign.com. Number of employees: 3. Approximate annual billing: $500,000. Design firm. Specializes in identities and visual branding, product packaging, print and web design, environmental graphics and signage. Majority of clients are government, corporations and nonprofits. Current clients include NOAA, Western Pacific Regional Fishery Management Council, Alexander & Baldwin, Inc.

NEEDS Approached by 5-10 illustrators and 10 designers/year. Works with 1-2 illustrators/year. Prefers freelancers with experience in multimedia. Uses freelancers mainly for multimedia projects and lettering. 5% of work is with print ads. 90% of design demands skills in Photoshop, Illustrator, Quark, Flash, Dreamweaver and InDesign.

FIRST CONTACT & TERMS Designers: Send query letter with web link. Illustrators: Send postcard sample of work or web link. Pays for design by the hour, $20-50. Pays for illustration by the project. Rights purchased vary according to project.

TIPS "Have a good sense of humor and enjoy life."

WORK

2019 Monument Ave., Richmond VA 23220. (804)358-9372. **Fax:** (804)355-2784. **Website:** worklabs.com. **Contact:** Cabell Harris, president/chief creative director. Estab. 1994. Number of employees: 10. Approximate annual billing: $44 million. Ad agency. Specializes in new product development and design, advertising, and strategic and creative problem solving. Current clients include Luck Stone, Snagajob.com, Macy's amd a variety of ad agencies. Client list available upon request. Professional affiliations Advertising Club of Richmond, AIGA.

NEEDS Approached by 25 illustrators and 35-40 designers/year. Works with 2-3 illustrators and 6-7 designers/year. Works on assignment only. Prefers freelancers with experience in animation, computer graphics, Macintosh. Uses freelancers mainly for new business pitches and specialty projects. Also for logos, mechanicals, TV/film graphics, posters, print ads, package design, and storyboards. 40% of work is with print ads. 95% of design work demands knowledge of FreeHand, Illustrator, Photoshop and QuarkXPress. 20% of illustration work demands knowledge of Free-Hand, Illustrator, Photoshop and InDesign.

FIRST CONTACT & TERMS Send query letter with photocopies, photographs, résumé, tearsheets, URL. Accepts e-mail submissions. Check website for formats. Samples are filed or returned. Responds only if interested. Request portfolio review in original query. Company will contact artist for portfolio review if interested. Portfolio should include b&w and color finished art, photographs, slides, tearsheets and transparencies. Pays freelancers usually a set budget with a buyout. Negotiates rights purchased. Finds freelancers through submissions, sourcebooks and word of mouth.

TIPS "Send nonreturnable samples (JPEGs or PDFs) of work with résumé. Follow up by e-mail."

YASVIN COMMUNICATIONS

P.O. Box 116, Hancock NH 03449. (603)525-3000. **Fax:** (603)525-3300. **E-mail:** info@yasvin.com. **Website:** yasvin.com. **Contact:** Creative Director. Estab. 1990. Number of employees: 3. Specializes in annual reports, brand and corporate identity, advertising, web design, commercials, corporate documentary films. Clients: corporations, colleges and non-profits.

NEEDS Approached by 10-15 freelancers/year. Works with 4 freelance illustrators and 2 designers/year. Uses freelancers for design, illustration, logos. Freelance work demands knowledge of Illustrator, InDesign, Photoshop and QuarkXPress.

FIRST CONTACT & TERMS Send postcard sample of work or e-mail with your URL. Pays for design by the project and by the day. Pays for work by the project. Rights purchased vary according to project.

SPENCER ZAHN & ASSOCIATES

2015 Sansom St., Philadelphia PA 19103. (215)564-5979. **Fax:** (215)564-6285. **E-mail:** szahn@erols.com.

Website: www.spencerzahn.com. **Contact:** Spencer Zahn, CEO; J. McCarthy, art director. Estab. 1970. Member of GPCC. 3 employees. Specializes in brand and corporate identity, direct mail design, marketing, retail and business to business advertising. POS. Clients: corporations, manufacturers, etc. Firm specializes in direct mail, electronic collateral, print ads.

NEEDS Works with freelance illustrators and designers. Prefers artists with experience in Macintosh computers. Uses freelancers for design and illustration; direct mail design; and mechanicals. Needs computer-literate freelancers for design, illustration and production. 80% of freelance work demands knowledge of Illustrator, Photoshop, FreeHand and QuarkXPress.

FIRST CONTACT & TERMS Send query letter with samples. Samples are not filed and are returned by SASE if requested by artist. Responds only if interested. Artist should follow up with call. Portfolio should include final art and printed samples. Buys all rights.

ZUNPARTNERS, INC.

676 N. La Salle Dr., Suite 426, Chicago IL 60654. (312)951-5533. **E-mail:** bill.ferdinand@zunpartners.com; hello@zunpartners.com. **Website:** www.zunpartners.com. **Contact:** William Ferdinand, partner. Estab. 1991. Number of employees: 9. Specializes in annual reports, brand and corporate identity, capability brochures, package and publication design, electronic and interactive. Clients: from Fortune 500 to Internet startup companies, focusing on high impact service firms. Current clients include Deloitte, Baker and McKenzie, Bracewell and Giuliani. Client list available upon request. Professional affiliations: AIGA, ACD, LMA.

NEEDS Approached by 30 freelancers/year. Works with 10-15 freelance illustrators and 15-20 designers/year. Looks for strong personal style (local and national). Uses illustrators mainly for editorial. Uses designers mainly for design and layout. Also uses freelancers for collateral and identity design, illustration; Web, video, audiovisual materials; direct mail, magazine design and lettering; logos; and retouching. Needs computer-literate freelancers for design, illustration, production and presentation. 90% of freelance work demands knowledge of Illustrator, Photoshop, InDesign.

FIRST CONTACT & TERMS Send postcard sample of work or send query letter with brochure or résumé. Samples are filed. Responds only if interested. Portfolios may be dropped off every Friday. Artist should follow up. Portfolio should include b&w and color samples. Pays for design by the hour and by the project. Pays for illustration by the project. Rights purchased vary according to project. Finds artists through reference books and submissions.

TIPS Impressed by "to the point portfolios. Show me what you like to do and what you brought to the projects you worked on. Don't fill a book with extra items (samples) for the sake of showing quantity."

ADVERTISING

SYNDICATES & CARTOON FEATURES

Syndicates are agents who sell comic strips, panels, and editorial cartoons to newspapers and magazines. If you want to see your comic strip in the funny papers, you must first get the attention of a syndicate. They promote and distribute comic strips and other features in exchange for a cut of the profits.

The syndicate business is one of the hardest markets to break into. Newspapers are reluctant to drop long-established strips for new ones. Consequently, spaces for new strips do not open up often. When they do, syndicates look for a "sure thing," a feature they'll feel comfortable investing more than $25,000 in for promotion and marketing. Even after syndication, much of your promotion will be up to you.

To crack this market, you have to be more than a fabulous cartoonist—the art won't sell if the idea isn't there in the first place. Work worthy of syndication must be original, salable, and timely, and characters must have universal appeal to attract a diverse audience.

Although newspaper syndication is still the most popular and profitable method of getting your comic strip to a wide audience, the Internet has become an exciting new venue for comic strips and political cartoons. With the click of your mouse, you can be introduced to *The Boiling Point* by Mikhaela Reid, *Overboard* by Chip Dunham, and *Strange Brew* by John Deering. (GoComics.com provides a great list of online comics.)

Such sites may not make much money for cartoonists, but it's clear they are a great promotional tool. It is rumored that scouts for the major syndicates have been known to surf the more popular comic strip sites in search of fresh voices.

HELPFUL RESOURCES

You'll get an excellent overview of the field by reading *Your Career in Comics* by Lee Nordling (Andrews McMeel), a comprehensive review of syndication from the viewpoints of the cartoonist, the newspaper editor, and the syndicate. *Successful Syndication: A Guide for Writers and Cartoonists* by Michael H. Sedge (Allworth Press) also offers concrete advice to aspiring cartoonists.

There are also several good sources of information online. Stu's Comic Strip Connection at www.stus.com/index2.htm provides links to most syndicates and other essential sources, including helpful books, courtesy of Stu Rees. The National Cartoonists Society at www.reuben.org provides history, expert advice, links to the major syndicates, and membership information.

HOW TO SUBMIT TO SYNDICATES

Each syndicate has a preferred method for submissions, and most have guidelines you can send for or access online. Availability is indicated in the listings.

To submit a strip idea, send a brief cover letter (fifty words or less is ideal) summarizing your idea, along with a character sheet (the names and descriptions of your major characters), and photocopies of twenty-four of your best strip samples on 8½×11 paper, six daily strips per page. Sending at least one month of samples shows that you're capable of producing consistent artwork and a long-lasting idea. Never submit originals; always send photocopies of your work. Simultaneous submissions are usually acceptable. It is often possible to query syndicates online by attaching art files or links to your website. Response time can take several months. Syndicates understand it would be impractical for you to wait for replies before submitting your ideas to other syndicates.

Editorial Cartoons

If you're an editorial cartoonist, you'll need to start out selling your cartoons to a base newspaper (probably in your hometown) and build up some clips before approaching a syndicate. Submitting published clips proves to the syndicate that you have a following and are able to produce cartoons on a regular basis. Once you've built up a good collection of clips, submit at least twelve photocopied samples of your published work along with a brief cover letter.

Payment and Contracts

If you're one of the lucky few to be picked up by a syndicate, your earnings will depend on the number of publications in which your work appears. It takes a minimum of about sixty interested newspapers to make it profitable for a syndicate to distribute a strip. A top strip such as *Garfield* may be in as many as 2,500 papers worldwide.

Newspapers pay in the area of $10–15 a week for a daily feature. If that doesn't sound like much, multiply that figure by 100 or even 1,000 newspapers. Your payment will be a percentage of gross or net receipts. Contracts usually involve a 50/50 split between the syndicate and cartoonist. Check the listings for more specific payment information.

Before signing a contract, be sure you understand the terms and are comfortable with them.

Self-Syndication

Self-syndicated cartoonists retain all rights to their work and keep all profits, but they also have to act as their own salespeople, sending packets to newspapers and other likely outlets. This requires developing a mailing list, promoting the strip (or panel) periodically, and developing a pricing, billing, and collections structure. If you have a knack for business and the required time and energy, this might be the route for you. Weekly suburban or alternative newspapers are the best bet here. (Daily newspapers rarely buy from self-syndicated cartoonists.)

☉ ARTIZANS.COM

11136 - 75A St. NW, Edmonton Alberta T5B 2C5, Canada. (780)471-6112; (877)700-8666. **E-mail:** submissions@artizans.com. **Website:** www.artizans.com. **Contact:** submissions editor. Estab. 1998. Artist agency and syndicate providing commissioned artwork, stock illustrations, political cartoons, gag cartoons, global caricatures and humorous illustrations to magazines, newspapers, websites, corporate and trade publications and ad agencies. Artists represented include Jan Op De Beeck, Chris Wildt, Jerry King, Roy Delgado and Dusan Petricic.

NEEDS Works with 30-40 artists/year. Buys 30-40 features/year. Needs single-image gag cartoons, political cartoons, illustrations and graphic art. Prefers established professional artists who create artwork regularly, and/or former professional artists who have an existing arhivc of cartoons, caricatures or illustrations.

FIRST CONTACT & TERMS Submission guidelines available online.

CITY NEWS SERVICE, LLC

P.O. Box 86, Willow Springs MO 65793-0086. (417)469-4476. **E-mail:** cns@cnsus.org. **Website:** www.cnsus.org. Estab. 1969. Editorial service providing editorial and graphic packages for magazines.

NEEDS Buys from 12 or more freelance artists/year. Considers caricatures, editorial cartoons, and tax and business subjects as themes; considers b&w line drawings and shading film.

FIRST CONTACT & TERMS Send query letter with résumé, tearsheets or photocopies. Samples should contain business subjects. "Send 5 or more b&w line drawings, color drawings, shading film or good line-drawing editorial cartoons." Does not want to see comic strips. Samples not filed are returned by SASE. Responds in 4-6 weeks. To show a portfolio, mail tearsheets or photostats. Pays 50% of net proceeds; pays flat fee of $25 minimum. "We may buy art outright or split percentage of sales."

TIPS "We have the markets for multiple sales of editorial support art. We need talented artists to supply specific projects. We will work with beginning artists. Be honest about talent and artistic ability. If it isn't there, don't beat your head against the wall."

CONTINENTAL FEATURES/CONTINENTAL NEWS SERVICE

501 W. Broadway, P.M.B. #265, Plaza A, San Diego CA 92101-3802. (858)492-8696. **E-mail:** continentalnewsservice@yahoo.com. **Website:** www.continentalnewsservice.com. **Contact:** Gary P. Salamone, editor-in-chief. Estab. 1981. Syndicate serving 3 outlets—house publication, publishing business, and the general public—through the Continental Newstime general interest news magazine. Features include Portfolio, a collection of cartoon and caricature art. Guidelines available for #10 SASE with first-class postage.

NEEDS Approached by up to 200 cartoonists/year. Number of new strips introduced each year varies. Considers comic strips and gag cartoons. Does not consider highly abstract, computer-produced or stick-figure art. Prefers single-panel with gagline. Maximum size of artwork: 8×10; must be reducible to 65% of original size.

FIRST CONTACT & TERMS Sample package should include cover letter and photocopies (10-15 samples), but cartoonists should have 2-3 years' worth of material in reserve. Samples are filed or are returned by SASE if requested by artist. Responds in 1 month, if interested or if SASE is received. No telephone calls please. To show portfolio, mail photocopies and cover letter. Pays 70% of gross income on publication. Rights purchased vary according to project. Minimum length of contract is 2-3 years. The artist owns the original art and the characters.

TIPS "We need single-panel cartoons and comic strips appropriate for an English-speaking international audience, including cartoons that communicate feelings or predicaments, without words. Do not send samples reflecting the highs and lows and different stages of your artistic development. *CF/CNS* wants to see consistency and quality, so you'll need to send your best samples."

HISPANIC LINK NEWS SERVICE

(202)234-0280. **Fax:** (202)234-4090. **E-mail:** charlie@hispaniclink.org. **Website:** www.hispaniclinkdc.org. **Contact:** Charles Ericksen. Estab. 1980. Syndicated column service to 250 newspapers and a newsletter serving 2,000 subscribers "movers and shakers in the Hispanic community in US, plus others interested in Hispanics." Guidelines available.

NEEDS Buys from a few freelancers/year. Considers single panel cartoons; b&w; pen & ink line drawings.

Work should have a Hispanic angle; "most are editorial cartoons, some straight humor."

FIRST CONTACT & TERMS Send query letter with résumé and photocopies to be kept on file. Samples not filed are returned by SASE. Responds in 3 weeks. Portfolio review not required. **Pays on acceptance**; $25 flat fee (average). Considers clients' preferences when establishing payment. Buys reprint rights and negotiates rights purchased. "While we ask for reprint rights, we also allow the artist to sell later."

TIPS Interested in seeing more cultural humor. "While we accept work from all artists, we are particularly interested in helping Hispanic artists showcase their work. Cartoons should offer a Hispanic perspective on current events or a Hispanic view of life."

KING FEATURES SYNDICATE

Hearst Corp., 300 W. 57th St., 15th Floor, New York NY 10019-5238. (212)969-7550. **Fax:** (646)280-1550. **Website:** www.kingfeatures.com. **Contact:** submissions editor.

FIRST CONTACT & TERMS Send (1): A cover letter that briefly outlines the overall nature of your comic strip. Your letter should include your full name, address and telephone number and shouldn't be much longer than a single page. (2): 24 b&w daily comic strips. You should reduce your comics to fit onto standard 8½×11 sheets of paper. Write your name, address and phone number on each page. Do not send your original drawings! Send photocopies instead. (3): A character sheet that shows your major characters (if any) along with their names and a paragraph description of each. "We do not accept work submitted via the Internet or on disk. Due to the extremely high volume of submissions we receive, it is easiest for us to receive, track, and account for the work if everything is sent in via regular mail or courier in the format described above. King Features is one of the world's largest syndicates. Each year, it gets more thousands of submissions of which only a few are chosen for syndication."

TIPS "The single best way of improving your chances for success is to practice. Only by drawing and writing cartoons do you get better at it. Invariably, the cartoonists whose work we like best turn out to be those who draw and write cartoons regularly, whether anyone sees their work or not. Another key to success it to read a lot. Read all sorts of things—fiction, magazines and newspapers. Humor is based on real life. The more you know about life, the more you have to humorously write about."

UNIVERSAL UCLICK

1130 Walnut St., Kansas City MO 64106. **E-mail:** submissions@amuniversal.com. **Website:** www.universaluclick.com. **Contact:** submissions editor. Estab. 1970. Print and online syndicate serving over 300 online clients daily. Art guidelines available on website.

NEEDS Approached by 200 cartoonists and 50 illustrators/year. Introduces about 15 new strips/year. Recent introductions include *Wumo*, *Heavenly Nostrils*, *Dark Side of the Horse*. Considers caricatures, single- or multi-panel cartoons, comic strips, puzzles/games. Looking for conservative and liberal political cartoons; unique puzzles, games and quizzes.

FIRST CONTACT & TERMS Send cover letter, character sheets and finished cartoons. Prefers to see 4 to 6 weeks worth of samples. Samples are not filed and are returned by SASE if requested by artist. Responds in 6-8 weeks. Will contact artist for portfolio review if interested. Pays on publication. "Royalties are based on negotiated rates, fees or licenses depending on content and distribution channels." Rights are negotiated. Artist owns original art and characters. Minimum length of contract: 3-year term is preferred; offers automatic renewal.

WASHINGTON POST WRITERS GROUP

1150 15th St. NW, Washington DC 20071. (202)334-5375; (800)879-9794, ext. 2. **E-mail:** cartoonsubmission@washpost.com; wpwgsales@washpost.com. **Website:** www.postwritersgroup.com. **Contact:** comics editor. Estab. 1973. Syndicate serving over 1,000 daily, Sunday and weekly newspapers in US and abroad. Submission guidelines available on website or for SASE with necessary postage.

NEEDS Considers comic strips, panel and editorial cartoons.

FIRST CONTACT & TERMS Send at least 24 cartoons. "You do not need to send color or Sunday cartoons in your initial submission; we will ask for those later if we require them. Of course if you do include color work, we are happy to review it." No fax submissions. Include SASE for reply only; cannot return materials. Submissions without SASE will not receive a reply. Responds whenever possible due to volume of submissions. Can submit by e-mail, but only if you can send it as a multi-page PDF with at least 2 dailies to a page.

TIPS "Use letter-sized paper for your submission. Make sure cartoons will reduce to standard sizes. Send only copies; never send originals."

ARTISTS' REPRESENTATIVES

///

Many artists find leaving promotion to a rep allows them more time for the creative process. In exchange for actively promoting an artist's career, the representative receives a percentage of sales (usually 25–30 percent). Reps generally focus on either the fine art market or commercial market, rarely both.

Fine art reps promote the work of fine artists, sculptors, craftspeople, and fine art photographers to galleries, museums, corporate art collectors, interior designers, and art publishers. Commercial reps help illustrators and graphic designers obtain assignments from advertising agencies, publishers, magazines, and other buyers. Some reps also act as licensing agents.

What Reps Do

Reps work with artists to bring their portfolios up to speed and actively promote their work to clients. Usually a rep will recommend advertising in one of the many creative directories such as *American Showcase* or *Workbook* so that your work will be seen by hundreds of art directors. (Expect to make an initial investment in costs for duplicate portfolios and mailings.) Reps also negotiate contracts, handle billing, and collect payments.

Getting representation isn't as easy as you might think. Reps are choosy about who they represent—not just in terms of talent but also in terms of marketability and professionalism. Reps will only take on talent they know will sell.

What to Send

Once you've gone through the listings in this section and compiled a list of art reps who handle your type and style of work, contact them with a brief query letter and nonreturnable copies of your work. Check each listing for specific guidelines and requirements.

AMERICAN ARTISTS REP, INC.

1 Chatsworth Ave. #518, Larchmont NY 10538. (212)682-2462. **Fax:** (212)582-0090. **Website:** www. aareps.com. Estab. 1930. Commercial illustration representative. Member of SPAR. Represents 40 illustrators. Markets include advertising agencies, corporations/client direct, design firms, editorial/magazines, paper products/greeting cards, publishing/books, sales/promotion firms.

HANDLES Illustration, design.

TERMS Rep receives 30% commission. "All portfolio expenses billed to artist." Advertising costs are split: 70% paid by talent; 30% paid by representative. "Promotion is encouraged; portfolio must be presented in a professional manner—8×10, 4×5, tearsheets, etc." Advertises in *American Showcase*, *The Black Book*, *RSVP*, *Workbook*, medical and Graphic Artist Guild publications.

HOW TO CONTACT Send query letter, direct mail flyer/brochure, tearsheets. Responds in 1 week if interested. After initial contact, drop off or mail appropriate materials for review. Portfolio should include tearsheets, slides. Obtains new talent through recommendations from others, solicitation, conferences.

ARTINFORMS

Martha Productions, 7550 W. 82nd St., Playa Del Rey CA 90293. (310)670-5300. **Fax:** (310)670-3644. **E-mail:** contact@artinforms.com; contact@marthaproductions.com. **Website:** www.marthaproductions.com/AI/ai.html. **Contact:** Martha Spelman, president. Estab. 2000. Commercial illustration representative. Specializes in illustrators who create informational graphics and technical drawings, including maps, charts, diagrams, cutaways, flow charts and more.

ARTISAN CREATIVE, INC.

(310)312-2062. **Fax:** (310)312-0670. **E-mail:** lainfo@artisancreative.com. **Website:** www.artisancreative.com. Estab. 1988. Represents creative directors, art directors, graphic designers, illustrators, animators (3D and 2D), storyboarders, packaging designers, photographers, web designers, broadcast designers and flash developers. Markets include advertising agencies, corporations/client direct, design firms, entertainment industry.

○ Additional locations in San Francisco, Chicago, New York and Indianapolis. See website for details.

HANDLES Web design, multimedia, illustration, photography and production. Looking for web, packaging, traditional and multimedia-based graphic designers.

TERMS 100% of advertising costs paid by the representative. For promotional purposes, talent must provide PDFs of work. Advertises in magazines for the trade, direct mail and the Internet.

HOW TO CONTACT For first contact, e-mail résumé to creative staffing department. "You will then be contacted if a portfolio review is needed." Portfolio should include roughs, tearsheets, photographs, or color photos of your best work.

TIPS "Have at least 2 years of working experience and a great portfolio."

ARTWORKS ILLUSTRATION

325 W. 38th St., Suite 1605, New York NY 10018. (212)239-4946. **Fax:** (212)239-6106. **E-mail:** artworksillustration@earthlink.net. **Website:** www.artworksillustration.com. Estab. 1990. Commercial illustration representative. Member of Society of Illustrators. Represents 30 illustrators. Specializes in publishing. Markets include advertising agencies, design firms, paper products/greeting cards, movie studios, publishing/books, sales/promotion firms, corporations/client direct, editorial/magazines, video games. Artists include Dan Brown, Dennis Lyall, Jerry Vanderstelt and Chris Cocozza.

HANDLES Illustration. Looking for interesting juvenile, digital sci-fi/fantasy & romance images.

TERMS Rep receives 30% commission. Exclusive area representation required. Advertising costs are split: 75% paid by artist; 25% paid by rep. Advertises in *American Showcase* and on www.theispot.com. *How to Contact* for first contact, send e-mail samples. Responds only if interested.

BERENDSEN & ASSOCIATES, INC.

5 W. Fifth St., Suite 300, Covington KY 41011. (513)861-1400. **Fax:** (859)980-0820. **E-mail:** bob@illustratorsrep.com; info@illustratorsrep.com. **Website:** www.illustratorsrep.com; www.photographersrep.com; www.designersrep.com; www.stockartrep.com. Estab. 1986. Commercial illustration, photography, design representative. Represents 70 illustrators, 15 photographers. Specializes in "high-visibility consumer accounts." Markets include advertising agencies, corporations/client direct, design firms, editorial/magazines, paper products/greeting cards, pub-

lishing/books, sales/promotion firms. Clients include Disney, CNN, Pentagram, F+W. Additional client list available upon request. Represents Bill Fox, Kevin Torline, Judy Hand, Frank Ordaz, Wendy Ackison, Jack Pennington, Ursula Roma, John Sledd, Richard Cowdrey, Corey Wolfe, John Margeson, Paul Lopez and Tony Randazzo.

HANDLES Illustration, photography and web design. "We are always looking for illustrators who can draw people, product and action well. Also, we look for styles that are metaphoric in content, and it's a plus if the stock rights are available."

TERMS Rep receives 30% commission. Charges "mostly for postage, but figures not available." No geographic restrictions. Advertising costs are split: 70% paid by talent; 30% paid by rep. For promotional purposes, "artist can co-op in our direct mail promotions, and sourcebooks are recommended. Portfolios are updated regularly." Advertises in *RSVP*, *Creative Illustration Book*, *Directory of Illustration* and *American Showcase*.

HOW TO CONTACT For first contact, send an e-mail with no more than 6 JPEGs attached; or send query letter and any nonreturnable tearsheets, slides, photographs or photocopies.

TIPS Artists should have "a proven style" with at least 10 samples of that style.

BERNSTEIN & ANDRIULLI

58 W. 40th St., 6th Floor, New York NY 10018. (212)682-1490. **Fax:** (212)286-1890. **E-mail:** info@ba-reps.com. **Website:** www.ba-reps.com. Estab. 1975. Commercial illustration and photography representative. Member of SPAR. Represents 100 illustrators, 52 photographers. Markets include advertising agencies, corporations/client direct, design firms, editorial/magazines, paper products/greeting cards, publishing/books, sales/promotion firms.

HANDLES Illustration, new media and photography.

TERMS Rep receives a commission. Exclusive career representation is required. No geographic restrictions. Advertises in *The Black Book*, *Workbook*, *Bernstein Andriulli International Illustration*, *CA Magazine*, *Archive*, *American Illustration/Photography*.

HOW TO CONTACT Send query e-mail with website or digital files. Call to schedule an appointment before dropping off portfolio.

JOANIE BERNSTEIN, ART REP

756 Eighth Ave. S., Naples FL 34102. (239)403-4393. **Fax:** (239)403-0066. **E-mail:** joanie@joaniebrep.com. **Website:** www.joaniebrep.com. Estab. 1984. Commercial illustration representative.

HANDLES Illustration. Looking for an unusual, problem-solving style. Clients include advertising, design, animation, books, music, product merchandising, developers, movie studios, films, private collectors.

TERMS Rep receives 25% commission. Exclusive representation required.

HOW TO CONTACT E-mail samples.

TIPS "I'd strongly advise an updated website. Also add 'What's New'—show off new work."

BLASCO CREATIVE ARTISTS

110 S. William St., Mount Prospect IL 60056. (312)782-0244. **E-mail:** jean@blascocreative.com. **Website:** www.blascocreative.com. **Contact:** Jean Blasco. Estab. 1988. Commercial illustration and photography/CGI. Represents 20+ internationally acclaimed illustrators and 3 celebrated photographers. Markets include advertising agencies; corporations; design firms; editorial/magazines; publishing/books; promotion and packaging. Clients include "every major player in the United States."

HANDLES Illustration. "We are receptive to reviewing samples by enthusiastic up-and-coming artists. E-mail samples and/or your website address."

TERMS Exclusive area representation is preferred. For promotional purposes, talent must provide printed promotional pieces and a well organized, creative portfolio. "If your book is not ready to show, be willing to invest in a new one." Advertises in *Workbook*, *Directory of Illustration*, *Folio Planet*, *Found Folios*, www.theispot.com.

HOW TO CONTACT For first contact, send samples via e-mail, or printed materials that do not have to be returned. Responds only if interested. Obtains new talent through recommendations from art directors, referrals and submissions.

TIPS "You need to be true to yourself as an artist..define your direction and style and don't bend to commercial whims. I like to see an artist who creates imagery not only for commissioned projects but also for his/her own personal fulfillment."

BROWN INK GALLERY

222 E. Brinkerhoff Ave., Palisades Park NJ 07650. (973)865-4966. **Fax:** (201)461-6571 (call first). **E-mail:** robert229artist@juno.com. **Website:** www.brownink gallery.com. **Contact:** Bob Brown, president/owner. Estab. 1978. Digital fine art publisher and distributor. Represents 5 fine artists, 2 illustrators. Specializes in advertising, magazine editorials and book publishing, fine art. Markets include advertising agencies, corporations/client direct, design firms, editorial/magazines, galleries, movie studios, paper products/greeting cards, publishing/books, record companies, sales/promotion firms.

HANDLES Fine art, illustration, digital fine art, digital fine art printing, licensing material. Looking for professional artists who are interested in making a living with their art. Art samples and portfolio required.

TERMS Rep receives 25% commission on illustration assignment; 50% on publishing (digital publishing) after expenses. "The only fee we charge is for services rendered (scanning, proofing, printing, etc.). We pay for postage, labels and envelopes." Exclusive area representation required (only in the NY, NJ, CT region of the country). Advertising costs are paid by artist or split: 75% paid by artist; 25% paid by rep. Artists must pay for their own promotional material. For promotional purposes, talent must provide a full-color direct mail piece, an 8½×11 flexible portfolio, digital files and CD.

HOW TO CONTACT For first contact, send bio, direct mail flier/brochure, photocopies, photographs, résumé, SASE, tearsheets, slides, digital images/CD, query letter (optional). Responds only if interested. After initial contact, call to schedule an appointment, drop off or mail portfolio, or e-mail. Portfolio should include b&w and color finished art, original art, photographs, slides, tearsheets, transparencies (35mm, 4½ and 8×10).

TIPS "Be as professional as possible! Your presentation is paramount. The competition is fierce, therefore your presentation (portfolio) and art samples need to match or exceed that of the competition."

⊙ CONTACT JUPITER, INC.

1410 William St., Montreal Quebec H3C 1R5, Canada. (514)572-0388; (646)290-5405. **E-mail:** oliver@con tactjupiter.com; info@contactjupiter.com. **Website:** www.contactjupiter.com. **Contact:** Oliver Mielenz, creative facilitator. Estab. 1996. Commercial illus-

tration representative. Represents 17 illustrators, 6 photographers. Specializes in creating images for advertising and publishing clients. Licenses illustrators and photographers. Markets include advertising agencies, paper products/greeting cards, record companies, publishing/books, corporations/client direct and editorial/magazines.

HANDLES Illustration, multimedia, music, photography, design.

TERMS Rep receives 15-25% and rep fee. Advertising costs are split: 90% paid by artist; 10% paid by rep. Exclusive representation required. For promotional purposes, talent must provide electronic art samples only. Advertises in *Directory of Illustration*.

HOW TO CONTACT Send query by e-mail with several low-res JPEGs, along with your information, target markets and experiences. "If we think you've got what we need, we'll be in touch."

TIPS "One specific style is easier to sell. Focus, focus, focus. Initiative, I find, is very important in an artist."

CORNELL & COMPANY, ILLUSTRATION AND DESIGN

44 Jog Hill Rd., Trumball CT 06611. (203)454-4210. **Fax:** (203)454-4258. **E-mail:** merial@cornellandco. com. **Website:** www.cornellandco.com. **Contact:** Merial Cornell. Estab. 1989. Member of SCBWI and Graphic Artists Guild. Cornell & Company (formerly Cornell & McCarthy, LLC) represents a diverse group of talented, professional artists specailizaing illustration of children's picutre books, educational materials, magazines, stationery, kids products, and toys. "Please visit our website for an overview of our group iillustrators. Cornell & Company also provides consulting, art buying services and support for large projects."

TERMS For first contact, send query letter, direct mail brochures or postcards, color copies. Samples are not returned. Will reply only if interested. Also interested in author/illustrators. Obtains new talent through recommendations from industry contacts, solicitation, submissions and conferences.

CWC INTERNATIONAL, INC.

330 Pearl St., #2B, New York NY 10038. (646)486-6586. **E-mail:** agent@cwc-i.com; contact@cwc-i.com. **Website:** www.cwc-i.com. Estab. 1999. Commercial ilustration representative. Represents 23 illustrators. Specializes in advertising, fashion. Markets include advertising agencies, corporations/client direct, de-

sign firms, editorial/magazines, galleries, paper products/greeting cards, publishing/books, record companies. Artists include Jeffrey Fulvimari, Stina Persson, Chris Long and Kenzo Minami.

HANDLES Fine art, illustration.

TERMS Exclusive area representation required.

HOW TO CONTACT Submission guidelines available online.

TIPS "Please do not call. When sending any image samples by e-mail, be sure the entire file will not exceed 2MB."

LINDA DE MORETA REPRESENTS

(510)769-1421. **E-mail:** linda@lindareps.com. **Website:** www.lindareps.com. Estab. 1988. Commercial illustration, calligraphy/handlettering, storyboards/comps, motion graphics and photography representative. Represents 10 illustrators, 2 photographers. Markets include advertising agencies; design firms; corporations/client direct; editorial/magazines; paper products/greeting cards; publishing/books. Represents Chuck Pyle, Pete McDonnell, Monica Dengo, James Yamasaki, John Howell, Shannon Abbey, Shan O'Neill and Mack Dee.

HANDLES Photography, illustration, lettering/title design, storyboards/comps, motion graphics, and animation.

TERMS Commission, exclusive representation requirements and advertising costs are according to individual agreements. Materials for promotional purposes vary with each artist. Advertises in *Workbook*, *Directory of Illustration*.

HOW TO CONTACT For first contact, e-mail samples or link to website. Responds to any inquiry in which there is an interest. Portfolios are individually developed for each artist.

TIPS Obtains new talent through client and artist referrals primarily, some solicitation. "We look for great creativity, a personal vision and well developed style combined with professionalism, and passion."

THE DESKTOP GROUP

420 Lexington Ave., 21st Floor, New York NY 10170. (212)916-0805. **Fax:** (212)867-1759. **E-mail:** info@desktopgroup.com. **Website:** www.thedesktopgroup.com. Estab. 1991. Specializes in recruiting and placing creative talent on a freelance basis. Markets include advertising agencies, design firms, publishers (book and magazine), corporations, and banking/financial firms.

HANDLES Artists with Mac and Windows software and multimedia expertise—graphic designers, production artists, prepress technicians, presentation specialists, traffickers, art directors, Web designers, content developers, project managers, copywriters, and proofreaders.

HOW TO CONTACT For first contact, e-mail résumé, cover letter and work samples.

TIPS "Our clients prefer working with talented artists who have flexible, easy-going personalities and who are very professional."

LIBBY FORD ARTIST REPRESENTATIVE

320 E. 57th St. 10B, New York NY 10022. (212)935-8068. **Website:** www.libbyford.com. Represents over 45 illustrators. Specializes in children's trade books, young adult and educational markets.

TERMS Portfolios samples should be sent electronically. Will contact you for additional materials.

ROBERT GALITZ FINE ART & ACCENT ART

166 Hilltop Court, Sleepy Hollow IL 60118. (847)426-8842. **E-mail:** robert@galitzfineart.com. **Website:** www.galitzfineart.com. **Contact:** Robert Galitz, owner. Estab. 1986. Fine art representative. Represents 100 fine artists (including 2 sculptors). Specializes in contemporary/abstract corporate art. Markets include architects, corporate collections, galleries, interior decorators, private collections. Represents Louis De Mayo.

HANDLES Fine art.

TERMS Agent receives 25-40% commission. No geographic restrictions; sells mainly in Chicago, Wisconsin, Indiana and Kentucky. For promotional purposes, talent must provide "good photos and slides." Advertises in monthly art publications and guides.

HOW TO CONTACT Send query letter, slides, photographs. Responds in 2 weeks. After initial contact, call for appointment to show portfolio of original art. Obtains new talent through recommendations from others, solicitation, conferences.

TIPS "Be confident and persistent. Never give up or quit."

● GRAHAM-CAMERON ILLUSTRATION

59 Hertford Rd., Brighton BN1 7GG, United Kingdom. +44(0)1273 385890. **E-mail:** enquiry@gciforillustration.com. **Website:** www.gciforillustration.com. **Contact:** Helen Graham-Cameron, art director. Estab. 1985. Commercial illustration representative. Represents 45 illustrators. Agency specializes in

Childrens' and Educational Illustration. Markets include designer firms and publishing/books.

HANDLES Illustration.

TERMS Rep receives 30% standard commission. Exclusive representation required. Advertising costs are 100% paid by representative. May occasionally be asked to supply an illustration to representative's brief.

HOW TO CONTACT For first contact, talent should send link to website. Responds in 3 months.

TIPS Obtains new talent through submissions.

ANITA GRIEN REPRESENTING ARTISTS

155 E. 38th St., New York NY 10016. (212)697-6170; (917)494-3826 (cell). **E-mail:** anita@anitagrien.com. **Website:** www.anitagrien.com. Representative not currently seeking new talent.

CAROL GUENZI AGENTS, INC.

865 Delaware St., Denver CO 80204. (303)820-2599; (800)417-5120. **E-mail:** art@artagent.com. **Website:** www.artagent.com. **Contact:** Carol Guenzi, president. Estab. 1984. Commercial illustration, photography, new media and film/animation representative. Represents 18 illustrators, 8 photographers, 4 film/animation developers, and 3 multimedia developers, copywriter. Specializes in a "worldwide selection of talent in all areas of visual communications." Markets include advertising agencies, corporations/client direct, design firms, editorial/magazines, paper products/greeting cards, sales/promotions firms. Clients: Miller/Coors, Celestial Seasonings, Audi, Northface, Whole Foods, Western Union, American Blue Ribbon Holding, Coca-Cola, Bacardi, First Data, Quiznos, Starbucks, Boston Market, Nike, etc. Client list available upon request. Represents Christer Eriksson, Bruce Hutchison, Kym Foster, Jeff Pollard, Kelly Hume and many more; Illustration, photography. Looking for "unique style application."

TERMS Rep receives 25-30% commission. Exclusive area representation is required. Advertising costs are split: 70-75% paid by talent; 25-30% paid by rep. For promotional purposes, talent must provide "promotional material; some restrictions on portfolios." Advertises in Directory of Illustration, Workbook, social marketing.

HOW TO CONTACT For first contact, e-mail PDFs or JPEGs with link to URL, or send direct mail flier/brochure. Responds only if interested. E-mail electronic files. Portfolio should include promotional material or electronic files. Obtains new talent through solicitation, art directors' referrals, and active pursuit by individual artists.

TIPS "Show your strongest style and have at least 12 samples of that style before introducing all your capabilities. Be prepared to add additional work to your portfolio to help round out your style. Have a digital background."

HOLLY HAHN & CO.

1852 W. Greenleaf, Chicago IL 60626. (312)371-0500. **E-mail:** holly@hollyhahn.com. **Website:** www.hollyhahn.com. Estab. 1988. Commercial illustration and photography representative.

HANDLES Illustration, photography.

HOW TO CONTACT Send direct mail flier/brochure and tearsheets.

HERMAN AGENCY

350 Central Park West, New York NY 10025. (212)749-4907. **E-mail:** Ronnie@hermanagencyinc.com. **Website:** www.hermanagencyinc.com. Estab. 1999. Literary and artistic agency for children's books. Member of SCBWI, Graphic Artists' Guild and Authors' Guild. Some of the illustrators represented: Michael Rex, Troy Cummings, Geoffrey Hayes. Currently not accepting new clients unless they have been successfully published by major trade publishing houses.

HANDLES Illustration. Looking for authors and artists with strong history of publishing in the children's market.

TERMS Offers written exclusive contract. Advertising costs are split: 75% paid by illustrator; 25% paid by rep.

HOW TO CONTACT For first contact, e-mail only. Responds in 8-16 weeks. For first contact, artists or author/artists should e-mail a link to their website with bio and list of published books as well as new picture book or dummy to Ronnie. We will contact you only if your samples are right for us. For first contact, authors of middle-grade should e-mail bio, list of published books and first ten pages. Finds illustrators and authors through recommendations from others, conferences, queries/solicitations.

TIPS "Check our website to see if you belong with our agency."

SCOTT HULL ASSOCIATES

3875 Ferry Rd., Bellbrook OH 45305. (937)433-8383. **Fax:** (937)433-0434. **E-mail:** scott@scotthull.com. **Website:** www.scotthull.com. **Contact:** Scott Hull. Estab. 1981. Specialized illustration representative. Represents 25+ illustrators.

HOW TO CONTACT Send e-mail samples or appropriate materials for review. No original art. Follow up with e-mail. Responds in 1 week.

TIPS Looks for interesting talent with a passion to grow, as well as a strong, in-depth portfolio.

VINCENT KAMIN & ASSOCIATES

(312)685-8834. **Fax:** (312)787-8834. **E-mail:** vinceka min@att.net. Estab. 1971. Commercial photography, graphic design representative. Member of SPAR. Represents 6 illustrators, 6 photographers, 1 designer, 1 fine artist (includes 1 sculptor). Markets include advertising agencies.

HANDLES Illustration, photography.

TERMS Rep receives 30% commission. Advertising costs are split: 90% paid by talent; 10% paid by representative. Advertises in *Workbook* and *Chicago Directory*.

HOW TO CONTACT Send tearsheets. Responds in 10 days. After initial contact, call to schedule an appointment. Portfolio should include tearsheets.

CLIFF KNECHT—ARTIST REPRESENTATIVE

309 Walnut Rd., Pittsburgh PA 15202. (412)761-5666. **E-mail:** cliff@artrep1.com. **Website:** www.artrep1. com. **Contact:** Cliff Knecht. Estab. 1972. Commercial illustration representative. Represents more than 20 illustrators. Markets include advertising agencies, corporations/client direct, design firms, editorial/ magazines, paper products/greeting cards, publishing/books, sales/promotion firms.

HANDLES Illustration.

TERMS Rep receives 25% commission. No geographic restrictions. Advertising costs are split: 75% paid by the talent; 25% paid by representative. For promotional purposes, talent must provide a direct mail piece. Advertises in *Graphic Artists Guild Directory of Illustration*.

HOW TO CONTACT Send résumé, direct mail flier/ brochure, tearsheets, and send JPEG samples by e-mail. Responds in 1 week. After initial contact, call for appointment to show portfolio of original art, tearsheets, slides, photographs. Obtains new talent directly or through recommendations from others.

SHARON KURLANSKY ASSOCIATES

192 Southville Rd., Southborough MA 01772. (508)733-2761. **Fax:** (508)480-9221. **E-mail:** sharon@ laughing-stock.com. **Website:** www.laughing-stock. com. **Contact:** Sharon Kurlansky. Estab. 1978. Commercial illustration representative. Represents illus-

trators. Clients: advertising agencies; corporations/ client direct; design firms; editorial/magazines; paper products/greeting cards; publishing/books; sales/promotion firms. Client list available upon request. Represents Tim Lewis, Blair Thornley, and Ronald Slabbers. Licenses stock illustration for 150 illustrators at www.laughing-stock.com in all markets.

HANDLES Illustration.

TERMS Rep receives 25% commission. Exclusive area representation is required. Advertising costs are split: 75% paid by talent; 25% paid by representative. "Will develop promotional materials with talent. Portfolio presentation formated and developed with talent also."

HOW TO CONTACT For first contact, e-mail with website address/online portfolio. Responds in 1 month if interested.

CRISTOPHER LAPP PHOTOGRAPHY

1211 Sunset Plaza Dr., Suite 413, Los Angeles CA 90069. (310)612-0040. **E-mail:** cristopherlapp.pho to@gmail.com. **Website:** www.cristopherlapp.com. **Contact:** Cristopher Lapp. Estab. 1994. Specializes in canvas transfers, fine art prints, hand-pulled originals, limited edition.

HANDLES Decorative art, fashionable art, commercial and designer marketing. Clients include: Posner Fine Art, Gilanyi Inc., Jordan Designs.

TERMS Keeps samples on file.

HOW TO CONTACT Send an e-mail inquiry.

MAGNET REPS

1783 S. Crescent Heights Blvd., Los Angeles CA 90035. **E-mail:** art@magnetreps.com. **Website:** www.mag netreps.com. Estab. 1999. Commercial illustration and art licensing agency. Represents 18 illustrators. Clients: advertising agencies, corporations/client direct, design firms, editorial/magazines, movie studios, publishing/books, record companies, character development and art licensing across all product categories. Represents: Red Nose Studio, Bella Pilar, Emiliano Ponzi, Yelena Bryksenkova, Graham Roumieu, Dinara Mirtalipova, Pieter Van Eenoge and Eleanor Grosch among others.

HANDLES Illustration. "Looking for artists with the passion to illustrate every day, an awareness of cultural trends in the world we live in, and a basic understanding of the business of illustration."

TERMS Exclusive representation required. Advertising costs are split. For promotional purposes, talent must provide a well-developed, consistent portfolio.
HOW TO CONTACT Submit a web link to online portfolio, or send 3 sample low-res JPEGs for review via e-mail only. Responds in approximately 1 month. "We do not return unsolicited submissions." Will contact artist via e-mail if interested.
TIPS "Be realistic about how your style aligns with our agency. We do not represent scientific, technical, medical, sci-fi, fantasy, military, hyper-realistic, story boarding, landscape, pin-up, cartoon or cutesy styles. We do not represent graphic designers or photographers, and we will not represent illustrators that imitate the style of a contemporary illustrator."

MARLENA AGENCY

278 Hamilton Ave., Princeton NJ 08540. (609)252-9405. **Fax:** (609)252-9408. **E-mail:** marlena@marlenaagency.com. **Website:** www.marlenaagency.com. Estab. 1990. Commercial illustration representative. Represents approx. 30 illustrators from France, Poland, Germany, Hungary, Italy, Spain, Canada and US. "We speak English, French and Polish." Specializes in conceptual illustration. Markets include advertising agencies, corporations/client direct, design firms, editorial/magazines, publishing/books, theaters.
HANDLES Illustration, fine art and prints.
TERMS Rep receives 30% commission; 35% if translation needed. Costs are shared by all artists. Exclusive area representation is required. Advertising costs are split: 70% paid by talent; 30% paid by representative. For promotional purposes, talent must provide e-mailed and direct mail pieces, 3-4 portfolios. Advertises in *Workbook*. Many of the artists are regularly featured in *CA* annuals, The Society of Illustrators annuals, and American Illustration annuals. Agency produces promotional materials for artists, such as wrapping paper, calendars, and brochures.
HOW TO CONTACT Send tearsheets or e-mail low-resolution images. Responds in 1 week, only if interested. After initial contact, drop off or mail appropriate materials. Portfolio should include tearsheets.
TIPS Wants artists with "talent, good concepts-intelligent illustration, promptness in keeping up with projects, deadlines, etc."

MARTHA PRODUCTIONS, INC.

7550 W. 82nd St., Playa Del Rey CA 90293. (310)670-5300. **Fax:** (310)670-3644. **E-mail:** contact@marthaproductions.com. **Website:** www.marthaproductions.com. **Contact:** Martha Spelman, president. Estab. 1978. Commercial illustration representative. Represents 45 illustrators. Also licenses the work of illustrators. Specializes in illustration in various styles and media. Markets include advertising agencies; corporations/client direct; design firms; developers; editorial/magazines; paper products/greeting cards; publishing/books; record companies; sales/promotion firms.
HANDLES Illustration. "Reps illustrators for assignment illustration in a range of styles."
TERMS Rep receives 30% commission. Advertising costs are split: 70% paid by talent; 30% paid by representative. For promotional purposes, talent must be on our website. Advertises in *Workbook*.
HOW TO CONTACT For first contact, e-mail a few small JPEG files. Responds only if interested. Portfolio shold include b&w and color samples. Obtains new talent through recommendations and solicitation.
TIPS "An artist seeking representation should have a strong portfolio with pieces relevant to advertising, corporate collateral or publishing markets. Check the rep's website or ads to see the other talent they represent to determine whether the artist could be an asset to that rep's group or if there may be a conflict. Reps are looking for new artists who already have a portfolio of salable pieces, a willingness to invest advertising of their own work and experience working in commercial art."

MB ARTISTS

775 Sixth Ave., #6, New York NY 10001. (212)689-7830. **E-mail:** mela@mbartists.com. **Website:** www.mbartists.com. **Contact:** Mela Bolinao. Estab. 1986. Juvenile illustration representative. Member of SPAR, Society of Illustrators and SCBWI. Represents over 45 illustrators. Specializes in illustration for juvenile markets. Markets include advertising agencies; editorial/magazines; publishing/books; toys/games.
HANDLES Illustration.
TERMS Exclusive representation required. Rep receives 25% commission. No geographic restrictions. Advertising costs are split: 75% paid by talent; 25% paid by representative. Advertises in *Picture Book*, *Directory of Illustration*, *Play Directory*, *Workbook*, folioplanet.com, and www.theispot.com.

HOW TO CONTACT E-mail query letter with website address or send portfolio with flier/brochure, tear sheets, published books if available, and SASE. Responds in 1 week. Portfolio should include at least 10-15 images exhibiting a consistent style.

TIPS Leans toward "highly individual personal styles."

MENDOLA ARTISTS

420 Lexington Ave., New York NY 10170. (212)986-5680. **Fax:** (212)818-1246. **E-mail:** info@mendolaart. com. **Website:** www.mendolaart.com. Estab. 1961. Commercial illustration representative. Member of Society of Illustrators, Graphic Artists Guild. Represents 60 or more illustrators. Markets include advertising agencies; corporations/client direct; design firms; editorial/magazines; sales/promotion firms. "Representing the industry's leading illustration talent worldwide, we work with the top agencies, magazine corporations, and publishers. Exclusive representation is usually required. Send us an e-mail with a link to your website or JPEGs. We will contact you if interested in seeing additional work."

MHS LICENSING

11100 Wayzata Blvd., Suite 550, Minneapolis MN 55305. (952)544-1377. **Fax:** (952)544-8663. **E-mail:** marty@mhslicensing.com; artreviewcommittee@ mhslicensing.com. **Website:** www.mhslicensing.com. **Contact:** Marty H. Segelbaum, president. Estab. 1995. Licensing agency. Represents over 30 fine artists, photographers, illustrators and brands. Markets include paper products/greeting cards, publishing/books and other consumer products including giftware, stationery/paper, tabletop, apparel, home fashions, textiles, etc. Artists include Al Agnew, Amy Hautman, Amylee Weeks, Audrey Jeanne Roberts, Christine Adolph, Collin Bogle, Corbert Gauthier, Cranston Collection, Darrell Bush, H. Hargrove, Hautman Brothers, James Meger, Josephine Kimberling, Judy Buswell, Julie Ingleman, Kathy Hatch, Lisa Weedn, Louise Carey, Luis Fitch, Marcie St. Clair, Paper D'Art, Patrick Reid O'Brien, Robin Roderick, Ron King, Stacey Yacula, Stephanie Ryan, Terry Doughty, Tina Higgins, Val Warner and Victoria Schultz. Brands include Buck Wear, Mamasana, Munki Munki, Museware by Sheree, Smirk, Sparky & Marie and The Girls.

HANDLES Fine art, illustration, photography and brand concepts.

TERMS Negotiable with firm.

HOW TO CONTACT Send query letter with bio, tearsheets, approximately 10 low-res JPEGs via e-mail. See submission guidelines on website. "Keep your submission simple and affordable by leaving all the fancy packaging, wrapping and enclosures in your studio. 8½×11 tearsheets (inkjet is fine) and your biography are all that we need for review." Responds in 6 weeks. "No phone calls, please." Send SASE for return of material.

TIPS "Our mutual success is based on providing manufacturers with trend-forward artwork. Please don't duplicate what is already on the market but think instead, 'What are consumers going to want to buy in 9 months, 1 year, or 2 years?' We want to learn how you envision your artwork being applied to a variety of product types. Artists are encouraged to submit their artwork mocked-up into potential product collections ranging from stationery to tabletop to home fashion (kitchen, bed and bath). Visit your local department store or mass retailer to learn more about the key items in these categories. And, if you have multiple artwork styles, include them with your submission."

MORGAN GAYNIN, INC.

149 Madison Ave., Suite 1140, New York NY 10016. (212)475-0440. **Fax:** (212)475-0598. **E-mail:** info@ morgangaynin.com; submissions@morgangaynin. com. **Website:** www.morgangaynin.com. **Contact:** Gail Gaynin. Estab. 1974. Currently not accepting submissions. See website for updates. Markets include advertising agencies; corporations/client direct; design firms; magazines; books;children's books; sales/promotion firms.

TERMS Rep receives 30% commission. Exclusive area representation is required. No geographic restrictions. Advertising costs are split: 70% paid by talent; 30% paid by representative. Advertises in directories, on the Web, direct mail.

HOW TO CONTACT Follow submission guidelines on website.

MUNRO CAMPAGNA ARTISTS REPRESENTATIVES

630 N. State St., #2109, Chicago IL 60654. (312)335-8925. **E-mail:** steve@munrocampagna.com. **Website:** www.munrocampagna.com. **Contact:** Steve Munro, president. Estab. 1987. Commercial illustration, photography representative. Member of SPAR, CAR (Chicago Artists Representatives). Represents 22 illustrators, 2 photographers. Markets include ad-

vertising agencies; corporations/client direct; design firms; publishing/books. Represents Pat Dypold and Douglas Klauba.

HANDLES Illustration.

TERMS Rep receives 25-30% commission. Exclusive area representation is required. Advertising costs are split: 75% paid by talent; 25% paid by representative. For promotional purposes, talent must provide 2 portfolios. Advertises in *The Black Book* and *Workbook*.

HOW TO CONTACT For first contact, send query letter, bio, tearsheets and SASE. Responds in 2 weeks. After initial contact, write to schedule an appointment.

THE NEWBORN GROUP, INC.

(212)989-4600. **E-mail:** joan@newborngroup.com. **Website:** www.newborngroup.com. Estab. 1964. Commercial illustration representative. Member of Society of Illustrators; Graphic Artists Guild. Represents 15 illustrators. Markets include advertising agencies, design firms, editorial/magazines, publishing/books. Clients include Leo Burnett, Penguin Putnam, Time Inc., Weschler Inc.

HANDLES Illustration.

TERMS Rep receives 30% commission. Exclusive area representation is required. Advertising costs are split: 70% paid by talent; 30% paid by representative. Advertises in *Workbook* and *Directory of Illustration*.

HOW TO CONTACT "Not reviewing new talent."

PAINTED WORDS

310 W. 97th St., Suite 24, New York NY 10025. **Fax:** (212)663-2891. **E-mail:** info@painted-words.com; submissions@painted-words.com. **Website:** www.painted-words.com. Estab. 1993. Literary agent for children's books. Represents 40 authors and illustrators. Markets include children's publishing and licensed products.

HANDLES Illustration and author/illustrators.

TERMS Exclusive area representation is required.

HOW TO CONTACT "An artist seeking representation is encouraged to send a link to his or her website. We are currently seeking illustrators to add to our children's publishing group, specifically those who have a talent for writing. Please do not e-mail manuscripts. If we are interested in the art style, we will request a writing sample. All samples and unsolicited manuscripts submitted via regular mail will be returned unopened."

DEBORAH PEACOCK PRODUCTIONS

P.O. Box 300127, Austin TX 78703. (512)970-9024. **E-mail:** photo@deborahpeacock.com. **Website:** www.deborahpeacock.com; www.art-n-music.com. **Contact:** Deborah Peacock. Booking, graphic design, public relations, photography and consultancy. Deborah Peacock Productions caters to businesses, products, actors and musicians, performing and visual artists; product photography, special events, videography and graphic/web design. Represents entertainers for private parties and special events.

HANDLES Considers all media and all types of prints.

MARIA PISCOPO

1684 Decoto Rd., #271, Union City CA 94587. (714)356-4260. **E-mail:** maria@mpiscopo.com. **Website:** www.mpiscopo.com. **Contact:** Maria Piscopo. Estab. 1978. Commercial photography representative. Member of SPAR, Women in Photography, Society of Illustrative Photographers. Market includes: advertising agencies, corporate and designer firms. Interested in reviewing illustration, photography, fine art and design. Representatives receive 25% commission.

TERMS Send query letter and samples via PDF to maria@mpiscopo.com. Do not call. Responds within 2 weeks, only if interested. E-mail for specifications of artwork.

TIPS Obtains new talent through personal referral and photo magazine articles. "Do lots of research. Be very businesslike, organized, professional and follow the above instructions!"

CAROLYN POTTS & ASSOCIATES, INC.

P.O. Box 6214, Evanston IL 60204. (312)560-6400; (847)864-7644. **E-mail:** carolyn@cpotts.com. **Website:** www.cpotts.com. Estab. 1976. Commercial photography representative and marketing consultant for creative professionals. 30 years experience in landing assignments for commercial photographers. Specializes in contemporary advertising and design. Markets include advertising agencies, corporations/client direct, design firms.

HANDLES Photography.

TERMS Rep receives 30-35% commission. Artists share cost of their direct mail postage and preparation. Exclusive representation is required. Advertising costs are split: 70% paid by artist; 30% paid by rep (after initial trial period wherein artist pays 100%). For promotional purposes, talent must have website and provide direct mail piece.

HOW TO CONTACT For first contact, send e-mail. Responds within 3 days. After initial contact, write to schedule an appointment. Portfolio should include examples of published work.

TIPS Looking for artists with high level of professionalism, awareness of current advertising market, professional presentation materials and website and a positive, proactive attitude.

CHRISTINE PRAPAS/ARTIST REPRESENTATIVE

8402 SW Woods Creek Court, Portland OR 97219. (503)245-9511. **Fax:** (503)245-9512. **E-mail:** christine@christineprapas.com. **Website:** www.christineprapas.com. Estab. 1978. Commercial illustration and photography representative. Member of AIGA and Graphic Artists Guild. "Promotional material welcome."

KERRY REILLY REPS

1826 Asheville Place, Charlotte NC 28203. (704)372-6007. **E-mail:** kerry@reillyreps.com. **Website:** www.reillyreps.com. **Contact:** Kerry Reilly. Estab. 1990. Commercial illustration and photography representative. Represents 16 illustrators, 2 photographers and animatics. Markets include advertising agencies; corporations/client direct; design firms; editorial/magazines. Clients include GM, VW, Walt Disney World, USPO.

○ Kerry Reilly Reps is partnering with Steven Edsey & Sons.

HANDLES Illustration, photography. Looking for computer graphics Photoshop, Illustrator, FreeHand, etc.

TERMS Rep receives 25% commission. Exclusive area representation is required. No geographic restrictions. Advertising costs are split 75% paid by talent; 25% paid by representative. For promotional purposes, talent must provide at least 2 pages printed leave-behind samples. Preferred format is 9×12 pages, portfolio work on 4×5 transparencies. Advertises in iSpot.

HOW TO CONTACT For first contact, send direct mail flier/brochure or samples of work. Responds in 2 weeks. After initial contact, call for appointment to show portfolio or drop off or mail tearsheets, slides, 4×5 transparencies.

TIPS "Have printed samples and electronic samples (in JPEG format)."

RETRO REPS

Martha Productions, 7550 W. 82nd St., Playa Del Rey CA 90293. (310)670-5300. **Fax:** (310)670-3644. **E-mail:** contact@marthaproductions.com. **Website:** www.retroreps.com. **Contact:** Martha Spelman, president. Estab. 1998. Commercial illustration representative. Represents 22 illustrators. Specializes in artists working in vintage or retro styles from the 1920s through 1970s.

LILLA ROGERS STUDIO

(781)641-2787. **E-mail:** info@lillarogers.com or via online contact form. **Website:** www.lillarogers.com. **Contact:** Susan McCabe or Jennifer Nelson, agents. Estab. 1984. Commercial illustration representatives. Represents 30+ illustrators. Markets include advertising agencies, corporations/client direct, design firms, editorial/magazines, paper products, publishing/books, prints and posters, sales/promotion firms, children's books, surface design. Artists include Lisa Congdon, Helen Dardik, Sarah Walsh, Jillian Phillips, Mike Lowery, Carolyn Gavin, Bonnie Dain, and Susy Pilgrim Waters.

○ The studio has launched a worldwide new e-course, "Make Art That Sells," and a global talent search, which is the primary way they find their next artist to represent. Visit www.lillarogers.com/school for more details.

HANDLES Illustration.

TERMS Exclusive representation required. Promotions include Surtex NYC trade show, Printsource NYC trade show, Licensing Expo and other events; also runs extensive direct mail and e-mail newsletter campaigns.

HOW TO CONTACT For first contact, e-mail 3-5 low-resolution JPEGs or a link to your website. Responds only if interested.

TIPS "It's good to check out the agency's website to see if you feel like it's a good fit. Explain in your e-mail why you want an agent and why you think we are a good match. No phone calls, please. The very best way to get represented is to enter our annual Global Talent Search."

ROSENTHAL REPRESENTS

3850 Eddingham Ave., Calabasas CA 91302. (818)222-5445. **Fax:** (818)222-5650. **E-mail:** elise@rosenthalrepresents.com; eliselicenses@earthlink.net. **Website:** www.rosenthalrepresents.com. **Contact:** Elise Rosenthal. Estab. 1979. Represents 25 artists and designers geared for creating products, such as: dinnerware, flags, gift bags, textiles (fabric), rugs, placemats, cutting boards, coasters, kitchen and bath textiles, bedding, wall hangings, children's and baby products, stationery, and more. Specializes in licensing, merchandising art. Markets include manufacturers of tabletop products (dinnerware), rugs, kitchen and bath textiles, paper products/greeting cards, and more. Handles product designers and artists. Must know Photoshop and other computer programs to help artist adapt art into product mockups.

TERMS Rep receives 50% as a licensing agent. Exclusive licensing representation is required. No geographic restrictions. "Artist contributes $1,000 once a year to exhibit with us at our 2 all important trade shows, Surtex and Licensing Shows." For promotional purposes, talent must provide CD of artwork designs and website link if available. "We advertise in Total Art Licensing. Only contact us if you have done product design and if you are willing to work hard. Must be willing to accept critiques and make corrections."

HOW TO CONTACT Send e-mail, computer link, JPEGs of your work, direct mail flyer/brochure, tearsheets, photocopies, and SASE. Responds in 1 week. After initial contact, call for appointment to show portfolio of tearsheets, photographs, photocopies. Obtains new talent through seeing their work in trade shows, in magazines and through referrels.

SALZMAN INTERNATIONAL

1751 Charles Ave., Arcate CA 95521. (212)997-0115 or (415)285-8267. **E-mail:** rs@salzint.com. **Website:** www.salzint.com. Estab. 1982. Commercial illustration representative. Represents 20 illustrators. 20% of artwork is children's book illustration. Staff includes Richard Salzman. Open to illustrators seeking representation. Accepting both new and established illustrators.

LIZ SANDERS AGENCY

2415 E. Hangman Creek Lane, Spokane WA 99224-8514. (509)993-6400. **E-mail:** liz@lizsanders.com; artsubmissions@lizsanders.com. **Website:** www.lizsanders.com. **Contact:** Liz Sanders, owner. Estab. 1985. Commercial illustration representative. Represents 10 illustrators. Specializes in marketing of individual artists "within an ever-evolving illustration world." Markets include advertising agencies, corporations/client direct, design firms, editorial/magazines, juvenile markets, paper products/greeting cards, publishing/books, record companies, sales/promotion firms.

HANDLES Interested in illustration. "Looking for fresh, unique talent committed to long-term careers whereby the agent/talent relationship is mutually respectful, responsive and measurably successful."

TERMS Rep receives 30% commission. Exclusive representation required. Advertises in *Picturebook*, *American Showcase*, *Workbook*, *Directory of Illustration*, direct mail material, traditional/electronic portfolio for agent's personal presentations; means to advertise—if not substantially, then consistently.

HOW TO CONTACT For first contact, send nonreturnable printed pieces or e-mailed web address. Responds only if interested. After initial contact, call to schedule an appointment, depending on geographic criteria. Portfolio should include tearsheets, photocopies and digital output.

TIPS "Concisely present a single, focused style supported by 8-12 strong samples. Only send a true portfolio upon request."

JOAN SAPIRO ART CONSULTANTS

138 W. 12th Ave., Denver CO 80204. (303)793-0792. **E-mail:** info@sapiroart.com. **Website:** www.sapiroart.com. **Contact:** Kay Brouillette, principal. Estab. 1980. Specializes in "corporate art with other emphasis on hospitality, health care and art consulting/advising to private collectors."

HANDLES All mediums of artwork.

TERMS Artist must be flexible and willing to ship work on consignment. Also must be able to provide sketches, etc., if commission piece involved. No geographic restrictions.

HOW TO CONTACT Mail JPEG images encompassing the range of your work identified with your name, title of work, medium, dimensions, and pricing contact information, pertinent information about your art and process. Optional inclusions: biography, CV or resume. Be willing to work on a commission basis. Please enclose a stamped, self-addressed envelope if you would like us to return your CD or printed images.

TIPS Obtains new talent through recommendations, publications, travel, research, university faculty.

FREDA SCOTT, INC.

302 Costa Rica Ave., San Mateo CA 94402. (650)548-2446. **E-mail:** freda@fredascott.com. **Website:** www.fredascott.com. **Contact:** Freda Scott, rep/president.

Estab. 1980. Commercial photography, illustration or photography, commercial illustration representative and licensing agent. Represents 12 photographers, 8 illustrators. Licenses photographers and illustrators. Markets include advertising agencies, architects, corporate/client direct, designer firms, developers, direct mail firms, paper products/greeting cards.

HANDLES Illustration, photography.

TERMS Rep receives 25% as standard commission. Advertising costs paid entirely by talent. For promotional purposes, talent must provide mailers/postcards. Advertises in *Workbook* and *American Showcase/Illustrators.*

HOW TO CONTACT Send link to website. Responds, only if interested, within 2 weeks. Rep will contact the talent for portfolio review, if interested.

TIPS Obtains new talent through submissions and recommendations from other artists, art directors and designers.

SUSAN AND CO.

(206)232-7873. **E-mail:** susan@susanandco.com. **Website:** www.susanandco.com. Estab. 1979. Artist representive for commercial illustrators. Represents 12 illustrators. Markets include advertising agencies, corporations, client direct, design firms and publishing/books.

HANDLES Looks for "current illustration styles."

TERMS Rep receives 25% commission. National representation is required. Advertising costs are split: 75% paid by talent; 25% paid by representative.

HOW TO CONTACT For first contact, send e-mail letter and samples. Responds in 2 weeks, only if interested. Portfolio should "be representative of unique style."

⊘ TAENDEM AGENCY

P.O. Box 47054, 15-555 W. 12th Ave., Vancouver British Columbia V5Z 4L6, Canada. (604)569-6544. **E-mail:** talent@taendem.com. **Website:** www.taendem. com. **Contact:** Corwin Hiebert, principal. Estab. 2006. International management agency. Represents a handful of designers and illustrators. Specializes in consulting with freelancers and assisting them with building and growing a successful small creative business. Also full-service business administration and marketing management for creative entrepreneurs. Offerings include: business planning, branding, marketing strategy, portfolio development, website development, social media planning, contract management, client management, project management, proposal writing, estimates and invoicing, itinerate speaking engagements, travel logistics, and production.

HANDLES Illustration, photography, fine art, design and videography.

TERMS Upon acceptance, we charge a minimum monthly retainer of $200 for access and management rights; for specific tasks we use project costing—quoted and applied upon talent's approval. Additional work is quoted and billed upon talent request/approval. Itinerate speaking commission rate is negotiated on a case-by-case basis. Management representation is nonexclusive. Business development consultation available to qualified talent only; full-service management representation is selectively offered at the discretion of the agency. 100% of advertising costs paid by talent. Standard offering includes no paid advertising. Talent must provide full contact information, current headshot, website link and a sample of their work. For photographers, we require 10 select portfolio images.

HOW TO CONTACT Send link to website and full contact information and a brief business description. Portfolio should include large thumbnails, videographers should provide demo reel (Vimeo or YouTube). A business manager will be in contact within 1 week.

TIPS Obtains new talent through submissions and recommendations from other artists. Keep e-mails short and friendly. No phone calls. "Creatives are more likely to generate demand when their business is well-organized and their marketing efforts elicit curiosity instead of trying to stand out in a crowd of talented peers. Growing your business network and developing your portfolio through personal and collaborative projects makes you more attractive to both reps and buyers. If you need help growing your creative small business, just remember: You are Batman. We are Robin."

THOSE 3 REPS

501 Second Ave., Suite A-600, Dallas TX 75226. (214)871-1316. **Fax:** (214)880-0337. **E-mail:** more info@those3reps.com. **Website:** www.those3reps. com. Estab. 1989. Member of Dallas Society of Visual Community. Represents illustrators and photographers. Specializes in commercial art. Clients: advertising agencies, corporations/client direct, design firms, editorial/magazines.

HANDLES Illustration, photography (including digital).

TERMS Rep receives 30% commission. Exclusive area representation is required. Advertising costs are split 70% paid by talent; 30% paid by representative. For promotional purposes, talent must provide 2 new pieces every 2 months, national advertising in sourcebooks and at least 1 mailer. Advertises in *Workbook*, own book.

HOW TO CONTACT For first contact, send query letter and PDFs. Responds in days or weeks only if interested. After initial contact, call to schedule an appointment, drop off or mail in appropriate materials. Portfolio should include digital prints.

TIPS Wants artists with "strong unique consistent style."

☺ THREE IN A BOX, INC.

67 Mowat Ave., Suite 045, Toronto Ontario M6K 3E3, Canada. (212)643-0896 (USA); (416)367-2446 (Canada). **E-mail:** info@threeinabox.com. **Website:** www.threeinabox.com. Estab. 1990. Commercial illustration representative. Member of Graphic Artists Guild. Represents 53 illustrators, 2 photographers. Specializes in illustration. Licenses illustrators and photographers. Markets include advertising agencies, corporations/client direct, design firms, editorial/magazines, paper products/greeting cards, publishing/books, record companies, sales/promotion firms.

HOW TO CONTACT For first contact, e-mail query letter and URL. Responds in 1 week. After initial contact, rep will call if interested. Send only links to website.

CHRISTINA A. TUGEAU: ARTIST AGENCY, LLC

3009 Margaret Jones Lane, Williamsburg VA 23185. **E-mail:** chris@catugeau.com. **Website:** www.catugeau.com. Blog: catugeau.wordpress.com. **Contact:** Christina Tugeau, owner; Christy Ewers, agent. Estab. 1994. Children's publishing market illustration representative (K-12). Member of SCBWI. Represents 30 illustrators. Specializes in children's book publishing and educational market and related areas. Represents Priscilla Burris, Christine Kornacki, Patrice Barton, Roger Motzkus, Melissa Iwai, Jason Wolff, John Kanzler, Martha Aviles, Ana Ochoa, Kelsey Garrity Riley, Lesley Withrow, Nicole Tadgell and Sarah Beise, among others artists of North America.

HANDLES Illustration. Must be proficient at illustrating children and animals in a variety of interactive situations, backgrounds, full color/b&w, and with a strong narrative sense.

TERMS Rep receives 25% commission. Exclusive US representation is required. For promotional purposes, talent must provide direct mail promo(s), 8-10 good "back-up" samples (multiples). North American artists only.

HOW TO CONTACT Christy@catugeau.com. "For first contact, e-mail a few JPEG samples and a live link to website. Responds immediately!"

TIPS "You should have a style uniquely and comfortably your own. Be a cooperative team player and be great with deadlines. Will consider young, new artists to the market with great potential and desire, and of course published, more experienced North American illustrators. Best to study and learn the market standards and expectations by representing yourself for a while when new to the market."

⊕ V PRODUCTIONS

81 N. Roosevelt Ave., Apt. 11, Pasadena CA 91107. **E-mail:** workshopsonlocation@gmail.com. **Website:** www.workshopsonlocation.com. **Contact:** Gina Vriens, principal producer. Estab. 2014. Workshop & event organizer. Represents photographers, illustrators, designers, fine artists. "V Productions allows creative individuals to focus on their craft, while leaving the rest to us. We not only produce workshops, but also provide on-site workshop support and marketing consulting." Markets include corporate/client direct, festival/conference.

HOW TO CONTACT E-mail link to website and bio. Responds in 1 week.

GWEN WALTERS ARTIST REPRESENTATIVE

20 Windsor Lane, Palm Beach Garden FL 33418. (561)805-7739. **E-mail:** artincgw@gmail.com. **Website:** www.gwenwaltersartrep.com. **Contact:** Gwen Walters. Estab. 1976. Commercial illustration representative. Represents 60+ illustrators. Clients: children's book publishing (trade & educational); editorial/magazines; paper products/greeting cards; publishing/books; sales/promotion firms. "I lean more toward book publishing." Represents Gerardo Suzan, Rosario Valderrama, Lane Gregory, Susan Spellman, Judith Pfeiffer, Yvonne Gilbert, Gary Torrisi, Larry Johnson, Pat Paris, Tom Barrett, Linda Pierce and many more.

HANDLES Illustration.

TERMS Rep receives 30% commission.

HOW TO CONTACT For first contact, e-mail portfolio. After initial contact, representative will call. Portfolio should include "as much as possible."

WATSON & SPIERMAN PRODUCTIONS

W+S+W Creative, 636 Broadway, Suite 1122, New York NY 10012. (212)431-4480. **E-mail:** info@wsw creative.com. **Website:** www.watsonspierman.com. Estab. 1992. Commercial illustration/photography representative. Represents 4 illustrators and 11 photographers. Specializes in general illustration, photography. Markets include advertising agencies, design firms, galleries, paper products/greeting cards, record companies, publishing/books, sales/promotion firms, corporations/client direct, editorial/magazines. Photographers include: Henrique Bagulho, Siri Berting, Chris Clor, George Kamper, Dale May, Kan Nakai, Zave Smith, Gandee Vasan, Michael Weschler, and Bret Wills. Illustrators include: Monica Lind, Meghann Powell, Paula Romani, and Ty Wilson. CGI: Plush Post Post Productions, Chris Clor, and Kan Nakai.

HANDLES Comercial, illustration, and photography.

TERMS Rep receives 30% commission. Exclusive representation required. Advertising costs are paid by artist. Artist must publish every year in a sourcebook with all Watson & Spierman talent. Advertises in *The Workbook*.

HOW TO CONTACT For first contact, send link to website. Responds only if interested. After initial contact, drop off or mail portfolio. Portfolio should include b&w, color, finished art, original art, photographs, tearsheets.

TIPS "We love to hear if an artist has an ad out or recently booked a job. Those are the updates that are most important to us."

THE WILEY GROUP

1535 Green St., Suite 301, San Francisco CA 94123. (415)441-3055. **Fax:** (415)520-0999. **E-mail:** info@ thewileygroup.com; david@thewileygroup.com. **Website:** www.thewileygroup.com. **Contact:** David Wiley, owner. Estab. 1984. Represents a broad spectrum of unique commercial artists. Over 29 years of experience in marketing, advertising and promotional work paired with a long-time fascination and appreciation of the arts, marketing and communication. David matches up US and worldwide agencies in ad-vertising, graphic design, publishing with illustrators who can best present their products in innovative, effective ways. Past clients have included Disney, Coca-Cola, Smithsonian, Microsoft, Nike, Oracle, Google, Random House, Eli Lilly Pharmaceuticals, National Geographic, Super Bowl XLII, Twinlab, FedEx, Nestle Corp. and Apple.

○ Mission statement: Building working relationships between illustrators and hiring professionals through individualized problem solving and creative processes.

TERMS Rep receives 25% commission with a bonus structure. No geographical restriction.

HOW TO CONTACT Actively seeking stop-motion, animation and 3D artists with solid illustration skills. "First and foremost, we receive an extensive numbers of inquiries, so responses might be be delayed. If you do not hear back within 20 days, please resubmit noting in the subject line that it is your second submission. Before submitting, please read the following: We *only* represent commercial illustrators, no photographers. It is important you familiarize yourself with our agency and the artists we represent, understanding the styles we currently manage and the work we do with our clients (also visit our blog or Facebook page). We are only interested in adding unique and well-developed styles that will fit within our portfolio of talent, so understanding our current portfolio is a big part of your submission process. Once you have done so, and feel there may be a fit, please e-mail your information. Be sure to include the following: Introduction (including who you are and your professional background), the style and medium that best describes you, a list of clients, sample images in JPEG format *only* (with a max total size of 3MB) and a link to your website, blog, Facebook page or other relevant professional information. We do not accept mailed printed samples and will not return them if sent without previous agreement."

DEBORAH WOLFE, LTD.

731 N. 24th St., Philadelphia PA 19130. (215)232-6666. **Fax:** (215)232-6585. **E-mail:** info@illustrationonline. com. **Website:** www.illustrationonline.com. **Contact:** Deborah Wolfe. Estab. 1978. Commercial illustration and animation representative. Member of Graphic Artist Guild. Represents 40 illustrators. Markets include advertising agencies, corporations/client direct,

design firms, editorial/magazines, publishing/books, animation.

HANDLES Illustration.

TERMS Rep receives 25% commission. Advertises in *Workbook*, *Directory of Illustration Picturebook* and *The Medical Sourcebook*.

HOW TO CONTACT For first contact, send an e-mail with samples or a web address. Responds in 3 weeks.

ART FAIRS

//

How would you like to sell your art from New York to California, showcasing it to thousands of eager art collectors? Art fairs (also called art festivals or art shows) are not only a good source of income for artists but an opportunity to see how people react to their work. If you like to travel, enjoy meeting people, and can do your own matting and framing, this could be a great market for you.

Many outdoor fairs occur during the spring, summer, and fall months to take advantage of warmer temperatures. However, depending on the region, temperatures could be hot and humid, and not all that pleasant! And, of course, there is always the chance of rain. Indoor art fairs held in November and December are popular because they capitalize on the holiday shopping season.

To start selling at art fairs, you will need an inventory of work—some framed, some unframed. Even if customers do not buy the framed paintings or prints, having some framed work displayed in your booth will give buyers an idea of how your work looks framed, which could spur sales of your unframed prints. The most successful art fair exhibitors try to show a range of sizes and prices for customers to choose from.

When looking at the art fairs listed in this section, first consider local shows and shows in your neighboring cities and states. Once you find a show you'd like to enter, visit its website or contact the appropriate person for a more detailed prospectus. A prospectus is an application that will offer additional information not provided in the art fair's listing.

Ideally, most of your paintings, prints, etc. should be matted and stored in protective wraps or bags so that customers can look through your inventory without damaging artwork and mats. You will also need a canopy or tent to protect yourself and your wares from the elements as well as some bins in which to store the prints. A display wall will allow you to show off your best framed prints. Generally, artists will have 100 square feet of space in which to set up their tents and canopies. Most listings will specify the dimensions of the exhibition space for each artist.

If you see the ☺ icon before a listing in this section, it means that the art fair is a juried event. In other words, there is a selection process artists must go through to be admitted into the fair. Many art fairs have quotas for the categories of exhibitors. For example, one art fair may accept the mediums of photography, sculpture, painting, metal work, and jewelry. Once each category fills with qualified exhibitors, no more will be admitted to the show that year. The jurying process also ensures that the artists who sell their work at the fair meet the sponsor's criteria for quality. So, overall, a juried art fair is good for artists because it means they will be exhibiting their work along with other artists of equal caliber.

Be aware there are fees associated with entering art fairs. Most fairs have an application fee or a space fee, or sometimes both. The space fee is essentially a rental fee for the space your booth will occupy for the art fair's duration. These fees can vary greatly from show to show, so be sure to check this information in each listing before you apply to any art fair.

Most art fair sponsors want to exhibit only work that is handmade by the artist, no matter what medium. Unfortunately, some people try to sell work that they purchased elsewhere as their own original artwork. In the art fair trade, this is known as "buy/sell." It is an undesirable situation because it tends to bring down the quality of the whole show. Some listings will make a point to say "no buy/sell" or "no manufactured work."

For more information on art fairs, pick up a copy of *Sunshine Artist* (www.sunshineartist. com) or *Art Calendar* (www.artcalendar.com), and consult online sources such as www. artfairsource.com.

4 BRIDGES ARTS FESTIVAL

30 Frazier Ave., Chattanooga TN 37405. (423)265-4282, ext. 106. **Fax:** (423)265-5233. **E-mail:** katdunn@avarts.org. **Website:** www.4bridgesartsfestival.org. **Contact:** Kat Dunn. Estab. 2000. Two-day fine arts & crafts show held annually in mid-April. Held in a covered, open-air pavilion. Accepts photography and 24 different mediums. Juried by 3 different art professionals each year. Awards: $10,000 in artist merit awards; the on-site jurying for merit awards will take place Saturday morning. Number of exhibitors: 150. Public attendance: 13,000. Public admission: $7/day or a 2-day pass for $10; children under 18 are free. Artists should apply at www.zapplication.org. Deadline for entry: early November (see website for details). Application fee: $40. Space fee: $450-550 for 10×12 ft.; $900-1,000 for 20×12 ft. Average gross sales/exhibitor: $2,923. For more information, e-mail, visit website or call. The event is held at First Tennessee Pavilion.

57TH STREET ART FAIR

1507 E. 53rd St., PMB 296, Chicago IL 60615. (773)234-3247. **E-mail:** info@57thstartfair.org. **Website:** www.57thstreetartfair.org. Estab. 1948. Fine art & craft show held annually in June. Outdoors. Accepts painting, sculpture, photography, glass, jewelry, leather, wood, ceramics, fiber, printmaking. Juried. Free to public. Apply via www.zapplication.org. Deadline for entry: January 15. Application fee: $35. Space fee: $300. Exhibition space: 10×10. For more information, e-mail or visit website.

AKRON ARTS EXPO

220 Balch St., Akron OH 44302. (330)375-2836. **Fax:** (330)375-2883. **E-mail:** PBomba@akronohio.gov. **Website:** www.akronartsexpo.org. **Contact:** Penny Bomba, artist coordinator. Estab. 1979. Held in late July. "The Akron Arts Expo is a nationally recognized juried fine arts & crafts show held outside with over 160 artists, ribbon and cash awards, great food, an interactive children's area, and entertainment for the entire family. Participants in this festival present quality fine arts and crafts that are offered for sale at reasonable prices. For more information, see the website." Application fee $10. Booth fee: $200. Event held in Hardesty Park.

ALEXANDRIA KING STREET ART FESTIVAL

270 Central Blvd., Suite 107B, Jupiter FL 33458. (561)746-6615. **Fax:** (561)746-6528. **E-mail:** info@artfestival.com. **Website:** www.artfestival.com. **Contact:** Malinda Ratliff, communications manager. Estab. 2003. Fine art & craft fair held annually in late September. Outdoors. Accepts photography, jewelry, mixed media, sculpture, wood, ceramic, glass, painting, digital, fiber, metal. Juried. Number exhibitors: 230. Number attendees: 150,000. Free to public. Apply online via www.zapplication.org. Deadline: see website. Application fee: $35. Space fee: $575. Exhibition space: 10×10 and 10×20.

For more information, artists should e-mail, call or visit website.

ALLEN PARK ARTS & CRAFTS STREET FAIR

16850 Southfield Rd., Allen Park MI 48101-2599. (734)258-7720. **E-mail:** applications@allenparkstreetfair.org. **Website:** www.allenparkstreetfair.org. **Contact:** Allen Park Festivities Commission. Estab. 1981. Arts & crafts show held annually the 1st Friday and Saturday in August. Outdoors. Accepts photography, sculpture, ceramics, jewelry, glass, wood, prints, drawings, paintings. All work must be of fine quality and original work of entrant. Such items as imports, velvet paintings, manufactured or kit jewelry and any commercially produced merchandise are not eligible for exhibit or sale. Juried by 5 photos (no slides) of work. Number of exhibitors: 200. Free to the public. Deadline: May 1. Application fee: $25. Space fee: $175-$200. Exhibition space: 10×10 ft. Apply via www.zapplication.org. Artists should call or see website for more information.

ALLENTOWN ART FESTIVAL

P.O. Box 1566, Buffalo NY 14205. (716)881-4269. **E-mail:** allentownartfestival@verizon.net. **Website:** www.allentownartfestival.com. **Contact:** Mary Myszkiewicz, president. Estab. 1958. Fine arts & crafts show held annually 2nd full weekend in June. Outdoors. Accepts photography, painting, watercolor, drawing, graphics, sculpture, mixed media, clay, glass, acrylic, jewelry, creative craft (hard/soft). Slides juried by hired professionals that change yearly. Awards/prizes: 41 cash prizes totaling over $20,000; includes Best of Show awarding $1,000. Number of exhibitors: 450. Public attendance: 300,000. Free to public. Artists should apply by downloading application from website. Deadline for entry: late January. Exhibition space: 10×13 ft. Application fee: $15. Booth fee $275. For more information, artists should e-mail, visit website, call or send SASE. Show held in Allentown Historic Preservation District.

TIPS "Artists must have attractive booth and interact with the public."

ALTON ARTS & CRAFTS EXPRESSIONS

P.O. Box 1326, Palatine IL 60078. (312)751-2500; (847)991-4748. **E-mail:** asoaartists@aol.com. **Website:** www.americansocietyofartists.org. **Contact:** Office personnel. Estab. 1979. Fine arts & crafts show held annually indoors in Alton IL, in spring and fall, usually March and September. Accepts quilting, fabric crafts, artwear, photography, sculpture, jewelry, glass works, woodworking and more. Please submit 4 images representative of your work you wish to exhibit, 1 of your display set-up, your first/last name, physical address, daytime telephone number—résumé/show listing helpful. "See our website for online jury information." Number of exhibitors: 50. Free to the public. Artists should apply by submitting jury materials. Submit to: asoartists@aol.com. If juried in, you will receive a jury/approval number. Deadline for entry: 2 months prior to show or earlier if spaces fill. Space fee: to be announced. Exhibition space: approximately 100 sq. ft. for single space; other sizes available. For more information, artsits should send SASE, submit jury material and submit jury material to ASA, P.O. Box 1326, Palatine IL 60078.

TIPS "Remember that when you are at work in your studio, you are an artist. But when you are at a show, you are a business person selling your work."

AMERICAN ARTISAN FESTIVAL

P.O. Box 41743, Nashville TN 37204. (615)429-7708. **E-mail:** americanartisanfestival@gmail.com. **Website:** www.facebook.com/theamericanartisanfestival. Estab. 1971. Fine arts & crafts show held annually mid-June, Father's Day weekend. Outdoors. Accepts photography and 21 different medium categories. Juried by 3 different art professionals each year. 3 cash awards presented. Number of exhibitors: 165. Public attendance: 30,000. No admission fee for the public. Artists should apply online at www.zapplication.org. Deadline for entry: early March (see website for details). For more information, e-mail or visit the website. Festival held at Centennial Park, Nashville TN.

AMERICAN FINE CRAFT SHOW NYC

P.O. Box 480, Slate Hill NY 10973. (845)355-2400; (845)661-1221. **Fax:** (845)355-2444. **E-mail:** show.director@americanartmarketing.com. **Website:** www.americanfinecraftshownyc.com. **Contact:** Richard Rothbard, director. Fine art & craft show held annually in October. Indoors. Accepts handmade crafts, basketry, ceramics, decorative fiber, furniture, glass, jewelry, leather, metal, mixed media, paper, wearable art, wood. Juried. Apply online. Deadline for entry: April 30. Application fee: $35. Space fee: $200. Exhibition space: varies. For more information, e-mail or visit website.

AMERICAN FOLK ART FESTIVAL

(707)246-2460. **E-mail:** gavitee@aol.com. **Website:** www.americanfolkartfestival.com. **Contact:** Susan Bartolucci. Arts & crafts show held annually in September. Indoors. Accepts handmade crafts, one-of-a-kind folk art, Americana & folk art antiques. Admission: $10. Apply online. Deadline for entry: see website. Application fee: see website. Space fee: see website. Exhibition space: see website. For more information, e-mail or visit website.

AMISH ACRES ARTS & CRAFTS FESTIVAL

1600 W. Market St., Nappanee IN 46550. (574)773-4188 or (800)800-4942. **E-mail:** amishacres@amishacres.com; beckymaust@amishacres.com. **Website:** www.amishacres.com. **Contact:** Becky Cappert, marketplace coordinator. Estab. 1962. Arts & crafts show held annually first weekend in August. Outdoors. Accepts photography, crafts, floral, folk, jewelry, oil, acrylic, sculpture, textiles, watercolors, wearable, wood. Juried by 5 images, either 35mm slides or e-mailed digital images. Awards/prizes: $5,000 cash including Best of Show and $1,000 purchase prizes. Number of exhibitors: 300. Public attendance: 60,000. Admission: $7; $6 seniors; Children under 12 free. Artists should apply by sending SASE or printing application from website. Deadline for entry: April 1. Exhibition space: 10×12, 15×12, 20×12 or 30×12 ft.; optional stable fee, with tent, also available. For more information, artists should e-mail, visit website, call or send SASE.

TIPS "Create a vibrant, open display that beckons to passing customers. Interact with potential buyers. Sell the romance of the purchase."

☯ ANACORTES ARTS FESTIVAL

505 O Ave., Anacortes WA 98221. (360)293-6211. **Fax:** (360)299-0722. **E-mail:** staff@anacortesartsfestival.com. **Website:** www.anacortesartsfestival.com. Fine arts & crafts show held annually 1st full weekend in August. Accepts photography, painting, drawings, prints, ceramics, fiber art, paper art, glass, jewelry, sculpture, yard art, woodworking. Juried by projecting 3 images on a large screen. Works are evaluated on originality, quality and marketability. Each applicant must provide 5 high-quality digital images, including a booth shot. Awards/prizes: festival offers awards totaling $3,600. Number of exhibitors: 250. We only accept online applications through zapplication.org. Application fee: $30. Deadline for entry: early March. Space fee: $325. Exhibition space: 10×10 ft. For more information, artists should see website. Show is located on Commercial Ave. from 4th to 10th St.

☯ ANN ARBOR STREET ART FAIR

721 E. Huron, Suite 200, Ann Arbor MI 48104. (734)994-5260. **Fax:** (734)994-0504. **E-mail:** production@artfair.org; mriley@artfair.org. **Website:** www.artfair.org. Estab. 1958. Fine arts & crafts show held annually 3rd Saturday in July. Outdoors. Accepts photography, fiber, glass, digital art, jewelry, metals, 2D and 3D mixed media, sculpture, clay, painting, drawing, printmaking, pastels, wood. Juried based on originality, creativity, technique, craftsmanship and production. Awards/prizes: cash prizes for outstanding work in any media. Number of exhibitors: 200. Public attendance: 500,000. Free to the public. Artists should apply through www.zapplication.org. Deadline for entry: January 13. Application fee: $35/40. Space fee: $650. Exhibition space: 10×12 ft. Average gross sales/exhibitor: $7,000. For more information, artists should e-mail, visit website, call.

☯ ANN ARBOR SUMMER ART FAIR

118 N. Fourth Ave., Ann Arbor MI 48104. (734)662-3382. **Fax:** (734)662-0339. **E-mail:** info@theguild.org; nicole@theguild.org. **Website:** www.theguild.org. Estab. 1970. Fine arts and craft show held annually on the third Wednesday through Saturday in July. Outdoors. Accepts all fine art categories. Juried. Number of exhibitors: 325. Attendance: 500,000-750,000. Free to public. Deadline for entry is January; enter online at www.juriedartservices.com. Exhibition space: 10×10, 10×13, 10×17 ft. For information, artists should visit the website, call, or e-mail. Show is located on University of Michigan campus and in downtown Ann Arbor.

⊕ ☯ THE ANNA MARIA ISLAND ARTS & CRAFTS FESTIVAL

270 Central Blvd., Suite 107B, Jupiter FL 33458. (561)746-6615. **Fax:** (561)746-6528. **E-mail:** info@artfestival.com. **Website:** www.artfestival.com. Fine art & craft fair held annually in mid-November. Outdoors. Accepts photography, jewelry, mixed media, sculpture, wood, ceramic, glass, painting, digital, fiber, metal. Juried. Number exhibitors: 106. Number attendees: 10,000. Free to public. Apply online via zapplication.org. Deadline: see website. Application fee: $15; free to mail in paper application. Space fee: $250. Exhibition space: 10×10 and 10×20. For more information, artists should e-mail, call or visit website.

☯ ANNUAL ARTS & CRAFTS ADVENTURE

American Society of Artists, P.O. Box 1326, Palatine IL 60078. (847)991-4748. **E-mail:** asoaartists@aol.com. **Website:** www.americansocietyofartists.org. Estab. 1991. Fine arts & crafts show held annually in May the Saturday before Mother's Day. Outdoors. Accepts fine art and handmade crafts. Juried. Number of exhibitors: 55. Free to the public. Apply be e-mailing asoaartists@aol.com or via mail with SASE. Send 4 images representative of your work you wish to exhibit, 1 of your display set-up, your first/last name, physical address, daytime phone number and résumé/show listing. Deadline for entry: varies. Space fee: $95 (price less or more for smaller or larger space). Exhibition space: 10×10 (smaller and larger spaces also available upon request). For more information, artists should visit website.

TIPS "Remember to present your work in a professional manner."

☯ APPLE ANNIE CRAFTS & ARTS SHOW

4905 Roswell Rd., Marietta GA 30062. **Fax:** (770)552-6420. **E-mail:** sagw4905@gmail.com. **Website:** www.st-ann.org/womens-guild/apple-annie. Estab. 1981. Handmade arts & crafts show held annually the 1st weekend in December. Juried. Indoors. Accepts handmade arts and crafts like photography, woodworking, ceramics, pottery, painting, fabrics, glass, etc. Number of exhibitors: 120. Public attendance: 4,000. Artists should apply by visiting website to print application form. Deadline: March 1 (see website for details). Application fee: $20, nonrefundable. Booth fee $200.

Exhibition space: 80 sq. ft. minimum, may be more. For more information, artists may visit website.

TIPS "We are looking for vendors with an open, welcoming booth, who are accessible and friendly to customers."

⊕ ○ APPLEWOOD ARTS

(303)797-9656. **Fax:** (303)797-9656. **E-mail:** knessso@aol.com. **Website:** www.applewoodartsandcrafts.com. **Contact:** Kathleen Ness. Estab. 1977. Arts & crafts show held annually 3 times in November. Indoors. Accepts original fine art & handmade crafts. Juried. Awards/prizes: 9 Most Original Booth prizes. Exhibitors: 100. Number of attendees: 4,000. Admission: $4. Artists should apply via website. Deadline for entry: mid June. Application fee: none. Space fee: $300. Exhibition space: 10×10; 12×12. For more information, artists should visit website.

⊕ ○ ARLINGTON FESTIVAL OF THE ARTS

270 Central Blvd., Suite 107B, Jupiter FL 33458. (561)746-6615. **Fax:** (561)746-6528. **E-mail:** info@artfestival.com. **Website:** www.artfestival.com. **Contact:** Malinda Ratliff, communications manager. Estab. 2013. Fine art & craft fair held annually in mid-April. Outdoors. Accepts photography, jewelry, mixed media, sculpture, wood, ceramic, glass, painting, digital, fiber, metal. Juried. Number exhibitors: 140. Number attendees: 50,000. Free to public. Apply online via www. zapplication.org. Deadline: see website. Application fee: $25. Space fee: $395. Exhibition space: 10×10 and 10×20. For more information, artists should e-mail, call or visit website.

○ Festival located at Highland St. in the Clarendon district of Arlington VA.

⊕ ○ ART & APPLES FESTIVAL

407 Pine St., Rochester MI 48307. (248)651-4110. **Fax:** (248)651-4757. **E-mail:** festivals@pccart.org. **E-mail:** lbates@pccart.org. **Website:** www.artandapples.com. **Contact:** Laura Bates, festival director. Estab. 1965. Fine arts & crafts show held annually in September. Outdoors. Accepts handmade crafts and fine art. Juried. Exhibitors: 290. Number of attendees: 125,000. Admission: $5. Apply online. Deadline for entry: see website. Application fee: see website. Space fee: see website. Exhibition space: see website. For more information, e-mail or visit website.

⊕ ○ ART-A-FAIR

P.O. Box 547, Laguna Beach CA 92652. (949)494-4514. **E-mail:** marketing@art-a-fair.com. **Website:** www. art-a-fair.com. Estab. 1967. Fine arts show held annually in June-August. Outoors. Accepts painting, sculpture, ceramics, jewelry, printmaking, photography, master crafts, digital art, fiber, glass, pencil, wood. Juried. Exhibitors: 125. Number of attendees: see website. Admission: $7.50 adults; $4.50 seniors; children 12 & under free. Apply online. Deadline for entry: see website. Application fee: $40 (per medium). Space fee: $200 + $35 membership fee. Exhibition space: see website. For more information, e-mail, visit website or call.

⊕ ○ ART BIRMINGHAM

118 N. Fourth Ave., Ann Arbor MI 48104. (734)662-3382. **Fax:** (734)662-0339. **Website:** www.theguild.org. Estab. 1981. Arts & crafts show held annually in May. Outoors. Accepts handmade crafts painting, ceramics, photography, jewelry, glass, wood, sculpture, mixed media, fiber, metal and more. Juried. Exhibitors: 150. Number of attendees: see website. Free to public. Apply online. Deadline for entry: see website. Application fee: see website. Space fee: see website. Exhibition space: see website. For more information, visit website or call.

⊕ ○ ART FAIR AT LAUMEIER SCULPTURE PARK

(314)615-5278. **E-mail:** artfair@laumeier.org. **Website:** www.laumeir.org. **Contact:** Sara Matthew, special events manager. Estab. 1987. Arts & crafts show held annually in May during Mother's Day weekend. Outdoors. Accepts fine handmade crafts, ceramics, fiber/textiles, glass, jewelry, mixed media 2D, printmaking/drawing, painting, photography/digital, sculpture, wood. Features regional food vendors, a wine garden, and live music. Juried. Awards/prizes: $5,000 in cash awards. Number of exhibitors: 150. Number of attendees: 15,000. Admission: $10 adults 12+; $5 children 6-11; children under 5 free. Apply via www.zapplication.org or visit www.laumeier sculpturepark.org/programs_events/art_fair/art ists. Deadline for entry: January 10. Application fee: $35 (per category). Space fee: $350 (open booth); $450 (tented booth). Exhibition space: 10×10. Average sales: $5,000. For more information, see website.

ART FAIR AT QUEENY PARK

GSLAA-Vic Barr, 1668 Rishon Hill Dr., St. Louis MO 63146. 636)724-5968. **Website:** www.artfair atqueenypark.com. Arts & crafts show held annually in August. Indoors. Accepts handmade crafts, clay, digital (computer) art, drawing/print, fiber (basketry, paper, wearable, woven), glass, jewelry, 2D/3D mixed media, oil/acrylic, photography, sculpture, water media, wood. Juried. Exhibitors: 140. Number of attendees: see website. Free to public. Apply online. Deadline for entry: see website. Application fee: $25; $50 for late application. Space fee: $225. Exhibition space: 10×8. For more information, visit website or call.

ART FAIR JACKSON HOLE

Art Association of Jackson Hole, P.O. Box 1248, Jackson WY 83001. (307)733-6379. **Fax:** (307)733-6694. **E-mail:** artistinfo@jhartfair.org. **Website:** www.jhart fair.org. Estab. 1965. Arts & crafts show held annually in July & August. Outoors. Accepts handmade crafts, ceramic, drawing, fiber, furniture, glass, graphics & printmaking, jewelry, leather, metalwork, 2D/3D mixed media, painting, photography, sculpture, toys & games, wearable fiber, wood. Juried. Exhibitors: 135. Number of attendees: 30,000. Free for art association members; $5 per day for non-members. Apply via www.zapplication.org. Deadline for entry: see website. Application fee: $35. Space fee: varies. Exhibition space: varies. For more information, e-mail, visit website or call.

ART FAIR OFF THE SQUARE

P.O. Box 1791, Madison WI 53701-1791. **E-mail:** wi artcraft@gmail.com. **Website:** www.artcraftwis.org/AFOS.html. Estab. 1965. Arts & crafts show held annually in July. Outoors. Accepts handmade crafts ceramics, art glass, painting, fiber, sculpture, jewelry, graphics, papermaking, photography, wood and more. Juried. Awards/prizes: Best of Category. Exhibitors: 140. Number of attendees: see website. Free to public. Apply via www.zapplication.org. Deadline for entry: see website. Application fee: $25. Space fee: $300. Exhibition space: 10×10. For more information, e-mail, visit website or call.

ART FAIR ON THE COURTHOUSE LAWN

P.O. Box 795, Rhinelander WI 54501. (715)365-7460. **E-mail:** assistant@rhinelanderchamber.com. **Website:** www.explorerhinelander.com. **Contact:** events coordinator. Estab. 1985. Arts & crafts show held an-

nually in June. Outdoors. Accepts woodworking (includes furniture), jewelry, glass items, metal, paintings and photography. Number of exhibitors: 150. Public attendance: 3,000. Free to the public. Space fee: $75-300. Exhibit space: 10×10 to 10×30 ft. For more information, artists should e-mail, call or visit website. Show located at Oneida County Courthouse.
TIPS "We accept only items handmade by the exhibitor."

ART FAIR ON THE SQUARE

227 State St., Madison WI 53703. (608)257-0158, ext 229. **E-mail:** artfair@mmoca.org. **Website:** www.mmoca.org. **Contact:** Annik Dupaty. Estab. 1958. Arts & crafts show held annually in July. Outoors. Accepts handmade crafts, ceramics, fiber, leather, furniture, jewelry, glass, digital art, metal, sculpture, 2D/3D mixed media, painting, photography, printmaking/graphics/drawing, wood. Juried. Awards/prizes: Best of Show; Invitational Award. Exhibitors: varies. Number of attendees: 150,000+. Free to public. Apply via www.zapplication.org. Deadline for entry: see website. Application fee: $35. Space fee: $495 (single); $1,050 (double). Exhibition space: 10×10 (single); 10×10 (double). For more information, e-mail, visit website or call.

ART FEST BY THE SEA

270 Central Blvd., Suite 107B, Jupiter FL 33458. (561)746-6615. **Fax:** (561)746-6528. **E-mail:** info@artfestival.com. **Website:** www.artfestival.com. **Contact:** Malinda Ratliff, communications manager. Estab. 1989. Fine art & craft fair held annually in early March. Outdoors. Accepts photography, jewelry, mixed media, sculpture, wood, ceramic, glass, painting, digital, fiber, metal. Juried. Number exhibitors: 340. Number attendees: 125,000. Free to public. Apply online via www.zapplication.org. Deadline: see website. Application fee: $25. Space fee: $415. Exhibition space: 10×10 and 10×20. For more information, artists should e-mail, call or visit website.
Fair located along A1A Between Donald Ross Rd. and Marcinski in Juno Beach FL.

ARTFEST FORT MYERS

1375 Jackson St., Suite 401, Fort Myers FL 33901. (239)768-3602. **E-mail:** info@artfestfortmyers.com. **Website:** www.artfestformyers.com. Fine arts & crafts fair held annually in February. Outdoors. Accepts handmade crafts, ceramics, digital, drawing/graphics, fiber, glass, jewelry, metal, 2D/3D mixed media, painting, photography, printmaking, sculpture, wearable, wood. Juried. Awards/prizes: $5,000 in cash. Exhibitors: 200. Number of attendees: 85,000. Free to public. Apply online. Deadline for entry: September 15. Application fee: $35. Space fee: $460.50. Exhibition space: 10×10. For more information, e-mail, visit website or call.

ART FESTIVAL BETH-EL

400 Pasadena Ave. S., St. Petersburg FL 33707. (727)347-6136. **Fax:** (727)343-8982. **E-mail:** info@art festivalbethel.com. **Website:** www.artfestivalbethel. com. Estab. 1972. Fine arts & crafts show held annually the last weekend in January. Indoors. Accepts photography, painting, jewelry, sculpture, woodworking, glass. Juried by special committee on-site or through slides. Awards/prizes: over $7,000 prize money. Number of exhibitors: over 170. Public attendance: 8,000-10,000. Free to the public. Artists should apply by application with photos or slides; show is invitational. Deadline for entry: September. For more information, artists should call or visit website. A commission is taken.

TIPS "Don't crowd display panels with artwork. Make sure your prices are on your pictures. Speak to customers about your work."

ART FESTIVAL OF HENDERSON

P.O. Box 95050, Henderson NV 89009-5050. (702)267-2171. **Website:** www.hendersonlive.com/special-events/art-festival-of-henderson#New_Artist. Arts & crafts show held annually in May. Outdoors. Accepts handmade crafts, paintings, pottery, jewelry, photography and much more. Juried. Exhibitors: varies. Number of attendees: 25,000. Free to public. Apply online. Deadline for entry: see website. Application fee: see website. Space fee: see website. Exhibition space: see website. For more information, visit website or call.

ARTFEST MIDWEST—"THE OTHER SHOW"

Stookey Companies, P.O. Box 31083, Des Moines IA 50310. (515)278-6200. **Fax:** (515)276-7513. **E-mail:** suestookey@att.net. **Website:** www.artfestmidwest. com. Fine art fair held annually in June. Indoors & outdoors. Accepts handmade fine art, ceramic, fiber, drawing, glass, jewelry, metal, 2D/3D mixed media, painting, photography, wood. Juried. Exhibitors: 240. Number of attendees: 30,000. Free to public.

Apply via www.zapplication.org. Deadline for entry: March. Application fee: $30. Space fee: varies. Exhibition space: see website. For more information, e-mail suestookey@att.net, visit website at www.artfestmidwest.com or call 515-278-6200.

ARTIGRAS FINE ARTS FESTIVAL

5520 PGA Blvd., Suite 200, Palm Beach Gardens FL 33418. (561)748-3946. **Fax:** (561)745-7519. **E-mail:** info@artigras.org; artists@artigras.org. **Website:** www.artigras.org. Estab. 1985. Fine arts & crafts fair held annually in February. Outdoors. Accepts handmade crafts, ceramics, fiber (wearable and non-wearable), digital art, drawing & printmaking, glass, jewelry, metal, mixed media, painting, photography, sculpture, and wood. Juried. Awards/prizes: $17,000 in cash awards and ribbons. Exhibitors: 300. Number of attendees: 85,000. Admission: $8 advance; $10 at gate; children 12 & under free. Apply online. Deadline for entry: September. Application fee: $40. Space fee: $450 +tax (single); $900+ tax (double). Exhibition space: 12×12 (single); 12×24 (double). For more information, e-mail, visit website or call.

ART IN BLOOM—CATIGNY PARK

EM Events, LLC, P.O. Box 4332, Naperville IL 60567. (630)536-8416. **E-mail:** emelloy@emevents.com. **Website:** www.cantigny.org/calendar/signature-events/art-in-bloom. Fine arts & crafts show held annually in June. Outdoors. Accepts handmade crafts ceramics, drawing, fiber non-functional, fiber wearable, paper non-functional, furniture, glass, jewelry, acrylic, oil, watercolor, pastel, sculpture, wood, mixed media, collage, photography, and printmaking. Juried. Exhibitors: 80. Number of attendees: 8,000. Free to public. Apply online. Deadline for entry: see website. Application fee: $10. Space fee: $285. Exhibition space: 10×10. For more information, e-mail, visit website or call.

ART IN THE BARN—BARRINGTON

Advocate Good Shepherd Hospital, Art in the Barn Artist Committee, 450 W. Highway 22, Barrington IL 60010. (847)842-4496. **E-mail:** artinthebarn@comcast.net. **Website:** www.artinthebarn-barrington. com. Estab. 1974. Fine arts & crafts show held annually in September. Indoors & outdoors. Accepts handmade crafts, ceramics, painting, jewelry, glass, sculpture, fiber, drawing, photography, digital media, printmaking, scratchboard, mixed media, wood.

Juried. Awards/prizes: Best of Show; Best of Medium; purchase awards. Exhibitors: 185. Number of attendees: 8,500. Admission: $5; children 12 & under free. Apply online. Deadline for entry: see website. Application fee: $20. Space fee: $100 (indoors); $85 (outdoors). Exhibition space: varies. For more information, e-mail, visit website or call.

ART IN THE PARK (ARIZONA)

P.O. Box 748, Sierra Vista AZ 85636-0247. (520)803-0584. **E-mail:** edieartist@cox.net. **Website:** www.artintheparksierravista.com. Estab. 1972. Oldest longest running Arts & crafts fair in Southern Arizona. Fine arts & crafts show held annually 1st full weekend in October. Outdoors. Accepts photography, all fine arts and crafts created by vendor. No resale retail strictly applied. Juried by Huachaca Art Association Board. Artists submit 5 photos. Returnable with SASE. Number of exhibitors: 203. Public attendance: 15,000. Free to public. Artists should apply by downloading the application www.artintheparksierravista.com. Deadline for entry: postmarked by late June. Last minute/late entries always considered. No application fee. Space fee: $200-275, includes jury fee. Exhibition space: 15×30 ft. Some electrical; additional cost of $25. Some RV space available at $15/night. For more information, artists should see website, e-mail, call or send SASE. Show located in Veteran's Memorial Park.

ART IN THE PARK (GEORGIA)

P.O. Box 1540, Thomasville GA 31799. (229)227-7020. **Fax:** (229)227-3320. **E-mail:** roseshowfest@rose.net; laura@thomasville.org. **Website:** www.downtownthomasville.com. **Contact:** Laura Beggs. Estab. 1998-1999. Art in the Park (an event of Thomasville's Rose Show and Festival) is a one-day arts & crafts show held annually in April. Outdoors. Accepts photography, handcrafted items, oils, acrylics, woodworking, stained glass, other varieties. Juried by a selection committee. Number of exhibitors: 60. Public attendance: 2,500. Free to public. Artists should apply by submitting official application. Deadline for entry: early February. Space fee varies by year. Exhibition space: 20×20 ft. For more information, artists should e-mail, call or visit website. Show located in Paradise Park.
TIPS "Most important, be friendly to the public and have an attractive booth display."

ART IN THE PARK (NEBRASKA)

Kearney Artist Guild, P.O. Box 1368, Kearney NE 68848-1368. (308)708-0510. **E-mail:** artintheparkkearney@charter.net. **Website:** www.kearneyartistsguild.com. Estab. 1971. Fine arts & crafts show held annually in July. Outdoors. Accepts handmade crafts, ceramics, drawing, fiber, mixed media, glass, jewelry, painting, photography, sculpture. Juried. Exhibitors: 90. Number of attendees: varies. Free to public. Apply online. Deadline for entry: early June. Application fee: $10. Space fee: varies. Exhibition space: varies. For more information, e-mail, visit website or call.

ART IN THE PARK (HOLLAND, MICHIGAN)

Holland Friends of Art, P.O. Box 1052, Holland MI 49422. **E-mail:** info@hollandfriendsofart.com. **Website:** www.hollandfriendsofart.com. **Contact:** Sarah Johnson, art fair chairperson. This annual fine arts and crafts fair is held on the first Saturday of August in Holland. The event draws one of the largest influx of visitors to the city on a single day, second only to Tulip Time. More than 300 fine artists and artisans from 8 states will be on hand to display and sell their work. Juried. All items for sale must be original. Public attendance: 10,000+. Entry fee: $90 (HFA members $80); includes a $20 application fee. Deadline: late March. Space fee: $160 for a double-wide space; $150 for a double-deep space. Exhibition space: 12×12 ft. Details of the jury and entry process are explained on the application. Application available online. Call, e-mail or visit website for more information. Event held in Centennial Park.
TIPS "Create an inviting and neat booth. Offer well-made quality artwork and crafts at a variety of prices."

ART IN THE PARK (PLYMOUTH, MICHIGAN)

P.O. Box 702490, Plymouth MI 48170. (734)454-1314. **Fax:** (734)454-3670. **E-mail:** info@artinthepark.com. **Website:** www.artinthepark.com. Estab. 1979. Arts & crafts show held annually in July. Outdoors. Accepts handmade crafts, paintings, sculpture, ceramics, jewelry, fiber, fine glass, woodwork, mixed media, photography, and folk art. Juried. Exhibitors: 400. Number of attendees: 300,000. Free to public. Apply online. Deadline for entry: see website. Application fee: $20. Space fee: $580. Exhibition space: 10×10. For more information, e-mail, visit website or call.

☥ ART IN THE PARK (VIRGINIA)

20 S. New St., Staunton VA 24401. (540)885-2028. E-mail: info@saartcenter.org; director@saartcenter.org. **Website:** www.saartcenter.org. **Contact:** Beth Hodges, exec. director. Estab. 1961. Fine arts & crafts show held annually every Memorial Day weekend. Outdoors. Juried by submitting 4 photos representative of the work to be sold. Award/prizes: $1,500. Number of exhibitors: 60. Public attendance: 3,000-4,000. Free to public. Artists should apply by sending in application. Exhibition space: 10×10 ft. For more information, artists should e-mail, call or visit website. Show located at Gypsy Hill Park.

☥ ART IN THE PARK FALL FOLIAGE FESTIVAL

P.O. Box 1447, Rutland VT 05701. (802)775-0356. E-mail: info@chaffeeartcenter.org; mbarros@chaffeeartcenter.org. **Website:** www.chaffeeartcenter.org. Estab. 1961. A fine arts & crafts show held at Main Street Park in Rutland VT annually in October over Columbus Day weekend. Accepts fine art, specialty foods, fiber, jewelry, glass, metal, wood, photography, clay, floral, etc. All applications will be juried by a panel of experts. The Art in the Park Festivals are dedicated to high-quality art and craft products. Number of exhibitors: 100. Public attendance: 9,000-10,000. Public admission: voluntary donation. Artists should apply online and either e-mail or submit a CD with 3 photos of work and 1 of booth (photos upon preapproval). Deadline for entry: early bird discount of $25 per show for applications received by March 31. Space fee: $200-350. Exhibit space: 10×12 or 20×12 ft. For more information, artists should e-mail, visit website, or call. Show located in Main Street Park.

TIPS "Have a good presentation, variety, if possible (in pricing also), to appeal to a large group of people. Apply early, as there may be a limited amount of accepted vendors per category. Applications will be juried on a first come, first served basis until the category is determined to be filled."

☥ ART IN THE PARK—FINE ARTS FESTIVAL

Swartz Creek Kiwanis, 5023 Holland Dr., Swartz Creek MI 48473. (810)635-2717. **E-mail:** aitp@hsaa. com. **Website:** www.swartzcreekkiwanis.org/art. Estab. 2008. Annual outdoor fine art festival held in August. Accepts all fine art. Juried by art professionals hired by the committee, monetary prizes given. Average number of exhibitors: 50. Average number of at-

tendees: 2,500-3,000. Free admission. Artists should apply by accessing the website. Deadline: early July. Space fee of $125; $175 for late applications. Space is 144 sq. ft. For more information artists should e-mail or visit the website. Festival held at Elms Park.

TIPS "Bring unique products."

➕ ☥ ART IN THE VILLAGE WITH CRAFT MARKETPLACE

270 Central Blvd., Suite 107B, Jupiter FL 33458. (561)746-6615. **Fax:** (561)746-6528. **E-mail:** info@artfestival.com. **Website:** www.artfestival.com. **Contact:** Malinda Ratliff, communications manager. Estab. 1991. Fine art & craft fair held annually in early June. Outdoors. Accepts photography, jewelry, mixed media, sculpture, wood, ceramic, glass, painting, digital, fiber, metal. Juried. Number exhibitors: 150. Number attendees: 70,000. Free to public. Apply online via zapplication.org. Deadline: see website. Application fee: $25. Space fee: $450. Exhibition space: 10×10 and 10×20. For more information, artists should e-mail, call or visit website.

💬 Show located at Legacy Village in Cleveland, OH.

➕ ☥ ART IN THE WILDS

214 Chemical Works Rd., Kane PA 16735. (814)837-7167. **E-mail:** mab@penn.com. **Website:** www.artinthewilds.org. **Contact:** Marilyn Blackmore. Estab. 2006. Arts & crafts show held annually in September. Outdoors. Accepts handmade crafts, drawing/pastels, metal, glass, clay/porcelain, photography, printmaking/graphics, mixed media, fabric/fiber, wood, leather, and jewelry. Juried. Awards/prizes: Best of Show; Excellence Award. Exhibitors: varies. Number of attendees: varies. Free to public. Apply online. Deadline for entry: see website. Application fee: $20. Space fee: varies. Exhibition space: varies. For more information, e-mail, visit website or call.

ARTISPHERE

16 Augusta St., Greenville SC 29601. (864)271-9398. **E-mail:** kerry@greenvillearts.com. **Website:** www.artisphere.us. Estab. 2004. Fine arts & crafts fair held annually in May. Outdoors. Accepts handmade crafts, ceramic, digital art, fiber, drawing, furniture, glass, jewelry, metal, 2D/3D mixed media, painting, photography, printmaking, sculpture, wood. Juried. Awards/prizes: Best in Show, 2nd Place, 3rd Place, 4 merit awards, Mayor's Choice Award. Exhibitors: 130. Number of attendees: varies. Free to public. Apply via

ART FAIRS

www.zapplication.org. Deadline for entry: early January. Application fee: $30. Space fee: $350. Exhibition space: 12×12. For more information, e-mail, visit website, or call.

◑ ART ON THE LAWN

Village Artisans, 100 Corry St., Yellow Springs OH 45387. (937)767-1209. **E-mail:** villageartisans.email@yahoo.com. **Website:** www.villageartisans.blogspot.com. Blog: www.villageartisans.blogspot.com. **Contact:** Village Artisans. Estab. 1983. Fine arts & crafts show held annually the 2nd Saturday in August. Outdoors. Accepts photography, all hand-made media and original artwork. Juried, as received, from photos accompanying the application. Awards: Best of Show receives a free booth space at next year's event. Number of exhibitors: 90-100. Free to public. Request an application by calling or e-mailing, or download an application from the website. Deadline for entry: July 31; however, the sooner received, the better the chances of acceptance. Jury fee: $15. Space fee: $75 before May; $85 until late July; $105 thereafter. Exhibition space: 10×10 ft. Average gross sales vary. For more information, artists should visit website, e-mail, call, send SASE or stop by Village Artisans at above address.

⊕ ◑ ART ON THE MALL

The Office of Alumni Relations, Mail Stop 301, The University of Toledo, 2801 W. Bancroft St., Toledo OH 43606-3390. (419)530-2586. **E-mail:** artonthemall@utoledo.edu. **Website:** www.toledoalumni.org. Art & craft show held annually in July. Outdoors. Accepts handmade crafts, ceramics, fiber, glass, jewelry, mixed media, photography, wood. Juried. Awards/prizes: Best of Show, 1st Place, 2nd Place, 3rd Place, Purchase Award. Number exhibitors: see website. Number attendees: 12,000. Free to public. Apply online. Deadline for entry: late April. Application fee: $25. Space fee: $100. Exhibition space: 10×10. For more information, e-mail, call or visit website.

⊕ ◑ ART ON THE SQUARE

P.O. Box 23561, Belleville IL 62223. (800)677-9255; (618)233-6769. **E-mail:** artonthesquarecompetition@gmail.com. **Website:** www.artonthesquare.com. Estab. 2002. Fine arts & crafts show held annually in May. Outdoors. Accepts handmade crafts, photography, glass, jewelry, clay, sculpture, fine craft, mixed media, wood and digital art. Juried. Awards/prizes:

over $30,000 in cash. Exhibitors: 105. Number of attendees: varies. Free to public. Apply online. Deadline for entry: see website. Application fee: see website. Space fee: see website. Exhibition space: see website. For more information, e-mail, visit website or call.

⊕ ◑ ART RAPIDS!

P.O. Box 301, Elk Rapids MI 49629. (231)264-6660. **E-mail:** art@mullalys128.com. **Website:** www.artrapids.org. **Contact:** Barb Mullaly. Arts & crafts fair held annually last Saturday in June. Outdoors. Accepts handmade crafts, ceramic, drawing, fiber, glass, jewelry, painting, photography, printmaking, sculpture, wood, metal, paper, or mixed media. Juried. Awards/prizes: Best of Show, Honorable Mention, People's Choice. Exhibitors: 70. Number of attendees: 4,000. Free to public. Apply online. Deadline for entry: early April. Application fee: $20. Space fee: varies. Exhibition space: 10×10. For more information, e-mail, visit website or call.

⊕ ◑ ART STAR CRAFT BAZAAR

E-mail: info@artstarphilly.com. **Website:** www.artstarcraftbazaar.com. Estab. 2003. Arts & crafts fair held annually in May. Outdoors. Accepts handmade crafts, fabric, clay, glass, wood, paper, paintings/drawings, sculpture and more. Juried. Exhibitors: varies. Number of attendees: varies. Free to public. Apply online. Deadline for entry: see website. Application fee: see website. Space fee: see website. Exhibition space: see website. For more information, artists should send e-mail or visit website.

⊕ ◑ ART UNDER THE ELMS

415 Main St., Lewiston ID 83501. (208)792-2726. **Fax:** (208)792-2850. **E-mail:** defitzgerald@lcsc.edu. **Website:** www.lcsc.edu/ce/aue. **Contact:** Debi Fitzgerald, director. Estab. 1984. Fine arts & crafts fair held annually in April. Outdoors. Accepts handmade crafts, ceramic, digital art, fiber, drawing, furniture, glass, jewelry, metal, 2D/3D mixed media, painting, photography, pre-packaged food, printmaking, wood. Juried. Awards/prizes: announced after jury. Exhibitors: 100. Number of attendees: varies. Free to public. Apply online. Deadline for entry: early January. Application fee: $20. Space fee: varies. Exhibition space: 10×10. For more information, artists should send e-mail, visit website or call.

ARTS & CRAFTS ADVENTURE

P.O. Box 1326, Palatine IL 60078. (312)751-2500.
Fax: (847)221-5853. **E-mail:** asoaartists@aol.com.
Website: www.americansocietyofartists.org. **Contact:** Office personnel. Estab. 1991. Fine arts & crafts
show held annually in early May and mid-September.
Outdoors. Event held in Park Ridge IL. Accepts photography, pottery, paintings, sculpture, glass, wood,
woodcarving, and more. Juried by 4 slides or photos
of work and 1 slide or photo of display; a résumé or
show listing is helpful. See our website for online jury.
To jury via e-mail: asoaartists@aol.com. Number of
exhibitors: 75. Free to the public. Artists should apply
by submitting jury materials. Submit to asoaartists@
aol.com. If juried in, you will receive a jury/approval
number. Deadline for entry: 2 months prior to show
or earlier if spaces fill. Space fee: to be announced.
Exhibition space: approximately 100 sq. ft. for single
space; other sizes available. For more information,
artists should send SASE, submit jury material. Show
located in Hodges Park.
TIPS "Remember that when you are at work in your
studio, you are an artist. But when you are at a show,
you are a business person selling your work."

AN ARTS & CRAFTS AFFAIR, AUTUMN & SPRING TOURS

P.O. Box 655, Antioch IL 60002. (402)331-2889. **E-mail:** hpifestivals@cox.net. **Website:** www.hpifestivals.com. **Contact:** Huffman Productions. Estab.
1983. An arts & crafts show that tours different cities and states. The Autumn Festival tours annually
October-November; Spring Festival tours annually
in March & April. Artists should visit website to see
list of states and schedule. Indoors. Accepts photography, pottery, stained glass, jewelry, clothing, wood,
baskets. All artwork must be handcrafted by the actual artist exhibiting at the show. Juried by sending in
2 photos of work and 1 of display. Awards/prizes: 4 $30
show gift certificates; $50, $100 and $150 certificates
off future booth fees. Number of exhibitors: 300-500
depending on location. Public attendance: 15,000-
35,000. Public admission: $8-9/adults; $7-8/seniors;
10 & under, free. Artists should apply by calling to
request an application. Deadline for entry: varies for
date and location. Space fee: $350-1,350. Exhibition
space: 8×11 ft. up to 8×22 ft. For more information,
artists should e-mail, call, or visit website.

TIPS "Have a nice display, make sure business name
is visible, dress professionally, have different price
points, and be willing to talk to your customers."

ARTS & CRAFTS FESTIVAL

Simsbury Woman's Club, P.O. Box 903, Simsbury
CT 06070. (860)658-2684. **E-mail:** simsburywomans
club@hotmail.com; swc_artsandcrafts@yahoo.com.
Website: www.simsburywomansclub.org. **Contact:**
Shirley Barsness, co-chairman. Estab. 1978. Arts &
crafts show held in mid-September. Juried. Outdoors
rain or shine. Original artwork, photography, clothing, accessories, jewelry, toys, wood objects and floral
arrangements accepted. Manufactured items or items
made from kits not accepted. Individuals should apply by submitting completed application, 4 photos or
JPEG files, including 1 of display booth. Exhibition
space: 11×14 ft. or 15×14 ft. frontage. Space fee: $160-
175; late applications $170-185. Number of exhibitors:
120. Public attendance: 5,000-7,000. Free to public.
Deadline for entry: August 15. For more information,
artists should e-mail swc_artsandcrafts@yahoo.com
or call Jean at (860)658-4490 or Shirley at (860)658-
2684. Applications available on website. Show located
in Simsbury Center.
TIPS "Display artwork in an attractive setting."

ARTS ADVENTURE

P.O. Box 1326, Palatine IL 60078. (312)571-2500
or (847)991-4748. **Fax:** (847)221-5853. **E-mail:**
asoaartists@aol.com. **Website:** www.americansociety
ofartists.org. Estab. 2001. American Society of Artists. Fine arts & crafts show held annually the end of
July. Event held in Chicago. Outdoors. Accepts photography, paintings, pottery, sculpture, jewelry and
more. Juried. Please submit 4 images representative
of your work you wish to exhibit, 1 of your display
set-up, your first/last name, physical address, daytime
telephone number (résumé/show listing helpful). See
our website for online jury. To jury: submit via e-mail
to asoaartists@aol.com or to the above address. Include a business-size (#10) SASE please. Number of
exhibitors: 50. Free to the public. If juried in, you will
receive a jury/approval number. Deadline for entry:
2 months prior to show or earlier if spaces fill. Entry
fee: TBA. Exhibition space: approximately 100 sq. ft.
for single space; other sizes available. For more information, artists should send SASE.

TIPS "Remember that when you are at work in your studio, you are an artist. But when you are at a show, you are a business person selling your work."

ART'S ALIVE

200 125th St., Ocean City MD 21842. (410)250-0125. **Website:** oceancitymd.gov/recreation_and_parks/specialevents.html. **Contact:** Brenda Moore, event coordinator. Estab. 2000. Fine art show held annually in mid-June. Outdoors. Accepts photography, ceramics, drawing, fiber, furniture, glass, printmaking, jewelry, mixed media, painting, sculpture, fine wood. Juried. Awards/prizes: $5,250 in cash prizes. Number of exhibitors: 100. Public attendance: 10,000. Free to public. Artists should apply by downloading application from website or call. Deadline for entry: February 28. Space fee: $200. Jury Fee: $25. Exhibition space: 10×10 ft. For more information, artists should visit website, call or send SASE. Show located in Northside Park.

TIPS Apply early.

ARTS, BEATS & EATS

301 W. Fourth St., Suite LL-150, Royal Oak MI 48067. (208)792-2726. **Fax:** (208)792-2850. **E-mail:** lisa@artsbeatseats.com. **Website:** www.artsbeatseats.com. **Contact:** Lisa Konikow, art director. Estab. 1997. Fine arts & crafts fair held annually in September. Outdoors. Accepts handmade crafts, ceramic, digital art, fiber, drawing, glass, jewelry, metal, 2D/3D mixed media, painting, photography, printmaking, wood. Juried. Awards/prizes: $7,500 in cash awards. Exhibitors: 145. Number of attendees: 400,000. Free to public. Apply online. Deadline for entry: March. Application fee: $25. Space fee: $490. Exhibition space: 10×10. For more information, artists should send e-mail, visit website or call

ARTS EXPERIENCE

P.O. Box 1326, Palatine IL 60078. (312)751-2500 or (847)991-4748. **E-mail:** asoaartists@aol.com. **Website:** www.americansocietyofartists.org. Estab. 1979. Fine arts & crafts show held in summer in Chicago. Outdoors. Accepts photography, paintings, graphics, sculpture, quilting, woodworking, fiber art, handcrafted candles, glass works, jewelry and more. Juried by 4 images representative of work being exhibited; 1 image of display set-up, résumé with show listings helpful. Submit to asoaartists@aol.com. Number of exhibitors: 50. Free to public. Artists should apply by submitting jury material and indicate you are interested in this particular show. When you pass the jury, you will receive jury approval number and application you requested. You may also submit to ASA, P.O. Box 1326, Palatine IL 60078. Include a SASE (business size, #10). Deadline for entry: 2 months prior to show or earlier if space is filled. Space fee: to be announced. Exhibition space: 100 sq. ft. for single space; other sizes are available. For more information, artists should send SASE to submit jury material.

TIPS "Remember that at work in your studio, you are an artist. When you are at a show, you are a business person selling your work."

ARTSFEST

P.O. Box 99, 13480 Dowell Rd., Dowell MD 20629. (410)326-4640. **Fax:** (410)326-4887. **E-mail:** info@annmariegarden.org. **Website:** www.annmariegarden.org. Estab. 1984. Fine arts & crafts fair held annually in September. Indoors & outdoors. Accepts handmade crafts, ceramic, digital art, fiber, drawing, furniture, glass, jewelry, metal, 2D/3D mixed media, painting, photography, printmaking, wood. Juried. Awards/prizes: Best of Show, Best Demonstration, Wooded Path Award, Best New Artsfest Artist Award. Exhibitors: 170. Number of attendees: varies. Admission: $6 adults; children 11 & under free; members free. Apply online. Deadline for entry: March. Application fee: $25. Space fee: varies. Exhibition space: varies. For more information, artists should send e-mail, visit website or call.

ARTS IN THE PARK

302 Second Ave. E., Kalispell MT 59901. (406)755-5268. **E-mail:** information@hockadaymuseum.com. **Website:** www.hockadaymuseum.org. Estab. 1968. Fine arts & crafts show held annually 4th weekend in July (see website for details). Outdoors. Accepts photography, jewelry, clothing, paintings, pottery, glass, wood, furniture, baskets. Juried by a panel of 5 members. Artwork is evaluated for quality, creativity and originality. Jurors attempt to achieve a balance of mediums in the show. Number of exhibitors: 100. Public attendance: 10,000. Artists should apply by completing the online application form and sending 5 images in JPEG format; 4 images of work and 1 of booth. Application fee: $25. Exhibition space: 10×10 or 10×20 ft. Booth fees: $170-435. For more information, artists should e-mail, call, or visit website. Show located in Depot Park.

⊙ ARTS ON THE GREEN

Arts Association of Oldham County, 104 E. Main St., LaGrange KY 40031. (502)222-3822. **Fax:** (502)222-3823. **E-mail:** maryklausing@bellsouth.net. **Website:** www.aaooc.org. **Contact:** Mary Klausing, director. Estab. 1999. Fine arts & crafts festival held annually 1st weekend in June. Outdoors. Accepts photography, painting, clay, sculpture, metal, wood, fabric, glass, jewelry. Juried by a panel. Awards/prizes: cash prizes for Best of Show and category awards. Number of exhibitors: 100. Public attendance: 7,500. Free to the public. Artists should apply online or call. Deadline for entry: April 15. Jury fee: $25. Space fee: $180. Electricity fee: $15. Exhibition space: 10×10 or 10×12 ft. For more information, artists should e-mail, visit website, call. Show located on the lawn of the Oldham County Courthouse Square.

TIPS "Make potential customers feel welcome in your space. Don't overcrowd your work. Smile!"

⊙ ARTSPLOSURE

313 S. Blount St., #200B, Raleigh NC 27601. (919)832-8699. **Fax:** (919)832-0890. **E-mail:** sarah@artsplosure.org. **Website:** www.artsplosure.org. **Contact:** Sarah Wolfe, art market coordinator. Estab. 1979. Annual outdoor art/craft fair held the 3rd weekend of May. Accepts ceramics, glass, fiber art, jewelry, metal, painting, photography, wood, 2D and 3D artwork. Juried event. Awards: 6 totaling $3,500 cash. Number of exhibitors: up to 170. Public attendance: 75,000. Free admission to the public. Applications available in October, deadline is late January. Application fee: $32. Space fee: $330 for 12×12 ft.; $660 for a double space. Average sales: $2,500. To apply, visit www.artsplosure.org.

⊕ ⊙ ARTSQUEST FINE ARTS FESTIVAL

Cultural Arts Alliance of Walton County, Bayou Arts Center, 105 Hogtown Bayou Lane, Santa Rosa Beach FL 32459. (850)622-5970. **E-mail:** info@culturalartsalliance.com. **Website:** www.artsquestflorida.com. Estab. 1988. Fine arts & crafts fair held anually in May. Outdoors. Accepts handmade crafts, ceramic, digital art, fiber, drawing, glass, jewelry, metal, 2D/3D mixed media, painting, photography, printmaking, sculpture, wood. Juried. Awards/prizes: Best in Show, Awards of Excellence and Awards of Merit. Exhibitors: 125. Number of attendees: varies. Free to public. Apply online. Deadline for entry: February. Application fee: $40. Space fee: $300. Exhibition space: 10×10.

For more information, artists should send e-mail, visit website or call.

⊙ ARTWORKS OF EAU GALLIE FINE ARTS FESTIVAL

1490 Highland Ave., Suite A, Melbourne FL 32935. (321)242-1456. **E-mail:** artworksfestival@gmail.com. **Website:** www.artworksofeaugallie.org. **Contact:** Link Johnsten, president. Estab. 1996. Fine art & fine crafts show held annually in November the weekend before Thanksgiving. Outdoors. Accepts photography, various mediums—original artists' works only. Juried. Awards/prizes: Art Awards, Demonstrators' Awards, Sponsor Purchase Program. Number of exhibitors: 80-100. Public attendance: 15,000-20,000. Free to public. Artists should apply online. Applications accepted beginning March 1. Deadline for entry: September 1. Space fee: $160. Exhibition space: 12×12 ft. Average gross sales/exhibitor varies. For more information, artists should visit website.

TIPS "Artists must be prepared to demonstrate their methods of work by creating works of art in their booths."

⊕ ⊙ ATLANTA ARTS FESTIVAL

P.O. Box 724694, Atlanta GA 31139. (770)941-9660. **Fax:** (866)519-2918. **E-mail:** info@atlantaartsfestival.com. **Website:** www.atlantaartsfestival.com. Estab. 2006. Fine arts & crafts fair held annually in September. Outdoors. Accepts handmade crafts, ceramic, digital art, fiber, drawing, glass, jewelry, metal, 2D/3D mixed media, painting, photography, printmaking, wood. Juried. Awards/prizes: Best in Category, Best in Show. Exhibitors: 200. Number of attendees: varies. Free to public. Apply online. Deadline for entry: April. Application fee: $25. Space fee: varies. Exhibition space: 10×10. For more information, artists should send e-mail, visit website or call.

⊕ ATOMIC HOLIDAY BAZAAR

801 N. Tamiami Trail, Sarasota FL 34236. **E-mail:** atomicholidaybazaar@gmail.com. **Website:** www.atomicholidaybazaar.com. **Contact:** Adrien Lucas, event producer. Estab. 2006. Arts & Crafts show held annually the 1st or 2nd weekend of December. Indoors. Accepts handmade crafts, vintage clothing, kitsch, vintage jewelry, art, paper products, body products & makeup, homemade canned goods, fine jewelry, silversmiths, shoe cobblers, T-shirt screen printing, artists and plushie makers. Exhibitors: 150. Number of attendees: 1,000. Admission: $5 adults; 12

& under free. Apply via website. Deadline for entry: mid September. Space fee: $90 table; $280 booth. Exhibition space: 8×3 (table); 12×8 (booth). For more information e-mail or see website.

⊕ ⊙ BARRINGTON ART FESTIVAL

Amdur Productions, P.O. Box 550, Highland Park IL 60035. (847)926-4300. **Fax:** (847)926-4330. **E-mail:** info@amdurproductions.com. **Website:** www.amdurproductions.com. Estab. 2009. Fine arts & crafts fair held annually in May. Outdoors. Accepts handmade crafts, ceramics, fiber, glass, jewelry, metal, photography, watercolors and wood. Juried. Awards/prizes: announced at awards party. Exhibitors: 125. Number of attendees: 122,000. Free to public. Apply online. Deadline for entry: early January. Application fee: $25. Space fee: $415. Exhibition space: see website. For more information, artists should send e-mail, visit website or call.

⊕ ⊙ BARTLETT FESTIVAL OF THE ART

118 W. Bartlett Ave., Suite 2, Bartlett IL 60103. (630)372-4152. **E-mail:** art@artsinbartlett.org. **Website:** www.artsinbartlett.org. Estab. 2002. Fine arts & crafts fair held annually in June. Outdoors. Accepts handmade crafts, paintings, photography, fiber, sculpture, glass, jewelry, wood and more. Juried. Exhibitors: see website. Number of attendees: 3,000. Free to public. Apply online. Deadline for entry: April. Application fee: see website. Space fee: $150. Exhibition space: 10×10. For more information, artists should send e-mail, visit website or call.

⊕ ⊙ BAYOU CITY ART FESTIVAL

(713)521-0133. **E-mail:** info@bayoucityartfestival. com. **Website:** www.artcolonyassociation.org/bayou-city-art-festival-memorial-park. Fine arts & crafts fair held annually in March. Outdoors. Accepts handmade crafts, ceramic, digital art, fiber, drawing, furniture, glass, jewelry, metal, 2D/3D mixed media, painting, photography, printmaking, sculpture, wood. Juried. Awards/prizes: Best of Show, 2nd Place, 3rd Place, Best Booth, Award of Excellence. Exhibitors: see website. Number of attendees: varies. Admission: $15 adults; $3 children 4-12; children 3 & under free. Apply online. Deadline for entry: November. Application fee: see website. Space fee: varies. Exhibition space: varies. For more information, artists should send e-mail, visit website or call.

⊕ ⊙ BEAVER CREEK ART FESTIVAL

270 Central Blvd., Suite 107B, Jupiter FL 33458. (561)746-6615. **Fax:** (561)746-6528. **E-mail:** info@artfestival.com. **Website:** www.artfestival.com. **Contact:** Malinda Ratliff, communications manager. Estab. 1988. Fine arts & crafts fair held annually in August. Outdoors. Accepts handmade crafts, clay, digital, fiber, glass, jewelry, mixed media, painting, photography, printmaking/drawing, sculpture, wood. Juried. Awards/prizes: announced after jury. Exhibitors: 150. Number of attendees: varies. Free to public. Apply online. Deadline for entry: see website. Application fee: $35. Space fee: $475. Exhibition space: 10×10 and 10×20. For more information, artists should send e-mail, visit website or call.

○ Festival located at Beaver Creek Village in Avon, CO.

⊕ ⊙ BERKSHIRES ARTS FESTIVAL

P.O. Box 480, Slate Hill NY 10973. (845)355-2400. **Fax:** (845)355-2444. **E-mail:** show.director@americanartmarketing.com. **Website:** www.berkshiresartsfestival. com. Estab. 1984. Fine arts & crafts fair held annually in July. Indoors & outdoors. Accepts handmade crafts, ceramic, digital art, fiber, drawing, encaustic, furniture, glass, jewelry, metal, 2D/3D mixed media, painting, photography, sculpture, wood. Juried. Exhibitors: see website. Number of attendees: varies. Admission: $13 adults; $11 seniors; $5 students; $14 weekend pass; children 10 & under free. Apply online. Deadline for entry: early January. Application fee: $35. Space fee: varies. Exhibition space: varies. For more information, artists should send e-mail, visit website or call.

⊕ ⊙ BEST OF THE NORTHWEST FALL ART & FINE CRAFT SHOW

Northwest Art Alliance, Suite 103, 7777 62nd Ave., NE, Seattle WA 98115. (206)525-5926. **E-mail:** info@nwartalliance.com. **Website:** www.nwartalliance. com. Fine art & craft show held annually in October & November. Indoors. Accepts handmade crafts, ceramics, paintings, jewelry, glass, photography, wearable art and other mediums. Juried. Number exhibitors: 110. Number attendees: varies. Admission: $5 online; $6 at door; children 12 & under free. Apply via Zapplication.org. Deadline for entry: May. Application fee: $35. Space fee: varies. Exhibition space: varies. For more information, artists should call, e-mail or visit website.

BEST OF THE NORTHWEST SPRING ART & FINE CRAFT SHOW

Northwest Art Alliance, Suite 103, 7777 62nd Ave., NE, Seattle WA 98115. (206)525-5926. **E-mail:** info@nwartalliance.com. **Website:** www.nwartalliance.com. Fine art & craft show held annually in March. Indoors. Accepts handmade crafts, ceramics, paintings, jewelry, glass, photography, wearable art and other mediums. Juried. Number exhibitors: 110. Number attendees: varies. Admission: $5 online; $6 at door; children 12 & under free. Apply via Zapplication.org. Deadline for entry: January. Application fee: $35. Space fee: varies. Exhibition space: varies. For more information, artists should call, e-mail or visit website.

BEVERLY HILLS ART SHOW

Beverly Gardens Park, 9450 N. Santa Monica Blvd., Beverly Hills CA 90210. (310)285-6836. **E-mail:** kmclean@beverlyhills.org. **Website:** www.beverlyhills.org/artshow. Estab. 1973. Fine arts & crafts show held biannually 3rd weekend in May and 3rd weekend in October. Outdoors, 4 blocks in the center of Beverly Hills. Accepts photography, painting, sculpture, ceramics, jewelry, glass, traditional printmaking and digital media. Juried. Awards/prizes: 1st place in category, cash awards, Best in Show cash award; Mayor's Purchase Award in May show. Number of exhibitors: 230-250. Public attendance: 30,000-50,000. Free to public. Deadline for entry: mid-February for the May show; mid-July for the October show. For more information, artists should e-mail, visit website, call or send SASE. Show located at historic Beverley Gardens. **TIPS** "Art fairs tend to be commercially oriented. It usually pays off to think in somewhat commercial terms. Personally, I like risky and unusual art, but the artists who produce esoteric art sometimes go hungry! Be nice and have a clean presentation."

BLACK SWAMP ARTS FESTIVAL

P.O. Box 532, Bowling Green OH 43402. (419)354-2723. **E-mail:** info@blackswamparts.org. **Website:** www.blackswamparts.org. The Black Swamp Arts Festival (BSAF), held early September, connects art and the community by presenting an annual arts festival and by promoting the arts in the Bowling Green community. Awards: Best in Show ($1,500); Best 2D ($1,000); Best 3D ($1,000); 2nd Place ($750); 3rd Place ($500); Honorable Mentions (3 awards, $200 each). Apply online at www.zapplication.org. Call, e-mail, or visit website for more information. Application fee: $35. Single booth fee: $275. Double booth fee: $550. Show located in downtown Bowling Green.

BLUEGRASS FESTIVAL & ARTIST MARKET

922 Main St., Stone Mountain GA 30083. (404)873-1222. **E-mail:** lisa@affps.com. **Website:** www.stonemountainvillage.com/ssim.html. **Contact:** Lisa Windle, festival director. Estab. 2011. Arts & crafts show held annually late March. Outdoors. Accepts handmade crafts, painting, photography, sculpture, leather, metal, glass, jewelry. Juried by a panel. Awards/prizes: ribbons. Number of exhibitors: 150. Number of attendees: 7,500. Free to public. Apply online at www.zapplication.com. Deadline for entry: February 14. Application fee: $25. Space fee: $200. Exhibition space: 10×10. For more information, see website.

BOCA FEST

270 Central Blvd., Suite 107B, Jupiter FL 33458. (561)746-6615. **Fax:** (561)746-6528. **E-mail:** info@artfestival.com. **Website:** www.artfestivalc.com. **Contact:** Malinda Ratliff, communications manager. Estab. 1988. Fine art & craft fair held annually in January. Outdoors. Accepts photography, jewelry, mixed media, sculpture, wood, ceramic, glass, painting, digital, fiber, metal. Juried. Number exhibitors: 210. Number attendees: 80,000. Free to public. Apply online via www.zapplication.org. Deadline: see website. Application fee: $25. Space fee: $395. Exhibition space: 10×10 and 10×20. For more information, artists should e-mail, call or visit website.

Festival located at The Shops at Boca Center in Boca Raton FL.

BOCA RATON FINE ART SHOW

Hot Works, P.O. Box 1425, Sarasota FL 34230. (941)755-3088. **E-mail:** info@hotworks.org; patty@hotworks.org. **Website:** www.hotworks.org. **Contact:** Patty Naronzny. Estab. 2008. The annual Boca Raton Fine Art Show brings high-quality juried artists to sell their artworks in the heart of downtown Boca Raton. "The event takes place in a premium location on Federal Highway/US-1 at Palmetto Park Road. In its 3rd year, the Boca Raton Fine Art Show was voted no. 68 in the country by *Art Fair Source Book*." All work is original and personally handmade by the artist. We offer awards to attract the nation's best artists. Our goal is to create an atmosphere that enhances the artwork and creates a relaxing environment for art lovers. All types of disciplines for sale including sculpture, paintings, clay, glass, printmaking, fiber, wood, jewelry, photography, and more. Art show also has artist demonstrations, live entertainment, and food. Awards: 2 $500 Juror's Awards and 5 $100 Awards of Excellence. "In addition to the professional artists, as part of our commitment to bring art education into the event, there is a Budding Artists Art Competition, sponsored by the Institute for the Arts & Education, Inc., the 501(c)(3) nonprofit organization behind the event." For more information, see www.hotworks.org.

⊕ ⨀ BONITA SPRINGS NATIONAL ART FESTIVAL

P.O. Box 367465, Bonita Springs FL 34136-7465. (239)992-1213. **Fax:** (239)495-3999. **E-mail:** artfest@ artinusa.com. **Website:** www.artinusa.com/bonita. **Contact:** Barry Witt, director. Fine arts & crafts fair held annually 3 times a year. Outdoors. Accepts handmade crafts, Paintings, glass, jewelry, clay works, photography, sculpture, wood and more. Juried. Awards/prizes: Best of Show, Best 2D, Best 3D, Distinction Award. Exhibitors: see website. Number of attendees: varies. Free to public. Apply online. Deadline for entry: early January. Application fee: $30. Space fee: $400. Exhibition space: 10×12. For more information, artists should send e-mail, visit website or call.

⊕ ⨀ BOSTON MILLS ARTFEST

Website: www.bmbw.com. Estab. 1971. Fine arts & crafts fair held annually in June & July. Outdoors. Accepts handmade crafts, ceramic, digital art, fiber, drawing, furniture, glass, jewelry, metal, 2D/3D mixed media, painting, photography, printmaking, wood. Juried. Awards/prizes: First in Category, Award of Excellence. Exhibitors: see website. Number of attendees: varies. Free to public. Apply online. Deadline for entry: see website. Application fee: see website. Space fee: see website. Exhibition space: see website. For more information, artists should send e-mail, visit website or call.

⨀ BRICK STREET MARKET

E-mail: info@zionsvillechamber.org. **Website:** www.zionsvillechamber.org. **Contact:** Dusky Loebel. Estab. 1985. Fine art, antique & craft show held annually the Saturday after Mother's Day. Outdoors. In collaboration with area merchants, this annual event is held on Main Street in the Historic Downtown of Zionsville IN. Please submit application found on line at www.zi

onsvillechamber.org and 3 JPEG images. All mediums are welcome. Artists are encouraged to perform demonstrations of their work and talk with visitors during the event. Tents will be provided. Artists may use their own white 10×10 ft. tents if space is available. Artists must supply display equipment. Committee will not accept catalog or mass-produced products. Number of exhibitors: 150-180. Public attendance: 8,000-10,000. Free to public. Space fee: see website.

⊕ ⨀ BROWNWOOD PADDOCK SQUARE ART & CRAFT FESTIVAL

270 Central Blvd., Suite 107B, Jupiter FL 33458. (561)746-6615. **Fax:** (561)746-6528. **E-mail:** info@ artfestival.com. **Website:** www.artfestival.com. **Contact:** Malinda Ratliff, communications manager. Estab. 1997. Fine art & craft fair held annually in mid April. Outdoors. Accepts photography, jewelry, mixed media, sculpture, wood, ceramic, glass, painting, digital, fiber, metal. Juried. Number exhibitors: 205. Number attendees: 20,000. Free to public. Apply online via www.zapplication.org or visit website for paper application. Deadline: see website. Application fee: $15. Space fee: $265. Exhibition space: 10×10 and 10×20. For more information, artists should e-mail, call or visit website. Festival located at Brownwood in The Villages, FL.

⊕ ⨀ BRUCE MUSEUM OUTDOOR ARTS FESTIVAL

1 Museum Dr., Greenwich CT 06830-7157. (203) 869-6786, ext. 336. **E-mail:** sue@brucemuseum.org. **Website:** www.brucemuseum.org. **Contact:** Sue Brown Gordon, festival director. Estab. 1981. Fine arts & crafts fair held annually in October. Outdoors. Accepts handmade crafts, painting, sculpture, mixed media, graphics/drawing (including computer-generated works), photography. Juried. Exhibitors: see website. Number of attendees: varies. Free to public. Apply online. Deadline for entry: June. Application fee: $20. Space fee: $350. Exhibition space: 10×12. For more information, artists should send e-mail, visit website or call.

⊕ ⨀ BUCKHEAD SPRING ARTS & CRAFTS FESTIVAL

4469 Stella Dr., Atlanta GA 30327. (404)873-1222. **E-mail:** lisa@affps.com. **Website:** www.buckheadarts festival.com. **Contact:** Lisa Windle, festival director. Estab. 2009. Annual arts & crafts show. Held mid May. Outdoors. Accepts handmade crafts, paintings, photography, sculpture, leather, metal, glass, jewelry. Juried. Awards/prizes: ribbons. Number of exhibitors: 185. Number of attendees: 40,000. Free to public. Apply online at www.zapplication.com. Deadline for entry: March 14. Application fee: $25. Space fee: $200. Exhibition space: 10×10 ft. For more information, artists should visit website.

✪ ◉ BUFFALO GROVE INVITATIONAL ART FESTIVAL

Amdur Productions, P.O. Box 550, Highland Park IL 60035. (847)926-4300. **Fax:** (847)926-4330. **E-mail:** info@amdurproductions.com. **Website:** www.amdurproductions.com. Estab. 2002. Fine arts & crafts fair held annually in July. Outdoors. Accepts handmade crafts, ceramic, digital art, fiber, drawing, furniture, glass, jewelry, metal, 2D/3D mixed media, painting, photography, printmaking, wood. Juried. Exhibitors: 120. Number of attendees: 20,000. Free to public. Apply online. Deadline for entry: see website. Application fee: $25. Space fee: $450. Exhibition space: 10×10. For more information, artists should send e-mail, visit website or call.

✪ BUFFALO RIVER ELK FESTIVAL

Jasper AR 72641. (870)446-2455. **Website:** www.theozarkmountains.com. **Contact:** Patti or Nancy, vendor coordinators. Estab. 1997. Arts & crafts show held annually in June. Outdoors. Accepts fine art & handmade crafts, photography, on-site design. Exhibitors: 60. Number of attendees: 6,000. Free to public. Artists should apply via website. Deadline for entry: June 1. Application fee: none. Space fee: $75. Exhibition space: 10×10. For more information, artists should visit website.

◉ BY HAND FINE ART & CRAFT FAIR

1 I-X Center Dr., Cleveland OH 44135. (216)265-2663. **E-mail:** rattewell@ixcenter.com. **Website:** www.clevelandbyhand.com. **Contact:** Rob Attewell, show manager. Estab. 2004. Fine arts & crafts show held annually in November. Indoors. Accepts photography, 2D, 3D, clay, digital, fiber, furniture, glass, jewelry, leather, metal, oil/acrylics, printmaking, sculpture, watercolor, wood, wearable art. Juried; group reviews applications and photos. Awards/prizes: ribbons, booths. Number of exhibitors: 150-200. Number of attendees: 20,000. Admission: free. Artists should apply via www.zapplication.org. Deadline: June 15. Application fee: $25. Space fee: $399 (8×10); $425 (10×10). Exhibition space: 10×10, 15×10, 20×10 ft. For more

information, artists should e-mail or go to www.zapplication.org.

◉ CAIN PARK ARTS FESTIVAL

40 Severance Circle, Cleveland Heights OH 44118-9988. (216)291-3669. **Fax:** (216)291-3705. **E-mail:** jhoffman@clvhts.com; artsfestival@clvhts.com. **Website:** www.cainpark.com. Estab. 1976. Fine arts & crafts show held annually 2nd weekend in July (3 day event). Outdoors. Accepts photography, painting, clay, sculpture, wood, jewelry, leather, glass, ceramics, clothes and other fiber, paper, block printing. Juried by a panel of professional artists; submit digital images online or mail CD. Awards/prizes: Artist to Artist Award, $450; also Judges' Selection, Director's Choice and Artists' Award. Number of exhibitors: 150. Public attendance: 15,000. Fee for public: $5; Free on Friday. "Applications are available online at our website www.cainpark.com." Artists should apply by requesting an application by mail, visiting website to download application or by calling. Deadline for entry: early March. Application fee: $50. Space fee: $450. Exhibition space: 10×10 ft. Average gross sales/exhibitor: $4,000. For more information, artists should e-mail, call or visit website. Show located in Cain Park. **TIPS** "Have an attractive booth to display your work. Have a variety of prices. Be available to answer questions about your work."

◉ CALABASAS FINE ARTS FESTIVAL

100 Civic Center Way, Calabasas CA 91302. (818)224-1657. **E-mail:** artscouncil@cityofcalabasas.com. **Website:** www.calabasasartscouncil.com. Estab. 1997. Fine arts & crafts show held annually in late April/early May. Outdoors. Accepts photography, painting, sculpture, jewelry, mixed media. Juried. Number of exhibitors: 150. Public attendance: 10,000+. Free to public. Application fee: $25. Artists should apply online through www.zapplication.org; must include 3 photos of work and 1 photo of booth display. For more information, artists should call, e-mail or visit website. Show located at the Commons at Calabasas and the Calabasas Civic Center.

◉ CAREFREE FINE ART & WINE FESTIVAL

15648 Eagles Nest Dr., Fountain Hills AZ 85268. (480)837-5637. **Fax:** (480)837-2355. **E-mail:** info@thunderbirdartists.com. **Website:** www.thunderbirdartists.com. **Contact:** Denise Colter, president. Estab. 1993. Fine arts & crafts show held annually 3 times a year (January, March, November). Outdoors. Accepts photography, paintings, bronzes, baskets, jewelry, stone, pottery. Juried; CEO blind juries by medium. Number of exhibitors: 175. Attendance: 30,000. Admission: $3. Applications available online at www.zapplication.org. Deadline for entry: mid-June (see website for specifics). Application fee: $30. Space fee: $430-$1,240. Exhibition space: 10×10 to 10×30 ft. For more information, artists should e-mail, call or visit website.

TIPS "A clean gallery-type presentation is very important."

⊕ ◯ CAROUSEL FINE CRAFT SHOW

OCA Renaissance Arts Center & Theatre, 1200 E. Center St., Kingsport TN 37660. (423)392-8414. E-mail: stephanos@kingsporttn.gov. **Website:** www.engagekingsport.com. **Contact:** Will Stephanos, show director. Estab. 2012. Fine art show held annually in March. Indoors. Accepts fine art & handmade crafts, photography, clay, fiber, paintings, furniture, wood, metal, jewelry, glass. Juried. Exhibitors: 38. Number of attendees: 5,000-8,000. Admission: $5 (one day pass); $7 (2 day pass). Artists should apply online. Deadline for entry: December 1. Application fee: none. Space fee: $250. Exhibition space: 10×10. For more information, artists should e-mail, visit website or call.

◯ CEDARHURST CRAFT FAIR

P.O. Box 923, 2600 Richview Rd., Mt. Vernon IL 62864. (618)242-1236, ext. 234. **Fax:** (618)242-9530. E-mail: linda@cedarhurst.org; sarah@cedarhurst.org. **Website:** www.cedarhurst.org. **Contact:** Linda Wheeler, staff coordinator. Estab. 1977. Arts & crafts show held annually on the 1st weekend after Labor Day each September. Outdoors. Accepts photography, paper, glass, metal, clay, wood, leather, jewelry, fiber, baskets, 2D art. Juried. Awards/prizes: Best of most category. Number of exhibitors: 125+. Public attendance: 12,000. Public admission: $5. Artists should apply by filling out online application form. Deadline for entry: March. Application fee: $25. Exhibition space: 10×15 ft. For more information, artists should e-mail, call or visit website.

◯ CELLULAR SOUTH GUMTREE FESTIVAL

P.O. Box 786, Tupelo MS 38802. (622)844-2787. E-mail: laura.gumtreemuseum@gmail.com. **Website:** www.gumtreemuseum.com. Annual fine arts & crafts festival held early May on the historic courtyard square in downtown Tupelo. "A Mother's Day weekend tradition." Considers all styles and genres. Past shows have included: graphics, photography, drawings, glass, jewelry, clay, sculpture, painting, traditional crafts, water color and mixed media. Juried; selection panel made up of 4 prominent representatives in the artist community, with one serving as an alternate. Artist attendance limited to 100 juried artists selected by a panel; the next 20 artists will be placed on a waiting list. Awards: Best in Show ($1,500 Festival Purchase Award); Merit Awards ($4,900 in 7 categories); Purchase Awards ($7,000 work selected by patrons). Public attendance: 30,000. Free admission to the public. Application form, and complete details, available online. Application fee: $35. Space fee: $200 for 10×10 ft. (double booth limited availability). For more information, e-mail or see website.

⊕ ◯ CENTERFEST: THE ART LOVERS FESTIVAL

Durham Arts Council, 120 Morris St., Durham NC 27701. (919)560-2787. E-mail: centerfest@durhamarts.org. **Website:** www.centerfest.durhamarts.org. Estab. 1974. Fine arts & crafts fair held annually in September. Outdoors. Accepts handmade crafts, clay, drawing, fibers, glass, painting, photography, printmaking, wood, jewelry, mixed media, sculpture. Juried. Awards/prizes: Best in Show, 1st place, 2nd place, 3rd place. Exhibitors: 140. Number of attendees: see website. Admission: $5 donation accepted at gate. Apply online. Deadline for entry: May. Application fee: see website. Space fee: $195 (single); $390 (double). Exhibition space: 10×10 (single); 10×20 (double). For more information, artists should send e-mail, visit website or call.

CENTERVILLE–WASHINGTON TOWNSHIP AMERICANA FESTIVAL

P.O. Box 41794, Centerville OH 45441-0794. (937)433-5898. **Fax:** (937)433-5898. E-mail: americanafestival@sbcglobal.net. **Website:** www.americanafestival.org. Estab. 1972. Arts, crafts and antiques show held annually on the 4th of July, except when the 4th falls on a Sunday and then festival is held on Monday the 5th. Festival includes entertainment, parade, food, car show and other activities. Accepts arts, crafts, antiques, photography and all mediums. "No factory-made items accepted." Awards/prizes: 1st, 2nd, 3rd places; certificates and ribbons for most attractive displays. Number of exhibitors: 275-300. Public attendance: 75,000. Free to the public. Exhibitors should send SASE for application form, or apply online. Deadline for entry: early June (see website for details). Space fee: $40-55 site specific. Exhibition space: 12×10 ft. For more information, artists should e-mail, call or visit website. Arts & crafts booths located on N. Main St., in Benham's Grove and limited spots in teh Children's Activity area.

TIPS "Moderately priced products sell best. Bring business cards and have an eye-catching display."

CHAMBER SOUTH'S ANNUAL SOUTH MIAMI ART FESTIVAL

Sunset Dr. (SW 72nd St.) from US 1 to Red Rd. (SW 57th Ave.), South Miami FL 33143. (305)661-1621. **Fax:** (305)666-0508. **E-mail:** art@chambersouth.com. **Website:** www.chambersouth.com/events/south-mi ami-art-festival. **Contact:** Arelis Ferro, art festival coordinator. Estab. 1971. Annual. Fine art & craft show held the 1st weekend in November. Outdoors. Accepts 2D & 3D mixed media, ceramics, clay, digital art, glass, jewelry, metalwork, painting (oil, acrylic, watercolor), printmaking, drawing, sculpture, textiles, wood. Juried by panel of jurors who meet to review work; includes artists and board members. Cash prizes, ribbons to display during event, exemption from jury in the following year's show. Average number of exhibitors: 130. Average number of attendees: 50,000. Admission: free. Artists should apply by www.zapplication.org. Deadline: July 31. Application fee: $25. Space fee: standard, $325; corner $375. Space is 10×10 (10×20 also available). For more information artists should e-mail, call or visit the website.

TIPS "Good, clean displays; interact with customers without hounding."

CHARDON SQUARE ARTS FESTIVAL

P.O. Box 1063, Chardon OH 44024. (440)285-8686; (440)285-3519. **E-mail:** sgipson@aol.com. **Website:** www.chardonsquareassociation.org. **Contact:** Jan Gipson, chairman. Estab. 1980. Fine arts & crafts show held annually in early August (see website for details). Outdoors. Accepts photography, pottery, weaving, wood, paintings, jewelry. Juried. Number of exhibitors: 105. Public attendance: 4,000. Free to public. Artists can find application on website. Exhibition space: 12×12 ft. For more information, artists should call or visit website.

TIPS "Make your booth attractive; be friendly and offer quality work."

CHARLEVOIX WATERFRONT ART FAIR

P.O. Box 57, Charlevoix MI 49720. (231)547-2675. **E-mail:** cwaf14@gmail.com. **Website:** www.charlevoix waterfrontartfair.org. "The Annual Charlevoix Waterfront Art Fair is a juried and invitational show and sale. Categories are: ceramics, glass, fiber; drawing; wood; painting; mixed media 2-D and 3-D; jewelry, fine and other; printmaking; photography; sculpture. To apply, each entrant must submit 4 digital images (3 images of your art work and one booth image) sized 1920 x 1920 pixels at 72 dpi for consideration by the jury (ZAPP images are acceptable). A non-refundable processing fee of $25.00, plus $15.00 for each additional category entered, must accompany the artist's application."

CHASTAIN PARK FESTIVAL

4469 Stella Dr., Atlanta GA 30327. (404)873-1222. **E-mail:** lisa@affps.com. **Website:** www.chastain-parkartsfestival.com. **Contact:** Lisa Windle, festival director. Estab. 2008. Arts & crafts show held annually early November. Outdoors. Accepts handmade crafts, painting, photography, sculpture, leather, metal, glass, jewelry. Juried by a panel. Awards/prizes: ribbons. Number of exhibitors: 175. Number of attendees: 45,000. Free to public. Apply online at www.zapplica tion.com. Deadline for entry: August 28. Application fee: $25. Space fee: $300. Exhibition space: 10×10. For more information, send e-mail or see website.

CHATSWORTH CRANBERRY FESTIVAL

P.O. Box 286, Chatsworth NJ 08019. (609)726-9237. **Fax:** (609)726-1459. **E-mail:** lgiamalis@aol.com. **Website:** www.cranfest.org. **Contact:** Lynn Giamalis. Estab. 1983. Arts & crafts show held annually in mid-October (see website for details). Outdoors. The festival is a celebration of New Jersey's cranberry harvest, the 3rd largest in the country, and offers a tribute to the Pine Barrens and local culture. Accepts photography. Juried. Number of exhibitors: 200. Public attendance: 75,000-100,000. Free to public. Artists should apply by sending SASE to above address (application form online). Requires 3 pictures of products and 1 of display. Deadline: September 1. Space fee: $225 for 2 days. Exhibition space: 15×15 ft. For more information, artists should visit website. Show located in downtown Chatsworth.

⊕ ⓪ CHRISTMAS CONNECTION

Ste. 223 Renaissance Arts Center, 1200 E. Center St., Kingsport TN 37660. (423)392-8415. **E-mail:** bethestep@kingsporttn.gov. **Website:** www.engage kingsport.com. **Contact:** Beth Estep, show director. Estab. 1978. Arts & crafts show held annually in November. Indoors. Accepts fine art & handmade crafts. Juried. Exhibitors: 148. Number of attendees: 10,000. Free to public. Artists should apply online. Deadline for entry: August 1. Application fee: none. Space fee: $195. Exhibition space: 10×10. For more information, artists should e-mail, visit website or call.

⓪ CHUN CAPITOL HILL PEOPLE'S FAIR

1290 Williams St., Suite 102, Denver CO 80218. (303)830-1651. **Fax:** (303)830-1782. **E-mail:** nicole anderson@chundenver.org. **Website:** www.peoples fair.com; www.chundenver.org. **Contact:** Nicole Anderson, operations manager. Estab. 1972. Arts & music festival held annually 1st full weekend in June. Outdoors. Accepts photography, ceramics, jewelry, paintings, wearable art, glass, sculpture, wood, paper, fiber, children's items, and more. Juried by professional artisans representing a variety of mediums and selected members of fair management. The jury process is based on originality, quality and expression. Awards/prizes: Best of Show. Number of exhibitors: 300. Public attendance: 200,000. Free to public. Artists should apply by downloading application from website. Deadline for entry: March. Application fee: $35. Space fee: $300-400, depending on type of art. Exhibition space: 10×10 ft. For more information, artists should e-mail, visit website or call. Festival located at Civic Center Park.

⓪ CHURCH STREET ART & CRAFT SHOW

Downtown Waynesville Association, P.O. Box 1409, Waynesville NC 28786. (828)456-3517. **E-mail:** info@ downtownwaynesville.com; downtownwaynesville@ charter.net. **Website:** www.downtownwaynesville. com. Estab. 1983. Fine arts & crafts show held annually 2nd Saturday in October. Outdoors. Accepts photography, paintings, fiber, pottery, wood, jewelry. Juried by committee: submit 4 slides or digital photos of work and 1 of booth display. Prizes: $100-400 Number of exhibitors: 100. Public attendance: 15,000-18,000. Free to public. Entry fee: $25. Space fee: $110 ($200 for 2 booths). Exhibition space: 10×12 ft. (option of 2 booths for 12×20 space). For more information

and application, see website. Deadline: mid-August. Show located in downtown Waynesville on Main St. **TIPS** Recommends "quality in work and display."

⓪ CITY OF FAIRFAX FALL FESTIVAL

10455 Armstrong St., Fairfax VA 22030. (703)385-7949. **Fax:** (703)246-6321. **E-mail:** leslie.herman@ fairfaxva.gov; mitzi.taylor@fairfaxva.gov. **Website:** www.fairfaxva.gov. **Contact:** Mitzi Taylor, special event coordinator. Estab. 1985. Arts & crafts festival held annually the 2nd weekend in October. Outdoors. Accepts photography, jewelry, glass, pottery, clay, wood, mixed media. Juried by a panel of 5 independent jurors. Number of exhibitors: 400. Public attendance: 25,000. Free to the public. Deadline for entry: mid-March. Artists should apply by contacting Mitzi Taylor for an application. Application fee: $12. Space fee: $160 10×10 ft. For more information, artists should e-mail. Festival located in historic downtown Fairfax.

⓪ CITY OF FAIRFAX HOLIDAY CRAFT SHOW

10455 Armstrong St., Fairfax VA 22030. (703)385-7949. **Fax:** (703)246-6321. **E-mail:** mitzi.taylor@fair faxva.gov; leslie.herman@fairfaxva.gov. **Website:** www.fairfaxva.gov. **Contact:** Mitzi Taylor, event coordinator. Estab. 1985. Arts & crafts show held annually 3rd weekend in November. Indoors. Accepts photography, jewelry, glass, pottery, clay, wood, mixed media. Juried by a panel of 5 independent jurors. Number of exhibitors: 247. Public attendance: 5,000. Public admission: $5 for age 18 and older. $8 for 2 day pass. Artists should apply by contacting Mitzi Taylor for an application. Deadline for entry: early March (see website for details). Application fee: $12. Space fee: 10×6 ft. $195; 11×9 ft. $245; 10×10 ft. $270. For more information, artists should e-mail.

⊕ ⓪ CITYPLACE ART FAIR

270 Central Blvd., Suite 107B, Jupiter FL 33458. (561)746-6615. **Fax:** (561)746-6528. **E-mail:** info@ artfestival.com. **Website:** www.artfestival.com. **Contact:** Malinda Ratliff, communications manager. Estab. 2011. Fine art & craft fair held annually in early March. Outdoors. Accepts photography, jewelry, mixed media, sculpture, wood, ceramic, glass, painting, digital, fiber, metal. Juried. Number exhibitors: 200. Number attendees: 40,000. Free to public. Apply online via www.zapplication.org. Deadline: see website. Application fee: $25. Space fee: $395. Exhibition

space: 10×10 and 10×20. For more information, artists should e-mail, call or visit website.

○ Fair located in CityPlace in downtown West Palm Beach FL.

⊕ ☺ COCONUT GROVE ARTS FESTIVAL

3390 Mary St., Suite 128, Coconut Grove FL 33133. (305)447-0401. **E-mail:** katrina@cgaf.com. **Website:** www.coconutgroveartsfest.com. **Contact:** Katrina Delgado. The Coconut Grove Arts Festival showcases the works of 360 internationally recognized artists who are selected from nearly 1,300 applicants. Jurors evaluate the artist's work and displays to select participants in such categories as mixed media, painting, photography, digital art, printmaking & drawing, watercolor, claywork, glass, fiber, jewelry & metalwork, sculpture and wood.

⊕ COCONUT POINT ART FESTIVAL

270 Central Blvd., Suite 107B, Jupiter FL 33458. (561)746-6615. **Fax:** (561)746-6528. **E-mail:** info@artfestival.com. **Website:** www.artfestival.com. **Contact:** Malinda Ratliff, communications manager. Estab. 2007. Fine art & craft fair held annually in late December/early January & February. Outdoors. Accepts photography, jewelry, mixed media, sculpture, wood, ceramic, glass, painting, digital, fiber, metal. Juried. Number exhibitors: 200-280. Number attendees: 90,000. Free to public. Apply online via www.zapplication.org. Deadline: see website. Application fee: $25. Space fee: $395-425. Exhibition space: 10×10 and 10×20. For more information, artists should e-mail, call or visit website.

○ Festival held at Coconut Point in Estero FL.

⊕ ☺ COLORADO COUNTRY CHRISTMAS GIFT SHOW

Denver Mart, 451 E. 58th Ave., Denver CO 80216. (800)521-7469. **Fax:** (425)889-8165. **E-mail:** denver@showcase.events.org. **Website:** www.showcaseevents. org. **Contact:** Kim Peck, show manager. Estab. 2003. Annual holiday show held early November. Indoors. Accepts handmade crafts, art, photography, pottery, glass, jewelry, fiber, clothing. Juried. Exhibitors: 400. Number of attendees: 25,000. Admission: see website. Apply by e-mail, call or website. Deadline for entry: see website. Space fee: see website. Exhibition space: 10×10. For more information e-mail, call, send SASE or see website.

☺ COLORSCAPE CHENANGO ARTS FESTIVAL

P.O. Box 624, Norwich NY 13815. (607)336-3378. **E-mail:** info@colorscape.org. **Website:** www.colorscape.org. Estab. 1995. A juried exhibition of art & fine crafts held annually the weekend after Labor Day. Outdoors. Accepts photography and all types of media. Juried. Awards/prizes: $6,000. Number of exhibitors: 115. Public attendance: 10,000-12,000. Free to public. Deadline for entry: see website for details. Application fee: $15 jury fee. Space fee: $175. Exhibition space: 12×12 ft. For more information, artists should e-mail, visit website, call or send SASE. Show located in downtown Norwich.

TIPS "Interact with your audience. Talk to them about your work and how it is created. People like to be involved in the art they buy and are more likely to buy if you involve them."

⊕ COLUMBIANA ARTIST MARKET

P.O. Box 624, 104 Mildred St., Columbiana AL 35051. (205)669-0044. **E-mail:** info@shelbycountyartscouncil.com. **Website:** www.shelbycountyartscouncil.com. Member artists gather to offer their original artwork. Work available include oil paintings, acrylic paintings, photography, jewelry, fabric arts, print making, pottery and more.

☺ CONYERS CHERRY BLOSSOM FESTIVAL

1996 Centennial Olympic Pkwy., Conyers GA 30013. (770)860-4190; (770)860-4194. **E-mail:** rebecca.hill@conyersga.com. **Website:** www.conyerscherryblossomfest.com. **Contact:** Jill Miller. Estab. 1981. Arts & crafts show held annually in late March (see website for details). Outdoors. The festival is held at the Georgia International Horse Park at the Grand Prix Plaza overlooking the Grand Prix Stadium used during the 1996 Centennial Olympic Games. Accepts photography, paintings and any other handmade or original art. Juried. Submit 5 images: 1 picture must represent your work as it is displayed; 1 must represent a workshop photo of the artist creating their work; the other 3 need to represent your items as an accurate representation in size, style, and quality of work. Number of exhibitors: 300. Public attendance: 40,000. Free to public. Space fee: $135. Exhibition space: 10×10 ft. Electricity fee: $30. Application fee: $10; apply online. For more information, artists should e-mail, call or visit website. Show located at the Georgia International Horse Park.

ART FAIRS

✚ CORAL SPRINGS FESTIVAL OF THE ARTS

270 Central Blvd., Suite 107B, Jupiter FL 33458. (561)746-6615. **Fax:** (561)746-6528. **E-mail:** info@ artfestival.com. **Website:** www.artfestival.com. "The Coral Springs Festival of the Arts has grown considerably over the years into a two-day celebration of arts and culture with a fine art show, contemporary craft festival, theatrical performances and full line-up of live music. Held in conjunction with the Coral Springs Art Festival Committee and the City, this event brings 250 of the nation best artists and crafters to South Florida. Stroll amidst life-size sculptures, spectacular paintings, one-of-a-kind jewels, photography, ceramics, a separate craft festival, Green Market and much more. No matter what you're looking for, you'll be sure to find it among the various array of artists and crafters participating in this arts and crafts fair."

✚ ◉ COTTONWOOD ART FESTIVAL

2100 E. Campbell Rd., Suite 100, Richardson TX 75081. (972)744-458. **E-mail:** serri.ayers@cor.gov. **Website:** www.cottonwoodartfestival.com. **Contact:** Serri Ayers. "The semi-annual Cottonwood Art Festival is a juried show. Jurors have selected over 240 artists from 800 submissions to exhibit their museum-quality work at the festival. The artists compete in 14 categories: 2D mixed media, 3D mixed media, ceramics, digital, drawings/pastels, fiber, glass, jewelry, leather, metalwork, painting, photography, sculpture and wood. Rated as one of the top art festivals in the United States, the prestigious show is the premier fine art event in North Texas."

✚ COUNTRY FOLK ARTS AND CRAFTS SHOW

E-mail: shows@countryfolkart.com. **Website:** www. countryfolkart.com. Country Folk Art Shows has grown to 17 shows in 5 states. Every participant is juried and hand selected for their outstanding workmanship and integrity of creative design. Some of the more popular decorating items found at our shows are handcrafted furniture, home and garden decor, jewelry, textiles, holiday decor, wearable art, handmade candles and soaps, quilts, paintings, framed art, florals, iron work, wood carvings, baskets, stained glass and much more.

◉ CRAFT FAIR AT THE BAY

38 Charles St., Rochester NH 03867. (603)332-2616. **Fax:** (603)332-8413. **E-mail:** info@castleberryfairs. com. **Website:** www.castleberryfairs.com. Estab. 1988. Arts & crafts show held annually in July in Alton Bay NH. Outdoors. Accepts photography and all other mediums. Juried by photo, slide or sample. Number of exhibitors: 85. Public attendance: 7,500. Free to the public. Artists should apply by downloading application from website. Deadline for entry: until full. Exhibition space: 100 sq. ft. For more information, artists should call, e-mail or visit website.

TIPS "Do not bring a book; do not bring a chair. Smile and make eye contact with everyone who enters your booth. Have them sign your guest book; get their e-mail address so you can let them know when you are in the area again. And, finally, make the sale—they are at the fair to shop, after all."

✚ ◉ CRAFTS AT PURCHASE

P.O. Box 28, Woodstock NY 12498. (845)331-7900. **Fax:** (845)331-7484. **E-mail:** crafts@artrider.com. **Website:** www.artrider.com. **Contact:** Laura Kandel, assistant director. Estab. 2012. Boutique show of fine contemporary craft held annually in late October or early November. Indoors. Accepts photography, fine art, ceramics, wood, mixed media, leather, glass, metal, fiber, jewelry. Juried. Submit 5 images of work and 1 of booth. Exhibitors: 100. Attendance: 3,500. Admission: $10. Artists should apply online at www.artrider.com or www.zapplication.org. Deadline for entry: end of May. Application fee: $45. Space fee: $545. Exhibition space: 10×10. For more information, artists should e-mail, visit website, call.

◉ CRAFTWESTPORT

P.O. Box 28, Woodstock NY 12498. (845)331-7484. **Fax:** (845)331-7484. **E-mail:** crafts@artrider.com. **Website:** www.artrider.com. Estab. 1975. Fine arts & craft show held annually in the 3rd weekend before Thanksgiving. Indoors. Accepts photography, wearable and nonwearable fiber, jewelry, clay, leather, wood, glass, painting, drawing, prints, mixed media. Juried by 5 images of work and 1 of booth, viewed sequentially. Number of exhibitors: 160. Public attendance: 5,000. Public admission: $10. Artists should apply online at www.artrider.com or at www.zapplication.org. Deadline for entry: end of May. Application fee: $45. Space fee: $525. Exhibition space: 10×10 ft. For more information, artists should e-mail, visit website call.

⊕ ◎ CROCKER PARK FINE ART FAIR WITH CRAFT MARKETPLACE

270 Central Blvd., Suite 107B, Jupiter FL 33458. (561)746-6615. **Fax:** (561)746-6528. **E-mail:** info@artfestival.com. **Website:** www.artfestival.com. **Contact:** Malinda Ratliff, communications officer. Estab. 2006. Fine art & craft fair held annually in mid-June. Outdoors. Accepts photography, jewelry, mixed media, sculpture, wood, ceramic, glass, painting, digital, fiber, metal. Juried. Number exhibitors: 125. Number attendees: 50,000. Free to public. Apply online via www.zapplication.org. Deadline: see website. Application fee: $25. Space fee: $395. Exhibition space: 10×10 and 10×20. For more information, artists should e-mail, call or visit website.

◎ Fair located in Crocker Park in Westlake/Cleveland OH.

CUSTER FAIR

P.O. Box 6013, Evanston IL 60204. (847)328-2204. **Fax:** (847)328-2295. **E-mail:** office@custerfair.com. **Website:** www.custerfair.com. Estab. 1972. Outdoor fine art craft show held in June. Accepts photography and all mediums. Number of exhibitors: 400. Public attendance: 70,000. Free to the public. Application fee: $10. Booth fee: $250-400. Deadline for entry: early May. Space fee varies, e-mail, call, or visit website for more details.

TIPS "Be prepared to speak with patrons; invite them to look at your work and discuss."

A DAY IN TOWNE

Boalsburg Memorial Day Committee, 163 Boal Estate Dr., Boalsburg PA 16827. (814)466-6210. **E-mail:** office@boalmuseum.com. **Website:** www.boalsburgvillage.com. Arts & crafts show held annually the last Monday in May/Memorial Day weekend. Outdoors. Accepts photography, country fabric & wood, wool knit, soap, jewelry, dried flowers, children, pottery, blown glass. Vendor must make own work. Number of exhibitors: 125-135. Public attendance: 20,000. Artists should apply by writing an inquiry letter and sending 2-3 photos; 1 of booth and 2 of the craft. Deadline for entry: January 1–February 1. Space fee: $75. Exhibition space: 10×15 ft.

TIPS "Please do not send fees until you receive an official contract. Have a neat booth and nice smile. Have fair prices—if too high, product will not sell here."

◎ DEERFIELD FINE ARTS FESTIVAL

3417 R.F.D., Long Grove IL 60047. (847)726-8669. **E-mail:** dwevents@comcast.net. **Website:** www.dwevents.org. **Contact:** D&W Events, Inc. Estab. 2003. Fine art show held annually end of May/beginning of June. Outdoors. Accepts photography, fiber, oil, acrylic, watercolor, mixed media, jewelry, sculpture, metal, paper, ceramics, painting. Juried by 3 jurors. Awards/prizes: Best of Show; 1st Place, awards of excellence. Number of exhibitors: 120-150. Public attendance: 20,000. Free to public. Free parking. Artists should apply via www.zapplication.com or our promoter website: www.dwevents.org. Exhibition space: 100 sq. ft. For more information artists should e-mail, visit website, call. Show located at Park Avenue and Deerfield Road adjacent to Jewett Park in Deerfield IL.

TIPS "Artists should display professionally and attractively, and interact positively with everyone."

◎ DELAWARE ARTS FESTIVAL

P.O. Box 589, Delaware OH 43015. **E-mail:** info@delawareartsfestival.org. **Website:** www.delawareartsfestival.org. Estab. 1973. Fine arts & crafts show held annually the Saturday and Sunday after Mother's Day. Outdoors. Accepts photography; all mediums, but no buy/sell. Juried by category panels who are also artists. Awards/prizes: Ribbons, cash awards, free booth for Best of Show the following year. Number of exhibitors: 160. Public attendance: 50,000. Free to the public. Submit 3 photographs per category that best represent your work. Your work will be juried in accordance with our guidelines. Photos (no slides) will be returned only if you provide a SASE. Artists should apply by visiting website for application. Jury fee: $10 per category, payable to the Delaware Arts Festival. Space fee: $140. Exhibition space: 120 sq. ft. For more information, artists should e-mail or visit website. Show located in historic downtown Delaware OH, just 2 blocks from the heart of Ohio Wesleyan University Campus.

TIPS "Have high-quality, original stuff. Engage the public. Applications will be screened according to originality, technique, craftsmanship and design. Unaffiliated professional judges are hired to make all prize award decisions. The Delaware Arts Festival, Inc. will exercise the right to reject items during the show that are not the quality of the media submitted with the applications. No commercial buy and resell merchandise permitted. Set up a good booth."

⊕ ◯ DELRAY MARKETPLACE ART & CRAFT FESTIVAL

270 Central Blvd., Suite 107B, Jupiter FL 33458. (561)746-6615. **Fax:** (561)746-6528. **E-mail:** info@artfestival.com. **Website:** www.artfestival.com. **Contact:** Malinda Ratliff, communications manager. Estab. 2013. Fine art & craft fair held annually in November. Outdoors. Accepts photography, jewelry, mixed media, sculpture, wood, ceramic, glass, painting, digital, fiber, metal. Juried. Number exhibitors: 100. Number attendees: 40,000. Free to public. Apply online via www.zapplication.org. Deadline: see website. Application fee: $25. Space fee: $350. Exhibition space: 10×10 and 10×20. For more information, artists should e-mail, call or visit website.

◗ Festival located at Delray Marketplace off West Atlantic Ave. in Delray Beach FL.

DICKENS CHRISTMAS SHOW & FESTIVAL

2101 N. Oak St., Myrtle Beach SC 29577. (843)448-9483. **Fax:** (843)626-1513. **E-mail:** dickensshow@sc.rr.com. **Website:** www.dickenschristmasshow.com. **Contact:** Samantha Bower, manager. Estab. 1981. Annual arts & crafts, seasonal/holiday show held in November. Indoors. Accepts all fine art. Average number of exhibitors: 350. Average number of attendees: 16,000. Admission: $8.50 (plus tax). Artists should apply by application. Deadline: see website. Space fee: $300-800. Space is 10×10. For more information artists should e-mail, call or visit the website. Show held at Myrtle Beach Convention Center.

TIPS "Make sure your products are good and your display is good."

⊕ ◯ DOLLAR BANK THREE RIVERS ARTS FESTIVAL

803 Liberty Ave., Pittsburgh PA 15222. (412)471-6070. **E-mail:** trafmarket@trustarts.org. **Website:** www.trustarts.org/traf. **Contact:** Melissa Franko, artist market manager. Estab. 1960. Fine art show held annually in June. Outdoors. Accepts fine art & handmade crafts, photography, clay, ceramics, fiber, paintings, furniture, wood, metal, leather, mixed media, jewelry, glass, sculpture, drawing, digital art, printmaking. Juried. Awards/prizes: $10,000 in awards/prizes given away. Exhibitors: 360. Number of attendees: 600,000. Free to public. Artists should apply via www.zapplication.org. Deadline for entry: February 1. Application fee: $35. Space fee: $360-485.

Exhibition space: 10×10. For more information, artists should visit website.

◯ ALDEN B. DOW MUSEUM SUMMER ART FAIR

1801 W. St. Andrews Rd., Midland MI 48640. **Fax:** (989)631-7890. **E-mail:** mills@mcfta.org. **Website:** www.mcfta.org. **Contact:** Emmy Mills, business manager/art fair coordinator. Estab. 1966. Fine art & crafts show held annually in early June. Outdoors. Accepts photography, ceramics, fibers, jewelry, mixed media 3D, painting, wood, drawing, glass, leather, sculpture, basket, furniture. Juried by a panel. Awards: $500 1st Place, $300 2nd Place, $100 3rd Place. Average number of exhibitors: 150. Public attendance: 5,000-8,000. Free to public. Artists should apply at www.mcfta.org/specialevents.html. Deadline for entry: late March; see website for details. Application fee: jury $25, second medium $5/each. Space fee: $195/single booth, $365/double booth. Exhibition space: approximately 12×12 ft. Average gross sales/exhibitor: $1,500. Artists should e-mail or visit website for more information. Event takes place at Midland Center for the Arts.

⊕ ◯ DOWNTOWN ASPEN ART FESTIVAL

270 Central Blvd., Suite 107B, Jupiter FL 33458. (561)746-6615. **Fax:** (561)746-6528. **E-mail:** info@artfestival.com. **Website:** www.artfestival.com. **Contact:** Malinda Ratliff, communications manager. Estab. 2003. Fine art & craft fair held annually in July. Outdoors. Accepts photography, jewelry, mixed media, sculpture, wood, ceramic, glass, painting, digital, fiber, metal. Juried. Number exhibitors: 150. Number attendees: 80,000. Free to public. Apply online via www.zapplication.org. Deadline: see website. Application fee: $35. Space fee: $475. Exhibition space: 10×10 and 10×20. For more information, artists should e-mail, call or visit website.

◗ Festival located at Monarch Street in Aspen CO.

⊕ ◯ DOWNTOWN DELRAY BEACH FESTIVAL OF THE ARTS

207 Central Blvd., Suite 107B, Jupiter FL 33458. (561)746-6615. **Fax:** (561)746-6528. **E-mail:** info@artfestival.com. **Website:** www.artfestival.com. **Contact:** Malinda Ratliff, communications manager. Estab. 2000. Fine art & craft fair held annually in mid-January. Outdoors. Accepts photography, jewelry, mixed media, sculpture, wood, ceramic, glass, paint-

ing, digital, fiber, metal. Juried. Number exhibitors: 305. Number attendees: 100,000. Free to public. Apply online via www.zapplication.org. Deadline: see website. Application fee: $25. Space fee: $395. Exhibition space: 10×10 and 10×20. For more information, artists should e-mail, call or visit website.

○ Festival located at Atlantic Ave. in downtown Delray Beach FL.

⊕ ○ DOWNTOWN DELRAY BEACH THANKSGIVING WEEKEND ART FESTIVAL

207 Central Blvd., Suite 107B, Jupiter FL 33458. (561)746-6615. **Fax:** (561)746-6528. **E-mail:** info@ artfestival.com. **Website:** www.artfestival.com. **Contact:** Malinda Ratliff, communications manager. Estab. 2000. Fine art & craft fair held annually in November. Outdoors. Accepts photography, jewelry, mixed media, sculpture, wood, ceramic, glass, painting, digital, fiber, metal. Juried. Number exhibitors: 150. Number attendees: 80,000. Free to public. Apply online via www.zapplication.org. Deadline: see website. Application fee: $25. Space fee: $395. Exhibition space: 10×10 and 10×20. For more information, artists should e-mail, call, or visit website.

○ Festival located at 4th Ave. & Atlantic Ave. in downtown Delray Beach FL.

⊕ ○ DOWNTOWN DUNEDIN ART FESTIVAL

270 Central Blvd., Suite 107B, Jupiter FL 33458. (561)746-6615. **Fax:** (561)746-6528. **E-mail:** info@ artfestival.com. **Website:** www.arfestival.com. **Contact:** Malinda Ratliff, communications manager. Estab. 1997. Fine art & craft fair held annually in January. Outdoors. Accepts photography, jewelry, mixed media, sculpture, wood, ceramic, glass, painting, digital, fiber, metal. Juried. Number exhibitors: 130. Number attendees: 40,000. Free to public. Apply online via www.zapplication.org. Deadline: see website. Application fee: $25. Space fee: $395. Exhibition space: 10×10 and 10×20. For more information, artists should e-mail, call or visit website.

○ Festival located at Main St. in downtown Dunedin FL.

○ DOWNTOWN FESTIVAL & ART SHOW

P.O. Box 490, Gainesville FL 32627. (352)393-8536. **Fax:** (352)334-2249. **E-mail:** piperlr@cityofgaines ville.org. **Website:** www.gvlculturalaffairs.org. **Contact:** Linda Piper, events coordinator. Estab. 1981. Fine arts & crafts show held annually in November (see website for more details). Outdoors. Accepts photography, wood, ceramic, fiber, glass, and all mediums. Juried by 3 digital images of artwork and 1 digital image of booth. Awards/prizes: $15,000 in cash awards; $3,000 in purchase awards. Number of exhibitors: 250. Public attendance: 100,000. Free to the public. Artists should apply by mailing 4 digital images. Deadline for entry: May. Space fee: $235, competitive, $215 noncompetitive. Exhibition space: 12×12 ft. Average gross sales/exhibitor: $6,000. For more information, artists should e-mail, visit website, call.

TIPS "Submit the highest quality digital images. A proper booth image is very important."

⊕ ○ DOWNTOWN SARASOTA CRAFT FAIR

270 Central Blvd., Suite 107B, Jupiter FL 33458. (561)746-6615. **Fax:** (561)746-6528. **E-mail:** info@ ArtFestival.com. **Website:** www.artfestival.com. **Contact:** Malinda Ratliff, communications manager. "This popular annual craft festival has garnered crowds of fine craft lovers each year. Behold contemporary crafts from more than 100 of the nation's most talented artisans. A variety of jewelry, pottery, ceramics, photography, painting, clothing and much more—all handmade in America—will be on display, ranging from $15 to $3,000. An expansive Green Market with plants, orchids, exotic flora, handmade soaps, gourmet spices and freshly popped kettle corn further complements the weekend, blending nature with nurture."

⊕ ○ DOWNTOWN SARASOTA FESTIVAL OF THE ARTS

270 Central Blvd., Suite 107B, Jupiter FL 33458. (561)746-6615. **Fax:** (561)746-6528. **E-mail:** info@art festival.com. **Website:** www.artfestival.com. Fine art & craft fair held annually in mid-February. Outdoors. Accepts photography, jewelry, mixed media, sculpture, wood, ceramic, glass, painting, digital, fiber, metal. Juried. Number exhibitors: 305. Number attendees: 80,000. Free to public. Apply online via www. zapplication.org. Deadline: see website. Application fee: $25. Space fee: $395. Exhibition space: 10×10 and 10×20. For more information, artists should e-mail, call or visit website. Festival located at Main St. at Orange Ave. heading east and ending at Links Ave. in Downtown Sarasota FL.

⊕ ☺ DOWNTOWN STEAMBOAT SPRINGS ART FESTIVAL ON YAMPA STREET, THE YAMPA ART STROLL

270 Central Blvd., Suite 107B, Jupiter FL 33458. (561)746-6615. **Fax:** (561)746-6528. **E-mail:** info@artfestival.com. **Website:** www.artfestival.com. **Contact:** Malinda Ratliff, communications manager. Estab. 2015. Fine art & craft fair held annually in August. Outdoors. Accepts photography, jewelry, mixed media, sculpture, wood, ceramic, glass, painting, digital, fiber, metal. Juried. Number exhibitors: see website. Number attendees: see website. Free to public. Apply online via www.zapplication.org. Deadline: see website. Application fee: $35. Space fee: $350. Exhibition space: 10×10 and 10×20. For more information, artists should e-mail, call, or visit website.

○ Festival located at Yampa Ave. in Steamboat Springs CO.

⊕ ☺ DOWNTOWN STUART ART FESTIVAL

270 Central Blvd., Suite 107B, Jupiter FL 34458. (561)746-6615. **Fax:** (561)746-6528. **E-mail:** info@artfestival.com. **Website:** www.artfestival.com. **Contact:** Malinda Ratliff, communications manager. Estab. 1991. Fine art & craft fair held annually in February. Outdoors. Accepts photography, jewelry, mixed media, sculpture, wood, ceramic, glass, painting, digital, fiber, metal. Juried. Number exhibitors: 200. Number attendees: 50,000. Free to public. Apply online via www.zapplication.org. Deadline: see website. Application fee: $25. Space fee: $395. Exhibition space: 10×10 and 10×20. For more information, artists should e-mail, call, or visit website.

○ Festival located at Osceola St. in Stuart FL.

⊕ ☺ DOWNTOWN VENICE ART FESTIVAL

270 Central Blvd., Suite 107B, Jupiter FL 33458. (561)746-6615. **Fax:** (561)746-6528. **E-mail:** info@artfestival.com. **Website:** www.artfestival.com. **Contact:** Malinda Ratliff, communications manager. Estab. 1987. Fine art & craft fair held annually in early March & mid-November. Outdoors. Accepts photography, jewelry, mixed media, sculpture, wood, ceramic, glass, painting, digital, fiber, metal. Juried. Number exhibitors: 130-200. Number attendees: 50,000. Free to public. Apply online via www.zapplication.org. Deadline: see website. Application fee: $25. Space fee: $350-395. Exhibition space: 10×10 and 10×20. For more information, artists should e-mail, call, or visit website.

○ Festival located at W. Venice Ave. in downtown Venice FL.

☺ DURANGO AUTUMN ARTS FESTIVAL

802 E. Second Ave., Durango CO 81301. (970)422-8566. **Fax:** (970)259-6571. **E-mail:** daaf@durangoarts.org. **Website:** www.durangoarts.org/programs. Estab. 1994. Fine arts & crafts show. Third weekend in September. Outdoors. Accepts photography and all mediums. Juried. Number of exhibitors: 90. Public attendance: 6,500. Free to public. Exhibition space: 10×10 ft. & 10×20 ft. Space fee $325 & $625. Application fee of $30. Apply via www.zapplication.org. For more information, artists should visit website.

☺ EDENS ART FAIR

P.O. Box 1326, Palatine IL 60078. (312)751-2500. **E-mail:** asoa@webtv.net; asoaartists@aol.com. **Website:** www.americansocietyofartists.com. **Contact:** Office personnel. Estab. 1995 (after renovation of location; held many years prior to renovation). American Society of Artists. Fine arts & fine selected crafts show held annually in mid-July. Outdoors. Event held in Wilmette IL. Accepts photography, paintings, sculpture, glass works, jewelry and more. Juried. Send 4 slides or photos of your work and 1 slide or photo of your display; #10 SASE; a résumé or show listing is helpful. Number of exhibitors: 50. Free to the public. Artists should apply by submitting jury materials. Please jury by submitting 4 images representative of your work you wish to exhibit, one of your display set-up, your first/last name, physical address, daytime telephone number—résumé/show listing helpful. Submit to: asoaartists@aol.com. If you pass jury you will receive a nonmember jury approval number. If juried in, you will receive a jury/approval number. Deadline for entry: 2 months prior to show or earlier if spaces fill. Entry fee: to be announced. Exhibition space: approximately 100 sq. ft. for single space; other sizes available. For more information, artists should send SASE, submit jury material.

TIPS "Remember that when you are at work in your studio, you are an artist. But when you are at a show, you are a business person selling your work."

⊕ ☺ EDINA ART FAIR

(952)922-1524. **Fax:** (952)922-4413. **Website:** www.edinaartfair.com. Fine arts & crafts fair held annually in June. Outdoors. Accepts handmade crafts, ceramics, enamel, fiber, glass, jewelry, mixed media, photography, sculpture, wearable art, wood. Juried. Awards/prizes: Best of Show, Best Display, Awards of Excellence, Merit Awards. Number exhibitors: 300. Number attendees: 165,000. Free to public. Apply online. Deadline for entry: February. Application fee: $35. Space fee: $425 (single); $850 (double). Exhibition space: 10×10 (single); 10×20 (double). For more information, artists should visit website or call.

EL DORADO COUNTY FAIR

100 Placerville Dr., Placerville CA 95667. (530)621-5860. **Fax:** (530)295-2566. **E-mail:** fair@eldorado countyfair.org. **Website:** www.eldoradocountyfair. org. Estab. 1859. County fair held annually in June. Indoors. Accepts photography, fine arts and handicrafts. Awards/prizes given, see entry guide on website for details. Number of exhibitors: 350-450. Average number of attendees: 55,000. Admission fee: $9. Deadline: mid-May. Application fee: varies by class, see entry guide. For more information, visit website. Fair held at El Dorado County Fairgrounds in Placerville CA. **TIPS** "Not a lot of selling at fair shows, competition mostly."

⊕ ⍟ ELK RIVER ARENA'S FALL CRAFT SHOW

1000 School St., Elk River MN 55330. (763)635-1145. **Fax:** (763)635-1144. **E-mail:** lestby@elkrivermn.gov. **Website:** www.elkriverarena.com. **Contact:** Laura Estby, office assistant. Estab. 1990. Annual fine arts & crafts show held early May. Indoors. Accepts handmade crafts, paintings, ceramics, photography, upcycled items. Juried. Exhibitors: 85+. Number of attendees: 1,200. Free to public. Apply online at elkriverarena.com. Deadline for entry: until filled. Space fee: $50-$75. Exhibition space: 90-126 sq. ft. For more information e-mail or see website.

⍟ ELMWOOD AVENUE FESTIVAL OF THE ARTS, INC.

P.O. Box 786, Buffalo NY 14213-0786. (716)830-2484. **E-mail:** directoreafa@aol.com. **Website:** www.elm woodartfest.org. Estab. 2000. Arts & crafts show held annually in late August, the weekend before Labor Day weekend. Outdoors. Accepts photography, metal, fiber, ceramics, glass, wood, jewelry, basketry, 2D media. Juried. Awards/prizes: to be determined. Number of exhibitors: 170. Public attendance: 80,000-120,000. Free to the public. Artists should apply by e-mailing

their contact information or by downloading application from website. Deadline for entry: April. Application fee: $25. Space fee: $295. Exhibition space: 10×15 ft. Average gross sales/exhibitor: $3,000. For more information, artists should e-mail, call or visit website. Show located on Elmwood Ave.
TIPS "Make sure your display is well designed, with clean lines that highlight your work. Have a variety of price points—even wealthy people don't always want to spend $500 at a booth where they may like the work."

⊕ ESSEX FALL CRAFT SHOW

P.O. Box 8139, Essex VT 05451. (802)879-6837. **E-mail:** info@vtcrafts.com. **Website:** www.vtcrafts. com. **Contact:** Kathy Rose, owner. Estab. 1981. Arts & crafts show held annually in October. Indoors. Accepts fine art & handmade crafts. Exhibitors: 200. Number of attendees: 10,000. Admission: $8. Artists should apply via website. Deadline for entry: see website. Application fee: none. Space fee: $525. Exhibition space: 10×10. For more information, artists should visit website.

⊕ ⍟ ESSEX SPRING CRAFT SHOW

P.O. Box 8139, Essex VT 05451. (802)879-6837. **E-mail:** info@vtcrafts.com. **Website:** www.vtcrafts. com. **Contact:** Kathy Rose, owner. Estab. 1997. Arts & crafts show held annually in May. Indoors. Accepts fine art & handmade crafts. Juried. Exhibitors: 120. Number of attendees: 8,000. Admission: $7. Artists should apply via website. Deadline for entry: see website. Application fee: none. Space fee: $350. Exhibition space: 10×10. For more information, artists should visit website.

⍟ ESTERO FINE ART SHOW

Hot Works, LLC, Miromar Outlets, 10801 Corkscrew Rd., Estero FL 33928. (941)755-3088. **E-mail:** patty@ hotworks.org. **Website:** www.hotworks.org. **Contact:** Patty Narozny, executive director. Estab. 2008. Biannual fine art show held for 2 days in early January and early November. Outdoors. "This event showcases artists from around the globe. Art includes glass, clay, wood, fiber, jewelry, sculpture, painting, photography, and metal. There is artwork for every budget. Focus is on technique/execution, quality and originality." Juried by art professionals in the industry. 3 images of work, 1 of booth. Awards: $1,500 distributed as follows; 2 $500 Juror's Award of Excellence (purchase awards) and 5 $100 Awards of Excellence. Number of exhibitors: 110. Average number of attendees: 10,000. Free admission and free parking. Application fee: $30. Space fee: $385. Space: 11×11. For more information, artists should e-mail, call, see website, or visit www.zapplication.org for details.

○ Show located at Miromar Design Center, 10800 Corkscrew Road, Estero FL 33928.

TIPS "Bring enough work to sell that people want to see—original work! Stay positive."

○ EVERGREEN FINE ARTS FESTIVAL

Evergreen Artists Association, 22528 Blue Jay Rd., Morrison CO 80465. (303)618-9834. **E-mail:** joshtrefethen@gmail.com. **Website:** www.evergreenfineartsfestival.com; www.evergreenartists.org. **Contact:** Josh Trefethen, festival director. Estab. 1966. Fine arts show held annually the 4th weekend in August. Outdoors in Historic Heritage Grove Venue, next to Hiwan Homestead. Accepts both 2D and 3D media, including photography, fiber, oil, acrylic, pottery, jewelry, mixed media, ceramics, wood, watercolor. Juried event with jurors that change yearly. Artists should submit online 3 views of work and 1 booth display by digital photograph high-res. Awards/prizes: Best of Show in 2D and 3D and 6 awards of excellence, monetary plus jury exempt next year. Number of exhibitors: 100. Public attendance: 6,000-8,000. Free to public. Deadline for entry: March 15. Application fee: $30. Space: $350 (upon acceptance). Exhibition space: 10×10 ft. Submissions only on www.zapplication.org begin in December and jurying completed in early April. "Currently ranked in the top 100 by Art Fair Source Book." For more information, artists should call or send SASE.

○ FAIRE ON THE SQUARE

117 W. Goodwin St., Prescott AZ 86303. (928)445-2000, ext. 112. **Fax:** (928)445-0068. **E-mail:** chamber@prescott.org; scott@prescott.org. **Website:** www.prescott.org. Estab. 1985. Arts & crafts show held annually Labor Day weekend. Outdoors. Accepts photography, ceramics, painting, sculpture, clothing, woodworking, metal art, glass, floral, home décor. No resale. Juried. Photos of work and artist creating work are required. Number of exhibitors: 170. Public attendance: 10,000-12,000. Free to public. Application can be printed from website or obtained by phone request. Deadline: spaces are sold until show is full. Exhibition space: $425; $460 for food booth; 10×15 ft. For more information, artist should e-mail, visit website, or call.

○ A FAIR IN THE PARK

6300 Fifth Ave., Pittsburgh PA 15232. **E-mail:** fairdirector@craftsmensguild.org. **Website:** www.afairinthepark.org. Estab. 1969. Contemporary fine arts & crafts show held annually the weekend after Labor Day outdoors. Accepts photography, clay, fiber, jewelry, metal, mixed media, wood, glass, 2D visual arts. Juried. Awards/prizes: 1 Best of Show and 4 Craftsmen's Guild Awards. Number of exhibitors: 105. Public attendance: 25,000+. Free to public. Submit 5 JPEG images; 4 of artwork, 1 of booth display. Application fee: $25. Booth fee: $350 or $400 for corner booth. Deadline for entry: see website. Exhibition space: 10×10 ft. Average gross sales/exhibitor: $1,000 and up. For more information artists should e-mail or visit website. Show located in Mellon Park.

TIPS "It is very important for artists to present their work to the public, to concentrate on the business aspect of their artist career. They will find that they can build a strong customer/collector base by exhibiting their work and by educating the public about their artistic process and passion for creativity."

⊕ ○ FALL CRAFTS AT LYNDHURST

P.O. Box 28, Woodstock NY 12498. (845)331-7900. **Fax:** (845)331-7484. **E-mail:** crafts@artrider.com. **Website:** www.artrider.com. Estab. 1984. Fine arts & crafts show held annually in early to mid September. Outdoors. Accepts photography, wearable and nonwearable fiber, jewelry, clay, leather, wood, glass, painting, drawing, prints, mixed media. Juried by 5 images of work and 1 of booth, viewed sequentially. Number of exhibitors: 275. Attendance: 14,000. Admission: $10. Artists should apply at www.artrider.com or www.zapplication.org. Deadline for entry: end of May. Application fee: $45. Space fee: $795-895. Exhibition space: 10×10 ft. For more information, artists should e-mail, visit website, call.

○ FALL FEST IN THE PARK

117 W. Goodwin St., Prescott AZ 86303. (928)445-2000 or (800)266-7534. **E-mail:** chamber@prescott.org; scott@prescott.org. **Website:** www.prescott.org. Estab. 1981. Arts & crafts show held annually in mid-October. Outdoors. Accepts photography, ceramics, painting, sculpture, clothing, woodworking, metal art, glass, floral, home décor. No resale. Juried. Photos

of work, booth, and artist creating work are required. Number of exhibitors: 150. Public attendance: 6,000 7,000. Free to public. Application can be printed from website or obtained by phone request. Deposit: $50, nonrefundable. Electricity is limited and has a fee of $15. Deadline: Spaces are sold until show is full. Exhibition space: $250; $275 for food booth; 10×15 ft. For more information, artists should e-mail, visit website or call.

FALL FESTIVAL OF ART AT QUEENY PARK

P.O. Box 31265, St. Louis MO 63131. (314)889-0433. **E-mail:** info@gslaa.org. **Website:** artfairatqueenypark.com. Estab. 1976. Fine arts & crafts show held annually Labor Day weekend at Queeny Park. Indoors. Accepts photography, all fine art and fine craft categories. Juried by 4 jurors; 5 slides shown simultaneously. Awards/prizes: 3 levels, ribbons, $4,000+ total prizes. Number of exhibitors: 130-140. Public attendance: 4,000-6,000. Admission: $5. Artists should apply online. Application fee: $25. Booth fee: $225; $250 for corner booth. Deadline for entry: mid-June, see website for specific date. Exhibition space: 80 sq. ft. (8×10) For more information, artists should e-mail or visit website.

TIPS "Excellent, professional slides; neat, interesting booth. But most important—exciting, vibrant, eye-catching artwork."

FALL FESTIVAL OF THE ARTS OAKBROOK CENTER

Amudr Productions, P.O. Box 550, Highland Park IL 60035. (847)926-4300. **Fax:** (847)926-4330. **E-mail:** info@amdurproductions.com. **Website:** www.amdurproductions.com. Estab. 1962. Fine arts & crafts fair held annually in September. Outdoors. Accepts handmade crafts, jewelry, ceramics, painting, photography, digital, printmaking and more. Juried. Number exhibitors: see website. Number attendees: varies. Admission: Free to public. Apply online. Deadline for entry: see website. Application fee: $25. Space fee: $460. Exhibition space: 10×10. For more information, artists should e-mail, call or visit website.

FALL FESTIVAL ON PONCE

Olmstead Park, North Druid Hills, 1451 Ponce de Leon, Atlanta GA 30307. (404)873-1222. **E-mail:** info@affps.com. **Website:** festivalonponce.com. **Contact:** Lisa Windle, festival director. Estab. 2010. Arts & crafts show held annually mid October. Outdoors. Ac-

cepts handmade crafts, painting, photography, sculpture, leather, metal, glass, jewelry. Juried by a panel. Awards/prizes: ribbons. Number of exhibitors: 125. Number of attendees: 45,000. Free to public. Apply online at www.zapplication.org. Deadline for entry: August 21. Application fee: $25. Space fee: $275. Exhibition space: 10×10. For more information, e-mail or see website.

FALL FINE ART & CRAFTS AT BROOKDALE PARK

473 Watchung Ave., Bloomfield NJ 07003. (908)874-5247. **Fax:** (908)874-7098. **E-mail:** info@rosesquared.com. **Website:** www.rosesquared.com. **Contact:** Howard Rose, vice president. Estab. 1998. Fine arts & crafts show held annually in mid-October. Outdoors. Accepts photography and all other mediums. Juried. Number of exhibitors: 160. Public attendance: 12,000. Free to public. Artists should apply on the website. Deadline for entry: mid-September. Application fee: $25. Space fee: varies by booth size. Exhibitor space: 120 sq. ft. See application form on website for details. For more information, artists should visit the website. **TIPS** "Have a range of products and prices."

FARGO'S DOWNTOWN STREET FAIR

Downtown Community Partnership, 210 Broadway N., #202, Fargo ND 58102. (701)241-1570; (701)451-9062. **Fax:** (701)241-8275. **E-mail:** fargostreetfair@downtownfargo.com. **Website:** www.downtownfargo.com. **Contact:** Stephanie Holland, street fair consultant. Estab. 1975. "This juried event is located in historic downtown Fargo on Broadway in July. It is a street fair that successfully combines arts & crafts, food, marketplace, music and entertainment. It attracts a large number of visitors from the tri-state region/Winnepeg and many vacationers. The locals also look forward to it every year! The show is largely made up of traditional crafts, jewelry, clothing and is focused on increasing its fine arts entries each year." Outdoors. Accepts food/culinary, mixed media, pottery/ceramic, wood furniture, glass, music, printmaking, wood other, jewelry, naturals/floral, recycled/found object/green, leather, painting, sculpture, metal, photography, textiles/fibers/clothing. Number of exhibitors: 300. Public attendance: 130,000-150,000. Free to public. "Artists should apply online and submit 3 photos for the jury: 3 images of your work, 1 image of booth, and 4 images of process." All JPEG photos must be 300 dpi and be at least

1,800×1,200 pixels. Deadline for entry: mid-February. Space fee: $325-700 depending on size and/or corner. Exhibition space: 11×11. For more information, artists should visit www.downtownfargo.com. Fair located in downtown Fargo.

FAUST HERITAGE FESTIVAL

15185 Olive Blvd., St. Louis MO 63017. (314)615-8328. **E-mail:** lritchey@stlouisco.com. **Website:** www.stlou isco.com/parks. **Contact:** Lori Ritchey, museum educator. Historic arts & crafts festival held annually in September. Outdoors. Accepts historic arts & crafts, watercolor, jewelry, wood , floral, baskets, prints, drawing, mixed media, folk art. Must be approved by staff to attend festival. Number exhibitors: 20-30. Number of attendees: 4,000. Admission: $5 adults; $2 children ages 4-12, 3 & under free. Apply by contacting festival coordinator. Deadline for entry: August. Space fee: 15% of gross sales. Exhibition space: varies; set up must be historically accurate with no plastic tents. For more information, artists should e-mail.

✚ FESTIVAL FETE

P.O. Box 2552, Newport RI 02840. (401)207-8115. **E-mail:** pilar@festivalfete.com. **Website:** www.festival fete.com. Fine arts & crafts fair held annually in July. Outdoors. Accepts handmade crafts, painting, sculpture, photography, drawing, fabric, crafts, ceramics, glass and jewelry. Juried. Awards/prizes: see website. Number exhibitors: 150. Number attendees: varies. Free to public. Apply online. Deadline for entry: see website. Application fee: see website. Space fee: $175. Exhibition space: 10×10. For more information, artists should email, visit website or call.

◯ FESTIVAL IN THE PARK

(704)338-1060. **E-mail:** festival@festivalinthepark. org. **Website:** www.festivalinthepark.org. Estab. 1964. Fine arts & crafts show held annually in late September (3rd Friday after Labor Day). Outdoors. Accepts photography and all arts mediums. Awards/ prizes: $4,000 in cash awards. Number of exhibitors: 180. Public attendance: 100,000. Free to the public. Artists should apply by visiting website for application. Deadline: July 15. Application fee: $45. Space fee: $345. Exhibition space: 10×10 ft. For more information, artists should e-mail, visit website, call.

✚ ◯ FIESTA ARTS FAIR

Southwest School of Art, 300 Augusta St., San Antonio TX 78205. (210)224-1848. **Fax:** (210)224-9337.

Website: www.swschool.org/fiestaartsfair. Art & craft market/show held annually in April. Outdoors. Accepts handmade crafts, Ceramics, paintings, jewelry, glass, photography, wearable art and other mediums. Juried. Number exhibitors: 125. Number attendees: 12,000. Admission: $16 weekend pass; $10 daily adult pass; $5 daily children pass; children 5 & under free. Apply via www.zapplication.org. Deadline for entry: November. Application fee: none. Space fee: varies. Exhibition space: varies. For more information, artists should call or visit website.

◯ FILLMORE JAZZ FESTIVAL

Steven Restivo Event Services, LLC, P.O. Box 151017, San Rafael CA 94915. (800)310-6563. **Fax:** (415)456-6436. **Website:** www.fillmorejazzfestival.com. Estab. 1984. Fine arts & crafts show and jazz festival held annually 1st weekend of July in San Francisco, between Jackson & Eddy Streets. Outdoors. Accepts photography, ceramics, glass, jewelry, paintings, sculpture, metal clay, wood, clothing. Juried by prescreened panel. Number of exhibitors: 250. Public attendance: 100,000. Free to public. Deadline for entry: ongoing; apply online. Exhibition space: 8×10 ft. or 10×10 ft. Average gross sales/exhibitor: $800-11,000. For more information, artists should visit website or call.

◯ FINE ART & CRAFTS AT ANDERSON PARK

274 Bellevue Ave., Upper Montclair NJ 07043. (908)874-5247. **Fax:** (908)874-7098. **E-mail:** info@ rosesquared.com. **Website:** www.rosesquared.com. Estab. 1984. Fine art & craft show held annually in mid-September. Outdoors. Accepts photography and all other mediums. Juried. Number of exhibitors: 160. Public attendance: 12,000. Free to the public. Artists should apply on the website. Deadline for entry: mid-August. Application fee: $25. Space fee varies by booth size; see application form on website for details. For more information, artists should visit the website. **TIPS** "Create a range of sizes and prices."

◯ FINE ART & CRAFTS AT VERONA PARK

542 Bloomfield Ave., Verona NJ 07044. (908)874-5247. **Fax:** (908)874-7098. **E-mail:** info@rosesquared.com. **Website:** www.rosesquared.com. **Contact:** Howard Rose, vice president. Estab. 1986. Fine arts & crafts show held annually in mid-May. Outdoors. Accepts photography and all other mediums. Juried. Number of exhibitors: 140. Public attendance: 10,000. Free to public. Artists should apply on the website. Deadline

for entry: mid-April. Application fee: $25. Space fee varies by booth size; see application form on website for details. For more information, artists should visit the website.

TIPS "Have a range of sizes and price ranges."

✚ ◯ FINE ART FAIR

Foster Arts Center Building, 203 Harrison St., Peoria IL 61602. (309)637-2787. **E-mail:** events@peoriaart guild.org. **Website:** www.peoriaartguild.org. **Contact:** special events coordinator. Estab. 1962. Fine arts & crafts fair held annually in September. Outdoors. Accepts handmade crafts, painting, sculpture, photography, drawing, fabric, crafts, ceramics, glass and jewelry. Juried. Number exhibitors: 150. Number attendees: varies. Admission: $7 adults; children 12 & under free; Peoria Art Guild members free. Apply online. Deadline for entry: see website. Application fee: see website. Space fee: see website. Exhibition space: see website. For more information, artists should e-mail, visit website or call.

✚ ◯ FIREFLY ART FAIR

Wauwatosa Historical Society, 7406 Hillcrest Drive, Wauwatosa WI 53213. (414)774-8672. **E-mail:** staff@ wauwatosahistoricalsociety.org. **Website:** www.wau watosahistoricalsociety.org. Estab. 1985. Fine arts & crafts fair held annually in August. Outdoors. Accepts handmade crafts, painting, sculpture, photography, ceramics, jewelry, fiber, printmaking, glass, paper, leather, wood. Juried. Number exhibitors: 150. Number attendees: varies. Free to public. Apply online. Deadline for entry: March. Application fee: $15. Space fee: $140. Exhibition space: 10×10. For more information, artists should email, visit website or call.

◯ FOOTHILLS ARTS & CRAFTS FAIR

2753 Lynn Rd., Suite A, Tryon NC 28782-7870. (828)859-7427. **E-mail:** info@blueridgebbqfestival. com. **Website:** www.blueridgebbqfestival.com. Estab. 1994. Fine arts & crafts show and Blue Ridge BBQ Festival/Championship held annually the 2nd Friday and Saturday in June. Outdoors. Accepts contemporary, traditional and fine art by artist only; nothing manufactured or imported. Juried. Number of exhibitors: 50. Public attendance: 15,000+. Public admission: $8; 12 and under free. Artists should apply by downloading application from website or sending personal information to e-mail or mailing address. See website for deadline for entry. Jury fee: $25, nonrefundable.

Space fee: $175. Exhibition space: 10×10 ft. For more information, artists should e-mail or visit website.

TIPS "Have an attractive booth, unique items, and reasonable prices."

◯ FOUNTAIN HILLS FINE ART & WINE AFFAIRE

15648 N. Eagles Nest Dr., Fountain Hills AZ 85268. (480)837-5637. **Fax:** (480)837-2355. **E-mail:** info@ thunderbirdartists.com. **Website:** www.thunderbird artists.com. **Contact:** Denise Colter, president. Estab. 2005. Fine arts & crafts show held annually in March. Outdoors. Accepts photography, paintings, bronzes, baskets, jewelry, stone, pottery. Juried; CEO blind juries by medium. Number of exhibitors: 125. Public attendance: 20,000. Public admission: $3. Apply online at www.zapplication.org. Deadline for entry: November (see website for specifics). Application fee: $30. Space fee: $430-1,240. Exhibition space: 10×10 to 10×30 ft. For more information, artists should e-mail, call or see website.

TIPS "A clean, gallery-type presentation is very important."

◯ FOURTH AVENUE STREET FAIR

434 E. Ninth St., Tucson AZ 85705. (520)624-5004 or (800)933-2477. **Fax:** (520)624-5933. **E-mail:** kurt@ fourthavenue.org. **Website:** www.fourthavenue.org. **Contact:** Kurt. Estab. 1970. Arts & crafts fair held annually in late March/early April and December (see website for details). Outdoors. Accepts photography, drawing, painting, sculpture, arts & crafts. Juried by 5 jurors. Awards/prizes: Best of Show. Number of exhibitors: 400. Public attendance: 300,000. Free to the public. Artists should apply by completing the online application at www.zapplication.org. Requires 4 photos of art/craft and 1 booth photo. $35 application fee. Booth fee $505, additional $150 for corner booth. Deadline for entry: see website for details. Exhibition space: 10×10 ft. Average gross sales/exhibitor: $3,000. For more information, artists should e-mail, visit website, call, send SASE. Fair located on 4th Ave., between 9th St. and University Ave.

◯ FOURTH STREET FESTIVAL FOR THE ARTS & CRAFTS

P.O. Box 1257, Bloomington IN 47402. (812)575-0484; (812)335-3814. **E-mail:** info@4thstreet.org. **Website:** www.4thstreet.org. Estab. 1976. Fine arts & crafts show held annually Labor Day weekend. Outdoors. Accepts photography, clay, glass, fiber, jewelry, painting, graphic, mixed media, wood. Juried by a 4-member panel. Awards/prizes: Best of Show ($750), 1st, 2nd, 3rd in 2D and 3D. Number of exhibitors: 105. Public attendance: 25,000. Free to public. Artists should apply by sending requests by mail, e-mail or download application from website at www.zapplication.org. Exhibition space: 10×10 ft. Average gross sales/exhibitor: $2,700. For more information, artists should e-mail, visit website, call or send for information with SASE. Show located at 4th St. and Grant St. adjacent to Indiana University.

TIPS Be professional.

◑ FRANKFORT ART FAIR

P.O. Box 566, Frankfort MI 49635. (231)352-7251. **Fax:** (231)352-6750. **E-mail:** fcofc@frankfort-elberta.com. **Website:** www.frankfort-elberta.com. **Contact:** Joanne Bartley, executive director. Fine art fair held annually in August. Outdoors. Accepts photography, clay, glass, jewelry, textiles, wood, drawing/graphic arts, painting, sculpture, baskets, mixed media. Juried by 3 photos of work, 1 photo of booth display and 1 photo of work in progress. Prior exhibitors are not automatically accepted. No buy/sell allowed. Artists should apply online website, e-mailing or calling. Deadline for entry: May 1 ($50 late fee). Jury fee: $25. Space fee: $125 for Friday and Saturday. Exhibition space: 12×12 ft. For more information, artists should e-mail or visit website. Fair located in Market Square Park.

◑ FREDERICK FESTIVAL OF THE ARTS

22 S. Market St., Suite 3, Frederick MD 21701. (301)662-4190. **Fax:** (301)663-3084. **E-mail:** info@frederickartscouncil.org. **Website:** www.frederickartscouncil.org. Juried 2-day fine arts festival held annually the 1st weekend of June along Carroll Creek Linear Park in downtown Frederick. Features approximately 110 artists from across the country, 2 stages of musical performances, children's crafts and activities, artist demonstrations, as well as interactive classical theater performances. For more information, including application deadlines and fees, visit website. Festival takes place in Carroll Creek Linear Park in downtown Frederick.

⊕ ◑ FRIENDS OF THE KENOSHA PUBLIC MUSEUMS ART FAIR

5500 First Ave., Kenosha WI 53140. (262)653-4140. **E-mail:** pgregorski@kenosha.org. **Website:** www.kenoshapublicmuseum.org. **Contact:** Peggy Grego-

rski, deputy director. Estab. 1964. Fine arts & crafts show held annually 3rd Sunday of July. Indoors & outdoors. Accepts handmade crafts. Juried. Awards/prizes: 5 awards totaling $2,000. Exhibitors: 125. Number of attendees: 7,000. Free to public. Apply online. Deadline for entry: May 1. Application fee: none. Space fee: $125-200. Exhibition space: 10×10 (indoors); 15×15 (outdoors). For more information, artists should send e-mail or visit website.

◑ FUNKY FERNDALE ART SHOW

Integrity Shows, P.O. Box 1070, Ann Arbor MI 48106. **E-mail:** info@integrityshows.com. **Website:** www.funkyferndaleartfair.com. **Contact:** Mark Loeb. Estab. 2004. Fine arts & crafts show held annually in September. Outdoors. Accepts photography and all fine art and craft mediums; emphasis on fun, funky work. Juried by 3 independent jurors. Awards/prizes: purchase and merit awards. Number of exhibitors: 120. Public attendance: 30,000. Free to the public. Application fee: $25. Booth fee: $295. Electricity limited; fee: $100. For more information, artists should visit our website.

TIPS "Show enthusiasm. Keep a mailing list. Develop collectors."

⊕ ◑ GAITHERSBURG-KENTLANDS DOWNTOWN ART FESTIVAL

270 Central Blvd., Suite 107B, Jupiter FL 33458. (561)746-6615. **Fax:** (561)746-6528. **E-mail:** info@artfestival.com. **Website:** www.artfestival.com. **Contact:** Malinda Ratliff, communications manager. Estab. 2015. Fine art & craft fair held annually in September. Outdoors. Accepts photography, jewelry, mixed media, sculpture, wood, ceramic, glass, painting, digital, fiber, metal. Juried. Number exhibitors: see website. Number attendees: see website. Free to public. Apply online via www.zapplication.org. Deadline: see website. Application fee: $25. Space fee: $450. Exhibition space: 10×10 and 10×20. For more information, artists should e-mail, call or visit website.

◐ Festival located at The Streets of Market and Main at Kentlands Downtown.

◑ GARRISON ART CENTER'S JURIED FINE CRAFTS FAIR

23 Garrison's Landing, P.O. Box 4, Garrison NY 10524. (845)424-3960. **E-mail:** info@garrisonartcenter.org. **Website:** www.garrisonartcenter.org. Outdoor, riverside fine crafts show held annually on the third weekend in August. 85 exhibitors are selected

to exhibit and sell handmade original work. Entries are judged based on creativity, originality and quality. Annual visitors 4,000-5,000. Visit our website for information, prospectus, and application. Fair located at Garrison's Landing.

TIPS "Have an inviting booth and be pleasant and accessible. Don't hide behind your product—engage the audience."

✚ ○ GASPARILLA FESTIVAL OF THE ARTS

P.O. Box 10591, Tampa FL 33679. (813)876-1747. **E-mail:** info@gasparillaarts.com. **Website:** www.gasparilla-arts.com. Estab. 1970. Fine arts & crafts fair held annually in March. Outdoors. Accepts handmade crafts, ceramic, digital, drawing, fiber, glass, jewelry, mixed media, painting, photography, printmaking, sculpture, watercolor and wood. Juried. Awards/prizes: $74,500 in cash awards. Number exhibitors: 300. Number attendees: 250,000. Free to public. Apply online. Deadline for entry: September. Application fee: $40. Space fee: $375. Exhibition space: 10×10. For more information, artists should email, visit website or call.

✚ ○ GATHERING AT THE GREAT DIVIDE

Mountain Art Festivals, P.O. Box 3578, Breckenridge CO 80424. (970)547-9326. **E-mail:** info@mountainartfestivals.com. **Website:** www.mountainartfestivals.com. Estab. 1975. Fine arts & crafts fair held annually in August. Outdoors. Accepts handmade crafts, painting, sculpture, photography, drawing, fabric, crafts, ceramics, glass and jewelry. Juried. Number exhibitors: see website. Number attendees: varies. Free to public. Apply online. Deadline for entry: April. Application fee: $35. Space fee: $500. Exhibition space: 10×10. For more information, artists should email, visit website or call.

○ GENEVA ARTS FAIR

8 S. Third St., Geneva IL 60134. (630)232-6060. **E-mail:** chamberinfo@genevachamber.com. **Website:** www.genevachamber.com. Fine arts show held annually in late-July (see website for details). Outdoors. Juried. "The unprecedented Geneva Arts Fair transforms downtown Geneva into a venue for over 150 esteemed artists and draws a crowd of more than 20,000. The juried show was voted a Top 200 Fine Craft Fair by *Art Fair SourceBook* and a previous winner of 'Best Craft or Art Show' by *West Suburban Living* magazine." Accepts photography, ceramics, fiber, printmaking, mixed media, watercolor, wood, sculpture and jewelry. Application deadline: early February. Please visit www.emevents.com to apply.

GERMANTOWN FESTIVAL

P.O. Box 381741, Germantown TN 38183. (901)757-9212. **Website:** www.germantownfest.com. Estab. 1971. Arts & crafts show held annually the weekend after Labor Day. Outdoors. Accepts photography, all arts & crafts mediums. Number of exhibitors: 400+. Public attendance: 65,000. Free to public. Artists should apply by sending applications by mail. Deadline for entry: until filled. Application/space fee: $200-250. Exhibition space: 10×10 ft. For more information, artists should e-mail, call or send SASE. Show located at Germantown Civic Club Complex 7745 Poplar Pike.

TIPS "Display and promote to the public. Price attractively."

✚ ○ GLAM INDIE CRAFT SHOW

E-mail: glamcraftshow@gmail.com. **Website:** www.glamcraftshow.com. Fine arts & crafts fair held annually in December. Outdoors. Accepts handmade crafts, painting, sculpture, photography, drawing, fabric, crafts, ceramics, glass and jewelry. Juried. Number exhibitors: varies. Number attendees: varies. Admission: $3 adults; children 10 & under free. Apply online. Deadline for entry: September. Application fee: see website. Space fee: varies. Exhibition space: varies. For more information, artists should email or visit website.

✚ ○ GLENCOE FESTIVAL OF ART

Amdur Productions, P.O. Box 550, Highland Park IL 60035. (847)926-4300. **E-mail:** info@amdurproductions.com. **Website:** www.amdurproductions.com. Fine arts & crafts fair held annually in August. Outdoors. Accepts handmade crafts, painting, sculpture, photography, drawing, fabric, crafts, ceramics, glass and jewelry. Juried. Number exhibitors: 120. Number attendees: 35,000. Free to public. Apply online. Deadline for entry: see website. Application fee: $25. Space fee: varies. Exhibition space: varies. For more information, artists should email or visit website.

✚ ○ GLENVIEW OUTDOOR ART FAIR

Glenview Art League, P.O. Box 463, Glenview IL 60025-0463. (847)724-4007. **E-mail:** glenviewartleague@att.net. **Website:** www.glenviewartleague.org. Fine arts & crafts fair held annually in July. Outdoors. Accepts handmade crafts, Paintings, sculpture, hand-pulled artist's prints (e.g., etchings), drawings, mixed media, ceramics, photography and jewelry. Juried. Awards/prizes: Best of Show, Awards of Excellence, Merit Awards. Number exhibitors: see website. Number attendees: varies. Free to public. Apply online. Deadline for entry: May. Application fee: $10. Space fee: varies. Exhibition space: 12×12. For more information, artists should email, call or visit website.

⊕ GLOUCESTER COUNTY SPRING CRAFT & HOME SHOW

P.O. Box 925, Millville NJ 08332. (856)765-0118. **Fax:** (856)765-9050. **E-mail:** bkenterprisenj@aol.com. **Website:** www.gloucestercraftfair.com. **Contact:** Kathy Wright, organizer. Estab. 2010. Arts & crafts show held annually 1st Saturday in May. Indoors & outdoors. Accepts fine art & handmade crafts, home & garden, food. Awards/prizes: $100 for Best Spring Booth. Exhibitors: 150. Number of attendees: 2,500. Free to public. Artists should apply via website. Deadline for entry: late September. Application fee: none. Space fee: $30 (one day). Exhibition space: 10×10. For more information, artists should e-mail, visit website or call.

⊕ GLOUCESTER WATERFRONT FESTIVAL

38 Charles St., Rochester NH 03867. (603)332-2616. **E-mail:** info@castleberryfairs.com; terrym@worldpath.net. **Website:** www.castleberryfairs.com. **Contact:** Terry Mullen, events coordinator. Estab. 1971. Arts & crafts show held the 3rd weekend in August in Gloucester MA. Outdoors in Stage Fort Park. Accepts photography and all other mediums. Juried by photo, slide or sample. Number of exhibitors: 225. Public attendance: 50,000. Free to the public. Artists should apply by downloading application from website. Deadline for entry: until full. Space fee: $375. Exhibition space: 10×10 ft. Average gross sales/exhibitor: "Generally, this is considered an 'excellent' show, so I would guess most exhibitors sell ten times their booth fee, or in this case, at least $3,500 in sales." For more information, artists should visit website. Show located in Stage Fort Park, Hough Ave., Gloucester NH.
TIPS "Do not bring a book; do not bring a chair. Smile and make eye contact with everyone who enters your booth. Have them sign your guest book; get their e-mail address so you can let them know when you are in the area again. And, finally, make the sale—they are at the fair to shop, after all."

⊕ ☺ GOLDEN FINE ARTS FESTIVAL

1010 Washington Ave., Golden CO 80401. (303)279-3113. **E-mail:** info@goldencochamber.org. **Website:** www.goldenfineartsfestival.org. Fine arts & crafts fair held annually in August. Outdoors. Accepts handmade crafts, ceramics, fiber, glass, jewelry, mixed media, 2D, painting, photography, and sculpture. Juried. Number exhibitors: see website. Number attendees: 40,000. Free to public. Apply online. Deadline for entry: April. Application fee: $25. Space fee: $350. Exhibition space: 10×10. For more information, artists should email, call or visit website.

GOLD RUSH DAYS

P.O. Box 774, Dahlonega GA 30533. **E-mail:** DahlonegaJayceesFestival@gmail.com. **Website:** www.dahlonegajaycees.com. Arts & crafts show held annually the 3rd full week in October. Accepts photography, paintings and homemade, handcrafted items. No digitally originated artwork. Outdoors. Number of exhibitors: 300. Public attendance: 200,000. Application fee of $25. Free to the public. Artists should apply online under "Gold Rush," or send SASE to request application. Deadline: March. Exhibition space: 10×10 ft. Artists should e-mail, visit website for more information. Show located at the public square and historic district.
TIPS "Talk to other artists who have done other shows and festivals. Get tips and advice from those in the same line of work."

☺ GOOD OLD SUMMERTIME ART FAIR

P.O. Box 1753, Kenosha WI 53141. (262)654-0065. **E-mail:** info@kenoshaartassociation.org. **Website:** www.kenoshaartassociation.org. Estab. 1975. Fine arts show held annually the 1st Sunday in June. Outdoors. Accepts photography, paintings, drawings, mosaics, ceramics, pottery, sculpture, wood, stained glass. Juried by a panel. Photos or slides required with application. Number of exhibitors: 100. Public attendance: 3,000. Free to public. Artists should apply by completing application form, and including fees and SASE. Deadline for entry: early April. Exhibition space: 12×12 ft. For more information, artists should e-mail, visit website or send SASE.
TIPS "Have a professional display, and be friendly."

○ GRAND FESTIVAL OF THE ARTS & CRAFTS

P.O. Box 429, Grand Lake CO 80447-0429. (970)627-3402. **Fax:** (970)627-8007. **E-mail:** glinfo@grandlakechamber.com. **Website:** www.grandlakechamber.com. Fine arts & crafts show held annually in June and September. Outdoors. Accepts photography, jewelry, leather, mixed media, painting, paper, sculpture, wearable art. Juried by chamber committee. Awards/prizes: Best in Show and People's Choice. Number of exhibitors: 60-75. Public attendance: 1,000+. Free to public. Artists should apply by submitting slides or photos. Deadline for entry: early June and early September. Application fee: $175; includes space fee and business license. No electricity available. Exhibition space: 10×10 ft. For more information, artists should e-mail or call. Show held at Town Square Park on Grand Ave.

GREAT LAKES ART FAIR

46100 Grand River Ave., Novi MI 48374. (248)348-5600, ext. 208. **Fax:** (248)347-7720. **E-mail:** info@greatlakesartfair.com. **Website:** www.greatlakesartfair.com. **Contact:** Andrea Picklo, event manager. Estab. 2009. Held in April. Accepts paintings, sculptures, metal and fiber work, jewelry, 2D and 3D art, ceramics and glass. Cash prizes are given. Number of exhibitors: 150-200. Public attendance: 12,000-15,000. Application fee: $30. Space fee: $400-800. Exhibition space: 10×12 ft.

TIPS E-mail, call, or visit website for more information.

○ GREAT NECK STREET FAIR

Showtiques Crafts, Inc., 1 Orient Way, Suite F, #127, Rutherford NJ 07070. (201)869-0406. **E-mail:** showtiques@gmail.com. **Website:** www.showtiques.com. Estab. 1978. Fine arts & crafts show held annually in early May (see website for details) in the Village of Great Neck. "Welcomes professional artists, craftspeople and vendors of upscale giftware." Outdoors. Accepts photography, all arts & crafts made by the exhibitor. Juried. Number of exhibitors: 250. Public attendance: 50,000. Free to public. Deadline for entry: until full. Space fee: $150-250. Exhibition space: 10×10 ft. For more information, artists should e-mail, visit website or call.

○ GREENWICH VILLAGE ART FAIR

711 N. Main St., Rockford IL 61103. (815)968-2787. **Fax:** (815)316-2179. **E-mail:** nsauer@rockfordartmuseum.org. **Website:** www.rockfordartmuseum.org/gvaf.html. **Contact:** Nancy Sauer. Estab. 1948. Juried. 2-day Outdoor fine art fair held annually in September. $4,500 in Best of Show and Judges' Choice Awards. Number of exhibitors: 155. Public attendance: 7,000. Application fee $30. Booth fee: $225. Deadline for entry: April 30. Exhibition space: 10×10 ft. Apply online through www.zapplication.org.

○ GUILFORD CRAFT EXPO

P.O. Box 589, Guilford CT 06437. (203)453-5947. **E-mail:** expo@guilfordartcenter.org. **Website:** www.guilfordartcenter.org. Estab. 1957. Fine craft & art show held annually in mid-July. Outdoors. Accepts photography, wearable and nonwearable fiber, metal and nonmetal jewelry, clay, leather, wood, glass, painting, drawing, prints, mixed media, sculpture. Juried by 5 images of work, viewed sequentially. Number of exhibitors: 180. Public attendance: 9,000. Public admission: $7 and $9. Artists should apply online at www.zapplication.org (preferred) or by downloading an application at www.guilfordartcenter.org. Deadline for entry: early January. Application fee: $40. Space fee: $680. Exhibition space: 10×10 ft. For more information, artists should e-mail, visit website, call.

⊕ ○ HALIFAX ART FESTIVAL

P.O. Box 2038, Ormond Beach FL 32175-2038. (386)304-7247; (407)701-1184. **E-mail:** pataberna thy2012@hotmail.com. **Website:** www.halifaxartfestival.com. Estab. 1962. Fine arts & crafts fair held annually in November. Outdoors. Accepts handmade crafts, ceramics, fiber, glass, jewelry, mixed media, 2D, painting, photography, and sculpture. Juried. Awards/prizes: Best of Show, Judges' Choice, Awards of Excellence, Awards of Distinction, Awards of Honor, Awards of Merit, Student Art Awards, Purchase Award, Patron Purchase Award. Number exhibitors: 200. Number attendees: 45,000. Free to public. Apply online. Deadline for entry: August. Application fee: $30. Space fee: $225 (competitive); $125 (non competitive). Exhibition space: see website. For more information, artists should e-mail, call, or visit website.

⊙ HERKIMER COUNTY ARTS & CRAFTS FAIR

100 Reservoir Rd., Herkimer NY 13350. (315)866-0300, ext. 8459. **Fax:** (315)866-1706. **E-mail:** fuhrerjm@herkimer.edu. **Website:** www.herkimer.edu/ac. **Contact:** Jan Fuhrer, coordinator. Estab. 1976. Fine art & craft show held annually in mid-November on Veterans Day weekend. Indoors. Accepts photography and all handcrafted artwork. Juried by a committee. Awards/prizes: ribbons. Number of exhibitors: 120+. Public attendance: 4,000. Admission: $4. Deadline: May 1 or until filled. Application fee: $10. Exhibition space: 10×6 ft. Space fee: $155. For more information, artists should call, e-mail, or send SASE.

⊙ HIGHLAND MAPLE FESTIVAL

P.O. Box 223, Monterey VA 24465. (540)468-2550. **Fax:** (540)468-2551. **E-mail:** highcc@cfw.com; info@highlandcounty.org. **Website:** www.highlandcounty.org. Estab. 1958. Fine arts & crafts show held annually the 2nd and 3rd weekends in March. Indoors and outdoors. Accepts photography, pottery, weaving, jewelry, painting, wood crafts, furniture. Juried by 5 photos or slides. Photos need to include one of setup and your workshop. Number of exhibitors: 150. Public attendance: 35,000-50,000. "Vendors accepted until show is full." Exhibition space: 10×10 ft. For more information, artists should e-mail, visit website, or call. **TIPS** "Have quality work and good salesmanship."

⊙ HIGHLANDS ART LEAGUE'S ANNUAL FINE ARTS & CRAFTS FESTIVAL

1989 Lakeview Dr., Sebring FL 33870. (863)385-5312. **E-mail:** director@highlandsartleague.org. **Website:** www.highlandsartleague.org. **Contact:** Martile Blackman, festival director. Estab. 1966. Fine arts & crafts show held annually first Saturday in November. Outdoors. Accepts photography, pottery, painting, jewelry, fabric. Juried based on quality of work. Awards/prizes: monetary awards. Number of exhibitors: 100+. Public attendance: more than 15,000. Free to the public. Artists should apply by calling or visiting website for application form. Deadline for entry: September 1. Exhibition space: 10×14 and 10×28 ft. Artists should e-mail for more information. Festival held in Circle Park in downtown Sebring.

⊕ ⊙ HILTON HEAD ISLAND ART FESTIVAL WITH CRAFT MARKETPLACE

270 Central Blvd., Suite 107B, Jupiter FL 33458. (561)746-6615. **Fax:** (561)746-6528. **E-mail:** info@artfestival.com. **Website:** www.artfestival.com. **Contact:** Malinda Ratliff, communications manager. Estab. 2009. Fine art & craft fair held annually in late May. Outdoors. Accepts photography, jewelry, mixed media, sculpture, wood, ceramic, glass, painting, digital, fiber, metal. Juried. Number exhibitors: 100. Number attendees: 60,000. Free to public. Apply online via www.zapplication.org. Deadline: see website. Application fee: $25. Space fee: $375. Exhibition space: 10×10 and 10×20. For more information, artists should e-mail, call, or visit website.

⊙ Festival located at Shelter Cove Harbour and Marina on Hilton Head Island.

⊙ HINSDALE FINE ARTS FESTIVAL

22 E. First St., Hinsdale IL 60521. (630)323-3952. **Fax:** (630)323-3953. **E-mail:** info@hinsdalechamber.com. **Website:** www.hinsdalechamber.com. Fine arts show held annually in mid-June. Outdoors. Accepts photography, ceramics, painting, sculpture, fiber arts, mixed media, jewelry. Juried by 3 images. Awards/prizes: Best in Show, President's Award and 1st, 2nd and 3rd place in 2D and 3D categories. Number of exhibitors: 140. Public attendance: 2,000-3,000. Free to public. Artists should apply online at www.zapplication.org. Deadline for entry: First week in March. Application fee: $30. Space fee: $275. Exhibition space: 10×10 ft. For more information, artists should e-mail or visit website.

TIPS "Original artwork sold by artist."

⊕ ⊙ HISTORIC SHAW ART FAIR

(314)773-3935. **E-mail:** greg@gobdesign.com. **Website:** www.shawartfair.org. **Contact:** Greg Gobberdiel, coordinator. Fine arts & crafts fair held annually in October. Outdoors. Accepts handmade crafts, ceramics, fiber, glass, jewelry, mixed media, painting, photography, and sculpture. Juried. Number exhibitors: see website. Number attendees: varies. Free to public. Apply online. Deadline for entry: April. Application fee: $25. Space fee: $280. Exhibition space: 10×10. For more information, artists should email, call or visit website.

⊕ ◯ HOBE SOUND FESTIVAL OF THE ARTS & CRAFT SHOW

270 Central Blvd., Suite 107B, Jupiter FL 33458. (561)746-6615. **Fax:** (561)746-6528. **E-mail:** info@ artfestival.com. **Website:** www.artfestival.com. **Contact:** Malinda Ratliff, communications manager. Estab. 2006. Fine art & craft fair held annually in February. Outdoors. Accepts photography, jewelry, mixed media, sculpture, wood, ceramic, glass, painting, digital, fiber, metal. Juried. Number exhibitors: 130. Number attendees: 70,000. Free to public. Apply online via www.zapplication.org. Deadline: see website. Application fee: $25. Space fee: $395. Exhibition space: 10×10 and 10×20. For more information, artists should e-mail, call, or visit website.

◯ Show located at A1A/Dixie Highway where the street intersects with Bridge Road in Hobe Sound FL.

◯ HOLIDAY CRAFTMORRISTOWN

P.O. Box 28, Woodstock NY 12498. (845)331-7900. **Fax:** (845)331-7484. **E-mail:** crafts@artrider.com. **Website:** www.artrider.com. Estab. 1990. Fine arts & crafts show held annually in early December. Indoors. Accepts photography, wearable and nonwearable fiber, jewelry, clay, leather, wood, glass, painting, drawing, prints, mixed media. Juried by 5 images of work and 1 of booth, viewed sequentially. Number of exhibitors: 165. Public attendance: 5,000. Public admission: $9. Artists should apply online at www.artrider.com or www.zapplication.org. Deadline for entry: end of May. Application fee: $45. Space fee: $545. Exhibition space: 10×10 ft. For more information, artists should e-mail, visit website, or call.

◯ HOLIDAY FINE ARTS & CRAFTS SHOW

60 Ida Lee Dr., Leesburg VA 20176. (703)777-1368. **Fax:** (703)737-7165. **E-mail:** lfountain@leesburgva. gov. **Website:** www.idalee.org. Estab. 1990. Arts & crafts show held annually the 1st full weekend in December. Indoors. Accepts handcrafted items only, including but not limited to: photography, jewelry, pottery, baskets, clothing, gourmet food products, wood work, fine art, accessories, pet items, soaps/lotions and florals. Juried. Number of exhibitors: 95. Public attendance: 2,500. Free to public. Artists should apply by downloading application from website. Deadline for entry: August 31. Space fee: $110-150. Exhibition space: 10×7 ft. and 10×10 ft. For more information, artists should e-mail or visit website.

◯ HOLLY ARTS & CRAFTS FESTIVAL

P.O. Box 64, Pinehurst NC 28370. (910)295-7462. **E-mail:** info@pinehurstbusinessguild.com. **Website:** www.pinehurstbusinessguild.com. Estab. 1978. Annual arts & crafts show held 3rd Saturday in October. Outdoors. Accepts quality photography, arts and crafts. Juried based on uniqueness, quality of product and overall display. Number of exhibitors: 200. Public attendance: 7,000. Free to the public. Submit 3 color photos, 2 of work to be exhibited, 1 of booth. Deadline: Late March. Application fee: $25 by separate check. Space fee: $75. Electricity fee: $5 Exhibition space: 10×10 ft. For more information, artists should call or visit website.

HOME, CONDO AND OUTDOOR ART & CRAFT FAIR

P.O. Box 486, Ocean City MD 21843. (410)213-8090. **Fax:** (410)213-8092. **E-mail:** events@oceanpromo tions.info. **Website:** www.oceanpromotions.info. Estab. 1984. Fine arts & crafts show held annually in March. Indoors. Accepts photography, carvings, pottery, ceramics, glass work, floral, watercolor, sculpture, prints, oils, pen and ink. Number of exhibitors: 50. Public attendance: 9,000. Public admission: $7/adults; $6/seniors & students; 13 and under free; military, fire and police free. Artists should apply by e-mailing request for info and application. Deadline for entry: until full. Space fee: $250. Exhibition space: 10×10 ft. For more information, artists should e-mail, visit website or call. Show held in the R.E. Powell Ocean City Convention Center.

HOME DECORATING & REMODELING SHOW

P.O. Box 230699, Las Vegas NV 89105-0699. (702)450-7984; (800)343-8344. **Fax:** (702)451-7305. **E-mail:** showprosadmin@cox.net. **Website:** www.nashville homeshow.com. Estab. 1983. Home show held annually in early September (see website for details). Indoors. Accepts photography, sculpture, watercolor, oils, mixed media, pottery. Awards/prizes: Outstanding Booth Award. Number of exhibitors: 350-400. Public attendance: 20,000. Public admission: $10 (discount coupon available on website); Seniors 62+ free on Friday; children 12 & under free with adult. Artists should apply by calling. Marketing is directed to middle and above income brackets. Deadline for entry: open until filled. Space fee: starts at $950. Exhibition space: 10×10 ft. or complements of 10×10 ft. For more information, artists should call or visit website.

HOT SPRINGS ARTS & CRAFTS FAIR

308 Pullman, Hot Springs AR 71901. (501)623-9592. **E-mail:** sephpipkin@aol.com. **Website:** www.hotspringsartsandcraftsfair.com. **Contact:** Peggy Barnett. Estab. 1968. Fine arts & crafts show held annually the 1st full weekend in October at the Garland County Fairgrounds. Indoors and outdoors. Accepts photography and varied mediums ranging from heritage, crafts, jewelry, furniture. Juried by a committee of 12 volunteers. Number of exhibitors: 350+. Public attendance: 50,000+. Free to public. Deadline for entry: August. Space fee: $125 (single); $250 (double). Exhibition space: 10×10 or 10×20 ft. For more information, and to apply, artists should e-mail, call or visit website. Fair located at Garland County Fairgrounds.

HYDE PARK ARTS & CRAFTS ADVENTURE

P.O. Box 1326, Palatine IL 60078. (312)751-2500, (847)991-4748. **Fax:** (847)221-5853. **E-mail:** asoaartists@aol.com. **Website:** www.americansocietyofartists.org. Estab. 2006. Arts & crafts show held once a year in late September. Event held in Chicago. Outdoors. Accepts photography, painting, glass, wood, fiber arts, hand-crafted candles, quilts, sculpture and more. Juried. Please submit 4 images representative of your work you wish to exhibit, 1 of your display set-up, your first/last name, physical address, daytime telephone number—résumé/show listing helpful. Number of exhibitors: 50. Free to the public. Artists should apply by submitting jury materials. Please submit to: asoaartists@aol.com. If juried in, you will receive a jury/approval number. See website for jurying online. Deadline for entry: 2 months prior to show or earlier if available. Entry fee: to be announced. Exhibition space: approximately 100 sq. ft. for single space; other sizes are available. For more information, artists should send SASE, submit jury material. Show located at University of Chicago's Hyde Park Shopping Center.

TIPS "Remember that when you are at work in your studio, you are an artist. But when you are at a show, you are a business person selling your work."

HYDE PARK SQUARE ART SHOW

P.O. Box 8402, Cincinnati OH 45208. (513)353-2045. **E-mail:** hpartshowinfo@aol.com. **Website:** www.hydeparksquare.org/hydeparkartshow.html. Fine arts

& crafts fair held annually in August. Outdoors. Accepts handmade crafts, ceramics, fiber, glass, jewelry, mixed media, 2D, painting, photography, and sculpture. Juried. Awards/prizes: Best of Show, 1st Place, 2nd Place, 3rd Place, Honorable Mention. Number exhibitors: see website. Number attendees: see website. Free to public. Apply online. Deadline for entry: March. Application fee: $35. Space fee: $125. Exhibition space: see website. For more information, artists should email, call or visit website.

STAN HYWET HALL & GARDENS OHIO MART

714 N. Portage Path, Akron OH 44303. (330)315-3255. **E-mail:** ohiomart@stanhywet.org. **Website:** www.stanhywet.org. Estab. 1966. Artisan crafts show held annually 1st full weekend in October. Outdoors. Accepts photography and all mediums. Juried via mail application. Awards/prizes: Best Booth Display. Number of exhibitors: 150. Public attendance: 15,000-20,000. Deadline varies. Application fee: $25, nonrefundable. Application available online. Exhibition space: 10×10 or 10×15 ft. For more information, artists should visit website or call.

IDAHO ARTISTRY IN WOOD SHOW

(208)466-4899. **E-mail:** marlies-schmitt@clearwire.net. **Website:** www.idahoartistryinwood.org. **Contact:** Marlies Schmitt, publicity chair. Estab. 2009. Fine arts & crafts show held annually last weekend of February. Indoors. Accepts handmade crafts, artwork made from wood or gourds. Awards/prizes: prize ribbons. Number exhibitors: 120 competitors; 7 vendors. Number of attendees: 1,000. Admission: $4; 12 & under free. Artists should apply online. Deadline for entry: February 15 for advance registration; registration can de done at exhibit site on day before show opens. Application fee: $3 per piece in advacne; $5 at the door. Space fee: $75. Exhibition space: 100 sq. ft. For more information artists should e-mail or visit website.

IMAGES—A FESTIVAL OF THE ARTS

E-mail: images@imagesartfestival.org. **Website:** www.imagesartfestival.org. Fine arts & crafts fair held annually in January. Outdoors. Accepts handmade crafts, ceramics, fiber, glass, jewelry, mixed media, 2D, painting, photography, and sculpture. Juried. Awards/prizes: $100,000 in awards and prizes. Number exhibitors: 225. Number attendees: 45,000. Free to public. Apply online. Deadline for entry: October.

Application fee: $40. Space fee: $250. Exhibition space: 11×12. For more information, artists should email, call or visit website.

⊕ INDIANA ART FAIR

650 W. Washington St., Indianapolis IN 46204. (317)233-9348. **Fax:** (317)233-8268. **E-mail:** cmiller@ indianamuseum.org. **Website:** www.indianamuseum.org. Estab. 2004. Annual art/craft show held the 2nd weekend of February. Indoors. Juried; 5-6 judges award points in 3 categories. 60 exhibitors; 3,000 attendees. $13 admission for the public. Application fee $25. Space fee $165; 80 sq. ft. Accepts ceramics, glass, fiber, jewelry, painting, sculpture, mixed media, drawing/pastels, garden, leather, surface decoration, wood, metal, printmaking, and photography.

TIPS "Make sure that your booth space complements your product and presents well. Good photography can be key for juried shows."

⊕ INDIAN WELLS ARTS FESTIVAL

78-200 Miles Ave., Indian Wells CA 92210. (760)346-0042. **Fax:** (760)346-0042. **E-mail:** info@indianwells artsfestival.com. **Website:** www.indianwellsartsfesti val.com. **Contact:** Dianne Funk, producer. "A premier fine arts festival attracting thousands annually. The Indian Wells Arts Festival brings a splash of color to the beautiful grass concourse of the Indian Wells Tennis Garden. This spectacular venue transforms into an artisan village featuring 200 judged and juried artists and hundreds of pieces of one-of-a-kind artwork available for sale. Enjoy special exhibits and demonstrations. Watch glass blowing, monumental rock sculpting, wood carving, pottery wheel, weaving and painting. Wine tasting, gourmet market, children's activities, entertainment and refreshments add to the festival atmosphere." Apply online at indianwellsartsfestival.com/artists.html. See website for more information.

⊕ INDIE SOUTH FAIR

660 N. Chase St., Athens GA 30601. **E-mail:** indie southfair@gmail.com. **Website:** www.indiesouth fair.com. **Contact:** Serra Ferguson, organizer. Estab. 2007. Arts & Crafts show held annually the 1st weekends of May & December. Outdoors. Accepts handmade crafts and all other mediums. Exhibitors: 100. Number of attendees: 3,000. Free to public. Apply via website. Deadline for entry: March 2 for Spring show; September 28 for holiday market. Application fee: $15.

Space fee: $175 (10×10); $90 (6×4). Exhibition space: 10×10; 6×4. Average sales: $800-1,200. For more information send e-mail.

⊕ INTERNATIONAL FOLK FESTIVAL

301 Hay St., Fayetteville NC 28302. (910)323-1776. **Fax:** (910)323-1727. **E-mail:** bobp@theartscouncil. com. **Website:** www.theartscouncil.com. Estab. 1978. Fine arts & crafts show held annually the last weekend in September. Outdoors. Accepts photography, painting of all mediums, pottery, woodworking, sculptures. Work must be original. Number of exhibitors: 120+. Public attendance: 85,000-100,000 over 2 days. Free to public. Artists should apply on the website. Exhibition space: 10×10 ft. For more information, artists should e-mail or visit website. Festival held in Festival Park/ downtown Fayetteville.

TIPS "Have reasonable prices."

⊕ ISLE OF EIGHT FLAGS SHRIMP FESTIVAL

P.O. Box 17251, Fernandina Beach FL 32035. (904)701-2786. **Website:** www.islandart.org. Estab. 1963. Fine arts & crafts show and community celebration held annually the 1st weekend in May. Outdoors. Accepts all mediums. Juried. Awards: $9,000 in cash prizes. Number of exhibitors: 300. Public attendance: 150,000. Free to public. Artists should apply by downloading application from website. Slides are not accepted. Digital images in JPEG format only must be submitted on a CD/DVD with application. Deadline for entry: January 31. Application fee: $30 (non-refundable). Space fee: $225. Exhibition space: 10×12 ft. Average gross sales/exhibitor: $1,500+. For more information, artists should visit website.

⊕ JOHNS HOPKINS UNIVERSITY SPRING FAIR

3400 N. Charles St., Mattin Suite 210, Baltimore MD 21218. (410)516-7692. **Fax:** (410)516-6185. **E-mail:** info@jhuspringfair.com; springfair.artsandcrafts@ gmail.com. **Website:** www.jhuspringfair.com. Estab. 1972. Fine arts & crafts, campus-wide festival held annually in April. Outdoors. Accepts photography and all mediums. Juried. Number of exhibitors: 80. Public attendance: 20,000+. Free to public. Artists should apply via website. Deadline for entry: early March. Application and space fee: $200. Exhibition space: 10×10 ft. For more information, artists should e-mail, visit website, or call. Fair located on Johns Hopkins Homewood Campus.

TIPS "Artists should have fun displays, good prices, good variety and quality pieces."

JUBILEE FESTIVAL

Eastern Shore Chamber of Commerce, P.O. Drawer 310, Daphne AL 36526. (251)621-8222; (251)928-6387. **Fax:** (251)621-8001. **E-mail:** lroberts@eschamber.com; office@eschamber.com. **Website:** www.eschamber.com. **Contact:** Liz Roberts. Estab. 1952. Fine arts & crafts show held in late September in Olde Towne of Daphne AL. Outdoors. Accepts photography and fine arts and crafts. Juried. Awards/prizes: ribbons and cash prizes total $4,300 with Best of Show $750. Number of exhibitors: 258. Free to the public. Jury fee: $20. Space fee: $100 for single; $200 for double. Exhibition space: 10×10 ft. or 10×20 ft. For more information, and application form, artists should e-mail, call, see website. Festival located in "Olde Towne" Daphne on Main St.

KALAMAZOO INSTITUTE OF ARTS FAIR

Kalamazoo Institute of Arts, 314 S. Park St., Kalamazoo MI 49007. (269)349-7775. **Fax:** (269)349-9313. **E-mail:** joeb@kiarts.org. **Website:** www.kiarts.org/artfair. **Contact:** Joe Bower. Estab. 1951. Fine jurored art fair held annually in June. Outdoors. "The KIA's annual art fair has been going strong for 64 years. Still staged in shady, historic Bronson Park, the fair boasts more hours, more artists and more activities. It now spans 2 full days. The art fair provides patrons with more time to visit and artists with an insurance day in case of rain. Some 190 artists will be invited to set up colorful booths. Numerous festivities are planned, including public art activities, musical performances, a beer garden and an artist dinner. For more information, visit www.kiarts.org/artfair." Apply via www.zapplication.org. Application fee: $30. Booth fee: $275.

KENTUCK FESTIVAL OF THE ARTS

503 Main Ave., Northport AL 35476. (205)758-1257. **Fax:** (205)758-1258. **E-mail:** kentuck@kentuck.org. **Website:** www.kentuck.org. **Contact:** Amy Echols, executive director. Call or e-mail for more information. General information about the festival available on the website. "Celebrates a variety of artistic styles ranging from folk to contemporary arts as well as traditional crafts. Each of the 250+ artists participating in the festival is either invited as a guest artist or is juried based on the quality and originality of their work. The guest artists are nationally recognized folk and visionary artists whose powerful visual images continue to capture national and international acclaim." Festival held at Kentuck Park.

KETNER'S MILL COUNTY ARTS FAIR

P.O. Box 322, Lookout Mountain TN 37350. (423)267-5702. **E-mail:** contact@ketnersmill.org. **Website:** www.ketnersmill.org. **Contact:** Dee Nash, event coordinator. Estab. 1977. Arts & crafts show held annually the 3rd weekend in October held on the grounds of the historic Ketner's Mills, in Whitwell TN, and the banks of the Sequatchie River. Outdoors. Accepts photography, painting, prints, dolls, fiber arts, baskets, folk art, wood crafts, jewelry, musical instruments, sculpture, pottery, glass. Juried. Number of exhibitors: 170. Number of attendees: 10,000/day, depending on weather. Artists should apply online. Space fee: $125. Electricity: $10 limited to light use. Exhibition space: 15×15 ft. Average gross sales/exhibitor: $1,500. Fair held at Ketner's Mill.

TIPS "Display your best and most expensive work, framed. But also have smaller unframed items to sell. Never underestimate a show: Someone may come forward and buy a large item."

KEY BISCAYNE ART FESTIVAL

270 Central Blvd., Suite 107B, Jupiter FL 33458. (561)746-6615. **Fax:** (561)746-6528. **E-mail:** info@artfestival.com. **Website:** www.artfestival.com. **Contact:** Malinda Ratliff, communications manager. Estab. 1964. Fine art & craft fair held annually in March. Outdoors. Accepts photography, jewelry, mixed media, sculpture, wood, ceramic, glass, painting, digital, fiber, metal. Juried. Number exhibitors: 125. Number attendees: 50,000. Free to public. Apply online via www.zapplication.org. Deadline: see website. Application fee: $25. Space fee: $395. Exhibition space: 10×10 and 10×20. For more information, artists should e-mail, call, or visit website.

Festival located at Village Green Park in Key Biscayne FL.

KINGS DRIVE ART WALK

Little Sugar Creek Greenway, Charlotte NC 28203. (704)338-1060. **E-mail:** festival@festivalinthepark.org. **Website:** www.festivalinthepark.org. **Contact:** Julie Whitney Austin, executive director. Estab. 1964. Fine art & craft show held annually in late April. Outdoors. Accepts photography. Juried. Number of exhibitors: 85. Public attendance: 35,000+. Free to public.

Artists should apply online at www.festivalinthepark.org/kingsdrive.asp. Deadline for entry: March 1. Application fee: $25. Space fee: $235. Exhibition space: 10×10 ft. For more information, artists should e-mail, call or visit website.

✿ KINGS MOUNTAIN ART FAIR

13106 Skyline Blvd., Woodside CA 94062. (650)851-2710. **E-mail:** kmafsecty@aol.com. **Website:** www.kingsmountainartfair.org. **Contact:** Carrie German, administrative assistant. Estab. 1963. Fine arts & crafts show held annually Labor Day weekend. Fundraiser for volunteer fire dept. Accepts photography, ceramics, clothing, 2D, painting, glass, jewelry, leather, sculpture, textile/fiber, wood. Juried. Number of exhibitors: 138. Public attendance: 10,000. Free to public. Deadline for entry: January 30. Application fee: $20 (online). Exhibition space: 10×10 ft. Average gross sales/exhibitor: $3,500. For more information, artists should e-mail or visit website.

TIPS "Located in Redwood Forest South of San Francisco. Keep an open mind and be flexible."

⊕ ✿ KPFA CRAFT FAIR

1929 MLK Jr. Way, Berkeley CA 94704. (510)848-6767 ext. 243. **E-mail:** events@kpfa.org. **Website:** www.kpfa.org/craftsfair/. **Contact:** Jan Etre, coordinator. Fine arts & crafts fair held annually in December. Indoors. Accepts handmade crafts, ceramics, fiber, glass, jewelry, mixed media, 2D, painting, photography, and sculpture. Juried. Number exhibitors: 200. Number attendees: see website. Admission: $10; disabled, 65+ and children under 17 free. Apply online. Deadline for entry: see website. Application fee: $20. Space fee: varies. Exhibition space: 10×10. For more information, artists should email, call or visit website.

✿ KRASL ART FAIR ON THE BLUFF

707 Lake Blvd., St. Joseph MI 49085. (269)983-0271. **Fax:** (269)983-0275. **E-mail:** info1@krasl.org. **Website:** www.krasl.org. **Contact:** Sara Shambarger; Colleen Villa. Estab. 1962. Fine arts & fine craft show held annually the 2nd weekend of July (see website for details). Outdoors. Accepts art in 19 media categories including photography, painting (oils, acrylics & watercolors), digital art, drawing, pastels, fibers (wearable and decorative), clay (functional and nonfunctional), glass, jewelry (precious and nonprecious), sculpture, printmaking and graphics, metals (mixed media 2D and 3D) and woods. Number of exhibitors:

200. Number of attendees: thousands. Free to public. Application fee: $30. Applications are available online through www.zapplication.org. Deadline for entry: early January. There is on-site jurying the same day of the fair and approximately 30% are invited back without having to pay the $30 application fee. Space fee: $275. Exhibition space: 10×10 to 15×15 ft. or $300 for 20×20 ft. (limited). "Krasl Art Fair on the Bluff is ranked: #10 in the *Sunshine Artist Magazine's* 200 Best for 2014; #8 on the Art Fair Calendar's new Best Art Shows List from their 2014 survey; #48 in the *Art Fair Source Book's* Top 100 shows." For more information, artists should e-mail or visit website.

✿ LAKE CITY ARTS & CRAFTS FESTIVAL

P.O. Box 1147, Lake City CO 81235. (817)343-3305. **E-mail:** info@lakecityarts.org; kerrycoy@aol.com. **Website:** www.lakecityarts.org. Estab. 1975. Fine arts/arts & craft show held annually 3rd Tuesday in July. One-day event. Outdoors. Accepts photography, jewelry, metal work, woodworking, painting, handmade items. Juried by 3-5 undisclosed jurors. Prize: Winners are entered in a drawing for a free booth space in the following year's show. Number of exhibitors: 85. Public attendance: 500. Free to the public. Space fee: $75. Jury fee: $10. Exhibition space: 12×12 ft. Deadline for submission: mid April. Average gross sales/exhibitor: $500-$1,000. For more information, and application form, artists should visit website. Festival located at the Lake City Town Park and along Silver St.

TIPS "Repeat vendors draw repeat customers. People like to see their favorite vendors each year or every other year. If you come every year, have new things as well as your best-selling products."

⊕ ✿ LAKEFRONT FESTIVAL OF ART

700 N. Art Museum Dr., Milwaukee WI 53202. (414)224-3853. **E-mail:** lfoa@mam.org. **Website:** www.mam.org/lfoa. **Contact:** Krista Renfrew, festival director. Estab. 1963. Fine art show held annually the 3rd week in June. Indoors & outdoors. Accepts printmaking, sculpture, wood, painting, jewelry, ceramics, digital, drawing/pastel, MM2, fiber-non, wearable fiber, glass, photography, metal, NM. Juried. Awards/prizes: Artist Awards (10), Honorable Mention (10), Sculpture Garden. Exhibitors: 176. Number of attendees: 25,000. Admission: $17 general; $10 members & advance; 12 & under free. Apply via Zapplication.org. Deadline for entry: November 25. Application fee: $35. Space fee: $500; $600 corner. Ex-

hibition Space: 10×10. For more information send e-mail or visit website.

⊕ ◐ LAKELAND CRAFT FESTIVAL, THE

270 Central Blvd., Suite 107B, Jupiter FL 33458. (561)746-6615. **Fax:** (561)746-6528. **E-mail:** info@artfestival.com. **Website:** www.artfestival.com. **Contact:** Malinda Ratliff, communications manager. Estab. 2013. Fine art & craft fair held annually in late March. Outdoors. Accepts photography, jewelry, mixed media, sculpture, wood, ceramic, glass, painting, digital, fiber, metal. Juried. Number exhibitors: 110. Number attendees: 18,000. Free to public. Apply online via www.zapplication.org or visit website for paper application. Deadline: see website. Application fee: $15. Space fee: $250. Exhibition space: 10×10 and 10×20. For more information, artists should e-mail, call or visit website. Festival located at Lakeside Village in Lakeland FL.

⊕ LAKE ST. LOUIS FARMERS AND ARTISTS MARKET

P.O. Box 91, Warrenton MO 63383-0091. (314)495-2531. **E-mail:** lakestlouisfarmersmarket@gmail.com. **Website:** www.themeadowsatlsl.com. Farmer & craft market held annually every Saturday, April-October. Outoors. Accepts handmade crafts, jewelry, art, pottery, soap, candles, clothing, wood crafts and other crafts. Exhibitors: varies. Number of attendees: varies. Free to public. Apply online. Deadline for entry: see website. Application fee: none. Space fee: $325 (full season); $25 (daily vendor). Exhibition space: 10×10. For more information, artists should send e-mail, visit website or call.

⊕ ◐ LAKE SUMTER ART & CRAFT FESTIVAL

270 Central Blvd., Suite 107B, Jupiter FL 33458. (561)746-6615. **Fax:** (561)746-6528. **E-mail:** info@artfestival.com. **Website:** www.artfestival.com. **Contact:** Malinda Ratliff, communications manager. Estab. 2010. Fine art & craft fair held annually in mid February. Outdoors. Accepts photography, jewelry, mixed media, sculpture, wood, ceramic, glass, painting, digital, fiber, metal. Juried. Number exhibitors: 205. Number attendees: 20,000. Free to public. Apply online via www.zapplication.org or visit website for paper application. Deadline: see website. Application fee: $15. Space fee: $265. Exhibition space: 10×10 and 10×20. For more information, artists should e-mail,

call or visit website. Festival located at Lake Sumter Landing in The Villages FL.

◐ LA QUINTA ARTS FESTIVAL

78150 Calle Tampico #215, La Quinta CA 92253. (760)564-1244. **Fax:** (760)564-6884. **E-mail:** helpline@lqaf.com. **Website:** www.lqaf.com. **Contact:** artists: Kathleen Hughes, events manager; photographers: Christi Salamone, executive director. Estab. 1983. Fine arts & crafts festival held annually. Outdoors. Accepts mixed-media 2D/3D, printmaking, photography, drawing and pastel, painting, jewelry, ceramics, fiber, sculpture, glass, wood. Juried over 3 days online by 5 jury members per each of the 11 media categories. Awards/prizes: cash, automatic acceptance into future show, gift cards from premier local restaurants, hotel package, ad in *SW Art*. Number of exhibitors: 230. Public attendance: 28,000+. Admission: $15-day pass; $20 multiday pass. Artists should apply via www.zapplication.org only. Deadline for entry: September 30. Jury fee: $50. Space fee: $275. Exhibition space: 12×12 ft. Average exhibitor sales: $13,450. For more information, artists should visit website.

TIPS "Make sure that booth image looks like an art gallery! Less is more."

⊕ ◐ LAS OLAS ART FAIR

270 Central Blvd., Suite 107B, Jupiter FL 33458. (561)746-6615. **Fax:** (561)746-6528. **E-mail:** info@artfestival.com. **Website:** www.artfestival.com. **Contact:** Malinda Ratliff, communications manager. Estab. 1988. Fine art & craft fair held annually in January, March and mid-October. Outdoors. Accepts photography, jewelry, mixed media, sculpture, wood, ceramic, glass, painting, digital, fiber, metal. Juried. Number exhibitors: 150. Number attendees: 70,000. Free to public. Apply online via www.zapplication.org. Deadline: see website. Application fee: $25. Space fee: $395. Exhibition space: 10×10 and 10×20. For more information, artists should e-mail, call, or visit website.

◐ Fair located on Las Olas Blvd. in Ft. Lauderdale FL.

⊕ LEAGUE OF NH CRAFTSMEN ANNUAL FAIR

League of NH Craftsmen, 49 S. Main St., Suite 100, Concord NH 03301-5080. (603)224-3375. **Fax:** (603)225-8452. **E-mail:** twiltse@nhcrafts.org. **Website:** www.nhcrafts.org/craftsmens-fair-overview.php.

Contact: Susie Lowe-Stockwell, executive director. "The Lansdowne Arts Festival is a weekend-long event featuring an array of creative and performing arts, including painting, crafts, sculpture, jewelry, live music, demonstrations, and children's events. Set in the historic suburb of Lansdowne, Pennsylvania, the festival has grown to include dozens of exhibiting artists and musical acts. All festival events will be held at the historic Twentieth Century Club at 84 S. Lansdowne Ave." See website for more information.

LEEPER PARK ART FAIR
22180 Sundancer Court, #504, Estero FL 33928. (574)276-2942. **Fax:** (574)272-8598. **E-mail:** Studio266@aol.com. **Website:** www.leeperparkartfair.org. **Contact:** Judy Ladd, director. Estab. 1968. Fine arts & crafts show held annually in June. Outdoors. Accepts photography and all areas of fine art. Juried. Awards/prizes: $3,700. Number of exhibitors: 120. Public attendance: 10,000. Free to public. Artists should apply by going to the website and clicking on "To Apply." Deadline for entry: early March. Space fee: $330. Exhibition space: 12×12 ft. Average gross sales/exhibitor: $5,000. For more information, artists should e-mail, call or visit website.

TIPS "Make sure your booth display is well presented and, when applying, slides are top notch!"

LEESBURG FINE ART FESTIVAL
Paragon Fine Art Festivals, 8258 Midnight Pass Rd., Sarasota FL 34242. (941)487-8061. **Fax:** (941)346-0302. **E-mail:** admin@paragonartfest.com. **Website:** www.paragonartevents.com/lee. **Contact:** Bill Kinney. Fine arts & crafts fair held annually in September. Outdoors. Accepts handmade crafts, ceramics, fiber, glass, jewelry, mixed media, painting, photography, and sculpture. Juried. Number exhibitors: 115. Number attendees: varies. Free to public. Apply online. Deadline for entry: July. Application fee: $30. Space fee: $395. Exhibition space: see website. For more information, artists should email, call or visit website.

LES CHENEAUX FESTIVAL OF ARTS
P.O. Box 147, Cedarville MI 49719. (517)282-4950. **E-mail:** lcifoa@gmail.com. **Website:** www.lescheneaux.net/?annualevents. **Contact:** Rick Sapero. Estab. 1976. Fine arts & crafts show held annually 2nd Saturday in August. Outdoors. Accepts photography and all other media; original work and design only; no kits or commercially manufactured goods. Juried by a committee of 10. Submit 4 slides (3 of the artwork; 1 of booth display). Awards: monetary prizes for excellent and original work. Number of exhibitors: 70. Public attendance: 8,000. Public admission: $7. Artists should fill out application form to apply. Deadline for entry: March 15. Booth fee: $75; Jury fee: $5. Exhibition space: 10×10 ft. Average gross sales/exhibitor: $5-500. For more information, artists should call, send SASE, or visit website.

LEVIS COMMONS FINE ART FAIR
The Guild of Artists & Artisans, 118 N. Fourth Ave., Ann Arbor MI 48104. (734)662-3382 ext. 101. **E-mail:** info@theguild.org; nicole@theguild.org. **Website:** www.theguild.org. **Contact:** Nicole McKay, artist relations director. Fine arts & crafts fair held annually in September. Outdoors. Accepts handmade crafts, jewelry, ceramics, painting, glass, photography, fiber and more. Juried. Number exhibitors: 130. Number attendees: 35,000. Free to public. Apply online. Deadline for entry: April. Application fee: $25 members; $30 non-members. Space fee: varies. Exhibition space: varies. For more information, artists should email, call or visit website.

LEWISTON ART FESTIVAL
P.O. Box 1, Lewiston NY 14092. (716)754-0166. **Fax:** (716)754-9166. **E-mail:** director@artcouncil.org. **Website:** www.artcouncil.org. Estab. 1966. Arts & crafts show held annually in August. Outdoors. Accepts handmade crafts, drawing, printmaking, computer generated art, 2D/3D mixed media, photography, ceramics, fiber, glass, jewelry, sculpture, wood. Juried. Exhibitors: 175. Number of attendees: 35,000. Free to public. Apply online. Deadline for entry: early May. Application fee: $15. Space fee: $175. Exhibition space: 10×10. For more information, artists should send e-mail, visit website.

LIBERTY ARTS SQUARED
P.O. Box 302, Liberty MO 64069. **E-mail:** staff@libertyartssquared.org. **Website:** www.libertyartssquared.org. Estab. 2010. Outdoor fine art/craft show held annually. Accepts all mediums. Awards: prizes totaling $4,000; Visual Arts for Awards $1,500; Folk Art for Awards $1,500; Overall Best of Show Award $500. Free admission to the public; free parking. Application fee: $25. Space fee: $200. Exhibition space: 10×10 ft. For more information, e-mail, or visit website.

ART FAIRS

⦾ LILAC FESTIVAL ARTS & CRAFTS SHOWS

26 Goodman St., Rochester NY 14607. (585)244-0951. **E-mail:** lyn@rochesterevents.com. **Website:** www.rochesterevents.com. Estab. 1985. Arts & crafts shows held annually in mid-May (see website for details). Outdoors. Accepts photography, painting, ceramics, woodworking, metal sculpture, fiber. Juried by a panel. Number of exhibitors: 120. Public attendance: 25,000. Free to public. Exhibition space: 10×10 ft. Space fee: $200. For more information, and to apply, artists should e-mail or visit website. Festival held at Highland Park in Rochester NY.

⊕ ⦾ LINCOLN ARTS FESTIVAL

E-mail: melissa@artscene.org. **Website:** www.artscene.org/lincoln-arts-festival. Fine arts & crafts fair held annually in September. Outdoors. Accepts handmade crafts, jewelry, ceramics, painting, glass, photography, fiber and more. Juried. Awards/prizes: $6,000 in awards & prizes. Number exhibitors: see website. Number attendees: varies. Free to public. Apply online. Deadline for entry: May. Application fee: $25. Space fee: $190 (10×10); $310 (10×20). Exhibition space: 10×10; 10×20. For more information, artists should email or visit website.

⊕ ⦾ LINCOLNSHIRE ART FESTIVAL

E-mail: info@amdurproductions.com. **Website:** www.amdurproductions.com. Fine arts & crafts fair held annually in August. Outdoors. Accepts handmade crafts, jewelry, ceramics, painting, glass, photography, fiber and more. Juried. Awards/prizes: given at festival. Number exhibitors: 130. Number attendees: 30,000. Free to public. Apply online. Deadline for entry: January. Application fee: $25. Space fee: $430. Exhibition space: 10×10. For more information, artists should email or visit website.

LIONS CLUB ARTS & CRAFTS FESTIVAL

Henderson Lions Club, P.O. Box 842, Henderson KY 42419. **E-mail:** lionsartsandcrafts@gmail.com. **Website:** www.lionsartsandcrafts.com. Estab. 1972. Formerly Gradd Arts & Crafts Festival. Arts & crafts show held annually 1st full weekend in October. Outdoors. Accepts photography taken by crafter only. Number of exhibitors: 100-150. Public attendance: 10,000+. Artists should apply by calling to be put on mailing list. Space fee: $100. Exhibition space: 15×15 ft. For more information, artists should e-mail, visit website, or call. Festival located at John James Audubon State Park.

TIPS "Be sure that only hand-crafted items are sold. No buy/sell items will be allowed."

⦿ LOMPOC FLOWER FESTIVAL

414 W. Ocean Ave., Lompoc CA 93436. (805)735-8511. **E-mail:** lompocvalle1@verizon.net. **Website:** www.lompocvalleyartassociation.com. **Contact:** Kathy Badrak. Estab. 1942. Sponsored by Lompoc Valley Art Association, Cyprus Gallery. Show held annually last week in June. Festival event includes a parade, food booths, entertainment, beer garden and commercial center, which is not located near arts & crafts area. Outdoors. Accepts photography, fine art, woodworking, pottery, stained glass, fine jewelry. Juried by 5 members of the LVAA. Vendor must submit 3 photos of their work and a description on how they make their art. Artists should apply by downloading application from website. Deadline for entry: early May. Space fee: $375 (single); $575 (double); $100 cleaning deposit (to be refunded after show-see application for details). Exhibition space: 12×16 ft. For more information, artists should visit website.

⊕ LONG GROVE ART FEST

Star Events, 1609 W. Belmont Ave., 2nd Floor, Chicago IL 60657. **E-mail:** info@starevents.com. **Website:** www.starevents.com/festivals/long-grove-art-fest. "More than 100 local artists will captivate festival goers with their inspirations talents in various art forms including oil, acrylic, watercolor, jewelry, sculpture, photography, wood, fiber, glass, paper, metal, and mixed media, all in the relaxed setting of the streets of Long Grove. Artists will also be able to submit their 2D and 3D creations in to the festival's annual art competition." See website for more information.

⊕ ⦾ LONG'S PARK ART & CRAFT FESTIVAL

Long's Park Amphitheater Foundation, 630 Janet Ave., Suite A-111, Lancaster PA 17601-4541. (717)735-8883. **Website:** www.longspark.org/art-craft-festival. Fine arts & crafts fair held annually Labor Day Weekend. Outdoors. Accepts handmade crafts, jewelry, ceramics, painting, glass, photography, fiber and more. Juried. Number exhibitors: 200. Number attendees: varies. Admission: see website. Apply online. Deadline for entry: February. Application fee: see website. Space fee: $510 (single); $645 (double). Exhibition space: 10×10 (single); 10×20 (double) . For more information, artists should call or visit website.

⊕ ◉ LOUISVILLE FESTIVAL OF THE ARTS WITH CRAFT MARKETPLACE AT PADDOCK SHOPS

270 Central Blvd., Suite 107B, Jupiter FL 33458. (561)746-6615. **Fax:** (561)746-6528. **E-mail:** info@artfestival.com. **Website:** www.artfestival.com. **Contact:** Malinda Ratliff, communications manager. Estab. 2008. Fine art & craft fair held annually in mid-June. Outdoors. Accepts photography, jewelry, mixed media, sculpture, wood, ceramic, glass, painting, digital, fiber, metal. Juried. Number exhibitors: 130. Number attendees: 50,000. Free to public. Apply online via www.zapplication.org. Deadline: see website. Application fee: $25. Space fee: $375. Exhibition space: 10×10 and 10×20. For more information, artists should e-mail, call or visit website.

◉ Show located at Paddock Shops on Summit Plaza Dr. in Louisville KY.

◉ LUTZ ARTS & CRAFTS FESTIVAL

(813)949-7060; (813)949-1937. Estab. 1979. Fine arts & crafts show held annually in December in Lutz FL. Outdoors. Accepts fine arts, jewelry, painting, photography, sculpture, crafts. Juried. Number of exhibitors: 250. Public attendance: 35,000. Admission fee: $2 per car (for parking). Deadline for entry: September 1 or until category is full. Exhibition space: 12×12 ft. For more information, artists should e-mail fsincich@gmail.com or call. Festival takes place at Lake Park.

⊕ ◉ MADEIRA BEACH THANKSGIVING WEEKEND CRAFT FESTIVAL

270 Central Blvd., Suite 107B, Jupiter FL 33458. (561)746-6615. **Fax:** (561)746-6528. **E-mail:** info@artfestival.com. **Website:** www.artfestival.com. **Contact:** Malinda Ratliff, communications manager. Estab. 2012. Fine art & craft fair held annually in November. Outdoors. Accepts photography, jewelry, mixed media, sculpture, wood, ceramic, glass, painting, digital, fiber, metal. Juried. Number exhibitors: 80. Number attendees: 13,000. Free to public. Apply online via www.zapplication.org or visit website for paper application. Deadline: see website. Application fee: $15. Space fee: $250. Exhibition space: 10×10 and 10×20. For more information, artists should e-mail, call or visit website. Festival located at Madeira Way between Gulf Blvd. & 150th Ave.

MADISON CHAUTAUQUA FESTIVAL OF ART

601 W. First St., Madison IN 47250. (812)265-6100. **Fax:** (812)273-3694. **E-mail:** georgie@madisonchautauqua.com. **Website:** www.madisonchautauqua.com. **Contact:** Georgie Kelly, coordinator. Estab. 1971. Premier juried fine arts & crafts show, featuring painting, photography, stained glass, jewelry, textiles pottery and more, amid the tree-lined streets of Madison's historic district. Held annually the last weekend in September. Stop by the Riverfront Food-Fest for a variety of foods to enjoy. Relax and listen to the live performances on the Lanier Mansion lawn, on the plaza and along the riverfront. Takes place in late September. Painting (2D artists may sell prints, but must include originals as well), photography, pottery, sculpture, wearable, jewelry, fiber, wood, baskets, glass, paper, leather. The number of artists in each category is limited to protect the integrity of the show. Festival held in Madison's National Landmark Historic District.

⊕ ◉ MAGNOLIA BLOSSOM FESTIVAL

Magnolia/Columbia County Chamber of Commerce, P.O. Box 866, Magnolia AR 71754. (870)901-2216; (870)693-5265. **E-mail:** jpate006@centurytel.net; jpate002@centurytel.net. **Website:** www.blossomfestival.org. Craft show held annually in May. Outdoors. Accepts handmade crafts, ceramics, paintings, jewelry, glass, photography, wearable art and other mediums. Juried. Number exhibitors: see website. Number attendees: varies. Free to public. Apply online. Deadline for entry: late March. Application fee: none. Space fee: varies. Exhibition space: varies. For more information, artists should call, e-mail or visit website.

⊕ ◉ MAIN STREET TO THE ROCKIES ART FESTIVAL

270 Central Blvd., Suite 107B, Jupiter FL 33458. (561)746-6615. **Fax:** (561)746-6528. **E-mail:** info@artfestival.com. **Website:** www.artfestival.com. **Contact:** Malinda Ratliff, communications manager. Estab. 2007. Fine art & craft fair held annually in mid-August. Outdoors. Accepts photography, jewelry, mixed media, sculpture, wood, ceramic, glass, painting, digital, fiber, metal. Juried. Number exhibitors: 100. Number attendees: 60,000. Free to public. Apply online via www.zapplication.org. Deadline: see website. Application fee: $35. Space fee: $475. Exhibition

ART FAIRS

space: 10×10 and 10×20. For more information, artists should e-mail, call, or visit website.

○ Festival located at Main St. in Downtown Frisco CO.

⊕ ○ MAINSAIL ARTS FESTIVAL

E-mail: artist@mainsailart.org. Website: www.mainsailart.org. Fine arts & crafts fair held annually in April. Outdoors. Accepts handmade crafts, ceramics, digital art, fibers, glass, graphics, jewelry, metal, mixed media, oil/acrylic, photography, sculpture, watercolor and wood . Juried. Awards/prizes: $60,000 in cash awards. Number exhibitors: 270. Number attendees: 100,000. Free to public. Apply online. Deadline for entry: December. Application fee: $35. Space fee: $275. Exhibition space: 10×10. For more information, artists should email or visit website.

⊕ ○ MANAYUNK ARTS FESTIVAL

4312 Main St., Philadelphia PA 19127. (215)482-9565. E-mail: info@manayunk.org. Website: www.manayunk.com. Contact: Caitlin Maloney, director of marketing & events. Estab. 1990. Arts & craft show held annually late June. Outdoors. Accepts handmade crafts, fiber, glass, ceramics, jewelry, mixed media, painting, photography, wood, sculpture. Juried. Awards/prizes: Best in each category; Best in Show. Exhibitors: 300. Number of attendees: 200,000. Free to public. Apply via www.zapplication.org. Deadline for entry: March 1. Application fee: $30. Space fee: $450. Exhibition Space: 10×10. Average sales: $2,000-7,000. For more information send e-mail or call.

⊕ ○ MARCO ISLAND FESTIVAL OF THE ARTS

270 Central Blvd., Suite 107B, Jupiter FL 33458. (561)746-6615. Fax: (561)746-6528. E-mail: info@artfestival.com. Website: www.artfestival.com. Contact: Malinda Ratliff, communications manager. Estab. 2014. Fine art & craft fair held annually in mid-March. Outdoors. Accepts photography, jewelry, mixed media, sculpture, wood, ceramic, glass, painting, digital, fiber, metal. Juried. Number exhibitors: 175. Number attendees: 40,000. Free to public. Apply online via www.zapplication.org. Deadline: see website. Application fee: $25. Space fee: $415. Exhibition space: 10×10 and 10×20. For more information, artists should e-mail, call, or visit website.

○ Festival located at Veteran's Park off N. Collier Blvd. in Marco Island FL.

⊕ ○ MARION ARTS FESTIVAL

1225 Sixth Ave., Suite 100, Marion IA 52302. Website: www.marionartsfestival.com. Fine arts & crafts fair held annually in May. Outdoors. Accepts handmade crafts, jewelry, ceramics, painting, photography, digital, printmaking and more. Juried. Awards/prizes: Best of Show, IDEA Award. Number exhibitors: 50. Number attendees: 14,000. Free to public. Apply via Zapplication.org. Deadline for entry: January. Application fee: $25. Space fee: $225. Exhibition space: 10×10. For more information, artists should visit website.

⊕ MARSHFIELD ART FAIR

New Visions Gallery, 1000 N. Oak Ave., Marshfield WI 54449. (715)387-5562. E-mail: newvisions.gallery@frontier.com. Website: www.marshfieldartfair.weebly.com. "Share a Marshfield tradition with family and friends at this FREE community celebration of the arts, held each year on Mother's Day. Marshfield Art Fair offers a wide variety of fine art and craft by more than 100 Midwestern artists. Musicians and performers entertain throughout the day. Hands-On-Art activities are available for kids." See website for more information.

○ MASON ARTS FESTIVAL

Mason-Deerfield Arts Alliance, P.O. Box 381, Mason OH 45040. (513)309-8585. E-mail: masonarts@gmail.com; info@the-arts-alliance.org. Website: www.masonarts.org. Fine arts & crafts show held annually in mid-September (see website for details). Indoors and outdoors. Accepts photography, graphics, printmaking, mixed media; painting and drawing; ceramics, metal sculpture; fiber, glass, jewelry, wood, leather. Juried. Awards/prizes: $3,000+. Number of exhibitors: 75-100. Public attendance: 3,000-5,000. Free to the public. Artists should apply by visiting website for application, e-mailing or calling. Deadline for entry: see website. Jury fee: $25. Space fee: $75. Exhibition space: 12×12 ft.; artist must provide 10×10 ft. pop-up tent.

○ City Gallery show is held indoors; these artists are not permitted to participate outdoors and vice versa. City Gallery is a juried show featuring approximately 30-50 artists who may show up to 2 pieces.

⊕ MCGREGOR SPRING ARTS & CRAFTS FESTIVAL

McGregor-Marquette Chamber of Commerce, P.O. Box 105, McGregor IA 52157. (800)896-0910; (563)873-2186. **E-mail:** mcgregormarquettecham ber@gmail.com. **Website:** www.mcgreg-marq.org. Fine arts & crafts fair held annually in May & October. Indoors & outdoors. Accepts handmade crafts, jewelry, ceramics, painting, photography, digital, printmaking and more. Number exhibitors: see website. Number attendees: varies. Free to public. Apply via online. Deadline for entry: see website. Application fee: none. Space fee: $75 outdoor; $100 indoor. Exhibition space: 10×10. For more information, artists should e-mail, call or visit website.

◉ MEMORIAL WEEKEND ARTS & CRAFTS FESTIVAL

38 Charles St., Rochester NH 03867. (603)332-2616. **Fax:** (603)332-8413. **E-mail:** info@castleberryfairs. com. **Website:** www.castleberryfairs.com. **Contact:** Sherry Mullen. Estab. 1989. Arts & crafts show held annually on Memorial Day weekend in Meredith NH. Outdoors. Accepts photography and all other mediums. Juried by photo, slide or sample. Number of exhibitors: 85. Public attendance: 7,500. Free to the public. Artists should apply by downloading application from website. Deadline for entry: until full. Space fee: $225. Exhibition space: 10×10 ft. For more information, artists should visit website. Festival held at Mill Falls Marketplace.

TIPS "Do not bring a book; do not bring a chair. Smile and make eye contact with everyone who enters your booth. Have them sign your guest book; get their e-mail address so you can let them know when you are in the area again. And, finally, make the sale—they are at the fair to shop, after all."

⊕ MENDOTA SWEET CORN FESTIVAL CRAFTER'S MARKET PLACE & FLEA MARKET

Mendota Area Chamber of Commerce, P.O. Box 620, Mendota IL 61342. (815)539-6507. **Fax:** (815)539-6025. **E-mail:** rfriedlein@mendotachamber.com. **Website:** www.sweetcornfestival.com. **Contact:** Roberta Friedlein, administrative assistant. Estab. 1979. Arts & crafts show held annually in August. Outdoors. Accepts handmade crafts, fine art, antiques, flea market items. Exhibitors: 200. Number of attendees: 55,000. Free to public. Apply by calling or sending e-mail.

Deadline for entry: until full. Application fee: none. Space fee: $70. Exhibition space: 10×10. For more information send e-mail, call or visit website.

⊕ MESA ARTS FESTIVAL

Mesa Arts Center, One E. Main St., Mesa AZ 85201. (480)644-6627. **Fax:** (480)644-6503. **E-mail:** shawn. lawson@mesaartscenter.com. **Website:** www.mesa artscenter.com. Fine arts & crafts fair held annually in December. Outdoors. Accepts handmade crafts, jewelry, ceramics, painting, photography, digital, printmaking and more. Number exhibitors: see website. Number attendees: varies. Free to public. Apply online. Deadline for entry: see website. Application fee: $25. Space fee: $250. Exhibition space: 10×10. For more information, artists should e-mail, call or visit website.

◉ MICHIGAN STATE UNIVERSITY HOLIDAY ARTS & CRAFTS SHOW

49 Abbot Rd., Room 26, MSU Union, East Lansing MI 48824. (517)355-3354. **E-mail:** uab@rhs.msu. edu; artsandcrafts@uabevents.com. **Website:** www. uabevents.com. **Contact:** Stephanie Bierlein. Estab. 1963. Arts & crafts show held annually the 1st weekend in December. Indoors. Accepts photography, basketry, candles, ceramics, clothing, sculpture, soaps, drawings, floral, fibers, glass, jewelry, metals, painting, graphics, pottery, wood. Selected by a committee using photographs submitted by each vendor to eliminate commercial products. They will evaluate on quality, creativity and crowd appeal. Number of exhibitors: 171. Public attendance: 15,000. Free to public. Artists should apply online. Exhibition space: 8×5 ft. For more information, artists should visit website or call.

◉ MICHIGAN STATE UNIVERSITY SPRING ARTS & CRAFTS SHOW

49 Abbot Rd., Room 26, MSU Union, East Lansing MI 48824. (517)355-3354. **Fax:** (517)432-2448. **E-mail:** artsandcrafts@uabevents.com. **Website:** www.uabev ents.com. **Contact:** Stephanie Bierlein. Estab. 1963. Arts & crafts show held annually the weekend before Memorial Day weekend in mid-May in conjunction with the East Lansing Art Festival. Both shows are free for the public to attend. Outdoors. Accepts photography, basketry, candles, ceramics, clothing, sculpture, soaps, drawings, floral, fibers, glass, jewelry, metals, painting, graphics, pottery, wood. Juried by a committee using photographs submitted by each vendor

to eliminate commercial products. They will evaluate on quality, creativity and crowd appeal. Number of exhibitors: 329. Public attendance: 30,000. Free to public. Artists can apply online beginning in February. Online applications will be accepted until show is filled. Application fee: $310 ($290 if apply online). Exhibition space: 10×10 ft. (double booth available, $600 or $580 online). For more information, artists should visit website or call.

MID-MISSOURI ARTISTS CHRISTMAS ARTS & CRAFTS SALE

P.O. Box 116, Warrensburg MO 64093. (660)747-6092. **E-mail:** rlimback@iland.net. Estab. 1970. Holiday arts & crafts show held annually in November. Indoors. Accepts photography and all original arts and crafts. Juried by 3 good-quality color photos (2 of the artwork, 1 of the display). Number of exhibitors: 50. Public attendance: 1,200. Free to the public. Artists should apply by e-mailing or calling for an application form. Entry form also available at www.midmissouriartists.webs.com. Deadline for entry: early November. Space fee: $50. Exhibition space: 10×10 ft. For more information, artists should e-mail or call.

TIPS "Items under $100 are most popular."

MIDSUMMER ARTS FAIRE

P.O. Box 24, Quincy IL 62306. (217)779-2285. **Fax:** (217)222-8698. **E-mail:** info@artsfaire.org. **Website:** www.artsfaire.org. **Contact:** Kris Eyler, coordinator. Fine art show held annually in June. Outdoors. Accepts photography, paintings, pottery, jewelry. Juried. Awards/prizes: various totaling $5,000. Exhibitors: 60. Number of attendees: 7,000. Free to public. Apply via www.zapplication.org. Deadline for entry: February 28. Application fee: $20. Space fee: $100. Exhibition space: 10×10. Average sales: $2,500. For more information, artists should e-mail, call, see Facebook page or visit website.

MILL VALLEY FALL ARTS FESTIVAL

P.O. Box 300, Mill Valley CA 94942. (415)381-8090. **E-mail:** mvfafartists@gmail.com. **Website:** www.mvfaf.org. "The Mill Valley Fall Arts Festival has been recognized as a fine art and craft show of high quality original artwork for over 55 years. The festival draws well-educated buyers from nearby affluent neighborhoods of Marin County and the greater San Francisco Bay Area. The event provides an exceptional opportunity for the sale of unique, creative and high-end work." Artists interested in participating must apply

via www.zapplication.org. Applications open mid-January and close mid-April. See website for more information.

MILWAUKEE DOMES ART FESTIVAL

Website: www.milwaukeedomesartfestival.com. Fine arts & crafts fair held annually in August. Indoors & outdoors. Accepts handmade crafts, jewelry, ceramics, painting, photography, digital, printmaking and more. Juried. Awards/prizes: $10,500 in awards and prizes. Number exhibitors: see website. Number attendees: varies. Free to public. Apply online. Deadline for entry: see website. Application fee: $35. Space fee: $250 outdoor; $450 indoor. Exhibition space: 10×10. For more information visit website.

MINNESOTA WOMEN'S ART FESTIVAL

E-mail: nlsiegal@aolc.om. **Website:** www.womensartfestival.com. "The mission of the Women's Art Festival is to provide a welcoming place for women artists to show and sell their creations and to provide a fun and festive atmosphere for guest to shop, gather and enjoy community. Supporting local women artists of all experience levels, from first time exhibitors to experienced professionals, we are a non-juried show with the expectation that all goods are of excellent quality, made and sold by local women. We do not accept dealers or importers and define local as any woman who wants to travel to Minneapolis for a day of fun, camaraderie, community and creativity. Now held at the Colin Powell Youth Leadership Center, 2924 4th Ave. S, in Minneapolis, the event has grown to include over 130 women artists working in a large variety of media. There is live music by women performers throughout the day and a women-owned coffee shop providing food, beverages and treats. Artists and guests alike comment on the quality of the artistic work, the fun and comfortable atmosphere, the caliber of the music and the wonderful addition of good food, good coffee and the chance to see good friends." See website for more information.

MISSION FEDERAL ARTWALK

2210 Columbia St., San Diego CA 92101. (619)615-1090. **Fax:** (619)615-1099. **E-mail:** info@artwalksandiego.org. **Website:** www.artwalksandiego.org. Fine arts & crafts fair held annually in April. Outdoors. Accepts handmade crafts, jewelry, ceramics, painting, photography, digital, printmaking and more. Juried. Number exhibitors: 350. Number attendees:

90,000. Free to public. Apply online. Deadline for entry: January. Application fee: none. Space fee: varies. Exhibition space: varies. For more information, artists should e-mail, call or visit website.

MONTAUK ARTISTS' ASSOCIATION, INC.

P.O. Box 2751, Montauk NY 11954. (631)668-5336. **E-mail:** montaukart@aol.com. **Website:** montauk artistsassociation.org; www.montaukchamber. com. **Contact:** Anne Weissman. Estab. 1970. 501(c) (3). Arts & crafts show held annually Memorial Day weekend; 3rd weekend in August. Outdoors. Accepts photography, paintings, prints (numbered and signed in bins), sculpture, limited fine art, jewelry and ceramics. Number of exhibitors: 90. Public attendance: 8-10,000. Free to public. Exhibition space: 12×12. For more information, artists should call or visit website.

✪ ◯ MONTE SANO ART FESTIVAL

706 Randolph Ave., Huntsville AL 35801. (256)653-3654. **E-mail:** curtisbenzle@gmail.com. **Website:** www.montesanoartfestival.com. **Contact:** Curtis Benzle, director. Estab. 1998. Annual arts & crafts show held in September. Outdoors. Accepts handmade crafts, painting, sculpture, photography, prints. Juried. Exhibitors: 130. Number of attendees: 4,000. Admission: $7. Apply via website. Deadline for entry: May 1. Application fee: $15. Space fee: $125. Exhibition space: 100 sq. ft. Average sales: $2,000. For more information see website.

✪ ◯ MOUNT DORA ARTS FESTIVAL

Mount Dora Center for the Arts, 138 East Fifth Ave., Mount Dora FL 32757. (352)383-0880. **Fax:** (352)383-7753. **Website:** www.mountdoracenterforthearts.org/arts-festival. "A juried fine arts festival, for art lovers, casual festival-goers and families, nothing compares to the Mount Dora Arts Festival. In addition to the endless rows of fine art, including oil paintings, watercolors, acrylics, clay, sculpture and photography, the festival features local and regional musical entertainment at a main stage in Donnelly Park." See website for more information.

◯ MOUNT GRETNA OUTDOOR ART SHOW

P.O. Box 637, Mount Gretna PA 17064. (717)964-3270. **Fax:** (717)964-3054. **E-mail:** mtgretnaart@comcast. net. **Website:** www.mtgretnaarts.com. Estab. 1974. Fine arts & crafts show held annually 3rd full weekend in August. Outdoors. Accepts photography, oils, acrylics, watercolors, mixed media, jewelry, wood, pa-

per, graphics, sculpture, leather, clay/porcelain. Juried by 4 professional artists who assign each applicant a numeric score. The highest scores in each medium are accepted. Awards/prizes: Judges' Choice Awards: 30 artists are invited to return the following year, jury exempt; the top 10 are given a monetary award of $250. Number of exhibitors: 250. Public attendance: 15,000-19,000. Public admission: $10; children under 12 free. Artists should apply via www.zapplication.org. Deadline for entry: April 1. Application fee: $25. Space fee: $350 per 10×12 ft. space; $700 per 10×24 ft. double space. For more information, artists should e-mail, visit website, call.

MOUNTAIN STATE FOREST FESTIVAL

P.O. Box 388, 101 Lough St., Elkins WV 26241. (304)636-1824. **Fax:** (304)636-4020. **E-mail:** msff@forestfestival.com; mwileman@forestfestival.com. **Website:** www.forestfestival.com. **Contact:** Cindy Nucilli, executive director. Estab. 1930. Arts, crafts & photography show held annually in early October. Accepts photography and homemade crafts. Awards/prizes: cash awards for photography only. Number of exhibitors: 50+. Public attendance: 75,000. Free to the public. Artists should apply by requesting an application form. For more information, artists should visit website, call, or visit Facebook page (search "Mountain State Forest Festival").

✪ MYSTIC OUTDOOR ARTS FESTIVAL

E-mail: Cherielin@MysticChamber.org. **Website:** www.mysticchamber.org/?sec=sec&s=44. "The annual Mystic Outdoor Art Festival has evolved in many ways from its humble beginnings. In 1957, Milton Baline and several other local business owners and art lovers proposed that Mystic pattern a festival after the famous Washington Square Festival in New York. That first show featured 105 artists and 500 paintings. Between 4,000 and 6,000 visitors came to admire and purchase art. Today the Mystic Outdoor Art Festival stretches over two miles and is the oldest of its kind in the Northeast. The Mystic Outdoor Art Festival has grown to over 250 artists who come from all corners of the United States and bring more than 100,000 works of art." See website for more information.

✪ ◯ NAMPA FESTIVAL OF ARTS

131 Constitution Way, Nampa ID 83686. (208)468-5858. **Fax:** (208)465-2282. **E-mail:** rec@cityofnampa.us. **Website:** www.nampaparksandrecreation. org. **Contact:** Wendy Davis, program director. Estab.

1986. Fine art & craft show held annually mid-August. Outdoors. Accepts handmade crafts, fine art, photography, metal, anything handmade. Juried. Awards/prizes: cash. Exhibitors: 180. Number of attendees: 15,000. Free to public. See website for application. Deadline for entry: July 10. Space fee: $40-90. Exhibition Space: 10×10, 15×15, 20×20. For more information send e-mail, call or visit website.

✪ NAPERVILLE WOMAN'S CLUB ART FAIR

(630)209-1246. **E-mail:** naperartfair@comcast.net. **Website:** www.napervillewomansclub.org. **Contact:** Roxanne Lang. "Over 100 local and national artists will be displaying original artwork in clay, fiber, glass, jewelry, mixed media, metal, painting, photography, sculpture and wood. Ribbons and cash prizes are awarded to winning artists by local judges and NWC. The Naperville Woman's Club Art Fair is the longest continuously running art fair in Illinois. Activities at this event include entertainment, a silent auction, artist demonstrations, the Empty Bowl Fundraiser to benefit local food pantries, and the Petite Picassos children's activities tent. This is the largest fundraiser of the year for the Naperville Woman's Club. Proceeds from the event help fund a local art scholarship and local charities. Admission and parking are free. For more information please email us at: naperartfair@comcast.net."

◉ NEW ENGLAND CRAFT & SPECIALTY FOOD FAIR

38 Charles St., Rochester NH 03867. (603)332-2616. **Fax:** (603)332-8413. **E-mail:** info@castleberryfairs.com. **Website:** www.castleberryfairs.com. Estab. 1995. Arts & crafts show held annually on Veterans Day weekend in Salem NH. Indoors. Accepts photography and all other mediums. Juried by photo, slide or sample. Number of exhibitors: 200. Public attendance: 15,000. Artists should apply by downloading application from website. Deadline for entry: until full. Space fee: $350-450. Exhibition space: 10×6 or 10×10 ft. Average gross sales/exhibitor: "Generally, this is considered an 'excellent' show, so I would guess most exhibitors sell 10 times their booth fee, or in this case, at least $3,000 in sales." For more information, artists should visit website. Fair is held at Rockingham Park Racetrack.

TIPS "Do not bring a book; do not bring a chair. Smile and make eye contact with everyone who enters your booth. Have them sign your guest book; get their e-mail address so you can let them know when you are in the area again. And, finally, make the sale—they are at the fair to shop, after all."

◉ ◉ NEW MEXICO ARTS AND CRAFTS FAIR

2501 San Pedro St. NE, Suite 110, Albuquerque NM 87110. (505)884-9043. **E-mail:** info@nmartsandcraftsfair.org. **Website:** www.nmartsandcraftsfair.org. Estab. 1962. Fine arts & craft show held annually in June. Indoors. Accepts decorative and functional ceramics, digital art, drawing, fiber, precious and non-precious jewelry, photography, paintings, printmaking, mixed media, metal, sculpture and wood. *Only New Mexico residents 18 years and older are eligible.* See website for more details.

NEW ORLEANS JAZZ & HERITAGE FESTIVAL

336 Camp St., Suite 250, New Orleans LA 70130. (504)410-4100. **Fax:** (504)558-6121. **Website:** www.nojazzfest.com. **Contact:** Mandy Dillon. Estab. 1970. This festival showcases music, cuisine, arts and crafts from the region and around the world. The Louisiana Heritage Fair is held at the Fair Grounds Race Course over the course of 2 weekends (late April/early May; see website for details). Apply online via www.zapplication.org. Must submit 5 images, 4 of artwork, 1 of booth. Application fee: $30. Deadline: late December (see website for details). Call or visit website for more information.

NEW SMYRNA BEACH ART FIESTA

City of New Smyrna Beach, 210 Sams Ave., New Smyrna Beach FL 32168. (386)424-2175. **Fax:** (386)424-2177. **E-mail:** kshelton@cityofnsb.com. **Website:** www.cityofnsb.com; nsbfla.com/index.cfm. **Contact:** Kimla Shelton. Estab. 1952. Arts & crafts show held annually in February. Outdoors. Accepts photography, oil, acrylics, pastel, drawings, graphics, sculpture, crafts, watercolor. Awards/prizes: $15,000 prize money; $1,600/category; Best of Show. Number of exhibitors: 250. Public attendance: 14,000. Free to public. Artists should apply by calling to get on mailing list. Applications are always mailed out the day before Thanksgiving. Deadline for entry: until full. Exhibition space: 10×10 ft. For more information, artists should call. Show held in the Old Fort Park area.

NEW WORLD FESTIVAL OF THE ARTS

P.O. Box 2300, Manteo NC 27954. (252)473-2838; (252)473-2133. **E-mail:** dareartsinfo@gmail.com. **Website:** www.townofmanteo.com. **Contact:** Edward Greene. Estab. 1963. Fine arts & crafts show held annually in mid-August (see website for details). Outdoors. Juried. Location is the Waterfront in downtown Manteo. Features 80 selected artists from Vermont to Florida exhibiting and selling their works. Application fee: $15. Space fee: $85.

NEWTON ARTS FESTIVAL

Piper Promotions, 4 Old Green Rd., Sandy Hook CT 06482. (203)512-9100. **E-mail:** staceyolszewski@yahoo.com. **Website:** www.newtownartsfestival.com. **Contact:** Stacey Olszewski. Fine arts & crafts fair held annually in September. Outdoors. Accepts handmade crafts, jewelry, ceramics, painting, photography, digital, printmaking and more. Juried. Number exhibitors: see website. Number attendees: varies. Admission: $5; children 12 & under free. Apply online. Deadline for entry: August. Application fee: none. Space fee: $105 (booth); $225 (festival tent). Exhibition space: 10×10. For more information, artists should e-mail, call or visit website.

NIANTIC OUTDOOR ART & CRAFT SHOW

P.O. Box 227, Niantic CT 06357. (860)739-9128. **E-mail:** artshowwoody@yahoo.com. **Website:** www.nianticartsandcraftshow.com. **Contact:** Craig Woody. Fine art & craft show held annually in July. Outdoors. Accepts handmade crafts, ceramics, fiber, glass, graphics, jewelry, leather, metal, mixed media, painting, photography, printmaking, sculpture, woodworking. Juried. Number exhibitors: 142. Number attendees: varies. Free to public. Apply online. Deadline for entry: March. Application fee: $20. Space fee: varies. Exhibition space: varies. For more information, artists should e-mail, call or visit website.

NORTH CHARLESTON ARTS FESTIVAL

P.O. Box 190016, North Charleston SC 29419-9016. (843)740-5854. **E-mail:** culturalarts@northcharleston.org. **Website:** www.northcharlestonartsfest.com. Fine arts & crafts fair held annually in May. Outdoors. Accepts handmade crafts, jewelry, ceramics, painting, photography, digital, printmaking and more. Juried. Number exhibitors: see website. Number attendees: 30,000. Admission: see website. Apply online. Deadline for entry: January. Application fee: see website. Space fee: see website. Exhibition space: see website. For more information, artists should e-mail, call or visit website.

NORTH CONGREGATIONAL PEACH & CRAFT FAIR

17 Church St., New Hartford CT 06057. (860)379-2466. **Website:** www.northchurchucc.com. **Contact:** K.T. "Sully" Sullivan. Estab. 1966. Arts & crafts show held annually in mid-August. Outdoors on the Green at Pine Meadow. Accepts photography, most arts and crafts. Number of exhibitors: 50. Public attendance: 500-2,000. Free to public. Artists should call for application form. Deadline for entry: August. Application fee: $60. Exhibition space: 11×11 ft.
TIPS "Be prepared for all kinds of weather."

NORTH SHORE FESTIVAL OF ART

Amdur Productions, P.O. Box 550, Highland Park IL 60035. (847)926-4300. **E-mail:** info@amdurproductions.com. **Website:** www.amdurproductions.com. Fine arts & crafts fair held annually in July. Outdoors. Accepts handmade crafts, jewelry, ceramics, painting, photography, digital, printmaking and more. Juried. Number exhibitors: 100. Number attendees: 84,000. Free to public. Apply online. Deadline for entry: see website. Application fee: $25. Space fee: $445. Exhibition space: 10×10. For more information, artists should e-mail, call or visit website.

NORTHERN VIRGINIA FINE ARTS FESTIVAL

(703)471-9242. **E-mail:** info@restonarts.org. **Website:** www.northernvirginiafineartsfestival.org. Fine arts & crafts fair held annually in May. Outdoors. Accepts handmade crafts, jewelry, ceramics, painting, photography, digital, printmaking and more. Juried. Number exhibitors: 200. Number attendees: varies. Admission: $5; children 18 & under free. Apply online. Deadline for entry: see website. Application fee: see website. Space fee: see website. Exhibition space: see website. For more information, artists should e-mail, call or visit website.

OAK PARK AVENUE-LAKE ARTS & CRAFTS SHOW

P.O. Box 1326, Palatine IL 60078. (312)751-2500; (847)991-4748. **E-mail:** asoaartists@aol.com. **Website:** www.americansocietyofartists.org. Estab. 1974.

Fine arts & crafts show held annually in mid-August. Event held in Oak Park IL. Outdoors. Accepts photography, painting, graphics, sculpture, glass, wood, paper, fiber arts, mosaics and more. Juried. Please submit 4 images representative of your work you wish to exhibit, 1 of your display set-up, your first/last name, physical address, daytime telephone number—résumé/show listing helpful. Number of exhibitors: 150. Free to the public. Artists should apply by submitting jury materials. To jury online, submit to: asoaartists@aol.com. If juried in, you will receive a jury/approval number. Deadline for entry: 2 months prior to show or earlier if spaces fill. Entry fee: $195. Exhibition space: approximately 100 sq. ft. for single space; other sizes available. For more information, artists should send SASE with jury material to the above address. Show takes place in Scoville Park (located in Oak Park).

TIPS "Remember that when you are at work in your studio, you are an artist. But when you are at a show, you are a business person selling your work."

OC FAIR VISUAL ARTS COMPETITION

88 Fair Dr., Costa Mesa CA 92626. (714)708-1718. **E-mail:** visualarts@ocfair.com. **Website:** www.ocfair.com/competitions. **Contact:** Barbara Thompson, program coordinator, visual arts. Annual fine art and craft show held from mid-July to mid-August. Indoors. Accepted media includes: photography, 2D media, sculpture, ceramics, graphic arts, fine woodworking and film. Juried event with cash and purchase awards. Digital submissions only. Over 2,000 exhibitors each year. 1.3 million attendees. 20,000 sq. ft. exhibition space. Fair admission fee: $12. Artists should apply online at www.ocfair.com/competitions after April 1. Deadline for entry: June 1. Application fee of $10 per entry. Open to California residents 19 and older; young adults 13-18. E-mail or visit website for more information.

OCONOMOWOC FESTIVAL OF THE ARTS

P.O. Box 651, Oconomowoc WI 53066. **Website:** www.oconomowocarts.org. Estab. 1970. Fine arts & crafts fair held annually in August. Outdoors. Accepts handmade crafts, jewelry, ceramics, painting, photography, digital, printmaking and more. Juried. Awards/prizes: $3,500 in awards & prizes. Number exhibitors: 140. Number attendees: varies. Admission: Free to public. Apply online. Deadline for entry: March. Application fee: $40. Space fee: $250. Ex-

hibition space: 10×10. For more information, artists should visit website.

OHIO MART

Stan Hywet Hall and Gardens, 714 N. Portage Path, Akron OH 44303. (330)836-5533; (888)836-5533. **E-mail:** info@stanhywet.org. **Website:** www.stanhywet.org. Estab. 1966. Fine arts & crafts fair held annually in October. Outdoors. Accepts handmade crafts, jewelry, ceramics, painting, photography, digital, printmaking and more. Juried. Number exhibitors: see website. Number attendees: varies. Admission: $9 adults; $2 youth. Apply online. Deadline for entry: see website. Application fee: see website. Space fee: see website. Exhibition space: see website. For more information, artists should call, e-mail or visit website.

OHIO SAUERKRAUT FESTIVAL

P.O. Box 281, Waynesville OH 45068. (513)897-8855, ext. 2. **Fax:** (513)897-9833. **E-mail:** waynesville@aol.com. **Website:** www.sauerkrautfestival.com. **Contact:** Barb Lindsay, office and event coordinator. Estab. 1969. Arts & crafts show held annually 2nd full weekend in October. Outdoors. Accepts photography and handcrafted items only. Juried by jury team. Number of exhibitors: 458. Public attendance: 350,000. Jury fee: $20. Space fee: $200 + $25 processing fee. Exhibition space: 10×10 ft. For more information, artists should visit website or call.

TIPS "Have reasonably priced items."

OKLAHOMA CITY FESTIVAL OF THE ARTS

Arts Council of Oklahoma City, 400 W. California, Oklahoma City OK 73102. (405)270-4848. **Fax:** (405)270-4888. **E-mail:** info@artscouncilokc.com. **Website:** www.artscouncilokc.com. Estab. 1967. Fine arts & crafts fair held annually in April. Outdoors. Accepts handmade crafts, jewelry, ceramics, painting, photography, digital, printmaking and more. Juried. Number exhibitors: 144. Number attendees: varies. Free to public. Apply online. Deadline for entry: see website. Application fee: see website. Space fee: see website. Exhibition space: see website. For more information, artists should call, e-mail, or visit website.

OLD CAPITOL ART FAIR

P.O. Box 5701, Springfield IL 62705. (405)270-4848. **Fax:** (405)270-4888. **E-mail:** artistinfo@yahoo.com. **Website:** www.socaf.org. **Contact:** Kate Baima. Estab. 1961. Fine arts & crafts fair held annually in May.

Outdoors. Accepts handmade crafts, jewelry, ceramics, painting, photography, digital, printmaking and more. Juried. Awards/prizes: 1st Place, 2nd Place, 3rd Place, Awards of Merit. Number exhibitors: see website. Number attendees: varies. Free to public. Apply online. Deadline for entry: November. Application fee: $35. Space fee: $300 (single); $550 (double). Exhibition space: 10×10 (single); 10×10 (double). For more information, artists should call, e-mail or visit website.

⊕ ○ OLD FOURTH WARD PARK ARTS FESTIVAL

592 N. Angier Ave. NE, Atlanta GA 30308. (404)873-1222. **E-mail:** info@affps.com. **Website:** oldfourth wardparkartsfestival.com. **Contact:** Lisa Windle, festival director. Estab. 2013. Arts & crafts show held annually late June. Outdoors. Accepts handmade crafts, painting, photography, sculpture, leather, metal, glass, jewelry. Juried by a panel. Awards/prizes: ribbons. Number of exhibitors: 130. Number of attendees: 25,000. Free to public. Apply online at www.zappli cation.org. Deadline for entry: late April. Application fee: $25. Space fee: $225. Exhibition space: 10×10. For more information, send e-mail or see website.

OLD TOWN ART FAIR

1763 N. North Park Ave., Chicago IL 60614. (312)337-1938. **E-mail:** info@oldtowntriangle.com. **Website:** www.oldtownartfair.com. Estab. 1950. Fine art festival held annually in early June (see website for details). Located in the city's historic Old Town Triangle District. Artists featured are chosen by an independent jury of professional artists, gallery owners and museum curators. Features a wide range of art mediums, including 2D and 3D mixed media, drawing, painting, photography, printmaking, ceramics, fiber, glass, jewelry and works in metal, stone and wood. Apply online at www.zappplication.org. For more information, call, e-mail, or visit website. Fair located in Old Town Triangle District.

⊕ ○ OLD TOWN ART FESTIVAL

Old Town San Diego Chamber of Commerce, P.O. 82686, San Diego CA 92138. (619)233-5008. **Fax:** (619)233-0898. **E-mail:** rob-vslmedia@cox.net; otsd@ aol.com. **Website:** www.oldtownartfestival.com. Fine arts & crafts fair held annually in September. Outdoors. Accepts handmade crafts, jewelry, ceramics, painting, photography, digital, printmaking and more. Juried. Number exhibitors: see website. Num-

ber attendees: 15,000. Free to public. Apply online. Deadline for entry: September 1. Application fee: $25. Space fee: varies. Exhibition space: varies. For more information, artists should call, e-mail or visit website.

⊕ ○ OMAHA SUMMER ARTS FESTIVAL

Vic Gutman & Associates, P.O. Box 31036, Omaha NE 68131. (402)345-5401. **Fax:** (402)342-4114. **E-mail:** ebalazs@vgagroup.com. **Website:** www.summerarts. org. Estab. 1975. Fine arts & crafts fair held annually in June. Outdoors. Accepts handmade crafts, jewelry, ceramics, painting, photography, digital, printmaking and more. Juried. Number exhibitors: 135. Number attendees: varies. Free to public. Apply online. Deadline for entry: see website. Application fee: see website. Space fee: varies. Exhibition space: varies. For more information, artists should call, e-mail or visit website.

○ ON THE GREEN FINE ART & CRAFT SHOW

P.O. Box 304, Glastonbury CT 06033. (860)659-1196. **Fax:** (860)633-4301. **E-mail:** info@glastonburyarts. org. **Website:** www.glastonburyarts.org. **Contact:** Jane Fox, administrator. Estab. 1961. Fine art & craft show held annually 2nd week of September. Outdoors. Accepts photography, pastel, prints, pottery, jewelry, drawing, sculpture, mixed media, oil, acrylic, glass, watercolor, graphic, wood, fiber, etc. Juried (with 3 photos of work, 1 photo of booth). Awards/prizes: $3,000 total prize money in different categories. Number of exhibitors: 200. Public attendance: 15,000. Free to public. Artists should apply online. Deadline for entry: early June. Jury fee: $15. Space fee: $275. Exhibition space: 12×15 ft. Average gross sales/exhibitor varies. For more information, artists should visit website. Show located at Hubbard Green.

⊕ ◐ ○ ONE OF A KIND CRAFT SHOW

10 Alcorn Ave., Suite 100, Toronto Ontario M4V 3A9. (416)960-5399. **Fax:** (416)923-5624. **E-mail:** jill@ oneofakindshow.com. **Website:** www.oneofakind show.com. **Contact:** Jill Benson. Estab. 1975. Fine arts & crafts fair held annually 3 times a year. Outdoors. Accepts handmade crafts, jewelry, ceramics, painting, photography, digital, printmaking and more. Juried. Number exhibitors: varies per show. Number attendees: varies per show. Free to public. Apply online. Deadline for entry: see website. Application fee: see website. Space fee: varies. Exhibition space: var-

ies. For more information, artists should call, e-mail or visit website.

➕ 🎧 ORANGE BEACH FESTIVAL OF ART

26389 Canal Road, Orange Beach AL 36561. (251)981-2787. **Fax:** (251)981-6981. **E-mail:** helpdesk@orange beachartcenter.com. **Website:** www.orangebeacharts festival.com. Fine art & craft show held annually in March. Outdoors. Accepts handmade crafts, ceramics, paintings, jewelry, glass, photography, wearable art and other mediums. Juried. Number exhibitors: 90. Number attendees: varies. Free to public. Apply online. Deadline for entry: See website. Application fee: see website. Space fee: varies. Exhibition space: varies. For more information, artists should call, e-mail or visit website.

🎧 ORCHARD LAKE FINE ART SHOW

P.O. Box 79, Milford MI 48381-0079. (248)684-2613. **E-mail:** info@hotworks.org. **Website:** www.hot works.org. **Contact:** Patty Narozny, executive director & producer. Estab. 2003. Voted in the top 100 art fairs nationwide the last 8 years in the row by *Sunshine Magazine* out of more than 4,000 art fairs. "The Orchard Lake Fine Art Show takes place in the heart of West Bloomfield, located on a street with high visibility from Orchard Lake Road, south of Maple Road, in an area that provides plenty of free parking for patrons and weekend access for local businesses. West Bloomfield MI is located adjacent to Bloomfiled Hills, listed as the #2 highest income city in the US, according to Wikipedia.org, and hoome of Cranbrook Art Institute. West Bloomfield has been voted one of *Money Magazine*'s 'Best Places to Live,' and is an upscale community with rolilng hills that provide a tranquil setting for beautiful and lavish homes. $5 admission helps support the Institute for the Arts & Education, Inc., a 501(c)(3) nonprofit organization whose focus is visual arts and community enrichment. 12 & under free. This event follows Ann Arbor, has great event hours and provides ease of move-in and move-out. All work must be original and personally handmade by the artist. There is $2,500 in professional artist awards. We accept all disciplines including sculpture, paintings, clay, glass, wood, fiber, jewelry, photography and more." Professional applications are accepted "manual" or via www.zapplication.org. Please include 3 images of your most compelling work, plus one of your booth presentation as you would set up at the show. Space fee: $375, 10×10; 10×15, $525; 10×20, $650; add

$75 for corner. "Generators are permitted as long as they do not bother anyone for any reason." Deadline to apply is March 15. "No buy/sell/import permitted. As part of our commitment to bring art education into the community, there is the Chadwick Accounting Group's Youth Art Competition for grades K-8 or ages 5-12, in which we encourage budding artists to create their original and personally handmade artwork that is publicly displayed in the show the entire weekend." $250 in youth art awards. The deadline to apply for youth art is July 1. More information can be found on the web at www.hotworks.org.

➕ 🎧 PA GUILD OF CRAFTSMEN FINE CRAFT FAIRS

Center of American Craft, 335 N. Queen St., Lancaster PA 17603. (717)431-8706. **E-mail:** nick@pacrafts.org. **Website:** www.pacrafts.org/fine-craft-fairs. **Contact:** Nick Mohler. Fine arts & crafts fair held annually 5 times a year. Outdoors. Accepts handmade crafts, jewelry, ceramics, painting, photography, digital, printmaking and more. Juried. Number exhibitors: varies per show. Number attendees: varies per show. Free to public. Apply online. Deadline for entry: January. Application fee: $25. Space fee: varies. Exhibition space: 10×10. For more information, artists should call, e-mail or visit website.

➕ 🎧 PALM SPRINGS FINE ART FAIR

HEG—Hamptons Expo Group, 223 Hampton Rd., Southampton NY 11968. (631)283-5505. **Fax:** (631)702-2141. **E-mail:** info@hegshows.com. **Website:** www.palmspringsfineartfair.com. Fine art fair held annually in February. Indoors. Accepts fine art from galleries. Juried. Number exhibitors: 60. Number attendees: 12,000. Admission: see website. Apply online. Deadline for entry: see website. Application fee: none. Space fee: varies. Exhibition space: varies. For more information, artists should e-mail, call or visit website.

➕ 🎧 PALMER PARK ART FAIR

Integrity Shows, P.O. Box 1070, Ann Arbor MI 48106. (207)725-5507. **E-mail:** info@integrityshows.com. **Website:** www.funkyferndaleartfair.com. **Contact:** Mark Loeb. Estab. 2014. Fine arts & crafts show held annually in May. Outdoors. Accepts photography and all fine art and craft mediums. Juried by 3 independent jurors. Awards/prizes: purchase and merit awards. Number of exhibitors: 80. Public attendance: 7,000. Free to the public. Apply online. Deadline for entry: see website. Application fee: $25. Booth fee: $295. Electricity limited; fee: $100. For more information, visit website.

PANOPLY ARTS FESTIVAL

The Arts Council, Inc., 700 Monroe St. SW, Suite 2, Huntsville AL 35801. (256)519-2787. **Fax:** (256)533-3811. **E-mail:** info@artshuntsville.org; vhinton@arts huntsville.org. **Website:** www.panoply.org. Estab. 1982. Fine arts show held annually the last weekend in April. Also features music and dance. Outdoors. Accepts photography, painting, sculpture, drawing, printmaking, mixed media, glass, fiber. Juried by a panel of judges chosen for their in-depth knowledge and experience in multiple mediums, and who jury from slides or disks in January. During the festival 1 judge awards various prizes. Number of exhibitors: 60-80. Public attendance: 140,000+. Public admission: $5/day or $10/weekend (children 12 and under free). Artists should e-mail, call, or go online for an application form. Deadline for entry: January. Space fee: $185. Exhibition space: 10×10 ft. (tent available, space fee $390). Average gross sales/exhibitor: $2,500. For more information, artists should e-mail or visit website. The festival is held in Big Spring International Park.

PARADISE CITY ARTS FESTIVALS

30 Industrial Dr. E, Northampton MA 01060. (800)511-9725. **Fax:** (413)587-0966. **E-mail:** artist@ paradisecityarts.com. **Website:** www.paradisecity arts.com. Estab. 1995. 4 fine arts & crafts shows held annually in March, May, October, and November. Indoors. Accepts photography, all original art and fine craft media. Juried by 5 digital images of work and an independent board of jury advisors. Number of exhibitors: 150-275. Public attendance: 5,000-20,000. Public admission: $12. Artists should apply by submitting name and address to be added to mailing list or print application from website. Deadlines for entry: April 1 (fall shows); September 9 (spring shows). Application fee: $30-45. Space fee: $855-1,365. Exhibition space varies by show, see website for more details. For more information, artists should e-mail, visit website, or call.

PARK FOREST ART FAIR

367 Artists Walk, Park Forest IL 60466. (708)748-3377. **Fax:** (708)748-9132. **E-mail:** tallgrass367@sbcglobal. net; jmuchnik@sbcglobal.net. **Website:** www.tallgrass arts.org. **Contact:** Janet Muchnik, president. Estab.

1955. Fine arts & crafts festival held annually 3rd weekend in September. Outdoors. Accepts photography and any media that would fit the criteria and meet the standards of fine art or craft. Juried by professional artists (representing several media). Jurying opens in January when "call for artists" is posted on website; closes at end of June. Jurying is done on a monthly basis so successful applicants can make plans to participate. Juried artists may also exhibit in the Tall Grass Gallery and Gift Shop. Awards/prizes: Best 2D work: $750; Best 3D work: $750; Best Jewelry: $750; 2 director's prizes: $100 each; Judge's Choice (any media); several purchase awards and 1 Purchase Prize for the Tall Grass Permanent Collection. Number of exhibitors: 70-100. Public attendance: 3,000-4,000. Free to the public. Artists should apply online. Submit 6 photographs of work by CD or e-mail. Deadline for entry: June 28. Jury fee: $35. Space fee: $175. Exhibition space: 12×10 ft. tent with space around it. "Some spaces are under an awning and do not require the use of a tent but should be requested early." For more information, artists should e-mail or visit website.

TIPS "A good display is a large key to sales; however, in recent years, fair attendees have also looked for a range of prices. This includes prints or smaller-size artworks. Exhibitors should be prepared (and willing) to talk about their artworks and techniques."

PARK POINT ART FAIR

(218)428-1916. **E-mail:** coordinator@parkpointart fair.org. **Website:** www.parkpointartfair.org. **Contact:** Carla Tamburro, art fair coordinator. Estab. 1970. Fine arts & crafts fair held annually in June. Outdoors. Accepts handmade crafts, jewelry, ceramics, painting, photography, digital, printmaking and more. Juried. Awards/prizes: $1,300 in awards. Number exhibitors: 120. Number attendees: 10,000. Free to public. Apply online. Deadline for entry: March. Application fee: $15. Space fee: $185. Exhibition space: 10×10. For more information, artists should e-mail, call, or visit website.

PATTERSON APRICOT FIESTA

P.O. Box 442, Patterson CA 95363. (209)892-3118. **Fax:** (209)892-3388. **E-mail:** patterson_apricot_fies ta@hotmail.com. **Website:** www.apricotfiesta.com. **Contact:** Jaclyn Camara, chairperson. Estab. 1984. Arts & crafts show held annually in May/June. Outdoors. Accepts photography, oils, leather, various handcrafts. Juried by type of product. Number of exhibitors: 140-150. Public attendance: 30,000. Free to the public. Deadline for entry: mid-April. Application fee/space fee: $225/craft, $275/commerical. Exhibition space: 12×12 ft. For more information, artists should call, send SASE. Event held at Center Circle Plaza in downtown Patterson.

TIPS "Please get your applications in early!"

PEND OREILLE ARTS COUNCIL

P.O. Box 1694, Sandpoint ID 83864. (208)263-6139; (208)255-1869. **E-mail:** art@sandpoint.net. **Website:** www.artinsandpoint.org. Estab. 1978. Arts & crafts show held annually, second week in August. Outdoors. Accepts photography and all handmade, non-commercial works. Juried by 8-member jury. Number of exhibitors: 120. Public attendance: 5,000. Free to public. Artists should apply by sending in application, available in February, along with 4 images (3 of your work, 1 of your booth space). Deadline for entry: April. Application fee: $15. Space fee: $185-280, no commission taken. Electricity: $50. Exhibition space: 10×10 ft. or 10×15 ft. (shared booths available). For more information, artists should e-mail, call or visit website. Show located in downtown Sandpoint.

PENTWATER FINE ARTS & CRAFT FAIR

Pentwater Jr. Women's Club, P.O. Box 357, Pentwater MI 49449. **E-mail:** pentwaterjuniorwomensclub@ yahoo.com. **Website:** www.pentwaterjuniorwomens club.com. "Always the 2nd Saturday in July, the fair is held on the beautiful Village Green located in downtown Pentwater MI, during the height of the summer resort season. The fair is held regardless of the weather, and space is limited for this juried show." Artists can apply via www.zapplication.org. See website for more information.

PETERS VALLEY FINE CRAFT FAIR

19 Kuhn Rd., Layton NJ 07851. (973)948-5200. **E-mail:** craftfair@petersvalley.org; info@petersvalley. org. **Website:** www.petersvalley.org. Estab. 1970. Fine craft show held annually in late September at the Sussex County Fairgrounds in Augusta NJ. Indoors/enclosed spaces. Accepts photography, ceramics, fiber, glass, basketry, metal, jewelry, sculpture, printmaking, paper, drawing, painting. Juried. Awards. Number of exhibitors: 150. Public attendance: 7,000-8,000. Public admission: $9. Artists should apply via www. zapplication.org. Deadline for entry: April 1. Application fee: $35. Space fee: $455 (includes electricity). Ex-

hibition space: 10×10 ft. Average gross sales/exhibitor: $2,000-5,000. For more information artists should e-mail, visit website, or call.

PIEDMONT CRAFTSMEN'S FAIR

(336)725-1516. **E-mail:** craftsfair@piedmontcrafts men.org. **Website:** www.piedmontcraftsmen.org/ programs/crafts-fair. **Contact:** Deborah Britton, fair coordinator. Estab. 1963. Annual showcase held 3rd weekend in November. Indoors. Open to public. Accepts clay, wood, glass, fibers, leather, metal, photography, printmaking, and mixed media. Number exhibitors: see website. Number attendees: see website. Admission: $7 adults; $6 students/seniors; children 12 & under free; weekend pass $11. Apply online. Deadline for entry: mid-April. Application fee: $35. Space fee: starts at $625. Exhibition space: see website. For more information, e-mail, visit website, or call.

PIEDMONT PARK ARTS FESTIVAL

1701 Piedmont Ave., Atlanta GA 30306. (404)873-1222. **E-mail:** lisa@affps.com. **Website:** www.pied montparkartsfestival.com. **Contact:** Lisa Windle, festival director. Estab. 2011. Arts & crafts show held annually in mid August. Outdoors. Accepts handmade crafts, painting, photography, sculpture, leather, metal, glass, jewelry. Juried by a panel. Awards/prizes: ribbons. Number of exhibitors: 250. Number of attendees: 60,000. Free to public. Apply online at www. zapplication.com. Deadline for entry: June 6. Application fee: $25. Space fee: $275. Exhibition space: 10×10. For more information artists should visit website.

PRAIRIE ARTS FESTIVAL

201 Schaumburg Court, Schaumburg IL 60193. (847)923-3605. **Fax:** (847)923-2458. **E-mail:** rben venuti@villageofschaumburg.com. **Website:** www. prairiecenter.org. **Contact:** Roxane Benvenuti, special events coordinator. Outdoor fine art & craft exhibition and sale featuring artists, food truck vendors, live entertainment and children's activities. Held over Saturday-Sunday of Memorial Day weekend. Located in the Robert O. Atcher Municipal Center grounds, adjacent to the Schaumburg Prairie Center for the Arts. Artist applications available in mid-January; due online or postmarked by March 6. 155 spaces available. Application fee: $110 (for 15×10 space); $220 (30×10 space). No jury fee. "With thousands of patrons in attendance, an ad in the Prairie Arts Festival program is a great way to get your business noticed. Rates are

reasonable, and an ad in the program gives you access to a select regional market. Sponsorship opportunities are also available." For more information, call, e-mail or visit the website.

TIPS "Submit your best work for the jury since these images are selling your work."

PUNGO STRAWBERRY FESTIVAL

P.O. Box 6158, Virginia Beach VA 23456. (757)721-6001. **Fax:** (757)721-9335. **E-mail:** pungofestival@aol.com. **Website:** www.pungostrawberryfestival.info. Estab. 1983. Arts & crafts show held annually on Memorial Day weekend. Outdoors. Accepts photography and all media. Number of exhibitors: 60. Public attendance: 120,000. Free to public; $5 parking fee. Artists should apply by calling for application or downloading a copy from the website and mail in. Deadline for entry: early March; applications accepted from that point until all spaces are full. Notice of acceptance or denial by early April. Application fee: $50 refundable deposit. Space fee: $200 (off road location); $500 (on road location). Exhibition space: 10×10 ft. For more information, artists should e-mail, visit website or call.

PYRAMID HILL ANNUAL ART FAIR

1763 Hamilton Cleves Rd., Hamilton OH 45013. (513)868-8336. **Fax:** (513)868-3585. **E-mail:** pyramid@pyramidhill.org. **Website:** www.pyramidhill.org. Art fair held the last Saturday and Sunday of September. Application fee: $25. Booth fee: $100 for a single, $200 for a double. Call, e-mail or visit website for more information. Fair located at Pyramid Hill Sculpture Park and Museum.

TIPS "Make items affordable! Quality work at affordable prices will produce profit."

◎ QUAKER ARTS FESTIVAL

P.O. Box 202, Orchard Park NY 14127. (716)667-2787. **E-mail:** opjaycees@aol.com; kelly@opjaycees.com. **Website:** www.opjaycees.com. Estab. 1961. Fine arts & crafts show held annually in mid-September (see website for details). 80% Outdoors, 20% indoors. Accepts photography, painting, graphics, sculpture, crafts. Juried by 4 panelists during event. Awards/prizes: over $10,000 total cash prizes, ribbons and trophies. Number of exhibitors: up to 300. Public attendance: 75,000. Free to the public. Artists can obtain applications online or by sending SASE. Deadline for entry: May 31 for returning exhibitors and then first come, first serve up to festival date (see website for de-

tails). Space fee: Before September 1: $185 (single) or $370 (double); after September 1: $210 (single) or $420 (double). Exhibition space: 10×12 ft. (outdoor), 10×6 ft. (indoor). For more information, artists should visit website or send e-mail.

TIPS "Have an inviting booth with a variety of work at various price levels."

RATTLESNAKE AND WILDLIFE FESTIVAL

P.O. Box 292, Claxton GA 30417. (912)739-3820. **E-mail:** rattlesnakewildlifefestival@yahoo.com; thall@claxtonevanschamber.com. **Website:** www.claxtonevanschamber.com; Facebook page: Rattlesnake & Wildlife Festival. Estab. 1968. Arts & crafts show held annually 2nd weekend in March. Outdoors. Accepts photography and various mediums. Number of exhibitors: 150-200. Public attendance: 15,000-20,000. Artists should apply by filling out an application. Click on the "Registration Tab" located on the Rattlesnake & Wildlife Festival home page. Deadline for entry: late February/early March (see website for details). Space fee: $100 (outdoor); $200 (indoor). Exhibition space: 10×16 (indoor); 10×10 (outdoor). For more information, artists should e-mail, visit website or call.

TIPS "Your display is a major factor in whether people will stop to browse when passing by. Offer a variety."

◎ RHINEBECK ARTS FESTIVAL

P.O. Box 28, Woodstock NY 12498. (845)331-7900. **Fax:** (845)331-7484. **E-mail:** crafts@artrider.com. **Website:** www.artrider.com. **Contact:** Stacey Jarit. Estab. 2013. Festival of fine contemporary craft and art held annually in late September or early October. 150 indoors and 40 outdoors. Accepts photography, fine art, ceramics, wood, mixed media, leather, glass, metal, fiber, jewelry, sculpture. Juried. Submit 5 images of your work and 1 of your booth. Public attendance: 10,000. Public admission: $10. Artists should apply online at www.artrider.com or www.zapplication.org. Deadline for entry: first Monday in January. Application fee: $45. For more information, artists should e-mail, visit website, or call. Application fees: $0 first time Artrider applicant, $40 mailed in or online, $65 late. Space fee: $495-545. Exhibition space: 10×10 and 10×20 ft. For more information, artists should e-mail, visit website, or call.

◎ RILEY FESTIVAL

312 E. Main St., Suite C, Greenfield IN 46140. (317)462-2141. **Fax:** (317)467-1449. **E-mail:** info@rileyfestival.com. **Website:** www.rileyfestival.com. **Contact:** Sarah

Kesterson, public relations. Estab. 1970. Fine arts & crafts festival held in October. Outdoors. Accepts photography, fine arts, home arts, quilts. Juried. Awards/prizes: small monetary awards and ribbons. Number of exhibitors: 450. Public attendance: 75,000. Free to public. Artists should apply by downloading application on website. Deadline for entry: mid-September. Space fee: $185. Exhibition space: 10×10 ft. For more information, artists should visit website.

TIPS "Keep arts priced for middle-class viewers."

RIVERBANK CHEESE & WINE EXPOSITION

6618 Third St., Riverbank CA 95367-2317. (209)863-9600. **Fax:** (209)863-9601. **E-mail:** events@riverbank cheeseandwine.org. **Website:** www.riverbankcheese andwine.org. **Contact:** Chris Elswick, event coordinator. Estab. 1977. Arts & crafts show and food show held annually 2nd weekend in October. Outdoors. Accepts photography, other mediums depends on the product. Juried by pictures and information about the artists. Number of exhibitors: 250. Public attendance: 60,000. Free to public. Artists should apply by calling and requesting an application. Applications also available on website. Deadline for entry: early September. Space fee: $300-500. Exhibition space: 12×12 ft. For more information, artists should e-mail, visit website, call or send SASE. Show located at Santa Fe & 3rd St., Riverbank CA.

TIPS Make sure your display is pleasing to the eye.

ROTARY KEY BISCAYNE ART FESTIVAL

270 Central Blvd, Suite 107B, Jupiter FL 33458. (561)746-6615. **Fax:** (561)746-6528. **E-mail:** info@ artfestival.com. **Website:** www.artfestival.com. Estab. 1963. "The annual Key Biscayne Art Fair benefits our partner and co producer, the Rotary Club of Key Biscayne. Held in Key Biscayne, an affluent island community in Miami-Dade County, just south of downtown Miami, the annual Key Biscayne Art Festival is one not to be missed! In fact, visitors plan their springtime vacations to South Florida around this terrific outdoor festival that brings together longtime favorites and the newest names in the contemporary art scene. Life-size sculptures, spectacular paintings, one-of-a-kind jewels, photography, ceramics, and much more make for one fabulous weekend." See website for more information.

ROYAL OAK CLAY GLASS AND METAL SHOW

Integrity Shows, P.O. Box 1070, Ann Arbor MI 48106. (207)725-5507. **E-mail:** info@integrityshows.com. **Website:** www.funkyferndaleartfair.com. **Contact:** Mark Loeb. Estab. 1994. Art show featuring works made of clay, glass or metal only held annually in June. Outdoors. Accepts clay, glass and metal only. We encourage demonstrations. Juried by 3 independent jurors. Awards/prizes: purchase and merit awards. Number of exhibitors: 120. Public attendance: 35,000. Free to the public. Apply online. Deadline for entry: see website. Application fee: $25. Booth fee: $295. Electricity limited; fee: $100. For more information, visit website.

ROYAL OAK OUTDOOR ART FAIR

211 Williams St., P.O. Box 64, Royal Oak MI 48068. (248)246-3180. **E-mail:** mail@royaloakartscouncil. com. **E-mail:** todg@ci.royal-oak.mi.us. **Website:** www.ci.royal-oak.mi.us. **Contact:** Recreation office staff. Estab. 1970. Fine arts & crafts show held annually in July. Outdoors. Accepts photography, collage, jewelry, clay, drawing, painting, glass, fiber, wood, metal, leather, soft sculpture. Juried. Number of exhibitors: 125. Public attendance: 25,000. Free to public. Free adjacent parking. Artists should apply with online application form at www.royaloakarts.com and 3 slides of current work. Space fee: $260 (plus a $30 nonrefundable processing fee per medium). Exhibition space: 15×15 ft. For more information, artists should e-mail, call, or visit website. Fair located at Memorial Park.

TIPS "Be sure to label your slides on the front with name, size of work and 'top.'"

SACO SIDEWALK ART FESTIVAL

P.O. Box 336, 12½ Pepperell Square, Suite 2A, Saco ME 04072. (207)286-3546. **E-mail:** sacospirit@hot mail.com. **Website:** www.sacospirit.com. Estab. 1970. Event held in late June. Annual event organized and managed by Saco Spirit, Inc., a nonprofit organization committed to making Saco a better place to live and work by enhancing the vitality of our downtown. Dedicated to promoting art and culture in our community. Space fee: $75. Exhibition space: 10×10 ft. See website for more details. Festival located in historic downtown Saco.

TIPS "Offer a variety of pieces priced at various levels."

SALT FORK ARTS & CRAFTS FESTIVAL

P.O. Box 250, Cambridge OH 43725. (740)439-9379. **E-mail:** director@saltforkfestival.org. **Website:** www. saltforkfestival.org. "The Salt Fork Arts & Crafts Festival (SFACF) is a juried festival that showcases high quality art in a variety of mediums, painting, pottery, ceramics, fiber art, metal work, jewelry, acrylics, mixed media, photography, and more. Between 90 and 100 artists come from all over the US, for this 3-day event. In addition, the festival heralds Heritage of the Arts. This program offers a look at Early American and Appalachian arts and crafts. Many of which are demonstrated by craftsmen practicing arts such as basket weaving, flint knapping, spindling, flute making, quilting, blacksmithing, and more. Area students are given the opportunity to display their work , visitors are entertained throughout the weekend by a variety of talented performing artists, concessionaires offer satisfying foods and there are crafts for kids and adults." See website for more information.

SALT LAKE'S FAMILY CHRISTMAS GIFT SHOW

South Towne Exposition Center, 9575 S. State St., Sandy UT 84070. (800)521-7469. **Fax:** (425)889-8165. **E-mail:** saltlake@showcaseevents.org. **Website:** www. showcaseevents.org. **Contact:** Kristine Vannoy, show manager. Estab. 1999. Seasonal holiday show held annually in November. Indoors. Accepts handmade crafts, art, photography, pottery, glass, jewelry, clothing, fiber. Juried. Exhibitors: 400. Number of attendees: 25,000. Admission: $11.50 (for all 3 days); 13 & under free. Apply via website or call or e-mail for application. Deadline for entry: October 31. Space fee: see website. Exhibition space: 10×10. For more information send e-mail, call, send SASE or visit website.

SAN FRANCISCO BAZAAR

1559B Sloat Blvd. #198, San Francisco CA 94132. (415)684-8447. **E-mail:** sf_info@sanfranciscobazaar. org. **Website:** www.sanfranciscobazaar.org. **Contact:** Jamie Chan, director. Estab. 2007. Handmade, independent DIY art & design festival held annually 5 times a year (see website for dates). Indoors & outdoors. Accepts handmade crafts, locally and domestically designed goods. Juried. Exhibitors: 150. Number of attendees: 10,000. Free to public. Apply online at www.sanfranciscobazaar.org/apply. Deadline for entry: varies (see website). Application fee: $0-$20 per show. Space fee: $90-$400. Exhibition space: 10×10 ft. For more information, artists should see website.

SANDY SPRINGS FESTIVAL

P.O. Box 422571, Atlanta GA 30342. (404)851-9111; (404)845-0793. **E-mail:** info@sandyspringsfestival. org; rmurphy@heritagesandysprings.org; patrick@ affps.com; randall@affps.com. **Website:** www.sandy springsfestival.com. Estab. 1985. Annual arts & crafts show held annually in mid-September. See website for details. Outdoors. Accepts photography, painting, sculpture, jewelry, furniture, clothing. Juried by artist committee. Awards/prizes: ribbons for Best in Show, 2nd Place, 3rd Place and Best Booth. Number of exhibitors: 135 maximum. Public attendance: 20,000. Public admission $5. Artists may apply via application on website or online at www.zapplication.org. Application fee: $25. Space fee: $250 for 10×10, $500 for 10×20. Average gross sales per exhibitor: $1,000. For more information, artists should e-mail or visit website.

TIPS "Many of the purchases made at Sandy Springs Festival are priced under $100. The look of the booth and its general attractiveness are very important, especially to those who might not know art."

SANTA CALI GON DAYS FESTIVAL

210 W. Truman Rd., Independence MO 64050. (816)252-4745. **E-mail:** lois@ichamber.biz. **Website:** www.santacaligon.com. Estab. 1973. Market vendors 4-day show held annually Labor Day weekend. Outdoors. Ranked in top 20 for vendor profitability. Accepts handmade arts & crafts, photography, and other mediums. Juried by committee. Number of exhibitors: 250. Public attendance: 300,000. Free to public. Artists should apply online. Application requirements include completed application, full booth fee, $20 jury fee (via seperate check), 4 photos of product/art and 1 photo of display. Exhibition space: 10×10 ft. For more information, artists should e-mail, visit website or call.

SANTA FE COLLEGE SPRING ARTS FESTIVAL

3000 NW 83rd St., Gainesville FL 32606. (352)395-5355. **Fax:** (352)336-2715. **E-mail:** kathryn.lehman@ sfcollege.edu. **Website:** www.springartsfestival.com. **Contact:** Kathryn Lehman, cultural programs coordinator. Fine arts and crafts festival held in mid-April (see website for details). "The festival is one of the 3 largest annual events in Gainesville and is known for its high-quality, unique artwork." Held in the downtown historic district. Public attendance: 130,000+. Call, e-mail or visit website for more information.

SARASOTA CRAFT FAIR

270 Central Blvd., Suite 107B, Jupiter FL 33458. (561)746-6615. **Fax:** (561)746-6528. **E-mail:** info@artfestival.com. **Website:** www.artfestival.com. **Contact:** Malinda Ratliff, communications manager. "Behold contemporary crafts from more than 100 of the nation's most talented artisans. A variety of jewelry, pottery, ceramics, photography, painting, clothing and much more—all handmade in America—will be on display, ranging from $15-3,000. An expansive Green Market with plants, orchids, exotic flora, handmade soaps, gourmet spices and freshly popped kettle corn further compliments the weekend, blending nature with nurture." See website for more information.

⊙ SAUSALITO ART FESTIVAL

P.O. Box 10, Sausalito CA 94966. (415)332-3555. **Fax:** (415)331-1340. **E-mail:** info@sausalitoartfestival.org. **Website:** www.sausalitoartfestival.org. Estab. 1952. Premiere fine art festival held annually Labor Day weekend. Outdoors. Accepts painting, photography, 2D and 3D mixed media, ceramics, drawing, fiber, functional art, glass, jewelry, printmaking, sculpture, watercolor, woodwork. Juried. Jurors are elected by their peers from the previous year's show (1 from each category). They meet for a weekend at the end of March and give scores of 1, 2, 4 or 5 to each applicant (5 being the highest). 5 images must be submitted, 4 of art and 1 of booth. Number of exhibitors: 280. Public attendance: 40,000. Artists should apply by visiting website for instructions and application. Applications are through Juried Art Services. Deadline for entry: March. Exhibition space: 100 or 200 sq. ft. Application fee: $50; $100 for late applications. Booth fees range from $1,425-3,125. Average gross sales/exhibitor: $7,700. For more information, artists should visit website. Festival located in Marinship Park.

⊕ SAWDUST ART FESTIVAL

935 Laguna Canyon Rd., Laguna Beach CA 92651. (949)494-3030. **E-mail:** info@sawdustartfestival.org. **Website:** www.sawdustartfestival.org. **Contact:** Tom Klingenmeier, general manager. Estab. 1967. Annual arts & crafts show held annually June-August (see website for dates; also has winter shows). Outdoors. Accepts handmade crafts, all art mediums. Awards/prizes: peer awards. Exhibitors: 210 (summer); 175

(winter). Number of attendees: 300,000 (summer); 20,000 (winter). Admission: $8.50, adults; $7, seniors; $4 children ages 6-12; children 5 & under free. Application release date varies (see website). Deadline for entry: varies (see website). Application fee: $30 per show. Space fee: $1,250+ (summer). Exhibition space: 10×8 ft. For more information, call, e-mail or see website.

⊙ SCOTTSDALE ARTS FESTIVAL

7380 E. Second St., Scottsdale AZ 85251. (480)874-2787; (480)994-2787. **Fax:** (480)874-4699. **Website:** www.scottsdaleartsfestival.org. Estab. 1970. Fine arts & crafts show held annually in March. Outdoors. Accepts photography, jewelry, ceramics, sculpture, metal, glass, drawings, fiber, paintings, printmaking, mixed media, wood. Juried. Awards/prizes: 1st, 2nd, 3rd places in each category and Best of Show. Number of exhibitors: 200. Public attendance: 40,000. Public admission: $10/single day; $15/2-day pass. Artists should apply through www.zapplication.org. Deadline for entry: October. Exhibition space: 100 sq. ft. For more information, artists should visit website.

⊕ ⊙ SCOTTSDALE CELEBRATION OF FINE ARTS

7900 E. Greenway Rd., Suite 101, Scottsdale AZ 85260-1714. (480)443-7695. **Fax:** (480)596-8179. **E-mail:** info@celebrateart.com. **Website:** www.celebrateart.com. "The Celebration of Fine Art™ is a juried show. We jury not only for quality but variety. This helps insure that direct competition is minimized and that you will have the best opportunity for success. All styles of art in all mediums are welcome. In addition to painting and sculpture we also have fine crafts such as furniture, jewelry, ceramics basketry and weaving. Only work created by the artist and handmade work is accepted. We do not allow manufactured goods of any kind. Artists who have previously been selected for the show will be juried in the 2 months following the current exhibit. Additional details, prices and other information are contained in the artist application packet." See website for more information.

⊕ ⊙ SHADYSIDE ART & CRAFT FESTIVAL

270 Central Blvd., Suite 107B, Jupiter FL 33458. (561)746-6615. **Fax:** (561)746-6528. **E-mail:** info@artfestival.com. **Website:** www.artfestival.com. **Contact:** Malinda Ratliff, communications manager. Estab. 1996. Fine art & craft fair held annually in

late May. Outdoors. Accepts photography, jewelry, mixed media, sculpture, wood, ceramic, glass, painting, digital, fiber, metal. Juried. Number exhibitors: 125. Number attendees: 60,000. Free to public. Apply online via www.zapplication.org. Deadline: see website. Application fee: $25. Space fee: $395. Exhibition space: 10×10 and 10×20. For more information, artists should e-mail, call, or visit website.

○ Festival located at Walnut St. in Shadyside (Pittsburgh PA).

SIDEWALK ART MART

Downtown Helena, Inc., Mount Helena Music Festival, 225 Cruse Ave., Suite B, Helena MT 59601. (406)447-1535. **Fax:** (406)447-1533. **E-mail:** jmchugh@mt.net. **Website:** www.downtownhelena.com. **Contact:** Jim McHugh. Estab. 1974. Arts, crafts and music festival held annually in June. Outdoors. Accepts photography. No restrictions except to display appropriate work for all ages. Number of exhibitors: 50+. Public attendance: 5,000. Free to public. Artists should apply by visiting website to download application. Space fee: $100-125. Exhibition space: 10×10 ft. For more information, artists should e-mail, visit website or call. Festival held at Women's Park in Helena MT.

TIPS "Greet people walking by and have an eye-catching product in front of booth. We have found that high-end artists or expensively priced art booths that had business cards with e-mail or website information received many contacts after the festival."

◎ SIERRA MADRE WISTARIA FESTIVAL

19 Suffolk Ave., Unit A, Sierra Madre CA 91024. (626)355-5111; (626)233-5524. **Fax:** (626)306-1150. **E-mail:** smadrecc@gmail.com. **Website:** www.sierramadrechamber.com/wistaria/photos.htm. Fine arts, crafts and garden show held annually in March. Outdoors. Accepts photography, anything handcrafted. Juried. Craft vendors send in application and photos to be juried. Most appropriate are selected. Awards/prizes: Number of exhibitors: 175. Public attendance: 12,000. Free to public. Artists should apply by sending completed and signed application, 3-5 photographs of their work, application fee, license application, space fee and 2 SASEs. Deadline for entry: late December. Application fee: $25. Public Safety Fee (nonrefundable) $25. Space fee: $185. Exhibition space: 10×10 ft. For more information, artists should e-mail, visit

website or call. Applications can be found on chamber website.

TIPS "Have a clear and simple application. Be nice."

⊕ ◎ SIESTA FIESTA

270 Central Blvd., Suite 107B, Jupiter FL 33458. (561)746-6615. **Fax:** (561)746-6528. **E-mail:** info@artfestival.com. **Website:** www.artfestival.com. **Contact:** Malinda Ratliff, communications manager. Estab. 1978. Fine art & craft fair held annually in April. Outdoors. Accepts photography, jewelry, mixed media, sculpture, wood, ceramic, glass, painting, digital, fiber, metal. Juried. Number exhibitors: 85. Number attendees: 40,000. Free to public. Apply online via www.zapplication.org. Deadline: see website. Application fee: $25. Space fee: $350. Exhibition space: 10×10 and 10×20. For more information, artists should e-mail, call, or visit website.

○ Festival located at Ocean Blvd. in Siesta Key Village.

SKOKIE ART GUILD FINE ART EXPO

Devonshire Cultural Center, 4400 Greenwood St., Skokie IL 60077. (847)677-8163. **E-mail:** info@skokieartguild.org; skokieart@aol.com. **Website:** www.skokieartguild.org. Outdoor fine art/craft show open to all artists (18+) in the Chicagoland area. Held in mid-May. Entrance fee: $20 (members), $30 (nonmembers). Awards: 1st, 2nd, 3rd place ribbons, Purchase Awards. Deadline for application: early May. Event held at Oakton Park.

TIPS Display your work in a professional manner: matted, framed, etc.

◎ SMITHVILLE FIDDLERS' JAMBOREE AND CRAFT FESTIVAL

P.O. Box 83, Smithville TN 37166. (615)597-8500. **E-mail:** eadkins@smithvillejamboree.com. **Website:** www.smithvillejamboree.com. **Contact:** Emma Adkins, craft coordinator. Estab. 1971. Arts & crafts show held annually the weekend nearest the Fourth of July holiday. Indoors. Juried by photos and personally talking with crafters. Awards/prizes: ribbons and free booth for following year for Best of Show, Best of Appalachian Craft, Best Display, Best New Comer. Number of exhibitors: 235. Public attendance: 130,000. Free to public. Artists should apply online. Deadline: May 1. Space fee: $125. Exhibition space: 12×12 ft. Average gross sales/exhibitors: $1,200+. For more information, artists should call or visit website. Festival held in downton Smithville.

⊕ Ⓖ SMOKY HILL RIVER FESTIVAL FINE ART SHOW

(785)309-5770. **E-mail:** sahc@salina.org. **Website:** www.riverfestival.com. Fine art & craft show held annually in June. Outdoors. Accepts handmade crafts ceramics, jewelry, fiber, mixed media, painting, drawing/pastels, glass, metal, wood, graphics/printmaking, digital, paper, sculpture, and photography. Juried. Awards/prizes: Jurors' Merit Awards, Purchase Awards. Number exhibitors: 90. Number attendees: 60,000. Admission: $10 in advance; $15 at gate; children 11 & under free. Apply via www.zapplication.org. Deadline for entry: February. Application fee: $30. Space fee: $275. Exhibition space: 10×10. For more information, artists should e-mail or visit website.

Ⓖ SOLANO AVENUE STROLL

1563 Solano Ave., #101, Berkeley CA 94707. (510)527-5358. **E-mail:** info@solanostroll.org. **Website:** www.solanostroll.org. **Contact:** Allen Cain. Estab. 1974. Fine arts & crafts show held annually 2nd Sunday in September. Outdoors. "Since 1974, the merchants, restaurants, and professionals, as well as the twin cities of Albany and Berkeley have hosted the Solano Avenue Stroll, the East Bay's largest street festival." Accepts photography and all other mediums. Juried by board of directors. Number of exhibitors: 150 spaces for crafts; 600 spaces total. Public attendance: 250,000. Free to the public. Artists should apply online in April, or send SASE. Space fee: $150. Exhibition space: 10×10 ft. For more information, artists should e-mail, visit website, or send SASE. Event takes place on Solano Ave. in Berkeley and Albany CA.

TIPS "Artists should have a clean presentation; small-ticket items as well as large-ticket items; great customer service; enjoy themselves."

⊕ SOUTH JERSEY PUMPKIN SHOW

P.O. Box 925, Millville NJ 08332. (856)765-0118. **Fax:** (856)765-9050. **E-mail:** sjpumpkinshow@aol.com. **Website:** www.sjpumpkinshow.com. **Contact:** Kathy Wright, organizer. Estab. 2003. Arts & crafts show held annually 2nd weekend in October. Indoors & outdoors. Accepts fine art & handmade crafts, wood, metal, pottery, glass, quilts. Awards/prizes: $100 for Fall Booth. Exhibitors: 175. Number of attendees: 10,500. Admission: $5/car (good all 3 days). Artists should apply via website. Deadline for entry: late September. Application fee: none. Space fee: $40

(one day); $100 (weekend). Exhibition space: 10×10. For more information, artists should e-mail, visit website or call.

THE SOUTHWEST ARTS FESTIVAL

Indio Chamber of Commerce, 82921 Indio Blvd., Indio CA 92201. (760)347-0676. **Fax:** (763)347-6069. **E-mail:** jonathan@indiochamber.org;swaf@indiochamber.org. **Website:** www.southwestartsfest.com. Estab. 1986. Featuring over 275 acclaimed artists showing traditional, contemporary and abstract fine works of art and quality crafts, the festival is a major, internationally recognized cultural event attended by nearly 10,000 people. The event features a wide selection of clay, crafts, drawings, glass work, jewelry, metal works, paintings, photographs, printmaking, sculpture and textiles. Application fee: $55. Easy check-in and check-out procedures with safe and secure access to festival grounds for setup and breakdown. Allow advance set-up for artists with special requirements (very large art requiring the use of cranes, forklifts, etc., or artists with special needs). Artist parking is free. Disabled artist parking is available. Apply online. For more information, artists should call, e-mail, or visit website. Show takes place in January.

⊕ Ⓖ SPANISH SPRINGS ART & CRAFT FESTIVAL

270 Central Blvd., Suite 107B, Jupiter FL 33458. (561)746-6615. **Fax:** (561)746-6528. **E-mail:** info@artfestival.com. **Website:** www.artfestival.com. **Contact:** Malinda Ratliff, communications manager. Estab. 1997. Fine art & craft fair held annually in January & November. Outdoors. Accepts photography, jewelry, mixed media, sculpture, wood, ceramic, glass, painting, digital, fiber, metal. Juried. Number exhibitors: 210. Number attendees: 20,000. Free to public. Apply online via www.zapplication.org or visit website for paper application. Deadline: see website. Application fee: $15. Space fee: $265. Exhibition space: 10×10 and 10×20. For more information, artists should e-mail, call or visit website. Festival located at Spanish Springs, The Villages, FL.

⊕ SPANKER CREEK FARM ARTS & CRAFTS FAIR

P.O. Box 5644, Bella Vista AR 72714. (479)685-5655. **E-mail:** info@spankercreekfarm.com. **Website:** www.spankercreekfarm.com. Arts & craft show held annually in the spring & fall. Outdoors & indoors. Accepts handmade crafts, ceramics, paintings, jewelry, glass, photography, wearable art and other mediums. Juried. Number exhibitors: see website. Number attendees: varies. Free to public. Apply online. Deadline for entry: see website for dates. Application fee: none. Space fee: varies. Exhibition space: varies. For more information, artists should call, e-mail or visit website.

SPRING CRAFTMORRISTOWN

P.O. Box 28, Woodstock NY 12498. (845)331-7900. **Fax:** (845)331-7484. **E-mail:** crafts@artrider.com. **Website:** www.artrider.com. Estab. 1990. Fine arts & crafts show held annually in March. Indoors. Accepts photography, wearable and nonwearable fiber, jewelry, clay, leather, wood, glass, painting, drawing, prints, mixed media. Juried by 5 images of work and 1 of booth, viewed sequentially. Number of exhibitors: 150. Public attendance: 5,000. Public admission: $9. Artists should apply online at www.artrider.com or at www.zapplication.org. Deadline for entry: January 1. Application fee: $45. Space fee: $495. Exhibition space: 10×10 ft. For more information, artists should e-mail, visit website, or call.

SPRING CRAFTS AT LYNDHURST

P.O. Box 28, Woodstock NY 12498. (845)331-7900. **Fax:** (845)331-7484. **E-mail:** crafts@artrider.com. **Website:** www.artrider.com. Estab. 1984. Fine arts & crafts show held annually in early May. Outdoors. Accepts photography, wearable and nonwearable fiber, jewelry, clay, leather, wood, glass, painting, drawing, prints, mixed media. Juried by 5 images of work and 1 of booth, viewed sequentially. Number of exhibitors: 275. Public attendance: 14,000. Public admission: $10. Artists should apply at www.artrider.com or can apply online at www.zapplication.org. Deadline for entry: January 1. Application fee: $45. Space fee: $775-875. Exhibition space: 10×10 ft. For more information, artists should e-mail, visit website, or call.

SPRINGFEST

Southern Pines Business Association, P.O. Box 831, Southern Pines NC 28388. (910)315-6508. **E-mail:** spbainfo@southernpines.biz. **Website:** www.southernpines.biz. **Contact:** Susan Harris. Estab. 1979. Arts & crafts show held annually last Saturday in April. Outdoors. Accepts photography and crafts. We host over 160 vendors from all around North Carolina and the country. Enjoy beautiful artwork and crafts including paintings, jewelry, metal art, photography, woodwork, designs from nature and other amazing creations. Event is held in conjunction with Tour de Moore, an annual bicycle race in Moore County, and is co-sponsored by the town of Southern Pines. Public attendance: 8,000. Free to the public. Deadline: March (see website for more details). Space fee: $75. Exhibition space: 10×12 ft. For more information, artists should e-mail, visit website, call, send SASE. Apply online. Event held in historic downtown Southern Pines on Broad St.

SPRING FESTIVAL, AN ARTS & CRAFTS AFFAIR

P.O. Box 655, Antioch IL 60002. (402)331-2889. **E-mail:** hpifestivals@cox.net. **Website:** www.hpifestivals.com. Annual tour takes place in Omaha (March & April), Minneapolis (March & April) and Chicago (April). Application available online. Artists should e-mail or see website for specifics on each location and exhibitor information.

SPRING FESTIVAL ON PONCE

Olmstead Park, North Druid Hills, 1451 Ponce de Leon, Atlanta GA 30307. (404)873-1222. **E-mail:** Lisa@affps.com. **Website:** festivalonponce.com. **Contact:** Lisa Windle, festival director. Estab. 2011. Arts & crafts show held annually early April. Outdoors. Accepts handmade crafts, painting, photography, sculpture, leather, metal, glass, jewelry. Juried by a panel. Awards/prizes: ribbons. Number of exhibitors: 125. Number of attendees: 40,000. Free to public. Apply online at www.zapplication.org. Deadline for entry: February 7. Application fee: $25. Space fee: $250. Exhibition space: 10×10. For more information, see website.

SPRING FINE ART & CRAFTS AT BROOKDALE PARK

473 Watchung Ave., Bloomfield NJ 07003. (908)874-5247. **Fax:** (908)874-7098. **E-mail:** info@rosesquared.com. **Website:** www.rosesquared.com. Estab. 1988. Fine arts & craft show held annually at Brookdale Park on the border of Bloomfield and Montclair NJ. Event takes place in mid-June on Father's Day weekend. Outdoors. Accepts photography and all other mediums. Juried. Number of exhibitors: 180. Public attendance: 16,000. Free to the public. Artists should apply by downloading application from website or call for application. Deadline: 1 month before show date. Application fee: $25. Space fee: varies by booth size. Exhibition space: 120 sq. ft. For more information, artists should e-mail, visit website, or call.

TIPS "Create a professional booth that is comfortable for the customer to enter. Be informative, friendly and outgoing. People come to meet the artist."

● ◎ SPRING GREEN ARTS & CRAFTS FAIR

P.O. Box 96, Spring Green WI 53588. **E-mail:** spring greenartfair@gmail.com. **Website:** www.spring greenartfair.com. Fine arts & crafts fair held annually June. Indoors. Accepts handmade crafts, glass, wood, painting, fiber, graphics, pottery, sculpture, jewelry, photography. Juried. Awards/prizes: Best of Show, Award of Excellence. Number exhibitors: see website. Number of attendees: varies per show. Admission: varies per show. Apply online. Deadline for entry: mid February. Application fee: $10-$20. Space fee: $150. Exhibition space: 10×10. For more information, artists should send e-mail or visit website.

● ◎ ST. ARMANDS CIRCLE CRAFT FESTIVAL

270 Central Blvd., Suite 107B, Jupiter FL 33458. (561)746-6615. **Fax:** (561)746-6528. **E-mail:** info@art festival.com. **Website:** www.artfestival.com. **Contact:** Malinda Ratliff, communications manager. Estab. 2004. Fine art & craft fair held annually in January & November. Outdoors. Accepts photography, jewelry, mixed media, sculpture, wood, ceramic, glass, painting, digital, fiber, metal. Juried. Number exhibitors: 180-210. Number attendees: 80,000-100,000. Free to public. Apply online via www.zapplication.org. Deadline: see website. Application fee: $25. Space fee: $415-435. Exhibition space: 10×10 and 10×20. For more information, artists should e-mail, call, or visit website. Fair held in St. Armands Circle in Sarasota FL.

◎ ST. CHARLES FINE ART SHOW

2 E. Main St., St. Charles IL 60174. (630)443-3967. **E-mail:** info@downtownstcharles.org. **Website:** www. downtownstcharles.org/fineartshow. **Contact:** Jamie Blair. Fine art show held annually in May during Memorial Day weekend. Outdoors. Accepts photography, painting, sculpture, glass, ceramics, jewelry, nonwearable fiber art. Juried by committee: submit 4 slides of art and 1 slide of booth/display. Awards/prizes: Cash awards in several categories. Free to the public. Artists can apply via website. Deadline for entry: early January. Jury fee: $35. Space fee: $375. Exhibition space: 10×10 ft. For more information, artists should e-mail or visit website.

◎ ST. GEORGE ART FESTIVAL

50 S. Main, St. George UT 84770. (435)627-4500. **E-mail:** artadmn@sgcity.org; gary.sanders@sgcity.org; leisure@sgcity.org. **Website:** www.sgcity.org/artfes tival. **Contact:** Gary Sanders. Estab. 1979. Fine arts & crafts show held annually Easter weekend in either March or April. Outdoors. Accepts photography, painting, wood, jewelry, ceramics, sculpture, drawing, 3D mixed media, glass, metal, digital. Juried from digital submissions. Awards/prizes: $5,000 Purchase Awards. Art pieces selected will be placed in the city's permanent collections. Number of exhibitors: 110. Public attendance: 20,000/day. Free to public. Artists should apply by completing application form via EntryThingy, nonrefundable application fee, slides or digital format of 4 current works in each category and 1 of booth, and SASE. Deadline for entry: January 9. Exhibition space: 10×11 ft. For more information, artists should check website or e-mail.

TIPS "Artists should have more than 50% originals. Have quality booths and set-up to display art in best possible manner. Be outgoing and friendly with buyers."

◎ ST. JAMES COURT ART SHOW

P.O. Box 3804, Louisville KY 40201. (502)635-1842. **Fax:** (502)635-1296. **E-mail:** mesrock@stjamescourt artshow.com. **Website:** www.sjcas.com. Estab. 1957. Annual fine arts & crafts show held the first full weekend in October. Accepts photography; has 17 medium categories. Juried in April; there is also a street jury held during the art show. Number of exhibitors: 270. Public attendance: 200,000. Free to the public. Artists should apply by visiting website and printing out an application or via www.zapplication.org. Deadline for entry: March 31 (see website for details). Application fee: $30. Space fee: $550. Exhibition space: 10×12 ft. For more information, artists should visit website. TIPS "Have a variety of price points."

● ◎ ST. JOHN MEDICAL CENTER FESTIVAL OF THE ARTS

(440)808-9201. **E-mail:** ardis.radak@csauh.com. **Website:** www.www.sjws.net/festival_of_arts.aspx. **Contact:** Ardis Radak. Art & craft show held annually in July. Outdoors. Accepts handmade crafts, ceramics, glass, fiber, glass, graphics, jewelry, leather, metal, mixed media, painting, photography, printmaking, sculpture, woodworking. Juried. Awards/prizes: Best of Show, 1st Place, 2nd Place, Honorable Mention.

Number exhibitors: 200. Number attendees: 15,000. Free to public. Apply via www.zapplication.org. Deadline for entry: May. Application fee: $15. Space fee: $300 (single); $600 (double). Exhibition space: 10×10 (single); 10×20 (double). For more information, artists should e-mail, call or visit website.

ST. LOUIS ART FAIR

225 S. Meramec Ave., Suite 105, St. Louis MO 63105. **E-mail:** info@culturalfestivals.com. **Website:** www.culturalfestivals.com. **Contact:** Laura Miller, director of operations. Estab. 1994. Fine art/craft show held annually in September, the weekend after Labor Day. Outdoors. Accepts photography, ceramics, drawings, digital, glass, fiber, jewelry, mixed-media, metalwork, printmaking, paintings, sculpture and wood. Juried event, uses 5 jurors using 3 rounds, digital app. Total prize money available: $21,000—26 awards ranging from $500-1,000. Number of exhibitors: 180. Average attendance: 130,000. Admission free to the public. 2014 Deadline for applications: March 22. $40 application fee. Space fee: $625-725. 100 sq. ft. space. Average gross sales for exhibitor: $8.500. Apply at www.zapplication.org. For more information, call, e-mail or visit website. Fair held in the central business district of Clayton MO.

TIPS "Look at shows and get a feel for what it is."

ST. PATRICK'S DAY CRAFT SALE & FALL CRAFT SALE

P.O. Box 461, Maple Lake MN 55358-0461. **Website:** www.maplelakechamber.com. **Contact:** Kathy. Estab. 1988. Arts & crafts show held biannually in March and early November. Indoors. Number of exhibitors: 30-40. Public attendance: 300-600. Free to public. Deadline for entry: 2 weeks before the event. Exhibition space: 10×10 ft. For more information or an application, artists should visit website.

TIPS "Don't charge an arm and a leg for the items. Don't overcrowd your items. Be helpful, but not pushy."

STEPPIN' OUT

Downtown Blacksburg, Inc., P.O. Box 233, Blacksburg VA 24063. (540)951-0454. **E-mail:** dbi@downtownblacksburg.com; events@downtownblacksburg.com. **Website:** www.blacksburgsteppinout.com. Estab. 1981. Arts & crafts show held annually 1st Friday and Saturday in August. Outdoors. Accepts photography, pottery, painting, drawing, fiber arts, jewelry, general crafts. All arts and crafts must be handmade.

Number of exhibitors: 170. Public attendance: 45,000. Free to public. Space fee: $175. An additional $10 is required for electricity. Exhibition space: 10×16 ft. Artists should apply by e-mailing, calling or downloading an application on website. Deadline for entry: early May.

TIPS "Visit shows and consider the booth aesthetic—what appeals to you. Put the time, thought, energy and money into your booth to draw people in to see your work."

STILLWATER ARTS FESTIVAL

P.O. Box 1449, Stillwater OK 74076. (405)747-8070. **E-mail:** stillwaterartsfestival@stillwater.org; rjanway@stillwater.org. **Website:** www.stillwater.org/stillwater_arts_festival/index.php. **Contact:** Rachel Janway. Estab. 1977. Fine art show held annually in April. Outdoors. Accepts photography, oil, acrylic, watercolor and multi media paintings, pottery, pastel work, fiber arts, jewelry, sculpture, glass art, wood and other. Juried. Awards are based on entry acceptance on quality, distribution and various media entries. Awards/prizes: Best of Show, $500; 1st Place, $200; 2nd Place, $150; 3rd Place, $100. Number of exhibitors: 80. Public attendance: 7,500-10,000. Free to public. Artists should apply via www.zapplication.org. Deadline for entry: early spring (visit website for details). Jury fee: $20. Booth fee $140; $240 for 2 booths. Exhibition space: 10×10 ft. For more information, artists should e-mail or call. Festival held at 8th & Husband Streets.

STOCKLEY GARDENS FALL ARTS FESTIVAL

801 Boush St., Suite 302, Norfolk VA 23510. (757)625-6161. **Fax:** (757)625-7775. **E-mail:** aknox@hopehouse.org. **Website:** www.stockleygardens.com. **Contact:** Anne Knox, development coordinator. Estab. 1984. Fine arts & crafts show held biannually in the 3rd weekends in May and October. Outdoors. Accepts photography and all major fine art mediums. Juried. Number of exhibitors: 135. Public attendance: 25,000. Free to the public. Artists should apply by submitting application, jury and booth fees, 5 slides. Deadline for entry: February and July. Exhibition space: 10×10 ft. For more information, artists should visit the website.

STONE ARCH BRIDGE FESTIVAL

(651)398-0590. **E-mail:** stacy@weimarketing.com; heatherwmpls@gmail.com. **Website:** www.stonearchbridgefestival.com. **Contact:** Sara Collins, manager. Estab. 1994. Fine arts & crafts and culinary arts show held annually on Father's Day weekend in the Riverfront District of Minneapolis. Outdoors. Accepts drawing/pastels, printmaking, ceramics, jewelry (metals/stone), mixed media, painting, photography, sculpture metal works, bead work (jewelry or sculpture), glass, fine craft, special consideration. Juried by committee. Awards/prizes: free booth the following year; $100 cash prize. Number of exhibitors: 250+. Public attendance: 80,000. Free to public. Artists should apply by application found on website or through www.zapplication.org. Application fee: $25. Deadline for entry: early April. Space fee: depends on booth location (see website for details). Exhibition space: 10×10 ft. For more information, artists should call (651)228-1664 or e-mail Stacy De Young at stacy@weimarketing.com.

TIPS "Have an attractive display and variety of prices."

✚ ⓠ STONE MOUNTAIN OKTOBERFEST & ARTIST MARKET

6655 James B Rivers Dr., Stone Mountain GA 30083. (404)873-1222. **E-mail:** lisa@affps.com. **Website:** www.stonemountainvillage.com/oktoberfest0809. html. **Contact:** Lisa Windle, festival director. Estab. 2011. Arts & crafts show held annually mid October. Outdoors. Accepts handmade crafts, painting, photography, sculpture, leather, metal, glass, jewelry. Juried by a panel. Awards/prizes: ribbons. Number of exhibitors: 150. Number of attendees: 7,500. Free to public. Apply online at www.zapplication.com. Deadline for entry: August 22. Application fee: $25. Space fee: $150. Exhibition space: 10×10. For more information, see website.

ⓠ STRAWBERRY FESTIVAL

2815 Second Ave. N., Billings MT 59101. (406)294-5060. **Fax:** (406)294-5061. **E-mail:** info@strawberryfun.com; natashap@downtownbillings.com. **Website:** www.downtownbillings.com. **Contact:** Natasha. Estab. 1991. Fine arts & crafts show held annually 2nd Saturday in June. Outdoors. Accepts photography and only finely crafted work. Handcrafted works by the selling artist will be given priority. Requires photographs of booth set up and 2-3 of work. Juried. Public attendance: 15,000. Free to public. Artists should apply online. Deadline for entry: April. Space fee: $155. Exhibition space: 10×10 ft. For more information, artists should e-mail or visit website. Show located at N. Broadway & 2nd Ave. N in downtown Billings.

ⓠ SUMMER ART IN THE PARK FESTIVAL

16 S. Main St., Rutland VT 05701. (802)775-0356. **E-mail:** info@chaffeeartcenter.org. **Website:** www.chaffeeartcenter.org. Estab. 1961. A fine arts & crafts show held at Main Street Park in Rutland VT annually in mid-August. Accepts fine art, specialty foods, fiber, jewelry, glass, metal, wood, photography, clay, floral, etc. All applications will be juried by a panel of experts. The Art in the Park Festivals are dedicated to high-quality art and craft products. Number of exhibitors: 100. Public attendance: 9,000-10,000. Public admission: voluntary donation. Artists should apply online and either e-mail or submit a CD with 3 photos of work and 1 of booth (photos upon preapproval). Deadline for entry: early bird discount of $25 per show for applications received by March 31. Space fee: $200-350. Exhibit space: 10×12 or 20×12 ft. For more information, artists should e-mail, visit website, or call. Festival held in Main Street Park.

TIPS "Have a good presentation, variety if possible (in price ranges, too) to appeal to a large group of people. Apply early as there may be a limited amount of accepted vendors per category. Applications will be juried on a first come, first served basis until the category is determined to be filled."

ⓠ SUMMER ARTS & CRAFTS FESTIVAL

38 Charles St., Rochester NH 03867. **E-mail:** info@castleberryfairs.com. **Website:** www.castleberryfairs.com. Estab. 1992. Arts & crafts show held annually 2nd weekend in August in Lincoln NH. Outdoors. Accepts photography and all other mediums. Juried by photo, slide or sample. Number of exhibitors: 100. Public attendance: 7,500. Free to the public. Artists should apply by downloading application from website. Application fee: $50. Space fee: $225. Exhibition space: 10×10 ft. For more information, artists should visit website. Festival held at Village Shops & Town Green, Main Street.

TIPS "Do not bring a book; do not bring a chair. Smile and make eye contact with everyone who enters your booth. Have them sign your guest book; get their e-mail address so you can let them know when you are in the area again. And, finally, make the sale—they are at the fair to shop, after all."

ⓠ SUMMERFAIR

7850 Five Mile Rd., Cincinnati OH 45230. (513)531-0050. **Fax:** (513)531-0377. **E-mail:** exhibitors@summerfair.org. **Website:** www.summerfair.org. Estab.

1968. Fine arts & crafts show held annually the weekend after Memorial Day. Outdoors. Accepts photography, ceramics, drawing, printmaking, fiber, leather, glass, jewelry, painting, sculpture, metal, wood and mixed media. Juried by a panel of judges selected by Summerfair, including artists and art educators with expertise in the categories offered at Summerfair. Submit application with 5 digital images (no booth image) through www.zapplication.org. Awards/prizes: $11,000 in cash awards. Number of exhibitors: 300. Public attendance: 20,000. Public admission: $10. Deadline: February. Application fee: $30. Space fee: $375, single; $750, double space; $75 canopy fee (optional—exhibitors can rent a canopy for all days of the fair). Exhibition space: 10×10 ft. for single space; 10×20 ft. for double space. For more information, artists should e-mail, visit website, call. Fair held at Cincinnati's historic Coney Island.

✚ ◯ SUMMIT ART FESTIVAL

Website: www.summitartfest.org. Fine arts & crafts fair held annually October. Outdoors. Accepts handmade crafts, jewelry, ceramics, painting, glass, photography, fiber and more. Juried. Awards/prizes: Best of Show, 2nd place, 3rd place, Mayor's Award, Juror's Merit Award. Number exhibitors: see website. Number attendees: varies. Free to public. Apply online. Deadline for entry: July. Application fee: $25. Space fee: $255. Exhibition space: 10×10. For more information, artists should visit website.

◯ SUN FEST, INC.

P.O. Box 2404, Bartlesville OK 74005. (918)331-0456. **Fax:** (918)331-3217. **E-mail:** sunfestbville@gmail.com. **Website:** www.bartlesvillesunfest.org. Estab. 1982. Fine arts & crafts show held annually in early June. Outdoors. Accepts photography, painting and other arts and crafts. Juried. Awards: $2,000 in cash awards along with a ribbon/award to be displayed. Number of exhibitors: 95-100. Number of attendees: 25,000-30,000. Free to the public. Artists should apply by e-mailing or calling for an entry form, or completing online, along with 3-5 photos showing your work and booth display. Deadline: April. Space fee: $125. An extra $20 is charged for use of electricity. Exhibition space: 10×10 ft. For more information, artists should e-mail, call or visit website.

◯ SURPRISE FINE ART & WINE FESTIVAL

15648 N. Eagles Nest Dr., Fountain Hills AZ 85268. (480)837-5637. **Fax:** (480)837-2355. **E-mail:** info@thunderbirdartists.com. **Website:** www.thunderbirdartists.com. **Contact:** Denise Colter, president. Estab. 2013. Fine arts & crafts show held annually in the winter. Outdoors. Accepts photography, paintings, bronzes, baskets, jewelry, stone, pottery. Juried; CEO blind juries by medium. Number of exhibitors: 100. Public attendance: 10,000. Public admission: $3. Apply online at www.zapplication.org. Deadline for entry: mid-June (see website for specifics). Application fee: $30. Space fee: $430-1,240. Exhibition space: 10×10 to 10×30 ft. For more information, artists should e-mail, call, or see website.

TIPS "A clean, gallery-type presentation is very important."

◯ SYRACUSE ARTS & CRAFTS FESTIVAL

115 W. Fayette St., Syracuse NY 13202. (315)422-8284. **Fax:** (315)471-4503. **E-mail:** lreed@downtownsyracuse.com. **Website:** www.syracuseartsandcraftsfestival.com. **Contact:** Laurie Reed, director. Estab. 1970. Fine arts & crafts show held annually in late July. Outdoors. Accepts photography, ceramics, fabric/fiber, glass, jewelry, leather, metal, wood, computer art, drawing, printmaking, painting. Juried by 4 independent jurors. Jurors review 4 digital images of work and 1 digital image of booth display. Number of exhibitors: 165. Public attendance: 50,000. Free to public. Artists should apply online through www.zapplication.org. Application fee: $25. Space fee: $280. Exhibition space: 10×10 ft. For more information, artists should e-mail, visit website, or call.

✚ ◯ TALUCA LAKE FINE ARTS FESTIVAL

West Coast Artists, P.O. Box 750, Acton CA 93510. (818)813-4478. **Fax:** (661)526-4575. **E-mail:** info@westcoastartists.com. **Website:** www.westcoastartists.com. "Open to all media of original fine art and fine crafts. All work will be juried. Categories will be limited. No commercial, manufactured, imported, mass produced or purchased for resale items will be accepted. No clothing. No representatives." See website for more information.

✚ ◯ TAOS FALL ARTS FESTIVAL

P.O. Box 675, Taos NM 87571. (575)758-4648. **E-mail:** tfafvolunteer@gmail.com. **Website:** www.taosfallarts.

com. **Contact:** Patsy S. Wright. Estab. 1974. "This festival is the oldest art festival in Taos, premiering in 1974 and only showcasing artist that reside in Taos County. It includes three major art shows: the curated exhibit titled 'Distinguished Achievement Award Series', a juried exhibit titled Taos Select, and the Taos Open, as its name implies, an exhibit open to all artists working in Taos County. The festival represents over 250 Taos County artists working in a variety of mediums. Each year a limited edition poster is printed to commemorate the arts festival. The proceeds from the shows will benefit art programs for Taos County children." See website for more information.

TARPON SPRINGS FINE ARTS FESTIVAL

111 E. Tarpon Ave., Tarpon Springs FL 34689. (727)937-6109. **Fax:** (727)937-2879. **E-mail:** scottie@ tarponspringschamber.org. **Website:** www.tarpon springschamber.com. Estab. 1974. Fine arts & crafts show held annually in late March. Outdoors. Accepts photography, acrylic, oil, ceramics, digital, fiber, glass, graphics, drawings, pastels, jewelry, leather, metal, mixed media, sculpture, watercolor, wood. Juried by CD or images e-mailed. Awards/prizes: cash, ribbons and Patron Awards. Number of exhibitors: 200. Public attendance: 20,000. Public admission: $5 (includes free drink ticket: wine, beer, soda or water); free-age 12 and under and active duty military. Artists should apply by submitting signed application, CD or e-mailed images, fees and SASE. Deadline for entry: late December. Jury fee: $30. Space fee: $230. Exhibition space: 10×12 ft. For more information, artists should e-mail, call or send SASE.
TIPS "Produce good CDs for jurors."

THREE RIVERS ARTS FESTIVAL

803 Liberty Ave., Pittsburgh PA 15222. (412)456-6666. **Fax:** (412)471-6917. **Website:** www.3riversartsfest. org. **Contact:** Sonja Sweterlitsch, director. Estab. 1960. "Three Rivers Arts Festival has presented, during its vast and varied history, more than 10,000 visual and performing artists and entertained millions of residents and visitors. Three Rivers Arts Festival faces a new turning point in its history as a division of the Pittsburgh Cultural Trust, further advancing the shared mission of each organization to foster economic development through the arts and to enhance the quality of life in the region." Application fee: $35. Booth fee: $340-410. See website for more informa-

tion. Festival located at Point State Park in downtown Pittsburgh.

TUBAC FESTIVAL OF THE ARTS

P.O. Box 1866, Tubac AZ 85646. (520)398-2704. **Fax:** (520)398-3287. **E-mail:** assistance@tubacaz.com. **Website:** www.tubacaz.com. Estab. 1959. Fine arts & crafts show held annually in early February (see website for details). Outdoors. Accepts photography and considers all fine arts and crafts. Juried. A 7-member panel reviews digital images and artist statement. Names are withheld from the jurists. Number of exhibitors: 170. Public attendance: 65,000. Free to the public; parking: $6. Deadline for entry: late October (see website for details). Application fee: $30. Artists should apply online and provide images on a labeled CD (see website for requirements). Space fee: $575. Electrical fee: $50. Exhibition space: 10×10 ft. (a limited number of double booths are available). For more information, artists should e-mail, call or visit website.

TULIP FESTIVAL STREET FAIR

(425)321-7433. **Fax:** (360)428-6753. **E-mail:** mvstreet faircoordinator@gmail.com. **Website:** www.mount vernondowntown.org. Estab. 1984. Arts & crafts show held annually 3rd weekend in April. Outdoors. Accepts photography and original artists' work only. No manufactured work. Juried by a board. Jury fee: $10 with application and prospectus. Number of exhibitors: 220. Public attendance: 30,000-35,000. Free to public. Artists should apply by downloading the prospectus (new vendors) or returning vendor application at www.mountvernondowntown.org/events/ tulipfest. Deadline for entry: mid December. Application fee: none. Space fee: $300. Exhibition space: 10×10 ft. Average gross sales/exhibitor: $2,500-4,000. For more information, artists should e-mail, visit website, call or send SASE.
TIPS "Keep records of your street fair attendance and sales for your résumé. Network with other artists about which street fairs are better to return to or apply for."

TULSA INTERNATIONAL MAYFEST

2210 S. Main St., Tulsa OK 74114. (918)582-6435. **Fax:** (918)517-3518. **E-mail:** comments@tulsamayfest.org. **Website:** www.tulsamayfest.org. Estab. 1972. Fine arts & crafts show annually held in May. Outdoors. Accepts photography, clay, leather/fiber, mixed media, drawing, pastels, graphics, printmaking, jewelry, glass, metal, wood, painting. Juried by a blind jurying process. Artists should apply online at www.zappli cation.org and submit 4 images of work and 1 photo of booth set-up. Awards/prizes: Best in Category and Best in Show. Number of exhibitors: 125. Public attendance: 350,000. Free to public. Artists should apply by downloading application in the fall. See website for deadline entry. Application fee: $35. Space fee: $350. Exhibition space: 10×10 ft. For more information, artists should e-mail or visit website.

⊕ ☺ TYSON WELLS SELL-A-RAMA

P.O. Box 60, Quartzsite AZ 85346. (928)927-6364. E-mail: tysonwells@tds.net. **Website:** www.tysonwells. com. Arts & craft show held annually in January. Outdoors & indoors. Accepts handmade crafts, ceramics, paintings, jewelry, glass, photography, wearable art and other mediums. Juried. Number exhibitors: see website. Number attendees: varies. Free to public. Apply online. Deadline for entry: see website for dates. Application fee: none. Space fee: varies. Exhibition space: varies. For more information, artists should call, e-mail or visit website.

⊕ ☺ UPPER ARLINGTON LABOR DAY ARTS FESTIVAL

(614)583-5000. **Website:** www.uaoh.net/egov/ docs/1389217117601.htm. Fine art & craft show held annually in September. Outdoors. Accepts handmade crafts, ceramics, fiber, glass, graphics, jewelry, leather, metal, mixed media, painting, photography, printmaking, sculpture, woodworking. Juried. Awards/ prizes: $1,350 in award. Number exhibitors: 200. Number attendees: 25,000. Free to public. Apply via www.zapplication.org. Deadline for entry: February. Application fee: see website. Space fee: varies. Exhibition space: varies. For more information, artists should call or visit website.

☺ UPTOWN ART FAIR

1406 W. Lake St., Lower Level C, Minneapolis MN 55408. (612)823-4581. **Fax:** (612)823-3158. **E-mail:** maude@uptownminneapolis.com; info@uptown minneapolis.com; jessica@uptownminneapolis.com; hannah@uptownminneapolis.com. **Website:** www.up townartfair.com. Estab. 1963. Fine arts & crafts show held annually 1st full weekend in August. Outdoors. Accepts photography, painting, printmaking, drawing, 2D and 3D mixed media, ceramics, fiber, sculpture, jewelry, wood and glass. Juried by 4 images of artwork and 1 of booth display. Awards/prizes: Best in Show in each category; Best Artist. Number of exhibitors: 350. Public attendance: 375,000. Free to the public. The Uptown Art Fair uses www.zapplication. org. Each artist must submit 5 images of his or her work. All artwork must be in a high-quality digital format. Five highly qualified artists, instructors, and critics handpick Uptown Art Fair exhibitors after previewing projections of the images on 6-ft. screens. The identities of the artists remain anonymous during the entire review process. All submitted images must be free of signatures, headshots or other identifying marks. Three rounds of scoring determine the final selection and waitlist for the show. Artists will be notified shortly after of their acceptance. For additional information, see the links on website. Deadline for entry: early March. Application fee: $40. Space fee: $550 for 10×10 space; $1,100 for 10×20 space. For more information, artists should call or visit website. Fair located at Lake St. and Hennepin Ave. and "The Mall" in Southwest Minneapolis.

☺ A VICTORIAN CHAUTAUQUA

1101 E. Market St., Jeffersonville IN 47130. (812)283-3728 or (888)472-0606. **Fax:** (812)283-6049. **E-mail:** hsmsteam@aol.com. **Website:** www.steamboatmu seum.org. **Contact:** Roger Fisher, festival chairman. Estab. 1993. Fine arts & crafts show held annually 3rd weekend in May. Outdoors. Accepts photography, all mediums. Juried by a committee of 5. Number of exhibitors: 80. Public attendance: 3,000. Exhibition space: 12×12 ft. For more information, artists should e-mail, call, or visit website.

VILLAGE SQUARE ARTS & CRAFTS FAIR

P.O. Box 176, Saugatuck MI 49453. **E-mail:** artclub@ saugatuckdouglasartclub.org. **Website:** www.sau gatuckdouglasartclub.org. Estab. 2004. The art club offers 2 fairs each summer. See website for upcoming dates. This fair has some fine artists as well as crafters. Both fairs take place on the 2 busiest weekends in the resort town of Saugatuck's summer season. Both are extremely well attended. Generally the vendors do very well. Booth fee: $95-140. Fair located at corner of Butler and Main Streets, Saugatuck MI. **TIPS** "Create an inviting booth. Offer well-made artwork and crafts for a variety of prices."

⊕ VIRGINIA BEACH DOWNTOWN ART FAIR

270 Central Blvd., Suite 107B, Jupiter FL 33458. (561)746-6615. **Fax:** (561)746-6528. **E-mail:** info@ artfestival.com. **Website:** www.artfestival.com. **Contact:** Malinda Ratliff, communications manager. Estab. 2015. Fine art & craft fair held annually in April. Outdoors. Accepts photography, jewelry, mixed media, sculpture, wood, ceramic, glass, painting, digital, fiber, metal. Juried. Number exhibitors: 80. Number attendees: see website. Free to public. Apply online via www.zapplication.org. Deadline: see website. Application fee: $25. Space fee: $395. Exhibition space: 10×10 and 10×20. For more information, artists should e-mail, call, or visit website.

▢ Festival located Main St. between Central Park Ave. and Constitution Dr.

VIRGINIA CHRISTMAS MARKET

The Exhibition Center at Meadow Event Park, 13111 Dawn Blvd., Doswell VA 23047. (804)253-6284. **Fax:** (804)253-6285. **E-mail:** bill.wagstaff@virginiashows. com. **Website:** www.virginiashows.com. Indoors. Virginia Christmas Market is held the last weekend in October at the Exhibition Center at Meadow Event Park. Virginia Christmas Market will showcase up to 300 quality artisans, crafters, boutiques and specialty food shops. Features porcelain, pottery, quilts, folk art, fine art, reproduction furniture, flags, ironwork, carvings, leather, toys, tinware, candles, dollcraft, wovenwares, book authors, musicians, jewelry, basketry, gourmet foods—all set amid festive Christmas displays. Accepts photography and other arts and crafts. Juried by 3 photos of artwork and 1 of display. Attendance: 15,000. Public admission: $7; children FREE (under 10). Artists should apply by calling, e-mailing or downloading application from website. Space fee: $335. Exhibit spaces: 10×10 ft. For more information, artists should call, e-mail, or contact through website.
TIPS If possible, attend the show before you apply.

◎ VIRGINIA SPRING MARKET

11050 Branch Rd., Glen Allen VA 23059. (804)253-6284. **Fax:** (804)253-6285. **E-mail:** bill.wagstaff@virginiashows.com. **Website:** www.virginiashows.com. **Contact:** Bill Wagstaff. Estab. 1988. Holiday arts & crafts show held annually 1st weekend in March at the Exhibition Center at Meadow Event Park, 13111 Dawn Blvd., Doswell VA. Virginia Spring Market will showcase up to 300 quality artisans, crafters, boutiques

and specialty food shops. Features porcelain, pottery, quilts, folk art, fine art, reproduction furniture, flags, ironwork, carvings, leather, toys, tinware, candles, dollcraft, wovenwares, book authors, musicians, jewelry, basketry and gourmet foods, all set amid festive spring displays. Accepts photography and other arts and crafts. Juried by 3 images of artwork and 1 of display. Public attendance: 12,000. Public admission: $7; children free (under 10). Artists should apply by calling, e-mailing, or downloading application from website. Space fee: $335. Exhibition space: 10×10 ft. For more information, artists should call, e-mail, or contact through website.
TIPS "If possible, attend the show before you apply."

⊕ ◎ VIRTU ART FESTIVAL

(401)596-7761. **Fax:** (401)596-2190. **E-mail:** lkonicki@ westerlychamber.org. **Website:** www.westerlychamber.org. **Contact:** Lisa Konicki, executive director. Estab. 1996. Arts & crafts show held annually in May. Outdoors. Accepts original fine art & handmade crafts, oils, acrylics, prints, wood, watercolor, pottery, glass, jewelry, sculpture. Juried. Exhibitors: 150. Number of attendees: 20,000. Free to public. Artists should apply via website. Deadline for entry: February 20. Application fee: none. Space fee: $200. Exhibition space: 12×12. For more information, artists should e-mail.

◎ WASHINGTON SQUARE OUTDOOR ART EXHIBIT

P.O. Box 1045, New York NY 10276. (212)982-6255. **Fax:** (212)982-6256. **E-mail:** jrm.wsoae@gmail.com. **Website:** www.wsoae.org. Estab. 1931. Fine arts & crafts show held semiannually Memorial Day weekend and Labor Day weekend. Outdoors. Accepts photography, oil, watercolor, graphics, mixed media, sculpture, crafts. Juried by submitting 5 slides of work and 1 of booth. Awards/prizes: certificates, ribbons and cash prizes. Number of exhibitors: 150. Public attendance: 100,000. Free to public. Artists should apply by sending a SASE or downloading application from website. Deadline for entry: March, spring show; July, fall show. Exhibition space: 5×10 ft. up to 10×10 ft., double spaces available. Jury fee of $20. First show weekend (3 days) fee of $410. Second show weekend (2 days) $310. Both weekends (all 5 days) fee of $525. For more information, artists should call or send SASE.
TIPS "Price work sensibly."

WATERFRONT FINE ART & WINE FESTIVAL

15648 N. Eagles Nest Dr., Fountain Hills AZ 85268. (480)837-5637. **Fax:** (480)837-2355. **E-mail:** info@thunderbirdartists.com. **Website:** www.thunderbirdartists.com. **Contact:** Denise Colter, President. Estab. 2012. Fine art/craft show held annually the 1st weekend in December. Outdoors. Accepts photography, paintings, bronzes, baskets, jewelry, stone, pottery. Juried; blind jury by CEO. Number of exhibitors: 125. Public attendance: 20,000. Public admission: $3. Apply online at www.zapplication.org. Deadline for entry: mid-August (see website for specifics). Application fee: $30. Space fee: $430-1,240. Exhibition space: 10×10 to 10×30 ft. For more information, artists should e-mail, call, or visit website.
TIPS "A clean, gallery-type presentation is very important."

☺ WATERFRONT FINE ART FAIR

P.O. Box 176, Saugatuck MI 49453. **E-mail:** artclub@saugatuckdouglasartclub.org. **Website:** www.saugatuckdouglassartclub.org. Fee is $135. This includes application fee, booth fee, and city license. Applications juried in early April. For information, e-mail, call, or visit the website. Fair held at Cook Park.
TIPS "Create a pleasing, inviting booth. Offer well-made, top-quality fine art."

☺ WESTMORELAND ART NATIONALS

252 Twin Lakes Rd., Latrobe PA 15650-3554. (724)834-7474. **E-mail:** info@artsandheritage.com; adam@artsandheritage.com. **Website:** www.artsandheritage.com. **Contact:** Adam Shaffer, executive director. Estab. 1975. Juried fine art exhibition & crafts show held annually in early July (see website for details). Juried art exhibition is indoors. Photography displays are indoors. Accepts photography, all handmade mediums. Juried by 2 jurors. Awards/prizes: $5,700 in prizes. Number of exhibitors: 190. Public attendance: 160,000. Free to public. Artists should apply by downloading application from website. Application fee: $25/craft show vendors; $35/art nationals exhibitors. Deadline for entry: early March. Space fee: $375-750. Exhibition space: 10×10 or 10×20 ft. For more information, artists should visit e-mail, call, or visit website. Please direct questions to our executive director.

☺ WHITEFISH ARTS FESTIVAL

P.O. Box 131, Whitefish MT 59937. (406)862-5875. **E-mail:** wafdirector@gmail.com. **Website:** www. whitefishartsfestival.org. Estab. 1979. High-quality art show held annually the 1st full weekend in July. Outdoors. Accepts photography, pottery, jewelry, sculpture, paintings, woodworking. Juried. Art must be original and handcrafted. Work is evaluated for creativity, quality and originality. Awards/prizes: Best of Show awarded $100 off booth fee for following year with no application fee. Number of exhibitors: 120. Public attendance: 3,000-5,000. Free to public. Entry fee: $29. Deadline: see website for details. Space fee: $215. Exhibition space: 10×10 ft. For more information, and to apply, artists should visit website.
TIPS Recommends "variety of price range, professional display, early application for special requests."

☺ WHITE OAK CRAFTS FAIR

P.O. Box 111, Woodbury TN 37190. (615)563-2787 or (800)235-9073. **E-mail:** mary@artscenterofcc.com. **E-mail:** carol@artscenterofcc.com. **Website:** www.artscenterofcc.com. Estab. 1985. Arts & crafts show held annually in early September (see website for details) featuring the traditional and contemporary craft arts of Cannon County and Middle Tennessee. Outdoors. Accepts photography; all handmade crafts, traditional and contemporary. Must be handcrafted displaying excellence in concept and technique. Juried by committee. Send 3 slides or photos. Awards/prizes: more than $1,000 cash in merit awards. Number of exhibitors: 80. Public attendance: 6,000. Free to public. Applications can be downloaded from website. Deadline: early July. Space fee: $120 ($90 for Artisan member) for a 10×10 ft. under tent; $95 ($65 for Artisan member) for a 12×12 ft. outside. For more information, artists should e-mail, call or visit website. Fair takes place along the banks of the East Fork Stones River just down from the Arts Center.

☺ WILD WIND FOLK ART & CRAFT FESTIVAL

P.O. Box 719, Long Lake NY 12847. (814)723-0707; (814)688-1516. **E-mail:** wildwindcraftshow@yahoo.com. **Website:** www.wildwindfestival.com. **Contact:** Liz Allen and Carol Jilk, directors. Estab. 1979. Traditional crafts show held annually the weekend after Labor Day at the Warren County Fairgrounds in Pittsfield PA. Barn locations and outdoors. Accepts traditional country crafts, photography, paintings, pottery, jewelry, traditional crafts, prints, stained glass. Juried by promoters. Need 3 photos or slides of work plus 1 of booth, if available. Number of exhibitors: 160. Public attendance: 9,000. Artists should apply by visiting website and filling out application request, calling or sending a written request. Festival held at the Warren County Fairgrounds, Pittsfield, PA.

⊕ WINNEBAGOLAND ART FAIR

South Park Ave., Oshkosh WI 54902. **E-mail:** osh koshfaa@gmail.com. Estab. 1957. Fine arts show held annually the second Sunday in June. Outdoors. Accepts painting, wood or stone, ceramics, metal sculpture, jewelry, glass, fabric, drawing, photography, wall hangings, basketry. Artwork must be the original work of the artist in concept and execution. Juried. Applicants send in photographs to be reviewed. Awards/prizes: monetary awards, purchase, merit and Best of Show awards. Number of exhibitors: 125-160. Public attendance: 5,000-8,000. Free to public. Deadline for entry: Previous exhibitors due mid-March; new exhibitors due late March. $25 late entry fee after March. Exhibition space: 20×20 ft. For more information, artists should e-mail or see website. The updated entry form will be added to the website in early January.

TIPS "Artists should send clear, uncluttered photos of their current work which they intend to show in their booth as well as a photo of their booth setup."

⊕ WOODSSTOCK MUSIC & ARTS FESTIVAL

(419)862-3182. **Website:** www.woodsstock.org. Fine art & craft show held annually in August. Outdoors. Accepts handmade crafts, ceramics, drawing, fiber, glass, jewelry, leather, metal, mixed media, painting, photography, sculpture, wood. Juried. Awards/prizes: Best of Show, Honorable Mention. Number exhibitors: see website. Number attendees: varies. Admission: $25 general; $45 VIP. Apply via www.zapplica tion.org. Deadline for entry: June. Application fee: $20. Space fee: $100 (single); $150 (double). Exhibition space: 10×10 (single); 10×20 (double). For more information, artists should visit website.

⊕ WYANDOTTE STREET ART FAIR

2624 Biddle Ave., Wyandotte MI 48192. (734)324-4502. **Fax:** (734)324-7283. **E-mail:** hthiede@wyan.org. **Website:** www.wyandottestreetartfair.org. **Contact:** Heather Thiede, special events coordinator. Estab. 1961. Fine arts & crafts show held annually 2nd week in July. Outdoors. Accepts photography, 2D mixed media, 3D mixed media, painting, pottery, basketry, sculpture, fiber, leather, digital cartoons, clothing, stitchery, metal, glass, wood, toys, prints, drawing. Juried. Awards/prizes: Best New Artist $500; Best Booth Design Award $500; Best of Show $1,200. Number of exhibitors: 300. Public attendance: 200,000. Free to the public. Artists may apply online or request application. Deadline for entry: early February. Application fee: $20 jury fee. Space fee: $250/single space; $475/double space. Exhibition space: 10×12 ft. Average gross sales/exhibitor: $2,000-$4,000. For more information, and to apply, artists should e-mail, visit website, call, or send SASE.

CONTESTS

Whether you're a seasoned veteran or a newcomer still cutting your teeth, you should consider entering contests to see how your work compares to that of other artists or graphic designers. The contests in this section range in scope from tiny juried county fairs to massive international competitions. When possible, we've included entry fees and other pertinent information in our limited space. Contact sponsors for entry forms and more details.

Once you receive rules and entry forms, pay particular attention to the sections describing rights. Some sponsors retain all rights to winning entries or even submitted images. Be wary of these. While you can benefit from the publicity and awards connected with winning prestigious competitions, you shouldn't unknowingly forfeit copyright. Granting limited rights for publicity is reasonable, but you should never assign rights of any kind without adequate financial compensation or a written agreement. If such terms are not stated in the contest rules, ask the sponsors for clarification.

If you're satisfied with the contest's copyright rules, check with contest officials to see what types of images won in previous years. By scrutinizing former winners, you might notice a trend in judging that could help when choosing your entries. If you can't view the images, ask what styles and subject matters have been popular.

440 GALLERY ANNUAL SMALL WORKS SHOW

440 Sixth Ave., Brooklyn NY 11215. (718)499-3844. **E-mail:** gallery440@verizon.net. **Website:** www.440gallery.com. **Contact:** Nancy Lunsford, director. Annual juried exhibition hosted by 440 Gallery, a cooperative run by member artists. An exhibition opportunity for US artists whose work is selected by a different curator each year. All work, including frames and mounting materials must be less than 12 inches in all directions. Open to all 2D and 3D media. Videos are considered if the monitor provided is also under 12 inches. Three prizes awarded with small cash awards: The Curator's Choice Award (decided by the juror), the 440 Award (decided by the members of the cooperative), the People's Choice Award (decided by "liking" images posted on our Facebook page). Deadline: early November. For more information about entering submissions, visit website in late September/early October, go to "Call for Entry" page.

440 GALLERY ANNUAL THEMED SHOW

440 Sixth Ave., Brooklyn NY 11215. (718)449-3844. **E-mail:** gallery440@verizon.net. **Website:** www.440gallery.com. **Contact:** Nancy Lunsford. National juried exhibition with a stated theme, and the subject varies from year to year. Past themes have been: animals, Brooklyn, text. An outside curator is invited to judge entries. All media and styles welcome. There is no size limitation, but extremely large work is unlikely to be chosen. Open to all US artists ages 18 and over. Deadline: mid-May. Interested artists should see website for more information.

🌑 AESTHETICA ART PRIZE

P.O. Box 371, York YO23 1WL, United Kingdom. **E-mail:** info@aestheticamagazine.com; artprize@aestheticamagazine.com. **Website:** www.aestheticamagazine.com. There are 4 categories: Photograpic & Digital Art, Three-Dimensional Design & Sculpture, Painting & Drawing, Video Installation & Performance. See guidelines at Artwork & Photography, Fiction, and Poetry. See guidelines at www.aestheticamagazine.com.

AMERICAN SOCIETY OF AVIATION ARTISTS INTERNATIONAL ART EXHIBITION

American Society of Aviation Artists, 581 Airport Road, Bethel PA 19507. (732)735-6545. **E-mail:** ASAAcontact@asaa-avart.org. **Website:** www.asaa-avart.org. **Contact:** Nanette O'Neal. Entry fee: $50/ entry for non-ASAA members. This annual contest is held to promote aerospace art. Several prizes will be awarded. Open to all skill levels. See website for more information including deadlines for submission.

ARTIST FELLOWSHIPS/VIRGINIA COMMISSION FOR THE ARTS

1001 E. Broad St., Suite 330, Richmond VA 23219. (804)225-3132. **Fax:** (804)225-4327. **E-mail:** arts@arts.virginia.gov; tiffany.ferreira@vca.virginia.gov. **Website:** www.arts.virginia.gov. The purpose of the Artist Fellowship program is to encourage significant development in the work of individual artists, to support the realization of specific artistic ideas, and to recognize the central contribution professional artists make to the creative environment of Virginia. Grant amounts: $5,000. Emerging and established artists are eligible. Open only to artists who are legal residents of Virginia and are at least 18 years of age. Applications are available in July. See Guidelines for Funding and application forms on the website or write for more information.

ARTISTIC DREAMS

159 N. Main St., Smithfield UT 84335. (435)713-4414. **Fax:** (435)713-4422. **E-mail:** editor@artisticdreams.net. **Website:** www.artisticdreams.net. **Contact:** Tom Worthen, Ph.D., editor. Annual contest to create a larger audience for artists and poets, and a place to record their work. Open to anyone living in the US or Canada, 18 year or older. Any art that can have a still digital image (not a photography contest) or any poem 21 lines or less is eligible. Rolling deadline, entries are judged as they are received. You will know 2-3 weeks after entering if your art/poetry is accepted to be published. When enough entries are accepted for a book, the artists and writers who are invited to be published will be notified. Entries can be entered online after registering an account. No mailed entries will be accepted. You may submit one art piece and one poem per theme. There are 3 art winners and 3 poetry winners per book. Each winner will receive $100 and a free copy of the anthology. No entry fee and open to all skill levels.

⚫ Contestants should see website for more information.

ARTISTS ALPINE HOLIDAY

Ouray County Arts Association, P.O. Box 167, Ouray CO 81427. (970)626-5513. **E-mail:** jbhazen@yahoo.com. **Website:** www.ourayarts.org. **Contact:** DeAnn

McDaniel, registrar. Cost: $30, includes up to 2 entries. Annual fine arts show. Juried. Cash awards for 1st, 2nd and 3rd prizes in all categories total $7,200. Best of Show: $750; People's Choice Award: $50. Open to all skill levels. Photographers and artists should call or see website for more information.

THE ARTIST'S MAGAZINE ALL-MEDIA

F+W, a Content + eCommerce Company, Competition Dept., 10151 Carver Rd., Suite 200, Blue Ash OH 45242. (715)445-4621, ext. 13430. **E-mail:** art-compe tition@fwmedia.com. **Website:** www.artistsnetwork. com/competitions/all-media-online-competition. **Contact:** Nicole Howard, customer service specialist. Cost: $25/entry. Annual contest held to recognize the best work being done in various mediums. Awards: the grand prize winner receives a $500 prize, as well as a subscription to *The Artist's Magazine* and $50 worth of North Light Books. All 8 first place winners receive $100, complimentary subscriptions to *The Artist's Magazine* and $100 worth of North Light Books. Honorable mentions receive complimentary subscriptions to *The Artist's Magazine* and $50 worth of North Light Books. Open to all skill levels. Deadline: October. E-mail or see website for more information.

THE ARTIST'S MAGAZINE OVER 60 COMPETITION

F+W, a Content + eCommerce Company, Competitions Dept., 10151 Carver Rd, Suite 200, Blue Ash OH 45242. (715)445-4621, ext.13430. **E-mail:** art-com petition@fwmedia.com. **Website:** www.artistsnet work.com/competitions/over-60-art-competition. **Contact:** Nicole Howard, customer service specialist. Cost: $25/slide or image. Annual contest for artists age 60+ working in all traditional art media. Entries can be submitted online using the online entry form. There is no limit to the number of images you may enter. You may mail all your entries in on one CD. You *must* include a cover sheet that lists the title, medium/media, and dimensions of each image. The titles of the images on the CD must match the titles on the sheet. Image files cannot exceed 5MG. The file format must be JPEG. If your work is selected for the top 10, we will contact you at a later date and ask that you provide a high-res replacement file. Incomplete entry forms and information sheets, and improperly marked CDs will be disqualified. See website for complete submission details. Awards: $1,000 in prizes; 10 winners each receive $100. Winners will be published in the March issue of *The Artist's Magazine* and on the website. Open to all skill levels; however, participants must be 60 years of age or older. Deadline: September. E-mail or see website for more information.

THE ARTIST'S MAGAZINE'S ANNUAL ART COMPETITION

F+W, a Content + eCommerce Company, Competition Dept., 10151 Carver Rd., Suite 200, Blue Ash OH 45242. (715)445-4621, ext. 13430. **E-mail:** art-compe tition@fwmedia.com. **Website:** www.artistsnetwork. com/competitions/the-artists-magazine-annual-art-competition. **Contact:** Nicole Howard, customer service specialist. Cost: All entries in the Student/Beginner Division (for artists age 16 and over who (1) have been enrolled in a posthigh school art program for no more than 4 years OR (2) have pursued art on their own or in workshops/lessons for no more than 4 years) are $15 per image. All others are $25 per image. Entries submitted after April 1 are $20 for students entries and $30 for all other entries. Held annually. "You may enter work in any and all categories; there is no limit to the number of images you may enter. Enter online. Image files cannot exceed 5MB. The file must be saved as a JPEG in RGB color mode (not CMYK). File names should include only letters, numbers and spaces. See website for complete submission details; and a list of eligible categories. Awards: More than $25,000 in cash prizes; 5 1st Place awards: $2,500 each; 5 2nd Place awards: $1,250 each; 5 3rd Place awards: $750 each; 15 Honorable Mentions: $100 each. Winners will be featured and finalists' names will be published in an upcoming issue of *The Artist's Magazine*. Nine finalists will be featured in the "Competition Spotlight" in *The Artist's Magazine*, 12 finalists will be featured as "Artist of the Month" on our website and the works of 12 finalists will be offered on our website as desktop wallpaper. All award winners and Honorable Mentions receive a 1-year membership to the North Light VIP Program. See website for prizes to be won in the Student/Beginner Division category. Open to all skill levels. Deadline: mid-April. E-mail or see website for more information.

⌂ ARTIST TRUST FELLOWSHIP AWARD

1835 12th Ave., Seattle WA 98122. (209)467-8734, ext. 11. **Fax:** (866)218-7878. **E-mail:** info@artisttrust.org. **Website:** www.artisttrust.org. **Contact:** Miguel Guillen, program manager. Fellowships award $7,500 to practicing professional artists of exceptional talent and demonstrated ability. The Fellowship is a merit-based, not a project-based award. Recipients present a Meet the Artist Event to a community in Washington state that has little or no access to the artist and their work. Awards 14 fellowships of $7,500 and 2 residencies with $1,000 stipends at the Millay Colony. Artist Trust Fellowships are awarded in two-year cycles. Applicants must be 18 years of age or older, Washington State residents at the time of application and payment, and generative artists.

◕ ARTSLINK PROJECTS AWARD

CEC Artslink, 291 Broadway, 12th Floor, New York NY 10007. (212)643-1985, ext. 23. **Fax:** (212)643-1996. **E-mail:** tmiller@cecartslink.org. **Website:** www.cec artslink.org. **Contact:** Tamalyn Miller, program director. Estab. 1962. "CEC ArtsLink is an international arts organization. Our programs encourage and support exchange of artists and cultural managers in the United States and abroad. We believe that the arts are a society's most deliberate and complex means of communication, and that artists and arts administrators can help nations overcome long histories of reciprocal distrust, insularity and conflict. CEC Arts-Link promotes communication and understanding through innovative, mutually beneficial collaborative projects. CEC was founded in 1962 to enable citizens of the United States and the Soviet Union to accomplish what their governments could not by opening doors, sharing ideas and building mutual trust. In today's transformed and complex world, citizen diplomacy is still urgently needed."

⊕ BUCKTOWN ARTS FEST POSTER CONTEST

2200 N. Oakley, Chicago IL 60647. **E-mail:** poster contest@bucktownartsfest.com. **Website:** www. bucktownartsfest.com/posters. **Contact:** Amy Waldon, committee member. Annual contest. "We hope you wil share your creativity and passion for the Bucktown Arts Fest by entering our poster contest! The purpose of the contest is to design a poster promoting the Bucktown Arts Fest. Just create an original artwork in your media that you think best exemplefies the Bucktown Arts Fest and submit it in JPEG format. The deadline for entries is March 31. There is no fee to enter. Winners will receive a prize and complimentary admission into the festival. Plus, your artwork will be used to promote the Fest, including the Bucktown Arts Fest website, festival merchandise

(posters, t-shirts, hangtags, postcards, program), collateral, press releases and signage." One winner will be selected. Winner will be announced May 31 via an e-mail blast.

CREATIVE QUARTERLY CALL FOR ENTRIES

244 Fifth Ave., Suite F269, New York NY 10001-7604. (718)775-3943. **E-mail:** coordinator@cqjournal. com. **Website:** www.cqjournal.com. Entry fee: varies. Quarterly contest. "Our publication is all about inspiration. Open to all art directors, graphic designers, photographers, illustrators and fine artists in all countries. Separate categories for professionals and students. We accept both commissioned and uncommissioned entries. Work is judged on the uniqueness of the image and how it best solves a marketing problem. Winners will be requested to submit an image of a person, place or thing that inspires their work. We will reprint these in the issue and select one for our cover image. *Creative Quarterly* has the rights to promote the work through our publications and website. Complete rights and copyright belong to the individual artist, designer or photographer who enters their work. Enter online or by sending a disc. Winners will be featured in the next issue of *Creative Quarterly* corresponding with the call for entries and will be displayed in our online gallery. Runners-up will be displayed online only. Winners and runners-up both receive a complimentary copy of the publication." Open to all skill levels. Deadline: Last Friday of January, April, July and October. See website for more information.

DIRECT ART MAGAZINE

SlowArt Productions, 123 Warren St., Hudson NY 12534. (518)828-2343. **E-mail:** slowart@aol.com. **Website:** www.slowart.com. **Contact:** Tim Slowinski, director. Cost: $35. Annual contest. "This contest is to select artists for publication in the annual edition of *Direct Art Magazine.*" Open to all skill levels. Awards: publication in *Direct Art Magazine*, front and back covers; 4-to-6 page coverage; full-page display awards. Value of awards: $22,000. Deadline: March 31, annually. E-mail or see website for more information.

DIRECT ART MAGAZINE PUBLICATION COMPETITION

SlowArt Productions, 123 Warren St., Hudson NY 12534. **E-mail:** slowart@aol.com; limnerentry@aol. com. **Website:** www.slowart.com. **Contact:** Tim Slowinski, director. Cost: $35. Annual contest. National magazine publication of new and emerging art in all medias. Cover and feature article awards. Open to all skill levels. Send SASE or see website for more information. SlowArt Productions presents the annual group thematic exhibition. Open to all artists, national and international, working in all media. All forms of art are eligible. *Entrants must be 18 years of age or older to apply.* 96 inch maximum for wall hung work, 72 inch for free-standing sculpture.

EMERGING ARTISTS

SlowArt Productions, 123 Warren St., Hudson NY 12534. (518)828-2343. **E-mail:** slowart@aol.com. **Website:** www.slowart.com. **Contact:** Tim Slowinski, director. Cost: $35. Annual contest. "This contest is dedicated to the exhibition, publication and promotion of emerging artists." Open to all skill levels. Awards: exhibition at the Limner Gallery; $1,000 cash; $2,200 in publication awards. Deadline: November 30, annually. E-mail or see website for more information.

EXHIBITIONS WITHOUT WALLS FOR PHOTOGRAPHERS AND DIGITAL ARTISTS

130 SW 20th St., Cape Coral FL 33991. (239)223-6824. **E-mail:** ewedman@exhibitionswithoutwalls.com. **Website:** www.exhibitionswithoutwalls.com. **Contact:** Ed Wedman, co-founder. Cost: $25 for up to 5 images, each additional image up to 10 is an additional charge of $4. Contest is held quarterly. Online international juried competitions for photographers and digital artists. Prizes vary, but a minimum of $900 in cash awards and additional prizes. Open to all skill levels. Deadline: 30 days after submissions open. Contestants should see website for more information.

HOW INTERACTIVE DESIGN AWARDS

F+W, a Content + eCommerce Company, Competition Dept., 10151 Carver Rd., Suite 200, Blue Ash OH 45242. (715)445-4612, ext. 13430. **E-mail:** HOWcompetition@fwmedia.com. **Website:** www.howdesign.com/interactivedesignawards. **Contact:** Nicole Howard. Annual contest to recognize the best in digital design. See website for complete submission details and a list of categories. Awards: All winning entries will be featured online at HOWInteractiveDesign.com, at the HOW Design Live event, at the HOW Interactive Design Conferences and receive a $100 discount to the HOW Design Conference. One "Best of Show" winner will get a free trip to the HOW Conference (round-trip airfare, hotel and registration) and will be prominently featured in the HOW July 2016 issue.

Open to all skill levels. **Deadline: November.** E-mail or see website for more information.

HOW INTERNATIONAL DESIGN AWARDS

F+W, a Content + eCommerce Company, Competition Dept., 10151 Carver Rd., Suite 200, Blue Ash OH 45242. (715)445-4612, ext. 13430. **E-mail:** how competition@fwmedia.com. **Website:** www.howdesign.com/internationaldesignawards. **Contact:** Nicole Howard. Annual contest to recognize the best graphic design work from around the world. Awards: All Outstanding Achievement entry winners will be featured in HOW's International Design Annual and get a $100 discount to the HOW Design Conference. One "Best of Show" winner will get a free trip to the HOW Design Conference (roundtrip airfare, hotel and registration), will be featured in the HOW Design Annual issue and will be showcased in the online design competition gallery. Open to all skill levels. **Deadline: mid-August.** E-mail or see website for more information.

HOW LOGO DESIGN AWARDS

F+W, a Content + eCommerce Company, Competition Dept., 10151 Carver Rd., Suite 200, Blue Ash OH 45242. (715)445-4612, ext. 13430. **E-mail:** how competition@fwmedia.com. **Website:** www.howdesign.com/logodesignawards. **Contact:** Nicole Howard. Annual contest. "There are no categories, and it doesn't matter if your logo was created for yourself, for work or just for fun…we want to see what you can do! So take this wide-open media and run with it! All logos must be submitted online at howdesign.com. The image size must not exceed 1280×1024 pixels. The image can be saved at a resolution that will enable us to zoom in to see details during judging, but the file size must not exceed 5MB." Cost: $45/logo. Awards: 10 winners will be featured on the HOW website, receive a prize pack of design books from HOW's official online store and receive a graphic to post on your website announcing your winning status. From the top 10 winners, visitors to HOWDesign.com will have a window of time to vote for one Reader's Choice Best of Show winner, which will receive additional attention as the featured project in Behind the Design, a column in HOW magazine. Open to all skill levels. **Deadline: July.** E-mail or see website for more information.

HOW POSTER DESIGN AWARDS

F+W, a Content + eCommerce Company, Competition Dept., 10151 Carver Rd., Suite 200, Blue Ash OH

45242. (715)445-4612, ext. 13430. **E-mail:** howcom petition@fwmedia.com. **Website:** www.howdesign. com/posterdesignawards. **Contact:** Nicole Howard. Annual contest. "There are no categories, and it doesn't matter if your poster was created for yourself, for work or just for fun…we want to see what you can do! So take this wide-open media and run with it! All posters must be submitted online at howdesign.com. The image size must not exceed 1280×1024 pixels. The image can be saved at a resolution that will enable us to zoom in to see details during judging, but the file size must not exceed 5MB." Awards: 10 winners will be featured on the HOW website, get $150 worth of HOW books and a 1-year subscription to *HOW* magazine, and receive a graphic to post on your website announcing your winning status. Open to all skill levels. **Deadline:early December.** E-mail or see website for more information.

HOW PROMOTION & MARKETING DESIGN AWARDS

F+W, a Content + eCommerce Company, Competition Dept., 10151 Carver Rd., Suite 200, Blue Ash OH 45242. (715)445-4612, ext. 13430. **E-mail:** self-promo-competition@fwmedia.com. **Website:** www.howdesign.com/design-competitions/promotion-marketing-design-awards. **Contact:** Nicole Howard, customer service specialist. Estab. 1988. Annual contest. HOW's longest-running design competition. "This is the only awards program to specifically recognize outstanding promotional work—whether it's a self-promo to showcase a design firm's capabilities, a project for a client's goods or services, an announcement or a student résumé or portfolio. HOW's Promotion & Marketing Design Awards celebrates design work that's engaging, memorable and effective at moving the viewer toward action." See website for complete submission details and a list of categories. Accepts actual samples of annual reports, brochures, catalogs, direct mail, book and magazine covers and interior pages, invitations, announcements, greeting cards, letterhead, logos, packaging, posters, print advertising, calendars, wearables, 3D objects interactive work and more. Designs may be entered in more than one category. Submit a separate entry and fee for each category. Awards: All winning entries will be featured in HOW's Self-Promotion Design Annual and winners will get a $100 discount to HOW Design Live. Best of Show awarded a free trip to the annual HOW Design Live (round-trip airfare, hotel and registration) and

an award to be presented at the conference. Open to all skill levels. **Deadline: March.** E-mail or see website for more information.

IN-HOWSE DESIGN AWARDS

F+W, a Content + eCommerce Company, Competition Dept., 10151 Carver Rd., Suite 200, Blue Ash OH 45242. (715)445-4612, ext. 13430. **E-mail:** howcom petition@fwmedia.com. **Website:** www.howdesign. com/in-howsedesignawards. **Contact:** Nicole Howard. Cost: Single entry—$115 (stationery systems count as single entries); campaign—$140 (3 or more pieces that function as a system or series). Payment must accompany entries. Entries received without payment will be disqualified. Entry fees are nonrefundable. Annual contest held to recognize the best creative work produced by designers working in corporations, associations and organizations. Submissions are evaluated by business category to ensure that a broad range of design work is represented. Accepts actual samples of annual reports, brochures, catalogs, direct mail, book and magazine covers and interior pages, invitations, announcements, greeting cards, letterhead, logos, packaging, posters, print advertising, calendars, wearables, 3D objects and other print projects. Also accepts color print-outs of workspaces, signage and other environmental graphic design. Does not accept videos, CDs, DVDs, websites or other interactive work, or digital images or slides of print work. Digital work is eligible in Interactive Design Awards. Designs may be entered in more than one category (see website for category listing). See website for complete submission details; and a list of eligible categories. Awards: Best of Show winner will receive: 2-page spread in *HOW*'s January issue; representation in the online gallery and archive; press release to the design community promoting your win; and a trip to the 2014 HOW Design Live Conference. Merit winners will receive publication in *HOW* magazine and a $100 gift certificate toward the HOW Design Live Conference. Open to all skill levels. Deadline: July. Call, e-mail or see website for more information.

KENTUCKY ARCHAEOLOGY MONTH POSTER CONTEST

109-A W. Poplar St., Elizabethtown KY 42701. (270)855-9780. **E-mail:** christywpritchard@gmail.com. **Website:** www.kyopa-org.org/kentucky_archae ology_month.html. **Contact:** Christy Pritchard, chair. Estab. 2014. Winning artwork and design will be used as the official poster for the first annual Kentucky Archaeology Month, "Celebrating Kentucky Archaeology." Calling all artists and graphic designers to submit poster designs that reflect their interpretation of Kentucky's rich heritage. The KAM steering committee will select 3 finalists from the designs submitted. Finalists will be e-mailed to the KyOPA membership and the winner will be selected by a membership vote. The official Kentucky Archaeology Month poster will be distributed to the Governor's office, members of Kentucky House, Kentucky Senate, as well as Kentucky libraries, schools, and various parks within the state. See website for submission deadline. Artists should submit proposed artwork in electronic, camera-ready format. Submitting artists must also complete the entry form. Submission must be original artwork. Submissions must be 2-dimensional artwork. No syndicated, copyrighted or clip art images may be submitted. Reproducibility will be a factor in the committee's decision. High contrast and bright colors are recommended, the estimated size of the poster will be 18×24. Selected artwork for the poster will be artistic, positive in approach and informative for use as a teaching tool. Selected artwork for the poster will commemorate Kentucky Archaeology Month celebrating the long history of archaeology and heritage studies in Kentucky. Selected artwork for the poster will have broad appeal to Kentuckians, educators, students, those considering Kentucky for travel and vacation, historians, artists and the general public. A committee will select 3 finalists from the artwork submitted. The selection committee will consist of members from KyOPA, the Kentucky Heritage Council, and the Office of State Archaeology. Artwork will be judged based upon: quality of artwork, creativity and originality of artwork, positive and thematically appropriate artwork, reproducibility. The winner will be selected by electronic vote, via e-mail, from the KyOPA membership. The Kentucky Organization of Professional Archaeologists will retain rights of ownership for all final artwork commissioned via this solicitation. The committee reserves the right to use the artwork for additional purposes, such as websites and print materials.

⊕ LONG ISLAND ARTISTS EXHIBITION

107 E. Deer Park Rd., Dix Hills NY 11746. (631)462-5400. **Website:** www.artleagueli.org. Cost: 2 images, $40; $5 each additional image up to 3. Total maximum 5 images; non-members: First 2 images , $50; $5 each additional image up to 3. Total maximum 5 images. Open to artists residing in Suffolk, Nassau, Brooklyn and Queens. 2D and 3D work in any medium may be submitted, including photography and fine craft. Prize/Award: $500 Awards of Excellence and Honorable Mentions of 1 year memberships in ALLI will be given at the discretion of the judge. Deadline for submissions: late February. Contestants should call or see website for more information.

LOS ANGELES CENTER FOR DIGITAL JURIED COMPETITION

1515 Wilcox Ave., Los Angeles CA 90028. (323)646-9427. **E-mail:** info@lacphoto.org. **Website:** www.lacphoto.org. The Los Angeles Center of Photography (LACP) is dedicated to supporting photographers and the phtographic arts. LACP provides high-caliber classes, local and travel workshops, exhibitions, screenings, lectures, and community outreach efforts, including grants, need-based scholarships, and focused programming for youth and low-income families.

LOVE UNLIMITED FILM FESTIVAL & ART EXHIBITION

100 Cooper Point Rd., Suite 140-136, Olympia WA 98502. **E-mail:** entries1@loveanddiversity.org; volunteers@loveanddiversity.org. **Website:** www.communitygardenlove.org. **Contact:** submissions administrator. Accepts art (ceramics, drawings, fiber, functional, furniture, jewelry, metal, painting, printmaking, digital or graphics, mixed media 2D, mixed media 3D, sculpture, watercolor, wood, other or beyond categorization (specify), photography, music, writing, photos and all types of designs, as well as film and scripts. Accepts poetry, hip-hop, spoken word and zine excerpts, autobiography/memoir, children's, fiction, horror, humor, journalism, mystery, nature, novels, short stories, nonfiction, poetry, romance, science fiction/fantasy, screenwriting, travel, young adult and other topic areas. We accept writing in all these topic areas provided these topic areas are directly, indirectly, literally or symbolically related to love. Awards: over $30,000 in cash and prizes and 120 given out during a red carpet gala event in Los Angeles and in Austin TX. Photos and videos of past events are online. Open to all skill levels. Deadlines: October for art, November for all other categories. See website for more information.

⊕ MICHIGAN ANNUAL XLIII (ART COMPETITION & EXHIBITION)

125 Macomb Place, Mt. Clemons MI 48043. (586)469-8666. **Fax:** (586)469-4529. **E-mail:** exhibitions@theartcenter.org. **Website:** www.theartcenter.org. **Contact:** Stephanie Szmiot, exhibition manager. Cost: $35.00 per artist for up to two entries to be juried. Annual statewide juried art competition. Open to resident Michigan artists ages 18 and older. No size or media restrictions. Featuring new guest juror each year. Up to 50 selected artworks are on display for about 4 weeks in main gallery. Prize/Award: 1st Place $1,000, 2nd Place $600, 3rd Place $400, in addition to five Honorable Mention Awards. Deadline for submissions: late December-early January. Contestants should write, send SASE, call, e-mail, and see website for more information.

⊕ NATIONAL ART ENCOUNTER COMPETITION

585 Park St., Naples FL 34102. (239)262-6517. **Fax:** (212)262-5404. **E-mail:** jack.obrien@naplesart.org. **Website:** www.naplesart.org/callforartistcat/exhibit-opportunities. **Contact:** Jack O'Brien, curator. Cost: $40. Bi-annual photography contest. Open to artists residing in the US. Enter artwork in either the 2D or 3D categories. Awards: 6 cash awards totaling $2,500. Open to all skill levels. Deadline: September 19, 2016. Photographers should visit website for more information.

NICKELODEON ARTIST PROGRAM

231 W. Olive Ave., Burbank CA 91502. (818)736-3663. **E-mail:** info.artist@nick.com. **Website:** www.nickartist.com. Annual program developed to broaden Nickelodeon's outreach efforts. Nickelodeon's Artist Program offers aspiring artists with diverse backgrounds and experiences the opportunity to hone their artistic skills while working on our 2D and CG animated television shows. The program provides a salaried position for up to 6 months. General Track participants will have hands-on interaction with established background designers, character designers and more, while Storyboard Track participants will receive hands-on experience working with lead storyboard artists. Submission period from March 1-April 1. Application information and submission guidelines are available on our website at www.nickartist.com. No entry fee. Open to intermediate and advanced creative artists. Follow us on Twitter @NickArtists; Like us on Facebook: www.facebook.com/NickArtist.

PASTEL 100

F+W, a Content + eCommerce Company, Competitions Dept., 10151 Carver Rd., Suite 200, Blue Ash OH 45242. (715)445-4621, ext. 13430. **E-mail:** PJedit@fwmedia.com. **Website:** www.artistsnetwork.com/pasteljournalcompetition. **Contact:** Anne Hevner. Cost: $25/image for early bird entries, $30/image after early bird deadline. Annual contest sponsored by *The Pastel Journal.* Offers cash, prizes and publicity to winners. Enter files online or via regular mail. "All digital files submitted via regular mail must be accompanied by an Official Entry Form or facsimilie. There is no limit to the number of images you may enter. If you mail all your entries in on one CD, please include a separate sheet that gives the title and dimensions of each image. Image files cannot exceed 5MB. The file format must be JPEG. If your work is selected for the top 100, we will contact you about sending a high-res replacement. Incomplete entry forms and information sheets, and improperly marked CDs will be disqualified. *Slides will not be accepted.* CDs will not be returned." See website for a listing of categories. Awards: More than $13,000 in cash prizes, including the Pastel Journal Grand Prize, $5,000; the Ruth Richeson/Unison Pastels Award, $2,000 value in sets of pastels and surfaces; Gold Medal Award, $2,500; Silver Medal Award, $1,500; and Bronze Medal Award, $1,000; plus category awards. All top prizewinners and placewinners will receive features in *The Pastel Journal.* Honorable mentions (70 awarded) will be featured in *The Pastel Journal.* See website for a complete list of awards. Open to all skill levels. Artists must be 16 or older. Work must be at least 80% soft pastel; no oil pastel. Nupastels and other "harder" pastels are considered soft pastels. The contest is open to artists in the US and abroad. All works must be original. Compositions based on published material or other artists' work are *not* considered original and are not eligible. See website for complete eligibility details. **Deadline: September.** E-mail or see website for more information.

PRINT'S REGIONAL DESIGN ANNUAL

F+W, a Content + eCommerce Company, Competition Dept., 10151 Carver Rd., Suite 200, Blue Ash OH 45242. (715)445-4612, ext. 13430. **Fax:** (715)445-4087. **E-mail:** printcomp@fwmedia.com. **Website:** www.

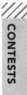

CONTESTS

regionaldesignannual.printmag.com/competition-details. **Contact:** Nicole Howard, customer service specialist. Cost: (see website for current rates/dates): Single entries: $95 each piece; campaigns and series: $120 (3 or more pieces in each submission). Ad campaigns, book cover series, corporate brochure series, or poster series will all be considered campaigns. Any packaging entry, whether a single package or a family of packages, will be considered a single entry (fee: $95). Any letterhead entry that consists of stationery, envelope, and business card will be considered a single entry. Held annually. "The *Regional Design Annual* is more than just a catalog of the best American design created over the year. For 30 years, this highly-anticipated collection of art and design has displayed the considerable breadth and depth of high-quality work being generated in every corner of the country. For many designers, the *RDA* symbolizes the pinnacle of design accomplishment, while at the same time directly reflecting the aesthetics and zeitgeist of the regions included." Enter online. You may submit up to 10 digital photos per entry (5MB per file). If your work is selected as a finalist you may be asked to send a sample. See website for complete submission details; and a listing of categories. Awards: Winners will be published in the December issue of *Print,* as well as featured in an online gallery. Open to all skill levels. **Deadline: early March** (see website for details). E-mail or see website for more information.

A SHOW OF HEADS

SlowArt Productions, 123 Warren St., Hudson NY 12534. (518)828-2343. **E-mail:** slowart@aol.com. **Website:** www.slowart.com. **Contact:** Tim Slowinski, director. Cost: $35. Annual contest. "This contest is to select artists for exhibition in The Show of Heads at Limner Gallery. The show features work based on the portrayal and interpretation of the human head." Open to all skill levels. Awards: exhibition at Limner Gallery; 3 artists receive publication in *Direct Art Magazine*; 1 artist receives 2 full pages; 2 artists receive 1 page. Value of awards: $2,200. Deadline: August 31, annually. E-mail or see website for more information.

SPLASH: THE BEST OF WATERCOLOR

F+W, a Content + eCommerce Company, Competition Dept., 10151 Carver Rd., Blue Ash OH 45242. (715)445-4612, ext. 13430. **Website:** www.splashwatercolor.com; www.artistsnetwork.com/splashwater

color. **Contact:** List manager. Cost: $30 for the first painting and $30 for each additional digital submission. Annual contest showcasing the finest watercolor paintings being created today. A new book in the series is published every year by North Light Books and features nearly 140 paintings by a wide variety of artists from around the world, each with instructive information about how it was achieved—including inspiration, tips and techniques. "We look for excellence in a variety of styles and subjects. The dominant medium must be transparent watercolor, though minor uses of other media are acceptable." Your digital images may be submitted online or on CD/DVD (please label the disks with your name and address). Mailed entries must be accompanied by a color printout and an entry form. Disks will not be returned. For judging purposes, these images must be high-quality, in RGB color mode, JPEG format, and 72 dpi. All digital files must be smaller than 5MB. Digital files submitted by mail must be labeled with your last name, first name, the entry number (should correspond to the number on the entry form), with no punctuation marks until the file extension (example: Wolf Rachel 3.jpg). Awards: winning paintings will be published in a beautiful hardcover book. Open to all skill levels. **Deadline: December.** E-mail or see website for more information.

STROKES OF GENIUS: THE BEST OF DRAWING

F+W, a Content + eCommerce Company, Competition Dept., 10151 Carver Rd., Suite 200, Blue Ash OH 45242. (715)445-4612, ext. 13430. **E-mail:** bestofnorthlight@fwmedia.com; art-competition@fwmedia.com. **Website:** www.artistsnetwork.com/competitions/strokes-of-genius. **Contact:** Nicole Howard, customer service specialist. Cost: $30 for the first drawing and $25 for each additional drawing. Annual contest showcasing the finest drawings being created today. A new book in the series is published every year by North Light Books and features nearly 140 drawings by a wide variety of artists from around the world, each with instructive information about how it was achieved—including inspiration, tips and techniques. Artwork can be in any dry medium, or wet medium applied in a linear fashion that would be traditionally considered drawing. Final judgment on whether a work of art fits into the "drawing" category will be determined by the editors. All submissions will be reviewed by Rachel Wolf and the editorial staff of

North Light Books. Art will be selected on the basis of general quality as well as suitability for this publication. Your digital images may be submitted online. For judging purposes, these images must be high-quality, in RGB color mode, JPEG format, and 72 dpi. All digital files must be smaller than 5MB. Awards: winning drawings will be published in a beautiful hardcover book. Open to all skill levels. **Deadline: April.** E-mail or see website for more information.

⊕ TALLAHASSEE INTERNATIONAL JURIED COMPETITION

530 W. Call St., Rm. 250FAB, Tallahassee FL 32306-1140. (850)644-3906. **Fax:** (850)644-7229. **E-mail:** tallahasseeinternational@fsu.edu. **Website:** www. mofa.cfa.fsu.edu/participate/tallahassee-internation al. **Contact:** Jean D. Young, coordinator. Cost: $20/2 images. Annual art contest. Artists worldwide, 18+ are eligible. All media and subject matter eligible for consideration. Juried by panel of FSU College of Fine Arts faculty. One entry/person. Awards: 1st- $1,000; 2nd- $500. Color catalog is produced. Open to all skill levels. Deadline: February 15, 2016. Photographers should e-mail or visit website for more information.

WATERCOLOR ARTIST'S WATERMEDIA SHOWCASE

F+W, a content and ecommerce company, Competition Dept., 10151 Carver Rd., Suite 200, Blue Ash OH 45242. (715)445-4621, ext. 13430. **E-mail:** waterme diashowcase@fwmedia.com. **Website:** www.artist snetwork.com/watermediashowcase. **Contact:** Nicole Florence, customer service specialist. Cost: $20/image for early bird entries (submitted on or before July 1). Entries submitted after July 1 are $25/image. Annual contest. You must enter online and all entries must be submitted as digital files. You may enter work in any and all categories; there is no limit to the number of images you may enter. If your work is selected as a winner, we may contact you about sending a high-res replacement. Incomplete entry forms and information sheets, and improperly named image files will be disqualified. See website for complete submission details. Award: Best of Show: $1,000; 2nd Place: $500; 3rd Place: $250; 4th Place: $100. Award winners will be published and Honorable Mentions' names will be listed in the April issue of *Watercolor Artist*. All winners and honorable mentions will receive a certificate suitable for framing. Open to all skill levels. **Deadline: August 1.** E-mail or see website for more information.

◐ FRED WHITEHEAD AWARD FOR DESIGN OF A TRADE BOOK

E-mail: tilsecretary@yahoo.com. **Website:** www.tex asinstituteofletters.org. Offered annually for the best design for a trade book. Open to Texas residents or those who have lived in Texas for 2 consecutive years. See website for guidelines. **Deadline: Early January;** see website for exact date.

WORKSHOPS & ART TOURS

Taking an art or design workshop or tour is one of the best ways to improve your creative skills. There is no substitute for the hands-on experience and one-on-one instruction you can receive at a workshop. Besides, where else can you go and spend several days with people who share your passion for art or design?

Plein air drawing and painting are perennial workshop favorites. Creativity is another popular workshop topic. You'll also find highly specialized workshops such as Celtic design and forensic art. Many tours specialize in a specific location and the great artistic opportunities that location affords.

As you peruse these pages, take a good look at the quality of workshops and the skill level the sponsors want to attract. It is important to know if a workshop is for beginners, advanced amateurs, or professionals. Information from a workshop organizer can help you make that determination.

These workshop listings contain only the basic information needed to make contact with sponsors and a brief description of the styles or media covered in the programs. We also include information on costs when possible. Write, call, or e-mail the workshop/tour sponsors for complete information. Most have websites with extensive information about their programs, when they're offered, and how much they cost.

A workshop or tour can be whatever the artist or designer wishes—a holiday from the normal working routine or an exciting introduction to new skills and perspectives on the craft. Whatever you desire, you're sure to find in these pages a workshop or tour that fulfills your expectations.

3 DAY COLOR INTENSIVE WITH KITTY WALLIS

10915 SW 37th Ave., Portland OR 97219. (503)307-1142 (cell). **E-mail:** walliscorp@yahoo.com. **Contact:** Kitty Wallis, artist and teacher. Students will learn about color as a tool for the artist. How to achieve light, and life in their work. Designed for pastel artists. Open to all skill levels. Three workshops held summer of 2015. Small classes limited to 5 students; scheduled over 3 day weekends. Cost: $360 including Wallis Archival Sanded Pastel Paper and some materials. Lodging and meals not included. Please write with SASE, call, or e-mail for more information.

ACADIA WORKSHOP CENTER

7 Bernard Rd., Bernard ME 04612. (207)460-4119. **E-mail:** awcmaine@gmail.com. **Website:** www.acadia workshopcenter.com. **Contact:** Gail Ribas, director/owner. 4-to 5 day workshops with top instructors in all painting media on the coast of Maine. Workshops are held during the summer and early fall. Interested parties should check the website for details.

ARROWMONT SCHOOL OF ARTS AND CRAFTS

556 Pkwy., Gatlinburg TN 37738. (865)436-5860. **Fax:** (865)430-4101. **E-mail:** bmay@arrowmont.org; info@arrowmont.org. **Website:** www.arrowmont.org. Offers weekend, 1- and 2-week workshops in photography, drawing, painting, clay, metals/enamels, kiln glass, fibers, surface design, wood turning and furniture. Residencies, studio assistantships, work-study, and scholarships are available. See individual course descriptions for pricing.

ART ESCAPES WORKSHOPS WITH DORY KANTER

E-mail: dory@dorykanter.com. **Website:** www.dory kanter.com. **Contact:** Dory Kanter, artist and workshop organizer. Next workshops: check website for dates. "Chronicling impressions with quick sketches and visual storytelling is an everyday practice for Dory Kanter, whose best-selling book *Art Escapes* provides daily exercises and inspirations for artists, to help them build confidence and cultivate creativity. Join Dory as she makes it easy to create art every day with original Art Escape projects designed to spark your creativity and capture the sights and scenes around you. Learn enlivening observational art projects to record your wanderings at home or on the road. Dory will demonstrate how to create luminous water-color mixes with her 4 color triads. All skill levels will experience both inspiration and success." E-mail and see website for more information.

ART IMMERSION TRIP WITH WORKSHOP IN NEW MEXICO

P.O. Box 1473, Cullowhee NC 28723. (828)342-6913. **E-mail:** contact@cullowheemountainarts.org. **Website:** www.cullowheemountainarts.org. **Contact:** Norma Hendrix, director. Cost: $1,379-$1,579 (includes lodging, 2-4 day workshop, breakfasts, 1 dinner, some transportation and museums). "Cullowhee Mountain Arts offers exceptional summer artist workshops in painting, drawing, printmaking, book arts, ceramics, photography and mixed media. Our distinguished faculty with national and international reputations will provide a week-long immersion in their topic supplemented with lectures, demonstrations or portfolio talks. Cullowhee Mountain Arts is committed to supporting the personal and professional development of every artist, whatever their level, by providing the setting and facilities for intense learning and art making, shared in community. We believe that are enlivens community life and that in a supportive community, art thrives best. Our studios are located on Western Carolina University's campus, surrounded by the natural beauty of the Blue Ridge Mountains in North Carolina." Upcoming workshops in New Mexico include: Debra Fitts (Ceramic Sculpture: Intermediate to Advanced), "The Spirit & The Figure"; Ron Pokrasso (Printmaking: All Levels), "Monotype and More: Mixed Media Printmaking"; Nancy Reyner (Acrylic: Intermediate, Advanced, Masters), "Acrylic Innovation: Inventing New Painting Techniques & Styles"; and Sandra Wilson (Painting: All Levels), "Acrylic Textures, Transfers and Layers." Call, e-mail, or see website for more detailed information including exact dates and locations.

ARTIST'S NETWORK UNIVERSITY

E-mail: service@artistsnetworkuniversity.com. **Website:** www.artistsnetworkuniversity.com. For more than 25 years, the experts at North Light Books have been publishing books designed to connect artists with ideas and inspiration. Now, Artist's Network University brings North Light Books' friendly, accessible style of fine are instruction to online art classes. Get personal instruction on your own schedule in the mediums/topics you want and at the skill level that best fits you wherever you are in art. Cost:

$159.99/$169.99. Classes start every Tuesday and run for 4 weeks. Send e-mail for more information.

⊕ ART WORKSHOPS

431 Hartford Ave., Wethersfield CT 06109. (860)436-9857. **E-mail:** info@wethersfieldarts.org. **Website:** www.wethersfieldarts.org. **Contact:** Betty Standish. Workshops held monthly. See website for more details. Open to all skill levels. Please e-mail with questions or interest.

ART WORKSHOPS IN GUATEMALA

4758 Lyndale Ave. S., Minneapolis MN 55419-5304. (612)825-0747. **E-mail:** info@artguat.org. **Website:** www.artguat.org. **Contact:** Liza Fourre, director. Estab. 1995. Art & cultural workshops held in Antigua, Guatemala. See website for a list of upcoming workshops.

COASTAL MAINE ART WORKSHOPS/ ROCKLAND AND BEYOND!

P.O. Box 845, Camden ME 04843. (207)594-4813. **E-mail:** info@coastalmaineartworkshops.com. **Website:** www.coastalmaineartworkshops.com. **Contact:** Lyn Donovan, director. Seasonal. Cost: Tuition in Maine includes free parking and 24 hour studio use. Costs for classes abroad vary depending on location and what is included. "Maine students make their own arrangements for lodging and meals; most establishments offer breakfast and there are many nearby options for great food." Workshops in Maine are held weekly early-July through early-October with nationally and internationally known instructors teaching 5-day Plein Air classes in watercolor and oils. "We have glorious scenery, a fine large studio and a reputation for lavish personal attention. Rockland and Belfast, our 2nd local site, are halfway up the coast of Maine and full of great art, friendly places to stay and terrific food. Our classes in Europe thru 'Paint Away: Art Classes Abroad!' are generally in the spring and fall." Both programs have classes for all skill levels. Artists should contact us directly or see website for more information.

EILEEN CORSE—PAINTING WITH PASSION

4144 Herschel St., Jacksonville FL 32210. (904)388-8205. **E-mail:** corsegalleryatelier@comcast.net. **Website:** corsegalleryatelier.com. **Contact:** Eileen Corse, owner. Eileen Corse teaches how to apply oil paint with a palette knife to create lively and colorful paintings. Each day, Corse will demonstrate her technique.

Open to all skill levels. One-day workshops held once a month. Tuition is $100. Interested parties should e-mail or see website for more information.

CREALDÉ SCHOOL OF ART

600 St. Andrews Blvd., Winter Park FL 32792. (407)671-1886. **E-mail:** pschreyer@crealde.org; rberrie@crealde.org. **Website:** www.crealde.org. **Contact:** Peter Schreyer, executive director; Robin Berrie, marketing manager. Crealdé School of Art is a community-based nonprofit arts organization established in 1975. It features a year-round curriculum of over 100 visual arts classes for students of all ages, taught by a faculty of over 40 working artists; a renowned summer art camp for children and teens; a visiting artist workshop series, 3 galleries, the contemporary sculpture garden, and award-winning outreach programs. Offers classes covering traditional and digital photography; b&w darkroom techniques; landscape, portrait, documentary, travel, wildlife and abstract photography; and educational tours. See website for more information and upcoming workshops.

CREATIVE ARTS WORKSHOP

80 Audubon St., New Haven CT 06511. (203)562-4927. **E-mail:** haroldshapirophoto@gmail.com. **Website:** www.creativeartsworkshop.org. **Contact:** Harold Shapiro, photography department head. A nonprofit regional center for education in the visual arts that has served the Greater New Haven area since 1961. Located in the heart of the award-winning Audubon Arts District, CAW offers a wide-range of classes in the visual arts in its own 3-story building with fully equipped studios and an active exhibition schedule in its well-known Hilles Gallery. Offers exciting classes and advanced workshops. Digital and traditional b&w darkroom. See website for more information and upcoming workshops.

CREATIVE COMPOSITION AND DEPTH WITH INSTRUCTOR LAURIE HUMBLE

Cheap Joe's Art Stuff, 374 Industrial Park Dr., Boone NC 28607. (800)227-2788 ext. 1123. **E-mail:** edwina@cheapjoes.com. **Website:** www.cheapjoes.com; www.lauriehumble.com. **Contact:** Edwina May, workshop coordinator. Workshop dates change annually. "Learn how to compose your work and use a sense of depth to draw the viewer in and hold their interest longer. Discover the key to editing reference material, whether you are working from photos or life. Laurie will provide subject matter for days 1, 2 and 3 while teaching you how to choose and make your subject work as a successful painting. On days 4 and 5, bring your own photo references or work from photos provided by Laurie. Both beginners and advanced painters will come away with a new understanding of how to create great design and achieve a sense of visual depth. Lessons learned can be applied to any painting style or skill level. There will be plenty of painting time, demos and individual instruction. You will be amazed at the new levels of dimension you create!" Workshop is held at Cheap Joe's Art Stuff. Call, e-mail, or see website for more information. Three, 4- and 5-day Artist Instructional Workshops available in watercolor, acrylic, oil, colored pencil and mixed media. In total, 25-30 workshops per year, May through October. For registration or more information, visit the website or contact Edwina. Terrific views from studio, covered porch with rocking chairs, many local attractions and discounted lodging rates for workshop participants. Classes are held in a spacious workshop studio with color correct lighting, individual adjustable artist tables, ergonomic adjustable chairs, separate demo area with camera and 70" TV screen/monitor, convenient parking, and no stairs to climb. Delicious full lunches provided Monday-Thursday, free coffee, hot tea, fresh fruit and other goodies. Free gift each morning, Retail outlet store next door for supplies, true southern hospitality, and the friendliest customer service in the world.

CREATIVE EXPLORATIONS IN MIXED MEDIA SERIES

E-mail: lisa@cyrstudio.com. Website: www.cyrstudio.com; www.artistsnetwork.com/art_online_seminars. Contact: Artist's Network. Recorded webinars available for download with Artist's Network. *Session 1—Collage Techniques for the Mixed-Media Artist*: This video covers an array of exciting collage techniques from gluing, sealing, tearing, scoring, punching, die-cutting, and custom inlays; to wrinkling, creasing, burning, peeling-back, stitching, weaving, embossing and debossing handmade, custom treated and machine-made papers, foils and ephemera. If you love working in collage, this recorded workshop with artist Lisa L. Cyr is for you (www.northlightshop.com/creating-explorations-in-mixed-media-digital-download-u7890)! *Session 2—Transforming the Surface With Mixed-Media Painting Techniques*: This video covers a striking array of creative approaches in which to alter and transform the mixed-media painting surface. Lushly painted passages and rich transitions employing resist, blotting, lift-off, dissolve, marbling, sponging, distressing, aging and printmaking techniques will be shown in inventive combinations. Utilizing both traditional and unconventional tools and techniques, this audiovisual presentation will certainly ignite the creative juices (www.northlightshop.com/transforming-the-surface-with-mixed-media-painting-techniques-download-u7891)! *Session 3—Assemblage Accents: Employing Faux Finishes and Patinas*: This video covers creatively customizing found objects, assemblage accents and sculptural creations with unique finishes and patinas. To enliven the mixed-media landscape, a diverse array of techniques and materials from repurposed and custom treated material and man-made elements are explored. With the addition of faux finishes and decorative techniques, the everyday object can be transformed into a one-of-a-kind accent, communicating a concept or illuminating a subject in a unique way. Working in bas-relief and dealing with the structural issues of assemblage accents and 3D work are also discussed (www.northlightshop.com/creative-explorations-mixed-media-digital-download-u7892). Cost: Each audivisual presentation is available for download for $20. See download links to purchase on Northlightshop.com.

CULLOWHEE MOUNTAIN ARTS SUMMER WORKSHOP SERIES

598 W. Main St., Sylva NC 28779. (828)342-6913. E-mail: contact@cullowheemountainarts.org. Website: www.cullowheemountainarts.org. Contact: Norma Hendrix, director (norma@cullowheemountainarts.org). Cost: $525-875 for 5-day tuition, lab fees and Sunday wine reception (housing and partial meal plans are available at an additional cost, ranging from $500-775 a week. Two catered meals can be purchased a la carte with prior registration). "Cullowhee Mountain Arts offers exceptional summer artist workshops in painting, ceramics, mixed media, encaustic, printmaking and book arts. The distinguished faculty with national and international reputations will provide an immersion in their topic supplemented with lectures, demonstrations or portfolio talks. Cullowhee Mountain Arts is committed to supporting the personal and professional development of every artist, whatever their level, by providing the setting and facilities for intense learning and art-making, shared in community. Upcoming workshops on the WCU campus include: Building Books & Imagery (book arts), Alice

Austin; Contemporary Dinnerware (ceramics), Jeff Oestreich and Pat Burns; Advanced Cold Wax and Oil Painting (painting), Rebecca Crowell; Introduction to Cold Wax (painting), Janice Mason Steeves; Encaustic Collagraphs (printmaking), Jane Nodine; Poetry, Plein Air and Otherwise (Creative Writing), Lola Haskins. Also offering workshops, trips and retreats to Santa Fe and Taos NM and spring and fall artist retreats at Lake Logan NC.

☯ DAWSON COLLEGE CENTRE FOR TRAINING AND DEVELOPMENT
4001 de Maisonneuve Blvd. W., Suite 2G.1, Montreal Quebec H3Z 3G4, Canada. (514)933-0047. **Fax:** (514)937-3832. **E-mail:** ctd@dawsoncollege.qc.ca. **Website:** www.dawsoncollege.qc.ca/ciait. Workshop subjects include imaging arts and technologies, computer animation, photography, digital imaging, desktop publishing, multimedia, and web publishing and design. See website for course and workshop information.

DRAWING FOR THE ABSOLUTE BEGINNER
Cincinnati OH. **E-mail:** mmwillenbrink@gmail.com. **Website:** www.shadowblaze.com. **Contact:** Mark or Mary Willenbrink. Mark Willenbrink, with his wife Mary, is the best-selling author of the *Absolute Beginner* series, which includes *Watercolor for the Absolute Beginner* and *Drawing for the Absolute Beginner*. Mark enjoys sharing the fundamentals of art in understandable terms, encouraging others to pursue their creative potential. He is a professional illustrator, a fine artist and he teaches art classes and workshops. For more information on his latest workshops and books, visit www.shadowblaze.com; like Mark's Facebook page at www.facebook.com/pages/ Mark-Willenbrink-Artist-Author-and-Illustrator/153942411304719.

DYNAMICS OF LIGHT-FILLED LANDSCAPE PAINTING
(808)873-0597. **E-mail:** julie@pleinairjourneys.com. **Website:** www.pleinairjourneys.com. **Contact:** Julie Houck. Annual workshops teaching the fundamentals of light on the landscape. Maui HI. Cost: $350, instruction only. All levels welcome.

ETRUSCAN PLACES LANDSCAPE PAINTING IN ITALY & IPSWICH, MA (USA)
10 Ashland St., Newburyport MA 01950. (212)780-3216. **E-mail:** info@landscapepainting.com. **Website:** www.landscapepainting.com. **Contact:** Maddine Insalaco, director. Annual workshop held May through October in Italy and May in USA. Intensive one-week plein-air landscape painting workshops in Tuscany and the Roman Campagna. Cost: $2,250-2,950 depending on location and occupancy. Fees include: workshop, most or all meals, equipment and all supplies except paint and brushes, trips, museum visits, accommodations and local transportation. Open-air landscape painting all the time, rain or shine. Open to all skill levels. Interested parties should call, e-mail or see website for more information.

EXPERIMENTAL PAINTING: INSPIRATIONAL APPROACHES IN MIXED MEDIA
E-mail: lisa@cyrstudio.com. **Website:** www.cyrstudio.com. **Contact:** Lisa L. Cyr. "This highly visual, hands-on workshop will investigate exploratory methodologies, techniques and approaches in mixed-media art. Throughout the workshop, many exciting in-depth demonstrations will be shown, providing an extensive array of visually-stimulating possibilities for artists to explore. Both 2D and 3D mixed-media techniques will be covered, including employing alternative working grounds, using custom tools, toning the painting surface in imaginative ways, creating a tactile ground, building the visual architecture and utilizing innovative mixed-media techniques to create intriguing effects. To assist artists in their own creative path, topics on nurturing the creative spirit, developing personal content through journalism, embracing a multidisciplinary mindset and creating message-driven art will also be discussed. For artists that are looking to push their work to a new level, this workshop will be a valuable resource and an ongoing source for creative inspiration. You can view the book that the workshop is based upon at www.cyrstudio.com/workasplay.html." See website for more information including dates and locations.

FINE ARTS WORK CENTER
24 Pearl St., Provincetown MA 02657. (508)487-9960, ext. 103. **Fax:** (508)487-8873. **E-mail:** workshops@fawc.org. **Website:** www.fawc.org. Estab. 1968. Faculty includes Connie Imboden, David Hilliard, Pam Houston, Nick Flynn, Shellburne Thurber, Salvatore Scibona, John Murillo, Joanne Dugan, Rob Swainston and many more.

FRANCISCAN LIFE PROCESS CENTER ART SCHOOL

11650 Downes, Lowell MI 49331. (616)897-7842, ext.352. **Fax:** (616)897-7054. **E-mail:** kbechtel@lifeprocesscenter.org. **Website:** www.lifeprocesscenter.org (click visual arts tab, and then adult workshops). **Contact:** Kathy Bechtel. Monthly workshops. Oil, painting and pastel. Open to all skill levels. Cost varies. See website for complete workshop schedule. Topics include figure painting, expressive portraits, alla prima figure and portrait painting, figure drawing, colored pencil and ink wash on canvas, plein air painting, woodcut with chine colle, and color and light. Interested parties should e-mail or visit website for more information.

HORIZONS: ARTISTIC TRAVEL

P.O. Box 634, Leverett MA 01054. (413)367-9200. **Fax:** (413)367-9522. **E-mail:** horizons@horizons-art.com. **Website:** www.horizons-art.com. **Contact:** Jane Sinauer, director. "Horizons offers one-of-a-kind small-group travel adventures in Southern Africa: Sea to Safari; Peru: the Inca Heartland; Ecuador: Andes to the Amazon; Southeast Asia: Burma and Laos (2014); and new for 2013, A Foodie's Italy: Parma and Bologna. As of 2013, our catalog will solely be online to ensure that you always have the most up-to-date information. If you would like a detailed itinerary for any trip or have specific questions, please let us know."

HUDSON RIVER VALLEY ART WORKSHOPS

P.O. Box 659, 11135 St. Rt. 32, Greenville NY 12083. (518)966-5219. **Fax:** (518)966-8754. **E-mail:** info@artworkshops.com. **Website:** www.artworkshops.com. **Contact:** Kim LaPolla, art workshops director. Cost: varies. Yearly schedule of classes: March-December. "We present about 40 workshops a year with professional instructors in a range of media: oil, pastel, watercolor, acrylic, collage, textiles, mixed media." Open to all skill levels. For more information call, e-mail or see website.

KRISTY KUTCH COLORED PENCIL WORKSHOPS

11555 W. Earl Rd., Michigan City IN 46360. (219)874-4688. **E-mail:** kakutch@earthlink.net. **Website:** www.artshow.com/kutch. Instruction focuses on using "traditional," water-soluble pencils, and water-soluble wax pastels to create painting-like works of art.

Multiple workshops throughout the year. Prices vary. See website for more details.

LANDSCAPE PAINTING IN SOUTHERN FRANCE

(808)280-6083. **E-mail:** juliehouck@gmail.com. **Website:** www.pleinairjourneys.com. **Contact:** Julie Houck. Learn the dynamics of landscape painting in the lovely Languedoc region of southwestern France. Fee $3,600. Includes lodging, instruction and most meals. Contact Julie Houck (808)280-6083 or julie@pleinairjourneys.com, or visit www.pleinairjourneys.com.

LIGHT & COLOR WORKSHOPS

10030 Fair Oaks Blvd., Fair Oaks CA 95628. (916)966-7517. **E-mail:** sarback@lightandcolor.com. **Website:** www.lightandcolor.com. **Contact:** Susan Sarback. These in-depth workshops focus on specific seeing and painting techniques based on the light and color of the Impressionists. Through painting a variety of subjects, the students learn the foundation needed to paint any subject—landscape, still life, portraiture, etc. Open to all skill levels. Interested parties should call or e-mail for more information.

THE MACDOWELL COLONY

100 High St., Peterborough NH 03458. (603)924-3886. **Fax:** (603)924-9142. **E-mail:** admissions@macdowellcolony.org. **Website:** www.macdowellcolony.org. Estab. 1907. Provides creative artists with uninterrupted time and seclusion to work and enjoy the experience of living in a community of gifted artists. Residencies of up to 8 weeks for writers, playwrights, composers, film/video makers, visual artists, architects and interdisciplinary artists. Artists in residence receive room, board and exclusive use of a studio. Average length of residency is 5 weeks. Ability to pay for residency is not a factor; there are no residency fees. Limited funds available for travel reimbursement and artist grants based on need. Application deadlines: January 15: summer (June-September); April 15: fall/winter (October-January); September 15: winter/spring (February-May). Visit website for online application and guidelines. Questions should be directed to the admissions director.

MADELINE ISLAND SCHOOL OF THE ARTS

978 Middle Rd., P.O. Box 536, LaPointe WI 54850. (715)747-2054. **E-mail:** misa@cheqnet.net. **Website:** www.madelineschool.com. **Contact:** Jenna J. Erick-

son, director of programs. Workshop tuition $425-760 for 5-day workshops. Lodging and meals are separate, both are provided on-site. Workshops held annually between May-October. Workshops offered in writing, painting, quilting, photography and yoga. Open to all skill levels. Interested parties should call, e-mail or see website for more information.

MAINE MEDIA WORKSHOPS

70 Camden St., P.O. Box 200, Rockport ME 04856. (207)236-8581 or (877)577-7700. **Fax:** (207)236-2558. **E-mail:** info@mainemedia.edu. **Website:** www.mainemedia.edu. "Maine Media Workshops is a non-profit educational organization offering year-round workshops for photographers, filmmakers and media artists. Students from across the country and around the world attend courses at all levels, from absolute beginner and serious amateur to working professional; also high school and college students. Professional certificate and low-residency MFA degree programs are available through Maine Media College." See website for the fall calendar.

⊕ NIGHTSCAPES: EXPLORING THE DARK SIDE IN PASTEL

(203)235-1417. **Fax:** (203)630_0503. **E-mail:** christine iversartist@gmail.com. **Website:** www.christineivers.com. **Contact:** Chris Ivers. Cost: varies. Workshops held throughout the year. This workshop will explore painting night cityscapes on textured black boards that students prepare the first day of the workshop. Color temperature, atmosphere perspective, drawing and the making of glowing lights are all part of the fun. This is a workshop or relaxation and encouragement. Demos & critiques are always included. Open to all skill levels. See website for complete workshop schedule. Interested parties should call, e-mail, or visit website for more information.

ONLINE WORKSHOP: CREATIVE EXPLORATIONS IN MIXED MEDIA: 2D, 3D AND BEYOND!

E-mail: lisa@cyrstudio.com. **E-mail:** service@artistsnetworkuniversity.com. **Website:** www.cyrstudio.com; www.artistsnetworkuniversity.com. **Contact:** Artist's Network University. Ongoing online workshop with Artist's Network University (www.artistsnetworkuniversity.com/courses/creative-explorations-in-mixed-media-2d-3d-and-beyond). This workshop will explore alternative, innovative ways of conceptualizing and creating content-driven mixed-

media art that is on the cutting-edge. Throughout the workshop, insightful and thought-provoking profiles of leading artists and illustrators accompany exciting, in-depth, step-by-step demonstrations, shedding light on signature processes and techniques. The workshop also provides insight into the historical influences behind contemporary thinking and approaches, investigating the origins of alternative, unconventional picture making throughout the decades. Offering a wide range of possibilities for exploration and experimentation, this workshop will reveal how alternative, mixed media aesthetics is uniting the disciplines of 2D, 3D, digital and new media art in inventive combinations. For those wanting to venture outside the norm, this workshop will be a valuable resource and an ongoing source for creative inspiration. Cost: $149.99 for 4 weeks, includes a downloadable copy of the book *Art Revolution* by Lisa L. Cyr. Open to all skill levels. E-mail or see website for more information.

ONLINE WORKSHOP: WITHIN THE LAYERS: INSPIRATIONAL MIXED MEDIA TECHNIQUES

E-mail: lisa@cyrstudio.com. **E-mail:** service@artistsnetworkuniversity.com. **Website:** www.cyrstudio.com; www.artistsnetworkuniversity.com. **Contact:** Artist's Network University. Ongoing online workshop with Artist's Network University (www.artistsnetworkuniversity.com/courses/within-the-layers-inspirational-mixed-media-techniques). This workshop investigates exploratory methodologies, techniques and approaches in mixed-media art. Throughout this mixed-media workshop, exciting in-depth demonstations will be shown, providing an extensive array of visually-stimulating mixed-media art project possibilities for artists to explore. Both 2D and 3D mixed-media techniques will be covered. For artists who are looking to push their mixed-media ideas and work to a new level, this workshop will be a valuable resource and an ongoing source for creative inspiration. Cost: $149.99 for 4 weeks, includes a downloadable copy of the book *Experimental Painting* by Lisa L. Cyr. You can view the video book trailer that the workshop is based upon at www.cyrstudio.com/workasplay.html. Open to all skill levels. E-mail or see website for more information.

⊕ THE PAINTERLY PORTRAIT, 3-DAY WORKSHOP

31 Main St., Newton CT 06470. (203)297-1399. E-mail: alain@picardstudio.com. Website: www. picardstudio.com. Contact: Alain J. Picard, artist/instructor. "Learn to develop life-like portrait paintings, whether working from the live model or photographic references. Using the live model as our reference, we'll learn all the techniques necessary to create stunning portraits in pastel and oil. Lighting and posing the model, photographing the model for reference, designing the portrait, creating lifelike skin tones, learning the painterly approach, and refining your portrait will all be covered in a relaxed and friendly environment. Alain will demonstrate each morning and students will work throughout the day to develop lifelike portraits. The workshops will conclude with an encouraging group critique. Medium: oil and pastel. Open to all skill levels. Artists should see website for more information and dates."

PAINTING IN PROVENCE

Website: ianroberts.com. Contact: Ian Roberts. Workshops focuses on painting. Two 4-hour sessions daily. The emphasis is on strong design and composition. All media and levels of experience welcome. Spectacular landscape. Gourmet food and wine. Double or single coccupancy $3,390-4,190. Covers all costs from time picked up in Avignon until dropped off again 10 days later. Workshops held annually. Workshops held annually. Interested parties should e-mail or visit website for more information.

PENINSULA SCHOOL OF ART

P.O. Box 304, 3900 County Rd. F, Fish Creek WI 54212. (920)868-3455. E-mail: info@peninsulaschool ofart.org. Website: www.peninsulaschoolofart.com. "With instruction in all media, and for every skill level, we've brought excellence to art education for 50 years. Within the inspirational setting of Door County WI, nationally-recognized artist educators lead 1- to 5-day workshops throughout the year. Themed gallery exhibitions of master artists' works, including the annual Door County Plein Air Festival, enhance the School's curriculum." Cost per workshop varies. Nearby lodging and meals not included in cost.

⊕ PENNELLATE D'ITALIA—ITALIAN ART SOJOURN WITH BRIAN KEELER

P.O. Box 397, Wyalusing PA 18853. (570)746-1187. E-mail: bkeeler@epix.net. Website: www.briankeeler. com. Contact: Brian Keeler, instructor/organizer. The workshop is a plein air landscape and studio figure painting workshop in Tuscany and Umbria. The art sojourn includes trips to several museums and many charming small towns plus Florence and Rome. Art history slide lecture too. Open to all skill levels. Held annually May-June. Cost is $3,450 and includes all ground transport, most lodging and meals. Interested parties should call, e-mail or see website for more information.

PETERS VALLEY SCHOOL OF CRAFT

19 Kuhn Rd., Layton NJ 07851. (973)948-5200. Fax: (973)948-0011. E-mail: info@petersvalley.org. Website: www.petersvalley.org. Offers workshops May, June, July, August and September; 2-5 days long. Offers instruction by talented photographers in a wide range of photographic disciplines—from daguereotypes to digital and everything in between. Also offers classes in blacksmithing/metals, ceramics, fibers, fine metals, weaving and woodworking. Located in northwest New Jersey in the Delaware Water Gap National Recreation Area, 70 miles west of New York. Artists and photographers should call for catalog or visit website for more information.

⊕ 🌀 PLEIN AIR PAINTING & SKETCHING IN SOUTHERN FRANCE

(985)809-6332. E-mail: art@alanflattmann.com. Website: www.alanflattmann.com. Contact: Alan Flattmann, artist/teacher. Cost: $3,700. 10 days of plein air painting and sketching in the beautiful Lot River Valley of Southern France. Open to all skill levels. See website for complete workshop schedule. Interested parties should call, e-mail or visit website for more information.

⊕ PLEIN AIR PAINTING FOR THE STUDIO ARTIST

(203)235-1417. Fax: (203)630_0503. E-mail: christine iversartist@gmail.com. Website: www.christineivers. com. Contact: Chris Ivers. Cost: varies. Workshops held throughout the year. This workshop is perfect for studio artists who are afraid to go outside to paint. We spend the mornings with our sketchbooks, cameras, smartphones, etc., gathering reference information from which we will work when we come back to the studio. Critical drawing, good note taking skills and more help us to create wonderful landscapes all within the safety and convenience of a studio. All mediums are welcome. Demos & critiques always included. Open to all skill levels. See website for complete workshop schedule. Interested parties should call, e-mail, or visit website for more information.

PLEIN AIR PAINTING WORKSHOPS (FRANCE, SPAIN, BELGIUM, SWITZERLAND)

French Escapade, 2389 Blackpool Place, San Leandro CA 94577. (510)483-5713. **E-mail:** contact@frenchescapade.com. **Website:** www.frenchescapade.com. **Contact:** Jackie Grandchamps. Cost: $2,640-3,590—includes lodging, most meals, painting classes and cultural visits. Held more than 5 times a year between April and October. See website for all upcoming workshops. "American teachers are running the art aspect of the workshop. Since the tours are limited to 7 guests, each participant will receive private consult from the teacher in addition the the demos and daily critiques. We stay in one accommodation for the 8 days and paint different sceneries, villages and flower fields each day. A bilingual guide will be accompanying you at all times so that you not only get the best experience in painting, but also in experiencing the fine cuisine and culture of the country." Open to all skill levels. See website for more information.

JULIE GILBERT POLLARD WATERCOLOR AND OIL WORKSHOPS AND CLASSES

(623)849-2504. **E-mail:** JulieGilbertPollard@cox.net. **Website:** www.juliegilbertpollard.com. **Contact:** Julie Gilbert Pollard. See website for upcoming schedule. "Julie Gilbert Pollard has taught watercolor and oil classes for some 30 years. While glowing, brilliant color in a format of painterly realism is her personal painting objective, her goal when teaching is to assist in the search for the individual artistic personality of each student, leaning heavily on the fundamentals of art as the gateway to fulfilling personal expression and intuitive painting." Most classes and workshops are open to all skill levels. Recurring theme: the components of a landscape with rocks, water and flowers figuring prominently—in both studio and plein air. See website for listings. Many venues with varying costs are available including: Cynthia's Art Asylum, Phoenix AZ; Scottsdale Artists' School, Scottsdale, AZ; Shemer Art Center, Phoenix AZ. Costs vary with venue and length of program; call, e-mail or see www.juliegilbertpollard.com for more information. Julie's textbook publications available for purchase include:

Brilliant Color, Watercolor Unleashed, Acrylic Unleashed (books and DVDs).

PORTRAIT AND STILL-LIFE WORKSHOPS WITH BEV LEE

645½ 30 Rd., Grand Junction CO 81504. **E-mail:** bleefinearts@gmail.com. **Website:** www.bevlee.com. **Contact:** Bev Lee. Held annually. See website for upcoming schedule. Emphasis for each workshop will be placed on drawing shapes and values to model form. For the portrait workshops, students will learn to map the face to capture a likeness. Color, composition, and pastel technique will also be explored. Work will be from live models with demos each morning. In the still life workshops, students will work from various live set-ups as they experiment with color composition and design. Challenging objects will be used to help get past that "I can't paint" feeling. Cost: $270 for 3-day plus model fee; $450 for 5-day plus model fee. Open to all skill levels. Artists should e-mail or see website for more information.

POSSIBILITIES

(623)487-4031. **E-mail:** nancy@nchristy.com. **Website:** www.nchristy.com. **Contact:** Nancy Christy-Moore, artist/instructor. Expanding your creativity and knowledge of mixed water-media techniques is this workshop's main focus. Cost: fees range from $85-100 per day and $200-275 for 2 or more days. No lodging or food is included. Open to all skill levels. Artists should call, e-mail or see website for more information.

RICE PAPER COLLAGE & MIXED MEDIA

(623)487-4031. **Fax:** (623)487-4031. **E-mail:** nancy@nchristy.com. **Website:** www.nchristy.com. **Contact:** Nancy Christy-Moore, artist/instructor. This workshop is an excellent venue for both beginners and advanced watercolorists, offering creative play with delicate rice papers combined with mixed media techniques with inks, enamels, oil pastels and more. After this workshop you will never again consider a failed watercolor anything but a new beginning. Taught locally at various venues throughout Arizona; scheduled at various times for art groups and art centers. Listings are updated frequently on website. Cost: fees range from $85-100 per day and $200-250 for 2 or more days. No lodging or food is included. Open to all skill levels. Artists should call, e-mail or see website for more information.

THE SCHOOL OF LIGHT & COLOR

10030 Fair Oaks Blvd., Fair Oaks CA 95628. (916)966-7517. **E-mail:** sarback@lightandcolor.com. **Website:** www.lightandcolor.com. **Contact:** Susan Sarback, artist/instructor. Workshops offer instruction on painting with oils or pastels. Workshops for all skill levels. Call, e-mail or see website for more information.

⊕ ◔ JEANNE ROSIER SMITH PASTEL PAINTING IN CROATIA WITH SLIKAMILINA PAINTING TOURS

#38 Racisce, Lumbarda 20263, Croatia. (385)98 974 5683. **E-mail:** slikamilina@yahoo.ca; jeannersmith@verizon.net. **Website:** www.slikamilina.ca. Cost: $3,000 CAD. Single occupancy including meals, lodging and transportation. Airfaire not included. "Join me on my next pastel painting trip to the beautiful island of Korcula, off the coast of Dubrovnik, Croatia. You'll fly into Dubrovnik, and we'll take a boat to the island. From our base there we will explore coastal towns, olive groves and mountain perches. This all-inclusive painting trip includes stunning coastal views, great food and wine, travel around the island, and a day tour of Dubrovnik. My painting trips include lots of specific pastel demonstration and instruction, plenty of individual attention at your easel in an enthusiastic, supportive atmosphere. Contact Jeanne or Lynda at Slikamilina for more information." Open to all skill levels. Interested parties should e-mail or visit website for more information.

SOHN FINE ART—MASTER ARTIST WORKSHOPS

6 Elm St., 1B-C, Stockbridge MA 01230. (413)298-1025. **E-mail:** info@sohnfineart.com. **Website:** www.sohnfineart.com. **Contact:** Cassandra Sohn, owner. Workshops held every 1-3 months, taught by our represented master artists. Cost: $100-500, depending on the workshop (meals and lodging not included). Frequent areas of concentration are unique workshops within the photographic field. This includes all levels of students: beginner, intermediate and advanced, as well as Photoshop and Lightroom courses, alternative process courses and many varieties of traditional and digital photography courses. Interested parties should call, e-mail, or see the website for more information.

SOUTH SHORE ART CENTER

119 Ripley Rd., Cohasset MA 02025. (781)383-2787. **Fax:** (781)383-2964. **E-mail:** info@ssac.org. **Website:** www.ssac.org. South Shore Art Center is a nonprofit organization based in the coastal area south of Boston. The facility features appealing galleries and teaching studios. Offers exhibitions and gallery programs, sales of fine art and studio crafts, courses and workshops, school outreach and special events. See website for more information and a list of upcoming workshops and events.

CARRIE STUART PARKS DRAWING WORKSHOPS

P.O. Box 73, Cataldo ID 83810. (208)682-4564. **Fax:** (208)682-4773. **E-mail:** carrie@stuartparks.com. **Website:** www.stuartparks.com. **Contact:** Carrie Stuart Parks. These workshops teach basic drawing skills, focusing on portrait drawing. As classes are constantly being added, artists should see website for information on upcoming workshops. Cost varies with each workshop but averages $695, depending on the location. Open to all skill levels. Artists should call, e-mail or see website for more information.

CARRIE STUART PARKS FORENSIC ART WORKSHOPS

P.O. Box 73, Cataldo ID 83810. (208)682-4564. **Fax:** (208)682-4773. **E-mail:** carrie@stuartparks.com. **Website:** www.stuartparks.com. **Contact:** Carrie Stuart Parks. Held monthly in various locations across the country. A variety of classes are offered to civilian and law enforcement. Each class is 40 hours (1 week) in length. As classes are constantly being added, artists should see website for information on upcoming workshops and a helpful FAQ section. Cost varies with each workshop, but averages $695. Open to all skill levels. Artists should call, e-mail or see website for more information.

CARRIE STUART PARKS WATERCOLOR WORKSHOPS

P.O. Box 73, Cataldo ID 83810. (208)682-4564. **Fax:** (208)682-4773. **E-mail:** carrie@stuartparks.com. **Website:** www.stuartparks.com. **Contact:** Carrie Stuart Parks. These workshops focus on general subjects and portraits. Cost varies with each workshop but averages $450, depending on the location. Open to all skill levels. Artists should call, e-mail or see website for more information.

TETON ARTS COUNCIL SUMMER ART WORKSHOP SERIES

P.O. Box 627, Driggs ID 83422. (208)354-4ART (4278). **E-mail:** info@tetonartscouncil.com. **Website:** www.

tetonartscouncil.com. Annual. "Teton Arts Council hosts several art workshops in Teton Valley for painters and digital photographers. The west side of the Bridger-Teton mountain range provides warm and high-quality sunlight during the long summer days. The workshop schedule varies each summer based on the teaching artists and grants available; see the website for scheduled workshops. All workshops include a welcome social, instruction anddemonstration, and a salon at the end of the workshop. Most workshops include guided excursions on conservation lands or back country. We work with local hotels and B&Bs to offer discounts to participants." Open to all skill levels. Cost: Ranges $35-165 per workshop; lodging and travel expenses are separate. Artists should see website for more information.

TRIPLE D GAME FARM

P.O. Box 5072, Kalispell MT 59903. (406)755-9653. **Fax:** (406)755-9021. **E-mail:** info@tripledgamefarm. com. **Website:** www.tripledgamefarm.com. **Contact:** Kathleen O'Neil, assistant manager. We raise wildlife and train our species for photographers, artists, and cinema. Wolves, bears, mountain lions, bobcats, lynx, tigers, snow leopards, coyotes, fox, fisher, otter, porcupine and more are available. Open to all skill levels. Interested parties should write, call, e-mail, or see website for more information.

TUCSON ART ACADEMY, GABOR SVAGRIK

E-mail: questions@tucsonartacademyonline.com. **Website:** www.svagrikfineart.com; www.tucson artacademyonline.com. **Contact:** Christine Svagrik, co-owner Tucson Art Academy. Refer to website for workshop dates. Gabor will guide all levels of landscape painters (oil, pastels or acrylics) to further their understanding of color, value and light in their outdoor and studio paintings. Each student will be taught the importance of composition through concise drawing and editing. Cost: $595 for a 4-week online workshop. See website for details. See the website or send an e-mail for more information.

WHIDBEY ISLAND FINE ART STUDIO

813 Edge Cliff Dr., Langley WA 98260. (360)637-4690. **E-mail:** info@whidbeyislandfas.com. **Website:** www. whidbeyislandfas.com. **Contact:** Cary Jurriaans, director. Cost varies by workshop; see website for details. Annual. Drawing and painting workshops from the still life, figure and landscape in studio and plein air. Individual attention and a personalized approach. Location: Langley; a shuttle will be provided, if needed, to pick up students from the ferry in Clinton. See website for dates. Open to all skill levels. Artists should call, e-mail or see website for more information.

THE HELENE WURLITZER FOUNDATION

P.O. Box 1891, Taos NM 87571. (575)758-2413. **Fax:** (575)758-2559. **E-mail:** hwf@taosnet.com. **Website:** www.wurlitzerfoundation.org. **Contact:** Michael A. Knight, executive director. Estab. 1954. The foundation offers residencies to artists in the following creative fields: visual and literary arts and music composition. There are 2 12-week sessions from mid-January through mid-April, early September-early December, and 1-10 week session from early June to mid-August. Application deadline: January 18 for following year. For application, request by e-mail or visit website to download.

YADDO

The Corporation of Yaddo Residencies, P.O. Box 395, 312 Union Ave., Saratoga Springs NY 12866-0395. (518)584-0746. **Fax:** (518)584-1312. **E-mail:** chwait@ yaddo.org. **Website:** www.yaddo.org. **Contact:** Candace Wait, program director. Estab. 1900. Two seasons: large season is May-August; small season is October-May (stays from 2 weeks to 2 months; average stay is 5 weeks). Accepts 230 artists/year. Accommodates approximately 35 artists in large season. Those qualified for invitations to Yaddo are highly qualified writers, visual artists (including photographers), composers, choreographers, performance artists and film and video artists who are working at the professional level in their fields. Artists who wish to work collaboratively are encouraged to apply. An abiding principle at Yaddo is that applications for residencies are judged on the quality of the artists' work and professional promise. Site includes four small lakes, a rose garden, woodland, swimming pool, tennis courts. Yaddo's nonrefundable application fee is $30, to which is added a fee for media uploads ranging from $5-10 depending on the discipline. Application fees must be paid by credit card. Two letters of recommendation are requested. All application materials, including contact information, résumé, work sample, and reference letter, must be submitted online. Applications are considered by the Admissions Committee and invitations are issued by March 15 (deadline: January

1) and October 1 (deadline: August 1). Information available on website.

GRANTS
State & Provincial

///

Arts councils in the United States and Canada provide assistance to artists in the form of fellowships or grants. These grants can be substantial and confer prestige upon recipients; however, only state or province residents are eligible. Because deadlines and available support vary annually, query first (with a SASE) or check websites for guidelines.

UNITED STATES ARTS AGENCIES

Alabama State Council on the Arts, 201 Monroe St., Montgomery AL 36130-1800. (334)242-4076. E-mail: staff@arts.alabama.gov. Website: www.arts.state.al.us.

Alaska State Council on the Arts, 161 S. Klevin St., Suite 102, Anchorage AK 99508-1506. (907)269-6601 or (888)278-7424. E-mail: aksca.info@alaska.gov. Website: www.eed.state.ak.us/aksca.

Arizona Commission on the Arts, 417 W. Roosevelt St., Phoenix AZ 85003-1326. (602)771-6501. E-mail: info@azarts.gov. Website: www.azarts.gov.

Arkansas Arts Council, 323 Center St., Suite 1500, Little Rock AR 72201-2606. (501)324-9766. E-mail: info@arkansasarts.com. Website: www.arkansasarts.org.

California Arts Council, 1300 I St., Suite 930, Sacramento CA 95814. (916)322-6555 or (800)201-6201. E-mail: info@arts.ca.gov. Website: www.cac.ca.gov.

Colorado Creative Industries, 1625 Broadway, Suite 2700, Denver CO 80202. (303)892-3802. E-mail: online form. Website: www.coloradocreativeindustries.org.

Connecticut Commission on Culture & Tourism, One Constitution Plaza, 2nd Floor, Hartford CT 06103. (860)256-2800. Website: www.cultureandtourism.org.

Delaware Division of the Arts, Carvel State Office Bldg., 4th Floor, 820 N. French St., Wilmington DE 19801. (302)577-8278 (New Castle County) or (302)739-5304 (Kent or Sussex counties). E-mail: delarts@state.de.us. Website: www.artsdel.org.

District of Columbia Commission on the Arts and Humanities, 200 I St. SE, Washington DC 20003. (202)724-5613. E-mail: cah@dc.gov. Website: www.dcarts.dc.gov.

Florida Division of Cultural Affairs, R.A. Gray Bldg., 3rd Floor, 500 S. Bronough St., Tallahassee FL 32399-0250. (850)245-6470. E-mail: info@florida-arts.org. Website: www.florida-arts.org.

Georgia Council for the Arts, 75 Fifth St., Suite 1200, Atlanta GA 30308. (404)685-2787. E-mail: gaarts@gaarts.org. Website: www.gaarts.org.

Guam Council on the Arts and Humanities, P.O. Box 2950, Hagatna GU 96932. (671)300-1204/1205/1206/1207/1208. E-mail: info@caha.guam.gov. Website: www.guam caha.org.

Hawai'i State Foundation on Culture & the Arts, 250 S. Hotel St., 2nd Floor, Honolulu HI 96813. (808)586-0300. Website: www.state.hi.us/sfca.

Idaho Commission on the Arts, P.O. Box 83720, Boise ID 83720-0008. (208)334-2119 or (800)278-3863. E-mail: info@arts.idaho.gov. Website: www.arts.idaho.gov.

Illinois Arts Council, James R. Thompson Center, 100 W. Randolph, Suite 10-500, Chicago IL 60601-3230. (312)814-6750 or (800)237-6994. E-mail: iac.info@illinois.gov. Website: www.arts.illinois.gov.

Indiana Arts Commission, 100 N. Senate Ave., Room N505, Indianapolis IN 46204. (317)232-1268. E-mail: IndianaArtsCommission@iac.in.gov. Website: www.in.gov/arts.

Iowa Arts Council, 600 E. Locust, Des Moines IA 50319-0290. (515)242-6194. Website: www.iowaartscouncil.org.

Kansas Creative Arts Industries Commission, 700 SW Jackson, Suite 1004, Topeka KS 66603-3774. (785)296-2178. E-mail: pjasso@kansascommerce.com. Website: www.kansascommerce.com/caic.

Kentucky Arts Council, Capital Plaza Tower, 21st Floor, 500 Mero St., Frankfort KY 40601-1987. (502)564-3757 or (888)833-2787. E-mail: kyarts@ky.gov. Website: www.artscouncil.ky.gov.

Louisiana Division of the Arts, P.O. Box 44247, Baton Rouge LA 70804-4247. (225)342-8180. E-mail: arts@crt.la.gov. Website: www.crt.state.la.us/cultural-development/arts.

Maine Arts Commission, 193 State St., 25 State House Station, Augusta ME 04333-0025. (207)287-2724. E-mail: MaineArts.info@maine.gov. Website: mainearts.maine.gov.

Maryland State Arts Council, 175 W. Ostend St., Suite E, Baltimore MD 21230. (410)767-6555. E-mail: msac@msac.org. Website: www.msac.org.

Massachusetts Cultural Council, 10 St. James Ave., 3rd Floor, Boston MA 02116-3803. (617)727-2700. E-mail: mcc@art.state.ma.us. Website: www.massculturalcouncil.org.

Michigan Council for Arts and Cultural Affairs, 300 N. Washington Square, Lansing MI 48913. (517)241-4011. E-mail: artsinfo@michigan.org. Website: www.themedc.org/arts.

Minnesota State Arts Board, Park Square Court, Suite 200, 400 Sibley St., St. Paul MN 55101-1928. (651)215-1600 or (800)866-2787. E-mail: msab@arts.state.mn.us. Website: www.arts.state.mn.us.

Mississippi Arts Commission, 501 N. West St., Suite 1101A, Woolfolk Bldg., Jackson MS 39201. (601)359-6030 or (800)582-2233. Website: www.arts.state.ms.us.

Missouri Arts Council, 815 Olive St., Suite 16, St. Louis MO 63101-1503. (314)340-6845 or (866)407-4752. E-mail: moarts@ded.mo.gov. Website: www.missouriartscouncil.org.

Montana Arts Council, P.O. Box 202201, Helena MT 59620-2201. (406)444-6430. E-mail: mac@mt.gov. Website: art.mt.gov.

National Assembly of State Arts Agencies, 1200 18th St. NW, Suite 1100, Washington DC 20036. (202)347-6352. E-mail: nasaa@nasaa-arts.org. Website: www.nasaa-arts.org.

Nebraska Arts Council, Burlington Bldg., 1004 Farnam St., Plaza Level, Omaha NE 68102. (402)595-2122. E-mail: nac.info@nebraska.gov. Website: www.nebraskaartscouncil.org.

Nevada Arts Council, 716 N. Carson St., Suite A, Carson City NV 89701. (775)687-6680. E-mail: infonvartscouncil@nevadaculture.org. Website: nac.nevadaculture.org.

New Hampshire State Council on the Arts, 19 Pillsbury St., 1st Floor, Concord NH 03301. (603)271-2789. Website: www.nh.gov/nharts.

New Jersey State Council on the Arts, 225 W. State St., 4th Floor, P.O. Box 306, Trenton NJ 08625. (609)292-6130. E-mail: feedback@sos.state.nj.us. Website: nj.gov/state/njsca/index.html.

New Mexico Arts, Dept. of Cultural Affairs, Bataan Memorial Bldg., 407 Galisteo St., 2nd Floor, Suite 270, Santa Fe NM 87501. (505)827-6490. Website: www.nmarts.org.

New York State Council on the Arts, 300 Park Ave. S., 10th Floor, New York NY 10010. (212)459-8800. Website: www.nysca.org.

North Carolina Arts Council, Cultural Resources Bldg., 109 E. Jones St., Raleigh NC 27601. (919)807-6500. E-mail: ncarts@ncdcr.gov. Website: www.ncarts.org.

North Dakota Council on the Arts, 1600 E. Century Ave., Suite 6, Bismarck ND 58503-0649. (701)328-7590. E-mail: comserv@nd.gov. Website: www.state.nd.us/arts.

Ohio Arts Council, 30 E. Broad St., Columbus OH 43215. (614)466-4494. Website: www.oac.state.oh.us.

Oklahoma Arts Council, Jim Thorpe Bldg., 2101 N. Lincoln Blvd., Suite 640, Oklahoma City OK 73105. (405)521-2931. E-mail: okarts@arts.ok.gov. Website: www.arts.ok.gov.

Oregon Arts Commission, 775 Summer St., NE, Suite 200, Salem OR 97301-1280. (503)986-0082. E-mail: oregon.artscomm@state.or.us. Website: www.oregonartscommission.org.

Pennsylvania Council on the Arts, 216 Finance Bldg., Harrisburg PA 17120. (717)787-6883. Website: www.pacouncilonthearts.org.

Institute of Puerto Rican Culture, P.O. Box 9024184, San Juan PR 00902-4184. (787)724-0700. E-mail: online form. Website: www.icp.gobierno.pr.

Rhode Island State Council on the Arts, One Capitol Hill, 3rd Floor, Providence RI 02908. (401)222-3880. E-mail: info@arts.ri.gov. Website: www.arts.ri.gov.

American Samoa Council on Arts, Culture and the Humanities, P.O. Box 1540, Pago Pago AS 96799. (684)633-4347. E-mail: ascach@samoatelco.com. Website: www.ashpo.org/index.php/cultural.html.

South Carolina Arts Commission, 1026 Sumter St., Suite 200, Columbia SC 29201. (803)734-8696. E-mail: info@arts.sc.gov. Website: www.southcarolinaarts.com.

South Dakota Arts Council, 711 E. Wells Ave., Pierre SD 57501. (605)773-3301. E-mail: sdac@state.sd.us. Website: www.artscouncil.sd.gov.

Tennessee Arts Commission, 401 Charlotte Ave., Nashville TN 37243. (615)741-1701. Website: www.tn.gov/arts.

Texas Commission on the Arts, E.O. Thompson Office Bldg., 920 Colorado, Suite 501, Austin TX 78701. (512)463-5535. E-mail: front.desk@arts.texas.gov. Website: www.arts.texas.gov.

Utah Division of Arts and Museums, 617 E. South Temple, Salt Lake City UT 84102. (801)236-7555. Website: heritage.utah.gov/utah-division-of-arts-museums.

Vermont Arts Council, 136 State St., Montpelier VT 05633-6001. (802)828-3291. E-mail: info@vermontartscouncil.org. Website: www.vermontartscouncil.org.

Virginia Commission for the Arts, 1001 E. Broad St., Suite 330, Richmond VA 23219. (804)225-3132. E-mail: arts@vca.virginia.gov. Website: www.arts.virginia.gov.

Virgin Islands Council on the Arts, 5070 Norre Gade, St. Thomas VI 00802-6876. (340)774-5984. Website: vicouncilonarts.org.

Washington State Arts Commission, 711 Capitol Way, S., Suite 600, Olympia WA 98501. (360)753-3860. E-mail: online form. Website: www.arts.wa.gov.

West Virginia Commission on the Arts, The Cultural Center, Capitol Complex, 1900 Kanawha Blvd., E., Charleston WV 25305-0300. (304)558-0220. Website: www.wvculture.org/arts.

Wisconsin Arts Board, P.O. Box 8690, Madison WI 53702. (608)266-0190. E-mail: artsboard@wisconsin.gov. Website: artsboard.wisconsin.gov.

Wyoming Arts Council, Barrett Bldg., 2nd Floor, 2301 Central Ave., Cheyenne WY 82002. (307)777-7742. E-mail: online form. Website: wyoarts.state.wy.us.

CANADIAN PROVINCES ARTS AGENCIES

Alberta Foundation for the Arts, 10708 - 105 Ave., Edmonton, Alberta T5H 0A1. (780)427-9968. E-mail: online form. Website: www.affta.ab.ca.

British Columbia Arts Council, P.O. Box 9819, Stn. Prov. Govt., Victoria, British Columbia V8W 9W3. (250)356-1718. E-mail: BCArtsCouncil@gov.bc.ca. Website: www.bcartscouncil.ca.

Canada Council for the Arts, 150 Elgin St., P.O. Box 1047, Ottawa, Ontario K1P 5V8. (613)566-4414, ext. 5060 or (800)263-5588. E-mail: info@canadacouncil.ca. Website: www.canadacouncil.ca.

Manitoba Arts Council, 525-93 Lombard Ave., Winnipeg, Manitoba R3B 3B1. (204)945-2237 or (866)994-2787. E-mail: info@artscouncil.mb.ca. Website: artscouncil.mb.ca.

New Brunswick Arts Board, 649 Queen St., 2nd Floor, Fredericton, New Brunswick E3B 1C3. (506)444-4444 or (866)460-2787. E-mail: online form. Website: www.artsnb.ca.

Newfoundland and Labrador Arts Council, P.O. Box 98, St. John's, Newfoundland A1C 5H5. (709)726-2212 or (866)726-2212 (within Newfoundland). E-mail: nlacmail@nlac.ca. Website: www.nlac.ca.

Nova Scotia Department of Communities, Culture, and Heritage, 1741 Brunswick St., 3rd Floor, Halifax, Nova Scotia B3J 2R5. (902)424-2170. E-mail: cch@gov.ns.ca. Website: www.gov.ns.ca/cch.

Ontario Arts Council, 151 Bloor St. W., 5th Floor, Toronto, Ontario M5S 1T6. (416)961-1660 or (800)387-0058. E-mail: info@arts.on.ca. Website: www.arts.on.ca.

Prince Edward Island Council of the Arts, 115 Richmond St., Charlottetown, Prince Edward Island C1A 1H7. (902)368-4410 or (888)734-2784. Website: www.peiartscouncil.com.

Quebec Council for Arts & Literature, 79 boul. René-Lévesque Est, 3e étage, Quebec, Quebec G1R 5N5. (418)643-1707 or (800)608-3350. E-mail: info@calq.gouv.qc.ca. Website: www.calq.gouv.qc.ca.

Saskatchewan Arts Board, 1355 Broad St., Regina, Saskatchewan S4R 7V1. (306)787-4056 or (800)667-7526. E-mail: info@artsboard.sk.ca. Website: www.artsboard.sk.ca.

Yukon Arts Section, Cultural Services Branch, Box 2703, Whitehorse, Yukon Y1A 2C6. (867)667-5036. E-mail: arts@gov.yk.ca. Website: www.tc.gov.yk.ca.

REGIONAL GRANTS & AWARDS

The following opportunities are arranged by state since most of them grant money to artists in a particular geographic region. Because deadlines vary annually, check websites or call for the most up-to-date information.

California

James D. Phelan Art Awards, Kala Art Institute, Don Porcella, 1060 Heinz Ave., Berkeley CA 94710. (510)549-2977. Website: www.kala.org. For artists born in California only.

Connecticut

Martha Boschen Porter Fund, Inc., 145 White Hallow Rd., Sharon CT 06064. For artists in northwestern Connecticut, western Massachusetts, and adjacent areas of New York (except New York City).

Idaho

See Betty Bowen Memorial Award, under Washington.

Illinois

Illinois Arts Council, Individual Artists Support Initiative, James R. Thompson Center, 100 W. Randolph, Suite 10-500, Chicago IL 60601. (312)814-6750. For Illinois artists only.

Kentucky

Kentucky Foundation for Women Grants Program, 1215 Heyburn Bldg., 332 W. Broadway, Louisville KY 40202. (502)562-0045 or (866)654-7564. E-mail: team@kfw.org. Website: www.kfw.org/grants.html. For female artists living in Kentucky only.

Massachusetts

See Martha Boschen Porter Fund, Inc., under Connecticut.

Minnesota

McKnight Artist Fellowships for Photographers, E-mail: gallery@mcad.edu. Website: mcad.edu. For Minnesota artists only.

New York

A.I.R. Gallery Fellowship Program, 111 Front St., #228, Brooklyn NY 11201. (212)255-6651. E-mail: info@airgallery.org. Website: www.airgallery.org. For female artists from New York City metro area only.

Arts & Cultural Council for Greater Rochester, 200 Ridge Rd., Suite 214, Rochester NY 14615. (585)473-4000. Website: www.artsrochester.org.

New York Foundation for the Arts: Artists' Fellowships, 20 Jay St., 7th Floor, Brooklyn NY 11201. (212)366-6900. E-mail: fellowships@nyfa.org. Website: www.nyfa.org. For New York artists only.

See Martha Boschen Porter Fund, Inc., under Connecticut.

Oregon
See Betty Bowen Memorial Award, under Washington.

Pennsylvania
Leeway Foundation—Philadelphia, Pennsylvania Region, The Philadelphia Bldg., 1315 Walnut St., Suite 832, Philadelphia PA 19107. (215)545-4078. E-mail: info@leeway. org. Website: www.leeway.org. For female artists in Philadelphia only.

Texas
Individual Artist Grant Program—Houston, Texas, Houston Arts Alliance, 3201 Allen Pkwy., Suite 250, Houston TX 77019-1800. (713)527-9330. E-mail: online form. Website: www.houstonartsalliance.com. For Houston artists only.

Washington
Betty Bowen Memorial Award, c/o Seattle Art Museum, 1300 First Ave., Seattle WA 98101. (206)654-3100. E-mail: bettybowen@seattleartmuseum.org. Website: www.seattle artmuseum.org/about-sam/art-submissions. For artists in Washington, Oregon and Idaho only.

RESIDENCIES & ORGANIZATIONS

RESIDENCIES

Artists' residencies (also known as communities, colonies, or retreats) are programs that support artists by providing time and space for the creation of new work. There are over 500 residency programs in the United States and approximately 1,000 worldwide. These programs provide an estimated $40 million in support to independent artists each year.

Many offer not only the resources to do artwork but also to have it seen by the public. While some communities are isolated in rural areas, others are located near urban centers and may provide public programming such as workshops and exhibitions. Spending time as a resident at an artists' community is a great way to network and cultivate relationships with other artists.

Alliance of Artists Communities: www.artistcommunities.org
　　Offers an extensive list of international artists' communities and residencies.
Anderson Ranch Arts Center: www.andersonranch.org
　　Nonprofit visual arts community located in Snowmass Village CO.
Arrowmont School of Arts and Crafts: www.arrowmont.org
　　Nationally renowned center of contemporary arts and crafts education located in Gatlinburg TN.
Bogliasco Foundation/Liguria Study Center for the Arts & Humanities: www.bfny.org
　　Located on the Italian Riviera in the village of Bogliasco, the Liguria Study Center provides residential fellowships for creative or scholarly projects in the arts and humanities.
Fine Arts Work Center: www.fawc.org

Nonprofit institution devoted to encouraging and supporting young artists, located in Provincetown MA.

Hall Farm Center

A 221-acre retreat in Townshend VT, that offers residencies, workshops, and other resources for emerging and established artists.

Kala Art Institute: www.kala.org

Located in the former Heinz ketchup factory in Berkeley CA, Kala provides exceptional facilities to professional artists working in all forms of printmaking, photography, digital media, and book arts.

Lower Manhattan Cultural Council: www.lmcc.net

Creative hub for connecting residents, tourists, and workers to Lower Manhattan's vast and vibrant arts community. Provides residencies, studio space, grants, and professional development programming to artists.

The MacDowell Colony: www.macdowellcolony.org

A 100-year-old artists' community consisting of 32 studios located on a 450-acre farm in Peterborough NH.

Santa Fe Art Institute: www.sfai.org

Located on the College of Santa Fe campus in Santa Fe NM, SFAI is a nonprofit organization offering a wide range of programs to serve artists at various stages of their careers.

Vermont Studio Center: www.vermontstudiocenter.org

The largest international artists' and writers' residency program in the United States, located in Johnson VT.

Women's Studio Workshop: www.wsworkshop.org

Visual arts organization in Rosendale NY, with specialized studios in printmaking, hand papermaking, ceramics, letterpress printing, photography, and book arts.

Yaddo: www.yaddo.org

Artists' community located on a 400-acre estate in Saratoga Springs NY, offering residencies to professional creative artists from all nations and backgrounds.

ORGANIZATIONS

There are numerous organizations for artists that provide resources and information about everything from industry standards and marketing tips to contest announcements and legal advice. Included here are just a handful of groups that we at *Artist's & Graphic Designer's Market* have found useful.

American Institute of Graphic Arts: www.aiga.org

AIGA is the oldest and largest membership association for professionals engaged in the discipline, practice, and culture of designing.

Art Dealers Association of America: www.artdealers.org

Nonprofit membership organization of the nation's leading galleries in the fine arts.

The Art Directors Club: www.adcglobal.org

The ADC is the premier organization for integrated media and the first international creative collective of its kind. Founded in New York in 1920, the ADC is a self-funding, not-for-profit membership organization that celebrates and inspires creative excellence by connecting visual communications professionals from around the world.

Artists Unite: www.artistsunite-ny.org

Nonprofit organization dedicated to providing quality arts programming and to helping artists of all genres collaborate on projects.

Association International du Film d'Animation (International Animated Film Association): www.asifa.net

International organization dedicated to the art of animation, providing worldwide news and information on chapters of the group, as well as conferences, contests, and workshops.

The Association of American Editorial Cartoonists: editorialcartoonists.com

Professional association concerned with promoting the interests of staff, freelance, and student editorial cartoonists in the United States.

The Association of Medical Illustrators: www.ami.org

International organization for anyone interested in the highly specialized niche of medical illustration.

The Association of Science Fiction and Fantasy Artists: www.asfa-art.org

Nonprofit association organized for artistic, literary, educational, and charitable purposes concerning the visual arts of science fiction, fantasy, mythology, and related topics.

Association Typographique Internationale: www.atypi.org

Not-for-profit organization run by an elected board of type designers, type publishers, and graphic and typographic designers.

Canadian Association of Professional Image Creators: www.capic.org

Not-for-profit association dedicated to safeguarding and promoting the rights and interests of photographers, illustrators, and digital artists working in the communications industry.

Canadian Society of Children's Authors, Illustrators, and Performers: www.canscaip.org

This organization supports and promotes all aspects of children's literature, illustration, and performance.

College Art Association: www.collegeart.org

CAA promotes excellence in scholarship and teaching in the history and criticism of the visual arts and in creativity and technical skill in the teaching and practices of art. Membership is open to all individuals with an interest in art, art history, or a related discipline.

The Comic Book Legal Defense Fund: www.cbldf.org

Nonprofit organization dedicated to the preservation of First Amendment rights for members of the comics community.

Graphic Artists Guild: www.gag.org

National union of illustrators, designers, production artists, and other creatives who have come together to pursue common goals, share experiences, and raise industry standards.

Greeting Card Association: www.greetingcard.org

Trade organization representing greeting card and stationery publishers, and allied members of the industry.

National Cartoonists Society: www.reuben.org

Home of the famed Reuben Awards, this organization offers news and resources for cartoonists interested in everything from caricature to animation.

New York Foundation for the Arts: www.nyfa.org

NYFA offers information and financial assistance to artists and organizations that directly serve artists, by supporting arts programming in the community, and by building collaborative relationships with others who advocate for the arts in New York State and throughout the country.

Society of Children's Book Writers and Illustrators: www.scbwi.org

With chapters all over the world, SCBWI is the premier organization for professionals in children's publishing.

Society of Graphic Designers of Canada: www.gdc.net

Member-based organization of design professionals, educators, administrators, students, and associates in communications, marketing, media, and design-related fields.

Society of Illustrators: www.societyillustrators.org

Since 1901, this nonprofit organization has been working to promote the interests of professional illustrators through exhibitions, lectures, and education, and by fostering a sense of community and open discussion.

Type Directors Club: www.tdc.org

Organization dedicated to raising the standards of typography and related fields of the graphic arts through research, education, competitions, and publications.

United States Artists: www.unitedstatesartists.org

Provides direct financial support to artists across all disciplines. Currently offers one grant program: USA Fellows.

US Regional Arts Organizations: www.usregionalarts.org

Six nonprofit entities created to encourage development of the arts and to support arts programs on a regional basis. Funded by the NEA, these organizations—Arts Midwest, Mid-America Arts Alliance, Mid Atlantic Arts Foundation, New England Foundation for the Arts, Southern Arts Federation, and Western States Arts Federation—provide technical assistance to their member state arts agencies, support and promote artists and arts organizations, and develop and manage arts initiatives on local, regional, national, and international levels.

PUBLICATIONS, WEBSITES, & BLOGS

///

In addition to the thousands of trade publications written for visual artists, there are now countless websites, blogs, and online artists' communities intended to connect, inspire, and support artists in their careers. Listed here are just a handful of books, magazines, and online resources to get you started; most will lead to additional sources, especially websites that provide links to other sites.

BOOKS

AIGA Professional Practices in Graphic Design, 2nd ed., edited by Tad Crawford (Allworth Press)

Art Marketing 101: A Handbook for the Fine Artist, 3rd ed. by Constance Smith (ArtNetwork)

The Artist-Gallery Partnership: A Practical Guide to Consigning Art, 3rd ed. by Tad Crawford and Susan Mellon (Allworth Press)

The Artist's Guide to Public Art: How to Find and Win Commissions by Lynn Basa (Allworth Press)

The Artist's Guide to Selling Work by Annabelle Ruston (A&C Black)

Breaking Into Freelance Illustration: The Guide for Artists, Designers and Illustrators by Holly DeWolf (HOW Books, F+W, a Content + eCommerce Company)

Breaking Into Graphic Design by Michael Jefferson (Allworth Press)

Build Your Own Brand by Robin Landa (HOW Books, F+W, a Content + eCommerce Company)

Business and Legal Forms for Fine Artists, 3rd ed. by Tad Crawford (Allworth Press)

Business and Legal Forms for Graphic Designers, 4th ed. by Tad Crawford and Eva Doman Bruck (Allworth Press)

Business and Legal Forms for Illustrators by Tad Crawford (Allworth Press)

The Business of Being an Artist by Daniel Grant (Allworth Press)

Career Solutions for Creative People: How to Balance Artistic Goals With Career Security by Dr. Ronda Ormont (Allworth Press)

Children's Writer's & Illustrator's Market edited by Chuck Sambuchino (Writer's Digest Books, F+W, a Content + eCommerce Company)

Comic Books 101: The History, Methods and Madness by Chris Ryall and Scott Tipton (IMPACT Books, F+W, a Content + eCommerce Company)

Comics and Sequential Art: Principles and Practices From the Legendary Cartoonist by Will Eisner (Poorhouse Press)

Create Your Art Career by Rhonda Schaller (Allworth Press)

Create Your Own Website Using WordPress in a Weekend by Alannah Moore (Focal Press)

The Creative Person's Website Builder by Alannah More (HOW Books, F+W, a Content + eCommerce Company)

Creativity for Graphic Designers by Mark Oldach (North Light Books, F+W, a Content + eCommerce Company)

The Designer's Guide to Business and Careers: How to Succeed on the Job or on Your Own by Peg Faimon (HOW Books, F+W, a Content + eCommerce Company)

The Designer's Guide to Marketing and Pricing: How to Win Clients and What to Charge Them by Ilise Benun and Peleg Top (HOW Books, F+W, a Content + eCommerce Company)

The Digital Creative's Survival Guide by Paul Wyatt (HOW Books, F+W, a Content + eCommerce Company)

The Fine Artist's Guide to Marketing and Self-Promotion by Julius Vitali (Allworth Press)

Fingerprint: The Art of Using Handmade Elements in Graphic Design by Chen Design Associates (HOW Books, F+W, a Content + eCommerce Company)

Freelance Design in Practice: Don't Start Work Without It by Cathy Fishel (HOW Books, F+W, a Content + eCommerce Company)

Graphic Artists Guild Handbook: Pricing & Ethical Guidelines (Graphic Artists Guild)

The Graphic Design Business Book by Tad Crawford (Allworth Press)

The Graphic Designer's Guide to Clients by Ellen Shapiro (Allworth Press)

Graphic Storytelling & Visual Narrative by Will Eisner (Poorhouse Press)

Guide to Getting Arts Grants by Ellen Liberatori (Allworth Press)

How to Draw and Sell Comics by Alan McKenzie (IMPACT Books, F+W, a Content + eCommerce Company)

How to Survive and Prosper as an Artist: Selling Yourself Without Selling Your Soul by Caroll Michels (Owl Books)

IdeaSelling: Successfully Pitch Your Creative Ideas to Bosses, Clients and Other Decision Makers by Sam Harrison (HOW Books, F+W, a Content + eCommerce Company)

Inside the Business of Graphic Design: 60 Leaders Share Their Secrets of Success by Catharine Fishel (Allworth Press)

Inside the Business of Illustration, by Steven Heller and Marshall Arisman (Allworth Press)

Legal Guide for the Visual Artist, 5th ed. by Tad Crawford (Allworth Press)

Licensing Art 101: Publishing and Licensing Your Artwork for Profit, 3rd ed. updated by Michael Woodward (ArtNetwork)

Licensing Art & Design: A Professional's Guide to Licensing and Royalty Agreements by Caryn R. Leland (Allworth Press)

Logo, Font & Lettering Bible: A Comprehensive Guide to the Design, Construction and Usage of Alphabets and Symbols by Leslie Cabarga (HOW Books, F+W, a Content + eCommerce Company)

Making Comics: Storytelling Secrets of Comics, Manga and Graphic Novels by Scott McCloud (HarperCollins)

Marketing and Buying Fine Art Online: A Guide for Artists and Collectors by Marques Vickers (Allworth Press)

New Markets for Artists by Brainard Carey (Allworth Press)

Selling Art Without Galleries: Toward Making a Living From Your Art by Daniel Grant (Allworth Press)

Starting Your Career as a Freelance Illustrator or Graphic Designer by Michael Fleishman (Allworth Press)

The Successful Artist's Career Guide by Margaret Peot (North Light Books, F+W, a Content + eCommerce Company)

Successful Syndication: A Guide for Writers and Cartoonists by Michael Sedge (Allworth Press)

What they Didn't Teach You in Design School by Phil Cleaver (HOW Books, F+W, a Content + eCommerce Company)

MAGAZINES

Advertising Age: www.adage.com
Weekly print magazine delivering news, analysis, and data on marketing and media. Website provides a database of advertising agencies as well as daily e-mail newsletters: Ad Age Daily, Ad Age's Mediaworks, and Ad Age Digital.

Art Business News: www.artbusinessnews.com

Monthly magazine that reports on art trends, news, and retailing issues. Offers profiles on emerging and established artists, as well as in-depth articles on merchandising and marketing issues.

Artforum: www.artforum.com

International magazine widely known as a decisive voice in its field. Features in-depth articles and reviews of contemporary art, as well as book reviews and columns on cinema and popular culture.

Art in America: www.artinamericamagazine.com

"The World's Premier Art Magazine," covering the visual art world both in the US and abroad, but concentrating on New York City. Provides news and criticism of painting, sculpture, photography, installation art, performance art, video, and architecture in exhibition reviews, artist profiles, and feature articles. Every August issue is the *Annual Guide to Museums, Galleries, and Artists.*

The Artist's Magazine: www.artistsnetwork.com/the-artists-magazine

Features color reproductions, interviews with artists, practical lessons in craft, and news of exhibitions and events.

ARTnews: www.artnews.com

Oldest and most widely circulated art magazine in the world. Reports on the art, personalities, issues, trends, and events shaping the international art world.

Art Papers: www.artpapers.org

Dedicated to the examination, development, and definition of art and culture in the world today.

Communication Arts Magazine: www.commarts.com

Leading trade journal for visual communications. Showcases the top work in graphic design, advertising, illustration, photography, and interactive design.

Creativity: creativity-online.com

Monthly magazine about the creative process. Website features what its editors believe to be the best video, print, and interactive ads.

Drawing: www.artistsnetwork.com/drawing-magazine

Each issue of *Drawing* provides working artists with information and inspiration regarding the foundation of all art: drawing. If you work with charcoal, graphite, pen, colored pencil, or any other drawing media, this is the magazine for you.

Eye: The International Review of Graphic Design: www.eyemagazine.com

Published in the United Kingdom, this quarterly print magazine is for anyone involved in graphic design and visual culture.

Grafik: www.grafikmagazine.co.uk

Based in London, this monthly magazine serves the international design community with essential information, independent-minded editorial, unflinching reviews, and outspoken opinion from industry personalities.

Graphic Design USA: www.gdusa.com

News magazine for graphic designers and other creative professionals.

Greetings etc.: www.greetingsmagazine.com

Official publication of the Greeting Card Association, featuring timely information for everyone doing business in the greeting card, stationery, and party goods markets.

HOW: www.howdesign.com

Provides graphic design professionals with essential business information, covers new technology and processes, profiles renowned and up-and-coming designers, details noteworthy projects, provides creative inspiration, and publishes special issues featuring the winners of its annual competitions. Website is a trusted source for business advice, creative inspiration, and tools of the trade.

JUXTAPOZ: www.juxtapoz.com

Monthly art and culture magazine based in San Francisco. Features profiles and exhibition announcements of "lowbrow" or "underground" artists—art establishment conventions do not apply here.

Pastel Journal: www.artistsnetwork.com/pastel-journal

The leading publication devoted to pastel artists of all skill levels, from the passionate amateur to the working professional. Each issue is packed with gorgeous artwork, insight and creative inspiration from top working artists.

PRINT: www.printmag.com

Bimonthly magazine about visual culture and design that documents and critiques commercial, social and environmental design from every angle.

Professional Artist: www.professionalartistmag.com

(Formerly named *Art Calendar.*) Business magazine devoted to connecting artists with income-generating opportunities and resources for a successful art career.

Southwest Art: www.southwestart.com

With more than 40 years of experience, *Southwest Art* is the leading magazine devoted to American Western art. Each issue puts readers in touch with the artists, galleries, and collectors that shape the market.

Target Marketing: www.targetmarketingmag.com

The authoritative source for hands-on, how-to information concerning all direct response media, including direct mail, e-mail and the Web. Readers gain insight into topics such as using databases and lists effectively, acquiring new customers, upselling and cross-selling existing customers, fulfillment strategies, and more.

Watercolor Artist: www.artistsnetwork.com/watercolor-artist

Go inside the studios of the best and brightest of today's watermedia artists. Learn about making art from the inside out—from inspiration to pinpointing materials and techniques. Each issue includes the most reliable information available on must-have painting tools and materials, from paint to paper to brushes and beyond.

WEBSITES & BLOGS

The Alternative Pick: www.altpick.com

"The best source for creatives on the Web." Allows artists to display samples of their work that can be searched by art buyers and directors. Offers industry news, classifieds, job postings, and more.

Animation World Network: www.awn.com

Comprehensive and targeted coverage of the international animation community has made AWN the leading source of animation industry news in the world. It provides an industry database, job postings, education resources, discussion forums, newsletters, and a host of other resources covering everything related to animation.

ArtBusiness.com: www.artbusiness.com

Provides art appraisals, art price data, news, articles, and market information for art collectors, artists and fine arts professionals. Also consults on marketing, promotion, public relations, website construction, Internet selling, and career development for artists at all stages.

ArtDeadline.com: www.artdeadline.com

"The Professional Artist's Resource," offering thousands of income and exhibition opportunities and resources for artists of all disciplines. Subscriptions start at $12/year, or you can get a one-day trial for $8.

Art Deadlines List: www.artdeadlineslist.com

Great source for calls for entries, competitions, scholarships, festivals, and plenty of other resources. Subscription is free, or you can purchase a premium edition for $12/year.

Artist Career Training: www.artistcareertraining.com

Offers valuable information to help you market your art and build your career. Sign up for a monthly newsletter and weekly tips.

Artist Help Network: www.artisthelpnetwork.com

Designed to help artists take control of their careers, the network assists artists in locating information, resources, guidance, and advice on a comprehensive range of career-related topics.

Artist's Market Online: www.artistsmarketonline.com

The Internet's most comprehensive guide to launching or growing your freelance creative career so that you can sell your art. The best reference guide for artists, designers and photographers who want to establish or grow a successful career in fine art, photography, illustration, cartooning or graphic design.

Artists Network: www.artistsnetwork.com

Offers art contests, art videos, online art classes, books for artists and more. Connect to *The Artist's Magazine*, *Watercolor Artist*, *Drawing*, and *Pastel Journal*, as well as other helpful resources.

Artists Network Television: www.artistsnetwork.tv

Online resource for art videos from leading contemporary artists. These streaming videos can be viewed 24/7 from any computer or hand-held viewing device with a high-speed Internet connection, making it easy to take these online art workshops from the comfort of your home.

Artlex Art Dictionary: www.artlex.com

Online dictionary that provides definitions, examples, and cross-references for more than 3,600 art terms.

Artline: www.artline.com

Offers news and events from eight reputable art dealer associations: Art Dealers Association of America, Art Dealers Association of Chicago, Art Dealers Association of Greater Washington, Association of International Photography Art Dealers, Fine Art Dealers Association, International Fine Print Dealers Association, San Francisco Art Dealers Association, and The Society of London Art Dealers.

Art Schools: www.artschools.com

Free online directory with a searchable database of art schools all over the world. Also offers information on financial aid, majors, and lots more.

Artsy: www.artsy.net

Artsy's mission is to make all the world's art accessible to anyone with an Internet connection. An online platform for discovering, discussing, and collecting art. Collection comprises 50,000+ artworks by 11,000+ artists from leading galleries, museums, private collections, foundations, and artists' estates spanning diverse cultures and time periods. Provides one of the largest collections of contemporary art available online.

Children's Illustrators: www.childrensillustrators.com

Online networking community for children's illustrators, agents, publishing houses, advertising agencies, and design groups from around the world.

The Comics Reporter: www.comicsreporter.com

Offers an overview of the history of comics, as well as resources and information about publishing comic books and syndicating comic strips.

Creative Talent Network

Online networking community of experienced animators, illustrators, designers, Web creators, production artists, and other creatives.

The Drawing Board for Illustrators: www.thedrawingboardforillustrators.com

Information and resources for illustrators, including pricing guidelines, marketing tips, and links to publications, organizations, and associations.

EBSQ: Self-Representing Artists: www.ebsqart.com

Online art association whose members represent their own work to the public. Membership is open to artists at all stages of their careers, and all media and styles are welcome.

Illustration Friday: www.illustrationfriday.com

Online forum for illustrators that offers a weekly challenge: a new topic is posted every Friday, and then participants have a week to submit an illustration of their own interpretation.

The Medical Illustrators' Home Page: www.medartist.com

A site where medical illustrators can display and market their work.

The Nose: www.the-nose.com

A place for caricature artists to showcase their work.

Talkabout Design: www.talkaboutdesign.com

Online forum and blog for the design community.

Theispot.com: www.theispot.com

Widely recognized as "the world's premier illustration site," allowing illustrators from all over the world to showcase and market their work.

UnderConsideration: www.underconsideration.com

A network of blogs (Speak Up, Brand New, Quipsologies, The Design Encyclopedia) dedicated to the progress of the graphic design profession and its practitioners, students, and enthusiasts.

Volunteer Lawyers for the Arts: www.vlany.org

Provides education and other services relating to legal and business issues for artists and arts organizations in every discipline.

WetCanvas: www.wetcanvas.com

Largest online community of visual artists, offering forums, critiques, art lessons and projects, marketing tools, a reference image library, and more—all for FREE!

GLOSSARY

Acceptance (payment on). An artist is paid for his/her work as soon as a buyer decides to use it.

Adobe Illustrator®. Drawing and painting computer software.

Adobe InDesign®. Revised, retooled version of Adobe PageMaker.

Adobe PageMaker®. Page-layout design software. Product relaunched as InDesign.

Adobe Photoshop®. Photo manipulation computer program.

Advance. Amount paid to an artist before beginning work on an assigned project. Often paid to cover preliminary expenses.

Airbrush. Small pencil-shaped pressure gun used to spray ink, paint, or dye to obtain gradated tonal effects.

Anime. Japanese word for animation.

Art director. In commercial markets, the person responsible for choosing and purchasing artwork and supervising the design process.

Artist's statement. A short essay, no more than a paragraph or two, describing an artist's mission and creative process.

Biannual. Occurring twice a year. See also *semiannual*.

Biennial. Occurring once every two years.

Bimonthly. Occurring once every two months.

Biweekly. Occurring once every two weeks.

Book. Another term for a portfolio.

Buyout. The sale of all reproduction rights (and sometimes the original work) by the artist; also subcontracted portions of a job resold at a cost or profit to the end client by the artist.

Calligraphy. The art of fine handwriting.

Camera-ready. Art that is completely prepared for copy camera platemaking.

Capabilities brochure. A brochure, similar to an annual report, outlining for prospective clients the nature of a company's business and the range of products or services it provides.

Caption. See *gagline*.

Caricature. An illustrated representation that distorts, exaggerates, or oversimplifies specific features.

Carriage trade. Wealthy clients or customers of a business.

Cartoon. A comical or satirical drawing.

CD-ROM. Compact disc read-only memory—nonerasable electronic medium used for digitized image and document storage and retrieval on computers.

Collateral. Accompanying or auxiliary pieces, such as brochures, especially used in advertising.

Color separation. Photographic process of separating any multi-color image into its primary component parts (cyan, magenta, yellow, and black) for printing.

Commission. 1) Percentage of retail price taken by a sponsor/salesman on artwork sold. 2) Assignment given to an artist.

Comprehensive. Complete sketch of layout showing how a finished illustration will look when printed; also called a comp.

Consignment. Arrangement by which items are sent by an artist to a sales agent (gallery, shop, sales rep, etc.) for sale with the understanding that the artist will not receive payment until work is sold. A commission is almost always charged for this service.

Copyright. The exclusive legal right to reproduce, publish, and sell the matter and form of a literary or artistic work.

Direct mail package. Sales or promotional material that is distributed by mail. Usually consists of an outer envelope, a cover letter, brochure or flier, SASE, and postpaid reply card, or order form with business reply envelope.

dpi. Dots per inch—the unit of measure used to describe the scanning resolution of an image or the quality of an output device. See also *resolution*.

Dummy. A rough model of a book or multipage piece, created as a preliminary step in determining page layout and length. Also, a rough model of a card with an unusual fold or die cut.

Edition. A set of identical prints published of one piece of art.

Engraving. A print made by cutting into the printing surface with a point. See also *etching*.

Environmental graphic design (EGD). The planning, designing, and specifying of graphic elements in the built and natural environment; signage.

EPS. Encapsulated PostScript—a computer format used for saving or creating graphics.

Estimate. A ballpark figure given to a client by a designer anticipating the final cost of a project.

Etching. A print made by the intaglio process, creating a design in the surface of a metal or other plate with a needle and using a mordant to bite out the design.

Exclusive area representation. Requirement that an artist's work appear in only one outlet within a defined geographical area.

Finished art. A completed illustration, mechanical, photo, or combination of the three that is ready to go to the printer. Also called camera-ready art.

Gagline. The words printed with a cartoon (usually directly beneath); also called a caption.

Giclée. Method of creating limited and unlimited edition prints using computer technology in place of traditional methods of reproducing artwork. Original artwork or transparency is digitally scanned, and the stored information is manipulated on screen using computer software (usually Photoshop). Once the image is refined on screen, it is printed on an Iris printer, a specialized ink-jet printer designed for making giclée prints.

GIF. Graphics Interchange Format—a computer format used for saving or creating graphics.

Gouache. Opaque watercolor with definite, appreciable film thickness and an actual paint layer.

Halftone. Reproduction of a continuous tone illustration with the image formed by dots produced by a camera lens screen.

Honorarium. Token payment—small amount of money and/or a credit line and copies of the publication in which an artist's work appears.

Informational graphics. Information, especially numerical data, visually represented with illustration and text; charts/graphs.

Intaglio. A printmaking process in which lines are incised into the suface of a plate or print form such as in engraving or etching.

IRC. International Reply Coupon—purchased at the post office to enclose with artwork sent to a foreign buyer to cover his/her postage cost when replying.

Iris print. Limited and unlimited edition print or giclée output on an Iris or ink-jet printer (named after Iris Graphics of Bedford, MA, a leading supplier of ink-jet printers).

JPEG. Joint Photographic Experts Group—a computer format used for saving or creating graphics.

Keyline. An outline drawing on completed art for the purpose of indicating its shape, position, and size.

Kill fee. Portion of an agreed-upon payment an artist receives for a job that was assigned, started, but then canceled.

Layout. Arrangement of photographs, illustrations, text, and headlines for printed material.

Licensing. The process whereby an artist who owns the rights to his or her artwork permits (through a written contract) another party to use the artwork for a specific purpose for a specified time in return for a fee and/or royalty.

Linocut. A relief print made from linoleum fastened to a wooden block. See also *relief*.

Lithograph. A print made by drawing on fine-grained porous limestone or on a zinc plate with greasy material, then wetting the stone or plate and applying greasy ink, which will adhere only to the drawn lines. Dampened paper is applied to the stone and is rubbed over with a special press to make the final print.

Logo. Name or design of a company or product used as a trademark on letterhead, direct mail packages, in advertising, etc., to establish visual identity.

Mechanicals. Preparation of work for printing.

Mezzotint. A method of engraving in which the artist works from dark to light. The entire painting surface is first covered with a regular fine scratching made by using a rocking tool called a cradle. This takes the ink and appears as a black background. The design is burnished onto it, does not take the ink, and therefore appears in white.

Multimedia. A generic term used by advertising, public relations, and audiovisual firms to describe productions involving a combination of media such as animation, video, Web graphics or other visual effects. Also, a term used to reflect the varied in-house capabilities of an agency.

Offset. Printing process in which a flat printing plate is treated to be ink-receptive in image areas and ink-repellent in nonimage areas. Ink is transferred from the printing plate to a rubber plate and then to the paper.

On spec. Abbreviation for "on speculation." See also *speculation*.

Overlay. Transparent cover over copy, on which instruction, corrections, or color location directions are given.

Panel. In cartooning, the boxed-in illustration; can be single panel, double panel, or multiple panel.

PDF. Portable Document Format—Adobe® file format for representing documents in a manner that is independent of the original application software, hardware, and operating system used to create those documents.

P-O-P. Point-of-purchase—in-store marketing display that promotes a product.

Print. An impression pulled from an original plate, stone, block screen, or negative; also a positive made from a photographic negative.

Production artist. In the final phases of the design process, the artist responsible for mechanicals and sometimes the overseeing of printing.

Publication (payment on). An artist is not paid for his/her work until it is actually published, as opposed to payment on acceptance.

QuarkXPress. Page layout computer program.

Query. Letter to an art director or buyer eliciting interest in a work an artist wants to illustrate or sell.

Quote. Set fee proposed to a client prior to commencing work on a project.

Relief. A composition or design made so that all or part projects from a flat surface.

Rendering. A drawn representation of a building, interior, etc. in perspective.

Resolution. The pixel density of an image, or the number of dots per inch a device is capable of recognizing or reproducing.

Retail. The sale of goods in small quantities directly to the consumer.

Roughs. Preliminary sketches or drawings.

Royalty. An agreed percentage paid by a publisher to an artist for each copy of a work sold.

SASE. Self-addressed, stamped envelope.

Self-publishing. In this arrangement, an artist coordinates and pays for printing, distribution, and marketing of her own artwork and in turn keeps all ensuing profits.

Semiannual. Occurring twice a year. See also *biannual*.

Semimonthly. Occurring twice a month.

Semiweekly. Occurring twice a week.

Serigraph. Silkscreen; method of printing in which a stencil is adhered to a fine mesh cloth stretched over a wooden frame. Paint is forced through the area not blocked by the stencil.

Simultaneous submission. Sending the same artwork to more than one potential buyer at the same time.

Speculation. Creating artwork with no assurance that a potential buyer will purchase it or reimburse expenses in any way; referred to as work "on spec."

Spot illustration. Small illustration used to decorate a page of type or to serve as a column ending.

Storyboard. Series of panels that illustrate a progressive sequence or graphics and story copy of a TV commercial, film, or filmstrip. Serves as a guide for the eventual finished product.

Tabloid. Publication whose format is an ordinary newspaper page turned sideways.

Tearsheet. Page containing an artist's published illustration, cartoon, design, or photograph.

Thumbnail. A rough layout in miniature.

TIFF. Tagged Image File Format—a computer format used for saving or creating graphics.

Transparency. A photographic positive film such as a color slide.

Type spec. Type specification; determination of the size and style of type to be used in a layout.

Unsolicited submission. Sample(s) of artwork sent to a buyer without being requested.

Velox. Photoprint of a continuous tone subject that has been transformed into line art by means of a halftone screen.

Wash. Thin application of transparent color or watercolor black for a pastel or gray tonal effect.

Wholesale. The sale of commodities in large quantities usually for resale (as by a retail merchant).

Woodcut. A print made by cutting a design in side-grain of a block of wood, also called a woodblock print. The ink is transferred from the raised surfaces to paper.

GEOGRAPHIC INDEX

COLORADO

GEORGIA

NORTH CAROLINA

NORTH DAKOTA

INTERNATIONAL INDEX

NICHE MARKETING INDEX

GENERAL INDEX

GENERAL INDEX

Ideas. Instruction. Inspiration.

Receive FREE downloadable bonus materials when you sign up for
our free newsletter at artistsnetwork.com/Newsletter_Thanks.

These and other fine North Light products are available at your
favorite art & craft retailer, bookstore, or online supplier.
Visit our websites at artistsnetwork.com and artistsnetwork.tv.

Get published and get paid with Artist's Market Online!

Go to ArtistsMarketOnline.com for up-to-date market news, contacts, and articles. Use the activation code at the front of this book to access your FREE subscription.

Follow us on the Artist's Network Facebook page for the latest market news and chances to win FREE BOOKS!